CONSTITUTIONAL LAW

Constitutional Law

2ND EDITION

MICHAEL FORDE

Published in 2004 by
First Law Limited
Merchant's Court,
Merchants Quay,
Dublin 8,
Ireland.
www.firstlaw.ie

Typeset by Gough Typesetting Services, Dublin.

ISBN 1-904480-19-5 Hardback
1-904480-15-2 Paperback

A catalogue record for this book
is available from the British Library.

Printed by Johnswood Press Ltd

DEDICATION

For Catherine

Foreword to the First Edition

The fiftieth anniversary of the Constitution of Ireland has evoked many responses and reactions. These have ranged from the shallow and uninformed to the knowledgeable and even profound. Dr Forde's response has been to write this excellent book. The book is closely written and wide ranging. One of its many merits is that it reminds the reader that Ireland does not live in a capsule isolated from the rest of the world. In his treatment of the various provisions of the Constitution he draws our attention to the relationship between these provisions and the provisions of other national Constitutions and of various international conventions to which Ireland is a party. This essay in comparative study will be of great benefit to all readers whether lawyers or lay people. By structuring the book to treat the Constitution under various headings which indicate the impact and effect it has upon various legislative and executive functions, as well as upon economic and social activities within the State, the author enables the reader who has not had a legal training to appreciate the importance and the pervasiveness of the Constitution through every aspect of political, social and economic life in our State.

The Constitution is fundamentally a public text and is the basic law of the State and of the government of the State. Taken as a unity the Constitution reflects certain overarching principles and the fundamental decisions to which individual provisions must be subordinate. Yet it is not intended to contain the prolixity of a legal code, but rather its nature is, as Chief Justice Marshall stated in respect of the United States Constitution, "that only its great outline should be marked, its important objects designated, and the minor ingredients which compose those objects themselves. To have prescribed the means by which government should in all future times execute its powers would have been to change entirely the character of the instrument and to give it the properties of a legal code." Chief Justice Marshall went on to point out that it would have been an unwise attempt to provide rules for exigencies which, if foreseen at all, must have been seen dimly and can best be provided for as they occur.

From time to time criticisms have been made that the Constitution of Ireland is too detailed. That does not bear close scrutiny. It is a shorter document than the Constitution of the United States, and very much shorter than the Constitutions of most, if not all, European States and other States which have written Constitutions. The whole of that portion of the Constitution which deals with fundamental rights is comprised in five articles.

A constitution is intended to endure for a very long time and must therefore be adaptable to the various movements and changes in human affairs. It is written in the present tense and is intended at all times to be interpreted and read as a contemporary law. The ultimate question remains always what do the words of the text mean in our time? This work sets out to show what it has been held to mean and, to some extent, what it could be held to mean in various departments and areas of life in Ireland. The Constitution has an inner unity and the meaning of any one part must be linked to that of other provisions. It reflects certain overriding principles and the decisions to which individual provisions are subordinate. But it cannot because of that be seen as unchanging except by formal amendment. The value of the Constitution is not based upon any static meaning it might have had fifty years ago, but in the adaptability of its fundamental principles to cope with current problems and current needs. The provisions of the Constitution are not designed only to meet passing occasions but are concerned also to provide for the future and for events of good or bad tendencies which nobody could have prophesied. Therefore the Constitution is not concerned with what has been but is concerned with what may be. It was not intended to preserve a pre-existing society but in effect to create a new one and to put in place new principles that an earlier generation, perhaps, had not sufficiently recognised.

The Constitution is in large measure a blueprint for government. One might say that where the text is not actually prescribing the form of government it is limiting the powers of government or imposing obligations upon it. It is not solely occupied with the scope of government but is also preoccupied with the relationship between the individual and the State and its organs of government. The text does however point to the supremacy of the human dignity of every person particularly in the specific provisions of the articles dealing with fundamental rights.

These rights are sometimes criticised because it is alleged they smack of a uniquely Catholic concept of fundamental rights being based upon natural law or natural rights. This stems from a mistaken assumption that natural law or natural rights are uniquely Catholic, which of course they are not. As Dr Forde pertinently observes the authors of the Declaration of the Rights of Man and of the Citizen in France in 1789 could scarcely have been regarded as pious Catholics. The Constitution of the United States of America and the European Convention on Human Rights and Fundamental Freedoms are themselves basically natural law or natural rights documents. Like the Irish Constitution they do not set out or claim to create fundamental rights but they recognise the pre-existence of fundamental rights which are inherent in man because he is man, and they guarantee to protect them. The history of the concept of natural law or natural rights in the Western European Greco-Roman tradition has been the subject of many learned works. The effect of the Roman philosophic conception, which had been borrowed from Greece, was that natural law was the sum of all those principles which ought to control human conduct because they were found in the very nature of man as a rational and social being. In contradiction to the positivist philosophy of law our courts have on more than one occasion pointed out that the rights guaranteed by the Constitution are not the fruit of law and that there are rights which are anterior to the law. This is recognised not only in the Constitutions I have referred to, but in the United Nations Charter and in the United Nations Universal Declaration of Human Rights. The latter document spoke of the 'recognition of the inherent dignity and of the equal and inalienable rights of all members of the human family' as the foundations of freedom, justice and peace in the world.

It is universally recognised that the family is the fundamental unit group of society. Many critics of our Constitution seem to labour under the impression that this claim is unique to our Constitution. One example of a modern European Constitution whose provisions demand protection for the family and marriage is the Constitution of the Federal Republic of Germany. Article 6 of that Constitution provides 'marriage and family shall enjoy the special protection of the State'. This was one of the foundations for a decision of the Federal Constitutional Court of that State, many years before *Murphy's Case,* striking down income tax laws discriminating against married couples. More recently the same provision has underpinned the decision of the same Court striking down Social Welfare laws which enabled an unmarried couple to receive more assistance than a married couple. It has even been alleged that the family provisions in the Irish Constitution necessitated the constitutional amendment dealing with adoption. The perceived necessity for that amendment had nothing whatever to do with the family provisions. It was based upon the fear that the Adoption Board would fall to be condemned under Article 37 of the Constitution lest the Board's functions and powers, if they were held to be of a judicial nature, would fall outside the limited scope given by Article 37 to the exercise of these by bodies other than courts. In view of the fact that the Board has no power to decide questions of the marital status of the applicants for adoption it would, perhaps, be prudent to provide for the direct participation of the High Court in the decision making.

This book should also help to clear up another popular but misconceived criticism of the Constitution. It is the oft repeated claim that it is excessively protective of private property interests. Except for the special provisions dealing with the taking of the property of religious denominations (as distinct from religious orders) and of educational institutions there is no reference whatever in the Constitution to the payment of compensation for the taking of property. The Constitutions of the United States and of the Federal Republic of Germany, and the French Declaration of the Rights of Man and of the Citizen, unlike the Irish Constitution do expressly provide for the payment of compensation. The Constitution acknowledges that man, in virtue of his rational being, has the natural right, antecedent to positive law, to the private ownership of external goods. The Constitution prohibits the State from passing any law to abolish the right of private ownership, which of course is quite distinct from deciding how much property a person may be entitled to own or to retain. It goes on to give a specific power to the State to delimit the exercise of this right in the interest of the common good and to regulate it by the principles of social justice. As the author has pointed out the case law on our Constitution has indicated quite clearly that a claim to compensation which can be sustained in the courts on the basis of a constitutional claim could be only a claim to just compensation. It does not permit of unjust enrichment nor does it, as has been pointed out by the Supreme Court, guarantee that in every case justice will require compensation. The recent observations of my colleague Mr Justice McCarthy in the course of his judgment in a case in the Supreme Court hinted that legislation which permitted unjustly large amounts of compensation to be awarded by statutory bodies might itself be unconstitutional. All of the complaints concerning the question of compensation for land taken or for the limitation of the use of land are properly to be directed at the Acts of the Oireachtas which determine these standards of compensation and not the Constitution. Relatively speaking there have been very few constitutional cases dealing with questions of property as compared with constitutional cases dealing with personal liberty and other subjects. The fact that our society is still largely agricultural has not greatly affected the matter. The objective and the result of the Land War indicated that the ownership of land provided not only the sustenance but also the means of economic independence and was a necessary precondition of political independence and expression. That is, however, very far removed from the view that stable property relationships constitute the highest aim of the law. Nowadays most people live their whole lives without any real prospect of the ownership of property in the traditional sense save perhaps the house they live in. Their economic existence depends not on the certainty of property ownership but upon employment contracts, unemployment benefit, social welfare, tax exemptions and such like. In the developing jurisprudence these may come to be established as property rights. What the Constitution says is that the citizen cannot be deprived of his inherent right to own a house as distinct from his economic ability to acquire one. Even this minimal right is not without its corresponding duties. But equally the Constitution tells him that in accord with the principles of social justice if the service of the common good so requires it he may not be permitted to accumulate property or to resist all efforts by the State to achieve a more equitable distribution of property or a more equitable beneficial use to the community of the property. Effectually it means that all property is given for use and not simply for enjoyment without use. In the appropriate context this may include being put to the use of others.

In one or two passages the learned author has suggested that "justice" is too vague a criterion when it comes to answering specific questions. By Article 40.3 of the Constitution, which is the guarantee of fair procedures, the question of whether or not there has been an injustice is committed to the courts in the last analysis to decide. This highlights the fact that the Judiciary, which is committed to apply the provisions of the Constitution to all public and private controversies, finds itself by reason of the constitutional provisions caught up in many social, economic, philosophical and political debates because all such questions are ultimately cast in the form of cases before the courts in an attempt to secure ultimate resolution by those courts. Thus every important aspect of the most fundamental issues confronting our society and state finally arrives before the courts. Constitutional interpretation by the Courts is for the most part obligatory. When litigants come to court looking for an answer the judges cannot avoid definite interpretations because they prefer not to penetrate the full meaning of constitutional provisions. Their function is to decide cases and not to enjoy the luxury of simply savouring whatever the constitutional question is. The fact that some persons may think that some provisions of the Constitution are over general or that the moral concepts which are given the force of law may be somewhat obscure as well as being illuminating means that there is something which calls for interpretation. In the last analysis that is the function of the Judiciary. The interpretations given by judges are by definition personal interpretations and are ones which have to be pronounced in public and are open to public criticism and scrutiny. It is often forgotten that it is not the judges who bring the cases. They are powerless to give any interpretation unless the litigants bring the cases to the courts. Then the judge has no alternative but to resolve the questions. It has been observed by the Supreme Court of the United States that the Justices of the Court are fully aware that they are not final because they are infallible but that they are infallible because they know they are final. The observation is equally applicable to our own Supreme Court. When the courts interpret the Constitution they speak for the whole community not simply for the courts alone. Therefore their decisions must be received as legitimate. To that extent the Constitution cannot be seen as unchanging except by a formal amendment. Formal amendments are difficult and costly procedures because they require referenda. Therefore as interpreters of the Constitution judges must adapt their interpretation to meet the changing circumstances of life and of society.

Our Supreme Court decided many years ago it is not rigidly bound by precedent in its constitutional interpretation, or other interpretation of the law. Therefore judges are in a position to undo their own constitutional mistakes. Nevertheless this is not done lightly or casually, because any tribunal which frequently changes its mind on fundamental questions can hardly expect others to respect its decisions. Chief Justice Marshall refused to punctuate his opinions with references to previous decisions but preferred a grander style of reasoning. Irish judges do not often have the opportunity to adopt such a magisterial approach. Even if they felt like availing of an opportunity to adopt such a course they would probably feel inhibited against so doing by knowledge, based on some experience, that their successors might lament the "absence of authority" for such a decision. Yet like Marshall they must always bear in mind that their task is to elucidate the Constitution and not simply to refine judicial doctrines.

In one of his chapters Dr Forde treats of the constitutional provision in times of emergency and the judicial experience in this field. In such situations the Judiciary is faced with the task of accommodating conflicting values. The circumstances that can endanger the safety of a nation are infinite and that is why the Constitution makes provision for such situations. The courts can never ignore the Constitution, even in the operation of those provisions for suspending parts or perhaps even all of the Constitution. Where the government and parliament may legitimately do so they cannot legitimately suspend their commitment to constitutionalism. It is difficult to conceive of a justification consonant with this commitment for the continuance of an Oireachtas' declaration of the existence of a national emergency for almost forty years after the armed conflict in question had ceased. Even in emergency situations certain basic requirements must continue to be observed. That view has already made its appearance in our constitutional jurisprudence.

The Constitution does not permit of discrimination between the citizens on the grounds of sex alone. To assert, as is sometimes thoughtlessly done, that the Constitution provides or expresses the view that 'a woman's place is in the home' is completely to misunderstand the text of the Constitution. The provision in Article 41.2 says that the State 'recognises that by her life within the home, woman gives to the State a support without which the common good cannot be achieved' The Constitution is acknowledging as a fact something which has never yet been challenged as such. The Constitution does not exclude from this recognition the woman who works outside the home as well as within it. What is most surprising however is that subsection (2) of that section has never been invoked in any litigation before our courts. This provides that "mothers shall not be obliged by economic necessity to engage in labour to the neglect of their duties in the home." The Constitution was almost fifty years old before the discrimination against married women in the income tax code was brought to court to be struck down. Neither the Constitution nor the courts can be blamed for people's failure to invoke provisions of the Constitution in appropriate cases.

A matter of great significance at present is non-governmental action. The author provides an interesting chapter on this subject. The duty or obligation not to infringe constitutionally protected fundamental rights has generally arisen in claims of a breach by some organ of state. However the Constitution does not speak to the State alone. It is capable of encompassing relationships between individuals or between groups as well as between them and the State. Constitutionally guaranteed rights are protected from infringement by individuals or groups of individuals. Such questions have already arisen and been decided in cases such as the *Educational Co. Ltd.* v. *Fitzpatrick, Meskell* v. *C.I.E., Murtagh Properties Ltd.* v. *Cleary, Murphy* v. *Stewart* and other cases. It is not difficult to envisage a whole range of situations, even in the field of contract, between individuals which restrict or infringe guaranteed rights; for example, restrictive covenants of a racist character or embodying nationality or religious discrimination, or against the acts of individuals or bodies who deprive or obstruct others in the exercise of their constitutional rights, particularly in the field of fundamental rights. This doctrine of third-party effect upon interpersonal or 'intersubjective' relations has grown in German constitutional jurisprudence and also in Austrian and Swiss jurisprudence. In those countries, where the distinction between public law and private law is much more rigidly drawn than in Ireland, the courts have tended to draw inspiration from the human rights principles embodied in their Constitution which were originally thought to apply to disputes only with public authorities. This is due in a large measure to the fact that structural innovations in contemporary society have in many instances obliged States to share their power with influential groups of individuals or large-scale private organisations who wield considerable economic or even political power, such as corporations, trade unions, political parties and other institutions. In Belgium and Italy the courts also appear prepared to take into consideration constitutional provisions when balancing interests between citizens in cases which concern religious, political or trade union freedom. The protection of individual rights against other social groups or powerful groups is not in itself a new development. What is significant is the introduction into the jurisprudence of these countries of the right of recourse to constitutional norms. If liberty is to be valued both as an end and as a means the Constitution must offer protection against the encroachment of powerful groups upon man's right to develop his faculties in accordance with the ideals of human dignity. Therefore it must ensure liberty and justice for all individuals. This covers liberty and justice in the economic field and in fields such as professional discipline, statutory monopolies and trade unions.

By bringing his readers to each of these areas, and many others besides, to show them the effects of the Constitution within these areas Dr Forde has made available to all his readers a greater understanding of the Constitution and of the significance and effect of its provisions in penetrating the many areas of national and everyday life already familiar to the citizen. He deserves our gratitude for having marked the Golden Jubilee of the Constitution in such a valuable and concrete way.

Brian Walsh,
The Supreme Court,
August, 1987.

Preface to the First Edition

The Constitution of Ireland was adopted fifty years ago and came into force on December 29, 1937. This book is an account of how the Constitution's requirements have been implemented by the legislature and interpreted by the courts. I would like to think of the book as a treatise on the constitutional law of Ireland but must leave it to the reader to decide if I have achieved that objective. To an extent the book is divided into four parts. Chapters I–III are introductory and deal with the drafting and adoption of the Constitution, some features of the State and its citizens and that vital characteristic of most modern constitutions, the judicial review of laws. Chapters IV–XI deal with the various institutions of government and with the activities of the State in the international arena and in relation to fiscal matters. Chapters XII to XXVII consider what may be termed the various civil liberties and human rights aspects of the Constitution and also state security restrictions on such liberties and rights. Chapter XXVIII deals very briefly with the various legal remedies for breaches of the Constitution.

The two existing published works on the Constitution — Professor John M. Kelly's prodigious article by article commentary (2nd ed., 1984) and David Morgan's excellent work which focuses mainly on the institutions of government (1985) have provided me with much assistance in completing this work. What I would hope that this book adds to the existing corpus of constitutional law literature is a somewhat more integrated and contextual account of the subject. Since Irish society, and most of its institutions, are much older than the present Constitution, I have felt it necessary in places to deal with major constitutional law events of the past, even events that preceded the Free State Constitution of 1922 and even preceding the Act of Union of 1800. Because some of those involved in drafting the present Constitution had extensive knowledge of foreign constitutions and also because the experience with constitutions in other countries throws considerable light on our own constitutional experience, I have attempted to deal with the subject in the context of some foreign constitutions, especially the Constitutions of the United States, France, Germany and the United Kingdom. Indeed, the Irish courts frequently look to foreign constitutions and constitutional law cases for guidance in interpreting the Constitution.

A particular difficulty in writing on Irish constitutional law, or indeed on any legal topic in Ireland, is the unreported judgment, by which I mean the written judgment which was given but which was never reported in any of the regular series of law reports. No doubt I have overlooked some of the more obscure of these flourishing creatures. As is explained in Chapter XIII, it would seem that the Constitution requires that the State's laws be accessible, so it would seem to follow that there is some constitutional obligation on the State to ensure that judgments, especially those of constitutional significance, are published. The law is stated on the basis of materials available to me as at July 1, 1987.

I am most grateful to those friends and colleagues who read drafts of various chapters for me; in particular, Ken Casey, B.C.L., Frank Clarke, S.C., Meliosa Dooge, B.L., Denis Forde, M.Sc., Richard Humphries of the L. & H., Patrick MacEntee, S.C., Q.C., Diarmaid McGuinness, B.L., Eanna Mulloy, B.L., Hugh O'Flaherty, S.C., Mary Ellen Ring, B.L., Dr. Yvonne Scannell, B.L. and Michael Staines, solicitor. Thanks also to John Spillane and to Mary Feehan of the Mercier Press for their particular tolerance during the terminal stages of the book. I must add a special word of gratitude to Eileen Dawson of the U.C.D. secretarial centre, to Eilis Barry B.L. and to Bernie Power of the Mercier Press. Since May 1986 Eileen has been typing and re-typing the manuscript so often that by now she must know it off by heart. Over the winter of 1986–87 Eilis Barry somehow managed to find the time from a busy law practice to take in hand what was very much a manuscript of incoherent and often inaccurate commentary; it is too embarrassing to recount the number of errors of law and syntactical barbarisms that she put right. Throughout the Spring and Summer of 1987, Bernie Power did much the same with the proofs. From the time he agreed to write the foreword, I was always conscious of Ireland's outstanding constitutional lawyer, Mr Justice Brian Walsh of the Supreme Court and of the European Court of Human Rights, taking an interest in the book. I wish to thank him for being an inspiration and for his gracious foreword. Finally this book would never have seen the light of day if it were not for the support and encouragement I received from Catherine, Patrick and Peter.

Michael Forde,
Rathmines,
Dublin 6.

Bastille Day, 1987

Preface to Second Edition

On delivering the last corrected proofs to the publishers yesterday, it was a tremendous relief that writing the 2nd edition of this book had at last come to an end. The first edition took about eighteen months in all to write, from conception to delivery, but this present version has been under way for what feels like years on end. If I ever needed confirmation that one slows down with age, this undertaking provides further evidence. In those intervening years, I would hope that I acquired a better understanding of the subject, especially from being involved in numerous constitutional cases in the High Court and the Supreme Court – with a mixed success rate.

This edition follows largely the sequence and approach in its predecessor. However, perhaps emboldened by experience, I have decided to be somewhat critical and have expressed disagreement with the outcomes in or reasoning (or absence of any or any coherent reasoning) in several of the cases discussed herein. Since there are few invariably correct answers to numerous constitutional issues, the reader should get a better grasp of what the law in this area is from a somewhat sceptical account of the subject. This is especially so when – unlike in the USA, Australia, Canada and Germany – Supreme Court decisions on the constitutionality of post-1937 statutes are circumscribed by the 'single judgment' rule and, at least in recent years in many other cases, the Supreme Court has an exceptional record of unanimity; memorable dissents are comparatively rare now (unlike e.g., Henchy and McCarthy JJ. in *Norris*). Some readers may find fault with my almost invariable use of the pronoun "he" rather than the more egalitarian "he or she" but, on the basis of previous experience, I have found the latter formulation quite difficult to write over extended passages.

Sine 1987 the Constitution has been amended on thirteen occasions and it has been subjected to extensive judicial interpretation – on one occasion, running to 357 pages of the Irish Reports (*Maguire v. Ardagh*). Given the volume of new material that has been generated in the last sixteen years, a fully comprehensive account of all constitutional developments would require a work of twice this length, which would tax the ingenuity of any book binder and the resources of most students. Consequently, I have been selective to an extent, focusing more on issues that take my interest than on others and endeavouring not to stray into closely related areas of administrative law, as well as eschewing topics that are dealt with comprehensively in other works. At times it has been difficult to draw the line; for instance, between the constitutional aspects of family law and Family Law. I have sought to state the law on the basis of materials available to me on October 1, 2003 but, in view of the enormous quantity of relevant material (statues, S.I.'s, cases etc.), there are bound to be several that I overlooked.

Three distinguished individuals who played roles in the previous edition have sadly died. Those are the Honourable Mr. Justice Brian Walsh, who wrote the foreword; Ms. Meliosa Dooge, B.L., who helped me with the chapter on the family; Captain Sean Feehan, the proprietor of Mercier Press, who published that edition. I also owe special debts of gratitude to three other remarkable persons who went out of their way to help me in earlier stages of my career and without whose assistance this book would never have seen the light of day. Those are Dr. Kadar Asmal, presently South Africa's Minister for Education, who in the late 1960's managed some of the time to keep me on the 'straight and narrow' when I was an undergraduate at T.C.D; Professor Paul O'Higgins, of Christs College, Cambridge, who support for and hospitality to Irish students in Cambridge is legendary; the Honourable Mr. Justice Hugh O'Flaherty, whose encouragement during my early years at the Bar was invaluable to me, not to mention his forewords to two of my books and leading me in my first case of any legal significance (*Cashman v. Clifford* – where a Cork "bookie" sued a Kerry "D.J.").

In completing this edition, I obtained assistance from several colleagues at the Bar, for which I am most grateful, most notably Richard Humphreys B.L., Finnbarr McElligott B.L., and Shane Murphy S.C. – none of whom are in any way responsible for such errors as I failed to detect. As on numerous occasions previously, Marie Armah Kwantran did an excellent job in deciphering my practically incomprehensible manuscripts, enabling me to deliver an almost impeccable typescript to the publishers. In her new freelance capacity, Therese Carrick oversaw the editorial work, operating against exceptionally tight time schedules. Bart Daly has taken over the "torch" from the late Captain Feehan. I wish to thank each of them sincerely for their time and dedication to this small enterprise. Throughout the entire writing ordeal, I have had the enduring cheerful support from Catherine, Patrick and Peter.

Michael Forde,
Mountain View Road,
Dublin 6.

Thanksgiving Day, 2003

Table of Contents

Table of Cases

Table of Legislation

Constitution of Ireland 1937—*contd.*

Constitution of Ireland 1937—*contd.*

Constitution of Ireland 1937—*contd.*

Constitution of Ireland 1937—*contd.*

INTERNATIONAL CONVENTIONS, DIRECTIVES, LEGISLATION AND TREATIES

CHAPTER 1

Introduction

Ireland is a large island off the west coast of Europe comprising about 32,000 square miles and with a population of over 5,000,000 persons. Unlike most islands of its size, Ireland is divided politically. The bulk of the island comprises what is popularly known as the Republic of Ireland but the six counties in the north-eastern corner of the island, occupying about 5,200 square miles and with a population of about 1,400,000 persons, is a part of the United Kingdom of Great Britain and Northern Ireland.[1] Writing in 1765, from an English perspective, the jurist William Blackstone described the legal relationship between the two countries as follows:

> "As to Ireland, that is still a distinct kingdom: though a dependent subordinate kingdom. It was only entitled to dominion or lordship of Ireland, and the king's style was no other than dominus Hiberniae, lord of Ireland, till the thirty-third year of king Henry the eighth; when he assumed the title of king, which is recognized by an act of parliament 35 Hen. VIII. c. 3. But, as Scotland and England are now one and the same kingdom, and yet differ in their municipal laws; so England and Ireland are, on the other hand, distinct kingdoms, and yet in general agree in their laws. The inhabitants of Ireland are, for the most part, descended from the English, who planted it as a kind of colony, after the conquest of it by King Henry the second and the laws of England were then received and sworn to by the Irish nation, assembled at the council of Lismore. And as Ireland, thus conquered, planted, and governed, still continues in a state of dependence, it must necessarily conform to, and be obliged by, such laws as the superior state thinks proper to prescribe."[2]

There was an Irish Parliament based in Dublin, with a House of Commons and a House of Lords, but it was subordinate to the Westminster Parliament until 1782, when it was granted considerable legal autonomy, which it retained for almost another 20 years.

---

[1] See generally, J.C. Beckett, *The Making of Modern Ireland, 1603–1923* (1966), L.M. Cullen, *The Emergence of Modern Ireland 1600–1900* (1981) and R.F. Foster, *Modern Ireland, 1600–1972* (1988).

[2] W. Blackstone, *Commentaries on the Laws of England* (1st ed., 1765), p.100 (2001, Cavendish ed., p.73). *Cf.* W. Holdsworth, *A History of English Law* (1938) Vol.11, pp.21 *et seq.* and W.N. Osborough, *Studies in Irish Legal History* (1999) ch.4.

By the Act of Union 1800[3] Ireland was absorbed into the United Kingdom of Great Britain and Ireland. According to Article 1, as from 1 January 1801 "and for ever," the Kingdom of Ireland and the Kingdom of Great Britain "shall be ... united into one kingdom, by the name of the United Kingdom of Great Britain and Ireland ...". For the next hundred and twenty years, the entire island was ruled from Westminster.[4] In accordance with Article 4 of the Act of Union, 100 Members of Parliament were elected to represent Irish constituencies, and four bishops and 28 lords temporal from Ireland became members of the House of Lords.[5] Many of modern Ireland's legal and administrative structures originated during this period, especially in the Victorian era. Among the most important political and social events during those years were Catholic Emancipation (1829), the Great Famine (1845–50), the Land War (1879–82) which culminated in the agrarian reforms of the 1880s, and the Home Rule movement which culminated in the Government of Ireland Act 1914. However, the advent of World War I caused the United Kingdom Government to defer implementation of this Act until the war was over.

But before the Great War ended, Irish nationalists staged an armed uprising at Easter 1916, mainly in Dublin. Those who organised this rebellion proclaimed an Irish Republic[6] and fought the British forces for a week. The uprising failed militarily and most of its leaders were shot. But the executions fanned anti-British sentiments and, within two years, most elected Irish Members of Parliament were refusing to take their seats in Westminster and instead participated in Dáil Éireann. In 1921 the Dáil declared independence[7] and purported to be the parliament of an independent Ireland.[8] At the same time, armed nationalists were carrying out attacks on the British forces and on the Royal Irish Constabulary in various parts of the country.[9] Nationalist military efforts were extremely effective in the south and west of the country and, by 1921, martial law had been declared in the counties of Cork, Kerry, Limerick and Tipperary,[10] where a guerrilla war was being conducted.[11] On

---

[3] 40 Geo. 3 ch. 67; see generally, G. Bolton, *The Passing of the Act of Union* (1966) and M. Brown *et. al.* (eds), *The Irish Act of Union* (2003).

[4] *Supra* n.1 and A. Jackson, *Ireland, 1798–1998*, W. Vaughan ed., *A New History of Ireland, V and VI, Ireland Under the Union – I: 1800–1870, – II: 1870–1921* (1989 and 1996) and P. O'Farrell, *England and Ireland Since 1800* (1975).

[5] Cf. *Earl of Antrim's Petition* [1967] 1 A.C. 691.

[6] Proclamation of April 24, 1916 by "The Provisional Government of the Irish Republic to the People of Ireland."

[7] Declaration of January 21, 1921, in Minutes of Dáil Éireann, 1919, 21 pp.14–16 (n.d.).

[8] See generally, A. Mitchell, *Revolutionary Government in Ireland: Dáil Éireann 1919–1922* (1995).

[9] See generally, M. Hopkinson, *The Irish War of Independence* (2002) and C. Townsend, *The British Campaign in Ireland: The Development of Political and Military Policies* (1975).

[10] Dublin Gazette, 10 Dec. 1920, proclamation by Viscount French; see generally, C. Campbell, *Emergency Law in Ireland, 1918 1925* (1994).

December 23, 1920, the United Kingdom Parliament enacted the Government of Ireland Act, which provided for "home rule" parliaments in Dublin and in Belfast, with provisions whereby both parliaments could merge if they chose to do so. A parliament for the six north-eastern counties of the island was established in Belfast and this "Stormont" parliament ruled that part of the country until it was disbanded in 1972.[12] Most elected representatives in the rest of the country refused to take part in a Dublin home rule parliament; their allegiance was to the Irish Republic and its Dáil.

The War of Independence was eventually brought to an end on December 6, 1921, by a treaty that was concluded between a delegation representing Great Britain, which included David Lloyd George, the Prime Minister, and Winston Churchill, and a delegation representing the Dáil, which included Arthur Griffith and Michael Collins. Under this treaty, Ireland was to become substantially independent, having a status similar to that of Canada, and would be known as the Irish Free State. Provision was made for the six north-eastern counties to opt out of the 1921 settlement and to continue to be governed from Stormont in accordance with the Government of Ireland Act 1920. Northern Ireland promptly chose to continue with that system and for the next fifty years was a veritable one-party state, being ruled throughout by the Unionist Party.[13]

On October 25, 1922 a majority of the elected representatives for the remainder of the island, sitting as a constituent assembly, adopted a constitution for the Irish Free State, to which the December 1921 treaty was annexed.[14] Around the same time the United Kingdom Parliament passed laws giving effect to this treaty and to the Free State Constitution – the Irish Free State (Agreement) Act 1922 and the Irish Free State Constitution Act 1922. However, a sizeable proportion of Irish nationalists opposed the terms of the 1921 treaty, principally because it gave the British monarch various powers and prerogatives in the Free State and it required all members of the Free State Parliament to take an oath of allegiance to the Crown. Opposition to the 1921 settlement eventually took the form of civil war and, between June 1922 and May 1923, forces of the Free State Government and forces known as Republicans engaged in combat.[15] Two of Ireland's main political parties trace their roots to the Civil War split: Fianna Fáil are successors of the Republicans and Fine Gael are successors of the then Free State Government and the Cumann na nGael party.

---

[11] See generally, T. Barry *Guerrilla Days in Ireland* (1949) and P. Hart, *The IRA and its Enemies: Violence and Community in County Cork, 1916–1923* (1998).
[12] *Infra*, p.83.
[13] See generally, M. Farrell, *Northern Ireland: The Orange State* (1976) and *infra*, pp.82 *et seq.*
[14] Constitution of the Irish Free State (Saorstát Éireann) Act 1922; *infra*, pp.7 *et seq.*
[15] See generally, M. Hopkinson, *Green Against Green: The Irish Civil War* (1988).

Although they lost the Civil War and refused to participate in the Free State Parliament, the bulk of the Republicans (Fianna Fáil) entered the Dáil in 1927 and, by 1932, succeeded in forming a government.[16] Under the leadership of Eamon de Valera, that Government proceeded to dismantle parts of the 1922 Constitution, such as the oath of allegiance to the Crown, the office of Governor General and appeals from Irish courts to the Privy Council in London. Eventually in 1937 a new Constitution, the Constitution of Ireland, was approved by the Free State Dáil and by a popular referendum. This Constitution came into force on December 29, 1937. To date, it has been amended on twenty two occasions, including in 1972 to enable the State to join the European Communities, and in 1987, 1992 and 2002 to permit radical extensions of the powers of the EC/European Union over Irish affairs.

Constitutions and Constitutional Law

Constitutions are the rules laid down for governing communities. Numerous private organisations, clubs and societies possess constitutions, *i.e.* rules regarding how they regulate their affairs. In registered companies, the memorandum and articles of association may be described as the shareholders' constitution. A trade union's constitution comprises principally the union's rule book. The term 'constitution' also connotes the ground rules that states adopt to determine how their affairs shall be run.[17] One of the most enduring national constitutions is that of the United States of America, which was adopted by a constituent assembly at Philadelphia in 1787 and which has remained in force since then despite the profound changes which have taken place in North America, although it has been amended on several occasions.[18] By contrast, during those 220 years France has had more than ten constitutions in all, the present one being that of the Fifth Republic adopted in 1958.[19] Canada's Constitution is eighty years younger than that of the United States, being embodied in the Constitution Act 1867,[20] but it was modified extensively by the Canada Act 1982. The Australian Constitution dates from the turn of the last century and is embodied in the Commonwealth of Australia Constitution

---

[16] See generally, R. Dunphy, *The Making of Fianna Fail Power in Ireland, 1923–1948* (1995).

[17] See generally, C. McIllwain, *Constitutionalism: Ancient and Modern* (rev. ed., 1958), L. Alexander ed., *Constitutionalism, Philosophical Foundations* (1998), D. Franklin & M. Baun eds. *Political Culture and Constitutionalism: A Comparative Approach* (1994), S.E. Finer ed., *Five Constitutions* (1979) and J. Cadart, *Institutions Politiques et Droit Constitutionnel* (2nd ed., 1979), 2 vols.

[18] See generally, L. Tribe, *American Constitutional Law* (3rd ed., 2000 and 2003), 2 vols.

[19] See generally, J. Bell, *French Constitutional Law* (1992).

[20] 30 & 31 Vic. c.3. See generally, P. Hogg, *Constitutional Law of Canada* (4th ed., 1997).

Act 1900.[21] The present German and Italian Constitutions were adopted shortly after the end of the last war,[22] and the present South African Constitution was enacted in 1996. [23]

Constitutional law is concerned with the legal features of constitutions. These are primarily political instruments, in the sense that they regulate many aspects of political action. Some constitutions are fiscal instruments as well, in the sense that they lay down basic rules regarding a state's financial affairs. For instance Part X of the German Constitution contains an elaborate set of rules which deal with questions such as apportionment of expenditure between the Federal Government and the Länder, customs duties, taxes and administration, budgetary provisions, increases in expenditure, procuring credit and the rendering of accounts. Constitutions are legal instruments to the extent that their provisions will be enforced in courts of law and analogous tribunals. The actual legal force of constitutional provisions varies in different countries. Virtually every provision of the Irish, the United States, the Canadian, the Australian and the German Constitutions have the direct force of law, in that the national courts will declare that they give rise to enforceable legal rights and obligations. By contrast, the former Soviet Union's Constitution[24] had relatively little legal significance in the traditional sense and was almost exclusively a political instrument. In France the Constitution is acquiring greater legal significance but laws, once promulgated, may not be invalidated there on the grounds of unconstitutionality.

In his seminal work on political institutions and constitutional law, Professor Jacques Cadart distinguishes between actual constitutions and formal constitutions. He defines the constitution *au sense matériel* as "the entirety of rules of law regardless of their forms that deal with the principal organs of state – how those organs were established, their authority, how they function and their relationships with each other. These legal rules are supplemented by various non-legal customs or usages that vitally affect the entire political mechanism. ... Consequently, the actual constitution is comprised of a great variety of legal rules: constitutional laws in the strict sense, ordinary laws, and governmental and other administrative regulations. But it also comprises internal parliamentary rules as well as customs that supplement written texts and which often are extremely important."[25] On the other hand, the constitution *au sens formel* is "a written document which was adopted in special circumstances and which contains legal rules that are more authoritative than all other legal rules."[26] The vast majority of national constitutions are set out

---

[21] 63 & 64 Vic. c.12.See generally, T. Blackshield & T. Williams, *Australian Constitutional Law and Theory* (3rd ed., 2002).

[22] See generally, D. Currie, *The Constitution of the Federal Republic of Germany* (1994).

[23] See generally, M. Chaskalson et al, *Constitutional Law of South Africa* (rev. ed., 1999).

[24] See generally, W.E. Butler, *Soviet Law* (1983), ch.8.

[25] *Supra*, n.17, pp.119–120.

[26] *Id.* at p.120.

in a single document; the United States Constitution runs to approximately 25 pages, the French Constitution covers approximately 30 pages and the German Constitution occupies nearly 70 pages. But the British Constitution is said to be an unwritten constitution. This does not mean that its terms have never been reduced to writing; there is hardly another constitution the terms of which have been written and indeed written about as much. Unlike the United States and many other constitutions, however, the British Constitution has never been encapsulated in a single authoritative document. As Professor de Smith observed, "[a]s every beginner knows, the United Kingdom has no 'constitution' in the narrower sense of the term. There is no document or group of documents called the British constitution. But since Britain has a regular system of government, with a complex of rules defining the composition, functions and inter-relationship of the institutions of government, and delineating the rights and duties of the governed, Britain does have a constitution and a body of constitutional law, if these terms are used in a broader sense."[27]

The Constitution of Ireland and many other constitutions contain the following common features.

Separation of Powers: The machinery of government is divided into three main parts, the legislature, the executive and the judiciary; the legislature enacts laws, the executive implements those laws and the courts decide disputes concerning matters of law.

Universal Suffrage: Virtually the entire adult population is entitled to vote in elections to determine who shall become legislators and govern the country, and also in referenda on proposed constitutional amendments.

Fundamental Rights: There are certain rights, such as personal liberty and freedom of expression, which must be respected by all the organs of government, and any laws or administrative measures which conflict with these fundamental rights are unconstitutional and invalid.

Judicial Review: Either the ordinary courts or special constitutional tribunals are empowered to decide if particular laws or administrative acts contravene the constitutional provisions, including those on fundamental rights.

Amendment: Particular mechanisms must be used in order to amend their provisions.

---

[27] S.A. de Smith, *Constitutional and Administrative Law* (5th ed., 1985) at p.18. The classic work on the British Constitution was A.V. Dicey, *Introduction to the Study of the Law of the Constitution* (10th ed., 1959), but some of this has been overtaken by the Human Rights Act 1998.

THE IRISH FREE STATE CONSTITUTION

The Constitution of the Irish Free State was adopted by the Dáil sitting as a constituent assembly on 25 October 1922, and came into force on 6 December 1922.[28] During its fifteen years existence it underwent substantial amendment, especially after 1932. Those who drafted that Constitution had numerous models to look to for guidance.[29] There was the Government of Ireland Act 1920,[30] which was a scheme for a form of devolved government in Ireland. Within the British Empire, there were the Canadian Constitution Act 1867,[31] the Commonwealth of Australia Constitution Act 1900,[32] and the South Africa Act 1909.[33] Additionally, there was the United States Constitution and constitutions of several continental European states.

Many features of the Free State Constitution were reproduced either in their entirety or substantially in the 1937 Constitution. The form of government was a parliamentary democracy; the parliament was comprised of two chambers, the Dáil and the Senate, and members of the more powerful chamber, the Dáil, were elected on a universal franchise under a system of proportional representation. The functioning of these chambers and their relationship with the executive followed very much the Westminster model. At the centre of the judicial system was the High Court, from which appeals could be taken to the Supreme Court; other first instance courts of local and limited jurisdiction were envisaged. Various civil liberties and fundamental rights were guaranteed, notably personal liberty (Article 6), inviolability of ones dwelling (Article 7), freedom of expression, assembly and of association (Article 9), free elementary education (Article 10), the right to vote (Article 14), non-retroactive penal laws (Article 43), trial in due course of law (Article 70) and jury trial for serious offences (Article 72). Pre-1922 laws were carried over into the Free State except where they conflicted with the Constitution (Article 73). The High Court was empowered to declare invalid any law the provisions of which contravened the Constitution (Article 65).

Dismantling the 1922 Settlement

Several provisions of the Free State Constitution were excised by amendments. One of the last of these was to abolish the Senate in 1936, but the new

---

[28] See generally, L. Kohn, *Constitution of the Irish Free State* (1932) and J.M. McNeill, *Studies on the Constitution of the Irish Free State* (1925).
[29] See generally, Farrell, "The Drafting of the Irish Free State Constitution" 5 *Irish Jurist* 115 and 343 (1970) and 6 *Irish Jurist* 111 and 345 (1971).
[30] 10 & 11 Geo. 5 c.67.
[31] 30 & 31 Vic. c.3, in Appendix I to Hogg, *supra* n.20.
[32] 63 & 64 Vic. c.12, in Appendix to Blackshield & Williams, *supra* n.21.
[33] 9 Edw. 7 c.9.

constitution nevertheless provided for a bi-cameral parliament, although one in which the Senate was not to be as independent and would have less power than its predecessor between 1922 and 1936.[34] Mr de Valera and most of his followers in the Fianna Fáil party had been opposed to features of the December 1921 treaty with Great Britain and to some provisions of the 1922 Constitution, and it was these articles which were the principal focus of amendment between 1932 and 1936.[35] The first of these was the oath of allegiance to the Crown; it was abolished by the Constitution (Removal of Oath) Act 1933. In that year also the Governor General was stripped of many of his functions by the Constitution (Amendment) No. 20 and No. 21 Acts. Appeals from the Irish courts to the Privy Council ended with the Constitution (Amendment) (No. 22) Act 1933. By 1936 the Crown was divested of all constitutional authority and functions within the Free State, but the Executive Authority (External Relations) Act 1936, enabled him to act on behalf of the Free State Government in foreign affairs. His role in this regard continued for over ten years after the adoption of the new constitution until Ireland declared itself to be a Republic in December 1948.[36]

Article 2A

From a primarily legal perspective, one of the most important features of the 1922 Constitution is how it applied to emergency measures that were taken to combat private armies and acts of violence aimed at undermining the authority of the State. During the first two years of its existence the State was involved in a civil war and resorted to martial law methods.[37] When the Civil War ended, a rump of the Republicans, calling themselves the Irish Republican Army, continued sporadic armed resistance to the State, which culminated in the murder of Kevin O'Higgins, the Minister for Justice, in July 1927.[38] When Fianna Fáil came to power in 1932, a rump of Cumann na nGael supporters organised their own private army, which became known as the Blue Shirts because they modelled themselves on Mussolini's Brown Shirts.[39] By the time the new constitution came into force in 1937 they were a spent force.

Article 50 of the Free State Constitution provided that the Constitution could be amended. Any proposed amendment would have to be passed by the Dáil and the Senate, and then be approved in a popular referendum. But for

---

[34] See generally, D. O'Sullivan, *The Irish Free State and its Senate* (1940).

[35] See generally, B. Sexton, *Ireland and the Crown, 1922–36: the Governor Generalship of the Irish Free State* (1989).

[36] Republic of Ireland Act 1948.

[37] See generally, Campbell, *supra* n.10.

[38] See generally, J. Bower Bell, *The Secret Army: A History of the IRA*, 1916–70 (1970).

[39] See generally, M. Manning, *The Blueshirts* (1970).

the first eight years in which the Constitution was in force, it was stipulated that its provisions could be amended by way of ordinary legislation. Shortly before this eight year period expired, the legislature amended Article 50 and stipulated that the period during which the Constitution could be amended by way of ordinary law should be extended to sixteen years from December 1922.[40] By the Constitution (Amendment No.17) Act 1931, the legislature sought to amend many of the Constitution's provisions by inserting into it the remarkable Article 2A.

Article 2A was a detailed code of measures which gave the police and the military sweeping powers to deal with any emergency declared by the Government. This law was entitled an "Act to amend the Constitution by inserting therein an Article making better provision for safeguarding the rights of the people and containing provisions for meeting a prevalence of disorder." Its provisions came into force whenever the Government desired that they should be effective, or as the Act put it, whenever the Government "is of opinion that circumstances exist which render it expedient." Among its provisions was authority for any member of the Garda Síochána (*i.e.* police) to interrogate persons being held in custody, failure to give the interrogator the required information was made an offence, and a military tribunal was empowered to try and convict persons charged with offences whether committed before or after the Act was adopted. This tribunal could order that anybody found guilty should suffer the death penalty. The then Chief Justice described some of these provisions as "the antithesis of the rule of law" and "within their scope, the rule of anarchy."[41] This Act's provisions were in conflict with the very structure of the 1922 Constitution and with many of its Articles, including personal liberty, no *ex post facto* offences, jury trial and trial in due course of law. However, the Act stipulated that the remainder of the Constitution, commencing with Article 3, was to be interpreted subject to these virtually unprecedented provisions.

In *State (Ryan) v. Lennon,*[42] it was held that this measure was a valid constitutional amendment and that, accordingly, the bulk of the Constitution was subject to its provisions. The applicants in that case had been charged with various offences before an Article 2A military tribunal; they sought to have the tribunal declared unconstitutional on the grounds that it contravened the separation of powers between the executive and the judiciary, and that it offended against many of the specific guarantees. A three-judge High Court and, on appeal, the Supreme Court rejected these contentions. Two main arguments were advanced by the applicants. One was that the amending Act, whereby the legislature sought to extend by a further eight years its power to amend the Constitution, was not itself a valid amendment; that it was implicit

---

[40] Constitution (Amendment) (No.16) Act 1929.
[41] *State (Ryan) v. Lennon* [1935] I.R. 170 at p.198.
[42] *Ibid.*

in Article 50 that the Constitution could never be amended by ordinary law once it had been in force for eight years. The other was that there were certain constitutional provisions that were so fundamental to the scheme for government adopted by the Dáil as a constituent assembly in October 1922 that they could not be excised from the Constitution, in particular, that they could not be so excised whenever the Government thought it expedient to do so. Kennedy C.J., in a vigorous dissenting judgment, agreed with these contentions.

According to FitzGibbon J., however, the fact that the Constitution expressly forbade amendments that conflicted with the December 1921 Treaty led to the conclusion that Article 50, the clause providing for amendments, could itself be amended; the existence of this express restriction

> "support[ed] the view that the Oireachtas was intended to have full power of legislation and amendment outside of the prohibited area, and, as there was no prohibition against amendment of Article 50, [the eight year extension was] within the powers conferred on the Oireachtas...
>
> [T]he object of Article 50 was to prescribe the method by which legislative sanction was to be given to those amendments of the Constitution which the Oireachtas was empowered to make, and the Oireachtas had full power during eight years, in the absence of any express prohibition, to alter, modify, or repeal the method prescribed. The extension of the period of eight years to sixteen was, in the absence of any such express prohibition, an amendment within the powers conferred. I can find no ... sound justification for the exclusion of Article 50 from the powers of amendment, which appear to me to exist in respect of every other Article of the Constitution except those which embody provisions of the Scheduled Treaty, and in respect even of those Articles so far as the amendments made to them are not repugnant to any provision of the Scheduled Treaty."[43]

Dealing with Article 2A, he concluded that the profound changes introduced by it nevertheless fell within Article 50's authority to amend the Constitution, in that the only express restriction on the amending power was that it should not be inconsistent with the 1921 treaty. Unlike some other national constitutions, there was no prohibition against amendments that cut down or abrogated rights, which are commonly described as fundamental or inalienable or inviolable. Because national conceptions of what rights are indeed fundamental differ from country to country, the judge rejected the contention that there exist rights which are "universal and inalienable." Indeed, he ventured to suggest that Article 2A may even be regarded as a manifestation of a uniquely

---

[43] *Id.* at p.227.

Irish conception of fundamental rights, in that it was introduced by the Cumann na nGael Government in 1931 and was roundly condemned by Fianna Fáil but, when that party entered government, it then began to make use of the Article's powers. Thus the near universal acceptance of Article 2A was "some evidence that none of those whose duty it is to make the laws see anything in it which they regard as exceptionally iniquitous, or as derogating from the standard of civilisation which they deem adequate for Saorstát Éireann."[44] Just as Magna Carta and the 1689 Bill of Rights embody English conceptions of fundamental rights, and the Amendments to the United States Constitution proclaim the American conception of such rights, the judge suggested that the various amendments to the Free State Constitution, in particular Article 2A, may very well enshrine those "conceptions of liberty and justice embraced by the Gael."[45]

This judgment, with its formidable critique of fundamental rights concepts, was handed down on 19 December 1934. By then, the Government was preparing a new constitution, one of the central features of which would be to provide for "fundamental human rights" which would be specially protected so as to be unalterable.

THE 1937 CONSTITUTION

The present Constitution of Ireland was approved by the Free State Dáil in June 1937, was approved by a majority of voters in a referendum on July 1, 1937, and came into force on December 29, 1937.[46] It was very much the creature of Mr de Valera, the then President of the Executive Council (Prime Minister), who had been one of the leaders of the Easter 1916 revolt and to an extent of the Republican side during the Civil War of 1922-23. At the time it was adopted, the Constitution was regarded by many of his political opponents as a peculiarly Fianna Fáil response to the exigencies of Irish politics and not as a constitutive instrument to which the entire population would have any special allegiance. Because it was formulated and proposed by one major political party and was opposed at the time by the main opposition parties, it was not regarded by the latter as the embodiment of a national consensus about the form and function of government appropriate to Irish conditions. On account of its partisan origins, it was not regarded in quite the same way as the Germans consider the Federal Republic's Constitution. Now that the 1937 Constitution has lasted for 65 years and the Fine Gael and Labour parties have governed on several occasions in accordance with its requirements, it is no

---

[44] *Id.* at p.235.
[45] *Ibid.*
[46] The definitive work for many years has been J.M. Kelly, *The Irish Constitution* (3rd ed., G. Hogan & G. Whyte (eds), 1994).

longer regarded as a partisan instrument; like de Gaulle's constitution of 1958, it is now generally considered to be a truly national constitution.

There are three principal ways in which constitutions are drafted.[47] One is what may be termed the democratic method, where elected representatives of the populace gather and, following consideration of numerous proposals and lengthy debate, they eventually agree on a constitution. Perhaps the best example is the United States Constitution, which was adopted at the constitutional convention in Philadelphia in 1787. At the other extreme is the authoritarian method, where one individual imposes his chosen constitution on a nation, such as Stalin's and Brezhniev's Soviet Constitutions of 1936 and 1977, respectively. The third method of constitution-making is the semi-authoritarian one, where one individual or a very small group of persons decide what the constitution ought to contain, and that constitution is then adopted by the populace in a referendum, as was Napoleon's Constitution of the Year VIII and de Gaulle's Constitution of the French Fifth Republic. The Constitution of Ireland is nearest to this third category.[48]

When Mr de Valera opposed the December 1921 treaty with Great Britain he produced before a private session of the Dáil his own proposals for settling the conflict with the British, which became known as Document no. 2. When his party came to power in 1932, he promised that those features of the Free State Constitution, which he found most objectionable, would be dismantled. In May 1934 he requested a committee of civil servants to examine the 1922 Constitution and ascertain which of its provisions could be regarded as fundamental, in the sense of safeguarding democratic rights, and to report on how those provisions could be specially protected against change. At the end of that year the Supreme Court's judgments in *State (Ryan) v. Lennon*[49] were handed down. By 1935 he had decided that there ought to be an entirely new constitution and in May 1935 he requested John J. Hearne, who was legal adviser at the Department of External Affairs, to draft the heads of a new constitution. In October 1936, a noted Irish scholar and official at the Department of Education, Michael Ó Griobhtha, was seconded to the Taoiseach's Department in order to work on the intended Constitution's Irish text. Whatever quibbles one may have with some of its clauses, the Constitution is a model of superb drafting. The heads of the new document were to contain three particular features. Firstly, "fundamental human rights" were to be specially protected so as to be unalterable, except by referendum and in cases of public emergency. There was to be a president who would fulfil all the functions that had been exercised by the King and the Governor General. However, the King was to be retained for the purpose of international relations.

---

[47] See generally, E. McWhinney, *Constitution Making: Principles, Process, Practice* (1981).
[48] Curiously, there is no published comprehensive account of the Constitution's drafting.
[49] [1935] I.R. 170.

Two major constitutional events occurred in 1936. On account of its opposition to various government Bills, the Free State Senate was abolished in May of that year. A committee was then established to examine the entire question of a bi-cameral legislature and it issued several reports. Among the members of this committee were the then Secretary of the Cabinet, Maurice Moynihan, and Mr Hearne who was also working on the new constitution. It was one of the minority report, which became the framework for the post-1937 Senate.[50] The other momentous event was the abdication of King Edward VIII in December 1936. On the very day he abdicated the Dáil was summoned by telegram, and it considered and passed a proposal that the King should be removed entirely from the then Constitution. Henceforth, it was the Chairman of the Dáil who would summon and dissolve the Dáil, and sign bills that were passed by the Dáil. At the same time, the Dáil passed the Executive Authority (External Relations) Bill, which provided that the King would continue to represent Ireland in the field of international relations.

By the middle of March 1937, the first set of proofs for the draft constitution became available and they were circulated to some members of the cabinet, the Attorney General, several leading civil servants and perhaps to some others. The strikingly ultra-montane religious clauses attracted considerable opposition and were amended. There also was some criticism of the first three articles which deal with "the nation." During April the draft was discussed at cabinet and it would seem that the proposed measure went through smoothly, although some of these cabinet meetings were unusually long. On May 1, over 1,000 copies of the agreed document in English were circulated to all the judges, bishops, members of the Dáil, prominent members of the Catholic clergy and to figures abroad. The proposed measure was then put before the Dáil; it had been formally introduced on 10 March and its second reading commenced on May 11. Parliamentary debate lasted eleven days, during which other legislative business and the ordinary business of the Dáil were also conducted. Fine Gael speakers vigorously opposed the proposed measure and Labour party deputies were hostile to some of its provisions. A matter that exercised John A. Costello KC, a former Attorney General who was later to become Taoiseach, was that the Dáil was a creature of the Free State Constitution and, accordingly, any new constitution could only take the form of an amendment to the 1922 Constitution. Mr de Valera's response was that "it is the people themselves who will enact" the new measure, and "[t]he people have power to determine from time to time who their rulers will be and also what their Government will be."[51]

---

[50] *Report of Second House of the Oireachtas Committee, 1936*: Minority Report of Dr D.A. Binchy and Ors.

[51] 67 *Dáil Debates*, Col. 416. In 1845 the French Constitution of 1875 was abrogated in a similar fashion. The 1990s transition in South Africa was considered in *Certification of*

Mr de Valera was anxious that the definitive text of the Constitution would be in Irish. Throughout the earlier drafting stage he had insisted that the English version be in plain non-legal language and he wanted the Irish version also to be devoid of legal jargon. Instead of having the Oireachtas staff translate the English version, he convened a group of recognised Irish scholars to write the Irish version, which was done in conjunction with preparing the English version. They had not completed their task when the English version was published in May 1937; it was not until a month later that their version was ready and it was discussed by the Dáil for only one day. On the following day, June 14, the proposed Constitution was approved by the Dáil. In a plebiscite of almost 76% of the electorate, the draft Constitution was approved by 685,105 votes to 526,945 votes against.

This Constitution contains all the features described above as the attributes of many national constitutions. It provides for three main organs of government, the Parliament, the Government and the Courts, and provision is also made for a President. Virtually the entire adult population is entitled to vote in periodic elections for members of the Parliament, for the President and in referenda; voting, other than in referenda, is by way of transferable votes, and parliamentary elections are conducted in accordance with proportional representation. Various fundamental rights are guaranteed; notably, trial in due course of law, jury trial for serious offences, equality, personal liberty, freedom of expression, of assembly and of association, education, property, religion and rights regarding the family. The Superior Courts are given the power of judicial review of laws. Amendments can be made with the approval of the citizens in a referendum.

Although it perpetuates many of the Free State Constitution's features, the present Constitution is significantly different in several respects. At the primarily political level, its evolution is not constrained by the terms of the December 1921 treaty and the British monarch has no role whatsoever to play in the constitutional scheme. Many of the functions previously performed by or for the Crown are allocated to the President. It does not characterise the Irish State as a republic but, by the Republic of Ireland Act 1948, the State is so described. The correct name of the State is Ireland and not the Republic of Ireland; in the Irish language the name of the State is Éire. The Constitution is far lengthier and a more detailed document than its predecessor of 1922, and its treatment of the subject matter is arranged more rationally under broad headings and sub-headings. Most of what may be termed the human rights provisions are collected in Articles 38–44, which are headed trial of offences, personal rights, the family, education, private property and religion. Finally, it

---

the *Constitution of the Republic of South Africa, Re* [1996] 4 S.A. 744 (S. Africa Constitutional Court). See generally, D. Greenberg *et al.*, *Constitutionalism and Democracy: Transitions in the Contemporary World* (1993) and S. Levinson, *Responding to Imperfection: The Theory and Practice of Constitutional Amend*ment (1995).

is a bi-lingual document and, in the event of conflict between both versions, that in the Irish language prevails.

PRE-1937 INSTITUTIONS, LAWS AND PREROGATIVES

Adopting the Constitution in 1937 did not bring about such profound changes in laws and institutions as, for example, accompanied the new Constitution during the 1789 French Revolution. There continued to be seven days in each week and twelve months in each year; the days of the week and months of the year continued to bear the same names; hurlers continued to take "21 yard frees;" motorists continued to drive on the left-hand side of the road; on Sundays one still had to travel three miles from ones home to be a "bona fide traveller."[52] But the new State's first President was elected, as was its first Senate. In accordance with Articles 54–56 of the Constitution, the Free State's Dáil, Government and civil service became the Dáil, the Government and the civil service of the new State. It was not until much later that the court structure envisaged by the Constitution was established; under Article 58 of the Constitution, the then Supreme Court, High Court, Circuit Court and District Court continued to function until, in 1961, they were replaced in a comprehensive Judiciary Act. Provision is made in Articles 49 and 50 of the Constitution for State succession and for pre-1937 laws and other forms of authority to continue in force.

State succession

State succession arises where one State is replaced by another in respect of sovereignty over a given territory, in conformity with international law. Often the precise extent of that succession is regulated by treaty; for instance, to what extent does the new State become owner of the former State's property, is responsible for the former State's debts and adhere to treaties to which the former State was a party. One of these questions was dealt with in the 1921 treaty, the extent of the Free State's liability for the United Kingdom's then public debt.[53] Article 80 of the Free State Constitution provided for succession to the Provisional Government's rights and liabilities, and to the functions of British Government departments. But there was uncertainty about some other questions, such as whether extradition agreements that had been made under the Extradition Act 1870, applied to the Free State.

---

[52] *Attorney General v. Brown* [1937] I.R. 125.
[53] Art.5; see too Art.7 of the Act of Union 1800.

Article 49.3 of the 1937 Constitution is a comprehensive state-succession clause, stipulating that "[t]he Government shall be the successors of the Government of (the Free State) as regards all property, assets, rights and liabilities." But this throws no light on the precise extent to which the Free State succeeded the Government of the United Kingdom of Great Britain and Ireland.

Pre-1937 laws

When the American colonies broke away from Britain 220 years ago, some of them sought to abolish English law from their jurisdictions and some even introduced legislation forbidding citation of English precedents in their courts.[54] A major goal of the French Revolutionaries was to sweep away the laws and legal institutions of the *Ancien Régime*, and replace them with more coherent and suitable arrangements, which resulted in Napoleon's *Code Civil, Code de Procédure Pénal* and his "new model" judiciary. Ireland's break from Great Britain in 1922 was not followed by any profound changes in laws or institutions. Perhaps the most significant change was the abolition of the grand jury,[55] which for many persons symbolised a moneyed elite dominating the criminal justice system, and also replacing magistrates with full time District Judges who had legal qualifications and experience.[56] Otherwise, most old laws continued in force until they were repealed or amended.

Article 73 of the Free State Constitution stipulated that the pre-1922 "laws in force ... shall continue to be of full force and effect", provided however that those laws were "not inconsistent with" that Constitution. Some of the pre-1922 laws ceased to have effect because they did not contemplate Ireland as being an independent State. Thus, in a dispute between an English-based and an Irish-based trade union over which union was entitled to call itself the Irish Transport and General Workers Union, it was held that a provision in the Trade Union Act 1876, which provides for mutual registration of trade unions between England, Scotland and Ireland, was no longer in force. That provision was based on the assumption that these three areas were part of the one political unit or State, which was no longer the case.[57] Similarly, in 1964 the House of Lords held that the then U.K. rules for extraditing persons to Ireland, in

---

[54] See generally, Stoebuck, "Reception of English Common Law in the American Colonies" 10 *William & Mary L. Rev.* 393 (1968).

[55] Courts of Justice Act 1924, ss.27 and 64; see generally, W.G. Hubbard, *Juries in Ireland* (1911).

[56] District Justices (Temporary Provisions) Act 1923; see generally, J. O'Connor, *The Irish Justice of the Peace* (2nd ed., 1916) 2 vols.

[57] *Irish Transport & General Workers Union v. Transport & General Workers Union* [1936] I.R. 471; similarly, *Performing Rights Soc. v. Bray U.D.C.* [1928] I.R. 506.

existence since 1851, could no longer be enforced because the Royal Irish Constabulary, named in the 1851 Act, had been replaced by an entirely new force, the Garda Síochána.[58] Some pre-1922 laws ceased to have effect because they contravened the 1922 Constitution's very provisions. But absent any inconsistency with that Constitution, the old laws remained in force. As O'Byrne J. stated in one instance, "It seems to me to have been intended to set up the new State with the least possible change in the previously existing law, and that Article 73 should be so construed as to effectuate this intention. ... (P)reviously existing laws should be regarded as still subsisting unless they are clearly inconsistent with the Constitution."[59]

In very much the same way, laws that were in force before December 1937 were continued in force by Article 50.1 of the 1937 Constitution, provided however that they were not inconsistent with the new Constitution. This Article 50.1 provides that "[s]ubject to this Constitution and to the extent to which they are not inconsistent therewith, the laws in force in (the Free State) immediately prior to ... the coming into operation of this Constitution shall continue to be of full force and effect until the same or any of them shall have been repealed or amended by enactment of the Oireachtas." Accordingly, for example, the Garda Síochána, which was established in 1924, remained lawfully constituted and continued to enforce the Road Traffic Act 1933, and other pre-1937 measures; pre-1937 land titles remained valid and existing contracts could be enforced in accordance with the pre-1937 law of contract. But pre-1937 laws and other measures that did conflict with the new Constitution were not carried forward. O'Byrne J.'s observation about Article 73 of the Free State Constitution is also true of Article 50.1 of the new Constitution.

Statutes

Numerous pre-1937 statutory provisions have been held to be inconsistent with the new Constitution and, accordingly, were not carried over by Article 50.1. Of measures enacted by the pre-1922 Union Parliament which were struck down, the best known instances perhaps were the part of the Petty Sessions (Ireland) Act 1851, regarding extradition between Ireland and other parts of the United Kingdom, which was held to infringe the fugitive's constitutional right to have an intended extradition's legality challenged in court;[60] the "Griffith" Valuation Acts 1852-64, which were held to have perpetuated an unfairly discriminatory method of valuing property for taxation and other purposes;[61] section 4 of the Vagrancy Act 1824, as amended, which contained

---

[58] *Metropolitan Police C'mr v. Hammond* [1965] A.C. 810.
[59] *State (Kennedy) v. Little* [1931] I.R. 391 at p.58.
[60] *State (Quinn) v. Ryan* [1965] I.R. 70.
[61] *Brennan v. Attorney General* [1981] I.L.R.M. 355.

the offence of being a suspected person.[62] Several Free State legislative provisions also have been struck down for inconsistency, such as the requirement in the Ministers and Secretaries Act 1924, to obtain the Attorney General's *fiat* before one can sue the Government or a Government Minister or Department;[63] and section 17 of the Criminal Law Amendment Act 1935, which forbade selling, advertising or importing contraceptives.[64] No pre-Act of Union law has been struck down[65] but the validity of the Habeas Corpus Act 1782, has been doubted by several judges.[66]

Common law

By common law is meant those principles and rules that judges have declared to be the law, including what is called equity. Before 1922, Irish and English common law and equity were practically identical; there were some minor differences between them. Articles 73 and 50.1 respectively carried over the pre-1922 and pre-1937 law. But some of these doctrines or rules have also been declared no longer to be in force because of inconsistency with the Constitution, most notably several rules that discriminated in favour of husbands, as against their wives; for instance, the irrebuttable presumption that any child born to a married woman was fathered by her husband[67] and the rule that a husband is not legally bound by his undertaking, made in a pre-marriage contract, to rear their children in a particular religion.[68] In one such instance, rather than merely holding the discrimination to be invalid, the Supreme Court held that wives should benefit from a rule that previously only benefited husbands and, in consequence, extended the ambit of liability for damages in the common law.[69] An issue that calls for extended discussion is the extent to which the courts should modify common law in order for it to be consistent with constitutional rules and also with circumstances prevailing at the beginning of the 21st century.[70]

Under what is known as the doctrine of *stare decisis*,[71] once the highest court in a legal system decides that the law on a particular point is such-and-

---

[62] *King v. Attorney General* [1981] I.R. 233.

[63] *Macauley v. Minister for Posts and Telegraphs* [1966] I.R. 345.

[64] *McGee v. Attorney General* [1974] I.R. 284.

[65] Cf. *Tivoli Cinema Ltd, Re* [1992] 1 I.R. 412.

[66] See *infra*, p.340.

[67] *S. v. S.* [1983] I.R. 68.

[68] *Tilson Infants, Re* [1951] I.R. 1.

[69] *McKinley v. Minister for Defence* [1992] 2 I.R. 333.

[70] Cf. Art. 39(2) of the South African Constitution, "when developing the common law ..., every court ... must promote the spirit, purport and objects of the Bill of Rights"; considered in *Carmichele v. Minister of Safety and Security*, 12 B.H.R.C. 60 (2001).

[71] See generally, R. Byrne & J. McCutcheon, *The Irish Legal System* (4th ed., 2001), ch.12 on precedents.

such, not alone are all inferior courts bound by that decision but the highest court itself is bound by its own decision; in later cases that court cannot depart from its previous view of the law. This doctrine is based on assumptions about the existence of ultimately correct answers to all questions and about judicial infallibility, and there is much to be said in its favour because it makes the law certain and predictable. Yet it also has drawbacks; most notably, it makes the law somewhat too rigid and inflexible. In fact, the doctrine was never invariably adhered to.[72] Eventually in 1965, the Supreme Court ruled that the doctrine no longer applies; in exceptional circumstances, that Court would set aside its own previous interpretation of the law.[73] Not long afterwards, the Law Lords in Britain announced that they too would no longer be constrained by *stare decisis*. As for the Judicial Committee of the Privy Council, it never regarded itself as being restricted in this manner. With the passing of rigid *stare decisis,* therefore, the questions whether the Irish courts are absolutely bound by decisions of the pre-1922 House of Lords and whether the post-1961 Supreme Court must follow the pre-1961 Supreme Court's, or even its own pronouncements, no longer arise. Indeed, on the question of when may foreign divorces be recognised, where a law was enacted in order prospectively to change what was regarded as the position at common law, it was then held that the pre-Act common law had also adapted to conform with the Constitution and the new statutory regime.[74]

Nevertheless, the Supreme Court will not readily depart from its previous decisions,[75] although it has done so, even in cases as important as interpreting the Constitution itself.[76] As an oracle of the Constitution, that Court does not claim to be infallible. Nor will it lightly depart from pronouncements about the law made by the pre-1961 Supreme Court or by the House of Lords. Even present-day decisions of the English, Scottish and Northern Ireland superior courts are treated with great respect by Irish judges.

Are the present High Court, Circuit Court and District Court bound by decisions of the pre-1961 Supreme Court and also of the House of Lords given before 1922, that have not been rejected by the present Supreme Court? This

---

[72] Compare *Allen v. Flood* [1898] A.C. 1 with *Quinn v. Leathan* [1901] A.C. 495.

[73] *Attorney General v. Ryan's Car Hire Ltd* [1965] I.R. 642, a stance adopted by the Australian High Court 50 years earlier: *Australian Agricultural Co. v. Federated Engine Drivers & Firemen's Ass'n* (1913) 17 C.L.R. 261. See generally, N. McCormick and R. Summers (eds), *Interpreting Precedents, A Comparative Study* (1997) and Harris, "Final Appeal Courts Overruling Their Own 'Wrong Precedents: The Ongoing Search for Principle'" 118 *L.Q.R.* 408 (2002).

[74] *W. v. W.* [1993] 2 I.R. 476.

[75] Byrne and McCutcheon, *supra,* n.71, pp.334 *et seq.*; e.g., *Mogul of Ireland Ltd v. Tipperary (N.R.) C.C.* [1976] I.R. 260, *O'Brien v. Mirror Group Newspapers Ltd* [2001] 1 I.R. 1, *Irish Hardware Ass'n v. South Dublin C.C.* [2001] 2 I.L.R.M. 291 and *D.H. v. Groarke* [2002] 3 I.R. 522; compare e.g. *Doyle v. Hearne* [1987] I.R. 601 and *Finucane v. McMahon* [1990] 1 I.R. 165..

[76] E.g., *Costello v. D.P.P.* [1984] I.R. 436.

is a question that has not yet been authoritatively answered, or at least has not been answered conclusively. As regards pre-1961 Supreme Court decisions, the question never seems to have been posed; issues of policy aside, there are arguments for and against the High Court and Circuit Court being so bound. As for decisions of the House of Lords made before the Free State was established, different judges have expressed conflicting views on the point, although much of the commentary was made at a time when rigid *stare decisis* still obtained in the Supreme Court and in the House of Lords. Even then, some judges baulked at slavishly following each and every English authority. According to Gavan Duffy J., who as a judge was quite an innovator, "English decisions which were followed here, are binding upon this Court only when they represent a law so well settled or pronounced. by so weighty a juristic authority that they may fairly be regarded, in a system built up upon the principle of *stare decisis*, as having become established as part of the law of the land before the Treaty ...".[77] That judge considered that he was not bound by pre-1922 decisions that, apart entirely from inconsistency with the Constitution, were "administered in a way so repugnant to the common sense of our citizens as to make the law look ridiculous", because "it is not in the public interest that we should repeat the mistake."[78] Walsh J. has expressed the view that the only laws that were carried over by Article 50.1 of the Constitution were statutes as opposed to judicial decisions regarding what the common law is.[79] Given that by its very nature the common law, or judge-made law, has always developed and adapted itself to changing circumstances, there is no question of Article 50.1 freezing the common law into its pre-1937 state. This question bears on the controversial issue of "horizontal effect" or "state action", *viz.* in what circumstances does the Constitution place legal obligations on private individuals and bodies.

Prerogative Rights and Powers

In the United Kingdom the State possesses certain rights, powers and privileges which, as a matter of legal principle, are vested in the Crown.[80] Some of these have been incorporated into statute, such as that the Crown is a preferential creditor when its debtors go bankrupt; some have been abolished, such as the Crown's immunity from suit in actions for breach of contract and in tort; some are regarded as anachronistic if not obsolete, for instance, the Crown's privileges in respect of certain swans and whales, and its right to impress persons into

---

[77] *Exham v. Beamish* [1939] I.R. 336 at p.348.
[78] *Ibid.*
[79] *Gaffney v. Gaffney* [1975] I.R. 133.
[80] See generally, A. Bradley and K. Ewing, *Constitutional and Administrative Law* (13 ed. 2003), Chap.12.

the naval service. Two important powers that are Crown prerogatives in Britain are the subject of statutory regulation in this country, viz., determining the extent of the State's territorial waters[81] and regulating the civil service.[82] Prerogative rights relating to property are the subject of Part III (ss.27–32) of the State Property Act 1954. What were the prerogative powers of the Crown regarding foreign affairs are covered by Article 29.4 of the Constitution, which assigns to the Government authority over "(t)he executive power of the State in or in connection with its external relations ...". Article 13.6 vests in the President what in Britain is the prerogative of pardons, and Article 13.2.2 gives the President the "absolute discretion" to refuse to dissolve the Dáil when the Government has lost its support.

Article 49 of the Constitution deals with State succession to prerogatives and related authority generally, and stipulates that all rights and prerogatives that formerly were exercisable by the Free State shall belong to the people; that "[a]ll powers, functions, rights and prerogatives whatsoever exercisable in or in respect of (the Free State) immediately before the 11th day of December, 1936, whether in virtue of the Constitution then in force or otherwise, by the authority in which the executive power of (the Free State) was then vested are hereby declared to belong to the people." This Article goes on to say that these powers and authorities can be exercised "only by or on the authority of" the Government except where legislation or the Constitution itself provides otherwise. Unlike the position as regards carrying over earlier laws, there was no provision in the Free State Constitution identical to Article 49, although there are some parallels in its Article 2. According to this Article, "(a)ll powers of government and all authority legislative, executive and judicial" shall be exercised in the manner provided by the Constitution. Perhaps the "powers of government" referred to here included residuary prerogatives and authorities. The main question arising out of Article 49 of the Constitution is precisely what "powers, functions, rights and prerogatives" were carried over from the Free State and, through it, from the *Ancien Régime?* In particular, did all of the royal prerogatives vest in the Free State Government, which throughout most of its existence had the Crown at its apex? And were all of those prerogatives absorbed by the new State in 1937? Or to put it the other way around, which of the old prerogatives were not carried over and why is that so?

One reason why some of them were not carried over is that they are based on the fact that they belong to a monarch. But the State is not a monarchy and, indeed, is described as a republic; even the Free State was not a monarchy. In *Byrne* v. *Ireland*,[83] which concerned the question of whether the State enjoys immunity in tort actions, Walsh J. explained that many of the prerogatives in

---

[81] Maritime Jurisdiction Acts 1959–64.
[82] Civil Service Regulation Act 1956.
[83] [1972] I.R. 241.

common law were founded on the principle that the State was personified in the King, and that it would be irrational if such an exalted authority could be sued by individuals in his courts:

> "The King enjoyed a personal pre-eminence; perfection was ascribed to him. These were the prerogatives pertaining to the royal dignity. It was under this heading that he was personally immune from civil or criminal proceedings. So far as the royal authority was concerned, the prerogative relating to this was a general one by virtue of which the King was the supreme head of the executive; he had the prerogative right to make treaties and alliances with foreign states and the power to declare war and to make peace, and he was regarded as the fountain-head of justice and the general conservator of the peace of the kingdom. In the early days the King sat in person to administer justice and all jurisdictions in the civil courts were derived from him, either mediately or immediately. To this very day in England every civil suit in the High Court commences in the form of a command by the sovereign to the defendant to enter an appearance. In criminal proceedings the Sovereign acts as a prosecutor, and the judges derive their appointments from the Sovereign."[84]

Under the Constitution, however, as Article 6 stipulates, all governmental powers, whether legislative, executive or judicial, "derive, under God, from the people" and not from any monarch. It therefore would contradict the very basis of public power in this State if the executive or the State enjoyed any of the prerogatives that are founded on the medieval principle that ultimate legal sovereignty vests in a monarch. The same reasoning applies to the Free State. As Walsh J. pointed out in the *Byrne* case, Article 2 of the Free State Constitution stated that all public power and authority "are derived from the people of Ireland;" the Free State's authority was not defined as deriving from the British monarch. The position of the King in the Free State Constitution was confined to a few express provisions and even those clauses were excised in 1933 when the oath of allegiance, the main powers of the Governor General and appeals to the Privy Council were ended, and in 1936 by the 26th Amendment to the Constitution. And "(w)hile the King had a limited place in the Constitution of Saorstát Éireann, he had no place in the present new republican form of constitution which was enacted in 1937 ....".[85]

Another reason why some of the old prerogatives were not carried over by Article 49 is that they are inconsistent with rights guaranteed by the Constitution. Indeed, some prerogatives may even have conflicted with rights guaranteed by the Free State Constitution. Although the courts have not yet

---

[84] *Id.* at p.272.
[85] *Id.* at p.283.

been called upon to pass judgment on the question, it may well be that the prerogative writ *ne exeat regno,* by which the monarch could command a subject not to leave the realm,[86] may very well no longer exist because it is an impermissible interference with the individual's general right to go abroad, not to mention the guarantee of freedom of movement within the European Community. A similar question applies to some of the prerogatives that have been given a statutory form, such as the Revenue Commissioners' preferential rights in bankruptcies. It would seem that the Civil Service Regulation Act 1956, does not give the Government as extensive a power to dismiss civil servants as exists under the prerogative in the United Kingdom.[87] The following former prerogatives call for some consideration.

Immunity from Suit

In *Byrne* v. *Ireland,*[88] the plaintiff sought to bring an action in tort against the State, naming as defendant Ireland and the Attorney General. She claimed that she had been injured in consequence of negligence and breach of duty on the part of employees of the Minister for Posts and Telegraphs. Because under the law at the time she could not have sued the Minister on the basis of vicarious liability,[89] she sought to have the State itself made liable. Its principal defence was that it had inherited the Crown's immunity from suit at common law and, accordingly, could not be rendered liable.

In the past, most states enjoyed a degree of immunity in one form or another. The legal position in the United Kingdom was embodied in the maxim "the King can do no wrong;" an action could not be maintained against the United Kingdom State in respect of torts committed in the course of public service.[90] However, the individual official who committed the tort could be held liable and so could his employer if it were a corporation capable of being sued. In the United States, the legal position was embodied in the maxim "sovereign immunity,"[91] with the vital difference that not only could individuals not sue the U.S. Government in tort but neither could they sue State governments nor many public corporations, and many individual officials could not be held liable for torts that they committed in the course of their duties.[92] The position in pre-Revolutionary France was very similar, where the maxim *le Roi ne peut mal faire* applied. However, most of these immunities have been abolished. Even in pre-1922 Britain and Ireland, there was a petition of right procedure

---

[86] *Cf. Al Nahkel for Contracting & Trading Ltd v. Lowe* [1986] 1 Q.B. 235.

[87] *Garvey v. Ireland* [1981] I.R. 75.

[88] [1972] I.R. 241.

[89] *Carolan v. Minister for Defence* [1927] I.R. 62.

[90] See generally, P. Hogg and P. Monahan, *Liability of the Crown* (3rd ed., 2000).

[91] *Cf.* 11th Amendment to U.S. Constitution, reversing *Chisholm v. Georgia* 2 U.S. (2 Dall.) 417 (1793).

[92] See generally, D. Dobbs, *The Law of Torts* (2000), Chap.15.

for claims against the Crown relating to property and for breach of contract;[93] and in the U.S.A. the Tucker Act of 1887 empowered the Court of Claims to hear similar claims against the U.S. Government. As regards tort, the U.S. Federal Tort Claims Act 1945 and the British Crown Proceedings Act 1947, virtually abolished immunity, and similar enactments were passed in Australia, Canada and New Zealand.[94] In France, the highest court in the famous *arrêt Blanco* of 1873[95] ruled that the State could be made liable in damages for the torts of its officials, servants and agents.

It was held by the Supreme Court in *Byrne* v. *Ireland* that State immunity in tort is not one of the prerogatives or common law rules that were carried over by Articles 49 and 50 of the Constitution, and indeed that they had not even been carried over by the parallel provisions of the Free State Constitution.[96] According *to* Walsh J., "the basis of the Crown prerogatives in English law was that the King was the personification of the State",[97] but that monarchic concept of the State was expressly repudiated by Article 6 of the 1937 Constitution and indeed by Article 2 of the Free State Constitution. Therefore, the only way that sovereign immunity could exist under the Constitution is if it can be inferred from the present constitutional structure or is a necessary attribute of a sovereign State. As regards the former, some immunity is expressly granted to the President and to members of both Houses of the Oireachtas, and diplomatic immunity could be inferred from Article 29. That Article 5 describes the State as sovereign does not mean that the State has immunity from suit; this Article's principal meaning is that "the State is not amenable to any external authority for its conduct."[98] Furthermore, it is not necessary for the State to enjoy complete immunity in order for it to function effectively, as is demonstrated by the rejection of tort immunity in Britain, the United States, France and elsewhere, and by legislative provisions of the Oireachtas, such as sections 3(9) and 118 of the Factories Act 1955, and section 59 of the Civil Liability Act 1961. These provide "ample support for (the) view that immunity from suit for wrong is not a necessary ingredient of State sovereignty."[99] In general, all legal persons, including the State, should be answerable in courts for their wrongs except where the Constitution allows for immunity from suit; "there is no power, institution, or person in the land free of the law save where such immunity is expressed, or provided for in the Constitution."[100] But there is nothing in the Constitution "envisaging the writing

---

[93] Petition of Right (Ireland) Act 1873, 36 & 37 Vic. c.69.

[94] See generally, Hogg & Monahan, *supra*, n.90.

[95] Trib. Conflicts, 8 Feb. 1873, [1873] *Dalloz* III, 71; see generally, D. Fairgrieve, *State Liability in Tort* (2003), pp.12–13 and 287–288.

[96] See generally, Osborough, "The Demise of the State's Immunity in Tort" 8 *Irish Jurist* 175 (1973).

[97] [1972] I.R. 272.

[98] *Id.* at p.264.

[99] *Id.* at p.269.

into it of a theory of immunity from suit of the State ...".[101] Accordingly, the plaintiff was not prevented from prosecuting her action against the State, the correct procedure being to sue the State and to join the Attorney General in order to effect service upon the Attorney for both parties.

Walsh J. agreed that the State could lay down particular statutory duties and at the same time provide in the very legislation that the State itself shall not be bound by those duties.[102] But it cannot exempt itself from duties deriving from the Constitution except where the Constitution either expressly or by implication allows for such immunity. Whether or not the State by legislation can exempt itself, its officials or agents from duties based on the common law has not yet been determined; part of Walsh J.'s judgment in *Byrne* seems to suggest that it cannot and other parts suggest that it can, at least in particular contexts.

In 1954 the Public Authorities Protection Act 1893,[103] which gave public authorities a degree of immunity from suit, was repealed. Section 2(1) of the Ministers and Secretaries Act 1924, has been interpreted as replacing the petition of right procedure and providing that the State may be sued for breach of contract. However, the general principles governing public sector contract liability have never been authoritatively spelled out, even though there are several reported cases dealing with contractual claims against Government Ministers. Ireland has not enacted legislation along the lines of the British Crown Proceedings Act 1947, or the U.S. Federal Tort Claims Act 1945.[104]

The State not bound by Statute

Statutes used to be interpreted as not binding upon the State or on public bodies except where the Act in question either expressly or by clear implication provides that the State and those bodies must abide by the requirements.[105] The principle that the State is exempted from statutory obligations, save where the Act in question overrides that exception, was sometimes explained as being founded on the royal prerogative, and on numerous occasions counsel conceded that this prerogative was carried over by the Free State and by the 1937 Constitutions. Whereas some of the old prerogatives were declared to apply no longer by virtue of the republican nature of the present Constitution, and indeed because the Crown was not even at the core of the Free State Constitution, in 1945 the principle that statutes *prima facie* do not bind the

---

[100] *Id*, at p.281.

[101] *Ibid.*

[102] *Id.*, at p.279 but *cf. Employment Equality Bill, Re* [1997] 2 I.R. 321.

[103] 56 & 57 Vic. c.61.

[104] See generally, G. Hogan & D. Morgan, *Administrative Law in Ireland* (3rd ed., 1998), Chap.15.

[105] F. Bennion, *Statutory Interpretation* (3rd ed., 1997), pp.139–145.

State was assumed, in a case before the Supreme Court concerning rating,[106] to have been carried over and one of the judges there endorsed the principle.

However, in *Howard* v. *Commissioners of Public Works*,[107] which concerned whether the defendant there was bound by planning legislation, the Supreme Court rejected this principle, on the grounds that its roots were in the royal prerogative, it conflicted with the guarantee of equality before the law and, under the separation of powers doctrine, it is wrong to confer any special status on the executive that is not expressly provided for in the Constitution. Denham J. there endorsed views expressed by the Australian High Court that,

> "once it is accepted that a legislative intention to bind the Crown may be disclosed notwithstanding that it could not be said that that intention was 'manifest from the very terms' of the statute or that the purpose of the statute would otherwise be 'wholly frustrated', fundamental principle precludes confinement of the general words which the Legislature has used in a way which will defeat that intention. Such a legislative intent must, of course, be found in the provisions of the statute – including its subject matter and disclosed purpose and policy – when construed in a context which includes permissible intrinsic aids. If such a legislative intent does appear from the provisions of a statute when so construed, it must necessarily prevail over any judge-made rule of statutory construction, including the rule relating to statutes binding the Crown."[108]

In the event, it was held that the planning legislation there applied to the defendant and to the "interpretative centre" it was in the course of constructing.[109]

Priority in Bankruptcy

At common law, when an individual or corporation became bankrupt the Crown was entitled to be repaid whatever was owing to it from the insolvent's estate before any other creditors could obtain payment. The origins and evolution of this prerogative are explained in formidable detail by Kingsmill Moore J. in *Irish Employers Mutual Insurance Assn. Ltd., Re*[110] But it was held by the Supreme Court in that case, upholding Gavan Duffy P. in *Re P.C.*[111] that since Article 61 of the Free State Constitution required all revenues of the State to

---

[106] *Cork C.C.* v. *Cmr for Public Works* [1945] I.R. 561.
[107] [1994] 1 I.R. 101.
[108] *Id.* at p.158 quoting from *Bropho v. Western Australia*, 171 C.L.R. 1 (1990) at pp.21–22.
[109] *Cf. Howard v. Cmr for Public Works (No.3)* [1994] 3 I.R. 394.
[110] [1955] I.R. 176.
[111] [1955] I.R. 306.

be paid into a central fund "for the purposes of the Irish Free State," as a matter of legal principle public revenues ceased to belong to the Crown. Accordingly, it was held, whatever prerogative to be paid in priority as existed in respect of money owing to the State had ceased; there was "no room for that part of the prerogative which gave Crown debts priority of demand."[112] As Kingsmill Moore J. put it, following an exhaustive survey of the Free State as compared with the practice in Britain and Canada, "the Central Fund of Saorstát Éireann did not possess the characteristics of a Royal Exchequer, ... the king owned no property in Ireland, and ... therefore the prerogative of priority payment which is dependent on the existence of a royal property, claim or title had ceased to exist."[113]

These conclusions were reinforced by the fact that the Finance Act 1924, contained a provision (section 38) that all taxes owing to the Central Fund shall be preferential debts in bankruptcy; enacting this section indicated that the Free State legislature was of the view that the priority arising under the common law had ceased in 1922. Section 38 was construed somewhat narrowly by the courts and was eventually repealed in 1967.[114] However, the Bankruptcy Acts, the Companies Acts, and the Finance Acts give the State somewhat restricted priorities in insolvency.[115] Whether preferring the State over individuals and companies in this way is consistent with the Constitution's substantive guarantees has never been determined.

Treasure Trove

Another of the traditional prerogatives of the Crown was in respect of treasure trove: any treasure that was found in the State belonged not to the finder nor to the owner of the land on which it was found, but was the property of the Crown. While searching in a bog about ten miles from Cashel, the plaintiffs in *Webb v. Ireland*[116] found what has become known as the Derrynaflan hoard. This consists of a chalice, a paten and some other artefacts dating from the ninth century, and are regarded as of great historic significance and are worth millions of euro. Although the hoard is a vitally important national relic, there was no legislation regulating the ownership or disposition of such items; the National Monuments Acts 1930-1954, dealt only with monuments in the nature of mounds, buildings and the like, although there were prohibitions against exporting items such as the hoard. The State claimed ownership of the hoard *inter alia* because it was treasure trove. Insofar as the State's entitlement to treasure trove derived from the ancient royal prerogative to that effect, it was

---

[112] [1955] I.R. 241.
[113] *Id.* at p.231.
[114] Finance Act 1967, Sch.19, pt II.
[115] See generally, M. Forde, *Bankruptcy Law* (1990), pp.153 *et seq.*
[116] [1988] I.R. 353.

held not to have been carried over into Irish law in 1922 for the same reasons as were stated in the *Byrne* and the *Irish Employers' Mutual* cases.

In this instance, however, the Supreme Court went on to hold that, by virtue of the Constitution, artefacts of that kind that form an important part of the national heritage vest in the State unless they have some identifiable owner. The State therefore is in a similar position as was the Crown under the old prerogative of treasure trove, albeit on a radically different conceptual basis. According to Finlay C.J., this is because "one of the most important national assets belonging to the people is their heritage and knowledge of its true origins and the buildings and objects which constitute keys to their ancient history."[117] Consequently, one of the ingredients of national sovereignty is "ownership by the State of objects which constitute antiquities of importance which are discovered and which have no known owner."[118]

Royal Charters

There are numerous bodies in the State that were constituted by royal charter.[119] The contention that, in view of what was held in the *Byrne* and the *Webb* cases, these bodies ceased to have a legal existence since 1922, was rejected by the Supreme Court in *Geoghegan* v. *Institute of Chartered Accountants*.[120] A distinction was drawn between the content of a rule and the source of a measure. All laws and institutions existing in the United Kingdom prior to 1922 were carried over then, save where the content of a particular rule contravened the Constitution. It does not matter that the measure carried over was first promulgated by a medieval monarch. Indeed by the Adaptation of Charters Act 1926, the Government was empowered to make such amendments to charters as may be necessary to render them fully effective in the State.

High Court of Parliament

The United Kingdom House of Commons and House of Lords constitute not alone a legislative body but also the High Court of Parliament, although with one exception (appeals from the Court of Appeal to the Judicial Committee of the House of Lords) they no longer exercise any truly judicial functions. These Houses have an inherent power to conduct enquiries into any matter of public concern, including where conclusions reached may gravely damage individuals' reputations and good names, but they no longer conduct investigations where the focus is alleged wrong-doing by particular individuals not involved in government; these are usually left to formal or informal tribunals of inquiry. In

---

[117] *Id.* at p.383.
[118] *Ibid. cf. La Lavia, Re* [1999] 3 I.R. 413.
[119] See generally, M. Forde, *Company Law* (3rd ed., 1999), pp.5–7.
[120] [1995] 3 I.R. 86.

Maguire v. *Ardagh*,[121] which concerned an Oireachtas Joint Committee's enquiry into the shooting dead of a civilian in 2000 by members of the Garda Síochána, it was accepted by all parties that whatever powers the Oireachtas had in this regard did not arise by way of the carry-over provisions; any such powers had to derive from the Constitution itself, expressly or impliedly, or from legislation. In the event, it was held that there was no implied constitutional authority to carry out the type of investigation as was envisaged there.

AMENDMENT

Constitutions generally are entrenched, in the sense that they are a form of super-law that cannot be changed in the same way as ordinary laws may be repealed or amended. In other words, in constitutional democracies, a simple majority of the political community, using the normal procedures of law-making, cannot alter constitutional provisions; insofar as these may be changed, additional steps must be taken. Indeed, some constitutions do not envisage any mechanism for their alteration; similarly, particular constitutional provisions may be declared immutable. Of course such stipulations are no cast iron guarantee against constitutional amendment or repeal, except that if some purported charge does take place, that would be through unconstitutional means, as occurred in the 1990s in Eastern Europe when the entire Communist political system was abandoned in favour of constitutional democracy not very different from the Irish system. South Africa's constitutional transition in the 1990s was not quite as radical, from a purely legal perspective. As already mentioned, a criticism made of the 1937 Constitution at the time by its opponents was that it was "illegitimate," in that it did not take the form of an amendment to the Free State Constitution.[122]

Most national constitutions specify procedures which must be followed in order to amend their provisions. Thus under Article 5 of the United States Constitution, any proposed amendment must receive the approval of either two-thirds of the State legislatures or of three-quarters of a specially convened constitutional convention. Under Article 89 of the French Constitution, any proposed amendment must either be approved in a popular referendum or, alternatively, secure the support of three-fifths of the Parliament convened as Congress. And under Article 79 of the German Constitution, a proposed amendment must secure the support of two thirds of the members of each House of the Federal Parliament.

Some constitutions stipulate that certain provisions shall be entrenched in the sense that they cannot ever be altered; for instance the various American

---

[121] [2002] 1 I.R. 385; *infra*, p.114.
[122] *Supra*, p.13.

States' equal suffrage in the U.S. Senate, the republican form of government in France and also in Italy, and the "basic rights" provisions of the German Constitution. In *State (Ryan)* v. *Lennon*[123] it was held that the Free State Constitution's Article 50, which dealt with amendment, could itself be amended in accordance with the procedures it laid down and, furthermore, that the only legal restriction on amending that Constitution was that it should not conflict with the December 1921 treaty with Britain. At times, constitutional interpretation by the courts may be perceived as a form of amendment, where what is widely regarded to be the present constitutional position is rejected by the courts.

Transitional Period

The procedure for amending the Constitution is laid down in Article 46 and also in Article 51. This latter provision deals only with the first four years of the Constitution's existence and, accordingly, is no longer applicable. Under it, during the three years immediately after the first President entered office, amendments to the Constitution could be made by way of ordinary legislation. Unlike the parallel provisions in the 1922 Constitution, Article 51 stipulated that itself could not be amended by legislation, that it would cease to have force once the first President was in office for three years and, during that period, the President was empowered to veto any proposed amendment by the legislature if he believed the proposal was "of such a character and importance that the will of the people thereon ought to be ascertained by referendum ...." Subject to these conditions, therefore, constitutional amendments could be made by the Oireachtas itself up to June 25, 1941 but not after then. It would seem that an Act passed during the transitional period would not be an effective amendment unless it plainly described itself as an amending measure. At least in *State (Burke)* v. *Lennon*,[124] where the constitutionality of the internment without trial provisions of the Offences Against the State Act 1939, was contested, Gavan Duffy J. observed that counsel for the defendants were "quite right" in not arguing that this Act amended the Constitution simply because it had been passed during the three year period.[125] Two sets of amendments were made under this transitional procedure.

Immediately after the outbreak of World War II in 1939, the definition of "time of war" in the Constitution's emergencies provision (Article 28.3) was supplemented. Thenceforth, time of war is to include a time when a war is being fought abroad but in respect of which both Houses of the Oireachtas

---

[123] [1935] I.R. 170; *supra*, p.9.
[124] [1940] I.R. 136.
[125] *Id.*, at p.143. Article 46.3 stipulates how legislation proposing a constitutional amendment should describe itself but Art. 51 contains no comparable provision.

have resolved that, arising out of it, "a national emergency exists affecting the vital interests of the State."[126] Emergency legislation which was adopted under cover of this amendment has been upheld by the courts. One possible flaw in the 1939 amendment, which was not raised in the cases, is that it was adopted only in the English language; Article 25.5.4 stipulates that where there is a conflict between the Constitution's Irish and English texts the former shall prevail. Since in 1939 there was no Irish version of the extended concept of "time of war", it would seem that only the original version of that concept was valid, although such a view conflicts with the undoubted intention of the legislature in 1939. When the Constitution was again amended in 1941, that amendment contained an Irish version of the 1939 measure. Whether this latter amendment cured any defect in the 1939 amendment has not been determined by the courts; because the concept of time of war was extended further in 1941, this question is no longer of any direct legal relevance.

The Second Amendment to the Constitution, which was adopted in May 1941, was a collection of alterations of different kinds. Many of them were changes to the Constitution's Irish text, which made it more consistent with the English version. Several others may be described as drafting improvements, which removed certain inconsistencies and resolved some other uncertainties. Three substantial amendments were made at this time. The definition of "time of war" in Article 28.3 was further supplemented to include the time following the Oireachtas' declaration of an emergency and until such declaration is rescinded.[127] Various changes were made to the form of *habeas corpus* procedure provided for in Article 40.4.[128] Thirdly, whenever it decides on the constitutionality of a Bill referred to it by the President, or of a law enacted by the Oireachtas, the Supreme Court is required to give only one judgment and even the existence of concurring or dissenting opinions may not be disclosed.[129]

Subsequent Amendments

Since 1941, the procedure for making amendments to the Constitution is that laid down in Article 46. It applies to "[a]ny provision of the Constitution" and, accordingly, it would seem that this Article can be the subject of amendment itself. Amendments can be "by way of variation, addition or repeal", and it has been held that this includes a "power to clarify or make more explicit anything already in the Constitution."[130]

---

[126] *Infra*, p.866.
[127] *Ibid*.
[128] *Infra*, p.338.
[129] *Infra*, p.64.
[130] *Finn v. Attorney General* [1983] I.R. 154 at p.164.

Any proposal for amendment must originate in the Dáil; therefore, it is only the members of the Dáil who can take the initiative for amendments. The Bill must describe itself as an "Act to Amend the Constitution." Subject to this, it would seem that there is nothing preventing the amendment from taking the form of Article 2A of the Free State Constitution,[131] *i.e.* the form of detailed rules but providing that, where they conflict with the existing Constitution, those rules shall be deemed to supplant the constitutional provisions. Yet an argument can be made that such a measure falls foul of the requirement that the proposed amendment "shall not contain any other proposal." It could be said that an Article 2A-type measure is primarily ordinary legislation and, consequently, is an "other proposal." It may well be that this clause was put in the Constitution in order to prevent there being any more Article 2As.

The Bill proposing an amendment must be passed or be deemed to have passed both Houses of the Oireachtas and must then be the subject of a referendum. If a majority of the votes cast in the referendum are in favour of the Bill, it is deemed to have been passed. In that event, the Bill will be signed by the President and duly promulgated as a law, at which stage it operates to amend the Constitution.

The conduct of referenda is governed primarily by the Referendum Act 1994.[132] Following the *McKenna* case[133] in the following year, concerning the expenditure of public money in support of one side of the argument in referenda campaigns, a Referendum Commission was established to deal with perceived difficulties arising from this decision.

Four amendments made concerned EC/EU membership and three others were on the question of abortion. Some proposed amendments were rejected by the electorate; notably the 1959 and 1968 proposals to abolish proportional representation,[134] one of the 1992 proposals regarding abortion,[135] which in very similar terms was again rejected in 2002,[136] and the 2001 proposal to approve adherence to the Treaty of Nice,[137] which was resubmitted with a provision on neutrality to the electorate in 2002 and passed.[138] A proposal to remove the ban on divorce was rejected in 1986[139] but was passed nine years later in a different form.[140] In 2001, at a very late stage, the Government

---

[131] *Supra*, p.8.
[132] *Infra*, p.605.
[133] *McKenna v. An Taoiseach (No.2)* [1995] 2 I.R. 1; *infra*, p.394.
[134] Referenda of June 17, 1959 and of October 16, 1968.
[135] Referendum of November 25, 1992.
[136] Referendum of March 6, 2002.
[137] Referendum of June 7, 2001.
[138] Article 29.4.7–9; *infra*, p.253.
[139] Referendum of June 26, 1986.
[140] Article 41.3.2; *infra*, p.717.

abandoned a referendum on proposals regarding judicial accountability,[141] when it failed to obtain cross-party support for them. Those post-transition amendments which were adopted are as follows:[142]

3rd Amendment, 1972: This adopted Article 29.4.3 to enable the State to join the then European Communities.[143]

4th Amendment, 1972: This amended Article 16.2 and reduced the voting age for Dáil elections from 21 to 18 years of age.[144]

5th Amendment, 1972: This deleted from Article 44 reference to the "special position" of the Catholic Church.[145]

6th Amendment, 1979: This introduced Article 37.2, in order to avert the possibility of the Adoption Board and orders made by it being declared invalid, on the basis that the Board had been exercising powers that could only be exercised by the courts.[146]

7th Amendment, 1979: This altered Article 18.4 concerning the election of senators representing third level institutions.[147]

8th Amendment 1983: This adopted Article 40.3.3.i restricting abortion. In 1992, the proposed 12th Amendment, to change this Article in view of how it had been interpreted in the controversial *"X"* case[148] was rejected in a referendum,[149] but two other changes to this Article were adopted then.

9th Amendment, 1984: This further amended Article 16.2 to enable the franchise in Dáil elections to be extended, particularly to citizens of States that permit Irish citizens to vote in their parliamentary elections, such as the United Kingdom.[150]

10th Amendment, 1987: This amended Article 29.4.3 (adopted in 1972) and authorised the State to ratify the Single European Act of 1986,[151] which had been blocked by the *Crotty* case.[152]

11th Amendment, 1992: This adopted Articles 29.4.4 and 11, authorising the State to ratify the Treaty on European Union of 1992 ("Maastricht") and

---

[141] 22nd Amendment of the Constitution Bill, 2001, which did not pass both Houses.
[142] The voting statistics are tabulated in J. Coakley and M. Gallagher (eds), *Politics in the Republic of Ireland* (3rd ed., 1999), p.372.
[143] *Infra*, p.252.
[144] *Infra*, p.594.
[145] *Infra*, p.617.
[146] *Infra*, p.709.
[147] *Infra*, p.101.
[148] *Attorney General v. X* [1992] 1 I.R. 1; *infra*, p.723.
[149] On November 25, 1992.
[150] *Infra*, p.595.
[151] *Infra*, p.252.
[152] *Crotty v. An Taoiseach* [1987] I.R. 513; *infra*, p.230.
[153] *Infra*, p.253.

the Treaty regarding Community Patents of 1989.[153]

13th Amendment, 1992: This qualified Article 40.3.3 on abortion, by preserving the right to travel.[154]

14th Amendment, 1992: This further qualified that Article, by preserving freedom to give and to obtain information about abortion services lawfully available abroad.[155]

15th Amendment, 1996: This altered Article 41.3.2, removing the ban on divorce and laying down the circumstances in which divorce would be permitted.[156]

16th Amendment, 1996: This adopted Article 40.4.7, enabling bail to be refused where that was considered necessary to prevent the individual committing other offences.[157]

17th Amendment, 1997: This adopted Article 28.2.4.3, lifting restrictions on Cabinet confidentiality[158] identified in the *Hamilton (No.1)* case.[159]

18th Amendment, 1998: this adopted Article 29.4.5, authorising the State to ratify amendments to the Treaty on European Union done at Amsterdam in 1997.[160]

19th Amendment, 1998: This amended Articles 2 and 3 and adopted Article 29.7 and 8, giving effect to the "Belfast Agreement" concluded on 10th April of that year.[161] An unusual feature of this amendment was that it was approved in a conditional form; it became fully effective only when certain aspects of that agreement were implemented.[162]

20th Amendment, 1999: This adopted Article 28A, setting a constitutional framework for local government.[163]

21st Amendment, 2002: This adopted Article 15.5.2, abolishing the death penalty.[164]

23rd Amendment, 2002: This adopted Article 29.9, permitting the State to ratify the Statute of the International Criminal Court.[165]

26th Amendment, 2002: This adopted Article 29.4.7–9, permitting the State to ratify the Nice Treaty.[166]

---

[154] *Infra*, p.725.
[155] *Infra*, p.726.
[156] *Infra*, p.717.
[157] *Infra*, p.355.
[158] *Infra*, p.123.
[159] *Attorney General v. Hamilton (No.1)* [1993] 2 I.R. 250.
[160] *Infra*, p.253.
[161] *Infra*, p.83.
[162] Declaration Under Article 29.7 of the Constitution (Extension of Time) Act 1999.
[163] *Infra*, p.128.
[164] *Infra*, p.307.
[165] *Infra*, p.483.
[166] *Infra*, p.253.

Constitutional review

Committees have been established from time to time in order to examine the Constitution and propose amendments to it. An Oireachtas inter-party committee was constituted for this purpose in 1966 and it published its report in December 1967.[167] The only amendment that it inspired was to have the "special position" of the Catholic Church removed in 1973. An expert committee was appointed by the Government in 1995, to again review the Constitution and to "establish areas where constitutional change may be desirable or necessary", but was left to take into account that certain topics were being separately considered by the Oireachtas all-party committee on the Constitution, viz. Articles 2 and 3, divorce, bail, cabinet confidentiality and votes for emigrants. Its lengthy report, with extensive appendices, was published in May 1996.[168]

An all party Oireachtas committee was established in 1997 "in order to provide focus to the place and relevance of the Constitution and to establish those areas where constitutional change may be desirable or necessary" and, to that end, to take account of the 1996 report. To date, it has published progress reports on the Seanad, the President, the courts and the judiciary, and abortion, referenda, the parliament and the Government, and a report on private property is presently being prepared.

---

[167] Pr.9817.
[168] Pn.1632

CHAPTER 2

Judicial Review

Undoubtedly, the most profound legal difference between the pre-1922 State, on the one hand, and the Irish Free State and the Republic, on the other, is that the pre-1922 parliament was supreme whereas after 1922, laws enacted could be reviewed by the courts and struck down as invalid if they were inconsistent with the Free State Constitution or, after 1937, the present Constitution. Many regard the judicial review of laws as an inextricable feature of so-called written constitutions, especially of constitutions that seek to guarantee civil liberties and human rights.[1] Nevertheless, there are constitutions which contain similar guarantees but which do not contemplate judicial review, notably the Constitutions of the French Third and Fourth Republics, the Italian Constitution of 1848 and the 'Weimar' German Constitution of 1919. Indeed, the United States Constitution does not expressly authorise judicial review, a matter that has given rise to considerable controversy about the propriety of the U.S. courts striking down federal legislation.[2]

Because judicial review permits judges to set aside laws enacted by popularly elected assemblies, it is sometimes regarded as anti-democratic and undesirable. At one time in England it was believed that the legislature could not depart unduly from the general principles of common law; as Lord Coke put it in *Bonham's* case, "in many cases, the common law will control acts of parliament, and sometimes adjudge them to be utterly void: for when an act of parliament is against common right and reason, or repugnant, or impossible, to be performed, the common law will control it and adjudge such act to be void."[3] Yet when the English adopted a Bill of Rights in 1689[4] they did not empower the courts to set aside laws that were inconsistent with the guarantees contained in that instrument.[5] The position there has since significantly changed with the enactment of the Human Rights Act 1998.[6]

---

[1] See generally, M. Cappelletti, *Judicial Review in the Contemporary World* (1971).

[2] There is a vast literature on this subject, e.g. Rostow, "The Democratic Character of Judicial Review", 66 *Harv. L. Rev.* 193 (1952) and Praksah and Yoo, "The Origins of Judicial Review", 70 *U. Chicago L. Rev.* 887 (2003).

[3] (1610) 8 Co. Rep. 113b.

[4] 1 Wm. & Mary sess. 2, c.2.

[5] Cf. Osborough, "The Failure to Enact an Irish Bill of Rights: A Gap in Irish Constitutional History" 33 *Irish Jurist* 392 (1998).

[6] See generally, Bonner *et al*, "Judicial Approaches to the Human Rights Act" 52 *Int'l & Comp. L.Q.* 549 (2003).

JUSTICIABILITY

The authority of the courts to strike down measures that are inconsistent with the Constitution is proclaimed explicitly and implicitly in several provisions. When dealing with these, one begins with the two core clauses. Under Article 50, all laws that were in force in the Free State at the end of 1937 are carried over into the new State provided that those laws are not inconsistent with the new Constitution.[7] As for legislation enacted since December 1937, Article 15.4.1 stipulates that the Oireachtas shall not enact any law which contravenes any of the Constitution's provisions.

Many constitutions which provide for judicial review of laws restrict considerably the tribunals that can consider constitutional questions; some even restrict the categories of persons who are permitted to raise these questions before those tribunals.[8] Thus, France, Germany, Italy and South Africa have what may be described as a centralised system of judicial review; in those countries, special constitutional tribunals (the *Conseil Constitutionnel,* the *Bundesuerfassungsgericht,* the *Corte Constituzionale* and the Constitutional Court) are assigned the task of deciding on the constitutionality of legislation.[9] In France, moreover, no individual or private organisation can initiate proceedings in the *Conseil Constitutionnel.* Any 60 deputies of the *Assemblée Nationale* or of the *Sénat* can challenge the constitutionality of an Act before that tribunal but once an Act is promulgated, its constitutionality can no longer be tested.[10] Australia, Canada and the United States, by contrast, have what is termed a fully decentralised system of judicial review, *i.e.* litigants in any case and in any court can raise the question of a law's constitutionality.[11]

Reference by the President

Article 26.1 of the Constitution empowers the President to refer a Bill that has passed both Houses of the Oireachtas to the Supreme Court in order to determine if any of its provisions would be inconsistent with the Constitution. It states that "[t]he President may ... refer any Bill to which this Article applies to the Supreme Court for a decision on the question as to whether such Bill or any specified provision or provisions of such Bill is or are repugnant to this

---

[7] *Supra,* p.16.

[8] See generally, Cappelletti, *supra,* n.1, pp.45–68 and V. Jackson & M. Tushnet, *Comparative Constitutional Law* (1999), ch.6.

[9] The South African Constitutional Court is the final arbiter on all "constitutional matters," which are defined as "includ[ing] any issue involving the interpretation, protection or enforcement of the Constitution": Art.167(7) of the Constitution.

[10] Art. 61 of the Constitution.

[11] Provided, of course, they meet the requirements regarding standing, ripeness and mootness etc.; see *infra,* pp.876 *et seq.*

Constitution or to any provision thereof."[12] Before referring a Bill under this procedure, the President is obliged to consult the Council of State, a body established under the Constitution to advise the President. Any such reference to the Court must be made within seven days of the President receiving the Bill for signature. Where the Court concludes that the Bill or any of its provisions are inconsistent with the Constitution, the President may not sign the Bill; otherwise, it must be signed.

Litigants raising constitutionality

The principal judicial review mechanism in the Constitution is mixed, in that aggrieved individuals and bodies can challenge the constitutionality of laws in virtually all kinds of litigation; the constitutional question will be determined there and then by the court which is hearing the case. According to Article 34.3 of the Constitution, "[t]he Courts of First Instance shall include a High Court invested with full original jurisdiction in and power to determine all matters and questions ... (T)he jurisdiction of the High Court shall extend to the question of the validity of any law having regard to the provisions of this Constitution." But this clause goes on to provide that it is only the High Court and the Supreme Court that can rule on the constitutional status of post-1937 legislation.[13] No particular procedure is laid down in the Constitution for raising constitutional issues.[14]

The High Court and the Supreme Court's authority to review laws and other matters in the light of the constitutional provisions and guarantees is entrenched and cannot be taken away by statute. The Supreme Court's jurisdiction in this regard is expressly entrenched by Article 34.4.4, which forbids enacting any law to reduce its authority to review on appeal post-1937 laws.[15] There is no similar provision for the High Court. However, Article 34.3 (above) gives it full jurisdiction to review pre-1937 and post-1937 laws, and Article 15.4.1 forbids the Oireachtas from enacting laws which are repugnant to any provision of the Constitution. These almost certainly would be interpreted as entrenching the Court's jurisdiction in all constitutional issues.[16] So far, no law has been enacted purporting to cut down the High Court or the Supreme Court's jurisdiction on these questions.

---

[12] *Infra*, p.91.
[13] *Infra*, p.144.
[14] RSC, O.60 requires the Attorney General to be notified when constitutional issues are being canvassed.
[15] *Infra*, p.158.
[16] *Infra*, p.151.

Unreviewable issues

There are certain questions which the Constitution provides cannot be reviewed by the courts and, by their very nature, certain other questions are inherently unreviewable. Some of these are dealt with only in outline at this stage. Unlike the position under the United States Constitution, the Supreme Court does not have any general discretion to decline to hear appeals from the High Court raising constitutional law issues.[17] Nor have the Irish courts ever declined to hear a case because of the drastic political ramifications of the likely decision; there is no recognised "political question" doctrine of judicial abstention.[18] Over and above the "directive principles" in Article 45, however, it has been held that certain constitutional provisions do not confer legally enforceable rights on individuals, most notably Article 29.3, which states that "Ireland accepts the generally recognised principles of international law as its rule of conduct in its relations with other States."[19] In contrast, however, it was held that individuals could enforce Article 5, which states that "Ireland is a sovereign, independent ... State."[20]

EC measures

Article 29.4.3–9 of the Constitution provides for Ireland's accession to the European Communities/Union. Article 29.4.10 then provides that neither the EC/EU treaties nor legislation adopted under those treaties, nor any measures that the State is obliged to adopt because of Ireland's membership of the EC/ EU, can be declared unconstitutional.[21]

Emergency laws

Article 28.3 of the Constitution deals with the State's involvement in wars and with national emergencies. One of its provisions is that, where both Houses of the Oireachtas have resolved that a national emergency exists, any law then enacted for the purpose of securing public safety and the like cannot be declared unconstitutional.[22]

---

[17] The discretionary *certiorari* system was adopted in the U.S. by the Judiciary Act, 1925.
[18] Cf. *Curtin v. Minister for Defence* [2002] 2 N.Z.L.R. 744 and *McBain, ex parte Australian Catholic Bishop's Conference, Re*, 76 A.L.J.L.R. 694 (2002). See generally, McDermott, "The Separation of Powers and the Doctrine of Non-Justiciability", 35 *Irish Jurist* 280 (2000).
[19] *Kavanagh v. Governor of Mountjoy Prison* [2002] 3 I.R. 97; *infra*, p.240.
[20] *Crotty v. An Taoiseach* [1987] I.R. 713; *infra*, p.230.
[21] *Infra*, p.262.
[22] *Infra*, p.867.

Conduct of the President

By virtue of Article 13.8.1 of the Constitution, the President is not answerable before any court for his official conduct.[23] The only way in which complaints of abuse of power by the President can be considered is through the impeachment procedure laid down in Article 12.10.

Provisions referred under Article 26

Where the Supreme Court upholds the provisions of a Bill referred to it by the President under the Article 26 procedure, described above, the constitutionality of those provisions can never again be challenged in the courts. It is provided by Article 34.3.3 of the Constitution that "[n]o court whatever shall have jurisdiction to question the validity *of* a law, or any provision of a law, the Bill for which shall have been referred ... under Article 26 ..., or to question the validity of a provision of a law where the corresponding provision in the Bill for such law shall have been referred ...under ...Article 26." It is possible that this clause refers to provisions of Bills which were upheld under this procedure only since the present Supreme Court was established in 1961.

Bills before the Oireachtas

Bills being considered by one or both Houses of the Oireachtas, or Bills about to be introduced into either House, cannot be challenged in the courts on the grounds that their provisions are inconsistent with those of the Constitution. So it was held in *Wireless Dealers' Assn. v. Fair Trade Commission,*[24] where the Supreme Court declined to enjoin the Minister from sponsoring in the Seanad a Bill that had passed the Dáil and which the plaintiffs claimed was unconstitutional. But once a Bill has passed both Houses, it appears that it can be the subject of a constitutional challenge,[25] although the argument may be made that such proceedings should not be entertained because they would have the practical effect of preventing the President from referring the Bill in question to the Supreme Court under Article 26.

Referenda

The substantive merits of a proposal to amend the Constitution, being put before the electorate in a referendum, cannot be challenged. No matter how obnoxious, eccentric, contradictory or inexplicable the proposal is, it is not a matter for the courts to pass judgment on; it is left to the people to decide what

---

[23] *Infra*, p.90.
[24] Unreported, High Court, March 14, 1956.
[25] *Westco Lagan Ltd v. Attorney General* [2002] 2 N.Z.L.R. 40.

their Constitution should contain.[26] But it would appear that any proposal for amendment that does not comply with the amending machinery contained in Article 46 may be challenged. In *Morris v. Minister for the Environment*,[27] concerning the 2002 abortion referendum, at the outset the defendant claimed that there was no jurisdiction to consider compatibility of the proposal with this Article but, in the event, he declined to pursue that contention. The manner in which referenda are conducted may be challenged under the petition procedure contained in Part IV (section 42–58) of the Referendum Act 1994.[28]

Money bills

Article 21 of the Constitution treats what are called "money bills" somewhat differently from other Bills introduced in the legislature. Disputes about whether a particular Bill is indeed a money bill are resolved by a special Committee of Privileges, whose decision is "final and conclusive."[29]

Impeachment

Article 12.10 contains a mechanism for impeaching the President[30] and Article 35.4 is the means of removing judges of the High Court and of the Supreme Court.[31] Both involve resolutions of each House of the Oireachtas. Whether the courts have any say in the procedure being followed by either House in those circumstances, or regarding the grounds being put forward for removal, is debateable.

Advisory opinions

Apart from the Article 26 procedure, whereby the President may refer a Bill to the Supreme Court for a ruling or its constitutionality, the courts will not determine a constitutional question that does not relate to an on-going legal dispute. They will not facilitate a genuinely interested individual or body by way of giving advice about whether some action or proposed measure would be constitutional.[32] They have adopted doctrines of *locus standi*, ripeness and mootness to ensure that parties will not use them for this purpose.[33]

---

[26] *Infra*, p.608.
[27] [2002] 1 I.R. 326; *infra*, p.606.
[28] *Infra*, p.605.
[29] *Infra*, p.104.
[30] *Infra*, p.95.
[31] *Infra*, p.162.
[32] E.g., *Thorpe v. The Commonwealth (No.3)* (1997) 71 A.L.J.L.R. 767.
[33] *Infra*, pp.876 *et seq.*

"Hands Off" issues

There are other issues that, although not made unreviewable by the Constitution's express or implied requirements, courts abstain from being involved in to some extent, on the grounds that they are uniquely or predominantly matters for either House to determine or for the Government or other executive agency to resolve. Where what is being challenged concerns the internal affairs of either or both Houses of the Oireachtas, the allocation of public funds, foreign relations and questions involving security or defence, at times the courts demonstrate considerable deference to the House in question or to the executive. But there is no fully coherent pattern in the case law and much depends on the composition of the Supreme Court from time to time. Often when the Court decides not to invalidate a decision of the Government that is being challenged, it refers to the respect that one "great organ of State owes to the other," a cliché signifying that the subject matter of the decision is highly political and the Court is loath to interfere with the political process.

That the decision or measure being challenged arises in a very political context has not prevented the Court from declaring it to be unconstitutional from time to time. Because legislation "repugnant to ... *any* provisions of the Constitution" (apart from Article 45) is invalid, all acts of the Government incompatible with them must also be invalid. Thus in *Crotty v. An Taoiseach*,[34] the decision to ratify the Single European Act was held to be incompatible with Article 5's stipulation that Ireland is a "sovereign, independent, democratic state." In *McKenna v. An Taoiseach (No.2)*[35] it was held that the Government's decision, concurred in by the Dáil, to spend £500,000 in support of a "yes" vote in the forthcoming referendum on divorce contravened Article 40.1's guarantee of "equality before the law." On the other hand, Article 29.1-3 of the Constitution has been consistently held not to grant rights to individuals, with the consequence that State action that is unlawful in international law will not be declared to be invalid or to be the basis of any other judicial remedy; this Article's requirements have been held to be merely "statements of principles or guidelines rather than binding rules on the Executive."[36]

On the basis of this reasoning about Article 29.1-3, it seems that the words "any provision" in Article 15.4.1 of the Constitution cannot mean what they would appear to mean but, instead, mean only those provisions as the courts conclude confer rights on individuals. In other words, it appears, at least some constitutional provisions are equivalent to private law rules and, unless a plaintiff can point to a violation to his own material and discrete detriment, there is no judicial remedy; the existence of the plaintiff's right and his *locus standi* to institute the proceedings are all the same. As a result of this logic, an

---

[34] [1987] I.R. 713.
[35] [1995] 2 I.R. 1.
[36] *Horgan v. An Taoiseach* [2003] 2 I.L.R.M. 357 at p.397.

Act of the Oireachtas that is repugnant to Article 29.1–3 would be unconstitutional but, because it does not offend against any individual's rights, it cannot be challenged in the courts other than through the Article 26 procedure. Further, although the President in this manner can prevent violations of Article 29.1-3 taking place, the Government and other executive authority have impunity to contravene public international law in any way they wish, unless of course in doing so they violate some other constitutional provision. Whether there are other comparable non-rights creating constitutional provisions remains to be seen. But for the *Crotty* decision, Article 5 of the Constitution also would seem to comprise "statements of principle as guidelines rather than binding rules...."[37]

THE PRESUMPTION OF CONSTITUTIONALITY

When determining the constitutional validity of legislation or a regulation, or of a Bill referred under the Article 26 procedure, the courts apply what is known as the presumption of constitutionality. Provisions of Acts of the Oireachtas being challenged or of Bills so referred by the President are presumed to be constitutional and the onus is on those who seek to establish their unconstitutionality. Further, if it is possible to decide the case in a manner that does not require addressing the constitutional issue at all, or if that issue can be avoided by way of statutory construction, generally the provision in question will be allowed to stand. An argument that the presumption does not apply in Article 26 references was rejected by the Supreme Court.[38] A variant of this presumption is that, where a particular provision is found to be invalid, the court will endeavour to "sever" it from its surrounding provisions, if the severed parts are capable of being operated and in the manner that the Oireachtas would have envisaged.[39] From time to time in recent years, Acts have been passed that expressly acknowledged that they may be unconstitutional in part but providing that they shall not be operative to that extent.[40]

Justifications

As applied to Acts of the Oireachtas which were passed since December 1937 and to Bills referred under Article 26, the primary justification for the presumption of constitutionality is that the courts should assume that, when

---

[37] *Ibid.*

[38] *Sections 5 and 10 of the Illegal Immigrants (Trafficking) Bill 1999, Re* [2000] 2 I.R. 360 at pp.367–370.

[39] *Infra*, p.892.

[40] *Infra*, p.291.

adopting the measure in question, the Oireachtas sought to comply with the Constitution. In Budd J.'s words, "the legislative body must be deemed to legislate with a knowledge of the Constitution and presumably does not intend by its measures to infringe it."[41] This justification his been described as the "respect which one great organ of State owes another."[42]

A second justification, which need not be confined to post-1937 laws, is that the courts should hesitate to strike down legislation because, by doing so, they may leave a legislative void which it is not within their power to fill. Indiscriminate invalidation of laws would disrupt orderly government and could result in considerable hardship for many persons. As Henchy J. explained, a court "unmakes what was put forth as a law by the legislature, but unlike the legislature, it cannot enact a law in its place;" accordingly if the power to strike down laws "were used indiscriminately it would tend to upset the structure of government...."[43]

Another justification for the presumption is the normal rule of evidence and procedure, that the burden of proof and onus of persuasion lies on the party who is making a particular claim; those who assert the unconstitutionality of laws or indeed of other measures carry the onus of establishing that proposition.

Another justification still is that the State is a parliamentary democracy which is based on the principle of majority rule and, while that principle is bounded by constitutional constraints, majority rule in a constitutional democracy demands that in a closely balanced case the majority's decision be given the benefit of the doubt.[44] If the majority indeed acted improperly, the next or second next Government may very well rectify matters. This is particularly the case with legislation regulating business and economic questions; the Oireachtas and not the courts are the best judges of what measures the economic situation calls for.[45] Ever since the mid-1930s, the United States Supreme Court has demonstrated a marked reluctance to strike down economic legislation no matter how unwise the measure appears to be.[46] When it allows State parties a wide "margin of appreciation" in determining how they limit the exercise of guaranteed rights for reasons such as public safety, national security and protecting the rights and freedoms of others, the European Court of Human Rights applies a principle which is similar to the presumption of constitutionality.

---

[41] *Educational Co. of Ireland Ltd v. Fitzpatrick (No. 2)* [1961] I.R. 345 at p.368.

[42] *Buckley v. Attorney General* [1950] I.R. 67 at p.80.

[43] *State (Woods) v. Attorney General* [1969] I.R. 385 at p.398.

[44] Because the US Constitution does not expressly authorise the invalidation of federal legislation, the US courts place special emphasis on this justification for the presumption.

[45] Chap.26 *infra* on "economic rights."

[46] *E.g.*, *Minnesota v. Clover Leaf Creamery Co.*, 449 U.S. 456 (1980).

Applications

The presumption of constitutionality manifests itself in several ways.

Onus of persuasion

As has just been stated, one application of this presumption is in requiring a party who is asserting unconstitutionality to establish his case. Sometimes unconstitutionality can be demonstrated on the basis of legal argument alone; on other occasions it is necessary to go into evidence. For instance in *Ryan v. Attorney General*,[47] which concerned the scheme to put fluoride into domestic water supplies, most of the 65 days trial involved giving testimony, much of it from expert witnesses. In the event, the plaintiff's claims were rejected. In *Norris v. Attorney General*,[48] where the plaintiff contended that provisions outlawing certain homosexual practices were unconstitutional, extensive expert evidence was given for the plaintiff but the State did not call any witnesses; nevertheless, the plaintiff lost his case.

Deciding on other grounds

If the case can be decided on grounds which do not involve considering a law's constitutional status, it will be determined on those grounds and the constitutional issues will not be addressed.[49] For instance, in *Irish Family Planning Association v. Ryan*,[50] the plaintiff launched an extensive constitutional attack on the laws regarding the censorship of publications. But the case was decided on the basis of the interpretation of a section in those Acts and, consequently, the constitutional issues did not require to be determined. Similarly in *Roche v. Minister for Industry and Commerce*,[51] the plaintiffs sought *inter alia* to have provisions of the Minerals Development Acts, 1940–79, declared invalid. However, the court found that the Minister had not complied with the procedures laid down in one of those Acts' sections and, consequently, the constitutional claims no longer called for determination.[52]

A variant of this approach is the case where a party is challenging both the validity of regulations issued under a law and the provisions which purport to authorise adoption of those regulations. If the regulations are *ultra vires* the Act in question, it is no longer necessary to deal with the issue of the Act's

---

[47] [1965] I.R. 294; *infra*, p.638.
[48] [1984] I.R 36; *infra*, p.661.
[49] See generally, H. Delaney & D. McGrath, *Civil Procedure in the Superior Courts* (2001), pp.486–488.
[50] [1979] I.R. 295; *infra*, p.551.
[51] [1978] I.R. 149; *infra*, p.736.
[52] Similarly see *M. v. An Bord Uchtála* [1977] I.R. 287.

constitutionality. For instance in *Cooke v. Walsh*,[53] the plaintiff contended that provisions of the Health Act 1970, and certain regulations issued under them violated the constitutional separation of powers. However, those regulations were found to be *ultra vires* the 1970 Act and therefore were invalid; consequently, it was not necessary to consider the Act's constitutional status.

Occasionally, the courts express a view on the constitutionality of an impugned provision where, in the circumstances, it was not essential for the case that they do so. At times this is done because it is in the general public interest to have constitutional doubts about particular measures laid to rest; on other occasions it may be done out of deference to the arguments made by counsel. In *Crotty v. An Taoiseach*,[54] where the Single European Act was claimed to be unconstitutional on its face, the High Court ruled that the plaintiff did not possess the *locus standi* to challenge that Act's validity on various grounds. Nevertheless, "[i]n deference ... to the able and elaborate arguments which have been advanced ... by counsel on both sides,"[55] the Court gave its view that the Act would withstand the challenge based on those grounds. However, on appeal the Supreme Court held that Part III of this measure was unconstitutional.

In *Murphy v. G.M.*,[56] where the freezing of money under the Proceeds of Crime Act 1996, was challenged on several non-constitutional grounds, as well as the Act itself being challenged, O'Higgins J. declined to deal first with the non-constitutional aspects and ruled that all the issues in the case should be dealt with at the one time, notwithstanding that this would lead to a very protracted hearing. His judgment does not record why he took this unusual step, which was urged on him by the plaintiff, an officer of the Criminal Assets Bureau.

Double construction

Where a provision is capable of two or more meanings, one of which would render it unconstitutional and the other is constitutionally acceptable, the provision will be given the latter meaning. For instance, dealing with provisions that purported to grant the lower courts extensive and perhaps excessive jurisdiction, O'Byrne J. observed that "if the statute can reasonably be construed as to comply with the provisions of the Constitution, such construction should be placed upon it."[57] And dealing with provisions restricting appeals to the Supreme Court perhaps excessively, Walsh J. said that "it must be assumed that the Oireachtas ... did not intend to violate the constitutional provisions

---

[53] [1984] I.R. 710; *infra*, p.177.
[54] [1987] I.R. 713.
[55] *Id.* at p.760.
[56] Unreported, High Court, June 4, 1999.
[57] *Grimes v. Owners of S.S. Bangor Bay* [1948] I.R. 350 at p.358.

referred to unless the statutory provision leads to no other possible construction."[58]

A striking example of this rule or practice is *J.H., Re*,[59] which concerned statutory powers to deprive parents of custody of their children. The Guardianship of Infants Act 1964, authorises the courts to grant custody to persons other than the child's parents in certain circumstances where doing so promotes the "welfare of the infant."[60] This latter term means how, from the child's point of view, its best interests are served. Article 42 of the Constitution, however, confers on married parents inalienable rights with regard to the custody and education of their children, which can be forfeited only in the most exceptional circumstances. It was held by the Supreme Court that, in deciding who shall have custody of married parents' children, the provisions of the 1964 Act must be construed in the light of this guarantee. Accordingly, those provisions cannot "be construed as meaning simply that the balance of the [child's] welfare ... must be the sole criterion for the determination by the Court of the issue."[61] Where the parents are married, those provisions "must be construed as involving a constitutional presumption that the welfare of the child ... is to be found within the family" unless exceptional circumstances or compelling reasons otherwise have been established to the court's satisfaction.[62] Where it is at all possible to construe an Act in a manner which is consistent with the Constitution, then the Act should be given that meaning. It is only where the statutory provisions obviously conflict with the Constitution that they will be struck down as invalid.

Discretionary authority

A variant of the double construction rule which is resorted to frequently is that, where a provision grants some degree of discretionary authority, it will be interpreted as only authorising action which is consistent with the constitutional requirements and, accordingly, must be construed as not sanctioning unconstitutional activity. Where the Oireachtas gives discretionary authority to the executive, it is presumed that the authority will be exercised in a manner that complies with constitutionally required fair procedures, will not be exercised in an arbitrary or capricious fashion and will not be used to violate individuals' personal rights. But it would appear, this particular aspect of the presumption of constitutionality is subject to exceptions, the ambit of which remains to be worked out.

---

[58] *People (Attorney General) v. Conmey* [1975] I.R. 341 at p.362.
[59] [1985] I.R. 375.
[60] Ss.16, 3 and 2.
[61] [1985] I.R. 394.
[62] *Id.* at p.395.

In those two leading cases on business regulation, *McDonald v. Bord na gCon*,[63] and *East Donegal Co-Operative Society v. Attorney General*,[64] Walsh J.'s judgments for the Supreme Court contain the definitive statement of this principle. In the *McDonald* case, dealing with provisions that on their face seemed to permit the most arbitrary use of investigatory procedures, Walsh J. held that "the wording of the provisions ... does not exclude the application of the principles of natural justice to these investigations. While the Board may determine the manner in which the investigation shall be carried out the clear words or necessary implication which would be required to exclude the principles of natural justice from such investigation are not present in the sections."[65] In the *East Donegal* case, dealing with provisions that seemed to give the Minister an unfettered discretion and accordingly would permit arbitrary decisions, it was held that those cannot be interpreted to that effect. On account of the presumption of constitutionality, decisions by the Minister must be made in accordance with fair procedures and be consistent with the general policies underlying the Act and its general structure. According to Walsh J., "the presumption of constitutionality carries with it not only the presumption that the constitutional interpretation or construction is the one intended by the Oireachtas but also that the Oireachtas intended that proceedings, procedures, discretions and adjudications which are permitted, provided for or prescribed by an Act ... are to be conducted in accordance with the principles of constitutional justice."[66]

Laws providing for the regulation of political activity also have been interpreted in this fashion. In *Loftus v. Attorney General*,[67] which concerned provisions for registering political parties, the contention that these powers could be exercised arbitrarily was rejected on the grounds that "[w]hile [the registrar] is given a discretion to register or not register, this is not an unfettered discretion. He is bound to act fairly and judicially in accordance with the Constitution. Accordingly he must consider every application on its merits. ..If the registrar exercised his discretion or his powers capriciously, partially or in a manifestly unfair manner, it would be assumed that this could not have been contemplated or intended by the Oireachtas and his action would be restrained and corrected by the Courts. Therefore, the absence (from the Act] of standards or criteria does not mean that the registrar has a discretion to ignore constitutional rights ...".[68]

Similarly with laws which grant the executive powers vis-à-vis the courts

---

[63] [1965] I.R. 217; *infra*, p.774.

[64] [1970] I.R. 317; *infra*, p.779.

[65] [1965] I.R. 217 at p.243.

[66] [1970] I.R. 317 at p.341.

[67] [1979] I.R. 221; *infra*, p.588.

[68] *Id.* at p.241; similarly *State (Lynch) v. Cooney* [1982] I.R. 337 at p.360.

and the judiciary; it is presumed that those powers will be exercised in a manner as *inter alia* respects the constitutional scheme for the separation of powers and the principle of judicial independence. In *Eccles v. Ireland*,[69] where it was contended that powers given to the Government regarding the appointment and remuneration of members of the Special Criminal Court contravened these principles, this argument was rejected on the grounds that it is to be presumed that those discretionary powers will be applied in a manner consistent with the Constitution.[70] But it is difficult to understand how an individual can get the information to ensure that judicial independence is always being maintained in making these appointments.

Why this presumption was not applied by the Supreme Court in *D.K. v. Crowley*[71] is not explained nor even adverted to in the judgment given by Keane C.J. It concerned the Domestic Violence Act 1996, s. 4(3) of which authorises the District or the Circuit Court to make *ex parte* "barring orders," compelling persons temporarily to leave their homes because they are likely to cause significant harm to persons there. Under the Circuit Court Rules, successful applicants for those orders had to further apply within eight days, on notice to the addressee of the orders, to have them extended; but there was no equivalent requirement for applications in the District Court. It was principally because District Court *ex parte* barring orders could continue for several weeks, without ever being reviewed, that s. 4(3) was declared invalid by the Supreme Court, even though this constitutional deficiency could easily be remedied by implying into the sub-section an obligation to promptly apply for an extension of such order as was granted. Indeed, the plaintiff's *locus standi* there is questionable because, within days of the *ex parte* order having been made, he applied to have it discharged but then declined to pursue his application on the day fixed for the hearing.

This presumption was adverted to in *Cox v. Ireland*[72] but no indication was given why it did not apply there. It concerned s. 34 of the Offences Against the State Act 1939, that operated to deprive public officials, who were convicted in the Special Criminal Court, of their jobs and their pension entitlements. Section 34(5) of this gave the Government an absolute discretion to remit, in whole or in part, the application of this section. Notwithstanding, the entire section 34 was declared invalid by the Supreme Court and subsection (5) "does not save the section from its constitutional invalidity."[73]

---

[69] [1985] I.R. 545; *infra*, p.854.
[70] *Id.* at p.544.
[71] [2002] 2 I.R. 744; *infra*, p.490.
[72] [1992] 2 I.R. 503; *infra*, p.795.
[73] *Id.* at p.524.

Pre-1937 measures

The justification most often advanced for the presumption of constitutionality and for the various applications of that principle is that it should be assumed that the Oireachtas sought to exercise its powers in accordance with the constitutional provisions. In Barrington J.'s words, "(t)his presumption arises from the respect which each of the great organs of state owes to each other. Each will assume that the other is attempting properly to perform its constitutional function ...".[74] The question, therefore, arises whether pre-December 1937 laws and regulations enjoy an equivalent presumption. On several occasions it has been held that Acts of the Free State Oireachtas and Acts of the pre-1922 Union Parliament "enjoy no such presumption in respect of the provisions of the Constitution ...".[75]

Some such presumption can be justified, however, on grounds other than the respect which should be paid to the present Oireachtas and, to that extent, pre-1937 laws and perhaps even pre-1922 laws enjoy some presumption of constitutionality. This may particularly be the case with laws enacted since 1922 and where a similar constitutional provision in question was also contained in the Free State Constitution, in that it is fair to assume that the Free State Oireachtas did not intend to contravene that provision.[76] The fact that pre-1937 laws were carried over into the new State by Article 50 suggests that, where it is reasonably possible to do so, all such laws should be given the benefit of the doubt.[77] Indeed the very first case in which the presumption was articulated, *Pigs Marketing Board v. Donnelly (Dublin) Ltd.*,[78] concerned a challenge to pre-December 1937 laws, the Pigs and Bacon Acts 1935-1937. Where pre-1937 provisions were amended by the present Oireachtas, it would seem that such action confers on the amended sections the fuller presumption enjoyed by post-1937 laws. Whether making those amendments also constitutes a post-1937 endorsement of the remainder of the Act is questionable.

PRINCIPLES OF CONSTITUTIONAL INTERPRETATION

The Constitution is a document which contains numerous general principles and rules, prescriptions and prohibitions. When a dispute arises as to whether a particular action or course of conduct is required or is forbidden by the Constitution, the answer is often patently obvious. To take some examples at random: the President's term of office is seven years from the date of taking

---

[74] *Crotty v. An Taoiseach* [1987] I.R. 713 at p.743.
[75] *de Burca v. Attorney General* [1976] I.R. 38 at p.45.
[76] *Cf. Garvey v. Ireland* [1981] I.R. 75.
[77] *E.g., Norris v. Attorney General* [1984] I.R. 36.
[78] [1939] I.R. 413; *infra*, p.768.

up the office; women are entitled to vote in Dáil, Seanad and Presidential elections and in referenda; the State may not charge fees for primary school education. Frequently, however, the correct answer to a particular question about a constitutional claim is not obvious from what the instrument says. Many of the Constitution's provisions are extremely vague and ideologically loaded, capable of sustaining a variety of meanings. To take the 1983 Amendment concerning the unborn's right to life and the question of abortion: it is anything but clear from the words used in what circumstance terminating a pregnancy is permissible under Article 40.3.3. Similarly, it is far from obvious exactly when discrimination between individuals is proscribed by Article 40.1 or when the compulsory acquisition of a person's property is forbidden by Article 40.3.2.

Where the correct answer to a constitutional problem is not obvious from the instrument's text, then the court or whoever else is called upon to resolve the question must resort to interpretation, *i.e.* decide what the words mean in context and with reference to the particular dispute. One of the main tasks of lawyers and courts is interpreting documents; virtually every day judges are called upon to determine what the terms of a contract, a will, a settlement, a regulation or an Act of the Oireachtas mean. Over the years courts have developed general principles regarding the interpretation of laws.[79] Some of the most ambiguous terms that commonly occur in statutes are defined or explained by the Interpretation Act 1937. How international treaties should be construed has for long been a source of some controversy until the proper approach was resolved by the Vienna Convention on the Law of Treaties;[80] according to Article 31, a treaty "shall be interpreted in good faith in accordance with the ordinary meaning to be given to the terms of the treaty in their context and in the light of its object and purpose ...". But there are no settled principles and rules of constitutional interpretation. In recent years, the proper approach to construing constitutions has generated a vast scholarly literature in the United States, with many eminent authors advocating different approaches to the question.[81]

When interpreting a contract or a deed, what the courts endeavour to do is to ascertain the parties' true intent when they used the words in question. Similarly, in statutory interpretation, the purpose is to find out what the Oireachtas intended when it chose certain words. But where those words are ambiguous, it is likely that different legislators would have attributed slightly different meanings to them if they had been asked about their own subjective intentions when voting on the measure. Accordingly, the purpose of

---

[79] See generally, F. Bennion, *Statutory Interpretation* (4th ed., 2002).

[80] Of May 23, 1969, 1155 UNTS 331.

[81] See generally, L. Tribe, *American Constitutional Law* (3rd ed., 2000), pp. 30 *et seq.* and Barak, "The Supreme Court – Foreword: A Judge on Judging: The Role of a Supreme Court in a Democracy" 116 *Harv. L. Rev.* (2002) at pp.62 *et seq.*

interpretation is to find some objective intention attributable to them. It is even more difficult with a constitution that has been adopted by the people as a whole, to determine what objectively they intended when a majority of them approved the instrument some 65 years ago. This task is not quite as daunting when looking for the true meaning of an amendment adopted more recently. As explained by an eminent Canadian judge,

> "The task of expounding a constitution is crucially different from that of construing a statute. A statute defines present rights and obligations. It is easily enacted and as easily repealed. A constitution, by contrast, is drafted with an eye to the future. Its function is to provide a continuing framework for the legitimate exercise of governmental power and, when joined by a Bill or Charter of Rights, for the unremitting protection of individual rights and liberties. Once enacted, its provisions cannot easily be repealed or amended. It must, therefore, be capable of growth and development over time to meet new social, political and historical realities often unimagined by its framers. The judiciary is the guardian of the constitution and must, in interpreting its provisions, bear these considerations in mind."[82]

The text

The most important principle of interpretation is the elementary rule that the ordinary meaning of the Constitution's words override all other considerations. Especially however when many of these words are open-ended and are capable of several specific meanings that could not be said to be wrong, ascertaining their "true" meaning is no easy endeavour. Unlike statutes, there are no well established principles and rules of construction to guide those who draw up constitutions. A particular requirement's proper or true meaning does not turn entirely on what dictionaries indicate but on the provision in question in its context, taking account of its provenance, and the overall objectives and structure of the Constitution. Moreover, what a provision may actually mean can vary over time, in the sense that developments in society may induce the courts to look again at it and conclude that, in the present day and age, it should not be confined to the meaning attributed to it previously. It is because full account must be taken of context, including current political and social conditions, that a provision's strict linguistic meaning may not be its proper legal meaning.

---

[82] *Hunter v. Southam Inc.* 11 D.L.R. 4th 641 (1984) at p.649.

Fundamental fairness in the common law

It would seem that where the Constitution's very terms are at variance with traditional conceptions of fundamental fairness at common law, its literal meaning nevertheless prevails. At least the Supreme Court has applied the literal meaning of the Constitution where that ran counter to a long-standing legal tradition and where probably those who drafted the Constitution did not intend to override that practice. In *People (D.P.P.) v. O'Shea*,[83] the issue was whether the prosecution in a criminal case could appeal to the Supreme Court against the defendant's acquittal in the High Court. To permit such an appeal would violate one of the fundamental principles of criminal justice, the rule against double jeopardy *(nemo bis in idem debet vexari)*. But Article 34.4.3° provides that the Supreme Court has appellate jurisdiction from "all decisions of" the High Court, subject to such exceptions and regulations as are prescribed by law. A divided Supreme Court held that the word "all" here must be given its literal meaning, even though that results in a situation which conflicts with what traditionally has been regarded as fair play in criminal procedure.

Henchy J. dissented vigorously from such ultra-literalism, observing that:

> "[t]he validity of this syllogism depends on the soundness of its major premise, *i.e.*, that an appeal lies from every decision of the High Court save those validly excepted by law. I agree that if the relevant sub-section of the Constitution is looked at in isolation and is given a literal reading, it would lend itself to that interpretation. But I do not agree that such an approach is a correct method of constitutional interpretation. Any single constitutional right or power is but a component in an ensemble of interconnected and interacting provisions which must be brought into play as part of a larger composition, and which must be given such an integrated interpretation as will fit it harmoniously into the general constitutional order and modulation. It may be said of a constitution, more than of any other legal instrument, that 'the letter killeth, but the spirit giveth life.' No single constitutional provision (particularly one designed to safeguard personal liberty or the social order) may be isolated and construed with undeviating literalness."[84]

Internal consistency

Where two or more provisions of the Constitution tend to point in different directions, they should be interpreted in such a way that they blend with each other; what is described as "horizontal balancing." In Henchy J.'s words, they "must be given such an integrated interpretation as will fit (them) harmoniously

---

[83] [1982] I.R. 384; *infra*, p.480.
[84] *Id.* at p.426.

into the general constitutional order and modulation."[85] An instance where the Court resolved apparent internal inconsistencies and confusion was *Tormey v. Ireland*,[86] which like *O'Shea,* also concerned a question of criminal procedure, *viz.,* whether or to what extent the High Court can be deprived of its jurisdiction to try cases by that jurisdiction being conferred exclusively on the Circuit Court. According to Article 34.3.1, the High Court has "full original jurisdiction in and power to determine all matters and questions, whether of law or fact ...". To give the Circuit Court exclusive jurisdiction over certain categories of case demonstrably conflicts with the literal meaning of this clause. However, Article 34.3.4° stipulates that other courts of first instance shall be established, such as the Circuit Court. It was held by the Supreme Court in *Tormey* that the former clause must be read alongside the latter and that their aggregate effect is that exclusive jurisdiction in particular categories of cases may be conferred on the Circuit Court, provided that the High Court retains a supervisory jurisdiction over that Court. Such an arrangement, it was held, is more consistent with fundamental fairness and equality before the law, because it would be most unfair if one party in a case invariably could insist that the trial must take place in the High Court. Dealing with the proper approach to constitutional interpretation,

Henchy J., for the Court, said that:

> "despite its unqualified and unambiguous term [the above clause] cannot be given an entirely literal construction. The rule of literal interpretation, which is generally applied in the absence of ambiguity or absurdity in the text, must here give way to the more fundamental rule of constitutional interpretation that the Constitution must be read as a whole and that its several provisions must not be looked at in isolation, but be treated as interlocking parts of the general constitutional scheme. This means that where two constructions of a provision are open in the light of the Constitution as a whole, despite the apparent unambiguity of the provision itself, the court should adopt the construction which will achieve the smooth and harmonious operation of the Constitution. A judicial attitude of strict construction should be avoided when it would allow the imperfection or inadequacy of the words used to defeat or pervert any of the fundamental purposes of the Constitution. It follows from such global approach that, save where the Constitution itself otherwise provides, all its provisions should be given due weight and effect and not be subordinated one to the other. Thus where there are two provisions in apparent conflict with one another, there should be adopted, if possible, an interpretation which will give due and harmonious effect to both

---

[85] *Ibid.*
[86] [1985] I.R. 289; *infra*, p.148.

provisions. The true purpose and range of a Constitution would not be achieved if it were treated as no more than the sum of its parts."[87]

Hierarchy of values

It is notorious that many of the settled rules of statutory construction contradict each other; so too, it would seem, do the principles of constitutional interpretation. For while the courts should try to harmonise apparently conflicting clauses, nevertheless there are some clauses that are more important than others, and those exceptional clauses take precedence over the more ordinary clauses. This is the process of what is described as "vertical-balancing." Perhaps the best example is in *O'B. v. S.*,[88] where a party contested the validity of a rule that if a person died intestate and was survived, on the one hand by a non-marital child and on the other by a brother or sister or an aunt or uncle, the non-marital child cannot inherit the intestate deceased's estate. Discrimination of this nature would appear to conflict with Article 40.1's guarantee of equality. But the Supreme Court held that account must also be had of Article 43's guarantees regarding the family based on marriage and that the discriminatory rule in the Succession Act 1965, was justifiable under this latter Article, which in a sense took precedence.

Some of the constitutional guarantees of individual rights are not expressly qualified and others are formulated as being subject to various qualifications. But many of these rights, it has been held, are subject to the general qualification that they must not be exercised in a manner that conflicts with the constitutional rights of others. Therefore, a balance frequently must be struck. Furthermore, where the case in question is a dispute between an individual and the State, the State is entitled to plead the necessity of protecting other individuals' rights and indeed the common good as justification for its *prima facie* unconstitutional action. According to Griffin J. in *People v. Shaw*,[89] which was another criminal procedure case:

"The existence in a Constitution of certain guaranteed civil, as distinct from natural, fundamental human rights does not mean that a person is entitled to insist on a particular guaranteed right to the exclusion or disregard of another person's guaranteed right, or of the common good. Indeed, many of the guaranteed personal rights under our Constitution are expressly limited in their application. But even where there is no such express limitation, it is a fundamental canon of construction, as well as being a phenomenon of every legal order, that rights, whether constitutional or merely legal, are prone to come into conflict with one

---

[87] *Id.* at pp.295–296.
[88] [1984] I.R. 316.
[89] [1982] I.R. 1.

another to such an extent that in particular circumstances one of them
must yield right of way to another. If possible, fundamental rights under
a Constitution should be given a mutually harmonious application, but
when that is not found possible, the hierarchy or priority of the conflicting
rights must be examined, both as between themselves and in relation to
the general welfare of society. This may involve the toning down or even
the putting into temporary abeyance of a particular guaranteed right so
that, in a fair and objective way, the more pertinent and important right
in a given set of circumstances may be preferred and given application."[90]

Of course, the great difficulty with two-tiered, and even more so with multi-
tiered, constitutional provisions is ascertaining which clauses have priority
over others. A possible source of guidance is the preamble, where the main
objectives of the entire constitutional enterprise are given as "promot(ing) the
common good, with due observance of prudence, justice and charity, so that
the dignity and freedom of the individual may be assured, true social order
attained ..". But these resounding generalisations supply little practical guidance
for finding the proper ranking of constitutional requirements and guarantees.
O'B. v. S. may stand for the principle that the more specific rights guaranteed
in Articles 41–44 take precedence over the broad equality and due process
guarantees in Article 40.1 and 3. In the *Shaw* case, Kenny J. suggested that
"[W]hen a conflict of constitutional rights arises, it must be resolved by having
regard to (a) the terms of the Constitution, (b) the ethical values which all
Christians living in the State acknowledge and accept and (c) the main tenets
of our system of constitutional parliamentary democracy."[91]

The Irish text

Some of the world's principal international treaties, most notably the United
Nations Charter, are in several different languages and each of those forms
part of the authentic text. The Rome Treaty, which established the European
Economic Community, presently has twelve authentic versions. Some national
constitutions have two or more authentic texts, for instance the Canadian
Constitution, the English and French versions of which are "equally
authoritative."[92] There are two authentic texts of the Constitution of Ireland,
the English and the Irish versions. Where, however, there is "a conflict between"
both texts, Article 25.5.4 stipulates that the Irish text shall prevail.[93]

---

[90] *Id.* at p.56.
[91] *Id.* at p.63.
[92] Constitution Act 1982, ss.56 and 57; see generally, P. Hogg, *Constitutional Law of Canada*
(4th ed. 1997), pp. 1295–1296.
[93] See generally, M. O'Cearuil, *Bunreacht na hÉireann: A Study of the Irish Text* (1999),

Although the Irish text must take precedence over the English, in no reported instance so far has a clear conflict between both versions been established. The courts have taken the position that, where it is reasonably possible to do so, both versions should be reconciled on the grounds, as Budd J. explained, that "[i]t is not to be thought that those who framed or enacted the Constitution would knowingly do anything so absurd as to frame or enact texts with different meanings in parts."[94] Any conflict between the two texts could only result from inadvertence. Accordingly, the courts do not search for discrepancies between the texts but seek to reconcile them. Thus, in *State (Gilliland) v. Governor of Mountjoy Prison*,[95] one of the issues was the correct meaning of the terms "*costas*" and "charge." Barrington J. held that "before admitting the existence of a conflict one must enquire if the words "charge" and "*costas*" have a common meaning. If there is a common meaning it is assumed that that is what was meant in both texts of the Constitution. If there is no common meaning a conflict may be inevitable and in that event the Irish text prevails."[96] On the other hand, the courts frequently examine the Irish text carefully in order to throw light on the English version.

Many of the apparent inconsistencies between the texts have been reconciled by the cases. Among those differences remaining to be resolved are the meaning of "war" in the provisions dealing with states of emergency.[97] Article 28.3.1 and 3 uses the term "*chogadh*" but Articles 38.4.1 and 40.4.6 use the term "*eisíthe*," while the term "war" is used throughout the English version. Indeed, the First Amendment to the Constitution, which extended Article 28.3.3 to incorporate an expanded definition of "time of war," was adopted in English only. However, the Second Amendment, which *inter alia* extended that definition further, also contained an Irish version of the earlier amendment.

Preparatory Work

An aid to statutory interpretation which courts in many countries use is the preparatory work for the legislation or provision in question, for instance, reports of official inquiries into the subject matter of the law in question, earlier and revised drafts of the law and its parliamentary history. But it has been held by the Supreme Court that only in very exceptional circumstances should resort be had to parliamentary debates in order to decide what a particular statutory provision means.[98] The Vienna Convention on the Law of Treaties permits

---

M. O'Cearuil, *Two Texts or Two Constitutions* (2002) and M. O'Cearuil, *Bunreacht na hÉireann: Divergences and Inconsistencies?* (2003).
[94] *O'Donovan v. Attorney General* [1941] I.R. 114 at p.131.
[95] [1987] I.R. 201.
[96] *Id.* at p.215.
[97] *Infra*, p.869.
[98] *Crilly v. T. & J. Farrington Ltd.* [2001] 3 I.R. 251.

resort to the *travaux préparatoires* when seeking to interpret treaties. Preparatory work for the United States Constitution is frequently resorted to by the U.S. courts, as is preparatory work for the European Convention on Human Rights by the Strasbourg court.

The only preparatory work on the Constitution that is a matter of public record is the Dáil Debates between May 11 and June 14, 1937. Those, however, are rarely cited by counsel in constitutional law litigation and are hardly ever referred to in the judgments given. The courts have never decided, as a matter of principle, the precise relevance of those debates to constitutional interpretation; there is no reported instance where those were decisive for the outcome of a case. In one of the very few reported instances where the debates were referred to, Henchy J., dissenting, observed that "[i]f one were to scrutinise the debates in Parliament and the records of the written and spoken arguments for and against the draft Constitution in 1937, I venture to think that one would not find the hint of an opinion, either from the proponents or opponents of the Constitution, that a verdict of not guilty emanating from a jury trial ... could be reopened by appeal or otherwise. Indeed, if such opinion had been expressed by any reputable person or body, it is to be arguably contended that the Constitution would never have been enacted by the people."[99]

Public Opinion and Law in 1937

What bearing has the public opinion of sixty five years ago on determining what the Constitution means? In *People v. O'Shea*,[100] Henchy J., dissenting, reasoned that the Constitution prohibits prosecutors from appealing a criminal conviction and that the people would not have voted for the Constitution in 1937 if they believed that it would allow appeals in those circumstances; that, accordingly, the Constitution cannot now be interpreted as providing for such appeals. In other words, the Constitution means what people in 1937 believed it to mean. This argument presents several difficulties. How do we know what people in 1937 believed a particular clause to mean? Even if we did find that out it does not follow that people voted for the Constitution just because they believed several of its clauses had particular meanings. Most voters either accepted or rejected the Constitution in its entirety and the vote was largely along party political lines.

On several occasions the courts have refused to construe vague provisions of the Constitution in a manner consistent with what probably was the public opinion in 1937, perhaps most notably in *McGee v. Attorney General*,[101] where the prohibition against importing and selling contraceptives was struck down.

---

[99] *People v. O'Shea* [1982] I.R. at p.433.
[100] [1982] I.R. 284.
[101] [1974] I.R. 284; *infra*, p.660.

Walsh J. observed that "from time to time the prevailing ideas of (prudence, justice and charity) may be conditioned by the passage of time; no interpretation of the Constitution is intended to be for all time."[102] McCarthy J., dissenting, in *Norris v. Attorney General*,[103] castigated the view that the Constitution embodies the mores of 1937. He:

> "f[ou]nd it philosophically impossible to carry out the necessary exercise of applying what I might believe to be the thinking of 1937 to the demands of 1983. It seems to me that ... this ... argument fails *in limine* – it would plainly be impossible to identify with the necessary degree of accuracy of description the standards or mores of the Irish people in 1937 – indeed, it is no easy task to do so today. If one had to seek, in testing the consistency or otherwise of a pre-1922 statute or a statute of Saorstát Éireann with the Constitution, to do so by reference to the presumed attitude of the Irish people in 1937 (however difficult that might be 45 years after the enactment of the Constitution), one must postulate the concept of doing so 145 years after its enactment. Suffice it to say that the Constitution is a living document; its life depends not merely upon itself but upon the people from whom it came and to whom it gives varying rights and duties ... In my view, it passes from the realm of legal fiction into the world of unreality if the test sought to be applied is one based on some such question as: 'Did the people of Saorstát Éireann in 1937 consider that the offence created by (some Victorian statute) should no longer be in force?' The only thing considered by those who voted for or against the Constitution in 1937 was whether or not they wanted a new Constitution."[104]

As the *McGee* case demonstrates, the fact that a law was enacted shortly before the Constitution was adopted does not mean that the law is consistent with the Constitution. The provisions which were struck down in that case had been enacted in 1935; O'Keeffe P. at first instance upheld them on the grounds that "the best test of the [constitutional] position is to be found in the views expressed when the section was being passed into law since, in point of time, this was so close to the enactment of the Constitution by the people."[105] But this method of constitutional analysis was rejected by the Supreme Court. In *O'Donovan v. Attorney General*,[106] and again in *McMahon v. Attorney General*,[107] where features of the electoral rules were challenged successfully, Budd J. and Pringle

---

[102] *Id.* at p.319.
[103] [1984] I.R. 36.
[104] *Id.* at p.319.
[105] [1974] I.R. 293.
[106] [1961] I.R. 114.
[107] [1972] I.R. 69.

J., respectively, rejected contentions that the impugned provisions were valid because the Free State's Electoral Acts contained similar rules.

The state of the law in 1937 used to be relevant in determining whether an offence is a "minor offence" that, therefore, can be tried summarily.[108] According to Ó Dálaigh C.J. in one instance, "[o]ne can have little doubt that the framers of the Constitution of Ireland, when in Article 38 they spoke of a minor offence, meant the kind of thing that had been generally understood to be such under the laws of Saorstát Éireann ... and since one may assume that 'minor offence' in both Constitutions was intended to mean the same thing, an examination of the statute role of Saorstát Éireann will throw a flood of light on where the line is to be fixed between minor and non-minor offences, so far at least as imprisonment is a factor which operates to change what at first and prima facie might be the one into the other."[109] However, in *State (Rollinson) v. Kelly*,[110] McCarthy J. stressed that the time which matters for these purposes is "the time the relevant convictions were recorded,"[111] and Henchy and Griffin JJ. observed that the state of the law and public opinion in the past has no great relevance to this question.

The Free State Constitution

In order to ascertain the true meaning of existing constitutions, courts occasionally look to previous constitutions and to established interpretations of their provisions. Many of the present Constitution's clauses are identical to or very similar to those of its predecessor of 1922; accordingly, cases dealing with the Free State Constitution can be relevant in interpreting that of 1937. It is reasonable to assume that those who drafted the present Constitution and included in it clauses identical to those of its predecessor of 1922 intended that those clauses would have the meaning given to them by the Free State courts. Thus, both Constitutions provide that the Supreme Court has "appellate jurisdiction from all decisions of the High Court." It was held in 1928[112] that this clause in the 1922 Constitution gave parties a constitutional right to appeal from all decisions of the High Court, without the need for any statutory grant of a right of appeal, and this clause in the 1937 Constitution has been interpreted in the same way.[113]

Perhaps the best example of an interpretation of the 1922 Constitution being carried on into the present Constitution is O'Higgins C.J.'s concurring

---

[108] *Infra*, p.428.
[109] *Melling v. O'Mathghamhna* [1962] I.R. 46.
[110] [1984] I.R. 248.
[111] *Id.* at p.267.
[112] *Warner v. Minister for Industry and Commerce* [1929] I.R. 582.
[113] *State (Browne) v. Feran* [1967] I.R. 147.

judgment in *State (D.P.P.) v. Walsh.*[114] This involved proceedings for criminal contempt of court on the grounds that remarks the defendants had published about a criminal trial "scandalised the court." Under Article 38.5 of the Constitution, persons who are being tried on a serious criminal charge are entitled to be tried with a jury. The alleged contempts in this case were serious criminal charges and the question, therefore, was whether the defendants were entitled to jury trial. The majority judgment of Henchy J. answered no, because the Constitution guarantees the independence of the judiciary and the courts and for, various reasons, judicial independence is best safeguarded if charges of contempt are generally dealt with by judges sitting without a jury. O'Higgins CJ. agreed with these conclusions, on the additional grounds that the Free State Constitution contained an identical guarantee of *jury* trial and in 1928 it was decided that this clause did not apply to criminal contempts.[115]

Comparative Constitutional law

Provisions of foreign constitutions and the decisions of foreign constitutional tribunals are sometimes resorted to as an aid to interpreting the Constitution.[116] In *State (Quinn) v. Ryan,*[117] where the pre-1965 arrangements for extradition to the United Kingdom were struck down, Walsh J. observed that looking to the practice of the U.S. Supreme Court is more appropriate to the post-1937 constitutional system than following the practice of the English courts. He "reject[ed] the submission that because upon the foundation of the State our Courts took over an English legal system and the common law that the Courts must be deemed to have adopted and should now adopt an approach to constitutional questions conditioned by English judicial methods and English legal training which despite their undoubted excellence were not fashioned for interpreting written constitutions or reviewing the constitutionality of legislation. In this State one would have expected that if the approach of any Court of final appeal of another State was to have been held up as an example for this Court to follow it would more appropriately have been the Supreme Court of the United States ...".[118]

As Walsh J. pointed out in *O'B. v. S.,*[119] however, which concerned the

---

[114] [1981] I.R. 412.

[115] *Attorney General v. Kelly* [1928] I.R. 308.

[116] See generally, McCrudden, "A Common Law of Human Rights? Transnational Judicial Conversations on Constitutional Rights," in K. O'Donovan & G. Rubin (eds), *Human Rights and Legal History* (2000), V. Jackson and M. Tushnet, *Comparative Constitutional Law* (1999) and Tushnet, "The Possibilities of Comparative Constitutional Law" 108 *Yale L.J.* 1225 (1999).

[117] [1965] I.R. 70.

[118] *Id.* at p.126.

[119] [1984] I.R. 316; *infra*, p.384.

intestate succession rights of non-marital children, because there are significant differences between the Irish and the U.S. Constitutions, the American cases must not be slavishly followed here. In that case, the statutory discrimination against the non-marital child might be invalid if the constitutional guarantee of equality stood on its own. But unlike the position under the U.S. Constitution, the Constitution of Ireland contains specific guarantees regarding the family based on marriage, to which the entitlement to equality is subordinate. In *People v. O'Shea*,[120] which concerned appeals against criminal acquittals, a divided Supreme Court would not follow the U.S. cases, which treat such appeals as contravening the constitutional prohibition against double jeopardy, on the grounds that the Irish Constitution expressly provides that "all decisions" of the High Court can be appealed from. In *State (D.P.P) v. Walsh*,[121] which concerned criminal contempt of court, the defendants' argument that they were entitled to be tried with a jury was based partly on modern U.S. cases, which hold that all serious contempt charges must be tried with a jury. This contention was rejected because, in the first place, the parallel provision in the Free State Constitution had been interpreted to deny jury trial in such cases. Henchy J. also pointed to "certain differences between the US Constitution and ours" and to the fact that "judges in [U.S.] state courts, by reason of the manner of their appointment and of their terms of tenure, do not fully correspond to our judges,"[122] as reasons for not following the U.S. case law.

Decisions of the Commonwealth courts are occasionally resorted to as an aid to interpretation, most notably the Australian cases on the separation of powers between the judiciary and the executive. The principal reported instance where the courts relied on decisions of Continental European constitutional tribunals was in the *Murphy* "Family Taxation" case,[123] where Hamilton J. and the Supreme Court on appeal found guidance in judgments of the Cypriot, the German and the Italian constitutional courts. In the *An Blascaod Mór Teo*.[124] litigation Budd J. took cognisance of a provision of a South African Constitution[125] and also of a decision of the French *Conseil d'Etat*.[126] And, in the *McKenna* case,[127] concerning State funding for one side in referenda, Denham J. took account of a decision of the German Constitutional Court.[128]

---

[120] [1982] I.R. 384; *infra*, p.480.

[121] [1981] I.R. 412.

[122] *Id*. at p.434.

[123] *Murphy v. Attorney General* [1982] I.R. 241; *infra*, p.670.

[124] [2000] 1 I.R. 6 and [2000] 3 I.R. 564; Budd J.'s important judgment of February 27, 1998 is not reported, other than in the briefest summary.

[125] Article 25.1 states that "[n]o one may be deprived of property except in terms of a law of general application ...".

[126] *Soc La Fleurette*, C.E. January 14, 1938; [1938] *Dalloz* 3, 41.

[127] *McKenna v. An Taoiseach (No.2)* [1995] 2 I.R. 1; *infra*, p.394.

[128] *Official Propaganda case*, 44 *BVerf GE* 125 (1977).

Public International Law

Article 29.3 of the Constitution provides that "Ireland accepts the generally recognised principles of international law as its rule of conduct in its relations with other States." The State is a party to several international treaties and conventions that deal with human rights, the most important of which perhaps is the European Convention on Human Rights.[129] But the precise extent to which rules of international law and the requirements of international treaties are relevant to construing the Constitution has never been determined. In *State (D.P.P.) v. Walsh,* Henchy J. observed that "[t]here is a presumption that our law in this respect is in conformity with the European Convention on Human Rights."[130] Apart from holding that certain representations made to the UN's High Commissioner for Refugees gave rise to a legitimate expectation that certain procedural steps will be followed in refugee cases,[131] international law has hardly influenced the Supreme Court, especially the major multilateral treaties on human rights.

On several occasions, it refused to strike down measures that contravened the European Convention on Human Rights, notwithstanding that there was no coercive reason for holding that this Convention's requirements were not complemented by those in the Constitution.[132] In *Kavanagh v. Governor of Mountjoy Prison*[133] it adopted the same stance with regard to the UN Covenant on Civil and Political Rights[134] and to how it was interpreted by the UN Human Rights Committee in a claim brought against the State by the plaintiff in that action.[135] In these instances the international standard was rejected because it had not been formally incorporated into domestic law, as envisaged by Article 29.6 of the Constitution. Article 29.3 cannot be invoked by litigants to hold the State to its obligations under these treaties or any fundamental principles of international law, such as that of equality, because it was held that Article 29.3 does not confer rights on individuals.

THE SINGLE JUDGMENT RULE

Normally, cases are tried in the High Court by one judge but exceptionally the High Court sits as a divisional court and is then comprised of three judges. Generally, the Supreme Court hears cases as a three-judge court but for

---

[129] Of November 4, 1950, 213 U.N.T.S. 221; *infra,* p.293.
[130] [1981] I.R. 440.
[131] *Fakih v. Minister for Justice* [1993] 2 I.R. 406.
[132] *E.g. Croke v. Smith (No. 2)* [1998] 1 I.R. 101; *infra,* pp.326.
[133] [2002] 3 I.R. 97; *infra,* pp.228 and 240.
[134] Of March 23, 1976, 999 U.N.T.S. 171.
[135] *Kavanagh v. Ireland,* Decision of April 4, 2001.

important cases it sits as a five-judge court and exceptionally with a larger bench. Where a court consists of more than one judge, the common law tradition is that each judge gives his own judgment, and the point of law decided by the court is contained in the judgments of the majority judges.[136] A distinctive feature of the common law tradition is dissenting judgments: where one or more of the judges disagree with their brethren's analysis of the case, they may give judgments that contradict the majority. Occasionally, particularly well argued dissenting judgments gain wider acceptance over time and eventually become acknowledged as the correct statement of the law. By contrast, most continental European courts and also the European Court of Justice at Luxembourg follow what may be termed the "single judgment" rule, by which courts give one judgment and even the existence of dissent among the judges or even differences of view among the majority judges are not revealed.[137] The German Constitutional Court and the European Court of Human Rights are notable exceptions to this pattern.

One of the changes made by the Second Amendment to the Constitution in 1941 was to apply the single judgment rule to the Supreme Court when deciding most constitutional cases. Where the President refers a Bill to the Court under the Article 26 procedure, it is provided that "[t]he decision ... of the Court ... shall be pronounced by such one of those judges as the Court shall direct, and no other opinion, whether assenting or dissenting, shall be pronounced nor shall the existence of any such other opinion be disclosed."[138] Article 34.4.5 of the Constitution contains a similar provision in respect of decisions by the Supreme Court regarding the "validity of a law having regard to the provisions of the Constitution," *i.e.* in cases where it is claimed that some provision of a post-1937 Act is unconstitutional. It has been held that decisions regarding the validity of some statutory instruments made under post-1937 laws also fall within this one judgment rule.[139]

On at least one instance, however, the Court has acted in a way that would not appear to be consistent with the latter article. That was in *Minister for Social Affairs v. Scanlon*,[140] where there was a judgment of Fennelly J. which, *inter alia*, expressed an opinion on a question as to the validity of the Social Welfare Acts, with which the Chief Justice and his three other colleagues concurred.

---

[136] In England, the Court of Appeal now often issues a composite judgment, to which all of the judges make a contribution; see generally, Munday, "All for One and One for All" 61 *Cam. L.J.* 321 (2002).

[137] See generally, Nadlemann, "Judicial Dissent: Publication *v.* Secrecy" 8 *American J. Comp. L.* 415 (1959).

[138] Art. 26.2.2.

[139] *State (Gilliland) v. Governor Mountjoy Prison* [1987] I.R. 201.

[140] [2001] 1 I.R. 64; *infra*, p.831.

CHAPTER 3

The State and its Authority

The Constitution of Ireland is designed to deal with the method of government of a particular group of people in one geographic area. Articles 1–11 distinguish between the Irish nation and the State of Ireland. They commence by proclaiming the "sovereign right" of the Irish nation to self-determination (Article 1). The next two Articles, which affect Northern Ireland, were amended in 1998 following the Belfast Agreement concluded on 10th April of that year. It then goes on to deal with questions such as the name of the State, which is Ireland (Article 4); the nature of, the State, which is "sovereign, independent [and] democratic" (Article 5); that its form of government is one that follows the traditional tripartite separation of powers (Article 6); the national flag (Article 7); the official languages (Article 8); citizenship (Article 9) and ownership of natural resources (Article 10).

THE NATION

At its very beginning, the Constitution makes a distinction between the "Nation" and the "State," although neither term is defined. At the start of his major work, *Institutions Politiques et Droit Constitutionnel,*[1] Professor Jacques Cadart observed that the state is different from the nation. The latter is a "fluid and imprecise, though extremely influential concept; a concept that is essentially sociological and historical, and cannot be judicially defined."[2] It is "a common consciousness, a common civilization that has evolved during a long common history."[3] In its use of the term "Nation", the Constitution envisages Irish people living anywhere, including those living in the six counties of Northern Ireland and abroad. The State, on the other hand, connotes the political unit or community that comprises the 26 counties, described as the Republic of Ireland. As regards these preliminary clauses of the Constitution, the Supreme Court has observed that "[o]ne of the theories held in 1937 by a substantial number of citizens was that a Nation, as distinct from a State, had rights; that the Irish people living in what is now called the Republic of Ireland and in Northern Ireland together formed the Irish Nation; that a nation has a right to unity of

---

[1] (2nd ed., 1979), 2 vols.
[2] *Id.* at p.53.
[3] *Ibid.*

territory in some form, be it as a unitary or federal state; and that the Government of Ireland Act 1920, though legally binding, was a violation of that national right to unity which was superior to positive law."[4]

Former Article 2 stipulated that "[t]he national territory consists of the whole island of Ireland ...." Objection was taken to this on the grounds that it purported to give the Republic some form of legal authority over Northern Ireland. Whether that indeed was the case hardly matters now because it was amended, to give effect to the Belfast Agreement of April 10, 1998. It now states that "[i]t is the entitlement and birthright of every person born in the island of Ireland, which includes its islands and seas, to be part of the Irish nation. That is also the entitlement of all persons otherwise qualified in accordance with law to be citizens of Ireland. Furthermore, the Irish nation cherishes its special affinity with people of Irish ancestry living abroad who share its cultural identity and heritage."

SOVEREIGN, INDEPENDENT AND DEMOCRATIC

Articles 1 and 5 of the Constitution emphasise the principle of self-determination. According to Article 1, '[t]he Irish nation hereby affirms its inalienable and indefeasible, and sovereign right to choose its own form of Government, to determine its relations with other nations, and to develop its life, political, economic and cultural, in accordance with its own genius and traditions." Article 5 adds that "Ireland is a sovereign, independent ... state" and, furthermore, is "a democratic state."

Emphasis here on sovereignty and independence does not mean that the State cannot enter into legally binding obligations with other States and entities, including joining various forms of international organisation. Article 29.4 authorises the Government to conduct "external relations," which includes treaty making, and authorises adherence to international bodies whose purpose is "international co-operation in matters of common concern." Where, however, those bodies are given extensive authority to make decisions and enter into engagements that profoundly affect the State and its people, the State cannot become part of them without explicit constitutional authority to do so. In *Crotty v. An Taoiseach*,[5] the Supreme Court enjoined adherence to the Single European Act of 1986, which significantly extended the authority of the European Communities, on the grounds that neither the then Article 29.4.3 (adopted in order to permit membership of those Communities) nor any other Article authorised so extensive a derogation from national independence. In consequence, that Article was amended in 1987, so that this E.C. measure

---

[4]   *Criminal Law (Jurisdiction) Bill, 1975, Re* [1977] I.R. 129 at p.147.
[5]   [1987] I.R. 713; *infra*, p.230.

could be ratified. Subsequent major alterations to the Communities' structure were the subject of amendments adopted in 1992 (the Maastricht treaty), in 1998 (the Amsterdam treaty) with regard to the European Union and in 2002 concerning the Nice Treaty. Whether the principle in *Crotty* inhibits membership of the United Nations has never been put to the test.

The democratic nature of the State is provided for in detail, principally in the provisions concerning Dáil, Seanad and Presidential elections,[6] referenda[7] and the conduct of parliamentary business.[8]

Unlike in the United States and several other constitutions, the State is not described as a republic or as having a republican form of government. However, section 2 of the Republic of Ireland Act 1948, stipulates that "[i]t is hereby declared that the description of the State shall be the Republic of Ireland."

NATIONALITY AND CITIZENSHIP

Article 9.1 of the Constitution provides that everyone who was a citizen of the Irish Free State in 1937 shall become and is an Irish citizen. This Article goes on to provide that the future acquisition and loss of Irish citizenship shall be regulated by law, subject only to the proviso that no person shall be excluded from citizenship on account of sex. Ireland is a party to the United Nations-sponsored Convention on the Nationality of Married Women of 1957,[9] which rejects the anachronistic "unity of the family headed by the husband" concept in nationality law and adopts the principle of equality between the sexes. Under it, wives shall not be forced to acquire their husbands' nationality, but Article 3 provides for "specially privileged naturalisation procedures" to be made available for a wife who wishes to acquire her husband's nationality. Article 9 of the UN Convention on the Elimination of All Forms of Sex Discrimination,[10] to which Ireland is a party, is very similar except that it does not expressly provide for specially privileged procedures for wives. Ireland is also a party to the European Convention on Multiple Nationality of 1963.[11]

There are very few Irish laws that treat aliens differently from Irish nationals; what discrimination exists is mainly in the political arena and as regards jury service, ownership of land in Ireland and also of Irish-registered ships and aircraft. Nationals of EC Member States and their dependants must be treated in the same way as Irish citizens in respect of the Rome Treaty's subject

---

[6] *Infra*, pp.590 *et seq.*
[7] *Infra*, pp.604 *et seq.*
[8] *Infra*, pp.101 *et seq.*
[9] Of February 20, 1957, 309 UNTS 65.
[10] Of December 18, 1979, 1249 UNTS 13.
[11] Of May 6, 1963, 634 UNTS 221.

matters.[12] As is explained below, in some respects Irish-registered companies, ships and aircraft are equated with nationals. Under international law, states have rights against other states with regard to their own citizens, but there must be some "genuine link" between the person in question and the state claiming the right of international protection.

Citizens

It was not until 1956 that a comprehensive measure was adopted dealing with citizenship,[13] the Irish Nationality and Citizenship Act 1956. All persons who at that time were Irish citizens retained their nationality, notwithstanding the 1956 Act's provisions. Following Ireland's ratification of the U.N. Sex Discrimination Convention, this Act was amended in 1986 in order to put the two sexes on a more equal footing as regards nationality. Because there has never been a great number of outsiders trying to get into Ireland until recently, these Acts were relatively generous as regards who can become citizens, until they were further amended in 1994 and in 2001.

Previously almost everyone born in Ireland (either in the Republic or in Northern Ireland) or on an Irish ship or aircraft automatically acquired Irish citizenship. And persons of non-Irish parentage who were born in Northern Ireland since 1922 acquired Irish citizenship merely by making or by having made for them the prescribed declaration. There was a widely held view that, by virtue or the original version of Article 2 of the Constitution, a person born anywhere in the island of Ireland was automatically entitled to become a citizen. The present version, which states *inter alia* that "[i]t is the entitlement and birthright of every person born in the island of Ireland ... to be part of the Irish nation ...", does not in terms confer citizenship on every person who is born on the island. Because it does not use the word "citizen," in contrast to other constitutional provisions that do so, an argument can be made that Article 2 does not confer any right of citizenship as such, which Article 9.1 stipulates is a matter for the Oireachtas to regulate. However, there is a widespread view that Article 2 confers entitlement to citizenship on those who are born on the island of Ireland and indeed many of those who in 1998 voted for this version of that Article were of the view that it had this very effect. Because it was conceded by the State that the minors in *L. v. Minister for Justice*,[14] who were born in the State in October and November 2001 were "entitled to claim Irish citizenship," the Supreme Court found it unnecessary to determine the effect of this Article.

---

[12] *Infra*, p.253.
[13] Replacing the Irish Nationality and Citizenship Acts 1935–37.
[14] Unreported, Supreme Court, January 23, 2003.

Acquiring citizenship

There are five main ways of becoming an Irish citizen provided for in the Irish Nationality and Citizenship Acts, 1956-2001. One is by the *ius soli* rule, *i.e.* place of birth. Since 2001, a person born anywhere in Ireland, either North or South, is *ipso facto* an Irish citizen from birth provided that he is not entitled to citizenship of another country.[15] Otherwise, persons born anywhere on the island become entitled to citizenship once they, or someone on their behalf, does "any act which only an Irish citizen is entitled to do." A child born on an Irish ship or aircraft is deemed to have been born in Ireland.[16] But a child of a non-national born on one of them, or in Ireland to a non-national parent who was entitled to diplomatic immunity, does not become a citizen unless a declaration of citizenship is made by it or on its behalf.[17] Where a declaration of alienage was made in respect of a child born in Ireland, he cannot acquire nationality until he makes a declaration of citizenship.[18]

Another mode of acquiring citizenship is by the *jus sanguinis* method, *i.e.* parentage. Previously, anyone who at birth had a mother or father possessing Irish citizenship was an Irish citizen, again subject to certain qualifications. Adoption by an Irish citizen in accordance with the procedures laid down in the Adoption Acts 1952-76, also confer Irish nationality. Since 2001, however, if the child is born outside of Ireland and the parent through whom it claims citizenship also was born outside of Ireland, it cannot become a citizen unless either the birth was registered under section 27 of the 1956 Act or, alternatively, that parent at the time was abroad in the public service of the State.[19] It is stipulated that this change in the rules shall neither confer citizenship on a person who in 2001 was not a citizen, nor deprive a person of citizenship if he was a citizen at that time.

Part III (sections 14–20) of the 1956 Act, as amended, lays down the procedure whereby adult aliens who have been resident in the State for more than four years and who intend to continue residing here can apply to the Minister for a certificate of naturalisation; the Minister has an "absolute discretion" as to whether a certificate should be issued.[20] The usual conditions for naturalisation can be waived in respect of certain categories of individuals connected with the State in different ways, and also where the applicant is a "refugee" or a "stateless person" within the internationally accepted definition of those terms.[21] When calculating periods of residence, account shall not be

---

[15] 1956 Act, s.6(1)–(3), as amended in 2001. Keane C.J. in *L.*, *supra* n.13, at pp.22–23, quotes the pre-amended (*i.e.* the original 1956 Act) version of s.6, which was no longer in force then.

[16] 1956 Act, s.13.

[17] 1956 Act as amended, s.6(4).

[18] *Id.* s.6(5).

[19] *Id.* s.7(3), as amended in 2001.

[20] *Id.* s.15, as amended in 1986.

[21] *Id.* s.16, as amended in 1986.

taken of a non-EC national's presence in the State without a residence permit, his being otherwise an alien without permission to be in the State or his being in the State for the purpose of study or seeking to be recognised as a refugee.[22]

A spouse of an Irish citizen[23] can acquire citizenship by naturalisation, provided the couple are of full age and of good character, the marriage is subsisting, they are living together as husband and wife, and intend to continue residing in Ireland.[24] Normally, the marriage must have existed for three years, the applicant must have at least one year's continuous residence in Ireland and, in the preceding four years, have lived on the island for at least two years. However, these requirements may be waived by the Minister where otherwise the person's bodily integrity or liberty would be seriously endangered. The same rules for calculating the duration of presence in the State, referred to above, apply.

Acquiring citizenship through marriage to an Irish national gave rise to constitutional litigation in 1979[25] and the rules regarding this were amended in 1986.[26] A spouse does not become an Irish citizen by the mere fact of marriage;[27] nor does marriage to an alien automatically lead to the loss of Irish citizenship, whether or not the citizen acquires the alien spouse's nationality.[28] Marriages taking place since June 2001 no longer enable spouses to become citizens but they may do so through naturalisation, as described above. For those who prior to then married an Irish citizen or a person who subsequently became a citizen, and who before June 2004 made a declaration under section 8 of the 1956 Act, the position is as follows.[29] That spouse has to lodge with the Minister or with any diplomatic or consular office a declaration in the prescribed form accepting Irish citizenship. It cannot be lodged until either the marriage has lasted for three years or the spouse has been an Irish citizen for three years, which ever is the longer period. Furthermore, the marriage must still be subsisting when the declaration is lodged, the couple must still be living together as husband and wife, and the Irish spouse must submit an affidavit to that effect. An alternative mode open to the spouse is to apply for naturalisation, and the Minister can waive the normal prerequisites for becoming naturalised, *inter alia*, where the applicant is married to an Irish citizen whether or not the spouse acquired citizenship by way of naturalisation.

Finally, the President can confer citizenship on an individual who, in the Government's opinion, "has done signal honour or rendered distinguished

---

[22] *Id.* s.16A, enacted in 2001.

[23] *Kelly v. Ireland* [1996] 3 I.R. 537.

[24] 1956 Act, s.15A, inserted by 2001 Act.

[25] *Somjee v. Minister for Justice* [1981] I.L.R.M. 324; *infra*, p.381.

[26] 1956 Act, s.8, as amended in 1986.

[27] 1956 Act, s.20.

[28] *Id.* at p.23.

[29] Irish Nationality and Citizenship Act 2001, s.4(2).

service to the nation," or to that person's child or grandchild.[30]

Irish law permits dual nationality and indeed many Northern Ireland residents and also persons born in Ireland before 1948 are both British subjects and Irish citizens.

Losing citizenship

Irish nationals cannot be deprived of their citizenship except where that status was acquired by way of naturalisation. In those cases, the Minister is authorised by section 19 of the 1956 Act to revoke a certificate of naturalisation if satisfied that one of the following occurred, *viz.* that the certificate was acquired by fraud, misrepresentation or concealment; that the person voluntarily acquired the citizenship of another State, otherwise than through marriage; that the individual failed in his duty of "fidelity to the nation and loyalty to the State;" that the person is also a citizen of another country at war with the State; extended residence outside the State without registering annually in the prescribed manner. Before the Minister can exercise this power, he is obliged to notify the person in question, stating the grounds on which he proposes to act. Provision is made for referring disputes arising to a Committee of Inquiry, chaired by someone with judicial experience. An informal way of losing citizenship is where the Minister declines to renew a passport.

Renouncing citizenship

Irish nationals may renounce their citizenship on becoming or in order to become citizens of another State but, in a time of war, cannot do so without the Minister's consent.[31]

European citizenship

The concept of citizenship of the European Union was incorporated into Articles 17-22 of the Treaty Establishing the European Community by the Maastricht Agreement of 1992.[32] Every national of an EC/EU Member State is deemed to be an EU citizen as well, and is given certain rights by those Articles — principally to move to and reside in any Member State's territory, and to vote and stand as a candidate in municipal elections there, and in elections to the European Parliament.

---

[30] *Id.* at p.12.
[31] *Id.* at s.21, as amended in 1986.
[32] See *infra*, p.253.

Companies

Registered companies and other corporations are not affected by the Irish Nationality and Citizenship Acts 1956–2001, and indeed there is no general statutory concept of an Irish company. But such a concept exists for certain limited purposes. Thus, the Mercantile Marine Act 1955, defines "Irish body corporate" as "a body corporate established under and subject to the law of the State and having its principal place of business in the State";[33] the Fisheries (Amendment) Act 1983, defines a "qualified body" as a body corporate which is controlled by or in which all the shares are beneficially owned by Irish nationals;[34] the Insurance Act 1936, defines "foreign company" as a company incorporated under the law of a foreign country.[35] For corporation tax purposes, an Irish company may be regarded as a company that is resident in the State, regardless of where it is registered.[36] Under Articles 43 *et seq.* of the EC Treaty, which deal with freedom of establishment, companies are assimilated to nationals of the EC States where they are formed and have their "registered office, central administration or principal place of business" within the EC.

Companies can be registered in the State under the Companies Acts 1963-2001. There is no great difficulty in registering such companies; their shareholders can be either individuals or other companies, and there are no restrictions on foreign nationals or corporations establishing Irish registered companies. Under international law, the nationality of companies is often determined by treaty, such as double taxation agreements; otherwise, attribution of nationality depends on all the circumstances of the case.

Ships

A ship is in a sense a national of the state whose flag it flies. Every state has its own conditions under which ships can fly the national flag. According to Article 5(1) of the 1958 Geneva Convention on the High Seas,[37] there must be a specific form of "genuine link" between ships and the state whose flag they fly. Under it, "[e]ach State shall fix the conditions for the grant of its nationality to ships, for the registration of ships in its territory, and for the right to fly its flag. Ships have the nationality of the State whose flag they are entitled to fly. There must exist a genuine link between the State and the ship; in particular, the State must effectively exercise its jurisdiction and control in administrative, technical and social matters over ships flying its flag." Although this condemns

---

[33] S.2(1).
[34] *Cf. Pesca Valentia Ltd v. Minister for Fisheries* [1985] I.R. 193.
[35] S.3.
[36] See generally, K. Corrigan, *Revenue Law* (2000), Vol.2, pp.778 *et seq.*
[37] Of April 29, 1958, 450 UNTS 82.

the practice of what is termed "flags of convenience," some states nevertheless permit registration of ships with which they have virtually no connection whatsoever.

The registration and some other aspects of Irish shipping are dealt with in the Mercantile Marine Act 1955. Irish ships are State-owned ships and ships that are wholly owned by Irish citizens or by Irish companies, provided that they are not registered in any other country; Irish ships are also ships that are registered in Ireland. There is a duty on Irish ship owners to register their ships in Ireland, subject to some exceptions. Irish registered ships or any share in such ships can be owned only by Irish citizens or companies; aliens and foreign companies cannot register ships in Ireland. Irish companies in the context of this Act mean companies that are registered under the Companies Acts 1963–2001, or otherwise established under Irish law and that also have their "principal place of business" in the State. Provision is made whereby the Government can permit citizens and Irish companies to register ships abroad and can permit nationals of a "reciprocating State" to register their ships in this country.

Aircraft

According to the Chicago Convention of 1944,[38] to which Ireland is a party, the nationality of aircraft is governed by their state of registration. Because this Convention places significant burdens on states of registration, the flags of convenience phenomenon has not extended to aircraft. The criteria for registering aircraft in Ireland are not laid down by statute; instead, section 11(d) of the Air Navigation and Transport Act 1946, under which the Convention came into operation in the State, authorises the Minister to issue regulations regarding registering aircraft in the State. The present rules are contained in the Air Navigation (Nationality and Registration of Aircraft) Order 1963.[39] Under these, in order to register an aircraft in Ireland, it must be owned by an Irish citizen or else by a company that is registered in and has its principal place of business in the State, and the chairman and two-thirds of the directors of which are Irish citizens. Aircraft registered in another country may not be registered in Ireland. Where an aircraft is owned by an alien who resides in or has a place of business in the State, or by a company that has its place of business in the State but otherwise does not satisfy the above-mentioned requirements, it may be registered here provided that it is not used as a public transport or an aerial work aircraft, and that it satisfies such other conditions as the Minister may lay down.

---

[38] Of December 7, 1944, 15 UNTS 295.
[39] S.I. No. 88 of 1963.

State Territory

The Constitution does not define the territorial extent of the State. Former Article 2 did so, as comprising "the whole island of Ireland, its islands and the territorial seas." In light of the 1998 amendment, the State's territory now would appear to consist of the entire island, minus Northern Ireland, as well as the 26 counties' adjoining islands and territorial seas.

Territorial Sea

By territorial sea or waters is meant the area of sea close to a state and over which, by virtue of international law, that state has extensive regulatory authority. Under international law states can exercise the following rights over their territorial seas, viz. jurisdiction over foreign ships of war and merchant vessels, police, customs and revenue functions, fishery rights, maritime ceremonial and establishment of defence zones. The 1982 U.N. Convention on the Law of the Sea[40] which reflects present-day customary international law, would seem to go even further than this, because its Article 1 stipulates that "[t]he sovereignty of a coastal State extends, beyond its land territory and internal waters ... to a belt of sea adjacent to its coast, described as the territorial sea. This sovereignty is exercised subject to the provisions of these articles and to other rules of international law." However extensive it is, the littoral state's sovereignty over the territorial sea is subject to the right of innocent passage for ships from other states.

How the extent of the territorial sea is to be measured is provided for in Articles 3–16 of the 1982 U.N. Convention and is governed by the Maritime Jurisdiction Acts 1959-1988.[41] These adopted the traditional "three miles" rule but in 1988 extended it to twelve nautical miles. That is to say, taking the low-water mark as the baseline, the territorial sea is the stretch of sea between it and twelve nautical miles out from there. There are detailed provisions in the 1959 Act about fixing base lines and it authorises the Government by order to prescribe straight base lines in respect of bays and mouths of rivers.

The 1959 Act designated the Irish territorial sea as an exclusive fishery area, the nature of which was set out in Part XIII (sections 221–224) of the Fisheries (Consolidation) Act 1959. Irish accession to the European Communities, however, has drastically transformed the position as regards fishing, and in 1976 the exclusive fishery zone was extended to 200 nautical miles.[42]

---

[40] Of December 10, 1982, 1833 U.N.T.S. 397; *cf.* [1998] Ir. T.S. No. 1 containing related material.

[41] See generally, C. Symmons, *Ireland and the Law of the Sea* (2nd ed., 2000).

[42] S.I. No. 320 of 1976.

Continental Shelf

By continental shelf is meant an area of the sea bed extending from the coast over which a state possesses certain exclusive rights, in particular, a right to the economic exploitation of that area. Whereas the territorial sea is a very ancient concept, that of the continental shelf only emerged over the last 60 years or so. According to Article 77 of the 1982 Law of the Sea Convention,[43] "[t]he coastal State exercises over the continental shelf sovereign rights for the purpose of exploring it and exploiting its natural resources. The(se) rights ... are exclusive in the sense that if the coastal State does not explore the continental shelf or exploit its natural resources, no one may undertake these activities, or make a claim to the continental shelf, without the express consent of the coastal State." This Convention contains criteria for determining the boundaries between adjacent continental shelves but is silent about the continental shelf's outer limits.

Under the Continental Shelf Act 1968,[44] the Government is empowered to designate an area or areas as the continental shelf, and any rights regarding exploring and exploiting the sea bed are vested in the Minister. That Act goes on to extend the State's criminal and civil jurisdiction over occurrences that take place on or near any installation within the continental shelf. The Minister is empowered to take certain measures to safeguard navigation and to protect installations in that area, and several legislative provisions are extended by this Act to the continental shelf. So far, the boundaries between the Irish and the French continental shelves have not been finally determined. That between Ireland and the United Kingdom was settled by an agreement made in 1988,[45] which establishes two boundary lines that run well beyond the 200 nautical miles limit, but the parties reserved their position as to the outer edge of the continental margin.

STATE PROPERTY

Within the territory of the Republic, the State in one guise or another is an extensive property owner.[46] Many of the State-owned or controlled corporations own land and other property, as do the various local authorities, health authorities, educational authorities and the like. Government ministers, as corporations sole, own land and other property; they have general statutory

---

[43] *Supra.* n.40.

[44] See generally, Symmons, *supra*, n.41.

[45] Of November 7, 1988, [1990] Ir. T.S. No.1; also Protocol of December 8, 1992 [1993] Ir. T.S. No.2.

[46] On the pre-1922 position, see *Irish Employers Mutual Insurance Association, Re* [1955] I.R. 176 at p.220.

authority to "acquire, hold and dispose of land for the purposes of the functions, powers or duties of" their Departments.[47] A State Property Act was passed in 1954[48] to deal with the State as the owner of property, which covers such matters as vesting land in the State, the transfer of land from one State authority to another, the powers of the State regarding such land, gifts to the State. Escheat and *bona vacantia* were abolished by section 73 of the Succession Act 1965, which replaced them with the similar rule that, where a person dies intestate but there is no one entitled to succeed to the estate, the State takes the estate as "ultimate intestate successor." As is explained later,[49] the State and may public agencies are empowered to compulsorily acquire property that is needed for some public purpose, usually on a payment of adequate compensation.

Natural resources

All natural resources and equivalent assets, not in private ownership, are vested in the State by Article 10 of the Constitution, according to which "natural resources, including the air and all forms of potential energy, within the jurisdiction of the (State) and all royalties and franchises within that jurisdiction belong to the State subject to all estates and interests therein for the time being lawfully vested in any person or body." This does not embrace all forms of property but only "natural resources" and "forms of potential energy," "royalties" and "franchises." Nor does this clause affect individuals' ordinary property rights in these resources etc. But subject to any existing private property rights, these resources etc. belong to the State. By virtue of the State Property Act 1954, which defines land to include *inter alia* mines and minerals, franchises and "other rights, privileges, liberties, advantages or benefits of whatsoever kind in, over, or in relation to land," most of these resources etc. which do not belong to others are vested in the Minister.[50]

National heritage

There is no express reference in the Constitution to cultural objects that form important features of the national heritage. However, in *Webb v. Ireland*,[51] which concerned who owned and who should be rewarded for finding the

---

[47] Ministers and Secretaries Act 1924, s.2(1).
[48] Replacing the State Lands Act 1924.
[49] *Infra*, p.732.
[50] See generally, A. Lyall, *Land Law in Ireland* (2nd ed., 2000), p.44.
[51] [1988] I.R. 353; *supra*, p.27. See generally, Lyall, *supra*, n.50, at pp.27–36.

"Derrynaflan hoard," the Supreme Court held that, arising from the "sovereign" nature of the State, the property belonged to the State where it did not have any other identifiable owner. According to Finlay C.J., an essential attribute of sovereignty is the "ownership by the State of objects which constitute antiquities of importance which are discovered and which have no known owner."[52] The view that persons who found those objects become their owners was rejected, as was the view that they belonged to the owner of the fee simple of property in which they were found. Walsh J. referred to "the fundamental duty of the State to safeguard all the national assets whether truly in the ownership of private individuals and more importantly, where the owner is not known or cannot be ascertained."[53] There are several important international conventions on the protection and preservation of cultural property, to which Ireland is not a party.

Legislative provisions to that end include the National Monuments Acts 1930-94,[54] the Heritage Act 1995, the National Cultural Institutions Act 1997, the Architectural Heritage (National Inventory) and Historic Monuments (Miscellaneous Provisions) Act 1999, the Wildlife (Amendment) Act 2000, and the Heritage Fund Act 2001. Political responsibility for these and related matters is vested principally in the Minister for Arts, Heritage, Gaeltacht and the Islands. A measure purportedly designed to preserve the national heritage was declared unconstitutional by the Supreme Court, namely the Blascaod Mór National Historic Park Act 1989.[55] Applying the logic underlying *Webb*, it was held by Barr J. in *La Lavia, Re*[56] that the rules regarding commercial salvage do not apply to ancient wrecks; in that instance, three wrecks from the Spanish Armada lying off-shore at Sreedagh, Co. Sligo. Unlike wrecks envisaged by the Merchant Shipping Act 1894,[57] very old wrecks lack commercial market value in practical terms and it is usually impossible to trace the successors in title of the owners and/or indemnifiers at the time of the loss. Rather, the position is that "[m]aritime archaeological wrecks and related artefacts found on or under the sea bed in Irish territorial waters, like similar objects discovered on land, are the property of the State which holds them for and on behalf of the people of Ireland as part of the historical and cultural heritage of the nation."[58]

---

[52] *Id.* at p.383.
[53] *Id.* at p.391.
[54] See generally, Lyall, *supra* n.50, pp. 36–38.
[55] *An Blascaod Mór Teo. v. Commissioners for Public Works (No.3)* [2000] 1 I.R. 6; *infra*, p.397.
[56] [1999] 3 I.R. 413.
[57] 57 & 58 Vic. c.60.
[58] [1999] 3 I.R. at p.467.

The Irish Language

Until well into the nineteenth century Irish was the predominant language of the people in Ireland and English was spoken mainly by the formally educated elite, as well as by the various agents of the London-based Government. Due to what was described as "immense pressure, compulsion in the schools, social, political and commercial force" around the turn of the 19th century,[59] however, most people began to use English and only a small minority communicated in Irish. Notwithstanding, Irish is given a special status by Article 25.5.4° of the Constitution in that, where its Irish and the English texts "conflict," the former takes precedence.[60] Additionally, by virtue of Article 8.1 and 2, "[t]he Irish language as the national language is the first official language," while English "is recognised as a second official language." This may be contrasted with the Free State,[61] the Canadian[62] and the South African Constitutions,[63] acknowledging two, two and eleven "official languages," respectively, none of which were/are afforded any legal precedence over the other. These and Article 8 of the Constitution are predicated on what the Canadian Supreme Court described as "the essential role that language plays in human existence, development and dignity. It is through language that we are able to form concepts; to structure and order the world around us. Language bridges the gap between isolation and community, allowing humans to delineate the rights and duties they hold in respect of one another, and thus to live in society."[64] On account of how the Irish language was discriminated against and virtually suppressed for over a century, those who framed the Constitution gave it priority over English in some respects.[65]

Article 8.3 goes on to say that "[p]rovision may, however, be made by law for the exclusive use of either of the said languages for any one or more official purposes, either throughout the State or in any part thereof." Apparently, this was designed to deal principally with Northern Ireland becoming part of the State at some time.[66] To date no law has been enacted, as envisaged here, providing for language exclusivity in one or another context. Nor was any general measure enacted dealing with the use of both official languages, as for instance was done in Canada, until the Official Languages Act was passed in 2003.

Most of the official business of the State is presently conducted in English,

---

[59] *Ó Foghludha v. McClean* [1934] I.R. 469 at p.482.

[60] *Supra*, p.56.

[61] Art. 4, considered in *Ó Foghludha, supra* n. 59

[62] Art. 16 of the Charter, considered *in e.g. Commissioner of Official Languages v. Lavigne*, 13 B.H.R.C. 151 (2002) (Can.).

[63] Art. 6.1; other languages are referred to in Art.5(5).

[64] The *Lavigne* case, *supra*, n.62 at pp.160–161.

[65] See generally, S. O'Tuathail, *Gaeilge Agus Bunreacht* (2002).

[66] *O'Beolain v. Fahy* [2001] 2 I.R. 279 at p.337.

for instance, published legislation, Dáil and Seanad debates, and proceedings in the courts.

Legal Proceedings

It is hardly surprising that the leading case on the subject, *O'Beolain v. Fahy*,[67] concerned legislation and legal proceedings. The plaintiff, who was being prosecuted for road traffic offences, wanted to conduct his defence in Irish. To that end, he sought to be provided with Irish translations of the relevant parts of the Road Traffic Acts and of the District Court Rules, but neither of these had been published nor were made available to him. It was held by the Supreme Court that he had a constitutional right to conduct his defence in Irish and, consequently, to be provided with Irish translations of these materials.

Article 25 of the Constitution does not set any time frame within which laws enacted in one of the official languages must be translated into the other. But no official translations of Acts had been published in the previous 20 years and, as McGuinness J. observed, the Acts in this case which were translated belatedly "would never have been translated were it not for the efforts of the applicant and his legal advisors."[68] There was no equivalent express requirement for regulations and other official documents but, it was held, Article 8 in conjunction with the guarantee of a "fair trial" entitled the applicant to an Irish translation of the rules. According to Hardiman J., except where so provided under Article 8.3, the Irish language "cannot ... be excluded from any part of the public discourse of the nation or the official business of the State or any of its emanations. Not can it be treated less favourably in these contexts than the second official language. Nor can those who are competent and desirous of using it as a means of expression or communication be precluded from or disadvantaged in so doing in any national or official context."[69] Thus, for example, in proceedings being conducted in English, a person giving evidence is entitled to do so in Irish, even if he understands English.[70] A party to proceedings may cross-examine witnesses in Irish, even though he has a knowledge of English.[71] Prior to the *O'Beolain* case, it had been held by O'Hanlon J. that there was an obligation on the State to make available an Irish version of the Rules of the Superior Courts.[72]

Unless there is express legislative provision to the contrary, however, a party to legal proceedings may not insist on the other side of the case conducting

---

[67] *Id.*
[68] *Id.* at p.308.
[69] *Id.* at p.340.
[70] *Ibid.*
[71] *An Stat (Mac Fhearraigh) v. MacGamhnia* (1982) T.E. 29.
[72] *Delap v. An tAire Dlí agus Cirt* (1990) T.E. 46.

it in Irish. On account of the official policy of bilingualism, an English speaking party cannot be compelled to participate other than in one of the official languages of his choosing.[73] Those who wish to conduct their arrangements through English are entitled to equality of treatment with the other official language.[74]

Nor is an accused entitled to trial by an all Irish-speaking jury. In *McCarthaigh v. Ireland*,[75] the Supreme Court rejected the plaintiff's claim that, in his forthcoming trial for robbery in the Circuit Court, he should have a jury that were able to follow the proceedings in Irish, rather than with the aid of translation. In the Dublin area, where the trial was to take place, the evidence indicated that only about 25% of the population had a good knowledge of spoken Irish and only about 10% could understand the discussion of difficult questions of criminal law in Irish. Because an all Irish-speaking jury would not be representative of the community where the trial was to take place, the prerequisites for a fair trial would not thereby be met.[76] Assuming for argument sake the Oireachtas provided for the choice of an all Irish-speaking jury, the question would then arise of reconciling this Article with Article 8.3. Nor is an accused entitled to a simultaneous translation of the proceedings. In *McCarthaigh v. Minister for Justice*,[77] Finnegan P. emphasised several disadvantages for accused persons in having the evidence and also the submissions translated simultaneously, and held that a sequential translation would suffice.

Section 8 of the Official Languages Act 2003, makes several provisions for proceedings before courts and tribunals: *inter alia*, a person is entitled to choose which of the two languages to use in any pleading or other court document, and is entitled to be heard and to give evidence in either language of his choice. To facilitate the proceedings, the court may make available either a simultaneous or a consecutive translation. Where the State or other public body is a party, it must use the language chosen by the other party.

Section 71 of the Courts of Justice Act 1924, provides that District Judges who are assigned to an area of the country where the Irish languages is in general use, normally should have sufficient knowledge of that language in order to conduct proceedings without needing an interpreter. Because, however, this requirement is qualified by the words "so far as may be practical having regard to all the relevant circumstances," it was held in *O'Monacháin v. An Taoiseach*[78] that this does not place an absolute obligation on those judges to conduct cases without an interpreter.

---

[73] *O'Beolain* [2001] 2 I.R. at p.342.
[74] *Attorney General v. Coyne* (1963) 101 I.L.T.R. 17 and *Ni Ceallaigh v. An tAire Comhshaoil* (1992) T.E. 52.
[75] [1999] 1 I.R. 200.
[76] *Infra*, p.449.
[77] [2002] 4 I.R. 8.
[78] [1986] I.L.R.M. 660.

By virtue of the Legal Practitioners (Qualifying) Act 1929, and the Solicitors Act 1954, section 3, passing an examination to demonstrate proficiency in the Irish language is a prerequisite for becoming a barrister or a solicitor in the State. Various Irish Legal Terms Orders were published from time to time under the Irish Legal Terms Act 1945. The Courts Services Board are required by section 7(d) of the Court Services Act 1998, to ensure that adequate and competent staff are available in the courts "to provide service through Irish as well as English [in view of] the Government policy on bilingualism."

Other contexts

The use of language in enacting Acts of the Oireachtas is dealt with in Article 25.4 and 5 of the Constitution. Bills may be passed in either of the official languages or, simultaneously, in both languages. If passed in one language, it is the authoritative text; if passed in both, then "[i]n case of conflicts between the texts," Irish prevails.[79] If passed in one language only, an official translation must be issued in the other language. It was held in the *O'Beolain* case[80] that these translations must be made available with reasonable expedition, following the Act being passed, that delays of years in doing so are unacceptable and that the onus to do so would appear to fall on the Minister who introduced the measure in question. Under section 7 of the 2003 Act, "as soon as may be" after an Act is passed, the text in both official languages must be published simultaneously.

Several other requirements regarding the two languages are contained in this Act. Members of either House of the Oireachtas may use either of the languages in any debate or other proceedings there. Specified documents must be published simultaneously in both languages. Sections 11–18 deal with drawing up and implementing schemes for use of both languages by public bodies. A Language Commissioner (*An Commisinéir Teanga*) is to be appointed, principally in order to monitor compliance with the Act, and is given extensive power to conduct investigations to that end.

A regional authority to administer services in the predominantly Irish-speaking areas, or "*Gaeltachts*," was established by Údaras na Gaeltachta Act 1979. Some members of this authority are appointed by the Minister; others are elected by residents in those areas, which for this purpose are divided into three constituencies — the Munster, the Connaught and the Donegal *Gaeltachts*.

Broadcasting television programmes in the Irish language is regulated by Part VI (sections 42–53) of the Broadcasting Act 2001. This is the responsibility of Telifís na Gaeilge, a body corporate, which is obliged to "establish and

---

[79] Art. 25.4.6°.
[80] *Supra*, n.66.

maintain a national television broadcasting service which shall have the character of a public service and be made available, in so far as it is reasonably practical, to the whole community on the island of Ireland."[81]

As well as for qualifying as a lawyer in the State, in order to obtain certain jobs in the public service a knowledge of Irish is required. But depending on the type of job involved, this may contravene the EC's rules against indirect discrimination on the basis of nationality of another EC Member State. It was held by the European Court of Justice in *Groener v. Minister for Education*[82] that it was permissible to require some knowledge of Irish from applicants to be teachers in a VEC-managed art school. Measures to encourage this language, however, "must not in any circumstances be disproportionate in relation to the aim pursued and the manner in which they are applied must not bring about discrimination against nationals of other Member States."[83]

NORTHERN IRELAND

The existence on the island of Ireland of that part of the United Kingdom comprising Northern Ireland is not expressly mentioned in the Constitution. But it is indirectly referred to in Article 29.7, concerning the Belfast Agreement of 10 April 1998, in Article 3, which was amended consequent on that Agreement, and in Article 2 regarding, *inter alia*, the "birthright" of persons born anywhere on the island.

When the State became independent in 1922, representatives of a majority of the people in the six counties in the North Eastern part of the country decided to stay out of this arrangement and opted to remain part of the United Kingdom (U.K.). Under the Government of Ireland Act 1920, in May 1921 a devolved parliament had been established for those counties. On December 5, 1922, the day the Free State's Constitution was enacted at Westminster, the 1920 Act was amended to confine itself to Northern Ireland, subject to some minor modifications. For 50 years thereafter, it was governed partly from Westminster and also by a Parliament at Stormont, which had extensive autonomy.[84] There was a Northern Ireland House of Commons and a Senate, a Government, a Prime Minister and Ministers of his Government, a court system under a Court of Appeal, and a Governor of the province. That Parliament was given all powers to "make laws for the peace, order and good government of ... Northern Ireland," except for matters expressly excluded by s. 4 of the 1920 Act. Section

---

[81] S.45(1).
[82] Case 379/87 [1989] E.C.R. 3967.
[83] *Id.* para.19.
[84] See generally, H. Calvert, *Constitutional Law in Northern Ireland* (1968) and T. Hennessy, *A History of Northern Ireland, 1920–1996* (1997).

5 of this Act prohibited establishing or endowing any religion, and also imposing any disability or disadvantage based on religious belief or ecclesiastical status. By virtue of section 75 of this Act, the "supreme authority" of the Parliament at Westminster was to "remain unaffected and undiminished over all persons, matters and things" there.

Sectarian violence broke out there in the late 1960s, which resulted in substantial numbers of British troops being deployed there in August 1969. Following disagreements between the British and the Northern Ireland Governments about security, the Stormont Parliament was prorogued in 1972 and ultimately abolished on 18 July 1973. For much of the time since then, the place was governed by "direct rule" from Westminster, through a Secretary of State for Northern Ireland. In between, there were several periods of devolved "power sharing" government. Arising from the Inter-Governmental Agreement made at Sunningdale in 1973,[85] the Northern Ireland Constitution Act 1973 was passed, providing for a unicameral assembly and an executive. But these led to a campaign of intimidation by the Ulster Workers' Council and were prorogued for a period in 1974, which was extended until they were dissolved in 1975. Another initiative in devolved government was attempted under the Northern Ireland Act 1982. An assembly was elected but was boycotted by nationalist interests. There were widespread protests following the Inter-Government Agreement at Hillsborough in 1985,[86] which led to the assembly being dissolved in June 1986. Direct rule from Westminster resumed until, under the Northern Ireland Act 1998, another assembly was elected and an executive appointed. This development was brought about by the Inter-Government Agreement made in Belfast on 10 April 1998 and the Multi-Party Agreement of the same date annexed to it.[87] This latter agreement is popularly referred to as the "Belfast" or the "Good Friday" Agreement.

In order to give effect in the State to aspects of these Agreements, the Constitution was amended to incorporate Article 29.7 and also to amend Articles 2 and 3. Article 29.7 authorised the State to "consent to be bound by" the Inter-Government Agreement and also the creation of cross-border bodies as envisaged by it. Old Article 2, which stated that the "whole island of Ireland" comprised the "national territory," [88] was replaced by a largely if not entirely aspirational statement, that "[i]t is the entitlement and birthright of every person born in the island of Ireland, which includes its islands and seas, to be part of the Irish nation. ..." It is widely accepted that the first sentence of this entitles

---

[85] Of December 9, 1973; of November 15, 1985; considered in *Boland v. An Taoiseach* [1974] I.R. 338.

[86] [1985] Ir. T.S. No.2, considered in *Ex p.Molyneaux* [1986] 1 W.L.R. 331.

[87] [2000] Ir. T.S. No.18. See generally, A. Morgan, *The Belfast Agreement* (2000) and C. Harvey ed., *Human Rights, Equality and Democratic Renewal in Northern Ireland* (2001). *Cf.* B. Dickson, *The Legal System of Northern Ireland* (4th ed., 2001).

[88] Considered in *McGimpsey v. Ireland* [1990] I.R. 110.

persons born anywhere on the island to become Irish citizens.[89] Whether "cherish[ing] special affinity with people of Irish ancestry" gives rise to any legally enforceable entitlements is questionable.

The new Article 3 provides as follows:

> "1. It is the firm will of the Irish nation, in harmony and friendship, to unite all the people who share the territory of the island of Ireland, in all the diversity of their identities and traditions, recognising that a united Ireland shall be brought about only by peaceful means with the consent of a majority of the people, democratically expressed, in both jurisdictions in the island. Until then, the laws enacted by the Parliament established by this Constitution shall have the like area and extent of application as the laws enacted by the Parliament that existed immediately before the coming into operation of this Constitution.
>
> 2. Institutions with executive powers and functions that are shared between those jurisdictions may be established by their respective responsible authorities for stated purposes and may exercise powers and functions in respect of all or any part of the island."

In other words, except where under general principles of international law they may so apply,[90] laws enacted in the State shall not apply to Northern Ireland. But it and the Republic may at any stage join and form part of the present State, provided that "a majority ... in both jurisdictions" vote for unity. What is envisaged here would appear to be aggregate majority, not separate majorities in each part of the island.[91] Finally, cross-border bodies may be established and carry on such functions as are authorised by the Oireachtas.

Proceedings to prevent the proposed 19th Amendment, incorporating these clauses, being put to a referendum were rejected by the Supreme Court in *Riordan v. An Taoiseach (No.2)*.[92] It was unsuccessfully contended that this amendment could not be adopted because its coming into operation was being suspended, contingent on the Government deciding that it was satisfied that the UK was implementing its side of the bargain struck in the 1998 Agreement. A twelve month period provided for making this declaration was extended for a further twelve months by the Declaration under Article 29.7 of the Constitution (Extension of Time) Act 1999. On December 7, 1999, the Government declaration to this effect was published in *Iris Oifigiúil*.

The Belfast or Good Friday Agreement does not appear to have any signatories. Negotiations or "talks" that led up to it involved not alone representatives of the two Governments but also representatives of most of the political

---

[89] *Supra*, p.68.
[90] Art.29.8, also adopted by the 19th Amendment.
[91] Compare Art. I(i) and (ii) of the Inter Governmental Agreement.
[92] [1999] 4 I.R. 343; *infra*, p.608.

parties in Northern Ireland, except for notably the Democratic Unionist Party (DUP). It sets out how the Assembly and Executive for Northern Ireland are to function, which was implemented by the Northern Ireland Act 1998. So far as the State is directly concerned, the Agreement provides for a North-South Ministerial Council, a British-Irish Council and a British-Irish Intergovernmental Conference. As well as providing for measures to safeguard human rights in Northern Ireland, it provides for "comparable steps" being taken by the Irish Government, including proposals that "draw on the European Convention on Human Rights and other international instruments in the field of human rights ...". A Human Rights Commission has been established[93] and the envisaged incorporation of the Convention into Irish law eventually took place in 2003.[94] Provision made in the Agreement for decommissioning illegally held weapons resulted in the Decommissioning Act 1997. Provision is also made for a review of the Offences Against the State Acts 1939-85, which took place in 2002.[95] Provision too is made for the release of certain prisoners, which was implemented by the Criminal Justice (Release of Prisoners) Act 1998.[96] Finally there are provisions for validation, implementation and review of this Agreement.

The reference in Article 3.2 to inter-jurisdictional institutions is amplified in Article 29.7.2, which states that:

> "[a]ny institution established by or under the Agreement may exercise the powers and functions thereby conferred on it in respect of all or any part of the island of Ireland notwithstanding any other provision of this Constitution conferring a like power or function on any person or any organ of Sate appointed under or created or established by or under this Constitution. Any power or function conferred on such an institution in relation to the settlement or resolution of disputes or controversies may be in addition to or in substitution for any like power or function conferred by this Constitution on any such person or organ of State as aforesaid."

What this appears to mean is that the fact that the Constitution requires any particular legislative, executive or judicial function to be performed by a designated organ of the State shall not operate as a bar on that function being exercised by any duly authorised cross-border body. Consequently, these bodies have potentially extremely wide powers and authority, but they are subject to all other provisions of the Constitution, at least where they affect persons in the State.

---

[93] Human Rights Commission Acts 2000–01.
[94] European Convention on Human Rights Act 2003.
[95] *Report of Committee to Review the Offences Against the State Acts 1939–1998* (2002).
[96] *Cf. O'Neill & Quinn v. Minister for Justice* (Peart J., March 27, 2002),which is under appeal.

On March 8, 1999, four agreements were made between the two Governments – establishing the North-South Council, the British-Irish Council and the Inter Governmental Conference, earlier envisaged, and also Implementation Bodies.[97] Some weeks later, the British-Irish Agreement Act 1999 was enacted to give effect to what had then been agreed on the cross-border "implementation bodies," as well as authorising members of the Government to participate in the North-South Council and in the British-Irish Council.

---

[97] [2000] Ir. T.S. Nos 26–30.

CHAPTER 4

The President

In some countries, most notably the United States and South Africa, the chief of the executive is also the formal head of State. But in many other countries, such as France, Germany, Italy, the United Kingdom and many Commonwealth countries, there is both a head of government (Prime Minister) and also a head of state (President or monarch). Throughout most of the Free State era, the British monarch, represented in Ireland by the Governor General, was the formal head of State. Under the 1937 Constitution, however, the President of Ireland, although not designated as such, is the head of State and exercises powers broadly similar to those of the German and the Italian Presidents.[1] Indeed, the President fulfils many of the functions that in Britain are exercised by the Queen. It is widely believed that the model for several features of the Irish presidency was that of the German Weimar Republic.

STATUS

According to Article 12.1 of the Constitution, "the President ... shall take precedence over all other persons in the State and ... shall exercise and perform the powers and functions conferred on the President by this Constitution and by law." For all formal occasions, therefore, the President has precedence over everybody else in the State.

On entering office, the President must make a public declaration before the members of both Houses of the Oireachtas, the judges of the Supreme Court and of the High Court, and other public personages in the following terms: "In the presence of Almighty God I ... do solemnly and sincerely promise and declare that I will maintain the Constitution of Ireland and uphold its laws, that I will fulfil my duties faithfully and conscientiously in accordance with the Constitution and the law, and that I will dedicate my abilities to the service and welfare of the people of Ireland. May God direct and sustain me."[2]

The President cannot be a member of either House of the Oireachtas, nor hold any paid office or position,[3] although Presidents invariably hold several honorary offices. President de Valera, for instance, was Chancellor of the

---

[1] See generally, S. Dooney & J. O'Toole, *Irish Government Today* (2nd ed., 1998), Chap.5.
[2] Art.12.8.
[3] Art.12.6.

National University of Ireland. The President's remuneration is determined by law. The Constitution forbids any "diminish(ment)" of the President's remuneration and allowances during the term of office,[4] thereby assuring that the President has a degree of financial independence. The President's official residence must be in or near the city of Dublin[5] and in fact is Áras an Uachtarán in the Phoenix Park, which was formerly the Vice Regent's lodge. A President must obtain the Government's consent before leaving the State at any time during his office.[6] Provisions regarding the President's official residence, remuneration, pension, secretary and staff are laid down in the Presidential Establishment Acts 1938-1991; the legal effect of the official seal is provided for in the Presidential Seal Act 1937.

ELECTION

The Presidential term of office is seven years[7] except, of course, where the President resigns (as Cearbhall Ó Dálaigh did in 1976), dies (as Mr Erskine Childers did in 1974), is removed from office or is permanently incapacitated in accordance with Article 14. Who can be elected President and the rules governing such elections are governed by Article 12 of the Constitution and by the Presidential Election Act 1993.

Candidacy

In order to contest a presidential election,[8] one must be an Irish citizen, of 35 years of age or more, and be otherwise eligible for election. By being otherwise eligible is meant, principally, that one is nominated for election in the manner laid down in Article 12.4. Former or retiring Presidents are entitled to nominate themselves; against that, they can stand for re-election only once. In 1983, Dr Hillery nominated himself for re-election, although in the event no candidate stood against him in that year, so that he was declared duly elected. Other aspirant candidates for the office must be nominated by at least twenty members of either House of the Oireachtas or, alternatively, by at least four County Councils or County Borough Councils.[9] Thus, aspirant Presidents need considerable support from established politicians before they can even contest an election.

---

4   Art.12.11.3.
5   Art.12.11.1.
6   Art.12.9.
7   Art.12.3.1.
8   Art.12.4.1.
9   Art.12.4.2.

Voting

Only citizens can vote in Presidential elections and every citizen entitled to vote in Dáil elections has the right to vote at elections for the President.[10] Unlike in France, there are no first and second rounds in the elections; unlike the U.S. position, the President is chosen directly by those voting[11] and not indirectly by an electoral college. Voting is by secret ballot and the system of voting is by way of the single transferable vote.[12] In other words, where more than two candidates stand, one can vote numbers 1,2, 3 etc. for them in order of ones choice; if ones chosen no. 1 candidate is eliminated, ones votes are then transferred to ones chosen number 2 candidate and so on until the winner emerges.[13]

POWERS

The Constitution confers several powers on the President. Additionally, the legislature is authorised to confer other powers but any such powers can only be exercised on the advice of the Government.[14] In British constitutional theory, foreign affairs is a matter that is primarily within the royal prerogative. When Ireland became a Republic in 1948, the Oireachtas authorised the President, on the Government's authority and advice, to act in the field of external relations.[15]

As regards the powers under the Constitution, the President has very little scope to take initiatives because Article 13.9 stipulates that most of those powers can only be exercised either with the Government's approval or having consulted the Council of State. According to this clause, "[t]he powers and functions conferred on the President by this Constitution shall be exercisable and performable by him only on the advice of the Government, save where it is provided by this Constitution that he shall act in his absolute discretion or after consultation with or in relation to the Council of State, or on the advice or nomination of, or on receipt of any other communication from, any other person or body." The most significant power that is not constrained in any way is the "absolute discretion" to reject a Taoiseach's request for a dissolution of the Dáil when that Taoiseach has lost majority support in the Dáil.[16]

It is provided that the President "shall not be answerable to ... any court"

---

[10] Art.12.2.2.
[11] Art.12.2.1.
[12] Art.12.2.3.
[13] See *infra*, p.597 on "PR" elections.
[14] Arts.13, 10 and 11.
[15] Republic of Ireland Act 1948, s.53.
[16] Art.13.2.2.

in respect of how he exercises his powers or performs his functions.[17] But this does not mean that each and every action of the President is entirely incapable of being reviewed in the courts. In *State (Walshe) v. Murphy*,[18] it was contended that the defendant had not been validly appointed as a temporary District Judge because he had not been a legal practitioner for the requisite qualifying period. One of the answers given to this argument was that the validity of his appointment could not be questioned in the courts because he had been appointed by the President and, by virtue of Article 13.8.1, the President cannot be made answerable to any court. It was held that being answerable here means being called before a court and answerable for one's actions – being "made or forced to answer or give account of his conduct to that person or institution."[19] But that was not the issue in the case, which was simply whether or not the defendant had the qualifications for appointment as a judge. If such questions could not be reviewed by the courts, then there would be numerous ways in which the executive could act illegally and unconstitutionally without ever having to defend what it did before the courts.

The Council of State

The Council of State, which the President is sometimes required to consult,[20] is comprised of senior political figures, judges and some others; it resembles somewhat the Privy Council which advises the Crown in Britain. While the Constitution requires that the President consult the Council of State on various issues, there is no express obligation on the President to act in accordance with whatever advice the Council gives. All that Article 32 of the Constitution provides is that the President shall not exercise any power that requires consulting the Council unless he has convened a meeting of its members and spoken on the matter to those who attend the meeting.

The composition of the Council of State is provided for in Article 31. It is comprised firstly of *ex officio* members, *viz.* the Taoiseach (Prime Minister), the Tánaiste (Deputy Prime Minister), the Chief Justice, the President of the High Court, the Chairman of the Dáil, the Chairman of the Seanad and the Attorney General. Secondly, it includes every former President, Taoiseach and Chief Justice who is able and willing to act as a member. Thirdly, the President has an "absolute discretion(ary)" power to appoint up to seven other members of the Council and these persons hold office until the President who appointed them is replaced in office. Any of these appointees can resign and the President can terminate the appointment of any one of them for such reason as seems

---

[17] Art.13.8.1.
[18] [1981] I.R. 275.
[19] *Id.* at p.282.
[20] See instances in Dooney & O'Toole, *supra*, n.1, pp.123–126.

sufficient. Every member of the Council of State must subscribe to a declaration in the form set out in Article 31.4.

Signing bills and promulgating laws

In order for them to become law, Bills that have passed or are deemed to have passed both Houses of the Oireachtas must first be signed by the President.[21] It is the Taoiseach who presents a Bill for signature[22] and, normally, it must be signed within one week of its being presented.[23] The President is also required to promulgate every Act once it is signed,[24] which is done by directing that a notice be inserted in *Iris Oifigiúil*.[25]

While the President has no general power to veto what the legislature has decided on, there are two circumstances where he can refuse at the outset to sign a Bill. As is explained below, one is where, under Article 26, he decides that the Bill should be referred to the Supreme Court for a decision about its constitutionality. The other is where the Dáil and Seanad are deadlocked over the Bill and, under Article 27, a majority of senators and some Dáil members request a referendum on the Bill's terms.

Referring bills to the Supreme Court

Article 26 lays down a procedure by which the President can decline to sign and promulgate a Bill that has been passed by both Houses and, instead, can refer it to the Supreme Court in order to have its constitutionality determined.[26] This Article applies to Bills other than Money Bills, proposed constitutional amendments and Bills enacted under the speedy emergency procedure provided for in Article 24. Before referring any such Bill to the Court, the President must consult with the Council of State but there is no stipulation that the Council's advice, if given, must be followed. Not more than seven days may elapse between the time that the Bill is presented for signature and its being referred to the Supreme Court. A five or more judge Court, after hearing argument for and against the Bill, must give its decision in a single judgment within sixty days of the reference. If the Bill or any provision of it is declared to be unconstitutional, the President must not sign it; otherwise, the Bill must be signed and duly promulgated.

---

[21] Art.13.3.1.
[22] Art.25.1.
[23] Art.25.2 and 3.
[24] Art.13.3.2.
[25] Art.25.4.2.
[26] See generally, A. Collins and J. O'Reilly, *Civil Proceedings and the State* (2nd ed., 2003), Chap.8 and instances in Dooney & O'Toole, *supra*, n.1, pp.127–129.

Referring bills for consultative referendum

Article 27 lays down a procedure, which has never been used, whereby the President can decline to sign and promulgate a Bill that has attracted extensive political opposition and, instead, make the Bill the subject of an actual or a *de facto* consultative referendum. This provision applies to any Bill, other than a proposed constitutional amendment (which in any event must be voted on in a referendum), about which the Dáil and the Seanad are deadlocked and which, in accordance with Article 23, is deemed nevertheless to have been passed by both Houses. The President does not have the initiating power as regards this procedure. What is required is that a joint petition be addressed to the President, by a majority of members of the Seanad and at least one-third of the members of the Dáil, requesting the President not to sign the Bill because it "contains a proposal of such national importance that the will of the people thereon ought to be ascertained." Such petition must be presented within four days of the Bill being deemed to have been passed by both Houses and it is required to contain a statement of "the particular ground or grounds on which the request is based ....". Even where a Bill has been referred to the Supreme Court under the Article 26 procedure and is pronounced to be not unconstitutional, it can still be made the subject of a consultative referendum in the manner described here. The President must consult with the Council of State but, as with Article 26, it would seem that there is no obligation to act on the Council's advice.

Where the President forms the view that the Bill is of national importance in the sense defined above, he will decline to sign it until one or other of the following takes place. One is that the Bill's terms are not rejected in a referendum. But a rejection here requires more than a bare majority of those voting against the Bill. According to Article 47, not alone must a majority of votes in the referendum have been cast against the Bill but those "no" votes must amount to at least one-third of the registered electors. This is to ensure that a Bill is not blocked in circumstances where a great majority of the population are indifferent about it. The alternative prerequisite before the President can sign the Bill is that the Dáil must be dissolved and fresh elections take place, and on reassembling the Dáil must have passed a resolution approving the Bill's contents; in other words, a *de facto* or quasi-referendum must have taken place.

Summoning and Dissolving the Dáil

It is the President who dissolves sessions of the Dáil and who summonses the next Dáil, but always on the advice of the Taoiseach (Prime Minister).[27] In

---

[27] Art.13.2.1.

contrast with some countries, the head of State cannot take the initiative in resolving deadlock between elected politicians by ordering that the legislature shall be dissolved, thereby precipitating a general election. However, a Taoiseach who has lost the support of the Dáil and who wants an election cannot insist on getting a dissolution; in those circumstances the President has the "absolute discretion" to decide that that Dáil shall continue in session, in anticipation of some other Taoiseach being selected.[28] Unlike the position in Britain, the President who refuses to grant a dissolution has no constitutional authority to "send for" some other leading political figure with a view to forming a new government.

Appointing the Taoiseach and Government members

It is the President who appoints the Taoiseach and the other members of the Government. But it is the Dáil that nominates the Taoiseach and the other members of the Government are nominated by the Taoiseach with the approval of the Dáil.[29] By contrast, in Britain, France and Italy (and Weimar Germany) the head of State has a discretion over who the head of government shall be, although in practice a person who is not expected to secure majority support in the legislature will not be offered that position.

Resignation and removal of Government members

Any member of the Government wishing to resign tenders his resignation to the President, who will accept the resignation where the Taoiseach advises so.[30] If the Taoiseach wishes to remove a member from the Government and cannot secure their resignation, it is the President on the Taoiseach's advice who removes that member.[31] In 1970 two Government Ministers, Charles Haughey and Neil Blaney, were removed from office in this manner over the "arms" affair; Brian Lenihan was removed from office in 1990 for reasons that were never made entirely clear. Unlike the position in some countries, the head of State has no independent power to remove the chief executive or any other member of the Government.

---

[28] Art.13.2.2.
[29] Art.13.1.1 and 2.
[30] Art.13.1.3.
[31] *Ibid.*

Pardons and commuting punishment

On the advice of the Government, the President may grant pardons and commute sentences.[32] But the Oireachtas may confer power to commute or remit sentences on "other authorities";[33] that has been done by section 23 of the Criminal Justice Act 1951, which authorises the Government to commute or remit any punishment, forfeiture or disqualification imposed by a criminal court, and that power may be delegated to the Minister for Justice. This provision does not apply to disqualification from holding a driving licence[34] which, therefore, can only be lifted by the President.

Other powers

The other powers conferred by the Constitution on the President are as follows. After consulting with the Council of State, the President can convene a meeting of either or both Houses of the Oireachtas.[35] After consulting with the Council of State and having received the Government's approval, the President can communicate with both Houses of the Oireachtas on "any matter of national or public importance"[36] and can also address a message to the entire nation at any time and on any matter.[37] Under Article 22, the President may convene a Committee of Privileges in order to determine if a Bill is a Money Bill[38] and, under Article 24, to abridge the time for legislative consideration of Bills that are urgent and immediately necessary as defined there.[39] Judges of the High Court, the Supreme Court, the Central Criminal Court, the Circuit Court and the District Court are appointed by the President on the advice of the Government,[40] and it is the President who removes any of these judges from office when both Houses of the Oireachtas have passed the appropriate resolutions.[41] Supreme command of the defence forces is vested in the President,[42] although military command and all executive and administrative functions over the defence forces are exercised by the Government through the Minister for Defence.[43] Subject to Government direction, the President

---

[32] Art.13.6.
[33] *Ibid.*
[34] Road Traffic Act 1961, s.124.
[35] Art.13.2.3.
[36] Art.13.7.1.
[37] Art.13.7.2.
[38] *Infra*, p.104.
[39] *Infra*, p.105.
[40] Art.35.1.
[41] Art.35.4.
[42] Art.13.4.
[43] Art.13.5 and Defence Acts 1954–1998.

can act "in or in connection with" the State's external relations.[44] Irish citizenship can be granted by the President as a token of honour.[45] And the President has statutory powers of appointment in respect of several major offices, such as the Ombudsman, the Governor of the Central Bank, the Chairman of the Agricultural Institute and An Coimisineir Teanga.

THE PRESIDENTIAL COMMISSION

Article 14 of the Constitution provides for the establishment of a Presidential Commission, which is authorised to exercise the President's powers when he either cannot or will not act. This Commission is comprised of the Chief Justice and the Chairmen of the Dáil and of the Senate; where any of these cannot act, the President of the High Court and the Deputy Chairmen of the Dáil and of the Senate, respectively, act in their place. This Commission can act by any two of its members and notwithstanding a vacancy in its membership. It is authorised to exercise the President's powers and functions in any of the following circumstances, *viz.* where the President is absent, is temporarily incapable of acting, is under a permanent incapacity, has died or resigned, has been removed from office, where the office is otherwise vacant and where he fails to perform any or all of the powers or functions of the office. Permanent incapacity must be established to the satisfaction of a five-judge Supreme Court[46] and the President can be removed from office only through the formal procedure under Article 12.10. In the event of circumstances arising concerning the President's powers and functions that are not provided for in Article 14, the Council of State is empowered to decided what shall be done.[47]

REMOVAL

Impeachment was the process whereby leading political figures who had fallen out of favour were tried by the legislature on charges of corruption or abuse of power. Some of the leading characters in English and Irish history have suffered impeachment, such as Sir Walter Raleigh, Thomas Wentworth – the Earl of Stafford, Archbishop Laud, Viscount Bolingbroke, James Butler – the Duke of Ormond and Warren Hastings, but no such trial has taken place in Britain since 1804. Impeachment is the procedure laid down in the U.S. Constitution for removing "the President, Vice-President and all civil officers of the US

---

[44] Republic of Ireland Act 1948, s.3.
[45] Irish Nationality and Citizenship Act 1956, s.12.
[46] Art.12.3.1.
[47] Art.14.4.

[on] conviction of Treason, Bribery, or other high Crimes and Misdemeanours."[48]

A similar procedure is laid down in Article 12.10 of the Irish Constitution as the exclusive way of dealing with presidential misbehaviour. According to Article 13.8.1, "the President shall not be answerable to either House of the Oireachtas or to any court for the exercise and performance of the powers and functions of his office or for any act done or purporting to be done by him in the exercise and performance of these powers and functions." Therefore, the courts cannot entertain claims that presidential powers have been exercised wrongfully or were or are being abused; the President's official conduct is beyond judicial review.[49] Nor, generally, is the President answerable to the legislature. Instead, the only mechanism provided whereby the behaviour of the President, may be brought under review is removal for "stated misbehaviour" in accordance with the procedures laid down in Article 12.10. Not alone has a President never been removed in this country but removal has never seriously been suggested. Indeed, Irish Presidents very rarely attract even mild criticism from politicians or the general public. The term "stated misbehaviour," especially when viewed against the US provision, suggests that a President can be impeached not alone for being involved in criminal offences but on other grounds as well. It remains to be seen whether what is meant by "stated misbehaviour" will be defined by the courts or whether that is exclusively a matter for the legislature to decide.

The machinery laid down in Article 12.10 is briefly as follows. At the outset, at least thirty members of either the Dáil or the Seanad must sign a notice of motion that the President shall be removed. That motion must secure the support of at least two-thirds of the total membership of the House of the Oireachtas in question before the process can commence and the resolution of that House must state "the charge." It is then the other House of the Oireachtas that investigates the charge, or causes it to be investigated. What precise form that investigation shall take is not laid down, other than that the President is entitled to appear and to be legally represented at the investigation. It will be remembered that during the attempt to impeach President Nixon and later President Clinton the Congress appointed a special prosecutor for that purpose. Any adverse finding against the President must take the form of a resolution of the House in which the charge was investigated, which requires a majority of two-thirds of that House's entire membership, and declaring as follows: "[t]hat the charge preferred against the President has been sustained and that the misbehaviour, the subject of the charge, was such as to render him unfit to continue in office …". The passing of such a resolution operates to remove the President from office.

---

[48] Art. II.4.
[49] *State (Walshe) v. Murphy* [1981] I.R. 275.

CHAPTER 5

The Legislature

As is the case in many democratic countries, the legislature in Ireland is comprised of two chambers or houses, called the Dáil and the Seanad.[1] Members of the Dáil are elected directly by the general public at least every five years whereas most of the senators are elected primarily by politicians, also at least every five years. Unlike the position in the United States and Italy, but like that in the United Kingdom, France and Germany, the so-called lower chamber, the Dáil, has far more power and authority than the other chamber. Under the Constitution, the Oireachtas is defined to comprise not only the Dáil and the Seanad but also the President.[2] The Oireachtas is given the "sole and exclusive power of making laws for the State. ..."[3] It was held by the Supreme Court in *Maguire v. Ardagh*,[4] concerning an Oireachtas enquiry into a Garda fatal shooting incident in 2000, that neither House of the Oireachtas is a successor to the pre-1922 Houses of the United Kingdom Parliament, in the sense that such powers and privileges as that Parliament had were not carried over into Irish law in 1922 nor in 1937. Whatever competences both Houses have arise either expressly or impliedly from the Constitution's provisions, as well as from legislation.

Article 15.2.2 of the Constitution permits the creation, or recognition, of "subordinate legislatures" and the conferring of powers on those bodies but this mechanism has never been availed of. Nor has the Oireachtas ever established "functional or vocational councils" as permitted by Article 15.3.

Since 1973 the Oireachtas' monopoly of law-making power has been significantly encroached upon by the European Communities/Union.[5] By virtue of Article 29.4.3–10 of the Constitution, certain very specific provisions of the Treaty Establishing the European Communities, and also Regulations and Directives enacted by the EC's institutions, are automatically part of domestic law, confer rights and impose reciprocal obligations, without having to be enacted in any manner by or under the Oireachtas.

---

[1] See generally, B. Chubb, *The Government and Politics of Ireland* (3rd ed., 1992), Chap.11 and S. Dooney & J. O'Toole, *Irish Government Today* (2nd ed. 1998), Chap.3.
[2] Art.15.1.
[3] Art.15.2.
[4] [2002] 1 I.R. 385.
[5] *Infra*, p.257.

THE DÁIL

That the Dáil possesses far more power and influence than the Seanad is reflected in the fact that the Government is responsible to the Dáil,[6] all but two of the members of the Government must be members of the Dáil,[7] the Government must resign if it loses the support of a majority in the Dáil,[8] financial issues are within the Dáil's virtually exclusive control[9] and the Dáil's assent must be obtained before war can be declared.[10] Dáil elections are governed principally by the Electoral Acts 1992–2002.[11] In 2003 there were 166 elected members of the Dáil; they are known as Teachtaí Dála, or TDs for short, and they represent 42 electoral constituencies.

Article 15.7–15 of the Constitution lays down the following rules which apply to both the Dáil and the Seanad. Each of these Houses is to sit in or near Dublin. Each House must hold at least one session every year and its sittings must be in public. In cases of "special emergency," however, and where two-thirds of the members present are in agreement, each House can hold a private sitting. Each House must select a chairman and deputy chairman, must lay down their powers and duties, and must make provision for a quorum. These matters are contained in both Houses' standing orders.[12]

Except where the Constitution makes special provision to the contrary, questions before each House are resolved by a majority of votes cast by the members present who vote.[13] Where there is an equality of votes, the chairman of the House or other presiding member has a casting vote.[14] A person cannot be a member of both Houses at any one time.[15] Provision must be made by law for members' allowances and travelling and other expenses, and for remunerating the chairman and deputy chairman of both Houses.[16] Overall management of the Dáil, and also of the Seanad, in provided for in the Houses of the Oireachtas Commission Act 2002, *inter alia*, paying of wages and expenses, overseeing expenditure, providing secretarial facilities, providing legal advice and involvement in legal proceedings. To this end, a Commission was established, comprising the chairman of the Dáil and of the Seanad, the Clerk of the Dáil, four ordinary members of the Dáil, three ordinary members of the Seanad and a representative of the Minister. Provisions regarding laying

---

[6] Art.28.4.1.
[7] Art.28.7.
[8] Art.28.10.
[9] Arts.21 and 22.
[10] Art.28.3.1.
[11] *Infra*, pp.590 *et seq.*
[12] Standing Orders of the Dáil (2002) and of the Seanad (1999).
[13] Art.15.11.1.
[14] Art.15.1.2.
[15] Art.15.14.
[16] Arts. 15.15 and 15.9.2.

documents before either or both Houses are contained in the Houses of the Oireachtas (Laying of Documents) Act 1966. The status, rights and obligations of civil servants who work in either House are regulated by the Staff of the Houses of the Oireachtas Act 1959.

The functions of modern legislatures, especially of the Dáil, may be itemised as (1) choosing the government, (2) dismissing the government, (3) making the government behave, (4) making laws and (5) making peace and war. Ireland has never since independence become a party to an international war. How the Dáil chooses and dismisses the Government is considered in the next chapter, which deals with the executive. As regards making the Government behave and enact laws, Professor Chubb observed that the Oireachtas is "sadly ineffective,"[17] and that as an institution it is not an important positive contributor to policy, largely because of the domination that the government has over it, a domination that is both accepted by all those involved and made the more effective by the habit of party loyalty and strict adherence to the party line in the voting lobbies. Other causes of the Oireachtas' comparative ineffectiveness include its procedures and techniques being archaic and ineffective, its staff and facilities available to members are meagre, and its members' education and experience and the view that they have of their job ill equip them to make the kind of enquiries that are necessary or to appreciate the kind of data that ought to be made available in order to judge performance.

THE SEANAD

A Senate was provided for in the Free State Constitution but was abolished in 1936.[18] Nevertheless, the present Constitution provides for a Seanad, the principal features of which are that it possesses relatively little political power, most Senators are chosen by politicians who were elected at central or at local government levels, there is special Seanad representation for university graduates and eleven senators are nominated by the Taoiseach. Only persons eligible to sit in the Dáil are entitled to become Senators.[19] As is the case in Dáil elections, voting for the Seanad is by way of secret ballot and the system of proportional representation is one of the single transferable vote but voting is by postal ballot.[20] Article 15.7–15 of the Constitution lays down various procedural rules that apply to both the Dáil and the Seanad.[21]

In his account of the Seanad, Professor Chubb observed that "Seanad Éireann is both singular in its composition and circumscribed in its powers. In considering a new senate, De Valera was attracted by one of the proposals of a

---

[17] *Supra*, n.1, p.199.
[18] See generally, D. O'Sullivan, *The Irish Free State and its Senate* (1940).
[19] Art.18.2 and Electoral Act 1992, s.41.
[20] Art.18.5.
[21] *Supra*, p.98.

commission set up to advise on the composition of a new house, a proposal for
a body selected on a vocational basis and obviously inspired by the principles
enunciated in the encyclical Quadragesimo Anno of Pius XI. However, he
recognised that the country was not sufficiently organised on vocational lines
to allow direct choice by vocational bodies, and he was also concerned not to
have a body that would be likely to oppose the government of the day."[22]

Of the 60 senators in all,[23] forty-three are selected in what may be termed
a quasi-vocational manner. That is to say, in order to become one of these
senators, one must be nominated for election by various organisations that are
divided into five broad panels.[24] There are panels for – (1) Irish language and
culture, literature, art, education and other professional interests; (2) Agriculture
and allied interests, and fisheries; (3) Labour, both organised and unorganised;
(4) Industry and commerce, including banking, finance, accounting,
engineering and architecture; (5) Public administration and social services,
including voluntary social activities. Rules regarding these panels are laid down
in the Seanad Electoral (Panel Members) Acts 1937–1954. In order to be
nominated for election by any of these panels, the aspiring senator must possess
"knowledge and practical experience of" the activity or activities that the panel
in question represents. Thus in one instance where the question of eligibility
for nomination by the labour panel arose, Pringle J. held that it was sufficient
if the person "has a reasonable amount of knowledge of the problems which
arise in our society between employee and employer and if he has also had a
reasonable amount of practical experience in dealing with these problems ...".[25]
It is not laid down in the Constitution how those nominated by these five
panels are to be elected; the matter is to be regulated by law.[26] Article 19
stipulates that the law may even provide for any vocational or functional group
directly electing senators, but that option has never been availed of. Under the
Seanad Electoral (Panel Members) Act 1947, the right to vote for those
nominated by these panels is given to all members of the in-coming Dáil, to all
the out-going senators, and to members of all city and county councils, and
borough councils. Thus, these are chosen by elected politicians rather than by
the general public or by vocational sectors of the public.

Another six senators are "elected" by the National University of Ireland
(which comprises the University Colleges of Cork, Dublin and Galway) and
by the University of Dublin (*i.e.* Trinity College, Dublin).[27] Each University
is represented by three senators, although the persons chosen do not have to
have any connection whatsoever with the University in question. As is the

---

[22] *Supra*, n.1, p.197.
[23] Art.18.1.
[24] Art.18.7.
[25] *Ormonde and Dolan v. McGabhann*, unreported, High Court, Pringle J., July 9, 1969.
[26] Art.18.10.1.
[27] Art.18.4.

case with the five nominating panels, the precise mode of university representation and election is regulated by law, which in this case is the Seanad Electoral (University Members) Act 1937. The right to vote in university senate elections is confined by this Act to graduates of the National University and graduates of Trinity College who are Irish citizens and who have reached at least eighteen years of age.[28] Article 18.4.2 of the Constitution, which was adopted in 1979, allows for extending senate representation to other institutions of higher education in the State; so far no such measure has been adopted which would permit, for example, senate representation for graduates of the Dublin City University and the University of Limerick or for the various regional colleges.

The remaining eleven senators are nominated by whoever the new Dáil chooses to be Taoiseach – the so-called "Taoiseach's eleven." Thus, with in-coming TDs being entitled (along with councillors) to vote for the five panels' nominees and with the "Taoiseach's eleven," the in-coming Government is practically guaranteed majority support in the Seanad, which largely explains why there has been so little conflict between both Houses of the Oireachtas since 1937 – in contrast with what occurred in the Free State. Conflict is more likely when a change of Government takes place without a general election having occurred.

LEGISLATION

The Oireachtas' primary function is to enact legislation. Most proposed laws emanate from the Government and are first introduced in the Dáil. Occasionally Bills, *i.e.* proposals for laws, are first introduced in the Seanad. At times Bills emanate from an opposition party or are sponsored by individual members, although these proposals rarely succeed in being adopted as legislation. Before it can be signed by the President, a Bill must have been passed by both Houses or be deemed to have been so passed. The contents of a Bill being considered by either House cannot be challenged in the courts,[29] nor it would seem can a Bill that has passed both Houses be so challenged,[30] other than by it being referred by the President to the Supreme Court under Article 26.

Legislative Procedure

Legislative proposals usually adopt the following procedure. The heads (*i.e.* main objectives and the means by which they shall be realised) of a Bill will

---

[28] Electoral (Amendment) Act 1973, s.3.
[29] *Wireless Dealers' Association v. Fair Trade Commission*, unreported, Supreme Court, March 7, 1956.
[30] But *cf. Westco Lagan Ltd v. Attorney General* [2001] 1 N.Z.L.R. 40.

be drawn up by the Government department which is sponsoring the Bill; often the contents of those heads will have been discussed with various interest groups affected in one way or another if the Bill were to become law. These heads are then discussed by the entire Government at cabinet and, if they are acceptable there, they go to the Attorney General's office in order to be translated into legislative form by the parliamentary counsel.[31] Subsequently, the draft Bill will be considered again in cabinet and, if the Government decide to go ahead with the proposal, the Bill will be introduced in the Dáil or exceptionally in the Seanad.

Once the Bill is introduced, the procedure, which follows the Westminster model, is that laid down in Standing Orders of 2002 (Dáil) and of 1999 (Seanad). There are five stages in all. The first stage is the formal introduction of the Bill in the House; the proposer is required to state its title and to provide a short description of its purpose. If the Bill gets through this stage, its contents will be printed at the State's expense and copies of it will be made available at the stationery office to the public. The second stage is a debate on the general principles that the Bill contains, after which it is regarded as having been approved in principle and is not subject to fundamental alteration. The third stage comprises a detailed consideration of the Bill's contents; it is examined section by section and amendments which alter its details but which do not affect its basic thrust may be made. Previously, this stage was conducted by the whole Dáil; now usually consideration of the details is consigned to a special committee of the Dáil, comprising mainly members with a special interest in or knowledge of the subject matter. In practice, however, many Bills go through without any serious scrutiny of their details and at times the burden is then thrown on the courts to find a solution where, under ordinary principles of statutory interpretation, the State would be on the losing side in a dispute. The fourth (report) stage consists merely of a review of how the Bill's details have fared at the preceding stage; thus the description "report." But amendments may be proposed so long as they arise out of the committee proceedings. The fifth and final stage, which in fact usually takes place immediately following the report stage, is a brief consideration of and a vote on the motion "that the Bill do now pass." Once that motion is carried, the Bill, together with such amendments as were made to it, will have been passed by the Dáil. Where a Bill is introduced first in the Seanad, it goes through the very same stages there. When a Bill goes from one House to the other – generally from the Dáil to the Seanad – it does not go through a "first stage" in the second House.

Professor Chubb described the basic structure of legislative procedure in these terms:

---

[31] See generally, Mooney, "The Work of the Office of the Parliamentary Counsel to the Government of Ireland" 22 *Statute L. Rev.* 163 (2001).

"The principles ... seem to be four. First, the house considers proposals
in an advanced stage of preparation. The idea that governs the legislative
procedures of many parliaments – namely, that a bill is only a proposal
to be investigated by a committee that will interrogate its authors and
hear interested parties before preparing its own version to present to the
full house – is alien to Irish parliamentary tradition. Second, the principles
of a bill are debated first and in full house and, having been agreed upon,
are not thereafter open to amendment. Third, it is ordinarily the job of
ministers to bring in bills and to sponsor them; the Oireachtas expects
this and is organized accordingly. Fourth, business is so arranged and
rules so framed that the government can get its bills passed without too
much delay, while at the same time the opposition has opportunities to
deploy its case against them. In doing so, the opposition will sometimes
be as much concerned to persuade the public outside the house that the
running of the country would be better placed in their hands at the next
election as to influence the government to alter its proposals (though at
the third stage particularly, much hard, detailed work is done – albeit by
a small minority of members – to amend details of bills and to improve
them technically). The orderly and timely passage of business is assured
by the government's majority and by the activities of the party whips,
who manage their respective parties, arrange the timetable in consultation
with each other and make sure that members are present to vote."[32]

Disagreement between the Dáil and Seanad

Constitutions providing for bicameral legislatures almost invariably lay down
a medium for resolving conflicts between both Houses as regards proposed
legislation. In the United Kingdom the House of Lords could block any Bill
coming from the House of Commons (and *vice versa*) until, under threat by
the monarch to create a host of additional peers, the Parliament Act 1911,[33]
was enacted which removed the Lords' complete veto. However, whereas the
Lords still come into conflict with the House of Commons, conflict between
the Seanad and the Dáil is virtually unheard of, principally because of the
manner in which senators are selected. Both Houses came into conflict on
only two occasions – in 1959 and 1964 – and the first of those instances
concerned proposed legislation for a constitutional amendment that would
remove proportional representation in Dáil elections and in favour of the "first
past the post" system.[34] That Bill eventually was passed but was rejected in a
referendum. On at least one occasion the Seanad disagreed with the Dáil on

---

[32] *Supra*, n.1, at p.195.
[33] 1 & 2 Geo. 5, c.13.
[34] The other occasion concerned the Pawnbrokers Bill 1964.

particular provisions in a Bill but in the event the Seanad accepted the Dáil's view on the Bill.

Except for two special categories of Bills (Money Bills and emergency Bills being put through under Article 24), the deadlock – resolving procedure laid down in Article 23 of the Constitution is as follows. Where the Bill was initiated and passed in the Dáil but does not secure the Seanad's approval, and at least ninety days have elapsed from when the Bill was first introduced in the Dáil, the Dáil can pass a resolution to the effect that the Bill shall be deemed to have passed both Houses. Consequently, the longest that the Seanad can block measures coming from the Dáil is three months. Where the Bill was first introduced in the Seanad but is then amended in the Dáil, the ninety day period commences from the time when the amended Bill is sent back from the Dáil to the Seanad. Article 23 does not expressly provide that the Dáil's resolution "deeming" the Bill to be passed also applies where the Seanad merely amends without rejecting in its entirety a Dáil Bill; presumably the Article's intention is that the Dáil can override the Seanad's amendment just as much as it can override the Seanad's outright rejection of a measure.

Money Bills

Most constitutions give the "lower house" special authority as regards financial matters. Even before 1911, by convention, Bills dealing wholly or mainly with public expenditure or taxation had to originate in the House of Commons and could not be amended by the House of Lords, and the Lords could not even amend the financial clauses of other Bills except where the House of Commons consented to that amendment. The procedure for "Money Bills" is laid down in Article 21 of the Constitution. These can only be initiated in the Dáil; they must be sent to the Seanad for its recommendations but the Dáil can choose to accept or reject those recommendations. Any such recommendation must be submitted to the Dáil within twenty days of the Bill having been sent by the Dáil to the Seanad.

Money Bills[35] may be described as Bills that impose a tax or related charge, or that deal with the receipt or expenditure of public funds. They are defined in Article 22.1 as "a Bill which contains only provisions dealing with all or any of the following matters, namely, the imposition, repeal, remission, alteration or regulation of taxation; the imposition for the payment of debt or other financial purposes of charges on public moneys or the variation or repeal of any such charges; supply; the appropriation, receipt, custody, issue or audit of accounts of public money; the raising or guarantee of any loan or the repayment thereof; matters subordinate and incidental to these matters or any

---

[35] See generally, "'A Tax by Any Other Name': Some Thoughts on Money Bills and Other Taxing Measures" 22 *Statute L. Rev.* 211 (2001) and 23 *Statute L. Rev.* 147 (2002).

of them." The reason for the word "only" being in this definition is to prevent non-fiscal provisions being "tacked on" to an essentially fiscal measure, with a view to preventing the Seanad from temporarily blocking those provisions. But a Bill dealing with any taxation, money or loan raised by "local authorities" or by bodies "for local purposes" is not a Money Bill.[36]

In the event of a dispute about whether a Bill falls within the above definition, the question is not resolved in the courts. Instead, under Article 22.2 the chairman of the Dáil certifies that it is such a Bill, and that certification is "final and conclusive" unless the Seanad passes a resolution requesting the President to have the matter sent to a Committee of Privileges for a determination. Where the Seanad so requests, the President must consult the Council of State and can then decide to send the question to that Committee. Members of that Committee will then be appointed by the President. An equal number are selected from members of the Dáil and of the Seanad, and a judge of the Supreme Court chairs the Committee. In the event of a tied vote, the judge has a casting vote. The Committee's decision is "final and conclusive." If the President decides against referring the question to this Committee or where the matter is sent to them but they do not come to a conclusion within the allocated 21 days, the original certificate of the chairman of the Dáil is declared to "stand confirmed." A dispute as to whether a Bill is a Money Bill has never been sent to this Committee; although in 1935 a Committee of Privileges was established under similar provisions of the Free State Constitution to consider the Land Purchase Guarantee Fund Bill, which dealt with defaults in the payment of land annuities.

Urgent Bills

Article 24 of the Constitution provides a mechanism whereby in cases of great urgency a Bill can be rushed through the legislature, although cause for resorting to this procedure has never yet arisen. It does not apply to proposed constitutional amendments, nor does it permit truncated consideration of Bills in the Dáil. It applies when a Bill has been passed by the Dáil and the Taoiseach certifies in writing to the President and to the chairman of the Dáil and of the Seanad that, in the Government's opinion, the measure is extremely urgent, in the following terms: "the Bill is urgent and immediately necessary for the preservation of the public peace and security, or by reason of the existence of a public emergency, whether domestic or international ...".

Where the Taoiseach has certified that the Bill is immediately necessary, as thus provided, and the Dáil resolves that the time for consideration of the Bill in the Seanad shall be abridged, and having consulted with the Council of State the President agrees with that abridgement, the amount of time that the

---

[36] Art.21.1.2.

Seanad has for considering the measure is whatever time the Dáil has stipulated in its resolution. If the Seanad rejects the Bill or amends it in a way that is not acceptable to the Dáil, the Bill is nevertheless deemed to have passed both Houses on expiry of the time specified in the Dáil resolution. However, a Bill that becomes law through this abridged procedure can remain in effect for only ninety days following its enactment; it can remain in force for a period after the ninety days expire provided that the Dáil and the Seanad agree that it shall continue in force.

Private Bills

From time to time the Oireachtas enacts private laws, which are sponsored by private individuals or groups,[37] for instance the Limerick Marts Act 1992, the Altamont (Amendment of Deed of Trust) Act 1993 and the Trinity College Dublin (Charters and Letters Patent Amendment) Act 2000. The procedure for passing these is contained in the joint Dáil and Seanad Standing Orders for Private Business (1939). Regulation 1 of these defines a private Bill as any Bill "promoted for the particular interest or benefit of any person or locality as distinguished from a measure of public policy ...". In the past this procedure was often availed of to assist railway, canal and water companies to get established. In the *An Blascaod Mór Teo* case,[38] Budd J. held that the Act in question there, which authorised the nationalisation of most of the Great Blasket Island, being enacted as a public Act, was not required to have gone through the private Bill procedure.

Signature and promulgation of laws

Article 25 of the Constitution contains the requirements regarding the signature and promulgation of laws. Once a Bill has been passed by or is deemed to have been passed by both Houses of the Oireachtas, it must be presented by the Taoiseach to the President for signature and promulgation. The Bill must be signed within five to seven days of it being presented for signature. But it can be signed earlier than the fifth day if the Government so requests and the Seanad concurs with the speedy signature. Bills which were passed under the Article 24 "urgent Bills" procedure must be signed on the day they are presented to the President; Bills providing for a referendum and a constitutional amendment must be signed when the President is satisfied that the amendment procedure laid down in Article 46 was duly complied with.

---

[37] See generally, A. Collins and J. O'Reilly, *Civil Proceedings and the State* (2nd ed., 2003), Chap.12.

[38] Unreported, High Court, February 27, 1998, at pp.92–93.

Every Bill which is signed must be promulgated, by which is meant that on the President's direction a notice must be inserted in the official gazette, called *Iris Oifigiúil*, stating that the Bill has become law. Following signature and promulgation, the signed text or texts of the Bill must be enrolled for record in the office of the Registrar of the Supreme Court. The enrolled text or texts are declared to be "conclusive evidence of the provisions of such law."[39] Most Bills are enacted in English and Irish translations must be made of them; likewise, where they are enacted in Irish, English translations must be made. Occasionally, a Bill is enacted in both of the official languages; where a Bill is enacted in the two languages, the Irish text prevails in the event of conflict between them.

Except where it provides otherwise, every Bill becomes law and comes into operation on the day on which it is signed by the President. Frequently, laws provide that they shall not come into effect or that certain of their provisions shall not come into effect until the Government or the appropriate Minister makes an order.[40] Sometimes the Minister or the Government's order in this context must secure the approval of one or both Houses of the Oireachtas; at times these orders are subject to a legislative veto. A notable example of complex procedures for bringing a law into force is section 13 of the Extradition (European Convention on the Suppression of Terrorism) Act 1987. A measure enacted in 1997 concerning procedures before committees of either House or joint committees, not alone provided that it would come into force in respect of either House when that House so resolved, but that the Act would cease to operate in respect of either House if that House so resolved.[41] Ordinarily, the courts will not direct the Government or the Minister, as the case may be, to make an order bringing an Act or provisions of an Act into force.[42]

LEGISLATIVE PRIVILEGE

Legislative privilege signifies the degree of legal autonomy that legislators possess for regulating their activities. In the United Kingdom this question is dealt with partly by parliamentary custom and partly by judicial decision.[43] At times the House of Commons claims privileges which are more extensive than would be recognised by the courts and, in the past, there has been conflict between the judges and the House of Commons over the scope of its privileges,[44] most notably an episode in the 1840s regarding Mr Stockdale

---

[39] Art.25.4.5.
[40] See generally, F. Bennion, *Statutory Interpretation* (3rd ed., 1997), pp.201–209.
[41] Committees of the Houses of the Oireachtas (Compellability, Privileges and Immunities of Witnesses) Act 1997.
[42] *Infra*, p.186.
[43] D. Limon *et al* ed.'s *Erskine May's Parliamentary Practice* (22nd ed., 1997).

who claimed that he had been libelled in a publication that had been ordered by the Commons. Most modern constitutions stipulate in some detail the extent to which legislators enjoy special privileges.

Legislative privilege is dealt with in Articles 15.10.12 and 13 of the Constitution, but numerous questions concerning its scope remain to be resolved. For instance, do those clauses contain an exhaustive statement of both Houses' privileges? To what extent is the British practice relevant in determining the content of those privileges? Who is the final arbiter of the scope of any privilege – the House in question or the courts? In the U.K. and some Commonwealth countries the courts have concluded that they have jurisdiction to determine questions of parliamentary privilege[45] and the United States Supreme Court regularly decides these questions.[46] Although Article 34.3.1 grants the High Court a very extensive jurisdiction, nevertheless the Constitution's separation of powers provisions may render each House the best judge of at least some features of its privileges.

Speech and debate

Since the Bill of Rights of 1689[47] it has generally been considered in the public interest that elected representatives can say in Parliament what cannot freely be said outside of either House because of libel laws and other restrictions; that public representatives should be entitled to speak bluntly and even harshly in the House. The ambit of this privilege was defined by the Australian legislature as follows: "[i]n proceedings in any court or tribunal, it is not lawful for evidence to be tendered or received, questions asked or statements, submissions or comments made, concerning proceedings in Parliament, by way of, or for the purpose of – (a) questioning or relying on the truth, motive, intention or good faith of anything forming part of those proceedings in Parliament; (b) otherwise questioning or establishing the credibility, motive, intention or good faith of any person; or (c) drawing, or inviting the drawing of, inferences or conclusions wholly or partly from anything forming part of those proceedings in Parliament."[48]

---

[44] See generally, Lock, "Parliamentary Privilege and the Courts: the Avoidance of Conflict" [1985] *Public Law* 64.

[45] E.g., *Reavy v. Century Newspapers Ltd* [2001] N.I. 187 and *Buchanan v. Jennings* [2002] 3 N.Z.L.R. 145.

[46] See generally, Reinstein & Silvergate, "Legislative Privilege and the Separation of Powers" 86 *Harvard Law Review* 1120 (1973). *Cf.* the *Green Party Exclusion* case, 70 BVerf G 324 (1986).

[47] 1 W. & M. 2 sess., c.2, Art.9, "That Freedom of Speech and Debates and Proceedings in Parliament ought not to be impeached or questioned in any court or place out of Parliament." *Cf. A. v. United Kingdom*, 36 E.H.R.R. 51 (2003).

[48] Parliamentary Privileges Act 1987, s.16(3), reversing *R. v. Murphy*, 64 A.L.R. 498 (1986).

Members of both Houses of the Oireachtas are legally free to say whatever they wish during the proceedings of the Dáil or the Seanad. Article 15.13 of the Constitution states that those members "shall not in respect of any utterance in either House, be amenable to any court or any authority other than the House itself." Accordingly, as regards what they say in either House, TDs and senators are legally insulated from the laws of libel and slander[49] and also from other laws that affect speech, such as blasphemy, sedition and the Official Secrets Act 1963. As Finlay C.J. pointed out, these provisions "constitute a very far-reaching privilege indeed to members of the Houses. ... They represent an absolute privilege and one which is clear may, in many instances, represent a major invasion of personal rights of the individual, particularly with regard to his or her good name and property rights. [This also] constitutes a significant restriction on the important public right associated with the administration of justice, of the maximum availability of all relevant evidence ...".[50] But this does not mean that there are no constraints on members saying what they like. For Dáil Standing Order 58(1) stipulates that "member[s] shall not make an utterance in the nature of being defamatory and where a member makes such an utterance it may be *prima facie* an abuse of privilege ...".[51] This Order then contains a mechanism for redressing grievances of individuals who believe that they have been defamed by what has been said in the House.

It would seem that members' professional bodies or trade unions, and perhaps even their private clubs, cannot discipline them for their parliamentary utterances. It would appear that what they have said in the House cannot even be challenged or relied on for the purpose of supporting legal proceedings based on events that happened outside the House; for example, if a TD or senator is sued for libel in respect of something said in a radio interview and in defence pleads "fair comment" or "qualified privilege," a plaintiff cannot use comments made in the House to show that the defendant was actuated by malice.[52] In *An Blascaod Mór Teo (No.4)*,[53] it was held that a claim for damages for misfeasance could not be brought against a Government Minister for allegedly misleading the Dáil when introducing legislation; such jurisdiction as the courts may have in this regard was ousted by Article 15.13. However, when they are relevant in proceedings, evidence may be adduced of statements made in either House; for example a statement made in the Dáil by the Minister

---

This Act, *inter alia*, authorises fines or imprisonment by order of either House for breach of its privilege and that warrants committing a person to prison for this purpose must set out particulars of the breach.

[49] *Cf. Dillon v. Balfour* (1887) 20 L.R. Ir. 600.

[50] *Attorney General v. Hamilton (No.2)* [1993] 3 I.R. 227 at p.270.

[51] *Cf. Maguire v. Ardagh* [2002] 1 I.R. 385 at p.684.

[52] *Buchanan v. Jennings* [2002] 3 N.Z.L.R. 145. Cf. *Laurance v. Katter* [2000] 1 Q'd R. 147 and *Rann v. Olsen* (2000) 76 S.A.S.R. 450.

[53] [2000] 3 I.R. 564.

for Justice regarding when Garda representative associations should be consulted.[54] In the *Blascoad Mór Teo* trial, the Dáil and Seanad debates were adduced in evidence by the plaintiffs.

It remains to be seen what is meant by the term "utterance in either House;" the phrase would appear to have a narrower meaning than the term "proceedings in Parliament" in British parliamentary practice. There was a view that the privilege prevented the courts from looking at parliamentary debates as an aid to interpreting legislation but that was rejected in 1993 by the House of Lords.[55]

What called for determination in *Attorney General v. Hamilton (No. 2)*[56] was whether the immunity attached to a statement made outside either House repeating what had been said there. It was held by the Supreme Court that, where in the circumstances it is clear that the speaker outside the House was consciously abandoning his privilege, then he loses the protection; otherwise, the privilege attaches. Three Dáil representatives had made allegations in the chamber of serious wrong-doing on the part of a major meat processing firm, which became the subject of a Tribunal of Inquiry, referred to popularly as the "Beef Tribunal." Subsequently, those deputies made statements to the Tribunal's chairman, repeating these allegations, and the question was whether in consequence they could be required by the Tribunal to disclose their sources of information. In making these statements, they had made it abundantly clear to the chairman that they did not wish to waive or abandon their immunity. Consequently, it was held, any attempt to force disclosure of their sources would contravene Article 15.13. As explained by O'Flaherty J., "[i]f [they] are questioned ostensibly on their written statements which they submitted to the Tribunal in reality they are being questioned on their utterances in the Dáil ... because the statements that they furnished were merely a reiteration of such utterances. ... If a Deputy was apparently disciplined for failing to elaborate on what was in such a statement he would, in reality, be punished because of his Dáil utterance and that would be ... in direct breach of [this] constitutional immunity ...".[57]

Except for repeating outside the House what was said there it appears that the immunity here cannot be waived. It was because the immunity granted in 1689 to members of the United Kingdom Parliament could not be waived, either by the representative in question or by Parliament itself, that the legislation on defamation was amended in 1996 to permit an MP or a Lord to waive the privilege in respect of what he stated in the House or what otherwise was done there with reference to him.[58]

---

[54] *Garda Representative Association v. Ireland* [1989] I.R. 193.

[55] *Pepper v. Hart* [1993] A.C. 593. Compare *Wilson v. First County Fruit Ltd (No.2)* [2003] 3 W.L.R. 568.

[56] [1983] 3 I.R. 227.

[57] *Id.* at p.292.

[58] Defamation Act 1966, s.13, considered in *Hamilton v. Al Fayed* [2001] 1 A.C. 315.

Legislation has been enacted rendering privileged all statements made and documents tendered in evidence to Committees of either or both Houses of the Oireachtas.[59]

Reports of proceedings

It has for long been regarded as being in the public interest that the business of each House of a legislature should be recorded thoroughly and fully reported, which was the cause of another Mr Stockdale incident in the 1830s[60] and the ensuing Parliamentary Papers Act 1840,[61] which gave reports of parliamentary proceedings extensive privilege in the law of defamation.[62] According to Article 15.12 of the Constitution, "[a]ll official reports and publications of the Oireachtas or of either House thereof and utterances made in either House wherever published shall be privileged." Therefore, all published reports of what was said in either House and all publications that have been authorised by either House cannot be the subject of a libel action. It has been held by the Supreme Court that the scope of the privilege here is not confined to defamation claims but extends to "any form of legal proceedings wherever [the words] may be published," is "extensive ... and is analogous to the immunity" in Article 15.13.[63]

Arrest

It has for long been regarded as being in the public interest that elected representatives should not be harassed by the police and the constitutions of some countries give public representatives very extensive immunity from law-enforcement action. Article 15.13 of the Constitution grants members of both Houses of the Oireachtas freedom from arrest when "going to and returning from and while within the precincts of either House." However, this freedom does not obtain in cases of treason, felony or breach of the peace. In Britain, by contrast, this privilege extends only to arrest in civil matters, such as refusal to comply with a maintenance order.

Internal autonomy/inherent powers

The privileges and immunities considered above are part of a wider principle

---

[59] *Infra*, p.113.
[60] *Stockdale v. Hansard* (1839) 9 A. & E. 1 and *Sheriff of Middlesex's case* (1840) 11 A. & E. 273.
[61] 3 Vic. c.9.
[62] Replaced by the Defamation Act 1961.
[63] *Attorney General v. Hamilton (No.2)* [1993] 3 I.R. 227 at pp.268 and 269.

that legislative assemblies should be permitted a considerable degree of autonomy in conducting their own affairs, without external intervention. Article 15.10 of the Constitution authorises each House of the Oireachtas to regulate its own internal affairs: that "[e]ach House shall make its own rules and standing orders, with power to attach penalties for their infringement, and shall have power to ensure freedom of debate, to protect its official documents and the private papers of its members, and to protect itself and its members against any person or persons interfering with, molesting or attempting to corrupt members in the exercise of their duties." Ultimately, it is the courts who are the actual arbiters of the extent of the autonomy so granted but they are most reluctant to involve themselves in the internal affairs of either House. Thus, when a TD sought to challenge a decision of the Ceann Comhairle, disallowing part of a question he put down for answering by a Government Minister, leave to seek judicial review of that decision was rejected.[64] Similarly, leave was refused to seek a declaration against Dáil Éireann where a Dáil seat had been vacant and a writ for a by-election to fill that vacancy had not been moved.[65] However, leave was given there as against the Government and the Attorney General, to agitate this issue but on the day before the case was to be heard, a writ was moved, thereby rendering the case moot. In Canada the courts have rejected a complaint that the standing orders of the Ontario Legislative Assembly contained unconstitutional religious discrimination,[66] because they provided for saying a Christian prayer at the commencement of each session. Once it was established that standing orders are necessary for the Assembly to function, the contents of those orders were held to be solely the prerogative of the Assembly.

Where a particular subject matter falls within the House's privileged domain, there remains the question of how alleged breaches of privilege are to be determined and what can be done to persons who are found to have contravened the House's rules. Both Houses have Committees of Procedure and Privileges, which under Standing Orders can investigate allegations and make recommendations. Must these Committees give the person being investigated a fair hearing or "natural justice"? It can hardly be doubted that either House can admonish and issue reprimands, and indeed suspend members. But they cannot expel them, nor can they imprison them. The House of Commons used to fine and imprison persons but has not done so since the nineteenth century.[67]

---

[64] O'Malley v. An Ceann Comhairle [1997] 1 I.R. 427. Compare Wuppesahl case, 80 BVerf GE 188 (1989).

[65] Dudley v. An Taoiseach [1994] 2 I.L.R.M. 321.

[66] Speaker of the Legislative Assembly v. Ontario H.R. Comm., 201 D.L.R. 4th 698 (2001).

[67] See generally, D. Clarke and G. McCoy, The Most Fundamental Legal Right (2000), Chap.9, "Contempt of the Legislature."

OIREACHTAS COMMITTEES

An important aspect of a legislature's activities is the work done by the numerous committees of either House or of joint committees, which investigate matters of public concern and report on their findings. In the Oireachtas these committees fall into three categories, *viz.* standing, select and special committees.[68] In 1970 and in 1994 legislation was enacted in respect of investigations being carried out by committees, namely the Dáil Committee on Public Accounts' so-called "Arms Inquiry"[69] and the Dáil Committee on Legislation and Security's inquiry into the circumstances in which a President of the High Court had been appointed.[70] Oireachtas Committees' status, powers and functions are now governed by the Committees of the Houses of the Oireachtas (Privilege and Procedure) Act 1976, by the Committees of the Houses of the Oireachtas (Compellability, Privileges and Immunities of Witnesses) Act 1997, and by the standing orders of the Dáil and of the Seanad. Under the Comptroller and Auditor General and Committees of the Houses of the Oireachtas (Special Provisions) Act 1998, the Dáil may require the Comptroller and Auditor General to carry out an investigation into circumstances that pose a "substantial risk to the revenues of the State."

What members say in Oireachtas committees is given the same protection by the 1976 Act as is provided for in Article 15.13 of the Constitution. And what is stated by them and by committee advisors, officials and agents, is deemed privileged, as are documents connected with a committee and its official reports and publications. The main features of the 1997 Act include authority conferred on the committee in question to require persons to give evidence, to produce documents and to make an affidavit discovering documents, and to give such other directions as are "reasonable and just." Evidence given or documents tendered to a committee are absolutely privileged, as if they were given in court proceedings. Statements or admissions so made are inadmissible against their maker in any subsequent criminal proceedings. Witnesses may be required to take an oath. Persons referred to or otherwise identified in proceedings before a committee are entitled to come and give evidence and call witnesses and, with the committee's consent, may cross-examine other witnesses and make submissions. Where a civil servant, member of the Garda Síochána or the Defence Forces gives evidence, he is not permitted to "question or express an opinion on the merits of any policy ... or on the ... objectives" of such policy of the Government or of any Minister or of the Attorney General.[71]

---

[68] See generally, Chubb, *supra*, n.1, pp.202–203.

[69] Committee of Public Accounts of Dáil Éireann (Privilege and Procedure) Act 1970.

[70] Select Committee on Legislation and Security of Dáil Éireann (Privilege and Immunity) Act 1994.

[71] S.15.

There are several circumstances in which persons may refuse to answer questions or tender documents and also mechanisms for resolving disputes as to whether those circumstances obtain. Judges are entirely exempted from the obligation to give evidence and tender documents, as is the President or any member of his office. So too are the Attorney General and the Director of Public Prosecutions, and any of their officials, with a restricted exception for proceedings before the Committee of Public Accounts. Members of either House cannot be questioned about the source of information contained in anything they said in the House or in any of its committees. Section 5 exempts questions concerning what may be described as sensitive topics and disputes relating to these may be referred to the High Court. Disputes about some of them, namely whether the information may prejudice State security or its relations with other States, or whether it may prejudice law-enforcement, may also be resolved by the Secretary of the Government. Objections may be made to the relevance of questions asked, which may be resolved by way of application to the High Court.

Extent of authority

To date the practice has been to establish Oireachtas committees by way of a resolution of the House in question, or by both Houses as the case may be, and the initiation of any investigation is done similarly. In *Maguire v. Ardagh*,[72] the principal issue was whether an investigation could be carried out by the Joint Committee on Justice, Equality and Defence of Women's Rights, into an incident in 2000 at Abbeylara, Co. Longford, in which a civilian was shot dead by one or more members of the Garda Síochána. Because that investigation might have resulted in a conclusion that one or more of those Gardaí may have unlawfully exceeded their power to use firearms, the Supreme Court held that the Committee had no inherent authority to conduct this investigation, even if it did have the powers conferred on it by the 1997 Act. It was left open by the Court whether that authority could be conferred on a committee by way of legislation.

It was accepted by all concerned that these committees could carry out inquiries relating to the legislative function. But there was no indication that the enquiry here was for any such function, other than in the general public interest. If the enquiry's objective was to formulate policy for legislative proposals, that should be made clear from the very outset. What was being objected to here was the Joint Committee's assertion that it was empowered to establish the truth of controverted facts about a past event and, if so, conclude that one or more individuals were responsible for an unlawful killing. This, it was held, could not be done for several reasons.

---

[72] [2002] 1 I.R. 385.

Neither the Constitution nor statute gave any express power to conduct that kind of enquiry, nor was the power carried over from the Westminster Parliament in 1922. The alleged basis for this power was that it was an inherent attribute of a Parliament in a constitutional democracy, with emphasis on the practice of the U.S. Congress to hold enquiries of this nature. However, the Congress is deemed to have inherited several attributes of the U.K. Parliament, which at least in the past was a High Court as well as a legislative assembly, as is exemplified by its power to try persons by way of impeachment. Additionally, because the executive in the U.S. does not control the legislature to the same extent and manner as in Ireland, there may be a greater need for this power in the U.S. Because parliamentary inquiries of this nature had become politically discredited at the beginning of the last century, being for all practical purposes replaced by inquiries under the Tribunals of Inquiry (Evidence) Act 1921, it is curious that these enquiries were not expressly provided for in 1922 if that had been the intention of those who drafted the Free State Constitution. Indeed its *travaux préparatoires* show that a proposal along these lines had been contemplated at the time, such a provision existed in the Government of Ireland Act 1920 (the Home Rule proposals) and was provided for inferentially in the Acts establishing Constitutions for Canada and Australia. In the light of historical and comparative analysis and the constitutional text, there was no implied power, as was contended for.

Additionally, there are express provisions in the Constitution that provide for findings of individual culpability – of the President, of judges and of members of either House. Legislation had to be enacted to enable these and other committees to compel the attendance of witnesses, which would not be necessary if there was an inherent power. In the circumstances, the Committee had available to it more than enough information to form policy with regard to the use of firearms by members of the Gardaí, and examining them and cross-examining them on the Abbeylara incident, in order to find individual culpability would hardly add anything of significance.

This was fortified by the separate ground that the activities of the Joint Committee, if not constrained, would permit it to make findings that gravely injured an individual's reputation and good name, with potentially catastrophic economic and social consequences for him. All persons have a constitutional right to protect their good name and even the Dáil's own Standing Orders circumscribe the freedom of members to say whatever they like about an individual in the course of proceedings in the House. There were ineffective safeguards in the Joint Committee's procedures to protect persons' reputations and, when the basis of the inquiry power is said to be inherent, there has to be counter-balanced against it the express guarantee of ones good name.

An additional factor was what was described as institutional bias; the enquiry that could result in findings of individual culpability was being carried on by full-time politicians. Because investigations of this nature can so easily become politicised, there was not the same protection for persons' good names as there would be in an enquiry conducted by a judge appointed under the 1921 Act. Given that this perfectly acceptable procedure existed for investigating concerns about individual wrongdoing, there was no practical necessity to imply that the Oireachtas itself could set up its own comparable machinery. Whether what was described as the institutional bias objection could be overcome by express legislative authority to set up an enquiry of this nature was left open, although it was pointed out that it was most unsatisfactory for politicians involved in these inquiries commenting in the meantime about how they were being or would be conducted.

Geoghegan J. added that a legitimate Oireachtas Committee enquiry into a proper legislative purpose might inevitably and unavoidably result in "implied blame" being attached to an individual. Were that to occur, it would not inevitably render the entire enquiry *ultra vires*.

Procedure

Oireachtas committees are empowered by section 13 of the 1997 Act to devise rules and guidelines for the conduct of their procedures. Any such rules must provide for fair procedures and it would seem that the courts may intervene if unfair procedures are being followed. These committees can take evidence on oath and, if they chose, conduct their hearings otherwise than in public. Sections 4 and 5 of the Official Secrets Act 1963, do not apply to evidence given or documents produced on a committee's direction. Precisely what procedures are fair depends on the nature and conduct of the enquiry in question, and committees would be allowed a degree of flexibility in this regard. Where, however, a person before a committee is more in the nature of a party or potential accused, as compared with any other witness, and witnesses have immunity in respect of their evidence, then that person is entitled to a reasonable means of defending himself. It was held in *Re Haughey*[73] that persons in this position should be given a copy of any evidence that reflected on their good name, be permitted through counsel to cross-examine their accuser or accusers, be allowed to give rebutting evidence and, finally, be permitted through counsel to address the committee in their defence.

That case arose from the turmoil in Northern Ireland at the end of the 1960s, where mobs carried out attacks on Catholic communities. Some Northern nationalist representatives sought funds, in order to buy arms for self-defence, and they managed to secure arms from sources in the Republic. Beyond these incontrovertible details, it is hard to know what exactly did happen except that two former government ministers were prosecuted, unsuccessfully, for illegally importing arms (the "Arms Trial").[74] The Committee of Public

---

[73] [1971] I.R. 217.
[74] *People v. Luyckx & Others*, unreported, Central Criminal Court, October 1970.

Accounts investigated the use of public funds which it was alleged were applied unlawfully to buy arms. Among those the Committee summoned to give evidence was Paraic Haughey – whose brother, a former Minister for Finance who subsequently became Taoiseach, was to be tried and acquitted on charges of illegally importing arms. Doubts about the Committee's legal authority to subpoena witnesses were resolved by the Committee of Public Accounts of Dáil Éireann (Privilege and Procedure) Act 1970, being enacted. All witnesses were given the same immunities and privileges that they would have in the High Court. When Mr Haughey came before the Committee he read a prepared statement disclaiming all knowledge of or connection with the subject matter of the investigation, and from then on declined to answer any questions. Section 3(4) of the 1970 Act anticipated witnesses not co-operating with the investigation by empowering the Committee to require that the High Court punish the recalcitrant for contempt. Mr Haughey was thereupon sent forward to the Court under this provision. However, the Supreme Court held that this form of sanction was unconstitutional because it in effect provided that an individual could be tried and convicted of a serious criminal offence without the benefit of a jury trial.[75] Under section 3(8) of the 1997 Act, refusal to cooperate with an Oireachtas committee in several ways is made an offence, for which the alleged offender is then tried in the normal manner.

It also was held in *Re Haughey* that the Committee's procedures were unfair and unlawful because, since Mr Haughey was more in the position of a party than a mere witness, they did not allow him to cross-examine persons who gave evidence adverse to him. Under the 1996 Act, any persons referred to or otherwise identified in the course of evidence may cross-examine witnesses if the committee in question so consents. One of the objections raised by the applicants in *Maguire v. Ardagh*[76] was that, since the members of the Gardaí there also were in a position equivalent to a party or accused, they should have been afforded full rights of cross-examination, rather than the very restricted role contemplated by the Committee. What the Committee envisaged was that there should be no cross examination until all the evidence in chief had been adduced and then the Gardaí were to be allowed only a limited time to challenge adverse witnesses. It was held by the Supreme Court that this was not a sufficient vindication of their constitutional right to protect their good name. Hardiman J. stressed that "the right to cross-examine one's accusers is a constitutional right and not a concession" and is an "essential constitutionally guaranteed aspect of fair procedures."[77] He added that "when a body decides to deal with matters as serious as those in question here, it cannot ... deny to persons whose reputations and livelihoods are thus brought into issue the full power to cross-examine fully, as a matter of right and without unreasonable hindrance."[78]

---

[75] *Infra*, p.411.
[76] [2002] 1 I.R. 385.
[77] *Id*. at p.705.
[78] *Id*. at p.707.

CHAPTER 6

The Executive

The executive is another branch in the traditional separation of powers. Article 28.2 of the Constitution provides that "[t]he executive power of the State shall, subject to the provisions of this Constitution, be exercised by or on the authority of the Government."

THE GOVERNMENT

Article 28 of the Constitution sets out the basic rules regarding the composition of the Government and its essential functions.[1] It consists of the Taoiseach, the Tánaiste and Government Ministers.

Taoiseach

Under Article 28.5 of the Constitution, at the head of the Government is the Taoiseach, or Prime Minister, who is appointed by the President on the Dáil's nomination.[2] The President has no say at all as to who shall form a Government; it is the Dáil alone that determines who forms and leads the Government. A Taoiseach who loses the support of a majority in the Dáil is obliged to resign from office there and then, except where the Dáil is dissolved and a general election is called, in which event the Taoiseach stays in office until the incoming Dáil decides who shall hold the office.[3] All Government Ministers are chosen by the Taoiseach, who also can decide to dismiss them, although the formal appointments and removals from office are the acts of the President.[4] One of the Taoiseach's constitutional functions is to "keep the President generally informed on matters of domestic and international policy."[5] There

---

[1] See generally, B. Chubb, *The Government and Politics of Ireland* (3rd ed., 1992), Chap. 10 and S. Dooney & J. O'Toole, *Irish Government Today* (2nd ed., 1998), Chaps 1 and 2. *Cf.* I. Jennings, *Cabinet Government* (1959).
[2] Art.13.1.1.
[3] Art.28.10.
[4] Art.13.1.2–3.
[5] Art.28.5.2.

is a separate civil service Department of the Taoiseach. The constitutional duties and functions of a Taoiseach have been summarised as follows:[6]

Duties flowing from the nomination and resignation or removal of certain office holders

– The nomination of Ministers (Article 13.1.2);

– acceptance of the resignation of a Minister (Article 28.9.2);

– nomination of members of the Seanad (Article 18.3 and Article 18.10.2);

– notification of the President of a resolution removing the Comptroller and Auditor General (Article 33.2)

– notification of the President of a resolution removing a judge of the Supreme Court or the High Court (Article 35.4.2);

– duties concerning the nomination and removal of the Attorney General (Article 30 and Article 30.5).

Advice to the President

– Advice to the President on the summoning and dissolution of the Dáil (Article 13.2.1);
– provision of information to the President on matters of domestic and international policy (Article 28.5.2).

Duties flowing from the passage of legislation and enrolment of the authentic text of the Constitution

– Certification of urgency for the purposes of abridging time for the consideration of a Bill by the Seanad (Article 24.1);

– presentation to the President of a Bill for signature (Article 25.1);

– signature of a message from the Government to the Dáil prior to any vote or resolution appropriating revenue or other public moneys (Article 17.2);

– the preparation and signature of the authentic text of the Constitution to be enrolled in the office of the Registrar of the Supreme Court (Article 25.5.1 and Article 25.5.2).

---

[6] *Riordan v. An Tánaiste* [1997] 3 I.R. 502 at pp.504–505.

Tánaiste

Article 28.6 of the Constitution requires a Government Minister, known as the Tánaiste or deputy Prime Minister, whose principal official function is to deputise for the Taoiseach when the latter is temporarily absent and to take the place of a Taoiseach who is permanently incapacitated or who dies, until another is appointed.[7] The Tánaiste is treated as just another Government Minister for all other purposes. There is no Department of the Tánaiste as such but Tánaisti usually occupy one of the more important Government Departments. As well as being a Minister, the Tánaiste must be a member of the Dáil, is *ex officio* a member of the Council of State and ranks next after the Taoiseach, before the Minister for Finance.

There is no constitutional obligation to assign a particular Department to the Tánaiste. Nor is there any restriction on assigning to the Tánaiste functions over and above what is stipulated in the Constitution. Nor is there any obligation on the Tánaiste to remain in the State at all times when the Taoiseach is abroad.[8] If, however, there were a constitutional duty for the Taoiseach to perform but he and the Tánaiste were not in the country, one of them would have to return in order to discharge that obligation.

Ministers and Departments

By Article 28 of the Constitution, the Government must comprise between seven and fifteen members.[9] Government Ministers are appointed by the President on the Taoiseach's nomination, lose office once the Taoiseach resigns and can be removed from office at the discretion of the Taoiseach.[10] As well as the Taoiseach, the Tánaiste and the Minister for Finance, all but two of these Ministers must be members of the Dáil; not more than two Ministers can be senators.[11] But all Ministers are entitled to attend and to be heard in either House of the Oireachtas.[12]

The general status, rights and obligations of Ministers are governed by the Ministers and Secretaries Act 1924, as amended. Section 1 of that Act provides that eleven Departments of State shall be established, which Departments are allocated responsibility for specified matters, and various public agencies are assigned to the charge of the different Departments. Since then, some Departments have been abolished (*e.g.* Posts and Telegraphs) or merged with

---

[7] Art.28.6.
[8] *Supra*, n.6.
[9] Art.28.1.
[10] Arts.13.2 and 3, and 28.9.4 and 11.
[11] Art.28.7.
[12] Art.28.7.

others (*e.g.* Fisheries) and new Departments have been created (*e.g.* the Public Service in 1973).

Each Minister's legal status is defined by section 2(1) of the 1924 Act as "a corporation sole ..., and shall have perpetual succession and an official seal ..., and may sue ..., and be sued ..., and may acquire, hold and dispose of land for the purposes of the functions, powers or duties of the Department ...". In other words, each Ministry possesses a separate legal personality of its own, which continues even though different individuals assume charge of the Department. Each Ministry may sue and be sued, and can acquire and dispose of land.

The Ministers and Secretaries (Amendment) (No.2) Act 1977, authorises the creation of a new category of Minister, called Minister of State, to be appointed by the Government on the Taoiseach's nomination. The maximum number of these Ministers has since been increased to fifteen. Ministers of State must be members of either House of the Oireachtas. They can be removed by the Government on the Taoiseach's recommendation and they must vacate their office whenever the Taoiseach resigns.[13] The 1977 Act permits statutory and other powers vested in a Minister of the Government to be delegated to a Minister of State subject to certain conditions and safeguards. These are, principally, that the Minister of State be assigned to a particular Government Department; any or all of the powers vested in the Minister in charge of that Department can be delegated to the Minister of State but those powers are exercisable subject to the Government Minister's "general superintendence and control" and to any condition contained in the delegation; finally, it is declared that the delegation "shall not remove or derogate from the responsibility of the Minister of the Government on whose request (the delegation) was made or ... as a member of the Government for the exercise or performance of the statutory powers and duties thereby delegated."[14] In this way it is hoped that any constitutional difficulty with this new category of Minister is overcome.

Governing through the legislature

Under the United States constitutional scheme, the Government is largely insulated from the legislature once the President's cabinet appointees secure Congressional approval. The Irish scheme of government in comparison is modelled on that in the United Kingdom, where the Prime Minister and cabinet govern through the legislature and are responsible to it. According to Article 28.4.1 and 2 of the Constitution, "[t]he Government shall be responsible to

---

[13] S.1(1).
[14] S.2(2)(f).

Dáil Éireann. The Government shall meet and act as a collective authority, and shall be collectively responsible for the Departments of State administered by the members of the Government."

Governments that lose the support of a majority in the Dáil must either leave office or face a general election.[15] Political scientists are better qualified than lawyers to comment on the actual practice and effectiveness of cabinet government through the legislature. What constitutes "collective responsibility" to the Dáil and whether Ministers bear "individual responsibility" to the Dáil for all that happens in their Departments is more a political than a juridical question.[16]

Whether Ministers are legally responsible in their personal capacities for what they or their subordinates do in the course of duty has never been clarified.[17] This issue is of little particular practical importance since section 2(1) of the Ministers and Secretaries Act 1924, permits actions to be brought against the Minister as a corporation sole; claims may also be brought against the State under the name of Ireland.[18]

Cabinet confidentiality

Although parties to litigation usually can obtain a court order that all relevant documentation connected with their dispute should be discovered to them by the opposing party, for the purpose of a proper hearing of the case (i.e. an order for "discovery"), occasionally as is explained below, this documentation may be withheld on the grounds of what may be called executive privilege. This privilege has a comparatively narrow ambit, the presumption being strongly in favour of disclosure. In appropriate circumstances, even cabinet documentation can be the subject of discovery orders.

During the course of the "Beef Tribunal," the question arose as to whether Government Ministers were free to give evidence concerning what occurred at meetings of the Government. There the sole member of that Tribunal indicated that he proposed questioning a former Minister for Energy about what had taken place at a cabinet meeting that made decisions about credit insurance for beef exported to Iraq. However, the Attorney General intervened, contending that any discussions that took place then were confidential and neither the Government of the day, let alone a Minister, could waive that confidentiality; it was contended that this was a fundamental aspect of the separation of powers and of cabinet Government under the Constitution. In

---

[15] Art.28.10 and 11.
[16] See, however, G. Hogan & D. Morgan, *Administrative Law in Ireland* (3rd ed., 1998), pp.53–63.
[17] Cf. *Decock v. Government of Alberta* 186 D.L.R. 265 (2002).
[18] *Byrne v. Ireland* [1972] I.R. 241.

Attorney General v. Hamilton[19] the Supreme Court, by a 3/2 majority, overruled O'Hanlon J. and endorsed the Attorney's argument. According to Hederman J.: "[i]f it were permissible to compel in any circumstances the disclosure of the content of discussions which take place at Government meetings the executive role of the Government as envisaged by the Constitution would be undermined, perhaps even de-stabilised."[20] On the assumption that the Dáil could not compel a Government Minister to disclose what had been said in Cabinet, O'Flaherty J. concluded that a Tribunal established by the Dáil and Seanad equally could not compel disclosure. In a powerful dissent, McCarthy J. pointed out that in no other comparable jurisdiction was there an absolute constitutional prohibition against ever disclosing what was said in Cabinet, that there was nothing in the general principle of cabinet responsibility that required so unqualified a prohibition. According to him, the question is whether it is in the public interest that the information being sought in any particular instance should be disclosed; it was the Tribunal that was the arbiter of this interest, subject to judicial review by the courts. No opinion was expressed on the desirability of disclosure here because the Attorney had contended for absolute confidentiality, regardless of the circumstances.

That holding was substantially reversed in a referendum held in 1999, which adopted Article 28.4.3 of the Constitution, endorsing the position taken by McCarthy J. According to it,

> "3 The confidentiality of discussions at meetings of the Government shall be respected in all circumstances save only where the High Court determines that disclosure should be made in respect of a particular matter—
>> i in the interests of the administration of justice by a Court, or
>> ii by virtue of an overriding public interest, pursuant to an application in that behalf by a tribunal appointed by the Government or a Minister of the Government on the authority of the Houses of the Oireachtas to inquire into a matter stated by them to be of public importance."

To date, this clause has not been considered by the courts.[21]

THE DEFENCE FORCES

According to Article 15.6.1 and 2 of the Constitution, only the Oireachtas can raise and maintain a defence force, it there being described as an "armed force";

---

[19] [1993] 2 I.R. 250.
[20] *Id.* at p.275.
[21] *Cf. Irish Press Publications Ltd v. Minister for Enterprise* [2002] 4 I.R. 110.

that "[t]he right to raise and maintain military or armed forces is vested exclusively in the Oireachtas. No military or armed force, other than (such a) force raised and maintained by the Oireachtas, shall be raised or maintained for any purpose whatsoever." Doubtless, this latter provision was inspired by the illegal private army tradition in Ireland, especially by the so-called Irish Republican Army. Article 13.4 and 5 places the President in charge of the armed forces, describing them as the "defence forces"; "[t]he supreme command of the Defence Forces is hereby vested in the President; (and) all commissioned officers of the Defence Forces shall hold their commissions from the President." While the President is the head of these forces, it is the Government, through the Minister for Defence, that has charge and control over them. According to section 17(1) of the Defence Act 1954, "[u]nder the direction of the President, and subject to the provisions of this Act, the military command of, and all executive and administrative powers in relation to, the Defence Forces ... shall be exercisable by the Government ... through and by the Minister."

Members of the forces' status, rights and duties are regulated principally by a very detailed code in the Defence Acts 1954-1998.[22] Only Irish citizens and aliens who are specially approved by the Minister can be appointed as officers.[23] In 1960 provision was made whereby members of these forces could be sent abroad to serve in conjunction with an international United Nations force.

Members of the defence forces are subject to military law in that sections 124–169 of the 1954 Act designate a whole host of acts to be offences under military law (*e.g.* ranging from unjustified cowardice in war, mutiny, insubordination and desertion, to the "ordinary law" offences of treason, murder, genocide, manslaughter and rape), and an accused can be tried for these offences by court martial. Military courts are provided for in Article 38.4 of the Constitution, and the courts martial established by the 1954 Act are comprised of at least five officers, with the Judge Advocate General in attendance.[24] The jurisdiction of courts martial is defined as "to try and punish any person for an offence against military law committed by such person while subject to military law as an officer or a man."[25] A Courts Martial Appeals Court was established in 1983.[26]

The principal military officers (the Chief of Staff, the Adjutant-General and the Quartermaster General) are appointed by and removable by the President.[27] Officers are also appointed by the President, who may, for any

---

[22] See generally, G. Humphreys & C. Craven, *Military Law in Ireland* (1997).
[23] Defence Act 1954, s.41.
[24] *Id.* ss.185-208.
[25] *Id.* s.192(1).
[26] Court Martial (Appeals) Act 1983.
[27] 1954 Act, ss.42 and 47(2).

prescribed reason, retire them or direct that they shall relinquish their commissions.[28] The President may dismiss an officer provided that reasons for the proposed dismissal are given and the officer has a reasonable opportunity of making representations.[29] The Minister is given extensive power to make regulations regarding these forces. Members cannot stand for parliamentary elections[30] and are disqualified from being members of any local authority;[31] any officer who becomes a member of either House of the Oireachtas thereupon relinquishes his or her commission.[32] Members of the permanent forces are forbidden to "join, or be a member of, or subscribe to, any political organisation or society or any secret society whatsoever."[33]

By the Defence (Amendment) Act 1990 provision was made whereby associations comparable to trade unions could be established to represent members' economic interests, but it was coupled with a prohibition against members joining a trade union or other similar body. These associations are required to be independent and, without the Minister's permission, may not affiliate to or be associated with any trade union or other body. Members are prohibited from endeavouring to persuade any member to join a trade union or other similar body.

THE GARDA SÍOCHÁNA

Ireland has a single national police force, the Garda Síochána, which was first established in 1923 and was merged with the Dublin Metropolitan Police in 1925. There is no express reference in the Constitution to policing.[34] The general status, rights and duties of the Gardaí are regulated principally by the Garda Síochána Act 1924, and Police Forces Amalgamation Act 1925, as amended.[35] In 1989 provision was made whereby members could be sent abroad to serve in conjunction with an international United Nations force. And in 1997 provision was made to facilitate compliance with the State's obligations under the Europol Convention and its protocols.

Decisions whether persons should be prosecuted for summary offences are almost entirely a matter for the Gardaí but authority to prosecute in respect of serious offences has been vested in the Attorney General and the Director of Public Prosecutions.[36] In addition to whatever powers of arrest they possess

---

[28] *Id.*, s.48(2).
[29] *Id.*, s.50.
[30] Electoral Act 1992, s.4(g) (Dáil).
[31] 1954 Act, s.104 and Local Government Act 2001, s.13(1)(g).
[32] *Id.*, s.48(6).
[33] *Id.*, s.103(1).
[34] Except in Art.61, the carry-over provision.
[35] See generally, D. Walsh, *The Irish Police* (1998).
[36] *Infra*, p.428.

at common law along with all other citizens, there is a vast body of legislation that authorises members of the Garda, sometimes members who are above a specified rank, to arrest, question, seize property and enter premises, usually on having a warrant but on certain occasions even without any warrant.[37] A member of the force acting in excess of his lawful powers will be held liable in damages, for instance, for false imprisonment or trespass to the person, or to goods or to land.[38] In 1984 legislative provision was made for a Garda Complaints Board, in order to deal with allegations of wrong-doing against members of the force but it did not come into operation until 1987. On two occasions "laws of validation" had to be passed to deal with irregularities in the way that the Government dealt with the force.[39]

The highest ranks of the force (the Commissioner, Deputy Commissioners, and Assistant Commissioners) are appointed by the Government and they "may at any time be removed from such office" by the Government.[40] However, the Government does not possess an absolute and unfettered discretion to remove these officers.[41] The Minister for Justice, Equality and Law Reform is empowered to make regulations governing virtually every aspect of the force. Gardaí are not eligible to be elected to or to sit in the Dáil or the Seanad,[42] and are forbidden by regulation to stand for public office or to take any other active part in politics.[43] Gardaí are not permitted to become members of a trade union,[44] although the 1924 Act provides for a trade union substitute in the form of single representative bodies for the major ranks.[45] These bodies must be independent of and not associate with any outside body of persons.

THE CIVIL SERVICE

The Government rely principally on the civil service in order to render effective the executive power of the State.[46] Apart from legislation on appointments, discipline and pensions, no Act of the Oireachtas regulating how the service should function existed until the Public Service Management Act 1997. Under section 4(1) of this Act, the head of each Department is known as the Secretary General, who is given "the authority, responsibility and accountability" for carrying on numerous enumerated functions, *inter alia*, managing the

---

[37] *Infra*, p.318.
[38] E.g., *Dunne v. Clinton* [1930] I.R. 366 and *Lynch v. Fitzgerald* [1938] I.R. 382.
[39] Acts of 1937 No. 5 and of 1979 No. 16; *infra*, p.290.
[40] 1925 Act ss. 6 and 7.
[41] *Garvey v. Ireland* [1981] I.R. 75.
[42] Electoral Act 1992, s.41(h)(Dáil).
[43] Garda Síochána (Discipline) Regulations, S.I. No. 94 of 1989, schedule, para.15.
[44] *Aughey v. Ireland* [1986] I.L.R.M. 206.
[45] S.13 as amended by the Garda Síochána Act 1977, s.1.
[46] See generally, Chubb, *supra*, n.1, Chap.13 and Downey & O'Toole, *supra*, n.1, Chap.6.

Department, implementing Government policies that affect it, advising the Minister, preparing strategy statements and progress reports, ensuring that functions are discharged in a cost effective manner and hiring and firing staff below the grade of principal. This authority is subject to any other statutory provision, direction of the Government and determination of "matters of policy" by the Minister. Further, the Secretary General is made accountable to his Minister, who may issue him with written instructions. Responsibility as provided for here is most unlikely to be construed as personal legal responsibility to one or more members of the public. Where requested to do so, a Secretary General must appear before a competent Committee of either House of the Oireachtas when considering a strategy statement prepared for his department.

Civil servants' appointments are governed by the Civil Service Commissioners Act 1956, the purpose of which is to ensure that the best persons are chosen using fair procedures. Their status, rights and responsibilities are governed by the Civil Service Regulations Act 1956.[47] According to section 5 of this Act, "[e]very established civil servant shall hold office at the will and pleasure of the Government." Nevertheless, a civil servant cannot be dismissed for any reason whatsoever and is entitled to a prior fair hearing if the dismissal is related to misconduct or may otherwise adversely reflect on his character.

Except where permitted to do so by their terms of employment, civil servants are incapable of being elected or sitting as members of the Dáil or of the Seanad.[48] No statutory provisions exist dealing with such controversial matters as the other political activities of civil servants but a departmental circular first issued in 1932 prohibits their political involvement, which is defined to include the following:

> "(i) An official shall not be a member of an Association or serve on a Committee having for its object the promotion of the interests of a political party or the promotion or the prevention of the return of a particular candidate to the Dáil.
>
> (ii) An official shall not support or oppose any particular candidate or party either by public statement or writing.
>
> (iii) An official shall not make any verbal statements in public (or which are liable to be published), and shall not contribute to newspapers or other publications any letters or articles, conveying information, comment or criticism on any matter of current political interest, or which concerns the political action or position of the Government or of any member or group of members of the Oireachtas."[49]

---

[47] See generally, M. Forde, *Employment Law* (2nd ed., 2001), Chap.13.
[48] Electoral Act 1992, s.41(h).
[49] Circular 21/1932, amended by circular 22/1974.

In 1974, most of these restrictions were lifted from industrial and clerical civil servants. Since 1982 strikes and other industrial action by civil servants are no longer automatically unlawful.[50]

LOCAL GOVERNMENT

A significant amount of public administration is carried on at local level, although the powers of local authorities are subject to extensive control by central government and most funding for local activities is provided by the Minister for Finance rather than raised locally.[51] Prior to 1999, when Article 28A was adopted, there were no constitutional provisions on regional and local government. Under this,

> "1. The State recognises the role of local government in providing a forum for the democratic representation of local communities, in exercising and performing at local level powers and functions conferred by law and in promoting by its initiatives the interests of such communities.
>
> 2. There shall be such directly elected local authorities as may be determined by law and their powers and functions shall, subject to the provisions of this Constitution, be so determined and shall be exercised and performed in accordance with law.
>
> 3. Elections for members of such local authorities shall be held in accordance with law not later than the end of the fifth year after the year in which they were last held.
>
> 4. Every citizen who has the right to vote at an election for members of Dáil Éireann and such other persons as may be determined by law shall have the right to vote at an election for members of such of the local authorities referred to in section 2 of this Article as shall be determined by law.
>
> 5. Casual vacancies in the membership of local authorities referred to in section 2 of this Article shall be filled in accordance with law."

To date, this clause has not been considered by the courts.

Local government is regulated principally by the Local Government Act 2001, which provides for local authorities in the prescribed local government areas. Under section 11(7) of this Act, each local authority is a body corporate, with perpetual succession and power to sue and be sued in its own name, can acquire, manage and dispose of land and has a seal. *Inter alia*, members of the Defence Forces, the Garda Síochána, the civil service and local authority

---

[50] Trade Disputes (Amendment) Act 1982.
[51] See generally, Chubb, *supra*, n.1, Chap.15 and Downey & O'Toole, *supra*, n.1, Chap.8.

employees above a certain grade cannot be elected to these bodies. Decision making power in local government is divided between the elected representatives and the full-time manager. Under Part 19 (sections 198–211) of this Act, local authorities can make bye-laws. Section 216 sets out the circumstances in which the Minister may remove the elected representatives from their office.

PUBLIC AGENCIES AND BODIES

The State's executive power is also rendered effective through a vast array of public agencies, boards, bodies, corporations and companies.[52] In addition to local and regional authorities, there are, to name some of them, the Ombudsman, the Central Bank, the Revenue Commissioners, the Director of Public Prosecutions, the Environmental Protection Agency, the Planning Board, the Competition Authority, the Equality Authority, the Radio Television Authority, the Film Censor, as well as Health Authorities. An almost complete list of these bodies is contained in the schedule to the Official Languages Act 2003. Some of these offices or bodies have a statutory guarantee of independence from executive interference. Many others are accountable to designated Government Ministers. The boards and chief officers of some of these bodies are insulated by legislation from removal except under specified circumstances and procedures.[53] One feature common to the statutes establishing many of these bodies is that members of the bodies' governing authorities or boards are forbidden from being members of either House of the Oireachtas or of the European Parliament.

There are several State-owned and managed enterprises that run a business, several of which are in a monopoly or near monopoly position. These are often referred to a "state-sponsored bodies" or "semi states." In recent years, some of these have been sold off to private investors and the State-owned industrial and commercial sector is much smaller now than it was prior to the 1980s. Especially in consequence of State-owned enterprises being privatised, in recent years agencies have been established to remove certain decision-making from the political domain. Significant economic choices that at times have considerable political ramifications are entrusted to "regulators," such as the Commission for Energy Regulation, established in 1999, the Commission for Aviation Regulation, established in 2001, the Commission for Communication Regulation, established in 2002, and the Irish Financial Services Regulatory Authority, established in 2003.

---

[52] See generally, Downey & O'Toole, Chap.9.
[53] *E.g.*, Planning and Development Act 2000, ss.105(15) and 106(15).

EXECUTIVE PRIVILEGE

Executive privilege signifies several things. It can mean some exemption from the ordinary rules of law; that certain legal rules, although generally applicable, do not bind the Government and its agents. This state of affairs was reflected somewhat in the principle, since repeated, of statutory construction to the effect that statutes do not bind the State except where the Act in question either expressly or by implication so provides.[54] Acting on the Government's instructions has never been a good defence to a criminal prosecution or civil action. Indeed, one of the fundamental principles of the common law has been that executive authorisation is never in itself a good defence in an action for a civil wrong.[55] A related connotation of executive privilege is that the executive possesses certain inherent powers to interfere with liberty or property, without having specific legislative authority to do so. That doctrine has always been rejected by the common law, and indeed the US Supreme Court has held that the executive there has no such right, at least when the State is not at war.[56]

Executive privilege also connotes that there are certain facts known to the Government or its agencies which are secret, and courts are not entitled to compel disclosure of that information.[57] While the Constitution provides expressly for legislative privileges, apart from Article 28.4.3 on cabinet confidentiality, there are no comparable provisions regarding the executive. Apart entirely from the Official Secrets Act 1963, there was a common law rule of evidence, known as "Crown privilege" or "public interest privilege", to the effect that the Government cannot be compelled to disclose documents recording facts that are privileged or that fall into a privileged category even though that information is relevant in proceedings and otherwise admissible in evidence. In the past the scope of this privilege was very extensive but it has been whittled down considerably in recent years. Indeed, at one time whenever a Government Minister objected to divulging information and swore an affidavit saying that disclosure would damage the public interest, that was the end of the matter and the courts would not go behind the claim of executive privilege.

A mere assertion by a Minister or other official of privilege will not be acceded to by the courts. In *Murphy v. Dublin Corporation*,[58] the Supreme Court held that, where any such claim is raised in a civil action, the court will insist on examining the documents and they will be excluded from the evidence only where the court is of the view that their disclosure would seriously damage the public interest. That case concerned an attempt by a local authority to

---

[54] Rejected in *Howard v. Commissioners for Public Works* [1994] 1 I.R. 101; *supra*, p.26.
[55] *Entick v. Carrington* (1765) 19 St. Tr. 1030.
[56] *Youngstown Sheet & Tube Co. v. Sawyer*, 343 U.S. 579 (1952).
[57] See generally, H. Delaney & D. McGrath, *Civil Procedure in the Supreme Courts* (2001), pp.298 *et seq.* and R. Canon & N. Neligan, *Evidence* (2002), pp.285 *et seq.*
[58] [1972] I.R. 215.

acquire compulsorily the plaintiff's land, which led to a public local inquiry, and the inspector who conducted the inquiry reported to the Minister. The plaintiff sought to have that report produced in evidence but the Minister objected on the grounds that disclosure of its contents "would be contrary to public policy and detrimental to the public interest and the service," the formula which for years had protected executive secrecy. On the grounds that the courts' constitutional function is to administer justice and to consider all relevant evidence, and the possibility that a claim of Ministerial privilege could very easily result in avoidable injustice being caused, the court refused to accede to that claim. Anybody claiming privilege would have to satisfy the court that the evidence ought in all the circumstances to be suppressed. According to Walsh J.:

"Under the Constitution the administration of justice is committed solely to the judiciary in the exercise of their powers in the courts set up under the Constitution. Power to compel the attendance of witnesses and the production of evidence is an inherent part of the judicial power of government of the State and is the ultimate safeguard of justice in the State. The proper exercise of the functions of the three powers of government set up under the Constitution, namely, the legislative, the executive and the judicial, is in the public interest. There may be occasions when the different aspects of the public interest 'pull in contrary directions' ... If the conflict arises during the exercise of the judicial power then, in my view, it is the judicial power which will decide which public interest shall prevail."[59]

And,

"As the legislative, executive, and judicial powers of government are all exercised under and on behalf of the State, the interest of the State, as such, is always involved. The division of powers does not give paramountcy in all circumstances to any one of the organs exercising the powers of government over the other. It is clear that when the vital interests of the State (such as the security of the State) may be adversely affected by disclosure or production of a document, greater harm may be caused by ordering rather than by refusing disclosure or production of a document. In such a case the courts would refuse the order but would do so on their own decision. The evidence that the courts might choose to act upon to arrive at that decision would be determined by the courts, having regard to the circumstances of the case. Again, taking the example of the safety of the State, it might well be that the court would be satisfied

[59] *Id.* at p.233.

to accept the opinion of the appropriate member of the executive or of the head of the Government as sufficient evidence of the fact upon a claim being made for non-disclosure or non-production, as the case may be, on that ground. I have referred to non-disclosure and non-production as distinct matters because in certain circumstances the very disclosure of the existence of a document, apart altogether from the question of its production, could in itself be a danger to the security of the State. ...

It is, however, impossible for the judicial power in the proper exercise of its functions to permit any other body or power to decide for it whether or not a document will be disclosed or produced. In the last resort the decision lies with the courts so long as they have seisin of the case."[60]

Once a particular document is relevant to a case, the party objecting to its disclosure must convince the court that divulging its contents would seriously damage the public interest.

It also was held in *Murphy* that there are no longer particular classes or categories of documents that *per se* are privileged. In Walsh J.'s words, "there can be no documents which may be withheld from production simply because they belong to a particular class of document. Each document must be decided upon having regard to the considerations which apply to that particular document and its contents. To grant or withhold the production of a document simply by reason of the class to which it belongs would be to regard all documents as being of equal importance notwithstanding that they may not be."[61]

An endeavour to overrule *Murphy* was rejected by the Supreme Court in *Ambiorix Ltd. v. Minister for the Environment*,[62] where the plaintiff sought discovery of documents concerning the formulation of policy for proposed legislation. Finlay C.J. there summarised the principles laid down in *Murphy* as follows:

"1. Under the Constitution the administration of justice is committed solely to the judiciary by the exercise of their own powers in the courts set up under the Constitution.

2. Power to compel the production of evidence (which, of course, includes a power to compel the production of documents) is an inherent part of the judicial power and is part of the ultimate safeguard of justice in the State.

3. Where a conflict arises during the exercise of the judicial power between the aspect of public interest involved in the confidentiality or

---

[60] *Id.* at pp.234–235.
[61] *Id.* at p.235.
[62] [1992] 1 I.R. 277.

exemption from documents pertaining to the exercise of the executive powers of the State, it is the judicial power which will decide which public interest shall prevail.

4 The duty of the judicial power to make that decision does not mean that there is any priority or preference for the production of evidence over other public interests, such as the security of the State or the efficient discharge of the functions of the executive organ of the government.

5 It is for the judicial power to choose the evidence upon which it might act in any individual case in order to reach that decision."[63]

He went on to say that these principles led to a number of practical conclusions where a claim of public interest privilege was made:

"(a) The executive cannot prevent the judicial power from examining documents which are relevant to an issue in a civil trial for the purpose of deciding whether they must be produced.

(b) There is no obligation on the judicial power to examine any particular document before deciding that it is exempt from production, and it can and will in many instances uphold a claim of privilege in respect of a document merely on the basis of a description of its nature and contents which it (the judicial power) accepts.

(c) There cannot, accordingly, be a generally applicable class or category of documents exempted from production by reason of the rank in the public service of the person creating them, or of the position of the individual or body intended to use them."[64]

THE ATTORNEY GENERAL

Countries of the common law tradition possess Attorneys General who perform broadly similar functions:[65] they are the Government's principal legal advisers, they have charge of litigation being brought by and against the State, they act as public prosecutors and they have authority to enforce various rights in which the public have a special interest. Before independence, these functions were carried out in Ireland by the Attorney General for Ireland and by the Solicitor General for Ireland.[66] Section 6 of the Ministers and Secretaries Act 1924, vested these officers' powers in the Attorney General of the Irish Free State. His functions were described by section 6 of the 1924 Act as:

---

[63] *Id.* at p.283.

[64] *Id.* at pp.283–284.

[65] See generally, J. Edwards, *The Attorney General, Politics and the Public Interest* (1984) and J. Edwards, *The Law Officers of the Crown* (1964).

[66] See generally, C. Smyth, *The Law Officers of Ireland* (1839).

"[exercising] the business, powers, authorities, duties and functions formerly vested in or exercised by [the predecessors] and the administration and control of the business, powers, authorities, duties and functions of ... the public services specified (*i.e.* Chief Crown Solicitor for Ireland, Chief State Solicitor's Department and all local State Solicitors, Treasury Solicitor for Ireland, Parliamentary Draftsman, Charities, Estates of illegitimates and deceased persons) and also the administration and business generally of public services in connection with the representation of the Government ... and of the public in all legal proceedings for the enforcement of law, the punishment of offenders and the assertion or protection of public rights and all powers, duties and functions connected with the same respectively, together with the duty of advising the [Government] and the several Ministers in matters of law and of legal opinion."

It is most exceptional for national constitutions to contain provisions dealing with officers who exercise these functions. However, Article 30 of the Constitution deals with the Attorney General – the Attorney's status, powers and responsibilities generally. Except where they conflict with this Article, the Attorney's "office" and remuneration are regulated by section 6 of the 1924 Act and other legislative provisions. [67]

Appointment and Status

Neither Article 30 nor the legislation lays down the qualifications for holding this office but the practice is to appoint a Senior Counsel. There is no requirement that the Attorney General be a member of either House of the Oireachtas, nor is such membership prohibited. It is the Taoiseach and not the Government who chooses the Attorney.[68] Although Attorneys frequently attend Government meetings, it is stipulated that the Attorney is not a member of the Government. The Attorney must retire whenever the Taoiseach resigns[69] but nevertheless may continue to carry out the duties of office until a new Taoiseach is appointed.[70] The Taoiseach can request an Attorney's resignation and can procure dismissal where the Attorney declines to resign.[71] However, the actual appointment is made by the President, and it is the President who receives any resignation and who terminates the appointment where the Taoiseach so advises.

---

[67] See generally, J. Casey, *The Irish Law Officers* (1996).
[68] Art.30.2.
[69] Art.30.4.
[70] Art.30.5.4.
[71] Art.30.5.

The Attorney General cannot be regarded as being a branch of the legislature, of the executive or of the courts but occupies a somewhat unique position. Kingsmill Moore J. described the Attorney as "in no way the servant of the Government but is put into an independent position. He is a great officer of State, with grave responsibilities of a quasi- judicial as well as of an executive nature";[72] Ó Dálaigh J. described the Attorney as "an independent constitutional officer."[73] According to Walsh J., "[b]y virtue of the Constitution he is an independent constitutional officer of state with powers and duties some of which are of a quasi-judicial nature and some of an executive nature. [H]e is not in any sense the servant of the executive, and any exercise by him of executive powers is not the exercise of the executive powers of the Government but rather those of the Attorney General himself."[74]

Powers and functions

According to Article 30.1 of the Constitution, the Attorney General "shall be the adviser of the Government in matters of law and legal opinion, and shall exercise and perform all such powers, functions and duties as are conferred or imposed on him by this Constitution or by law." The only function expressly designated in the Constitution is being the Government's legal adviser; additional powers and functions are set out in section 6 of the 1924 Act and in several other legislative provisions. Some of the powers formerly exercised by the Attorney have been declared unconstitutional, notably the power to block litigation being brought against the State or a Government Minister by denying his *fiat* to the plaintiff[75] and the power to send forward for trial on indictment an accused person, whom a District Judge refused to send for trial.[76] The former power was struck down because it was inextricably linked to sovereign immunity; the latter power because it permitted outside interference with the exercise of judicial functions.[77] Most of the Attorney's functions in connection with prosecuting persons charged with offences have been transferred to the Director of Public Prosecutions.[78]

It was held that the Attorney's decision to prosecute or not to prosecute individuals will not be reviewed by the Courts.[79] In *Macauley* v. *Minister for Posts and Telegraphs*,[80] the reason why Kenny J. struck down the provision

---

[72] *McLoughlin* v. *Minister for Social Welfare* [1958] I.R. 1 at p.17.
[73] *Id.* at p.25.
[74] *Byrne* v. *Ireland* [1972] I.R. 241 at p.287.
[75] *Macauley* v. *Minister for Posts and Telegraphs* [1966] I.R. 345.
[76] *Costello* v. *D.P.P.* [1984] I.R. 434; *infra*, p.202.
[77] This procedure was abolished by the Criminal Justice Act 1999; *infra*, p.433.
[78] Prosecution of Offences Act 1974.
[79] *State (Killian)* v. *Attorney General* (1958) 92 I.L.T.R. 182.
[80] [1966] I.R. 345.

in section 2(1) of the Ministers and Secretaries Act 1924, regarding the Attorney's *fiat*, was that the decision whether or not to grant it was not susceptible to judicial review; that "on any construction of it, the Attorney General may refuse his *fiat* for any reasons which seem to him to be sufficient and which may be mistaken" and that "no proceedings to review his decision can successfully be brought in the Courts."[81] It is debatable whether the courts today would rule that decisions of the Attorney are inherently incapable of judicial review.[82]

Government's legal adviser

The Attorney General's specific constitutional function is to "be the adviser of the Government in matters of law and legal opinion."[83] He advises the Government on proposed legislation, regulations, treaties and on legal disputes in which the State is involved. Exceptionally, the Attorney personally represents the Government before the courts. Parliamentary Counsel, respsonsible for drafting legislation and other measures, are attached to the Attorney's office. Legal advice given by the Attorney to the Government is subject to legal professional privilege and ordinarily cannot be the subject of an order for discovery.[84]

Criminal prosecutions

Before 1974, control of major criminal prosecutions was vested in the Attorney. He was the principal prosecutor for most indictable offences but private individuals and members of the Garda Síochána could and still can prosecute summary offences as "common informers." Article 30.3 of the Constitution provides that "[a]ll crimes and offences prosecuted in any court constituted under Article 34 ... other than a court of summary jurisdiction shall be prosecuted in the name of the People and at the suit of the Attorney General or some other person authorised in accordance with law to act for that purpose." Thus, it is permissible for the Oireachtas to authorise somebody other than the Attorney to prosecute indictable offences.

Several Acts empower the relevant Minister or other relevant authority to prosecute summarily in respect of offences under those Acts, for instance the Director of Corporate Enforcement. By virtue of the Prosecution of Offences Act 1974, a new statutory officer was created, the Director of Public Prosecutions (or D.P.P.), who is empowered to exercise most of the Attorney's

---

[81] *Id.* at pp.359 and 356.
[82] *Infra*, p.429 on reviewing discretion of the D.P.P. regarding prosecutions.
[83] Art.30.1.
[84] *Society for the Protection of Unborn Children (Ireland) Ltd* v. *Grogan (No.3)* [1992] 2 I.R. 471.

functions regarding criminal prosecutions.[85] According to section 3 of this Act, "[s]ubject to the provisions of this Act, the Director shall perform all the functions [hitherto] capable of being performed in relation to criminal matters … by the Attorney General." It is not clear whether this section purports to deprive the Attorney of authority to prosecute most offences and other authority in criminal matters, or whether the Attorney still retains that authority; in the light of the presumption of constitutionality, section 3 most likely has the latter meaning. Walsh J. has observed that "[t]he constitutional right of the Attorney General to prosecute in courts set up under Article 34 of the Constitution other than courts of summary jurisdiction cannot be removed by statute," although the right to prosecute can also be conferred on others by law.[86] In any event, where it is "expedient in the interests of national security to do so", the Government can order that functions transferred to the D.P.P. be exercised only by the Attorney.[87]

One of the traditional functions of the Attorney, which the D.P.P. is empowered to exercise, is to enter a *nolle prosequi, i.e.* to order that criminal proceedings in being shall cease.[88] One of the Attorney's statutory functions, which the D.P.P. now exercises, is to make the formal application for transferring a criminal trial from the Circuit Court or the Central Criminal Court to the non-jury Special Criminal Court.[89]

The 1974 Act provides that the Attorney's consent must always be obtained for prosecutions under the Genocide Act 1973, the Geneva Conventions Act 1962, and the Official Secrets Act 1963.[90] It also provides that the Attorney must certify a point of law for the purpose of appealing a criminal conviction to the Supreme Court and that it is the Attorney who decides if the acquittal of an accused person shall be referred to the Supreme Court, in order to resolve a question of law without prejudice to the accused.[91]

Party to litigation involving the State

Where the State is suing somebody or it is being sued, the Attorney General is often a party to the proceedings – either as plaintiff, defendant or notice party.[92]

Where the State itself – as distinct from a Government Minister or some other public body or official – is bringing suit, the action is brought by the Attorney in his own name. Proceedings to recover taxes may be brought by

---

[85] *Infra*, p.428.
[86] *State (Collins) v. Rune* [1984] I.R. 105 at p.118.
[87] 1974 Act, s.5.
[88] *Infra*, p.437.
[89] Offences Against the State Act 1939, s.46(2).
[90] S.3(5).
[91] S.3(4).
[92] See generally, H. Delaney & D. McGrath, *Civil Procedure in the Superior Courts* (2001), pp.164 *et seq.*

the Attorney,[93] although usually those are brought by Revenue officials in their own name. Where a claim is brought against the State itself, *i.e.* against Ireland, the procedure is to join the Attorney as a defendant. As Walsh J. advised in *Byrne v. Ireland*,[94] where it was held that the State does not enjoy general sovereign immunity, "the correct procedure would be to sue the State and to join the Attorney General in order to effect service upon the Attorney General for both parties. In effect the Attorney General would be joined in a representative capacity as the law officer of the State designated by the Constitution. If the claim should succeed, judgment would be again the State and 'not against the Attorney General.'"[95]

In most civil actions brought against public authorities the defendant is some public officer or corporation, such as the relevant Minister. All of the major public corporations have their own legal advisers and most if not all the government departments also have their own legal advisers. Nevertheless, even where no questions of constitutional law arise, the Attorney is frequently joined as a defendant.

Guardian of the public interest

The Attorney General exercises some diverse functions, which may be subsumed under the loose heading of guardian of the public interest. Section 6 of the Ministers and Secretaries Act 1924, transferred to the Attorney functions in respect of charities and the estates of non-marital children and of deceased persons.[96] Requests for extradition to the United Kingdom must be cleared by the Attorney before being processed in the normal manner.[97] He may direct a coroner to hold an inquest.[98] He may institute proceedings to have a person punished for contempt of court, for instance for breaking the *in camera* rule.[99] Where somebody is persistently breaking a rule, which is backed by a criminal sanction, the Attorney is generally entitled to apply to court to have that conduct enjoined.[100] Where for one reason or another statutory sanctions cannot be applied, at the Attorney's application the court may grant an injunction in place of the deficient sanction.[101] He may bring proceedings in order to enforce

---

[93] Taxes Consolidation Act 1997, s.998.
[94] [1972] I.R. 241.
[95] *Id.*, at p.298.
[96] *Cf.* Charities Act 1961, ss.24-26.
[97] Extradition Act 1965, ss.44A-44D; *cf. Wheeler v. Culligan* [1989] I.R. 344.
[98] Coroners Act 1962, s.24; *cf. Farrell v. Attorney General* [1998] 1 I.R. 203.
[99] Since 1974, contempt can also be punished at the suit of the D.P.P., *e.g. State (D.P.P.) v. Walsh* [1981] I.R. 412.
[100] E.g., *Attorney General v. Paperlink Ltd* [1984] I.L.R.M. 373. Cf. *Imperial Tobacco Ltd v. Attorney General* [1981] A.C. 718.
[101] *E.g., Attorney General v. Lee* [2001] 1 I.L.R.M. 553.

rights of the public generally, such as against nuisances and in respect of public rights of way and public fisheries.[102]

Under Order 60 of the Rules of the Superior Courts, where the constitutionality of a provision of any law is being challenged, the party with carriage of the case is obliged to notify the Attorney of the fact unless the Attorney is already a party to the proceedings. In any other case where a question regarding interpretation of the Constitution arises, the court may direct that the Attorney be notified. These notices must "state concisely the nature of the proceedings" and the party or parties' contentions. On being so notified, the Attorney becomes entitled to appear in the action and to become a party to it as regards the constitutional questions.

There are several statutory provisions that permit the Attorney to intervene in litigation between private parties, where the State has an indirect interest in the outcome. Additionally, where a particular public interest is involved in any kind of proceedings between private parties, the Attorney may be permitted to intervene in them in order to protect that interest.[103] Intervention may be permitted on an appeal where the Attorney was not involved in the trial.[104] But where a trial has taken place, in which the Attorney was not involved and the parties do not appeal the decision, the Attorney cannot then intervene for the purpose of prosecuting an appeal.[105]

Under what is known as the "relator action" procedure,[106] an individual may be allowed to being legal proceedings in the Attorney's name (*i.e.* at his relation) where the Constitution or the general law is being contravened and thereby acquire *locus standi* where otherwise that person might not have standing.[107]

---

[102] *E.g.*, *Moore v. Attorney General (No.2)* [1930] I.R. 560.

[103] *T. D.I. Metro Ltd v. Delap (No.1)* [2000] 4 I.R. 337.

[104] *Ibid.*

[105] *G. McG. v. D.W.* [2000] 4 I.R. 1.

[106] See generally, A. Collins and J. O'Reilly, *Civil Proceedings and the State* (2nd ed., 2003), Chap.9.

[107] *E.g.*, *Attorney General (Society for the Protection of Unborn Children (Ireland) Ltd v. Open Door Counselling Ltd* [1988] I.R. 593.

CHAPTER 7

The Courts

The final branch in the scheme of separation of powers is the courts and in a constitutional system, where the courts can strike down laws on the grounds of unconstitutionality, the judges play a vital role. According to Article 34.1, "[j]ustice shall be administered in courts established by law by judges appointed in the manner provided by this Constitution. ..." Many countries have a multiple court structure. Thus, federal states like Australia, Canada, Germany and the United States have federal courts and also separate state courts, although the exact relationship between the federal and the state tribunals differs from country to country. In most continental European countries there is one set of courts which deal with ordinary civil cases and an entirely separate court structure for dealing with disputes between individuals and the State, *i.e.*, there are wholly distinct administrative or public law courts, with their own courts of final appeal. In continental Europe, moreover, most of the highest constitutional tribunals are not part of the ordinary private law or even the public law court structures. Under the Constitution of Ireland, by contrast, the entire court structure is a distinctly unitary one.

COURT STRUCTURES

Ireland's present court structure can be traced back to the major judicial reorganisations of the 1870s and 1920s that were brought about by the Supreme Court of Judicature (Ireland) Act 1877, [1] and the Courts of Justice Act 1924. [2] In descending order of formal importance, the principal components of this system are the Supreme Court, the Court of Criminal Appeal and the Courts Martial Appeal Court, the High Court, the Circuit Court and the District Court. As is explained in the next chapter, Article 37 of the Constitution permits bodies other the courts to exercise non-criminal "limited functions and powers of a judicial nature;" this Article is the constitutional foundation for the many administrative tribunals that decide a wide range of disputed issues. The Labour Court, Coroners' inquests and judicial tribunals of inquiry are not courts as such, and the Special Criminal Court is an exceptional tribunal that can be set up in extraordinary circumstances. [3]

---

[1] 40 & 41 Vic. c.57.
[2] See generally, H. Delany, *The Courts Acts 1924–1997* (2nd ed., 2000).
[3] Offences Against the State Act 1939, Pt V; see *infra*, p.850.

The 1961 Acts

Shortly after the Free State came into existence, a Judiciary Act was passed providing that there shall be established a Supreme Court (of three judges), a High Court (of not more than six judges), a Court of Criminal Appeal, a Circuit Court (for which there were eight Circuits) and a District Court. The Courts of Justice Act 1924 was amended on numerous occasions, notably by the Courts of Justice Act 1936, which provided *inter alia* for an increase in the size of the Supreme Court to five judges and that the High Court should hold regular sittings outside Dublin to hear appeals from the Circuit Court and to transact other business. No Judiciary Act was passed immediately following the adoption of the 1937 Constitution. However, in 1951 in the *Killian* case,[4] the then Supreme Court conceded that the very terms of Article 34.1 (above) contemplated the enactment of such a measure and ten years later new courts were established by the Courts (Establishment and Constitution) Act 1961.

According to section 2(1) of this Act, "on the commencement of this Act, the Court of First Instance referred to in Article 34 of the Constitution as An Ard Chúirt (the High Court) shall stand established." There are similar provisions for the other four courts[5] and a Courts Martial Appeal Court was established in 1983.[6] This 1961 Act was immediately followed by the Courts (Supplemental Provisions) Act 1961, which, as is envisaged by Article 36 of the Constitution, deals with the qualifications for appointment of judges, their remuneration, pensions and age of retirement, the tenure of judges of the Circuit Court and of the District Court, the detailed organisation of the new courts, the distribution of jurisdiction and business among them and matters of procedure.

In principle the courts established in 1961 are entirely different from their predecessors but in fact the old structures were continued and the new courts had the very same personnel, powers and procedures as their predecessors.

The Circuit Court and the District Court

Article 34.3.4 of the Constitution gives the High Court full original jurisdiction of first instance but it goes on to provide that "[t]he Courts of First Instance shall also include Courts of local and limited jurisdiction with a right of appeal as determined by law." This clause does not require that all courts of first instance have local and limited jurisdiction; it suffices if some of the first instance courts possess these features. As Walsh J. explained, the Oireachtas "is free to set up as many courts of first instance as it sees fit, but is not free to

---

[4] *State (Killian) v. Minister for Justice* [1954] I.R. 207.
[5] Ss.1, 3, 4 and 5.
[6] Courts Martial Appeals Act 1983.

bestow on them, or on any statutory appellate court, the constitutional review functions of the High Court or the Supreme Court."[7] Thus the Oireachtas could establish courts of first instance other than the District Court and the Circuit Court: for instance, centralised special cartel courts and tax courts as exist on the Continent, and the former Restrictive Practices Court in Britain.

On the authority of this clause, sections 4 and 5 of the Courts (Establishment and Constitution) Act 1961, provided that "Court(s) of First Instance which shall be called ... The Circuit Court (and) The District Court ... shall stand established." Both the Circuit Court and the District Court are courts of record,[8] meaning that the accuracy of their formal orders cannot subsequently be called into question but, being inferior courts, may only commit for contempts committed in open court.

Circuit Court judges (of whom in 2003 there were 31) and District Judges (formerly called Justices) (of whom in 2003 there were 53)[9] are appointed by the President and must make the declaration set out in Article 34.5 of the Constitution.[10] Unlike the position regarding judges of the High Court and of the Supreme Court, the Oireachtas determines Circuit Court and District Judges' terms of appointment, as well as their remuneration, pension and retirement ages.[11] These are dealt with principally in Parts III and IV (sections 15–44) of the Courts (Supplemental Provisions) Act 1961, as amended. Section 23 of that Act contains special provisions regarding the Cork Circuit Court (and the since-abolished Cork Local Admiralty Court and the Cork Local Bankruptcy Court) and sections 35-44 of that Act contain special provisions concerning the Dublin Metropolitan District Court.

Although the powers and authority of the District Court are restricted in many ways, in one sense it is the most important court in the country because it is the court with which most people who are involved in litigation have direct experience. District Judges are all experienced barristers or solicitors who have become full-time professional judges – unlike the position with their pre-independence counterparts, the magistrates, or indeed the lay magistrates in England. As Gannon J. observed "(o)ur District Courts are now administered by fully competent and qualified lawyers, whose independence as judges, not only from the executive but even from their judicial colleagues, must be respected."[12]

---

[7] *State (Boyle) v. Neylon* [1986] I.R. 551 at p.555.
[8] Courts (Supplemental Provisions) Act 1961, s.21 and Courts Act 1971, s.13.
[9] Courts and Courts Officers Act 2002, ss.26 and 27, amending ss.10 and 11 of the Courts Act 1995.
[10] Art.35.1.
[11] *Infra*, p.163.
[12] *Clune v. D.P.P.* [1981] I.L.R.M. 17 at p.20.

"Local and limited jurisdiction"

The jurisdiction of the High Court and some of the jurisdiction of the Supreme Court derive directly from the Constitution and, to that extent, cannot be diminished except by way of a constitutional amendment.[13] But the jurisdiction of the Circuit Court and of the District Court derive exclusively from statute. At present, comparatively trivial cases are dealt with in the District Court, more serious cases are decided by the Circuit Court but the most serious questions can be resolved only by the High Court. The compulsory jurisdiction of the District Court in criminal cases is confined by the Constitution to minor offences;[14] at present, by law, the Circuit Court cannot try charges of treason, murder, piracy, genocide or rape.[15] As for civil claims, the Circuit Court now has jurisdiction in most family disputes and also in actions founded on contract and in the majority of tort actions, where the amount claimed does not exceed €100,000.[16] The Circuit Court used to have jurisdiction over winding up companies but that was removed in 1936.[17] Awards up to €20,000 may be made by the District Court.[18]

In an Admiralty case decided in the late 1940s,[19] the Supreme Court stressed that the District Court and the Circuit Court's jurisdiction must be both limited and local: there must be some limit on the gravity or nature of the case that those courts can try and, it would seem, there must be some connection between the case and the District or Circuit in which it is being tried. The limited nature of these courts' jurisdiction is patently obvious from the various Courts Acts that define the kinds of cases they have authority to try. Their jurisdiction in one sense is not local because there is only one Circuit Court and only one District Court, and each court's jurisdiction extends throughout the entire country. But the local requirement is usually satisfied in that each judge assigned to an area only has jurisdiction over cases that have a specified connection with the circuit or district in that area. In *State (Boyle) v. Neylon*,[20] it was held that the Constitution's requirement of a local jurisdiction is satisfied even where a trial is transferred from outside Dublin to the Dublin Circuit in the manner provided for in section 31 of the Courts Act 1981. According to Walsh J., for the Supreme Court, the purpose of the "local and limited" requirement in Article 34.3.4, which is identical to Article 64 of the Free State Constitution, is to provide local and cheaper venues for litigants than would be the case if they had to go to the High Court in Dublin. The whole structure of the Circuit

---

[13] *I. O'T. v. B.* [1998] 2 I.R. 321 at p.340.

[14] Art.38; *infra*, p.420.

[15] See generally, D. Walsh, *Criminal Procedure* (2002) at pp.56–57.

[16] Courts and Courts Officers Act 2002, s.13.

[17] Courts of Justice Act 1963, s.18.

[18] Courts and Courts Officers Act 2002, s.14.

[19] *Grimes v. Owners of S.S. Bangor Bay* [1948] I.R. 350.

[20] [1986] I.R. 551.

Court, as established first in 1924 and again in 1961, is based upon the exercise of jurisdiction locally, the localities being the circuits which are themselves created by statute and the boundaries of which have from time to time been altered by statute. But within a highly regionalised court structure, it is permissible to place some qualification on local jurisdiction in order that justice may be administered more effectively, and section 31 of the 1981 Act was one such qualification. Within the general framework of localised jurisdiction laid down by the Courts (Supplemental Provisions) Act 1961, "the Oireachtas may ... provide that in certain cases another locality would be properly available for the trial of a case whether civil or criminal. ... Experience has shown that justice itself would require a provision of this kind to avoid the risk of an injustice to one party or another by reason of local circumstances or conditions. The ability to transfer ... a case from one locality to another does not alter the essential local exercise of a jurisdiction of the Circuit Court. The constitutional provision in referring to 'local ... jurisdiction' does not mean that it must be local in the sense of being particularly connected with the place of residence of one party or another."[21]

Constitutional questions

Article 34.3.2 gives the High Court and the Supreme Court exclusive authority to determine the constitutionality of post-1937 legislation and goes on to provide that the possible unconstitutionality of such a law shall never be considered by any other court; that "no such question shall be raised (whether by pleading, argument or otherwise) in any Court established under this or any other Article of this Constitution other than the High Court or the Supreme Court." Thus, the Circuit Court and the District Court cannot refuse to be bound by post-1937 legislation on the grounds that it is invalid– except of course where the Act in question has already been struck down by one of the superior courts. Post-1937 laws are presumed to comply with the Constitution unless their invalidity has been established in accordance with Articles 34.3.2 and 34.4.4. But the Circuit Court and the District Court are not precluded from deciding the constitutional status of pre-1937 Acts.[22] Whether these courts may rule on the constitutionality of statutory instruments made under Acts of the post-1937 Oireachtas is very much an open question.[23]

Prohibiting these courts from considering the constitutionality of a post-1937 law arising "by pleading, or argument or otherwise" was held by O'Hanlon J. in *Minister for Labour v. Costello*[24] to prevent such a question being referred by either of these courts to the High Court or the Supreme Court to be

---

[21] *Id.* at p.557.

[22] *D.P.P. (Stratford) v. O'Neill* [1998] 2 I.R. 383.

[23] *Cf. Minister for Agriculture v. Brennan* [1999] 3 I.R. 228, 233.

[24] *Minister for Labour v. Costello* [1988] I.R. 235.

determined by way of case stated. Notwithstanding that a party claiming unconstitutionality wants to have the issue sent up to the superior court to be decided, the District Judge or Circuit Judge is required to "proceed on the assumption that powers conferred on him by Act of the Oireachtas, enacted subsequent to the enactment of the Constitution of 1937 may be lawfully exercised by him unless and until the statute has been successfully impugned in proceedings appropriate for that purpose."[25] A challenge to a post-1937 law must be brought by way of a separate action in the High Court.[26] However, a judge of one of these courts can adjourn a case where legislation that is central to the proceedings is being challenged before the High Court in another case.[27] He is not obliged to adjourn a prosecution whenever the legislation in question is being challenged in the higher courts by some other defendant; there is a judicial discretion to adjourn but it depends on the circumstances of the case whether that discretion has been correctly exercised in any particular instance.[28]

A stipulation that has become common in laws of validation, which legalises a pre-existing unlawful state of affairs, is that if a provision of that law "would, but for the provisions of this subsection conflict with the constitutional rights of any person, [they] shall be subject to such limitation as is necessary to secure that it does not so conflict …".[29] Where a provision of this nature is being applied by the District Court or the Circuit Court, it has been held that this does not involve the court considering the constitutional status of the law, as prohibited by Article 34.3.2°.[30]

Apart from the above prohibition, the District and the Circuit Courts are obliged to ensure that individuals' constitutional rights are respected. They must apply constitutionally – mandated fair procedures[31] and refuse to make orders that would result in a party's constitutional rights being invaded, including orders for extradition to another State where it is demonstrated that those rights would be infringed abroad.[32]

Appeals

According to Article 34.3, from these courts there shall be a "right of appeal as determined by law." It was held by the Supreme Court in *Todd v. Murphy*[33] that this proviso is not confined to determining the ambit or nature of an appeal

---

[25] *Id.* at p.241.
[26] *People (D.P.P.) v. Dougan* [1996] 1 I.R. 544.
[27] *State (Attorney General) v. Mangan* [1961] Ir. Jur. 17.
[28] *State (Llewllyn) v. ua Donnchadha* [1973] I.R. 151.
[29] *E.g.* Interpretation (Amendment) Act 1977, s.1(4).
[30] *Grealis v. D.P.P.* [2001] 3 I.R. 144; *infra*, p.291.
[31] *Coughlan v. Patwell* [1993] 1 I.R. 31.
[32] *Ellis v. O'Dea* [1989] I.R. 530.
[33] [1999] 2 I.R. 1.

but concern conferring any right of appeal. There the court refused to strike down a provision enabling a Circuit Judge to refuse a request to transfer a criminal trial to a different Circuit, which stipulated that any such decision "shall be final and unappealable." However, Geoghegan J. in the High Court expressed the view that there may be a constitutional right of appeal with regard to certain questions, notably against a criminal conviction or sentence imposed.[34] International human rights standards guarantee a right of appeal in criminal cases.[35]

On most questions, statute provides a general right of appeal by way of re-hearing from the District Court to the Circuit Court; similarly, provision is made for appeals from the latter to the High Court.[36] Provision is also made for stating a case, either by way of appeal or for consultation, from the District Court to the High Court and from the Circuit Court to the Supreme Court. An appeal from the District Court to the Circuit Court is final and so too is an appeal from the Circuit Court to the High Court,[37] except where the Oireachtas has stipulated otherwise.

The High Court

According to Article 34.3.1 of the Constitution, the High Court is one of "the Courts of First Instance invested with full original jurisdiction in and power to determine all matters and questions whether of law or fact, civil or criminal." The present High Court was established by section 2 of the Courts (Establishment and Constitution) Act 1961, and section 8(1) of the Courts (Supplemental Provisions) Act 1961 provides that "the High Court shall be a superior court of record with such original and other jurisdiction as is prescribed by the Constitution." This court is very different from many continental European constitutional tribunals in that, in addition to resolving constitutional law disputes, it deals with everyday civil and criminal cases in which no constitutional issues arise. It also is different from the Federal Court of Canada because the latter's jurisdiction covers constitutional questions and questions arising under federal legislation but not disputes concerning common law and equitable claims.

The High Court's jurisdiction is defined by the 1961 Courts Act partly in terms of the pre-independence High Court of Justice in Southern Ireland. It has the jurisdiction that the pre-1923 Court had or was capable of exercising and also which the pre-1961 High Court had or was capable of exercising; it is also given jurisdiction over cases of lunacy and cases involving minors, and

---

[34] *Id.* at p.5.
[35] Art.14(5).
[36] *Infra*, pp.477 and 512.
[37] Courts of Justice Act 1936, s.39; *e.g. Blackhall v. Grehan* [1995] 3 I.R. 208 and *L.P. v. M.P.* [2002] 1 I.R. 219.

other questions that pre-1961 statutes had vested in the old High Court.[38] In other words, its original jurisdiction embraces most prosecutions for indictable offences, most common law and equity actions and many disputes concerning statutory rights. Its jurisdiction is far more extensive, however, being held to exceed the aggregate of the jurisdictions vested in it by the 1961 Acts and other Acts; the term "full ... jurisdiction" in Article 34.3.1 must be given its ordinary meaning. That was in *The Fritz Raabe*[39] where the issue was whether the High Court could hear a dispute about a ship mortgage that had not been duly registered. Before the former Admiralty Court could hear a statutory action *in rem* on a ship mortgage, the mortgage had to be registered. Since the mortgage in this case was not registered, it was contended that, by virtue of the 1961 Act, the High Court could not try the case. But that view was rejected by the majority. According to Walsh J., "the fact that in former times courts of limited jurisdiction, such as the Admiralty Court, had no jurisdiction in certain types of justiciable controversies does not in any way restrict the jurisdiction of the High Court to adjudicate in any justiciable controversy ... It could scarcely be argued that the High Court could not adjudicate in a claim in respect of a mortgage of a ship which was not registered simply because the old Court of Admiralty could not have done so."[40]

Thus, by virtue of the Constitution itself and as is provided by section 8(1) of the 1961 Act (above), the High Court has authority to hear every kind of justiciable controversy, regardless of how insignificant the issue is. If it is justiciable, then a party is entitled to have it considered by the High Court. In *R.C. v. C.C.*,[41] Barron J. granted a divorce, on the basis of the recently adopted Article 41.3.2 of the Constitution, notwithstanding that the Family Law (Divorce) Act 1996, had not yet come into force. Constitutional law issues apart, however, it has been held that the High Court is not invariably obliged to try each and every dispute that comes before it, even though it possesses jurisdiction over the case; further, that the Oireachtas can grant lower courts exclusive jurisdiction to try certain categories of case,[42] provided however that the High Court retains its traditional supervisory jurisdiction over those courts generally exercised in the form of a judicial review application.

Criminal jurisdiction

When it exercises its original criminal jurisdiction, *i.e.* when it tries criminal cases, the High Court is known as the Central Criminal Court.[43] At present

---

[38] Courts (Supplemental Provisions) Act 1961, ss.8 and 9.
[39] *R.D. Cox Ltd v. Owners of the M.V. Fritz Raabe*, unreported, Supreme Court, August 1, 1974.
[40] *Id.* at p.13.
[41] [1997] 1 I.R. 334.
[42] *Tormey v. Ireland* [1985] I.R. 289; *infra*, p.148.
[43] Courts (Supplemental Provisions) Act 1961, ss.11 and 25(2).

this court has exclusive jurisdiction to try prosecutions for treason and related offences, murder and related offences, piracy, genocide rape and the major offences created by the Offences Against the State Act 1939, i.e. usurping the Government and obstructing the Government or the President. In *Tormey v. Ireland*,[44] the Supreme Court concluded that, at least as regards criminal cases, there is no constitutional prohibition against the Oireachtas giving the Circuit Court exclusive jurisdiction to try categories of indictable offences and thereby depriving the High Court of the authority to try those cases, provided, however, that it retains its supervisory jurisdiction over the court of trial.

In *Tormey,* the accused was returned for trial in the Dublin Circuit Court. He sought to have his trial transferred to the Central Criminal Court, which he could have done previously but, since the Courts Act 1981, that option was no longer available to accused persons. Because the Constitution gives the High Court "jurisdiction in and power to determine all matters," he contended that the 1981 Act's provision contravened Article 34.3.1. This argument was rejected because the rule of literal interpretation must "give way to the more fundamental rule ... that the Constitution must be read as a whole and that its several provisions must not be looked at in isolation, but be treated as interlocking parts of the general constitutional scheme."[45] Henchy J., for the court, pointed to the fact that the Constitution itself deprives the High Court of original jurisdiction over several matters, notably as regards summary offences, military offences and Special Criminal Court offences. But does not the maxim *expressio unius* suggest that, apart from these exceptions, the High Court has jurisdiction to try all other crimes? According to Henchy J., Article 34.3.1 is satisfied where, even though it cannot try the charge, the High Court can exercise its traditional supervisory jurisdiction over criminal trials in the form of *habeas corpus*, *certiorari*, prohibition, *mandamus*, *quo warranto*, injunction and a declaratory action, and even more so when there is a statutory right of appeal. "Full original jurisdiction" in this context, therefore, means not jurisdiction to try the case but extensive supervisory jurisdiction over the trial. It has been held that the Constitution itself does not grant convicted persons a right of appeal from the Circuit Court to the High Court.[46]

Civil jurisdiction

The original civil jurisdiction of the High Court is most extensive. It has not been finally determined whether the Oireachtas can confer on the lower courts exclusive jurisdiction over categories of claims concerning common law and equitable rights. In the light of what was held in the *Tormey* case, the position would seem to be that exclusive jurisdiction over specified civil claims can be

---

[44] [1985] I.R. 289.

[45] *Id.* at p.296.

[46] *State (Hunt) v. O'Donovan* [1975] I.R. 39; *infra*, p.478.

conferred on the Circuit Court and perhaps also on the District Court, provided that these courts' decisions can be reviewed by the High Court. The leading authority on this question is some *obiter dicta* in *R. v. R.*[47] But that case concerned jurisdiction in cases involving statutory rights and obligations, and the assumption underlying what was said there is undermined by what was held in *Tormey.*

The issue in *R. v. R.* was whether the Oireachtas can give the lower courts jurisdiction over disputes that hitherto was exercised exclusively by the High Court: in that instance, jurisdiction over several family law questions, the custody of children and maintenance. It was contended that provisions of the Guardianship of Infants Act 1964, the Family Law (Maintenance of Spouses and Children) Act 1976, the Family Law (Protection of Spouses and Children) Act 1976, and the Courts Act 1981, were unconstitutional because they gave the Circuit Court power to try cases of this nature and implicitly withdrew that jurisdiction from the High Court. Gannon J. found that the provisions in question did not have this effect: while they conferred jurisdiction on the Circuit Court, they did not seek to prevent the High Court from hearing these cases. Although the High Court has jurisdiction to try them, it could decline to hear any such case and order that the dispute should be tried in the lower court.[48] The High Court was not constitutionally obligated to try each and every one of these cases: "where, and so long as, (the lower courts') concurrent but limited jurisdiction exists, the High Court would not ... be compellable to provide any person, as a matter of constitutional right, with access to the High Court so as to enable him to have recourse to the High Court at his choice in lieu of recourse to the other court of first instance established by law and having the jurisdiction sought to be invoked."[49] McMahon J. reached a similar conclusion in *Ward v. Kinihan Electrical Ltd,*[50] where the constitutionality of provisions in the Courts of Justice Acts, that authorised the High Court to remit certain actions to the lower courts, were upheld.

In *R. v. R.* Gannon J. expressed the view that the Oireachtas is not constitutionally competent to give the courts of local and limited first instance jurisdiction the exclusive authority to try various categories of civil case; that the High Court cannot be deprived of its extensive jurisdiction in civil controversies by providing that some civil actions can be tried only in the lower courts, even where no question of constitutional right is involved. According to him:

"The basic principle in relation to the question of access to the Courts appears to be that in justice no wrong (using that word in the wide general

---

[47] [1984] I.R. 296.
[48] *Cf. O'R. v. O'R.* [1985] I.R. 367.
[49] [1984] I.R. 309.
[50] [1984] I.R. 292.

sense) should be without a remedy. What is called the right of access to the Courts is essentially a right to have recourse to justice and to have judicial determination in matters or questions of a disputable nature whether civil or criminal ...

In pursuing the objectives of promoting the common good and attaining true social order, the Oireachtas necessarily makes laws which confer rights, impose duties, create offences and prescribe sanctions in the form of penalties and punishments. In so far as such laws give rise to disputable questions of law or fact, civil or criminal, for judicial determination, it can be said that they create new jurisdiction.

Changes in social requirements and patterns and standards of behaviour which occur in the normal growth of the State and over a period of time may give rise, without intervention of legislation, to new and further matters and disputable questions of fact or law which were not in existence in 1937 but which require judicial determination. In my view, it would be inconsistent with the provisions of Article 34, section 3, sub-1, (as interpreted by the Supreme Court in the *Fritz Raabe* case) if there could be no jurisdiction in any court in such matters unless and until a jurisdiction was conferred by enactment of the Oireachtas. From the amplitude of jurisdiction with which the High Court is invested by Article 34 of the Constitution, it follows that the Oireachtas does not add to or increase the jurisdiction of the High Court by legislation. It follows also that the Oireachtas cannot create validly, in accordance with the Constitution, a new juridical jurisdiction and withhold it from the High Court; nor can it reduce, restrict or terminate any jurisdiction of the High Court."[51]

Following the *Tormey* decision, this analysis would seem to be wrong. The correct position would appear to be that exclusive jurisdiction can indeed be given to the Circuit Court provided that the High Court remains capable of reviewing the Circuit judge's decision. How extensive that power of review must be is unclear. Must it be (as is the position in 2003) a power to hear an appeal that involves an entire re-hearing of the evidence, or would a less extensive power of review suffice?

Where an Act of the Oireachtas (or statute carried over under Article 50) confers a right on an individual, it would appear that it is permissible to therein stipulate the manner in which claims to that right may be affected, including that disputes arising from those claims be decided by a court of local and limited jurisdiction, or by an administrative tribunal. It has not been determined whether such exclusion of jurisdiction must be stated in those very terms but it would appear that providing for a non-court remedy by inference excludes

---

[51] *Id.* at p.308.

direct redress through the courts.[52] Further it would appear that the Oireachtas is not obliged to confer any right of appeal from such a tribunal. This too applies where the Act in question imposes some novel form of obligation on individuals.

However, where the nature of the right/obligation in question is one that can have particularly profound consequences for the person in question, it may not be a "limited" administrative matter that can be confined to administrative tribunals[53] but, instead, can only be dealt with in the courts. A possibly acceptable compromise in cases of this nature is permitting the issue to be dealt with first by tribunals but subject to an extensive right of appeal to the courts.

Constitutional questions

Most High Court cases do not raise questions of constitutional law. But the High Court also hears cases in which the central argument or one of the contentions being made is that some Act, regulation, action, decision or transaction is unconstitutional. These questions can arise when the court is exercising its original jurisdiction, either civil or criminal, or when it is hearing appeals, or when it is exercising jurisdiction over lower tribunals by way of judicial review. Where a litigant contends that some Act passed since December 1937 is unconstitutional, then the court's jurisdiction derives from Article 34.3.2, according to which "the jurisdiction of the High Court shall extend to the question of the validity of any law having regard to the provisions of this Constitution ...". Where a party is contending that some pre-December 1937 Act, or some common law rule or doctrine, or some regulation, action, decision or transaction is unconstitutional, the court's authority derives from Article 34.3.1, which is the principal source of its general jurisdiction.

For most purposes, it does not matter that jurisdiction arises under clause 2, when the case involves the constitutionality of a post-1937 Act, whereas in other cases jurisdiction arises under clause 1. Indeed, it has not strictly been decided that jurisdiction over one category of case arises under clause 2 and over the other category arises under clause 1. But the special meaning of clause 2 (*i.e.* applying only to post-1937 Acts) follows from what was decided about Article 40.4.3 in *State (Sheerin) v. Kennedy*.[54] Article 40.4 entrenches in the Constitution a form of *habeas corpus* procedure. Clause 3 of this Article deals with the situation where an individual is being detained in accordance with some law but that law has been found by the High Court to be unconstitutional. It provides that the High Court can refer the question of the law's constitutionality to the Supreme Court; that where the High Court "is satisfied

---

[52] *Barraclough v. Brown* [1897] A.C. 615.
[53] Under Art.37.1; *infra*, p.193.
[54] [1966] I.R. 379.

that ... such law is invalid having regard to the provisions of this Constitution [it] shall refer the question of the validity of such law to the Supreme Court ...". "Law" in this context was held to mean some post 1937 Act. Walsh J. contrasted how this clause formulates the issue of unconstitutionality with similar formulae in other clauses. Those are Article 50, which concerns carrying over into the State laws that are not "inconsistent with" the Constitution, and Article 26, which deals with the President's power to refer Bills to the Supreme Court in order to determine if any of their provisions are "repugnant to" the Constitution. Since Bills that have passed both Houses of the Oireachtas but have not been signed and promulgated are not laws, they do not have any legal effect in the sense of affecting rights or imposing obligations. Accordingly, questions of a Bill's validity by definition cannot arise. Because they do not even purport to be laws, Bills cannot conceivably be invalid or be invalidated by the Constitution. At most, their provisions can be inconsistent with or repugnant to the Constitution. If Acts of the Free State Oireachtas or of the pre-1922 Parliament are consistent with the Constitution, then they were carried forward by Article 50 and cannot be invalid. But if their provisions are not in accordance with the Constitution, then they were never carried over by Article 50 and therefore could never be valid or invalid under the Constitution. It is only the legislative organ established by a particular constitution that can enact measures that are laws but which nevertheless are invalid with reference to that constitution. As Walsh J. explained:

> "Articles 34 and 40, where the law referred to is not expressly referred to as a law of the Oireachtas, in my view must be treated as meaning that the validity in question is a validity to be determined by the provisions of the Constitution in respect of something purporting to have been done within the terms of the Constitution and within the powers conferred by the Constitution. I think it is clear from these various provisions of the Constitution that the laws referred to are statutory provisions, as distinct from non-statutory law, and the validity of any statute can only be examined in the light of the powers of the parliament, which enacted it. The Oireachtas established by the Constitution is the only parliament which is, or was, subject to the provisions of the Constitution and therefore the question of determining the validity of a law having regard to the provisions of the Constitution can only refer to laws enacted by the Oireachtas established by the Constitution."[55]

Since, according to the *Tormey* case, it is constitutionally permissible for the Oireachtas to deprive the High Court of its original jurisdiction over particular categories of cases, the question arises of whether this power extends to cases

---

[55] *Id.* at p.386.

involving the constitutionality of a pre-1937 law or even of a post-1937 law. Article 34.3 of the Constitution contains no provision similar to that in Article 34.4.4, which entrenches the Supreme Court's constitutional jurisdiction in respect of post-1937 laws.[56] It could be argued that, since the Supreme Court's primary function is to hear appeals from the High Court, any attempt to deprive the High Court of jurisdiction regarding the validity of post-1937 laws would subvert the Supreme Court's entrenched jurisdiction and, accordingly, is not permitted. It could also be argued that the term "(s)ave as otherwise provided by this Article" implies that the High Court's jurisdiction to strike down post-1937 laws shall not be diminished by statute. Furthermore, since the other courts of first instance are not even permitted to consider the constitutionality of a post-1937 law, a diminishment of the High Court's jurisdiction in this regard would undermine the requirement of Article 15.4, which forbids the Oireachtas from enacting measures that contravene the Constitution and provides that any such measure shall be invalid. Consequently, the power of the Oireachtas as recognised in *Tormey* is subject to the High Court's entrenched jurisdiction with regard to deciding on the constitutionality of post-1937 laws. But the Constitution itself creates several exceptions to the High Court's jurisdiction regarding these matters, *viz.* laws that had been referred by the President to the Supreme Court under the Article 26 procedure, EC measures as defined in Article 29.4.3, emergency laws as defined in Article 28.3, Bills before the Oireachtas, proposed constitutional amendments and the President's official conduct.

It is not entirely clear whether all statutory instruments made under powers contained in a post-1937 Act are "laws" for the purpose being considered here. In *State (Gilliland) v. Governor* of *Mountjoy Prison*,[57] by the narrowest of margins the Supreme Court held that one kind of statutory instrument is a law for these purposes. These are statutory instruments made under Part II of the Extradition Act 1965, which simply stipulate that the provisions of Part II of that Act shall apply to a named country or countries with which Ireland has concluded extradition arrangements. The reason given by Finlay C.J. is that these instruments "are the machinery expressly created in that Act for the application of Part II of it ...".[58] It therefore may be that the more common kind of statutory instrument, which sets out in considerable detail the scope of some general requirement laid down in an Act, is not a law in this context. As McCarthy J., dissenting, pointed out, if they are laws then they would enjoy the privilege of the "one judgment" rule in the Supreme Court, a privilege that even laws of the Free State legislature do not enjoy. Additionally, if they are laws questions regarding their constitutionality could not be raised in the District Court or in the Circuit Court.

---

[56] *Infra*, p.158.
[57] [1987] I.R. 201.
[58] *Id.* at p.229.

The Supreme Court

Article 34.4 of the Constitution provides for a Supreme Court; that "[t]he Court of Final Appeal shall be called the Supreme Court (which) shall, with such exceptions and subject to such regulations as may be prescribed by law, have appellate jurisdiction from all decisions of the High Court, and shall also have appellate jurisdiction from such decisions of other courts as may be prescribed by law ... (and its) decision ... shall in all cases be final and conclusive." The present Supreme Court was established by section 1 of the Courts (Establishment and Constitution) Act 1961, and according to section 7(1) of the Courts (Supplemental Provisions) Act 1961, "the Supreme Court shall be a superior court of record with such appellate and other jurisdiction as is prescribed by the Constitution." This court's jurisdiction is primarily appellate.

Original jurisdiction

The Supreme Court has an original, or non-appellate, jurisdiction under Article 26 (reference of Bills by the President)[59] and Article 12.3.1 (President's incapacity)[60] of the Constitution. Because the Constitution describes the Supreme Court as an appellate tribunal, is it constitutionally permissible for the Oireachtas to confer an original or first instance jurisdiction on it?[61] In *People (A.G.) v. McGlynn*,[62] the court itself raised this point and answered it in the affirmative. While some of its jurisdiction is entrenched by the Constitution and cannot be taken away, there is nothing to prevent the Oireachtas from augmenting its jurisdiction. The issue in that case was whether the Supreme Court could exercise a consultative jurisdiction in a case stated before the Circuit Court had ruled on the issue, and it was held that the court could do so.

It was because the Supreme Court's only original statutory jurisdiction is to decide issues of law presented to it by way of case stated, and also because its decisions are final, that it declined to entertain a motion to discharge a permanent injunction it had upheld the varied where there had been a radical change in the legal and constitutional position in the meantime.[63] To what extent can the court decide on matters that were not raised, argued nor were the subject of evidence in the court from which an appeal is being taken? Ordinarily the court will not do so but in exceptional cases it has departed from this principle.[64]

---

[59] *Supra*, p.91.
[60] *Supra*, p.95.
[61] Which was the net issue in *Marbury v. Madison*, 5 U.S. 137 (1 Cranch) (1803).
[62] [1967] I.R. 232.
[63] *Attorney General (ex rel. Society for the Protection of Unborn Children (Ireland) Ltd) v. Open Door Counselling Ltd* [1994] 2 I.R. 333.
[64] *Infra*, pp.513–514.

Appellate jurisdiction

The Supreme Court's appellate jurisdiction derives both from the Constitution and from statute. In *State (Browne) v. Feran*,[65] it was held its appellate jurisdiction is not founded exclusively on statute but also derives from the Constitution itself; this is acknowledged in section 7(1) of the Courts (Supplemental Provisions) Act 1961 (above). As Walsh J. explained, the reference in Article 34.4 to "the appellate jurisdiction from decisions of the High Court is in terms which clearly indicate that this appellate jurisdiction derives directly from the Constitution itself and does not depend upon an Act of the Oireachtas."[66] Therefore, subject to one major qualification, a party has a constitutional right to appeal from any decision of the High Court.

What is a "decision" of the High Court for these purposes has been given an expansive interpretation and includes, for example, the findings of a judge on hearing an election petition[67] and rulings made in the course of a civil action.[68] Because the appellate jurisdiction under this Article applies to "all decisions of the High Court," it has even been held that the prosecutor can appeal against an acquittal by a criminal jury on the direction of a High Court judge[69] at the time since there was no post-1937 law providing that such matters shall not be the subject of an appeal. But it is doubtful if purely administrative directions given to an officer of the Court constitute decisions which can be appealed.[70] By virtue of this Article, in deciding a civil appeal the court may make such order as the justice of the case requires, for instance, substituting a different sum for the amount of damages awarded by a jury.[71] In contrast, in criminal appeals against acquittals and in the absence of any statutory authority to do so, the court held that it had no jurisdiction to order a re-trial.[72]

The Oireachtas is permitted to regulate the exercise of the Supreme Court's appellate jurisdiction and also to deprive it of that jurisdiction in those categories of cases as it deems ought not to be appealed. Although the appellate jurisdiction derives from the Constitution, Article 34.4.3 expressly authorises the Oireachtas to carve out exceptions. Several types of provision prohibiting or restricting appeals from decisions of the High Court exist. Sometimes appeals are confined to points of law only and sometimes that restriction is extended by requiring leave of the High Court, or of the Supreme Court itself, to appeal. Many decisions of the High Court in the areas of immigration, planning and

---

[65] [1967] I.R. 147.
[66] *Id.* at p.156.
[67] *Dillion-Leetch v. Calleary*, unreported, Supreme Court, July 25, 1973.
[68] *Green v. Blake* [1948] I.R. 242.
[69] *People v. O'Shea* [1982] I.R. 384; *infra*, p.480.
[70] *Re McGovern* [1971] I.R. 149.
[71] *Holohan v. Donohue* [1986] I.R. 45.
[72] *People (D.P.P.) v. Quilligan (No. 2)* [1989] I.R. 46.

compulsory purchase of property may be appealed only with the leave of that court and then only where its decision "involves a point of law of exceptional public importance and that it is desirable in the public interest that an appeal should be taken ....".[73] A judge's refusal to give leave to appeal under a provision of this nature cannot itself be appealed. But decisions regarding the constitutionality of any law are not so restricted.[74]

It is only in the most exceptional circumstances that statutory preclusion of appeals along these lines would be declared invalid. As the Supreme Court pointed out in *Illegal Immigrants (Trafficking) Bill, 1999, Re,* "the constitutional provision allows the legislature in the exercise of its discretion to restrict appeals ... and unless some constitutional defect is established as to the manner in which the legislature uses that power, it is not a matter for the courts to review the policy grounds upon which the legislature so decided."[75] Most circumstances where the right of appeal is restricted in the above manner involve decisions by administrative tribunals, which have been appealed to the High Court or have been challenged there in judicial review proceedings.

In order to prevent the Supreme Court from hearing appeals, the relevant provision must be contained in an Act of the Oireachtas. It was held in *State (Browne) v. Feran,*[76] that an Act of the Free State legislature or of the pre-1922 United Kingdom legislature that has been carried over by Article 50 will not suffice to deprive the Supreme Court of its constitutionally-based appellate jurisdiction.[77] The issue there was whether there could be an appeal from a decision of the High Court to grant an order of *habeas corpus* and it was a long-standing rule of case law that those orders could not be appealed against.[78] Because this preclusion of appeals was not embodied in an Act of the Oireachtas, it was held that the State was entitled under Article 34.4 to appeal against the order being granted. It was held in *Dillon-Leetch v. Calleary,*[79] where the plaintiff sought to appeal an election petition, that statutory preclusion of appeals from the High Court must be contained in a post-1961 Act, *i.e.* in an Act that was passed following the present Supreme Court's establishment in 1961. But this point has never been reiterated by the court. In one case Finlay C.J. observed that "exceptions to ... the right of appeal can only arise by virtue of a law or laws enacted subsequent to the coming into force of the Constitution."[80]

Provisions restricting the right of appeal are strictly construed and any

---

[73] *E.g.* Planning and Development Act 2000, s.50(4)(f)(i).
[74] *Jackson Way Properties Ltd v. Minister for the Environment* [1999] 4 I.R. 609.
[75] [2000] 2 I.R. 360 at p.400.
[76] [1967] I.R. 147.
[77] *Infra,* p.352.
[78] *E.g., State (Burke) v. Lennon* [1940] I.R. 136.
[79] Unreported, Supreme Court, July 25, 1973
[80] *Holohan v. Donohoe* [1986] I.R. 45 at p.48.

ambiguity will be interpreted in favour of allowing an appeal. As summarised by Hamilton C.J. in *Hanafin v. Minister for the Environment*,[81] which concerned the petition challenging the result of the 1995 divorce referendum, "(i)f it is the intention of the legislature to oust, except from or regulate the appellate jurisdiction of this Court to hear and determine appeals ..., such intention must be expressed in clear and unambiguous terms and it is a matter for interpretation by the court as to whether or not any provision of any law which purports to except from or regulate the appellate jurisdiction of this Court is effective to so do."[82] There the statutory words were held not to be sufficiently clear to prevent an appeal being taken from the decision of the High Court.[83] In the area of immigration, there is a short period within which administrative decisions may be challenged, which is extendable, and the High Court's determination on the challenge cannot be appealed unless the judge certifies that the issues are appropriate for an appeal. In *A.B. v. Minister for Justice*[84] it was held by the Supreme Court that this restriction on appealing applied only to decisions on the merits of the challenge and not to decisions refusing to extend the time for bringing that challenge. While it was difficult to understand why the legislation should make this distinction, the court's function is not to remedy a *casus omissus* and the provision was sufficiently ambiguous as to warrant an interpretation favouring the right of appeal on the time issue, which was completely distinct from the underlying merits in the judicial review application.

Another exception to the constitutional right of appeal to the Supreme Court is decisions of the High Court to refer a question to the European Court of Justice at Luxembourg under the procedure provided for in Article 234 (former 177) of the Treaty of Rome. In *Campus Oil Ltd. v. Minister for Industry and Energy*,[85] the Supreme Court said that the right of appeal deriving from Article 34 of the Constitution is qualified by Article 29.4.3, which deals with the E.C./E.U. Consequently, the judge who is seized of the case "has an untrammelled discretion as to whether he will or will not refer questions for a preliminary ruling under Article 177."[86] Moreover, by virtue of the status that the Rome Treaty enjoys under Article 29.4.3, the Oireachtas is not permitted to pass legislation, which would restrict the judge's discretion whether or not to refer a matter to the Luxembourg Court, such as providing for an appeal to the Supreme Court.

---

[81] [1996] 2 I.R. 321.
[82] *Id.* at p.389.
[83] Compare *Irish Asphalt Ltd v. An Bord Pleanála* [1996] 2 I.R. 179 and *Irish Hardware Association v. South Dublin C.C.* [2001] 2 I.L.R.M. 291 *Cf. Brick v. Burke* [2002] 2 I.L.R.M. 427 permitting an appeal in exceptional circumstances.
[84] [2002] 1 I.R. 296.
[85] [1983] I.R. 82.
[86] *Id.* at p.86.

In addition to its constitutional appellate jurisdiction, the Oireachtas may grant the Supreme Court other jurisdictions which would be exclusively statutory jurisdictions and which the legislature could withdraw from it at any time. As Walsh J. stated, the Oireachtas "may add jurisdictions to those jurisdictions already derived from the Constitution."[87] An example would be a right to hear appeals directly from the Circuit Court or from the District Court, assuming that this jurisdiction would not infringe the High Court's "full original jurisdiction."

Constitutional questions

Questions of constitutional law come before the Supreme Court in the course of its exercising original and appellate jurisdiction, and Article 26 of the Constitution authorises the President to refer Bills that have passed both Houses of the Oireachtas for the court's consideration. Its jurisdiction to hear appeals from the High Court is entrenched where the case raises the question of the constitutionality of a post-1937 law, so that the Oireachtas cannot deprive the court of this jurisdiction. According to Article 34.4.4, "[n]o law shall be enacted excepting from the appellate jurisdiction of the Supreme Court cases which involve questions as to the validity of any law having regard to the provisions of this Constitution." For the reasons given in *State (Sheerin) v. Kennedy*,[88] "law" in this context would appear to mean legislation enacted since December 1937. If "law" here does indeed mean that, then the Oireachtas is not prevented from providing that questions concerning the constitutionality of pre-1937 measures shall be determined only in the High Court and that its decisions cannot be appealed to the Supreme Court. Where the constitutionality of a post-1937 Act is at issue, the Constitution imposes the "single judgment" rule.[89]

Finality

While this Court's decision in "all cases (is) final and conclusive," it does not consider that it is fettered by the *stare decisis* maxim, *i.e.* that the Court can never subsequently hold that its previous decision no longer represents the law.[90] Although the Court is understandably reluctant to depart from its previous decisions and from the decisions of the pre-1961 Court, it has done so on several occasions.

Ordinarily, once the Supreme Court has decided a case and drawn up its order in those proceedings, that is the end of the matter; it is *res judicata* and

---

[87] *State (Browne) v. Feran* [1967] I.R. 147 at p.157.
[88] [1966[I.R. 379.
[89] Article 34.4,5; *supra*, p.63.
[90] *Supra*, p.19.

can never be re-opened by the parties.[91] There is no procedure, as exists elsewhere, for the court to review its own civil judgments but, since 1993, persons convicted on indictment can apply to the Court of Criminal Appeal to have their convictions reviewed.[92] Judgments in civil cases will be set aside where it is demonstrated that they were obtained by fraud.[93] Additionally, in its inherent jurisdiction to protect constitutional rights, the Court will set aside its own judgments in "special and usual circumstances," in "rare and exceptional cases."[94] But in the two leading cases on this question, the court rejected the contentions that the applicants' right to a fair hearing[95] and right to an impartial hearing,[96] respectively, had been contravened.

Criminal and Courts Martial appeals

The Constitution makes no express reference to the Court of Criminal Appeal, which was originally established by section 28 of the Courts of Justice Act 1924, and was again established by section 3 of the Courts (Establishment and Constitution) Act 1961. By virtue of section 12 of the Courts (Supplemental Provisions) Act 1961, this Court is a superior court of record and possesses all the statutory jurisdiction hitherto exercised by the pre-1961 Court of Criminal Appeal. Subject to some qualifications, persons convicted of an offence by either the Circuit Court or by the Central Criminal Court can appeal to the Court of Criminal Appeal; the appeal can be against conviction or against sentence. At one time there were some doubts as to whether the 1961 Courts Acts successfully secured their declared objective of establishing a Court of Criminal Appeal but those were put to rest by the Supreme Court in *People v. Conmey*.[97] O'Higgins C.J., for the court, pointed out that, while there is a constitutional right to appeal from the High Court to the Supreme Court, the Constitution does not prohibit the Oireachtas from establishing other courts with jurisdiction to hear appeals from the High Court or from the Circuit Court; that Article 34 "gives authority to the Oireachtas to establish such courts as it may think fit but subject to the mandatory provisions which relate to the High Court and the Supreme Court."[98]

There is no constitutional right of appeal from the Court of Criminal Appeal to the Supreme Court; whether such appeals can be made and the scope and conditions of those appeals is entirely a matter for statutory regulation.[99]

---

[91] *E.g. Open Door* case, *supra*, n.63.
[92] Criminal Procedure Act 1993.
[93] *Tassan Din v. Banco Ambrosiano S.P.A.* [1991] 1 I.R. 569.
[94] *Infra*, p.515.
[95] *Re Greendale Developments Ltd (No. 3)* [2000] 2 I.R. 514; *infra*, p.516.
[96] *Bula Ltd v. Tara Mines Ltd* (No 6) [2000] 4 I.R. 412; *infra*, p.516.
[97] [1975] I.R. 341. See too *State (Woods) v. Attorney General* [1969] I.R. 385.
[98] *Id.* at p.349.
[99] *Infra*, p.478.

By the Courts Martial Appeals Act 1983, a Courts Martial Appeal Court was established and was given jurisdiction to hear appeals from courts martial conducted under the Defence Act 1954.

Court Services

Formerly, the back-up administration of the courts system was the responsibility of the Minister for Justice. This was unsatisfactory in several respects and perhaps objectionable in principle in a constitutional system, which places considerable emphasis on the separation of powers. Following recommendations of a working group that had been established to deal with the question, the Court Services Act 1998 was passed, which transferred administrative responsibilities to an independent Courts Commission, of which serving judges are the majority of the members.

THE JUDICIARY

The courts are comprised of judges and other judicial officers, such as the master of the High Court, the taxing master, the official assignee, the accountant, the examiner and the various registrars. Judges are appointed from solicitors and barristers of a specified experience. In continental Europe, by contrast, virtually all judges are persons who embarked on a judicial career when they graduated from law school. It is because the continental judiciary are generally regarded as civil servants that the power to strike down laws for being unconstitutional often is not granted to the ordinary courts there but is reserved to special constitutional tribunals.

Appointment

Judges of the Supreme Court, the High Court, the Circuit Court, the District Court, and the Criminal Appeals Courts must be appointed by the President on the Government's advice.[100] With severable notable exceptions, until very recently judicial appointments were based largely on party political patronage. In order to overcome problems arising from this practice, a judicial appointments board was established in 1995[101] but it did not remove the party political element from the entire process. It should not be overlooked that there also is a significant political element in choosing United States Supreme

---

[100] Art.35.1.
[101] Courts and Courts Officers Act 1995, Pt IV (ss.12–33). Cf. Kentridge, "The Highest Court: Selecting the Judges", 62 *Cam. L.J.* 55 (2003).

Court judges and other judges there, and in selecting members of the continental European constitutional tribunals.

The form of declaration that must be made on taking judicial office is set out in Article 34.5.1 of the Constitution: any judge who declines or neglects to make that declaration is deemed to have vacated the office.[102]

There is no constitutional requirement concerning eligibility for judicial office: the requisite qualifications are entirely statutory. In one instance[103] it was contended that the Oireachtas did not have authority under the Constitution to lay down the eligibility requirements for these offices but that view was rejected. Article 36, which provides that numerous aspects of the courts and the judiciary shall be regulated in accordance with law, does not expressly mention qualifications for becoming a judge but this does not mean that the legislature cannot prescribe requisite criteria. Indeed, if the Oireachtas could not determine judges' qualifications, who then would decide those questions: the executive or the judiciary itself?

In *State (Walshe) v. Murphy*,[104] the central issue was the exact meaning of the term a "practising barrister" of certain years' standing in this context. The applicant, who had been convicted of a driving offence, sought to have his conviction set aside on the grounds that the temporary District Judge who tried the case was not qualified to hold the office. That judge had been called to the Bar in 1962, had been a subscriber to the Law Library and had practised in Dublin and on Circuit for eight years and three months. Thereafter, until his appointment as a temporary judge, he was employed as a full time legal assistant in the Attorney General's office and then as an examiner of titles in the Land Commission. The question was whether he was a "practising barrister ... of ten years standing at least at the date of appointment ...".[105] Finlay P. held that this provision does not mean a person who had been called to the Bar for longer than ten years. What the Oireachtas meant was "to provide a minimum standard of competence and skill for a person eligible for appointment;" accordingly, the above requirement means "a person who is a practising barrister at the time of his appointment and whose aggregate practice as a barrister at that time is not less than ten years."[106] In other words, the appointee must have in fact practised at the Bar for longer than ten years and be practising at the time of the appointment.

Working full time in the Government's legal service does not constitute practice at the Bar for these purposes because such persons do not, and indeed cannot, offer themselves at hazard to take legal work from anybody through a solicitor. As Finlay P. put it:

---

[102] Art.35.1.
[103] *State (Walshe) v. Murphy* [1981] I.R. 375.
[104] *Ibid.*
[105] Courts of Justice Act 1936, s.51(1).
[106] [1981] I.R. 289.

"The term 'practising barrister' ... refers to a person who, having the legal degree of barrister-at-law and having been called to the Bar, offers himself on hazard to take work (whether as an advocate or as an adviser) from persons who, through the agency of a solicitor, seek his services in the field in which he practises. A person who is employed as a legal assistant in the office of the Attorney General is clearly inhibited, by virtue of that employment, from carrying out legal work either in an advisory form or as an advocate for any person other than the Government. He is not in a position to accept instructions from any solicitor other than, possibly, the Chief State Solicitor. In any ordinary sense of the word, he could not be said to be on hazard and offering himself as a barrister to the public at large. In my view, similar considerations apply to a person who holds the office of examiner of titles and I consider the fact that that office involved appearances before the lay commissioners of the Land Commission (always on the instructions of the Land Commission itself and never to act for any other client) irrelevant to a consideration of this question."[107]

Tenure

In order to ensure their independence from the Government of the day, most Constitutions provide that judges cannot be removed easily from office. The tenure of Supreme Court and High Court judges is expressly protected by Article 35.4, according to which, "[a] judge of the Supreme Court or the High Court shall not be removed from office except for stated misbehaviour or incapacity, and then only upon resolutions passed by Dáil Éireann and by Seanad Éireann calling for his removal." This guarantee of tenure *quam diu se bene gesserint* derives from the Act of Settlement of 1701[108] and comprises two parts. One is the mechanism for dismissal, which is a resolution calling for removal and passed by both the Dáil and the Seanad. Those grounds on which judges can be so removed are confined to "misbehaviour or incapacity" and the resolutions calling for removal must state the grounds for moving against the judge in question. Several unresolved questions arise under this clause, such as what amounts to "misbehaviour," the extent of detail that must be contained in the stated grounds for removal whether a joint resolution for removal is reviewable by the courts and can a resolution be set aside if the court is satisfied that the judge did not get a fair hearing from the legislators or that the asserted grounds are a sham?[109] A related issue is the relevance of

---

[107] *Id.* at p.290.
[108] 12 & 13 Will. 3, c.2, s.2, re-enacted by the Irish Parliament as 21 & 22 Geo. 3 c.50. See generally, S. Shetreet, *Judges on Trial* (1996).
[109] *Cf. Therrien v. Minister for Justice* 200 D.L.R. 4th 1 (2000).

British precedents in determining these questions. The only judge ever to be removed since 1700 in Ireland or Britain under this kind of procedure was Sir Jonah Barrington in 1830, who was dismissed for his handling of the wards of court funds.

The Constitution does not have similar provisions with respect to other judges, although it contains a general guarantee of judicial independence. However, the Oireachtas has applied the *quam diu se bene gesserint* principle to Circuit Court Judges and District Judges. Ever since 1924, Circuit Court judges have enjoyed the "same tenure" as superior court judges[110] and that protection was extended to District judges in 1946.[111] The Courts Acts provide that, on the Minister's request, the Chief Justice must appoint a judge to investigate the condition of a District Judge's health, either physical or mental, or to inquire into a District Judge's conduct, either generally or on a particular occasion.[112] Where the Chief Justice is of the view that a District Judge's conduct would "bring the administration of justice into disrepute," he is authorised to interview the judge and to inform him of that opinion.[113] There are no parallel disciplinary provisions for other judges. Government proposals to amend the Constitution in 2000, making provision for disciplining judges, were at an advanced stage but were abandoned following objections from the opposition parties.

At one time most judges, once appointed, held their offices for the remainder of their lives. Indeed, in pre-Revolutionary France judicial offices could even be sold or inherited; Montesquieu's judgeship in the *Parlement* of Bordeaux was inherited. In nearly every country today judges must retire on attaining stipulated ages, the principal exception being Justices of the United States Supreme Court who hold office for life unless they are removed by way of impeachment.[114] It is an open question whether reducing the retirement age of already-appointed judges and compelling them to retire when they reach that age would contravene the above tenure guarantee.[115] When reducing judicial retirement ages, the convention is to exempt existing judges from the proposed reduction – which is why the Court of Exchequer in Ireland lasted 20 years after the great judicial reorganisation of 1877.

---

[110] Courts of Justice Act 1924, s.39.

[111] Courts of Justice (District Court) Act 1946, s.20.

[112] *Id.*, s.21.

[113] Courts (Supplemental Provisions) Act 1961, s.10(4).

[114] *Cf.* "Judicial Independence and Accountability" 61 *Law & Contemp. Problems* No.3 (1998), concerning other U.S. federal and State judges

[115] *Cf. Mackin v. New Brunswick*, 209 D.L.R. 4th 564 (2002).

Remuneration

Judges' remuneration is dealt with in the Constitution in two ways. Provision is made regarding remuneration for work done other than as judges of the courts established by the 1961 Act; according to Article 35.3, "no judge shall ... hold any other office or position of emolument." That is to say, a judge shall not hold any other job that pays remuneration. But it would seem that the clause does not forbid a judge from performing a particular task or series of tasks for which payment is made, for instance, acting as an arbitrator. The term "position" here would seem to have a meaning somewhat similar to that of "office;" the term used in the Irish text is "post."

Judges are protected from direct financial intimidation by the State in that, by virtue of Article 35.5, once appointed their remuneration cannot be reduced: that '[t]he remuneration of a judge shall not be reduced during his continuance in office." But there is no constitutional guarantee that judges' remuneration shall keep pace with that of comparable professional groups who, for various reasons, are in a better position to maintain their earnings in line with inflation. Over the last hundred years judges' relative salaries have fallen dramatically, although presently their salaries must be raised whenever remuneration in the civil service is increased. It was held by the Supreme Court in *McMenamin v. Ireland*[116] that the Government are obliged by the Constitution to keep judges' remuneration under review, so as to ensure that they do not fall so out of line with remuneration elsewhere as to jeopardise judicial independence.

There the applicant, a District Judge, challenged the manner in which his pension was determined, along with his lump sum retirement gratuity. At the time the relevant rules were introduced in 1961, there was nothing particularly unfair about them but, with the passage of time, the real value of the pension fell significantly. It was not suggested that this state of affairs was permitted to occur in order to make judges more amenable to the Government. A majority of the Court rejected the argument that the State was constitutionally obliged to ensure that judges' pension rights were not irrational or inequitable and, accordingly, did not strike down the rules in question. However, because those rules, as applied over time, did not achieve what they originally were intended to secure, there was an injustice that ought to be remedied. The Court declined to make a formal declaration to this effect because it was satisfied that, once the anomaly was drawn to the Government's attention, appropriate steps would be taken to remedy the situation. O'Flaherty J. endorsed the conclusion of the trial judge, that "[i]f for instance a salary for a District Court judge as fixed by statute became so eroded in real terms by reason of inflation that, having regard to salary movements in the community generally, it was totally out of line and so low as to undermine the secure independence of the judiciary, there would

---

[116] [1996] 3 I.R. 100.

be a breach of the constitutional obligation. As a pension is nothing more than deferred remuneration, the same principle would apply to pension rights."[117]

In *O'Byrne v. Minister for Finance*,[118] it was contended that subjecting judges' salaries to income tax constituted an impermissible reduction in their remuneration and contravened Article 68 of the Free State Constitution, which stated that a judge's remuneration "may not be diminished." The Supreme Court accepted that subjecting salaries to taxation did indeed "diminish" them. But it was held that the constitutional provision ought to be interpreted in the light of its objective, which was to ensure judicial independence. Since a non-discriminatory tax on judges' remuneration could not constitute a threat to their independence, the tax was not forbidden. Referring to similar provisions in foreign constitutions and constitutive laws, Kingsmill Moore J. observed that:

> "The object was to secure the independence of the judges and the impartial administration of justice. The legislation was for the protection of the people, not for the interests of the judges. A judge who was subject to removal or to have his salary reduced would be under temptation to be subservient to the wishes of those in whose power it was to ensure his removal or reduce his salary. Any discrimination by tax or otherwise against a judge or judges as a body, having the effect of reducing his or their salary would be equally objectionable. But I fail to see how a tax which is non-discriminatory against judges can assail the judicial independence. It is not and cannot be imposed by way of punishment to the judiciary for an assertion of independence. With certain exceptions, it is common to all. It is an unfortunate vicissitude of life from which the judiciary cannot claim to be immune."[119]

Furthermore:

> "But in no way does the legislation governing income tax discriminate against the judges or the judges' salaries as such. Judges are subject to the same liabilities as any other recipient of a fixed salary, no more and no less. If the object of the constitutional provision is to safeguard the independence of the judiciary from pressure or interference by the executive, this object is attained so long as the tax is not used to discriminate against the judges as such. If, as is suggested, persons assessed in respect of a fixed salary under Schedule E pay a disproportionate share of the burden of income tax when compared with those assessed under

---

[117] *Id.* at pp.140–141, *Cf. Conférence des Juges du Quebec v. Quebec*, 196 D.L.R. 4th 533 (2000) and *Bodner v. Alberta*, 222 D.L.R. 4th 284 (2002).
[118] [1959] I.R. 1.
[119] *Id.* at p.64.

other schedules, this incidental result of the framework of the income tax code cannot have been intended to operate, nor can it operate in such a way as to imperil the independence of the judiciary."[120]

Judges' remuneration is determined by sections 31 and 32 of the Oireachtas (Allowances to Members) and Ministerial, Parliamentary and Judicial Offices (Amendment) Act 1998, which fixes the salaries of the various judges and then provides that these amounts shall be increased correspondingly whenever there is a general increase in the Civil Service's remuneration. Judicial pensions are regulated by the second schedule to the Courts (Supplemental Provisions) Act 1961, as amended.

Independence

Judicial independence has for long been regarded as an essential ingredient of the rule of law and an unduly politicised judiciary was a substantial cause of the French and American Revolutions of the eighteenth century, and of the English Revolution of 1688. In order to ensure that judges are independent, the Constitution provides that they shall not be eligible for membership of either House of the Oireachtas, that they shall not hold any other paid post, that their remuneration shall not be reduced and that superior court judges can only be removed by both Houses of the Oireachtas. Ineligibility for membership of either House is self-explanatory, and the provisions against reduction of remuneration and on tenure are considered above. Most Western European constitutions contain provisions for judges' security of tenure and protecting judges' salaries but many of them add a general affirmation of judicial independence. Article 35.2 of the Constitution is very similar, providing that "[a]ll judges shall be independent in the exercise of their judicial functions and subject only to this Constitution and the law." This presumably means that judges shall not alone be independent of the executive but that they shall be independent of parties to litigation before them and, moreover, that neither the executive nor the legislature shall act in such a way as would undermine judicial independence. The courts have not yet pronounced on the precise meaning of this clause.

Although enquiries established under the Tribunals of Inquiry (Evidence) Acts 1921–2002, need not be chaired by or be conducted by serving judges, the practice has grown up of having these enquiries conducted in this manner. It was contended in *Haughey v. Moriarty*[121] that this practice was unconstitutional, on the grounds that judicial independence was thereby prejudiced,

---

[120] *Id.* at p.73.
[121] [1999] 3 I.R. 1 at p.64.

but that was rejected by the Supreme Court. Provided the President of the court in question agrees and "undue strain" is not placed on the work of the court, the Taoiseach or the Government are entitled to invite a judge to become either a member or the sole member of one of these enquiries.[122]

Immunity

At common law judges enjoyed immunity from suit in the sense that they could not be held liable in damages or otherwise in respect of what they did while acting within their jurisdiction.[123] As one judge stated, "[i]t is a principle of our law that no action will lie against a judge of one of the superior courts for a judicial act, though it be alleged to have been done maliciously and corruptly."[124] It has not been determined if this immunity exists under the Constitution. In *Byrne v. Ireland*,[125] where it was held that the principle "the King can do no wrong" was not carried over by Article 73 of the Free State Constitution nor by Article 50 of the present Constitution, the Supreme Court condemned all forms of blanket immunities from being sued except for immunities required by the Constitution, either expressly or by implication. Legislative privileges are an example of expressly required immunity[126] and diplomatic privilege or immunity was suggested to be impliedly required by Article 29 of the Constitution. Walsh J.'s judgment in the *Byrne* case did not mention judicial immunity. This suggests that the former immunity of judges may not have survived 1937 in its entirety. Nevertheless, the Constitution's guarantee of judicial independence may assure to the judges a degree of immunity from suit, *i.e.* sufficient immunity as is necessary to protect their independence; the extent of that immunity remains to be seen.[127] At common law judges lose their immunity when they act outside of their jurisdiction.

It is conceivable that the State itself may be held liable for undoubted wrongs committed by judges in the performance of their judicial functions even though those judges cannot be held personally liable. French and German law have instituted a system of liability of the State for damage done to an individual arising from wrong-doing by a judge in the discharge of judicial duties,[128] thereby providing a remedy for victims of judicial wrongs while at the same

---

[122] *Riordan v. An Taoiseach (No. 1)* [1999] 4 I.R. 321 at p.338.

[123] See generally, A. Olowofoyeku, *Suing Judges: A Study of Judicial Immunity* (1993).

[124] *Fray v. Blackburn* (1863) 3 B. & S. 576 at p.578.

[125] [1972] I.R. 241.

[126] *Supra*, p.107.

[127] *Cf. Desmond v. M.C.D. Management Services Ltd* [2000] 1 I.R. 505, extending absolute privilege in defamation to coroners.

[128] See generally, Capelletti, "Who Watches the Watchmen: A Comparative Study of Judicial Responsibility," 31 *American J. Compar. L.* 1 (1983).

time protecting individual judges from harassment by suits instituted against them by aggrieved litigants. It would appear that at common law judges were not immune from being prosecuted for offences they committed in the discharge of their office.[129] An endeavour to hold the State liable for alleged judicial wrong-doing was rejected by Flood J. in *Deighan v. Ireland*,[130] on the grounds that the judge had acted within his jurisdiction and could not be held personally liable and, accordingly, there could not be any vicarious liability. However, the plaintiff there was a lay litigant and it does not appear that he argued that, as in France, direct liability of the State may arise on the basis of *faute de service*, as contrasted with the individual judge's *faute personnel*.

---

[129] *Cf. R. v. Murphy* 5 N.S.W.L.R. 18 (1986) and *Gravel v. United States* 408 U.S. 606 at p.627 (1972).

[130] [1995] 2 I.R. 56.

CHAPTER 8

Separation of Powers

Constitutions deal with who is to govern and how those rulers are to exercise their powers; they say who takes what decisions, the procedures that must be followed before certain decisions can be made and any substantive limits to decision-making authority. Some constitutions confer virtually limitless powers on a single individual, such as a dictator. There are constitutions that seek to spread political power throughout the entire populace. Perhaps the most distinctive feature of most modern constitutions is that they classify power into three different categories, *viz.* standards-setting, implementation of standards that have been duly set and deciding disputes about the particular circumstances in which those standards apply. In other words, they classify power as legislative, executive and judicial, although the scope of power consigned to each of these branches and the relationship between them varies considerably from constitution to constitution.[1] Demarking the zones within which each of the three key organs of state may function also is a basis for certain fundamental rights, for instance against executive sentencing, against protracted detention in several circumstances, against some inequalities in the application of laws and against irrebuttable presumptions of fact.

SYSTEMS OF SEPARATED POWERS

The theory of the separation of powers is generally associated with Charles-Louis de Secondat (1689–1755), who 300 years ago became a leading judge in Bordeaux and at the same time acquired the name of Montesquieu; at the age of 27 he inherited the high judicial office of *Président à mortier* at the *Parlement* of Bordeaux. *Parlements* were the courts of last resort for the major regions of France, the leading one being the *Parlement* of Paris; they were all dissolved at an early stage of the 1789 Revolution. His contribution to modern constitutionalism lies not in how he performed his official duties but in a book he had published in 1748, the celebrated *De l'Esprit des Loix,* in which he paints an idealised picture of the English Constitution of the day.[2]

---

[1] See generally, M. Vile, *Constitutionalism and the Separation of Powers* (2nd ed. 1998), W. Gwynn, *The Meaning of the Separation of Powers* (1965) and D. Morgan, *The Separation of Powers in the Irish Constitution* (1997).

[2] See generally, Vile, *id.*, Chap.4.

A central feature of Montesquieu's theory of the State was the separation of powers; that all public powers should not be concentrated in one person's hands nor in one institution, but should be allocated between different branches of government. According to him:

> "In every State political power can be divided into three categories: the legislative power, the power to implement norms deriving from international law and the power to implement norms deriving from the civil law. As regards the first of these, the prince or the magistrate determines the law either for the time being or for always, and amends and abrogates laws that have been made. The second of these powers involves making peace and war, sending and receiving ambassadors, making the State more secure and preventing invasions. The third power is to punish those who commit crime and to resolve disputes that arise between individuals."[3]

His main argument was that:

> "Whenever the legislative power and the power to take action are united in the one individual or institution, there is no liberty because there is always the grave danger that the monarch or senate will not alone make tyrannical laws but will execute laws in a tyrannical manner. ...
>
> There is no liberty whenever the power to judge is not separated from the powers to legislate and to implement laws. If the power to judge could be exercised by the legislature, the citizens' lives and liberties would be greatly at risk, because the judge would also be the legislature. And if the executive exercised the judicial power, the judge could easily become an oppressor. Everything would be lost if the same individual or group or institution wielded the three powers; the powers to make laws, to execute the laws, and to judge those accused of crimes and disputes between individuals."[4]

Precisely what form of government Montesquieu favoured does not matter now. But his advocacy of the tripartite separation of powers, with its implicit criticism of the *Parlements'* structure, became dogma for the French revolutionaries of 1789 and for the "Founding Fathers" of the United States. Thus, in its penultimate clause, the Declaration of the Rights of Man and of the Citizen of 1789 proclaims that "a society without ... the separation of powers established is a society without a constitution." The great bulk of the United States Constitution of 1787 is comprised of Articles I-III; Article I

---

[3] (1973, ed.) Garnier Freres, book xi ch.vi (author's own translation).
[4] *Ibid.*

deals with "all legislative powers," Article II with "the executive power" and Article III with "the judicial power of the United States ...."

There is a fourth and frequently overlooked dimension to the allocation of power in any State and that is private ordering. In numerous respects public goals are not secured by the combination of the traditional three organs of state but, instead, by permitting private sector bodies regulate the particular area of concern. For instance, standards-setting and enforcement in many of the professions is done by professional bodies themselves rather than by State agencies. In the past, social welfare was largely provided by private charities and churches had a predominant role in education. At times, regulatory authority is shared between the State and private bodies, as in what are described as public/private partnerships, or when penal sanctions are imposed for contravention of privately-made rules. Under the State Authorities (Public and Private Partnership Arrangements) Act 2002, State authorities and private bodies can co-operate in securing certain public objectives.

While most modern constitutions incorporate a tripartite separation of powers, they differ considerably as regards how much power each of the three organs of State possesses, the extent to which each organ can exercise powers more usually associated with another organ, and whether any one or more organs can interfere with the activities of another. Indeed, the U.S. constitutional scheme is often described as more a system of checks and balances than a strict separation of powers.[5] France has had numerous constitutions since Montesquieu's day and every one of them has embodied different conceptions of *séparation des pouvoirs*.[6] The Irish Constitution stipulates in Article 6.1 that '[a]ll powers of government, legislative, executive and judicial, derive, under God, from the people (and t)hese powers of government are exercisable only by or on the authority of the organs of State established by this Constitution." Ireland, however, diverges from the United States model and, like countries such as France, Germany, Italy and the United Kingdom, has a fourth organ of State, *viz.*, a head of State, known as the President, who is neither a member of the executive nor of the legislature, but who nevertheless has several important constitutional functions.

Under most modern constitutions, there is a legislature, which is empowered to enunciate general rules of conduct for the community. According to Article 15.2.1 of the Irish Constitution, "[t]he sole and exclusive power of making laws for the State is hereby vested in the Oireachtas: no other legislative authority has power to make laws for the State." A second element of the traditional tripartite scheme is the executive; Article 28.2 of the Constitution states that "[t]he executive power of the State shall, subject to the provisions

---

[5] See generally, Sharp, "The Classic American Doctrine of the Separation of Powers", 2 *U. Chicago L. Rev.* 395 (1935) and Vile, *supra*, n.1, Chap.6.

[6] See generally, Neuborne, "Judicial Review and the Separation of Powers in France and the United States", 57 *New York L. Rev.* 363 (1982) and Vile, *supra*, n.1, Chap.9.

of this Constitution, be exercised by or on the authority of the Government." Constitutions, thirdly, establish courts, which shall exercise the judicial power of the State; as Article 34.1 of the Constitution provides, "[j]ustice shall be administered in courts established by law by judges appointed in the manner provided by this Constitution." That is to say, it is for the courts to resolve disputes between individuals, and between individuals and the State; they ascertain the underlying facts and decide what constitutional principle or rule that the legislature devised, or common law rule or equitable principle, should govern the circumstances.

Most modern constitutions do not give each of these three organs of State a monopoly over the standards-setting, disputes-resolution and executive powers. Some overlapping of powers is usually permitted. In Ireland the executive must be appointed from elected members of the legislature and it can be removed at any time by the legislature; most importantly, many major governmental decisions must be approved by the legislature before they can have legal effect. In the United States, by contrast, no member of the government may sit in the Congress, except for the Vice President who chairs the Senate. There, the chief executive (President) can select virtually anybody to join the government, but subject to the chosen person being approved by committees of both Houses of the Congress; the President can veto Bills that have passed both Houses, although it is possible to override that veto; and the President's term of office is not dependent on having the continued support of a Congressional majority. In France, neither the President, Prime Minister nor Cabinet Ministers may be members of the *Assemblée* or of the *Sénat*. Perhaps the most striking feature of the French *séparation des pouvoirs* is that the Constitution empowers the Parliament to enunciate general rules governing certain questions, such as civil rights, nationality, matrimony, crimes and misdemeanours, criminal penalties, taxes, currency, education and social security. But without any parliamentary approval, the Government can enunciate general rules regarding matters that are not itemised in Article 34 of the Constitution. Thus, the law-making power is parcelled out between the legislature and the executive, and the executive there possesses extensive standards-setting autonomy.[7]

While Article 6.1 of the Constitution proclaims the tripartite separation of powers and that scheme of government is reiterated in Article 15.2.1, Article 34.1 and Article 28.2, this separation is far from being a rigid one. In the words of Walsh J., the Constitution "does not give paramountcy in all circumstances to any one of the organs exercising the powers of government over the other."[8] Kenny J. observed that "the framers of the Constitution did

---

[7] See generally, Nicholas, "Loi, Reglement and Judicial Review in France" [1970] *Public L.* 251 and Lowenstein, "The Balance Between Legislative and Executive Power: A Study in Comparative Constitutional Law", 5 *U. Chicago L. Rev.* 566 (1938).

[8] *Murphy v. Dublin Corp.* [1972] I.R. 215 at p.234.

not adopt a rigid separation between legislative, executive and judicial powers."[9] Apart from Ó Dálaigh C.J.'s observation that the tripartite system was adopted to some extent because of "our previous experience under an alien government whose parliament was omnipotent and in whose executive lay wide reserves of prerogative power,"[10] there has been no judicial articulation of what generally the Constitution's version of the separation principle was designed to achieve.

EXECUTIVE LAW MAKING

The function of legislatures is to make laws, *i.e.* set down the standards of conduct expected of individuals, and what rights and responsibilities persons and bodies have, that may be sanctioned by the force of law. When they enter into contracts, individuals in a sense make a special law for their relationships within the context of those contracts. By executive law making is meant the Government, its Ministers or public officials, promulgating binding rules of conduct in the form of a statutory instrument, bye-law, decree, regulation or the like.

It is not practical that each and every question requiring standards-setting must be the subject of explicit provisions in an Act of the Oireachtas. Statutes would be unwieldy and virtually incomprehensible if they contained enormous chunks of technical material, for example the regulations regarding how civil aircraft must be operated. Many Acts require elaborate procedures for their implementation and, since some of these procedures may have to be amended occasionally, it can be more convenient if those rules are laid down by the executive in accordance with guidelines set out in an Act in question, rather than having them embodied in full in an Act. Examples include the regulations issued under the Diseases of Animals Act 1966, concerning farm animals suspected of having tuberculosis and brucellosis. Although an Act may address one particular problem, often new contingencies will arise that cannot be predicted at the time of enactment; the sensible thing may be to authorise the executive to make certain changes in the Act's scheme in order to deal with those contingencies. A comparatively recent innovation is regulated industries, where "regulators," having a degree of independence from Government Ministers, can lay down rules pertaining to particular sectors, such as financial services, telephony and electricity. In times of grave emergency, where circumstances are likely to change very rapidly and drastically, it may be necessary to give the Government extensive powers to deal with the situation but it may not be possible to spell out in any detail the nature of those powers

---

[9] *Abbey Films Ltd v. Attorney General* [1981] I.R. 39.
[10] *Melling v. O Mathghamhna* [1962] I.R. 1 at p.39.

and in what particular circumstances they can be exercised, as occurred during World War II with the Emergency Powers Acts. It has always been regarded as preferable to allow local authorities to issue bye-laws to deal with problems peculiar to their own areas than to have those issues regulated directly by the national legislature. Procedural rules for the conduct of court cases have always been drawn up by committees of judges and members of the legal profession, subject to being approved by the Minister.

Resort to subordinate legislation, however, has not been without its critics. In the 1930s an English Lord Chief Justice painted a picture of a bureaucratic conspiracy to wrest power from Parliament in favour of an executive, which had a vast authority to issue regulations,[11] but his account was promptly discredited as unsupported "by the smallest shred of evidence."[12] Among the major criticisms of delegated executive rule-making is that it is rarely examined and debated adequately by elected public representatives and, accordingly, it is undemocratic. One particular abuse has been conferring on Ministers a virtually unbounded discretion to issue whatever regulations they deem expedient or appropriate. Another was resort to what are called Henry VIII clauses, *i.e.* legislative authority to a Minister to amend the substantive provisions of an Act, in effect transforming the Minister from being an administrator to a legislator. A variant of such a clause is contained in some employment legislation, in which can be found a provision authorising the Minister to amend the Act in question in such way as is necessary to bring the State into compliance with its international legal obligations.[13]

What may be described as the "democratic deficit" argument is usually met by requiring the text of proposed rules to be laid before one or more of the Houses of the Oireachtas and, at times, to be voted on by one or both of them. Potential constitutional challenges are occasionally anticipated by a requirement that the rules in question are embodied in, or are expressly endorsed by an Act of the Oireachtas.[14] A feature of some recent Acts is that, in order to prevent a possible constitutional challenge, they list out a series of statutory instruments and stipulate that those shall have the force of law.[15]

The extent to which legislatures are permitted to delegate standards-setting power to the executive has been the subject of extensive litigation in most countries whose constitutions embody the tripartite separation of powers. Two preliminary questions arise, however. One is that of statutory construction, *viz.* does the regulation being challenged fall within the powers that the legislature sought to delegate to the executive? If the answer is no, then the regulation in question is *ultra vires* the Act. Second, was the regulation drawn

---

[11] Lord Hewart, *The New Despotism* (1929).

[12] *Report of the Committee on Ministers' Powers* (1932; Cmd. 4060), p.59.

[13] *E.g.*, Unfair Dismissals Act 1977, s.16(5).

[14] *E.g.*, Restrictive Trade Practices Act 1953, s.9.

[15] *E.g.*, Immigration Act 1999, s.2.

up in accordance with the procedures laid down in the governing Act and were those (if any) who were entitled to be heard before the regulation was issued in fact heard? If the answer is no, then the regulation again is *ultra vires* the Act. It is only when the answer to both questions is yes that the more difficult issue arises., *viz.* did the Oireachtas contravene Article 15.2.1 by seeking to delegate excessive powers?

Statutory Instruments

Many subordinate rules take the form of statutory instruments as defined in the Statutory Instruments Acts 1947-55, and must fulfil the requirements of these Acts.[16] Every measure that is governed by them must be printed and published by the Government Publications Office, and be assigned a number as of the year in which it is made. A notice must be placed in the *Iris Oifigiúil* of that fact, stating where copies of the instrument are to be obtained, and copies must then be kept at that place. Within seven days of the instrument being made, copies must be deposited in the following places: the National Library of Ireland, the Law Library at the Four Courts, the Kings Inns Library, the Law Society's Library, the Southern Law Association and at the Dublin, Cork, Limerick, Waterford and Galway Chambers of Commerce.

An intended regime that must be treated in this manner is defined in a complex way by the 1947 Act, as "an order, regulation, rule, scheme or bye-law made in exercise of a power conferred by statute," be it a post or pre-1937 statute;[17] in brief, an order, however described, issued under statutory authority. But that order must have been made after January 1948[18] by either the Government or any member of the Government, any Parliamentary Secretary, the President, a rules of court committee or any other agency discharging a public function in the sense that it "exercise(s) throughout the State any function of government, or discharge(s) throughout the State any public duties in relation to public administration."[19] Thus, bye-laws issued by local and regional authorities are excluded from the definition. Provision is made whereby the Attorney General can certify that a particular person or body exercises a public function for these purposes. Further, the statute in question must require that the order be laid before either or both Houses of the Oireachtas or, alternatively, the order must "affect the public generally or any particular class or classes of the public."[20] The 1947 Act does not indicate how one determines what is a

---

[16] See generally G. Hogan & D. Morgan, *Administrative Law in Ireland* (3rd ed., 1998), pp.23 *et seq.*
[17] S.1.
[18] S.2.
[19] S.2(1)(b)(v).
[20] S.2(1)(c)(ii).

class of the public, except that the Attorney General can certify that a particular class of persons possesses that character.

Some of the orders that satisfy this definition are nevertheless exempted from the 1947–55 Acts' requirements of publicity and deposit in the above-mentioned places. There is an exemption where the Act in question requires that the entire order be published in the *Iris Oifigiúil*. There also is an exemption where the Attorney General has certified that either a particular order or a class of order should not be so deposited by reason of "its merely local or personal application or its temporary operation or its limited application or for any other reason …".[21] It is provided that the validity or effect of any statutory instrument is not affected because these requirements regarding publicity or depositing copies were not adhered to.[22] Nevertheless, a person charged with breach of a duty imposed in a regulation that did not comply with any of these requirements has a good defence unless the prosecutor satisfies the court that "reasonable steps had been taken for the purpose of bringing the purport of (that) instrument to the notice of the public or of persons likely to be affected by it or of the defendant."[23]

Even though they are made by executive authority, the Oireachtas has at least a potential say in the content of most statutory instruments, in that the Act authorising their making usually provides that they shall be laid before one or both Houses. In that event, legislators have the opportunity of considering the proposed contents of the measure. Where the instrument in question touches on matters of general importance, usually the governing Act will provide that it be laid before one or both Houses and be subject to the negative resolution procedure, which means that the instrument shall not be effective if one or both Houses passes a resolution rejecting it. Where the instrument in question is of particular general importance, usually the Act will make it subject to the affirmative resolution procedure, by which is meant that it cannot take effect until one or both Houses, as the case may be, passes a resolution approving its contents. Incidental features of the different "laying" procedures are dealt with in the Houses of the Oireachtas (Laying of Documents) Act 1966. Despite the existence of such requirements, it is very rarely that newly made statutory instruments engender political debate. Perhaps the most controversial one of recent years was the annual "gagging order" made until 1994 under the Broadcasting Acts, prohibiting Radio Telefís Éireann from broadcasting certain matters.[24] A Joint Oireachtas Committee on Legislation reviews the content of draft instruments.

---

[21] S.2(4).

[22] S.3(3). Cf. *D.P.P. v. Collins* [1981] I.L.R.M. 447.

[23] S.3(2).

[24] S 31 of the Broadcasting Authority Act 1960, as amended; *post*, p.539.

Ultra vires

Whenever a regulation is the subject of a constitutional attack, the court will endeavour to avoid that issue by ascertaining whether it may be invalidated on other grounds, being whether it is *ultra vires* the rule-making authority in question. Where the basis for challenge is that the Act in question delegated excessive powers to the rule making body, O'Higgins C.J. explained that the proper approach is that, where reasonably possible to do so, the statutory provision delegating the power should be interpreted restrictively, so that by its terms it does not delegate excessive powers:

> "the consideration of any question involving the validity of a statute or a section thereof should, in appropriate circumstances be postponed to the consideration of any other question, the resolution of which will determine the issue between the parties. It is therefore, proper in this case that the question of *ultra vires,* apart from any question of constitutionality, should first be considered. In the consideration of such question, however, the validity of the section must be presumed and it must be interpreted in accordance with the existence of such a presumption, This means that if the section is capable of being interpreted in two ways, one of which would give a meaning which is consistent with what is permitted by the Constitution and the other of which would not, that meaning which is so consistent must be adopted ...
>
> It is necessary to seek a meaning for the words, which absolve the National Parliament from any intention to delegate its exclusive power of making or changing the laws. Needless to say, if such a meaning is not possible then the invalidity ... would be established. *Prima facie,* therefore, these words are to be interpreted in such a manner as to authorise only exclusions which the Act itself contemplates."[25]

Thus in *Cooke v. Walsh,*[26] it was argued that regulations issued under section 72 of the Health Act 1970 were *ultra vires* or, if those regulations were *intra vires* this Act, then section 72 contravened the separation of legislative and executive powers. The regulations there dealt with compensation for victims of road traffic accidents and the problem of collateral benefits; they provided that persons injured in those accidents and who stood to receive compensation under an insurance policy would not be eligible under the Health Acts for free medical treatment for their injuries. The 1970 Act does not provide for universal free treatment; infants and persons with insufficient means are entitled to all

---

[25] *Cooke v. Walsh* [1984] I.R. 710 at pp.728 and 729.
[26] *Ibid.*

hospital services without charge, and persons insured under the Social Welfare Acts qualify for some hospital services without charge. The effect of the impugned regulations was to shift a major item in the cost of compensating serious road traffic accident victims from the shoulders of the public health service on to the insurers, and ultimately on to the motorists who pay insurance premiums. Section 72 of the Act provides that

> "(1) The Minister may make regulations applicable to all Health Boards or to one or more than one Health Board regarding the manner in which and the extent to which the Board or Boards shall make available services under this Act and generally in relation to the administration of those services.
> (2) Regulations under this section may provide for any service under this Act being made available only to a particular class of the persons who have eligibility for that service."

It was argued that if section 72 did indeed purport to authorise the Minister to alter the eligibility rules for free hospital services, then it was an excessive delegation of legislative authority, for the section would be seeking to enable the Minister to bring about profound changes in the entire statutory scheme. But before addressing the constitutional issue, it was contended that section 72 did not in fact purport to authorise the Minister to alter eligibility in so drastic a manner; that it only authorised him to issue regulations concerning less vital and purely administrative aspects of the health service. The Supreme Court concluded that section 72 gave only this restricted authority and that the regulations, rendering a large class of otherwise eligible patients ineligible for free treatment when they were injured in a road traffic accident, were *ultra vires* the 1970 Act. Consideration of the constitutional question, therefore, was not required.

Except where that authority is clearly stated in the Act in question, it is presumed that the Oireachtas did not confer on the executive power to issue regulations that are unreasonable, arbitrary or unfairly discriminatory. Thus, in *Cassidy v. Minister for Industry and Commerce*,[27] where the plaintiff contested the legality and constitutionality of regulations made for controlling liquor prices in the Dundalk area, the Supreme Court held that the Prices Act 1958, did not authorise certain features of those regulations; that "Parliament cannot have intended that the Minister would exercise in such an arbitrary and unfair way" the power to make price control regulations.[28] But the regulations there were not declared *ultra vires*; instead, they were construed as applying otherwise than in the unfair manner. Regulations under the since-repealed Farm

---

[27] [1978] I.R. 297.
[28] *Id.* at p.312.

Tax Act 1985, that operated to bring farmers owning over 150 acres immediately into the tax net, but not other farmers, were declared invalid for being unfairly discriminatory.[29] Several regulations in the social welfare area were condemned on similar grounds, such as the exclusion of divorced women from entitlement to an unmarried mother's allowance,[30] the withdrawal of a blind pension on the person qualifying for a non-contributory old age pension[31] and the exclusion of persons receiving an unmarried mother's allowances from entitlement to disability benefit.[32] In the latter case, McCarthy J. observed that "[i]f a regulation is demonstrably lacking in logic and unfair it cannot be sustainable within the framework of the scheme; it cannot be a proper application of the statutory power to make regulations."[33]

Unconstitutional delegation

How much rule-making authority may be conferred by legislatures on the executive is of considerable political moment. If legislatures could not delegate extensive standards-setting powers, the kind of interventionist/welfare state that has grown up in Ireland and other Western European countries would never have developed. A large and finely tuned public service, or bureaucracy, requires considerable flexibility within which to set and adjust standards to meet the exigencies of complex and rapidly changing circumstances. Accordingly, the political opponents of the interventionist/welfare state tend to condemn delegated legislation, especially in the economic field.

With two notable exceptions, challenges to statutory provisions on the grounds that they unconstitutionally delegated excessive rule-making authority to the executive have been unsuccessful. In one instance, the *An Blascaod Mór Teo.* case,[34] the question was raised of the propriety of delegating authority to a private company, which could be authorised to manage aspects of an intended national park. That arrangement was upheld by Budd J. because there was no case law saying that public power could never be delegated to a private body and, further, under the 1989 Act being considered any such delegation could be vetoed by either House of the Oireachtas. It remains to be determined how extensive powers may be entrusted to industry "regulators" who enjoy a degree of insulation from the ordinary political processes. In one instance, section 5 of the Solicitors Act 1954, was challenged; it empowers the Law

---

[29] *Purcell v. Attorney General* [1995] 3 I.R. 287.
[30] *State (Kenny) v. Minister for Social Welfare* [1986] I.R. 693.
[31] *Harvey v. Minister for Social Welfare* [1990] 2 I.R. 232.
[32] *McHugh v. Minister for Social Welfare* [1994] 2 I.R. 139.
[33] *Id.* at p.156.
[34] *An Blascaod Mór Teo v. Commissioners for Public Works* Budd J., February 27, 1998.

Society of Ireland to make regulations for the solicitors profession, which must be laid before both Houses, who have no veto on them.[35] In the event, McGuinness J. found it unnecessary to deal with this point as she held for the applicant there on other grounds.

Provided that the basic policy choices are contained in the Act in question and it lays down the essential structure and orientation of the particular scheme, it is permissible to leave it to the executive to fill in the details. How specific an Act is required to be will often turn on the very nature of the legislation involved. There is no simple rule to determine when a delegation contravenes Article 15.2.1. As McMahon J. observed in the *AnCO* case, which for many years was the leading case, "(i)t is apparent from the authorities ... that there is no universal and apt formula to determine the extent to which legislative power may be delegated. The subject matter of regulation may be so fluid that a detailed prescription of standards could make effective administration impossible and delegated powers would have to include wide areas of judgment and discretion."[36] According to O'Higgins C.J. there, the test of a measure's constitutionality is "whether that which is challenged as an unauthorised delegation of parliamentary power is more than a mere giving effect to principles and policies which are contained in the statute itself. If it be, then it is not authorised; for such would constitute a purported exercise of legislative power by an authority, which is not permitted to do so under the Constitution. On the other hand, if it be within the permitted limits -if the law is laid down in the statute and details only are filled in or completed by the designated Minister or subordinate body -there is no unauthorised delegation of legislative power."[37] When deciding whether a particular delegation is or is not unconstitutional, account is taken of a number of issues. One is the extent to which, under the Act in question, the legislature must scrutinise the particular rules being challenged. At times, rules that are expected to be particularly controversial are required by the Act to be approved by a vote of one or both Houses before they can enter into force. In an evenly balanced case, the existence of a "legislative veto" in one of these forms would tend to save the measure from being held to be invalid. Another relevant consideration is the nature of the interest that the challenged rule affects and the way in which that interest is affected.

The principal instance where a statutory provision was struck down for delegating excessive authority to the executive was *Laurentiu v. Minister for Justice*,[38] where the Supreme Court declared section 5(1)(e) of the Aliens Act 1935, to be unconstitutional. It would be difficult to find a more extensive a delegation of power than section 5(1)(e), which concerned the control of aliens

---

[35] *Cf. Carroll v. Law Society* [2000] 1 I.L.R.M. 161.
[36] *Cityview Press Ltd v. An Chomhairle Oiliúna* [1980] I.R. 381 at p.389.
[37] *Id.* at p.399. *Cf.* the *Kalkar* case, 49 BVerfGE 89 (1978).
[38] [1999] 4 I.R. 26.

and the exclusion and deportation of aliens, stipulating that "[t]he Minister may, if and whenever he thinks proper, do by order ... all or any of the following things in respect either of all aliens or of aliens of a particular nationality or otherwise of a particular class, or of particular aliens, that is to say – make provision for the exclusion or the deportation and exclusion of such aliens from Saorstát Éireann and provide for and authorise the making by the Minister of orders for that purpose." No criteria of any kind were contained in the 1935 Act with regard to how these powers were to be exercised nor the procedures that should govern their exercise. But orders made under section 5(1)(e) had to be laid before either House of the Oireachtas, which could vote to revoke them. Under the Aliens Order 1936, the Minister gave himself an extremely wide discretion to deport aliens; he could do so "if he deems it to be conducive to the public good," subject to "any conditions [he] may think proper."[39] Once such an order is made in respect of an alien, he was obliged to leave and remain out of the State. In the 1980s an informal administrative procedure was adopted for dealing with refugee applications, to ensure that the State complied with its international legal obligations in that regard.

Having come to Ireland from Romania and being unsuccessful with his application for refugee status, the plaintiff was ordered by the Minister to be deported. He challenged this decision, contending *inter alia* that section 5(1)(e) was invalid. Although the constitutionality of parts of the Aliens Act 1935, had previously been contested in other cases, this glaring anomaly appears to have been overlooked until then. For the purposes of the argument, it was accepted that the Minister followed fair procedures before making the deportation decision and that he was not being so arbitrary or unfair as to bring the case within the *Cassidy* principle. For the Minister, it was contended that a power to deport aliens was traditionally an executive function that does not need legislative sanction,[40] that section 5(1)(e) of the 1935 Act confirmed this principle and that the policy of that section (an unfettered discretion of the Minister to deport) was embodied in the 1936 Order, which brought it within the "principles and policies" test articulated in the previous cases on this general topic. On account of the wide variety of circumstances and problems that may arise in controlling the admission of aliens, it was argued that the only practical way of addressing the whole question is to confer a wide discretion on the Minister; that section 5(1)(e) simply endorsed the legal position obtaining before the Act was passed.

Keane J. accepted that the power to expel aliens was intrinsically an executive power which, in the absence of any legislation, could be exercised by the Government or one of its Ministers. But when that power becomes the subject of legislation, the principles governing its exercise ought to be set out

---

[39] Reg.13(1).
[40] Cf. *Kanaya v. Minister for Justice* [2000] 2 I.L.R.M. 503.

in the Act in question. He rejected the argument that the principles in the 1935 Act were that the Minister could have a complete discretion as to who to deport and who should not be deported, thus bringing section 5(1)(e) within the criteria for constitutionality. In substance, section 5(1)(e) "permitted the Minister for Justice to legislate for deportation,"[41] which was not permissible.

The only other instance of a statutory provision being invalidated on these grounds was in *McDaid v. Sheehy*,[42] except that prior to the case being heard, legislation was enacted to validate the regulations in question. Under the Imposition of Duties Act 1957, the Government were given an extremely wide discretion to impose, vary and terminate customs and excise duties. As in *Laurentiu*, this Act contained no principles or policies whatsoever, other than that a most extensive discretion could be exercised by the executive. On account however of the subsequent validating Act, the Supreme Court held that Blayney J.'s finding of unconstitutionality should be regarded as *obiter*, as it was not necessary for the determination of the case.

Most of the other cases where "separation of power" challenges were unsuccessful concerned property rights and the regulation of business. *Planning and Development Bill 1999, Re*[43] concerned an endeavour to facilitate persons buying houses who otherwise would not be able to afford them, by requiring local authorities to adopt a housing strategy that significantly restricted the freedom developers otherwise would possess. This Bill was challenged principally on the grounds that it unduly interfered with property rights. It also was contended that section 93(3)(b) of the Bill was an excessive delegation of power; in determining eligibility for the purpose of such schemes, the authorities were required to take account of "any other financial circumstances" of applicants and of persons who might reasonably be expected to reside with them. Because the general policy of the Act was to assist persons of limited means to buy housing, as described in the definition of "eligible persons" in section 93(1), the Supreme Court held that subsection (3)(b) "does no more than allow the planning authority to take into account other financial circumstances of particular persons who might come within [that]definition."[44]

Under section 4(2) of the Competition Act 1991, the Competition Authority is authorised to grant licences permitting certain agreements, decisions and practices that offend against subsection (1), provided these meet criteria set out in subsection (2). Not surprisingly, a separation of powers attack on it was rejected by Barrington J.[45] Under section 6(2) of the Urban Renewal Act 1986, in addition to the Customs House Docks area, the Minister is empowered to designate other areas for renewal "where he is satisfied that there is a special

---

[41] [1999] 4 I.R. 92.
[42] [1991] 1 I.R. 1.
[43] [2000] 2 I.R. 321.
[44] *Id.* at p.359.
[45] *Cronin v. Competition Authority* [1998] 1 I.R. 265.

need to promote urban renewal therein ...". Again not surprisingly, a similar attack on it was rejected by Lynch J.[46]

Quite extensive discretionary powers may be delegated to the executive for the purpose of regulating particular industries, especially with regard to issues of pricing and quality control. In the first case where the non-delegation argument was advanced, concerning the since-repealed Pigs and Bacon Acts 1935-37, a Board established to regulate the bacon curing industry, comprising elected representatives of that industry, was authorised to fix prices for purchasing pigs which, in its opinion "would, under normal circumstances, be a proper price." In rejecting the challenge to these Acts, Hanna J. in the *Pigs Marketing Board* case[47] stressed the fact that, unless legislatures were permitted to delegate powers to the executive, especially in the field of regulating business, the legislatures' objectives could never be fully realised; accordingly, economic regulators can be entrusted with extensive standards-setting powers.[48] As for the power in question, to fix prices from time to time, which reflect what the normal market price should be, that was not exercising legislative powers but was simply giving effect to specific policy determined by the Oireachtas. Later in the *AnCO* case,[49] the system in the Industrial Training Act 1967 for imposing levies on various industrial sectors was upheld by the Supreme Court. The entire levy mechanism was contained in that Act and all that was delegated was power to determine exactly what form the levy for each industry should take. Emphasis was placed on the Act's obligation that, before a levy could be imposed on any particular industry, representatives of employers, employees and educational interests in that industry must be consulted and, further, the requirement that every order imposing a levy be subject to parliamentary supervision and could be blocked by either House of the Oireachtas where it felt that the order was inappropriate for one reason or another.

Radio and television broadcasting is an industry that always has been and remains regulated by the State. Formerly, it was entirely controlled by the Minister for Posts and Telegraphs, under the Wireless Telegraphy Act 1926, and in order to participate in the industry persons were required to hold an appropriate licence from the Minister. This Act authorised the Minister to make regulations setting out the form of those licences, their duration, when they would be revoked, their terms and conditions and such other matters as the Minister considered to be necessary or desirable. In the *Carrigaline T.V.* case,[50] Keane J. rejected a separation of powers challenge to these on the basis of the reasoning in the *Harvey* case,[51] although subsequently that judge observed

---

[46] *Ambiorix Ltd v. Minister for the Environment* [1992] 2 I.R. 37.
[47] *Pigs Marketing Board v. Donnelly (Dublin) Ltd* [1939] I.R. 413.
[48] *Infra*, p.773.
[49] *Supra*, n.36.
[50] *Carrigaline Community T.V. Broadcasting Co. Ltd v. Minister for Transport* [1997] 1 I.L.R.M. 241.
[51] *Harvey v. Minister for Social Welfare* [1990] 2 I.R. 232.

that the reasoning in that case is not "universally applicable to such cases."[52]

Mention already has been made of what at times are described as "Henry VIII clauses," being provisions authorising a Minister, or an official or body, to make regulations that amend the very terms of all or part of the Act in question. It was contended in *Harvey v. Minister for Social Welfare*[53] that section 75(1) of the Social Welfare Act 1952, was invalid for being such a provision; sub (1) authorised the Minister to make regulations concerning several social welfare benefits and allowances "for adjusting any [such] benefit, personal allowance or assistance (including disallowing payment thereof wholly or partly) that may be payable to such person." However, the Supreme Court rejected the challenge to this on the grounds that it was implied that the Minister will not contravene the separation of powers and endeavour to do something as radical as alter part of the 1952 Act. The Court went on to hold that the particular regulation in issue, that purported to withdraw a blind person's pension on qualifying for a non-contributory old age pension, was *ultra vires* section 75(1) because it was so unreasonable. Accordingly, clauses of this nature are not *per se* invalid but they will be struck down where, by their terms, it is "necessary and inevitable" that content of the statute will be changed.[54] Similarly, in the *An Blascaod Mór* case,[55] Budd J. upheld section 5(4) of the 1989 Act in question, which authorised the Minister to make orders containing "such ancillary or subsidiary provisions as [he] considers necessary or expedient including provisions adapting provisions of this Act." This was principally because subsection (4), in context, referred only to limited functions conferred by the Act on the Commissioners for Public Works.

The "principles and policies" approach articulated in the *AnCo* case are equally applicable to national regulations giving effect to EC/EU measures. Where the EC/EU rule in question embodies the principles and policies of what is being addressed, it was held by the Supreme Court on two occasions[56] that those can then be implemented by statutory instrument rather than by way of primary legislation. But where the indigenous requirement in question is not readily referable to what the EC Regulation or Directive stipulates, then it is *ultra vires* either entirely or to the extent to which it goes beyond filling in details of what the measure calls for. In these it was held that aspects of procedures to enforce the regime against growth-promoters in cattle and features of the regime governing milk quotas, respectively, embodied in statutory instruments, went no further than implementing in detail requirements contained in several EC Regulations on those subjects.

---

[52] *Laurentiu v. Minister for Justice* [1999] 4 I.R. 26 at p.88.
[53] [1990] 2 I.R. 232.
[54] *Supra*, n.52 at p.50.
[55] *Supra*, n.34.
[56] *Meagher v. Minister for Agriculture* [1994] 1 I.R. 358 and *Maher v. Minister for Agriculture* [2001] 2 I.R. 139; *infra*, pp.259 and 260.

EXECUTIVE LAW NULLIFICATION

There would seem to be three principal ways in which laws might be set aside by executive action. One is where the Act in question expressly provides that it shall cease to have effect in circumstances to be determined, either by the Government, some Minister or an official. Another is where the executive either declines to enforce a law or ceases enforcing it. That occurred in 1987 when the Government decided not to collect any further taxes for that year, under the Farm Tax Act 1985, and the Minister stated that it was intended to repeal this Act. In *Purcell* v *Attorney General*,[57] the plaintiff who owned a farm of approximately 650 acres was assessed for this tax for the previous year but, in the light of the Government decision, refused to pay it. Barron J. held that this *de facto* repeal of the Act was an unconstitutional interference with the will of the Oireachtas and, further, when "legislation is interfered with unlawfully, then what remains cannot be the will of the Oireachtas [and] ceases to be enforceable not only for the future, but for the past also."[58] On appeal, the plaintiff shifted ground, contending that the way in which the tax was to be collected in 1986 was so full of anomalies as to give rise to gross and unacceptable inequalities in the manner in which the 1985 Act was being applied; in particular, farmers were discriminated against on the basis of the size of their farms. It was held by the Supreme Court that the Oireachtas could not have intended that the 1985 Act be implemented in this manner and, consequently, the plaintiff was not liable to pay the tax for the year in question. Blayney J., for the Court, observed that the Government's *de facto* repeal of the Act "did not prevent the tax from being valid in respect of the farms on which it was imposed"[59] but, because the regulations for its implementation unlawfully discriminated, the tax was not recoverable.

However, the courts hesitate to oblige the State to enforce a law that it is not willing to apply. In *Duggan v. An Taoiseach*,[60] the plaintiffs were civil servants assigned to the Farm Tax Office. When in 1987 the Government decided not to collect this tax, they challenged their re-grading when they were re-assigned to their previous positions. Hamilton P. held that their "legitimate expectation" to retain these grades had been unlawfully interfered with and ordered that they be paid compensation. But he held that they did not have *locus standi* to seek a declaration that the Government's decision "was null and void and of no legal effect," or orders requiring the Government to take such steps as may be necessary to ensure that the tax will be collected, principally by giving the Farm Tax Commissioner the necessary resources for doing so.

---

[57] [1995] 3 I.R. 287.
[58] [1990] 2 I.R. 405 at p.408.
[59] [1995] 3 I.R. 287 at p.291.
[60] [1989] I.L.R.M. 610.

Frequently when laws are passed, the time for their implementation is deferred until such time as the Government or the responsible Minister makes an order putting the Act in question into force. Where a significant amount of time elapses since an Act was passed but no order is made putting it or part of it into effect, the question arises whether aggrieved persons have any legal remedy. This was considered in *State (Sheehan) v. Government of Ireland*[61] with regard to section 60 of the Civil Liability Act 1961, which provides that a road authority shall be liable in damages arising from any loss caused by its failure to maintain a public road adequately. In subsection (7) this stipulated that it was not to come into operation until so ordered by the Government, and in any event, not before April 1967. Having broken a leg when walking on a footpath in 1983, the plaintiff sued the local authority for damages. Anticipating that a defence of non-feasance might succeed, he then sought an order requiring the Government to give effect to section 60 of the 1961 Act and succeeded before Costello J., who was overruled on appeal. At the outset Henchy J. pointed out that, even if the plaintiff succeeded, that would be of no practical benefit to him because the section only applies to damage caused subsequent to its being put into operation. Henchy J. concluded that section 60(7), "by vesting the power of bringing the section into operation in the Government rather than in a particular Minister, and the wording used, connoting an enabling rather than a mandatory power or discretion, would seem to point to the parliamentary recognition of the fact that the important law reform to be effected by the section was not to take effect unless and until the Government became satisfied that, in the light of factors such as the necessary deployment of financial and other resources, the postulated reform could be carried into effect. The discretion vested in the Government to bring the section into operation on a date after the 1st April, 1967, was not limited in any way, as to time or otherwise."[62]

There may however be circumstances where a court would declare that the failure to put an Act or part of an Act into force is unlawful, as section 60 of the 1961 Act was somewhat unique. It introduced a significant law reform of general application, which would have placed a considerable financial burden on local authorities but those bodies are largely dependent on central Government for their resources. That dependency increased in 1984 when the system for assessing agricultural rates was declared unconstitutional. Where no reasonable grounds are given for not bringing legislation into effect, the separation of powers principle does not prevent a court from making a declaration accordingly.[63]

---

[61] [1987] I.R. 550.
[62] *Id.* at p.561. *Cf. Rooney v. Minister for Agriculture* [1991] 2 I.R. 539 and *Abidi v. Minister for Justice* [2002] 4 I.R. 234.
[63] *R. (Fire Brigades Union) v. Secretary of State* [1995] 2 A.C. 513.

EXECUTIVE ADJUDICATION

The function of courts is to resolve disputes about the application of laws. Those disputes fall into three principal categories, being criminal prosecutions, civil actions and, thirdly, claims between the State and individuals, frequently in the nature of judicial review applications, including challenges to the constitutionality of laws, regulations and decisions. Individuals at times enter into contracts establishing their own dispute-resolution procedure, either arbitration clauses or agreements that their dispute shall be the subject of third party valuation.

The administration of justice, through exercise of what for convenience may be termed "plenary" judicial powers, is consigned by the Constitution to the courts established and judges appointed under the Constitution.[64] Subject to the qualifications explained below, judicial power of this nature cannot be exercised by the executive. To over-simplify, it is for the judges and not civil servants to try cases. Plenary judicial power must be exercised by either the judges of the Supreme Court, the High Court, the Circuit Court, the District Court, the Court of Criminal Appeal or the Courts Martial Appeals Court; the Special Criminal Court is in a category of its own.

What may be described as "non-plenary" judicial power, on the other hand, can be exercised by executive and other officials, and these powers are frequently vested in what are known as administrative tribunals and agencies. Examples include public local inquiries where it is proposed to acquire land compulsorily, planning inquiries into objections against grants of planning permission and adjudications by the appeals tribunals established under the Social Welfare Acts. A considerable amount of public administration is performed in this manner.[65] But once a particular power falls within the "plenary" judicial category, it cannot be exercised by administrative tribunals and must be vested in the courts. For instance, in *Cowan v. Attorney General*,[66] the plaintiff had been declared elected to Dublin Corporation but an election petition was lodged to have his election declared void on the grounds that he was disqualified. The then procedure for dealing with local government election petitions was to have an experienced barrister appointed to investigate into and rule on the matter. It was held that a barrister's powers in these circumstances fell into the "plenary" judicial category, which accordingly could only be exercised by the courts – as had been the case before 1882.

What then is meant by "plenary" judicial power? – a term that the Constitution does not use but which provides a convenient short hand for explanation. In answering this difficult question, the courts have had little assistance from the United States cases because many of them deal with the

---

[64] Art.34.1.
[65] See generally, Hogan & Morgan, *supra*, n.16, Chap.6.
[66] [1961] I.R. 411.

complexities of Article I and Article III courts.[67] As one commentator observed, the US Supreme Court's "quest for a principled distinction between Article III adjudicative power and all other kinds of dispute – resolving authority, like Diogenes' search for an honest man, has taken many roads. The Court has enjoyed little more success than Diogenes."[68] The question usually arises when some official or body is empowered to decide certain disputes and it is claimed that, by virtue of the Constitution, the power to decide those issues can only be entrusted to the courts.

"Judicial"

A comprehensive definition of judicial power for the purpose of determining what kinds of decisions can be made only by the courts has not yet been found. In the leading case, *Solicitors Act, 1954, Re*[69] which concerned a system for disciplining solicitors, Kingsmill Moore J. observed, having considered several Australian authorities, that "[f]rom none of the (numerous) pronouncements as to the nature of judicial power ... can a definition at once exhaustive and precise be extracted, and probably no such definition can be framed. The varieties and combinations of powers with which the legislature may equip a tribunal are infinite, and in each case the particular powers must be considered in their totality and separately to see if a tribunal so endowed is invested with powers of such nature and extent that their exercise is in effect administering that justice which appertains to the judicial organ, and which the constitution indicates is properly entrusted only to the judges."[70] That an official or body is authorised to act in somewhat the same way as the courts, or exercise some powers similar to those possessed by the courts, does not mean that judicial powers are being exercised. In that case, Kingsmill Moore J. cited some "negative propositions" on the subject of what is judicial: "1. A tribunal is not necessarily a Court in the strict sense because it gives a final decision. 2. Nor because it hears witnesses on oath. 3. Nor because two or more contending parties appear before it between whom it has to decide. 4. Nor because it gives decisions which affect the rights of subjects. 5. Nor because there is an appeal to a Court. 6. Nor because it is a body to which the matter is referred by another body."[71] He put these propositions in another way: "[t]he fact that the powers entrusted to a tribunal must be exercised judicially does not in itself make their exercise an exercise of the judicial power. ... Nor does the fact that the tribunal may incidentally have to determine legal questions involve the

---

[67] See generally, L. Tribe, *American Constitutional Law* (3rd ed., 2000) Vol. 1, pp.285 *et seq.*
[68] L. Tribe, *Constitutional Choices* (1985), p.85.
[69] [1960] I.R. 239.
[70] *Id.* at p.271.
[71] *Id.* at p.265, quoting from *Shell Co. of Australia v. Federal Tax Comm.* [1931] A.C. 275.

conclusion that it is exercising judicial power. ... Nor is it material that the tribunal surrounds itself with the "trappings of Courts" or follows the usual procedure of a trial."[72] So much for what judicial power is not. But how is it to be recognised?

Kingsmill Moore J. adopted the following definitions, which have again and again been cited with approval. One is from Kennedy C.J. in *Lynham v. Butler (No.2)*,[73] a case that concerned the Land Commission's Lay Commissioners and the separation of powers under the Free State Constitution:

> "In the first place, the Judicial Power of the State is, like the Legislative Power and the Executive Power, one of the attributes of sovereignty, and a function of government. ... It is one of the activities of the government of a civilised state by which it fulfils its purpose of social order and peace by determining in accordance with the laws of the State all controversies of a justiciable nature arising within the territory of the State, and for that purpose exercising the authority of the State over person and property. The controversies, which fall to it for determination, may be divided into two classes, criminal and civil. In relation to the former class of controversy, the Judicial Power is exercised in determining the guilt or innocence of persons charged with offences against the State itself and in determining the punishments to be inflicted upon persons found guilty of offences charged against them, which punishments it then becomes the obligation of the Executive Department of Government to carry into effect. In relation to justiciable controversies of the civil class, the Judicial Power is exercised in determining in a final manner, by definitive adjudication according to law, rights or obligations in dispute between citizen and citizen, or between citizens and State, or between any parties whoever they be and in binding the parties by such determination which will be enforced if necessary with the authority of the State. Its characteristic public good in its civil aspect is finality and authority, the decisive ending of disputes and quarrels, and the avoidance of private methods of violence in asserting or resisting claims alleged or denied. It follows from its nature as I have described it that the exercise of the Judicial Power, which is coercive and must frequently act against the will of one of the parties to enforce its decision adverse to that party, requires of necessity that the Judicial Department of Government have compulsive authority over persons as, for instance, it must have authority to compel appearance of a party before it, to compel the attendance of witnesses, to order the execution of its judgments against persons and property."[74]

---

[72] *Id.* at pp.265–266.
[73] [1933] I.R. 74.
[74] *Id.* at p.74.

Another definition is from an Australian case concerning a power of interrogation (coupled with a duty to answer) that was conferred on a public official:

> "the words, 'judicial power' as used in (the Australian) Constitution mean the power which every sovereign authority must of necessity have to decide controversies between its subjects, or between itself and its subjects, whether the rights relate to life, liberty or property. The exercise of this power does not begin until some tribunal, which has power to give a binding, and authorative decision (whether subject to appeal or not) is called upon to take action. ' ... To erect a tribunal into a "Court" or "Jurisdiction" so as to make its determinations judicial, the essential element is that it should have power, by its *determination* within jurisdiction, to impose liability or affect rights. By this I mean that the liability is imposed, or the right affected by the determination only, and not by the fact determined, and so that the liability will exist, or the right will be affected, although the determination be wrong in law or in fact ... But where the determination binds, although it is based on an erroneous view of facts or law, then the power authorising it is judicial."[75]

In *McDonald v. Bord na gCon,*[76] a case concerning disciplining persons involved in the greyhound racing industry, Kenny J. described the administration of justice as having five characteristic features:

> "1. A dispute or controversy as to the existence of legal rights or a violation of the law:
> 2. The determination or ascertainment of the rights of parties or the imposition of liabilities or the infliction of a penalty:
> 3. The final determination (subject to appeal) of legal rights or liabilities or the imposition of penalties:
> 4. The enforcement of those rights or liabilities or the imposition of a penalty by the Court or by the executive power of the State which is called in by the Court to enforce its judgment:
> 5. The making of an order by the Court which as a matter of history is an order characteristic of Courts in this country."[77]

In the present context, a distinction may be drawn between a function that

---

[75] [1960] I.R. 269, quoting from *Attorney General for Australia v. The Queen* [1957] A.C. 288, quoting in turn from *R. (Wexford C.C.) v. Local Government Board* [1902] 2 I.R. 349 at p.373.

[76] [1965] I.R. 217.

[77] *Id.* at p.231.

must be discharged in a judicial fashion, *i.e.* hear both sides of the argument and not be biased, and a judicial function. Of course, whenever a judicial function is being exercised, the maxims *audi alteram partem* and *nemo iudex in sua causa* must be adhered to.[78]

Examples of decisions that were held not to be exercises of judicial functions in this context include the issue by Peace Commissioners of search warrants authorising the search of dwellings and containing a power of arrest;[79] the Director of Public Prosecutions substituting counts in an indictment where a person had been sent forward for trial by the District Court;[80] the raising of assessments by an inspector of taxes;[81] the calculation by the Minister of how much *ex gratia* "compensation [he] considers reasonable" ought to be paid to a civil servant ceasing to hold office;[82] the decision of the Registrar of Friendly Societies to appoint an inspector to investigate the affairs of a building society, where the society in question bears part of the costs of that investigation;[83] the discretion of the Government to release from custody a person found "guilty but insane," which strictly is an acquittal rather than a conviction;[84] the decision of a social welfare officer to revise a previous such officer's decision concerning an individual's entitlement to benefit.[85]

It was held by the Supreme Court in *Goodman International v. Hamilton*[86] that the carrying out of enquiries under the Tribunals of Enquiry (Evidence) Acts 1921-2002 is not a judicial function even though the enquiry there was chaired by a senior High Court judge (the President of the Court), practically everyone who came before it got legal representation that subsequently was paid for by the State, and the focus was alleged serious wrong-doing on behalf of parties involved in the beef industry. With the possible exception of item 1 in the characteristics identified in the *McDonnell* case, none of the others existed; it even was arguable that, on account of the "inquisitorial nature" of the enquiry, it was "not accurate to speak of a controversy concerning the violation of the law."[87] Nor could there be any question of the second characteristic being met. Finlay C.J. observed that "[i]t is no part, and never has been any part of the function of the judiciary in our system of law, to make a finding of fact in effect, *in vacuo*, and to report it to the legislature,"[88] which

---

[78] *Infra*, pp.435 and 489.
[79] *Byrne v. Grey* [1988] I.R. 31, *Farrell v. Farrelly* [1988] I.R. 201 and *Berkeley v. Edwards* [1988] I.R. 217.
[80] *O'Shea v. D.P.P.* [1988] I.R. 655.
[81] *Kennedy v. Hearne* [1988] I.R. 481 and *Deighan v. Hearne* [1990] 1 I.R. 499.
[82] *O'Cleirigh v. Minister for Agriculture* [1998] 4 I.R. 15.
[83] *State (Plunkett) v. Register of Friendly Societies* [1998] 4 I.R. 1.
[84] *Lundy v. Minister for Social Welfare* [1993] 3 I.R. 406.
[85] *Minister for Social Affairs v. Scanlon* [2001] 1 I.R. 64 at p.87.
[86] [1992] 2 I.R. 542.
[87] *Id.* at p.589.
[88] *Id.* at p.590.

is the very purpose of tribunals of enquiry. McCarthy J. explained that the "critical factor is adjudication, not enquiry," rejecting the contention that "the determining of truth or falsity is necessarily a judicial act in the sense that it may only validly be performed by judges. It does require the application of judicial standards, but it is an everyday occurrence that a variety of tribunals, collegiate or otherwise, have to decide disputes of fact. The added circumstance that the resolution of a dispute of fact in a particular way may involve a statement of fact amounting to offences under the Income Tax Acts, the Larceny Acts or the Criminal Justice Act 1951, does not amount to a finding of guilt."[89]

Criminal matters

While the distinction between criminal and non-criminal disputes is usually patently obvious, the courts have not yet spelled out precise criteria for determining which side of this line particular decisions fall.[90] In the *Solicitors Act* case, Kingsmill Moore J. observed that a "a characteristic feature of criminal matters is the infliction of penalties, a consideration which gives weight to the submission that a tribunal which is authorised to inflict a penalty, especially a severe penalty, even in cases where the offence is not strictly criminal, should be regarded as administering justice."[91] And in *McDonald v. Bord na gCon*, Kenny J. adopted the following definition of what is criminal: "[i]n order that a matter may be a criminal cause or matter it must, I think, fulfil two conditions which are connoted by and implied in the word 'criminal'. It must involve the consideration of some charge of crime, that is to say, of an offence against the public law ... and that charge must have been preferred or be about to be preferred before some Court or judicial tribunal having or claiming jurisdiction to impose punishment for the offence or alleged offence; and if the matter is one the direct outcome of which may be trial of the applicant and his possible punishment for an alleged offence by a Court claiming jurisdiction to do so, the matter is criminal."[92] In a different context, the Proceeds of Crime Act 1996, was held by the Supreme Court to be a civil rather than a criminal law.[93]

Peace commissioners carry out certain administrative functions ancillary to the administration of criminal justice and their powers to issue search and arrest warrants have withstood constitutional attack on separation of powers grounds.[94] But in *O'Mahony v. Melia*[95] their power to refuse bail and, instead,

---

[89] *Id.* at p.607. Similarly, *Haughey v. Moriarty* [1999] 3 I.R. 1.
[90] See *infra*, p.408.
[91] [1960] I.R. at p.263.
[92] [1965] I.R. at p.232.
[93] *Murphy v. G.M.* [2001] 4 I.R. 113; *infra*, p.414.
[94] *Supra*, n.79.
[95] [1989] I.R. 35.

remand persons in custody was declared invalid by Keane J., since it was a judicial power; in making these decisions, commissioners were required to hear the contentions of both parties and any evidence adduced.

Prosecutions in the District Court are commenced by a summons being issued in the name of that Court. A practice grew up of the clerk of the Court issuing and signing such summonses, without reference to the judge. Although this practice was not challenged on separation of powers grounds, in *State (Clarke) v. Roche*,[96] the Supreme Court suggested that it may very well be unconstitutional, especially in view of what previously had been said about peace commissioners remanding persons in custody.

Sentencing convicted persons is an exercise of criminal jurisdiction[97] although, in respect of a handful of offences, the judge has no discretion over what sentence shall be imposed. But Article 13.6 of the Constitution permits the Oireachtas to empower "other authorities" to commute or remit any punishment imposed by a court."[98]

Limited judicial functions and powers

The ever increasing amount and complexity of legislation and regulations engenders an enormous number of potential disputes between individuals and the State. In the 19th century, when the State apparatus was far less complex than it is today, most issues of this nature were resolved by magistrates and the discipline of judicial review grew out of the need for the Superior Courts to supervise the activities of the then lay magistracy. Most modern legislation provides for some tribunal, agency or official as the appropriate authority for resolving disputes that arise with regard to the proper application of the Act in question, for instance the Appeals Commissioners who deal with disputed tax assessments, and the Social Welfare Appeals Officers, who deal with differences about social welfare entitlements and obligations. Like delegated legislation, administrative adjudication is an inextricable feature of the modern interventionist/welfare state. It should be noted, however, that many of the determinations that are made by administrative tribunals in Ireland and in Britain are made by special administrative courts in the continental European countries. Article 6.1 of the European Convention on Human Rights requires that any tribunal that decides disputes about persons' "civil rights and obligations" must conform with the standards of independence, openness and fairness provided for there.[99]

Under the Constitution, the courts do not possess a complete monopoly of

---

[96] [1989] I.R. 619.
[97] *Infra*, p.473.
[98] *Infra*, p.475.
[99] *Cf. R(Alconbury Development Ltd) v. Secretary of State* [2001] 2 W.L.R. 1389.

judicial power. According to Article 37, "[n]othing in this Constitution shall operate to invalidate the exercise of limited functions and powers of a judicial nature, in matters other than criminal matters, by any person or body of persons duly authorised by law to exercise such functions and powers, notwithstanding that such person or such body of persons is not a judge or a court appointed or established as such under this Constitution." That is to say, in non-criminal disputes, individuals and bodies other than courts can exercise "limited functions and powers" of a judicial nature. Article 37 was adopted in order to ensure that many issues could be determined by administrative tribunals and by officials, rather than have the ordinary courts being clogged up dealing with those questions.

Under Article 37, persons or bodies other than courts may "exercise limited functions and powers of a judicial nature. ..." The classic formulation of what is encompassed by this phrase is that of Kingsmill Moore J. in *Solicitors Act 1954, Re*:

> "It is not a question of. 'limited jurisdiction' whether the limitation be in regard to persons or subject matter. ... It is the 'powers and functions' which must be 'limited', not the ambit of their exercise. Nor is the test of limitation to be sought in the number of powers and functions, which are exercised. The Constitution does not say 'powers and functions limited in number'. Again it must be emphasised that it is the powers and functions, which are in their own nature to be limited. A tribunal having but a few powers and functions but those of far-reaching effect and importance could not properly be regarded as exercising 'limited' powers and functions. ... The test as to whether a power is or is not 'limited', lies in the effect of the assigned power when exercised. If the exercise of the assigned powers and functions is calculated ordinarily to affect in the most profound and far-reaching way the lives, liberties, fortunes or reputations of those against whom they are exercised they cannot properly be described as limited."[100]

That is to say, the test of what is "limited" in this context is not that the decision-making authority affects only a limited category of persons, or concerns a very limited subject-matter, or that the decision-maker has very limited powers. The true test lies in the impact of the decision and of any powers assigned to the decision-maker. If these can have a profound and enduring effect on a person's legal rights, freedom, wealth or good name, then the power is not a limited one. Moreover, it would seem that where the decision in question is one that traditionally has been taken by the courts and not by executive agencies, especially where the decision-maker in question is given most of the powers

---

[100] [1960] I.R. 263–264.

exercised by courts and the decision can drastically affect individuals in the manner just described, then it will tend not to be regarded as a 'limited' power for the purposes of Article 37. Beyond this, it is hard to generalise about limited judicial powers and it is best to consider the principal contexts in which difficulties in applying this administrative adjudication Article arise.

Adoption

In the 1970s the view gained currency among some lawyers and politicians that the Adoption Board, An Bord Uchtála, exercised "plenary" judicial powers when making adoption orders and, accordingly, it was acting unconstitutionally and all orders made by it were invalid. This view was misconceived. As Walsh J. pointed out in one instance,[101] the Board does not adjudicate on anything approximating to a dispute between parties; its functions are the purely administrative ones of supervising placements for adoption. Nevertheless, it was decided that the Constitution should be amended in 1978[102] lest it ever be found that the Board exercised non-limited judicial powers. Article 37.2 provides that all adoptions made since December 1937 under the State's adoption laws shall be valid even though the adoption order was not made by a duly appointed judge.

Professional discipline

One category of case where there is a parallel with criminal trials is professional discipline. In *Solicitors Act 1954, Re*[103] the disciplinary procedure established by the Solicitors Act 1954, was held to contravene the separation of powers principle because of some unique features of that scheme and the position of solicitors. These features were that the Disciplinary Committee established under that Act was given the very same procedural powers as the High Court; further, the Committee could strike a solicitor off the rolls, which is a most severe penalty and which historically was a power exercised only by judges; additionally, the Committee could order that a solicitor make full restitution to aggrieved clients, which was essentially the same as awarding damages for fraud or for negligence.

However, in *M. v. The Medical Council*,[104] the Supreme Court found that the disciplinary procedures under the Medical Practitioners Act 1978, were sufficiently different from those considered in the *Solicitors Act* case as not to amount to the administration of justice – in the "plenary" sense. For, under this Act, the power to strike a doctor from the register of practitioners or to

---

[101] *G. v. An Bord Uchtála* [1980] I.R. 32 at pp.72–73.
[102] The 6th Amendment.
[103] [1960] I.R. 239; *infra*, p.784.
[104] [1984] I.R. 485; *infra*, p.788.

impose other very severe sanctions for professional misconduct is not conferred on the Medical Fitness to Practice Committee; all that this Committee is authorised to do is to make findings as to whether there was misconduct and it then is for the Medical Council to apply to the High Court to impose a severe sanction.

Occupational discipline is not inherently a matter reserved to the courts and in *McDonald v. Bord na gCon*,[105] the Supreme Court upheld provisions in the Greyhound Industry Act 1958, empowering Bord na gCon and the Coursing Club to discipline individuals involved in the greyhound racing business. Indeed, it was held that the disciplinary powers there not alone were not judicial in the full sense but were not even "limited" judicial powers as contemplated by Article 37. Challenges on these grounds to the procedures for disciplining members of the Institute of Chartered Accountants in Ireland and also for disciplining members of the Garda Síochána were rejected by the Supreme Court. Because the relationship between accountants and their Institute is based on contract and not on legislation, it was held that the Institute's disciplinary activity is not the administration of justice.[106] Because disciplining Gardaí was not historically a court function and the internal Garda enquiry is more in the nature of an investigation than a contest between parties, it was held that the Garda Disciplinary Tribunal does not administer justice for these purposes.[107]

Expropriation

Another category of case, where the parallel is with civil actions, is formal determinations as to whether a person's property should be acquired compulsorily for some public purpose, such as for constructing roads, building houses, dividing up extensive tracts of land under the Land Acts scheme. *Fisher v. Irish Land Commission*[108] was a case involving powers that the Land Commission had to remove judicial tenants from land vested in the Commission. There is a parallel between *Fisher* and the *Solicitors Act* case in that the decision to remove tenants on Land Commission property in the past was vested in Judicial Commissioners, who were High Court judges.[109] But under the Act in question, it was for Lay Commissioners, who were civil servants, to make that decision. The plaintiff contended that deciding whether the plaintiff should be removed from his land was a question that must be determined by the courts. It was argued that the test of what may be described as a "plenary" judicial

---

[105] [1965] I.R. 217; *infra*, p.774.
[106] *Geoghegan v. Institute of Chartered Accountants in Ireland* [1995] 3 I.R. 86; *infra*, p.788.
[107] *Keady v. Commissioner An Garda Síochána* [1992] 2 I.R. 197; *infra*, p.793.
[108] [1948] I.R. 3.
[109] Land Law (Ireland) Act 1881, 44 & 45 Vic. v.49, s.5.

decision is "(i)f the order of the tribunal is in itself effective to deprive a man of his property, without any further act being necessary to implement such order, and if the order is operative *per se* and not by virtue of any special force or effect given to it by statute;"[110] that the Lay Commissioners' decision here satisfied this definition. It was contended that their powers were not limited because those "are of the widest nature, and the sphere in which they are to exercise these powers, although limited, is an important one."[111] But it was held that the Lay Commissioners' powers were not judicial in the sense that they can only be exercised by the courts.

According to Gavan Duffy J., their function was to decide essentially questions of policy, rather than of legal right between the Land Commission and tenants, and the fact that a property interest was affected did not entitle the tenants to exceptional procedural protection, even though private property is the subject of guarantees in Article 43 of the Constitution. In his words:

> "When (the Land Commission) was told to consider whether lands should be taken from private use for specified public purposes, its primary trust was to make decisions on policy; emphatically it was not being commissioned to dispense justice. In resolving an issue between an individual and the public, it was not to adjudicate upon any *lis inter partes*. Since public policy was to be its guiding light, it was not being asked to determine any conflict of legal rights, and so its honest decision, within jurisdiction, would involve no legal wrong. The legal title of the proprietor stood unquestioned, but it might be required to yield to a paramount claim of expediency, as understood by the Land Commission. The legal right of a proprietor is to have an honest endeavour by the Land Commissioner to exercise as fairly as possible a discretion belonging to the sphere of economics and politics (in the original sense of that word), not to the judicial sphere; he has no legal right to a favourable decision upon an agglomeration of facts that might lead one expert to one opinion and another to a different one ...
>
> The fundamental issue ... is whether our Legislature is competent to make the expropriation of private property in land depend in the main on the opinion as to public policy of a non-judicial organ of government. The procedure is held up to odium as an invasion of a private right, unlawful as committing the final adjudication of a justiciable controversy to an extra judicial authority. But, when the process of expropriation is made by statute to pivot mainly upon extra-judicial considerations, the issue is at once invested with an extra-judicial character, and to dub it "justiciable" because it may result in the suppression of a private right is

---

[110] [1948] I.R. 21.
[111] *Ibid.*

to ignore the paramount importance of the fact that the expropriatory measure has been deliberately ascribed by the Legislature to the politico-economic sphere."[112]

Maguire C.J.'s judgment for the Supreme Court is based on similar reasoning.[113]

Therefore, where the decision-maker's function is to apply policy, those decisions are not judicial except in respect of criminal matters. But this is hardly a sufficient criterion for determining what is judicial, since virtually all kinds of civil adjudication done by the courts can be regarded as implementing policy. The law of tort, for instance, is nothing but a collection of policies that can easily be explained in "politico-economic" terms, as can the policies underlying the law of contract or labour law, or other branches of the law.

In most comparable countries, the assessment of how much compensation shall be paid to persons whose property has been expropriated by the State is carried out by the courts and, under several national constitutions, express provision exists to that effect. In Ireland, however, this function is carried out by what is known as a "property arbitrator," who is appointed by the State under the Acquisition of Land (Assessment of Compensation) Acts 1919-1960. In the *An Blascaod Mór* case,[114] Budd J. held that this "arbitrator" administers justice but it was only a limited judicial function and power, within Article 37.

LEGISLATIVE ADJUDICATION

Although their principal function is to enact laws, the Houses of the Oireachtas are authorised by the Constitution to determine certain disputes that might be regarded as the exercise of plenary (as opposed to "limited") judicial powers, namely Article 12.10 on removing a President and Article 35.4 on removing judges from office. In the past the United Kingdom Parliament exercised a general power to impeach by trying any public representative or official on charges of misconduct, but it has not been availed of for a century and a half. In view of what was decided in *Maguire v. Ardagh*,[115] there is no equivalent power in either House of the Oireachtas. There the Supreme Court held that there was no inherent power to conduct an investigation into a fatal shooting incident, involving members of the Garda Síochána, that might end in a finding that one or more of those Gardaí were culpable of unlawful killing, even though that conclusion would not have any direct legal effect. The Court left over the question whether it would be constitutionally permissible for the Oireachtas

---

[112] *Id.* at pp.13 and 14.
[113] *Infra*, p.744.
[114] High Court, February 27, 1998.
[115] [2002] 1 I.R. 385; *supra*, p.114.

by legislation to give itself, or one of its Houses or committees, authority of this nature, which has obvious separation of powers as well as other implications.

What were known as Bills of Attainder are Acts of Parliament imposing penalties on a named individual or individuals,[116] perhaps the most notorious being that of 1513 commanding the execution of the Bishop of Rochester's cook by being boiled in oil.[117] One of the contentions made in the *An Blascaod Mór (No. 3)*[118] case was that the 1989 Act involved there, which was targeted almost exclusively at the plaintiffs' lands, was in substance a Bill of Attainder. In the event, that Act was held to contravene the guarantee in Article 40.1 of equality before the law.

JUDICIAL ADMINISTRATION

Is there any constitutional limit to the tasks that the Oireachtas may assign to the courts? As has been observed, the Government or the Taoiseach inviting judges to be members of or to constitute tribunals of inquiry has been upheld.[119] So too has the exercise of administrative functions that are related to the ordinary administration of justice.[120] In *O'Donoghue v. Ireland*[121] the plaintiff, who was an undischarged bankrupt, challenged section 21 of the Bankruptcy Act 1988, under which he could be examined in the High Court about his assets and activities. It had previously been held that this procedure did not constitute the administration of justice because it did not involve the resolution of a dispute, nor was it incidental to such a process.[122] Because however, it was an aspect of bankruptcy proceedings already in the Court and it was a procedure that the courts have exercised for well over a century, it was held to be sufficiently related to the administration of justice as not to contravene the separation of powers. According to Kearns J., "[t]he unbroken thread extending over centuries whereby the examination of witnesses in the context of bankruptcy is seen and perceived as forming part of the administration of justice" strongly supported this conclusion.[123] Moreover, the examination of witnesses "could be described as an administrative function or a judicial function ...".[124]

---

[116] See *infra*, p.293.
[117] 22 IIen. 8 ch.9.
[118] [2000] 1 I.R. 6.
[119] *Haughey v. Moriarty* [1999] 3 I.R. 1 at p.64.
[120] *Countyglen plc, Re* [1995] 1 I.R. 220.
[121] [2000] 2 I.R. 168.
[122] *Re Redbreast Preserving Co.*, 91 I.L.T.R. 12 (1996).
[123] [2000] 2 I.R. 181.
[124] *Id.* at p.182.

INTERFERENCE WITH THE ADMINISTRATION OF JUSTICE

Justice must be administered only by judges in the courts (except for non-criminal "limited" judicial powers) and neither the legislature nor the executive can interfere with the courts' administration of justice. The right of the courts to try disputes without interference from the other organs of State was affirmed in strong terms in *Buckley v. Attorney General*,[125] where the Oireachtas sought to intervene directly in a case that was coming on for trial in the High Court. The courts have condemned legislative interference with criminal and civil trials by laying down irrebuttable evidentiary presumptions[126] and they have condemned provisions enabling the executive to decide what sentence shall be imposed on persons found guilty of an offence.[127] A distinction may be drawn between direct legislative action with regard to a particular case and provisions that apply in all circumstances that affect how courts should carry out their functions.

Buckley, usually referred to as the *Sinn Féin Funds* case, concerned a controversy that had existed since the 1920s over the ownership of funds that were held by trustees of the Sinn Féin organisation, a body that was most influential in securing Irish independence but which subsequently split into many factions. The trustees temporarily resolved the issue by placing the funds in a bank account in the organisation's name. Following the death of the last surviving trustee, a representative action was brought by the plaintiffs on behalf of themselves and all members of the organisation, claiming ownership of those funds and an order that the funds should be paid over to them. Defences were filed by the Attorney General. Subsequently, the Oireachtas sought to resolve the controversy by passing the Sinn Féin Funds Act 1947, which provided that all further proceedings in the pending suit shall be stayed, that the High Court should dismiss that action without costs and that the Court should direct that the funds be paid to a board established under the Act which would then administer them. The 1947 Act was held to be both an unjustifiable interference with private property[128] and a violation of the separation of powers. According to O'Byrne .J.: "[i]n bringing these proceedings the plaintiffs were exercising a constitutional right and they were, and are, entitled to have the matter in dispute determined by the judicial organ of the State. The substantial effect of the Act is that the dispute is determined by the Oireachtas and the Court is required and directed by the Oireachtas to dismiss the plaintiffs' claim without any hearing and without forming any opinion as to the rights of the respective parties to the dispute. ... (T)his is clearly repugnant to the provisions

---

[125] [1950] I.R. 67.
[126] *Maher v. Attorney General* [1973] I.R. 140; *infra*, p.466.
[127] *Deaton v. Attorney General* [1963] I.R. 170; *infra*, p.473.
[128] *Infra*, p.735.

of the Constitution, as being an unwarrantable interference by the Oireachtas with the operations of the Courts in the purely judicial domain."[129]

What may be described as "laws of validation" are not uncommon;[130] these are laws that declare lawful what hitherto has been unlawful and that operate retrospectively to validate an illegal state of affairs. Their constitutionality was upheld by Lynch J. in *Howard v. Commissioners for Public Works (No 3)*,[131] provided what is being validated is not otherwise unconstitutional and with the broad caveat that they do not cause injustice. In 1993 it was held by Costello J. and by the Supreme Court that development being carried on in connection with an "interpretive centre" at Mullaghmore, Co. Clare, was unlawful, as being done without having appropriate planning permission.[132] Prior to then it had been widely assumed that public authorities did not have to obtain planning permission. Within a week of Costello J.'s decision, there was enacted the State Authorities (Development and Management) Act 1993, which retrospectively exempted those authorities from to need to have planning permission, by stipulating that they "shall have, and be deemed always to have had, power" to carry out development of different kinds. There was a rider, that now usually features in validating laws, *viz*, that if any part of the Act should "conflict with the constitutional right of any person," that part "shall be subject to such limitations as are necessary to secure that [it does] not conflict but shall otherwise be of full force and effect." Unless struck down, this Act in a sense reversed the judgment that had been given and pre-empted the Supreme Court's decision. But unlike in the *Buckley* case, it did not endeavour to compel the court to decide the case before it in a particular manner, nor did it purport to override the injunction given by Costello J. against the development in question; the caveat ensured that it would be applied subject to *inter alia* the *Sinn Féin Funds* case principle. Consequently, Lynch J. could not find what particular injustice the Act caused the plaintiffs, who had also been the plaintiffs in the earlier case. They contended that the injustice was that Costello J.'s decision "is not to be upheld or to inure to the plaintiff's benefit as a logical extension on the determination on *ultra vires*",[133] which the judge found to be singularly uninformative. It might be different if there was some good basis for saying that the Oireachtas could not have previously exempted public authorities from the requirement to seek planning permission. In any event, the 1993 Act could not authorise the Commissioners to actually carry out its intended development at Mullaghmore as the plaintiff had a permanent injunction restraining such activity. All that the Act did in practice was to

---

[129] [1950] I.R. 84.
[130] *Infra*, p.290.
[131] [1994] 3 I.R. 394.
[132] *Howard v. Commissioners for Public Works* [1994] 1 I.R. 101.
[133] [1994] 3 I.R. 406.

validate existing unauthorised developments, subject to that injunction and any other injunctions given in other similar proceedings.

Most of the cases which concern interference with the administration of justice are best considered in context – in the chapters on criminal and on civil procedures. But one decision requires consideration at this juncture because it suggests that in recent years the courts have become even more determined to protect the judicial domain from intervention by the other organs of State. In *Costello v. D.P.P.*,[134] the Supreme Court went so far as to overrule its predecessor's decision[135] that upheld section 62 of the Courts of Justice Act 1936. Persons being prosecuted for an indictable offence must be first brought before a District Judge who, prior to 1999, conducted a preliminary examination of the charges and the evidence.[136] If in consequence the Judge found that "there is a sufficient case to put the accused on trial," he was to be returned for trial to the Circuit Court, or to the Central Criminal Court in the case of the most serious offences. But if "a sufficient case" was not established, the Judge had to order that the accused be discharged. Under section 62 of the 1936 Act, however, where a Judge in these circumstances did not return an accused for trial the Attorney General, and subsequently the Director of Public Prosecutions, could nevertheless direct that the accused must stand trial. Was this provision unconstitutional?

In *State (Shanahan) v. Attorney General*,[137] it was upheld by the Supreme Court, overruling Davitt P. In a short judgment, Walsh J., for the Court, reasoned that, since the Oireachtas would be entitled to dispense entirely with preliminary examination, in prosecutions for indictable offences and simply provide that accused persons be put on trial directly, the Oireachtas therefore is free to lay down the extent to which accused persons are to be protected by any preliminary proceedings. Accordingly, since the Oireachtas granted the accused a procedural protection to which he was not constitutionally entitled, the Oireachtas is permitted to stipulate the circumstances in which that protection shall not be absolute. Secondly, in deciding to return an accused for trial in these circumstances, the Attorney does not interfere with the District Judge's function. Once the Judge refused to return an accused for trial, the Attorney did not interfere with the judicial function because that was the end of that particular judicial controversy. The Attorney's direction that the accused nevertheless shall be tried is the "initiation of a different justiciable controversy, namely the trial upon indictment ... whose object is to determine the guilt or innocence of the accused person."[138] Twenty-two years later, however, this conclusion was overruled.

---

[134] [1984] I.R. 436.
[135] *State (Shanahan) v. Attorney General* [1964] I.R. 239.
[136] *Infra*, p.432.
[137] [1964] I.R. 239.
[138] *Id.* at p.258.

Giving judgment for the Supreme Court in *Costello*, O'Higgins C.J. did not indicate the extent that the Constitution may entitle accused persons to some preliminary examination of the charges being brought against them. According to the Chief Justice, the governing principle in the present context is that the District Judge exercises judicial power and any attempt by the executive to in effect reverse his determination is an impermissible interference with the judicial function; that "in conducting the preliminary examination ... the Justice was exercising the judicial power of the State as conferred by law on the District Court in accordance with the Constitution ... When, in the exercise of such judicial power, there is a determination of these justiciable issues, that determination cannot be set aside or reversed by any other authority. Such action would constitute an invasion of the judicial domain and an attempt to exercise the judicial power of government otherwise than by the organ of State established for this purpose by the Constitution. ... Any statutory provision which purports to authorise such an interference is *ipso facto* repugnant to the Constitution as invalid."[139] The Judge's decision not to return an accused for trial was a judicial determination that, in the circumstances, the accused should not be tried on indictment for the purpose of determining guilt or innocence. But the intended effect of a direction under section 62 of the 1936 Act "is to render this determination nugatory and without force and thereby to frustrate" the Court's order discharging an accused.[140] The power given to a non-judicial authority to come to a conclusion contrary to that of the Judge and to enforce that conclusion by compelling an accused to stand trial was "an impermissible intervention in the controversy between the people and the (accused)."[141]

The extent to which the courts are insulated from executive interference is most vividly illustrated by *State (McEldowney) v. Kelleher*.[142] This concerned permits that must be obtained under the Street and House to House Collections Act 1962, by persons and bodies who wish to solicit funds from the general public. Under this Act, everybody who wants to raise funds by way of street or door-to-door collections must obtain a permit from a Garda Chief Superintendent. The Superintendent can refuse to issue a permit on various stipulated grounds and is forbidden to issue one where he is of opinion that any of the proceeds will be used for an illegal or an immoral purpose, or to benefit an unlawful organisation. A disappointed applicant is entitled to appeal to the District Court against the refusal of a permit. But in any such appeal, where a Garda swore that the grounds for refusal is that money collected will be used for an illegal or immoral purpose or organisation, section 13(4) of the 1962 Act provided that the judge must dismiss the appeal. Once the Garda

---

[139] [1984] I.R. 454 and 457.
[140] *Id.* at p.456.
[141] *Id.* at p.457.
[142] [1983] I.R. 289.

swore that the refusal was on these grounds, there was an obligation to disallow the appeal. Overruling Costello J., the Supreme Court held that this provision contravened the separation of powers. According to Walsh J., for the Court, the 1962 Act could very well have given no right of appeal from a refusal by a Garda Superintendent; the only mode of redress open to aggrieved permit-seekers then would be an application for judicial review. However, the Oireachtas chose to grant a right of appeal to the court, thereby rendering the issue of granting a permit a justiciable one. But under this Act, where an applicant was to be refused a permit on the grounds that money collected would be used for an illegal or immoral purpose, the existence of those facts was not to be determined in accordance with the ordinary rules of evidence. Instead, the Judge was obliged to refuse a permit once a Garda said on oath that there were reasonable grounds for believing that the funds would be used in the forbidden manner; regardless of whether other evidence existed, that oath determined the entire issue. This, it was held, is an impermissible interference with the judicial function. As Walsh J. stated "[t]he statute creates a justiciable controversy and then purports to compel the court to decide it in a particular way upon a particular statement of opinion being given upon oath as to whether or not a statutory reason for refusing the permit exists, whatever opinion the court may have formed on the issue in question, or might have formed if it had heard any evidence upon it."[143]

---

[143] *Id.* at p.306; applied in *Cashman v. Clifford* [1989] I.R. 121.

CHAPTER 9

Public Finance

Regulating a state's financial affairs, such as taxation, government borrowing and public expenditure, is an important feature of some national constitutions. Ireland's fiscal system follows closely the structure, which has evolved in Britain over the last four hundred years.[1] As Kingsmill Moore J. observed in his masterly account of how the system has developed over the centuries, "American and European authorities have extolled the British system of public finance as at once the most elastic and the most efficient which has yet been devised. In its developed form it achieves three important political objects. The initiative in finance lies with the executive, the control with the popular house of the legislature, the auditing and examination is entrusted to an official who is independent of politics and whose tenure of office is analogous to that of the judiciary."[2] As compared with, for example, the Federal German Constitution, the Constitution of Ireland contains relatively few clauses that deal directly with fiscal questions. Its only provision that expressly contains a substantive requirement for public finance is Article 44.2.2, which is a guarantee "not to endow any religion".

In two significant respects Ireland no longer enjoys fiscal autonomy in that, with the advent of the Euro in 2002, it no longer issues its own currency and, under the rules of the European Monetary Union, the State is no longer free to borrow whatever sums it regards is needed. Value added tax was introduced in 1972, in conjunction with entry into the EC, and was significantly reformed in 1978 to give effect to an EC Council Directive of the previous year. To date the EC has not significantly affected other taxes, apart from customs and excise duties that directly concern the "common market", and taxes that create a barrier to free movement within the EC.[3] However, endeavours are being made to bring income tax and corporation tax rates more into line across the Communities and suggestions have been mooted of an EC tax on incomes, in order to fully achieve the "single market."

---

[1] See generally, J. O'Connell, *The Financial Administration of Ireland* (1961) and K. Corrigan, *Revenue Law* (2000), 2 vols. Cf. T. Daintith and A. Page, *The Executive in the Constitution* (1999), Chaps 4–6.

[2] *Irish Employers' Mutual Insurance Association, Re* [1955] I.R. 176 at p.212.

[3] See generally, Corrigan, *ibid.*, pp.129 *et seq*. Cf. *Metallgesellschaft Ltd v. Inland Revenue* (Cases C–397 and 410/98) [2001] Ch. 620.

THE CENTRAL FUND

The principle that all public revenues should be collected in a single fund, followed two hundred years ago when the Consolidated Fund was first established, is now incorporated into Article 11 of the Constitution; that "[a]ll revenues of the State from whatever source arising shall, subject to such exception as may be provided by law, form one fund. ..." What exactly is encompassed by the term "revenues of the State" here has not been judicially determined, in particular whether the term is confined to taxes and similar revenues (*e.g.* charges for services and payments for materials and property sold), or has it a wider application. All receipts that fit the description must be channelled into the one fund, which is known as the Central Fund. This is based in the Central Bank, in the sense that lodgements to it and disbursements from it are made from the "exchequer account" which is kept at the Central Bank; there are several subsidiary exchequer accounts there, most notably the Revenue Commissioners' account. Government expenditures are made from this fund and the Government can raise loans on the security of the fund.

LEGISLATIVE CONTROL OF FINANCE

The principle that the legislature controls the public finances was established in the English Bill of Rights of 1689,[4] which proclaimed that only Parliament could authorise the imposition of taxes and similar charges, and that all substantial public expenditure requires parliamentary approval. The first branch of this principle is not spelled out in the Constitution but, as is explained below, it is a long standing principle of common law that all taxes and the like require specific legislative approval. The second branch is incorporated into several constitutional provisions, which give the Dáil the predominant role in regulating public expenditure.

The estimates

At least once a year, the Dáil must be given the opportunity to review the State's financial circumstances by considering detailed estimates of revenues and expenditure for the financial year, which is co-extensive with the calendar year. According to Article 28.4.3 of the Constitution "[t]he Government shall prepare Estimates of the Receipts and Estimates of the Expenditure of the State for each financial year, and shall present them to Dáil Éireann for consideration." And according to Article 17, "[a]s soon as possible after the

---

[4]   1 Will. & Mary, sess 2, c.2.

presentation to [the] Dáil … of [these] Estimates …, Dáil Éireann shall consider such Estimates." The estimates are contained in a document entitled the White Paper on Receipts and Expenditure, which is usually published just before the annual budget. Under Dáil Standing Order No. 152, these must be presented to the Dáil and circulated to members of the Dáil not later than the 30th day of the financial year, and not less than seven days before the annual budget. The annual Appropriation Acts authorise the expenditure envisaged in the estimates, as approved by the Dáil. Frequently, government departments spend more than they had estimated, in which event they must present supplementary estimates to the Dáil.

Authority to tax

Taxation is the principal source of public funds; the other main sources are borrowing, charges for various public services and sales of public assets. There is no express authority conferred by the Constitution on the Oireachtas to levy taxes, or to impose charges, borrow or sell State assets. Such authority, however, is implicit in the constitutional scheme, *inter alia*, in the reference to money bills, which the Seanad cannot amend, and has never been questioned by the courts.

Ever since the Bill of Rights, it has been accepted that the executive do not possess any inherent authority to levy taxes; one of the principles declared by the Parliament then was that "the levying of money for the use of the Crown, by pretence of prerogative, without grant of Parliament, for longer time, or in other manner, than the same is or shall be granted, is illegal."[5] Thus in *Bowles v. Bank of England*,[6] the plaintiff challenged the Bank's decision to deduct income tax from dividends to be paid to him on the grounds that there was no specific legislative sanction for that deduction. Income tax is an annual tax, then being imposed from April 6 to the following April 5. He was due to be paid a dividend on July 1, 1912. Although the Finance Act for that year had not been yet passed, the House of Commons in accordance with its long standing procedures had passed a resolution assenting to income tax at a given rate for that financial year. The Bank claimed that, in the circumstances, this resolution empowered it to deduct the income tax. But it was held that this was not so; that ever since 1689 it "was finally settled that there could be no taxation in this country except under authority of an Act of Parliament" and that, with regard to power to levy taxes, no resolution of the House Committee of Ways and Means or of the House itself "has any legal effect whatsoever"; they cannot

---

[5] Art.14 of the French Declaration of the Rights of Man and of the Citizen is to the same effect.

[6] [1913] 1 Ch. 57.

justify "levying a tax before such tax is actually imposed by Act of Parliament."[7] Although the Bill of Rights did not by its terms apply to Ireland, it cannot be doubted that this principle reflects the legal and indeed the constitutional position in this country.[8]

There are some statutory qualifications to this principle. Under the Provisional Collection of Tax Act 1927, the very procedure, which was condemned in the *Bowles* case, was given statutory effect. This Act provides that a resolution of the Dáil to impose a new tax, or to continue a tax which is expiring, or to increase a permanent tax "shall ... have statutory effect as if contained in an Act of the Oireachtas" for a limited period. Accordingly, once proposals for taxes in the budget are approved by a Dáil resolution, those taxes can be collected forthwith pending enactment of the annual Finance Act. Furthermore, under the Imposition of Duties Act 1957, originally introduced as an emergency measure, certain duties (customs and excise duty and stamp duty) can be imposed by a Government order, although that order lapses at the end of the following year unless it is confirmed by legislation. In *McDaid v. Sheehy*,[9] the Supreme Court found it unnecessary to rule on the constitutionality of this Act, which had been challenged on separation of powers grounds, because the disputed Ministerial order imposing a levy had subsequently been validated by section 46 of the Finance Act 1976.

Where the Oireachtas delegates powers to some official or agency, there is a strong presumption that power to levy taxes has not been delegated.[10] Indeed, by virtue of Articles 21 and 22, there are good grounds for the view that the Oireachtas cannot delegate any authority to levy a tax, or not to levy one, as distinct from delegating a power to vary the rate of a tax already imposed.[11]

Nor will the courts over-generously interpret tax legislation to extend the tax net wider than the very terms of the measure in question. In one instance where the Revenue sought to rely on the doctrine of "fiscal nullity" in order to defeat a sophisticated tax avoidance scheme, that was lawful under the literal meaning of the law strictly interpreted, the Supreme Court refused to condemn that scheme. To do so would "constitute the invasion by the judiciary of the powers and functions of the legislature, in plain breach of the constitutional separation of powers."[12]

---

[7] *Id.* at pp.84–85.
[8] Cf. *Attorney General v. Wilts United Dairies*, 38 T.L.R. 781 (1922) and *Commonwealth v. Colonial Combining, Spinning and Weaving Co.*, 31 C.L.R. 421 (1922).
[9] [1991] 1 I.R. 1.
[10] *R. v. Richmond on Thames L.B.C., ex p. McCarthy & Stone (Developments) Ltd* [1992] 2 A.C. 48 and *Humphreys v. Minister for the Environment* [2001] 1 I.R. 263 at pp.293–294.
[11] Morris, "'A Tax by Any Other Name': Some Thoughts on Money Bills and Other Taxing Measures", 22 *Statute L. Rev.* 211 (2001) and 23 *Statute L. Rev.* 147, 163 (2002).
[12] *McGrath v. McDermott* [1988] I.R. 258 at p.276.

Exemption from taxes

The tax code contains a wide variety of exceptions from taxation, for example what is often referred to as the "artists' exemption" from income tax. In determining what categories of individuals, bodies and activities should be exempted from tax and the scope of any such exemptions, the State has an extremely wide discretion, with which the courts will not readily interfere. One of the unsuccessful arguments for the unconstitutionality of the (since-repealed) residential property tax concerned the form of exemption extended to low-income occupiers of those premises.[13]

In 1988 and again in 1993 the Oireachtas adopted a partial "tax amnesty" for defaulters under which, on declaring unpaid tax due from them and paying a certain proportion of what was then due, they were exempted from paying the remainder.[14] In 2001, without express legislative authority, a similar arrangement was adopted by the Revenue Commissioners, except that the exemption applied only to a part of the interest and penalties that otherwise would have been payable by persons who kept undeclared income and gains in undisclosed accounts with Irish banks.[15]

At times the Oireachtas abolishes particular taxes, such as the residential property tax that was in force between 1983 and 1997 and the anti-speculative property tax that existed between 2000 and 2001. In 1987 the Minister for Finance announced that the Government did not intend collecting the farm tax that had been introduced two years previously. A Farm Tax Commission office had been established for the purpose of collecting this tax and civil servants in the Land Commission had been assigned to that office. Suspension of this tax led to their being re-assigned to their previous posts, which resulted in a dispute about exactly what their status then should be; they claimed a "legitimate expectation" to retain certain seniority they had obtained on being transferred to the tax office. That contention was upheld by Hamilton P. in *Duggan v. An Taoiseach*,[16] who found that the Government had acted unlawfully in suspending collection of the tax, without having introduced legislation to repeal the Farm Tax Act 1985. That decision had contravened the Government's obligation to take care that the laws of the State are faithfully executed. Those applicants were held to be entitled to compensation for their expectation being unlawfully infringed but were held not to have *locus standi* to seek orders that the farm tax should continue to be collected until such time as the 1985 Act remained in force.

This very question came for consideration in *Purcell v. Attorney General*,[17]

---

[13] *Madigan v. Attorney General* [1986] I.L.R.M. 136.
[14] See generally, Corrigan, *supra*, n.1, pp.463 *et seq.*
[15] Statement of Practice, SP–GEN 1.01.
[16] [1989] I.L.R.M. 710.
[17] [1995] 3 I.R. 287; *infra*, p.400.

where the plaintiff had been assessed for the tax before the Minister's announcement of the suspension but he then refused to pay it. He challenged the constitutionality of the Act itself but, in view of its *de facto* repeal, that question did not have to be considered. It was held, however, that the Government's decision was unlawful and that he did not have to pay the tax.

Recovery of taxes

Ensuring that taxes which are due are paid is principally the responsibility of the Revenue Commissioners and, in particular, the Collector General. The Commissioners are somewhat of a legal anomaly, being a group of individuals appointed by the Minister for Finance; they are not a corporate body. In 1849 the Commissioners for Excise and the Commissioners for Stamps and Taxes were merged to form the Commissioners of Inland Revenue, and their general administrative functions were set out in the Inland Revenue Regulation Act 1890.[18] In 1924 the Department of Finance was established for *inter alia* "the collection and expenditure of the revenues of [the State]" and to supervise the activities of the Revenue Commissioners.[19] Every annual Finance Act gives the Commissioners the responsibility of the "care and control" of the taxes imposed therein.

Assessment

The principal taxes are raised by way of assessment. Where a revenue official is dissatisfied with what a person estimates are the taxes he must pay or if no estimate is put in, the usual procedure is for the official to raise an assessment on that person. It may be appealed to independent Appeals Commissioners, under the procedures set out in Part 40 (sections 932-949) of the Taxes Consolidation Act 1997; there is a further right of appeal from them to the Circuit Court and additionally, by way of case stated, to the High Court. There is also the Valuation Tribunal, established in 1988,[20] which determines disputes about the value of property subject to taxation; its decision on points of law can be appealed to the High Court.

It was contended unsuccessfully in *Kennedy v. Hearne*[21] and later in *Deighan v. Hearne*[22] that the system, whereby a person's tax liabilities can be determined by way of a tax inspector raising an assessment, was unconstitutional. The argument was that, by doing so, the inspector imposes a legally

---

[18] 53 & 54 Vic. c.21.
[19] Ministers and Secretaries Act 1924, s. 1(ii).
[20] Replaced by the Valuation Act 2001.
[21] [1988] I.R. 481.
[22] [1990] 1 I.R. 499.

enforceable liability on the individual and, in consequence, is exercising a truly judicial function, which is the sole prerogative of the courts. But it was held that an assessment as such does not create a liability; rather, that occurs when it has not been appealed and the individual defaults in payment. It does not matter that an assessment is capable of giving rise to a state of affairs where legal liability would be triggered for what could be a very considerable sum. Where, however, as in *Kennedy*, the inspector made an error in his assessment and there has not been any default, "then the courts are empowered to intervene immediately ... and to stop and set aside any action by way of recovery which has already taken place." [23] This includes a power to award damages in an appropriate case and, therefore, it cannot be said that the assessment procedure ousts the jurisdiction of the courts. In *Deighan*, by contrast, the plaintiff was unsuccessful because the entire 12 months allowed for appealing the assessment had gone by but he never availed of the opportunity. It was reiterated, however, that "[t]he courts can still intervene if an inspector were to act capriciously or in a wholly unreasonable fashion" in rejecting an application to extend time for appealing. [24]

Proceedings

Prior to 1922, although Revenue officials could bring proceedings to recover certain penalties and forfeitures, proceedings to recover taxes were brought by the Attorney General in the name of the Crown because, in British constitutional theory, tax revenues are the personal property of the Crown.[25] Under section 16 of the Finance Act 1923, authority to sue for the recovery of taxes was conferred on the Attorney General, except where provision is made to the contrary. It would seem that recovery proceedings cannot be brought in the names of the Revenue Commissioners as such; the right of the Attorney to sue, coupled with the authorisations subsequently given to individual tax inspectors to sue, would appear to render it unnecessary to also authorise the Commissioners to do so.

In 1924 authority was given to individual tax inspectors to sue in their own name in the District Court or the Circuit Court for the recovery of unpaid taxes.[26] In 1958 a similar power was given to them to sue by way of summary proceedings in the High Court.[27] In any such proceedings the inspectors are permitted to prove certain aspects of their case by proffering certificates, for instance that the sum in question is due and owing and that demand for payment

---

[23] [1988] I.R. 481 at p.489.
[24] [1990] 1 I.R. 505.
[25] *Supra*, n.2, pp.211–214.
[26] Finance Act 1924, s.11.
[27] Finance Act 1958, s.54.

was duly made prior to the proceedings. These certificates are evidence of the facts in question unless the contrary is proved.[28]

Extra-judicial modes

Unpaid taxes also can be recovered through extra-judicial procedures, both of which have survived oblique constitutional attacks. Since 1923 the Collector General could do so by sending a certificate to the sheriff or county registrar, stating the amount due and owing, which then could be levied by way of execution on the defaulter's property.[29] And since 1988 taxes can be recovered by the Commissioners sending to the assessed person's creditor (*e.g.* his bank but not his employer) a certificate which has the effect of attaching such monies as are due to that person, up to the sum assessed.[30] The constitutionality of this latter procedure was challenged unsuccessfully in *Orange v. Revenue Commissioners*[31] but Geoghegan J. accepted that, on the particular facts there, resort to attachment might constitute an unconstitutional abuse of power. Earlier, in *Kennedy v. Hearne*,[32] resort to the sheriff was challenged in the context of employers' duty to deduct and pay over employees' PAYE. Because the mechanism prescribed for estimating what was so due and owing and for meeting demands for such payments was found to be reasonable, this mode of recovery was upheld. But the plaintiff was compensated for the manner in which there had been resort to it by the Revenue.

The only successful constitutional challenge to tax-recovery procedures was *Daly v. Revenue Commissioners*,[33] which concerned a withholding tax on fees paid to professional persons. Under that system, a sum equal to income tax at the standard rate had to be withheld from such fees and was assessed on the gross amount of those fees, without making any allowance for deductible expenses. Subsequent amendments were made to this system, regarding years of assessment and set-offs, that resulted in the amount of tax withheld exceeding what ultimately was payable, reducing the funds available to the individual to discharge his liabilities and not permitting sums withheld being set off against tax payable. As a result, the individual had to suffer a double tax payment on the same income in any one year. Costello J. concluded that these amendments might be acceptable if they dealt entirely with a transitional situation, *i.e.* overcoming a windfall gain obtained in one year due to a change in the rules. Although they were so intended, as operated they imposed "a *permanent* measure which involves a permanently unfair method of collecting tax" as to

---

[28] *Ibid.*
[29] Finance Act 1923, s.7.
[30] Finance Act 1988, s.73.
[31] [1995] 1 I.R. 517.
[32] [1988] I.R. 481.
[33] [1995] 3 I.R. 1.

constitute an unfair and disproportionate infringement of the plaintiff's property rights.[34] The withholding system there was not "rationally connected to the objective" but was "arbitrary, unfair or based on irrational considerations" and also did not "impair the plaintiff's right as little as possible."[35]

Penalties imposed on tax defaulters, without any criminal conviction, have been held to contravene the European Convention on Human Rights.[36] But in *McLoughlin v. Tuite*,[37] the Supreme Court rejected the contention that these penalties are intrinsically criminal sanctions rather than civil obligations.

Unconstitutional taxes

Courts in Ireland and abroad have demonstrated a marked reluctance to find particular taxes or methods of determining what taxes should be paid to be constitutionally unacceptable. Taxes that unduly interfere with freedom of movement within the EC contravene the Treaty of Rome and are invalid. As indicated above, potentially unfair aspects of tax assessment and recovery procedures usually are met by upholding the procedure in question, with the caveat that its use in particular circumstances may still be remediable by the courts. The *Daly* case is something of an exception to this because the applicable rules did not allow for the exercise of any discretion; the only way that the injustice there could have been prevented was by invalidating the very rules. But when it comes to broader questions of tax policy, considerable deference is paid to the legislative choice, on the grounds that it is not the function of the courts to decide what taxes are good or bad. As stated in *Madigan v. Attorney General*,[38] involving an unsuccessful attack on the since-repealed residential property tax, courts are disinclined to invalidate tax laws because they "are in a category of their own and very considerable latitude must be allowed to the legislature in the enormously complex task of organising and directing the financial affairs of the State."[39]

The constitutional basis for most challenges to tax laws is that they impermissibly contravene property rights. By their very nature, taxes are the equivalent of expropriation. Because, however, most public services for which individual taxpayers are eligible are available to them, it rarely if ever can be said that tax constitutes expropriation without any compensation. Some very unique feature of the tax in question must be identified before it would be struck down.

---

[34] *Id.* at p.12.

[35] *Id.* at p.11.

[36] *Georgiou v. United Kingdom* [2001] S.T.C. 80 and *Han v. Customs and Excise Commissioners* [2001] 1 W.L.R. 2253.

[37] [1989] I.R. 83; *supra*, p.417.

[38] [1986] I.L.R.M. 136.

[39] *Id.* at p.151.

In many of the constitutional challenges, the argument made is that the tax in question or the manner of its application contravenes the guarantee in Article 40.1 of equality before the law – what in France is referred to as the principle of *égalité devant les charges publiques*. But in order to succeed, there must be something glaringly oppressive with the manner in which the tax in question draws the distinctions. In *Madigan*, the above-mentioned feature of the residential property tax was held not to be "offensive to principles of justice or fair play." The manner in which motor cars are taxed as benefit-in-kind was challenged in *Browne v. Attorney General*[40] on the grounds that it affected the plaintiffs' (salesmen) right to work and also because it discriminated against them who, unlike most working people, had to use cars in order to earn their living. But it was held by Murphy J. that such anomalies as that system contained were largely the consequence of how the plaintiffs managed their own affairs, rather than the scheme of things itself, and he refused to strike down those provisions. The system by which the incomes of married couples were aggregated for the purpose of income tax, without each of them enjoying separate substantial allowances, was held by Hamilton P. in *Murphy v. Attorney General*[41] to contravene the equality guarantee. The Supreme Court overruled him on this point, but it upheld the contention that the plaintiffs' rights under the guarantee of the family had been contravened. Similarly in *Muckley v. Attorney General*,[42] although the combination of income tax and social welfare rules created a disparity between the way that unmarried mothers and certain married couples with children are treated, the Supreme Court rejected a challenged to it under the equality guarantee, emphasising that Article 40.1 entitles the Oireachtas to differentiate between individuals and groups on the basis of "capacity, physical and moral, and of social function."

The only tax legislation to be invalidated because it unfairly discriminated was in *Brennan v. Attorney General*,[43] which concerned the system of valuation for determining *inter alia* liability for agricultural rates established in the 1850s and known as the Griffith Valuation. Although reasonably satisfactory for its time, with the major changes in agricultural markets and methods in the intervening 100 years, it gave rise to more and more extreme discrepancies. Some farmers with quite valuable lands could find themselves paying comparatively low rates whereas others, with less valuable lands, could be paying much more to their local authority. The Supreme Court held that there has to be some reasonable degree of uniformity in the administration of any particular system of taxation. As stated by O'Higgins C.J., "[i]n the assessment of a tax such as a county rate, reasonable uniformity of valuation appears essential to justice. If such reasonable uniformity is lacking, the inevitable

---

[40] [1991] 2 I.R. 58.
[41] [1982] I.R. 241; *infra*, p.670.
[42] [1985] I.R. 472.
[43] [1984] I.L.R.M. 355; *supra*, p.752.

result will be that some ratepayer is required to pay more than his fair share ought to be. This necessarily involves an attack upon his property rights which by definition become unjust."[44]

Tax systems that unduly discriminate against families, as compared with non-family unions, have been declared to be invalid, as contravening Article 41. In *Murphy v. Attorney General*,[45] the Supreme Court struck down ss. 192-197 of the Income Tax Act 1967, which provided that a husband and a wife's income shall be aggregated for the purpose of determining their tax liability, with the result that an unmarried couple living together and sharing overheads would have to pay far less tax than a husband and a wife in similar circumstances were required to pay.

Retrospective taxation, in the sense of imposing a new tax on transactions that already had concluded, is generally regarded as unsatisfactory. Taxing measures are construed to apply prospectively only, except where express and clear provision is made to the contrary.[46] What circumstances may render retrospective tax legislation unconstitutional have not been determined.

Where a tax is imposed by virtue of a statutory instrument that *prima facie* is authorised by an enabling Act, it must not operate in an unfair and in-discriminate manner. A 2% cent levy imposed on butchers and on exporters of cattle was held by the Supreme Court in *Doyle v. An Taoiseach*[47] to be *ultra vires* on account of the particularly unfair way it actually operated.

Other revenue-raising

Although in certain contexts a levy may not strictly be a tax,[48] the same requirement of unequivocal legislative (or E.C. Regulation or Directive) authorisation is required for imposing levies.There are no express restrictions or limitations in the Constitution on the State's power to borrow or in the manner in which that power may be exercised. At the time of high inflation in the 1980's, a "balanced budget" amendment was mooted but it obtained little political support. Following economic and monetary union in the EC-EU, however, there now are external constraints on the State's borrowing power, principally under Article 104 of the EC Treaty, on "excessive government deficits".

Whether the State or a public body may borrow without express legislative authority to do so remains to be determined. The statutes constituting most if not all State corporations expressly authorise them, *inter alia*, to borrow for

---

[44] *Id.* at p.365.
[45] [1982] I.R. 241.
[46] See generally, F. Bennion, *Statutory Interpretation* (3rd ed., 1997), p.623 and *Dublin Corporation v. Ashley* [1986] I.R. 781.
[47] [1986] I.L.R.M. 693; *infra*, p.399.
[48] *Byrne v. Conroy* [1998] 3 I.R. 1.

the purpose of their objectives. In 1992 legislation was enacted in order to prevent the possibility of some public sector borrowings being declared *ultra vires* and irrecoverable by the lenders,[49] following a controversial decision of the English House of Lords concerning local authorities financing their activities through "interest swaps."[50] Under the National Treasury Management Agency Act 1990, a specialised agency was established to manage the national debt in a variety of ways, subject to such directions as may be given by the Minister for Finance. And under the National Development Finance Agency Act 2002, a body was established to raise finance for priority infrastructure projects, including public-private partnership arrangements, in conjunction with this agency.

There are no express restrictions or limitations in the Constitution on the State's power to sell public assets, nor does there appear to be any authority on when there must be express legislative authorisation to dispose of such property. All of the major privatisations in recent years have been backed by legislation.[51]

There are numerous statutory provisions authorising the State or other public authorities to charge for services they supply to members of the public. Notwithstanding how the legislation in question may describe it, an imposition of any kind will be considered to be a tax where it is compulsory, is imposed by or under statute, is made by a public authority and for a public purpose, is enforceable by law and is not a payment for services rendered.[52] Moreover, a fee for services rendered will be deemed to be a tax unless it bears a reasonable relationship to the cost of whatever service is being provided or otherwise is not unreasonable, having regard to the statutory purpose.[53] Thus in *Humphrey v. Minister for the Environment*,[54] Murphy J. held that imposing a fee for taxi licences, which was measured by reference to the capital value of a taxi plate rather than to the cost of administering the licensing system, was a tax and accordingly, *ultra vires* the Minister because he had not been given explicit authority to levy it.[55] Power given to Dublin Corporation in 1983 to charge for water supplied for domestic purposes "by ... instalments" was held not to authorise requiring payment in a single sum.[56]

Another significant source of finance for the State, the issue of currency (a form of borrowing), ceased to be possible in 2002 when the Euro was adopted as the national currency.

---

[49] Financial Transactions of Certain Companies and Other Bodies Act 1992.

[50] *Hazell v. Hammersmith & Fulham L.B.C.* [1992] 2 A.C. 1.

[51] *E.g.*, A.C.C. Bank Act 2001, Irish National Petroleum Corporation Ltd Act 2001 and Trustee Savings Bank (Amendment) Act 2001.

[52] *Eurig's Estate, Re*, 165 D.L.R. 4th 1 (1998) and Morris, *supra*, n.11 at pp.235–236.

[53] *Ibid.*

[54] [2001] 1 I.R. 263.

[55] Compare *Airservices Australia v. Canadian Airlines Int'l Ltd*, 202 C.L.R. 133 (1999).

[56] *Dublin Corporation v. Ashley* [1986] L.R. 781.

Expenditure

Article 29.5.2 of the Constitution stipulates that "[t]he State shall not be bound by any international agreement involving a charge upon public funds unless the terms of the agreement shall have been approved by Dáil Éireann."[57] Although international law generally is not a part of domestic law, where the State becomes a party to an international treaty it is obliged under public international law to honour the terms of the treaty. The purpose of this provision is to prevent government from entering into financial commitments with other states without the sanction of the Dáil. Whether this applies to agreements with foreign banks and private financial consortia has never been determined; the Irish version "connradh idáisiúnta" suggests that it is confined to agreements with foreign states and probably with international organisations. Approval can take the form of a resolution of the Dáil but frequently takes the legislative form. In *State (Gilliland) v. Governor of Mountjoy Prison*,[58] which concerned the Ireland-United States Extradition Treaty of 1983, it was held that Dáil approval must be secured whenever the very "terms of the agreement itself ... involve such a charge", and what must be approved is not merely the charge but the terms of the international agreement in question.

Article 11 of the Constitution embodies the principle that all State expenditure requires explicit legislative sanction; that "[a]ll revenues of the State ... shall be appropriated for the purposes and in the manner and subject to the charges and liabilities determined and imposed by law." Every year the Oireachtas passes an Appropriation Act, which approves most categories of government expenditure for the year in question. In 2002, for example, expenditure for supply of €29 billion was approved in this manner; about two-thirds of this sum was in respect of the costs of social welfare, health, education and environment.

Expenditure approved by the annual Appropriation Acts is in respect of what may be termed the ordinary government services, both current and capital, which in financial jargon are known as "supply services"; the expenditure on them is called "voted expenditure." Because the Appropriation Acts are passed at the end of the financial year (the 2002 Act is dated December 13), it is necessary to have legislative approval for "supply" made in the intervening period. That is granted by the Central Fund (Permanent Provisions) Act 1965, which permits the Minister for Finance to authorise issuing from the Central Fund sums not in excess of four-fifths of the previous year's estimate for each government department. Expenditure on other items, called "non-voted" expenditure, is sanctioned by more permanent legislation, such as the State's contribution to the EC budget, the President's establishment, judicial salaries

---

[57] *Infra*, p.225.
[58] [1987] I.R. 201.

and pensions, and advances to local authorities and to State-owned bodies in respect of capital projects.

Article 11 does not prevent the courts from giving judgment against the State in circumstances where, as yet, funds to satisfy the judgment have not been appropriated. [59] And it has been observed that the courts can, by order of *mandamus*, compel a Minister to apply to the Oireachtas for an appropriation of funds to meet the amount of a judgment.[60]

One of the issues that arose in *McKenna v. An Taoiseach (No.2)*,[61] where the plaintiff challenged the decision of the Government to spend public funds in support of its proposal to amend the Constitution abolishing the ban on divorce, was whether it was unlawful because the funds in question had never been appropriated to the Minister for Justice, Equality and Law Reform, whose functions do not include securing amendments to the Constitution. In the event, the Supreme Court did not address this contention, holding that those payments infringed Article 40.1's equality guarantee, which *inter alia* does not permit public funds to be expended in support of one side of the argument in a referendum on a proposed constitutional amendment.

PREDOMINANT ROLES OF THE DÁIL AND THE GOVERNMENT

In the regulation and supervision of the State's financial affairs, the Constitution gives the Dáil a predominant role, which reflects the British constitutional tradition that the most representative house of the legislature should have the decisive say in financial issues. As has already been explained, only the Dáil can initiate Money Bills and the Seanad has no authority to amend those Bills,[62] the annual Estimates must be presented to and considered by the Dáil, treaties purporting to impose a charge on public funds must secure the Dáil's approval and the Minister who has charge of the Department of Finance must be a member of the Dáil. [63] The Comptroller and Auditor General, whose function is to control all payments from State funds and to audit the State accounts, is nominated by the Dáil and must report to the Dáil. [64] The Dáil's Standing Orders on financial procedures (Orders 147-157) provide for the appointment of a Dáil Committee of Public Accounts, whose function is to "examine and report to the Dáil ... upon the accounts showing the appropriation of the sums granted," and to "suggest alterations and improvements in the form of the Estimates submitted to the Dáil."[65]

---

[59] *Byrne v. Ireland* [1972] I.R. 241 at p.289.
[60] *Maunsell v. Minister for Education* [1940] I.R. 213.
[61] [1995] 2 I.R. 10; *supra*, p.394.
[62] *Supra*, p.104.
[63] Art.28.7.1.
[64] Art.33.
[65] S.O. No. 156.

Government monopoly

The Constitution and the Dáil's Standing Orders reflect constitutional patterns in many countries by giving only the Government of the day a decisive say in many financial questions; the Government has the exclusive authority to propose what public expenditure should be incurred and what taxes should be imposed. Article 17.2 of the Constitution provides that, before the Dáil can agree on the appropriation of public funds, "the purpose of the appropriation" must have been recommended to it by the Government. Under Standing Orders, only the Government, or one of its members, are permitted to introduce Bills or propose amendments to Bills, which principally involve public expenditure, *i.e.* which "involve the appropriation of revenue or other public moneys ...".[66] Thus no private member, nor even the main opposition party nor the only opposition party (as the case may be), can introduce proposed measures the principal purpose of which is public expenditure. Standing Orders also deal with taxation, which is described as "a charge upon the people"; only the Government, or one of its members, are permitted to introduce Bills or propose amendments to Bills which have the effect of imposing or increasing such charges. [67]

Dáil Committee of Public Accounts

The Dáil Committee of Public Accounts, which is established under Dáil Standing Order Number 156, is an exception to the predominant role played by the Government of the day regarding the State's finances. For no member of the Government or Parliamentary Secretary may be a member of this Committee. Subject to that requirement, its members must be "impartially representative of the Dáil." This Committee's functions are to "examine and report" to the Dáil on the accounts regarding public expenditure and it must "suggest alterations and improvements" in the Estimates. The Dáil has given the Committee power to "send for persons, papers and records", and much of the Committee's time is involved in examining individuals on various matters relating to the public accounts. One of this Committee's most successful ventures was the inquiry it conducted in 2000 into evasion of deposit interest retention tax ("DIRT") through several banks and other financial institutions in the State.

The parliamentary privilege that Article 15.12 and 13 of the Constitution confers on what is said in either House of the Oireachtas and in reports of what was said there, and to the Oireachtas' own reports and publications, is

[66] S.O. No. 149.
[67] S.O. No. 148.

supplemented by the Committees of the Houses of the Oireachtas (Privilege and Procedure) Act 1976. Extensive powers and privileges are conferred by the Committees of the Houses of the Oireachtas (Compellability, Privileges and Immunities of Witnesses) Act 1997.

COMPTROLLER AND AUDITOR GENERAL

Article 33 of the Constitution provides that there shall be a Comptroller and Auditor General, whose functions are defined as "to control on behalf of the State all disbursements and to audit all accounts of moneys administered by or under the authority of the Oireachtas." This constitutional office-holder is appointed by the President, on the Dáil's nomination, and has the same security of tenure as that possessed by High Court judges. As well as controlling State expenditure and auditing the accounts, the Comptroller is required to report to the Dáil at such periods as are determined by law, which at present is not later than October 31 in the year after the year to which the appropriation accounts related. Where the Dáil passes a resolution requesting an investigation, on the basis of "*prima facie* evidence of substantial risk to the revenues of the State," the Comptroller is given extensive powers to carry out thorough enquires by the Comptroller and Auditor General and Committees of the Houses of the Oireachtas (Special Provisions) Act 1998.

The full nature and scope of his functions have never been judicially defined, in particular what exactly is involved in "control[ling] disbursements" and which funds are "administered under the authority of the Oireachtas." On the other hand, what "audit[ing] all accounts" requires is reasonably clear. Subject to Article 33, the Comptroller's position and functions are regulated principally by the Comptroller and Auditor General Acts 1866–1998.

In *Comptroller and Auditor General v. Ireland*,[68] it was held that the Comptroller's constitutional audit functions on the revenue side were at least those practised in 1937 by his predecessor. According to Laffoy J. there, his functions in auditing the accounts of the Revenue Commissioners "in addition to requiring ... a financial audit in the sense of establishing that the books of accounts and records ... gave a true and fair view of the transactions in the relevant accounting period and the state of affairs at the end of that period, requires him to carry out a systems audit to check the effectiveness of the procedures operated generally by the Commissioners for the assessment and collection of taxes and to carry out a regularity audit for the purpose of establishing that the underlying transactions comply with authority. ...[69]

This case concerned the extent to which the Comptroller was entitled to

---

[68] [1997] 1 I.R. 248.
[69] *Id*. at p.262.

monitor the effectiveness of the Revenue Commissioners' procedures generally, using information supplied in the 1993 "tax amnesty". The legislation there provided for confidentiality and, to that end, segregated the ordinary Revenue from the division administering the amnesty. In the course of his audit, the Comptroller took a sample of 200 persons who had taken the amnesty and sought to match that information with data on the central Revenue computer; if there were reasonable grounds for supposing that a person so located also was one of those who got the amnesty, the information he gave to the "special collector" would be compared with that on the central computer. Under section 7(5) of the Waiver of Certain Taxes, Interest and Penalties Act 1993, information acquired by the Comptroller during his audit could only be used in order to ensure that the "special collector' had properly discharged his functions under that Act. But it added a proviso that this "shall not prevent the Comptroller ... from carrying out his functions. ..." It was held that the cumulative effect of these was that the Comptroller was precluded for the time being from using the computer data in order to confirm whether indeed a sample of individuals qualified for the amnesty. Where, however, a dispute arose between any one of them and the Revenue as to whether he properly qualified for the amnesty, at that stage the Comptroller would be entitled to all the embargoed information. This arrangement, it was held, did not contravene Article 33.

CHAPTER 10

International Relations

Ireland has relations with many states, especially with its nearest neighbour the United Kingdom and also with the United States of America, which countries were the destination of the great majority of Irish emigrants in the past and which still have very substantial populations who were born in Ireland or of direct Irish descent. Under the Belfast Agreement of 1998 between Ireland and the UK, provision is made for the governance of Northern Ireland and other aspects of Ireland-UK relations.[1] In 1950 Ireland concluded a Treaty of Friendship, Commerce and Navigation with the USA.[2] Since 1972 Ireland has been a member of the European Communities/Union.[3] Prior to then, there was a common travel area between the State and the UK and also free trade agreement.[4]

Ireland joined the League of Nations in 1930 but was not admitted into membership of the United Nations until 1955, at which time it subscribed to the Statute of the International Court of Justice. But the State has not accepted what is called the "optional clause" in this Court's Statute, Article 36(2), under which accepting states agree that that Court has jurisdiction over disputes to which they are parties and involving questions of international law. Ireland is a party to many of the world's major multilateral treaties and has ratified many of the major international human rights treaties, in particular the UN Covenant on Civil and Political Rights[5] and the European Convention on Human Rights.[6] Article 29.9 of the Constitution, adopted in 2002, authorises the State to ratify the Rome Statute for an International Criminal Court.[7]

CONDUCT OF INTERNATIONAL RELATIONS

Conducting international relations is predominantly a function of the Government, over which the legislature has only limited direct control, apart

---

[1] *Supra*, p.83.
[2] Treaty of January, 21 1950, with Protocol of June 24, 1992.
[3] *Infra*, Chap.11.
[4] See generally, Ryan, "The Common Travel Area Between Britain and Ireland", 64 *Mod. L. Rev.* 855 (2001) and Agreement of December 14, 1965 [1965] Ir. No. 10.
[5] Of March 23, 1976, 999 UNTS 171; *infra*, p.272.
[6] Of November 4, 1950, 213 UNTS 221; *infra*, p.273.
[7] Of July 17, 1998, 37 I.L.M. 999 (1998). *Cf.* International Criminal Court Bill 2003.

from its general ability to render Governments accountable. Executive authority in this regard is restricted principally in that only the Dáil may declare war,[8] legislation is required for treaties to become part of Irish law[9] and Dáil approval is required for treaties that impose a charge on public funds.[10] Although the courts allow the Government freedom of action within the authority conferred on it, such action is not entirely beyond constitutional constraint. It is debatable whether or to what extent Article 29.1-3 can be invoked to restrain, by court order, the manner in which the executive conducts itself in the international arena.

Article 29.4.1 of the Constitution provides that the State's executive power regarding external relations shall be "exercised by or on the authority of the Government" in accordance with Article 28. That power is normally exercised through the Minister for Foreign Affairs and, in particular, through the Irish embassies and consulates and in numerous international organisations.

The President is empowered by section 3 of the Republic of Ireland Act 1948, on the Government's authority and advice, to "exercise the executive power or any executive function of the State in or in connection with its external relations;" it only exceptionally that the President personally acts under this provision.

Co-Operation in Diplomacy

Article 29.4.2 endorsed the practice that prevailed until 1948 whereby, under the Executive Authority (External Relations) Act 1936, the British Crown represented Ireland in foreign affairs for some purposes; that function ceased with the enactment of the Republic of Ireland Act 1948. According to this Article "[f]or the purpose of the exercise of any executive function of the State in or in connection with its external relations, the Government may to such extent and subject to such conditions, if any, as may be determined by law, avail of or adopt any organ, instrument, or method of procedure used or adopted for the like purpose by the members of any group or league of nations with which the State is or becomes associated for the purpose of international co-operation in matters of common concern." This permits the State to be represented abroad through groups or leagues of states that are "associated for the purpose of international co-operation in matters of common concern", such as the Council of Europe.

Its limitations, however, were pointed out by Walsh J. in *Crotty v. An Taoiseach*,[11] which held that the Constitution would have to be amended before

---

[8] Art.28.3.1.
[9] *Infra*, p.236.
[10] *Infra*, p.225.
[11] [1987] I.R. 713; *infra*, p.230.

Ireland could ratify the Maastricht Treaty of 1992 on the European Union. Article 29.4.2 "simply provides for the adoption of any organ or instrument or method of procedure for the exercise of the executive functions of the State."[12] But it does not "require prior consultation with any other State as to the policy itself [and also] provides that there must be enabling legislation;" it "refrain[s] from granting to the Government the power to bind the State by agreement with such groups of nations as to the manner or under what conditions that executive functions of the State would be exercised."[13] Indeed, it is questionable whether membership of the United Nations is authorised by this Article, although such membership may come within Article 29.1–3.

Concluding international agreements

Article 29.5 does not use the term treaty but instead speaks of international agreement. Some constitutions, notably the US Constitution, differentiate between treaties as such and executive agreements with foreign states; section 8 of the Extradition Act 1965 distinguishes an "international agreement or convention" from some other kinds of understanding between the Government and a foreign state. A question that arises is precisely what kind of agreements are caught by Article 29.5; the courts have not yet pronounced on this issue. According to Article 2(1)(a) of the Vienna Convention on the Law of Treaties, "'treaty' means an "international agreement concluded between States in written form and governed by international law, whether embodied in a single instrument or in two or more related instruments and whatever its particular designation." Thus, an inter-governmental exchange of notes can be a treaty. Agreements between a State and an international organisation or other entity with legal personality under international law can be a treaty, although the Vienna Convention's own provisions do not apply to such agreements. It would seem that agreements between the State and individuals or organisations not possessing international legal personality are not caught by Article 29.5.

Under the United Nations Charter, Ireland is obliged to register with the UN secretariat all treaties to which it becomes a party; the UN publishes the text of all treaties registered with it in the United Nations Treaty Series (UNTS). Most treaties to which Ireland is a party are published by the Department of Foreign Affairs in its own treaty series.

The Crown and, through it, the Government in the United Kingdom has full authority to conclude treaties, and neither the Australian nor the Canadian Constitutions require their legislatures to play any part in treaty-making.[14] By

---

[12] *Id.* at p.783.
[13] *Ibid.*
[14] See generally, Opeskin, "Constitution Modelling: The Domestic Effect of International Law in Commonwealth Countries" [2000] *Public L.* 607, [2001] *Public L.* 97.

contrast, in the United States treaties must secure the Senate's approval by a two-thirds majority.[15] The French, German and the Italian Constitutions require virtually all treaties of major domestic significance to be ratified by legislation. Under Article 29.5 of the Irish Constitution, the Dáil has a significant role in treaty-making in two respects.

Lay before the Dáil

In the first place and except for "technical and administrative" agreements, every treaty that is concluded by the State must be laid before the Dáil; according to Article 29.5.1, "[e]very international agreement to which the State becomes a party shall be laid before Dáil Éireann." The legal consequences of a treaty not being laid before the Dáil have never been determined. It would appear that a treaty is to be regarded as effective in international law despite its not having been laid before the Dáil, because this clause speaks of the State being a "party" to the treaty and, significantly, it does not stipulate that the treaty shall not be binding unless it is duly laid. It is nevertheless conceivable that a treaty that is not duly laid before the Dáil cannot be relied upon by the State as the basis of authority of any kind for the purpose of domestic law.

Dáil approval where there is a charge on public funds

The second constitutional requirement is that the Dáil must give its consent to the very terms of most treaties that impose a direct charge on the State's finances. Except for "technical and administrative" treaties, according to Article 29.5.2, "the State shall not be bound by any international agreement involving a charge upon public funds unless the terms of the agreement shall have been approved by Dáil Éireann." Sometimes the requisite approval is embodied in legislation, for instance, the International Financial Corporation Act 1958, which stipulates that "the terms of the (relevant) agreement are hereby approved" and which then goes on to authorise that payments be made to the Corporation from the Central Fund; also the International Development Association (Special Action Account) Act 1978 and the International Common Fund for Commodities Act 1982. On other occasions, approval is signified by way of a formal Dáil resolution.

As a matter of public international law, it is not clear whether or not a treaty that is signed on behalf of or ratified by the State is legally binding when it involves a charge on public funds but that treaty has not yet been approved by the Dáil. Differences of view exist about the effect of constitutional limitations on a state's treaty-making powers, and most discussion of the question centres on constitutional requirements that were not met before the treaty was signed or ratified. According to Article 46 of the Vienna Convention

---

[15] US Constitution Art.VI(2).

on the Law of Treaties, a "State may not invoke the fact that its consent to be bound by a treaty has been expressed in violation of a provision of its internal law regarding competence to conclude treaties as invalidating its consent unless that violation was manifest and concerned a rule of its internal law of fundamental importance. A violation is manifest if it would be objectively evident to any State conducting itself in the matter in accordance with normal practice and in good faith." Also relevant to the issue is Article 27 of this Convention, which says that, subject to Article 46, "[a] party may not invoke the provisions of its internal law as justification for its failure to perform a treaty." The position, therefore, would appear to be that not having secured Dáil approval does not prevent the State from being bound in international law by a treaty where the State did not even attempt to secure that approval. But where a genuine endeavour was made to secure Dáil approval and that was not forthcoming, then the treaty is not binding.

It was held by the Supreme Court in *State (Gilliland) v. Governor of Mountjoy Prison*,[16] that once a treaty is of a non-technical and administrative' nature and it purports to impose a charge on public funds, it is legally ineffective within Ireland unless the requisite Dáil approval has been obtained. In order to have someone extradited from the State (other than to the UK), section 8(1) of the Extradition Act 1965 requires that there exists an extradition treaty or arrangement with the country that is seeking the fugitive and that the Government has made an order applying Part II of the 1965 Act to the requesting country. In July 1983 such a treaty was concluded between Ireland and the USA and by an order (S.I. No.300 of 1984), Part II of the Act was declared to apply to the USA. Extradition proceedings were instituted against the applicant, who contended successfully that the treaty involved a charge on public funds but, because it had never received formal Dáil approval, it was ineffective and accordingly Part II did not apply to the USA.

The first question posed there was whether the 1983 treaty 'involve(d) a charge upon public funds'. In answering this, the crucial test is the terms of the treaty itself, viz. whether those very terms involve a charge. According to Finlay C.J., the mere fact that the State must incur certain costs in fulfilling its obligations under a treaty does not mean that Dáil approval must be secured; "purely incidental or consequential expenses which may fall on some of the organs of the State by reason of the adherence of the State to an international agreement but which are not created by one or other of the terms of that agreement itself, would make such agreements fit into the category of international agreements which shall be laid before Dáil Éireann (provided that they are not merely administrative or technical) but not within the category of those the terms of which require approval from Dáil Éireann."[17]

---

[16] [1987] I.R. 201.
[17] *Id.* at p.236.

Thus, the fact that Article XVI(2) of the 1983 treaty stipulates that the Attorney General would provide for representing US interests in giving effect to the treaty, which would necessarily involve the expenditure of public funds, does not mean that the treaty imposes a charge as envisaged by Article 29.5.2. That clause merely imposes "an obligation on a constitutional officer ... to advise and assist and represent or provide for the representation of [US] interests in connection with extradition."[18] However, Article XVII of the 1983 treaty, which is headed "Expenses," stipulates that the requested State "shall bear all ... expenses arising out of an extradition request" and that that State "shall make no pecuniary claim against" the requesting State arising out of implementing the treaty. This, it was held, unequivocally involves a charge on public funds because, where the US sends a request for extradition to Ireland, the State has "entered into a binding commitment to the US to bear certain expenses ...."[19] Those expenses, inevitably, must be borne out of public funds, and "the right of the US to call upon this State to pay them arises by the direct and express terms" contained in the treaty.[20] Moreover, were it not for Article XVII, the expenses of processing US requests for extradition "could presumably be claimed against the US...".[21]

Since therefore public funds would be charged by Article XVII, the next issue posed was what is meant by "the terms of the agreement (being) approved by" the Dáil? The Dáil must approve of, not merely the existence of the treaty in question nor of the charge that the treaty imposes, but of the very terms of the treaty itself. Because the requisite Dáil approval had not been obtained at the time, what was the legal standing of the 1983 treaty and of S.I. No. 300 of 1984 purporting to apply Part II of the Extradition Act to the USA.? The statutory instrument was held to be invalid having regard to the provisions of Article 29.5.2; the Court did not comment on the legal status of the treaty itself in the light of that provision.

International arbitration and adjudication

Usually the State manages to resolve its differences with other States through negotiations and, where those fail, arbitration may be resorted to. To date the major political or economic international dispute to which Ireland is a party that has been referred to arbitration is the question of whether the UK has complied with that is described as the OSPAR Convention of 1992, arising from its nuclear facilities at Sellafield.[22] Ireland has not acceded to the International Court of Justice's optional protocol but is a party to the UN

---

[18] *Id.* at p.237.
[19] *Ibid.*
[20] *Ibid.*
[21] *Ibid.*
[22] *Ireland v. United Kingdom* 41 I.L.M. 40 (2002).

Covenant on Civil and Political Rights and the European Convention on Human Rights, including the individual's right of petition/complaint to the Court of Strasbourg and to the UN's Human Rights Committee, respectively.

According to Article 29.2 of the Constitution, "Ireland affirms its adherence to the principle of the pacific settlement of international disputes by international arbitration or judicial determination." Four principal questions arise from this clause, the first three of which concern what is envisaged by the terms "international disputes," "international arbitration" and "international judicial determination." These were addressed by the Supreme Court in *Kavanagh v. Governor of Mountjoy Prison*,[23] where the applicant was seeking redress in consequence of his successful claim against the State before the Human Rights Committee (the "UNHRC").[24] It had been held by the UNHRC that his trial before the Special Criminal Court had contravened Article 26 of the 1966 Covenant's guarantee of "equal before the law." He sought to have his conviction quashed, or to be released or at least to be paid compensation, based *inter alia* on that finding. He contended that "Article 34.1 must be read not in isolation but in conjunction with Article 29.2, which is in the nature of a *lex specialis* referring to a very limited category of judicial administration viz. international arbitrations and judicial determinations," and, further that "if the State's argument were correct, then legislative provisions enabling foreign judgments to be enforced here would be invalid."[25] Finnegan J. concluded that the views of the UNHRC were not a judicial determination and constituted no more than an expression of views carrying moral authority. On appeal, Fennelly J., for the Court, disagreed, holding that Article 29.2 did apply to these views. However, he rejected the claim being made on the ground that such views could not prevail against a judgment of an Irish court, in view of Article 34 of the Constitution.

JUDICIAL REVIEW OF INTERNATIONAL RELATIONS

Apart from questions of consistency with the requirements of Article 29 of the Constitution, to what extent are dealings between the Government and other States amenable to judicial review? Courts in Britain did not consider the validity of treaties as such and, when an attempt was made by Unionist politicians to have the Anglo-Irish "Hillsborough" Agreement of 1985 declared invalid, their claim was rejected as beyond the jurisdiction of the court.[26] In

---

[23] [2002] 3 I.R. 97.

[24] Decision of April 4, 2001.

[25] Para.27 of written submissions.

[26] *Molyneaux, ex parte* [1986] 1 W.L.R. 331; similarly, *R. (Rees Mogg) v. Secretary of State* [1994] Q.B. 552. See generally, Collins, "Foreign Relations and the Judiciary", 51 *Int'l & Comp. L.Q.* 485 (2002) and F.A. Mann, *Foreign Affairs in English Courts* (1986).

the United States, by contrast, the courts have considered attempts to challenge executive orders made in pursuance of the US-Iranian Agreements of 1981, which nullified attachments of Iranian assets in US banks; in the event the challenges were rejected.[27] But the courts there refused to consider the merits of an action concerning termination of the US-China defence treaty.[28] Arguably the most important Italian decision on this question is the 1982 case[29] which concerned a law implementing the Concordat with the Vatican, which, *inter alia*, provided that Catholic Church annulments of church marriages performed by a priest shall have automatic civil effect; that provision was declared to contravene the constitutional guarantee of fair procedures. In Germany the Federal Constitutional Court was called on to pronounce on the *Ostpolitik*, i.e. "Eastern Treaties" of 1970-73, in which the Federal Republic accepted the existing borders with its eastern neighbours and provided for friendly relations and co-operation. That Court upheld those agreements against charges that they unconstitutionally sought to diminish the national territory.[30] The French Constitution even provides that treaties entered into by the Government can be referred to the *Conseil Constitutionnel* for a ruling as to whether the treaty's terms contravene any constitutional provision.[31]

An instance somewhat similar to the German controversy is *Boland v. An Taoiseach*,[32] where part of the Anglo-Irish "Sunningdale" Agreement of 1973 was challenged unsuccessfully. Following negotiations between the British and the Irish Governments and some Northern Irish public representatives, it was agreed that a power-sharing executive (*i.e.* comprised of representatives of the Nationalist and Unionist communities) should be established in the North, that there should be a Council of Ireland and several other matters, in the hope that some solution to the sectarian conflict in the North could be reached. At the conclusion of the negotiations, an "agreed communiqué" was issued by all the parties setting out what had been agreed. The plaintiff challenged the constitutionality of clause 5 of this communiqué, which stipulated that the Irish Government "fully accepted and solemnly declared that there could be no change in the status of Northern Ireland until the majority of the people of Northern Ireland desired a change in that status." According to the plaintiff, this recognised the *de jure* position of Northern Ireland as a part of the United Kingdom, which conflicted with (the then) Articles 2 and 3 of the Constitution. It was argued that, although this was contained in a mere communiqué, once it

---

[27] *Dames & Moore v. Regan*, 453 US 654 (1981). See generally, L. Henkin, *Foreign Affairs and the US Constitution* (2nd ed., 1996) and T. Franck, *Political Questions Judicial Answers: Does the Rule of Law Apply to Foreign Affairs* (1992).

[28] *Goldwater v. Carter*, 444 US 966 (1979).

[29] [1982] Giur. Const. 138. *Cf.* the German *Condcordat* case, 6 BVerfGE 309 (1957).

[30] The *Inter-German Basic Treaty* case 36 BVerfGE 1 (1973).

[31] Art.54.

[32] [1974] I.R. 338.

was registered at the United Nations it would become a treaty and be binding in international law, and thus a legally binding surrender of the national territory. These contentions were rejected by a unanimous Supreme Court.

Slightly different approaches were adopted by the judges. Accord to FitzGerald C.J., whatever about other parts of the communiqué, clause 5 did not even constitute an agreement; it was a mere statement of policy, a mere reference to the *de facto* position in the North. By virtue of the separation of powers, the courts have no jurisdiction whatsoever to contradict policy statements emanating from the executive. Even if clause 5 did declare that Northern Ireland was legally part of the UK, Budd J. appears to have taken the view that the courts still could not interfere since that clause was not embodied in legislation or even draft legislation. It was a mere declaration of policy and a matter exclusively for the executive, which is responsible to the Dáil. As Griffin J. pointed out, if the clause had the meaning attributed to it by the plaintiff, before it could have any legal effect under the Constitution it would have to be approved by the Dáil since it involved a charge on public funds. If it were to be embodied in legislation, it most likely would be referred by the President to the Supreme Court under the Article 26 procedure; if that were not done, somebody would contest its validity under the usual Article 34.3 procedure. That was the stage at which the Court should consider the constitutional issue. O'Keeffe P. disagreed with this proposition, holding that an acknowledgement by the Government that the State had no *de jure* claim over Northern Ireland would "be clearly not within the competence of the Government having regard to the terms of the Constitution."[33] But he read clause 5 as having the meaning attributed to it by the Chief Justice.

The extent to which actions by the executive in the field of foreign relations are subject to judicial review came up again for consideration in *Crotty v. An Taoiseach,* [34] which concerned the Single European Act (SEA) of 1986. As is explained in the next chapter, Community law is given a special status by Article 29.4.10 of the Constitution. The SEA is a treaty concluded by the EC Member States, which dealt with two distinct matters. In its "Title II" it provided for various amendments to the treaties constituting the Communities and is aimed principally at facilitating decision-making within the Communities' institutions, bringing about more rapidly achievement of several of the EC's policies on economic integration and related harmonisation of laws. Title II's terms were confirmed by the European Communities Act 1986. It was contended that Title II and this Act were unconstitutional because they involved a significant departure from the existing EC structures. That was rejected because not alone did (present) Article 29.4.10 authorise the State to join the Communities but it authorises changes that might be made in the various EC mechanisms, provided that they did not depart radically from the original

---

[33] *Id.* at p.363.
[34] [1987] I.R. 713.

structure. As Finlay C.J. summed up the position, this Article authorises the State "to join in amendments to the [EEC] Treaties so long as such amendments do not alter the essential scope or objectives of the Communities" but the changes being made by Title II did not "alter the essential character of the Communities'. [35]

It is the Court's decision regarding Title III of the SEA that has most relevance for the question of judicial review of foreign policy. During the 1970s the EC Member States commenced some informal co-operation in foreign policy, which by the late 1980s came to be referred to as European foreign policy co-operation. The various governments would often consult with each other before adopting major foreign policy positions. What Title III sought to do was to place such co-operation on a formal basis, by having the methods and scope of co-operation spelled out in a binding treaty and by giving the entire enterprise a quasi-institutional embodiment under the name European Political Co-operation. For this purpose there would be Political Directors, a Political Committee, a European Correspondents Group, Working Groups and a secretariat based in Brussels. Title III did not by its very terms oblige the State Parties invariably to adopt a common position in foreign policy matters. But it required consultation and taking full account of other State Parties' views before adopting any final position, it strongly exhorted convergence of positions and joint action, and it obliged refraining from impeding consensus. Unlike Title II, this Title was not embodied in an Act of the Oireachtas; it was a treaty that had been signed on behalf of the State and its terms had been approved by a resolution of the Dáil. By a majority of 3 to 2, the Supreme Court found that its ratification would be unconstitutional unless the Constitution was suitably amended.

As in the *Boland* case, a preliminary question was to what extent executive acts and resolutions of the Dáil regarding foreign affairs can be made subject to judicial scrutiny. All of the judges were in agreement that the Government is subject to the Constitution even where it is exercising the foreign affairs powers. But according to Finlay C.J., dissenting, the courts will only intervene in foreign affairs where an individual's constitutional rights are being invaded or threatened; that "where an individual person comes before the Courts and establishes that action on the part of the executive has breached or threatened to breach one or other of his constitutional rights [then] the Courts must intervene to protect those rights …".[36] Save in such circumstances, the courts ought not to intervene because '[t]here is nothing in the provisions of Articles 28 and 29 of the Constitution … from which it would be possible to imply any right in the Courts in general to interfere in the field or area of external relations with the exercise of an executive power."[37] It could be said that the majority

---

[35] *Id.* at pp.767 and 770.
[36] *Id.* at p.774.
[37] *Ibid.*

did not contest this analysis, except that they adopted a more expansive view of what an individual's constitutional rights are. As in other cases where it was held that individuals are entitled to contest the constitutionality of electoral boundaries and of voting arrangements that are inconsistent with the Constitution's provisions regarding Dáil elections,[38] it was held that an individual is entitled to challenge in the courts Government action that is inconsistent with other constitutional provisions, such as those on national sovereignty. Referring to Articles 29.4.1 and 28.2, Henchy J. concluded that "in the conduct of the State's external relations, as in the exercise of the executive power in other respects, the Government is not immune from judicial control if it acts in a manner or for a purpose which is inconsistent with the Constitution."[39] The principal reason why the Court refused to grant the declarations that were sought in the *Boland* case was that what was being challenged was merely an agreed statement of policy by two governments; it was not a treaty giving rise to legal obligations in international law. But in an appropriate case the courts will intervene where the Government embodies its foreign policy in a treaty which is binding on the State in international law, even if at some later stage the treaty is found to be unconstitutional. As Walsh J. pointed out, "in international law the State in entering into a treaty must act in good faith. … If some part or all of [a particular] Treaty was subsequently translated into domestic legislation and found to be unconstitutional it would avail the State nothing in its [international] obligations. ..It would still be bound by the Treaty. … It is not for other States to the Treaty to satisfy themselves that the Government of Ireland observed its own constitutional requirements."[40]

The question then was on what grounds will the courts interfere with foreign policy that is embodied in a treaty. Because, under the dualism principle,[41] most interferences by the executive with an individual's rights and freedoms at the very outset require explicit legislative sanction, judicial scrutiny of such interferences is expressly authorised by several Articles of the Constitution.[42] An example of what might constitute such interference that does not require legislative sanction is the Government permitting some foreign government to expropriate an Irish citizen's property located abroad without demanding adequate compensation from that government. Possibly such failure by the Government would be amenable to judicial review, although it does not follow that it would always be declared to be unconstitutional.[43] Whether or to what extent citizens have a legally enforceable right to international protection by the State while they are abroad is an open question.[44] So too is that of the

---

[38] *Infra*, p.592.
[39] [1987] I.R. 786.
[40] *Id.* at p.780.
[41] *Infra*, p.235.
[42] E.g., *State (Trimbole) v. Governor of Mountjoy Prison* [1985] I.R. 550.
[43] Cf. *Dames and Moore v. Regan*, 453 US 654 (1981).
[44] Cf. *R. (Abassi) v. Secretary of State* 42 I.L.M. 358 (2003).

extent to which the State is permitted to cede part of the "national territory" or to give foreign states rights in respect of that territory. As has already been pointed out, the Anglo-Irish Agreement of 1986 spoke of no change in the status of Northern Ireland without indicating precisely what that status is. In the *Crotty* case it was held that the Constitution does not permit the State by agreement to abdicate its freedom of action to conduct foreign policy. While almost all international treaties operate to restrict the parties' freedom of action to some degree, and to that extent are unexceptional, the Government is not permitted to sign away its general freedom of action in dealing with foreign states and their nationals. As Walsh J. put it, "the Constitution ... confer[s] full freedom of action upon the Government to decide matters of foreign policy and to act as it thinks fit on any particular issue so far as policy is concerned and as, in the opinion of the Government, the occasion requires. ... [T]his freedom does not carry with it the power to abdicate that freedom or to enter into binding agreements with other States to exercise that power in a particular way or to refrain from exercising it save by particular procedures, and so to bind the State in its freedom of action in its foreign policy."[45]

The central issue in *Crotty* was the extent to which the State may become a party to international institutional arrangements whereby its freedom to deal with other states becomes extensively circumscribed. Participation in global, as contrasted with regional, organisations may very well be authorised by Article 29.1–3 of the Constitution. There is also Article 29.4.2, which authorises participation in international organisations, but such participation must be given legislative approval, thereby bringing it within the Court's explicit jurisdiction. Regarding this Article, Walsh J. observed that those adopting it "clearly foresaw the possibility of being associated with groups of nations for the purpose of international co-operation in matters of common concern and they provided for the possibility of the adoption of a common organ or instrument. Equally clearly they refrained from granting to the Government the power to bind the State by agreement with such groups of nations as to the manner or under what conditions that executive function of the State would be exercised."[46] Ireland's participation in the United Nations and in the Council of Europe is not covered by this Article because there is no enabling legislation providing for it. Whether Ireland's obligations to the UN and the Council of Europe amount to having obligations "as to the manner or under what conditions" foreign policy will be exercised is debatable; the answer is probably no because each of these organisations trench on freedom of action in foreign policy to a very limited extent.

What the Supreme Court found in *Crotty* was that Title III of the SEA involved a drastic transformation in the nature of the European Communities,

---

[45] [1987] I.R. 786 at p.783.
[46] *Ibid.*

rendering them no longer an essentially economic union and instead crossing the threshold of a political community, within which Ireland's foreign policy would no longer be guided as previously by the national interest. Consequently, in its international relations Ireland would cease to be a fully "sovereign state", as it is described in Article 5 of the Constitution. Such a dilution in national sovereignty was unconstitutional. Henchy J. summed up the effect of this part of the SEA as follows:

> "As a treaty, Title III is not designed in static terms. It not alone envisages changes in inter-state relations, but also postulates and requires those changes. And the purpose of those changes is to erode national independence in the conduct of external relations in the interests of European political cohesion in foreign relations. As I have pointed out, the treaty marks the transformation of the European Communities from an organisation, which has so far been essentially economic to one that is to be political also. It goes beyond existing arrangements and practices, in that it establishes within the framework of the Communities new institutions and offices (such as European Political Co-Operation, the Political Director and the Political Committee) and charts a route of co-ordination, by means such as working parties, a secretariat and regular meetings, so as to give impetus to the drive for European Unity.
>
> All this means that if Ireland were to ratify the Treaty it would be bound in international law to engage actively in a programme, which would trench progressively on Ireland's independence and sovereignty in the conduct of foreign relations. Ireland would therefore become bound to act in a way that would be inconsistent with the Constitution."[47]

According to Walsh J., "the essential nature of sovereignty is the right to say yes or say no", and that right was "materially qualified" by the SEA.[48] He stressed the fact that the foreign policy co-operation required under this Title even extended to the State's participation in the United Nations and the Council of Europe; that the Title could even require the State to combine with other EC Member States within these organisations. Furthermore, the somewhat ambiguous references in the Title to the Atlantic Alliance could very well be read as requiring the State never to impede co-operation among NATO Member States in the field of security. Before the Government could ratify Title III it would be necessary to amend the Constitution. In the event, it was amended in May 1987.

The extent to which in 2003 the State facilitated the United States transporting troops and arms to prosecute its war against Iraq was challenged

---

[47] *Id.* at p.788.
[48] *Id.* at p.781.

in *Horgan v. An Taoiseach.*[49] But Kearns J. rejected the contention that permitting the U.S. military to use Shannon Airport and to over-fly the country went further than had been authorised by a Dáil resolution of March 20, 2002 and, in any event, did not involve participating in a war as envisaged by Article 28.3.1 of the Constitution. In so far as that authorisation may have contravened the State's obligations under international law as a neutral, it was held that that was something which the courts could not remedy because, subject to exceptions as described below, international law is not part of domestic law.

INTERNATIONAL OBLIGATIONS AND IRISH LAW

There are two polar opposite approaches to the relevance of international law in municipal or national law, *viz.* "monism" and "dualism."[50] At the political and philosophical level, the monist sees the world community of states, organisations and individuals as part of a single world legal order, although one that allows for the delegation to individual countries and other geographic and personal communities of extensive law-making and adjudicative powers. In purely legal terms, monism means that a country's own laws include international law standards, especially the rules contained in treaties that a state has adhered to. While quite a number of countries are monist in this sense, very few states incorporate into their national legal systems all of customary international law and every rule contained in treaties that they have ratified.

"Dualism," which is the political-legal tradition in Britain and in Ireland,[51] may be described as a doctrine of legal insularity. What sent Anglo-Irish law down the dualist road is a matter of speculation. Dualism distinguishes sharply between international law and municipal law, and holds that international legal standards become part of national law only when they are incorporated by legislation into the state's legal system. The fact that a state becomes bound by a particular treaty has no significance for its own laws; for the treaty's standards to become part of state law requires that legislation be enacted that contains the treaty provisions. While dualism may be criticised for its parochial view of the world, there are certain advantages in its approach, in that it provides greater legal certainty than does monism as it is practised, and it leaves far less room for judicial discretion. Article 29.6 incorporates one element of dualism into the Constitution, *viz.*, the primacy of domestic legislation over international treaties; that "[n]o international agreement shall be part of the domestic law of the State save as may be determined by the Oireachtas." In contrast under

---

[49] [2003] 2 I.L.R.M. 357; *infra*, p.874.
[50] See generally, I. Brownlie, *Principles of Public International Law* (5th ed., 1998), Chap.2 and A. Cassese, *International Law* (2001), Chap.8.
[51] See generally, Opeskin, *supra*, n.14.

Article 29.4.3–10, the EC/EU Treaties, Regulations and Directives made under them are effective and have supremacy in Irish law, even overriding the Constitution itself.[52] There is no constitutional provision on the domestic status of customary international law.

Legislative implementation of treaties

Where a treaty calls for restrictions on or interference with an individual's legal rights, then by virtue of Article 29.6 (the "dualism" clause) in order for it to take effect within the State, an Act of the Oireachtas must be passed that incorporates the treaty or its requirements into Irish law. Sometimes the very terms of the treaty itself are made part of domestic law, such as the Vienna Convention on Diplomatic Relations.[53] In an instance where the International Convention Relating to the Arrest of Seagoing Ships 1952, had been fully incorporated into domestic law, without adaptation,[54] Barr J. held that the arrest under its provisions of two Georgia-registered "sister" ships was unlawful. That was because Georgia was not a party to that Convention which, accordingly, could not impose obligations on non-parties, except where the ship in question was contravening that Convention's substantive requirements. On other occasions, the legislature spells out in its own language the requirements contained in the relevant treaty, for instance the European Convention on Extradition.[55]

Once it has ratified a treaty that purports to confer rights or impose obligations on individuals, a State has an international law obligation to the co-signatories to enact appropriate legislation in order to give effect to the treaty requirements. Mere signature to a treaty ordinarily places no such obligation on a State, except in the rare case where the very terms of the treaty in question call for implementation once it is signed. Accordingly in *Hutchinson v. Minister for Justice*,[56] Blayney J. refused to order the State to take steps towards enacting the requirements of the Council of Europe's Convention on Transfer on Sentence of Prisoners, which Ireland signed but had not yet ratified because, "[i]n the case of a treaty which is subject to ratification, this act, which is absolutely discretionary, makes the treaty definitely binding. Thus, until ratification, the signature to the treaty leaves the contracting parties free to choose between acceptance and rejection of the text as it stands."[57] It is

---

[52] *Infra*, p.262.
[53] Of April 18, 1961, 500 UNTS 95, implemented by the Diplomatic Relations and Immunities Act 1967.
[54] *The Kapitan Labunets* [1995] 1 I.R. 164.
[55] Of December 13, 1957, 359 UNTS 273, implemented by the Extradition Act 1965.
[56] [1993] 3 I.R. 567.
[57] *Id.* at p.570.

questionable whether an order such as was sought there would be made if the Convention had been ratified by the State, although failure to incorporate its requirements into legislation may in special circumstances give rise to a "legitimate expectation" which aggrieved individuals may invoke.

When interpreting domestic legislation, some cognisance will be given to treaties binding on the State, although the precise extent to which treaties are relevant to statutory construction remains very much an open question.[58] In *Bourke v. Attorney General*,[59] where the plaintiff sought to block his extradition to England on the grounds that the offences in respect of which he was sought were connected with a "political offence," Ó Dálaigh C.J. referred extensively to the European Convention on Extradition and to this Convention's *travaux préparatoires*. Part II of the Extradition Act 1965 was modelled on this Convention, which also incorporates the concept of "political offence," and the Convention was deemed relevant to interpreting the meaning of such offence in Part III of the Act. Generally, legislation enacted in order to give effect to the State's treaty obligations will be construed so far as is reasonably possible so as to give full effect to those obligations, as envisaged by the treaty.

The issue that arose in *Travers v. O'Siochana*[60] was whether the bilateral double taxation agreement between Ireland and the UK, which was implemented by way of a statutory instrument, should be construed in a manner consistent with the OECD's Model Convention of 1977, around which that agreement was designed. In particular, should the term "local authority" have the meaning attributed to it in the Model? Because it was not a multilateral convention but only a proposed ideal for such treaties, Carroll J. held that the ordinary meaning of that term prevailed over what was envisaged in the Model.

Customary international law

Except where they conflict with statute or with the Constitution itself, the rules of customary international law are part of the common law of Ireland. It was stated by Davitt P. in *Ó Láighléis, Re* (a case involving treaty law) that "[a]part from any provision of the Constitution, the position would appear to be that the rules of the international law are not part of the domestic law, except in so far as they have been made so by legislation, judicial decision or established usage. To that extent its rules may be applied by the courts so long as they are not in conflict with an enactment of the legislature or a rule of the common law."[61]

The accuracy of this statement was contested in *ACT Shipping Ltd. v.*

---

[58] See generally, F. Bennion, *Statutory Interpretation* (3rd ed., 1997), pp.523 *et seq.*
[59] [1972] I.R. 36.
[60] [1994] 3 I.R. 199.
[61] [1960] I.R. 93 at p.103.

Minister for the Marine,[62] a salvage case where it was contended that the Minister had refused refuge to a stricken vessel, contrary to its right of refuge under customary international law. It was contended by the Minister that international law rules could only become part of domestic law if so incorporated by way of legislation, as envisaged by Articles 15.2 and 29.6 of the Constitution. But that argument was rejected by Barr J., who held that Article 15.2 does not inhibit the evolution of international customary law into domestic law. That Article was concerned with "making" laws, but "customary law is not made in the sense envisaged (there but) evolves from a practice or course of conduct which in time has become widely accepted."[63] Even if this were not correct and that Article constituted a barrier, it was held that the custom in question in the case had been absorbed into domestic law prior to 1937 and accordingly was carried over by Article 50. Barr J. then went on to consider whether the Minister also had a right in the circumstances to refuse the vessel entry into Irish territorial waters, in view of the risks its condition posed, and concluded that he had. Perhaps the commonest judicial application of customary international law in recent years has been the principle of sovereign immunity in several contexts.

Where, however, the State in dealing with other States acts contrary to customary international law, it appears that aggrieved individuals have no legal redress against such conduct. In *Horgan v. An Taoiseach*,[64] concerning U.S. use of Shannon Airport and over-flights during its 2003 war against Iraq, even if the State was thereby in breach of its obligations under international law as a neutral, Kearns J. held that it was legally free in domestic law to do so for the reasons explained below.

General principles of international law

Article 29.3 of the Constitution provides that "Ireland accepts the generally recognised principles of international law as its rule of conduct in its relations with other States." The dividing line between rules of customary international law and generally recognised principles of international law, if that line exists, is a difficult one. For many years it was taken for granted that no legally enforceable rights could be derived from Article 29.3 because it concerned exclusively inter-State relations and also on account of Article 29.6, the "dualist" clause. In *Ó Láighléis, Re*[65] it was contended that this clause did not prevent international treaties from having some legal effect within the State; in particular, that the administrative detention powers contained in the Offences

---

[62] [1994] 3 I.R. 232.
[63] *Id.* at p.422.
[64] [2003] 2 I.L.R.M. 357.
[65] [1960] I.R. 93.

Against the State (Amendment) Act 1940, were unconstitutional because *inter alia* they contravened the European Convention on Human Rights.[66] The essence of the applicant's argument there was that the Constitution is primarily monist. But this view was rejected as flying in the face of Article 29.6 and also of Article 15.2.1, which states that "the sole and exclusive power of making laws for the State is hereby vested in the (legislature); no other legislative authority has power to make laws for the State." Maguire C.J. explained that "[n]o argument can prevail against the express command of section 6 of Article 29 of the Constitution before judges whose declared duty it is to uphold the Constitution and the laws. The Court accordingly cannot accept the idea that the primacy of domestic legislation is displaced by the State becoming a party to the Convention. ... Nor can the Court accept the contention that the Act of 1940 is to be construed in the light of, and so as to produce conformity with a convention entered into ten years afterwards."[67] The Chief Justice observed that these clauses "clearly refer only to relationships between states and confer no rights on individuals."[68]

Subsequently in *State (Summers Jennings) v. Furlong*,[69] where it was sought to have extradition arrangements declared unconstitutional because they did not provide for "specialty," which is a near universal practice in extradition treaties, Henchy J. stressed that Article 29.3 "was not enacted and is not to be interpreted in these Courts, as a statement of the absolute restriction of the legislative powers of the State by the generally recognised principles of international law. As the Irish version makes clear, the section merely provides that Ireland accepts the generally recognised principles of international law as a guide (*ina dtreoir*) in its relations with other states."[70] This analysis was reiterated by the Supreme Court on numerous occasions since.

At the time when *Ó Láighléis* was decided (December 1958), however, individuals were not regarded as the subjects of international law and, for that reason alone, Article 29.3 could not be of assistance to them in the courts. Further, at that time there were no generally recognised principles of international law that conferred rights on individuals; principles such as diplomatic immunity and *pacta sunt servanda* conferred rights only on States and, consequently, made Article 29.3 even more redundant for individuals. But at present, individuals are regarded as having certain rights (as well as duties) under international law.[71] Further, there are now generally recognised principles of international law that confer rights on them, such as the principle of equality before the law, acknowledged in the *South West Africa case (2nd*

---

[66] *Id.* at p.124.
[67] [1960] I.R. 125.
[68] *Id.* at p.124.
[69] [1966] I.R. 183.
[70] *Id.* at p.190.
[71] See generally, A. Cassese, *supra*, n.50, pp.77 *et seq.*

Phase)[72] and, arguably, that persons should not be extradited to face the death sentence and that children should not be extradited in certain circumstances. In contrast, the "specialty" rule in *Summers Jennings'* case is not one that confers rights on individuals but is a customary right enjoyed by sending states in extradition arrangements. Consequently, the international law foundations for *Ó Láighléis* no longer exist. If the Oireachtas passed an Act that contravened an individual's rights under the general principles of international law, it would seem that the Act must be declared unconstitutional because Article 15.4 prohibits the enactment of a law which is "repugnant to ... *any* provision of the Constitution" (other than the "directive principles" in Article 45). In 1973 the Irish judges and counsel who contributed to the *Law Enforcement Commission Report*[73] came to a different conclusion from that in *Ó Láighléis*. Dealing with the question of whether the Constitution would permit enactment of a law that provides for the extradition of political offenders, Walsh J., Henchy J., Doyle SC, and Quigley BL, concluded that they "cannot advise that the Government of Ireland could legally enter into any agreement or that the legislature could validly enact any legislation affecting its relations with other states which would be in breach of the generally recognised principles of international law. For so long as these generally recognised principles forbid the extradition of .... political offen(ders) these members cannot advise that any agreement or legislation designed to produce this result would be valid."[74]

However, in *Kavanagh v. Governor of Mountjoy Prison*,[75] the Supreme Court rejected the contention that, because the international general principle of equality before the law conferred rights on individuals against States, in virtue of Article 29.3, that principle (as applied in a decision of the UN Human Rights Committee) was binding on the State. For the Court, Fennelly J. identified the "essential reliefs" being sought as quashing the plaintiff's conviction (which the UNHRC had found to contravene Article 26 of the Covenant) and a declaration that section 47(2) of the Offences Against the State Act 1937 was invalid, as contravening Article 29.3. But the plaintiff alternatively sought his early release and/or compensation. What was found to be fatal to his case was the words "its rule of conduct in its relations with other States." It was held that "[i]t is patent that this provision confers no rights on individuals" and that "[n]o single word in the section even arguably expresses an intention to confer rights capable of being invoked by individuals."[76]

It was argued for the plaintiff that, because in the *Crotty* case the Court invalidated measures that contravened Articles 1 and 6.1 of the Constitution, neither of which in terms purport to confer rights on individuals, and since

---

[72] [1966] I.C.J.R. 300.
[73] Prl. 3832.
[74] At p.42 (para.68).
[75] [2002] 3 I.R. 97.
[76] *Id.* at p.126. *Cf. R. v. Lyons* [2002] 3 W.L.R. 1562.

Article 15.4 condemns any law "repugnant to ... *any* provision of the Constitution", there no longer was good reason to conclude that individuals could never enforce Article 29.3. It further was argued that, by adhering to the UN Covenant and to the UNHRC mechanism for resolving disputes about compliance with the Covenant, Ireland has pledged to other states that it will respect rights conferred by the Covenant on Irish nationals and others; that failure to respect those rights was a departure from the "rule of conduct" referred to in Article 29.3. Fennelly J. described Article 15.2 as an obstacle to incorporating the international obligation. But this case was not an instance of some purported legislature pretending to enact a law. If Article 29.3 permits persons to enforce certain international law rights, it was argued that Article 15.2 cannot stand in the way. Similarly with Article 29.6; it is concerned with the automatic domestic effect of all categories of treaties but, it was argued, where Article 29.3 has the effect as just described, it then takes precedence as a *lex specialis*. None of these contentions were addressed by the court.

Relying heavily on *Kavanagh*, in *Horgan v. An Taoiseach*[77] Kearns J. held that because Article 29.1.3 contains merely "statements of principles or guidelines rather than binding rules on the Executive", in other words was an "aspirational or declaratory provision which cannot be made the subject matter of binding legal norms", it does not "impose binding public law obligations on the Executive towards its own citizens",[78] at least in the conduct of foreign affairs. Consequently, the courts were powerless to intervene in how the U.S. authorities were assisted by the State in the 2003 Iraq war, even if that assistance contravened the international law rules concerning neutrality.[79]

Legitimate expectation

In recent years there has evolved the doctrine of "legitimate expectation" in administrative law[80] under which, where a public authority leads a person to believe that it will follow a particular course of conduct, it can then be compelled to adopt that course even though, as a matter of strict law, an aggrieved individual has no right to enforce the expectation in question. The basis of this doctrine is fairness to the individual but, in appropriate circumstances, the public authority may be released from complying with the expectation in question. How broad and deep this principle is remains to be determined, such as when does it apply to "substantive" as opposed to procedural expectations, is there a distinction between duties not to act in a certain way as opposed to

---

[77] [2003] 2 I.L.R.M. 357.

[78] *Id.* at pp.397–398.

[79] Kearns J. also rejected the contention that the State had "participated" in that war, contrary to Article 28.3.1 of the Constitution.

[80] See generally, H. Delany, *Judicial Review of Administrative Action* (2001), Chap.4.

positive action, and the circumstances in which courts will permit expectations to be resiled from.

Many foreign jurisdictions that have a "dualist" legal tradition, notwithstanding in appropriate cases require public authorities to respect legitimate expectations created by international treaties the State has ratified but has not (or not fully) implemented. There are decisions of the Australian,[81] New Zealand,[82] English[83] and Hong Kong[84] courts to this effect, principally with regard to the UN Conventions on the Rights of the Child and on the Status of Refugees. In *Fakih v. Minister for Justice*[85] O'Hanlon J. held that a letter sent in 1985 by a senior civil servant to a representative of the UN Commissioner for Refugees, regarding the procedures that would be followed in refugee applications, created a legitimate expectation that those procedures would be adhered to, which the courts would enforce notwithstanding *Ó Láighléis*. This analysis appears to have been endorsed by the Supreme Court in another refugee case, *Gutrani v. Governor Training Unit*.[86]

In the light of these developments, it was further contended in *Kavanagh v. Governor of Mountjoy Prison*[87] that the State's adherence to the UN Covenant and to its First Protocol's mechanism for determining individual complaints gave rise to a legitimate expectation that, where the UNHRC found that the State had contravened the Covenant and in consequence was obliged to remedy that breach, appropriate steps would be taken to provide a remedy. Although Fennelly J. for the Supreme Court said that what the plaintiff there sought "in essence" was to have his conviction by the Special Criminal Court invalidated, he also sought, *inter alia*, a direction that he be released from the remainder of his sentence, as well as compensation. It was held that the legitimate expectation doctrine could not be relied on to have the conviction quashed, in view of Article 29.6, without any reference to the other remedies being sought. While the Court was prepared to assume that by entering into an international agreement, the State may create a legitimate expectation that its agencies will "respect its terms," it "could not accept such an obligation so as to affect either the provision of a statute or the judgment of the courts without coming into conflict with the Constitution."[88]

---

[81] *Minister of State v. Teoh*, 183 C.L.R. 273 (1995).
[82] *Tavita v. Minister of Immigration* [1994] 2 N.Z.L.R. 257.
[83] *R. v. Uxbridge Magistrates Court, ex p. Adimi* [2001] Q.B. 667.
[84] *Chan v. Director of Immigration*, 40 I.L.M. 88 (2001).
[85] [1993] 2 I.R. 406.
[86] [1993] 2 I.R. 427.
[87] [2002] 3. I.R. 97.
[88] *Id.* at p.129.

Immunities

For centuries accredited diplomats, foreign heads of state and foreign states as such have enjoyed immunity from being sued or being prosecuted in the receiving state or other state, as the case may be. More recently, similar immunities have been conferred on international organizations and their agents. Immunity from suit for accredited diplomats is provided for in the Diplomatic Relations and Immunities Act 1967, under which several international treaties are given the force of law in the State, notably the Vienna Convention on Diplomatic Relations.[89] Article 31(1) of the first of these Conventions provides for diplomatic immunity; that "a diplomatic agent shall enjoy immunity from the criminal ... and [the] civil and administrative jurisdiction, except in (certain cases)." But the sending state may waive a diplomat's immunity and it does not extend to the sending state's own criminal and civil jurisdiction. Article 105 of the United Nations Charter confers immunity on the UN and its representatives in all member states. Under a protocol to the Treaty Establishing the European Community, as amended, members of the European Parliament and the property and personnel of the various EC institutions are afforded a variety of immunities. Ireland has not ratified the European Convention on Sovereign Immunity.[90]

Ireland does not possess legislation, along the lines of that in several countries, giving immunity to foreign states and state agencies as such. In recent years the trend has been to considerably restrict those immunities, for instance in Britain, Canada and in the United States of America.[91] On several occasions, however, the Supreme Court has declined to curtail that immunity in any respect and has held it to be a complete defence to claims for deceit[92] and for unfair dismissal.[93] In *McElhinney v. Williams*,[94] where the plaintiff claimed that he had been assaulted by an on-duty British soldier who accidentally happened to be in County Donegal, the Court rejected the contention that the principles in *Byrne v. Ireland*[95] prevented recognition of this immunity in those circumstances. That was notwithstanding that a similar immunity would not be afforded in the British courts if it was claimed that an on-duty Irish soldier had assaulted someone in Britain. On account of Article 29.3's reference to the "generally accepted principles of international law", Hamilton C.J. concluded that "the State should not be concerned with the

---

[89] Of April 18, 1961, 500 U.N.T.S. 95. See generally, E. Denza, *Diplomatic Law* (2nd ed. 1998).

[90] Of May 16, 1972, E.T.S. No. 74.

[91] See generally, H. Fox, *The Law of State Immunity* (2002).

[92] *Schmidt v. Home Secretary* [1997] 2 I.R. 121.

[93] *Government of Canada v. Employment Appeals Tribunals* [1992] 2 I.R. 484.

[94] [1995] 3 I.R. 382; *infra*, p.301.

[95] [1972] I.R. 241.

attitude of other States with regard to similar immunities."[96] In other words, it is permissible for a State to claim sovereign immunity in the Irish courts in circumstances where that State rejects the very same immunity if claimed in its own courts; a State whose legislation contravenes a rule of international law is nevertheless entitled to assert that very rule in other States' courts. A challenge to this decision, contending that it contravened Ireland's obligations under Article 6(1) of the European Convention on Human Rights, was rejected by the Strasbourg Court.[97]

In another case decided at the same time, that Court held that this Article did not bar immunity claims by a State which was being sued for damages for torture.[98] The House of Lords in the *Pinochet* case[99] held that a former head of a foreign State (Chile), who at the time was not an accredited diplomat, was not entitled to immunity against being prosecuted for torture allegedly carried out under his instructions. In contrast, the ICJ has held that a serving Foreign Affairs Minister of a State (the Congo) was immune from being prosecuted in Belgium for torture.[100]

Certain decisions made by foreign public authorities cannot be challenged in the Irish courts notwithstanding the direct impact they may have on persons in the State. In *Adams v. D.P.P.*[101] the Supreme Court held that a direction made by the British Home Secretary, on foot of an Irish statutory instrument, was not reviewable, on the grounds that his decision-making power in this regard derived from the law of the UK and not from that instrument.

EXTRA-TERRITORIALITY

Three principal questions arise with regard to the Constitution and the issue of extra-territoriality, *viz.* the extent to which the Constitution creates obligations on the State with regard to persons, property and events outside the State; the extent to which the State is authorised by legislation to regulate individuals' affairs beyond the State the extent to which the acts of foreign agencies and tribunals will be given recognition in the State.

Ambit of the Constitution

Practically no judicial guidance exists on the question of whether or to what

---

[96] [1995] 3 I.R. 382 at p.405.
[97] *McElhinney v. Ireland* 34 E.H.R.R. 322 (2002).
[98] *Al Adsani v. United Kingdom* 34 E.H.R.R. 273 (2002).
[99] *R. v. Bow Street Magistrate, ex p. Pinochet Ugarte* [2001] 1 A.C. 147.
[100] *Democratic Republic of the Congo v. Belgium*, 41 I.L.M. 536 (2002)
[101] [2001] 1 I.R. 47.

extent the Constitution imposes obligations on the State with regard to persons, property and events situate abroad.[102] Case law in the United States holds that its Constitution has a very limited extra-territorial reach, although some of the arguable foreign violations of constitutional rights in those cases would be remediable in Ireland under the "abuse of process" principle.

"Long Arm" jurisdiction

To what extent can the Oireachtas regulate what happens beyond the land, sea and air territory of the State, *i.e.* outside of the 26 southern counties and the adjacent islands, seas and air space? This question requires to be answered on three levels. To begin with practicalities: the State is virtually powerless to regulate most of what occurs abroad simply because most persons abroad would ignore Irish rules that sought to apply to them. However, it is possible to require persons who are in or who come to Ireland to account for what they have done abroad, either by way of a criminal prosecution or by means of a civil action. Next, there is the issue of whether the regulation in question by its terms applies to the extra-territorial situation in question. There is a well established principle of statutory construction that laws, especially those that impose burdens on individuals, do not apply outside the jurisdiction except where they expressly or by clear implication manifest a contrary intention.[103] Assuming the Act is so applicable, the question then arises as to whether it complies with international law and comes within the State's legislative competence.

Legislative competence

One of the amendments made following the conclusion of the "Belfast Agreement" of April 10, 1998, was to adopt Article 29.8, which expressly authorises extra-territorial prescription; that "[t]he State may exercise extra-territorial jurisdiction in accordance with the generally recognised principles of international law." This removes any doubts there may be about the State's extra-territorial competence. Whether it (in conjunction with Article 29.3) also imposes a limit on that competence is debatable; the word "may" could be permissive or could mean "may only." In *Donegal Fuel & Supply Ltd. v. Londonderry Harbour Commissioners*,[104] which concerned financial obligations under an Act of 1847 affecting a pier in Donegal, Costello J. found that the Free State Oireachtas was competent to enact extra-territorial measures, subject to the general principles of international law. This would suggest that Article 29.8 embodies a similar restriction.

---

[102] *Cf. Attorney General v. "X"* [1992] 1 I.R. 1, where Costello J. granted an *ex parte* injunction forbidding a young girl in England from having an abortion there.

[103] F. Bennion, *Statutory Interpretation* (3rd ed., 1997), pp.283 *et seq.*

[104] *Donegal Fuel & Supply Co. v. Londonderry Harbour Commissioners* [1994] 1 I.R. 24.

With regard to non-criminal forms of extra-territorial regulation, there must be some significant connection between the subject matter of the regulation and the State that is extending its "long arm" to events taking place abroad, but the precise nature of these connections are unclear. In the *Donegal Fuel* case, the impugned measure was an obligation placed on the defendant, a public authority outside the State, to maintain the pier at Carrickrory, Co. Donegal, in good and adequate repair, to be funded out of taxes raised in Co. Derry. It was held that this contravened the general principles of public international law.

Extra-territorial offences

As regards criminal jurisdiction, under international law, a State is not permitted to punish persons for what they have done abroad unless those persons are its own nationals or the offence had some other significant connection with the State which seeks to impose the punishment;[105] for instance, where the offence has occurred on a ship or on an aircraft registered in that State, or the offence has damaged nationals of that State or was injurious to its national security. There are some offences, such as piracy, genocide and war crimes, which any State is permitted to punish. At common law, persons can only be convicted of offences which were committed by them within the State's own territory and not when the events took place abroad, even if the defendant is an Irish citizen. For these purposes, the State's territory is its land area, rivers, lakes, estuaries and bays, but not the territorial sea.[106] Where the legislature creates a new offence, in the absence of indications to the contrary, the prohibition is presumed not to apply to occurrences outside the State.[107] But the Oireachtas has created a substantial number of extra-territorial offences, the basic outlines of which can only be indicated here. Two related matters are the questions of what may be termed "trans-national" offences. *i.e.* where some ingredients of the offence occur abroad and others occur within the State[108] and, secondly, the question of "venue," *i.e.* precisely which court or courts have jurisdiction to try alleged offenders.[109]

In 1878 criminal jurisdiction in respect of indictable offences was extended to the territorial sea[110] and, according to s. 10(1) of the Maritime Jurisdiction

---

[105] See generally, I. Brownlie, *General Principles of International Law* (5th ed. 1998), Chap.15.

[106] *R. v. Keyn* (1876) 2 Ex. D. 63.

[107] *E.g. Swifte v. Swifte* [1910] 2 I.R. 140 and Bennion, *supra*, n.103.

[108] See generally, Hirst, "Jurisdiction Over Cross-Frontier Offences", 97 *L.Q.R.* 80 (1981) and Lew, "The Extraterritorial Jurisdiction of the English Courts", 27 *Int'l & Comp. L.Q.* 168 (1978).

[109] See generally, Williams, "Venue and the Ambit of the Criminal Law", 81 *L.Q.R.* 276, 395 (1965).

[110] Territorial Waters Jurisdiction Act 1878, 41 & 42 Vic. c.73.

Act 1959, which replaced the 1878 Act, "[e]very offence committed within the territorial seas or internal waters is an offence within the jurisdiction of the State and may be dealt with by a court of competent jurisdiction although committed on board or by means of a foreign ship and a person who commits such offence may be tried and punished accordingly." Section 3(1) of the Continental Shelf Act 1968, extends the State's criminal jurisdiction to occurrences at or near installations on the continental shelf. According to the first part of that section, "[a]ny act or omission which -(i) takes place on an installation in a designated area or any waters (near) such installation, and (ii) would, if taking place in the State, constitute an offence under the law of the State, shall be deemed for all purposes relating to the offence to take place in the State." Section 686(1) of the Merchant Shipping Act 1894,[111] extends the State's territory for the purposes of criminal jurisdiction to include what occurs on Irish ships and what Irish nationals do on foreign ships or in foreign ports: "[where] any person, being (an Irish) subject, is charged with having committed any offence on board any (Irish) ship on the high seas, or in any foreign port or harbour or on board any foreign ship to which he does not belong, or, not being an (Irish) subject, is charged with having committed any offence on board any (Irish) ship on the high seas, and that person is found within the jurisdiction of any (Irish) court …, that court shall have jurisdiction to try the offence …". Similar provision exists with respect to Irish aircraft; section 62(1) of Air Navigation and Transport Act 1936, provides that "any offence whatever committed on an (Irish) aircraft, shall, for the purpose of conferring jurisdiction, be deemed to have been committed in any place where the offender may for the time being be." The actual techniques used in these provisions to extend the State's criminal jurisdiction differ considerably, giving rise to some uncertainty about their precise effect.

There are numerous statutory provisions giving the State extra-territorial jurisdiction in respect of specific offences, such as section 9 of the Offences Against the Person Act 1861 (murder and manslaughter), section 57 of the same Act (bigamy), section 8 of the Perjury Act 1911, sections 2 and 3 of the Criminal Law Amendment Act 1885 (procuring women for the purposes of having sex, prostitution etc.), sections 4 and 20(3) of the Criminal Law (Jurisdiction) Act 1976, (explosives), section 31(11) of the Criminal Justice Act 1994 (money laundering) and also the provisions of the Sexual Offences (Jurisdiction) Act 1996, and the Criminal Justice (Theft and Fraud Offences) Act 2001. In the latter three instances, the circumstances must also constitute an offence under the law of the State where they occurred. Section 20 of the Misuse of Drugs Act 1977, creates an exceptionally extensive jurisdiction, in that it makes it an offence under Irish Law to become involved in the contravention of the drugs laws of any country where those laws correspond with the 1977 Act, as amended.

---

[111] 57 & 58 Vic. c.60.

Many extra-territorial offences have been created in order to give effect to international conventions to which the State is a party, for instance under the Genocide Act 1973 (genocide), the Geneva Conventions Acts 1962–98 (war crimes), the Air Traffic and Navigation Acts 1973–75 (aircraft hijacking and comparable acts), the Sea Pollution Acts 1991–99 (sea pollution), the Chemical Weapons Act 1997, the Criminal Justice (United Nations Conventions Against Torture) Act 2000, the Criminal Justice (Safety of United Nations Workers) Act 2000. The main provisions of the Criminal Law (Jurisdiction) Act 1976 were passed in order to get around the "political offence" exception to extradition, especially with reference to the violence taking place in Northern Ireland at the time.

Assisting the application of foreign laws

Over the last quarter of a century there has been an enormous increase in the range of measures and extent to which States are prepared to enforce, within their own borders, the rules and regulations of foreign States, usually on the basis of reciprocity.[112] In the past the principal example was extradition but in recent times cooperation has extended to other aspects of criminal law, fiscal affairs, enforcing foreign civil judgments and awards, and assistance in securing evidence for use in foreign investigations and procedures.

Courts in most states will enforce judgments rendered by courts in other countries provided that those judgments satisfy various procedural and substantive requirements. But in the absence of express legislative authority to apply them, foreign penal and revenue laws, and judgments that conflict with Irish public policy, will not be enforced in this country. Thus in *Peter Buchanan Ltd v. McVey*,[113] when a Scottish company that owed substantial moneys to the Scottish Revenue went into liquidation, the Revenue there appointed a liquidator, who then sought to recover from the defendant in Ireland money he had taken from the company that it ought to have paid in taxes. It was clear from the evidence that the liquidator "worked in every respect hand in glove" with the Revenue authorities in an effort to "chase the tax [and t]hat was the task for which he had been selected."[114] To permit him to prosecute proceedings in the State aimed in substance at recovering the tax owed to the Scottish authorities contravened the long recognised principle that one State's courts will not enforce another State's revenue laws, whether directly or indirectly. As Kingsmill Moore J. explained, "enforcement must not depend merely on the form in which the claim is made. It is not a question whether the

---

[112] See generally, D. McClean, *International Cooperation in Civil and Criminal Matters* (2002).
[113] [1954] I.R. 89.
[114] *Id.* at p.95.

plaintiff is a foreign State or the representative of a foreign State or its revenue authority. In every case, the substance of the claim must be scrutinised and if it then appears that it is really a suit brought for the purpose of collecting the debts of a foreign revenue, it must be rejected."[115] Costello J. followed this principle in *Bank of Ireland v. Meeneghan*,[116] where in the course of a prosecution by the English Revenue, an order was made against the first-named defendant freezing money he had in a bank account in the State. It was held that this order could not operate within the State so as to prevent him from withdrawing his money from that account, because the only way that order could have legal effect in Ireland is by having it enforced in the courts here.[117] However, by virtue of regulations adopted in 2002,[118] tax liabilities to other EC Member States can be enforced in the State as if the tax in question were owed to the Minister for Finance.

Many countries are parties to reciprocal bilateral and also multilateral treaties governing recognition and enforcement of judgments rendered in the State parties' courts. Ireland is a party to and has implemented several such agreements, principally the Brussels Convention on Jurisdiction and the Enforcement of Foreign Judgments of 1968,[119] as amended, the Lugano Convention on the same subject matter of 1988,[120] the New York Convention on the Recovery of Maintenance of 1956[121], the Hague Convention on the Civil Aspects of Child Abduction of 1980[122] the Luxembourg Convention on the Recognition and Enforcement of Decisions Concerning Custody of Children of 1980,[123] the Rome Convention on Procedures for the Recovery of Maintenance Payments of 1990,[124] the Hague Convention on Parental Responsibility and the Protection of Children of 1996.[125] The recognition of foreign divorces is affected by Article 41.3.3 of the Constitution, as well as legislation and an EC Directive.[126]

In *Reilly, Re*,[127] which concerned provisions that purported to give force

---

[115] *Id.*, at p.107. Similarly, *Attorney General of Canada v. R.J. Reynolds Tobacco Holdings Inc.*, 268 F. 3d 103 (2001).

[116] [1994] 3 I.R. 111.

[117] Cf. *Larkins v. National Union of Mineworkers* [1985] I.R. 671.

[118] European Communities (Mutual Assistance etc. re Taxes and Other Measures) Regulations, S.I. No. 462 of 2002.

[119] Of September 27, 1968, which has been replaced by E.C. Regulation No. 44 of 2001 on Jurisdiction and the Recognition and Enforcement of Judgments in Civil and Commercial Matters, O.J. No. L12/1 (2002).

[120] Of September 16, 1988, O.J. No. L319/9 (1988).

[121] Of June 20, 1956, 268 U.N.T.S. 32.

[122] Of October 25, 1980, 1343 U.N.T.S. 89.

[123] Of May 20, 1980, Eur. T.S. No. 105.

[124] Of November 6, 1990.

[125] Of October 19, 1996.

[126] *Infra*, p.719.

[127] [1942] I.R. 416.

in Ireland to orders made by English courts in bankruptcy proceedings, the Supreme Court held that the Constitution does not prevent the Oireachtas from enacting measures along these lines. According to Meredith J., "[i]t is very convenient that certain reciprocal rights and powers should exist between specified authorities in different countries, and the recognition of such rights and powers has never been regarded as a derogation of status as they only exist by agreement and can be repealed immediately. Reciprocal recognition of adjudications in bankruptcy is an instance."[128] This point was considered again in *A.C.W. v. Ireland*,[129] concerning the Child Abduction and Enforcement of Custody Orders Act 1991, which gives effect to the 1980 Hague Convention on Child Abduction. Under this, when a child is wrongly taken from one State-party to this Convention to another such State, the authorities in the latter are required to return the child and can obtain court orders to this end. It was contended that the effect of this was to deprive the Irish courts of jurisdiction to safeguard the constitutional rights of the child but, as Keane J. pointed out, section 3 of the 1991 Act requires the courts to give paramountcy to the welfare of the individual child, thereby enabling his rights to be fully protected.

It also was contended in *A.C.W.* that the effect of the 1991 Act was to deprive the Irish courts of jurisdiction to determine who is entitled to custody of a child, including one who is an Irish citizen, as the underlying premise of the Hague Convention is that issues of this nature are to be determined entirely by the courts of the State from where the child has been unlawfully taken. According to Keane J. this "is a common feature of conventions of this nature and is in accordance with well-established principles of international law"[130] and that "[g]iving effect in legislation to provisions of such conventions is clearly in accordance with Ireland's acceptance [in Article 29.3] of the generally recognised principles of international law and in harmony with one of the aims of the Constitution, as stated in the Preamble, to establish concord with other nations."[131] Apart entirely from this Article, it was held that it is within the competence of the Oireachtas "to give effect in domestic law to a convention which conferred jurisdiction in cases with an international dimension to foreign courts with the object of protecting the interests of children in this and other countries."[132]

Extradition is the practice of delivering up to the police authorities in other countries persons who are in the State but who are wanted for prosecution or punishment in respect of alleged crimes committed in the requesting countries.[133] Extradition usually exists on a reciprocal basis and its constitutional

---

[128] *Id.* at p.460. *Cf.* Bankruptcy Act 1988, s.142.
[129] [1994] 3 I.R. 232.
[130] *Id.* at p.242.
[131] *Id.* at p.243.
[132] *Id.* at p.244.
[133] *Infra*, p.336.

justification is similar to that for enforcing the judgments and orders of foreign courts. Whether the Constitution permits extradition to a state which does not afford reciprocal facilities to Ireland has never been determined; dicta in *Re Reilly*[134] suggest that reciprocity is not an essential feature of international judicial co-operation.

Section 51 of the Criminal Justice Act 1994 is a mechanism whereby *inter alia* the police authorities of a foreign State may request the Minister for Justice to obtain evidence they seek for the purpose of a criminal investigation. If the Minister accedes to this request, the matter is then sent to a District Court Judge for the evidence in question to be taken. It was held by the Supreme Court in *de Gotardi v. Smithwick*[135] that the hearing before the District Judge is "not the administration of Justice"[136] and, accordingly, the public may be excluded from it. It does not appear to have been contended there that, since under the separation of powers doctrine the function of the courts is to administer justice, conferring an exclusively investigatory function on the courts is unconstitutional. In subsequent proceedings between the same parties,[137] McGuinness J. held that witnesses in these applications do not have a general right to silence but, where they refuse to answer questions put to them, there is no power to punish them for contempt if they refuse to answer.[138]

---

[134] [1942] I.R. 416.
[135] [1999] 4 I.R. 223.
[136] *Id.* at p.229.
[137] [2000] 2 I.R. 553.
[138] *de Gotardi v. Smithwick (No.2)* [2000] 2 I.R. 553.

CHAPTER 11

The European Community/ European Union

In 1951 six Western European states (France, Germany, Italy, Belgium, The Netherlands and Luxembourg) established the European Coal and Steel Community[1] with a view to rationalising their coal and steel industries. Six years later, the same States concluded the Euratom Treaty,[2] which established a common mechanism for dealing with questions of atomic energy. At the same time they concluded what is commonly referred to as the Treaty of Rome, which established the European Economic Community.[3] In 1965, in what is known as the Merger Treaty,[4] those States agreed that these three institutions should have a single system of government, i.e. one Commission, one Council and one Assembly, and these became the European Communities (EC). Under the 1951 Treaty, the Coal and Steel Community was to last for 50 years and it has since ceased to exist.

In 1972 the Constitution was amended, incorporating what is Article 29.4.3, authorising the State to become part of these Communities and giving legal precedence to measures adopted by them or enacted in order to comply with the obligations of membership. By the Treaty of Accession of 22 January 1972,[5] Ireland became a member of the EC as from December 31, 1972, along with the United Kingdom and Denmark. Membership of the EC was subsequently extended by Treaties of Accession with Greece (1979), with Spain and Portugal (1985), with Sweden, Finland, Iceland, Austria and Liechtenstein (1992). At the time of writing, several Eastern European States have ratified further Treaties of Accession (Czech Republic,Cyprus, Estonia, Hungary, Latvia, Lithuania, Malta, Poland, Slovenia and Slovakia).

Originally conceived as a common market, the very nature as well as composition of the Communities has transformed radically to such extent that they now have many of the features of a federal State. The original treaties of 1957 were amended significantly by the Single European Act of 1986,[6] the

---

[1] Treaty of Rome, April 18, 1951, 261 UNTS 141.
[2] Treaty of Rome, March 25, 1957, 298 UNTS 3.
[3] Treaty of Rome, March 25, 1957, 298 UNTS 11.
[4] Signed in Rome, April 8, 1965, O.J. No. 152/2 (1967).
[5] O.J. L73, special ed. March 27, 1972.
[6] Of February 17, 1986, O.J. L169/1 (1987).

Maastricht Agreement of 1992,[7] the Treaty of Amsterdam of 1997[8] and the Treaty of Nice of 2001.[9] It was necessary to further amend Article 29.4 of the Constitution in 1987, 1992, 1998 and 2002 to give effect to each of these treaties, as well as the Community Patent Agreement of 1989. At present the Member States are in the process of negotiating a new constitution for this political arrangement.

The European Communities (EC) consists of the institutions and competences of the Economic Community and Euratom, established in 1957, along with the dissolved Coal and Steel Community. Under the Maastricht Agreement, what technically is a new entity was brought into being, namely the European Union (EU). It comprises the very same institutions and Member States. According to Article 1 of this Agreement, officially known as the Treaty on European Union, the Union is "founded on the European Communities, supplemented by the policies and forms of cooperation established by this Treaty. Its task [is] to organise, in a manner demonstrating consistency and solidarity, relations between the Member States and between their peoples." In law there are two communities, with one set of institutions, and their powers vary depending on which treaty is the basis for their actions. As described by the author of a leading book on the subject, the EU "may be regarded as the legal and political concept which gives expression to this underlying unity."[10]

OBJECTIVES AND INSTITUTIONS

The objectives of the EC are predominantly economic and are set out in Articles 2 and 3 of the EC Treaty (as amended) as follows:

"1. For the purposes set out in Article 2, the activities of the Community shall include, as provided in this Treaty and in accordance with the timescale set out therein:

(a) the prohibition, as between Member States, of customs duties and quantitative restrictions on the import and export of goods, and of all other measures having equivalent effect;

(b) a common commercial policy;

(c) an internal market characterised by the abolition, as between Member States, of obstacles to the free movement of goods, persons, services and capital;

---

[7] Of February 7, 1992, O.J. No. C224/1 (1992).

[8] Of October 2, 1997, O.J. No. C340/3 (1997).

[9] Of February 26, 2001, O.J. No. C80/1 (2001).

[10] T.C. Hartley, *The Foundations of European Community Law* (5th ed., 2003), p.9. See generally, Hartley, "The Constitutional Foundations of the European Union", 117 *L.Q.R.* 225 (2001).

(d) measures concerning the entry and movement of persons as provided for in Title IV;

(e) a common policy in the sphere of agriculture and fisheries;

(f) a common policy in the sphere of transport;

(g) a system ensuring that competition in the internal market is not distorted;

(h) the approximation of the laws of Member States to the extent required for the functioning of the common market;

(i) the promotion of coordination between employment policies of the Member States with a view to enhancing their effectiveness by developing a coordinated strategy for employment;

(j) a policy in the social sphere comprising a European Social Fund;

(k) the strengthening of economic and social cohesion;

(l) a policy in the sphere of the environment;

(m) the strengthening of the competitiveness of Community industry;

(n) the promotion of research and technological development;

(o) encouragement for the establishment and development of trans-European cultures of the Member States;

(p) a contribution to the attainment of a high level of health protection;

(q) a contribution to education and training of quality and to the flowering of the cultures of the Member States;

(r) a policy in the sphere of development cooperation;

(s) the association of the overseas countries and territories in order to increase trade and promote jointly economic and social development;

(t) a contribution to the strengthening of consumer protection;

(u) measures in the spheres of energy, civil protection and tourism.

2. In all the activities referred to in this Article the Community shall aim to eliminate inequalities, and to promote equality, between men and women."

Formerly, in order to achieve any of these objectives, there had to be unanimity among the several Member States. But with the expansion in membership, systems of qualified majorities were adopted for many issues. A degree of flexibility in the scheme of things exists, with States being permitted to "opt out" of certain aspects of the arrangements — most notably the United Kingdom and Denmark with regard to the common currency.

The objectives of the EU are political as well as economic and are set out in Article 2 of the Maastricht Treaty as follows:

"– to promote economic and social progress and a high level of employment and to achieve balanced and sustainable development, in particular through the creation of an area without internal frontiers, through the strengthening of economic and social cohesion and through the establishment of economic and monetary union, ultimately including a single currency in accordance with the provisions of this Treaty;

- to assert its identity on the international scene, in particular through the implementation of a common foreign and security policy including the progressive framing of a common defence policy, which might lead to a common defence, in accordance with the provisions of Article 17;
- to strengthen the promotion of the rights and interests of the nationals of its Member States through the introduction of a citizenship of the Union;
- to maintain and develop the Union as an area of freedom, security and justice, in which the free movement of persons is assured in conjunction with appropriate measures with respect to external border controls, asylum, immigration and the prevention and combating of crime;
- to maintain in full the *acquis communautaire* and build on it with a view to considering to what extent the policies and forms of cooperation introduced by this Treaty may need to be revised with the aim of ensuring the effectiveness of the mechanisms and the instructions of the Community."

Title V of this Treaty provides for a "common foreign and security policy" and Title VI provides for cooperation in "criminal matters." Most major decisions under these headings must be unanimous, in that each Member State wields a veto.

    In order to secure the various objects set out in these treaties, several institutions are established, principally, the Commission, the Council, the Parliament and the Court of Justice. There also is an Economic and Social Committee, a Committee of the Regions, a Court of First Instance and a Court of Auditors.

The Commission

The European Commission comprises nominees of each Member State, the larger States having two nominees for the present. But Commissioners are required to be independent of their own State and they must not represent their national interest while in that office; they "shall in the general interest of the Community, be completely independent in the performance of their duties."[11]

---

[11] Art.211(2) of the EC Treaty.

It takes decisions by way of simple majority vote but always endeavours to secure as much unanimity as is reasonably possible. All policy initiatives come from it for consideration by the Parliament and ultimate acceptance or rejection by the Council. Through its *fonctionnaries*, it oversees implementation of policies that have been adopted.

The Council

Each Member State's interests are catered for principally in the European Council, which contains representatives of their Governments. Its principal function is to determine which policy initiatives from the Commission should be implemented in the form of binding law, as an EC Regulation or an EC Directive. Many of its decisions are taken by way of qualified majority, with votes weighted depending on the size of each member's population but this weighting is slanted somewhat in favour of the smaller States. In 2003, Germany, Italy and the United Kingdom each had ten votes, and Ireland, Denmark and Finland each had three votes, and Luxembourg only two.

The Parliament

Since 1976 the European Parliament, which sits in Brussels and also in Strasbourg, has consisted of representatives who were directly elected from each of the Member States. Unlike most parliaments, it is not the ultimate arbiter of whether legislative proposals should or should not have the force of law; that is the Council's prerogative. But the Parliament is entitled to be consulted about proposed measures, by way of a reference from the Council for its opinion on every intended Regulation or Directive. The Commission is accountable to the Parliament, which can remove the entire body of the Commissioners from office by way of a vote of censure. But individual Commissioners are not vulnerable in this manner. Proposed sanctions against any Member State require the Parliament's approval, as does the admission of any new Member State. Elections to it are regulated by the European Parliament Elections Acts 1997–2002.

The Court

The European Court of Justice sits at Luxembourg, with jurisdiction over a considerable variety of disputes affecting the Communities. As well as hearing cases brought by the Commission against a Member State or by one such State against another, for breach of its Community obligations, about half of the Court's workload consists of dealing with requests under Article 234 of the

EC Treaty for "preliminary rulings" by the ordinary courts in each Member State. Judges of the Court are nominated by each of the Member States. There is also a Court of First instance, which deals with certain specialised fields.

Legislation

There are three principal types of what may be described as EC legislation, which, under Article 29.4.10 of the Constitution, take precedence over Acts of the Oireachtas and measures adopted under them.

Treaty provisions

Although much of the EC Treaty consists of rules regarding institutions, policy formulation and goals, it contains several very specific and unambiguous requirements addressed to the EC world at large; for instance, Article 141 on equal pay for equal work, as between men and women. Stipulations of this nature have been held to impose legally enforceable obligations and will result in the beneficiary of the rule in question obtaining legal redress against any party to whom they are addressed.[12] That party may be a private individual or body, as well as a Member State or organ or agency of the State.

Regulations

Community policies are implemented principally by way of Regulations, adopted by the Council after having consulted with the Parliament. According to Article 249 of the EC Treaty, a regulation "shall have general application. It shall be binding in its entirety and directly applicable in all Member States."

Directives

The other principal technique for implementing Community policies is Directives, also adopted by the Council after having consulted with the Parliament. According to Article 249 of the EC Treaty, a Directive "shall be binding, as to the result to be achieved, upon each Member State to which it is addressed, but shall leave to the national authorities the choice of form and methods." In other words, unlike Regulations, Directives are not intended to have automatic effect in the Member States but require those Governments to adopt discrete measures under their own law-making processes to give effect to their contents, for instance by passing an Act or making a statutory instrument. States have a discretion as to the exact "form and methods" they will use in order to render effective what Directives require of them.

---

[12] *Defrenne v. SABENA* (Case 43/75) [1976] E.C.R. 455.

Joint actions and common positions

Decisions made by the Union take the form of "joint actions" or "common positions", under Articles 14 and 15 of the Maastricht Treaty. In the case of the former they "commit Member States in the position they adopt"; in the case of the latter, those States "shall ensure that their national positions shall conform" to them.

IMPLEMENTING EC MEASURES

Because membership of the EC and later of the EU would involve a major concession of national sovereignty to a supra-national regional organisation, it was necessary to amend the Constitution on several occasion, as described above. That getting these amendments through was essential rather than an exercise in good government was confirmed by the Supreme Court in *Crotty v. An Taoiseach*,[13] which held that the State could not ratify the Single European Act of 1986 without explicit constitutional authority to do so.

In order to give full effect in Irish law to the EC Treaties and measures adopted by the EC institutions, the European Communities Act 1972, was passed. By virtue of section 2 of this Act, "[f]rom the 1st day of January 1973, the treaties governing the European Communities and the existing and future acts adopted by the institutions of those Communities shall be binding on the State and shall be part of the domestic law thereof under the conditions laid down in those treaties." The rationale for this was explained by Barrington J. in *Crotty* as follows:

"To make Ireland an effective member of [the EC] as of the 1st January 1973, it was necessary to make the Treaty part of the domestic law of Ireland. To achieve this it was necessary to pass an Act of the Oireachtas (i.e. the 1972 Act) pursuant to the provisions of Article 29.6 making the Treaty of Rome part of the domestic law of Ireland and giving the institutions of the Community a status in Irish domestic law. Had the Oireachtas not passed the European Communities Act 1972, Ireland might still have been a member of the Community in international law but it would have been in breach of its obligations in international law under the Treaty of Rome, and under the Treaty of Accession. This, however, would not have been a matter in relation to which the domestic courts of this country would have had any competence because the Treaty would not have been part of the domestic law."[14]

This Act has been amended on numerous occasions.

[13] [1987] I.R. 713.
[14] *Id.* at p.767. See generally, A. Collins and J. O'Reilly, *Civil Proceedings and the State* (2nd ed., 2003), Chap.10.

Community law applies within Ireland in four different ways. One is by way of legislation enacted by the Oireachtas to give effect to EC obligations, for instance, Part III (sections 18–27) of the Employment Equality Act 1998. Another is by way of the "statutory regulations" made by the Minister as provided for in the 1972 Act. Thirdly, Community Regulations are as effective in Ireland as are laws enacted by the Oireachtas. Finally those provisions of the EC Treaty and also of Directives which have "direct effect" have full force of law in the State; even though they are not embodied in an Act of the Oireachtas or an EC Regulation or a regulation made by the Minister under the 1972 Act, some provisions of the Treaty itself and also of Directives are immediately enforceable in the Irish courts. Which provisions in the Treaty and in Directives have "direct effect" is a complicated matter; oversimplifying the position, provisions that are clear and unambiguous, that are unconditional, and that are not dependent on any further action by the Member States can be directly enforceable in domestic law.

In order to make the incorporation of EC law into Irish law most effective, the 1972 Act empowers a Minister to make the necessary regulations,[15] which usually take the form of statutory instruments. It is provided that these regulations shall "have statutory effect"[16] but shall "not create an indictable offence."[17] These regulations may contain incidental and consequential provisions "repealing, amending or applying, with or without modification, other law exclusive of this Act."[18] A challenge to these provisions, on the grounds that they contravened the separation of powers, because they authorised adopting measures in the form of statutory instruments and not as primary legislation, was rejected by the Supreme Court in *Meagher v. Minister for Agriculture*.[19] On account of the large number and the diverse nature of EC measures that require domestic implementation, it was held that a broad authority of that nature was justified. But it was accepted there that, in principle, implementation of some particular measure could require an Act of the Oireachtas rather than subordinate legislation.

The issue that then arose in *Meagher* was whether the impugned parts of the statutory instrument there were invalid because they were not contained in an Act. Provisions in 1988 and 1990 statutory instruments, giving effect to certain EC Directives aimed at combating the use of "growth promoting" substances on cattle, were challenged on the grounds that they should have been contained in an Act. It was accepted by the plaintiff that the great bulk of those regulations were properly in that form, because they were expressly envisaged by the Directives, which contained the relevant "principles and

---

[15] 1972 Act, s.3.
[16] *Id.*, s.4, as amended by s.1 of the European Communities (Amendment) Act 1973.
[17] *Id.*, s.3(3).
[18] *Id.*, s.3(2).
[19] [1994] 1 I.R. 358.

policies;" in consequence, it was consistent with the separation of powers to give effect to them by way of statutory instrument. But, it was contended, two particular stipulations in the regulations were not warranted on this basis, namely authority to issue search warrants in order to search farms for proscribed substances and, secondly, permitting prosecutions to be brought in the District Court within two years (and not just six months) of the offence being committed. Because the Directives required the competent authorities to ensure that appropriate investigations are made, it was held that this could not be done "without creating a power to enable a compulsory search to be made of farms where animals are kept",[20] thus justifying the search warrants provision.

As for extending the period for bringing prosecutions to two years, this was held to be justified by the overriding obligation to ensure that the Directives were fully implemented. It was accepted that, by virtue of the Directives, breach of their requirements could be made criminal offences by way of a statutory instrument and not an Act. That being so, according to Blayney J., "it must follow logically that the implementation required in addition that the offences could be effectively prosecuted. So the regulations had to be in a form to enable this to be done and if it was necessary for this purpose to allow a period of two years, the Minister clearly had power to allow such a period."[21] Because the general rule for summary prosecutions was that they must commence within six months, unless the Act in question provides otherwise, and there was nothing in the Directives stipulating the relevant period, it was contended that the six months rule continued to apply unless it was amended by an Act. But it was held that such incidental amendments were expressly authorised by section 3(2) of the 1972 Act.

A similar challenge to provisions in a statutory instrument, giving effect to the EC Regulations on Milk Quotas, was rejected by the Supreme Court in *Maher v. Minister for Agriculture.*[22] Normally, Regulations are directly applicable in Irish law without the need for any indigenous implementing measure but, occasionally, Regulations leave certain aspects to be determined by the Member States themselves. Under the EC's Common Agriculture Policy, milk producers are guaranteed a minimum price for their milk, which eventually led to vast over-production of milk. In order to curb those, milk quotas were introduced in 1984, as a temporary measure but they remain in existence. These quotas were in a sense attached to the land. In order to deal with the problem of persons not actually involved in milk production holding quotas and also to regulate the circumstances in which quotas may be transferred, the EC adopted Regulations in 1999 giving effect to what is described as "*Agenda 2000.*" They conferred certain discretions on Member States as to how effect should be given to these changes. So far as the plaintiffs were concerned, the statutory

---

[20] *Id.* at p.358.
[21] *Ibid.*
[22] [2001] 2 I.R. 139.

instrument implementing the revised regime operated to deprive them of the quotas they owned.

Because the precise manner in which these changes were to be brought about was not set out in the EC Regulations, they contended that the new regime adopted by the State could only be put into effect by way of an Act of the Oireachtas. As Fennelly J. pointed out there, among the options expressly made available to Member States by the Regulations was to "break the link between land and milk quotas,"[23] which is what the statutory instrument did, subject to certain exceptions. In doing this, it was held, "the State is acting as a delegate of the Community in making the choice to separate land and milk quotas [and] the fact that Community regulations authorise the member states to exercise discretion does not take action of the latter kind outside the scope of the Community regime."[24]

In contrast, provisions of a 1998 statutory instrument giving effect to an EC Regulation on fisheries conservation were held to be invalid in *Browne v. Attorney General*[25] because they purported to create indictable offences. They were not made under the 1972 Act, which expressly prohibits regulations made under it from creating such offences. Instead, they were made under section 223A of the Fisheries Act 1959, which had been enacted in 1983; this authorises the Minister to adopt "measures of conservation of fish stocks and measures of rational exploitation of fisheries", but did not expressly authorise making contravention of these measures indictable offences. Nor did it contain any express stipulation or other indication that it was intended to be the vehicle for implementing EC measures. It was to be contrasted with section 224B of that Act, enacted at the same time, which authorised adopting measures to give effect to the EC's exclusive fishery limits, breach of which could be prosecuted on indictment; further, this power is declared to be "without prejudice to the generality of" section 3(1) of the 1972 Act. Consequently, the Supreme Court held that the 1998 S.I., insofar as it purported to create indictable offences was *ultra vires* section 233A of the 1959 Act because, on its true construction, this section had not been intended by the Oireachtas as a mechanism for giving effect to EC Regulations and Directives. Additionally, in 1972 the Oireachtas had adopted a firm rule that any such implementation measures should not create indictable offences except where primary legislation gave express authority to do so. According to Denham J., section 3(2) of the 1972 Act "recognises the significance of indictable offences and that they should be established by the Irish Parliament" and that "any statute purporting to give a power to the Minister to create an indictable offence should set out such power in plain and clear language."[26]

---

[23] *Id.* at p.257.
[24] *Id.* at pp.257–258.
[25] June 16, 2003, Supreme Court.
[26] At p.24.

SUPREMACY AND CONSTITUTION-PROOFING

Where EC law and the law of a Member State are in conflict, in particular, where the national measure in question is a provision of its written constitution, which of them takes precedence? There is nothing in the Treaties that says Community law shall prevail over national law. But it could be argued that, but virtue of Article 249 of the EC Treaty that renders Regulations directly applicable, these have a certain degree of supremacy.[27] It has been held by the European Court that Community law must always prevail over national law[28] but some Member States' own courts do not accept this as an unqualified proposition. In Germany, in Denmark and in Britain, it has been held that EC law has precedence only insofar as the national laws so permit.[29]

Provided that they are "necessitated by the obligations of membership", Article 29.4.10 of the Constitution grants the EC regime precedence over Irish law and even over the Constitution itself. According to it, "[n]o provision of this Constitution invalidates laws enacted, acts done or measures adopted by the State which are necessitated by the obligations of membership of the European Union or of the Communities, or prevents laws enacted, acts done or measures adopted by the [EU] or by the [EC] or by institutions thereof, or by bodies competent under the Treaties establishing the [EC], from having the force of law in the State." Whether this clause precludes amending the Constitution, in order to establish a somewhat different relationship between the State and the EC/EU, is debatable; it would appear to be subject to Article 46, which permits "[a]ny provision of the" Constitution to be amended in a referendum carried out in the manner stated there.

Four principal questions arise with reference to Article 29.4.10. One of these, which was considered in the *Meagher*, *Maher* and *Browne* cases, named what measures are called for by an EC Regulation or Directive with regard to the actual mode of implementation; in particular, whether by way of an Act of the Oireachtas or a statutory instrument. The Supreme Court takes a generous view of what being so "necessitated" involves. But enforcing an EC standard by making its breach an indictable offence requires unambiguous statutory authorisation.

There also arose in *Maher* the question of whether the substance of an EC requirement was unconstitutional; whether the manner in which the plaintiffs' lands were separated from their former milk quotas contravened the

---

[27] *Costa v. E.N.E.L.* (Case 6/64) [1963] E.C.R. 585 at p.594.

[28] *Simmenthal* case (Case 106/77) [1978] E.L.R. 629. See generally, Hartley, *supra,* n.10 at pp.191 *et seq.* and K. Peter, *Establishing the Supremacy of European Law* (2001).

[29] *Brunner v. European Union Treaty* [1994] 1 C.M.L.R. 57, *Carlsen v. Rasmussen* [1999] 3 C.M.L.R. 854 and *Thorburn v. Sunderland District Council* [2003] Q.B. 151. See generally, Hartley, *supra,* n.10, Chap.8 and Hartley, "International Law and the Law of the European Union – A Reasessment", 72 *Brit. Y.B. Int'l L.* 1 (2001).

Constitution's private property guarantee. In the event, it was concluded that this guarantee would not have been infringed[30] and, consequently, the issues of whether the measure was so "necessitated" and of supremacy did not arise. A similar conclusion was reached by Murphy J. in *Lawlor v. Minister for Agriculture*[31] but he added that, if the milk quota rules in issue there did contravene constitutional property rights, those rules nonetheless would prevail by virtue of (now) Article 29.4.10.

The third question is whether the EC Regulation or Directive in question is indeed duly authorised by the Treaties themselves, either because it does not comply with the prescribed procedures for lawmaking, or the content goes beyond the competences conferred on the Communities, including the requirement of subsidiarity. This leads into the critical question, *viz.* who is the final arbiter of whether the EC rule is *ultra vires* the Treaties – the Court in Luxembourg or the Supreme Court of Ireland? It was said in the *Crotty* case that it is the ECJ (European Court of Justice) that has the last word on this question; that its decisions "on the interpretation of the Treaty [of Rome] and on questions covering its implementation take precedence, in case of conflict, over the domestic law and the decisions of national courts of Member States."[32] It was conceded on behalf of the State that enactment of the 1986 Act was not necessitated at the time by EC membership and accordingly that Act was not constitution-proof. The Court went on to find that the changes in the existing EC structures and activities envisaged by Maastricht Title II did not "alter the essential character of the Communities" nor did they "create a threat to fundamental constitutional rights."[33] Accordingly, the 1986 Act, which embodied Title II, was not unconstitutional. In the event, the constitutional status of the entire Single European Act was put beyond doubt by the Tenth Amendment to the Constitution.

Potential clashes between Community requirements and fundamental rights guarantees in the Constitution may be averted by EC law itself accepting that the powers of the EC institutions are circumscribed by the obligation to have respect for human rights. Occasionally, Community measures have been declared invalid because they conflicted with human rights. According to Article 6 of the Treaty of Maastricht, the EU is "founded on the principles of liberty, democracy, respect for human rights and fundamental freedoms, and the rule of law ...". It adds that the Union "shall respect fundamental rights as guaranteed" in the European Convention on Human Rights and "as they result from the constitutional traditions common to the Member States, as general principles of Community law." In 2000 at Nice, the Commission, Council and Parliament adopted the Charter of Fundamental Rights for the European

---

[30] *Infra*, p.742.
[31] [1991] 1 I.R. 356.
[32] [1987] I.R. at 713 p.769.
[33] *Id.* at p.770.

Union[34] but, to date, it is non-binding and it does not contain any mechanism for securing compliance with its provisions.

A possible clash between Community law and the Constitution was avoided in 1991, with regard to publishing information in the State concerning abortion services legally available in other Member States. An interlocutory injunction had been granted against several students and students' organisations publishing such information, on the grounds that doing so contravened Article 40.3.3 on the right to life of the unborn. In a reference on a preliminary issue, the ECJ ruled that the defendants' activities there could not involve EC rules regarding the free provision of services because they had no economic link with bodies in the U.K. that provided an abortion service.[35] In view of this, Morris P. granted a permanent injunction against disseminating that information.[36]

---

[34] O.J. No. 364/1 (2000).

[35] *Society for the Protection of Unborn Children (Ireland) Ltd v. Grogan (No.2)* (Case 159/90) [1991] E.C.R. 4685.

[36] *Society for the Protection of Unborn Children (Ireland) Ltd v. Grogan (No.4)* [1994] 1 I.R. 46.

CHAPTER 12

Fundamental/Human Rights

The term civil liberties connotes certain freedoms that individuals in many countries enjoy, such as freedom from arbitrary arrest, freedom of speech and of association. The concept of fundamental rights is closely related to civil liberties: it means freedoms and rights that are almost universally regarded as so important that governments should not be permitted to infringe on such rights. Another term for those rights, which has gained currency in Ireland where natural law is widely accepted, is "natural rights". The range of these rights is more extensive than the traditional civil liberties, although precisely which rights are fundamental or natural is a matter of great controversy.[1] For instance the United States Constitution has been interpreted to give pregnant women the right to have an abortion[2] but the Irish Constitution guarantees the "right to life of the unborn,"[3] and while some constitutional instruments place great stress on the right to own and dispose of private property, this right is not embodied in other constitutions and analogous instruments.[4] Human rights is another name for fundamental rights, and freedoms and rights that make up civil liberties and fundamental rights are now almost universally referred to as human rights.

A considerable degree of confusion exists about what are, and indeed what is the very nature of, human rights – or fundamental rights or natural rights. As Myers McDougal and his collaborators explain in their seminal work, *Human Rights and World Public Order*:

> "It is in the substantive definition of human rights that the greatest confusion and inadequacy prevail. Little effort has been made to create a comprehensive map of the totality of human rights, and there has been little discussion of the detailed content of particular rights. Often even the very concept of human rights is left obscure. Sometimes no specification is offered of what is meant by human rights. When specification is attempted, it commonly exhibits a broad range of

---

[1] The literature on human rights and civil liberties generally is enormous. Excellent overviews include L. Henkin, *The Rights of Man Today* (1978), M. McDougal *et al.*, *Human Rights and World Public Order* (1980), L. Henkin *et al.*, *Human Rights* (1999) and H. Steiner and P. Alston, *International Human Rights in Context* (2nd ed., 2000).

[2] *Roe v. Wade*, 410 U.S. 113 (1973).

[3] Art.40.3.3.

[4] *Infra*, p.727.

confusions. Sometimes human rights are conceived in terms of natural law absolutes and buttressed by transempirical justifications, both theological and metaphysical. At other times human rights are confined to the demands, which particular peoples make at particular times in their particular, unique communities. Still again, human rights are often conceived as merely the rights, which a particular system of law in a particular state in fact protects. Sometimes this positivist conception is not even extended to all individual rights, but is limited only to certain specified rights distinguished by arbitrary criteria. Characteristically, the particular rights regarded as human rights are not explicitly related to the value features and institutional features of social process, and no procedures are specified for ascribing an empirical reference to the different categories of rights. Human rights are, further, often discussed as operative within a national or sub-national context, without appropriate reference being made to any relevant larger community context, global or regional. Similarly, it is not always recognized that the honouring of certain rights may require limitations of other rights. No intellectual procedures are devised, much less employed, for calculating the costs and benefits in terms of value consequences of a particular option in decision. The assumption is far too common that inherited technical, legal terms for the description of human rights can carry a reasonably precise and consistent empirical reference ascertainable by all."[5]

At the level of international law there is the Universal Declaration of Human Rights.[6] The United Nations and the Council of Europe have sponsored numerous human rights treaties, the most important ones for Ireland being the UN Covenant on Civil and Political Rights[7] and the European Convention on Human Rights[8], each of which have mechanisms for adjudicating on claims by individuals that the rights guaranteed there have been contravened by the State-Parties to them. By the European Convention on Human Rights Act 2003, the Convention was made part of Irish law but not to the extent that Acts of the Oireachtas that are incompatible with its guarantees are rendered invalid. A Charter of Fundamental Rights for the European Union was adopted in 2000 by the EC/EU institutions[9] but it is non-binding and contains no enforcement or monitoring mechanism. A State agency to promote and to

---

[5] (1980), pp.64–66.

[6] Of December 10, 1948, reproduced in I. Brownli and G.S. Goodwin Gill, *Basic Documents on Human Rights* (4th ed., 2002), p. 18 (hereinafter "*Basic Documents*").

[7] Of December 16, 1966, 999 UNTS 171 and *Basic Documents,* p.182; see generally, D. McGoldrick, *The Human Rights Commission* (1994) and P. Alston and J. Crawford (eds), *The Future of U.N. Human Rights Treaty Monitoring* (2000).

[8] Of November 4, 1950, 213 UNTS 221 and *Basic Documents,* p.398; see generally, D. Harris *et al., Law of the European Convention on Human Rights* (1995).

[9] Of December 7, 2000, O.J. No. 364/1 (2000) and *Basic Documents,* p.547; see generally,

encourage compliance with human rights was established by the Human Rights Commission Act 2000. It defines human rights as "the rights, liberties and freedoms conferred on or guaranteed to persons by the Constitution and ... by any agreement, treaty or convention to which the State is a party and which has been given the force of law," including the European Convention.[10]

NATURAL LAW AND INALIENABLE RIGHTS

Those freedoms and rights guaranteed by the Constitution reflect two near-universal theories of human rights. One is the historical approach to what are the individual rights that states should respect and, in order to determine what those rights are, it takes the evolution of human rights concepts through the ages as its guide. This tradition is proclaimed in the English Bill of Rights of 1689,[11] the preamble to which stipulates that the Lords and the Commons "(as their Ancestors in like case have usually done) for the vindication and asserting their ancient Rights and Liberties Declare" several particular rights. The Constitution's draftsmen would have drawn inspiration from the prevailing national concepts of fundamental rights, such as those embodied in that Bill of Rights in the American Constitution and its amendments,[12] in the 1789 French Declaration of the Rights of Man and of the Citizen,[13] and also the concepts of fundamental rights in continental European constitutions.

The other theory of human rights reflected in it is the natural law tradition.[14] According to this, individuals possess certain basic rights because of the mere fact that they are human beings and no state has authority to contravene those rights. Some of the very terms of the Constitution's guarantees embody this approach, for instance, the equality clause which provides that citizens "shall, as human persons, be held equal," and in the private property clause which speaks of "man, in virtue of his rational being, ha[ving] natural rights antecedent to positive law, to the private ownership of external goods." Several of the other guarantees have been explained in terms of natural law. Thus in one instance Walsh J. observed that "Articles 41, 42 and 43 emphatically reject the theory that there are no rights without laws, no rights contrary to the law and

---

Leonarts and de Smijter, "A Bill of Rights for the European Union", 38 *Comm. Mkt L. Rev.* 273 (2001) and P. Alston *et al.* ed.'s *The EU and Human Rights* (1999).

[10] S.11(3), as amended.

[11] 1 Wm. & M. c.2. See generally, J. Gough, *Fundamental Law in English Constitutional History* (1955).

[12] Of December 15, 1791 (1st ten Amendments); there are subsequent Amendments, *inter alia* of 1865 (against slavery), 1868 (due process and equal protection), 1870 (voting-race), 1920 (voting-sex) and 1971 (voting-age).

[13] Of August 26, 1789, reproduced in Henkin *et al, supra,* n.1 at p.32.

[14] See generally, J. Finnis, *Natural Law and Natural Rights* (1980), R. George, *In Defence of Natural Law* (1999) and Clarke, "The Role of Natural Law in Irish Constitutional Law", 27 *Irish Jurist* 187 (1982).

no rights anterior to the law. They indicate that justice is placed above the law and acknowledge that natural rights, or human rights, are not created by law but that the Constitution confirms their existence and gives them protection. The individual has natural and human rights over which the State has no authority; and the family, as the natural primary and fundamental unit group of society, has rights as such which the State cannot control ...".[15]

That natural law is the foundation for human rights is particularly strong in the Catholic intellectual tradition and, since Ireland is a predominantly Catholic country, it is no coincidence that the natural law tradition is endorsed by the Constitution and by many of the judges who interpret it. Natural law, however, is by no means a uniquely Catholic concept of fundamental rights, as is shown by the preamble and terms of the 1789 Declaration, the authors of which can by no stretch of the imagination be regarded as pious papists. It describes the objective of political institutions as "the preservation of the natural and imprescriptible rights of man," describes freedom of expression as "one of the most precious rights of man" and private property as an "inviolable and sacred right."

Myers McDougal and his collaborators explained the natural law approach to human rights as follows:

> "The natural law approach begins with the assumption that there are natural laws, both theological and metaphysical, which confer certain particular rights upon individual human beings. These rights find their authority either in divine will or in specified metaphysical absolutes. The natural law constitutes a "higher law" which is "the ultimate standard of fitness of all positive law, whether national or international," decisions by state elites which are taken contrary to this law are regarded as mere exercises of naked power.
>
> The great historic contribution of the natural law emphasis has been in the affording of this appeal from the realities of naked power to a higher authority which is asserted to require the protection of individual rights. The observational standpoint assumed by those who take this approach has commonly been that of identification with the whole of humanity.
>
> A principal emphasis has been upon a common human nature that implies comparable rights and equality for all. For many centuries this approach has been an unfailing source of articulated demand and of theoretical justification for human rights. Its pre-eminent contribution to both constitutional and international law, and especially to the protection of individual rights ... has been many times recorded."[16]

---

[15] *McGee v. Attorney General* [1974] I.R. 284 at p.310.
[16] *Supra*, n.1 at pp.68–69.

In its Preamble, the Constitution strikes a resoundingly Christian note: it begins by stating that "In the Name of the Most Holy Trinity, from Whom is all authority and to Whom, as our final end, all actions both of men and States must be referred," and that the people adopt the Constitution "Humbly acknowledging all our obligations to our Divine Lord, Jesus Christ, Who sustained our fathers through centuries of trial. ..." Article 6 states that all public powers "derive, under God, from the people." And the Constitution concludes with the words *inter alia "Dochum Glóire De," i.e.* for the glory of God.

Several judges have concluded from these provisions and from the general tenor of the Constitution that it embodies the Christian natural law tradition and, that in order to ascertain whether certain alleged rights exist and to determine the proper scope of such rights, the courts should consider what light this tradition throws on the subject. Thus according to Walsh J.:

> "The natural or human rights to which I have referred earlier in this judgment are part of what is generally called the natural law. There are many to argue that natural law may be regarded only as an ethical concept and as such is a reaffirmation of the ethical content of law in its ideal of justice. The natural law as a theological concept is the law of God promulgated by reason and is the ultimate governor of all the laws of men. In view of the acknowledgment of Christianity in the preamble and in view of the reference to God in article 6 of the Constitution, it must be accepted that the Constitution intended the natural human rights I have mentioned as being in the latter category rather than simply an acknowledgment of the ethical content of law in its ideal of justice. What exactly natural law is and what precisely it imports is a question which has exercised the minds of theologians for many centuries and on which they are not yet fully agreed. While the Constitution speaks of certain rights being imprescriptible or inalienable, or being antecedent and superior to positive law, it does not specify them."[17]

In one instance Kenny J. said that in order to ascertain what rights are guaranteed by Article 40.3 of the Constitution, the courts should be guided by "the Christian and democratic nature of the State,"[18] and went on to find in a Papal Encyclical support for the existence of a right of bodily integrity. On the other hand, the courts have not been deterred by Papal condemnation of contraception from holding that laws which prevent married persons from obtaining contraceptives are unconstitutional because those laws contravene the individual's right to privacy in marital affairs.[19]

---

[17] *McGee v. Attorney General* [1974] I.R. 284 at pp.317–318.
[18] *Ryan v. Attorney General* [1965] I.R. 294 at p.312.
[19] The *McGee* case [1974] I.R. 284.

While it is widely accepted that the Constitution adopts a natural law approach to human rights, it cannot be said that there is universal agreement among those whose job it is to interpret the Constitution as to what exactly is required by natural law. It would seem that the natural law interpretation does not mean a uniquely Catholic view of human rights, although some of the Constitution's provisions have a particularly Catholic flavour, notably, the former prohibition against introducing laws that would permit divorce. But it would seem that generally, where the main Christian churches are at one on a particular question, the Constitution will be given an interpretation which is consistent with those churches' attitude; this was one of the reasons given by a majority of the Supreme Court for upholding legislative provisions that forbade certain homosexual practices.[20] Irish judges from other religious backgrounds tend not to invoke natural law as a justification for their decisions.

In his account of natural law as envisaged by the Constitution, Walsh J. has stressed that it does not embody a sectarian concept of rights because the State, as established by the Constitution, is a pluralist one:

"In a pluralist society such as ours, the Courts cannot as a matter of constitutional law be asked to choose between the differing views, where they exist, of experts on the interpretation by the different religious denominations of either the nature or extent of these natural rights as they are to be found in the natural law. The same considerations apply also to the question of ascertaining the nature and extent of the duties which flow from natural law. ... In this country it falls finally upon the judges to interpret the Constitution and in doing so to determine, where necessary, the rights which are superior or antecedent to positive law or which are imprescriptible or inalienable. In the performance of this difficult duty there are certain guidelines laid down in the Constitution for the judge. The very structure and content of the Articles dealing with fundamental rights clearly indicate that justice is not subordinate to the law. In particular, the terms of section 3 of Article 40 expressly subordinate the law to justice. ... The judges must ... as best they can from their training and their experience interpret these rights in accordance with their ideas of prudence, justice and charity. It is but natural that from time to time the prevailing ideas of these virtues may be conditioned by the passage of time; no interpretation of the Constitution is intended to be final for all time."[21]

---

[20] *Norris v. Attorney General* [1984] I.R. 36.
[21] *McGee v. Attorney General* [1974] I.R. 284 at pp.318–319.

INTERNATIONAL HUMAN RIGHTS

Public international law is the legal system that governs principally relations between nation states. Much of it is customary in origin: the customary standards of inter-state relations that are universally accepted as binding legal norms. Today most of it is based on treaties – the vast web of bilateral inter-state agreements and the multilateral treaties and conventions, with the United Nations Charter at the apex. In the past human rights were very much a peripheral and indirect concern of international law, although one of the principles of customary international law is that states must provide a minimum amount of protection and justice for aliens within their jurisdiction.[22] This legal duty regarding aliens was not owed to them as individuals, however, but was owed to the states of which they were nationals; if those states chose not to take steps to protect their nationals abroad, that was the end of the matter insofar as the law was concerned.

Before the Second World War a number of treaties existed that addressed specific human rights concerns. Under some of the earliest of these, states undertook to respect the religious convictions of defeated nations, for instance, the civil articles of the Treaty of Limerick of 1691,[23] in which it was agreed by William III not to discriminate against Catholics in Ireland. By the end of the nineteenth century international concern about slavery led to the Brussels Agreement of 1890[24] being concluded, in which the principal European powers undertook to put an end to that practice. Witnesses to the carnage of the Napoleonic wars spent years lobbying to civilise the laws of warfare, ultimately leading to a series of Geneva and Hague conventions being adapted to that end.[25] A major feature of the Peace Treaties entered into following the First and Second World Wars were guarantees that various minorities in some of the defeated belligerents would be protected against discrimination.[26] In the Final Act of the Helsinki Conference on Security and Co-operation in Europe of 1975,[27] in which the borders drawn after World War II were formally ratified, the state parties agreed to "respect" and to "promote and encourage the effective exercise of" human rights — some of these being detailed in the annex on co-operation in humanitarian and other fields.

---

[22] See generally, M. McDougal *et al.*, *supra*, n.1, Appendix.

[23] Of October 3, 1691, reproduced in J. G. Simms, *The Treaty of Limerick* (1961), pp.19–24.

[24] 82 Brit. & Foreign State Papers, 1889–90 (1896), p.55; see generally, M. McDougal *et al.*, *supra*, n.1, pp.473 *et seq.*

[25] See generally, Symposium: The Hague Peace Conferences, 94 *Am. J. Int'l L.* 1 (2000) and Merox, "The Humanisation of Humanitarian Law", 94 *Am. J. Int'l L.* 239 (2000).

[26] See generally, W. McKeon, *Equality and Discrimination in International Law* (1983), Chaps 1 and 2.

[27] Of August 1, 1975, *Basic Documents*, p.557.

The United Nations system

The United Nations Charter is the constitution of the world, and one of the central declared objectives of the nations that adhere to it is to "reaffirm faith in fundamental human rights, in the dignity and worth of the human person, in the equal rights of men and women" and to "promote social progress and better standards of life in larger freedom."[28] One function of the UN is to "promote ... universal respect for, and observance of, human rights and fundamental freedoms ...".[29] In 1948 the UN adopted the Universal Declaration of Human Rights,[30] which is an itemisation of what are generally accepted to be human rights. Although its provisions are formulated in broad terms and it was not proclaimed as binding law but as "a common standard of achievement for all peoples and all nations," it is now widely regarded as forming part of customary international law. If the Declaration's requirements often go unobserved, it is not because they are not law but on account of inadequate enforcement machinery in the international arena.

In 1990 Ireland became a party to the two major international conventions that articulate in greater detail the standards proclaimed by the 1948 Declaration and contain machinery for securing a degree of compliance with them, which were promulgated by the UN, the International Covenant on Civil and Political Rights of 1966[31] (hereinafter referred to as the UN Covenant) and the International Covenant on Economic, Social and Cultural Rights[32] of the same year. The State has accepted the jurisdiction of the UN Human Rights Committee to investigate and rule on individual complaints that obligations under the first of these were not being adhered to. Ireland also is a party to UN-sponsored conventions on genocide, slavery, refugees and stateless persons, on the rights of the child, and on the elimination of discrimination against women and racial discrimination.

The European system

Ireland is a member of the Council of Europe and is a party to numerous human rights conventions sponsored by this body, including those on torture, on automatic data processing, on the legal status of children born outside marriage and a social charter. The international human rights treaty of greatest practical relevance to Irish citizens and residents is the Convention for the

---

[28] Preamble, in *Basic Documents*, p.2.
[29] Art.55(c)
[30] *Supra*, n.6.
[31] *Supra*, n.7 and [1990] Ir. T.S. No.9 (with reservations).
[32] Of December 16, 1966, 993 U.N.T.S. 3 and [1990] Ir. T.S. No.10 (with reservations).

Protection of Human Rights and Fundamental Freedoms,[33] which is popularly known as the European Convention on Human Rights (hereinafter referred to as the European Convention). It has what may be described as quasi-constitutional status in that it is a subject of the 1998 "Good Friday" Agreement, which was endorsed by a referendum that adopted the 19th Amendment to the Constitution. By the European Convention on Human Rights 2003, it was made part of Irish law and it is also referred to in the EC/EU treaties.

Adopted in Rome on November 4, 1950, Ireland was one of its twelve original signatories. Ireland moreover has accepted the First, Fourth, Sixth and Seventh Protocols to this Convention, which deal with substantive rights. Certain minimum rights are set out in it, which describes itself modestly as one of the "first steps for the collective enforcement of certain rights" that are proclaimed in the UN's Universal Declaration. In brief, the Convention guarantees the right to life (Article 2), not to be tortured or degraded (Article 3), not to be enslaved and the like (Article 4), liberty and personal security (Article 5), proper criminal and civil trials (Article. 6), no *ex post facto* criminal offences (Article. 7), privacy and family autonomy (Article 8), freedom of thought, conscience and religion (Article 9), freedom of expression (Article 10), freedom of assembly and to join trade unions (Article 11), marriage and founding a family (Article 12), non-discrimination (Article 14), private property, education and free elections (1st Protocol), not to be imprisoned for inability to pay debts and freedom of movement in several respects (2nd Protocol), abolition of the death penalty (6th Protocol), protection for aliens, the right to appeal criminal convictions and to compensation for wrongful conviction, no double jeopardy and equality between spouses (7th Protocol).

Ireland has entered reservations to the Convention and its Protocols. According to Article 6(3)(c) of the Convention, "everyone charged with a criminal offence has the following minimum rights ... (c) to defend himself in person or through legal assistance ... to be given it free when the interests of justice so require." The Irish Government in 1950 did not want to introduce free legal aid for criminal cases and therefore entered the reservation that "they do not interpret (this) Article as requiring the provision of free legal assistance to any wider extent than is now provided in Ireland."[34] Whether this is consistent with Article 64 of the Convention, which governs reservations, is now of academic interest only since the Criminal Justice (Legal Aid) Act 1962, came into force. Article 2 of the First Protocol guarantees the right to education. However, when signing this, the Government put on record their view that the right to education "is not sufficiently explicit in ensuring to parents the right to provide education for their children in their homes or in schools of the parents' own choice, whether or not such schools are private schools or are

---

[33] *Supra*, n.8.
[34] Ir. T.S. No.12 (1953).

schools recognised or established by the State."[35] Articles 2–4 of the Fourth Protocol guarantee freedom of movement within a state and between states in several respects. When it signed this, the Government stipulated that "the reference to extradition contained in paragraph 21 of the Report of the Committee of Experts on this Protocol and concerning paragraph 1 of Article 3 ... includes also laws providing for the execution in the territory of one Contracting Party of warrants for arrest issued by the authorities of another Contracting Party."[36] In other words, laws providing for the backing of warrants issued abroad, such as Part III of the Extradition Act 1965, are to be treated in the same way as laws dealing with extradition in the full sense.

Disputes about compliance with the Convention and its Protocols are determined principally by the European Court of Human Rights, which is based in Strasbourg. Ireland has accepted the right of aggrieved individuals to bring proceedings there against it for breach of its Convention obligations. On ten occasions to date, complaints against Ireland have been upheld by the Strasbourg court.[37] To date, however, the Irish courts have demonstrated enormous reluctance to give indirect force to this Convention by construing several of the Constitution's guarantees along the lines of how similar provisions of the Convention have been interpreted.[38] But this attitude to the Convention is unlikely to last, especially in view of the 2003 legislation giving effect to it and the fact that for several years courts in the United Kingdom have been applying the Convention against public authorities there.

The European Convention on Human Rights Act 2003

Except where prevented from during so by the clear and unambiguous terms of the Act, regulation or common law rule applicable, every "organ of the State" is obliged by sections 2 and 3 of the European Convention on Human Rights Act 2003, to exercise its powers and to discharge its duties in a manner that is compatible with this Convention and its four scheduled Protocols' requirements.[39] Where there is some ambiguity in the governing rule, section 2 of the 2003 Act acquires that it should be interpreted "in so far as is possible, subject to the rules of ... interpretation and application ... in a manner compatible with the ... Convention." It remains to be seen how the courts will

---

[35] Ir. T.S. No.3 (1954).

[36] Ir. T.S. No.11 (1968).

[37] See generally, O'Connell "Ireland" in R. Blackburn and J. Polakiewicz eds., *Fundamental Rights in Europe* (2001).

[38] *E.g., Murphy v. G.M.* [2001] 4 I.R. 113, which completely disregards the Strasbourg Court decisions on what is a criminal matter but relies extensively on U.S. Supreme Court decisions on the question.

[39] See generally, A. Collins and J. O'Reilly, *Civil Proceedings and the State* (2nd ed., 2003), Chap.11.

discharge their interpretive obligation in this regard and whether they will adopt approaches similar to those taken by the British and Northern Ireland courts under an equivalent provision there.[40]

Where an "organ of the State" has contravened the Convention in circumstances plainly required by an existing law, regulation or other rule applicable and where "no other legal remedy is adequate and available," section 5 of this Act authorises the High Court to make a declaration of incompatibility. But a declaration of incompatibility "shall not affect the validity, continuing operation or enforcement" of the rule in question. Consequently, notwithstanding that the rule there contravenes the Convention's guarantees, it remains effective in law and what has been done under it remains valid and fully effective. In such circumstances, however, an aggrieved party may be paid *ex gratia* compensation by the State. Additionally, a copy of the declaration of incompatibility must be laid before each House of the Oireachtas.

For the above purposes, an organ of the State is defined in section 1(1) as "includ[ing] a tribunal or any other body ... established by law or through which any of the legislative, executive or judicial powers of the State are exercised." But the definition excludes "the President or the Oireachtas or either House of the Oireachtas or a Committee of either such House ... or a Joint Committee of both such Houses." Also excluded from the definition is "a court," which means that the only remedy against judicial infringement of the Convention is to bring proceedings against Ireland before the Strasbourg Court. On several occasions, inordinate delays by senior Irish judges in deciding cases have been referred to that Court.[41] To what extent this definition embraces strictly private bodies that exercise quasi-public functions remains to be seen.

UNSPECIFIED RIGHTS

As well as guaranteeing various specific rights, such as personal liberty, trial in due course of law, freedom of expression and private property, the Constitution has been held to guarantee other rights which are not expressly referred to or are not obviously a part of the expressly referred to rights. These additional rights have been termed "unspecified" or "unenumerated" rights. Article 40.3.1 and 2 of the Constitution guarantee several rights and it has been held that their enumeration is not exhaustive. According to these provisions:

> "1. The State guarantees in its laws to respect, and, as far as practicable, by its laws to defend and vindicate the personal rights of the citizen.

---

[40] See generally, Edwards, "Reading Down Legislation Under the Human Rights Act" [2000] *Legal Studies* 353. *Cf. Re King's Application* [2003] N.I. 43.

[41] E.g. *Doran v. Ireland*, decision of July 31, 2003 by the court's third section, holding that the state had been in breach of Article 6(1) of the Convention.

2. The State shall, in particular, by its laws protect as best it may from unjust attack and, in the case of injustice done, vindicate the life, person, good name, and property rights of every citizen.

These are the principal constitutional bases for the unspecified or unenumerated rights. Their existence was first acknowledged by Kenny J. in the *"Fluoridation* case where he observed that "the personal rights which may be invoked to invalidate legislation are not confined to those specified in Article 40 but include all those rights which result from the Christian and democratic nature of the State. It is, however, a jurisdiction to be exercised with caution."[42] These views were endorsed by Ó Dálaigh C.J., who stated that "[t]he Court agrees ... that the personal rights mentioned in [Article 40.3] are not exhausted by the enumeration of "life, person, good name and property rights" as is shown by the use of the words "in particular" [there]; nor by the more detached treatment of specific rights in the subsequent sections of the Article. To attempt to make a list of all the rights which may properly fall within the category of "personal rights" would be difficult and, fortunately, is unnecessary in this present case."[43] Parallels have been drawn between Article 40.3.1 and 2 and the Ninth Amendment to the United States Constitution, according to which "(t)he enumeration in the Constitution, of certain rights, shall not be construed to deny or disparage others retained by the people." Indeed, this provision has a distinctly natural law flavour; that people have certain guaranteed rights over and above those spelled out in the Constitution, and the State shall not contravene those rights.

Precisely how these unspecified rights are to be "discovered" is not indicated in the Constitution, nor by the courts.[44] This raises the broader question of the proper approach to constitutional interpretation and what is described as "judicial activism." In what circumstances is a court justified in going beyond the strict letter of the Constitution and condemning some measure because it infringes some unspecified constitutional right? In *T.D. v. Minister for Education*,[45] Keane C.J. urged restraint in "identifying new rights of this nature" and urged fuller consideration of "the criteria by which the unenumerated rights are to be identified."[46] In the United States, invoking the unspecified right to privacy in order to strike down anti-abortion statutes has been the subject of prolonged and occasionally bitter controversy.[47]

For the purpose of discovering unspecified rights, Kenny J. invoked the

---

[42] *Ryan v. Attorney General* [1965] I.R. 294 at p.312.
[43] *Id.* at pp.344–345.
[44] Cf. Murphy, "An Ordering of Constitutional Values" 53 *So. Cal. L. Rev.* 703 (1980).
[45] [2001] 4 I.R. 259.
[46] *Id.* at p.282.
[47] E.g. *Planned Parenthood of Southeastern Pennsylvania v. Casey*, 505 U.S. 833 (1992).

"Christian and democratic nature of the State"[48] as one guide, which can be helpful in particular contexts. An indicator invoked by Walsh J. is "justice,"[49] which perhaps is the ideal criterion for ascertaining fundamental rights except that it is extremely vague when it comes to answering specific questions; such as does justice demand recognition of a fundamental right to travel abroad or a right not to be extradited for politically-motivated offences? Other possible criteria include tradition and consensus. Even assuming that it is possible to ascertain precisely what tradition demands or what the national consensus requires, the difficulty at times with these indicia is that there are some traditions which today would be regarded as profoundly unjust, and there can be a national consensus on various matters that can also be most unjust. Some judges resort to natural law in order to find unspecified rights, but it is debatable how useful in practice non-sectarian natural law can be, even though natural law concepts have had a powerful influence in the evolution of human rights. A perhaps more enlightening source of inspiration are the international human rights standards, especially those conventions to which Ireland is a party and which provide for some authoritative interpretation of their contents.

---

[48] *Supra,* n.43.
[49] *McGee v. Attorney General* [1974] I.R. 284 at pp.318–319.

CHAPTER 13

Legality and the Rule of Law

A society founded on anarchy is the very opposite of one that adheres to the principle of legality and the rule of law. Where anarchy prevails there are no set norms of conduct; persons are free to do what they like to themselves or to others, provided of course that they can get away with it. Anarchy has no room for rules or courts, or for governing principles such as equality, due process and substantive individual rights, The principle of legality and the rule of law connotes principally that persons are governed by general and prospective rules that must be enforced through courts; they are not subject to edicts that are arbitrary and inconsistent and, at times, incomprehensible or have retroactive effect. As F.A. Hayek described the rule of law, "[s]tripped of all technicalities this means that government in all its actions is bound by rules fixed and announced beforehand – rules which make it possible to foresee with fair certainty how the authority will use its coercive powers in given circumstances, and to plan ones individual affairs on the basis of this knowledge."[1]

In his well-known book on the British Constitution of the Victorian era, A.V. Dicey described the rule of law as a fundamental constitutional principle comprising the following features:

> "the 'rule of law', then, which forms a fundamental principle of the (British) constitution, has (these) meanings, or may be regarded from (these) different points of view.
>
> It means, in the first place, the absolute supremacy or predominance of regular law as opposed to the influence of arbitrary power, and excludes the existence of arbitrariness, of prerogative, or even of wide discretionary authority … .
>
> It means, again, equality before the law, or the equal subjection of all classes to the ordinary law of the land administered by the ordinary law courts; the 'rule of law' in this sense excludes the idea of any exemption of officials or others from the duty of obedience to the law which governs other citizens or from the jurisdiction of the ordinary tribunals … ."[2]

---

[1] *The Road to Serfdom* (1944) p.54. Cf. L. Fuller, *The Morality of Law* (rev. ed. 1973).
[2] *The Law of the Constitution* (10th ed. 1959) pp. 202–203 (first published 1885).

Dicey's rule of law, therefore, requires that government must have legal authority for its actions, that the law must not grant government unduly extensive discretionary powers, that as a general rule laws confer benefits and impose burdens on everybody, as opposed to benefiting and burdening discrete groups, and that the government's agents are answerable in the ordinary courts whenever they violate the law.

Another feature of Dicey's rule of law is that all legal rights are based on legislation and on settled common law, and not on vague constitutional guarantees, such as personal liberty, freedom of expression and assembly etc. But this feature was peculiar to the British Constitution of his day and is not generally regarded as a component of legality and the rule of law. On the other hand, essential features that Dicey did not expressly advert to are that laws must be accessible, comprehensible and generally not have retroactive effect.

The rule of law does not mean that the legal system or any particular law is just, in the sense that it must further the public interest or respect substantive values such as human dignity and freedom. The rule of law only ensures that the government will act with a degree of regularity and reliability. As one commentator has pointed out:

> "The rule of law is a political ideal which a legal system may lack or may possess to a greater or lesser degree. That much is common ground. It is also to be insisted that the rule of law is just one of the virtues which a legal system may possess and by which it is to be judged. It is not to be confused with democracy, justice, equality (before the law or otherwise), human rights of any kind or respect for persons or for the dignity of man. A non-democratic legal system, based on the denial of human rights, on extensive poverty, on racial segregation, sexual inequalities and religious persecution may, in principle, conform to the requirements of the rule of law better than any of the legal systems of the more enlightened western democracies. This does not mean that it will be better than those western democracies. It will be an immeasurably worse legal system, but it will excel in one respect: in its conformity to the rule of law." [3]

Some constitutions place greater emphasis than others on legality and the rule of law. For instance, the United States Constitution does not contain any express provision resembling Article 40.4.1 of the Irish Constitution, according to which "no citizen shall be deprived of his personal liberty save in accordance with law." The French Declaration of 1789 is pervaded with references to legality, for example, that liberty can only be restricted by legislation (art. 4), that one is free to act unless forbidden by legislation (art. 5), that one can be

---

[3]   Raz, "The Rule of Law and its virtue", 93 *L.Q.R.* 195 (1977) p.196. Cf. Craig, "Formal and Substantive Conceptions of the Rule of Law [1977] *Public L.* 467.

arrested and detained only in accordance with legislation (art. 7) and be punished only by virtue of legislation (art. 8). Authority under law is constantly stressed in the European Convention on Human Rights, especially in the guarantees contained in Articles 8-11, all of which can be restricted in various ways provided *inter alia* that the qualifications are "prescribed by law."

LAWFUL AUTHORITY

The very minimum that legality requires is that, before persons' liberty and other common law rights can be taken away from them, there must be express lawful authority to do so.[4] As regards personal liberty, this principle is stated in Article 40.4.1 of the Constitution. For this purpose, "law" includes the common law as well as legislation. Procedures that must be followed for enacting legislation, the extent to which government may act under delegated legislation and the extent to which pre-1937 statutes and the common law have been carried over by Articles 49 and 50 of the Constitution have been dealt with earlier on in this book.

Statutory Offences

What constitutes the offence of treason is defined in Article 39 of the Constitution but incidental and procedural aspects of that offence are governed by the Treason Act 1939. Many crimes are statutory offences, *i.e.* it is some statutory provision, of a pre-1937 or a post-1937 Act, that proscribes the conduct in question.[5]

When dealing with prosecutions for statutory offences the courts interpret the prohibitions strictly.[6] In other words, where there is some uncertainty as to whether the accused's proven behaviour is forbidden by the Act's very terms, the accused is given the benefit of the doubt. It is because of the ferocity of the penal system two hundred years ago, when individuals convicted of relatively trivial offences were sentenced to the most severe punishments, that the courts construed criminal statutes strictly. While courts today might not interpret penal statutes in the pedantic manner of their predecessors, the prevailing judicial view would seem to be summed up in the words that "a man is not to be put in peril upon an ambiguity, however much or little the Act appeals to the predilection of the Court."[7] The construction of modern penal legislation has

---

[4] See generally, F. McAuley & J. McCutcheon, *Criminal Liability* (2001) pp. 42–56 and A. Simester & G. Sullivan, *Criminal Law* (2000) pp. 28–33.

[5] See generally, F. McAuley & J. McCutcheon, *supra* and P. Charleton *et al.*, *Criminal Law* (1999).

[6] See generally, A. Ashworth, *Principles of Criminal Law* (2nd ed. 1995) pp.76–78.

[7] *London & North East Rly. v. Berriman* [1946] A.C. 278 at p.313.

been explained by Walsh J. as follows: "[s]o far as the construction of penal statutes is concerned ... they must be fairly construed according to the legislative intent as expressed in the enactment, and persons liable to a penalty should be entitled to the benefit of any genuine doubt or ambiguity as distinct from spurious doubts and ambiguities. Punishment should not be extended to cases which are not clearly embraced in the statutory provisions."[8]

Dealing with the Offences Against the State Act 1939, O'Higgins C.J. has observed that "(t)he Act of 1939 must be strictly construed. It is legislation of a penal kind which was passed for a special purpose and which has the effect of interfering with the normal rights and liberties of citizens."[9] And in *King v. Attorney General*,[10] where a provision of the Vagrancy Act 1824, was held to contravene constitutional guarantees, Kenny J. stated that "a person may be convicted of a criminal offence only if the ingredients of, and the acts constituting, the offence are specified with precision and clarity. ... It is a fundamental feature of our system of government by law (and not by decree or diktat) that citizens may be convicted only of offences which have been specified with precision by the judges who made the common law, or of offences which, created by statute, are expressed without ambiguity. ... In my opinion (the 'sus' provisions) are so uncertain that they cannot form the foundation for a criminal offence."[11]

Common Law Offences

Certain forms of conduct are criminal offences not because of any specific statutory prohibition but by virtue of the common law, most notably, murder, manslaughter, kidnapping, rape and arson. In recent years the Oireachtas has abolished numerous common law offences and replaced them with statutory offences, for instance rout, unlawful assembly and affray;[12] assault, battery, kidnapping and false imprisonment;[13] larceny, burglary, robbery, cheating (except in relation to the public revenue), extortion under colour of office and forgery.[14] In continental European countries there are no common law offences because the entire criminal law there is codified.

The common law is not static: through the ages it has developed and expanded, especially in the non-criminal field. Many acts that three hundred years ago would have been perfectly lawful are today actionable under the law

---

[8] *People v. Murray* [1977] I.R. 377; also *People v. McHugh* [2002] 1 I.R. 352.
[9] *People v. Farrell* [1978] I.R. 13 at 25.
[10] [1981] I.R. 233.
[11] *Id.* at p.263. *Cf. State (Dixon) v. Martin* [1985] I.L.R.M. 240, rejecting a contention that a statutory offence was void for uncertainty.
[12] Criminal Justice (Public Order) Act 1924.
[13] Non Fatal Offences Against the Person Act 1997.
[14] Criminal Justice (Theft and Fraud Offences) Act 2001.

of tort or are not allowed by general equitable principles. With regard to common law criminal offences, it would seem that in Britain the courts will no longer create new offences.[15] On the other hand existing offences, most notably the offence of conspiracy, has been expanded in Britain to cover new situations. Thus, in the famous "Ladies Directory" case, *Shaw v. D.P.P.*,[16] the defendant was convicted for having published a directory of London prostitutes, an action which was not forbidden by any statute or by existing case law. Nevertheless, it was held that his conduct amounted to the offence of conspiracy to corrupt public morals. And in *R. v. R.*[17] a husband was convicted of raping his wife, notwithstanding the common law principle that the offence could not be committed by a husband.

Whether or to what extent the Constitution permits the courts to expand the scope of common law offences has not been determined. In *Attorney General (ex rel. Society for the Protection of Unborn Children Ireland Ltd.) v. Open Door Counselling Ltd.*[18] where the plaintiff sought declarations and injunctions against the defendant for counselling pregnant women about abortion, Hamilton P. endorsed the continued existence of criminal conspiracy in Irish law, relying extensively on the modern English authorities, including *Shaw.* He stated that "the offence of conspiracy to corrupt public morals may be committed even when the agreement between two or more persons is to assist in the commission of a lawful act. ... The words corrupt public morals suggest conduct which a jury might find to be destructive of the fabric of society."[19] In any particular case, it is for a jury to decide whether what the defendant is proved to have done indeed tends to corrupt public morals. In the *S.P.U.C.* case, because a jury could very well conclude that what the defendants had been doing did not amount to this offence, Hamilton J. declined to make a declaration that their activities constituted the offence.[20] More recently, however, Geoghegan J. pointed out that the Constitution may form a barrier to the evolution of offences of this nature.[21] There is no reported instance of persons being convicted since 1937 of conspiracy to corrupt public morals.

Common Law Power to Detain and to Enter on Property

At common law, members of the Garda Síochána and also private individuals are entitled to stop and arrest persons who are about to commit, or who they

---

[15] See generally, Ashworth, *supra* n.6, pp. 59–63.
[16] [1962] A.C. 220.
[17] [1992] 1 A.C. 599.
[18] [1988] I.R. 593.
[19] *Id.* at p.613, referring to *Knuller v. D.P.P.* [1973] A.C. 435.
[20] *Id.* at p.615.
[21] *Myles v. Sreenan* [1994] 4 I.R. 294.

believe have committed, certain crimes.[22] In *D.P.P.* v *Fagan*[23] the Supreme Court held that Gardaí also have a common law power to conduct random stops of motor vehicles even though the driver is not suspected of committing any criminal offence. As is abundantly clear from Denham J.'s dissent, there was no good legal basis whatsoever for this conclusion, which has been rejected in other comparable jurisdictions.[24]

A similar example of that Court finding a common law power that manifestly did not exist at all, was *McMahon v. McDonald*,[25] where the plaintiff was being sought for extradition to England. Considerable force was used by the Gardaí in order to gain access to where he was living at the time, which was not authorised by the Extradition Act 1965. Because many other comparable Acts expressly authorise the use of reasonable force in order to enter a premises or a dwelling, it was contended that resort to force in this particular instance was not authorised and therefore was unlawful. Nor were the circumstances there such as were contemplated in the seminal *Semayne's* case,[26] where the ambit of the common law power of forcible entry was defined. Because the common law does not grant any power to extradite, it seems absurd to conclude that the common law authorises forcible entry of a dwelling for that purpose. Again, as in *Fagan*, but without citing any authority to support the proposition, it was held *ex tempore* that force was allowed here by the common law.[27]

ACCESSIBLE AND COMPREHENSIBLE LAWS

Article 25.1–4 of the Constitution sets out the procedures regarding signing and promulgating laws.[28] A Bill that has been passed by both Houses of the Oireachtas must be presented to the President for signature and for promulgation by inserting a notice in the *Iris Oifigiúil*. The required text, which is conclusive evidence of the law's provisions, must be enrolled for record in the office of the Registrar of the Supreme Court. The Statutory Instruments Acts 1947–80 seek to ensure that many forms of delegated legislation are published and made reasonably accessible to the public.

Judgments of the High Court and of the Supreme Court that are considered to be of general significance are published by the Incorporated Council for Law Reporting in Ireland, which is is made up of Government representatives, judges and representatives of both branches of the legal profession. Unlike the position in continental European countries, however, every High Court

---

[22] *Post*, p.319.
[23] [1994] 3 I.R. 265; *post*, p.320.
[24] *E.g. Ran v. Boudreau*, 196 D.L.R. 4th 53 (2001).
[25] Sup. Ct, July 27, 1988.
[26] (1604) 5 Co. Rep. 91a.
[27] Compare *R. (Rothman) v. C'mr Metropolitan Police* [2002] 2 W.L.R. 1315.
[28] *Ante*, p.106.

and Supreme Court judgment is not published in the official reports and indeed some very important decisions on the Constitution itself have gone un-reported.[29] There also are numerous *ex tempore* judgments of this court, of which no official record is kept.

It has not been decided in this country that laws must be reasonably accessible to those to whom they are addressed and be understandable by them. An argument to this effect finds support in the European Court of Human Rights *Sunday Times Case*.[30] The English Attorney General obtained an injunction against newspaper publishers restraining publication of articles on the thalidomide tragedy on the grounds that those articles were likely to prejudice a forthcoming trial where damages were being claimed against manufacturers of the drug. If those articles were published the publishers would be in contempt of court. The publishers claimed that Article 10 of the European Convention gave them the right to publish. But the British Government's response was that the contempt of court rule was a restriction on freedom of expression "prescribed by law" as envisaged by Article 10(2) of the Convention. In the event the court found that the injunction contravened Article 10. Dealing with restrictions on freedoms that are "prescribed by law", the Court observed that "[f]irstly the law must be adequately accessible: the citizen must be able to have an indication that is adequate in the circumstances of the legal rules applicable in a given case. Secondly, a norm cannot be regarded as a law unless it is formulated with sufficient precision to enable the citizen to regulate his conduct: he must be able – if need be with appropriate advice – to foresee, to a degree that is reasonable in the circumstances, the consequences which a given action may entail."[31] Some of the judges castigated the uncertainty of the English common law on contempt of court. The position in Britain has since changed with the Contempt of Court Act 1981; contempt in Ireland is still governed by the common law similar to that which obtained in England.

One of the grounds on which the constitutionality of the Proceeds of Crime Act 1996 was challenged was on account of its lack of precision. What constitutes "proceeds of crime" for the purpose of that Act is defined extremely broadly, to cover practically every item of property in the State (in view of this Act's retrospective application). All such property is subject to being confiscated by order of the High Court except where the Court "is satisfied that there would be a serious risk of injustice." The "void for vagueness" argument against this was rejected by the Supreme Court in *Murphy v. G.M.*[32] in one short paragraph, on the grounds that the onus of proof is on the Garda

---

[29] *E.g. An Blascaod Mór Teo v. C'mrs for Public Works*, Budd J., February 27, 1998; the Supreme Court decision on one aspect of this case is reported [2000] 1 I.R. 6.

[30] 2 E.H.R.R. 245 (1979).

[31] *Id.* at p.271. Similarly, *Malone v. United Kingdom*, 7 E.H.R.R. 14 (1984), *McLeod v. United Kingdom*, 27 E.H.R.R. 493 (1998) and *Lucas v. R.*, 157 D.L.R. 4th 423 (1998).

[32] [2001] 4 I.R. 113.

officer claiming that the property is the proceeds of crime. According to Keane
C.J. for the court, while the defence of a serious risk of injustice "is undoubtedly
wide in its scope, that can only be in ease of the individuals whose rights may
be affected and the court, in applying these provisions, will be obliged to act
in accordance with the requirements of constitutional and natural justice."[33]
But this does not address at all the contention that individuals ought to be in a
position to know in advance in what circumstances property they possess, that
comes within the very wide concept of proceeds of crime, is likely to be
confiscated, rather than them having to undergo protracted and at times
expensive High Court proceedings to that end; that the criterion "injustice" is
far too vague and amorphous a standard in this context. Comparable laws in
other countries stipulate with a degree of precision when property of this nature
will not be confiscated.

RETROACTIVE LAWS

An element of legality is the principle that, ordinarily, laws should operate
prospectively and not retroactively and, in particular, that laws should never
declare something to be a crime which was not an offence when the act in
question was done. A criticism that has often been levelled against the
Nuremberg trials of leading Nazis after World War II was that the defendants
were prosecuted for acts which were not criminal offences at the time they
occurred. But the tribunal there concluded that war crimes and crimes against
humanity were indeed violations of international law.

The principle of *nullum crimen sine lege*, that the criminal law should not
have retroactive effect, is endorsed by Article 15.5 of the Constitution, which
extends the legality requirement beyond crimes. It states that "[t]he Oireachtas
shall not declare acts to be infringements of the law which were not so at the
date of their commission." Article 7 of the European Convention and Article
15 of the U.N. Covenant forbid retrospection but not quite as extensively, as
they are confined to crimes. The Covenant adds that a penalty may not be
imposed which is heavier than the one obtaining when the offence in question
was committed and, further, that persons are entitled to benefit from any
subsequent reduction of the penalty for the offence. Article 9 of the U.S.
Constitution forbids both the federal and the state governments from enacting
any *"ex post facto* law." Non-retroactivity is a fundamental principle of E.C.
law in the words of the European Court of Justice, "in general, the principle of
legal certainty precludes a Community measure from taking effect from a point
in time before its publication. ..."[34]

---

[33] *Id.* at p.156.
[34] *Racke v. Hauptzollamt Mainz* (Case 98/78) [1979] E.C.R. 69 at p.86 and *Marks and Spencer p.l.c. v. Customs & Excise C'mrs* (Case 62/00) [2003] 2 W.L.R. 665.

There also is a general principle of statutory interpretation, that laws are presumed to be prospective only and, especially where they impose burdens on persons, will not be construed as applying retroactively unless so required by express words or very clear implication.[35] It was contended in *Murphy v. G.M.*[36] that the Proceeds of Crime Act 1996 should not be applied retrospectively because there was no express provision to that effect and it did not contain any limitation provision, in contrast with comparable laws in other countries; that the definition of "proceeds of crime" in s. 1(1) of this Act lent force to this argument because the reference to any "offence" there was not qualified by the words "before or after the passing of this Act", which words qualified only the phrase "property obtained or received" in that definition; that there are instances where one could obtain or receive property prior to 1996 which can be connected with a post 1996 crime, such as borrowing the price of buying property before 1996 and subsequently stealing money to pay off the loan. However, Keane C.J., for the Supreme Court, could "find no ambiguity" in the definition and, without referring to the example just given, concluded that any other construction would be "fanciful and artificial."[37] He was "satisfied that the definition in plain and unambiguous language extends to property obtained or received at any time before ... 1996 ... by or as a result of or in connection with the commission of an offence."[38]

Retroactive Crimes

It depends on the very terms of the penal legislation in question whether or not it operates retroactively; the mere fact that it may have some retrospective application as a matter of procedure is not enough to have it declared invalid. Thus in *Abbey Films Ltd. v. Attorney General*,[39] it was contended that ss. 14 and 15 of the Restrictive Practices Act 1972 were unconstitutional on the grounds, *inter alia*, that they contravened the non-retroactive clause. Those provisions dealt with how allegations of restrictive practices can be investigated. Authorised officers were empowered to enter and inspect business premises, to take and copy documents found there. But the owner of the premises, when confronted by such an officer, was entitled to apply to the High Court for a declaration that an entry and search should not be conducted. Where this

---

[35] See generally, F. Bennion, *Statutory Interpretation* (3rd ed. 1997), pp. 235–243. Recent applications of this principle include *Kenny v. An Bord Pleanála (No. 1)* [2001] 1 I.R. 565, *D.P.P. v. Murphy* [2001] 1 I.R. 171, *McInerney v. Minister for Agriculture* [1995] 3 I.R. 449, *Kelly v. Scales* [1994] 1 I.R. 42, *O'H. v. O'H.* [1990] 2 I.R. 448; also *Ulster Bank v. Carter* [1999] N.I. 93.

[36] [2001] 4 I.R. 113.

[37] *Id.* at p.129.

[38] *Id.* at p.130.

[39] [1981] I.R. 158.

declaration was made, the statutory right to enter etc. ceased; otherwise, it was an offence to refuse entry to or to obstruct the officer in question. It was contended that this procedure created a retroactive offence on the grounds that an owner, who refused to let an officer enter the premises, did not know if he was committing an offence until the court either made or refused the declaration. Denial of access was merely one ingredient of the offence, which was completed when the court declined to make the declaration. This argument was rejected on the basis that the offence was committed once entry was refused or the officer was obstructed. There was no question of conduct that in 1971 was lawful being declared in 1972 to have been an offence.

In times of grave emergency legislatures are tempted to criminalise acts retrospectively. The most striking example from modern Irish history is s. 16(1) of the Public Safety Act 1927, which was considered in *Attorney General v. McBride*.[40] Kevin O'Higgins, the Minister for Justice, was murdered in July 1927 and within a month this Act had become law. Section 16 of it empowered District Justices to order the detention of persons whom a Garda superintendent declared to be "suspect(ed) of being or having been engaged or concerned in the commission" of any of the offences set out in that Act's schedule; one such offence was the murder of a Government Minister. At that time the 1922 Constitution was effectively suspended[41] and, as a result, this provision could not be struck down on the grounds that it contravened the separation of powers principle or that it operated retrospectively. But it was contended by the defendant that it is a fundamental principle of statutory construction that criminal legislation is presumed not to apply retrospectively, unless such application is plainly and unambiguously called for by the Act. And since by its very terms section 16 did not announce that it was to apply to murders committed before 11 August 1927, it was urged that the section did not apply to persons who were suspected of a murder that occurred before that date. Hanna J. rejected that argument on the grounds that the section clearly referred to past acts. While it is debatable whether a provision like section 16 would not fall foul of Article 15.5 of the present Constitution, because the section does not stipulate that murders occurring before its enactment are a new category of criminal offence, undoubtedly the section violates the spirit of this Article. But the section would probably be struck down for some of the reasons which the Vagrancy Act's "sus" provision were condemned.

King v. Attorney General[42] concerned section 4 of the Vagrancy Act 1824, as amended by section 15 of the Prevention of Crimes Act 1871. Section 4 creates numerous disparate offences, such as fortune-telling, exposing wounds or deformities while begging, exposing obscene or indecent matter and

---

[40] [1928] I.R. 451. See too cases on World War II emergency powers orders, *People v. Shribman* [1946] I.R. 431 and *Minister for Agriculture v. O'Connell* [1942] I.R. 600.
[41] *Ante*, p.8.
[42] [1981] I.R. 433.

abandoning ones wife or child so that they become charges on the parish. One offence is being a "suspected person" frequenting any street or highway with intent to commit a felony. A major difficulty that prosecutors had with this offence was in proving the requisite felonious intent. Section 14 of the 1871 Act eased this burden considerably, by stipulating that intent could be proved from the accused's "known character" – in other words, from the accused's previous convictions. Consequently, persons who had been convicted of a felony could later be convicted under section 4 of the Vagrancy Act if a member of the Garda Síochána found them on any street or highway and suspected them of intending to commit a felony. All that was necessary for a conviction was to incur the Garda's suspicion and to have a previous conviction; there was no need for any overt act to indicate felonious intent at the time of the arrest. It was held by the Supreme Court that this offence was unconstitutional for several reasons, one being the offence's quasi-retrospective nature, in that a conviction could be obtained primarily on the basis of offences committed by an accused before ever arousing a Garda's suspicion under section 4. In Henchy J.'s words, the offence was "singularly at variance with both the explicit and implicit characteristics and limitations of the criminal law as to the onus of proof and mode of proof. ..."[43]

Other Retroactive Measures

Article 15.5 of the Constitution is not confined to criminal offences, as it applies to "declar[ing] acts to be infringements of the law. ..." In *Re Heffron Kearns Ltd. (no. 1)*,[44] Murphy J. inclined to the view it applied to what is now section 297A of the Companies Act 1990, the civil wrong of "reckless trading." Under this, substantial damages may be awarded against a defendant who was knowingly involved in carrying on a company's business in a reckless manner. Murphy J. pointed out that "in practical terms, a citizen might have as much and more reason to be aggrieved if his actions which at the time of their performance were wholly innocent were to attract substantial civil liability than he would be if the same actions were to be transmuted into a criminal activity punishable by a nominal fine."[45] Accordingly, the section there was interpreted as not applying retrospectively, thereby saving it from invalidity.[46]

In contrast, in *Chestvale Properties Ltd. v. Glackin*,[47] a challenge to Part II (section 7–24) of the Companies Act 1990, which expanded considerably the powers of court-appointed examiners, was rejected by Murphy J. This was

---

[43] *Id.* at p.257.
[44] [1993] 3 I.R. 177.
[45] *Id.* at p.187.
[46] Followed in *Jones v. Gunn* [1997] 3 I.R. 1.
[47] [1993] 3 I.R. 35.

because "in no sense [did it] declare any act to be an infringement of the law which was not so at the date of its commission."[48] Similarly in *Haughey v. Moriarty*,[49] concerning the Tribunals of Inquiry (Evidence) (Amendment) Act 1979, which *inter alia* empowered tribunals of enquiry to order that persons should pay costs where they knowingly provide false or misleading information. Geoghegan J. held that this power would only apply to information supplied after 1979 and, consequently, was not affected in any way by Article 15.5.

An instance that came closer to the line was *Minister for Social Affairs v. Scanlon*,[50] where since 1954 the Social Welfare Acts provided that persons who had incorrectly (but not fraudulently) claimed and been paid benefits would not be obliged to repay them if any time later the error was discovered. This was repealed in 1991/92 and proceedings were brought to recover £43,088, the equivalent of contributory disability benefit that had been paid erroneously to the defendant since he had stopped working as a C.I.E. signalman in 1985. Fennelly J., who gave the only judgment, did not address the contention that this change in the law "imposes a retrospective penalty if it permits the plaintiff to recover benefits already received"[51] and was no different in substance from the liability imposed by s. 297A of the Companies Act 1990. This omission is more remarkable when the judge went on to reject as "devoid of merit" a suggestion that the administrative scheme for imposing the liability to repay those benefits contravened the separation of powers.[52]

Retrospective non-penal laws may very well be unconstitutional because they contravene some other provision of the Constitution, although there are no reported instances of this happening. It has been a legislative convention that tax laws should not normally operate retroactively; although some tax laws may be upheld despite their retrospective nature, others may very well be struck down where non-payment of tax is a criminal offence[53] or as unjust attacks on private property.[54] For most of his working life before he was forced to retire, the defendant in *Scanlon* and his employer paid social welfare contributions which covered, *inter alia*, disability benefits. He argued that clawing back the disability benefit that had been erronously paid to the defendant over the previous nine years, when at the time the Social Welfare Acts had stipulated that it was not recoverable, contravened the Constitution's property guarantee. Fennelly J.'s response, was that "[t]he bar on recovery contains at most a statutory concession that the [benefits] already paid should not be recoverable ... even though it has [since] been established through the

---

[48] *Id.* at pp. 44–45.
[49] [1999] 3 I.R. 1.
[50] [2001] 1 I.R. 64.
[51] *Id.* at p.85.
[52] *Id.* at p.87; see *ante*, p.63 on the single judgment rule.
[53] *Doyle v. An Taoiseach* [1986] I.L.R.M. 693, at p.715.
[54] *E.g. Untermyer v. Anderson*, 276 U.S. 440 (1928).

[administrative] machinery that it had been wrongly paid in the first place."[55] Consequently, he could not "identify any constitutional right to retain the benefit of a concession of that sort [because] the right to receive benefit in the first place or retain benefit wrongly paid derive from statute and do not partake of the nature of a property right."[56]

LAW OF VALIDATION

Another form of retroactive law is a law of validation, *i.e.* a statute which declares conduct or measures lawful that were unlawful at the time they took place. Acts of Indemnity are often passed following revolutions and civil wars, such as those passed in 1923 and 1924,[57] General Pinochet's 1978 Amnesty Decree in Chile and South Africa's 1995 Truth and Reconciliation Act. There was a tax amnesty in 1988 and again in 1993.[58] Another comparable law is one that declares valid and effective statutory instruments that otherwise may be held to be unconstitutional on separation of powers grounds, for instance section 2 of the Immigration Act 1999, which was passed following the *Laurentiu* decision of the Supreme Court.[59] It was held by that court in *McDaid v. Sheehy*[60] that provisions of this nature operate to validate such orders by placing them on a statutory footing.

Another of these laws is one which stipulates that, despite a judicial finding that something was unlawful, the normal consequences of invalidity shall not apply. One of these was enacted in 1960 to deal with what were regarded by the visitors as illegal practices in University College, Dublin,[61] and two such laws were passed affecting the Garda Síochána.[62] Another was the Garda Síochána Act 1979, which was passed following the Supreme Court's decision in *Garvey v. Ireland*,[63] that the dismissal of Commissioner Garvey from the head of the police force was illegal and invalid. This Act validated the appointment of his successor and all the actions that the new commissioner had taken in the intervening period. The Courts (No. 3) Act 1986 was passed in response to a Supreme Court decision that a host of District Court summonses

---

[55] [2001] 1 I.R. at p.87.
[56] *Ibid.*
[57] Indemnity (British Military) Act 1923, Indemnity Act 1923, and Indemnity Act 1924. See generally, Dicey, *supra* n.2, pp. 232–237.
[58] *Ante*, p.209.
[59] *Laurentiu v. Minister for Justice* [1999] 4 I.R. 26; *ante*, p.180. Similarly s.5 of the European Communities (Amendment) Act 1993, following the High Court's decision in *Meagher v. Minister for Agriculture* [1994] 1 I.R. 329.
[60] [1991] 1 I.R. 1.
[61] University College Dublin Act 1960, s.3.
[62] 1937 No. 5 and 1979 No. 16.
[63] [1981] I.R. 75.

had not been issued lawfully.[64] Section 6 of the Local Government (Planning and Development) Act 1982, declared valid a planning permission that had been found by the Supreme Court to be *ultra vires* the Minister for Local Government.[65] The Electoral (Amendment) (No. 2) Act 2002, was a response to a finding by the High Court that certain permitted expenditure in general elections was unconstitutional.[66]

Because laws of this nature are expected to give rise to constitutional difficulties, in recent times the practice has been to stipulate that they do not purport to validate anything that otherwise would be unconstitutional. For instance, section 2(2) of the Immigration Act 1999, states that "[i]f subsection (1) would, but for this subsection, conflict with a constitutional right of any person, the operation of that subsection shall be subject to such limitation as is necessary to secure that it does not so conflict but shall be otherwise of full force and effect." The constitutionality of provisions of this nature was upheld in *Grealis v. D.P.P.*,[67] concerning section 1(4) of the Interpretation Act 1997, which purported to give retroactive effect to newly created criminal offences. It was held that the clause there operated to exclude prosecutions commenced prior to the 1997 Act coming into force. Consequently, this Act was not invalid (as it otherwise would be) because, but for the proviso, the effect of the Act would have been to render criminal activities that were not crimes at the time when they took place, offending against the principle of *nullum crimen sine lege*. It was contended that the proviso there was itself invalid because, in its application, often a District Judge would have to take a view on whether the 1997 Act was unconstitutional, a function which is the exclusive prerogative of the Superior Courts.[68] But this was rejected on the grounds that, in applying the proviso, the District Judge does not determine the validity of the statute in the same way as the High Court would. As described by Denham J. under the proviso the court's function is "to determine whether the operation of [the Act] conflicts with the constitutional right of the individual before the court".[69] If the answer is "yes", then the judge is deciding that the Act is unconstitutional but that is deemed to be different from deciding that the Act is invalid because the processes are "not similar". Why they are not similar is not explained and the argument for unconstitutionality is hardly addressed at all, other than stating

---

[64] *State (Clarke) v. Roche* [1986] I.R. 619.

[65] *Pine Valley Developments Ltd v. Minister for Environment* [1987] 1.R. 23.

[66] *Kelly v. Minister for the Environment* [2002] 4 I.R. 191.

[67] [2001] 3 I.R. 144.

[68] *Ante*, p.144.

[69] [2001] 3 I.R. 144 at p.187 Neither Keane C.J. and Hardiman J. address this very logical contention, which had succeeded in the High Court. This case was heard at the same time as in *Grealis* and it is curious why the contention here was not addressed by the Court in *Grealis* at [2001] 3 I.R. 144 at pp.160–163, especially as O'Donovan J. had declared the proviso invalid on those very grounds.

the obvious fact that District Judges have a duty to uphold persons' constitutional rights.

It was held by that court in *Shelly v. McMahon*[70] and again in *Glavin v. Governor of Mountjoy Prison*[71] that the Courts (No. 2) Act 1988, could not validate certain decisions taken by a former District Judge at a time when he continued inadvertently to act as such but he no longer was eligible to be a judge. There the judge reached his retirement age in January 1984 but he continued to carry out judicial functions for several years later until he realised that he should have retired earlier. In *Shelly* a conviction he imposed in that period was set aside and in *Glavin*, where he had returned the applicant for trial before the Circuit Court, the conviction handed down there also was set aside. This was not a question of those respective applicants having a constitutional right to be tried by a judge below a certain age or of having an entrenched right to a preliminary enquiry. Under the Constitution, they were entitled to the fundamental principle of legality, *i.e.* to be tried in due course of law. Under the law obtaining when Shelly was convicted, the "judge" no longer had any authority to try him and, accordingly, his conviction was a nullity. Similarly with Glavin's return for trial; the judge no longer had any authority to send him forward for trial in the Circuit Court and, in consequence, his trial in that court was fatally flawed. As O'Flaherty J. put it, "once it is realised that the holding of the preliminary examination and the trial are inexorably bound together then it must follow that, if there has been a failure to have a proper preliminary examination, the trial or anything that happens after a purported return for trial is not in accordance with the Constitution; there is a failure of due process."[72]

In 1993, in proceedings concerning a "visitors' centre" being built in the Burren in Co. Clare by the Commissioners for Public Works, it was held that its construction was *ultra vires* the Commissioners and unlawful because the requisite planning permission had not been obtained.[73] A perpetual injunction was granted restraining any further building there. Within a week of the High Court's decision to this effect, the State Authorities (Development and Management) Act 1993, was passed, which stipulated *inter alia* that a "State authority (*e.g.* the Commissioners) shall have and be deemed always to have had power" to, *inter alia*, construct facilities of that nature. It also contained the caveat that it was not to apply to such extent as would infringe any person's constitutional rights. It was contended in *Howard v. Commissioners for Public Works (No. 3)*[74] that this Act was repugnant to the Constitution because it purported to nullify a decision made by the courts regarding what the

---

[70] [1990] 1 I.R. 36.
[71] [1991] 2 I.R. 421.
[72] *Id.* at p.436.
[73] *Howard v. Commissioners for Public Works* [1994] 1 I.R. 101.
[74] [1994] 3 I.R. 394.

Commissioners were empowered and authorised to do. Because of the caveat, however, this Act had no effect on the injunction that had been obtained against building in the Burren. Subject to that, the Act simply enlarged the legal authority of the Commissioners, extending it beyond what the courts had found it to be. Doing this did not prejudice any right of the plaintiffs, unless there is a right against the law ever being changed, which does not exist other than for retrospective penalties and liabilities.

As Lynch J. explained, the earlier holding that the Commissioners lacked the power and authority to construct the "visitors' centre" stands and "[t]he Oireachtas cannot alter or reverse that finding or the declaration and injunction made on foot of the same. To attempt to do so would contravene the constitutional separation of powers ... in that the legislature would be trespassing on and into the judicial domain."[75] However, it was never suggested in those proceedings, "nor could it rationally be suggested, that any of the three legislatures existing since the creation of the [Commissioners] could not have conferred such powers by appropriate legislation in the past. Why [then] should it be impossible for the Oireachtas to do so now by the Act of 1993?"[76]

INDIVIDUALISED LAWS

Laws are supposed to be couched in general terms in the sense that they must not be aimed solely against a particular individual or a small group of individuals. The great bulk of legislative provisions are general. However, statutory provisions exceptionally refer to particular individuals or entities – more often to confer benefits on them than to subject them to burdens. Laws occasionally empower the executive to decide that particular individuals or bodies shall not be subject to the general requirements of those very laws.

Bills of Attainder

The most extreme form of law imposing burdens on named individuals, known as Bills of Attainder, were laws decreeing that a named person, or a group so narrowly defined as almost to be nameable, be put to death for high crimes. A much cited example is the Act of 1513 commanding that Richard Rose, the Bishop of Rochester's cook, be executed by boiling in oil and without benefit of clergy.[77] Another is the Act of 1569 that attainted Shane O'Neill.[78] It was called "an Act for the Attainder of Shane Oneile, and the extinguishment of the name Oneile, and the entitling of the Queen's Magestie, her Heyres and

---

[75] *Id.* at p.407.
[76] *Ibid.*
[77] 22 Hen. 8, c. 9.
[78] 11 Eliz. c. 1.

Successours to the country of Tyrone, and to other Countries and Territories in Ulster." Following a long preamble giving the English version of O'Neill's resistance to the occupying Elizabethan forces, the Act stipulated in section 1 that "the said Shane O'Neyle shall be of these treasons attainted, and that he shall forfit unto your Magestie his goods, lands and tenements, rents and possessions, and his blood corrupt and disabled for ever, and that he should be reputed, had, named, and declared a false traytor to your Magestie, your crowne and dignitie, and that all his tyrannie, acts, feates, and false opinions, shall be avoided, abated, adnuled, destroyed, and put out of remembrance for ever. ..."

In the modern context, Bills of Attainder have been described as "legislative punishments, of any form of severity, of specifically designated persons or groups." [79] It has been pointed out that the objection to these laws, "is rooted in the desirability of legislative disclosure of its purposes. When one branch (of government) may both enact and apply, it may more easily veil its real motive and even its true target. ... Thus, separating policy-making from application has the additional virtue of requiring relatively clear and candid articulation of the legislative purpose. By requiring the legislature to expose its purpose for observation the political processes are given a fuller opportunity to react to it. And the judiciary is better able to judge the validity of the purpose and to assure that it violates no constitutional restrictions." [80] In the *"Sinn Fein Funds"* case,[81] concerning an Act the substantial effect of which was that an existing legal dispute about the ownership of a sum of money "is determined by the Oireachtas and the Court is required and directed ... to dismiss the plaintiff's claim without any hearing and without forming any opinion as to the rights of the respective parties",[82] it was held that the Act was an unwarrantable interference by the Oireachtas with the operation of the courts in the purely judicial domain. This Act could also have been challenged as a Bill of Attainder: of all the disputes before the courts, why pick out this one? That argument was made in the *An Blascaod Mór* case,[83] concerning the An Blascaod Mór National Historic Park Act 1989, which enabled the State to compulsorily acquire all of the land on the Great Blasket Island owned by the plaintiffs but practically none of the land there owned by others, nor land on any other of the islands making up the Blasket archipelago. In the event the Act was condemned by the Supreme Court as contravening the guarantee of equality in Article 40.1 of the Constitution.

---

[79] *United States v. Brown*, 381 U.S. 437 (1965) at p.447; *e.g. Liyanage v. The Queen* [1967] A.C. 259 and *Kable v. Director of Public Prosecutions*, 189 C.L.R. 51 (1996).

[80] Note, "The Bonds of Legislative Specification: A Suggested Approach to the Bill of Attainder Clause", 72 *Yale L.J.* 330 (1962) at pp. 346–347.

[81] *Buckley v. Attorney General* [1950] I.R. 67; *ante*, p.200.

[82] *Id.* at p.84.

[83] *An Blascaod Mór Teo v. Commissioners for Public Works (No.3)* [2000] 1 I.R. 6; *post*, p.397.

Dispensing Powers

A dispensing power is a statutory provision authorising the executive to decree that a named individual or entity shall not be bound by the legislative requirement. One of the grievances in the Petition of Right of 1688 was James II's claim to dispensing powers. An excellent example of such a power can be found in *East Donegal Co-Operative Society Ltd. v. Attorney General*,[84] which concerned the Livestock Marts Act 1967. This Act gives the Minister extensive discretionary powers to regulate the operation of livestock marts; all marts have to hold a licence and the Minister can insert whatever conditions are deemed fit into the licence. Section 4 of the Act was a dispensing power: it purported to enable the Minister "if he so thinks fit", *inter alia*, to exempt any named individual or enterprise from the Act's requirements. But the Supreme Court struck down the provision as an unconstitutional violation of the equality guarantee. As Walsh J. stated, "[t]he constitutional right of the Oireachtas in its legislation to take account of difference of social function and difference of capacity, physical and moral, does not extend to delegating that power to members of the Executive, to the exclusion of the Oireachtas, in order to decide as between individuals (all of whom are, by the terms of the Act, bound by it) which of them should be exempted from the application of the Act. ..."[85] The court, however, went on to hold that circumstances can arise where dispensing powers are constitutionally permissible, where it is necessary to have such a power in order to prevent legislation from otherwise being declared unconstitutional. According to Walsh J., this power would be permissible where "such exemption were necessary to avoid an infringement of the constitutional rights of such individuals which infringement, because of circumstances peculiar to them, would necessarily result from the application of the statutory provision without such exemption."[86] No instance of such a law was given; but the circumstances of the 1967 Act in question disclosed no such constitutional need to provide for individualised exemptions from that Act's requirements.

In the passage quoted above, Walsh J. spoke of an Act containing a dispensing power "to the exclusion of the Oireachtas." This suggests that where a law grants a dispensing power it would not be constitutionally objectionable if the Act requires each particular dispensation to be approved by a resolution of both (or perhaps one) Houses of the Oireachtas.

---

[84] [1970] I.R. 317.
[85] *Id.* at p.350. *Cf. City of New Orleans v. Dukes*, 427 U.S 297 (1976).
[86] *Id.* at p.350.

THE RIGHT OF ACTION

Legality and the rule of law require not only that all interferences with individual liberty and rights be authorised by law and that those laws possess certain minimum structural features, but also that everybody who interferes with another's rights and freedoms be answerable to the courts. In Dicey's words, the "equal subjection of all classes to the ordinary law of the land administered by the ordinary law courts; ... exclud(ing) the idea of any exemption of officials or others from ... the jurisdiction of the ordinary tribunals."[87] Dicey did not mention that the State itself should be answerable before the courts because he wrote in the era when sovereign immunity was still the norm, although individual ministers and officials were personally answerable before the courts for whatever they did in the course of their duties.[88] But the rule of law under the Constitution means that not alone are private individuals and organisations, and public officials and agencies, answerable before the courts whenever they interfere with another's freedom or rights, but that the State itself – Ireland, represented by the Attorney General – can also be sued and held accountable. In *Byrne v. Ireland*,[89] the Supreme Court held that the common law principle of sovereign immunity, encompassed in the maxim that "the King can do no wrong", was not carried over into the law of the Free State, let alone into the law of the Republic. Accordingly, if the State, through its instrumentalities, has done something to an individual or body that would be unlawful if it were done by anyone else, there is nothing to preclude the injured party from suing the State; it is not shielded by legal immunity from suit. At present, there are no general statutory provisions that purport to exempt the State from liability in tort or for breach of contract or of trust; as is explained below, all that exists is a very limited immunity in respect of several public services.

Some modern constitutions, such as the German, Italian and South African Constitutions, expressly stipulate that persons in dispute with public authorities are entitled to go to court to have their disputes resolved, even where it is not being claimed that the plaintiff's constitutional rights were violated.[90] Such a right has been inferred from the French Constitution[91] but not from the United States Constitution.[92] This difference in approach may result from the fact that nearly all continental European countries have special administrative courts for dealing with disputes arising between individuals and the State or its organs and agents. Article 13 of the European Convention and Article 2(3)(a) of the

---

[87] *Supra* n. 2 pp. 202–203.

[88] *E.g. Entick v. Carrington* (1765) 19 St. Tr. 1030.

[89] [1972] I.R. 241.

[90] Articles 19(4), 113, and 34 respectively.

[91] *Minister for Agriculture v. Dame Lamotte*, Cons dEtat, February 17, 1950 [1950] *Dalloz* Jur. 282.

[92] *Johnson v. Robinson*, 415 U.S. 361 (1974).

U.N. Covenant guarantee an "effective remedy" against violation of the numerous guarantees contained therein. Additionally, Article 6(1) of the European Convention and Article 14(1) of the U.N. Covenant guarantee, *inter alia*, a "fair hearing" by independent and impartial tribunals in respect of persons "[civil] rights and obligations." These have been interpreted by the Strasbourg Court and by the U.N. Human Rights Committee as including a right of access to the courts so that an individual's dispute with, *inter alia*, the State is determined, as well as the manner of its determination.[93]

Constitutional Rights

Where a person is being unlawfully deprived of his liberty, Article 40.4 of the Constitution entitles him or someone on his behalf to apply to the High Court to secure a prompt hearing with a view to having him released. Apart from this, a more general right of access to the courts has been recognised in case law, culminating in *Byrne v. Ireland*. It was not directly concerned with an Act of the Oireachtas purporting to prevent or obstruct the plaintiff from going to court, seeking a determination that the State had contravened one or more of her constitutional rights. However, Walsh J.'s judgment there contains observations on legislative interferences with individuals' attempts to assert their constitutional rights in court. Generally, those provisions would be unconstitutional. Thus,

> "In several parts in the Constitution duties to make certain provisions for the benefit of the citizens are imposed on the State in terms which bestow rights upon the citizens and, unless some contrary provision appears in the Constitution, the Constitution must be deemed to have created a remedy for the enforcement of these rights. It follows that, where the right is one guaranteed by the State, it is against the State that the remedy must be sought if there has been a failure to discharge the constitutional obligation imposed. The Oireachtas cannot prevent or restrict the citizen from pursuing his remedy against the State in order to obtain or defend the very rights guaranteed by the Constitution in the form of obligations imposed upon the State; nor can the Oireachtas delegate to any organ of state the implementation of these rights so as to exonerate the State itself from its obligations under the Constitution. The State must act through its organs but it remains vicariously liable for the failures of these organs in the discharge of the obligations, save where expressly excluded by the Constitution."[94]

---

[93] *E.g. Osman v. United Kingdom*, 29 E.H.R.R. 245 (1998); see generally, Gearty, "Unravelling Osman", 64 *Mod. L. Rev.* 159 (2001). Compare *Matthews v. Ministry of Defence* [2003] 2 W.L.R. 435.

[94] [1972] I.R. 241 at p.264.

And:

> "the provisions of the Constitution obliging the State to act in a particular manner may be enforced in the Courts against the State as such. If, in particular cases, the State has already by law imposed on some organ of State or some servant of the State the duty to implement the right or protection guaranteed by the Constitution then, in cases of default, it may be sufficient and adequate in particular instances to bring proceedings against the person upon whom the duty has been so imposed; but that does not absolve the State upon which the primary obligation has been imposed, from responsibility to carry out the duty imposed upon it. If under the Constitution the State cannot do any act or be guilty of any omission save through one or more of its organs or servants, it is nonetheless answerable".[95]

Moreover:

> "a wrong which arises from the failure to honour an obligation must be capable of remedy, and a contest between the citizen and the State in the pursuit of such a remedy is a justiciable controversy cognisable by the Courts save where expressly excluded by a provision of the Constitution if it is in respect of obligations and rights created by the Constitution."[96]

In conclusion:

> "Where the People by the Constitution create rights against the State or impose duties upon the State, a remedy to enforce these must be deemed to be also available. It is as much the duty of the State to render justice against itself in favour of citizens as it is to administer the same between private individuals. The investigation and the adjudication of such claims by their nature belong to the judicial power of government in the State, designated in Article 6 of the Constitution of Ireland, which is vested in the judges and the courts appointed and established under the Constitution in accordance with the provisions of the Constitution.
>
> In my view, the whole tenor of our Constitution is to the effect that there is no power, institution, or person in the land free of the law save where such immunity is expressed, or provided for, in the Constitution itself."[97]

While these observations are all *obiter dicta*, they were endorsed by Ó Dalaigh

---

[95] *Id.* at p.265.
[96] *Id.* at pp. 279–280.
[97] *Id.* at p.271.

C.J. They are also consistent with a decision of the Supreme Court in 1964 in the *Quinn* case and a decision of Kenny J. in 1966 in the *Macauley* case.

In *State (Quinn) v. Ryan*,[98] the Supreme Court proclaimed the constitutional right of individuals to go to court, in order to have their right to liberty vindicated, and held that the legislature cannot deprive them of that right. There, the English police wanted to extradite the applicant from Ireland for trial on charges in England. The then extradition procedure (or strictly, backing of warrants procedure) was contained in the Petty Sessions (Ireland) Act 1851,[99] and provided that once Garda officers in Ireland received an arrest warrant from any United Kingdom police authority, the person sought could be arrested and forthwith surrendered to those authorities. No provision was made allowing the person being sought to contest the legality of his arrest before being handed over to the U.K. police. The applicant was arrested on foot of an English warrant, he applied for *habeas corpus* and the court held that the warrant was invalid. However, the Gardaí had a second and apparently valid warrant to arrest him, and when he was leaving the confines of the court they arrested him and brought him immediately to the border with Northern Ireland, where he was handed over to the police. In further *habeas corpus* proceedings, the Supreme Court held that the extradition provisions in the 1851 Act were unconstitutional because they denied persons the opportunity to go to court to challenge the validity of their arrest and detention. According to Ó Dalaigh, C.J., "[t]he claim made on behalf of the police to be entitled to arrest a citizen and forthwith to bundle him out of the jurisdiction before he has an opportunity of considering his rights is the negation of law and a denial of justice. ... It was not the intention of the Constitution in guaranteeing the fundamental rights of the citizen that these rights should be set at nought or circumvented. The intention was that rights of substance were being assured to the individual and that the Courts were the custodian of these rights."[100] And according to Walsh J., "a right to apply to the High Court or any Judge thereof is conferred on every person who wishes to challenge the legality of his detention. It must follow that any law which makes it possible to frustrate that right must necessarily be invalid. ..."[101] Following this judgment, new extradition procedures were adopted in the Extradition Act 1965.

A right of access to the court to have all questions of constitutional right determined was endorsed by Kenny J. in *Macauley v. Minister for Posts and Telegraphs*,[102] where it was held that the Attorney General could not prevent an individual from suing the Government by denying his *fiat*. According to Kenny J., "there is a right to have recourse to the High Court to defend and

---

[98] [1965] I.R. 70.
[99] 14 & 15 Vic. c.93.
[100] [1965] I.R. 70 at pp.122 and 123.
[101] *Id.* at p.124.
[102] [1966] I.R. 345.

vindicate a legal right and ... it is one of the personal rights of the citizens ... (T)he citizens have a right to have recourse to the Courts to question the validity of any law having regard to the provisions of the Constitution or for the purpose of asserting or defending a right given by the Constitution for if it did not exist, the guarantees and rights in the Constitution would be worthless." [103]

Immunity from Suit

It does not follow from what was decided in *Macauley* and in *Byrne* that there is a constitutional right to go to court to assert each and every non-constitutional claim. In the first place, the position may be different depending on whether the right being asserted arises under the common law or by way of statute. The plaintiff's claim in *Byrne* was one arising at common law, the tort of negligence, and the whole tenor of Walsh J.'s judgment is to condemn doctrines and provisions that seek to prevent individuals asserting their common law rights against the State. In *Macauley* the plaintiff's claim also was one arising at common law, for breach of contract: it was a dispute between the plaintiff and the Minister for Posts and Telegraphs about the bad telephone service he was getting. He sought to sue the Minister but, under section 2(1) of the Ministers and Secretaries Act 1924, it was essential to get the Attorney General's *fiat*, or consent, before an action against the Minister could be proceeded with. The Attorney would not grant his *fiat* in respect of the plaintiff's action, who then claimed that section 2(1) of the Act was unconstitutional. Kenny J. held that the Attorney's unfettered and unreviewable power to block all kinds of litigation against the State contravened the constitutional right of access to the courts. He did not mention legislative provisions seeking to exclude the State from liability under specific common law heads or rules, such as tort, breach of contract or breach of equitable obligations. But in the *Byrne* case Walsh J. suggested that the courts would not readily uphold such provisions. He remarked that "the observations which I have made as to the question of the prerogatives apply with even greater force to causes of action which are not based upon statutory provision"[104] and, having emphasised that what he had said did not imply that the State could never exempt itself from general statutory duties, he added that "(t)his case is concerned with the ability of the plaintiff to maintain a common-law action against the State for the tortious acts of its employees."[105]

The rule of law as conceived by Dicey was hostile not alone to the executive being given power to dispense individuals from the necessity of complying with the law, but it also condemned laws that granted individuals and

---

[103] *Id.* at p.359.
[104] [1972] I.R. 241 at p.275.
[105] *Id.* at p.279.

organisations broad immunity from being sued in the courts. Dicey's response to the Trade Disputes Act 1906,[106] which granted trade unions some immunity from suit, was to proclaim that "(t)he rule of law is in England now exposed to a new peril" because the legislature had "thought fit ... to confer extraordinary immunities on combinations both of employers and of workmen ... "[107] Nevertheless, and as Walsh J. pointed out in *Byrne v. Ireland*, the Constitution itself expressly provides for some immunities from suit, *viz.* Article 13.8.1, regarding the exercise and performance of the President's functions, and Article 15.12–13, regarding legislative privilege and freedom of members of the Oireachtas from arrest. Moreover, the Constitution may very well require granting other immunities, such as diplomatic immunity and foreign sovereign immunity, and it is conceivable that other immunities may still be justifiable in the light of the Constitution's underlying policies.

Parliamentary Immunity

Article 15.13 of the Constitution grants members of both Houses of the Oireachtas extensive immunity in respect of whatever they say in either chamber; these have been extended by statute.[108] In the *An Blascaod Mór Teo (No.4)* case,[109] Budd J. held that in an appropriate case the State itself could be held liable in damages for losses incurred by enacting an unconstitutional law, but that the Government Minister or member who sponsored the measure in question could not be held similarly liable on account of this immunity.

Diplomatic and Sovereign Immunity

One of the general principles of international law is that foreign States, their heads of State and Ministers of Government enjoy immunity from being sued in other States, as do accredited diplomats in the receiving State.[110] Extensive immunities are provided for in the Diplomatic Relations and Immunities Act 1967. In the *McElhinney* case[111] it was held that these immunities are not unconstitutional and they have been upheld by the Strasbourg Court as being consistent with the European Convention.[112]

Judicial Immunity

At common law judges enjoyed immunity from suit in that they could not be

---

[106] 6 Edw. 7 c.47.
[107] *Supra* n. 2 at pp. 204n.
[108] *Supra*, p.108.
[109] *An Blascaod Mór Teo v. Commissioners for Public Works (No.4)* [2000] 3 I.R. 565.
[110] *Supra*, p.243.
[111] *McElhinney v. Williams* [1995] 3 I.R. 382; *ante*, p.243.
[112] *McElhinney v. Ireland*, 34 E.H.R.R. 322 (2002).

held liable in respect of what they did while acting within their jurisdiction.[113] It has never been determined if this immunity is consistent with the Constitution and it is intriguing that Walsh J. in the *Byrne* case made no reference to judicial immunity. This immunity may very well be required by Article 35.2 of the Constitution, which guarantees judicial independence.[114] Section 53 of the Offences Against the State Act 1939 confers immunity on members of the Special Criminal Court in respect of the exercise of their judicial functions. Although judges in most continental European countries enjoy a similar immunity, circumstances can arise where the State will be held liable for the egregious wrong-doing of judges – for *faute de service judiciare*. There appears to be no good reason in principle why that should not also be the case in Ireland.

Witnesses' and Lawyers' Immunity

At common law witnesses in legal proceedings enjoy absolute immunity from suit for everything they say in the course of their evidence. It was contended in *Fagan v. Burgess*[115] that so extensive and unqualified an immunity was unconstitutional and, at minimum, there ought to be some civil remedy in damages where the witness deliberately gave false testimony. O'Higgins J. in his judgment does not address this argument at all, but dismissed the action in the light of *obiter dicta* from a Supreme Court case where this contention appears not to have been made.[116] Nor does it seem to have been urged in *E. O'K. v. D.K.*,[117] where the Supreme Court held that the common law immunity extends to expert witnesses.

Formerly lawyers could not be held liable in negligence for errors committed when conducting a case in court[118] but it is an open question whether this exception from the normal principles of professional liability would be upheld today.[119]

Public Services Immunities

The circumstances and extent to which the ordinary principles of civil liability in tort (or extra-contractual liability) apply to bodies providing public services is a perennial source of controversy, because at times the public service-provider is different in some significant respects from service-providers in the private

---

[113] *Supra*, p.167.
[114] *Supra*, p.166.
[115] [1999] 3 I.R. 306.
[116] *Looney v. Bank of Ireland* [1996] 1 I.R. 157.
[117] [2001] 3 I.R. 568.
[118] *Rondel v. Worsley* [1969] 1 A.C. 191.
[119] Compare *Hall & Co. v. Simons* [2002] 1 A.C. 615 with *Lai v. Chamberlains* [2003] 2 N.Z.L.R. 374.

sector.[120] Additionally, a handful of statutory provisions exist that exempt some public agencies and even professional associations from liability arising out of the defective performance or the non-performance of their functions. For more than a century the Post Office has enjoyed some immunity from suit and this is provided for in section 64(1) of the Postal and Telecommunication Services Act 1983, according to which An Post is "immune from all liability in respect of any loss or damage suffered by a person in the use of a postal service by reason of" not providing the service, or suspending, restricting or interrupting the service. The precise scope of the immunity does not appear to have been considered by the courts, nor does its constitutionality appear to have been challenged. The fire services are given a somewhat more restricted immunity by section 36 of the Fire Services Act 1981, which states that no action for damages may be brought against those responsible for the fire services "in respect of injury to persons or property alleged to have been caused or contributed to by the failure to comply with any functions conferred by this Act." The Central Bank is exonerated by section 9(5) of the Central Bank Act 1972, from liability in respect of "any losses incurred through the insolvency or default" of a holder of a banking licence. Immunities are conferred by statute on several regulatory authorities, for instance section 36 of the Solicitors (Amendment) Act 1994, which exempts the Law Society from liability where it shows that, in the circumstances, it acted reasonably and in good faith.[121] A more extensive immunity is conferred on some of these agencies.

In *Ryan v. Attorney General*,[122] the Supreme Court rejected the argument that the State is immune from liability for injuries received by serving soldiers in the course of hostilities. There the plaintiff had been injured in action in the Lebanon while serving with the U.N. Force, under the control of Irish officers. Finlay C.J., for the court, refused to follow British, Australian and U.S. case law, that allows immunity in such circumstances and is based on a view that civil liability might impede national defence, adding that U.N. service does not involve defence of the State. He pointed out that Article 28 of the Constitution provides the "most ample and unrestricted powers ... to legislate to secure public safety and the preservation of the State in time of war ... or armed rebellion",[123] and any immunity from suit conferred in legislation of that nature cannot be the subject of a constitutional challenge.

It would appear that the Attorney General, the Director of Public Prosecutions and the Garda Síochána enjoy extensive immunity from liability

---

[120] See generally, B. McMahon & W. Binchy, *The Law of Torts* (3rd ed. 2000), Chaps 9 and 38, D. Fairgrieve, *State Liability in Tort* (2003) (comparing England and France) and D. Dobbs, *The Law of Torts* (2000) Chap.15 (the U.S.A.).

[121] Similarly, *e.g.* Investment Intermediaries Act 1995, s.53, Stock Exchange Act 1995, s.53(1) and Irish Takeover Panel Act 1997, s.17.

[122] [1989] 1 I.R. 77.

[123] *Id.* at p.182.

in negligence with regard to decisions they take to either prosecute individuals or seek their extradition, or not to do so.[124] But the Gardaí would not seem to have a blanket immunity from negligence claims arising from their investigating crimes.[125] There are long-established torts of malicious prosecution and of misfeasance in public office.

Quasi Immunities

A number of other statutory provisions, which give the State or public institutions and officials virtual immunity from suit or other distinct advantages in litigation, call for mention. One of these, the Public Autorities Protection Act 1893,[126] which, *inter alia*, reduced the limitation period for actions against public bodies to six months, was repealed in 1954.[127] By virtue of s. 3(1) of the Statute of Limitations 1957, this Act "appli(ies) to proceedings by or against a State authority in like manner as if that State authority were a private individual", although exceptions are made for certain revenue and customs cases, and for tax claims. Proceedings arising from action taken under the Defence Act 1954 must be instituted in the High Court within six months of the alleged wrong taking place.[128]

Civil proceedings may not be brought in respect of anything purportedly done under the Mental Health Act 2001, without the prior permission of the High Court. Permission will be refused if the court is satisfied that the claim is "frivolous or vexatious", or that "there are no reasonable grounds for contending that the [intended defendant] acted in bad faith or without reasonable cause."[129] Previously, permission to bring such proceedings would be refused unless the court was satisfied that there were "substantial grounds for contending that [the intended defendant] acted in bad faith or without reasonable care."[130] Several Acts that grant bodies licensing and other regulatory powers stipulate that those bodies cannot be held liable for losses arising from the exercise of their powers where they demonstrate that they acted reasonably and/or in good faith.[131] Even apart from these provisions, public bodies and officials will not be held liable for any financial losses arising from their activities unless it is shown that they acted *mala fides* or recklessly, and not just negligently.[132]

---

[124] *W. v. Ireland (No. 2)* [1997] 2 I.R. 141.

[125] *Osman* case, *supra*, n.93.

[126] 56 & 57 Vic. c.61.

[127] Public Authorities (Judicial Proceedings) Act 1954.

[128] S.111.

[129] S.73.

[130] Mental Health Act 1945, s.260; *cf. Blehein v. Murphy (No. 2)* [2000] 3 I.R. 359, *Murphy v. Greene* [1990] 2 I.R. 566 and *O'Dowd v. North Western Health Board* [1983] I.L.R.M. 186.

[131] *Supra*, p.303.

[132] *Glencar Explorations Ltd v. Mayo C.C.* [2002] 1 I.R. 84 and *supra*, n.120.

In order to challenge the decisions of public authorities, to have them declared unlawful, it is often necessary to follow the "judicial review" procedure, which involves first applying to the High Court for leave to commence the action.[133] Ordinarily this is an *ex parte* application and the threshold for obtaining leave is quite low, the *prima facie*/arguable case test.[134] There are several statutory provisions that require leave applications to be made within a comparatively short period after the decision being challenged was taken, on notice to the decision-maker, and where the threshold for getting leave is that there are "substantial grounds for contending" that the decision is unlawful. A constitutional challenge to one such provision was rejected by the Supreme Court in *Re ss. 4 and 10 of the Illegal Immigrants (Trafficking) Bill 1999*.[135]

That plaintiffs may be required by the courts in appropriate cases to furnish security for defendants' costs in defending the action has been held not to be unconstitutional.[136] A challenge to the requirement that litigants in the Superior Courts pay certain court fees was rejected by the Supreme Court, principally because there was insufficient evidence adduced to warrant striking down the statutory instrument and also because the plaintiff there could have availed of the civil legal aid system.[137] In exceptional circumstances not covered by that system or by what is known as the Attorney General's scheme, persons seeking to sue the State or its agencies have a constitutional right to legal aid.[138]

Trade Union Immunity

At common law, members of unions of workers or employers and others engaged in industrial action in respect of wages and working conditions were subject to the same liabilities as anyone else who takes equivalent action. But the Trades Disputes Act 1906[139] conferred extensive immunities on them, which at the time caused Dicey considerable disquiet, especially section 4 which gave unions and employers' associations a virtual blanket immunity from liability in tort. But it was held that these do not provide legal protection for breach of constitutional rights[140] and they were narrowed somewhat by the Industrial Relations Act 1990. Former section 4 (now section 13 of the 1990 Act) is now confined to torts committed "in contemplation or furtherance of a trade dispute."[141] In 1982 in France a blanket trade union immunity was held to be unconstitutional.[142]

---

[133] R.S.C. Order 84; *post*, p.519.
[134] *G. v. D.P.P.* [1994] 1 I.R. 374.
[135] [2000] 2 I.R. 360; *post*, p.486.
[136] *Salih v. General Accident Fire & Life Assur. Ltd* [1987] I.R. 628.
[137] *Murphy v. Minister for Justice* [2001] 1 I.R. 95.
[138] *Kirwan v. Minister for Justice* [1994] 2 I.R. 417; *post*, p.493.
[139] 6 Edw. 7 c.47.
[140] *Crowley v. Ireland* [1980] I.R. 102; *post*, p.811.
[141] See generally, M. Forde, *Industrial Relations Law* (1991) pp. 190–191.
[142] Conseil Constitutionnel, October 22, 1982 [1983] *Dalloz* Jur. 189.

CHAPTER 14

Life and Human Dignity

The most fundamental of all rights is the right to life. Article 40.3.2 of the Constitution provides that "[t]he State shall ... by its laws protect as best it may from unjust attack and, in the case of injustice done, vindicate the life ... of every citizen." Life is expressly guaranteed by the principal international human rights instruments, most notably Article 2 of the European Convention and Article 6 of the UN Covenant, as well as in many post World War II Constitutions. The preamble to the Constitution, as well as the Constitutions of Germany and of South Africa, and the Canadian Bill of Rights, make express reference to upholding human dignity as a fundamental principle. Most human rights instruments adopted prior to 1945 make no express reference to life or to dignity but, in 1765, in his account of the "absolute rights of individuals," Blackstone placed first on his list the "right of personal security consist[ing] in a person's legal and uninterrupted enjoyment of his life, his limbs, his body, his health and his reputation."[1]

Article 40.3.2 of the Constitution contains no indication of the circumstances in which the taking of human life is permissible nor, indeed, does it cast any light on what is to be regarded as an "unjust attack" on life or on what measures may be needed for its vindication against attack. The "right to life of the unborn," which is guaranteed by Article 40.3.3, has been held to be concerned only with abortion and is qualified by the need to have "due regard to the equal right to life of the mother ...".

GENOCIDE

In the wake of the German Nazi atrocities and the Nuremberg war crimes trials, the UN General Assembly in 1948 adopted the Convention on the Prevention and Punishment of the Crime of Genocide,[2] with a view to deterring similar atrocities. Genocide is defined in Article 2 of this Convention as "any of the following acts committed with intent to destroy in whole or in part, a national, ethnical, racial or religious group as such, [*inter alia*] killing members of the group." Genocide also includes causing serious bodily or mental harm

---

[1] W. Blackstone, *Commentaries on the Laws of England* (1st ed., 1765), p.129.
[2] December 9, 1948, 78 UNTS 277. See generally, W. Schabas, *Genocide in International Law* (2000).

to members of the group, deliberately inflicting on them conditions calculated to induce their physical destruction, preventing births within the group and forcibly transferring their children to another group. Provision is made for extraterritorial criminal jurisdiction over persons accused of genocide and for their extradition.[3] Ireland gave effect to the Convention's requirements in the Genocide Act 1973.

DEATH PENALTY

A major constitutional controversy for many years in the United States has been the circumstances in which persons convicted of serious offences may be subjected to capital punishment.[4] A similar question has bedevilled the Privy Council, mainly in appeals from West Indies States where the death penalty was imposed on convicted murderers.[5] In 1995, the Constitutional Court of South Africa unanimously struck down the death penalty as a form of "cruel, inhuman or degrading punishment" not permitted by its Constitution.[6] Both Article 2 of the European Convention and Article 6 of the UN Covenant permit capital punishment as a penalty for crimes; in the latter case, only for "the most serious crimes" and not where the guilty person is under eighteen years of age or is a pregnant woman. But the European Convention's 6th Protocol of 1983 prohibits the death penalty except in time of war or of imminent threat of war.

Article 15.5.2 of the Constitution, adopted in 2002, prohibits capital punishment; it states that "[t]he Oireachtas shall not enact any law providing for the imposition of the death penalty" and this prohibition obtains even during a time of war or armed rebellion contemplated by Article 28.3.3. Since 1954 every sentence of death imposed was commuted by the President under Article 13.6. The death penalty for murder was abolished by the Criminal Justice Act 1964, but remained principally for the murder of a member of the Garda Síochána in the course of his duty as well as for treason, until it was abolished entirely by section 1 of the Criminal Justice Act 1990.

Since 1965 persons could not be extradited to another country where, if found guilty, they would be executed.[7] Extradition in those circumstances

---

[3] *Cf. Nulyarimma v. Thompson*, 8 B.H.R.C. 135 (1999) (Australia) and the *Guatemala Genocide* case, 42 I.L.M. 686 (2003) (Spain).

[4] See generally R. Hood, *The Death Penalty, A Worldwide Perspective* (3rd ed., 2002) and A. Sarat, *Why the State Kills, Capital Punishment and the American Condition* (2001).

[5] Culminating in *Reyes v. The Queen* [2002] 2 A.C. 235, *R.. v. Hughes* [2002] 2 A.C. 259 and *Fox v. The Queen* [2002] 2 A.C. 284. Cf. *Re Constitution of Lithuania*, 6 B.H.R.C. 283 (1998).

[6] *S. v. Makwanyane* [1995] 1 L.R.C. 269.

[7] Extradition Act 1965, s.19.

was condemned by the European Court of Human Rights and by constitutional courts of other countries where the death penalty is not expressly prohibited.[8] It is debatable whether a person would be deported from Ireland in circumstances where he is likely to suffer the death penalty in the receiving State.

EXTRA-LEGAL EXECUTIONS

To deliberately kill another person, without legal authority to do so, is the criminal offence of murder, which carries the mandatory sentence of life imprisonment.[9] No distinction is drawn between killing done by agents of the State and by private individuals, although murder of a member of the Garda Síochána or a prison officer, or certain others, carries a minimum sentence of forty years imprisonment.[10]

In exceptional circumstances the State is permitted to use deadly force in order to save life and, perhaps, to keep the peace but exactly what the Constitution requires in this regard has never been considered by the courts. In a notorious case in the 1930s, Hanna J. held that, under the common law, "the armed forces can fire on an unlawful or riotous assembly only where such a course is necessary as a last resort to preserve life."[11] It was held by the Strasbourg Court in *McCann v. United Kingdom*[12] that the killing by SAS soldiers of suspected Irish terrorists in Gibraltar in 1998 in the circumstances contravened their right to life as guaranteed by Article 2 of the European Convention.

Under section 17 of the Coroners Act 1962, a coroner is obliged to hold an inquest where a person is found dead in his district and he is of the opinion that the death may have occurred *inter alia* "in a violent or unnatural manner, or suddenly and from unknown causes ...". To date the courts have not addressed the question whether the present system for coroners' inquests meets the obligation implicit in Article 40.3.2 that violent and other suspicious deaths should not go uninvestigated. It was held by the Strasbourg Court in *Shanaghan v. United Kingdom*[13] that Article 2 of the European Convention requires public authorities to carry out a thorough investigation of such deaths.[14] However, where a joint committee of the Oireachtas sought to investigate the

---

[8] *Soering v. United Kingdom* [1989] 11 E.H.R.R. 439, *United States v. Burns*, 195 D.L.R. 4th 1 (2001) and *Mohamed v. South Africa* 11 B.H.R.C. 374 (2001).
[9] See generally P. Charleton *et al*, *Criminal Law* (1999), Chap.7.
[10] Criminal Justice Act 1990, s.3.
[11] *Lynch v. Fitzgerald* [1938] I.R. 382 at p.405.
[12] E.H.R.R. 97 (1995).
[13] Unreported, May 4, 2001.
[14] Applied in *R. (Amin) v. Secretary of State* [2003] 3 W.L.R. 1169. Compare *Jordan's Application for Judicial Review, Re* [2002] N.I. 151.

circumstances in which in 2000 a young man was shot dead by members of the Garda Síochána, it was held by the Supreme Court that they had no legal authority to carry out an inquiry of that nature.[15] This incident is presently being investigated by a statutory tribunal of enquiry.

There is little authority on the question of what constitutional obligation the State has to take appropriate steps in order to prevent persons being killed or their lives being significantly endangered — either by agents of the State or by third parties. Where persons are in the custody of the State, for instance being imprisoned or held in Garda custody, there is a common law duty on the State to safeguard their lives and their welfare. Where pre-trial discovery of documents or adducing evidence in court would put a person's life at significant risk, the court will endeavour to alleviate that risk. Thus, in *Burke v. Central Independent Television plc*,[16] where the plaintiff was suing for defamation, the defendant contended that, if the identities of its sources of information were disclosed, it was very likely that the information would be passed on to terrorists and thereby put those persons' lives at risk. Affidavit evidence in support of this claim was accepted. Notwithstanding the plaintiff's constitutional right to his good name and to have it vindicated in court, the Supreme Court held that those sources' right to life took precedence and that the material need not be discovered.[17] Because the plaintiff's claim could thereby be prejudiced to an extent, the defendant was required to make certain amendments to the defence to counteract any prejudice: namely withdraw the plea of fair comment and be permitted instead to plead justification (i.e. the truth of the allegations) as a defence. It had been suggested by the defendant that, as a compromise, the plaintiff's lawyers would be permitted to view the disputed material, without revealing its contents to their client, but the court found this not to be acceptable. O'Flaherty J. observed that the documents in question did not appear to be relevant to what was actually in dispute and consequently did not need to be discovered at all to the plaintiff.

It depends on all the circumstances whether a court would prevent a person being either extradited or deported to a country where there is a significant risk that he may suffer extra-legal execution. But the Supreme Court has upheld a decision to deport a pregnant woman to Nigeria where the infant mortality rate is far higher that it is in Ireland.[18]

---

[15] *Maguire v. Ardagh* [2002] 1 I.R. 385; *supra*, p.114.
[16] [1994] 2 I.R. 61.
[17] Cf. *A's application for Judicial Review, Re* [2001] N.I. 335.
[18] *Baby O. v. Minister for Justice* [2002] 2 I.R. 169; *infra*, p.720.

RIGHT TO DIE

Whether or in what circumstances there is a constitutional right to die presents acute moral difficulties.[18] Where a person is extremely ill, is suffering excruciating pain or discomfort and has no real prospect of ever recovering, is he entitled to be assisted in taking his own life? If yes, what form may that assistance take? And if the person is in a virtual vegetative state and is not capable of expressing a desire to die, in what circumstances is it permissible to put an end to his life? Closely related to these is the question of euthanasia.

The common law offence of suicide was abolished in 1993[20] but it remains an offence to assist another person to kill himself. An adult of sound mind is entitled to refuse to undergo medical treatment that is necessary to save his life[21] but it would appear that parents are not entitled to prevent their children being administered life-saving treatment.[22]

Where a person is being kept alive on life-support, the circumstances in which that machine may be turned off and he be left to die were considered by the Supreme Court in *A Ward of Court (withholding medical treatment) (No.2), Re*.[23] In the course of a minor operation involving a general anaesthetic, a young woman suffered three cardiac arrests, resulting in very serious brain damage and for nearly 22 years was extensively handicapped, bed-ridden; she was practically in a persistent or permanent vegetative state, possessing an extremely minimal cognitive capacity. Insofar as she may have had some cognitive ability, realisation of her catastrophic condition would be a "terrible torment" to her and there was no prospect of her condition ever improving. For several years she was being fed through a gastronomy tube but her family eventually requested the hospital where she was to remove this tube.

As Hamilton C.J. emphasised, the issues there were "not about euthanasia and are not about putting down the old and the infirm, the mentally defective or the physically infirm but are about the question whether ... artificial feeding and antibiotic drugs may be withheld from a [person] who is and has been for more than twenty three years in a coma and has no hope of recovery, when it is accepted that if that is done, the [person] will shortly thereafter die."[24] Because she had been made a ward of court, the contention that in the circumstances the views of her family should be deferred to was rejected. What mattered were the best interests of the ward in the circumstances, against the backdrop of the constitutionally guaranteed right to life. This right imposes a "strong

---

[19] See generally D. Madden, *Medicine, Ethics and the Law* (2002), Chap.11 and H. Biggs, *Euthanasia, Death with Dignity and the Law* (2001).
[20] Criminal Law (Suicide) Act 1993.
[21] *A Ward of Court (Withholding Medical Treatment) (No. 2), Re* [1996] 2 I.R. 79 at p.124.
[22] *Infra*, p.695.
[23] [1996] 2 I.R. 79.
[24] *Id.* at p.120.

presumption in favour of taking all steps capable of preserving [life], save in exceptional circumstances [and t]he problem is to define such circumstances."[25] Because "the process of dying is part and an ultimate, inevitable consequence of life, the right to life necessarily implies the right to have nature take its course and to die a natural death and, unless the individual concerned so wishes, not to have life artificially maintained by the provision of nourishment by abnormal artificial means, which have no curative effect and which is intended merely to prolong life."[26] But that right "does not include the right to have life terminated or death accelerated and is confined to the natural process of dying."[27]

A further consideration here was the woman's right to bodily integrity and privacy, and that her being fed by a gastronomy tube "constitute[ed] an interference with the integrity of her body and cannot be regarded as a normal means of nourishment."[28] Were she a terminally ill competent adult, she would have "the right to forego or discontinue life saving treatment."[29] It was argued, however, that it was not open to others or to the courts to make that decision on her behalf, in view of her incapacity. That was rejected, on the grounds that persons should not be deprived of their constitutional rights where they are no longer capable of seeking to have them vindicated; for the court not to make the decision on her behalf would contravene her right to privacy, coupled with equality before the law. In all the circumstances, it was permissible to withdraw the tube, "thus ceasing to prolong her life to no useful purpose and allowing her to die."[30]

It would seem that it is not constitutionally permissible to take steps, other than withdrawing medical treatment that preserves life in similar circumstances, with the intention of ending a person's life, even if that person wants to die. As stated by Hamilton C.J., "[n]o person has the right to terminate or to have terminated or to accelerate or to have accelerated his or her death."[31] In *Pretty v. United Kingdom*,[32] the Strasbourg Court came to a similar conclusion.[33] Neither of these cases, however, concerned legislation that permitted euthanasia and, if such a law were passed by the Oireachtas, the *obiter dicta* in *A Ward, Re* would not be conclusive on the question. Laws in the U.S.A. (as in Ireland) that render physician-assisted suicide a crime have been upheld by the Supreme Court there against constitutional challenges.[34]

---

[25] *Id.* at p.123.
[26] *Id.* at p.124.
[27] *Ibid.*
[28] *Id.* at p.125.
[29] *Ibid.*
[30] *Id.* at p.128.
[31] *Id.* at p.124.
[32] 35 E.H.R.R. 1 (2002).
[33] Compare *Re A (Conjoined Twins: Surgical Separation)* [2001] 2 W.L.R. 480.
[34] *Washington v. Glucksberg*, 521 U.S. 702 (1997) and *Vacco v. Quill*, 521 U.S. 793 (1997).

TORTURE AND DEGRADING TREATMENT

Although there has been no judicial decision to the effect, there can be no doubt that torture and comparable forms of degrading treatment contravene Article 40.3.2 of the Constitution. Article 3 of the European Convention condemns "torture [and] inhuman or degrading treatment or punishment." Article 7 of the UN Covenant additionally condemns "cruel" treatment or punishment and stipulates that "no one shall be subjected without his free consent to medical or scientific experimentation." In *Ireland v. United Kingdom*,[35] the European Court of Human Rights concluded that the manner in which Republican detainees and prisoners were treated by the Northern Ireland police authorities and by the British army in the early 1970s constituted inhuman or degrading treatment but did not amount to torture, which that court defined as "deliberate inhuman treatment causing very serious and cruel suffering."[36] For the purposes of the Convention, conduct amounting to inhuman treatment can take a variety of forms, such as physical assault, using psychological interrogation techniques, detaining persons in inhuman conditions or extraditing or deporting them to places where they will face such conditions. Degrading treatment is conduct that grossly humiliates them; consideration will be given to the person in question's sex, age, health, normal sensibilities and other relevant circumstances.

The UN General Assembly adopted the Convention Against Torture and Other Cruel, Inhuman or Degrading Treatment or Punishment,[37] which requires State Parties to take effective action against torture inflicted by or instigated, or acquiesced in by, a public official or other person acting in an official capacity. It defines torture as "any act by which severe pain or suffering, whether physical or mental, is intentionally inflicted on a person for such purposes as obtaining from him or a third person information or a confession, punishing him for an act he or a third person has committed or is suspected or having committed, or intimidating or coercing him or a third person, or for any reason based on discrimination of any kind ....".[38] Under this Convention, State-sponsored torture must be made a criminal offence and provision is made for extra-territorial criminal jurisdiction and extradition in respect of those crimes.[39] Ireland gave effect to this Convention by the Criminal Justice (United Nations Convention Against Torture) Act 2000. Under section 4 of this Act, a person shall not be deported or extradited to another State where the Minister forms the view that there are substantial grounds for believing he would be in danger

---

[35] 2 E.H.R.R. 25 (1978).

[36] *Id.* at p.107.

[37] Of December 10, 1984, 1465 UNTS 85.

[38] Art. 1(1). *Cf. Public Committee Against Torture v. Israel*, 7 B.H.R.C. 31 (1991).

[39] *Cf. Reg. v. Bow Street Magistrate, ex p. Pinochet Ugarte (No. 3)* [2000] 1 A.C. 147.

of being tortured.[40] In this regard, the Minister must take account of all relevant circumstances, including the existence of a consistent pattern of gross, flagrant or mass violation of human rights. Depending on the circumstances, it may be impermissible to deport persons where they are most likely to receive ill treatment that is less severe than actual torture as defined in the 2000 Act.[41]

Several forms of degrading treatment are criminal offences and are also actionable torts at common law. Where such treatment is caused by private individuals or bodies, circumstances can exist where the State or one of its agents may be held liable in damages.[42] But foreign states who are sued for damages by the victims of torture carried out by their officials are entitled to have those proceedings dismissed on the basis of sovereign immunity.[43] In 2000, the Commission to Enquire Into Child Abuse Act was passed, which set up a formal enquiry into allegations of sex abuse practised on children in numerous institutions, principally, schools, industrial schools, reformatories, hospitals and children's homes. Also in the same year a Statute of Limitations (Amendment) Act was passed to extend the period during which victims of sexual abuse could bring civil proceedings for compensation against those responsible for their abuse.

---

[40] *Cf. Suresh v. Minister of Citizenship*, 208 D.L.R. 4th 1 (2002) and *Elmi v. Austria*, 6 B.H.R.C. 433 (1999).

[41] *Cf. Bensaid v. United Kingdom*, 33 E.H.R.R. 10 (2001), *Hilal v. United Kingdom*, 33 E.H.R.R. 2 (2001) and *Mamatkulov v. Turkey*, 14 B.H.R.C. 149 (2003).

[42] *Carmichele v. Minister for Safety and Security*, 12 B.H.R.C. 60 (2001).

[43] *Al Adsani v. United Kingdom*, 32 E.H.R.R. 273 (2002).

CHAPTER 15

Personal Liberty

"Freedom of the individual" is identified in the preamble to the Constitution as an overriding principle and personal liberty is implicit in several of its more specific guarantees. In 1765, in his account of the "absolute rights of individuals," Blackstone placed second on his list "personal liberty consist[ing] in the power of locomotion, of changing situation, of removing ones person to whatsoever place ones own inclinations may direct; without imprisonment or restraint, unless by due course of law."[1] In the 1789 Declaration of the Right of Man and of the Citizen, personal liberty is described as one of the "natural and imprescriptible rights of man" and that document commences by saying that "[i]n respect of their rights ... men are born and remain free ...." Article 5(1) of the European Convention and Article 9(1) of the UN Covenant stipulate that "[e]veryone has the right to liberty and to security of person."

Although Article 40.4.1 of the Constitution addresses liberty in terms of legality, by guaranteeing that "[n]o citizen shall be deprived of his personal liberty, save in accordance with law," it has long been accepted that laws that unacceptably curtail such liberty are invalid. Persons may not be deprived of their liberty for reasons that are inconsistent with the Constitution, for instance on account of the opinions, their religion or their sex or race. Nor may persons be deprived of their liberty through a procedure or in a manner that is unconstitutional. It is implicit in the constitutional scheme that persons may only be deprived of their liberty for good reasons embodied in law and in accordance with fair procedures. The European Convention goes somewhat further than the Constitution and the UN Covenant, in that it itemises the various grounds on which persons may be detained against their will and stipulates that detention on any other grounds contravenes the Convention. According to Article 5(1), "[n]o one shall be deprived of his liberty save in the following cases and in accordance with a procedure prescribed by law ..."; it then proceeds to enumerate six categories ((a)–(f)) of grounds on which personal liberty can be constrained.

---

[1] W. Blackstone, *Commentaries on the Laws of England* (1st ed., 1765), p.134.

PERMISSIBLE DETENTIONS

Apart from the requirements of what may be termed constitutional legality, Article 40.4.1 does not stipulate the grounds on which or procedures through which persons may be deprived of their liberty, with one exception, viz. persons cannot be imprisoned or otherwise punished for crimes without being convicted in a criminal trial. One of the major grievances addressed in the Petition of Right of 1628[2] was imprisonment at the behest of the executive without there being any legal basis other than the whim of the monarch. This led to the enactment of *habeas corpus* laws and a procedure for challenging unlawful detentions is now entrenched in Article 40.4.2–4 of the Constitution. A distinction should be drawn between detention by order of a court and administrative detentions, which can be challenged in the courts. Constitutional objections to the administrative detention of persons of unsound mind and of aliens facing deportation have been rejected by the Supreme Court.[3] Internment of suspected subversives by executive order, without trial, was upheld in 1940 on a view of Article 40.3.1 that is no longer accepted.[4] Administrative internment may not now be permissible unless done under the "state of emergency" powers in Article 28.3.3,[5] for instance section 2 of the Emergency Powers Act 1976, when this Act is operative. It is convenient to deal with internment and equivalent powers separately when considering State security and emergencies.

Article 9(1) of the UN Covenant condemns "arbitrary arrest or detention," as well as deprivation of liberty "except on such grounds and in accordance with such procedure as are established by law." Article 5(1) of the European Convention is extremely important in this respect because it goes further and sets out the only grounds that, under this Convention, justify detention, namely:

"(a) the lawful detention of a person after conviction by a competent court;

(b) the lawful arrest or detention of a person for non-compliance with the lawful order of a court or in order to secure the fulfilment of any obligation prescribed by law;

(c) the lawful arrest or detention of a person effected for the purpose of bringing him before the competent legal authority on reasonable suspicion of having committed an offence or when it is reasonably considered necessary to prevent his committing an offence or fleeing after having done so;

---

[2]   3 Car. c.1.
[3]   *Infra*, pp.326 and 330.
[4]   *Offences Against the State (Amendment) Bill, 1940, Re* [1940] I.R. 470.
[5]   *Infra*, pp.858 *et seq.*

(d) the detention of a minor by lawful order for the purpose of educational supervision or his lawful detention for the purpose of bringing him before the competent legal authority;

(e) the lawful detention of persons for the prevention of the spreading of infectious diseases, of persons of unsound mind, alcoholics or drug addicts, or vagrants;

(f) the lawful arrest or detention of a person to prevent his effecting an unauthorised entry into the country or of a person against whom action is being taken with a view to deportation or extradition."

Following Conviction

Detention is permissible following a conviction by a competent court, provided that the offence in question is not unconstitutional and that the conviction was not secured by unconstitutional methods. There are four systems for holding convicted persons in detention. One is what may be called the ordinary imprisonment regime, which is governed principally by the Prisons Acts 1826-1980, and Rules for the Government of Prisons 1947.[6] Another is the detention of young persons. Section 13 of the Criminal Justice Act 1960 empowers the court dealing with persons between the ages of 17 and 21, who have been convicted of an offence that warrants imprisonment, to order instead that they be detained in St. Patrick's Institution.[7] Under the Children Act 2001,[8] children (*i.e.* under 18 years of age) who are convicted in the Children's Court may be detained by order in a detention school or centre that has been specified for this purpose, where the court is satisfied that detention is the only suitable outcome and, if the child is under 16 years of age, that a place exists to hold him. Finally, adult convicted persons may be detained in a mental hospital. The Prisons Act 1970 empowers the Minister, in order to promote the rehabilitation of offenders, to provide other places for detaining persons being held in prison and in St Patrick's Institution. Provision is made by the Transfer of Sentenced Persons (Amendment) Act 1997, to transfer convicted prisoners to serve their sentences in prisons in their own states and also to accept Irish prisoners who have been transferred from those states.

By virtue of their very detention, prisoners are not entitled to exercise certain constitutional rights[9] or to the same extent as persons who are free.[10] But the fact of their detention does not deprive them of all constitutional rights. As summed up by Costello J. in *Kearney v. Minister for Justice*,[11] which involved

---

[6] See generally, P. McDermott, *Prison Law* (2000).

[7] See generally, D. Walsh, *Criminal Procedure* (2002), pp.1050 *et seq.*

[8] Ss.142 and 143.

[9] *Murray. v. Attorney General* [195] I.R. 532; *infra*, p.678.

[10] *Breathnach v. Ireland* [2001] 3 I.R. 230; *infra*, p.596.

[11] [1986] I.R. 116.

interference with the plaintiff's correspondence, "[w]hen the State lawfully exercises its power to deprive a citizen of his constitutional right to liberty, one of the consequences is a deprivation of the right to exercise many other constitutionally protected rights. Those that may still be exercised are those which do not depend on the continuance of his personal liberty and which are compatible with the reasonable requirements of the place in which he is imprisoned."[12] Prisoners should not be subjected to conditions that amount to degrading punishment or treatment, and they are entitled to have their freedom of expression, religion and privacy respected, within limits.[13] Under Article 37 of the UN Convention on the Rights of the Child,[14] child detainees "shall be separated from adults unless it is considered in [their] best interest not to do so" and are entitled "to maintain contact with [their] family through correspondence and visits, save in exceptional circumstances."

Breach of Court Order or of Specific Obligation

Imprisonment or detention is permitted by Article 5(1)(b) of the European Convention "in order to secure the fulfilment of any obligation prescribed by law," which has been held to mean the contravention of some very specific legal obligations. Detention is permissible as a sanction for flouting the lawful order of a court, such as an injunction or a barring order. The authority of the courts to issue injunctions is founded mainly on the general principles of equity,[15] which is a system of law that used to be administered by the Chancery Courts before the various courts were merged in 1877. There are numerous statutory provisions that authorise the courts to make orders equivalent to injunctions. Under the general principles of contempt of court,[16] the courts possess extensive inherent authority to order that persons who refuse to comply with court orders be detained.

Imprisonment or detention "merely on the grounds of inability to fulfil a contractual obligation," including not paying contractually incurred debts, is forbidden by the European Convention's Fourth Protocol and by Article 11 of the UN Covenant. This principle was anticipated by section 5 of the Debtors (Ireland) Act 1872,[17] according to which "no person shall ... be arrested or imprisoned for making default of a debt contracted ...". But prior to 1967, a person could be imprisoned, without any court order, for non-payment of

---

[12] *Id.* at pp.118–119.
[13] *Supra*, p.313.
[14] November 20, 1989, 1577 UNTS 3.
[15] See generally, H. Delaney, *Equity and the Law of Trusts in Ireland* (2nd ed., 1999), Chap.13.
[16] *Infra*, p.527.
[17] 3 & 4 Vic. c. 105.

assessed taxes.[18] So too may absconding officers and contributaries of companies that have been put into liquidation.[19] Under sections 6 and 7 of the 1872 Act, absconding debtors and those who simply refuse to pay their debts may be imprisoned by order of the court. Where a creditor has obtained a judgment against a debtor and the latter does not have property against which execution can be levied, under the Enforcement of Court Orders Acts 1926-1940, a District Judge may order that the debtor be examined as to his means. If the debtor does not co-operate with the examination, or does not satisfy the judge that the debt cannot be paid even by instalments, an order will be made requiring that the debt be paid. Non-payment can lead to the judge ordering that the debtor be imprisoned for at most three months on the grounds of wilful refusal or culpable neglect to pay. An imprisoned debtor must be released as soon as payment of the debt is tendered to the prison governor or to the District Court clerk. The Minister has an overriding discretion to order that the debtor be released at any time.

Arrest

It is permitted by Article 5(1)(c) of the European Convention to deprive persons of their liberty by arresting them in accordance with law in the context of investigating a suspected criminal offence.[20] Whether it is constitutionally permissible to arrest persons in order to question them about offences, especially where they are not suspects, remains to be determined but would appear to contravene the European Convention. Every form of deprivation of personal liberty is not an arrest. Arrest has been described as "a step in the criminal process; the apprehending or restraining of a person in order that he may be forthcoming to answer an alleged or suspected crime, made in the lawful exercise of an asserted authority, with the intention to bring the person within the criminal process ....".[21] In Walsh J.'s words, arrest is "simply a process of ensuring the attendance at court of the person so arrested."[22]

Warrants

At times, in order to effect a lawful arrest, the member of the Garda Síochána or other designated official must possess a valid arrest warrant issued by a judge or a peace commissioner, or sometimes by a senior Garda officer. Issuing arrest warrants by peace commissioners has been held not to contravene the

---

[18] Repealed by Income Tax (No. 2) Act 1997.
[19] Companies Act 1963, s.247 as amended in 2001.
[20] See generally, D. Walsh, *Criminal Procedure* (2002), Chap.4 (hereinafter *Walsh*).
[21] E. Ryan & P. Magee, *The Irish Criminal Process* (1983), p.85.
[22] *People v. Shaw* [1982] I.R. 1 at p.29.

separation of powers.[23] When applying for an arrest warrant, some specifics must be furnished that justify the officer's suspicions regarding the alleged offence; the issuing authority is no mere rubber stamp responding to the recitation of a statutory formula.[24] A warrant may stipulate the duration within which it is effective; otherwise, District Court warrants expire after six months, unless renewed.[25] Committal warrants are deemed to have expired where there has been undue delay in executing them.[26]

Warrant-Less

At common law, private individuals as well as members of the Garda Síochána are empowered to arrest persons, without having obtained an arrest warrant, provided they reasonably suspect the individual in question of having committed treason or what was a felony, or a continuing or imminent breach of the peace.[27] This is superseded by section 4 of the Criminal Law Act 1997, which authorises anyone to arrest a person reasonably suspected of committing an "arrestable offence" and authorises a Garda officer to arrest anyone he reasonably suspects of having committed such an offence – being an offence that can attract a sentence of imprisonment for five years or more. There are numerous other statutory provisions that authorise members of the Garda Síochána to arrest persons without having a warrant to do so. Section 15 of the Criminal Law Act 1976 empowers members of the Defence Forces to arrest persons they reasonably suspect of having committed one or more of the offences specified in section 8 of that Act.

Entering Property

Generally, in order to enter on private property without the owner's consent to effect an arrest, there must be lawful authority to do. In *D.P.P. v. McCreesh*,[28] the Supreme Court held that such statutory authority must be express. According to Hederman J., "[i]f it had been intended by the Oireachtas to confer on a member of the Garda the power to make inroads on the property rights of citizens which are recognised and protected by the common law, and to enter on private property against the will of the owner and there arrest the owner, express provision should have been made for such power."[29] However, in *Freeman v. D.P.P.*,[30] Carney J. declined to follow this principle and concluded

---

[23] *Supra*, p.191.
[24] *People v. Balfe* [1998] 4 I.R. 50.
[25] *Healy v. Governor Cork Prison* [1998] 2 I.R. 93.
[26] *Dutton v. O'Donnell* [1989] 2 I.R. 218.
[27] See generally Ryan & Magee, *supra*, n. 21, pp.97–98.
[28] [1992] 2 I.R. 239.
[29] *Id.* at p.254.
[30] [1996] I.R. 565.

that there could be implied statutory authorisation for a Garda to enter on property to effect an arrest of someone actually committing an offence there, as contrasted with a person suspected of having offended; that in those circumstances, going on to the property must be necessary in order to make an arrest.

Consent to enter on property for this purpose may be implied as well as express.[31] In *D.P.P. v. Forbes*[32] it was held by the Supreme Court that it is "axiomatic that any householder gives an implied authority to a member of the Garda to come onto the forecourt of his premises to see to the enforcement of the law or prevent a breach thereof."[33] Accordingly, a Garda could follow a suspected offender onto the driveway of his house and, unless told to leave the property, is deemed to have been authorised to be there. Entry into a person's dwelling for any purpose brings into consideration Article 40.5 of the Constitution, according to which "[t]he dwelling of every citizen is inviolable and shall not be forcibly entered save in accordance with law."[34]

Arrest for Questioning

Common law and statutory powers of arrest cannot normally be used in order to hold persons against their will for reasons other than to charge them with some offence. Generally, it is not permissible to arrest for the purpose of questioning or, for instance, until it is possible to initiate extradition or deportation proceedings.[35] According to Walsh J. in *People v. Shaw*, "[n]o person may be arrested (with or without a warrant) for the purpose of interrogation or the securing of evidence from that person. If there exists a practice of arresting persons for the purpose of 'assisting the police in their inquiries', it is unlawful. ... (T)here is no such procedure permitted by the law as 'holding for questioning' or detaining on any pretext except pursuant to a court order or for the purpose of charging and bringing the person detained before the court. Any other purpose is unknown to the law and constitutes a flagrant and unwarranted interference with the liberty of citizens."[36]

Detention or arrest simply for the purpose of questioning is forbidden by the European Convention except during a state of emergency and where the State in question has derogated from Article 5. In *Lawless v. Ireland (No.3)*,[37] the Strasbourg Court observed that Article 5(1)(c) and (3) of the Convention allow the arrest and detention of a person "solely for the purpose of bringing

---

[31] *D.P.P. v. Lynch* [1998] 4 I.R. 437.
[32] [1994] 2 I.R. 542.
[33] *Id.* at p.548.
[34] *Infra*, p.641.
[35] *State (Trimbole) v. Governor Mountjoy Prison* [1985] I.R. 550; *infra*, p.324.
[36] [1985] I.R. 29.
[37] 1 E.H.R.R. 15 (1961).

him before a judge," a view which the court reiterated in *Ireland v. United Kingdom.*[38] According to the Court in the *Lawless* case, Article 5(1)(c) and (3) must be construed together and that they:

> "[P]ermit deprivation of liberty only when such deprivation is effected for the purpose of bringing the person arrested or detained before the competent judicial authority, irrespective of whether such person is a person who is reasonably suspected of having committed an offence, or a person whom it is reasonably considered necessary to restrain from committing an offence, or a person whom it is reasonably considered necessary to restrain from absconding after having committed an offence. [This interpretation] is fully in harmony with the purpose of the Convention which is to protect the freedom and security of the individual against arbitrary detention or arrest."[39]

In both of these instances powers of arrest under section 30 of the Offences Against the State Act 1939, and similar provisions under the Northern Ireland Special Powers Act 1922, respectively, were sustained because Ireland and the United Kingdom had derogated from Article 5 at the relevant times.

It was held by the Supreme Court in *People v. Quilligan (No.3)*[40] that section 30 of the 1939 Act, which confers a draconian power of arrest and detention[41] and could be construed as authorising arrests for questioning, does not confer such a power. The protracted custody of the detainee envisaged by that section was held to be in order that he may not disrupt any ongoing investigation into the alleged offence. Comparable extensive arrest and detention powers are conferred by section 4 of the Criminal Justice Act 1984, and by section 2(1) of the Criminal Justice (Drug Trafficking) Act 1996, *inter alia* "for the proper investigation of the offence" in question.[42] In view of what was held in *Quilligan*, it is most unlikely that these will be interpreted to confer a right to arrest simply for the purpose of interrogating the person. Of course, a person arrested under any statutory provision may be questioned about the alleged offence for so long as he is prepared to put up with questioning. Instead, he may choose not to answer any questions posed, relying on his right of silence, although certain inferences may be drawn from remaining silent in some contexts.[43]

---

[38] 2 E.H.R.R. 25 (1978).
[39] [1961] 1 E.H.R.R. 15, 27–28.
[40] [1993] 2 I.R. 305.
[41] See generally *Walsh*, pp.240 *et seq.*
[42] *Id.*, pp.225 *et seq* and 248 *et seq.*
[43] *Infra*, p.456.

Arrest Procedure

Under the common law and also Article 5(2) of the European Convention and Article 9(2) of the UN Covenant, once a person is arrested, he must be "informed promptly ... of the reason for his arrest and of any charge against him." Even where a person is being stopped and searched, as opposed to being formally arrested, it was held by O'Hanlon J. in *D.P.P. v. Rooney* that he is "entitled to be informed of the nature and description of the statutory power which is being invoked."[44]

A person who has been arrested in order to be charged with an offence, is required by Article 5(3) of the Convention and Article 9(2) of the Covenant to be "brought promptly before a judge or other officer authorised by law to exercise judicial power." A requirement to this effect is contained in section 15 of the Criminal Justice Act 1951; an arrested person must be brought "as soon as practicable" before a judge of the District Court who has jurisdiction. If after 5 p.m. in the evening a person is arrested under a warrant or, if there is no warrant, he is charged, and a District Judge is due to sit before noon on the following day, it suffices that the person is brought before that judge at the commencement of that sitting. That person may then either be remanded in custody by the court or granted bail, or be released entirely, as the case may be.

There are several statutory provisions, however, that permit arrested persons to be detained in Garda custody for a protracted period, for the purpose of investigation, before they must be brought before the District Court or else released. The prototype is section 30 of the Offences Against the State Act 1939, as amended in 1998, and similar powers are given by section 4 of the Criminal Justice Act 1984 and by section 2 of the Criminal Justice (Drug Trafficking) Act 1996. Under these, the initial period of detention (24, 6 and 6 hours respectively) may be extended for further periods at the direction of a senior Garda officer[45] and may be further extended for a period by order of a District Judge. A person so detained must be informed of his right to contact and speak to a solicitor, which is a constitutional as well as a statutory entitlement. How persons so detained under the 1984 Act are to be dealt with is also governed by the Criminal Justice Act 1984 (Treatment of Persons in Custody in Garda Stations) Regulations 1987.[46] That these regulations may not have been strictly complied with in all respects will not invariably render the detention unlawful or any admissions made while being detained inadmissible in evidence at the person's trial. At the expiry of detention under these sections, there are restrictions on the circumstances in which the person may be re-arrested.

---

[44] [1992] 2 I.R. 7 at p.10; also *Farrelly v. Devally* [1998] 4 I.R. 76.
[45] *Cf. People v. Byrne* [1987] I.R. 363.
[46] S.I. No. 119 of 1987; see generally *Walsh*, pp.256 *et seq.*

Legal Advice

It was held by the Supreme Court in *D.P.P. v. Healy*[47] that, where a person is being detained in Garda custody and either he or someone on his behalf requests a solicitor, he has a constitutional right to see and take advice from that solicitor. If in those circumstances the Gardaí deliberately restrict his access to the solicitor, any inculpatory statement he made will ordinarily be rendered inadmissible against him at a subsequent trial. There, while being detained under section 30 of the Offences Against the State Act 1939, the defendant asked to see her solicitor but, on arriving at the Garda station, the solicitor was not allowed to speak to his client for some time until the client made admissions. According to Finlay C.J., "[t]he undoubted right of reasonable access to a solicitor enjoyed by a person who is in detention must be interpreted as being directed towards the vital function of ensuring that such person is aware of his rights and has the independent advice which would be appropriate in order to permit him to reach a truly free decision as to his attitude to interrogation or to the making of any statement, be it exculpatory or inculpatory. The availability of advice from a lawyer must ... be seen as a contribution at least towards some measure of equality in the position of the detained person and his interrogations."[48] But the court made it clear that it was not deciding the question of whether, prior to interrogating a suspect, he must be given a *Miranda*-style caution that he is entitled to have a solicitor present, either retained or appointed, prior to making any statement.[49]

This right of access to a solicitor is not absolute; it is one of reasonable access and its full contours remain to be delineated. Several of these questions are addressed in the 1987 regulations made for the statutory provisions that allow for prolonged detentions. Where a person being detained asks to see his solicitor, the Gardaí must make *bona fide* endeavours to make contact with that solicitor and allow reasonably prompt access as soon as he arrives at the Garda station. But there is no constitutional prohibition against questioning the person prior to the solicitor arriving,[50] nor is the solicitor entitled to be present when his client is being so interviewed, nor to prescribe how and where any such interview is to be conducted, nor it would seem is he entitled to see any of the interview notes prior to a charge being preferred.[51]

Unlawful/Unconstitutional Arrests

Persons who have been arrested for some purpose, other than to be charged with an offence, can bring a civil action for false imprisonment;[52] on a *habeas*

---

[47] [1990] I.L.R.M. 313.
[48] *Id.* at p.317.
[49] *Infra*, p.458.
[50] *People v. Buck* [2002] 2 I.R. 268.
[51] *Lavery v. Member in Charge* [1999] 2 I.R. 390.
[52] See generally, B. McMahon & Binchy, *Law of Torts* (3rd ed., 2000), pp.626 *et seq.*

corpus application, those persons may be ordered to be released;[53] depending on the circumstances, statements they made to the Gardaí during that arrest may not be admitted into evidence against them.[54]

In *State (Trimbole) v. Governor of Mountjoy Prison*,[55] the Supreme Court held that persons cannot be lawfully arrested under section 30 of the 1939 Act when the real reason for their arrest does not relate to an offence under that Act or a scheduled offence. The applicant was a leading figure in Australian organised crime and was wanted there for trial on several serious charges, including the murder of a politician who had sought to expose an illicit narcotics ring there. He left Australia and eventually came to live in Ireland. At the time, no extradition treaty existed between Ireland and Australia but section 8(1) of the Extradition Act 1965, permits the State to make informal extradition arrangements with any country on a reciprocal basis. While such an arrangement was in the process of being concluded between the Irish and the Australian authorities, in anticipation of a request being made to have him extradited, he was arrested by the Gardaí under section 30 of the 1939 Act on a charge of possessing a firearm and ammunition. On the following day, Egan J. ordered his release, being satisfied that, in the circumstances, the Gardaí could not genuinely have suspected that he was guilty of firearms offences and that this was merely a pretext for holding him. He was arrested again outside of the immediate precincts of the court but this time under a provisional warrant as provided for in section 27 of the Extradition Act 1965. On the same day, the Irish-Australian extradition arrangement became effective.

He contended, unsuccessfully, that the Extradition Act did not permit his being sent back to Australia. In addition, he argued that on account of his original arrest he had been in unlawful detention throughout and, accordingly, that the extradition proceedings against him could not be completed until he is first released. According to Egan J., "[t]here was a gross misuse of section 30 which amounted to a conscious and deliberate violation of constitutional rights (and t)here were no extraordinary excusing circumstances. ... [His] present detention is tainted by the illegality of his original arrest. It is the ultimate result of a conscious and deliberate violation of constitutional rights and is accordingly unlawful."[56] The Supreme Court agreed that he must be released immediately. Finlay C.J. observed that section 30 of the 1939 Act "is part of a code intended to protect the State against its enemies and those seeking to overthrow it by unlawful means"[57] but Trimbole could never be considered as falling within that category of person. As McCarthy J. stated, "(a)t the time of the arrest there was no possibility of holding (him) lawfully – it was therefore

---

[53] *Infra*, p.338.
[54] *Infra*, p.469.
[55] [1985] I.R. 550.
[56] *Id.* at pp.566–567.
[57] *Id.* at p.575.

a form of kidnapping to make him available to face" impending extradition proceedings.[58]

Preventive Detention

In addition to arrest for the purposes of bringing someone before a judicial authority, Article 5(1)(c) of the European Convention also permits administrative detention "when it is reasonably considered necessary to prevent [a person] committing an offence" and also where it is reasonably necessary to prevent a person fleeing after having committed an offence. Since the 16th amendment was adopted in 1996, it has been constitutionally permissible to refuse bail to persons charged with an offence on the grounds that they are likely to commit a "serious" offence if they are conditionally released.[59] Power to intern suspected subversives without trial, in order to safeguard the security of the State, was upheld by the Supreme Court in 1940[60] but it is questionable whether the court would reach the same conclusion today unless the power was being exercised in a state of emergency contemplated by Article 28.3.3. In the absence of a derogation, such a power would contravene the European Convention.

In *Connors v. Pearson*,[61] it was held that, apart from explicit statutory authority, the Gardaí have no power to hold potential witnesses in custody against their will, so as to safeguard them against apprehended violence and intimidation. According to Gibson J., "(i)mprisonment of a possible witness *quia timet* to protect him without his consent from unknown malefactors or intimidation is not within any common law principle of justification ...".[62] It would seem that, under Article 5(1) of the Convention, detention on those grounds is not permitted even if authorised by statute.

Juveniles

Article 5(1)(d) of the European Convention permits the detention of juveniles on two grounds. One is in order to bring them before a "competent legal authority," which, it would seem, means that minors can be detained to be brought before a court in order to remove them from harmful surroundings and protect them from falling into criminal ways. The other permitted purpose, of "educational supervision," envisages detention in reformatories and similar institutions. Article 37(b) of the UN Convention on the Rights of the Child,

---

[58] *Id.* at p.579. Compare *Criminal Assets Bureau v. Craft* [2001] 1 I.R. 121.
[59] *Infra*, p.355.
[60] *Supra*, n. 4 and *infra*, p.861.
[61] [1921] 2 I.R. 51.
[62] *Id.* at p.71.

requires that the "arrest [or] detention ... of a child ... shall ... be used only as a measure of last resort and for the shortest appropriate period of time," and children detained should be held separately from adult detainees and they should be enabled to maintain contact with their families.

Under the Children Act 2001, (when in force) persons under 18 years of age convicted of offences may only be detained in a prescribed children's detention school or centre.[63] Part VI (sections 55–70) of this Act contains a detailed code for the treatment of child suspects being held in Garda custody. This Act also adopted Part IVA (sections 23A–23N) of the Child Care Act 1991, whereby health boards are obliged to seek "special care orders" from courts, where they are of the view that such care is required in the circumstances. Members of the Gardaí also are empowered, to prevent a real and substantial risk to children who are not receiving adequate care or protection, to endeavour to deliver the child to the custody of a health board. For this purpose, health boards are authorised to maintain special care units or to arrange with others to maintain those units. On being found guilty of an offence, a child may no longer be detained in one of the units. In addition to complying with their other constitutional rights, persons detaining juveniles must comply with Article 41 of the Constitution, which concerns the family, and with Article 42, which deals mainly with the rights of parents regarding their children's education.[64]

The Diseased, Insane, Addicts and Vagrants

Article 5(1)(e) of the European Convention permits the administrative detention of categories of persons who are somewhat similar, *viz*. persons with an infectious disease, persons of unsound mind, drug addicts, alcoholics and vagrants. The Medical Treatment Act 1945, provided for the detention of only two of these groups on the authority of medical officers and, notwithstanding that they plainly contravened the European Convention, those provisions were upheld by the Supreme Court in *Croke v. Smith (No.2).*[65] In order to bring domestic practice into line with the Convention's requirements,[66] as well as to otherwise modernise the regime, the Mental Health Act 2000 was passed.

In the *Croke* case the main contention was that the 1945 Act did not contain adequate safeguards for persons who had been taken into a mental institution on the recommendation of two registered medical practitioners; in particular, that there should be some independent body to regularly review all detentions, such as was provided for in the Mental Treatment Act 1981 which had never come into force. How the court should approach constitutional challenges in this context was summed up by Hamilton C.J. as follows:

---

[63] See generally *Walsh*, pp.1058 *et seq.*
[64] *Infra*, p.695.
[65] [1998] 1 I.R. 101.
[66] *Cf. Benjamin v. United Kingdom* 36 E.H.R.R. 1 (2003).

"The right to liberty is, of course, not an absolute right and its exercise is
in fact and in many different ways restricted by perfectly valid laws,
both common law and statutory. Adjudication on a challenge to restrictive
laws will be helped by considering the object and justification advanced
in support of the law. It is obvious that if the object of the law is to
punish criminal behaviour different considerations will apply than when
the impugned law has a totally different object, such as the welfare of
the person whose liberty is restricted.

The reasons why the Act of 1945 deprives persons suffering from
mental disorder of their liberty are perfectly clear. It does so for a number
of different and perhaps overlapping reasons – in order to provide for
their care and treatment, for their own safety, and for the safety of others.
Its object is essentially benign. But this objective does not justify any
restriction designed to further it. On the contrary, the State's duty to
protect the citizens' rights becomes more exacting in the case of weak
and vulnerable citizens, such as those suffering from mental disorder.
So, it seems to me that the constitutional imperative to which I have
referred requires the Oireachtas to be particularly astute when depriving
persons suffering from mental disorder of their liberty and that it should
ensure that such legislation should contain adequate safeguards against
abuse and error in the interests of those whose welfare the legislation is
designed to support."[67]

While a system to independently review continued detentions "may be
desirable," the court held that the 1945 Act contained sufficient safeguards
against continued unnecessary detention, to which can be added the right under
Article 40.4 of the Constitution to challenge the legality of continued detention
in the High Court and the jurisdiction of the President of the High Court to
inquire into any complaint made to him of unnecessary continued detention.
Although not expressly provided for, it was held that "inherent in" section 172
of the 1945 Act was a requirement that the resident medical superintendent of
the institution in question shall "regularly and constantly review a patient in
order to ensure that he or she has not recovered and is still a person of unsound
mind and is a proper person to be detained under care and treatment."[68] There
was "no suggestion that such a review is not carried out,"[69] Hamilton C.J.
added, observing that "[i]f such review is not regularly carried out in accordance
with fair procedures and rendering justice to the patient then the intervention
of the court can be sought ...".[70] In the USA, the detention of persons whose

---

[67] [1998] 1 I.R. at p.118, quoting from Costello P. in *R.T. v. Director of the Central Mental
Hospital* [1995] 2 I.R. 65 at p.78.
[68] *Id.* at p.131.
[69] *Id.* at pp.131–132.
[70] *Id.* at p.131.

mental condition causes them to be a very serious risk to the public but are untreatable was upheld by the Supreme Court there.[71]

Sections 9 and 12 of the Mental Health Act 2001, (when in force) provide for placing persons in approved mental institutions against their will. What constitutes "mental disorder" for the purpose of this Act is defined in some detail in section 3, which involves either "mental illness," "severe dementia" or "significant intellectual disability." But persons may not be involuntarily detained merely because they are suffering from a personality disorder, are socially deviant or are addicted to drugs or intoxicants.[72] Under section 9, an application to the institution in question may be made by the person's spouse or individual of the opposite sex who was cohabiting with him for the previous three years, a relative (as defined therein), a member of the Garda Síochána, an officer duly authorised by a Health Board or any other person; subs. (2) disqualifies certain persons. An applicant for involuntary admission must have observed the person in question in the preceding 48 hours. That person also must have been examined within the next 24 hours by a registered medical practitioner who, if satisfied that the person is suffering from a mental disorder, shall recommend that he be detained. Provision is made for ensuring that the person is then taken to the institution in question, where he is again medically examined and, if found to be so suffering, shall be detained at first for 21 days, which may be renewed for periods not exceeding three months. Part III (sections 31–55) provides for regular reviews.

Under section 12 of the 2001 Act, a member of the Garda Síochána may take a person into custody and may forcibly enter any dwelling or other premises for that purpose if he reasonably believes that a person is suffering from a mental disorder and, as a result, there is a serious likelihood of him causing immediate serious harm to himself or to others. That Garda may then apply to have the person admitted to an institution as provided for in section 9 of this Act. A provision in the 1945 Act similar to section 12 of the 2001 Act was upheld by the Supreme Court in *Philip Clarke, Re*,[73] where the court described it as a section "carefully drafted so as to ensure that the person, alleged to be of unsound mind, shall be brought before and examined by responsible medical officers with the least possible delay."[74] It could not be "construed as an attack on the personal rights of the citizen" but "[o]n the contrary [is] designed for the protection of the citizen and for the promotion of the common good."[75]

---

[71] *Kansas v. Hendricks*, 521 U.S. 346 (1997); also *Anderson v. Scottish Ministers* [2002] 3 W.L.R. 1460.
[72] S.8(2).
[73] [1950] I.R. 235.
[74] *Id.* at p.247.
[75] *Ibid.*

Extradition

Article 5(1)(t) of the European Convention permits the administrative detention of persons with a view to extraditing them. Extradition is the response of states to the international mobility of criminals and suspected criminals; it is a formal process based on international agreement whereby a person, who is in one country and who is wanted in another country to stand trial or to serve imprisonment there, is handed over by the former country to officials of the latter. This process is regulated principally by the Extradition Acts 1965-2001.[76] Extradition to the United Kingdom – to be exact, rendition to Northern Ireland, England, Scotland, Wales, the Isle of Man and the Channel Islands – is governed by Part III (sections 41–55) of the 1965 Act; extradition to all other places is governed by Part II (sections 8–40) of that Act, which since 2001 contains a speedier and more simplified procedure for extraditing persons to designated State-parties to the EU Treaty on Simplified Extradition Procedures of 1995.[77]

The detention procedure under these Acts is as follows. This entire process commences with the Commissioner of the Garda Síochána receiving a request from a "judicial authority" in the United Kingdom, Isle of Man or Channel Islands (U.K. for short) to have someone extradited to the UK. Alternatively, the Minister for Justice receives a request from one of the designated Part II country's "accredited diplomats" or by the Central Authority of a designated European Convention country, to have someone extradited. In the former case, the Garda Commissioner merely endorses the arrest warrant for the wanted person; in the latter case, a District Judge will issue an arrest warrant for the person wanted in one of the other countries. That person can then be arrested by any member of the Garda Síochána and must be brought before the High Court, which will decide whether or not an extradition order should be made. Where that order is made, the person being held can apply to the High Court and argue that the order should be set aside on several specified grounds, such as that the offence in question is a political or a military offence, double jeopardy or inexcusable delay, or that there has been some underlying abuse of process, as occurred in the *Trimbole* case.[78]

Sections 27 and 49 of the Extradition Act 1965 provide for the "provisional arrest" of persons whose extradition is being sought but the formal request for extradition has not yet arrived in Ireland. Both procedures are virtually identical. Section 49 deals with provisional arrest for the purposes of extradition to the UK. A warrant to arrest a person will be issued by the High Court on the sworn information of an inspector of the Garda Síochána or Garda officer of higher rank. That Garda must swear that he has reason to believe that a UK judicial authority has issued a warrant to arrest the person in question for trial,

---

[76] See generally, M. Forde, *Extradition Law* (2nd ed., 1995).
[77] March 10, 1995, O.J. No. C78/1 of March 30, 1995.
[78] [1985] I.R. 550.

sentence or conviction but the warrant is not yet in the Garda's possession, that the relevant UK police authority wants that person arrested "on the ground of urgency," that the Garda has reason to believe that the person sought is in Ireland and, where the person sought has been convicted, that the purpose of the arrest is to bring him before the court for sentence or to undergo imprisonment. The provisional warrant procedure applies only to indictable offences and the person sought may not be arrested more than five days after the warrant is issued. On being duly arrested, that person must be brought before the High Court, which may remand him either in custody or on bail for not more than seven days. If during this time the UK arrest warrant is not produced the person detained must be released. Provisional arrest warrants issued under Part II of the 1965 Act remain effective for the ensuing 18 days, by which time the person must be released unless a proper extradition request has been received by the Minister.

Excluding and Deporting Aliens

Article 5(1)(f) of the European Convention permits administrative detention to prevent unauthorised entry into the country and also with a view to deportation. Authority to detain aliens who were not allowed to enter the State is contained in regulation 5(5) of the Aliens Order 1946;[79] they can be held "only until such time (being as soon as practicable) as he is removed from the State" under regulation 7 of that order, meaning for at least two months after being detained.[80] Persons applying for refugee status may be detained by an immigration officer or member of the Garda Síochána in specified circumstances, but must "as soon as practicable" then be brought before the District Court, which may order the person's continued detention, or that he be released subject to certain conditions, for instance that he resides or remains in a particular place.[81]

Authority to detain aliens in order to deport them is now contained in sections 3(1A) and 5 of the Immigration Act 1999. They may be arrested without a warrant by a member of the Garda Síochána and thereafter detained if a deportation order has been made in respect of the individual in question and the Garda has reasonable cause for suspecting either of the following, *viz.* the person failed to comply with a requirement in that order or in a notice furnished advising the Minister's intention to make such an order; he intends to avoid being deported; without lawful authority he intends to leave the State and go to another State; he destroyed his identity documents or has forged identity

---

[79] Aliens (Amendment) Order, S.I. No. 128, 1975, reg.3, amending reg.5 of Aliens Order 1946, S.R. & O. No. 395.

[80] *Lau v. Minister for Justice* [1993] 1 I.R. 116.

[81] Refugee Act 1996, s.9(8)–(10).

documents. Any person so arrested and held may be put on any aircraft, ship, train or other vehicle leaving the State and, until it "leaves the State," he is deemed to be in lawful custody. No provision is made for holding a person so detained for a minimum period, so that he may have an opportunity to challenge in the courts his removal from the State, presumably because there is perhaps adequate opportunity to contest the proposed making of deportation orders. But where a person in the very process of being deported wishes to challenge the Minister's order, it would seem that he should not be entirely denied that opportunity and may be held in custody pending his application for leave to contest the order.

Persons may not be detained under section 5 of the 1999 Act for longer than eight weeks in aggregate, subject to certain extensions. This power of administrative detention was upheld by the Supreme Court in *Sections 5 and 10 of the Illegal Immigrants (Trafficking) Bill 1999, Re.*[82] As in the *Croke (No.2)*[83] case, where detention of persons of unsound mind was sustained, it was held that circumstances could warrant so holding intended deportees because "there will always be cases where an immigrant who has gone through, or had an opportunity to go through, all the application and appeal procedures for asylum or for leave to remain in the country on humanitarian grounds will still attempt to evade the execution of a deportation order. Depending on the country of origin, travel arrangements may be extremely difficult to put in place and powers of detention between the making of the deportation order and in advance of the deportation itself may well be necessary in some instances."[84] Additionally, although there was no mechanism provided to monitor the need for protracted detention, several legal procedures exist which ensured that it would not be abused. One such abuse would be where it was "quite clear that deportation could not be carried out within the eight weeks."[85] It has been held permissible in England to detain persons whose application for asylum is being processed and who are awaiting a final decision whether or not they may remain in the country.[86]

RESTRICTIONS ON MOVEMENT

Personal liberty is not confined to not being held in unlawful custody but extends to freedom of movement generally, either within the State and also to both enter and to leave the State.

---

[82] [2000] 2 I.R. 360.
[83] *Supra*, p.326.
[84] [2000] 2 I.R. 410.
[85] *Id.* at p.411.
[86] *R.. (Saadi) v. Secretary of State* [2002] 1 W.L.R. 3131.

Within the State

Article 2(1) of the European Convention's Fourth Protocol provides that
"[e]veryone lawfully within the territory of a State shall, within that territory,
have the right to liberty of movement and freedom to choose his residence,"
but this can be made subject to restrictions that are "provided by law, are
necessary to protect national security, public order (*ordre public*), public health
or morals, or the rights and freedoms of others, and are consistent with the
other rights recognised. ..." There are numerous statutory provisions that
authorise members of the Garda Síochána to stop, question and search
individuals who are reasonably suspected of having committed an offence or
of being about to commit an offence,[87] for instance section 23 of the Misuse
of Drugs Act 1977. This provision was upheld by the Supreme Court in
O'Callagahan v. Ireland[88] against a claim that it contravened the guarantees
of equality and of respect for the personal rights of the citizen. According to
Finlay C.J., for the court, the damage that the use and distribution of illegal
drugs causes to society was sufficient justification for the Oireachtas conferring
such a power on the Gardaí. That comparable powers in other legislation are
expressly circumscribed did not mean that section 23 of the 1977 Act was
invalid because it did not contain equivalent safeguards. Finlay C.J. emphasised,
however, that powers of this nature must be exercised in a constitutional manner
and that, where the "purported exercise of [them] expose [a]ny person to
unnecessary harassment, distress or embarrassment, it would be an abuse of
the powers and an unconstitutional violation of that person's rights ....".[89]
Persons who are stopped under provisions of this nature must be told exactly
what power the Garda in question is relying on.[90]

In *D.P.P. v. Fagan*[91] it was held by the Supreme Court that the Gardaí had
equivalent powers at common law, although there was no authority of any
kind to support this conclusion, which was rejected by Denham J. in her dissent.
As she remarked, "[i]f such a power exists at common law then it is surprising
that the legislature spelled out the right to stop in so many statutes, but limited
it to situations where the nominated person had a reasonable suspicion" that
the individual either had offended or was about to offend.[92]

Persons' freedom of movement within the State may be restricted by a
court order. A person who has been convicted of an offence may be bound
over to keep the peace and, where charged with an offence, he may have been
granted bail on terms that restrict where he is permitted to go. Under the

---

[87] See generally *Walsh*, pp.359 *et seq.*
[88] [1994] 1 I.R. 554.
[89] *Id.* at p.563.
[90] *D.P.P. v. Rooney* [1992] 2 I.R. 7.
[91] [1994] 3 I.R. 265.
[92] *Id.* at p.285. Accord *R. v. Boudreau* 196 D.L.R. 4th 53 (2001).

Domestic Violence Act 1996, "safety orders" and "barring orders" may be obtained, preventing a parent, spouse or person in a comparable position from going to or being in the vicinity of where the applicant for such order resides. It would seem that orders made under section 16 of the Sex Offenders Act 2001 can include restrictions on movement. Under its general equity jurisdiction, courts may enjoin a person from "watching and besetting" particular premises, for instance, persons unlawfully picketing in the context of an industrial dispute with employers. Any such restrictions, however, are subject to the guarantee in Article 40.6.1.ii of freedom of assembly.

The free movement of aliens or "non-nationals" (not EU nationals or their dependants) within the State may be restricted by orders made by the Minister under the Aliens Act 1935; they may be required to remain in and to reside at particular places, and also to comply with provisions on registration, change of abode, travelling, employment and other like matters. Applicants for refugee status may be required by an immigration officer to reside or remain in particular areas. Movement of persons into and out of areas affected with diseases subject to the Diseases of Animals Act 1996, may be regulated by the Minister for Agriculture.

Entering the State

The State is prohibited by the European Convention's Fourth Protocol from preventing any of its own nationals from entering the State; Article 12(2) of the UN Covenant forbids "arbitrary" exclusion of nationals. Under the EC Treaties and regulations made under them, nationals of EC Member States and their dependants are entitled to enter and remain in the State.[93] But non-nationals (other than EU nationals and their dependants) can be so prevented, as can EU nationals in restricted circumstances.

Section 5(1)(a), (b) of the Aliens Act 1935, permits the Minister, "if and whenever he thinks proper," to order that a non-national be prohibited from landing in or entering the State. How broad a discretion the Minister has in this regard has not been determined.[94] Further, under section 4 of the Immigration Act 1999, the Minister may make such an order where he "considers it necessary in the interest of national security or public policy." Subject to this power, authority to exclude non-nationals is circumscribed by sections 8 and 9 of the Refugee Act 1996, which entitles a person who arrives at the frontiers of the State, who seeks asylum or who does not want to be expelled for fear of being persecuted, to apply to the Minister for refugee

---

[93] See generally, Ryan, "The Free Movement of Persons and Ireland" in M.C. Lucey and C. Keville (eds), *Irish Perspectives on EC Law* (2003).

[94] *Cf. Guylas v. Minister for Justice* [2001] 3 I.R. 216 and *R.. (Farrakhan) v. Secretary of State* [2002] Q.B. 391.

status and, to that end, to be interviewed as soon as practicable after arrival. That person must then be permitted to enter the State and remain there until either he withdraws his application or it is refused, or is transferred to what is described as a designated Dublin Convention country. He may, however, be excluded from the State and may not apply for refugee status where he is already the subject of an exclusion or deportation order under section 5 of the Aliens Act 1935, made for reasons of "national security or public policy (*ordre public*)." Refugee applications are then investigated by the Refugee Commissioner, whose decision may be appealed to the Refugee Appeal Board.

Leaving the State

Article 2(2) of the European Convention's Fourth Protocol provides that "[e]veryone shall be free to leave any country, including his own," but this right can be restricted in the same manner as intra-State movement may be regulated. Non-nationals (not EU nationals or their dependants) may be prohibited by the Minister from leaving the State, or restrictions or conditions may be imposed on when they may leave the State.[95] Applicants for refugee status are forbidden to leave the State without the Minister's consent.[96]

Officers and contributories of registered companies that are being wound up, who are about to leave the State, may by court order be arrested and detained until such further order;[97] so too may "absconding officers" of companies that are in liquidation.[98] There used to be a creditors' remedy, the writ *ne exeat regno*, which enabled a court to prohibit a person from leaving the country.[99] But it has not been determined whether it remains part of Irish law; there is no reference to it in the Rules of the Superior Courts. In 2002, Kearns J. made an *ex parte* order restraining persons from leaving the State.[100] In what is popularly known as *"X"* case,[101] the Supreme Court refused to make an order preventing a teenage pregnant girl from going abroad in order to have an abortion, in circumstances where there was a distinct likelihood that she would commit suicide on account of the circumstances in which she was made pregnant. Article 40.3.3 of the Constitution was subsequently amended, entrenching a right to travel in order to have an abortion abroad.[102]

In order to leave the State to get to countries other than the United Kingdom,

---

[95] Aliens Act 1935, s.5(1)(c), (d).
[96] Refugee Act 1996, s.9(4)(a).
[97] Companies Act 1963, s.247 as amended in 2001.
[98] *Supra*, n.19.
[99] *Al Nahkel Trading Ltd v. Lowe* [1986] 1 Q.B. 235.
[100] *O'Neill v. O'Keeffe* [2002] 2 I.R. 1.
[101] *Attorney General v. X* [1992] 1 I.R. 1; *infra*, p.723.
[102] *Infra*, p.725.

carriers by air or by sea often insist on the person having a valid passport; so too do immigration authorities at the destination. The circumstances in which an Irish citizen may be refused a passport, thereby impeding his freedom to travel, do not appear to have been extensively considered by the courts. In *Lennon v. Ganly*,[103] O'Hanlon J. held that there is a constitutional right to travel abroad; in that instance, the judge refused to grant an injunction forbidding the defendants from travelling to South Africa in order to play rugby there in the era of apartheid. A provision of the Adoption Acts was declared unconstitutional in *State (M) v. Attorney General*,[104] because it prevented young non-marital children from being brought out of the country regardless of how compelling the reason might be for taking them abroad. According to Finlay P., a child has a "constitutional right to travel in the manner and for a purpose consistent with its welfare chosen by its mother."[105] He observed that the right to travel abroad was one of the Constitution's unspecified rights and this right includes being given a passport in order to travel; that "a citizen has a right to a passport permitting him or her to avail of such facilities as international agreements existing at any given time afford to the holder of such a passport. To that right there are obvious and justified restrictions ....".[106]

Whether, under Article 40.3 of the Constitution, citizens have a legally enforceable right to protection by the State when they run into difficulties with foreign governments has never been determined.

Expulsion from the State

The State is prohibited by the European Convention's Fourth Protocol from "expell[ing], by means either of an individual or a collective measure," any of its own nationals from the State. Article 13 of the UN Covenant provides that "[a]n alien lawfully in the territory ... may be expelled therefrom only in pursuance of a decision reached in accordance with law and shall, except where compelling reasons of national security otherwise require, be allowed to submit the reasons against his expulsion and to have his case reviewed by, and be represented for the purpose before, the competent authority." Ireland is a party to the Geneva Convention on the Status of Refugees and its 1967 Protocol,[107] and also to the Dublin Convention[108] concerning which EC State is responsible for dealing with asylum applications. Two mechanisms exist for removing persons from the State, namely extradition and deportation.

---

[103] [1981] I.L.R.M. 84.
[104] [1979] I.R. 73.
[105] *Id.* at p.82.
[106] *Id.* at p.87.
[107] July 28, 1951 and January 31, 1967 and 606 UNTS 267 189 UNTS 150.
[108] Now EC Regulation 343/2003, O.J. L50/03, and Refugee Act 1996 (Section 22) Order 2003, S.I. No. 423.

Extradition

Regardless of their nationality, persons who are wanted abroad to be tried for alleged criminal offences, or to be imprisoned after having been convicted there, may be extradited by court order to that State if appropriate extradition arrangements exist between it and Ireland.[109] There are comprehensive extradition schemes between the State and the United Kingdom (and also the Channel Islands and the Isle of Man), with the State-parties to the European Convention on Extradition, and with Australia and the United States of America. In more limited circumstances, extradition also can take place to many other State-parties to multilateral conventions to which Ireland has adhered, for instance concerning aircraft hijacking and related acts, drug trafficking, torture, nuclear materials and offences against UN personnel. Persons can be extradited to be tried by the International War Crimes Tribunal at the Hague.

The Extradition Acts 1965-2001 set out certain circumstances in which persons may not be extradited and these may be supplemented by additional circumstances in the relevant extradition treaty, for instance where the offence in question is "political" or is connected with such an offence,[110] is a military offence, or where the penalty is capital punishment or where, if extradited, the person is likely to be victimised on account of his politics, race, religion or nationality, or is likely to be tortured. Additionally, Irish nationals may not be extradited in particular circumstances but must instead be then tried in the State for the offence in question. It was held in *State (Quinn) v. Ryan*,[111] that, even where there is express statutory authority to do so, persons cannot be handed over to a foreign police or judicial authority without having an opportunity to challenge in the High Court the legality and constitutionality of their detention. This case concerned the pre-1965 backing of warrants procedure for extradition between the UK and Ireland, which has been replaced by Part III (section 41–55) of the 1965 Act.

A method that is not infrequently used in some countries, to send wanted persons to be tried elsewhere when the extradition rules do not permit their being delivered up, is simply to deport them to the country where they are wanted – "disguised extradition." It has not been established whether an Irish court would set aside a deportation order where it is established that the real reason for deportation was to have the alien tried on charges in the State to which he is being deported, but it would be surprising if such steps were held to be lawful. The use of deportation powers in order to deliver up persons for trial in other countries has been condemned by the European Commission of Human Rights.[112] Nor has it been determined whether the courts here would

---

[109] *Supra*, n.76.
[110] *Infra*, p.613.
[111] [1965] I.R. 7.
[112] *Bozano v. France* 9 E.H.R.R. 297 (1986).

try and convict a person whose presence in Ireland was the result of disguised extradition from abroad; they have a discretion not to try the accused in those circumstances.[113]

Deportation

The State has an inherent power to deport aliens, which does not require statutory basis but is now governed principally by the Immigration Act 1999 enacted following the *Laurentiu* decision,[114] which held that the regime obtaining under orders made under the Aliens Act 1935 contravened the separation of powers between the Oireachtas and the executive. Nationals of EC member-States and their dependants may be deported only in exceptional circumstances.[115] Otherwise, the Minister has a wide discretion as to who he will deport, *inter alia*, where in his opinion that "would be conducive to the common good" and also where a person's asylum application has been refused. Aliens resident in the State for at least five years and who are economically active may not be deported unless they are serving a term of imprisonment, or a court has recommended that they be deported or they have been given at least three months notice by the Minister of their intended deportation.

Ireland's obligations under the Geneva Convention on the Status of Refugees and its 1967 Protocol were implemented by the Refugee Act 1996, which sets out the criteria and procedures for determining asylum applications. Those seeking refugee status may not be deported while their applications are pending. Persons may not be deported where they are likely to be victimised on account of their politics, race, religion nationality, membership of a particular social group, or where they are likely to be subject to serious assault or to be tortured.

Aliens do not have a constitutional right not to be deported and such rights as they enjoy in this regard are limited. As stated by Keane C.J., "in the sphere of immigration, its restriction or regulation, the non-national or alien constitutes a discrete category of persons whose entry, presence and expulsion from the State may be the subject of legislative and administrative measures which would not, and in many of its aspects could not, be applied to its citizens."[116] But in particular circumstances, deportation may contravene their rights to life and against degrading treatment,[117] and also their family rights under Article 43.1 of the Constitution.[118] Article 10 of the UN Convention on the Rights of the

---

[113] *R. v. Horseferry Road Magistrates Court, ex p.Bennett* [1994] 1 A.C. 42.
[114] [1999] 2 I.R. 26; *supra*, p.180.
[115] EC Treaty Article 39.3 permits deportation on grounds of "public policy, public security and public health". See generally, Ryan, *supra*, n.93, pp.334 *et seq.*
[116] *Sections. 5 and 10 of the Illegal Immigrants (Trafficking) Bill, 1999, Re* [2000] 2 I.R. 360 at p.383.
[117] *Supra*, p.312.
[118] *Infra*, p.686.

Child[119] gives children and their parents a qualified entitlement to enter and leave the State for the purpose of family reunification. The mechanism for challenging deportation orders, including several other decisions that precede the making of such orders, were upheld by the Supreme Court in *Sections 5 and 10 of the Illegal Immigrants (Trafficking) Bill 1999, Re*,[120] as was the power to detain for up to eight weeks persons whose deportation has been ordered and who fall into one of several categories.

HABEAS CORPUS AND THE ARTICLE 40.4 INQUIRY

Habeas corpus is the name given to the speedy procedure whereby the lawfulness of a person's existing detention is determined by a court.[121] It is embodied principally in Article 40.4 of the Constitution, according to which:

> "Upon complaint being made by or on behalf of any person to the High Court or any judge thereof alleging that such a person is being unlawfully detained, the High Court and any and every Judge thereof to whom such complaint is made shall forthwith enquire into the said complaint and may order the person in whose custody such person is detained to produce the body of such person before the High Court on a named day and to certify in writing the grounds of his detention, and the High Court shall, upon the body of such person being produced before that Court and after giving the person in whose custody he is detained an opportunity of justifying the detention, order the release of such person from such detention unless satisfied that he is being detained in accordance with the law."

This procedure is frequently invoked by or on behalf of persons claiming that they are being illegally detained, such as by the Gardaí or by an immigration officer, or in a mental hospital or in jail. It has for long been regarded as an essential complement to the principles of legality and liberty. If a complaint is made to any High Court judge that a person is being unlawfully detained, that judge will inquire promptly into the allegation, order whoever is holding the detainee to produce that person before the court and to explain the legal justification for the detention, the onus being on the party having custody to justify it. If it transpires that the law does not authorise the detention, the judge will order his immediate release. A remedy for unlawful detention along these lines is required by Article 5(4) of the European Convention and by Article 9(4) of the UN Covenant. But Article 40.4 cannot be invoked to invalidate any

---

[119] November 20, 1989, 1577 UNTS 3.
[120] *Supra*, n.116.

law enacted to secure public safety and preserve the State during a "national emergency" envisaged by Article 28.3.3.

The Habeas Corpus Acts

Although they have not been repealed and procedures under them are provided for in Order 84, rules 1–13 of the Rules of the Superior Courts, the Habeas Corpus Acts of 1782 and of 1816[122] are now virtually obsolete, having been supplanted by the entrenched and more flexible mechanism for vindicating personal liberty. *Habeas corpus* is a common law writ and these Acts merely regulate the manner in which applications for the writ should be made and responded to. One of the grievances listed in the Petition of Right, 1628,[123] was widespread disregard of this writ, which led to enacting the English Habeas Corpus Acts of 1640 and 1679;[124] the former abolished the capacity of the monarch to order persons' detention without legal authorisation to do so, the latter contained the procedure for granting the writ. On numerous occasions thereafter, sweeping powers of executive detention were sanctioned by Parliament, which often had the effect of "suspending" these Acts, for instance what became know as the "Irish Coercion Acts" of 1833 and 1881.[125] It was the ease and frequency of those suspensions occurring that caused Article I.9.2 of the U.S. Constitution to be adopted, which states that "[t]he privilege of the writ of *habeas corpus* shall not be suspended, unless when in cases of rebellion or invasion the public safety may require it." Until it was amended in 2001 to take all extradition proceedings out of the District Court, the procedure expressly provided for challenging extradition orders made by that court on several grounds was a *habeas corpus* application.

In the past jurists and men of public affairs tended to extol the virtues of *habeas corpus* to an extravagant extent. Perhaps the best known of these ecomia is that of Bolingbroke in 1734, who described it as "that noble badge of liberty, which every subject of Britain wears, and by which he is distinguished so eminently, not from slaves alone but even from the free men of other countries."[126] Just over a century later, Dicey could confidently assert that "[a]t the present day ... the securities for personal freedom in England are as

---

[121] See generally, R. Sharpe, *The Law of Habeas Corpus* (2nd ed., 1989) and D. Clarke & G. McCoy, *The Most Fundamental Legal Right* (2000).

[122] Habeas Corpus (Ireland) Act 1782, 22 Geo. 3 c.11 and Habeas Corpus Act 1816, 56 Geo. c.100; see generally J. Gabbett, *A Treatise on the Criminal Law* (1842), vol.2, pp.181–193.

[123] 3 Car. c.1.

[124] Act of Car. c. 10 and Act of Car. II c. 2; see generally W. Blackstone, *Commentaries on the Laws of England* (1st ed., 1768), vol.3, pp.131–138.

[125] 3 & 4 Will IV c. 4 and Peace Preservation (Ireland) Act 1881, 44 & 45 Vic. c.49.

[126] Clark & McCoy, *supra*, n.121, p.38.

complete as laws can make them,"[127] and he castigated as almost worthless guarantees of personal liberty embodied in entrenched constitutions. But this exaggerated view of the remedy hardly explains why the 1782 and 1816 Acts have not been repealed, since they provide no greater protection than exists under Article 40.4.

At times judges have adverted to differences between the constitutional and the statutory provisions. The extent if any to which Article 40.4 has replaced these Acts has yet to be determined. Walsh J. has stated that:

> "The application to challenge the legality of the deprivation of someone's personal liberty is enshrined as a constitutional right in respect of which the whole procedure is set out in the Constitution itself. It is outside the competence of any rule-making authority to make any rules whatever to regulate this procedure. Indeed, it is questionable, as it has been previously questioned, whether the (traditional) method of a conditional order followed by the procedure of an order absolute is the appropriate procedure -however convenient it may appear to be. The Rules of the Superior Courts which refer to *habeas corpus* do not refer to the constitutional procedure and are not applicable thereto but would refer to such provisions as are still operative of the Habeas Corpus Acts and the procedures thereunder."[128]

Judicial Review Alternative

From time to time the courts have cautioned against resort to Article 40.4/ *habeas corpus* where some other procedure (principally appeal or judicial review) is more appropriate, although where exactly the dividing line is to be drawn is not entirely clear. The only real difference between *habeas corpus* and judicial review is that proceedings under the former may be commenced before any judge of the High Court at any time. Judicial review applications must commence before a judge assigned to hear such cases and during normal court hours and, in some instances, on notice to the intending respondent rather than *ex parte*.[129] Although in *habeas corpus* the onus of establishing the legality of the detention is on the respondent, that often makes little practical difference. Nor does it matter that much that the court in *habeas corpus* must release a person found to be unlawfully detained whereas in judicial review the court has some discretion as to whether to grant the reliefs being sought even though

---

[127] A.V. Dicey, *An Introduction to the Study of the Law of the Constitution* (10th ed., 1959), p.220.

[128] *State (Aherne) v. Cotter* [1982] I.R. 188 at p.200. See too *Re Singer* 97 I.L.T.R. 130 at p.139 (1963).

[129] *Infra*, p.486.

the applicant has succeeded. Judicial reviews are dealt with comparatively slowly but, if the applicant is challenging the very legality of his detention, there is no reason why his case would be permitted to drag on for longer as a review than it would a *habeas corpus* application. In principle the *habeas corpus* judge has more procedural flexibility than if he were dealing with a judicial review but judges have not devised any major procedural innovations in the last sixty years in cases under Article 40.4, that could not be adopted in judicial reviews.

At the end of the day, *habeas corpus* is just another mode of judicial review, albeit one expressly entrenched in the Constitution. Notwithstanding the absence of major differences between the two procedures, some judges behave as if *habeas corpus* was so important a remedy that it should be availed of only in exceptional cases rather than in virtually all instances where the underlying issue is the legality of a person's detention. A motivation behind their caution is that the High Court must give precedence to Article 40.4 enquiries, conducting them with all possible dispatch, and some aggrieved litigants may seek to "jump the queue" in the court's list by formulating their claim as one for *habeas corpus*. Thus, in *McGlinchey v. Governor of Portlaoise Prison*,[130] where the applicant sought to challenge his imprisonment on foot of a conviction by the Special Criminal Court, Finlay C.J. stated that the Article 40.4 procedure "is not subject to any special procedures; it is not subject to any special rules and deals only with the question of the legality of the detention of the person who applies. It is therefore important that it should not be debased by being used for purposes for which it was not intended."[131] Yet in *Sheehan v. Reilly*,[132] where the applicant challenged the sentence imposed on him in the District Court, which on the face of the order exceeded that court's jurisdiction, Finlay C.J. stated that "[a]pplications which clearly in fact raise an issue as to the legality of the detention of a person must be treated as an application under Article 40, no matter how they are described."[133]

Where an applicant under this procedure obtains bail, that takes much of the urgency out of the case and should be a sufficient answer to any queue-jumping objection. In one instance O'Higgins J. held that an Article 40.4 enquiry should be discontinued, once the person being held gets bail, but that proposition is out of line with long-established case law[134] and was not endorsed by the Supreme Court on appeal.[135]

---

[130] [1988[I.R. 671.

[131] *Id.* at p.701.

[132] [1993] 2 I.R. 81.

[133] *Id.* at p.89. *Cf. Bennett v. Superintendent Rimutaka Prison* [2002] I.N.Z.L.R. 616 and *R. v. Oldham Justices, ex p.Cawley* [1997] Q.B. 1.

[134] *E.g., State (Aherne) v. Cotter* [1982] I.R. 188 and *R. v. Secretary of State, ex p.Launder (No.2)* [1998] Q.B. 994.

[135] *Bolger v. Commissioner of Garda Síochána* [2000] 1 I.L.R.M. 136.

Substance and Scope of Inquiry

When an application is made to a judge under Article 40.4 (or under the 1782–
1816 Acts) the question to be determined is whether the person in detention is
being held lawfully. By this is meant whether, at the time the complaint was
made, the person was being held in accordance with statutory authority or
some common law authority, and any such authority must not be
unconstitutional. Thus, where the law requires a warrant to arrest someone in
particular circumstances, a warrant-less arrest in those circumstances is not
authorised by law and, on an application, the court will order that the person
detained be released immediately. In *State (Quinn) v. Ryan*,[136] it was held that
the extradition provisions of the Petty Sessions (Ireland) Act 1851,[137] were
unconstitutional; accordingly, the applicant's detention under that Act had been
without any legal authority and his immediate release was ordered. And in
State (Trimbole) v. Governor of Mountjoy Prison,[138] where the applicant was
arrested under section 30 of the Offences Against the State Act 1939, but the
real reason for detaining him was to await implementation of extradition
arrangements being concluded with Australia, it was held that his detention
was not authorised by section 30 and his immediate release was ordered. Claims
for damages will not be entertained in proceedings of this nature but, where it
is found that a person is being held under a warrant or court order that was
unlawfully issued or made, the court will direct that it be quashed "in aid" of
the *habeas corpus*. Frequently, parallel judicial review proceedings are
instituted in order to obtain orders of *certiorari* quashing such authorities as
exist for the applicant's detention.

    It has not been determined by the courts how searching the inquiry under
Article 40.4 must be, other than that the judge does not have to confine the
hearing entirely to the issues raised by the applicant. Kingsmill Moore J.
observed in an extradition case that was decided four years before the 1965
Act came into force, that "a very wide field of enquiry is open to the court on
an application for *habeas corpus* and, where the detention is by an act of the
executive, the court can enquire into all the circumstances. It is concerned not
only to see that the documents are correct in form; it can investigate whether
the necessary conditions exist to justify the execution of such documents and
can enquire whether they have been executed by mistake or whether their
execution has been procured by fraud. Moreover the court can enquire if the
executive has misused its powers."[139] There does not appear to be any
comparable summary of the ambit of enquiry where the applicant is being
held under a court order. The scope of the inquiry required by Article 5(4) of

---

[136] [1965] I.R. 70.
[137] 14 & 15 Vic. c.93.
[138] [1985] I.R. 550.
[139] *State (Hully) v. Hynes* (1966) 100 I.L.T.R. 145 at p.163.

the European Convention was described by the Strasbourg Commission as follows:

> "It is ... only the legality of the detention itself which must be judicially controlled under Art. 5(4). The judicial control of the lawfulness of the detention is to be seen as a strict requirement. Its purpose is to safeguard the liberty of the individual and to prevent arbitrary measures of detention. ... [T]he procedure ... must cover the substantive grounds for detention. ... This does not mean, however, that ... the court must have unlimited powers of review. The question how far the review must extend may vary according to the kind of deprivation of liberty in question .... Thus the court ... does not have to review the correctness of a criminal conviction, under Art. 5(1)(a), while it must be able to ascertain whether a person is of unsound mind under Art. 5(1)(e)."[140]

Article 40.4 requires that the detainee be released unless the judge is satisfied that the detention is lawful. In *Application of Woods*,[141] it was held that the judge, as well as the Supreme Court on appeal, is not confined to an examination of the illegality complained of by the applicant but both are required to be alert to other grounds which could render the detention unlawful.

Because the sole focus of these enquiries is to ascertain whether the detention in question is lawful, not alone should the court not go beyond matters directly related to this question but, if at any stage the individual is released, the enquiry must forthwith be concluded. Thus in an instance where the respondents' custody of a young baby was contested by a Health Board and, at a very early stage they surrendered the child to the Board, the Supreme Court held that the enquiry should have been brought to an end there and then, since there could no longer be an issue of the respondents unlawfully detaining the child.[142]

Private Detentions

Article 40.4 is available where a person is being held in custody by a private individual or body, as well as being detained by an agency of the State. Disputes about the custody of children are at times commenced as enquiries under Article 40.4.

---

[140] *Caprino v. United Kingdom* 4 E.H.R.R. 91 (1982).
[141] [1970] I.R. 154.
[142] *Eastern Health Board v. E.* [2000] 1 I.R. 430.

Executive Detentions

Article 40.4 is used principally to challenge detentions by order of a minister or some public official, without the authority of a formal court order made after an *inter partes* hearing; for example, where a person has been arrested by a member of the Garda Síochána or is being held by the Gardaí without being formally arrested, or where he is being detained by an immigration officer or is being held in some mental institution. A leading case in 1939 concerned a person being interned without trial by order of the Minister.[143]

Traditionally persons challenged their pending deportation by way of *habeas corpus* and, if they made out a good case, they would be released and any deportation order would be quashed.[144] Under section 5(1) of the Illegal Immigrants (Trafficking) Act 2000, deportations and decisions leading up to those orders may only be challenged by way of judicial review, as provided for in Order 84 of the Rules of the Superior Courts. This, however, does not displace the jurisdiction under Article 40.4 to enquire into the legality of the detention of any intended deportee. As Keane C.J. stated in the *Illegal Immigrants' Bill* reference, "[i]t is not within the competence of the Oireachtas to circumscribe or abridge the right protected ... by that article [and] it must be presumed that it was not the intention of the Oireachtas in enacting this provision to amend or circumscribe that right in any way."[145] He added, however, that an unchallenged deportation order may be a sufficient answer to any Article 40.4 application; that "[t]he fact that the deportation order has previously been unsuccessfully challenged in judicial review or had not been challenged at all within time permitted by section 5 may be sufficient to constitute the deportation order as a lawful basis for that person's detention."[146] Where a deportation order is relied on in any such application, the prudent albeit cumbersome course is to then challenge that order by way of judicial review, which may require an extension of time to commence the proceedings, and both cases would then be heard concurrently.

Where the applicant is being held in custody on foot of any other kind of executive order that appears to be valid on its face, the person who made that order ought also to be made a party to the proceedings. Depending on the nature of the objection being made to his order, it may be necessary to challenge it in parallel judicial review proceedings even though this may involve unnecessary duplication of pleadings and affidavits.

---

[143] *State (Burke) v. Lennon* [1940] I.R. 136; *infra*, p.858.
[144] *E.g., Secretary of State v. O'Brien* [1923] A.C. 603; compare *R. v. Secretary of State ex p. Muboyayj* [1992] 1 Q.B. 244.
[145] *Supra*, n.116 at p.401.
[146] *Ibid.*

Court Ordered Detentions

Remands in custody by the District Court, the Circuit Court or the Special Criminal Court are often the subject of Article 40.4 applications. Prior to them being taken over by the High Court in 2001, remands by the District Court in extradition cases were perhaps the commonest of these cases. Depending on the nature of the objection being raised, an applicant may be required to institute parallel judicial review proceedings challenging the court's order, even though his may involve unneccessary duplication.

A person detained in a mental institution, having been found "guilty but insane" by the High Court, can challenge his continued detention under Article 40.4 on the grounds that he no longer suffers from the mental disability.[147] Where a convicted prisoner's sentence has expired but through oversight or otherwise he has not been released, it too would appear to be the appropriate mode of redress. It was held by the Supreme Court in *Sheehan v. Reilly*[148] that, where an inferior court passes a sentence of imprisonment that plainly exceeds its jurisdiction, the challenge to the prisoner's continued detention should proceed in this manner and not by way of judicial review. The applicant there had been convicted in the District Court of unlawful trespass with intent to steal, and also of stealing from the premises in question, and was sentenced to consecutive sentences amounting to 26 months, which was plainly in excess of that court's jurisdiction under section 12 of the Criminal Justice Act 1984. Earlier observations by the Supreme Court, that Article 40.4 is not the proper method for challenging convictions, were described by Finlay C.J. as not to be "read as a statement of the law which either can be relied upon to justify detention which clearly has not got a legal base nor to restrict or diminish the immediacy of the right of release provided by Article 40.4 ...".[149] Where a prisoner sought to challenge his conviction in the Circuit Court, long after the time for appealing had expired, on the grounds that the offence in question did not exist in law at the time of his trial, he was permitted to proceed by way of Article 40.4.[150] Where a prisoner claimed that he was entitled to be released because he had been detained long enough to qualify for the one-fourth remission of sentence, no objection was made to his application being made under Article 40.4 and the Supreme Court ordered that he be released.[151]

The *Sheehan* case was distinguished unconvincingly by the Supreme Court in *McSorley v. Governor of Mountjoy Prison*.[152] When the applicant was being tried in the District Court, the judge gave him no advice about obtaining legal representation or as to the availability of legal aid, notwithstanding that the

---

[147] *Gallagher v. Director Central Mental Hospital* [1996] 3 I.R. 1.
[148] [1993] 2 I.R. 81.
[149] *Id.* at p.91.
[150] *O'C. v. Governor Curragh Prison* [2002] 1 I.R. 66.
[151] *O'Brien v. Governor Limerick Prison* [1997] 2 I.L.R.M. 348.
[152] [1997] 2 I.R. 258.

judge was contemplating a custodial sentence. It was held that the matter should not have been aired as an Article 40.4 enquiry but, instead, because the judge's conduct was being questioned, it should have proceeded in the form of a judicial review application, with that judge being put on notice of the proceedings. Yet there is no good reason whatsoever why that judge could not have been made a notice party to the Article 40.4 enquiry and the case going ahead in that form. It has not been determined whether claims of entitlement to be released from prison under a scheme, such as that in the "Good Friday Agreement," may be brought in this manner or must instead proceed by way of judicial review.

In *State (Comerford) v. Governor of Mountjoy Prison*,[153] Barrington J. observed that "the *habeas corpus* procedure is designed to vindicate individual liberty and it should not be debased by being used as a vehicle to obtain other forms of relief. ... *Prima facie* ... such procedure ... should not be permitted by the court to become a vehicle by way of special, informal and expeditious procedure for the pursuit of other remedies."[154] There the applicant, a remand prisoner, was detained under exactly the same conditions as convicted offenders are held, which contravened the very letter of the Prison Rules. The reasons for holding him in that manner were entirely administrative and security considerations. It was held that, although the manner of his detention was irregular, that irregularity "was not such as to make [his] detention unlawful or to entitle him to an absolute order of *habeas corpus*."[155] Barrington J. there appears to confuse the appropriate procedure for asserting the illegality of a detention with whether, on the facts, the applicant has made out a good case. Where the focus of the challenge is the actual conditions in the prison, ordinarily that should be brought by way of judicial review.[156]

Procedure

The traditional *habeas corpus* procedure[157] has been by way of an *ex parte* application made on affidavit before a judge for a conditional order. If granted, that order would require whoever is holding the person in detention to produce him before the court, certify in writing the legal basis for the detention and explain to the court why the detention is lawful. If a satisfactory justification is not forthcoming, the detainee's immediate release would be ordered. As was mentioned above, Article 40.4 does not in fact incorporate this procedure but it nevertheless is normally followed.

---

[153] [1981] I.L.R.M. 86.

[154] *Id.* at p.90.

[155] *Ibid.*

[156] *State (McDonagh) v. Frawley* [1978] I.R. 131 and *State (Boyle) v. Kelly* [1974] I.R. 259.

[157] RSC, O.84 and A. Collins and J. O'Reilly, *Civil Proceedings and the State* (2nd ed., 2003), Chap.3.

Applicant

Usually it is the detainee, through counsel, who makes the application. But somebody else can apply on his behalf, although the court will not entertain every such application.[158] In *Woods, Re,*[159] the applicant was one of Mr Woods' fellow-prisoners. And in *State (Quinn) v. Ryan,*[160] although the proceedings were in Mr Quinn's own name, at the time he was in the hands of the English police and it was his solicitor who applied for *habeas corpus* on his behalf.

Respondent

Usually the person who is holding the detainee is named as respondent; in many of the reported cases he is the governor of a prison or of a detention centre, or an immigration officer. On occasion, however, somebody exercising indirect control over the detainee may be named as respondent, for instance a Health Authority, where a child who is the subject of the proceedings has been put in somebody's care, or the Adoption Board, where a child has been adopted. Sometimes the detainee is no longer under the named respondent's control but has been handed over to someone else. In *State (Quinn) v. Ryan* Davitt P. rejected the proposition that "if the court is satisfied that the body whose production is asked is not in the custody, power or control of the person to whom it is sought to address the writ, a writ of *habeas corpus* is not the proper remedy, though there was an original illegal taking or detention."[161] The correct position is "where shortly before a writ of *habeas corpus* was issued the person to whom it was directed had the body of the person named in the writ in illegal custody, it was not a good return to the writ to state that before its issue he had handed over custody to someone else, and therefore could not produce the body in obedience to the writ because he no longer had it in his custody, power or control, unless the person to whom he had handed over custody had himself a legal right to such custody."[162] Teevan J. accepted this proposition as correct as regards custody of children and the like, where there is a distinct probability that, under the pressure of the court process, the respondent could obtain the return of the person previously detained. But he held it was a sufficient return to the conditional order there to say that the applicant had been arrested under an English arrest warrant and had been delivered to the English police.[163]

---

[158] *Cf. Coalition of Clergy v. Bush,* 42 I.L.M. 396 (2003) (USA), *Odah v. United States,* 42 I.L.M. 408 (2003) and *Victorian Council for Civil Liberties v. Minister for Immigration* [2002] 11 L.R.C. 189.

[159] [1970] I.R. 154.

[160] [1965] I.R. 70.

[161] *Id.* at p.87, quoting from *Ex. p. O'Brien* [1923] 2 K.B. 361.

[162] *Id.* at pp.85–86.

[163] *Id.* at pp.105–106. *Cf. Quigley v. Chief Constable RUC* [1893] N.I. 238 and *Quigley, re* [1983] N.I. 245.

"Forthwith Enquire"

Under the procedure set out in the 1782 Act, where the application discloses a *prima facie* or arguable case, the judge will make a conditional order of *habeas corpus* and the respondent is thereby required to produce the detainee before the court and certify the lawfulness of the detention. Article 40.4.2 states that, when an application is first made, the judge "shall forthwith enquire into the said complaint" and he "may order" production of the body and a written statement of the grounds for detention. At this initial stage, before forming even a tentative view as to the lawfulness of the detention, the judge may "make inquiries of a speedy and, if necessary informal nature to try and ascertain the facts."[164] On several occasions judges have adverted to these somewhat different procedures without spelling out the full implications of the differences.

If on the initial application the judge concludes that there are no grounds for making a conditional order, it would seem that he can dismiss the application there and then. In *State (Whelan) v. Governor of Mountjoy Prison,*[165] Barrington J. described the court's function as, "once the enquiry is entered on and, provided the urgency and importance of the proceedings are kept in mind, the Court is entitled, after hearing the views of the prosecutor, the respondent and their legal representatives, to conduct the enquiry in the manner which the Court thinks best calculated to resolve the issues of law and fact raised in the proceedings, and to achieve the interest of justice. ... The duty ... 'forthwith to enquire' ... stresses the importance and the urgency of *habeas corpus* proceedings. But it does not mean that the High Court should skimp its enquiry or proceed on an inadequate understanding of the law or the facts."[166] And he observed that, at the preliminary stage, the court could "be satisfied that the complaint was groundless and could dismiss the application without calling on the (detainer) to produce the body or certify the grounds of the detention."[167]

Frequently, the next stage of the enquiry is a very short and simple affair; often a respondent will produce some warrant or court order plainly justifying the detention or, not infrequently, the basis proffered for the detention is so manifestly untenable that the enquiry is concluded in next to no time. At times, however, an applicant will want to "go behind" the warrant or order being relied on, *i.e.* contend that it was not properly granted or made and that, when the circumstances of its being obtained are fully investigated, it will be demonstrated that it is legally deficient.

Some judges tend to view production of a warrant or court order authorising detention as a sufficient answer to an Article 40.4 enquiry and that any ensuing attack on the warrant or order should proceed by way of a judicial review. But

---

[164] *Sheehan v. Reilly* [1993] 2 I.R. 81 at p.90.
[165] [1983] I.L.R.M. 52.
[166] *Id.* at p.403.
[167] *Id.* at p.55.

the constitutional enquiry procedure is not discretionary; once the circumstances justifying its commencement exist, it must be carried out to a full conclusion, although the overall circumstances of the case will dictate the precise manner and pace. This was emphasised in *Sheehan v. Reilly*,[168] where the High Court judge had declined to direct an Article 40.4 inquiry into the basis for a prisoner's detention and, instead, ordered that the proceedings should take the form of a judicial review. As put by Finlay C.J. there, "[a]lthough the application brought before the High Court ... was stated ... as being "for a conditional order of *habeas corpus* ... and for an enquiry [under] Article 40.4," it should ... have been regarded as an application for an enquiry as to the legality of the detention of the applicant pursuant to Article 40.4. ... Such an application in its urgency and importance must necessarily transcend any procedural form of application for judicial review or otherwise. Applications which clearly, in fact, raise an issue as to the legality of the detention of a person must be treated as an application under Article 40, no matter how they are described."[169]

The speed with which the full enquiry should be conducted depends on the nature of the issues, especially how long is required to have all the relevant facts before the court. Where they arise, disputes about discovery of documents almost invariably cause considerable delays. If in the meantime an applicant obtains bail, that will take at least some of the urgency out of the case. In the *Whelan* case, Barrington J. said that the word "forthwith" in Article 40.4.2 refers to the preliminary proceedings, *i.e.* proceedings in the nature of an application for a conditional order. It is unlikely, however, that by this he meant that the next stage of the enquiry may proceed at a leisurely pace. Guidelines as to the duration of proceedings of this nature have been laid down by the European Court of Human Rights.[170] In one instance where it was contended that an enquiry lasted an unacceptably long time in the High Court, the argument was rejected by the Supreme Court in an *ex tempore* judgment,[171] which did not endeavour to lay down any guidance on what priority should be given to such cases.

While Article 40.4 would appear to permit a single-stage inquiry, it was held in *State (Rogers) v. Galvin*,[172] that a prisoner's release cannot be ordered unless a two-stage procedure is followed, *i.e.* a procedure that puts the respondent on notice that the detention must be justified in court and gives him an opportunity to do so. There the applicant had been brought before the Special Criminal Court to be charged with capital murder and a firearms offence. His counsel requested the presiding judge to sit as a High Court judge for the purpose of a *habeas corpus* application and, having heard the evidence,

---

[168] [1993] 2 I.R. 81.
[169] *Id.* at p.89.
[170] *E. v. Norway* 17 E.H.R.R. 30 (1994).
[171] *Quinlivan v. Governor of Portlaoise Prison*, July 22, 1997,
[172] [1983] I.R. 249.

the judge ordered that he be released. It was held by the Supreme Court that such a single stage procedure should not have been followed because it did not afford the respondent an adequate opportunity to justify the detention. It was suggested by the Supreme Court in *Application of Zwann*,[173] that the 1782 Act is unconstitutional to the extent that it permits a judge to order a detainee's release without requiring a respondent to justify the detention. O'Higgins C.J. stated that "at first sight, and to the extent that its provisions permit the granting of an absolute order of *habeas corpus* without allowing an opportunity to justify the detention complained of, it would appear difficult to reconcile" the 1782 Act's provisions with those of Article 40.4.2.[174]

Successive Applications

Where one judge of the High Court has refused to grant a conditional order requiring the respondent to justify a detention, there is no rule prohibiting the detainee from applying to another judge for relief, although counsel are expected to inform that judge that another has already refused to grant the conditional order. But where the respondent supplies the reasons for the detention and the judge discharges the conditional order, it would seem that the matter is *res judicata* and cannot then be the subject of another application. So it was held in *State (Dowling) v. Kingston (No.2)*,[175] which was decided under the Free State Constitution and in which the authorities were exhaustively reviewed.

Where, however, the detainee finds new grounds for challenging the detention, which were not addressed or were not considered adequately in previous proceedings, it was held by the Supreme Court that a fresh application will be entertained. As Ó Dálaigh C.J. stated in *Application of Woods*:

> "neither the High Court nor the Supreme Court warrants, by its decision in an application for *habeas corpus*, that every possible ground of complaint has been considered and ruled. ... (It) will not preclude an applicant from later raising a new ground even though that ground might have been, but was not, put forward on the first application. ...
>
> [T]he court should entertain a complaint which bears on the question of the legality of the detention – even though in earlier proceedings the applicant might have raised the matter but did not do so. The duty of the Courts, to see that no one is deprived of his personal liberty save in accordance with law, overrides considerations which are valid in litigation *inter-partes*."[176]

---

[173] [1981] I.R. 395.
[174] *Id.* at p.403.
[175] [1937] I.R 699.
[176] [1970] I.R. 154 at p.162.

What was held there and also in the *Sheehan* case was neither adverted to nor distinguished by Lynch J., who gave the judgment for the Supreme Court in *Bolger v. Commissioner of An Garda Síochána.*[177] The applicant had been arrested under an English extradition warrant several years after a previous application to have him extradited for the same matter had been dismissed by the District Court and was never appealed. He obtained a conditional order around 11.15 a.m., while he was in Garda custody and before he had been brought to any court. The certificate for the return stated that he was being detained under the Prisons Acts, which Laffoy J. held was a good return and that was appealed unsuccessfully to the Supreme Court. The State then sought to have the conditional order set aside, principally on the grounds that his having in the meantime obtained bail meant that he was no longer "in custody." Notwithstanding the abundance of authority against this proposition, it was upheld by O'Higgins J. On the appeal against this, in a brief judgment that contains no reference to authority of any kind, it was held that the earlier rejection of the appeal against the certificate had put an end to the proceedings and, consequently, the applicant was thereby precluded from "going behind" the extradition warrant by way of Article 40.4. It was held that his case was "an attempt to avail of a fast track procedure ... where the appropriate remedies are by way of judicial review proceedings which are in being or even plenary proceedings"; the Article 40.4 case was an "abuse of what is a very important remedy provided by the Constitution."[178]

Re-Arrest

A person released following *habeas corpus* or Article 40.4 proceedings can be re-arrested on some other charge. Where the order for release was granted because there had been some technical defect in the detention, the detainee can be arrested again on the same charge. Where release was ordered because an arrest warrant was improperly served or on account of some procedural defect following the arrest, the detainee can be re-arrested under the same warrant. In *Singer (No.2), Re*[179] Walsh J. rejected as absurd the proposition that "once a person has been released on *habeas corpus* no matter what the reason he can never again be apprehended or detained in custody in respect of the charges which were pending against him at the time of his release."[180] While section 5 of the 1782 Act would appear to prohibit re-arrest following release on the order of the court, it was held by Barrington J. that this section did not have this meaning; all it requires is that persons who have applied to

---

[177] [2000] 1 I.L.R.M. 136.
[178] *Id.* at p.147.
[179] 98 I.L.T.R. 112 (1960).
[180] *Id.* at p.125 and *Quinlivan v. Governor of Portlaoise Prison* [1998] 1 I.R. 456.

the court for *habeas corpus* and have been released on bail must not be re-committed to prison in respect of the same charges.[181] Nevertheless, the detainee must first be set free and allowed to leave the precincts of the court before any re-arrest may occur.[182]

Appeal

Where the High Court or a judge of that Court refuses to grant the order, the detainee can appeal to the Supreme Court. In the past a respondent could not appeal against the granting of such an order.[183] However, in *State (Browne) v. Feran*,[184] it was held that, by virtue of the extensive appellate jurisdiction of the Supreme Court under Article 34 of the Constitution, a constitutional right of appeal exists against the grant of an order of *habeas corpus*. Under this Article, the Supreme Court "has appellate jurisdiction from all decisions of the High Court" and it was held that the term "all decisions" must be given its literal meaning,[185] which in this context means that a respondent who did not satisfy a judge that the detainee was being lawfully held can appeal. If it wished, the Oireachtas could deprive the detainee or the respondent, or both, of their right of appeal, but that right cannot be taken away if the case involves any question of the constitutionality of a post-1937 law.

Apart entirely from what was held in the *Browne* case, Article 40.4.3 of the Constitution provides for an appeal by the respondent where the detention is held to be unlawful because a provision of some post-1937 Act authorising that detention is found to be unconstitutional. This clause was adopted in 1941 after Gavan Duffy J. had held that the internment without trial provisions in the Offences Against the State Act 1939 were unconstitutional and ordered the applicant's release, and the Supreme Court had held that the order for release could not be appealed against.[186]

It would seem that a person whose release has been ordered by a judge cannot be detained pending the outcome of an appeal against the order. But that is not the case in an appeal under Article 40.4.3, where the judge has declared a provision of a post-1937 law to be unconstitutional. This clause expressly authorises the court to grant bail pending the appeal, which signifies that there is no automatic right to be released in those circumstances.

---

[181] *State (McFadden) v. Governor Mountjoy Prison (No. 2)* [1981] I.L.R.M. 121.
[182] *Id.* at p.124.
[183] *State (Burke) v. Lennon* [1940] I.R. 136, following *Cox v. Hakes* (1890) 15 App. Cas. 506.
[184] [1967] I.R. 147.
[185] See *supra*, p.53.
[186] *Supra* n. 183. See too *State (Gilliland) v. Governor Mountjoy Prison* [1987] I.L.R.M. 278.

BAIL

Persons who are charged with serious offences are often released on bail pending their trial.[187] Release on bail recognises the principle that accused persons are presumed innocent until they are proved guilty and that great injustice would be done if accused persons were detained but then acquitted at their trial. That those accused of crimes ought generally to be released on bail is implicit in the Eighth Amendment to the United States Constitution, which stipulates that "excessive bail shall not be required," and in the Sixth Amendment's requirement of a "speedy trial." Article 5(3) of the European Convention on Human Rights contains a similar stipulation, that "[e]veryone arrested ... shall be entitled to trial within a reasonable time or to release pending trial. Release may be conditioned by guarantees to appear for trial." According to Article 9(3) of the UN Covenant, "[i]t shall not be the general rule that persons awaiting trial shall be detained in custody, but release may be subject to guarantees to appear for trial ...".

The Right to Bail

The High Court has an original inherent jurisdiction to grant bail and there are no offences in respect of which that court can never give bail or must always give bail (except for misdemeanours under section 2 of the Habeas Corpus Act 1781). The District Court's authority regarding bail is regulated by statute: it cannot grant bail where the detainee is accused of treason or murder, or some other very serious offence; it has a discretion whether or not to grant bail in all other felonies and in various other misdemeanours. A form of bail is provided for in section 5(5) of the Immigration Act 1999.

In *People v. O'Callaghan*,[188] the Supreme Court held that accused persons have a constitutional right to bail, which can be denied only in exceptional circumstances, and that the terms of the bail shall not be excessive. As Walsh J. pointed out, the right to bail derives from the right to personal liberty and from the presumption of innocence until proven guilty in due course of law. This presumption "is a very real thing and is not simply a procedural rule taking effect only at the trial."[189] Detaining persons who are awaiting trial or an appeal can have a profound effect on their private lives, especially on their families who may well be deprived of a breadwinner. Additionally, it can be far more difficult for persons held in jail to arrange for their defence.

It was held by the Supreme Court in *People v. Gilliland*,[190] that the approach

---

[187] See generally, D. Walsh, *Criminal Procedure* (2002), Chap.10.
[188] [1966] I.R. 501.
[189] *Id.* at p.513.
[190] [1985] I.R. 643.

to bail set out in *O'Callaghan* applies equally where the detainee is being held with a view to being extradited to a country with which the State has a treaty providing for extradition. The key question is the likelihood of the detainee absconding if released on bail; if there is a strong likelihood of absconding then bail will be refused. While the State may have treaty obligations to grant extradition, those duties "must operate in a way that will not conflict with the fundamental right to personal liberty of a person who stands unconvicted of an offence. ..."[191]

In *McAllister, Re*[192] Kenny J. struck down a provision of a bankruptcy law that authorised the court to order a person, who refused to answer satisfactorily questions that were put, to be detained without being entitled to bail. He observed that he did not believe that even the Oireachtas could stipulate that an accused person shall never be entitled to bail.

Criteria for Bail

In the *O'Callaghan* case, Walsh J. conducted an extensive review of the various criteria governing decisions to grant bail. The fundamental criterion is, as has been stated, the likelihood of the detainee absconding: "the probability of the applicant evading justice."[193] Several of the specific criteria are merely aspects of this "fundamental test." But some of the criteria being used before 1966 were rejected there.

One is the likelihood of the prisoner facing personal danger if released, such as at the hands of the victim of the crime or of others incensed by it. As Walsh J. stated, "a bail motion cannot be used as a vehicle to import into the law the concept of protective custody for an unwilling recipient."[194] On the other hand, where the court is satisfied that, if the prisoner is released on bail, he will be subjected to such violence or intimidation as will deter him from standing trial then it may refuse bail. According to Finlay J. in *Application of Dolan*, "if a Court were properly led to the conclusion that the accused would not properly stand his trial because he would be prevented by violence or threats of violence from doing so rather than by his wish ... the Court should exercise its discretion against granting bail."[195]

Another criterion rejected in *O'Callaghan* was the possibility of a speedy trial. While this has some relevance to the bail decision, nevertheless, "the prospect of a speedy trial is not a ground for refusing bail where it ought otherwise be granted."[196]

---

[191] *Id.* at p.646.
[192] [1973] I.R. 238.
[193] [1966] I.R. 501 at p.513.
[194] *Id.* at p.515.
[195] Unreported, November 5, 1973.
[196] [1966] I.R. 501 at p.513.

Another inapplicable criterion was the likelihood of the detainee committing further offences if released – which is a consideration that may be taken into account under the Council of Europe guidelines. According to Walsh J., however, this considerations is not admissible under the Constitution because it is "alien to the true purposes of bail" and is "a form of preventive justice which has no place in our legal system. ..."[197] It is only in situations of grave emergency and in order to preserve the peace, order and safety of the State itself that preventive detention can be justified under the Constitution. Additionally, "an attempt to predict who is likely to commit an offence while awaiting trial on bail can never be more than speculation."[198] In 1996, however, the Constitution was amended to reverse this principle. According to Article 40.4.7, "[p]rovision may be made by law for the refusal of bail by a court to a person charged with a serious offence where it is reasonably considered necessary to prevent the commission of a serious offence by that person." Provision to this effect was made by section 2 of the Bail Act 1997, which sets out considerations that should be taken into account in this regard and adds that "it shall not be necessary for a court to be satisfied that the commission of a specific offence by that person is apprehended."

The matters that should be taken into account in determining whether a detainee shall be released on bail are as follows: the first four of these are particular aspects of the fundamental test of likelihood to abscond:

(i) The nature and seriousness of the charge. The more serious the charge, the more likely it is that the accused will abscond.

(ii) The nature and cogency of the evidence supporting the charge. The more cogent the evidence, again the greater the likelihood that the accused will abscond.

(iii) The likely sentence to be imposed if the accused is convicted. Again, the heavier the likely sentence, the greater the possibility of absconding. In order to estimate the likely sentence, the accused's criminal record, if any, can be put before the court.

(iv) The accused's failure to answer bail on previous occasions.

(v) The fact that the accused was caught red-handed.

(vi) The likelihood of the accused interfering with witnesses, disposing of property believed to be stolen and the like.

(vii) The accused has been charged with a serious offence and there is a significant likelihood that, if released on bail, he will commit a serious offence.

(viii) The objections of the Director of Public Prosecutions and of the police authorities. Any such objections must relate to the grounds

---

[197] *Id.* at p.516.
[198] *Id.* at p.517.

on which bail may properly be refused, and must be supported by sufficient evidence as lends credibility to the objections.

(ix) The substance and reliability of whoever is standing bail. While whoever is standing bail must be independent, there is no requirement that they be householders or that they own their own houses; although owning a house can be relevant to the question whether the bailsman has the financial ability to meet the demands of the bail.

Excessive Bail

One of the grievances that the 1689 English Bill of Rights[199] sought to redress was insistence on excessive bail terms. While that Act was never made part of the law of Ireland, Walsh J. said in *O'Callaghan* that its prohibition against excessive bail was declaratory of the common law that also obtained in Ireland. What the prohibition means is that the amount of bail demanded must not be so great that the accused cannot find somebody to meet it.

L'Henryenat v. Attorney General[200] concerned provisions in the Fisheries Acts whereby a District Judge is empowered to release a boat that has been seized, while allegedly being used for illegal fishing, provided that adequate security is given; the security must be sufficient to cover the maximum fine that can be made, the costs of the proceedings and the estimated value of any forfeitures. One of the plaintiff's contentions was that this provision was unconstitutional because it in effect imposed excessive bail. But the Supreme Court held that the section did not refer to bail and, accordingly, was not invalid on that ground.

---

[199] 1 Wm. & M. c.2.
[200] [1983] I.R. 193.

CHAPTER 16

Equality and Non-Discrimination

Equality as a fundamental principle governing rule-making and rule-application plays a central role in most modern constitutions and international human rights instruments.[1] The "Fundamental Rights" section of the Irish Constitution commences with a proclamation of equality in Article 40.1, that "[a]ll citizens shall, as human persons, be held equal before the law. This shall not be held to mean that the State shall not in its enactments, have due regard to differences of capacity, physical and moral, and of social function." Article 40.2 then addresses an archaic form of social stratification, by providing that "[t]itles of nobility shall not be conferred by the State" and that the prior approval of the Government is required before any citizen may accept any "title of nobility or of honour."

Egalité was one of the proclaimed goals of the French Revolution and in the first clause of the 1789 Declaration of the Rights of Man and of the Citizen it is declared that "[m]en are born and remain free and equal in respect of rights. Social distinctions shall be based solely upon public utility."[2] The Fourteenth Amendment to the United States Constitution, which was adopted to entrench the outcome of the Civil War but has since been applied to discrimination in areas other than race, stipulates that "[n]o State shall ... deny to any person within its jurisdiction the equal protection of the laws." In Bills of Rights adopted since the Second World War the formulation of the equality ideal has changed to an affirmation of equality coupled with a proscription against discrimination on certain grounds. Thus, Article 3 of the German Federal Republic's Basic Law provides that:

"1. All persons shall be equal before the law.
2. Men and women shall have equal rights.
3. No one may be prejudiced or favoured because of his sex, his parentage, his race, his language, his homeland and origin, his faith or his religious or political opinion."

In the major international human rights instruments the trend has been the

---

[1] See generally, P. G. Polyviou, *The Equal Protection of the Laws* (1980) and R. Dworkin, *Sovereign Virtue: The Theory and Practice of Equality* (2000).
[2] See too Art.6 of the Belgian Constitution of 1831 and Preamble to the Constitution of Bavaria of 1818.

opposite – from proscriptions against discrimination on defined grounds to more general affirmations of equality. Thus, the concluding substantive clause in the European Convention, Article 14, provides that "[t]he enjoyment of the rights and freedoms set forth in this Convention shall be secured without discrimination on any ground such as sex, race, colour, language, religion, political or other opinion, national or social origin, association with a national minority, property, birth or other status." But the UN Covenant, which was adopted in 1966, stipulates in Article 26 that "[a]ll persons are equal before the law and are entitled without any discrimination to the equal protection of the law. In this respect, the law shall prohibit any discrimination and guarantee to all persons equal and effective protection against discrimination on any ground such as race, colour, sex, language, religion, political or other opinion, national or social origin, property, birth or other status." Article 5 of the European Convention's Seventh Protocol and Article 24(4) of the U.N. Covenant call for equality between spouses in connection with their marriage and children.

Equality is a major component of most theories of justice. For some philosophers, the very touchstone of justice is equality. Aristotle stated that "equality and justice are synonymous: to be just is to be equal, to be unjust is to be unequal."[3] And the concept of justice advocated by John Rawls was summed up as follows:

> "First principle – Each person is to have an equal right to the most extensive total system of equal basic liberties compatible with a similar set of liberty for all.
>
> Second principle -Social and economic inequalities are to be arranged so that they are both: (a) to the greatest benefit of the least advantaged, consistent with the just savings principle, and (b) attached to offices and positions open to all under conditions of fair equality of opportunity."[4]

But there are others who take the view that equality has little or no place in a theory of justice. Among the ringing phrases of critics and sceptics that stand out are Fitzjames Stephens, an English conservative lawyer and utilitarian, that "equality is a word so wide and vague as to be by itself almost unmeaning;"[5] and Archibald Cox, a liberal American law professor, remarked that "(o)nce loosed, the idea of Equality is not easily cabined."[6] One impressive analysis of the topic goes almost so far as to suggest that equality provisions be excised

---

[3] J. Barnes ed., *The Complete Works – Nicomachean Ethics* (1984) v3 (1131a).
[4] *A Theory of Justice* (1971), p.302.
[5] *Liberty, Equality and Fraternity* (1873), p. 201.
[6] "Foreword: Constitutional Adjudication and the Promotion of Human Rights", 80 *Harv. L. Rev.* 91 (1996).

from constitutional documents – that "(e)quality as an idea should be banished from moral and legal discourse as an explanatory norm."[7]

Some of the major social transformations in history were inspired by egalitarianism, for instance, the end of feudalism, the end of slavery and serfdom, the extension of the franchise to all adult citizens, the modern feminist movement and the welfare state system. As a political ideal, equality has connoted change and for some "levelling" and even "confiscation." Ideology aside, serious flaws exist in equality as a criterion of justice. Its classic formulation by Aristotle is that "equality in morals means this: things that are alike should be treated alike, while things that are unalike should be treated unalike in proportion to their unalikeness."[8] But this, some say, is circular and a tautology. By what moral standard are we to measure "things" in order to ascertain their likeness or difference? Furthermore, by what standard are we to determine what identical or differential treatment is to be meted out? A simple answer to the ideological point is that constitutional instruments adopt equality as an overriding norm and, therefore, content must be given to that principle until such time as it is excised by the proper constitutional procedure. As for the philosophers' and the logicians' critique, in the first place their case against equality is not accepted by many other persons with the same calling. Moreover, it should not be overlooked that those responsible for framing some of the world's major constitutional instruments were not trained in formal philosophy and logic. And if the "almost unmeaning" norm of equality is to be abandoned, ought not liberty or freedom, which similarly lack substantive content, be excised from constitutional instruments?

CONNOTATIONS OF EQUALITY

Not only does the equality principle possess a number of different meanings, but it also forms a significant component of separate constitutional doctrines and fundamental rights.

"Structural" Equality

By "structural" equality is meant constitutional provisions that do not prescribe certain substantive outcomes but rather require that legislation be enacted, executive measures be adopted and judicial decisions be reached in a certain

---

[7] Westen, "The Empty Idea of Equality", 95 *Harv. L. Rev.* 537 (1982), at p.542; modified in Peters, "Equality Revisited", 110 *Harv. L. Rev.* 1210 (1997).

[8] *Supra*, n.3. In his *Politics* III 9 (1280a) he says "[f]or example, justice is thought by them to be, and is, equality – not, however, for all, but only for equals. And inequality is thought to be, and is, justice; neither is this for all, but only for unequals."

way. Sometimes these provisions generate separate specific rights. Thus, the democratic nature of the State virtually dictates a "one person, one vote" standard, and that political parties and candidates have every reasonable opportunity to present their messages to the electorate and to participate in elections.[9] And the adversary nature of criminal procedure suggests that all citizens have a "right to counsel" in serious controversies, because injustice could result if the contest between prosecutor and defendant is fought on unequal terms.[10]

Even the separation of powers doctrine serves egalitarian goals. An objection to Bills of Attainder and their modern equivalent is that, in them, the legislature does not lay down a general standard that all must respect but singles out one individual or a very discrete number of persons for adverse treatment. In the *"Sinn Fein Funds"* case,[11] where the Oireachtas sought to prevent a particular dispute about money from being tried by the courts, Gavan Duffy J. observed that "[J]ustice involves due process of law, and that law, to recall the monumental declaration of Daniel Webster, is the general law, a law which hears before it condemns, which proceeds upon inquiry and renders judgment only after trial, so that every citizen shall hold his life, liberty, and property and immunities under the protection of the general rules which govern society; arbitrary executions of power under the forms of legislation are thus excluded and no organ of the State can deny to the citizen the equal protection of the law"." [12] One of the contentions in the *An Blascaod Mór (No.3)* case[13] was that the An Blascaod Mór National Historic Park Act 1989, targeted the plaintiffs and practically no one else and, consequently, was in substance a Bill of Attainder.

A major reason for insisting on separating the legislative and executive powers is to prevent officials possessing too much discretion, which is open to abuse; in other words, to ensure a degree of "formal" equality. Thus, the unsuccessful parties' main grievance in the *Pigs Marketing Board*,[14] and the *East Donegal Co-Op*[15] cases was that the impugned legislation gave officials a very broad discretion; in the former, the law was challenged as contravening the separation of powers principle and, in the latter, as contravening equality.

Another kind of law that might be vulnerable to an equality-based challenge is one conferring a significant privilege on one individual or organisation but not on similar persons or entities. In the *East Donegal Co-Op* case the Supreme Court found it unnecessary to answer the question, "what would be the effect

---

[9] *O'Donovan v. Attorney General* [1961] I.R. 114; *infra* p.599.

[10] *State (Healy) v. Donoghue* [1976] I.R. 325; *infra*, p.439.

[11] *Buckley v. Attorney General* [1950] I.R. 67; *supra*, p.200.

[12] *Id.* at p.70.

[13] [2000] 1 I.R. 6; *infra* p.397.

[14] *Pigs Marketing Board v. Donnelly (Dublin) Ltd* [1939] I.R. 413; *infra*, p.768.

[15] *East Donegal Co-Op. Livestock Mart Ltd v. Attorney General* [1970] I.R. 317; *infra*, p.779.

if the Oireachtas itself in the statute named individuals who were to be exempted from the application of the law?"[16] But the court went on to hold unconstitutional a "dispensing" power, *i.e.* a delegated authority to exempt a particular individual or entity from the scope of a statute. A power, of their nature it was held, is valid only where, in the absence of such power, the law would be disproportionately over-inclusive in the light of the individual interests it affected.[17]

"Complementary" Equality

By "complementary" equality is meant aspects of substantive rights guaranteed in constitutions that have a distinct egalitarian thrust. The "Fundamental Rights" provisions of the Constitution contain some express references to "non-discrimination", which is the equivalent of equality. Thus, laws regulating the guaranteed "liberty (to) exercise (the) rights" of free expression, assembly and association must "contain no political, religious or class discrimination."[18] In guaranteeing religious freedom, the State undertakes, *inter alia,* not to make "any discrimination" on the ground of religion and, in providing aid for schools, not to "discriminate between" schools managed by different religious denominations.[19]

A requirement of equal treatment stands at the very core of some traditional civil liberties. Take for example freedom of expression, a right that has not greatly preoccupied our courts. In American constitutional law that right connotes, among other things, that the State may not hinder or favour one form of expression over another. In one instance where a law that prohibited politically motivated picketing, in a situation where labour picketing would have been permissible, was struck down,[20] Justice Marshall remarked that:

> "Above all else, the First Amendment means that government has no power to restrict expression because of its message, its ideas, its subject matter, or its content. To permit the continued building of our politics and culture, and to assure self-fulfilment for each individual, our people are guaranteed the right to express any thought, free from government censorship. The essence of the forbidden censorship is content control. ...
>
> Necessarily, then, under the Equal Protection Clause, not to mention the First Amendment itself, government may not grant the use of a fo-

---

[16] *Id.* at p.350.
[17] *Ibid.*
[18] Art. 40.6.1 and 2.
[19] Art. 40.3.3, and 4.
[20] *Police Dept. of Chicago v. Mosley*, 408 U.S. 92 (1972).

rum to people whose views it finds acceptable, but deny use to those wishing to express less favoured or more controversial views. And it may not select which issues are worth discussing or debating in public facilities. There is an 'equality of status in the field of ideas' and government must afford all points of view an equal opportunity to be heard …".[21]

Another specific right with a marked egalitarian content is the right to vote. In *O'Donovan v. Attorney General*,[22] which concerned the way in which electoral constituency boundaries should be drawn, Budd J. observed that "the primary aim and object" of Article 16.2 of the Constitution is "to achieve equality of ratio and representation",[23] and equality in that sense is confirmed by several other constitutional provisions:

"Article 5 provides *inter alia* that Ireland is a democratic State. Article 16.1.4, provides that no voter may exercise more than one vote at an election for Dáil Éireann. Article 40.1, provides that all citizens shall, as human persons, be held equal before the law. There is an explanatory addition to this Article, not relevant to what I am dealing with here. A 'democratic state' is one where government by the people prevails. In modern usage of the words I believe it to be correct to say a 'democratic state' denotes one in which all citizens have equal political rights. That the words should be given such a meaning in our Constitution seems to be supported by the other two Articles I have referred to as to the restriction of voting power to one vote per person and the equality of all before the law. That equality is not maintained if the vote of a person in one part of the country has a greater effect in securing parliamentary representation than the vote of a person in another part of the country ….There are thus contained in the Constitution other Articles the spirit of which demands equality of voting power and representation. The Articles I have just referred to admittedly have reference to equality of voting power, but are relevant in construing sub-clause 2.3 of Article 16 to this extent, that if it be established, as I believe it is, that the spirit and intendment of these other Articles is that the notion of equality in political matters is to be maintained, it would be illogical to find a different and inconsistent principle adumbrated elsewhere in the Constitution."[24]

Another example of this is private property. Across-the-board confiscation is not permissible in Ireland but, subject to the payment of compensation, pieces

---

[21] *Id.* at pp.95–99.
[22] [1961] I.R. 114.
[23] *Id.* at p.138.
[24] *Id.* at p.137.

or parcels of property may be expropriated in the public interest.[25] On the other hand, the State is entitled to levy taxation, either on income, goods or property. The principal contention in *Blake v. Attorney General*,[26] was that Parts II and IV of the Rent Restriction Act 1960, and related statutes violated the Constitution's guarantees of property rights under Articles 43 and 40.3, and also the equality clause. Part II of the 1960 Act, encompassing the rent-limiting provisions, was struck down principally because of its confiscatory nature, which might have been enough to dispose of the matter. However, the Supreme Court invoked discriminatory features of the Act in support of its conclusion of unconstitutionality. Only lettings of houses within a certain valuation or built before 1941 fell within the Act's scope. According to the court, no plausible basis for selecting these lettings was put forward: "apart from the fact that rent control existed only in such cases in the previous temporary legislation, no reason was advanced by counsel for the Attorney General", and "(n)o reason for this selection is apparent from the impugned legislation ...".[27] Additionally, local authority lettings were not subject to a similar regime. Neither the means nor needs of landlords nor of tenants were relevant to the determination whether a letting should be controlled or in determining the rent. And the control system, originally intended to be a temporary measure, had become a permanent institution. These features, coupled with the absence of an "adequate compensatory factor", made the conclusion "(in)escape(able)" that the legislation was "unfair and unjust" and "arbitrary."[28] Similarly in *Brennan v. Attorney General*,[29] which concerned the old "Griffith" valuations for land which were used for taxation and other purposes, it was the great inconsistencies that those valuations gave rise to which led to them being held to be an arbitrary interference with property rights.

"Formal" Equality

It is necessary to distinguish between formal equality, or equality *before* the law, and material equality, or equality *in* the law. Formal equality is concerned primarily with judicial and administrative discretion, and means that law-applying agencies must apply specific laws only to those to whom they are addressed. It is, therefore, nothing more than the most elementary principle of statutory construction and of administrative law, that law-applying agencies take account only of the distinctions between persons that are contained in the

---

[25] Art.43.
[26] [1982] I.R. 117; *infra*, p.759.
[27] *Id.* at p.138.
[28] *Id.* at pp.138 and 139.
[29] [1984] I.L.R.M. 355; *infra*, p.752.

statute being applied. Formal equality is sometimes derided as the emptiest of all ideals, signifying "the majesty equality ... that forbids the rich as well as the poor to sleep under bridges, to beg in the streets and to steal bread."[30]

The extent to which laws may be invalid for inconsistency with formal equality has been the subject of some confusion. The *East Donegal Co-op* case[31] concerned the Livestock Marts Act 1967, which empowers the Minister "at his discretion" to grant, refuse to grant and to revoke licences that are necessary to carry on the business of a livestock market. He is authorised, as well, at the time of granting a licence, to attach to it "such conditions as he shall think proper" and, "if he so thinks fit," to amend or revoke any of those conditions. Breach of a condition attached to a licence is made a criminal offence. No clear criteria are specified as to what the licence conditions should contain and, in contrast to the powers to refuse to grant and to revoke licences, no procedure is laid down for determining and varying conditions. Echoing a Diceyian view of equality, O'Keeffe P. held that the provisions on conditions violated equality on account of the "uncontrolled discretion" conferred on the Minister. This, he said, was because "[c]onditions need not be uniform for all licences: indeed the Act is framed in such a manner as to imply that they will not be. When it comes to attaching additional conditions to licences, there is no power to object and no obligation to consider objections and no machinery for review of the Minister's decision. That this is so can hardly be accidental ... (O)ne is compelled to accept that it was intended that the conditions might be arbitrarily imposed, and that such arbitrary imposition of conditions was carefully left free from review. In this respect ... the legislation *can* be operated within its lawful limits so as to differentiate between citizens in a manner which does not reflect differences of capacity, physical or moral, or of social function. ..."[32]

But this reasoning was rejected by the Supreme Court, because it was based on the assumption that an Act could be implemented outside the general framework of statutory construction, administrative law and criminal procedure. Moreover, its discriminatory application was not demonstrated and should not be readily presumed. Only the express power granted to exempt individual businesses from the 1967 Act was struck down.[33]

The principle to be deduced from this decision – that laws, however vague the standards they formulate and however wide the discretion they entrust to delegates are not inconsistent with the equality clause – has been held to be subject to at least one exception. A criminal law containing a standard that is so vague as to render it virtually impossible for persons to know whether or

---

[30] Anatole France, *The Red Lily* (tran. 1898), p.117.

[31] [1970] I.R. 317.

[32] *Id.*, at p.339.

[33] *Id.*, at p.351.

not they violate it, and which deals with a matter where arbitrary enforcement is endemic or inevitable, promotes unacceptable inequalities. In *King v. Attorney General*,[34] the Supreme Court invalidated Ireland's "sus law", section 4 of the Vagrancy Act 1824,[35] which created the offence of "loitering with intent", the principal ingredients of which were being a "suspected person, frequenting ... any street, highway, or place adjacent, with intent to commit a felony." Felonious intent could be inferred from the accused's previous convictions. Section 4 was struck down because, in addition to contravening the "due course of (criminal) law" guarantee[36] and material equality, it was "so prone to make a man's lawful occasions become unlawful and criminal by the breadth and arbitrariness of the discretion that is vested in both the prosecutor and the judge ...".[37]

Material Equality

Material equality, or equality *in* the law, by contrast, requires that laws themselves must take account of meaningful differences between persons; that persons who in fact are equal should be treated equally but that unequals in appropriate circumstances be treated differently. This version of equality itself possesses different connotations: as not embodying substantive values but merely requiring non-arbitrary or reasonable differentiations between persons; as embodying an egalitarian conception of society and accordingly demanding redistribution in order to ensure true equality; or a somewhat in-between meaning, as requiring that persons be treated with equal respect. Although Article 40.1 of the Constitution speaks in terms of "equal(ity) before the law", the rider that laws may "have due regard to (certain) differences" suggests that it was intended to guarantee some degree of material equality as well. In any event, this is how it has been construed by the courts.

While the "material" equality standard can be articulated in a handful of words – that persons who in fact are equals be treated equally – its actual application gives rise to a host of difficulties. In approaching any controversy concerning alleged unequal treatment, it is first necessary to ascertain whether in the context the persons being compared stand in similar or in dissimilar situations. But often sameness or difference may not be capable of empirical demonstration. Furthermore, dissimilar treatment of equals or similar treatment of unequals may be justifiable on other grounds, even on broader egalitarian grounds, for instance taxation. In one sense, persons are taxed unequally by requiring those with higher incomes or more assets to pay a greater share than

---

[34] [1981] I.R. 233.
[35] 5 Geo. 4, c.83.
[36] Art.38.1.
[37] [1981] I.R. 233 at p.257.

those who earn or who own less. Yet it is almost universally accepted that true equality in taxation demands that taxes be progressive.[38] Indeed, the questions of essential similarity of circumstances and justifiability of differential treatment are not entirely separate; for if different treatment is justifiable then the groups concerned cannot truly be in the same position.

Judicial application of the material equality standard concerns mainly legislation. But legislation by its very nature requires classification and the drawing of distinctions; laws specially tailored to the individual needs and circumstances of every person are neither ideal nor practicable. When adopting legislation, the Oireachtas almost invariably attempts to accommodate claims made by major interest groups who stand to be affected. Leaving aside groups against which there is considerable popular prejudice and those who in law and practice are excluded from the ordinary political processes, and perhaps the "targets" of core criminal laws, there always will be others who feel that they are unfairly disadvantaged by laws; that identical groups are accorded benefits not granted to those aggrieved, or that the aggrieved are subjected to disabilities not imposed on similar groups. In its role of guarantor of fundamental rights, a court cannot allow itself to become a forum for resolving the grievances of factions that have lost out in the ordinary political process. Such a role would duplicate the legislative function, would drastically affect the court's workload and, most importantly, would be anti-democratic. The usual standard of review in equality disputes, accordingly, is whether the classification is "relevant" or is "rationally related" to the legislative object.[39]

Under-Inclusion

A law is under-inclusive where it imposes burdens on one group but not on another essentially similar group; or which, in allocating certain benefits, it grants them to one group but not to another which, in the light of the law's objective, is in a similar situation. The classic formulation of the objection to under-inclusive classifications in laws and the under-inclusive administration

---

[38] *E.g.*, Art.13 of the 1789 Declaration of the Rights of Man and of the Citizen.

[39] The various review standards used by courts have been itemised as follows, *inter alia*:
1. That between classification and legislative objects there must be *some nexus*,
2. that classification must be based on an *intelligible differentiation*,
3. that classification must be based upon some *real and substantial distinction*,
4. that classification must be *relevant to the object of* the legislation,
5. that classification must be *rationally related to the object*,
6. that classification must be fairly related to the object,
7. that classification must not be capricious or invidious,
8. that classification must *not be arbitrary*,
9. that classification must be *reasonable*,
10. that classification must be *just*.

of laws is that of the American judge, Justice Jackson, who said that "[t]here is no more effective practical guaranty against arbitrary and unreasonable government than to require that the principles of law which officials would impose upon a minority must be imposed generally. Conversely, nothing opens the door to arbitrary action so effectively as to allow those officials to pick and choose only a few to whom they will apply legislation and thus to escape the political retribution that might be visited upon them if larger numbers were affected. Courts can take no better measure to assure that laws will be just than to require that laws be equal in operation."[40] Cases involving under-inclusive laws include *Blake v. Attorney General*,[41] which concerned the old rent restrictions system governing a narrowly defined category of lettings. In *King v. The Attorney General*,[42] the "sus" provisions were struck down, *inter alia*, because they were "so indiscriminately contrived to mark as criminal conduct committed by one person in certain circumstances when the same conduct, when engaged in by another person in similar circumstances, would be free of the taint of criminality."[43]

Yet if legislative classifications are to be broad and their administration is to admit of no exception, laws run the danger of being condemned for being the very opposite of under-inclusive, *i.e.* being over-inclusive. Among the cases where challenges to under-inclusive provisions failed is *Norris v. Attorney General*,[44] where the statutory provisions outlawing gross indecency were objected to because *inter alia* they "discriminate(d) between male homosexual citizens and female homosexual citizens and between homosexual and heterosexual citizens."[45] Another is *Condon v. Minister for Labour*,[46] where the statutory restriction on wage increases negotiable by bank employees were challenged because *inter alia* "the Acts single out these bank officials for special punitive treatment which is not applied to other classes of workers."[47]

Where a law is challenged for being impermissibly under-inclusive, the outcome will depend on how "fundamental" the interest adversely affected is and whether there is unjust inconsistency in applying the law to one class or classes but not to others. Current perceptions of fairness will determine the result of this exercise. An excellent example is *State (Nicolaou) v. An Bord Uchtála*,[48] which concerned the consent provisions of the Adoption Act 1952. There, the argument of sex discrimination *per se* having been rejected, the

---

[40] *Railway Express Agency Inc. v. New York*, 336 U.S. 106 (1949), at p.111.
[41] [1982] I.R. 117; *infra*, p.752.
[42] [1981] I.R. 233; *supra*, p.281.
[43] *Id.* at p.257.
[44] [1984] I.R. 36; *infra*, p.661.
[45] *Id.* at p.43.
[46] McWilliam J., 11 June 1980; *infra*, p.762.
[47] *Id.* at p.7.
[48] [1966] I.R. 567; *infra*, p.711.

Supreme Court addressed itself to the question of whether denying a veto over adoption to persons other than the child's mother, guardian or custodian was inconsistent. It held that it was not because:

> "In relation to the adoption of a child (these three groups) can be regarded as having, or capable of having ... a moral capacity or social function which differentiates (them) from persons who are not given such rights. When it is considered that an illegitimate child may be begotten by an act of rape, by a callous seduction or by an act of casual commerce by a man with a woman, as well as by the association of a man with a woman in making a common home without marriage in circumstances approximating to those to married life, and that, except in the latter instance, it is rare for a natural father to take any interest in his offspring, it is not difficult to appreciate the difference in moral capacity and social function between the natural father and (these three groups)."[49]

Because the father's interest in the non-marital child was not a "natural right", and in the light of the facility available to fathers to obtain a custody order over such children, it was held that the applicant failed to discharge the onus of establishing the law's unconstitutionality. While one may disagree with the stereotyping which led to these conclusions and a similar view most likely would not be taken today,[50] the reasoning demonstrates the general approach to under-inclusive laws.

Over-Inclusion

A law is over-inclusive where it imposes burdens on various groups, some of whom are not in fact within the "mischief" the law was designed to combat; alternatively, where the law grants benefits, *inter alia*, to groups who in fact should not be beneficiaries in the light of the law's overriding goals. The Bible supplies one much-cited example of over-inclusive burdens, where Herod ordered the death of all male children born on a certain day because he feared that one of them would some day bring about his downfall.

Long before the widespread acceptance of minority rights philosophies, a dilemma that faced all developed legal systems was that of over-inclusive rules. In the private law sphere those rules led to an institutional counter-balance, the Court of Chancery and its equity doctrines, and on the continent they gave rise to the "general clauses." The dilemma was outlined by von Ihering,[51] the famous German jurist, as follows:

---

[49] *Id.* at p.643.
[50] Cf. *W. O'R. v. E.H.* [1996] 2 I.R. 248 at pp.277–280.
[51] R. von Ihering, *L'Esprit du droit Romain* (1877).

"Take the example of civil and political personal capacity (majority and electoral right). Suppose that a legislator wishes to regulate this legally and he comes forth with this idea: he who has the judgment and stability of character required to regulate his own affairs will be of full age; he who possesses the capacity and wishes to contribute to the good of the state will be an eligible elector. As just as this idea is, it would be absurd to institute it as a law in abstract form, as one would suffer infinite pains to determine in each case the existence of these conditions. This legislator would create an inexhaustible source of controversies and would give free reign to the arbitrariness of the judge. The most irreproachable application of his law would not be safe from the objection of partiality, which the legislator would have provoked by his own action. How can the legislator avoid this stumbling block? Instead of these conditions, he will fix others, which have with the first a certain correlation, although not a one-to-one correspondence, but which have the advantage over them of being more easily and surely recognised in a concrete manner; for example, the attainment of 25 years for majority, the possession of a certain wealth, the practice of certain professions, etc. for the right of elector. This deviation from the original legislative idea, this abandonment of a more exact hypothesis in an abstract form, in favour of a less exact and less adequate one more easily recognised in practice, is required by one of the law's own purposes – by the desirability of facility and certainty in its functioning. It is possible here and there in applying this law that mistakes will occur, that majority or electoral rights will be granted or refused in particular cases where they wouldn't be under the abstract terms; yet this concrete mode of procedure is nonetheless preferable, in view of the necessities of life. This point of view, in law, is the only determinant."[52]

Like Dicey, von Ihering preferred the hard and fast rule, the formal solution, as opposed to a principle or policy to be implemented by delegates. Jurists in those days had not such confidence in administrative law as the Supreme Court demonstrated in the *East Donegal Co-Op* case.[53] The objection to "rules" is that sometimes they can be in the nature of blunderbuss measures in that, in order to ensure that the net is sufficiently widely cast, persons not in fact within the policy they seek to implement are adversely affected by them, such as Herod's "innocents."

Most laws that classify persons in order to secure the statutory purpose tend to have both under-inclusive and over-inclusive features. An example can be seen in the *Nicolaou* case,[54] which concerned provisions of the Adoption

---

[52] Vol.1 at pp.51–52.
[53] [1970] I.R. 317.
[54] [1966] I.R. 567.

Act 1952, under which virtually all fathers of non-marital children were in effect denied a veto over the decision of whether their child should be adopted. In the *An Blascaod Mór (No.3)* case,[55] concerning an Act for the nationalisation of most of the land on the Great Blasket Island, Barrington J. observed that the legislative "classification appears to be at once too narrow and too wide."[56] On account of *locus standi* restrictions on access to the courts, it is difficult to locate cases illustrative of over-inclusive distributions of benefits.

In determining the constitutional status of over-inclusive provisions, the net question is much the same as for under-inclusive ones, which is, whether a particularly "fundamental" interest is being burdened unjustly. Account should be taken of whether the law's objectives could have been secured by less drastic classificatory means. An illustration of this approach is *State (M.) v. Minister for Foreign Affairs*,[57] which concerned the rule in the Adoption Act 1952, that it was unlawful to remove or aid the removal of a non-marital child under one year of age from the State. There was no machinery whereby such removal could be effected lawfully, "no matter how dominant the advantage may appear and no matter how clearly the welfare of the child may be served by an early removal from the State …".[58] For instance, it may have been necessary for the child to go abroad to obtain medical treatment or, as was the case in *M.*, the choice was between the dark skinned child remaining in an institution or home in Ireland and, instead, him "becom(ing) a member of a family unit in (his father's) country as soon as possible."[59] Finlay P. concluded that the no-removal rule did not contravene the equality guarantee because "in the generality of cases the mother of an illegitimate child may be subjected to strains, stresses and pressures arising from economic and social conditions which fully justify the legislature in making special provisions with regard to the welfare of that child, which provisions are not considered necessary for the welfare of a legitimate child."[60] That rule nevertheless was held to be unconstitutional because of "the absence of any discretion vested in a court or otherwise for exceptional cases" so as to enable a young child to leave the State.[61] What principally saved the sections on naturalisation of spouses of the Irish Nationality and Citizenship Act 1956, in *Somjee v. Minister for Justice*[62] was the discretion the Minister possessed to waive the residence and notice requirements where the male applicant was married to an Irish citizen.

---

[55] [2000] 1 I.R. 6.
[56] *Id.* at p.19.
[57] [1979] I.R. 73.
[58] *Id.* at p.82.
[59] *Ibid.*
[60] *Id.* at p.79.
[61] *Id.* at p.82.
[62] [1981] I.L.R.M. 324; *infra*, p.381.

AMBIT OF ARTICLE 40.1

As once interpreted by the Supreme Court, the equality guarantee is of very limited application, concerning only what has been called "the essentials of human personality"[63] or "essential attributes as persons which make them human beings ...".[64] Thus in *Brennan v. Attorney General*,[65] O'Higgins C.J. for the court, held that "[i]n the view of the court a complaint that a system of taxation imposed on occupiers of land which has proved to be unfair, even arbitrary or unjust, is not cognisable under the provisions of Article 40.1. This section deals, and deals only, with the citizen as a human person and requires for each citizen as a human person, equality before the law.".[66] Further, "[t]he inequality of which the plaintiffs complain in this case does not concern their treatment as human persons. It concerns the manner in which as occupiers and owners of land their property is rated and taxed. Each person who owns or occupies the land in question will be treated in exactly the same way because the tax is related not to the person but to the land which, irrespective of who he may be, he occupies.".[67] This limitation is derived from the text of the Article, that citizens shall "as human persons" be held equal. But apart from differentiating between these essentials and "trading activities", it has not been suggested what these characteristics are. Nor has it been decided that wholly "invidious", "arbitrary" or "capricious" distinctions, that do not bear on these "essential characteristics", never violate equality.

It is conceivable, however, that the reference to "human persons" in Article 40.1 may be intended not as a restriction on the scope of the guaranteed equality but, instead, as a statement of the reason why the Constitution guarantees equality. Equality is guaranteed because all individuals are essentially equal and ought to be treated equally in identical circumstances. Article 43.1.1, similarly, embodies the justification for guaranteeing private property. Walsh J. in *Quinn's Supermarkets Ltd. v. Attorney General*[68] suggested that Article 40.1 is not confined to the "essentials of human personality." In his judgment, he stated that:

> "this provision is not a guarantee of absolute equality for all citizens in all circumstances but it is a guarantee of equality as human persons and (as the Irish text of the Constitution makes quite clear) is a guarantee

---

[63] *Murphy v. Attorney General* [1982] I.R. 241 at p.283, describing the Article as "relat[ing] to those attributes which make us human; it is concerned with the essentials of human personality."

[64] *Educational Co. of Ireland Ltd v. Fitzpatrick (No.2)* [1961] I.R. 345 at p.344.

[65] [1984] I.L.R.M. 355

[66] *Id.* at pp.364–365.

[67] *Id.* at pp.364–365.

[68] [1972] I.R. 1.

related to their dignity as human beings and a guarantee against any inequalities grounded upon an assumption, or indeed a belief, that some individual or individuals, or classes of individuals, by reason of their human attributes or their ethnic or racial, social or religious background, are to be treated as the inferior or superior of other individuals in the community. This list does not pretend to be complete; but it is merely intended to illustrate the view that this guarantee refers to human persons for what they are in themselves rather than to any lawful activities, trades or pursuits which they may engage in or follow."[69]

By endorsing this rationale for Article 40.1 in the *An Blascaod Mór (No.3)* case,[70] the Supreme Court appears to have rejected the view that this Article's ambit is confined to those "essential" attributes.

The equality guarantee in the European Convention, Article 14, is not confined to the very essentials of human personality. Once it is established that the right claimed by an applicant falls within the scope of the Convention, even if the conduct complained of is not a violation of the Article in question, it nevertheless can amount to a violation when that Article is read in conjunction with Article 14. In the *National Union of Belgian Police* case[71] the Strasbourg Court explained the place of this Article in the Convention's scheme in the following terms:

"Although Art. 14 has no independent existence, it is complementary to the other normative provisions of the Convention and Protocols: it safeguards individuals, or groups of individuals, placed in comparable situations, from all discrimination in the enjoyment of the rights and freedoms set forth in those provisions.

A measure which in itself is in conformity with the requirements of the Article enshrining the right or freedom in question may therefore infringe this Article when read in conjunction with Article 14 for the reason that it is of a discriminatory nature. It is as though Article 14 formed an integral part of each of the Articles laying down rights and freedoms whatever their nature.

These considerations apply in particular where a right embodied in the Convention and the corresponding obligation on the part of the State are not defined precisely, and consequently the State has a wide choice of the means for making the exercise of the right possible and effective. ..."[72]

---

[69] *Id.* at p.14.
[70] [2000] 1 I.R. 6.
[71] 1 E.H.R.R. 578 (1979).
[72] *Id.* at p.592 (para.44).

It is generally accepted that the inclusive term, "such as," in Article 14 means that some distinctions made on grounds other than those enumerated here are proscribed. But the Article does not forbid every difference in treatment in the exercise of the rights and freedoms recognized. In the seminal *Belgian Linguistics* case[73] that court set out the following broad criteria for applying the clause, holding that "the principle of equality of treatment is violated if the distinction has no objective and reasonable justification. The existence of such a justification must be assessed in relation to the aim and effects of the measure under consideration, regard being had to the principles which normally prevail in democratic societies. A difference of treatment in the exercise of a right laid down in the Convention must not only pursue a legitimate aim: Art. 14 is likewise violated when it is clearly established that there is no reasonable relationship of proportionality between the means employed and the aim sought to be realized."[74]

SOME CLASSIFICATIONS

Under international law and under some national constitutions, there are certain categories of persons whom laws may place at a disadvantage for only the most compelling of reasons; laws that affect those persons are carefully examined to ascertain if they are being unfairly treated. Thus the term "suspect classification." The identity of those groups depends very much on the nature of the society in question. In the United States, for example, with its long history of racial discrimination, colour has become the most "suspect" classification. Other such criteria are sex, being born outside marriage and alienage; although the US courts show a greater tolerance for differentiations based on sex, and even more so on other bases than it does for race-based distinctions. The 1989 Act authorising nationalisation of the Great Blasket Island excluded land owned by any descendant of a person who had lived there in or prior to 1953.[75] According to Barrington J., for the Supreme Court, this distinction "is based on a principle of pedigree – which appears to have no place (outside the law of succession) in a democratic society committed to the principle of equality. This fact alone makes the classification suspect."[76]

There are two major grounds for determining what classifications should be suspect under the equality clause: the irrelevance in general of certain characteristics to any legitimate social policy and the relative political powerlessness, and hence vulnerability, of certain social groups. An underlying goal of democratic societies is the protection and assurance of human dignity.

---

[73] 1 E.H.R.R. 241 and 252 (1979).

[74] *Id.* at p.284 (para.10).

[75] An Blascaod Mór National Historic Park Act 1989, s. 4(2).

[76] *An Blascaod Mór Teo v. Commissioners of Public Works (No.3)* [2000] 1 I.R. 6, 19 .

This objective is contained in the Preamble to the Constitution: "(a)nd seeking to promote the common good … so that the dignity … of the individual may be assured. …" The very core of dignity is that persons should be treated for what they are and, in particular, they should not be disadvantaged for possessing morally irrelevant traits or characteristics; that is to say, attributes that say nothing about a person's inherent worth, abilities or activities -in other words, characteristics that can have no bearing on "capacity, physical or moral, or social function", as the rider to Article 40.1 puts it. To take an extreme example, the colour of peoples' eyes or of their hair; that all blue-eyed adults should be prevented from voting or red-haired children be prevented from attending schools is an affront to those persons' dignity, since it is patently obvious that the colour of eyes or hair has no bearing whatsoever on their need or ability to vote or to learn.

The second ground for denoting certain criteria as suspect is that those minorities, who are politically unpopular and who have relatively little influence in the ordinary political process, need special protection against adverse treatment by the majority. The nature of the society would suggest the identity of these minorities. One of the first vulnerable groups in the United States to be protected against adverse discrimination, over one hundred years ago, were West Coast Chinese immigrants.[77] Recently the South African Constitutional Court found that persons who were HIV positive were a particularly vulnerable minority, who were subjected to systemic prejudice and discrimination.[78] Aliens who are legally in the State may fall into this category but, once their entitlement to remain has been ended, there are very narrow constitutional constraints on their being deported.[79]

Article 26 of the UN Covenant prohibits discrimination on grounds such as a person's "race, colour, sex, language, religion, political or other opinion, national or social origin, property, birth or other status;" Article 14 of the European Convention adds "association with a national minority" to this list. Discrimination in employment and in the provision of services is now subject to comprehensive legislative prohibition, in the Employment Equality Act 1998 and in the Equal Status Act 2000. These outlaw discrimination on the grounds of a person's sex, marital status, family status, sexual orientation, religious belief, age, disability, membership of the traveller community and also race, colour, nationality or ethnic or natural origins or any combination of these factors.

---

[77] *Yick Wo v. Hopkins*, 118 U.S. 356 (1886).
[78] *Hoffman v. South African Airways*, 10 B.H.R.C. 571 (2000).
[79] Unless of course they are nationals of an EC/EU Member State or a dependant.

Sex

Until comparatively recently, the law permitted extensive discrimination against women in most European countries, including Ireland. Discrimination on the grounds of sex is presently proscribed by statutes in a number of areas, most notably, exercising any public function or entering and carrying on any profession,[80] ownership of property,[81] acquiring nationality,[82] employment[83] and the provision of services.[84] While the Constitution contains no express blanket proscription on sex discrimination, there are certain provisions in it that prohibit distinctions on the grounds of sex, viz., in relation to nationality and citizenship;[85] eligibility for membership of, and to vote in elections for, the Dáil and the Seanad;[86] in the Directive Principle of Social Policy that "citizens (all of whom, men and women equally, have the right to an adequate means of livelihood) may (earn);"[87] also indirectly in the various EC requirements regarding equal pay and equal treatment in the workplace. Sex discrimination is prohibited by Article 14 of the European Convention and by Articles 2 and 26 of the UN Covenant, and in 1986 Ireland ratified the UN Convention on the Elimination of All Forms of Discrimination Against Women,[88] subject to reservations. Ireland also is a party to the earlier UN Conventions on the Political Rights of Women[89] and on the Nationality of Married Women.[90] On several occasions the courts have struck down legislation that permitted and also that in effect required sex-discriminatory practices.

Ambit of Protection

In order to determine what forms of sex discrimination are proscribed, first there is the question of what interests or claims may not be the subject of adverse discrimination. For instance, in *Murtagh Properties Ltd v. Cleary*[91] Kenny J. suggested that unequal remuneration structures for men and women

---

[80] Sex Disqualification (Removal) Act 1919.

[81] Married Women's Status Act 1957.

[82] Irish Nationality and Citizenship Act 1986.

[83] Employment Equality Act 1998; see generally M. Bolger and C. Kimber, *Sex Discrimination Law* (2000).

[84] Equal Status Act 2000; see generally Bolger & Kimber, *op cit*, Chap.13.

[85] Art.9.1.3.

[86] Arts.45.2.1.

[87] Art.45.2.1.

[88] December 18, 1979, 1249 UNTS 13. See generally, Mc. McDougal *et al.*, *Human Rights and World Public Order* (1980), Chap.10 and K. Askin & D. Koenig eds. *Women and International Human Rights Law* (2 vols., 1999).

[89] December 20, 1952, 193 UNTS 135.

[90] Of February 20, 1957; 309 UNTS 65.

[91] [1972] I.R. 330.

in the civil service might not be unconstitutional.[92] The 1979 UN Convention in Article 1 describes the discrimination that it strikes at in broad terms as "any distinction, exclusion or restriction made on the basis of sex which has the effect or purpose of impairing or nullifying the recognition, enjoyment or exercise by women, irrespective of their marital status, on a basis of equality of men and women, of human rights and fundamental freedoms in the political, economic, social, cultural, civil or any other field." Articles 7-16 of this Convention set out in some detail the ways in which these rights and freedoms may not be the subject of discrimination, such as for example 11(1)(d) on "(t)he right to equal remuneration, including benefits, and to equal treatment in respect of work of equal value, as well as equality of treatment in the evaluation of the quality of work."

In *de Burca v. Attorney General*,[93] the Supreme Court upheld the contention that the provision of the Juries Act 1927, whereby all women were excluded from jury service save where they exercised an option to serve, was unconstitutional. Henchy and Griffin JJ. addressed the matter almost entirely from the point of view of Article 38.5, which states that "no person shall be tried on any criminal charge without a jury." In their view, a fundamental attribute of the system of jury trial is that jury panels should be representative of a cross-section of the community, and that "a system of jury selection which operates so that there is a total absence of women from juries amounts to a denial of the right to trial by jury."[94] Another case, *Murtagh Properties Ltd. v. Cleary*,[95] was an application by publicans for an interim injunction against threatened picketing of their premises and the motion was treated as a trial of the action. The intended picket was to compel the plaintiffs to dismiss female bar workers from employment, because they were not union members, but the union did not accept female workers into its membership. Kenny J. held that the reference to "men and women equally, hav(ing) the right to an adequate means of livelihood" in the Directive Principles means that "each citizen has the right to earn a livelihood" and that this right "is one inherent in men and women."[96] Accordingly, "a policy or general rule under which anyone seeks to prevent an employer from employing men or women on the ground of sex only is prohibited by the Constitution ... (For example), a demand backed by a threat of a picket that women should not be employed at all in any activity solely because they are women ... is a breach of this right."[97] But he added that, since the right to work that triggered the Article 40.1 right not to be

---

[92] *Id.* at p.336. Of course, it is now prohibited by equal pay legislation as well as by Art.141 of the EEC Treaty.
[93] [1976] I.R. 38.
[94] *Id.* at p.77.
[95] [1972] I.R. 330.
[96] *Id.* at p.336.
[97] *Ibid.*

discriminated against on the grounds of sex was based on a Directive Principle, that right cannot provide that basis for striking down laws enacted by the Oireachtas.

The concurring judgment of Walsh J. in the *de Burca* case adopts a fundamentally different approach to these questions. Henchy and Griffin JJ. in *de Burca* and Kenny J. in *Murtagh Properties* first looked for a specific right guaranteed by the Constitution (to jury trial and to work, respectively) and then considered if the exclusion of women was consistent with that very right; the equality guarantee played only a subsidiary role in their decisions. Walsh J.'s approach focused almost solely on equality and in effect adopts the "suspect classification" rationale of the American law. In his view, while it is permissible to exempt certain classes of persons, including certain categories of women, from jury service, the 1927 Act:

> "is undisguisedly discriminatory on the ground of sex only. It would not be competent for the Oireachtas to legislate on the basis that women, by reason only of their sex, are physically or morally incapable of serving and acting as jurors. The statutory provision does not seek to make any distinction between the different functions that women may fulfil and it does not seek to justify the discrimination on the basis of any social function. It simply lumps together half of the members of the adult population, most of whom have only one thing in common, namely, their sex. In my view, it is not open to the State to discriminate in its enactments between the persons who are subject to its laws solely upon the ground of the sex of those persons. If a reference is to be made to the sex of a person, then the purpose of the law that makes such a discrimination should be to deal with some physical or moral capacity or social function that is related exclusively or very largely to that sex only."[98]

The only instance of a provision of an Act of the Oireachtas being struck down on the grounds of unconstitutional sex discrimination is *O'G v. Attorney General*,[99] which concerned a provision in the Adoption Acts that treated widows and widowers differently as adoptive parents; widowers had to satisfy more onerous burdens than widows in order to adopt a child. McMahon J. described the provision as one "founded on the idea of difference in capacity between men and women which has no foundation in fact", and consequently it was an "unwarranted denial of human equality …".[100]

Some common law rules have been held to be invalid on these grounds, even to the extent of extending the scope of a person's liability for causing

---

[98] *Id.* at p.71. Similarly, the *Nocturnal Employment* case 85 BVerfGE 191 (1992).
[99] [1985] I.L.R.M. 61.
[100] *Id.* at p.65.

personal injury. In one instance,[101] where the point "was reached without argument and as a moot",[102] the Supreme Court held that the common law presumption, that a wife was coerced by her husband in her presence to commit a crime, was incompatible with Article 40.1. As and from July 1986, the Oireachtas abolished the common law rule of a wife's dependent domicile, i.e., that her domicile invariably was that of her husband.[103] Two years later, in *C.M. v. T.M. (No. 2)*,[104] Barr J. held that, on account of Article 40.1 of the Constitution, this rule had not been carried over into law in 1937. He described the rule as "a relic of matrimonial female bondage which was swept away by principles of equality before the law and equal rights in marriage as between men and women which are enshrined in the Constitution ...".[105] Four years later, in *W. v. W.*,[106] this was approved by the Supreme Court.

Another such rule to meet this fate was that whereby a husband could recover damages for loss of his wife's "consortium", where she was seriously injured, but wives had no comparable remedy. In *McKinley v. Minister for Defence*,[107] a narrowly divided Supreme Court held that the common law should be extended to enable wives to recover damages in comparable circumstances. O'Flaherty J. based his decision "not only on the equality provisions of the Constitution but also on the fact that the Constitution gives marriage a special recognition .... That highlights the need to afford equal rights to both spouses."[108] It had been conceded by the defendant there that the common law rule contravened Article 40.1 but it was argued that, in consequence, the rule was never carried over in 1937 on account of that incompatibility. Finlay C.J. and Egan J., dissenting, agreed with this reasoning but they concluded that the effect of the validity was to extinguish the rule, on account of its archaic foundations.

Although preventing the adverse treatment of women is the main focus of anti-sex discrimination laws, unjustifiable discrimination against men also can fall foul of them.[109] Because Irish political life has always been dominated by males, understandably there are few provisions that significantly disadvantage them for no good reason. To date, no such measure has been held to have contravened the Constitution. In instances involving naturalisation[110] and social welfare benefits,[111] challenges to statutory provisions that discriminated against

---

[101] *State (D.P.P.) v. Walsh* [1981] I.R. 412.
[102] McCarthy J. in *McKinley v. Minister for Defence* [1992] 2 I.R. 333 at p.353.
[103] Domicile and Recognition of Foreign Divorces Act 1986.
[104] [1990] 2 I.R. 53.
[105] *Id.* at p.63.
[106] [1993] 2 I.R. 476.
[107] [1992] 2 I.R. 333.
[108] *Id.* at p.358.
[109] *Infra* p.381.
[110] *Somjee v. Minister for Justice* [1981] I.L.R.M. 324; *infra* p.381.
[111] *Lowth v. Minister for Social Welfare* [1998] 4 I.R. 321; *infra* p.382.

men were rejected, as being justifiable in the circumstances. Subsequently, however, the law in those very areas was amended to put an end to those discriminations.

Impact

The next question is the complex one of discrimination by impact, *i.e.* of laws that do not by their very terms disadvantage a particular sex but which nonetheless in their effect place that sex at a significant disadvantage. Discrimination by impact is proscribed by the 1979 UN Convention, Article I referring to "(a)ny distinction (etc.) which has the effect … of impairing (etc.)." In *Murphy v. Attorney General*,[112] where the aggregation of married couples' incomes for income tax purposes was struck down, it could have been argued that the aggregation provisions in the Income Tax Act 1967 unconstitutionally discriminated against women in their impact. Given that jobs in which women tend to work pay less than so-called male jobs and the still common assumption at that time that the mother's, if not the woman's, place is in the home and not in paid employment, it can hardly be doubted that those provisions discouraged married women from remaining employed, at least to the same extent that they "attack(ed)" the family by discouraging marriage. This contention may not have been pressed because it had been rejected previously in *Nicolaou v. An Bord Uchtála*,[113] where adoption provisions that unquestionably discriminated in their impact were sustained. The 1998 and 2000 legislation on equality prohibits, *inter alia*, indirect discrimination.

Separate But Equal

Depending on the society in question, "separate but equal" facilities can constitute adverse discrimination. Whether such facilities unfairly discriminate is essentially a factual question. The 1979 UN Convention does not expressly proscribe separate but equal education for men and women; indeed, the UNESCO-sponsored Convention Against Discrimination in Education[114] permits sex-segregated schools provided that the facilities are truly equal.

Sexual Orientation

Constitutional challenges have been made in several countries against laws that discriminated on the basis of sexual orientation.[115] In *Norris v. Attorney*

---

[112] [1982] I.R. 241; *infra*, p.668.
[113] [1966] I.R. 567.
[114] December 14, 1960, 429 UNTS 93.
[115] See generally, Norris, "Constitutional Challenges to Sexual Orientation Discrimination" 49 *Int'l & Comp. L.Q.* 755 (2000).

General,[116] a divided Supreme Court upheld section 11 of the Criminal Law (Amendment) Act 1885,[117] which made it an offence for a man to commit "any act of gross indecency with another male person." While admitting that the section was "unsatisfactory in many respects" and that there were "difficult(ies) in ascertaining the limits to be placed on the right to equal treatment and to the stage at which discrimination becomes invidious or arbitrary", McWilliam J. in the High Court sustained the validity of the section on grounds that "[i]t seems ... perfectly constitutional to say that certain activities shall be unlawful and subject to penalties when committed by groups of people who by reason of trade, profession or otherwise have special opportunities for engaging in such activities. ... The class of persons affected by (s. 11) is that of men, all men, and gross indecency may obviously take quite different forms when committed by men than when committed by women. This is one of the matters which ... the legislature may reasonably take into account in deciding what activities should be declared to be unlawful."[118] This particular aspect of the case was not squarely addressed by the Supreme Court on appeal.

The plaintiff there then took his case to the Strasbourg Court, which held that the provision contravened his right to privacy under Article 8 of the European Convention.[119] In 1993 the criminalisation of homosexual acts between adults in private was ended[120] and the 1998 and 2000 legislation on equality prohibits, *inter alia*, discrimination on the grounds of sexual orientation.

Justification

To date the Irish courts have not addressed the circumstances when, if ever, discrimination against women would be justified under the Constitution. In neither the *de Burca* nor the *Murtagh Properties* cases was any serious endeavour made to justify excluding women from jury service or from bar work, respectively; indeed under the Juries Act 1927, women could elect for jury service. There do not appear to be any remaining statutory provisions that directly discriminate against women and any constitutional challenge in the future will concern laws that discriminate against them indirectly, by impact. That abrogating the common law rule about a wife's domicile being always the same as that of her husband "might create some uncertainty for spouses and others who may have been affected by the rule in times past" was held not

---

[116] [1984] I.R. 36.
[117] 48 & 49 Vic. c.69.
[118] [1984] I.R. 50.
[119] *Norris v. Ireland* 13 E.H.R.R. 186 (1991).
[120] Criminal Law (Sexual Offences) Act 1993.
[121] *C.M. v. T.M. (No. 2)* [1990] 2 I.R. 52 at p.63.

to justify that rule.[121] And that abrogating the common law rule that permitted only husbands to sue for loss of consortium, would have the effect of significantly extending liability for a wrong by giving wives similar redress, was also held not to be a sufficient justification for the Supreme Court not to allow it to stand.[122]

On several occasions, laws that directly discriminated against men have been upheld by the courts as justifiable. Indeed in *Norris v. Attorney General*,[123] concerning the criminalisation of "gross indecency" between males, the State did not adduce any evidence to contradict the persuasive evidence given by the plaintiff's witness. Nonetheless, the prohibitions there were upheld because they were regarded as being consistent with the State's Christian ethos and the long standing tradition of hostility to homosexuality.

Another instance of discrimination against men being sustained was *Somjee v. Minister for Justice*,[124] which concerned the since-repealed provisions of the Irish Nationality and Citizenship Act 1956, dealing with the acquisition of nationality on marrying an Irish national. Under section 16 of that Act, the Minister possessed a discretionary power to dispense with the normal one-year notice and five-year residence requirements, but under section 8 an alien woman who married an Irish citizen was given the facility of automatically acquiring citizenship by virtue of her marriage. The plaintiff, a male of Pakistani nationality, on marrying an Irish citizen applied to the Minister to have the five-year residence and the notice requirements waived in his favour. Because the time for him was reduced to two years rather than waived entirely, he sought a declaration that he had been discriminated against contrary to Article 40.1. His claim was unsuccessful, partly on account of "severance" difficulties,[125] but also because what he was being denied was said to be more in the nature of a privilege than a right and, as well, because he failed to establish that the male/female distinction as applied to his circumstances was "invidious" or "unfairly discriminatory." The evidence suggested that, in making the distinction, the Oireachtas was having regard to the social, economic and political conditions which might prevail in the various jurisdictions from which alien aspirants for citizenship might come. And there was evidence that in some of those countries "the likelihood of females being engaged in any of the activities which might be relevant in considering an application for citizenship was sufficiently remote to justify the automatic granting of citizenship to female aliens upon their marriage to Irish citizens."[126] Accordingly, it was held by Keane J., "the distinction thus drawn is not necessarily invidious."[127] However, in 1986 the Nationality Act was amended to remove all

---

[122] *McKinley v. Minister for Defence* [1992] 2 I.R. 333.
[123] [1984] I.R. 50; *infra*, p.661.
[124] [1981] I.L.R.M. 326.
[125] *Infra*, p.894.
[126] [1981] I.L.R.M. p.326.
[127] *Ibid*.

discrimination on the basis of sex,[128] thereby bringing the Irish law into line with the 1979 UN Sex Discrimination Convention.

In still another instance, *Dennehy v. Minister for Social Welfare*,[129] the plaintiff, whose wife had deserted him, contended that a provision of the Social Welfare (Consolidation) Act 1981, was unconstitutional in that it provided benefits for deserted wives but gave no equivalent benefit to deserted husbands. Many United States decisions on sex discrimination were considered by Barron J., but he declined to be guided by them because "they were decided upon a different Constitution and on the basis of a different constitutional jurisprudence."[130] According to him, the test of constitutionality here was whether it was unjust, unreasonable or arbitrary to exclude men from these payments. And he concluded that in the circumstances it was not so unjust because the deserted wives' benefit was introduced when there was a serious problem of husbands leaving their wives and children, whereas desertion by wives of their husbands and children was most infrequent.[131] Additionally, mothers who have been caring for children almost invariably have lost out in the labour market and, accordingly, are in much greater need of financial support from the State than husbands, who would usually have careers of their own. Fourteen years later in *Lowth v. Minister for Social Welfare*[132] a deserted husband's challenge to these provisions was rejected by the Supreme Court on similar grounds; there was sufficient evidence to show that the Oireachtas had "ample grounds ... to conclude that deserted wives were in general likely to have greater needs than deserted husbands so as to justify legislation providing for social welfare, whether in the form of benefits or grants or a combination of both to meet such needs."[133] It was further held that the EC Directive 79/7 on the Principle of Equal Treatment for Men and Women in Matters of Social Security did not apply to this kind of benefit.

In *State (Nicolaou) v. An Bord Uchtála*[134] the Supreme Court upheld a provision that discriminated against males by impact, *viz.* section 14(1) of the Adoption Act 1952, which stipulates that an adoption order "shall not be made without the consent of every person being the child's mother or guardian or having charge or control over the child. ..." The contention that this discriminated on the grounds of sex, because it did not mention the natural father, was rejected because the father was not absolutely denied a veto. As explained by Walsh J., "[u]nder the provisions ... of the Act certain persons are given rights and all other persons are excluded. Whether or not the natural

---

[128] Irish Nationality and Citizenship Act 1986.
[129] Unreported, High Court, Barron J., July 26, 1984.
[130] At p.16.
[131] At p.17
[132] [1998] 4 I.R. 321.
[133] *Id.* at p.342.
[134] [1966] I.R. 567.

father is excluded depends upon the circumstances whether or not he comes within the description of a person who is given a right, and he may or may not come within some such description. If he is in fact excluded it is because in common with other blood relations and strangers he happens not to come within any such description. There is no discrimination against the natural father as such."[135] There certainly was sex discrimination in the law's impact or effect but this was held, in the circumstances, to be constitutionally permissible. In 1987 and again in 1998, following a decision by the European Court of Human Rights,[136] this regime was substantially modified to remove most restrictions on fathers.[137]

Reverse Discrimination

There is the question of so-called "reverse" discrimination, which in this context means preferring qualified women to equally qualified men in order to promote overall equality. The 1979 UN Convention's response is to permit these practices within limits; that "[a]doption by States Parties of temporary special measures aimed at accelerating *de facto* equality between men and women shall not be considered discrimination as defined in the present Convention, but shall in no way entail as a consequence the maintenance of unequal or separate standards; these measures shall be discontinued when the objectives of equality of opportunity and treatment have been achieved. Adoption ... of special measures ... aimed at protecting maternity shall not be considered discriminatory."[138]

Race

Race and colour-based discrimination is prohibited by Article 14 of the European Convention and by Articles 2 and 26 of the UN Covenant. Ireland has ratified the UN Convention on the Elimination of all Forms of Racial Discrimination.[139] Discrimination on the grounds of race, colour and ethnic origin is proscribed by the 1998 and 2000 equality legislation in the areas of employment and services.[140] The issue of racially discriminatory legislation

---

[135] *Id.* at p.641.

[136] *Keegan v. Ireland*, 18 E.H.R.R. 342 (1994).

[137] Adoption Act 1998.

[138] Art. 4. See generally, Fredman, "Reversing Discrimination", 113 *L.Q.R.* 575 (1997).

[139] December 21, 1965, 660 UNTS 195. See generally, M. McDougal et al., *Human Rights and World Public Order* (1980), Chap.9.

[140] Employment Equality Act 1998 and Equal Status Act 2000. *Cf.* EC Directive 43/2000 on Equal Treatment Between Persons Irrespective of Racial or Ethnic Origin, OJ 2000, L180/22.

or administrative practices has never come before the courts, at least insofar as the reported case law goes.[141] The judgments of Henchy and Griffin JJ. in *de Burca v. Attorney General*[142] might be held to imply that, since non-whites comprise a very small proportion of the citizenry, a Juries Act that confined jury service to "Caucasians only" would not be unconstitutional. At least, the grounds those judges invoked for striking down the 1927 Act would carry little weight when only a small minority is excluded from serving on juries. And following Kenny J.'s analysis in the *Murtagh Properties* case,[143] picketing to prevent the employment of non-whites might equally be held constitutionally permissible in so far as the constitutional provision relied on in that case was interpreted expressly to forbid merely sex discrimination in employment. But if, as is more likely Walsh J.'s view of the thrust of the equality guarantee represents the law, then laws and practices that adversely discriminate on the grounds of race are unconstitutional.

Status at Birth

Discrimination on the grounds of "birth, or other status" is prohibited by Article 14 of the European Convention and by Article 26 of the UN Covenant. Ireland has ratified the UN Convention on the Rights of the Child[144] and also the European Convention on the Legal Status of Children Born out of Wedlock.[145] Discrimination on the basis of status at birth is not dealt with in the 1998 and 2000 equality legislation.

There has been a tendency in the courts to reject claims by non-marital children that they have been put at an unfair disadvantage as compared with what used to be described as "legitimate" offspring. Even where there is no suggestion of competing claims from such offspring, the courts have refused to strike down disadvantages on the grounds of unfair discrimination being placed on non-maritals.[146] In *O'B. v. S.*[147] the Supreme Court held that legislative discrimination against those children, with the objective of favouring members of the family who are linked by or through marriage, can never contravene Article 40.1 because supporting and assisting the family based on marriage is an obligation on the State under Article 41 of the Constitution. As explained in Chapter 24, the case concerned sections 67 and 69 of the Succes-

---

[141] The closest perhaps is *Schlegell v. Corcoran* [1942] I.R. 19, a dispute between a landlord and his tenant.
[142] [1976] I.R. 38.
[143] [1972] I.R. 330.
[144] November 20, 1989, 1577 UNTS 3.
[145] October 15, 1975, 1138 UNTS 303.
[146] *E.g., State (M) v. Minister for Foreign Affairs* [1979] I.R. 73; *infra*, p.705.
[147] [1984] I.R. 316.

sion Act 1965, the effect of which prevents a deceased's non-marital child from inheriting any part of his estate where the deceased died intestate; the estate instead went to the deceased's brothers and sisters. It was contended that ss. 67 and 69 were unfairly discriminatory. Walsh J., giving the Court's judgment, agreed that the discrimination there was not based on any differences of physical or moral capacity, nor was there any question of non-marital children having a different social function in this context. He observed that "(i)ndeed, it could not be claimed that illegitimacy can, in itself, attribute any particular social function to the illegitimate person."[148] However, the provisions in question were "aimed at maintaining the primacy of the family as the fundamental unit group of society",[149] which is the policy underlying Article 41 of the Constitution. Accordingly, it cannot be maintained that distinctions drawn in order to secure an express constitutional objective are unconstitutionally discriminatory under Article 40.1. As Walsh J. put it, "the object and the nature of the legislation concerned must be taken into account, and ... the distinctions or discriminations which the legislation creates must not be unjust, unreasonable or arbitrary and must, of course, be relevant to the legislation in question. ... If legislation can be justified under one or more Articles of the Constitution, when read with all the others, it cannot be held to be unjust within the meaning of any Article. ... Having regard to the constitutional guarantees relating to the family, the Court cannot find that the differences created by the Act of 1965 are necessarily unreasonable, unjust or arbitrary."[150] He referred to various US decisions, in which provisions that discriminated against non-marital children were held to contravene the Fourteenth Amendment's equal protection clause, but found that it was not necessary to consider these cases in any detail because the U.S. Constitution contains no clause similar to Article 41 on the family. Moreover, it was "unnecessary to speculate upon what would be the position under Article 40.1, ... if Article 41 did not exist."[151] The Court also found that a decision of the European Court of Human Rights, holding that discrimination against non-marital children contravened Articles 8 and 14 of the Convention,[152] was not directly relevant because it concerned very different facts.

Yet it would be wrong to read *O'B. v. S.* as permitting all forms of discrimination against children who were born outside of marriage. What the case permits is this discrimination where the objective is to bolster the family based on marriage and it is a question of fact whether the legislative provision in question has that purpose.

---

[148] *Id.*, at p.333.
[149] *Id.*, at p.334
[150] *Ibid.*
[151] *Id.*, at p.336.
[152] *Marckx v. Belgium*, 2 E.H.R.R. 330 (1980).

Nationality

Nationality-based discrimination is prohibited by Article 14 of the European Convention and by Articles 2 and 26 of the UN Covenant; the former extends to association with a national minority. Certain forms of adverse action against aliens is forbidden by customary international law.[153] Within the EC/EU, many forms of discrimination against nationals of Member States and their dependants are outlawed.[154] There is a Treaty of Friendship, Commerce and Navigation between Ireland and the United States of America that disallows types of discriminatory treatment of each State's nationals.[155] Discrimination on the grounds of nationality is proscribed by the 1998 and 2000 equality legislation in the areas of employment and of services.

The enumerated "personal rights" in the Constitution, including equality, are guaranteed to "the citizen" but the rights classified under the Family, Education, Private Property and Religion are not so confined expressly. Nevertheless, nationality-based distinctions do not fit easily within the rider to the equality guarantee, that laws may take account of differences of "capacity, physical and moral, and of social function." Apart from laws that regulate the entry of aliens into the State and deportation, and what they may and may not do while in the State, there are very few legislative provisions that address the position of aliens as such; principally, certain rules regarding political participation,[156] jury service,[157] becoming an officer in the defence forces,[158] and the ownership of land in Ireland,[159] of Irish-registered ships and aircraft and of shares in companies owning such property.[160]

Prescribing a 14 days but extendable period within which aliens seeking to challenge decisions that could result in their deportation, was upheld by the Supreme Court.[161] There are several other comparable provisions in different contexts and the requirement here was held to be justified by the need to "bring about at an early stage legal certainty" concerning the alien's position.[162]

It was held by the Supreme Court in *Electoral Amendment Bill, 1983, Re,*[163]

---

[153] See generally, M. McDougal et al., *Human Rights and World Public Order* (1980), ch.14 and B. Sunderg-Weitman, *Discrimination on the Grounds of Nationality* (1977). Cf. *A. v. Secretary of State* [2003] 2 W.L.R. 564.

[154] E.g. *Bloomer v. Incorporated Law Society of Ireland* [1995] 3 I.R. 14.

[155] January 21, 1950, with Protocol of June 24, 1992.

[156] *Infra*, p.595.

[157] Juries Act 1976, s.6.

[158] Defence Act 1954, s.41.

[159] Land Act 1965, s.45.

[160] *Supra*, p.72.

[161] *Re ss. 5 and 10 of the Illegal Immigrants (Trafficking) Bill, 1999* [2000] 2 I.R. 360, *infra*, p.486.

[162] *Id.* at p.403.

[163] [1984] I.R. 268.

that excluding aliens from certain political rights was not alone consistent with the Constitution but was in fact required by it. The issue was whether it was permissible by legislation to permit aliens who satisfied certain conditions regarding reciprocity to vote in Dáil elections. What motivated the proposed legislation was that, since Irish citizens can vote in parliamentary elections in Britain, British citizens should be allowed to vote in Dáil elections. However, several of the Constitution's provisions on political participation stipulate that "all citizens" who fulfil certain qualifications are eligible to vote in and to stand as candidates in the election in question. Thus "(e)very citizen" (over 35 years of age) is eligible to be elected as President, "(e)very citizen" (over 21 years of age) is eligible to be a member of the Dáil or of the Seanad, "(e)very citizen" (over 18 years of age) is entitled to vote in Dáil elections, and "(e)very citizen" so entitled to vote has a vote in presidential elections and in referenda. It was contended that the effect of these provisions not alone gave citizens a right to vote in and to stand as candidates in the elections in question, but confined that right to citizens only; if any of these rights were to be extended to aliens that could only be done by an appropriate constitutional amendment. The court accepted this argument as regards Dáil elections, and the same principle presumably applies to presidential and Seanad elections and referenda. According to O'Higgins C.J., for the court, concerning Article 16 which deals with the Dáil, the Article's entire provisions "would appear to form a constitutional code" for holding Dáil elections and there is a clear intention to confine voting rights to Irish citizens.[164] Shortly afterwards, the Constitution was amended to permit extending the franchise in Dáil elections to nationals of EC Member States which permit Irish citizens to vote in their parliamentary elections. [165]

Disability

Neither Article 14 of the European Convention nor Articles 2 and 26 of the UN Covenant make any reference to disabled persons, perhaps because it is unusual to have laws that provide for discrimination against them. Discrimination on the grounds of disability is proscribed by the 1998 and 2000 equality legislation in the areas of employment and of services. Unless positive steps are taken to assist the disabled, on account of their physical or mental handicap, they will often be at a considerable disadvantage *vis-à-vis* their able-bodied brethren. Accordingly, for most practical purposes, it is necessary to take action in order to reduce if not eliminate discrimination against the disabled.[166] Apart from cases on the guarantee in Article 42.2 of free primary

---

[164] *Id.*, at p.75. Similarly, the *Foreign Voters* case (1990) 83 BVerfGE 37.

[165] The 9th Amendment, now Art. 16.2.ii.

[166] *Cf. Eldridge v. British Columbia*, 151 D.L.R. 4th 577 (1997).

education,[167] the disabled have not had a particularly encouraging experience in the courts. But an agency to promote the interests of disabled persons in several ways was established by the National Disability Authority Act 1999.

In *Draper v. Attorney General*,[168] it was contended by the plaintiff, a severely disabled woman, that the Electoral Acts unconstitutionally discriminated against her on the grounds that they did not allow her to vote by post. She wished to vote but her disability prevented her from going to her polling station. Her argument was that because voting is such a fundamental right, it was unfairly discriminatory not to permit her to vote in the only way that she could. But the Supreme Court rejected that contention. According to O'Higgins C.J., for the court, while the State is obliged to have laws that make the right to vote "operative and effective", the State's obligation is only to act reasonably and it was not unreasonable to deny handicapped persons the opportunity to vote by postal ballot because that form of voting is so open to abuse. As he put it, "(p)ostal voting may, without extraordinary and complex safeguards, be open to abuse", and to grant postal votes to the disabled "obviously contains a very high risk of abuse which could not easily be countered or controlled."[169] Such discrimination against the handicapped as existed here was entirely by way of impact and "the fact that some voters are unable to comply with (the law's) provisions does not of itself oblige the State to tailor that law to suit their special needs. The State may well regard the cost and risk involved in providing special facilities for particular groups as not justified, having regard to the numbers involved, their wide dispersal throughout the country and the risks of electoral abuses."[170]

The evidence that the court cited to support its conclusion that the legislature had not acted unreasonably is not very convincing. It was a report of a joint Oireachtas Committee on electoral law in 1962, which rejected the proposal to grant postal votes to persons other than members of the Garda Síochána and the defence forces. As the court observed, that Committee did not expressly advert to disabled persons who could not leave their homes. That such persons can vote by post in other democratic countries was not considered by the court. Indeed, apart from the 1962 report, it would seem that no other evidence of what is reasonable and practical with regard to electoral laws was given in the two-day hearing before McMahon J. However, in 1986 the Electoral Acts were amended to enable disabled people to vote through the post and no abuses of this system have come to light.

The principal net issue in *Employment Equality Bill, 1996, Re*,[171] was whether a law designed to combat discrimination on a variety of grounds in

---

[167] *E.g. Sinnott v. Minister for Education* [2001] 2 I.R. 545; *infra*, p.816.
[168] [1984] I.R. 277.
[169] *Id.* at p.290.
[170] *Ibid.*
[171] [1997] 2 I.R. 321.

employment can itself be repugnant to the anti-discrimination guarantee or other provisions in the Constitution. This Bill, which subsequently in an amended form became the Employment Equality Act 1998, consisted of three principal parts. Part III dealt with sex discrimination and replicated the EC requirements on equal pay and on equal treatment on the grounds of sex; Part IV dealt with discrimination on the other enumerated grounds, in respect of which several exceptions were made to the non-discrimination rule; the remainder dealt with the enforcement of these requirements, including the activities of the Equality Authority. In its entirety the Bill was referred to the Supreme Court by the President under Article 26 of the Constitution, which upheld its provisions against age discrimination and discrimination on the grounds of religion.

But "despite their laudable intention", parts of the Bill dealing with disability discrimination were declared to be repugnant for two main reasons. One is that they required most employers to incur what could be significant expenditure in order to meet the statutory requirements, by constructing facilities to enable disabled employees to carry out their work; this burden might be particularly onerous for small employers. Against that, some sections of the public service were exempted entirely from these requirements, notably the Garda Síochána and the Defence Forces, even with regard to desk work that was materially no different from ordinary office work. Hamilton C.J., for the court, contrasted the Bill with legislation to protect workers' health and safety, that also obliged employers to incur expenditure; it "is entirely proper that the State should insist that those who profit from an industrial process should manage it as safely, and with as little danger to health as possible [because] the cost of doing the job safely and in a healthy manner is properly regarded as part of the industrialist's cost of production." [172] He compared such legislation with the view that polluters should pay for the costs incurred by their polluting activities. The objection here, however, was that the Bill "attempts to transfer the cost of solving one of society's problems on to a particular group",[173] namely employers, who must bear the cost of providing special treatment or facilities and the exemption it contained for "undue hardship" was held to be unduly restrictive. Under the presumption of constitutionality, one would think that this proviso, which included "the financial circumstances of the employer", would have saved the measure from being deemed repugnant.

Religion

Article 44.2.3 of the Constitution forbids the State to "impose any disabilities or make any discrimination on the ground of religious profession, belief or

---

[172] *Id.* at p.367.
[173] *Ibid.*

status." In the *Equality Bill 1996* reference[174] the main attack on the exceptions made to the non-discrimination rule for certain kinds of jobs focused on Article 44.[175] Discrimination on the grounds of religion is proscribed by the 1998 and 2000 equality legislation in the areas of employment and of services.

FUNDAMENTAL INTERESTS

Article 40.3.1 and 2 of the Constitution may be regarded as a broad "substantive due process" guarantee that "[t]he State guarantees in its laws to respect, and, as far as practicable, by its laws to defend and vindicate the personal rights of the citizen. The State shall, in particular, by its laws protect as best it may from unjust attack and, in the case of injustice done, vindicate the life, person, good name, and property rights of every citizen." As has already been explained, it has been held that certain interests or claims not expressly referred to in the "personal rights" section are given constitutionally-protected status by these provisions, for example, bodily integrity, marital privacy, work and travel.[176] Where a claim is accorded the status of a "personal right", then any *prima facie* discriminatory treatment by the State, in regard to that right, carries a heavy burden of justification if the discrimination is to be upheld. In some of the decisions up to now, however, there is a tendency to consider allegations of differential treatment regarding these rights not in the light of the equality clause but solely in the context of the very interest claimed to be constitutionally protected.

Perhaps the best example of this non-comparativist tendency is *O'Brien v. Keogh*,[177] which concerned different limitation periods in the Statute of Limitations, 1957. The plaintiff, an infant, sued for damages resulting from injuries suffered in a car accident. According to the relevant statutory provisions, three years was the limitation period for personal injury actions brought by adults but the period for plaintiffs under a disability (including infants) was six years, except for infants who at the time the right of action accrued were in the custody of a parent. It was argued that, as between infants, the six year rule was impermissibly under-inclusive, *i.e.* one category of infant was unfairly excluded from it. This contention was rejected by the Supreme Court because "Article 40 does not require identical treatment of all persons without recognition of differences in relevant circumstances. It only forbids invidious discrimination. (And here, f)ar from effecting inequality, the purpose of the provision would appear to attempt to establish equality between the two groups

---

[174] [1997] 2 I.R. 321.
[175] *Infra*, p.631.
[176] *Supra*, p.275.
[177] [1972] I.R. 144.

(those in and not in parental custody)."[178] The matter did not end here, however. The court observed that the exclusion of all infants in parental custody from the six year rule could, in some instances, lead to injustice, such as where the parents subsequently die as a result of injuries suffered in the same accident and where the infant sues a parent, who then invokes the three year limitation period in defence. Accordingly, said Ó Dálaigh C.J., the provision was unfair in establishing an irrebuttable presumption that all infants in parental custody at the time the right of action accrued are adequately safeguarded; "the broad division into infants ... in parental custody and infants not in such custody is not calculated to bring up for consideration the matters that should be borne in mind if infants' rights are to be given reasonable protection."[179] Therefore, it was concluded, it "has been demonstrated" that the provision "fails to match up to the guarantee ... to protect (and) vindicate ... property rights of the citizen."[180]

Like the Henchy and Griffin JJ. judgments in *de Burca*,[181] Ó Dálaigh C.J.'s judgment here demonstrates some discomfort with the equality norm. The outcome in *O'Brien v. Keogh* could easily have been reached on the basis of the equality principle. As the 1957 Act admits, some persons under age need lengthy limitation periods. Accordingly, to draw a blanket distinction between infants in parental custody and those not in parental custody, at the time a right of action accrues, is unfair discrimination because in a significant number of contexts infants in parental custody are in objectively no different a position, for the purposes of the principles underlying peremptory limitation periods, than infants not in such custody.

This decision should be contrasted with that reached in a very similar case, *O'Brien v. Manufacturing Engineering Co.*,[182] which was decided – or at least handed down -on the same day. Briefly, under the now-repealed Workmen's Compensation Acts, where an injured worker accepted workmen's compensation for the injury, the limitation period for bringing a common law action for damages was reduced from three years to one year (or to two years in special circumstances). Walsh J., for the Supreme Court, focused principally on the equality clause. Having stated that the equality principle does not proscribe all differentiations but only "invidious discrimination", he went on to demonstrate that the different limitation periods for injured persons, who accepted workmen's compensation and those who did not accept it, is not discriminatory treatment of equals and in the circumstances is reasonable. He then went on to say that, for essentially the same reasons, the provision was not an unjustifiable interference with the "property right" to litigate claims.

---

[178] *Id.* at p.156.
[179] *Id.*, at p.157.
[180] *Id.*, at p.158.
[181] [1976] I.R. 38; *supra* p.376.
[182] [1973] I.R. 334.

This confusion as to whether the basis for challenge should be the equality principle or the substantive interest being claimed, as well as having some philosophical justification, may be explained partly by reference to *locus standi.* In *O'Brien v. Keogh* the plaintiff was an infant who had been in parental custody at the time the right of action accrued but he was not one of those infants unjustly affected by the three year rule in the ways the court described. He, therefore, would have been hard pressed to demonstrate that he was effectively in the same position as children who were not in parental custody who, it is fair to assume, would frequently have their rights of action extinguished by prescription on account of guardians who were ignorant of the law. Only infants whose parents subsequently die or whose parents invoke the three-year period against them would be in a comparable position to infants not in parental custody.

Liberty

When deciding who should and who should not be extradited or deported , the State must treat like circumstances in the same way. In *McMahon v. Leahy*,[183] the Supreme Court refused to order that the applicant be extradited to Northern Ireland in circumstances where numerous persons in virtually identical circumstances had not been extradited. When endeavours were made to extradite those persons, they would claim the "political offence" exemption and, up to then, that claim was never contested by the State. Consequently, it was held, the State contravened the guarantee of equality by contesting a similar claim in the applicant's case. O'Higgins C.J. observed that "[s]uch discriminatory treatment of one individual appears unfair, smacks of injustice and certainly requires explanation."[184] In the absence of any satisfactory explanation, he asked, "could it be said that all these [individuals] had been held equal before the law?."[185]

Administration of Justice

A feature of the right to a fair hearing guaranteed by Article 6 of the European Convention is "equality of arms", meaning that neither side in litigation should be given any undue procedural advantage over the other. The power of the Director of Public Prosecutions to prosecute persons for any offence in the Special Criminal Court, without ever being required to justify his decisions, was held by the UN Committee on Human Rights to contravene Article 26 of the UN Covenant.[186] In contrast, the Supreme Court saw nothing objectionable

---

[183] [1984] I.R. 525.
[184] *Id.*, at p.537.
[185] *Id.*, at p.538.
[186] *Kavanagh v. Ireland*, UNHRC, April 4, 2001.

in this entirely arbitrary method of administering justice[187] and, when the applicant there sought redress arising from the UN Committee's decision, the court declined to grant redress of any kind, not even compensation.[188] Nor in *Murphy v. G.M.*[189] did that court see anything objectionable about a procedure whereby only plaintiffs could adduce opinion, which could be accepted by the judge as evidence. This discrimination was held to be justifiable, as explained by Keane C.J., on the grounds that defendants in cases under the Proceeds of Crime Act 1996, should "normally be ... in a position to give evidence ... as to its (*i.e.* the property's) provenance without calling in aid opinion evidence."[190] Many of those defendants, however, are not in a position to prove that the property is not the proceeds of crime and at best can only prove how they obtained the property.

Having different time limits for bringing appeals in broadly similar proceedings was upheld in *Dornan Research and Development Ltd v. Attorney General.*[191] Employees who contend that they were subjected to sexual harassment, leading to their constructive dismissal, have alternative remedies; they may either apply to the Labour Court or else institute a claim in the Employment Appeals Tribunal. If they lose in the Labour Court, they have a limited right of appeal to the High Court; if instead, they lose in the Tribunal, they have a full appeal to the Circuit Court and, as well, another full appeal from its decision to the High Court. This difference in treatment was upheld by Geoghegan J. because "[t]he two Acts are dealing with different problems and there is nothing wrong or unconstitutional in there being different procedures for dealing with them."[192] Because these Acts overlap in certain circumstances, such as here, does not mean that both must provide for identical procedures. Further, if the court were to declare that s. 26(1)(e) of the Employment Equality Act 1977, was invalid, that would result in the applicant there and others in similar circumstances having no right of appeal from the Labour Court at all.

Political Participation

Equality for those participating in the political process is expressly provided for by several clauses in the Constitution; for instance that there shall be no sex discrimination in entitlement to vote in Dáil, Seanad and Presidential elections, and in referenda;[193] that those entitled to vote have only one vote in

---

[187] *Kavanagh v. Government of Ireland* [1996] 1 I.R. 321; *infra*, p.852.
[188] *Kavanagh v. Governor of Mountjoy Prison* [2002] 3 I.R. 97, *supra*, pp.228, 240 and 242.
[189] [2001] 4 I.R. 113; *infra*, p.509.
[190] *Id.*, at p.155.
[191] [2001] 1 I.R. 223.
[192] *Id.*, at p.227.
[193] *Infra*, pp.594 and 604.

these elections and in referenda;[194] that there should be consistency in the ratio between eligible voters in all constituencies.[195] Additionally, as Budd J. pointed out in *O'Donovan v. Attorney General*.[196] Article 5's stipulation that Ireland is "a democratic State" signifies that it is "one in which all citizens have equal political rights."[197]

Equality in the political sphere was resoundingly endorsed in *McKenna v. An Taoiseach (No.2)*,[198] where the Supreme Court held that the Government contravened Article 40.1 of the Constitution by allocating funds in support of the case for amending the Constitution in order to remove the ban on divorce. Following an earlier decision by Costello J.,[199] Keane J. in the High Court held that disputes about how public money should be spent are intrinsically political controversies, in which the courts should not get involved; both described the plaintiff's complaint as one of "*political* misconduct on which this court can express no view. ..."[200] No reference was made by them to Article 40.1 at all. In the appeal, it was contended by the State that the only way in which the plaintiff could impugn the decision of Dáil Éireann to vote monies to the Minister would be if the procedure laid down in Articles 28 and 17 for the appropriation of public funds had not been followed. She did make that argument as well[201] but the court decided to grapple with the more fundamental constitutional issue, namely the decision by the Government and endorsed by the Dáil (on the strength, *inter alia*, of Costello J.'s 1992 decision) to spend £500,000 on pro-divorce publicity during the referendum campaign.

Because neither the Constitution nor the Referendum Act 1994 give the Government any role in the conduct of referenda, Hamilton C.J. concluded that the Government's actions in this regard were not "in the exercise of the executive power of the State;" that "any activity of the Government is not *per se* an activity which assumes the character of the exercise of the executive power of the State."[202] But the Oireachtas and the Government "are both creatures of the Constitution and are not empowered to act free from [its] restraints. ..."[203] He accepted that the Government were entitled to present factual information about the subject matter of the referendum, to express its views on the point and to urge the electorate to endorse those views. When voting in a referendum to alter the Constitution, however, "the People, by virtue of the democratic nature of the State ... are entitled to be permitted to

---

[194] *Infra*, pp.597 and 604.
[195] *Infra*, p.598.
[196] [1961] I.R. 114.
[197] *Id.* at p.137.
[198] [1995] 2 I.R. 10.
[199] *McKenna v. An Taoiseach (No.1)* [1995] 2 I.R. 1.
[200] [1995] 2 I.R. 1 at p.18.
[201] *Id.* at p.20.
[202] *Id.* at p.38.
[203] *Id.* at p.40.

reach their decision free from unauthorised interference by any of the organs of State that they ... have created by the enactment of the Constitution."[204] Allocating the £500,000 here was an improper interference with this process because it "infringe[d] the concept of equality which is fundamental to the democratic nature of the State."[205] O'Flaherty J. stressed that "if we were to uphold the legitimacy of the present proposal, there would be a temptation for Government in an election atmosphere to stray in other directions with further inducements and thus sully the right of the people to decide freely and fairly on what is put before them in the referendum without any inducements – aside from verbal inducements, which are the essence of any voting campaign."[206] Denham J. added that public funds should not be used to finance one side in a general election. Notwithstanding the declaration of unconstitutionality made there, about seven weeks later the Minister for Finance paid the PR agency that had disseminated the pro-divorce publicity for the Government,[207] an action that elicited practically no public comment.

Subsequently, Radio Telefís Éireann's coverage of the divorce referendum campaign was challenged in *Coughlan v. Broadcasting Complaints Commission*,[208] where it was established that slightly more airtime had been given to those who advocated a "yes" vote than was given to those opposed to the proposed amendment. That happened principally because the various political parties were allowed separate broadcasts and, by way of coincidence, they all supported the proposal. But the Supreme Court held that this was not a sufficient justification for the disparate treatment of the two sides in the argument and, consequently, RTE had contravened its statutory obligation in "matters which are either of public controversy or the subject of current public debate [to be] fair to all interests concerned. ..."[209]

Not providing facilities to enable severely disabled persons to vote was held by the Supreme Court in *Draper v. Attorney General*[210] not to be unconstitutional. That court reached a similar conclusion in *Breathnach v. Ireland*,[211] with regard to the practical impossibility of convicted prisoners being able to vote. According to Keane C.J., "given that [prisoners'] incapacity to vote is the result of their own voluntary actions, ... the restriction thus imposed on their right to exercise their vote is at least as reasonable as the restriction on the disabled which existed" prior to 1986.[212] Insofar as prisoners have a constitutional right to vote, it was held that it goes into suspension for

---

[204] *Id.* at p.42.
[205] *Ibid.* Similarly, the *Official Propaganda* case, 44 BVerfGE 125 (1977).
[206] *Id.* at p.45.
[207] *Dáil Debates*, January 23, 1995, Vol.460, cols 388–395.
[208] [2000] 3 I.R. 1; *infra*, p.585.
[209] Broadcasting Act 1960, s.18(1)(b).
[210] [1984] I.R. 277; *supra*, p.388.
[211] [2001] 3 I.R. 216; *infra*, p.596.
[212] *Id.* at p.238.

so long as they are being detained and the State is not obliged to adopt appropriate measures in order that they are able to vote.

Requiring intending candidates in general and in European Parliament elections to pay a comparatively modest deposit, which might be forfeited, was declared invalid in *Redmond v. Minister for the Environment*.[213] It was argued by the State that the £300 deposit was a justifiable method of protecting the electoral system "from abuse by frivolous or vexatious persons, and from commercial or other improper exploitation."[214] But Herbert J. concluded that no evidence had been adduced to indicate a tendency to abuse the electoral system if the deposit requirement were abolished. Additionally, alternative means exist whereby potential abuses could be discouraged, for example a candidate having to be nominated and/or supported by a significant number of persons. What was so objectionable about deposits was that the discrimination was based on wealth or the absence of wealth, similar to the property-owner qualification for jury service that the Supreme Court had condemned in *de Burca*.[215] According to the judge, "a law which has the effect, even if totally unintended, of discriminating between human persons on the basis of money is an attack upon the dignity of those persons as human beings who do not have money", and it was "exactly the type of discrimination for which the framers of the first sentence of Article 40.1 of the Constitution were providing."[216] On the basis of the evidence heard, he held that it could not be justified under the second sentence in this Article.

Subjecting candidates for election to the Dáil and the European Parliament to slightly different regimes about how much they may spend, depending on whether they are or are not existing members of either House of the Oireachtas, was held to be invalid by the Supreme Court in *Kelly v. Minister for the Environment*.[217] In fixing the ceiling on how much a candidate may spend, the Electoral Act 1997 excluded any payment, service or facility provided by public funds to a member of either House; for example, free postage and telephone facilities. According to McKechnie J., "the principle of equality must apply to all candidates seeking election or re-election, as the case may be. This does not however necessarily mean that uniformity must follow in all circumstances. Where there is a difference, [it] must be legitimately based and must be justified on both objective and reasonable grounds."[218] Because the evidence showed that this disparity of treatment resulted in a great distortion between incumbents and non-incumbents but no justification of any kind for it was offered, the exemption for existing members was held to be unconstitutional.

---

[213] [2001] 4 I.R. 61.
[214] *Id.* at p.83.
[215] [1976] I.R. 38.
[216] [2001] 4 I.R. 61 at p.80. Similarly, the *Party Tax Deduction* case, 8 BVerfGE 51 (1958).
[217] [2002] 4 I.R. 191.
[218] *Id.* at p.200.

Family Relationships

Several common law rules that treated husbands and their wives differently have been declared invalid, for example, the presumption that a wife was coerced by her husband to commit a criminal offence,[219] the doctrine that a wife's domicile was entirely dependent on that of her husband[220] and that only husbands could recover damages for loss of the "consortium" of a spouse.[221] But providing social welfare benefits to wives who are deserted by their husbands, while not providing those benefits to husbands where wives desert them, was upheld by the Supreme Court.[222] And having a different regime for wives acquiring Irish nationality, from that for husbands, was upheld by Keane J.[223] Both of these discriminations were subsequently ended by the Oireachtas.

Property

Laws for the compulsory acquisition of property by the State must not unfairly discriminate, even where provision is made for adequately compensating the property-owner. In *An Blascaod Mór Teo v. Commissioners for Public Works (No. 3)*,[224] the Supreme Court declared invalid the An Blascaod Mór National Park Act 1989, which provided for the compulsory acquisition of practically all the land on the Great Blasket Island, on account of that island's cultural significance. Several well-known authors had lived there in the past and had described island life in their books, some of which were in the Irish language. The plaintiffs were the owners of practically all of the land on the island, which they had purchased from time to time in the 1950s and the 1960s. They contended that the 1989 Act was in substance a Bill of Attainder because it was targeted at them and their land. If indeed the island had the cultural importance being attached to it, they contended that the Act should have applied to all comparable culturally significant land in the State, especially the other islands in the Blasket archipelago. Further, at very minimum all land on the Great Island should have come within the Act. Excluded from its ambit was land owned by any descendant of someone who lived on the island in or before 1953, when its remaining inhabitants had been evacuated. Additionally, it was contended that it is most extraordinary to acquire land because it was inhabited by writers, that the plaintiffs had always endeavoured to preserve the amenity

---

[219] *State (D.P.P.) v. Walsh* [1982] I.R. 412.
[220] *W. v. W.* [1993] 2 I.R. 476.
[221] *McKinley v. Minister for Defence* [1992] 2 I.R. 333.
[222] *Lowth v. Minister for Social Welfare* [1998] 4 I.R. 321.
[223] *Somjee v. Minister for Finance* [1981] I.L.R.M. 324.
[224] [2000] 1 I.R. 6.

on the island and that, had they been asked to sell the land to the State before the 1989 Bill had been published, they may very well have agreed to do so.

It was because the 1989 Act discriminated between owners of land on the Great Island on the basis of descent, or "pedigree," that it was declared invalid. As Budd J. pointed out, "the actual aims of the 1989 Act could be better achieved by dealing with the property as an entity without fragmentation of ownership on a criterion of lineage."[225] This was because the land outside the scope of the Act was in tiny parcels scattered indiscriminately across the eastern side of the island. No coherent justification was offered for permitting descendants of pre-1953 owners to retain their interest in those parcels and, at the same time, to expropriate the plaintiffs, who had devoted considerable time and energy to the upkeep of the island in succeeding years. Budd J. concluded that:

> "It is difficult to see what steps were taken by the State to vindicate the plaintiffs' property rights. Evidence was given that officials of the State had no less than 43 meetings with members of the Foundation[226] before June 1989, which rather contrasts with the lack of meetings with the Plaintiffs, who owned more than 3/5ths of the Great Blasket; nor was any written explanation sent to the Plaintiffs' Solicitors setting out the rationale for compulsory purchase legislation nor was any initiative taken to seek co-operation to achieve the cultural objectives with which the Plaintiffs were clearly in sympathy. They had, out of their own resources, taken steps to preserve buildings in the village, they had kept open a guesthouse so as to assist visitors' access and they had cleared up the rubbish on the island.
>
> I conclude therefore that, in the absence of any real legitimate legislative purpose requiring the difference in treatment of the Plaintiff landowners and the exempted folk, the discrimination in the 1989 Act cannot be justified as the interests of the common good do not necessitate such measures. Furthermore, as the difference of treatment between the two categories of landowners created by the Act bears no relation to the quality of the actual difference between the two categories of landowners the discrimination is disproportionate and invidious. The requirement of proportionality has not been respected. Finally, the treatment of the Plaintiffs by the State authorities with regard to the legislation and the manner in which the State attempted to enforce the regime constitutes a failure by the State to protect the property rights of the Plaintiffs from unjust attack, to vindicate those rights or to regulate them where injustice has been done in breach of Article 40.3.2, and to regulate them in

---

[225] At p.137; it is difficult to understand why Budd J.'s very detailed judgment was never published in the official law reports.
[226] Which it was envisaged would manage the island.

accordance with the principles of social justice, and to delimit by law the exercise of the rights guaranteed and recognised by the Constitution in accordance with the exigencies of the common good contrary to Article 43.2.3 of the Constitution."[227]

The State's appeal against this decision was rejected. According to Barrington J., for the Supreme Court, the 1989 Act's "classification appears to be at once too narrow and too wide."[228] Using descent or "pedigree" as a criterion, outside of the law of succession, was "suspect." Rather, "a constitution should be pedigree blind just as it should be colour blind or gender blind except when those issues are relevant to a legitimate legislative purpose."[229] In this instance, the court could see no such purpose and had no doubt but that the discrimination between the plaintiffs and those descended from pre-1953 owners of land on the island was unfair.

As is explained in Chapter 25 on property rights, exceptionally tax laws will be declared invalid because they discriminate unfairly, the principal instance being *Brennan v. Attorney General*.[230] There the Griffith Valuation system, which fixed the value of agricultural land for the purpose of rates and several other charges, was held to have become so outmoded and arbitrary as to unfairly discriminate between comparable landowners; it lacked any "reasonable degree of uniformity. ..."[231]

Even-handedness is also required in the administration of tax laws. Thus in *Doyle v. An Taoiseach*,[232] a temporary 2 per cent levy in respect of cattle that were slaughtered or were exported from the State was held to be so arbitrary and unfair in the manner of its operation as to be *ultra vires* the powers of the Government to impose duties. This was because, on account of widespread opposition to this levy, butchers and exporters found it impossible to pass on the levy to those who sold them animals, as had been envisaged in the regulations. Had the levy been imposed at the place and time farmers sold their animals for exportation or slaughter, that problem could not have arisen. But on account of how the levy was structured – exporters paid it on the basis of the value of the animal at the pier head but that could be different from the original sale price and, further, often they could not identify the original sellers – it frequently was impossible for them to recoup what they had to pay. As described by Henchy J., the regulations "purported to impose a levy as a tax on the prime procedures of live cattle, [but] the ordinary operation of the levy in the context of market forces and other commercial realities had the effect

---

[227] At pp. 137–138.
[228] [2001] 1 I.R. p.19.
[229] *Ibid*.
[230] [1984] I.L.R.M. 355; *infra*, p.752.
[231] *Id.* at p.365. Similarly, the *Interest Tax* case, 84 BVerfGE 239 (1991).
[232] [1986] I.L.R.M. 693.

that the prime producer frequently escaped liability for the levy, in whole or in part, so that it fell to that extent on the exporter or butcher. ..."[233] He described this result as "so untargeted, indiscriminate and unfair, so removed from the primary policy of the levy",[234] as to be *ultra vires* the legislation it was adopted under.

A similar outcome was reached in *Purcell v. Attorney General*.[235] The plaintiff had been assessed for tax under the Farm Tax Act 1985, which proved to be highly unpopular. Its administration was slow in that lists were being compiled of all farms, depending on their size, and by 1986, only lists of the largest farms had come into existence. In that year, assessments were raised in respects of those farms, including on the plaintiff. Then in 1987 the Minister announced that the tax would no longer be collected, with the consequence that owners of the smaller farms, for which lists had not yet been drawn, would not receive any assessments. It was held by the Supreme Court that the Oireachtas could not have intended "to discriminate between farmers according to the respective size of their farm" and that "to construe the Act as meaning that the tax would be imposed on some farms within the ambit of the Act before it was imposed on others would be ... to make the Act unconstitutional. ..."[236] Consequently, on a proper construction, no assessments should have been raised until arrangements existed for assessing all farmers affected by the Act. The Minister's decision to tax owners of large farms before owners of small farms could be taxed, said Blayney J., "was to discriminate unfairly against the owners of farms in excess of 150 adjusted acres because the tax was imposed on them alone and did not affect the owners of other farms within the ambit of the Act."[237]

As also is explained in Chapter 25 on property rights, laws regulating the use persons may make of their property must not unfairly discriminate, the principal instance being the several Rent Restrictions Acts that severely limited what rent a comparatively small number of house-owners could charge their tenants, regardless of the financial circumstances of those owners or their tenants.[238]

Occupation

In *Murtagh Properties Ltd v. Cleary*,[239] it was held that picketing by a trade union, that did not allow women to become members, in support of a demand

---

[233] *Id.* at p.715. Cf. the *Coal Penny* case, 91 BVerfGE 186 (1994).
[234] *Ibid.*
[235] [1995] 3 I.R. 287.
[236] *Id.* at pp.293–294.
[237] *Id.* at p.294.
[238] *E.g., Blake v. Attorney General* [1982] I.R. 117; *infra*, p.759.
[239] [1972] I.R. 330.

that employers hire only union members, contravened the constitutional guarantee of equality. Most forms of unfair discrimination in the workplace are now outlawed by the Employment Equality Act 1998. Its provisions were upheld by the Supreme Court in *Employment Equality Bill 1997, Re*,[240] with the exception of those regarding disability, vicarious criminal liability and the use of certificates in order to prove certain facts in criminal trials. In particular, it was held that the Bill's provisions regarding discrimination on the grounds of age and of religious profession or belief were a reasonable balance between the Oireachtas' objective and the legitimate interests of employers.

It was held by the Supreme Court in *Riordan v. An Taoiseach*[241] that the guarantee of equality did not require that vacancies for posts in the public sector should be advertised, so that all those interested in getting the job in question would have adequate opportunity to apply for it. There the plaintiff challenged the decision of the Government to recommend a former Supreme Court judge to be a director of the European Investment Bank. According to Keane C.J., "even the most expansive construction of Article 40.1 could not support the proposition that the guarantee of equality required the imposition of such constraints on the executive in making recommendations of this nature."[242] Having different qualification periods for entitlement to pensions, as between judges of the District Court and of the Circuit Court, was upheld by the Supreme Court in *McMenamin v. Ireland*.[243]

On the other hand, liquor price control regulations that applied to the town of Dundalk but not to its surrounding areas, and which also treated lounge bars and public bars on the same footing, were declared invalid by the Supreme Court in *Cassidy v. Minister for Industry and Commerce*.[244] Because the legislation there did not expressly authorise the drawing of those distinctions, Henchy J. concluded that the Oireachtas "cannot have intended that the Minister would exercise in such an arbitrary and unfair way the legislative powers of price control vested in him."[245]

EQUALISING UP

Where the court finds that a particular rule or requirement unfairly discriminates, it must then address the appropriate remedy.[246] Where the provision in question imposes a burden on the plaintiff, a declaration of

---

[240] [1997] 2 I.R. 321.
[241] [2000] 4 I.R. 537.
[242] *Id.* at p.549.
[243] [1996] 3 I.R. 100.
[244] [1978] I.R. 297, *supra*, p.178.
[245] *Id.* at p.312.
[246] *Infra*, p.889.

invalidity will have the effect of removing that imposition. Difficulties arise where the plaintiff's contention is that he has not been given the benefit of a rule, from which others in comparable circumstances to him benefit. For instance, in *Lowth v. Minister for Social Welfare*,[247] a man whose wife had deserted him contended that paying a deserted spouse's social welfare benefit only to deserted wives contravened the equality guarantee. If the court had upheld this contention, a declaration of invalidity would only have the effect of a "equalising down" and thereby putting wives in as bad a legal position as the plaintiff. Under the separation of powers principle, the courts could not direct the Oireachtas to enact a law extending those benefits to deserted husbands.

An example of "equalising down" occurring was in *Bloomer v. Incorporated Law Society of Ireland*,[248] where Belfast-based law students contended that regulations of the Law Society exempting graduates of several universities in the Republic from having to sit qualifying examinations, was unlawful discrimination incompatible with EC law. Laffoy J. upheld the discrimination argument, although it does not appear to have been contended that, because most of the plaintiffs there would have been eligible to become Irish citizens, the rule in question did not discriminate against them indirectly on nationality grounds. In the light of her finding on the merits, the judge concluded that she had no choice but to declare the rule invalid.[249] This outcome was of no benefit at all to the successful plaintiffs but it operated to deprive graduates of the Republic's universities of an extremely valuable exemption.[250] It does not appear to have been contended there that, where a provision is held to contravene EC anti-discrimination requirements, the appropriate remedy under EC law is to "equalise up" rather then down.

On at least two occasions, however, the Supreme Court has equalised up when dealing with anomalous common law rules. A question that arose in *W. v. W.*,[251] where it was held that the doctrine of the married woman's dependent domicile contravened the guarantee of equality, was whether this should affect circumstances existing prior to 1986. That was because, in the Domicile and Recognition of Foreign Divorces Act 1986, that doctrine was repealed but only with prospective effect. Because common law rules are judge-made and not immutable, and because the question of the circumstances in which a foreign divorce would be recognised should be answered in the light of current policy, the Supreme Court held that a divorce would be recognised if granted by a court where either spouse had been domiciled at the time. While accepting that the common law rule contravened the equality clause, Hederman J.

---

[247] [1998] 4 I.R. 321.
[248] [1995] 3 I.R. 14.
[249] *Id.* at pp.55–59.
[250] *Cf. Abrahamson v. Law Society* [1996] 1 I.R. 403.
[251] [1993] 2 I.R. 476.

dissented on the consequences, because in 1986 the Oireachtas had addressed this very issue and made it clear that the pre-1986 regime was to apply to all divorces that had taken place by then. He observed that "[i]t may well be thought that the legislation should have gone further, the fact is that it cannot and this court cannot legislate."[252]

In the previous year, however, that judge was one of the majority who equalised up in *McKinley v. Minister for the Defence*.[253] This concerned the common law right of action for damages for loss of "consortium", a claim that could only be brought by husbands. In this instance, the plaintiff was the injured party's wife and both sides agreed that "[s]uch a right was inconsistent with the guarantee of equality ... and in that form, therefore, could not have been carried forward and be of full force and effect, pursuant to Article 50. ..."[254] A bare majority of the court held that, in consequence, the common law rule should be extended, enabling wives to recover damages. According to McCarthy J., "[t]he simpler solution is to make the common law conform to the Constitution, by declaring that the established right of the husband still exists and to deny such right to the wife would be an infringement of Article 40. In ruling in that fashion, the Court would not be legislating in matters of social policy; it would be removing discrimination."[255] Finlay C.J., and Egan J., dissenting, rejected this approach on account of the entirely anomalous basis for the common law rule, which is that a wife is part of a husband's property and, where she is injured, he ought to be compensated for the damage caused to his property.

How courts in Canada and in South Africa sometimes deal with this question is to declare the rule in the Act or regulation to be invalid, because it unfairly discriminates, but put a stay for say six or twelve months on the declaration becoming effective, in order that the legislature may enact an appropriate amending measure, which takes account of what was said in the judgment.[256]

---

[252] *Id.* at p.490.
[253] [1992] 2 I.R. 333.
[254] *Id.* at p.342.
[255] *Id.* at p.354.
[256] E.g. *Trocuik v. Attorney General of British Columbia*, 14 B.H.R.C.563 (2003) at p.573; compare *J. v. Director General*, 14 B.H.R.C. 575 (2003) at p.582.

CHAPTER 17

Criminal Procedure

Criminal law concerns conduct that is prohibited by penal sanctions. Ordinarily, alleged offenders may be tried for the offence in the criminal courts and, in the case of a serious offence, before a jury. It would appear that the State has a very broad discretion concerning what types of conduct should be punished by the criminal law and the ambit of criminal proscriptions expands inexorably from year to year. Provided the law in question complies with the minimum requirements of legality, or the "rule of law,"[1] and does not impermissibly discriminate nor unduly interfere with the various constitutional guarantees, the conduct in question can be made the subject of penal sanctions. To date the Irish courts have not addressed the question of whether the Constitution imposes additional constraints on criminal laws, regarding absolute and strict liability offences, and the *mens rea* required for very serious offences. But in *Employment Equality Bill, 1996, Re,*[2] the Supreme Court held that persons could be made vicariously criminally responsible for the actions of others only in limited circumstances; that the offence in question should be essentially regulatory in character and apply where the person has a particular privilege (such as a licence) or be under an obligation to maintain public standards (such as regarding health and safety, the environment or consumer protection). A provision that would have made employers vicariously responsible for a variety of discriminatory actions on the part of their employers, with a maximum penalty of a £15,000 fine or two years imprisonment, was held to be repugnant to the Constitution.

Criminal procedure is concerned with how persons suspected of having committed criminal offences are brought before and are dealt with by the courts.[3] To the extent that it involves arrest and detention for trial, and imprisonment if there is a conviction, the right to fair criminal procedures is an integral part of the right to personal liberty. Long before modern concepts of fundamental rights developed, many legal systems aspired to having fair criminal procedures, *i.e.* that regardless of their substantive content, criminal laws should be administered in a reasonable manner. From the mid-sixteenth

---

[1] *King v. Attorney General* [1981] I.R. 223, declaring invalid provisions of the Vagrancy Acts.

[2] [1997] 2 I.R. 321.

[3] See generally, D. Walsh, *Criminal Procedure* (2002) (hereafter "*Walsh*") and E. Ryan & P. Magee, *The Irish Criminal Process* (1983).

century onwards in continental Europe there was great interest in civilising criminal procedures, as is exemplified by the famous German Carolina of 1532 and the French Ordinance of Villers Cotterets of seven years later.[4] By the seventeenth century the English courts began developing concepts of natural justice, which have since evolved into the general principles of judicial impartiality *(nemo iudex in sua causa)* and the right of defence *(audi alteram partem).*[5] Other widely accepted principles of fair procedure have a more recent origin, such as entitlement to legal representation, the right to open and public proceedings and equality before the law.

Some constitutions place great stress on fair criminal procedures. One of the most significant features of the United States Bill of Rights is that much of it *(i.e.* the 4th, 5th and 6th Amendments) is comprised of a detailed enumeration of procedures, *viz.* requiring warrants in order to arrest persons and to search them, presentment before a grand jury, prohibition of double jeopardy and of self-incrimination, speedy trials and trial before a jury.[6] Similar detailed guarantees can be found in the Canadian Constitution.[7] Modern continental European constitutions, on the other hand, do not contain comparable provisions. Perhaps the most striking difference between the 1789 Declaration of the Rights of Man and of the Citizen and the US Amendments adopted in 1791 is that the former instrument makes no express reference to criminal procedure. Why there should be such a disparity of emphasis has not been satisfactorily explained; it is not as if the continental European legal tradition, which is inquisitorial in nature, is one that was indifferent to procedural protection for those accused of crimes.[8]

In its approach to criminal procedure the Constitution resembles continental constitutions in that it contains very few specific guarantees, the only ones being that trials shall be held in public and that there shall be jury trial for non-minor offences. Apart from these, any procedural protections have to be derived from the vague "due process" clause in Article 38.1, that "no person shall be tried on any criminal charge save in due course of law," and also from the more general provisions that "justice" is administered in the courts, that the judges shall be independent and that all procedures must conform with the scheme for the separation of powers.

In determining what particular procedural protections exist under the Constitution, a significant pointer is tradition, *i.e.* what protections the common

---

[4] See generally, A. Esmein, *A History of Continental Criminal Procedure* (1914) pp.314–322 and 145–174 and J. Langbein, *Torture and the Law of Proof* (1977).

[5] See generally, W. Blackstone, *Commentaries on the Laws of England* (1st ed., 1769), vol.4, ch.19 *et seq.* Irish criminal procedure in the 19th century is covered in W. Gabbett, *A Treatise on the Criminal Law* (1842), vol. 2.

[6] See generally, A. Amar, *The Constitution and Criminal Procedure: First Principles* (1997) and W. La Fave *et al, Criminal Procedure* (3rd ed., 2000).

[7] See generally, P. Hogg, *Constitutional Law of Canada* (4th ed., 1997) Chaps 48–51.

[8] *Supra* n. 4 and M. Damaska, *The Faces of Justice and State Authority* (1986).

law regards as the very minimal requirements of fair procedure. Among the principles that can be traced to this tradition are jury trial, speedy trial and the prohibitions against double jeopardy and forced self-incrimination. However, the common law was not unduly solicitous towards criminal defendants.[9] In *State (Healy) v. Donoghue*,[10] where the accused claimed a right to free legal aid, O'Higgins C.J. warned against confining procedural protections within the traditional concepts of fairness, observing that "[t]he general view of what is fair and proper in relation to criminal trials has always been the subject of change and development. Rules of evidence and rules of procedure gradually evolved as notions of fairness developed. The right to speak and to give evidence, and the right to be represented by a lawyer of ones choice were recognised gradually. To-day many people would be horrified to learn how far it was necessary to travel in order to create a balance between the accuser and the accused."[11]

Another pointer is the European Convention and the UN Covenant, in particular their Articles 6 and 14 respectively. In the *Healy* case O'Higgins C.J. cited Article 6(3)(c) of the Convention, in respect of which the Irish Government has entered a reservation, as "demonstrat(ing) clearly that it was (in 1950) recognised throughout Europe that, as one of his minimal rights" an accused person who had no money was to free legal aid.[12]

In seeking to discover the safeguards demanded by "due process," judges also rely on their intuitive sense of justice and fair play, which naturally is greatly influenced by their own experience with the criminal law or lack of it. Thus in the *Healy* case O'Higgins C.J. appealed to the sense of fairness, human dignity and to tradition:

> "the concept of justice, which is specifically referred to in the preamble in relation to the freedom and dignity of the individual, appears again in the provisions of Article 34 which deal with the Courts. It is justice which is to be administered in the Courts and this concept of justice must import not only fairness, and fair procedures, but also regard to the dignity of the individual ...
>
> (T)he words 'due course of law' in Article 38 make it mandatory that every criminal trial shall be conducted in accordance with the concept of justice, that the procedures applied shall be fair, and that the person accused will be afforded every opportunity to defend himself. If this were not so, the dignity of the individual would be ignored and the State would have failed to vindicate his personal rights. What then does justice

---

[9] See generally, Langbein, "The Criminal Trial Before the Lawyers", 45 *U. Chicago L. Rev.* 263 (1978).
[10] [1976] I.R. 325; *infra*, p.439.
[11] *Id.* at p.350.
[12] *Id.* at p.351.

require in relation to the trial of a person on a criminal charge? A person charged must be accorded certain rights (notably) to be adequately informed of the nature and substance of the accusation, to have the matter tried in his presence by an impartial and independent court or arbitrator, to hear and test by examination the evidence offered by or on behalf of his accuser, to be allowed to give or call evidence in his defence, and to be heard in argument or submission before judgment be given. By mentioning these I am not to be taken as giving a complete summary, or as excluding other rights such as the right to reasonable expedition and the right to have an opportunity for preparation of the defence.

It seems to me that this puts very clearly what one would expect to be the features of any trial which is regarded as fair. However, criminal charges vary in seriousness. There are thousands of trivial charges prosecuted in the District Courts throughout the State every day. In respect of all these there must be fairness and fair procedures, but there may be other cases in which more is required and where justice may be a more exacting task-master. The requirements of fairness and of justice must be considered in relation to the seriousness of the charge brought against the person and the consequences involved for him."[13]

The European Convention's criminal procedure guarantees are contained principally in Article 6:

"1. In the determination of … any criminal charge against him, everyone is entitled to a fair and public hearing within a reasonable time by an independent and impartial tribunal established by law. Judgment shall be pronounced publicly but the press and public may be excluded from all or part of the trial in the interest of morals, public order or national security in a democratic society, where the interests of juveniles or the protection of the private life of the parties so require, or to the extent strictly necessary in the opinion of the court in special circumstances where publicity would prejudice the interests of justice.

2. Everyone charged with a criminal offence shall be presumed innocent until proved guilty according to law.

3. Everyone charged with a criminal offence has the following minimum rights:
    (a) to be informed promptly, in a language which he understands and in detail, of the nature and cause of the accusation against him;
    (b) to have adequate time and facilities for the preparation of his defence;

---

[13] *Id.* at pp.348 and 349–350.

    (c) to defend himself in person or through legal assistance of his own choosing or, if he has not sufficient means to pay for legal assistance, to be given it free when the interests of justice so require;

    (d) to examine or have examined witnesses against him and to obtain the attendance and examination of witnesses on his behalf under the same conditions as witnesses against him;

    (e) to have the free assistance of an interpreter if he cannot understand or speak the language used in court."[14]

But this is not an exhaustive list of the Convention's procedural requirements. In the words of the Strasbourg Commission in the *Pataki-Dunshirn* cases,

> "Article 6 … does not define the notion of a fair trial in a criminal case. Para. 3 of the Article enumerates certain specific rights which constitute essential elements of that general notion, and para. 2 may be considered to add another element. The words 'minimum rights', however, clearly indicate that the five rights specifically enumerated in para. 3 are not exhaustive, and that a trial may not conform to the general standard of a 'fair trial', even if the minimum rights guaranteed by para. 3 – and also the right set forth in para. 2 – have been respected."[15]

Among the other unspecified components of fair procedure, it was said is "what is generally called the equality of arms, that is the procedural equality of the accused with the Public Prosecutor. …"[16]

Article 14 of the UN Covenant resembles Article 6 of the Convention but contains several additional entitlements, in particular the rights to silence, to appeal against a conviction and to have a conviction set aside if subsequently it is shown that there was a miscarriage of justice. Silence has been held to be an aspect of Article 6 and those other entitlements are provided for in the Convention's Seventh Protocol.

CRIMINAL CHARGE

The guarantees in the Constitution regarding criminal procedure apply where one is facing a "criminal charge" but it does not define this term. Where what is involved is intrinsically criminal, then the sanction can be imposed only in a prosecution that complies with the several criminal procedure guarantees, such as the presumption of innocence. Usually it will be obvious that a person is

---

[14] See generally, B. Emmerson & A. Ashworth, *Human Rights and Criminal Justice* (2001).
[15] (1963) 6 Y. B'k E.C.H.R. 414 at p.730.
[16] *Id.* at p.732.

being tried on a criminal charge. Occasions nevertheless arise where a person is being penalised in some other way and a question may be asked whether that sanction can only be imposed on being convicted by a duly established criminal court. For instance, firms that contravene the EC's rules on fair competition can be fined by the EC Commission without ever being charged, tried and convicted of a crime.[17] Is this procedure consistent with the obligation to channel the administration of the criminal law through the criminal courts? Two main categories of case arise in this context. One is where, as a sanction, a person's liberty is significantly impaired otherwise than by being imprisoned or similarly incarcerated,[18] for instance, by being prevented from travelling abroad,[19] by being confined to a particular area on account of anti-social behaviour[20] or by being held in a mental institution due to apprehension that he may commit serious offences if released.[21] The other is where monetary penalties are imposed either by administrative decree or in ostensibly civil proceedings,[22] for instance, exceptional taxes or revenue penalties,[23] damages far in excess of the extent of the loss incurred[24] or the forfeiture of property derived from a crime.[25]

In the 1970s several continental European countries pursued a policy of de-criminalisation, *i.e.* categorised various forms of proscribed behaviour as no longer criminal, in the ordinary sense, but as administrative offences, and persons accused of having committed those acts were dealt with by administrative agencies rather than by the criminal courts. Among those to be de-criminalised in this manner in Germany were the less serious road traffic offences. However, in *Ozturk v. Germany*,[26] the European Court of Human Rights ruled that road traffic administrative offences are crimes for the purposes of the Convention and, accordingly, persons accused of those wrongs must be dealt with through the normal criminal procedures. Notwithstanding that it is characterised in domestic law as civil or administrative and not criminal, a process will be deemed to be criminal for the purpose of Article 6 of the Convention depending on the nature of the conduct in question and the severity of the sanction being imposed; that the process does not have the usual trappings of a criminal prosecution does not put it outside the criminal category.[27]

---

[17] Regulation 17/62, J.O. 204/62, Article 15.
[18] See generally, Robinson, "Punishing Dangerousness: Cloaking Preventive Detention as Criminal Justice", 114 *Harv. L. Rev.* 1429 (2001).
[19] *E.g., Gough v. Chief Constable Derbyshire* [2002] 3 W.L.R. 289.
[20] *E.g., R. (McCann) v. Manchester Crown Court.*
[21] *E.g., Kansas v. Hendricks*, 521 UN 246 (1997).
[22] See generally, Mann, "Punitive Civil Sanctions: The Middle ground Between Criminal and Civil Law", 101 *Yale L.J.* 1795 (1992).
[23] *E.g., Dept. of Revenue v. Kurth Ranch*, 511 US 767 (1994).
[24] *E.g., United States v. Halper*, 490 US 435 (1989).
[25] *E.g., Austin v. United States*, 509 US 602 (1993).
[26] [1984] 6 E.H.R.R. 409.
[27] *E.g., Ezeh v. United Kingdom* 35 E.H.R.R. 28 (2002).

For forty years the leading authority on what, under the Constitution, will be treated as intrinsically criminal was *Melling v. Ó Mathghamhna.*[28] It arose out of charges of smuggling that were preferred against the plaintiff and, in respect of which he would have to pay a substantial penalty if convicted. In the event, it was held that those proceedings involved criminal charges because virtually every feature of the statutory procedure replicated normal criminal procedures. The case contains some general observations on the nature of criminal charges although none of the judges ventured a comprehensive definition of the concept. As Kingsmill Moore J. observed, "(t)he anomalies which still exist in the criminal law and the diversity of expression in statutes make a comprehensive definition almost impossible to frame."[29] Having quoted definitions from some of the textbooks, Kingsmill Moore J. set out "features, which are regarded as indicia of crimes":

"(i)   They are offences against the community at large and not against an individual. Blackstone defines a crime as a violation of the public rights and duties due to the whole community, considered as a community.

(ii)   The sanction is punitive, and not merely a matter of fiscal reparation ... and failure to pay, even where the offender has not the means, involves imprisonment.

(iii) They require *mens rea* for the act must be done 'knowingly' and 'with intent to evade the prohibition or restriction'... *Mens rea* is not an invariable ingredient of a criminal offence, and even in a civil action of debt for a penalty ... where the act complained of is an offence 'in the nature of a crime' but where *mens rea* is made an element of an offence it is generally an indication of criminality."[30]

This quasi-definition was given with reference to the smuggling offence in the *Melling* case and it is not clear whether or not, under the Constitution, there can be a criminal charge where the sanction is exclusively financial and where no question of imprisonment for non-payment of the fine or penalty arises. Lavery J. remarked that he did "not consider it necessary in order to establish the criminal character of the charge to find that imprisonment may be imposed as a primary punishment,"[31] which suggests that imprisonment for non-payment of the fine must be a secondary punishment. As Ó Dálaigh J. pointed out, however, refusal to pay damages awarded in what undoubtedly is a civil action can lead to the defaulting defendant being imprisoned.[32]

---

[28] [1962] I.R. 1.
[29] *Id.* at p.24.
[30] *Id.* at p.25 (citations omitted).
[31] *Id.* at p.11.
[32] *Id.* at p.40, referring to the Enforcement of Court Orders Act 1926.

Loss of Liberty

In 1939 administrative interment without trial of suspected subversives was held to be unconstitutional because, *inter alia*, in substance it involved the administration of criminal justice otherwise than by way of a prosecution and trial on a criminal charge. As was explained by Gavan Duffy J., in *State (Burke) v. Lennon*,[33] the authority conferred on the Minister by section 55 of the Offences Against the State Act 1939 to intern, "is an authority, not merely to act judicially, but to administer justice and an authority to administer criminal justice and condemn an alleged offender without charge or hearing and without the aid of a jury. But ... the administration of justice is a peculiarly and distinctly judicial function, which, from its essential nature, does not fall within the executive power and is not properly incidental to the performance of the appropriate functions of the executive; consequently, a law endowing a Minister of State, any Minister, with these powers is an invasion of the judicial domain and as such is repugnant to the Constitution."[34] However, in the following year, dealing with a modified internment without trial regime, the Supreme Court for all practical purposes overruled this decision, on the grounds that the object of internment was "not in the nature of punishment, but is a precautionary measure taken for the purpose of preserving the public peace and order and the security of the State."[35]

It is not essential for the process in question to have all the trappings of a criminal prosecution in order for it to be regarded as a trial on a criminal charge for these purposes. *Re Haughey*[36] concerned an investigation which was being conducted by the Dáil Committee of Public Accounts into how money that had been voted for Northern Ireland relief had been spent. In addition to its authority under the Dáil's standing orders, this Committee was given various powers by the Committee of Public Accounts of Dáil Éireann (Privilege and Procedure) Act 1970, such as to summon and examine witnesses, and to require them to produce any documents which were under their control. Section 2(4) of this Act established a mechanism for imposing sanctions on witnesses who refused to testify before the Committee or who did anything else which would constitute contempt of court if the Committee were a court of record. Any witness who disobeyed the Committee, as just described, would have "the offence" certified by the Committee's chairman and the matter would then be referred to the High Court, where it would be dealt with in the same way as if the witness had committed contempt of court. According to this section, where the witness disobeyed the Committee, "the committee may

---

[33] [1940] at p.136.
[34] *Id.* at p.152.
[35] *Re Offences Against the State (Amendment) Bill, 1940* [1940] I.R. 470; *infra*, p.861.
[36] [1971] I.R. 217.

certify the offence of that person ... to the High Court and the High Court may, after such inquiry as it thinks proper to make, punish or take steps for the punishment of that person in like manner as if he had been guilty of contempt of the High Court." When the applicant came before the Committee, he read a prepared statement, disclaiming all knowledge of or connection with the subject matter of the investigation, and then declined to answer any questions because he had been advised that, by answering them, he would be leaving himself open to being sued for defamation. His name and a statement of these circumstances was then forwarded by the Committee to a three -judge High Court, which decided that he should serve six months imprisonment. But that decision was overruled by the Supreme Court on the grounds that the procedure followed was unconstitutional.

It was held that section 2(4) of the 1970 Act created a criminal offence of disobeying the Committee's orders and that, since the penalty which could be imposed was unlimited (the court being able to penalise in the same way as for contempt of court), it was a major offence. It therefore should be the subject of trial with a jury, as required by Article 38.5. According to his counsel, there are two constitutional ways whereby witnesses can be compelled to co-operate with an administrative inquiry. One is by providing that failure to co-operate should be a minor offence punishable summarily.[37] The other is to provide that those conducting the inquiry should certify to the High Court that, in their view, the person in question has unlawfully failed to co-operate; then the High Court should be empowered to investigate the entire matter, hear that person and then punish in the same manner as if the person had committed contempt of court.[38] But under the procedure provided for in section 2(4), the Dáil Committee was empowered to find that a witness had committed an offence and the court's function was merely to determine the punishment. In the light of section 2(4)'s very terms, of how it had been regarded by the Dáil Committee and set against similar provisions for punishing persons who refused to co-operate with statutory inquiries, it was held that the section's most likely meaning was to authorise the Committee to find the witness guilty of a statutory offence and the court's function was to determine the appropriate sanction. This procedure flew in the face of the separation of powers. As Ó Dálaigh C.J. for the court explained, "the trial of a criminal offence is an exercise of judicial power and is a function of the Courts, not of a committee of the Legislature. [Accordingly] a statute that conferred on a committee of the Legislature a power to try a criminal offence would be repugnant to the Constitution and invalid. ... Moreover, under the Constitution the Courts cannot be used as appendages or auxiliaries to enforce the purported convictions of other tribunals. The Constitution ... reserves exclusively to the Courts the power to

---

[37] *Infra*, p.420.
[38] As in *e.g.* Solicitors (Amendment) Act 1960, s.15(2).

try persons on criminal charges. Trial, conviction and sentence are indivisible parts of the exercise of this power."[39]

Monetary Deprivations

A fine or other monetary penalty, a forfeiture and a tax all have the characteristics of being exactions made by the State other than in order to pay compensation. On several occasions challenges to Revenue penalties, as being intrinsically criminal, have been rejected by the courts, principally because they did not require any element of *mens rea* in order to be applicable.[40] Black J. remarked once that there is a long-standing tradition, which is "wholly illogical," that proceedings in respect of Revenue offences are civil in nature.[41]

A penalty commonly imposed on persons convicted of one or more particular offences is the forfeiture of property – often the instruments with which the offence was committed or the gain derived from the offence. Part II (sections 4-11) of the Criminal Justice Act 1994 goes much further where an accused has been convicted and sentenced for drug trafficking, money laundering or any other offence. When these proceedings have concluded, the court is empowered to decide whether the person "benefited from drug-trafficking" or has "benefited from" the offence for which he was convicted, or that offence along with any other offence. If it is established on the standard of proof in civil proceedings that the person did so benefit, an order may be made confiscating that benefit, in accordance with criteria set out in that Act. It was held by McCracken J. in *Gilligan v. Criminal Assets Bureau*[42] that the confiscation procedure here does not involve trying a person on a criminal charge because it cannot commence until the criminal trial has concluded and, unlike in a comparable procedure in Britain,[43] the confiscation is not made part of the sentence to be imposed. Because it did not form part of the criminal trial or sentence, he held that the process could not take place in the Special Criminal Court, which has an exclusively criminal jurisdiction.

The system for confiscating the proceeds of criminal activity contained in the Proceeds of Crime Act 1996, involves ostensibly civil proceedings but has many features closely associated with enforcing the criminal law. Under section 4 of this Act, where it can be shown that property is the "proceeds of crime," broadly defined, a court order can be obtained for its confiscation; there is a defence where that order would create a "serious risk of injustice." Although there are numerous statutory provisions authorising confiscating specific

---

[39] [1971] I.R. 250.
[40] *Infra*, p.417.
[41] *State (Gettings) v. Fawcett* [1945] I.R. 183 at p.210.
[42] Unreported, High Court, McCracken J., November 8, 2002.
[43] *Cf. Phillips v. United Kingdom* 11 B.H.R.C. 280 (2001).

property following conviction of an offence, no conviction is needed – of either the defendant or of any other party – in order to have property confiscated under the 1996 Act. There are comparable provisions in the United States which the courts there have held to be criminal for some purposes but not for others.[44]

It was contended in *Murphy v. G.M.*[45] that the 1996 Act was an ersatz civil law that intrinsically was a criminal measure because, *inter alia*, the plaintiff in those proceedings was a senior police officer attached to the Criminal Assets Bureau; no provision was made in the Act to compensate anyone, not even the victim of the alleged crime; the Act's purpose was predominantly punitive, as part of the State's "war against crime"; that the entire focus of the Act was crime, relief being predicated on the property in question deriving from crime. Further, criminal law arrest and search powers had been relied on in order to build up the case against the defendants and an *ad hoc* legal aid scheme had been devised for defendants, modelled on that for criminal legal aid. In its case, the State emphasised that proceedings under the 1996 Act contained none of the usual trappings of a criminal trial, that they were not designed to punish but intended to operate a civil *in rem* forfeiture and that, on several occasions, similar procedures were upheld in the USA. Moreover, forty years earlier, the Supreme Court had rejected a challenge to provisions in a customs and excise law for the forfeiture of unlawfully imported or exported goods.[46] Regarding to criteria in the *Melling* case, the defendants argued that the 1996 Act was aimed at wrongs against the community at large, *viz.* profitable criminal activity and, in particular, money laundering. Both the Dáil and Seanad debates and evidence adduced showed that this Act was regarded as an important instrument in the battle against crime, especially organised crime. Secondly, the detriment imposed was punitive, being the confiscation of property; in this instance £300,000, which was no different from a large fine. It could not be regarded as providing for reparation because it contained no provision to that effect. Thirdly, because all proceeds of crime came within the Act, regardless of whether or not they were legitimately obtained by the defendant, but confiscation would be withheld where that would cause "a serious risk of injustice," there was provision for *mens rea*.

According to Keane C.J., for the court, the criteria set out by Kingsmill Moore J. in *Melling* are not the exclusive test for determining what is criminal; reliance by the defendants on them was "misplaced" because, in an earlier case concerning tax penalties, Finlay C.J. referred to other considerations as well, notably the usual process surrounding criminal proceedings.[47] Few of these trappings existed under the 1996 Act, such as arrest, bail, indictment

---

[44] See *supra* ns. 22–25 and J. Gurule & S. Guerra, *The Law of Asset Forfeiture* (1998).
[45] [2001] 4 I.R. 113.
[46] *Attorney General v. Southern Industrial Trust Ltd* (1960) 94 I.L.T.R. 161; *infra*, p.417.
[47] *McLoughlin v. Tuite* [1989] I.R. 82; *infra*, p.417.

and imprisonment for failure to pay a penalty. Accordingly, it would appear that the constitutional criterion of what is criminal is a procedure that possesses most of the usual trappings of criminal procedures. In contrast, in the US and in the Strasbourg court, in appropriate criminal procedures, which have the outward appearance of civil claims, will nonetheless be held to be truly criminal, for instance a swingeing "tax" imposed on persons previously convicted of possessing marijuana.[48] For Keane C.J., the substance of the matter is determined predominantly if not exclusively by its form.

Additionally, it was held, the *mens rea* prerequisite did not obtain here and reliance by the defendants on it was "fundamentally misconceived."[49] This was because an order to confiscate the property in question could be made "even though it has not been shown … that there was no *mens rea* on the part of" the defendant, meaning that he was not "involved in any criminal activity" and was not "aware that the property constituted the proceeds of crime."[50] However, if the defendant was not involved in the crime in question and neither knew nor should have known that the property was the proceeds of crime, it would seem that in most instances an injustice would be caused if his property were confiscated, for instance where he was a *bona fide* purchaser for value. There may be exceptional cases where confiscation in those circumstances would not produce a serious risk of injustice and the possibility of that happening in some instances was held sufficient to show that the 1996 Act did not contain a *mens rea* requirement. The court purported to follow earlier cases on Revenue forfeitures and penalties, where liability was automatically imposed in all cases no matter how defendants got themselves involved.[51] Because *mens rea* could never be relevant in the Acts considered in those cases, they were held by Keane C.J. to be comparable to an Act where, in a small minority of cases, lack of *mens rea* would not be a good defence.[52]

It would seem that awarding punitive damages in civil proceedings would not be regarded as penalising defendants on a "criminal charge." Whereas practically all of the procedures involved in the *Melling* case were those of the criminal law, those involved in *O'Keefe v. Ferris*[53] were civil. There the plaintiff contended that, notwithstanding, the civil claim for damages being made against him for fraudulent trading, contrary to section 297A of the Companies Act 1963, was in essence a trial on a criminal charge. Under section 297A, where a company's insolvency is caused by the fraudulent trading of one of its directors, the company's liquidator can sue him for that wrong and he can be held liable for all of the company's unpaid debts. It was contended that those

---

[48] *Supra*, n.23.
[49] [2001] 4 I.R. 148
[50] *Ibid.*
[51] E.g., *Southern Industrial Trust, infra* p.417.
[52] *Cf. International Transport Roth v. Secretary of State* [2002] 3 W.L.R. 344.
[53] [1997] 3 I.R. 463.

proceedings were punitive, that liability depended on a *mens rea* of intending to defraud and that the conduct affected is an offence against the community at large; indeed, section 297 of that Act makes equivalent conduct also a criminal offence. Therefore, it was said, section 297A was an ersatz civil proceeding that intrinsically was criminal. Because, however, section 297A contained none of the usual trappings of criminal proceedings, because fraud is remediable in civil as well as in criminal law and, most importantly, the object of proceedings under the section is to recover compensation rather than to punish, it was held not to satisfy the test propounded in *Melling* for a criminal proceeding. Indeed, depending on the circumstances, a defendant in these proceedings will not be held liable for all of the company's unpaid debts but only for such amount as can be attributed to his wrongdoing.[54]

Revenue Cases

Exceptionally, what purports to be a tax can be in substance a criminal sanction.[55] In the past the Revenue Commissioners had very extensive powers for dealing with persons who contravened revenue law, one being to arrest defaulters and imprison them without any trial, which was repealed in 1967.[56] Their power to select which of several penalties should be imposed on persons convicted of revenue offences was declared unconstitutional in 1962, as contravening the separation of powers.[57]

Melling v. Ó Mathghamhna[58] involved proceedings under section 186 of the Customs Consolidation Act 1876,[59] and the central issue was whether those constituted a trial for non-minor offences. If (as is explained below) they possessed this character, they should have been conducted on indictment and before a jury. On account of the very nature of the procedure laid down in the 1876 Act, the Supreme Court was unanimous that the proceedings were in respect of criminal offences. The alleged smuggler had been arrested, detained in the Bridewell, cautioned, charged, put in the dock, remanded on bail and had his belongings searched. If he were convicted but did not pay the penalty imposed under the Act, he could have been imprisoned for up to six months. As Lavery J. observed,

> "it seems ... clear that a proceeding, the course of which permits the detention of the person concerned, the bringing of him in custody to a Garda Station, the entry of a charge in all respects in the terms appropriate

---

[54] *Re Hunting Lodges Ltd* [1985] I.L.R.M. 75.
[55] *Supra*, n.23.
[56] Income Tax (Amendment) Act 1967.
[57] *Deaton v. Attorney General* [1963] I.R. 170; *infra*, p.473.
[58] [162] I.R. 1.
[59] 39 & 40 Vic. c.36.

to the charge of a criminal offence, the searching of the person detained and the examination of papers and other things found upon him, the bringing of him before a District Justice in custody, the admission to bail to stand his trial and the detention in custody if bail be not granted or is not forthcoming, the imposition of a pecuniary penalty with the liability to imprisonment if the penalty is not paid has all the *indicia* of a criminal charge. The penalty is clearly punitive in character, being £100 or treble the duty-paid value of the goods." [60]

Four years earlier the Supreme Court decided *Attorney General v. Southern Industrial Trust Ltd*,[61] which concerned forfeiting goods found to have been illegally exported or imported. Under this procedure, contained in section 207 of the Customs Consolidation Act 1876, if persons sought to export an item, without having obtained a licence, the Attorney General could bring proceedings against them to have that item forfeited and condemned. The court concluded that those proceedings were not of their nature criminal. Lavery J. pointed out that they were *in rem* and not *in personam,* that no question of *mens rea* or of fraud arose, nor could the proceedings either directly or indirectly lead to a person's imprisonment, nor even to the imposition of a financial penalty. The statute provided that goods illegally imported or exported shall automatically be forfeited and the action was simply a civil procedure to have the goods in question condemned. The entire form of the procedure here was fundamentally different from that in the (subsequent) *Melling* case.

A revenue proceeding that lies somewhere in between those considered in these two cases is where the Act in question obliges a person to do something and stipulates a penalty, if he has not done what is required. Part 47 (sections 1052-1086) of the Taxes Consolidation Act 1997 imposes various penalties for failure to make tax returns or for making incorrect returns. The mode of imposing or recovering those penalties is laid down in section 1061 of that Act, which is described as "civil proceedings" brought by an officer of the Revenue Commissioners, and it is stated that the action shall be governed by the High Court's rules on civil proceedings. In *McLoughlin v. Tuite*,[62] it was contended that these proceedings are essentially criminal in nature. Applying the "indicia of crimes" referred to in *Melling*, the Supreme Court held that tax penalties lacked any requirement of *mens rea*; regardless of the circumstances and whatever deserving explanation the individual may have, failure to put in a return when called upon to do so attracted the statutory penalty and the courts had no power to mitigate the sum in question. Moreover, proceedings to recover penalties contained none of the usual trappings of the criminal law.

---

[60] *Id.*, at p.9.
[61] (1960) 94 I.L.T.R. 161. Cf. *Gora v. Customs and Excise Commissioners* [2003] 3 W.L.R. 160.
[62] [1989] I.R. 82.

Carroll J., in the High Court, suggested that the first of the *Melling* tests also might not be met; that "no person would regard failure to fill in a form and send it to the Revenue authorities as an offence."[63]

Challenges on these grounds to revenue penalties were rejected on at least two other occasions. In one, the penalty was for not sending the Revenue the statement, declaration and certificate required of employers;[64] in the other, it was for not paying the excise duty imposed on bookmakers.[65] But the European Court of Human Rights has held that imposing substantial penalties for dishonest tax (VAT) evasion was intrinsically criminal for the purposes of Article 6 of the Convention.[66]

Professional Discipline

In *Solicitors Act 1954, Re*,[67] Kingsmill Moore J. observed that a "characteristic feature of criminal matters is the infliction of penalties, a consideration which gives weight to the submission that a tribunal which is authorised to inflict a penalty, especially a severe penalty, even in cases where the offence is not strictly criminal, should be regarded as administering justice."[68] But it has never been argued, let alone it ever been held, that professional disciplinary procedures involve trials of criminal charges for the purpose of Article 38 of the Constitution.[69] Where the procedure in question concerns professional discipline or is a disciplinary mechanism for members of a group possessing some special status, they do not involve criminal charges for the purposes of the European Convention even though they concern adjudication of allegations of the most serious misconduct.[70] Military discipline, authorised by Article 38.4 of the Constitution, is carried out by way of court martial, where the accused has all the protection of criminal procedures, other than a jury.

Relator Action

Another instance in which the question of criminal or non-criminal proceedings has arisen concerns the common law power of the Attorney General to apply for an injunction restraining the commission of an offence. Where a person commits a statutory offence, the Attorney is entitled to bring proceedings in

---

[63] [1986] I.R. 235 at p.244.

[64] *Downes v. DPP* [1987] I.R. 139.

[65] *DPP v. Boyle* [1994] 2 I.R. 221.

[66] *Georgiou v. United Kingdom* [2001] S.T.C. 80.

[67] [1960] I.R. 239; *infra*, p.784.

[68] *Id.* at p.263.

[69] See *infra*, p.784 on various aspects of professional discipline.

[70] *Engle v. Netherlands*, 1 E.H.R.R. 647 (1979).

the High Court to have continued breach of the Act in question enjoined.[71] Furthermore, there is what is known as the relator procedure whereby persons, who are suffering a particular loss as a result of another committing a public wrong, can request the Attorney to lend his name to an action for the commission of the offence to be enjoined.[72] In *Attorney General v. Paperlink Ltd.*,[73] where the Attorney sought an injunction restraining the defendant from contravening the Post Office's statutory monopoly of carrying the mails, it was contended that, because breach of the monopoly was an offence under the Post Office Act 1908, the only mode of recourse that the Constitution permits against those in breach of it is to prosecute them on a criminal charge. Costello J. rejected this argument because the relevant section of that Act provided for several penalties for its breach, one being a prosecution where the maximum fine was £5 and the other was forfeiture of £100 for every week in which the breach occurs. Accordingly, it was held, since the exclusive sanction under the Act was not prosecution, "the defendants cannot complain that it is unjust that the issues in dispute between them and the Minister should be tried in a civil court where the onus of proof is different to that in a criminal court. (Consequently i)f the civil remedy (of forfeiture) is ineffective then there can be no objection to the Attorney General exercising in the public interest his right to apply to stop statutory breaches by means of a High Court injunction. …"[74] It remains to be seen whether the outcome would be the same if the only sanction for breaching the Act was prosecution on a criminal charge.

In *Attorney General (ex rel. Society for the Protection of Unborn Children Ireland Ltd.) v. Open Counselling Ltd.*,[75] where the plaintiffs sought *inter alia* an injunction against the defendants for counselling pregnant women with regard to abortion facilities in Britain, Hamilton P. indicated that an injunction of this nature would be given in a clear case of the criminal law being broken. However, because he was not entirely convinced that a jury would convict the defendants of conspiracy to corrupt public morals, he declined to declare that their conduct was a crime and, in consequence, enjoin that conduct. Since the central issue in that offence involves public morals or standards, which are to be determined by a jury and not by a judge, the relator was refused a declaration and an injunction. Hamilton P. was "not satisfied that there was no risk in [his] treating conduct as criminal when a jury might consider it otherwise."[76] In both the *Paperlink* and the *SPUC* cases the defendants admitted all the factual

---

[71] *E.g., Attorney General (O'Duffy) v. Appleton* [1907] 1 I.R. 252.
[72] See generally, A. Collins & J. O'Reilly, *Civil Proceedings and the State in Ireland* (2nd ed., 2003), Chap.7.
[73] [1984] I.L.R.M. 373.
[74] *Id.* at p.392.
[75] [1988] I.R. 593.
[76] *Id.* at p.615.

allegations made against them; perhaps where the essential facts are in dispute the issue can only be resolved by way of a trial with a jury.

MINOR OFFENCES

Traditionally, what were described as "petty offences" were dealt with rapidly, in the form of "bench trials" by magistrates.[77] All other offences, be they either felonies or misdemeanours, were tried on indictment with a jury. This distinction between minor and serious offences is given constitutional status in Article 38.3 of the Constitution, which envisages criminal trials before a jury but an exception is made from this principle in respect of "minor offences," which "may be tried by courts of summary jurisdiction";[78] the Special Criminal Court[79] and military tribunals[80] are dealt with separately. There is a somewhat comparable provision in the Australian Constitution[81] and United States constitutional jurisprudence also maintains this distinction.[82]

If the charge is of a minor offence, the defendant cannot insist on having a jury trial on indictment in the Circuit Court or in the Central Criminal Court. Instead, the trial can take place in the District Court, a court of summary jurisdiction, where the matter is disposed of rapidly by a District Judge sitting alone. As was explained earlier,[83] the District Judges are the successors of the old magistrates and are empowered to try persons in respect of selected statutory offences. Summary trials were described by Gannon J. as follows:

> "A summary trial is a trial which could be undertaken with some degree of expedition and informality without departing from the principles of justice. The purpose of summary procedures for minor offences is to ensure that such offences are charged and tried as soon as reasonably possible after their alleged commission so that the recollection of witnesses may still be reasonably clear, that the attendance of witnesses and presentation of evidence may be procured and presented without great difficulty or complexity, and that there should be minimal delay in the disposal of the work-load of minor offences."[84]

---

[77] See generally, W. Blackstone, *Commentaries on the Laws of England* (1769), vol.4, Chap.20.

[78] Art. 38.2 and 5.

[79] Art. 38.3; *infra*, p.850.

[80] Art. 38.4; *infra*, p.482.

[81] S. 80; *cf. Kingswell v. The Queen*, 159 C.L.R. 264 (1985) and *Cheng v. The Queen*, 203 C.L.R. 248 (2000).

[82] *Blanton v. City of North Las Vegas*, 489 U.S. 538 (1989).

[83] *Supra*, p.142.

[84] *Clune v. DPP* [1981] I.L.R.M. 17 at 20.

"Minor"

The classification of an offence as minor for these purposes does not turn on how it is characterised in the Act in question; even though the Act may render the offence triable in the District Court, if the offence truly falls into the non-minor category that court is not constitutionally permitted to try it summarily and without a jury, at least where the accused objects. What determines the character of the offence in this context is the moral quality of the act in question and the severity of the penalty to be imposed but, with regard to these, there are no definite criteria. A degree of discretion is permitted to the Oireachtas in this respect and it is only where the offence undoubtedly cannot be regarded as a minor one that, notwithstanding its summary designation, it cannot be tried without a jury if the accused so insists. As Geoghegan J. stated in *People v. Dougan*, "[a]n enactment that provided for the summary trial of an offence which can legitimately be argued to be minor but which some might equally legitimately regard as non-minor would not ... be declared void having regard to the Constitution. It would be only if on any reasonable view the offence was non-minor that the courts would declare the enactment to be unconstitutional."[85]

On the other hand, an offence may indeed be a minor one but the legislation in question may nevertheless provide that it shall be tried on indictment and before a jury. It is permissible for the Oireachtas to provide for jury trial of offences that, under the Constitution, need not be tried in this way. Where an accused pleads guilty, then it would seem that it is constitutionally permissible to dispose of the entire matter in the District Court. In one instance Walsh J. observed that "there is no constitutional difficulty in giving the District Court power to pass sentences of any duration upon a person who pleads guilty to an offence which is by law within the jurisdiction of the District Court. Indeed, it appears to me that there is no constitutional difficulty in giving the District Court power to deal with every criminal offence upon a plea of guilty."[86]

Where the legislation in question provides for a summary trial and the accused is prosecuted in the District Court, the judge is obliged to proceed with the trial unless he is prohibited from doing so by order of the High Court.[87] He may not even state a case to that court as to whether he is prohibited by the Constitution from holding the trial, unless the offence in question was created prior to 1937.[88] But he may adjourn the trial to enable the accused to challenge the process in the High Court.

Where, having decided that the offence is a minor one, the judge embarks on the trial but then, when sentencing arises, concludes that it cannot be a

---

[85] [1996] 1 I.R. 544 at p.554.
[86] *State (Sheerin) v. Kennedy* [1966] I.R. 379 at at p.393.
[87] *Colman v. Pinewood Developments Ltd* [1994] 3 I.R. 360.
[88] *People v. Dougan* [1996] 1 I.R. 544.

minor offence in view of the sentence to be imposed, he cannot then abandon the trial so that the accused can be charged on indictment. That occurred in *Feeney v. Clifford*,[89] where when it came to sentencing, the judge was informed that the defendant was in custody with seventeen months remaining of his sentence to serve. Because the judge was of the view that the charges before him warranted a sentence of two years, he abandoned the trial so that the accused could be tried on indictment. This was held by the Supreme Court not to be permissible because, once the guilty plea was entered, there could be no going back on the conviction; the judge "cannot hold the plea in some form of forensic limbo, until he has heard the evidence material to penalty."[90]

Nature of the Wrong

Henchy J. has observed that there are "certain offences (random examples of which are treason, genocide, murder, rape) which, because of the moral heinousness or the grave social evil inherent in them, can never be accounted minor no matter what penalty is attached to them …"[91] Apart from this principle, there is little judicial guidance as to what intrinsic features of the wrong distinguish a non-minor crime. The courts have taken the position that if a particular offence would normally fall into the minor category, but in a particular instance is committed in an exceptionally reprehensible manner, the unusual circumstances of its commission do not take it out of the minor category. As Walsh J. stated when dealing with the offence of drunken driving, "(t)he moral aspect of an offence can only be judged or stated in relation to the minimum legal requirements necessary to establish that offence in law …".[92] Presumably because of the moral opprobrium traditionally attached to them, crimes such as kidnapping and arson would be regarded as non-minor offences. But what of manslaughter and dangerous driving causing death? This raises the question of the criteria for determining whether a particular category of offence is regarded by the entire community as a serious wrong. The most reliable indicator is the penalties that attach to that offence. In all the leading cases on the minor/non-minor offence distinction, it has been stressed that the principal criterion for determining which side of the line a particular offence falls is the penalty.

Severity of the Penalty

In *Melling v. O'Mathghamhna*[93] Kingsmill Moore J. reasoned that, since one

---

[89] [1989] I.R. 668.

[90] *Id.* at p.679.

[91] *State (Rollinson) v. Kelly* [1984] I.R. 248 at p.260.

[92] *Conroy v. Attorney General* [1965] I.R. 411 at p.435.

[93] [1962] I.R. 1.

of the main objects of Article 38 is to protect jury trial and individuals have traditionally regarded the jury as a guarantee against executive abuses, the question of what is a minor offence ought to be approached from this perspective; that "[r]egarded from the point of view of the citizen offender the difference between a minor offence and a major offence depends chiefly on the punishment which is meted out to the convicted criminal. It is this which stamps an offence as serious or not serious in his eyes."[94] These views were endorsed by Ó Dálaigh J. in the same case and by many other judges subsequently. But there has been some divergence of opinion about how severe a particular penalty must be in order to bring the crime into the non-minor category.

Loss of Liberty: A criterion of severity, regarding imprisonment, is what customarily has been the maximum sentence that would be imposed if convicted in summary proceedings, which is twelve months imprisonment.[95] But there has been no determination to date that twelve months is the benchmark, although there are *dicta* that a shorter sentence than that signifies a minor offence and offences with a six months maximum have consistently been treated as minor. Where an accused is being sentenced in the District Court for an indictable offence which is triable summarily, the maximum penalty is 12 months imprisonment; where he is sentenced to consecutive periods of imprisonment in respect of two or more offences, the aggregate period to be served cannot exceed two years,[96] which is a form of legislative endorsement of a 12 months maximum as being the criterion. In *Mallon v. Minister for Agriculture*,[97] the State did not appeal the finding by Costello P. that a sentence of two years imprisonment took the offence outside of the non-minor category, a conclusion emphatically endorsed by the Supreme Court. And it was held in *Re Haughey*[98] that an indefinite period of imprisonment also takes the offence out of this category.

Detention of juveniles is treated differently. It was held in *J. v. Delap*[99] that a power to order that juveniles be detained in a reformatory did not take the offence in question out of the minor category. There the applicant, who was under seventeen years of age, was convicted in the District Court of malicious damage and, under the Children Act 1908, the judge ordered that he be detained for three years in a certified industrial training school maintained by the Department of Education, the Trinity House School. Because that school

[94] *Id.* at p.34.
[95] *Kingswell v. The Queen*, 159 C.L.R. 264 (1985).
[96] Criminal Justice Act 1951, s.5 as amended; upheld in *Meagher v. O'Leary* [1998] 1 I.L.R.M. 211.
[97] [1996] 1 I.R. 517.
[98] [1971] I.R. 217.
[99] [1989] I.R. 167.

was staffed by trained teachers and social workers, and had no connection with the prison service or the Department of Justice, Barr J. held that detention there was not equivalent to being imprisoned. Further the period of detention was "in the main related to the function of the school as a place of instruction and correction," rather than the "gravity of the offence which gave rise to it and the character of the convict."[100]

Monetary Deprivations: There is no clear judicial guidance about how large a fine must be in order to take the offence outside the non-minor category. In the past, a fine equivalent to €2,000 for smuggling was held to render the offence a minor one,[101] but a fine equivalent to €130,000 for large-scale illegal fishing was held to render the offence non-minor.[102] No criteria have been endorsed as indicative of where the line may be drawn, except perhaps the present day equivalent of what in 1937 was generally regarded as being the maximum fine for summary offences. Possible criteria include the District Court's jurisdiction to award damages in civil cases[103] or the average annual industrial wage.

Range of Possible Penalties: The offence may be one in respect of which there is no fixed penalty but where the Act in question lays down a range of penalties from which the judge is to select the appropriate sanction in the light of the circumstances of the case. If, as often occurs, the accused has been tried, convicted and sentenced, should not the category of the offence turn on the sentence that the District Judge decided to impose? This question has not been answered authoritatively. In *Haughey, Re*[104] it was said by Ó Dálaigh C.J. that the test relates not to the penalty imposed but to the penalty authorised by law. But the penalty provided for in that case was not of the kind just described – the Act which was considered there authorised imprisonment for an indefinite period and fine without any prescribed maximum or minimum whatsoever. Similarly in the *Rollinson* case,[105] the Act in question did not lay down a range of penalties: it provided for a fixed £500 penalty and there was another statute giving the judge a discretion to mitigate that amount to not less than £125. Henchy J. was of the view that the "true position" is that the maximum penalty is £500 and the minimum is £125;[106] O'Higgins C.J. disagreed, saying that "it is the penalty prescribed by the legislation which must be considered."[107] Because the maximum penalty there did not take the

---

[100] *Id.* at p.170.
[101] *Melling v. O'Mathghamhna* [1962] I.R. 1.
[102] *Kostan v. Ireland* [1978] I.L.R.M. 12.
[103] Up to €20,000: Courts and Court Officers Act 2002, s.13.
[104] [1971] I.R. 217.
[105] *State (Rollinson) v. Kelly* [1984] I.R. 248.
[106] *Id.* at p.261.
[107] *Id.* at p.257.

offence out of the minor category, it was not necessary to answer the question posed above.

Nevertheless, Griffin J. expressed the view that the test is the sentence which was passed: "the determining factor in deciding whether an offence is a minor offence should be the penalty imposed and not the maximum penalty which might have been imposed."[108] But this test was rejected by Hederman J., referring to the *Haughey* case where it was decided that "(t)he question was not what penalty the offence might attract before a jury but what penalty it might attract before a non-jury court," and as having "rejected the test of the penalty actually imposed."[109] Hederman J. found that the test is "the sentence that the offence can attract before the tribunal that does in fact try (the case)."[110] O'Higgins C.J. and McCarthy J. declined to express any view on this question. While he favoured the actual penalty test, Henchy J. would not commit himself on the question, remarking that "the test ... would seem normally to depend on the effective penalty validly imposed," but then adding that "the court of trial cannot convert a major offence into a minor one merely by imposing a penalty appropriate to a minor offence."[111]

Secondary Penalties: The question of what has been termed "secondary" penalties also has to be considered. For instance, several driving offences carry the penalty of imprisonment or a fine and, in addition, the offender may also be banned from driving for a prescribed period; several offences involving licensed establishments (such as public houses, betting shops and some restaurants) carry not alone the usual penalties but the licence may be endorsed and even forfeited; persons convicted of fraud and related offences are disqualified from acting as company auditors and may even be prohibited by the court from taking part in the management of any company. In *Conroy v. Attorney General*,[112] which concerned drunken driving, the Supreme Court held that what matters is the "primary punishment" of imprisonment or fine, or both; that resulting disqualification from driving and the like were "unfortunate consequences (which) are too remote in character to be taken into account in weighing the seriousness of an offence. ..."[113]

The secondary sanction in the *Rollinson* case was the possible review and withdrawal of the convicted person's bookmaker's licence. Henchy J. held that this sanction could never have applied in the circumstances of the case; O'Higgins C.J. and McCarthy J. held that possible review of the certificate "was too remote a consideration."[114] These views nevertheless suggest that

---

[108] *Id.* at p.263.
[109] *Id.* at p.266, referring to [1971] I.R. 247 at 248.
[110] *Id.* at p.266
[111] *Id.* at p.260.
[112] [1965] I.R. 411.
[113] *Id.* at p.441. See also *State (Pheasantry) v. Donnelly* [1982] I.L.R.M. 512.
[114] [1984] I.R. 257 at 260–261, and 267.

the secondary sanction is not an irrelevant consideration; that where such a sanction was imposed, or will or most likely will be imposed, account should be taken of it in determining the gravity of the offence. None of the cases so far have considered the secondary sanctions of dismissal from a job or disbarment from practising a profession that almost certainly would follow some convictions.

But it was held by Hamilton P. in *Cullen v. Attorney General*[115] that a power to award an unlimited amount of compensation, in addition to a fine not exceeding €100 or imprisonment for up to six months, was part of the penalty and, accordingly, was unconstitutional. There persons convicted of a road traffic offence could be ordered, in addition to the fine or imprisonment, to pay the injured party the equivalent to the amount of damages he would be entitled to if he had sued the accused for compensation. *Conroy* was distinguished because, in this instance, the provision purported to increase the penalty to be imposed to a sum not quantifiable until the trial had concluded.

Forfeiture: A penalty that is imposed in respect of some offences is forfeiture of property – for instance, unlawfully held drugs or firearms, unlawfully imported goods or stolen goods. *Kostan v. Ireland*,[116] concerned an offence under the Fisheries Acts and in respect of which the penalty imposed was forfeiture of fish and fishing gear, in that instance to the value of £102,040. McWilliam J. expressed no reservations about concluding that the offence fell outside of the minor category when it carried such a severe punishment. But in *O'Sullivan v. Hartnett*,[117] where the accused was convicted of being in possession of 900 unlawfully captured salmon and where the penalty included forfeiture of the catch, McWilliam J. rejected the contention that the offence was a non-minor one on the grounds that, since the accused was never lawfully in the possession of the fish, their forfeiture was not in reality a penalty. In the Supreme Court, however, it was held that the offence was a non-minor one because the potential fines that could have been levied amounted to around £10,000, the accused would be deprived of a vast quantity of valuable fish and, moreover, the accused could have received a sentence of imprisonment of up to six months.

Where, however, what will or may be forfeited are things that are "inherently designed for the commission of a criminal offence," it was held by Murphy J. in *Cartmill v. Ireland*,[118] that this does not take an otherwise minor offence out of that category. There the plaintiff was about to be prosecuted for operating illegal slot machines, contrary to the Gaming and Lotteries Act 1956. The primary penalty was a fine of no more than £100 or up to three months

---

[115] [1979] I.R. 394.
[116] [1978] I.L.R.M. 12.
[117] [1983] I.L.R.M. 79.
[118] [1987] I.R. 192.

imprisonment, with the possibility of losing a gaming licence. Additionally, any gaming instrument used in committing the offence could be forfeited and it was accepted that the equipment involved here had a very considerable value. Offences of the type involved here could only be prosecuted summarily. In refusing to enjoin the prosecution, it was said that there can be "good executive and administrative reasons for depriving a citizen of the right to use equipment or to exercise functions which are themselves valid and proper because [he] has displayed an incapacity or unwillingness to use the equipment or to discharge the functions in a proper manner."[119]

Where the Fine is Not Paid: A question which arises in cases where the penalty is a fine is how relevant is the sanction for non-payment of that fine. In the *Rollinson* case Henchy J. referred to the fact that under section 76 of the Courts of Justice Act 1936, persons who do not pay a revenue penalty can be imprisoned for up to six months but the judge did not comment on its significance in weighing the seriousness of an offence. On several occasions it has been held that a sentence of six months imprisonment for not paying a fine does not put an offence into the non-minor category. In the *Melling* case, the two dissenting judges held that the revenue offence in question was a non-minor one because persons who did not pay the appropriate penalties could be imprisoned for up to nine months.

Ability to Pay the Fine: Another question is the accused's ability to pay the fine or penalty. Where the judge can choose from a range of fines, almost invariably account will be taken of the convicted person's financial circumstances. Where the penalty is a fixed one, Ó Dálaigh J. stated in the *Melling* case that "regard has to be had to the burden which a fine of a particular amount would impose upon the ordinary or average citizen, with, if anything, ... a leaning in the direction of people of humbler circumstances. ..."[120]

Charged With Many Minor Offences: The fact that the accused was charged with a large number of offences, each of which individually is a minor offence, does not transform them into non-minor offences for these purposes. As Hederman J. stated in the *Rollinson* case, where the accused had been convicted on 56 charges and was fined a total of £6,750, "(t)he fact that when all these offences are added together the total amount of the penalties is a considerable amount of money which, if it were the penalty imposed for one of these convictions, would be sufficient to carry it out of the minor category does not ... change the essential character of each of the offences whose combined penalties reach such a sum. Each offence must be regarded as a separate

---

[119] *Id.* at p.199.
[120] [1962] I.R. 43.

offence."[121] However, because the point was not argued, Henchy J. declined to express a view on whether it was constitutionally permissible to enter such a large number of convictions for separate minor offences at the one time.[122] In one instance, it was conceded by the State that it would be an abuse to multiply charges in respect of substantially the same circumstances in the expectation or hope that the judge would impose consecutive sentences.[123]

Pre-1937 Public Opinion: If the offence existed before 1937 another matter that used to be considered was the state of law and public opinion when the offence was created and when the Constitution was adopted.[124] This may be of some relevance when considering the nature of the wrong, although ascertaining the public opinion of sixty-five years or more ago presents considerable practical difficulties. In any event, this criterion has no particular bearing on considering the penalty. In the *Rollinson* case McCarthy J. stressed that the time which matters is *"the time the relevant convictions were recorded,"*[125] and Henchy and Griffin JJ. observed that the state of the law and public opinion when the Act was enacted or when the Constitution was adopted have no particular relevance to the question.[126]

PROSECUTION

Prosecution is the formal process of bringing criminal charges against an individual or body and taking the essential steps necessary to ensure a conviction.[127] According to Article 30.3 of the Constitution, "[a]ll crimes and offences prosecuted in any court ... other than a court of summary jurisdiction shall be prosecuted in the name of the People and at the suit of the Attorney General or some other person authorised in accordance with law to act for that purpose." While this clause does not preclude the possibility of private prosecutions, it is clear from its very terms that it is for the Oireachtas to decide who shall prosecute in respect of indictable offences.

Since the Prosecution of Offences Act 1974 was enacted, most indictable offences have been prosecuted by the Director of Public Prosecutions (DPP), an independent civil servant who took over most of the Attorney General's functions in relation to prosecutions. There remain some offences that cannot be prosecuted without the Attorney's or the Director's consent. Many statutes

---

[121] [1984] I.R. 267. See also *State (Wilson) v. Neilan* [1985] I.R. 89.
[122] *Id.* at p.261.
[123] *Meagher v. O'Leary* [1998] 4 I.R. 33.
[124] *Conroy v. Attorney General* [1965] I.R. 411.
[125] [1984] I.R. 267, emphasis in the original.
[126] *Id.* at pp.260 and 263.
[127] See generally, *Walsh*, Chap.12.

that create summary offences designate some other public body as the prosecuting authority for those offences, for instance, a particular Minister or a local authority, or the agency or official with overall responsibility for the offending conduct, such as the Competition Authority, the National Authority for Occupational Health and Safety and the Director of Corporate Enforcement.

There is no legal obligation on the Director to prosecute every offence brought to his attention, not even where there appears to be sufficient evidence to obtain a conviction. To date, the courts have never ordered him to prosecute in any particular instance. Further it is entirely up to him to decide what a person should be charged with and whether he should be indicted or prosecuted summarily.[128] He also can put an end to a trial by entering a *nolle prosequi*. But doing this does not provide complete protection against the person being re-charged and tried,[129] although in particular circumstances that may be impermissible, as an abuse of the process.[130]

Challenging the Director's Decisions

It is only in the most exceptional circumstances that the courts will review the Director of Public Prosecutions' decision whether or not to prosecute an indictable offence or whether or not to take over a privately initiated prosecution.[131] However, adoption by the Director of a general policy not to prosecute certain offences may very well be unlawful. The governing principles were stated by Finlay C.J. in *State (McCormack) v. Curran*[132] as follows: "In regard to the DPP I reject the submission that he has only got a discretion as to whether to prosecute or not to prosecute in any particular case related exclusively to the probative value of the evidence laid before him ... [T]here are many other factors which may be appropriate and proper for him to take into consideration. ... If, of course, it can be demonstrated that he reached a decision *mala fide* or influenced by an improper motive or improper policy then his decision would be reviewable by a court."[133] In that case the court refused to interfere with the Director's decision not to bring a particular prosecution, under the Criminal Law (Jurisdiction) Act 1976, in respect of offences allegedly committed in Northern Ireland.

These principles were applied by the Supreme Court in *H. v. Director of Public Prosecutions*,[134] where the Director had declined to prosecute the

---

[128] *K.M. v. DPP* [1994] 1 I.R. 514.
[129] *Kelly v. DPP* [1996] 2 I.R. 596.
[130] *State (O'Callaghan) v. O'Huadhaigh* [1977] I.R. 42.
[131] *State (Ennis) v. Farrell* [1966] I.R. 107.
[132] [1987] I.L.R.M. 225.
[133] *Id.* at p.237.
[134] [1994] 2 I.R. 589.

applicant's husband for alleged sexual offences against their son. She contended that the real reason he was not prosecuted was because he was a member of the Garda Síochána. She sought an order that she be supplied with copies of statements taken by the Gardaí and other relevant documentation, so that she could commence a private prosecution. But it was held that there was no evidence before the court of the Director's *mala fides* or other impropriety and, indeed, several aspects of the case made it a "par excellence example" of one that should not result in a prosecution. For instance, there had been a long history of family strife, the case was an old one and it was most unlikely that the son who was in England would give evidence. Because the Director's discretion is not subject to the full rigours of judicial review, he was held not to be under an obligation to give reasons even where his decision is being challenged in High Court proceedings.[135] O'Flaherty J. added that, in general, reasons should never be furnished because, if they were given in some cases, persons would seek reasons in many other cases.[136] But where the Director informs a person that he will not be prosecuted but subsequently, without further evidence coming to light, he initiates a prosecution, he may in the circumstances be restrained from doing so.[137]

The Director has been held to have an equally wide discretion about sending cases for trial before the non-jury Special Criminal Court,[138] although exempting him from having to give any reason for these decisions was condemned by the UN Committee on Human Rights.[139]

In England the courts have set aside a decision of the Director there not to prosecute, because it flew in the face of the policy contained in the Code for Crown prosecutions.[140] And in a case where a prisoner was killed and the prison officers allegedly responsible were not prosecuted, it was held that the fundamental right to life of all persons required the Director there to explain his decision, unless there were compelling grounds to the contrary.[141] At a coroner's inquest, where those officers had been legally represented, the jury returned a unanimous verdict of unlawful killing. More recently, the House of Lords closely scrutinised the Director's decision to prosecute certain terrorist offences, ultimately upholding his decision.[142]

---

[135] Applied in *e.g. Landers v. Garda Síochána Complaints Board* [1997] 3 I.R. 347 and in *DPP v. Brennan* [1998] 4 I.R. 67.

[136] [1994] 2 I.R. 589 at p.603.

[137] *Eviston v. DPP* [2002] 3 I.R. 260.

[138] *Kavanagh v. Government of Ireland* [1996] 1 I.R. 321.

[139] *Kavanagh v. Ireland*, Decision of April 4, 2001.

[140] *R.(C.) v. DPP* [1995] 1 Cr. App. R. 136.

[141] *R. (Manning) v. DPP* [2001] Q.B. 330.

[142] *R. (Kebilene) v. DPP* [2000] 2 A.C. 326.

Private Prosecutions

Before independence anybody could bring a prosecution in respect of every offence. One of the principal changes in legal administration introduced in 1924 was the abolition of private prosecutions for indictable offences. According to section 9(1) of the Criminal Justice (Administration) Act 1924, "[a]ll criminal charges prosecuted upon indictment in any court shall be prosecuted at the suit of the Attorney General (or the Director of Public Prosecutions)." Thus, as regards offences that are triable on indictment, which means most serious offences, private individuals cannot bring a prosecution to conclusion; the State possesses a monopoly of the right to prosecute. But private individuals were permitted to initiate prosecutions for indictable offences up to the receiving of information and to the very point of return for trial by a District Judge, but at that stage the prosecution concluded unless it was taken over by the DPP.[143] Without the Director's intervention, the prosecution could go no further.

Private individuals may prosecute most summary offences as "common informers," *i.e.* as members of the public who are capable of giving information in respect of the commission of an offence. Indeed, when members of the Garda Síochána prosecute summary offences, they do so as common informers. Power to prosecute certain summary offences is reserved to various named Ministers, bodies or individuals, and to the DPP. A person seeking to commence a prosecution for criminal libel must get the prior authorisation of the High Court.[144]

Preserving and Disclosing Evidence

In the course of their investigating alleged crimes, the Gardaí have a duty to preserve any evidence they obtain that may be favourable to any accused person. Depending on the circumstances, failure to do this may result in a prosecution being stayed by the trial judge or being enjoined by the High Court.[145]

Where a person is being prosecuted, the Director (or other prosecuting authority) is obliged to furnish the defence not alone with full details of the evidence the prosecution will call but with details of all other evidence he or the Gardaí possess relevant to the case, especially any material that might assist the defence. Failure to do so may result in the trial being stayed or in a conviction being set aside.[146] Where, however, the accused is being tried

---

[143] *State (Ennis) v. Farrell* [1996] I.R. 107.

[144] *E.g., Hilliard v. Penfield Enterprises Ltd* [1990] 1 I.R. 138.

[145] *E.g., Dunne v. DPP* [2002] 2 I.R. 305.

[146] *People v. Meleady* [1995] 2 I.R. 517.

summarily rather than on indictment, the same extent of disclosure is not required.[147] Preservation and disclosure of evidence favourable to the defence is part of the "equality of arms" guaranteed by Article 6.1 of the European Convention.[148]

RETURN FOR TRIAL

Minor offences are usually tried by way of a summons to appear before the District Court.[149] Except where the accused is pleading guilty, offences other than minor offences must be tried on indictment before a jury. An indictment is the formal charge, stating what offence or offences the accused is being charged with, together with some particulars indicating the basis for the accusation;[150] the appendix to the Criminal Justice (Administration) Act 1924, contains forms of indictment for many of the serious offences.

Prior to its being abolished in 1999, where a person was being charged with an indictable offence, there had first to take place what was called a "preliminary examination" in the District Court.[151] This procedure was described by Finlay C.J. as "a judicial exercise of considerable importance in a criminal matter to the accused person as well as to the public. It [was] the only method by which, in the absence of a waiver of it by an accused person fully informed and capable of waiving it, a person [could] be put on indictment in any court other than the Special Criminal Court."[152] The purpose of this procedure was to ensure that there was a good *prima facie* case against the accused before he could be tried and also to enable him to know what evidence would be brought in support of the prosecution. Gannon J. explained the function of this procedure as the:

> "investigation in open court before the public on notice to, and in the presence of, the accused (upon his denial of the criminal offence with which he has been charged) of the nature and cogency of the evidence intended to be proffered in support of the charge, and it is effected by an examination of the record of that evidence as previously furnished to the accused. So much of the evidence as may be taken orally before such examination must be sworn and recorded in the form of a deposition before completion of the investigation. Following his consideration of the completed record, the District Justice is required to take the steps

---

[147] *DPP v. Doyle* [1994] 2 I.R. 286.
[148] *I.L.J. v. United Kingdom*, 33 E.H.R.R. 11 (2000).
[149] See generally, *Walsh*, Chap.13.
[150] See generally, *Walsh*, Chap.15.
[151] See generally, E. Ryan & P. Magee, *The Irish Criminal Process* (1983), Chap.9.
[152] *O'C. v. Judges of the Dublin Metropolitan District Court* [1994] 3 I.R. 246 at p.251.

prescribed in section 8 of the Act of 1967 according to whatever opinion may be reached by him. By sub-s. 5 of section 8, the District Justice is obliged to direct the discharge of the accused from either custody or his recognizance on bail to answer the charge, if the District Justice does not form an opinion that there is sufficient case to put the accused on trial."[153]

Where at the conclusion of this examination the District Judge declined to return the accused for trial, his decision could not be overridden by the Attorney General or Director of Public Prosecutions; endeavouring to do so was held by the Supreme Court to contravene the separation of powers between the executive and the judicial organs of the State,[154] reversing an earlier ruling to the contrary.[155] The power of the executive, where it was found that an accused was unfit to plead, without any order of the court to thereupon remove him and place him in a mental institution, was also held to contravene the separation of powers.[156] On several occasions it was held that there is no constitutional right to a preliminary examination, which did not exist for persons being charged before the Special Criminal Court.[157]

Preliminary examinations were replaced in the Criminal Justice Act 1999, by the procedure contained in Part 1A (sections 4A–4Q) of the Criminal Procedure Act 1967, as amended.[158] Where an accused is now charged before the District Court, he cannot be sent forward for trial without the prosecutor's consent and he must be sent for trial unless the case is being tried summarily, he is unfit to plead or he is pleading guilty under section 13 of that Act. At any time thereafter, however, he may apply to the trial court to dismiss one or more of the charges, which it will do if there is "not a sufficient case to put [him] on trial"; this decision may be appealed by the prosecution. After an accused has been sent forward, specified documents regarding the charges and the evidence must be served on him prior to being tried. If the trial court so directs, sworn depositions may be taken in the District Court, which may be subject to cross-examination and to re-examination. Provision is made for excluding the public from any of these proceedings before the District Court and for restricting their reporting.

---

[153] *Costello v. DPP* [1984] I.R. 436 at p.451. *Cf. Hynes v. The Queen*, 206 D.L.R. 4th 483 (2001).
[154] *Ibid.*
[155] *State (Shanahan) v. Attorney General* [1964] I.R. 239.
[156] *State (C.) v. Minister for Justice* [1967] I.R. 147.
[157] *Sloan v. Special Criminal Court* [1993] 3 I.R. 528.
[158] See generally, *Walsh*, Chap.14.

Venue

Venue concerns the place where the trial is to occur. Provisions regarding venue are contained in the constitutions of some federal states.[159] The jurisdiction of the High Court derives primarily from the Constitution; according to Article 34.3.1. it has "full original jurisdiction in and power to determine all matters and questions whether of law or fact. ..." A question that therefore arises is whether it is competent for the Oireachtas to provide that trials for certain categories of indictable offences, or indeed all indictable offences, must take place in the Circuit Court and cannot take place in the High Court. The argument against granting the Circuit Court exclusive jurisdiction is that the above clause should be given its literal meaning – that "full original jurisdiction" includes jurisdiction to try charges of indictable offences. The Supreme Court has held that, where a constitutional provision has a plain and unambiguous meaning, then it must be interpreted in accordance with that meaning even though that meaning runs against traditional concepts of fair procedure.[160] In 1974, the Supreme Court held that the Oireachtas could not deprive the High Court of its "full original jurisdiction" in Admiralty cases by stipulating that certain kinds of claims cannot be brought before it.[161] As was explained earlier, however, in *Tormey v. Attorney General*,[162] the Supreme Court held that, in the circumstances, the literal meaning of Article 34.3.1 must give way to other constitutional provisions and to practical considerations and, therefore, the Oireachtas may give the Circuit Court exclusive jurisdiction to try indictable offences and thereby deprive the High Court of its erstwhile jurisdiction to try them.

The Courts Acts require an alleged offence to have a specified connection with a particular district or circuit before it can be the subject of a trial in the District Court or in the Circuit Court.[163] Summary offences can be tried only by the judge assigned to the District where the offence is said to have occurred or where the defendant has been arrested or resides. Similarly with indictable offences being tried in the Circuit Court; only the judge of the circuit where the offence is said to have taken place or where the defendant has been arrested or resides can try the case. There are qualifications or exceptions to these rules in respect of a limited category of offences. Once a case is returned for trial to a particular Circuit Court outside Dublin, either the accused or the prosecution can apply to have the trial transferred to the Dublin Circuit Court.[164] Certain

---

[159] *E.g.*, 6th Amendment to the US Constitution, Art.80 of Australian Constitution and Art.101(1) of the German Constitution.

[160] *People v. O'Shea* [1982] I.R. 384; *supra*, p.53.

[161] *R.D. Cox Ltd v. Owners of M.V. Fritz Rabel* (1 Aug. 1974); *supra*, p.147.

[162] [1985] I.R. 289; *supra*, p.148.

[163] Courts (Supplemental Provisions) Act 1961, s.25(3).

[164] Courts and Courts Officers Act 1995, s.32.

very serious offences must be tried in the Central Criminal Court, *i.e.* by the High Court exercising its criminal jurisdiction, *viz.* treason, genocide, murder, piracy, rape and some offences under the Offences Against the State Act 1939.

INDEPENDENT AND IMPARTIAL TRIBUNAL

Article 6(1) of the European Convention and Article 14(1) of the UN Covenant require that criminal charges be determined by "an independent and impartial tribunal established by law." This means that the tribunal must not be influenced by the executive in making its decisions and, in addition, must be sufficiently independent of the executive so as not to be capable of being influenced by it unduly.[165] A similar principle is contained in the Constitution's scheme of the separation of powers and the Article 35.2 requirement, that "judges shall be independent in the exercise of their judicial functions," also embodies a similar principle. It may be summed up in the maxim *nemo iudex in sua causa, i.e.* that nobody should be judge of their own case. Article 14(1) of the UN Covenant also requires the tribunal to be "competent."

A conviction will be set aside where it is shown that the judge had a pronounced bias against the accused or otherwise lacked impartiality or, indeed, because in the circumstances there was far too great a risk of the judge not being impartial.[166] Where a trial is conducted by the judge in a significantly unfair manner, a conviction will be quashed on the grounds that justice must not only be done but must be seen to be done.[167]

Juries are equally subject to the principle against bias or the distinct likelihood of bias. Thus in *People v. Singer*,[168] the accused's conviction, on a fraud charge, was quashed because the foreman of the jury had been an investor in the company which had been the vehicle for the fraud and, consequently, there was too great a risk that he was not impartial. In *People v. Tobin*,[169] where the accused was convicted of rape and sexual assault, one member of the jury disclosed to the others that she had been sexually abused during her childhood but assured them that this would not cloud her objectivity. Because there was a real possibility that these events might have caused unconscious prejudice, the conviction was quashed, with a direction for a re-trial. The Court of Criminal Appeal observed that a considered and carefully worded direction by the judge to the jury might sufficiently counteract the danger of possible bias and render it unnecessary to discharge the jury in similar circumstances.

---

[165] *E.g., Starrs v. Procurator Fiscal*, 8 B.H.R.C. 1 (1999) (Scotland).
[166] *Sweeney v. Judge Brophy* [1993] 2 I.R. 202; see *infra*, p.488 for civil cases.
[167] *Dineen v. Judge Delap* [1994] 2 I.R. 228.
[168] [1975] I.R. 408.
[169] [2001] 3 I.R. 469.

The particular composition of the Special Criminal Court was challenged in *Eccles v. Ireland*,[170] on the grounds that it contravened this principle. But the Supreme Court held that, where possible, the law establishing the Special Criminal Court should be given a constitutional construction and that the Constitution itself exempted that court from the scope of Article 35.2.

DOUBLE JEOPARDY

The principle against double jeopardy, which is encapsulated in the maxim *nemo bis in idem debet vexari,* means that a person who has been tried in respect of a particular offence shall never be tried again for that offence.[171] This principle is intended to protect individuals from being harassed by spurious prosecutions and also to ensure that prosecutors prepare their cases adequately, in that they are not allowed a second chance to bring any case. This principle is an aspect of the general policy of the law, civil as well as criminal, that once a case is decided its merits shall not again be reopened: *res judicata*/abuse of process. At common law the pleas of *autrefois acquit* (previously acquitted) or *autrefois convict* (previously convicted) are complete answers to an indictment; if the defendant previously was either acquitted or convicted of the charge that is now being brought, the case will not be permitted to go ahead.[172] In order to come within these, the accused must have been in peril or jeopardy of conviction on the previous occasion, the previous verdict must have been final and, thirdly, the second indictment must be for the same offence or for an offence of which the accused might have been found guilty at the previous trial, or be based on identical facts.

Double jeopardy is prohibited by the Fifth Amendment to the United States Constitution: "nor shall any person be subject for the same offence to be twice put in jeopardy ...". Article 14(7) of the UN Covenant provides that "[n]o one shall be liable to be tried or punished again for an offence for which he has already been finally convicted or acquitted in accordance with the law and penal procedure'; a similar provision is contained in Article 4(1) of the European Convention's seventh protocol. The Constitution does not contain an equivalent clause and it remain to be determined in what circumstances, and subject to what safeguards, if any, the Oireachtas may derogate from the principle against double jeopardy.[173]

It was held by Finlay P. in *State (O'Callaghan) v. Ó hUadhaigh,*[174] that

---

[170] [1985] I.R. 545; *infra*, p.854.

[171] See generally, M. Freedland, *Double Jeopardy* (1969).

[172] See generally, *Walsh*, p.784 *et seq.* and P. McDermott, *Res Judicata and Double Jeopardy* (1999), Chaps 21–34.

[173] *Cf. State v. Boyle* [2002] L.R.C. 774 (Trinidad & Tobago).

[174] [1977] I.R. 42.

there is a limited constitutional guarantee against double jeopardy. When the applicant was prosecuted on several charges in the Circuit Court, a jury was sworn but, before he was given into their charge and following legal argument, the trial judge struck out most of the charges against him. Whereupon counsel for the DPP entered a *nolle prosequi* on all counts but stated that the accused would be re-arrested and charged again with the same offences. At common law a person who is discharged in consequence of a *nolle prosequi* could not plead *autrefois aquit.* In this case the accused had been remanded in custody for longer than six months, had undergone preliminary examination in the District Court, was returned for trial, the trial had been adjourned on several occasions and was then transferred to Dublin; all of these steps were taken at the instigation of the DPP. By the time the trial came on, the judge found that the accused could be proceeded against on only one count. What the DPP then sought was to revive the entire proceedings from the very beginning – the consequence of which would be to deny the accused of any procedural advantages he had secured in the meantime. On the other hand, the accused had no power to abort a trial and have the proceedings commence again. Because it would be most unfair and in a sense discriminatory, if the DPP could prosecute the accused all over again in these circumstances, Finlay P. held that the court could not re-try that case. To permit a fresh prosecution would be "to create such an extraordinary imbalance between the rights and powers of the prosecution and those of the accused respectively, and to give the Director such a relative independence from the decision of the court in any trial, would be to concur in a position of law which signally failed to import fairness and fair procedure. ..."[175]

On the other hand, it was held in *People v. O'Shea*[176] that, on account of the Constitution's express terms, the prosecution could appeal to the Supreme Court against an acquittal verdict in the Central Criminal Court even though traditionally prosecutors could not appeal against acquittals because that involves a degree of double jeopardy. Article 34.4.3 of the Constitution gives the Supreme Court jurisdiction to hear appeals from "all decisions" of the High Court and, it was held, this provision must be given its literal meaning, which is that the Supreme Court has jurisdiction over appeals – against acquittals as well as against convictions. However, the Oireachtas is free to preclude appeals in cases where the constitutionality of a post-1937 law is not in issue.[177] The appeal in *O'Shea* was against an acquittal at the direction of the trial judge and not an acquittal by the jury having considered the entire evidence. An acquittal that was secured by flagrantly improper means may very well fall within the *autrefois acquit* rule at common law but it is hardly

---

[175] *Id.* at p.54. Compare *Claffey v. DPP* [1993] 3 I.R. 582.
[176] [1982] I.R. 384.
[177] *Supra*, p.155.

protected by whatever implicit right against double jeopardy as exists under the Constitution.

A person who, on being convicted, admits to being guilty of other offences which are taken into account in determining the sentence, cannot later be charged in respect of those offences.[178] Section 17 of the Extradition Act 1965 applies the double jeopardy principle to extradition to countries other than to the United Kingdom and the Channel Islands and section 15 of the Criminal Law (Jurisdiction) Act 1976, has a similar requirement with regard to conviction or acquittal of any offence under the law of Northern Ireland. A significant statutory qualification of the principle is section 5 of the Courts of Justice Act 1928, which permits the Court of Criminal Appeal or, on appeal from it, the Supreme Court to reverse a conviction and to order that the accused be tried again for the same offence. But the ambit of this has been restricted to "when the quashed conviction resulted not from the inadequacy of the prosecution case but from a faulty trial (e.g. misdirection, inadmissible evidence, procedural irregularity) which, but for such fault, might have led to a supportable conviction."[179]

LEGAL REPRESENTATION

Article 6(3)(c) of the European Convention stipulates that an accused is entitled, "to defend himself in person or through legal assistance of his own choosing" and, additionally "if he has not sufficient means to pay for legal assistance, to be given it free when the interests of justice so require." Article 14(3)(d) of the UN Covenant is similarly phrased but adds that the accused must be informed of his right to defend himself or through counsel; sub (b) adds a right to "communicate with counsel of his own choosing" when preparing his defence. One of the rights guaranteed by the Sixth Amendment to the United States Constitution is for an accused to "have the assistance of Counsel for his Defence." Although it is not expressly guaranteed in the Constitution, it has been held that there is an implied constitutional right to obtain legal advice and representation and, in the case of persons who cannot afford to hire the services of a lawyer, to be provided with legal representation at the trial.

It was not until 1836 that accused persons were given the right to be legally represented in their own defence.[180] In circumstances where an accused has hired counsel, it can be unfair for a trial to proceed in the temporary absence

---

[178] Criminal Justice Act 1951, s.8.

[179] *People v. Griffin* [1974] I.R. 416 at p.420. *Cf. People v. Quilligan (No.2)* [1989] I.R. 46.

[180] Prisoners' Counsel Act 1836, 6 & 7 Will. 4, c.114. *Cf.* Langbein, "The Prosecutorial Origins of Defence Counsel in the Eighteenth Century: The Appearance of Solicitors", 58 *Cam. L.J.* 314 (1999).

of counsel. Thus in *O'Callaghan v. Clifford*,[181] where the accused was charged with revenue offences and the principal evidence against him was a certificate signed by a Revenue official, at the outset counsel applied to adjourn the case because the accused had been delayed in attending court and counsel required full instructions before proceeding. An adjournment was refused and the accused was convicted. It was quashed by the Supreme Court on account of the unfairness of the proceedings. While it is principally for the trial judge to determine whether adjournments were warranted, it was held that the circumstances here justified overruling his decision. In *Dawson v. Hamill*,[182] at the end of a one-day trial, the District Judge said he would give judgment on the following day and indicated that it would not be necessary for counsel to attend then. Counsel for the accused did not attend on that day but, before judgment was given, the prosecution were permitted to adduce further evidence and the accused was convicted. Lynch J. quashed the conviction in view of the accused being effectively denied representation but ordered the case to be remitted to be heard by a different District Judge.

When Ireland signed the European Convention in 1951, it entered a reservation in respect of this right of individuals, who cannot afford legal representation in criminal cases, to be provided with representation at the State's expense. Before it was recognised as having a constitutional basis, in 1962 the Oireachtas established a scheme whereby impecunious criminal defendants would be provided with representation at the State's expense, the Criminal Justice (Legal Aid) Act 1962.[183]

In 1976 the Supreme Court ruled in *State (Healy) v. Donoghue*[184] that a right of this nature is also guaranteed by the Constitution where the accused is on risk of losing his liberty or of some other serious penalty; the right is an integral part of trial "in due course of law." This case arose out of the legal aid strike, when solicitors were refusing to act under the legal aid scheme that existed then. The applicants were brought before the Children's Court on a charge, pleaded guilty and were sentenced to imprisonment. They were not legally represented and had not been informed then of their right to apply for legal aid. Some time later they were charged with another offence and were offered legal aid, but in the event no solicitor appeared for them, they pleaded guilty and were sentenced to six months detention. Their convictions were set aside on the grounds that they had not been given the opportunity to obtain legal assistance at the State's expense. According to O'Higgins C.J., procedural fairness under the Constitution, especially when viewed against the European Convention, requires that persons in the accused's position be given free legal aid:

---

[181] [1993] 3 I.R. 603.
[182] [1989] I.R. 275.
[183] See generally, *Walsh*, Chap.11.
[184] [1976] I.R. 325.

"Where a man's liberty is at stake, or where he faces a very severe penalty which may affect his welfare or his livelihood, justice may require more than the application of normal and fair procedures in relation to his trial. Facing, as he does, the power of the State, which is his accuser, the person charged, may be unable to defend himself adequately because of ignorance, lack of education, youth or other incapacity. In such circumstances his plight may require, if justice is to be done, that he should have legal assistance. In such circumstances, if he cannot provide such assistance by reason of lack of means, does justice under the Constitution also require that he be aided in his defence? In my view it does ... If the right to be represented is now an acknowledged right of an accused person, justice requires something more when, because of a lack of means, a person facing a serious criminal charge cannot provide a lawyer for his own defence. In my view the concept of justice under the Constitution, or constitutional justice requires that in such circumstances the person charged must be afforded the opportunity of being represented.

This opportunity must be provided by the State. Only in this way can justice be done, and only by recognising and discharging this duty can the State be said to vindicate the personal rights of the person charged. To hold otherwise would be to tolerate a situation in which the nature and extent of a man's ability to defend himself, when accused, could depend on the nature and extent of his means; that would be to tolerate injustice."[185]

The Chief Justice described the 1962 Act as a measure which implemented the implied constitutional right to legal aid, and he held that the trial judge's function is more than to apply that Act in a perfunctory manner. Once the statutory grounds for getting a legal aid certificate have been established, the judge must not only grant the certificate but should ensure that a qualified accused is informed of the right to apply for a certificate.

Where an undefended accused pleads guilty and it then becomes apparent from the circumstances that the likely sentence will be imprisonment, he must be informed by the judge of his right to legal aid.[186] And where he avails of that right and then decides to change his plea to not guilty, he should be permitted by the judge to do so.[187] When a certificate has been granted, the judge must ensure that the accused is not tried without the benefit of legal aid – unless he chooses to dispense with assistance.[188] Where the Director of Public Prosecutions or the Criminal Assets Bureau obtain an injunction freezing

---

[185] *Id.* at p.350.
[186] *Cahill v. Judge Reilly* [1994] 3 I.R. 547.
[187] *Byrne v. Judge McDonnell* [1997] 1 I.R. 392.
[188] *O'Callaghan v. Judge Clifford* [1993] 3 I.R. 603.

an accused's or defendant's assets, provision is made for varying those orders so that he can pay for legal advice and assistance.[189]

If the accused is able to pay for his legal representation, it would seem that he is entirely free to select a duly qualified solicitor and/or barrister. But where he is reliant on legal aid, he does not have that option and the court has a discretion to designate a particular solicitor, who can then engage the services of counsel of his choice and who is available to act for the accused.[190]

It would appear that, to date, no accused has had his conviction set aside on the grounds that his lawyer had acted incompetently. However, it was accepted by the Court of Criminal Appeal in *DPP v. McDonagh*[191] that, in an appropriate case, seriously negligent legal representation was a good ground of appeal. According to Keane C.J., "exceptionally, where the decision in question was taken either in defiance of or without proper instructions or when all the 'promptings of reason and good sense' pointed the other way, it might be open to an appellate court to set aside the verdict."[192] But the mere fact that counsel made a mistaken decision, or one that in retrospect was mistaken, is rarely a good ground of appeal. Although counsel there had made what appeared to have been the wrong decision, having taken the brief very shortly before the trial was due to start, his error was held to be not sufficiently egregious to have the conviction set aside.

TRIAL IN ABSENTIA

Article 14(3)(d) of the UN Covenant entitles an accused person "to be tried in his presence." There is no similar express guarantee in the European Convention but Article 6 has been held to prohibit some trials *in absentia*.[193] In *O'Callaghan v. Clifford*,[194] where the accused was being tried for failing to deliver a tax return and the prosecution were relying largely on a certificate in order to prove their case, the Supreme Court held that the judge was wrong in permitting the trial to go ahead in the accused's absence. He was represented by counsel, who sought an adjournment so that his client could give evidence disputing the contents of the certificate but that was refused. According to Denham J., in the circumstances "there was an absence of due process in ... proceeding with the trial in the absence of the" accused.[195]

---

[189] *Customs & Excise Commissioners v. Norris* [1991] 2 Q.B. 293 and *Solicitor General v. Panzer* [2001] 1 N.Z.L.R. 224
[190] *State (Royle) v. Kelly* [1974] I.R. 259.
[191] [2001] 3 I.R. 411.
[192] *Id.* at pp.425–426.
[193] *Cf. R. v. Jones* [2002] 2 W.L.R. 524.
[194] [1993] 3 I.R. 603.
[195] *Id.* at p.613.

Speedy Trial

Article 5(3) of the European Convention and Article 9(3) of the UN Covenant stipulate that "[e]veryone arrested or detained ... shall be entitled to trial within a reasonable time or else to release pending trial." Another of the criminal procedure rights guaranteed by the Sixth Amendment to the United States Constitution is the right to a "speedy trial."

Over 250 years ago the Irish Parliament passed an Act entitled "an Act for the more speedy trial of criminals in the county of the city of Dublin, and county of Dublin."[196] Today the speedy trial of summary offences is partly secured by usually having a six months limitation period for making the requisite complaint in respect of those offences.[197] But this principle does not apply to indictable offences and, unlike the position in most continental European countries and in the USA, there are no statutes of limitation for crimes; theoretically, one can be convicted of an indictable offence no matter how long ago the act in question occurred. One of the common law royal prerogatives was *nullum tempus occurrit regi, i.e.* time does not run against the Crown, meaning that a prosecution can be brought for an indictable offence at any time.

Where however there has been undue delay in bringing a prosecution that prejudices the accused's opportunity of a fair trial, the case will not be allowed to proceed.[198] In *State (O'Connell) v. Fawsitt,*[199] the Supreme Court held that there had been undue delay in bringing the accused for trial and that the appropriate remedy, in those circumstances, was an order prohibiting the DPP from proceeding with the prosecution. The applicant was charged in July 1982 and was returned for trial in the Circuit Court but the date for the trial was not fixed until late 1984. Because of confusion the case was adjourned until 1985. In the meantime, the accused had gone to work in England and a key witness for his defence became no longer available. Finlay C.J. endorsed Murphy J.'s formulation of the governing principles in those instances, that "the Constitution guarantees to every citizen that the trial of a person charged with a criminal offence will not be delayed excessively or to express the same proposition in positive terms, that the trial will be heard with reasonable expedition .... The nature of the delay must be considered, as has been already pointed out, having regard to the circumstances of the case."[200] Among the relevant circumstances, according to Murphy J.:

"I[]t is material to consider whether the delay is being measured between

---

[196] 3 Geo. III c. 15 (1729).
[197] Petty Sessions (Ireland) Act 1851, s.10(4). *Cf. DPP v. Logan* [1994] 3 I.R. 254.
[198] *Cf. H.M. Advocate v. R.* [2003] 2 W.L.R. 317.
[199] [1986] I.R. 362.
[200] *Id.,* at p.378.

the period when the charge is first brought and when the trial occurs or whether a retrial is to be conducted in accordance with the directions of an appellate court. It is equally obvious that consideration must be given to the nature of the charge itself. Minor offences can and should be dealt with summarily. Serious charges will take longer to present. Clearly there are many charges which of their nature tend to be complex and involve numerous witnesses and documentation. That charges such as were presented in the *Singer* matter[201] would require considerable time for preparation would be understandable and of necessity acceptable. Again, it would be important to consider whether the accused was detained in custody or not. Another factor, which may be of very considerable importance in many cases, is the attitude of the accused. Not infrequently the accused seeks or acquiesces in an adjournment of his trial either to postpone the day of reckoning or for other reasons. At the end of the day the test will be whether in all the relevant circumstances reasonable expedition was achieved."[202]

A balance must be struck between the State's interest in having offences prosecuted and the individual's right to a fair trial, the outcome depending on the circumstances of each case. Among the factors to be taken into account in striking this balance are "(i) [the length of] the delay in the case; (ii) the reason or reasons for the delay; (iii) the accused's actions in relation to the events in issue; (iv) the accused's assertion of his constitutional rights; (v) actual prejudice to the accused; (vi) pre-trial incarceration of accused; (vii) the length of time of pre-trial anxiety and concern of the accused; (viii) limitations or impairment of defence; (ix) circumstances which may render the case into a special category."[203] In the fifteen years since *O'Connell* was decided, the issue of delay has been before the Court of Criminal Appeal and the Supreme Court on numerous occasions. Many of these have involved allegations of child sexual abuse committed decades prior to the prosecution being commenced. It has been held that there is a higher onus on defendants in these cases to establish that, on account of the lengthy delay, they would not get a fair trial.[204]

---

[201] *Singer (No. 2), Re* (1964) 98 I.L.T.R. 112.

[202] [1986] I.R. 371.

[203] *B. v. DPP* [1997] 3 I.R. 140 at p.195.

[204] *E.g., Ibid* (lapse of 20 years), *J.L. v. DPP* [2000] 3 I.R. 122 (lapse of 21 years), *P. O'C. v. DPP* [2000] 3 I.R. 87 (lapse of 15 years), *J. O'C. v. DPP* [2000] 3 I.R. 478 (lapse of 16 years) and *P. M. v. Malone* [2002] 2 I.R. 560 (lapse of 20 years). See generally, Lewis & Mullins, "Delayed Criminal Prosecutions in Childhood Sexual Abuse: Ensuring a Fair Trial", 115 *L.Q.R.* 265 (1999).

Public Trial

A public trial means that the general public are free to attend the trial.[205] The principal object of requiring trials to be held in public is to ensure that the State cannot persecute its enemies secretly in some kind of Star Chamber. One of the few specific criminal procedure rights expressly mentioned by the Constitution is to a public trial; according to Article 34.1, "[j]ustice … save in such special and limited cases as may be prescribed by law, shall be administered in public." Article 6(1) of the European Convention stipulates that persons are entitled to a "public hearing" of the charges against them and that "[j]udgment shall be pronounced publicly but the press and public may be excluded from all or part of the trial in the interests of morals, public order or national security in a democratic society, where the interests of juveniles or the protection of the private life of the parties so require, or to the extent strictly necessary in the opinion of the court in special circumstances where publicity would prejudice the interests of justice." Article 14(1) of the UN Covenant is in similar terms. Another of the rights guaranteed by the United States Constitution's Sixth Amendment is the right to a "public trial." Related to the question of public trials is that of pre-trial publicity that may be regarded as prejudicing a fair trial and also criticism of how a trial is being conducted by the judge, which touch on the separate constitutional guarantee of freedom of speech and of expression.

The constitutional right to a public trial is not an unqualified one; it can be overridden or curtailed by any statutory provision in "special and limited cases." To date it has not been determined what features a case must possess for it to come within this exception but it is likely that the criteria in the European Convention will provide guidance. Provision is made for *in camera* hearings in cases involving major offences under the Official Secrets Act 1963, and also in cases of incest, rape and certain other sexual offences, but the verdict and any sentence must be given in public.[206] Judges have been given a discretion to exclude members of the public in prosecutions involving evidence of an indecent or obscene nature. However, *bona fide* representatives of the press are permitted to attend at these trials but any reports they publish must ensure that the parties' anonymity is preserved. There also are restrictions on reporting proceedings before the District Court when an accused is being considered for sending forward for trial on indictment and also where depositions are being taken for pending trials.[207] And there are restrictions on disclosing the identity of officers of the Criminal Assets Bureau who may give evidence

---

[205] See generally, J. Jaconelli, *Open Justice: A Critique of the Public Trial* (2002).
[206] See generally, *Walsh* p.952 *et seq.* and *Irish Times Ltd v. Ireland* [1998] 1 I.R. 359 at p.393.
[207] Criminal Procedure Act 1967, s.41 (as amended in 1999).

or otherwise.[208] It has been held that the taking of evidence in the District Court for the purpose of a foreign criminal investigation is not the administration of justice and accordingly, it does not have to take place in public.[209] Frequently, trial judges prohibit publication of evidence given in the *voir dire*, until the trial has concluded, in order to ensure principally that members of the jury do not become aware of evidence tendered that has been ruled inadmissible.

Although there is no general statutory provision authorising judges in specified circumstances to bar or limit press reporting, it was held by the Supreme Court in *Irish Times Ltd. v. Ireland*[210] that a trial judge has a discretion to impose reporting restrictions for the purpose of ensuring a fair trial. But this is a power that should only be exercised in extreme circumstances. Press reporting is a vital medium for the public to be aware of how justice is being administered and there is always the possibility that potential witnesses would learn of the proceedings in the press and then come forward and give evidence for the defence. Further, as Hamilton C.J. stressed, potentially adverse contemporaneous reporting of trials ordinarily can be countered by giving appropriate directions to the jury. In those exceptional circumstances where the judge is not confident that a jury will understand and follow his directions, discharging the jury and ordering a re-trial is preferable to severe restrictions on reporting the proceedings. It is only where contemporaneous reporting would pose a real risk to a fair trial, which cannot be redressed by instructing a jury, that restrictions may be imposed. There a Circuit Court judge trying a major drugs trafficking case ordered that there should be no contemporary media reporting of the proceedings other than that the trial was proceeding in open court, the names and addresses of the accused parties, the nature of the offences involved and where the trial was taking place. While the circumstances there warranted the judge being apprehensive about how the case might be reported, it was held that they did not pose so obvious a threat to a fair trial to warrant that embargo.

It does not seem to have been contended in the *Irish Times* case that, unless press reporting of criminal trials in particular circumstances is prohibited in circumstances "prescribed by law," *i.e.* by an Act of the Oireachtas or pre-1937 legislation, there is no lawful power to ban or to restrict reporting, no matter how desirable the ban would be. Criminal justice being "administered in public" appears to have been considered as meaning in a court that is open to the public and no more; that reporting of the proceedings is an entirely different matter, involving an appropriate balance between the rights to a free trial and to freedom of the press. Accordingly, it would seem that restrictions

---

[208] Criminal Assets Bureau Act 1996, s.10(6) & (7).
[209] *de Gotardi v. Smithwick* [1994] 4 I.R. 223.
[210] [1998] 1 I.R. 359. Also *Independent Star Ltd v. O'Connor* [2002] 4 I.R. 166.

on reporting can also be ignored for other compelling reasons, apart from fair trial considerations.[211]

Jury Trial

Jury trial in serious criminal cases is guaranteed by Article 38.5 of the Constitution; that "[s]ave in the case of the trial of offences [which are minor offences, or are tried by the Special Criminal Court or by military tribunals] no person shall be tried on any criminal charge without a jury." One of the most distinctive features of the common law tradition is jury trial, *i.e.* subject to the judge's directions, jurors who are chosen at random from the general populace determine the accused's guilt or innocence.[212] Jury trial is referred to in the Magna Carta[213] and one of the criminal procedure provisions in the 1689 Bill of Rights[214] is that "Jurors ought to be duly empanelled and returned, and Jurors which pass upon men in trials for High Treason ought to be Freeholders." Trial by an impartial jury of the State and district where the crime was committed is guaranteed by the United States Constitution's Sixth Amendment.[215] The only criminal procedure provision in the Australian Constitution is section 80's guarantee of "trial by jury."[216] But jury trial in the traditional common law sense hardly exists in continental Europe[217] and as a result there is no reference to it in the European Convention nor in the UN Covenant, although the guarantee of equality in the latter was held to signify that an accused is entitled to a trial by jury where other accused persons in comparable circumstances are so tried.[218] By far the principal difference between trials on indictment in the Special Criminal Court and elsewhere is that in the former case there is no jury; instead there are three judges.

Jury trial in criminal cases serves several ends, the most important perhaps being to ensure that the criminal justice system does not become unduly biased in favour of the government of the day. As Kingsmill Moore J. remarked in one instance, "(r)ightly or not, trial by jury had for centuries been regarded

---

[211] *Cf. R. v. Mentuck*, 205 D.L.R. 4th 512 (2001) and *Vancouver Sun v. Attorney General of Canada*, 205 D.L.R. 4th 542 (2001).

[212] See generally, P. Devlin, *Trial by Jury* (rev. ed., 1966), W.R. Cornish, *The Jury* (1968) and N. Vidmar ed., *World Jury Systems* (2000) (which contains a chapter on the Irish jury by J. Jackson *et al.*).

[213] Art.39: "No freeman shall be taken or [and] imprisoned or diseissed or exiled ... except by the lawful judgment of his peers ...".

[214] 1 Wm. & M. c.2.

[215] See generally, King in Vidmar ed., *supra*, n.212.

[216] See generally, Chesterman in *ibid.*

[217] See generally, Mannheim, "Trial by Jury in Modern Continental Criminal Law", (1937) 53 *L.Q.R.* 99, 388 (1937).

[218] *Kavanagh v. Ireland*, UNHR Committee decision of April 4, 2001.

popularly as a most important safeguard for the individual, a protection alike against the zeal of an enthusiastic executive or the rigidity of an ultra conservative judiciary. Especially was this so in the history of Ireland."[219] Henchy J. has spoken of "(t)he bitter Irish race-memory of politically appointed and executive-oriented judges … of packed juries and sometimes corrupt judge and prosecutors …"[220] Jury trial ensures that the criminal justice system remains in keeping with general values and beliefs in the community. It also ensures that a single judge is not left with the entire responsibility for deciding the truth of two or more conflicting versions of the facts. In the past that decision often determined whether or not the accused was to be executed.

Article 38.5 prohibits trial of non-minor offences "without a jury" (save for the excepted circumstances). This clause, however, does not define the meaning of jury trial. It undoubtedly signifies that the trial must broadly accord with the form of jury trial as existed in 1937 and with certain other requirements but it is not clear how far the Oireachtas may deviate from the 1937 model of the criminal jury. For instance, would it be permissible to have juries comprised of less than twelve persons and, if so, what is the constitutional minimum size for juries?[221] May the jury be allowed to separate once they have retired for the purpose of considering their verdict?[222] May the accused waive his right to trial by jury?[223] To what extent, if any, may the traditional secrecy of jury deliberations be encroached upon?[224] Would it be allowed, as happens in some continental European countries, for the trial judge or judges to retire with the jury when they consider their verdict? Is jury vetting, which easily could give rise to jury packing, constitutionally permissible? Can the traditional rights of the defence to challenge prospective jurors be taken away?

Composition

It was held by the Supreme Court in *de Burca v. Attorney General*[225] that the jury must be representative of the entire adult population and that a jury selection system that excluded women and also those who did not pay rates from jury panels was unconstitutional. As is explained above, Walsh J. based his conclusions regarding excluding women principally on the prohibition of unfair discrimination in Article 40.1; the jury selection system was "undisguisedly

---

[219] *Melling v. O'Mathghamnha* [1962] I.R. 1 at p.34.
[220] *People v. O'Shea* [1982] I.R. 384, 432.
[221] *Cf. Brownlee v. The Queen*, 207 C.L.R. 278 (2001) and *Fittock v. The Queen*, 77 A.L.J.L.R. 961 (2003).
[222] *Ibid.*
[223] *Cf. Brown v. The Queen*, 160 C.L.R. 171 (1986).
[224] *Cf. Pan v. The Queen*, 200 D.L.R. 4th 577 (2001).
[225] [1976] I.R. 38.

discriminatory on the ground of sex only."[226] Henchy and Griffin JJ., on the
other hand, founded their judgments on the principle that a crucial feature of
the traditional jury system is its representative nature – "the jury must be drawn
from a pool broadly representative of the community so that its verdict will be
stamped with the fairness and acceptability of a genuinely diffused community
decision,"[227] and "the jury should be a body which is truly representative, and
a fair cross section, of the community."[228]

The then jury selection system also excluded citizens who did not satisfy a
minimum rating qualification, *i.e.* who did not own property which was valued
for rating purposes at more than a given amount. Their exclusion too was
struck down in the *de Burca* case. According to Henchy J., the test of whether
a jury selection system is unconstitutionally unrepresentative "is whether, by
intent or operation, there is an exclusion of any class or group of citizens
(other than those excluded for reasons based on capacity or social function)
who, if included, might be expected to carry out their duties as jurors according
to beliefs, standards, or attitudes not represented by those included."[229] The
minimum rating requirement contravened this test because it "exclude(d) a
range of mental attitudes which, because they will be absent from the jury box
and the jury-room, will leave an accused with no hope of the contribution they
might make in the determination of guilt or innocence."[230] For instance, the
excluded group may very well have profoundly different views regarding
offences involving damage to property.

Under section 6 of the Juries Act 1976, every citizen aged between 18 and
70 years is qualified and liable for jury service, and only persons convicted of
certain serious offences are disqualified. The first schedule to this Act declares
various categories of persons to be ineligible for jury service, *e.g.* members of
the permanent defence forces, members of the Garda Síochána and practising
barristers and solicitors. Part II of that schedule declares an extensive cross
section of individuals excusable as of right, *e.g.* persons aged more than 65
years, whole-time students and practising doctors, dentists, nurses, vets and
pharmacists.

It is not clear whether the jury panel must come from the locality that has
some connection with the accused or with the alleged offence. Henchy J. has
expressed the view that "(t)here must, for a constitutional jury, be a valid nexus
between juror and jury district. This is needed to ensure that the jury's verdict
will have the quality of a community decision, for a jury so constituted will
reach its verdict in the knowledge that, in a real and special sense, its members

---

[226] *Id.* at p.71; *supra*, p.377.
[227] *Id.* at pp.75 and 82.
[228] *Id.* at p.76.
[229] *Ibid.*
[230] *Id.* at p.76.

will have to live with that decision. ...."[231] But in *State (Hughes) v. Neylon*,[232] where the accused complained about his trial being transferred from outside of Dublin to the Dublin Circuit Court, Finlay P. rejected the contention that there is a constitutional "right of an accused person to be tried by a jury drawn from a particular locality."[233]

Because the pending trial of former Taoiseach Mr. Haughey in 2000, for obstructing the working of "McCracken" tribunal that was investigating payments made to him, had attracted considerable publicity, the trial judge proposed to submit a questionnaire to the jury panel, designed to assist weeding out those whose views were likely to have been unduly affected by media comment. He prepared a list of fifteen questions, principally addressing issues that had come up in that tribunal and also in the "Flood" tribunal that was investigating corruption in the planning system. This approach was resisted by the prosecution and in *DPP v. Haugh*,[234] a Divisional Court held that it was unlawful. According to Carney J., the Juries Act 1976 is a "self-contained and all-embracing code relating to juries both civil and criminal" and that "[w]hatever needs to be ascertained now relating to juries ought to be found in [it]."[235] Section 15(3) of that Act, which requires the judge to invite jurors who feel they are not qualified to serve, to communicate directly with him if selected, is the mechanism provided for affording protection in this kind of case and there was no inherent jurisdiction to devise an alternative procedure. Laffoy J. declined to infer, from the provisions of the 1996 Act, authority to administer that questionnaire because doing so would depart from the principle that jury selection should be subject to public scrutiny and the long-standing practice that does not allow the interrogation of jurors who would appear to be qualified. Also, because there was no sanction for incorrectly answering any of the questions posed, there was no reason to believe that the questionnaire approach would be effective. Subsequently, the trial was stayed by the trial judge on account of concern that the jury would be prejudiced by the publicity.

An endeavour by a defendant, who intended conducting his case in Irish, to have a jury who understood that language without the need for an interpreter, was rejected by the Supreme Court in *MacCarthaigh v. Ireland*.[236] It was common knowledge that there were not many people who understood legal matters in the Irish language, without the need for an interpreter, and to accede to the request here would depart from the overriding principle that a jury should be representative of the community at large.

---

[231] *State (Byrne) v. Frawley* [1978] I.R. 326 at 347.
[232] [1982] I.L.R.M. 108.
[233] *Id.* at p.111.
[234] [2000] 1 I.R. 84.
[235] *Id.* at p.191.
[236] [1999] 1 I.R. 100.

Functioning

In the *de Burca* case, Walsh J. described the "essence of trial with a jury as follows: "the trial should be in the presence, and under the authority, of a presiding judge having power to instruct the jury as to the law and to advise them as to the facts, and the jury should be free to consider their verdicts alone without the intervention or presence of the Judge or any other person during their deliberations. I think it also imports an element of secrecy."[237] According to Henchy J. in another case, the constitutional right to trial with a jury is "essentially a right to the evolved and evolving common law trial by jury, that is to say, a trial before a judge and jury, in which the judge would preside, ensure that all conditions necessary for a fair and proper trial of that nature are complied with, decide all matters deemed to be matters of law, and direct the jury as to the legal principles and rules they are to observe and apply; and in which the jury ... would be the arbiter, under the governance of the judge, of all disputed issues of fact and, in particular, the issue of guilt or innocence."[238] Within this general framework, both judges made it clear that the nature and function of the jury need not replicate every feature of the 1937 model.

Majority verdicts, introduced by the Criminal Justice Act 1984, were upheld by the Supreme Court in *O'Callaghan v. Attorney General*.[239] Under section 25 of this Act, a verdict is effective provided there are at least eleven jurors and at least ten agree on their verdict. Because "[t]he essential feature of a jury trial is to interpose between the accused and the prosecution people who will bring their experience and common sense to bear on resolving the issue of ... guilt or innocence," O'Flaherty J. for the court concluded that unanimity is not essential for this purpose.[240] Nor were there any grounds for finding that majority verdicts would affect jury confidentiality and the principle that "the nature of the deliberation of a jury in a criminal case should not be revealed or be inquired into."[241] However, if the majority were substantially lowered from that provided for in the 1984 Act, it was indicated that this might depart unduly from the constitutional guarantee. Around the same time as this decision was handed down, the Australian High Court held that unanimity was a fundamental feature of trial by jury, both historically and as a matter of principle, and that to introduce majority verdicts there would contravene section 80 of their Constitution.[242]

A trial judge cannot direct the jury to bring in a guilty verdict. In *People v.*

---

[237] [1976] I.R. 67.
[238] *People v. O'Shea* [1982] I.R. 384 at p.431.
[239] [1993] 2 I.R. 17.
[240] *Id.* at p.25.
[241] *Id.* at p.26.
[242] *Cheatle v. The Queen*, 177 C.L.R. 541 (1993).

Davis[243] an accused who was convicted in those circumstances had his conviction set aside by the Supreme Court. On being arraigned on a murder charge, he pleaded "not guilty of murder, guilty of manslaughter." At the conclusion of the prosecution evidence, he elected not to give evidence in his defence and he did not call any witness. At the conclusion of his summing up to the jury, having emphasised that the question to be decided was one of fact, Costello J. said that "no reasonable jury could find that the accused was guilty of manslaughter, and so I must direct you as a matter of law that on the facts of this case you must return a verdict of murder." While a trial judge is entitled in appropriate circumstances to direct that an accused should be acquitted, Finlay C.J. for the court said that the corollary was not consistent with the constitutional guarantee. Trial judges are entitled to direct juries on the law concerning defences that may be open on the evidence adduced, and may even venture their opinion that a guilty verdict is the only one which would be reasonable or proper on the evidence but, ultimately, it is for the jury and not the judge to decide what their verdict will be. As Henchy J. observed in an earlier case, "[t]he use of the power to err in favour of the accused is left to the consciences of the jurors [and] what may seem to judges to be a perverse verdict of acquittal may represent the layman's rejection of a particular law as being unacceptable. So it is that such verdicts have often led to the reform of the criminal law."[244]

It was held in *Curtis v. Attorney General*[245] that every disputed issue of fact must be decided by the jury and not by the presiding judge. The plaintiff had been charged with a smuggling offence. Under the relevant legislation, the value of the goods alleged to have been smuggled is to be determined by the judge and, on conviction, the fine is treble the value of those goods. It was held that the goods' value also was a material issue in determining guilt or innocence and, accordingly, evidence regarding their value should have been left to the jury. Both offences require *mens rea* and Carroll J. was "satisfied that a jury would be entitled to take into account the value of the goods in deciding if there were such *mens rea*."[246]

Where the admissibility of particular evidence turns on issues of fact, traditionally those issues are decided by the judge in a *voir dire* and not by the jury. In 1981 the Supreme Court held that those should be determined by the jury instead.[247] But that view did not gain wide acceptance by trial judges and in *People v. Conroy*[248] it was effectively overruled, principally for reasons of practicability. Finlay C.J. noted that in particular the trial of a separate issue during the course of cases had "created immense difficulties," to the extent

---

[243] [1993] 2 I.R. 1.
[244] *People v. O'Shea* [1982] I.R. 384 at p.438.
[245] [1985] I.R. 458.
[246] *Id.* at p.463.
[247] *People v. Lynch* [1982] I.R. 64.
[248] [1986] I.R. 460.

that the advantages of having them resolved by a jury were overwhelmed by the disadvantages, creating a "risk of real injustice" to the accused.[249]

If in the circumstances there are grounds to be reasonably apprehensive that one or more of the jurors are biased, the jury should be discharged and replaced. And if the accused were convicted in those circumstances, his conviction will be set aside and a new trial ordered. According to the Court of Criminal Appeal in *People v. Tobin*,[250] the test to be applied is the very same one for determining whether a judge should recuse himself, *viz.* the test is objective. It is whether a reasonable person in the circumstances would have a reasonable apprehension that the accused would not receive a fair trial of the issues. It was held that "*a fortiori* therefore, it applies to the case of a challenge alleging bias in a jury."[251] Where the judge becomes aware of a possible bias during the trial, that may be rectifiable by him giving appropriate directions to the jury. In this case, involving alleged rape and sexual assault, one of the jurors disclosed that she had a personal experience of sexual abuse but the foreman of the jury assured the judge that it did not affect her impartiality in any way. On the strength of that assurance, the judge rejected an application to discharge the jury. But the conviction was set aside on appeal because there were reasonable grounds to apprehend bias. In an earlier instance, where the foreman of the jury had been an investor in the very company the accused was being tried for defrauding, the conviction was set aside.[252] In a case where an Asian defendant had been convicted in Birmingham and there was evidence of one juror having made racist jokes, the European Court of Human Rights held that the accused had not obtained a fair trial as required by Article 6(1) of the Convention.[253]

Prejudicial Publicity

Where it is shown that pre-trial publicity is very likely to significantly influence the jurors against the accused, his trial will not be allowed to proceed, either at the time scheduled or at all. An accused's right to a fair trial takes precedence over the State's interest in prosecuting those believed to have committed offences. It is principally for the trial judge to decide whether in all the circumstances the trial should proceed, in view of the publicity there has been. But his decision can be challenged by way of judicial review where the case is before a court other than the Central Criminal Court. At times, it may be possible by appropriate directions for the trial judge to alleviate the prejudicial effect

---

[249] *Id.* at pp.473 and 472.
[250] [2001] 3 I.R. 469.
[251] *Id.* at p.478.
[252] *People v. Singer* [1975] I.R. 408.
[253] *Sander v. United Kingdom*, 31 E.H.R.R. 1003 (2000).

of publicity. Additionally, there is what is described as the "fade factor," meaning that the prejudicial effect of publicity usually fades out with the passage of time.

Certain cases inevitably attract enormous publicity, on account of their very circumstances or the identity of the accused, but its mere existence is no reason why the trial should not proceed. Thus in *Z. v. DPP*.[254] the father of the alleged rape victim in the highly controversial "X" case failed to stop his trial on that charge notwithstanding the massive publicity surrounding that case. It was held by the Supreme Court that whatever prejudice as may exist could be dealt with suitably by the trial judge's directions to the jury. Finlay C.J. was "satisfied that a jury so fully and amply instructed will be able to bring to the trial of the case an impartial mind and will be particularly scrupulous about preventing themselves or indeed, in a sense preventing each other, from deciding the case based on any view arising from [the] general publicity or controversy."[255]

Like the question of delay prejudicing the fairness of a trial, the cases on pre-trial publicity turn very much on their own facts, as is illustrated graphically by the first of the comparatively recent cases on the question, *D. v. DPP*.[256] There the accused's trial for indecent assault on a boat off the Donegal coast had to end twice, with the jury being discharged, on the second instance on account of publicity the trial had attracted. Before his new trial commenced, the Sunday Tribune published on its front and inside pages a lengthy interview with the complainant, headed "Rape: it began when I was eleven," and containing a graphic account of her five years ordeal of "assault, pregnancy, a child …".By a majority of one, the Supreme Court held that, notwithstanding, the trial could go ahead. In contrast, in *DPP v. Haugh (No. 2)*,[257] the trial judge stayed, until further order, the trial of the former Taoiseach, Mr. Haughey, on a charge of obstructing the "McCracken" tribunal that had investigated his financial affairs. The basis for this decision was not merely the publicity that the conclusions of this tribunal had attracted but also potentially prejudicial remarks made by the Tánaiste when the trial was about to start and, as well, a massive poster campaign around Dublin for a "Jail the Corrupt Politicians" rally. The decision to stay the trial was unsuccessfully challenged in the High Court, where Carroll J. held that it is principally for the trial judge to decide whether, in view of all the circumstances, a fair trial can be had.

Where there has been prejudicial publicity in the course of a trial, which was not then halted, and the accused is convicted, that publicity may have been so damaging as to require the conviction to be set aside. An additional

---

[254] [1994] 2 I.R. 476.
[255] *Id.* at p.508. Similarly, *Redmond v. DPP* [2002] 4 I.R. 133.
[256] [1994] 2 I.R. 465.
[257] [2001] 1 I.R. 163.

consideration here, however, is the weight of the evidence against the accused. Thus in *People v. Davis*,[258] where there had been prominent newspaper photographs of a man accused of murder being brought into the court in shackles, handcuffed and chained to a prison officer, the Court of Criminal Appeal deprecated that kind of publicity. But in view of all the evidence, the court held that the jury's verdict was safe.

Onus of Proof

That it is for the prosecution to establish the accused's guilt is proclaimed in Article 6(2) of the European Convention and Article 14(2) of the UN Covenant, according to which "[e]veryone charged with a criminal offence shall have the right to be presumed innocent until proved guilty according to law." The traditional common law principle, endorsed by Article 9 of the 1789 Declaration of the Rights of Man and the Citizen, goes further and requires that the accused's guilt must be proved not just on the balance of probabilities but beyond reasonable doubt. It was held in *Hardy v. Ireland*[259] that a presumption of the accused's innocence is part of the "due course of law" in Article 38.1 of the Constitution. But it has not been determined whether the traditional high standard of proof is embodied in this Article.

There are numerous statutory provisions to the effect that, once the prosecution gives evidence tending to establish certain facts that are essential ingredients of the offence, then those facts are deemed to be proved unless the accused demonstrates or adduces evidence to the contrary. For instance, under section 24 of the Offences Against the State Act 1939, if an "incriminating document" is found on a person charged with membership of a proscribed organisation, that without any more constitutes evidence of membership unless the contrary is shown. In other words, if it is proved that the accused had an incriminating document, he is likely to be convicted of membership unless "the contrary is proved." A distinction is made between provisions that impose a legal onus on the defence and those that impose a less exacting evidentiary onus, although it may not always be clear from the provision in question which onus is involved. A legal onus requires the accused to establish his innocence in that, once the onus-shifting elements have been proved, the accused must satisfy the court on the balance of probabilities to the contrary. In contrast, an evidential onus means that, once the onus-shifting elements have been proved, the accused must adduce evidence to raise a reasonable doubt on the issue but, having done this, the prosecution must satisfy the jury as to that matter beyond reasonable doubt in the normal way.

---

[258] [2001] 1 I.R. 146.
[259] [1994] 2 I.R. 550.

Two and at times three aspects of imposing a legal onus on the accused run counter to traditional principles of fair procedure that are expressly recognised in many constitutions. One is that the accused is required to disprove essential facts of the offence with which he is charged. Another is that he is liable to be convicted notwithstanding his having raised a reasonable doubt about those facts. Additionally, depending on what those facts are, the accused may be in effect compelled to give evidence himself in order to avoid being convicted. In several Commonwealth countries it has been held that a reverse legal burden of proof is unconstitutional because it is a disproportionate means of achieving the objective of making the prosecution's task easier.[260]

This issue came before the Supreme Court in *O'Leary v. Attorney General*,[261] where the plaintiff had been convicted of possessing incriminating documents and, by virtue of that and no evidence to the contrary having been adduced by him, he was convicted of membership of the Irish Republican Army, a proscribed organisation. He contended that section 24 of the 1939 Act was unconstitutional, as contravening the presumption of innocence, relying particularly on a decision of the Canadian Supreme Court which found that a comparable provision infringed the presumption of innocence in the Constitution there.[262] O'Flaherty J., for the Court, held that the formulation in the Canadian law was so different from that contained in section 24, that this case was of no assistance.[263] He rejected the contention that the words "until the contrary is proved" in section 24 means that the legal onus was thrown on the accused to prove that he was not a member of an unlawful organisation, meaning in effect that he was not guilty of the offence. This, it was said, was because "[i]t is clear that such possession is to amount to *evidence* only; it is not to be taken as proof and so the probative value of the possession of such a document might be shaken in many ways: by cross examination; by pointing to the mental capacity of the accused or the circumstances by which he came to be in possession of the document, to give some examples."[264] The judge added that "[t]he important thing to note ... is that there is no mention of the burden of proof changing, much less that the presumption of innocence is to be set to one side at any stage."[265] In other words it appears, if the accused tenders evidence that raises a reasonable doubt about his alleged membership, then his having been in possession of the material in question is no longer sufficient to demonstrate guilt. This judgment concludes with an outline of what should be the judge's summing up to a jury in a case where section 24 is

---

[260] *E.g., Little Sisters Book and Art Emporium v. Minister for Justice*, 193 D.L.R. 4th 193 (2000) and *Singo v. State*, 12 B.H.R.C. 702 (2002) (South Africa).

[261] [1995] 1 I.R. 254.

[262] *The Queen v. Oakes*, 26 D.L.R. 4th 200 (1986).

[263] [1995] 1 I.R. at p.263.

[264] *Id.* at p.265.

[265] *Ibid.*

being relied on to prove membership and where, not alone the accused gave no evidence, but the prosecution witnesses were not cross-examined. Of course practically all such cases are tried before the non-jury Special Criminal Court.

Accordingly, it would appear that any ambiguity in the statutory language will cause the courts to construe what may appear to be the reverse onus instead as an evidentiary rather than a legal onus and that, in general, imposing a reverse evidentiary onus is not unconstitutional.[266] It remains to be seen what circumstances, if any, would justify imposing a reverse legal onus on an accused.

SILENCE

A right to silence and against self-incrimination existed in the common law[267] ever since Lord Chief Justice Coke checked the powers of inquisitorial courts in the early seventeenth century, holding that they could not compel accused persons to take the *ex officio* oath and answer interrogation, because that would "make one thereby to subject himself to the danger of a penal law."[268] This right was incorporated into the Fifth Amendment to the United States Constitution, that no one "shall be compelled in any criminal case to be a witness against himself," which gave rise to the expression, that gained currency in the 1950s, of "pleading the Fifth." Although it makes no express reference to it, the European Convention has been held to guarantee the right to silence and against self-incrimination. Article 14(3)(g) of the UN Covenant stipulates that "everyone shall be entitled [n]ot to be compelled to testify against himself or to confess guilt."

Entitlement to remain silent and not answer questions has been held by the Supreme Court to be a corollary of the guarantee of freedom of expression in Article 40.6 of the Constitution. It accordingly is not an absolute right but can be curtailed for legitimate purposes by proportionate means.[269] Perhaps if the court had not anchored silence in the right to free expression, which has received scanty protection, the court might have taken a more robust attitude when facing provisions that directly or indirectly require individuals to make inculpatory statements. A more appropriate basis is the implied right of privacy. Article 38.1's guarantee of a trial "in due course of law" means, *inter alia*, that answers given under compulsion, whether physical or legal, will not be admitted into evidence against the person who gave them; in particular, coerced confessions will not be taken into account.

---

[266] *E.g., R. (Kebilene) v. D.P.P.* [2000] 2 A.C. 326, *R. v. Lambert* [2002] 2 A.C. 545 and *R. v. Greenaway* [2003] N.I. 5. *Cf. Phillips v. United Kingdom*, 11 B.H.R.C. 280 (2001).
[267] L.W. Levy, *Origins of the Fifth Amendment* (1968) and Langbein, "The Historical Origins of the Privilege Against Self-Incrimination at Common Law", 92 *Mich. L. Rev.* 1047 (1994).
[268] *Burrowes v. High Commission* (1616) 81 Eng. Rep. 42.
[269] *Heaney v. Ireland* [1996] 1 I.R. 580.

Not Giving Evidence

Before 1898 an accused person was not permitted to give evidence in his own defence,[270] although he could defend himself without having the benefit of legal representation and, up to 1984, he could make an unsworn statement from the dock. But he cannot be obliged to give evidence in his defence. His right to silence is safeguarded by section 1(a), (b) of the Criminal Justice (Evidence) Act 1924, according to which "a person so charged shall not be called as a witness ... except on his own application" and his "failure ... to give evidence shall not be made the subject of any comment by the prosecution." Nor should failure to testify be adversely commented on by the judge. As put by Keane C.J., "the exercise by an accused person of his right not to give evidence in his own defence, cannot lead to any inference adverse to him being drawn by the court and, in the case of a trial by jury, the jury must be expressly so advised by the trial judge."[271]

Not Answering Questions

Except where there is legislation to the contrary or the circumstances come within one of the exceptions to the principle, witnesses in any criminal, civil or administrative proceedings are entitled to refuse to answer particular questions or furnish particular documents when doing so would cause them to admit their involvement in crime. In *Gilligan v. Criminal Assets Bureau*,[272] McGuinness J. expressed concern about making orders under section 9 of the Proceeds of Crime Act 1996, where respondents can be directed by the High Court to swear an affidavit setting out their assets, and also their income and sources of income over the previous ten years. Even if the plaintiff (a senior police officer) in proceedings of this nature were prepared to give an undertaking that the information in those affidavits would not be used in order to seek the deponent's conviction, the judge pointed out that there could be practical difficulties in giving effect to that undertaking in view of who the plaintiff is in these cases.

Caution

Under what are described as the "Judges' Rules," whenever a Garda officer decides to charge a person or whenever that officer desires to question a person being held in custody, the "usual caution" should be administered. This requires the subject or detainee to be told that he is "not obliged to say anything unless

---

[270] Criminal Evidence Act 1898, 61 & 62 Vic. c.36.
[271] *People v. Finnerty* [1999] 4 I.R. 364 at p.376.
[272] [1998] 3 I.R. 185 at p.243; also *M. v. D.* [1998] 3 I.R. 175.

you wish to do so, but whatever you say will be taken down in writing and may be used in evidence." A statement made without this caution being given is usually not admissible in evidence against the person at his trial. These "Rules" were described by O'Higgins C.J. as "not rules of law [but] rules for the guidance of persons taking statements."[273] Professor Walsh has observed that "the Irish judges display a distinct reticence to exercise their discretion to exclude" statements obtained in contravention of this requirement,[274] which perhaps explains the description given by the former Chief Justice.

Whether or to what extent these "Rules" have any constitutional basis, in the sense of the Oireachtas not being capable of abolishing or diluting them, remains to be determined. In the well-known *Miranda* case,[275] a comparable admonishment was held to be required by the US Constitution and a later legislative endeavour to abolish that was held to be unconstitutional there.[276] Indeed, *Miranda* not alone insists on the detainee being informed of his right to remain silent but also that he is entitled to have a lawyer present, either retained or appointed, and if at any stage he indicates that he wishes to consult his lawyer, there can be no further questioning until he obtains legal advice. Further, if he is alone and indicates in any manner that he does not want to be questioned, there can be no further questioning. Given the frequency with which disregard of the Judge's Rules is not sanctioned by the courts, it is most unlikely that they would be given a constitutional status, let alone ever be judicially extended to incorporate the *Miranda* safeguards against oppressive questioning of suspects being held in police custody.[277]

Compelled Disclosure

There are numerous statutory provisions that require persons to disclose information about themselves, many of which carry a penalty for failure to give the relevant information or for supplying false information. There also are provisions that require persons to answer questions put to them, notwithstanding that by their answers they may incriminate themselves, which usually add that the answers given may not be used against them in any subsequent prosecution, other than one for committing perjury when giving those answers. For instance, section 21(4) of the Bankruptcy Act 1988, which deals with interrogating bankrupts or others about the bankrupt's affairs, provides that any person who is examined under this section shall not be entitled to refuse to answer any question put to him, on the ground that his answer

---

[273] *People v. Farrell* [1978] I.R. 13 at p.21.
[274] *Walsh*, p.288.
[275] *Miranda v. Arizona*, 384 US 436 (1966).
[276] *Dickerson v. United States*, 530 US 428 (2000).
[277] E.g., *Mohammad v. State* [1999] 2 A.C. 111; compare *Lieu v. The Queen*, 177 D.L.R. 4th 302 (1999).

might incriminate him. But none of those answers shall be admissible in evidence against him in any other proceedings, civil or criminal, except in the case of any criminal proceedings for perjury in respect of any such answer. Other examples include section 29 of the Company Law Enforcement Act 2001 and section 5 of the Tribunals of Enquiry (Evidence) (Amendment) Act 1979. It does not appear to have been contended that a general statutory requirement to answer questions should be construed as not extending to answers that would incriminate unless express provision to that effect is made.

In *People v. Cummins*,[278] where the accused had made a statement to the Gardaí in circumstances of legal compulsion, the Supreme Court concluded that it was not voluntary and should not have been admitted into evidence against him. There, the accused was tried for the larceny of a car. When he was arrested, he was questioned by a Garda officer with reference to section 107 of the Road Traffic Act 1961, and answered that he had been using the car at the relevant time. Under section 107, a person commits an offence if he fails to give any information in his power relating to the identity of a person using a vehicle, if so required by a member of the Gardaí. Before the accused was questioned here, he was informed of the penalty.[279]

Within limits, the Oireachtas may compel persons to answer questions notwithstanding that those answers may be self-incriminatory but any answers so obtained may not be used in a criminal trial as evidence against the person who made them unless given voluntary. *National Irish Bank (No. 1), Re,*[280] concerned sections 10 and 18 of the Companies Act 1990, which empowers inspectors appointed under that Act to question individuals and provides that any answers given, when being so interviewed, "may be used in evidence against any person making or concurring in making" them. On the basis of earlier authority, the Supreme Court held that it was permissible to enact this provision, as the State had a legitimate interest in thoroughly investigating wrongdoing in the banking sector. But it was held that section 18 of that Act would not be construed as permitting answers given in those circumstances to be used in evidence later in a criminal trial of the person questioned; the contrary construction would have the effect of rendering it unconstitutional, as authorising the use of coerced admissions in criminal trials. In other words, the unqualified stipulation that answers "may be used in evidence against" must be given the meaning that they may *not* be used in criminal proceedings – which the draftsman hardly intended was the meaning, especially in an Act that radically extended the criminalisation of Company Law. The correctness

---

[278] [1972] I.R. 312.
[279] Similarly, *R. v. White* [1999] 174 D.L.R. 4th 111; compare *Brown v. Stott* [2001] 2 W.L.R. 817, *R. v. Kearns* [2002] 1 W.L.R. 2815 and *R. v. Jarvis* 219 D.L.R. 4th 233 (2002).
[280] [1999] 3 I.R. 145.

of this decision is questionable, as is the rationale given for section 10 of the 1990 Act, because it applies to all kinds of investigations by inspectors and not just into bank frauds.

It was distinguished in *Dunnes Stores Ireland Co. v. Ryan*[281] on the basis that breach of section 10 of that Act (i.e. refusal to cooperate) was not automatically wrongful; instead, the recalcitrant interviewee could be brought before the High Court and be appropriately dealt with there. In contrast, section 19 of that Act (which in the meantime had been repealed) rendered non-cooperation automatically a criminal offence. According to Kearns J., "[u]nder section 10 a person who is unwilling or refuses to answer still has the opportunity of having the reasonableness of that stance tested as an issue by the court [and] it is scarcely to be anticipated that the court will direct that unreasonable ... questions be answered."[282] On the basis of this reasoning, the test of constitutionality is the reasonableness or relevance of each question posed; if a question is reasonable and relevant, then the privilege cannot be relied upon. But unless given voluntarily, the answer cannot be used subsequently in a prosecution of the interviewee. Where the provision in question does not permit consideration of reasonableness, before non-cooperation is sanctioned, it is unconstitutional.

A similar conclusion was reached by the European Court of Human Rights in *Saunders v. United Kingdom*,[283] where the applicant underwent interrogation by officials empowered to investigate alleged wrongdoing in the management of a company and, when he was later prosecuted for those wrongs, his explanations were adduced in evidence against him. Allowing his answers to be used in that manner was found to have contravened his Article 6(i) right to a fair trial.

Adverse Consequences

In appropriate circumstances, it is permissible to stipulate that an accused's failure to answer questions may result in adverse inferences being drawn in a subsequent criminal trial. A challenge to one such provision was rejected by the Supreme Court in *Rock v. Ireland*,[284] namely sections 18 and 19 of the Criminal Justice Act 1984. Under section 18, where a person who is arrested by a member of the Garda Síochána and is found to be in possession of any object that the Garda reasonably believes to be attributable to his involvement in a criminal offence, and he then refuses to explain to the Garda how he came to have that object, at his subsequent trial an unfavourable inference may be drawn from his silence; the court "may draw such inferences from [his] failure

---

[281] [2002] 2 I.R. 60.
[282] *Id.* at p.122.
[283] 23 E.H.R.R. 313 (1997); also *I.J.L. v. United Kingdom*, 33 E.H.R.R. 11 (2001).
[284] [1997] 3 I.R. 484.

or refusal as may appear proper." According to Hamilton C.J., for the Supreme Court, this was a legitimate and proportionate response to the need to combat crime, which came within the Oireachtas' authority to balance individual rights with the general public interest. He observed that '[i]n this situation, the function of the court is not to decide whether a perfect balance has been achieved, but merely to decide whether, in restricting individual constitutional rights, the legislature have acted within the range of what is permissible."[285] He emphasised that any inference that is drawn from the accused's failure to furnish the Garda with an explanation cannot form the basis of a conviction without there being other inculpatory evidence and, further, the trial judge could refuse to permit an inference to be drawn in circumstances where its prejudicial effect would wholly outweigh its probative value as evidence.[286]

Unless permitted by express legislative provision, however, an accused's silence while in Garda custody and his refusal to answer any questions put to him then must not be taken into account in determining whether he is guilty of the offence charged. In *People v. Finnerty*,[287] where the trial judge made adverse comments to the jury on the accused's silence while being detained as a rape suspect, the Supreme Court set aside his conviction. The accused had been detained under section 4 of the Criminal Justice Act 1984, and, as Keane J. pointed out, sections 18 and 19 of that Act permit adverse inferences to be drawn in specified circumstances. But there was no provision that inferences may be drawn from the suspected person's silence, while being detained, and consequently he was fully entitled to remain silent and not suffer any adverse consequences for doing so.

Section 52 of the Offences Against the State Act 1939, which is a far more drastic encroachment on the right to silence, was upheld by the Supreme Court in *Heaney v. Ireland*[288] but was found by the European Court of Human Rights in *Quinn v. Ireland*[289] to contravene Article 6.1's fair trial guarantee. Under section 52 of this Act, if a person who is being held in Garda custody "fails or refuses to give ... a full account of his movements and actions during any specified period," he commits an offence carrying a penalty of up to six months imprisonment. Neither the law report nor the only judgment given by O'Flaherty J. contains any indication of the arguments made for the plaintiff, other than reference to 19th century cases that describe silence as a "most important right," "a sacred right" and the like. According to the judge, these "related to a time when, as far as criminal trials were concerned, an accused was not competent to give evidence in his or her own defence. ..."[290] There is no reference to the

---

[285] *Id.* at p.501.
[286] Similarly, *Averill v. United Kingdom*, 31 E.H.R.R. 839 (2000).
[287] [1999] 4 I.R. 364.
[288] 33 E.H.R.R. 12 (2000).
[289] Unreported, July 3, 2001.
[290] [1996] 1 I.R. at p.589.

Strasbourg case law, nor to Walsh J.'s judgment in the *Cummins* case, concerning statements made under legal compulsion. Having itemised many statutory provisions requiring individuals to disclose information and observed that section 52 of the 1939 Act is only in force when the Government have made a declaration that the ordinary courts are not adequate to administer justice, O'Flaherty J. observed out that "the innocent person has nothing to fear from giving an account of his or her movements,"[291] a proposition that is far from self-evident. It, however, forms the basis for the court's conclusion that "the *prima facie* entitlement of [innocent] citizens to take such a stand must yield to the right of the State to protect itself. *A fortiori*, the entitlement of those with something relevant to disclose concerning the commission of a crime to remain mute must be regarded as of a lesser order," and consequently section 52 of the Act achieves "proper proportionality."[292]

This reasoning did not impress the Strasbourg Court, which explained the rationale for a right to silence as protecting the accused "against improper compulsion by the authorities, thereby contributing to the avoidance of miscarriages of justice"; that "the prosecution in a criminal case [should] seek to prove their case against the accused without resort to evidence through methods of coercion or oppression in defiance of the will of the accused."[293] Under section 52 of the 1939 Act, the accused "had to choose between, on the one hand, remaining silent, a criminal conviction and potentially a six month prison sentence and, on the other, forfeiting his right to remain silent and providing information to police officers investigating serious offences at a time when [he] was considered to have been "charged" with those offences. ..."[294] Moreover, it was at a time when, under Irish law, "it was unclear whether ... any section 52 statements made by him would have been later admissible or not in evidence against him."[295] In these circumstances, "the degree of compulsion imposed on [him] by the application of section 52 of the 1939 Act ... in effect destroyed the very essence of his privilege against self-incrimination and his right to remain silent."[296] Security and public order concerns of the Government were held insufficient to justify a provision which "extinguishes the very essence of" these related rights.

---

[291] *Id.* at p.590.
[292] *Ibid.*
[293] Para.40.
[294] Para.54.
[295] *Ibid.*
[296] Para.56.

WITNESSES/EVIDENCE

Article 6(3)(d) of the European Convention and Article 14(3)(e) of the UN Covenant provide that the accused can "examine or have examined witnesses against him and obtain the attendance and examination of witnesses on his behalf under the same conditions as witnesses against him." Another of the accused's right guaranteed by the United States Sixth Amendment is the right "to be confronted with the witnesses against him; to have compulsory process for obtaining witnesses in his favor." It can hardly be doubted that the rights of compulsory process and confrontation, which are recognised in the general rules of criminal procedure, feature among the components of "due course of law" in Article 38.1 of the Constitution.

Orality

Evidence in criminal trials is given *viva voce* rather then in writing, contained in affidavits. One of the points that arose in *Haughey, Re*,[297] which concerned an inquiry being conducted by the Dáil Committee of Public Accounts and the applicant's subsequent trial in the High Court, was that in criminal trials evidence must be given orally save where statute or regulations provide otherwise. Certain kinds of evidence may only be given orally and documentary or other evidence is not sufficient. In *Employment Equality Bill, 1996, Re*,[298] the Supreme Court held that provisions allowing the tendering of a document summarising the events in question, to be *prima facie* evidence of what had occurred, contravened the "due process of law" guarantee. Under section 63 of the Bill being considered there, it would be an offence to obstruct or impede the court, the Director of Equality or an equality officer, or not to comply with a requirement demanded by any of them. In proceedings for breach of this section, a document either sealed by the court or certified by the Director, "relating to the circumstances in which the offence is alleged to have occurred," could be accepted as *prima facie* evidence of the facts stated in it. It was contended by the State that this procedure was acceptable because it was still open to the accused to contest the contents of the document and that the weight to be attached to it was a matter for the trial judge. Against that, it was argued that this procedure had the effect of admitting otherwise inadmissible hearsay evidence and denying the accused the opportunity to cross-examine his accusers. Although the State contended that, where the contents of a certificate are put in dispute, the court could require the attendance of the persons involved at the time so that they could be cross-examined, the Bill made no provision to that end.

---

[297] [1971] I.R. 217.
[298] [1997] 2 I.R. 321.

According to Hamilton C.J., for the court, evidence of this nature is permissible for processes "of a technical nature and there are other issues before the court."[299] But the document envisaged here would go to the very core of the offence, possibly not necessitating any other evidence being called of the alleged obstruction or non-compliance. There was nothing in the social policy of the 1996 Bill nor in the nature of the rights to be granted under it that rendered it necessary that evidence should be adduced in so unorthodox a manner. In consequence, resorting to this mode of proof was an irrational and a disproportionate interference with the right of a trial in due course of law.

Resort to certified documentary evidence for limited purposes was upheld by the Supreme Court in *DPP (Ivers) v. Murphy*.[300] When a person is first charged in the District Court, the prosecution could rely on a certificate by a Garda stating that at a specified time and place he arrested, charged and cautioned the accused. As O'Flaherty J. for the court pointed out, this dealt with "a purely procedural matter, antecedent to the holding of any trial," so that questions of "the burden of proof and so forth are of little or no relevance to the issue in debate."[301]

Cross-Examination

Cross-examination is the process of challenging a witness' evidence by confronting him in the witness box, in an endeavour to establish that what he has said is unreliable. Cross-examining witnesses on evidence they have given has been described as "beyond doubt the greatest legal engine ever invented for the discovery of truth."[302] Entitlement to cross-examine witnesses was identified in *Re Haughey*[303] as fundamental right of an accused. According to Ó Dálaigh C.J., "an accused person has a right to cross-examine every witness for the prosecution, subject, in respect of any question asked, to the court's power of disallowance on the ground of irrelevancy."[304] As emphasised more recently by Hardiman J., "the right to cross-examine one's accusers is a constitutional right and not a concession."[305]

---

[299] *Id.* at p.383.
[300] [1999] 1 I.R 98.
[301] *Id.* at p.105. Compare the *Kramer* case, 57 BVerfGE 250 (1981).
[302] Wigmore, *Evidence* (3rd ed., 1940), Vol.5, p.29 (s.1367).
[303] [1971] I.R. 217.
[304] *Id.* at p.261.
[305] *Maguire v. Ardagh* [2002] 1 I.R. 385 at p.705.

Hearsay

Hearsay is what may be described as second-hand evidence, which is not under oath and often cannot be adequately tested in cross-examination. Under what is known as the rule against hearsay, out-of-court statements may not be used to demonstrate the truth of what was asserted in them; these statements may not be introduced to persuade the court that their contents are substantively true.[306] There are several well-established exceptions to this rule and other exceptions have been created by statute from time to time. Part II (sections 4-9) of the Criminal Evidence Act 1992, permits documents to be admitted as evidence of the truth of their contents, where they were compiled in the ordinary course of business by a person with personal knowledge of their contents, subject however to several safeguards. It remains to be determined the extent to which the Oireachtas may create exceptions to this rule.

TV Link Up

A recent departure from the traditional method of giving evidence from the witness box is testifying through a live television link with the court. Section 13 of the Criminal Evidence Act 1992, permits evidence to be given in this manner in prosecutions for a sexual offence or an offence involving violence or a threat of violence, where the witness is under eighteen years of age (unless the court sees good reason to the contrary) or otherwise with leave of the court. Evidence given in this manner must be video recorded. Section 29 of this Act, which originally was confined to taking evidence from witnesses outside the State, was amended in 2001 to permit evidence *via* a live television link in any criminal proceedings or extradition application, where the witness is not the accused and provided the court grants leave. This evidence also must be video recorded.

Resort to evidence *via* a television link in a charge of sexual assault of a boy, who was under seventeen when he gave evidence, was upheld by the Supreme Court in *Donnelly v. Ireland*.[307] Hamilton C.J., for the court, rejected the contention that in all cases the accused is entitled to a direct face to face confrontation with his accusers; he held that what is guaranteed by fair procedures is a "rigorous testing by cross examination of the evidence against him or her."[308] Since it was "generally accepted that young persons under the age of 17 are likely to be traumatised by the experience of giving evidence in court"[309] and the objective of the legislation was to minimise trauma, this

---

[306] See generally, R. Cannon & N. Neiligan, *Evidence* (2002), ch.11 and A. Choo, *Hearsay and Confrontation in Criminal Trials* (1996).

[307] [1998] 1 I.R. 321; also in *White v. Ireland* [1995] 2 I.R. 268.

[308] *Id.* at p.356.

[309] *Ibid.*

procedure was found to be not unduly unfair because there were numerous protections for the accused. For instance, the witness must take the oath, a prior statement of his evidence is available to the accused, the witness can be cross-examined and his answers and demeanour will be visible to the judge and jury. The court would not accept the assertion that it is more difficult for a witness to tell lies in the accused's presence. Although it accepted that child witnesses are more easily manipulated by others into making false accusations, there still were sufficient safeguards and, in appropriate circumstances, the trial judge can insist on a face-to-face confrontation with the witness.

Presumptions

An evidentiary presumption is where the law deems a certain state of affairs to constitute a particular fact. Occasionally these presumptions are irrebuttable but they mostly may be rebutted by contradictory evidence. It has been held unconstitutional for the Oireachtas to stipulate that one form of proof of certain facts shall be conclusive evidence that those were indeed the facts. In *Maher v. Attorney General*,[310] the Supreme Court struck down on these grounds a provision of the Road Traffic Acts which dealt with proofs required to show that an accused was driving with more than a specified concentration of alcohol in his blood. According to the relevant section, the prosecution must prove in the ordinary way that the accused was driving, or had attempted to drive, and that there was alcohol in the accused's body. But with regard to the prohibited concentration of alcohol, a certificate by the Garda Medical Bureau, following analysis of a blood or urine sample taken from him, was conclusive evidence that the accused had alcohol of that concentration. Thus the question of whether the accused in fact had the proscribed concentration was "remove(d) altogether from the area of contestable facts"; in effect, the accused was "not free to contest the determination of the concentration of alcohol set out in the certificate" and the trial judge was "preclude[d] from exercising his judgment in respect of this matter. ..."[311] This entire approach to proving essential facts of the case was held to contravene the separation of powers principle. As Fitzgerald C.J., stated:

> "The administration of justice, which in criminal matters is confined exclusively by the Constitution to the courts and judges set up under the Constitution, necessarily reserves to those courts and judges the determination of all the essential ingredients of any offence charged against an accused person. In so far as the statutory provision in question here purports to remove such determination from the judges or the courts

---

[310] [1973] I.R. 140.
[311] *Id.* at p.145.

appointed and established under the Constitution, it is an invalid infringement of the judicial power. ... As far as this case is concerned, the offending element of the provision is the evidential conclusiveness given to the certificate. If the word 'conclusive' had not been in the paragraph, it would not be open to the objection, which has now been taken. By giving the certificate this evidential quality, the Oireachtas has invalidly impinged upon the exercise of the judicial power and to that extent the statutory provision is invalid having regard to the provisions of the Constitution."[312]

This case was distinguished in *Sloan v. Special Criminal Court*,[313] where the plaintiff had been charged with membership of a proscribed organisation, the Irish Republican Army (or IRA). Under powers given to it by section 19 of the Offences Against the State Act 1939, the Government designated the IRA as being an unlawful organisation and, by section 19(4) of the Act, that order was made conclusive evidence for all purposes that the IRA was unlawful. According to Costello J., once a proscription order has been made, "then the justiciable dispute which may be before the court is whether an accused is a member of an illegal organisation and not whether the organisation itself is illegal."[314] He added that, even if section 19(4) were unconstitutional, no evidence had been adduced to show that, on the facts of the case, the Special Criminal Court did not have jurisdiction to conduct the trial.[315]

Maher was similarly distinguished in *Hardy v. Ireland*,[316] where the plaintiff had been convicted of possessing an explosive substance, namely sodium chlorate. On its own, that very substance is not explosive but a Statutory Instrument of 1992 designated it as an explosive substance. Flood J. held that the effect of this S.I. was "to make it a matter of law that sodium chlorate is an explosive substance; just as the original statute made it a matter of law that gun powder was an explosive substance."[317] This particular aspect of the case does not seem to have been pursued in the appeal.

As has already been explained in the account of the onus of proof,[318] it is constitutionally permissible, where the prosecution have proved certain key facts, to shift the onus on to the accused to adduce evidence that raises a reasonable doubt either about those facts or his guilt generally. But it would not appear to be permissible to shift what has been described as the "legal onus" on to the accused.

---

[312] *Id.* at p.146. See also *State (McEldowney) v. Kelleher* [1983] I.R. 289.
[313] [1993] 3 I.R. 528.
[314] *Id.* at p.532.
[315] *Id.* at p.534.
[316] [1994]
[317] *Id.* at p.557.
[318] *Supra*, p.454.

Privileged Information

That certain information relevant to the issues in dispute and otherwise admissible in evidence is privileged, and consequently disclosure of it cannot be compelled in court, has been referred to in connection with the questions of self-incrimination,[319] and also of legislative privilege and executive privilege.[320] This latter privilege is very narrow. In *Murphy v. Dublin Corp.*,[321] where Walsh J. defined its scope, the judge stressed that he was dealing with a civil action and not with a prosecution. Deeming evidence to be privileged and thereby inadmissible means that the interest that the privilege protects is more compelling than the community's as well as the parties' interest in all relevant facts being disclosed to the court.

In *People v. Eccles*,[322] the Court of Criminal Appeal accepted that, in the light of what was held in the *Murphy* case, the Gardaí no longer can claim privilege over all their internal memoranda. Nevertheless, it was held that the Garda Chief Superintendent there was entitled to claim privilege regarding his source of information concerning the accused. He had been arrested under section 30 of the Offences Against the State Act 1939 in connection with the murder of a Garda Officer of which he was convicted. The arrest was extended by the Chief Superintendent for a further 24 hours, on the grounds that he had obtained information that warranted the prolonged detention. When asked to reveal the source or the nature of the source of this information, the Chief Superintendent claimed privilege. It was held that this was privileged because of the information's sensitive and confidential nature. According to Hederman J., for the court, "(n)ormally, a member of the Garda Síochána cannot claim privilege in respect of information received from a fellow member of the force simply by virtue of its being such a communication."[323] But in the exceptional circumstances of the case there, the Chief Superintendent was held entitled to refuse to say even whether his source was within the police or was a civilian.

Withholding information on the basis of the informers' privilege is subject, however, to the "innocence at stake" exception. This arises where disclosing an informer's identity is "necessary or right" in order to establish the accused's innocence. In those circumstances, the overriding public policy is "that which says that an innocent man is not to be condemned when his innocence can be proved. ..."[324] Accordingly, potentially relevant documentation that would disclose the identity of an informer should be given to the trial judge, so that

---

[319] *Supra*, p.456.
[320] *Supra*, pp.107 and 130.
[321] [1972] I.R. 215; *supra*, p.130.
[322] (1986) 3 Frewen 36.
[323] *Id.* at p.63; similarly *People v. Reddan* [1995] 3 I.R. 560 at p.571.
[324] *Marks v. Beyfus* (1890) 25 Q.B.D. 494 at p.498.

he can determine whether it would be so useful to the defence that the privilege should be overridden. In *DPP v. Special Criminal Court*,[325] the judges there proposed that the documentation should be given to the accused's legal advisors for that purpose, on the basis that its contents would not be disclosed to the accused himself, without further order of the court. But that approach to the problem was overruled by the Supreme Court, rejecting the argument that it is impractical and unrealistic to expect the trial judge to evaluate the significance of the material when he does not know what the accused's instructions are or the nature of any investigations that have been carried out on his behalf. The proposed approach could undermine the relationship between the lawyers and their client, if they were aware of issues that they could not disclose to him. Also there could be practical difficulties in conducting the defence. O'Flaherty J. emphasised that prosecuting counsel had an important role in this regard, in assisting the court to ascertain which material might indeed be particularly useful to the defence; State counsel's role is not exclusively to secure a conviction but to "assist in ensuring a fair and just trial."[326]

Formerly, spouses could not be compelled to give evidence against their partners but this was radically changed by Part IV (sections 20-26) of the Criminal Evidence Act 1992. However, these provisions do not "affect any right of a spouse or former spouse in respect of marital privacy," which is a constitutionally guaranteed entitlement.[327] Communications with priests-confessors are also constitutionally protected against forced disclosure.[328] Whether or to what extent what is known as legal professional privilege is so protected remains to be determined,[329] as does the question of whether it too is subject to an "innocence at stake" exception.

Unconstitutionally Obtained Evidence

Where information that is relevant to the issues and otherwise admissible in evidence has been obtained unlawfully, can it be used by the prosecution? The argument for admitting this evidence is that all information that is relevant to the case should be made available to the court. On the other hand, it is considered improper that the prosecution should benefit by contravening the law; that illegally obtained evidence should be excluded in order to deter the police from acting unlawfully when investigating crime. At times a distinction is drawn between tangible physical evidence and a confession or other admission made by the accused. What should be done with illegally obtained

---

[325] [1999] 1 I.R. 60.
[326] *Id.*, at p.88.
[327] *Infra*, p.669.
[328] *Infra*, p.632.
[329] *Infra*, p.650.

evidence has puzzled courts in most jurisdictions.[330] At common law the position was that, except for certain self-incriminating admissions that were not made voluntary, the courts had no power to exclude evidence simply on account of the manner in which it was obtained.

According to Kingsmill Moore J. in *People v. O'Brien*,[331] there is no hard and fast rule either rendering all illegally obtained evidence admissible or, on the contrary, excluding all such evidence. Instead, the governing principle is the "intermediate solution", where the trial judge in each particular case takes into account the nature of the crime being investigated, the nature and extent of the illegality in question, and determines whether or not, in the light of all the circumstances, the evidence in question should be excluded. A balancing exercise of this nature is required because "a choice has to be made between desirable ends which may be incompatible. It is desirable in the public interest that crime should be detected and punished. It is (also) desirable that individuals should not be subjected to illegal or inquisitorial methods of investigation and that the State should not attempt to advance its ends by utilising the fruits of such methods. (One should) lay emphasis not so much on the alleged fairness to the accused as on the public interest that the law should be observed even in the investigation of crime."[332] Therefore, it is for the trial judge in each instance to decide, in the light of the conflicting policies and all the circumstances of the case, whether or not to exclude the evidence.

In countries with constitutions that guarantee certain basic rights, like personal liberty, bodily integrity, inviolability of the home, privacy and the right to silence, the additional question arises of whether or in what circumstances can otherwise relevant admissible evidence obtained in contravention of these guarantees be admitted against an accused. On this question the United States courts have generated a complex case law, interpreting the Fourth Amendment's stipulation that "(t)he right of the people to be secure in their persons, houses, papers and effects against unreasonable searches and seizures, shall not be violated," and the Fifth Amendment's provision that "(n)o person … shall be compelled in any criminal case to be a witness against himself …". Article 40.5 of the Constitution is very similar to the US guarantee of security in the dwelling[333] but the Constitution contains no express provision similar to the Fourth and Fifth Amendments' rights against unreasonable search and seizures, and against self-incrimination. What is involved here is whether the public interest in placing all information relevant

---

[330] See generally, Dawson, "The Exclusion of Unlawfully obtained Evidence: A Comparative Study", 31 *Int'l & Comp. L.Q.* 513 (1982) and Davies, "Exclusion of Evidence Illegally or Improperly Obtained", 76 *Australian L.J.* 170 (2002).

[331] [1965] I.R. 142.

[332] *Id.* at p.160.

[333] *Infra*, p.641.

to the accused's guilt before the court should be outweighed by fundamental values protected by the Constitution.[334]

In *People v. O'Brien*,[335] the Gardaí having got what they believed was a warrant to search the accused's home, searched it and found incriminating evidence there. However, the warrant was made out erroneously for a different address – it was to search 118 Cashel Rd. and not, as required, 118 Captain's Rd. Accordingly, the search was unlawful and, moreover, in contravention of Article 40.5, which declares that the "dwelling of every citizen is inviolable." The question that therefore arose was whether that unconstitutionally obtained evidence should have been admitted at his trial. The Supreme Court held that, in the circumstances, it was proper to admit the evidence because the accused's constitutional rights had not been contravened intentionally. Where evidence is obtained in breach of an accused's constitutional rights, the governing principle is that it should not be admitted where the State or its agents made a "deliberate and conscious violation" of those rights, unless special and extraordinary circumstances exist which necessitate admitting the evidence. Walsh J. formulated the governing principle as follows:

> "When the illegality amounts to infringement of a constitutional right the matter assumes a far greater importance than is the case where the illegality does not amount to such infringement. The vindication and the protection of constitutional rights is a fundamental matter for all Courts established under the Constitution. That duty cannot yield place to any other competing interest. In Article 40 of the Constitution, the State has undertaken to defend and vindicate the inviolability of the dwelling of every citizen. The defence and vindication of the constitutional rights of the citizen is a duty superior to that of trying such citizen for a criminal offence. The Courts in exercising the judicial powers of government of the State must recognise the paramount position of constitutional rights and must uphold the objection of an accused person to the admissibility at his trial of evidence obtained or procured by the State or its servants or agents as a result of a deliberate and conscious violation of the constitutional rights of the accused person where no extraordinary excusing circumstances exist, such as the imminent destruction of vital evidence or the need to rescue a victim in peril. A suspect has no constitutional right to destroy or dispose of evidence or to imperil the victim. I would also place in the excusable category evidence obtained by a search incidental to and contemporaneous with a lawful arrest although made without a valid search warrant."[336]

---

[334] See generally, *Walsh*, Chap.9.
[335] [1965] I.R. 142.
[336] *Id.* at p.170.

The admissibility of confessions and other admissions of guilt by accused persons has given rise to considerable controversy, especially where the accused alleges that the confession was made only in consequence of having been detained by the police for long periods and being maltreated by them. As summed up by Keane C.J. in *People v. Buck:*[337]

"Three propositions are firmly established in our law:

(1) a confession, whether made to a police officer or any other person, will not be admitted in evidence unless it is proved beyond reasonable doubt to have been voluntarily made;

(2) even where voluntarily made, a trial judge retains a residual discretion to exclude such a statement where it is made to a police officer otherwise than in accordance with certain procedures, accepted in Ireland as being embodied in the English Judges' Rules;

(3) such a statement will also be excluded where it has been obtained as a result of a conscious and deliberate violation of the accused's constitutional rights."[338]

Those circumstances that amount to a conscious and deliberate violation of constitutional rights and exceptional special circumstances warranting admitting evidence notwithstanding such violation, are the subject of extensive case law turning on the facts of each particular instance.

SENTENCE

Where the accused is convicted, sentence is pronounced by the presiding judge.[339] Usually there is a range of possible sentences within which the one most appropriate to the circumstances and to the accused's condition is selected. The principal forms of sentence that are imposed are imprisonment,[340] community service, a fine, a compensation order, forfeiture of property connected with the offence, disqualification from holding a driving licence or certain other licences, a probation order. A person convicted of a breach of the peace may also be required to enter into recognisances of good behaviour and a person convicted of an offence where imprisonment is a penalty may, in the circumstances, have that sentence suspended. Special provisions exist for young

---

[337] [2002] 2 I.R. 268

[338] *Id.* at p.277.

[339] See generally, *Walsh*, Chap.21 and T. O'Malley, *Sentencing Law and Practice* (2000), especially Chap.4 on the "constitutional context."

[340] See generally, P. McDermott, *Prison Law* (2000).

offenders. Capital punishment was abolished by statute in 1990, as was corporal punishment in 1997.

The only references in the Constitution to sentencing are Article 15.5.2, abolishing capital punishment (in 2002), and Article 13.6, empowering the President, on the advice of the Government, to grant pardons, and also to commute and remit sentences, which power may be conferred by law on other authorities. Because the District Court may only try minor offences,[341] there is an implied constitutional restriction on the sentence that can be imposed there. Where their likely sentence is imprisonment, indigent accused persons have a constitutional right to legal assistance at their trial at public expense.[342] On several occasions the European Court of Human Rights has stressed that the executive should not be given a role in determining how long a person should be held in custody following conviction, which is tantamount to the length of sentence being determined by the executive and not by the courts.[343]

Judicial Function

Deciding what sentence is to be imposed in individual instances has been held to be an intrinsically judicial function that can be exercised only by judges in the courts and in which the executive should play no significant role. In *Deaton v. Attorney General*,[344] where the plaintiff had been convicted of certain smuggling offences, the sentence prescribed was either a fine of £100 or a forfeit of treble the value of the goods concerned, including the duty to be paid on them. But it was for the Revenue Commissioners and not the presiding judge to determine which of these sanctions was to be applied in each instance. The Supreme Court held that giving the Revenue authority to choose the penalty contravened the separation of powers principle. By tradition and by its very nature, determining what sentence should be applied in criminal cases is a judicial function and, therefore, a task that only can be performed by duly appointed judges. According to Ó Dálaigh C.J.:

> "Traditionally, … choice (of penalty) has lain with the Courts. Where the Legislature has prescribed a range of penalties the individual citizen who has committed an offence is safeguarded from the Executive's displeasure by the choice of penalty being in the determination of an independent judge. The individual citizen needs the safeguard of the Courts in the assessment of punishment as much as on his trial for the

---

[341] *Supra*, p.420.
[342] *Supra*, p.438.
[343] E.g., *Stafford v. United Kingdom*, 35 E.H.R.R. 1121 (2002), applied in *R. (Anderson) v. Secretary of State* [2002] 3 W.L.R. 1800.
[344] [1963] I.R. 170.

offence. The degree of punishment which a particular citizen is to undergo for an offence is a matter vitally affecting his liberty: and it is inconceivable to my mind that a Constitution which is broadly based on the doctrine of the separation of powers – and in this the Constitution of Saorstát Éireann and the Constitution of Ireland are at one – could have intended to place in the hands of the Executive the power to select the punishment to be undergone by citizens. It would not be too strong to characterise such a system of government as one of arbitrary power."[345]

This reasoning was relied on by Barron J. in *Murphy v. Wallace*[346] to invalidate section 90 of the Excise Management Act 1827, under which certain tax defaulters could be imprisoned by order of the District Court but they could be released at any time on the direction of the Revenue Commissioners. It does not appear to have been argued there that the power given to the Revenue in this regard was to "commute or remit punishment," as envisaged by Article 13.6.

A similar instance arose in *State (O) v. O'Brien*[347] concerning section 103 of the (since repealed) Children Act 1908, which empowered the court to sentence a young offender found guilty of murder to "be detained during His Majesty's pleasure." If this section meant that the offender could be held in prison for as long as the Minister or some other executive authority deems appropriate then, in the light of the *Deaton* case, it was unconstitutional because it would in effect empower the executive to determine what sentence should be served. In Walsh J.'s words, "once there is an element of selection or discretion (in sentencing), then … it falls within the judicial sphere and cannot be characterised as an executive function."[348] However, the Supreme Court held that this was not the proper construction of the section in the light of the Free State and the present Constitutions,[349] and of the Adaptation of Enactments Act 1922. In the present constitutional scheme, section 103 was held to mean that the courts could impose an indeterminate sentence, which could be remitted in accordance with Article 13.6 of the Constitution.

In *State (Woods) v. Attorney General*,[350] the Supreme Court held that there was no contravention of the separation of powers principle where the judge imposed one sentence but added that the sentence will be reduced if the offender complies with prison discipline for a specified period. Even though many of the prison rules are extremely vague and there is a considerable degree of

---

[345] *Id.* at p.183.
[345] [1993] 2 I.R. 138.
[346] [1973] I.R. 50
[347] *Id.* at p.67. *Cf. DPP v. Mollison* [2003] 2 W.L.R. 1160.
[348] [1969] I.R. 385.
[349] Especially, Art.49.
[350] [1969] I.R. 385.

discretion in their application, the actual imposition of sentence remained "entirely within the judicial domain."[351]

Commuting and Remitting Punishments

Over the years it became almost common practice for convicted persons to petition the Minister for Justice to exercise the power under section 23 of the Criminal Justice Act 1951, to commute or remit their sentences; these requests frequently were supported by politicians. These were often acceded to even though there were nothing particularly exceptional in the convicted persons' circumstances other than that, if they had been drawn to the trial judge's attention, he might very well have taken them into account in determining the sentence. In *Brennan v. Minister for Justice*,[352] Geoghegan J. rejected the contention that the power to commute or remit a sentence was an exclusively judicial power. Traditionally it has been an executive function (one of the Crown prerogatives), it does not fit the well-established criteria for what constitutes the administration of justice and Article 13.6 is consistent with this view. That power is "the executive administration of mercy rather than the judicial administration of justice. ..."[353] However, the judge went on to hold that the practice of acceding to petitions of this nature had become so widespread that it was equivalent to the operation of a parallel fall-back system for the administration of justice. That state of affairs went beyond what was envisaged by section 23 of the 1951 Act and was *ultra vires*; this section was designed to deal with "exceptional cases," where the Minister believed that the judge's decision was "wholly unsupportable." A more appropriate mode of redress is to appeal the sentence to the Circuit Court and, if unsuccessful there, to seek to judicially review the sentence imposed on grounds of irrationality. Section 23 would seem to contemplate principally exceptional circumstances that come to light after the sentence has been passed and after the time for appealing has expired.

An extensive discretion is conferred by statute on the Minister to order the temporary release of prisoners for whatever periods and subject to such circumstances as he deems appropriate.[354]

When imposing a sentence for certain drug-trafficking offences, the judge may direct that it may be reviewed by the court when at least half of the period imposed has been served, which may result in the remainder of the sentence being suspended in the light of how the prisoner has behaved in the meantime. But it was held by the Supreme Court in *People v. Finn*[355] that, in the absence

---

[351] *Id.* at p.412.
[352] [1995] 1 I.R. 612.
[353] *Id.* at p.626.
[354] *E.g., Kinihan v. Minister for Justice* [2001] 4 I.R. 454.
[355] [2001] 2 I.R. 25.

of a comparable statutory power, the courts could not take it on themselves to provide for the review of sentences in this manner. Under Article 13.6 of the Constitution, the power to commute or remit punishment is vested in the President and can also be "conferred by law on other authorities." This power was given to the executive by section 23 of the 1951 Act, as described above. Accordingly, "the remission power, despite its essentially judicial character, once vested under the Constitution in an executive organ, cannot without further legislative intervention, be exercised by the courts."[356] Keane C.J. added that reservation of a review power by the judiciary also appeared to contravene the procedure for dealing with appeals stipulated in the Rules of the Superior Courts.

Mandatory Sentences

It was accepted as a basic premise in the *Deaton* and in the *State (O)* cases that, although the selection of punishment is an integral part of the administration of justice, it would not be unconstitutional for the Oireachtas to prescribe fixed mandatory sentences for particular offences. A mandatory sentence, according to Ó Dálaigh C.J. in *Deaton*, "is the statement of a general rule which is one of the characteristics of legislation; this is wholly different from the selection of a penalty to be imposed in a particular case ... The Legislature does not prescribe the penalty to be imposed in an individual citizen's case; it states the general rule, and the application of that rule is for the Courts. If the general rule is enunciated in the form of a fixed penalty then all citizens convicted of the offence must bear the same punishment."[357] However, this does not mean that mandatory sentences never contravene other constitutional provisions, notably the guarantee of equality in the law or some principle requiring proportionality in sentencing.

Excessive Punishments

Article 3 of the European Convention prohibits "inhuman or degrading ... punishment," as does Article 7 of the UN Covenant, which also condemns "cruel ... punishment [i]n particular medical or scientific experimentation." Inflicting "cruel and unusual punishments" and imposing "excessive fines" are prohibited by the United States Constitution's Eighth Amendment, and occasionally the U.S. courts have struck down mandatory fines or forfeitures for being excessive. According to Article 8 of the 1789 Declaration of the Rights of Man and of Citizen, "[t]he law must impose no penalties other than

---

[356] *Id.* at p.46.
[357] [1963] I.R. 170 at p.182.

those which are absolutely and clearly necessary. ..." Irish courts may no longer impose the death penalty or corporal punishment. The most severe punishment they presently may impose is a mandatory minimum of forty years imprisonment for intentional murder of a member of the Garda Síochána or a prison officer on duty, or of certain others.[358]

Prison Conditions

Notwithstanding their incarceration, prisoners have constitutional rights but it has been held permissible to deprive them of certain rights, most notably to have conjugal visits with a view to having children[359] and to vote in general and other elections.[360] But they are not to be treated in any manner incompatible with their human dignity. For instance, it has been held that publishing photographs of a prisoner coming to and from court shackled to prison officers may amount to a contempt of court.[361] There are numerous decisions by the Strasbourg court holding that a variety of prison conditions contravened the European Convention.[362]

APPEAL/REVIEW

Article 2(1) of the European Convention's 7th Protocol and Article 14(5) of the UN Covenant stipulate that "[e]veryone convicted of a crime shall have the right to his conviction and sentence being reviewed by a higher tribunal according to law." Although the Constitution grants a right of appeal from the Central Criminal Court/High Court to the Supreme Court, that right is one that can be regulated and indeed taken away entirely by the Oireachtas, except where the constitutionality of post-1937 legislation is in issue. Both the European Convention's 7th Protocol and the UN Covenant provide that persons whose convictions are later overturned, because there was "a miscarriage of justice," must be compensated. In addition to the statutory rights of appeal as exist, convictions in the District Court and in the Circuit Court also can be challenged on limited grounds by way of application for judicial review or, exceptionally, for *habeas corpus*.

---

[358] Criminal Justice Act 1999, s 3. *Cf. Morrisey v. R.*, 191 D.L.R. 4th 86 (2000); *Latimer v. The Queen*, 193 D.L.R. 4th 577 (2001), *R.. v. Lichniak* [2002] 3 W.L.R. 1834 and *Life Imprisonment case*, 45 BVerfGE 187 (1977) (Germany).

[359] *Murray v. Ireland* [1991] I.L.R.M. 465; *infra*, p.678.

[360] *Breathnach v. Ireland* [2001] 3 I.R. 461; *infra*, p.596.

[361] *People v. Davis* [2001] 1 I.R. 146.

[362] *E.g., Keenan v. United Kingdom*, 33 E.H.R.R. 38 (2001) and *Price v. United Kingdom*, 39 E.H.R.R. 53 (2002); also *R. (Hirst) v. Secretary of State* [2002] 1 W.L.R. 2929.

Appeal

A comprehensive and thorough system of appellate review is a long-standing feature of continental European criminal procedure. Appeals in criminal cases are a comparatively modern phenomenon in common law countries; it is only since 1924 that convictions in jury trials could be appealed.[363] The right of appeal was exclusively a matter of statute: if there was no statutory grant of an appeal, then no appeal could be taken. Under the present procedure,[364] persons convicted in the District Court can appeal to the Circuit Court and those convicted in the Circuit Court or the Central Criminal Court can appeal to the Court of Criminal Appeal. An accused can only appeal from the latter Court to the Supreme Court in limited circumstances.

Judges have given different answers to the question of whether the Constitution itself grants a right of appeal to the High Court in criminal cases. In 1973, when this issue was first brought to the Supreme Court, in a remarkable judgment of just two sentences length, the court declined any comment on the issue. That was *State (Hunt) v. O'Donovan*,[365] where the accused pleaded guilty in the District Court to charges of indictable offences and was sent forward for sentence to the Circuit Court. He then sought to appeal against the sentence but, at that time, the Criminal Procedure Acts gave him no right of appeal in those circumstances. He contended that the Constitution entitled him to appeal to the High Court and that those Acts were unconstitutional insofar as they sought to deprive him of any appeal. Contrasting the terms of Article 34.4 (on the Supreme Court) with Article 34.3, Finlay P. concluded that the latter Article did not "confer a universal right of appeal" to the High Court.[366] Article 34.3.4 provides that there shall be "a right of appeal as determined by law" from courts of local and limited jurisdiction, such as the Circuit Court. Accordingly, it was held that the Oireachtas cannot establish subordinate courts from which no appeal whatsoever can be taken to the High Court. But it is constitutionally permissible for the Oireachtas to stipulate that certain decisions made by subordinate courts are not appealable, for instance the sentence given by the Circuit Court there. If the Constitution had intended that all Circuit Court and District Court decisions were to be appealable, it would not have stipulated that appeals from them shall be "determined by law," which in the context means an Act of the post-1937 Oireachtas.

By virtue of Article 34.4.3 of the Constitution and in the absence of clear and unambiguous legislative provision to the contrary, there is a constitutional

---

[363] Courts of Justice Act 1924; see generally, R. Pattenden, *English Criminal Appeals, 1844–1994* (1996).

[364] See generally, *Walsh*, Chap.22.

[365] [1975] I.R. 39.

[366] *Id.* at p.48.

right of appeal to the Supreme Court from a verdict of the Central Criminal Court; there is "appellate jurisdiction from all decisions" of the High Court. In *People (A. G.) v. Conmey*[367] the Supreme Court held that "all decisions" means literally all decisions. The accused, who had been convicted by the Central Criminal Court, appealed first to the Court of Criminal Appeal and then sought to appeal to the Supreme Court. It was held that, had he not chosen to appeal to the Court of Criminal Appeal, he would have had a constitutional right of appeal to the Supreme Court. But having brought his case to the Court of Criminal Appeal, which rejected his appeal, he had completely exhausted the High Court's power over the case; accordingly, there was no longer a High Court judgment that could be appealed. In *People v. Lynch*,[368] the accused, who was convicted by the Central Criminal Court, appealed directly to the Supreme Court, which held that it had a constitutional obligation to hear the appeal. In both of these cases the Supreme Court stressed that, except for cases raising a question of the validity of any law under the Constitution, Article 34.4.3 permits the Oireachtas to regulate or to deprive it of its jurisdiction to hear appeals from the High Court. Any legislative provision cutting down this jurisdiction "would of necessity have to be clear and unambiguous."[369]

A provision to this effect is contained in section 11 of the Criminal Procedure Act 1993, which "abolished" the right of appeal to the Supreme Court from the Central Criminal Court, except where the constitutionality of some law is in issue or, as provided for in section 34 of the Criminal Procedure Act 1967, which enables the prosecution to appeal in limited circumstances without affecting the actual verdict. There is a right of appeal from the Court of Criminal Appeal where either that court, or the Attorney General, has certified that the decision "involves a point of law of exceptional public importance and that it is desirable in the public interest" that an appeal should be taken.[370]

Appealing Against Acquittals

Formerly, prosecutors could not appeal to the Circuit Court or to the Court of Criminal Appeal against an acquittal. But they have since been given extensive appeal rights from the District Court and sentences imposed by the Circuit Court or by the Central Criminal Court can be reviewed by the Court of Criminal Appeal on the grounds that they are "unduly lenient." To date, no endeavour has been made to permit acquittals in jury trials to be appealed. A partial exception is section 34 of the Criminal Procedure Act 1967, which enables the Attorney General, if the accused is acquitted on the trial judge's direction,

---

[367] [1975] I.R. 341.
[368] [1982] I.R. 64.
[369] [1975] I.R. 341 at p.360; *supra*, p.157.
[370] Criminal Justice Act 1924, s.29.

to "refer a question of law" to the Supreme Court but without prejudice to the verdict.

In *People v. O'Shea*,[371] the Supreme Court affirmed *dicta* in the *Conmey* case to the effect that, not alone does an accused who is convicted by the Central Criminal Court have a qualified constitutional right of appeal to the Supreme Court, but the prosecution also have a right of appeal against an acquittal there. Traditionally, prosecutors never had redress against acquittals: once an accused was acquitted, the verdict could not be impeached or appealed against, and an accused could never be prosecuted again for the same offence because of *autrefois acquit*. In strong dissents, Finlay P. and Henchy J. contended that to permit prosecutors to appeal against acquittals would violate the integrity of the jury's verdict and contravene the fundamental principles of jury trial and double jeopardy. In an eloquent paragraph, Henchy J. declared that he was:

> "[s]atisfied that the indissoluble attachment to trial by jury of the right after acquittal to raise the plea of *autrefois acquit* was one of the prime reasons why the Constitution of 1937 (like that of 1922) mandated trial with a jury as the normal mode of trying major offences. The bitter Irish race-memory of politically appointed and Executive-oriented judges, of the suspension of jury trial in times of popular revolt, of the substitution therefore of summary trial or detention without trial, of cat-and-mouse releases from such detention, of packed juries, and sometimes corrupt judges and prosecutors, had long implanted in the consciousness of the people, and, therefore, in the minds of their political representatives, the conviction that the best way of preventing an individual from suffering a wrong conviction for an offence was to allow him to 'put himself upon his country', that is to say, to allow him to be tried for that offence by a fair, impartial and representative jury, sitting in a court presided over by an impartial and independent judge appointed under the Constitution, who would see that all the requirements for a fair and proper jury trial would be observed, so that, amongst other things, if the jury's verdict were one of not guilty, the accused could leave the court with the absolute assurance that he would never again be vexed for the same charge."[372]

But the majority in *O'Shea* took the position that the plain and unambiguous terms of the Constitution must be given their literal meaning even if that might offend against traditions in criminal procedure. According to O'Higgins C.J., "the clear words of the Constitution cannot be limited or restricted by advertence to what had been the law, the policies or the procedures formerly recognised

---

[371] [1982] I.R. 384.
[372] *Id.* at p.432.

or practised."[373] He added that permitting prosecutors to appeal against acquittals would not be grossly unfair or unjust because accused persons today have access to State-financed legal representation. Moreover, any claim by the accused to fair treatment would have to be viewed in the light of the State's duty under the Constitution "to detect and suppress crime."[374] In response to the contention that allowing prosecutors to appeal undermines the principle of jury trial, Walsh J, stated that such a "most valuable safeguard for the liberties of the citizen ... must ... be permitted to operate properly."[375] To take an extreme example, the law should allow some means whereby acquittal verdicts that were secured by grossly improper means could be set aside; that "[i]t would be totally abhorrent if a conviction which had been obtained by improper means, such as the corruption or coercion of a jury, should be allowed to stand. It should be equally abhorrent if an acquittal obtained by the same methods should be allowed to stand. If attempts to sway the verdicts of jurors by intimidation or other corrupt means were allowed to go unchecked, they could eventually bring about the destruction of the jury system of trial."[376]

A statutory provision entitling the prosecution to appeal to the Circuit Court against an acquittal in the District Court was upheld in *Considine v. Shannon Regional Fisheries Board*.[377] According to Hamilton C.J., for the Supreme Court, Article 34.3.4 provides that any appeal from those courts shall be "determined by law," which was clear and unambiguous, and there was no constitutional provision that prevented State appeals being permitted. He pointed out that in the past appeals by prosecutors could exist where there was very clear statutory language to that effect. But since at that time there were no constitutional constraints on the legislature, that only stated the obvious and lends nothing to the reasoning.

Judicial Review

Convictions and sentences in the District Court and in the Circuit Court can be challenged by the accused and also by the prosecution by way of an application for judicial review by the High Court, but on very limited grounds.[378] The procedure is contained in Order 84 of the Rules of the Superior Courts and the remedy almost invariably sought is an order of *certiorari* quashing the order being contested. In very exceptional circumstances, convictions may be challenged in the form of an Article 40.4/*habeas corpus*

---

[373] *Id.* at p.403.
[374] *Id.* at p.405.
[375] *Id.* at p.418.
[376] *Ibid.*
[377] [1997] 2 I.R. 404.
[378] *Cf. Buckley v. Kirby* [2000] 3 I.R. 431 and *Blanchfield v. Harnett* [2002] 3 I.R. 207.

enquiry. Where the convicted person's case falls within the scope of these non-appellate avenues of redress, they usually will be preferred because they are speedier than an appeal and they lead to conclusive results. In the *Tormey* case[379] the Supreme Court held that the High Court's traditional supervisory jurisdiction over the lower courts is part of that court's "full original jurisdiction" within Article 34.3.1 of the Constitution. Consequently, the Oireachtas cannot deprive the court of this jurisdiction.

JUVENILE JUSTICE

There are no constitutional provisions dealing in terms with the trial of juveniles on criminal charges. Ireland is a party to the Convention on the Rights of the Child,[380] Article 40 of which contains guarantees in respect of criminal laws and procedures. Many of these are given effect in the Children Act 2001, which applies to persons under 18 years of age. It, *inter alia*, lifted the age of criminal responsibility to 12, and further to 14 but subject to a rebuttable presumption; it also deals with treatment of suspects in Garda custody and the Children's Court.

MILITARY JUSTICE

Traditionally, discipline within the armed forces is maintained through a system of court-martials, whereby members of the forces accused of wrongdoing are tried by a bench of army officers.[381] Article 38.4 of the Constitution maintains this system by providing that:

> "1. Military tribunals may be established for the trial of offences against military law alleged to have been committed by persons while subject to military law ...
> 2. A member of the defence forces not on active service shall not be tried by any court martial or other military tribunal for an offence cognisable by the civil courts unless such offence is within the jurisdiction of any court-martial or other military tribunal under any law for the enforcement of military discipline."

Where there is a "state of war or armed rebellion," civilians may be tried by court martial.[382]

---

[379] [1985] I.R. 289; *supra*, p.148.
[380] November 20, 1989, 1577 UNTS 3.
[381] *Cf. Loving v. United States*, 517 U.S. 748 (1996) and *Minister of Defence v. Potsane* [2001] 3 L.R.C. 579 (S. Afr.).
[382] Art. 38.4.1; *infra*, p.865.

Part V (sections 118–251) of the Defence Act 1954, deals with liability to military law, offences against military law and court-martials.[383] A right of appeal from these tribunals was established by the Courts-Martial Appeals Act 1983, against conviction or sentence, with a restricted right of further appeal to the Supreme Court.

INTERNATIONAL CRIMINAL COURT

Article 29.9 of the Constitution permits the State to ratify the Rome Statute for the International Criminal Court[384] and in 2003 the Government published a Bill to give effect to its obligations under this statute.

---

[383] See generally, G. Humphries & C. Craven, *Military Law in Ireland* (1997).

[384] Of July 17, 1998, 37 I.L.M. 999 (1998), *Cf.* Statute of International Criminal Court decision, Cons. Constitutional, January 22, 1999; also, International Criminal Court Bill, 2003.

CHAPTER 18

Civil and Other Procedures

Most national constitutions and all of the general international human rights instruments contain guarantees of fair procedures; that individuals will not be adversely affected by the State without them being given an opportunity to have a fair hearing of their case before an impartial tribunal. The extent of protected procedural fairness depends on the subject matter and kind of decision being taken, and the general nature of the decision-making process in question. More rigorous procedural protections exist in civil litigation than for administrative adjudications and determinations. Contempt of court is a somewhat difficult process to classify and has close affinities with criminal procedure.

CIVIL LITIGATION

Civil procedure concerns the manner in which civil trials are conducted.[1] There is no express constitutional provision for civil trials that resembles the "due process of law" requirement for criminal trials. But it is implicit in Article 34.1 of the Constitution's requirement, that "(j)ustice shall be administered in courts," that civil procedure should be fair; additionally, fair civil procedures are required by Article 40.3 of the Constitution. In *S. v. S.*,[2] a case concerning evidence of paternity, O'Hanlon J. observed that the "combined effect of (these) constitutional provisions appears ... to guarantee *(inter alia)* something equivalent to the concept of 'due process' under the American Constitution in relation to causes and controversies litigated before the Courts," and that "(j)ust as parties have a right to access to the Courts when this is necessary to defend or vindicate life, person, good name or property rights, so they have a constitutional entitlement to fair procedures when they get to court."[3] Article 6(1) of the European Convention and Article 14(1) of the UN Covenant, which deal with the "determination of [ones] civil rights and obligations" as well as criminal charges, provide that persons are "entitled to a fair and public hearing within a reasonable time by an independent and impartial tribunal" and, subject to exceptions, "[j]udgment shall be pronounced publicly. ..."

---

[1] See generally, H. Delany & D. McGrath, *Civil Procedure in the Superior Courts* (2001) (hereafter, "*Delany & McGrath*") and J. Jolowicz, *On Civil Procedure* (2000).
[2] [1983] I.R. 68.
[3] *Id.* at pp.79 and 80.

Under the Constitution, the "distribution of jurisdiction and business among the said Courts and judges, and all matters of procedure (must) be regulated in accordance with law ..."[4] By virtue of the separation of powers principle, neither the executive nor the legislature can interfere with the actual administration of justice, as is exemplified in the *"Sinn Fein Funds"* case.[5] There the Oireachtas attempt to prevent a case from being heard and to determine who should own funds that were the subject matter of a court case, was declared unconstitutional. Questions of procedure are governed primarily by the Rules of Court – the Rules for the Superior Courts, for the Circuit Court and for the District Court – and there are also numerous statutory provisions that deal with procedures. Courts also have an "inherent jurisdiction" of somewhat uncertain ambit to make procedural improvisations.[6]

Access to Justice

That everyone with a legitimate grievance should have a reasonable opportunity to have their claim determined fairly is the fundamental objective of civil procedure. What the rules of procedure endeavour to achieve is to regulate that access in such a manner as is compatible with the legitimate interests of defendants and of third parties, and with the not unlimited resources of the court system. Accordingly, it is not each and every civil claim that the courts will entertain and indeed there are a vast number of disputes that can only be determined by administrative tribunals rather than by the courts. Where the claim being made is plainly unstateable from the outset, it will be dismissed without a full hearing, as an abuse of the process;[7] there are parallels here with the procedure in the District Court for filtering criminal prosecutions with little real prospect of ever succeeding. Claims may also be dismissed at the outset where they involve in substance relitigating issues that have already been decided in earlier proceedings between the very same parties; the doctrine civil *res judicata*[8] resembles criminal double jeopardy. As was explained above, there are several circumstances where an otherwise good claim will not succeed because the defendant in question enjoys immunity.[9]

In order to bring proceedings of certain kinds, prior application must be made to the High Court for authorisation to commence them – principally proceedings regarding actions taken under the Mental Health Act 2001, appli-

---

[4] Art.36. iii.
[5] *Buckley v. Attorney General* [1950] I.R. 67; *supra*, p.200.
[6] See generally, Dockray, "The Inherent Jurisdiction to Regulate Civil Proceedings", 113 *L.Q.R.* 120 (1997).
[7] See generally, *Delany & McGrath*, Chap.12.
[8] See generally, *id.*, Chap.24 and P. McDermott, *Res Judicata* (1999).
[9] *Supra*, p.300.

cations for judicial review of deportations and related orders, and challenges to compulsory purchase orders and planning permissions. It was held by the Supreme Court in *Sections 5 and 10 of the Illegal Immigrants (Trafficking) Bill, 1999, Re*,[10] that it is constitutionally permissible to require challenges to a variety of decisions concerning refugee applications and deportations to be brought by way of judicial review, on notice to the other party of the leave application, within tight time limits and where substantial grounds for obtaining leave must be demonstrated. For the court, Keane C.J. pointed out that the Oireachtas had a reasonably free hand in laying down the mode for contesting decisions taken by public authorities and, especially as this Bill did not seek to restrict any particular ground of challenge, "judicial review as such is not an inadequate remedy."[11] Because the fourteen days time limit laid down for commencing proceedings could be extended by the court in appropriate cases, it was not unduly restrictive. "Substantial grounds" for challenging decisions in this context means "reasonable, arguable and weighty," as contrasted with "trivial or tenuous" grounds,[12] and it was permissible for the Oireachtas in cases of this nature to restrict the right to a full hearing of an applicant's case until substantial grounds for the claim are first established to the satisfaction of the High Court. Because decisions of several other categories of public officials could only be challenged in a similar manner, these limitations on access to the courts were not unfairly discriminatory.

Litigants cannot be required to pay excessive fees and charges as a precondition of being permitted to bring proceedings, either against the State or against private parties. No stamp duty or other charge is imposed on applicants who seek *habeas corpus* orders under Article 40.4 of the Constitution. In *Murphy v. Minister for Justice*,[13] the Supreme Court rejected a contention by the plaintiff that it was unconstitutional to require him to pay fees of £17 in all in order to apply for judgment against another party who failed to file his defence. Because all public services must be funded by money raised from the public, principally either by way of taxes or charges for services, there was no constitutional ban on imposing some charge on litigants even though it may inhibit to an extent their decision to go to court. But "unreasonable charges" could not be imposed.[14] On their face, the charges there did not seem to be unduly excessive and, further, there was insufficient evidence before the court to show that, in the circumstances of this case, the plaintiff had insufficient resources and was not able to obtain legal assistance elsewhere, for instance from the State legal aid scheme. For the court, Murphy J. expressed doubts about the plaintiff's *locus standi* to mount the constitutional challenge.

---

[10] [2000] 2 I.R. 360.
[11] *Id.* at p.388.
[12] *Id.* at p.395.
[13] [2001] 1 I.R. 103.
[14] *E.g., Ndyanabo v. Attorney General* [2002] 3 L.R.C. 541 (Tanzania).

In special circumstances, plaintiffs can be required to lodge a sum by way of security for the defendant's costs, in the event of their claim being ultimately dismissed.[15] The contention that this was unconstitutional was rejected by O'Hanlon J.[16] Whether or in what circumstances what are described as "pay first, argue later" statutory requirements do not accord with the Constitution's implicit guarantee of access to justice remains to be determined.[17]

A major deterrent against vindicating one's rights in litigation is the cost of court proceedings, especially in the High Court where (as in Britain) legal costs are far higher than in most if not all continental European countries. For some aggrieved parties who are indigent this difficulty is resolved by the provision of legal aid.[18] But in addition to a non-aided litigant's own legal costs, ordinarily he is required to pay the costs of the other party in the event that he loses the case. Exceptionally, however, when the case involves a major issue of public importance and the State is one of the parties, it will be obliged to pay the other's costs regardless of the outcome.[19]

Where proceedings are pending in the District Court or the Circuit Court, then unless the court does not have jurisdiction to deal with the question, ordinarily the High Court will not grant an order prohibiting the hearing from going ahead. If there are circumstances that indicate that the case ought to be adjourned, at minimum an adjournment application should first be made to the trial judge. In *Colmey v. Pinewood Developments Ltd.*[20] it was held by Carroll J. that "[t]he District Court should not be injuncted from exercising its jurisdiction conferred by statute. This Court must assume that the District Court Judge will administer justice in accordance with the law. The balance of convenience lies in preserving free access to the District Court."[21] Earlier in *State (Llewellyn) v. Ua Donnchadha*,[22] a District Judge had rejected an application to adjourn a prosecution notwithstanding that the legislation in question was being challenged in the High Court by other parties. It was held by the Supreme Court that he had a jurisdiction to decide whether or not to grant that adjournment, which should not be interfered with by an order of prohibition. In view of the presumption of constitutionality, the District Judge must act on the basis that the law in question is valid. Often, however, adjournments are granted in those circumstances, until the constitutional challenge has been concluded.

---

[15] See generally, *Delany & McGrath*, Chap.10.
[16] *Salih v. General Accident Assur. Corp.* [1987] I.R. 628.
[17] *Cf. Metcash v. Com'r for South African Revenue*, 11 B.H.R.C. 497 (2000).
[18] *Infra*, p.492.
[19] *E.g.*, in *Horgan v. An Taoiseach* [2003] 2 I.L.R.M. 3357 the State was ordered to pay half of the unsuccessful plaintiff's costs.
[20] [1994] 3 I.R. 360.
[21] *Id.* at p.365.
[22] [1984] I.R. 525.

Venue

By venue in this context is meant where the trial takes place. As was explained earlier when considering the jurisdiction of the High Court, at one time it was believed that the Oireachtas could not deprive that court of jurisdiction to try civil cases.[23] But, following *Tormey v. Ireland*,[24] it would seem that it can confer exclusive jurisdiction to try particular categories of case on the Circuit Court and perhaps even on the District Court, provided that the High Court retains its traditional jurisdiction to supervise the workings of those courts by way of judicial review.

Venue in civil cases used to be dealt with by statute but is now regulated primarily by the Rules of Court.[25] Provision is made for remitting or transferring actions to a higher court or to a lower court, or from one circuit to another. Where the case has a significant international element, the Irish courts may not have jurisdiction or, in certain circumstances where they have jurisdiction, they may decline to exercise it on grounds of *forum non-conveniens*.[26]

Independent and Impartial Tribunal

Not alone must judges be independent of the legislature and the executive,[27] but they must also be independent of the parties. At common law a judge should not try a case where, because of some relationship with one of the parties, there is an apparent likelihood of bias – the maxim of *nemo iudex in sua causa*. A distinction is drawn between actual bias, which automatically disqualifies, and objective bias, meaning circumstances that may create a risk of bias. It was held by the Supreme Court in *Bula Ltd. v. Tara Mines Ltd. (no. 6)*[28] that the test for objective bias is "whether a reasonable person in the circumstances would have a reasonable apprehension that the [litigant] would not receive a fair trial of the issues."[29] A "real danger of bias" as the test was rejected because it does not take sufficient account of the need to ensure that public confidence in the judicial system should be maintained. The premise for the "reasonable apprehension" test is that "public confidence in the administration of justice is more likely to be maintained if the Court adopts a test that reflects the reaction of the ordinary reasonable member of the public

---

[23] *Supra*, p.148.
[24] [1985] I.R. 289.
[25] See generally, *Delany & McGrath*, Chap.12.
[26] *E.g. Analog Devices B.V. v. Zurich Ins. Co.* [2002] 1 I.R. 272.
[27] *Supra*, p.166.
[28] [2000] 4 I.R. 412.
[29] *Id.* at p.439.

to the irregularity in question."[30] Obvious examples are where the judge is related to one of the parties or has some financial interest in one of them.

In the *Bula* case it was contented that two Supreme Court judges who heard the appeal there had, previously as barristers, acted for one of the parties. It was held that the mere fact that a judge once had acted for a party as his legal advisor or his advocate is insufficient to disqualify him in this regard; indeed if this were not the case, many judges would not be able to try cases in which the State was a party. Additional aspects of the relationship between them may tip the balance in favour of disqualification; these were held not to obtain in *Bula*, where, *inter alia*, more than twenty years had elapsed since those judges had acted for the party and the issues subsequently before the court did not arise at that time. Additionally, the applicant had not asked the judges to recuse themselves at the outset but applied to have their judgment set aside some time after it had been handed down. In *Rooney v. Minister for Agriculture*,[31] the Supreme Court again held that the objective test had not been satisfied where one of the judges on that court, which had dismissed the plaintiff's appeal, had much earlier when a member of the Bar given certain advices to one of the respondents on a different issue.

On the other hand, the test was held to have been satisfied in *Dublin Wellwoman Centre Ltd. v. Ireland*.[32] It concerned the provision of information relating to abortion and the judge there had been chair of the Commission on the Status of Women in 1992 when that Commission published a statement supportive of such information being published. Denham J. observed that the question of abortion and related issues were "perhaps the most emotive and divisive topics in our community" then and especially in cases "where many reasonable people in our community hold strong opinions, it is of particular importance that neither party should have any reasonable reason to apprehend bias in the courts of justice."[33] In *O'Reilly v. Cassidy (No.2)*,[34] where the Circuit Court judge was the father of the barrister who represented the State in licensing proceedings, Flood J. quashed his decision although, at the hearing, no application had been made to the judge to recuse himself.

Ex parte Determinations

Occasionally a party is permitted to obtain an *ex parte* order against another party, without the latter being heard. Orders of this nature are objectionable in principle because they offend against the fundamental tenet of *audi alteram*

---

[30] *Id.* at p.440.
[31] [2001] 2 I.L.R.M. 37. Also, *Curran v. Finn* [2001] 4 I.R. 248.
[32] [1995] 1 I.L.R.M. 408.
[33] *Id.* at p.423.
[34] [1995] 1 I.L.R.M. 311.

partem. Ordinarily, these orders are made only in circumstances of particular urgency and where the applicant would be severely handicapped if notice and adequate opportunity to respond were to be given to the other side. Normally, the applicant is required to provide adequate security to cover the loss that would be occasioned to the other party if, in the event, it transpired that the applicant did not have a good case and in consequence the *ex parte* order should never have been made. State applicants for *ex parte* orders, under several statutory provisions, appear not to be asked to furnish security of this nature but whether that practice accords with the Constitution is questionable, especially where the other party is forced to incur substantial losses following the order being made against him.

Ordinarily, *ex parte* orders will only be permitted to last for a very short period, at which stage the party against whom the order was made is given a full opportunity to dispute the basis for making that order and its continuance. It was because the Domestic Violence Act 1996 contained no procedure for ensuring a prompt *inter partes* hearing, following the making of an interim barring order under section 4 of that Act, that in *D.K. v. Crowley*,[35] section 4(3) was declared unconstitutional by the Supreme Court. This Act is designed to protect spouses, children and others in comparable circumstance from violence in the home. Under it, aggrieved parties are able to get orders for their protection and also orders barring a violent respondent from, *inter alia*, going to or near where the applicant resides. Frequently, the effect of these is to prevent respondents from living in their own homes. Under section 4(3), where there were "reasonable grounds for believing there [was] an immediate risk of significant harm," an applicant could obtain *ex parte* an order directing the respondent to leave the home and not to re-enter it. This order could take effect even where a copy of the formal court application and supporting documentary evidence was not served on the respondent; where all he got at the time was notification that the interim barring order had been made. This order ceased to have effect when the court heard and determined the case for a permanent barring order but the respondent could apply under section 3 of the Act to have it discharged in the meantime. Breach of such order is a criminal offence, resulting in up to 12 months imprisonment, and can also constitute contempt of court.

On November 6, 1998, an interim order was made by the District Court against the plaintiff who three days later applied under section 3 to have it discharged. But on November 23, the day assigned to hear that application, he declined to proceed. Because he abandoned this comparatively early endeavour to have the interim order set aside, Kelly J. held that his constitutional claim concerning section 4(3) of the 1996 Act lacked merit. In the appeal, the State contended that, on account of what may be described as the "presumption of

---

[35] [2002] 2 I.R. 744.

propriety" identified in the *East Donegal* case, section 4(3) should not be declared invalid because section 4 was capable of being operated in a constitutionally acceptable manner, since there was nothing in it precluding designating an early date to hear an application for the discharge of an interim order. Indeed, under the Rules of the Circuit Court, applicants were required to apply for a hearing within the next eight days of their motion to maintain the order but there was no equivalent rule for District Judges. There was nothing in the Act expressly authorising the District Court to set an early date for hearing an application to continue the order, although in view of the presumption of constitutionality there does not appear to be any good reason why the Rules Committee could not confer such a jurisdiction on those judges. However, the court concluded that the fact that section 4 of the Act, with appropriate rules, was capable of being operated in a constitutional manner did not save it from invalidity.

Keane C.J. emphasised the vagueness of the statutory criteria for making interim orders, the profound effect they can have on respondents and, in view of the sanction, their quasi-criminal nature. He accepted that, in circumstances involving domestic violence, it was constitutionally permissible to provide for *ex parte* relief. Nonetheless, especially because applicants for these orders did not have to furnish any security, in the event of their ultimately not succeeding, and also that breach of an order is a criminal offence notwithstanding that subsequently it may transpire that it never should have been made, the balance was unduly tilted in favour of applicants. Accordingly, "[s]een in that context, the failure of the legislation to impose any time limit on the operation of an interim barring order, even when granted *ex parte* in the absence of the respondent, other than the provision that it is to expire when the application for an interim barring itself is determined, is inexplicable."[36] Because section 4 did not require the court that made an order to fix an early date, so that it can be reviewed in an *inter partes* hearing, the procedure was held to be fundamentally unfair. That respondents may apply to discharge such orders is insufficient protection for them; there should be an onus on the court to ensure that the order will cease unless there is a prompt *inter partes* hearing.

A somewhat analogous procedure that has been challenged from time to time but has not yet been ruled on are provisions enabling the Revenue to enforce their own tax assessments without obtaining any prior or subsequent confirmatory court order, even in circumstances where it remains open to the taxpayer to appeal those assessments. Under section 962 of the Taxes Consolidation Act 1997, once thirty days have expired from an assessment being raised, the Collector General may send a certificate to the sheriff, which authorises him forthwith to enforce that assessment. And under section 1002 of that Act, in similar circumstances, the Revenue Commissioners may send a

---

[36] *Id.* at p.440.

notice to a taxpayer's debtor, attaching that debt and requiring it to be paid over to the Revenue, in discharge of the assessed tax. Yet the taxpayer has a further 12 months, from the expiry of the thirty days, to appeal assessments for income tax and most other taxes. In *Kennedy v. Hearne*[37] and again in *Deighan v. Hearne*,[38] challenges to the predecessor of section 962 on the basis of separation of powers were rejected by the Supreme Court, which would not accept the contention that in making tax assessments a tax inspector is exercising intrinsically judicial powers. In *Deighan*, section 962's predecessor also was challenged on the grounds that it was "unjustly harsh" but, since the plaintiff there never endeavoured to appeal the assessments raised against him in the thirteen months available to him, he did not succeed. A challenge to the predecessor of section 1002 was rejected in *Orange v. Revenue Commissioners*,[39] but there the plaintiff did not dispute his liability to the Revenue for V.A.T. Geoghegan J. accepted that, where there was such a dispute, the section might constitute an unconstitutional attack on property rights contrary to Article 40.3. He additionally observed that resort to the statutory attachment procedure in particular circumstances could amount to an unconstitutional attack on those rights.

Making very serious allegations against individuals in open court in *ex parte* applications, which can be fully reported in the press without ever being libellous, may constitute contempt. As O'Hanlon J. observed in *Desmond v. Glackin (No. 1)*, "it seems to conflict with some of the basic principles of fair play if all these heavy blows can be delivered in open court on an *ex parte* application, and be duly reported on a nationwide basis accompanied by a commentary form ... public relations advisers, while denying the right to [the target of the accusations] to reply immediately in equally forthright terms in defence of their own good name and reputation."[40]

Legal Representation

Both branches of the legal profession have the right of audience in every court and in principle anybody is entitled to call on the services of any solicitor or barrister. Those who cannot afford legal representation may be entitled to either legal aid under what is known as the Attorney General's Scheme for a limited category of case or else under the Civil Legal Aid Act 1995. This Act replaced an *ad hoc* scheme established by the Minister for Justice at the end of 1979, which was one consequence of *Airey v. Ireland*[41] decided by the Strasbourg

---

[37] [1988] I.R. 481.
[38] [1990] 1 I.R. 499.
[39] [1995] 1 I.R. 517.
[40] [1993] 2 I.R. 43.
[41] 2 E.H.R.R. 305 (1979).

Court, where the complete absence of any civil legal aid in Ireland was held to contravene Article 6(1) of the European Convention. According to that court:

> "The Convention is intended to guarantee not rights that are theoretical and illusory but rights that are practical or effective. This is particularly so of the right of access to the courts in view of the prominent place held in a democratic society by the right to a fair trial. ...
>
> [W]hilst Article 6(1) guarantees to litigants an effective right of access to the courts for the determination of their 'civil rights and obligations', it leaves to the State a free choice of the means to be used towards this end. The institution of a legal aid scheme – which Ireland now envisages in family law matters – constitutes one of those means but there are others such as, for example, a simplification of procedure. In any event, it is not the Court's function to indicate, let alone dictate, which measures should be taken; all that the Convention requires is that an individual should enjoy his effective right of access to the courts in conditions not at variance with Article 6(1).
>
> The (existence of some right to free legal aid) does not therefore imply that the State must provide free legal aid for every dispute relating to a 'civil right'. To hold that so far-reaching an obligation exists would, the Court agrees, sit ill with the fact that the Convention contains no provision on legal aid for those disputes, Article 6(3)(c) dealing only with criminal proceedings. However, despite the absence of a similar clause for civil litigation, Article 6(1) may sometimes compel the State to provide for the assistance of a lawyer when such assistance proves indispensable for an effective access to court either because legal representation is rendered compulsory, as is done by the domestic law of certain Contracting States for various types of litigation, or by reason of the complexity of the procedure or of the case."[42]

It is debatable how extensive is the constitutional duty to provide legal aid other than in cases where a person's liberty is at stake. In *D.P.P. v. Governor of the Training Unit*,[43] it was held by Finnegan J. that persons arrested on foot of deportation orders are entitled to be given legal advice but that the legislation there was not unconstitutional merely because it made no express provision for State-funded legal aid. Even in hearings before administrative tribunals that affect a person's liberty, there can be a duty on the State to provide some legal aid.[44] But in *M.C. v. Legal Aid Board*,[45] where an indigent respondent in divorce proceedings could not get prompt legal assistance from the Legal Aid

---

[42] *Id.* at p.317.
[43] [2001] 1 I.R. 493.
[44] *Kirwan v. Minister for Justice* [1994] 2 I.R. 417.
[45] [1994] 3 I.R. 1.

Board, due to the large volume of work the Board was then handling, it was held that there was no constitutional obligation on the State to provide her with legal aid, which could be enforced by way of an order of *mandamus* against the Board. According to Gannon J., "[t]he duty of administering justice and adjudicating by due process does not create any obligation on the State to intervene in any private civil litigation so as to ensure that one party is as well equipped for their dispute as is the other. The fact that the existence of fundamental personal rights is expressly recognised by the Constitution does not impose on the State any duty to intervene in aid of a party involved in any private civil dispute in relation to any such personal rights."[46]

Speedy Trial

One of the commonest category of case before the European Court of Human Rights is a claim that civil proceedings have gone on for an unduly protracted period. In *Doran v. Ireland*,[47] the Strasbourg Court held that the delays in the High Court and in the Supreme Court in dealing with the applicant's case were so lengthy and unjustifiable as to contravene Article 6(1)'s guarantee of a fair trial. The applicants had agreed to buy a site, to build their home, but on account of differences concerning planning permission and maps, commenced High Court proceedings in 1991 before Hamilton P. (as he then was). Eventually, in October 1998, they were awarded substantial damages. Various justifications offered by the Government were rejected, as not warranting a delay of over seven years.

Excessive delay in bringing and in prosecuting civil claims is dealt with in two ways. Under the Statutes of Limitations 1957–2000, most categories of claim must be commenced within a specified period. Secondly, the courts have an inherent jurisdiction to dismiss a claim that is not being pursued with sufficient expedition, thereby endangering the prospect of a fair trial.

Limitation of Actions

Most civil claims must be commenced within a specified period of time or, otherwise, they become "statute-barred."[48] While rules of this nature strictly do not debar a plaintiff from suing and indeed from having his claim heard and determined, the proceedings will be struck out if the defendant pleads and establishes that they are statute-barred. These provisions' objective was described by Finlay C.J. as:

"to protect defendants against stale claims and avoid the injustices which

---

[46] *Id.* at p.55.
[47] Decision of July 31, 2003.
[48] See generally, J. Brady & A. Kerr, *The Limitation of Actions* (2nd ed., 1994).

might occur to them were they asked to defend themselves from claims which were not notified to them within a reasonable time.

Secondly, they are designed to promote as far as possible expeditious trials of action so that a court may have before it as the material upon which it must make its decision oral evidence which has the accuracy of recent recollection and documentary proof which is complete, features which must make a major contribution to the correctness and justice of the decision arrived at.

Thirdly, they are designed to promote as far as possible and proper a certainty of finality in potential claims which will permit individuals to arrange their affairs whether on a domestic, commercial or professional level in reliance to the maximum extent possible upon the absence of unknown or unexpected liabilities."[49]

The periods within which most civil claims must be brought are laid down in the Statutes of Limitations, 1957–2000. Actions for breach of contract and for some torts must be commenced within six years of the cause of action accruing, but claims for slander, negligence involving personal injury, nuisance and breach of statutory duty must be brought within three years of the right of action accruing. These are subject to various qualifications and there are rules for numerous other causes of action. Section 49 of the 1957 Act provides for an extension of the normal limitation periods where the plaintiff is an infant or is of unsound mind, and amendments made in 1991 and 2000 authorise the courts to allow otherwise late claims in certain types of case.

In determining whether a particular limitation period is unconstitutional, the overall approach has been described by Finlay C.J. as "[t]he counter-balance to the [above] objectives is the necessity as far as is practicable, or as best it may, for the State to ensure that such time limits do not unreasonably or unjustly impose hardship. Any time limit statutorily imposed upon the bringing of actions is potentially going to impose some hardship on some individual. What this Court must do is to ascertain whether the extent and nature of such hardship is so undue and so unreasonable having regard to the proper objectives of the legislation as to make it constitutionally flawed."[50] A distinction is to be drawn between adults who are fully capable of looking after their own affairs and persons who are or were under a disability.

Not Under a Disability

Persons who are not under a disability in this context are adults who are entirely capable of managing their own affairs – as opposed to children and young persons, the mentally ill and those suffering from some other incapacity or

---

[49] *Touhy v. Courtney* [1994] 3 I.R. 1 at p.48.
[50] *Ibid.*

handicap that prevents them from expeditiously looking after their affairs. It was held in *O'Brien v. Manufacturing Engineering Co.*[51] that a limitation period within which it is reasonable to expect that the victim of a wrong has had adequate opportunity to obtain legal advice and to arrange for proceedings to be brought is sufficient time for the purposes of the Constitution. Under the now repealed Workmen's Compensation Acts, all workers injured in the course of their employment were automatically entitled to compensation where they were injured at work, the amount to be calculated in the prescribed manner. Compensation was to be paid regardless of whether or not the employer had been negligent or the worker had been contributorily negligent. A worker who accepted the guaranteed compensation was not precluded from suing the employer for negligence or breach of duty, but these Acts prescribed that in such cases the limitation period shall be two years from the time when the injury occurred. It was held that this period was not unconstitutional. According to Walsh J., for the Supreme Court, even where injured workers are not paid their compensation, a two year or indeed a one year limitation period would not be impermissibly short: "a period of 12 months or, where there are substantial grounds for not initiating (an action) within 12 months, a period of 24 months is not unreasonably short to enable a person not suffering from any disability to ascertain whether or not he has a common-law action and to institute that action."[52]

The six year limitation period, within which actions for breach of contract and many torts must be brought, was upheld by the Supreme Court in *Touhy v. Courtney*,[53] which was a professional negligence claim against a solicitor. It was only after the six years had expired that the plaintiff learned that his solicitor had been negligent. Notwithstanding, it was held for reasons that are not articulated that, in the circumstances, six years "can be supported by just and reasonable policy decisions and is not accordingly a proper matter for judicial intervention."[54] The court rejected the contention that, if the limitation there were struck down, defendants would have ample protection against stale claims under the courts' inherent jurisdiction to stay proceedings when their prosecution can be shown to be oppressive for defendants. For under that jurisdiction, there would have to be a trial on the preliminary issue of undue delay, which then could be appealed. As Finlay C.J., for the Court, explained, "[t]o mount such a plea in an action of substance is a burdensome and expensive process. ... The time scale of such proceedings is quite extensive and the period of anxiety and uncertainty for the defendant even if eventually he or she is successful will frequently be very great. ..."[55]

---

[51] [1973] I.R. 334.
[52] *Id.*, at p.366. Compare *Moise v. Transitional Local Council* 11 B.H.R.C. 474 (2001) (S. Africa).
[53] [1994] 3 I.R. 1.
[54] *Id.* at p.50.
[55] *Id.* at p.49.

Under a Disability

Usually, persons under a disability benefit from lengthier limitation periods but special circumstances can justify even affording them somewhat short periods. The only instance in which such periods were struck down as unconstitutional was in *O'Brien v. Keogh*,[56] where the plaintiff, an infant who had been injured in a road traffic accident in 1963, commenced proceedings in 1968 claiming damages for negligence and breach of duty. Although the limitation period for these claims is normally three years from when the accident occurred, an exception is made where the plaintiff is under age but that exception did not obtain where the young person was in either of its parents' custody at the time of the accident. The reason for treating categories of young persons differently was that those who were not in a parent's custody are far more in danger of their right of action lapsing because of uncaring guardians; whereas it is reasonable to assume that, if the injured young person was with a parent, the father or mother would ensure that an action for damages is instituted promptly. Nevertheless, the Supreme Court struck down section 49(2)(ii) of the 1957 Act because several circumstances could arise where it would operate unfairly. For instance, both parents and the child could be injured in the accident and shortly afterwards both parents die; or the negligent driver may be one of the parents who then invokes the three year limitation period to escape liability. Eight years later in *Cahill v. Sutton*,[57] the court refused to declare section 11(2)(b) of the 1957 Act unconstitutional because the plaintiff's principal contentions were founded on the *ius tertii*.[58] Yet the decision in *O'Brien v. Keogh* was not founded entirely on *ius tertii* considerations because the second defendant in that case was the plaintiff's father, who had been driving the car in which the plaintiff was injured, and the claim against the father had been commenced more than three years following the time of the accident.

An example of special circumstances which warrant having limitation periods that are shorter than usual is *Moynihan v. Greensmyth*,[59] the circumstances there being the need to have deceased persons' estates administered with reasonable expedition. The facts of this case have parallels with *O'Brien v. Keogh* in that the plaintiff was an infant who had been injured in a road traffic accident; but in this instance the defendant had been killed in the accident. Following *O'Brien v. Keogh,* the normal limitation period under the 1957 Act for infants claiming damages in respect of personal injuries on the grounds of negligence or breach of duty, is three years from the time they reach their majority. Since, however, the defendant in the *Moynihan* case was dead, the matter was governed not by the 1957 Act but by section 9 of the

---

[56] [1972] I.R. 144.
[57] [1980] I.R. 269; *sinfra*, p.877.
[58] See *infra*, p.883.
[59] [1977] I.R. 55.

Civil Liability Act 1961; this section abolished the common law rule that causes of action in tort lapse where the defendant dies – *actio personalis moritur cum persona*. Section 9 provides that all tort actions shall survive against the deceased's estate, but proceedings must be brought against the estate within two years of the cause of action arising. It was held by the Supreme Court that, even as regards infant plaintiffs, a two year limitation period in these circumstances was fair and reasonable. According to O'Higgins C.J., for the court, "[b]earing in mind the State's duty to others (than plaintiffs) – in particular those who represent the estate of the deceased, and beneficiaries -some reasonable limitation on actions against the estate was obviously required. If the (entire) period of infancy were to form part of the period ..., then the danger of stale claims being brought would be very real and could constitute a serious threat to the rights of beneficiaries of the estate of a deceased. The alternative was to apply a period of limitation, which would have general application. It had to be either one or the other; and it does not appear that any compromise was possible."[60]

Judicial Review

Proceedings for the judicial review of administrative decisions must be commenced within three months or, in applications for *certiorari*, within six months. In appropriate circumstances, however, claims will be allowed outside of these periods.[61] Challenges to certain decisions, most notably in the areas of immigration, planning and compulsory purchase, must be begun much sooner; for many decisions regarding deportation and refugees, within fourteen days of the person being notified of the decision in question. Again, however, proceedings may be instituted later than this with the leave of the High Court if there are "good and sufficient reasons for extending the period."[62] An exceptionally short limitation period, which cannot be extended in particular cases under any circumstances, would be unconstitutional. In *Brady v. Donegal County Council*,[63] where the Act then in force stipulated an inflexible two month period within which planning decisions may be challenged, the plaintiff did not contest the decision in issue there within this time because he had no knowledge of it then. Costello J. expressed the view that "if the plaintiff's ignorance of his rights during the short limitation period is caused by the defendant's own wrongdoing and the law still imposes an absolute bar unaccompanied by any judicial discretion to raise it there must be very compelling reasons indeed to justify such a rigorous limitation on the exercise

---

[60] *Id.* at p.72.
[61] *de Roiste v. Minister for Defence* [2001] 1 I.R. 190.
[62] Illegal Immigrants (Trafficking) Act 2000, s.5(2)(a).
[63] [1989] I.L.R.M. 182.

of a constitutionally protected right."[64] He concluded that the two rigid months "cannot reasonably be justified. Unmodified, the subsection is unreasonable; being unreasonable, it is unconstitutional ...".[65]

Those views were endorsed by Ó Caoimh J. in *White v. Dublin Corporation*,[66] who declared invalid the rigid two month limitation period in the 1992 planning legislation for challenging the grant of planning permission, where the plaintiffs were not aware that the permission there had been granted until more than two months had elapsed. Very compelling reasons are required to justify so short a time limit, which in no circumstances whatsoever could be extended by a court. That developers should be absolutely secure that planning permissions they hold are unimpeachable, once two months have elapsed, regardless of the circumstances of the case, was "so restrictive as to render access to the courts impossible for persons in the position of the applicants and [consequently was] unreasonable and therefore unconstitutional."[67] By the time this case was decided the law had been changed to give objectors eight weeks to challenge a variety of planning and related decisions but which could be extended by the High Court on showing that "there is good and sufficient reason for doing so."[68]

A two week limitation period for challenging decisions related to immigration, but which could be extended, was upheld by the Supreme Court in *Sections 5 and 10 of the Illegal Immigrants (Trafficking) Bill, 1999, Re*.[69] The justification for such a short period, said Keane C.J. for the court, is that "administrative decisions, particularly those taken pursuant to detailed procedures laid down by law, should be capable of being applied or implemented with certainty at as early a date as possible and that any issue as to their validity should accordingly be determined as soon as possible."[70] Early finality here was necessary "in the interests of the proper management and treatment of persons seeking asylum or refugee status .... The early implementation of decisions duly and properly taken would facilitate the better and proper administration of the system governing seekers of asylum for both those who are ultimately successful and ultimately unsuccessful."[71] And the court's discretion to extend the stipulated time was "ample enough to avoid injustice where an applicant has been unable through no fault of his or hers, or for other good and sufficient reason, to bring the application" in time.[72]

---

[64] *Id.* at p.289.
[65] *Ibid.*
[66] Unreported, High Court, June 21, 2002.
[67] *Id.* at p.46. Similarly, *Plaintiff S157/2002 v. Commonwealth*, 77 A.L.J.L.R. 454. (2003)
[68] Planning and Development Act 2000, s.50(4).
[69] [2000] 2 I.R. 360.
[70] *Id.* at p.392.
[71] *Id.* at pp.392–393.
[72] *Id.* at p.393. *E.g.,. S. v. Minister for Justice* [2002] 2 I.R. 163.

Strike Out

Where there has been an excessive delay in bringing a case for trial, it will be struck out by the court for want of prosecution.[73] Thus in *Ó Domhnaill v. Merrick*,[74] the Supreme Court struck out a personal injuries claim arising out of an accident that occurred when the plaintiff was three years old but which was not commenced until some sixteen years later. Having considered the entire circumstances of the case, Henchy J. was "driven to the conclusion that not only was the delay in this case inordinate and inexcusable, but that there are no countervailing circumstances which would justify a disregard of this delay."[75] Not alone would holding the trial following such a delay be unfair to the defendant, but it was "incompatible with the contingencies which insurers of motor vehicles could reasonably be expected to provide against," and the delayed trial "would be apt to give an unjust or wrong result …".[76]

Under section 3 of the Proceeds of Crime Act 1996, the plaintiff (usually a senior Garda officer) can obtain an "interlocutory order" restraining any dealing in property shown to be the proceeds of crime and, once seven years have elapsed from the date of this order, under section 4 of this Act he can apply to the court for an order confiscating that property. It was contended in *Murphy v. G.M.*[77] that deferring for over seven years the trial of the net issue in proceedings of this nature, *viz.* whether the property ought to be confiscated, could not be justified at all and was unconstitutional. However, notwithstanding that the Act itself describes section 3 applications as "interlocutory" and, as defined in all legal dictionaries and in that court's own precedents it would be interlocutory, the Supreme Court concluded that those applications were in substance the trial of the action. As Keane C.J. for the court, put it, "[a]s to the claim that the period of seven years which must elapse before a disposal order is made is unduly oppressive, that rests on the misconception that the application (under section 4) for a disposal order can in some sense be equated to the trial of an action in respect of which the legislation earlier provides for interlocutory orders being made. That is clearly not the nature of the scheme provided for in the Act."[78] Prior to this conclusion being announced, High Court judges who heard applications under section 3 as well as all counsel for the plaintiffs in such cases and as counsel for defendants had acted on the "misconception"

---

[73] See generally, *Delany & McGrath*, ch.11.
[74] [1984] I.R. 151.
[75] *Id.* at p.157.
[76] *Id.* at p.158. Similarly, *Primor p.l.c. v. Stokes Kennedy Crawley* [1996] 2 I.R. 459 and *Anglo Irish Beef Processors Ltd v. Montgomery* [2002] 3 I.R. 510.
[77] [2001] 4 I.R. 113.
[78] *Id.* at p.154. Compare the concept of "interlocutory" as endorsed *inter alia* by Keane C.J. in *Minister for Agriculture v. Arte Leipzigel* [2000] 4 I.R. 32, as meaning all orders other than the final order disposing of an issue in the proceedings (e.g. other than the "disposal order" under s.4 of the 1996 Act).

that orders, expressly characterised by the Oireachtas as "interlocutory" and not the final order envisaged in the legislation, were indeed interlocutory.

Public Trial

The requirement states that justice should be administered in public and not behind closed doors, in some kind of Star Chamber, is considerably qualified. Article 34.1 of the Constitution states that "[j]ustice ... save in such special and limited cases as may be prescribed by law, shall be administered in public." Article 6(1) of the European Convention and Article 14(1) of the UN Covenant stipulate that "[j]udgment shall be pronounced publicly but the press and public may be excluded from all or part of the trial in the interest of morals, public order or national security in a democratic society, where the interests of juveniles or the protection of the private life of the parties so require, or to the extent strictly necessary in the opinion of the court in special circumstances where publicity would prejudice the interests of justice." To date, there has been no constitutional challenge to an *in camera* requirement in any law and it remains to be seen what kind of case is not sufficiently "special and limited" to justify a finding that it must be heard in public, notwithstanding the Oireachtas' direction to the contrary. Presumably guidance will be taken from the exceptions in Article 6(1) of the European Convention. Some statutory provisions require that cases be heard *in camera*; others empower the court to direct that the case shall be so heard, either entirely or partly. Additionally, it has been held in several criminal cases that the fundamental right to a fair trial may, in appropriate circumstances, justify some restrictions on public access to or knowledge about the proceedings. Perhaps it is because of the reference to "special and limited" cases that there are no rules of court giving the court discretion to insist on all or aspects of particular proceedings being heard *in camera*.

In the absence of an express statutory provision or perhaps a serious risk of the trial being rendered unfair, all aspects of proceedings must be conducted in open court. It remains to be determined whether an *in camera* requirement or anonymity for the parties or the witnesses can be imposed by way of statutory instrument. Even in circumstances where one of the parties has what may be regarded as a justifiable reason for preserving his anonymity, he will not be permitted to participate in the proceedings with a fictitious name and address. Thus in *Roe v. Blood Transfusion Service Board*,[79] the plaintiff, who had contracted Hepatitis C from contaminated blood supplied by the first defendant, sought to sue for damages under the name "Roe" and using her solicitors' address; she was anxious to keep her true identity out of the public domain. All but one of the defendants knew who she was, her name and address were

---

[79] [1996] 3 I.R. 67.

on the court file and she accepted that, if her claim were not settled, the trial would have to take place in public. Objection by the defendants to hearing proceedings in this manner were upheld by Laffoy J., on the grounds that "[t]he Constitution removed any judicial discretion to have proceedings heard other than in public."[80] She followed a decision of Hamilton P. to the same effect in a similar case, that proceedings include all pleadings, affidavits and exhibits, as well as oral testimony.[81] There was no suggestion here that disclosure of the plaintiff's name would result in an unfair trial. Similarly, in *Ansbacher (Caymen) Ltd., Re*,[82] where the applicants sought to challenge parts of the High Court's "Ansbacher Report" that referred to them, on the grounds that those references prejudiced their right to a good name and to privacy, it was held that they could not bring those proceedings anonymously. As McCracken J. there observed, when the question of anonymity was being determined, that gave "rise to a difficult chicken and egg situation," which caused him to permit the application on the point to be made in the name of the applicant's solicitors rather than in their own name. But he concluded that the substantive dispute could not proceed in that manner because the requirement of a public trial took precedence over privacy and reputational interests.

Following *dicta* of the Supreme Court in a case concerning imposing restrictions on press reporting of a criminal trial,[83] McCracken J. accepted that there were certain constitutional rights, such as a fair trial, that can outweigh the requirement that justice shall be administered in public. Another such right might be a person's (party or witness) right to life. However, that case was not strictly concerned with an *in camera* requirement because there was no question of members of the public not being permitted to attend the trial, nor of information concerning it being released to other members of the public. It would appear that the reference to "prescribed by law" in this Article is being taken to mean, *inter alia*, required in order to protect other more important constitutional interests, giving the court a broad discretion to determine what those interests are. If this is correct, there is no reason why, in special circumstances, a person's right to privacy should not be protected by an *in camera* order, as is permissible under Article 6(1) of the European Convention. Furthermore, if "balancing" of this nature is permissible, then Laffoy J.'s categorical but on the face of things correct analysis in *Roe* is wrong.

Even if this point had been raised, it would not have been necessary for the Supreme Court to decide it in *de Gotari v. Smithwick*,[84] where the applicant sought to judicially review a ruling made by a District Judge in the course of a

---

[80] *Id.* at p.70.
[81] *The Claimant v. Board of St. James' Hospital* (10 May 1989).
[82] [2002] 2 I.R. 517.
[83] *Irish Times Ltd v. Ireland* [1998] 1 I.R. 359; *supra*, p.445.
[84] [1994] 4 I.R. 223.

hearing that did not have to be conducted in public. That was under section 51 of the Criminal Justice Act 1994, for the purpose of assisting a criminal investigation being conducted by a French *juge d'instruction*. Because French law requires these investigations to be carried out in secret, it was contended that, as a matter of international comity, the judicial review equally should be held *in camera*; there was no suggestion that a fair trial of the applicant might be prejudiced. But it was held that comity was not always a satisfactory guide for determining whether the courts should apply a foreign law and that there was no principle of public international law that obliged Ireland to respect the French requirement of secrecy. Because, however, the process under section 51 of the 1994 Act does not constitute the administration of justice (since all it involves is recording statements being made by individuals, who are not even witnesses), there is no constitutional obligation that it take place in public.

Mandatory in camera

Among those proceedings where an *in camera* hearing is mandatory are many cases involving family law disputes, where most of the relevant Acts stipulate that "proceedings under this Act shall be heard otherwise in public." Every rehearing of a tax appeal in the Circuit Court "shall be heard *in camera*."[85] High Court proceedings to prevent a doctor, dentist or nurse from practising "shall be heard otherwise than in public."[86]

What is described as a "McKenzie friend" is a person who goes to court in order to assist a lay litigant in the conduct of his case. In exceptional circumstances lay litigants may be permitted to avail of such a person's assistance in *in camera* hearings. However, in *R.D. v. McGuinness*,[87] Macken J. held that a District Judge had not acted wrongfully in excluding a "McKenzie friend" from proceedings under the Domestic Violence Act 1996. That was because the party in question was a very articulate person, the court was very experienced in protecting lay litigants and there was no evidence to suggest that the party would be prejudiced and denied a fair hearing if he had to present his case without the "friend" being present.

None of the above provisions provide for any sanction where the *in camera* requirement has been breached. But it is a contempt of court to disseminate any information derived from proceedings of this nature, without prior judicial authority to do so. Persons whose legitimate interests are prejudiced by any unauthorised disclosure may seek appropriate orders to safeguard their privacy. Further, of its own motion, the court can take whatever steps appear to it to be necessary to ensure that there shall be no unauthorised disclosures. For instance,

---

[85] Taxes Consolidation Act 1997, s.942(9).
[86] *E.g.* Nurses Act 1985, s.44(2).
[87] [1999] 2 I.R. 411.

in *M.P. v. A.P.*,[88] as part of a settlement of matrimonial proceedings, the parties agreed that any future differences that they may have about access would first be submitted to the applicant, a consultant psychologist. But the husband became unhappy with the manner in which the applicant was dealing with one dispute and sent a complaint of professional misconduct to the applicant's professional body, including with it much of the documentation from the proceedings. Laffoy J. held that this was a breach of the *in camera* rule and, unless the husband undertook to withdraw from his complaint all documentation concerning the proceedings and not to disseminate that documentation to the professional body or to any third party, she would order him to do so.

In those cases where the *in camera* requirement is discretionary, in appropriate circumstances the court will permit embargoed material to be released, subject to safeguards. It would appear that there is no equivalent discretion where the rule is formulated in mandatory terms. In *R.M. v. D.M.*[89] Murphy J. refused to permit disclosure to the barristers' disciplinary body, of papers in divorce proceedings, following a complaint to that body of professional misconduct in the manner in which counsel had conducted his client's divorce case. The rule as formulated in the divorce and judicial separation context was held to "imply an absolute embargo on the production, in subsequent proceedings, of information which derives from or was introduced in proceedings protected by the rule."[90]

Optional in Camera

Perhaps the principal discretionary *in camera* provision is section 45(1) of the Courts (Supplemental Provisions) Act 1961 which states that:

> "[j]ustice *may* be administered otherwise than in public in any of the following cases–
>
> (a) applications of an urgent nature for relief by way of habeas corpus, bail, prohibition or injunction;
> (b) matrimonial causes and matters;
> (c) lunacy and minor (*i.e.* children) matters;
> (d) proceedings involving the disclosure of a secret manufacturing process."

Proceedings under the Proceeds of Crime Act 1996, may if "the Court considers it proper, be heard otherwise than in public;" applications for interim orders under this Act must be heard *in camera*.[91] Proceedings for "oppression" under

---

[88] [1996] 1 I.R. 144.
[89] [2000] 3 I.R. 373.
[90] *Id.* at p.386.
[91] S.8(3).

section 205 of the Companies Act 1963, will be heard *in camera* "[i]f in the opinion of the court, the hearing ... would involve the disclosure of information the publication of which would be seriously prejudicial to the legitimate interests of the company ...".[92]

Occasionally issues of major legal principle and indeed major political significance may be involved in proceedings that ordinarily would be *in camera*. Notwithstanding, the courts tend to insist that the actual hearing of the case, of the legal submissions as well as the evidence, shall take place in private, but permitting the judgment that will be delivered to be published, excising from it any material that would tend to identify persons involved in the case. Orders of this nature were made in, *inter alia*, in the "X case,"[93] the "Baby A" case[94] and in *Re A Ward of Court (withholding medical treatment) (No. 1)*.[95] In "oppression" proceedings under section 205 of the Companies Act 1963, the Supreme Court has stressed that the prerequisites for an *in camera* hearing must be strictly complied with. As Walsh J. put it in *Re R.*,[96] the court must be satisfied "that not only would the disclosure of information be seriously prejudicial to the legitimate interests of the company, but it must also be shown that a public hearing of the whole or of that part of the proceedings which it is sought to have heard other than in a public court would fall short of the doing of justice."[97]

In appropriate circumstances, courts permit the release of material subject to the *in camera* rule. In *Eastern Health Board v. Fitness to Practise Committee*,[98] complaints had been made to the Medical Council of misconduct by a doctor, who had been involved in a professional capacity in several cases of alleged sexual abuse of children, all of which had been heard *in camera*. An application by the Council for the release of papers related to these cases was acceded to because it was held that the public interest in the full investigation of these complaints took precedence over the children and others' interests in non-disclosure. In his order, Barr J. placed stringent conditions on the Council and on any others who would have access to these papers in the course of any investigations, and any subsequent fitness to practise enquiry. Disclosure to the press of the identity of a leading participant in a controversial case concerning a baby was permitted by McGuinness J. in the *"Baby A"* case, the name of an unincorporated adoption agency that had been at the centre of the dispute.[99] But she would not allow any other information relating to the case to be so published.

---

[92] S.205(7).
[93] *Attorney General v. X.* [1992] 1 I.R. 1.
[94] *Eastern Health Board v. E. (No.1)* [2002] 1 I.R. 430.
[95] [1996] 2 I.R. 73.
[96] [1989] I.R. 126.
[97] *Id.* at p.137. See *Irish Press Ltd v. Ingersoll Irish Publications Ltd* [1994] 1 I.R. 176.
[98] [1998] 3 I.R. 399.
[99] *Eastern Health Board v. E. (No.2)* [2000] 1 I.R. 451.

Not Administering Justice

There also are certain kinds of hearings in the courts that have been held not to constitute the administration of justice and, accordingly, need not be heard in public. Examinations by company liquidators of creditors and others connected with (often insolvent) companies, under what presently is section 245 of the Companies Act 1963, was held by the Supreme Court to fall into this category.[100] This is also the case where, under section 51 of the Criminal Justice Act 1984, evidence is being taken in the District Court for the purpose of a foreign criminal investigation.[101] Applications to the High Court for directions by inspectors appointed under Part II of the Companies Act 1990, were held by Murphy J. to fall into this category too.[102] On the other hand, Laffoy J. has held that an application by a liquidator under section 231 of the Companies Act 1963 for leave to continue proceedings that had been commenced by the company, which could involve an *inter partes* contest, fell outside this category and consequently had to be made in open court.[103]

Jury Trial

Formerly, disputes of fact in the common law courts were determined by a jury, in much the same way as in criminal trials, and it was the existence of the jury that explains many of the differences between common law procedures and procedures followed in continental European courts. However, Chancery cases, judicial reviews and several other categories of case were tried without a jury. By the beginning of the 21st century, jury trials of civil actions have been almost abolished, being confined to High Court actions where, prior to 1924 there could be a jury but excluding several categories of claim – actions for a liquidated sum, for breach of contract, for the recovery of land[104] and for personal injuries other than intentional trespass to the person and false imprisonment.[105] Unlike the position under the Seventh Amendment to the United States Constitution, there is no express constitutional guarantee of a jury trial in civil actions. It was held by McWilliam J. in *Murphy v. Hennessy*[106] that there is no implied constitutional right to a civil jury trial.

---

[100] *Re Redbreast Preserving Co.* (1957) 91 I.L.T.R. 12.
[101] *de Gotardi v. Smithwick* [1999] 4 I.R. 223.
[102] *Countyglen p.l.c., Re* [1995] 1 I.R. 220.
[103] *Greendale Developments Ltd (N. 1), Re* [1997] 3 I.R. 540.
[104] Courts of Justice Act 1924, s.94. See generally, Getzler, "The Fate of the Civil Jury in Late Victorian England" in K.O'Donovan & G. Rubin eds., *Human Rights and Legal History* (2000).
[105] Courts Act 1988, s.1.
[106] [1984] I.R. 378.

Onus of Proof

It was held permissible to place the entire onus of proof on defendants in appropriate cases. Under section 4 of the Proceeds of Crime Act 1996, at the hearing of the plaintiff's application to have the property in question confiscated, the onus is placed on the defendant to prove that it is not the proceeds of crime or to demonstrate other circumstances why it would be unjust to take the property from him. This was upheld by the Supreme Court in *Murphy v. G.M.*,[107] on the grounds that there is nothing inherently unconstitutional in reversing the onus of proof in civil cases, especially as the defendants in cases of this nature are more likely to know the actual provenance of the property in question and whether it constituted the proceeds of crime.

Witnesses/Evidence

Witnesses in civil proceedings often give their evidence in the form of sworn affidavits rather than orally from the witness box. Ordinarily, however, their evidence can be challenged by cross-examining the deponent. It has been held to infringe the constitutional separation of powers to forbid the court from hearing witnesses it may regard as having relevant evidence on the matter in question.[108]

Orality

That evidence usually is adduced *viva voce* from the witness box is largely the legacy of the jury system. But in cases commenced by way of special summons, summary summons, petition or originating motion, the evidence is adduced by affidavit, except where the court directs that there should be oral testimony. Using certificates in order to prove certain facts was upheld in *Verit Hotel & Leisure (Ireland) Ltd, Re.*[109] This concerned the procedure in Part VII (sections 149–169) of the Companies Act 1990 for imposing restrictions on directors of insolvent companies that were wound up and are insolvent. Under section 149(1) of the this Act, these provisions apply where either it is proved that the company was insolvent when it was wound up or, at any time thereafter, it is either proved or the liquidator certifies that the company is insolvent. Here the liquidator commenced proceedings against the company's directors, to have them restricted, and tendered a certificate stating that the company was insolvent. Carroll J. held that the certificate alone cannot be conclusive evidence

---

[107] [2001] 4 I.R. 113 at p.155.
[108] *Cashman v. Clifford* [1989] I.R. 121.
[109] [1996] 3 I.R. 300.

of insolvency. Further, the certificate is simply a device "to trigger off the application of" this part of the Act and the necessity for the court to be satisfied under section 150 that the directors concerned acted honestly and responsibly, which is the central issue in this type of proceedings. Thus, the certificate was "a preliminary step [and] there is nothing in the section which would prevent a director from raising any issue in relation to the insolvency of the company or adducing evidence in order to satisfy the court that he or she acted "honestly and responsibly ..."[110]

Cross-Examination

One of the principal techniques for defeating a party's case is by challenging his witnesses in cross-examination. On several occasions the Supreme Court has emphasised the importance of cross-examination, which is a "constitutionally guaranteed right and not a concession."[111] It remains to be determined what circumstances, if any, would justify a party being denied the opportunity to cross-examine his opponent's witness where there is a serious dispute about the accuracy of the evidence that was given.

Hearsay

On account of its second hand nature, it not strictly being an oath and often incapable of being properly tested in cross-examination, hearsay evidence is not the most reliable. Hearsay has always been permitted in interlocutory hearings but not at trials, subject to certain limited exceptions.[112] In was contended in *Murphy v. G.M.*,[113] that hearsay should not be permitted in applications for "interlocutory" asset-freezing orders under section 3 of the Proceeds of Crime Act 1996, because the trial judge had concluded that these applications were equivalent to the trial, albeit strictly interlocutory. On appeal it was contended that, insofar as section 3 by implication (as so construed) entirely abolished the hearsay rule in such applications, it was unconstitutional. But that was rejected by the Supreme Court, Keane C.J. simply stating, without any discussion whatsoever of the issues, that "[n]or is the provision for the admission of hearsay evidence of itself unconstitutional: it was a matter for the court hearing the application to decide what weight should be given to such evidence."[114]

---

[110] *Id.* at p.305.
[111] *Maguire v. Ardagh* [2002] 1 I.R. 385 at p.705.
[112] See generally *Delaney & McGrath*, pp.494 *et seq.*
[113] [2001] 4 I.R. 113.
[114] *Id.* at p.155.

Equality

It also was contended in *Murphy v. G.M*[115] that section 8(1) of that Act contravened the "equality of arms" principle, because it permitted the plaintiff to adduce certain opinion evidence in support of his case, when no equivalent concession was given to defendants. Under section 8(1), the plaintiff could call a senior police officer to state his "belief" that the property in question was the proceeds of crime, which opinion the court could accept as evidence if there were reasonable grounds for that belief; respondents were given no equivalent entitlement. The claim that this disparate treatment of the parties to what purports to be civil proceedings is hardly addressed at all in the Supreme Court's judgment, other than the bald assertion by Keane C.J. that "the court is satisfied that no such inequality has been demonstrated: the respondents ... will normally be ... in possession or control of the property and should be in a position to give evidence to the court as to its provenance, without calling in aid opinion evidence."[116]

Presumptions

Irrebuttable presumptions in statutes may fall foul of the Constitution because they constitute an interference by the legislature in the administration of justice and are an infringement of fair procedures. In *S. v. S.*[117] O'Hanlon J. held invalid the rule at common law, whereby it was conclusively presumed that a child born to a married woman was fathered by her husband. In that case the plaintiff left her husband in May 1980 to go and live with another man and in February 1981 she gave birth to a child, which, she said, was fathered by that other man. Indeed, her husband did not even claim to be the father but, because of the common law presumption, the Registrar General of Births and Deaths insisted on registering her husband as the child's father. In striking down the presumption, O'Hanlon J. described it as "repugnant to modern thinking," as the "lone survival of those narrow and outmoded rules of procedure" at common law that have since been changed by the legislature, and as "calculated to defeat the due and proper administration of justice;"[118] it was inconsistent with the guarantee of fair procedure and, therefore, was not carried over by Article 50 of the Constitution.

As has already been explained, in *State (McEldowney) v. Kelleher*,[119] the Supreme Court declared unconstitutional a similar provision of the Street and House-to-House Collections Act 1962. It provided that, where an applicant was appealing to the District Court against a Garda Inspector's refusal to issue

---

[115] [2001] 4 I.R. 113.
[116] *Id.* at p.155.
[117] [1983] I.R. 68.
[118] *Id.* at p.79.
[119] [1983] I.R. 289; *supra*, p.203.

a licence for collecting money, the sworn statement of a Garda that the proceeds from any such collection would be used for illegal or immoral purposes was conclusive evidence of that fact and that, consequently, the judge must disallow the appeal. This was held to be an excessive intrusion into the administration of justice, which is exclusively the judge's function.[120] The court there distinguished *State (O'Rourke) v. Kelly*,[121] which concerned the procedure for issuing warrants authorising repossession of dwellings under the Housing Act 1966, notably section 62(1), which says that a District Judge must issue a warrant if satisfied that a demand for repossession "has been duly made." A contention that this provision was unconstitutional was rejected, O'Higgins C.J. describing it as "no different to many of the statutory provisions which, on proof of certain matters, make it mandatory on a court to make a specified order."[122] It still required proof, in the normal manner, that the statutory formalities had been complied with and it was entirely for the judge to adjudicate on the issue.

Privileged Information

Although ascertaining the truth through all available evidence is the main objective of trials, at times this gives way to other values and purposes: for instance, in criminal trials, the prosecution may be prevented from relying on evidence that was unconstitutionally obtained. Information will not be admitted into evidence in civil trials because it is privileged[123] and some of these privileges are protected by the Constitution, not merely by existing practice and procedure. Parties to civil actions are not obliged to give evidence themselves, although their failure to testify in particular circumstances may warrant adverse inferences being drawn. Mention has already been made of the privilege against self-incrimination,[124] and also of legislative privilege[125] and executive privilege,[126] although the scope of the latter has been considerably restricted since *Murphy v. Dublin Corporation*[127] was decided. Certain communications between spouses[128] and also between a person and his priest-confessor[129] appear to be constitutionally protected, and perhaps also what is known as legal professional privilege.[130]

---

[120] Similarly, *Tinnelly v. United Kingdom*, 27 E.H.R.R. 249 (1999).
[121] [1983] I.R. 58.
[122] *Id.* at p.61.
[123] See generally *Delany & McGrath*, Chap.8.
[124] *Supra*, p.456.
[125] *Supra*, p.107.
[126] *Supra*, p.130.
[127] [1972] I.R. 215; *supra*, p.130.
[128] *Infra*, p.669.
[129] *Infra*, p.632.
[130] *Infra*, p.650.

Reasons

In the past there was a view that there was no legal obligation on judges to give reasons for their decisions although furnishing reasons, frequently in considerable detail, has been the practice in nearly all courts. Reasons especially should be given where a right of appeal exists because, without knowing why he lost his case, the party may not be able to evaluate his prospects of a successful appeal. Further, for many practical purposes, the appeal tribunal becomes a forum of first instance when it does not know the grounds in law or on the facts why the appellant lost. Notwithstanding, from time to time High Court judges decline to give reasoned decisions, even in cases involving complex issues of law and considerable dispute about the facts.[131]

Several continental European Constitutions expressly oblige all judges to give reasons[132] and the "fair trial" requirement in Article 6(1) of the European Convention has been construed to this effect. This obligation is now accepted in most common law countries[133] and failure to give any or any adequate reasons is now a free-standing ground of appeal in England.[134] In *Uphahlele v. First National Bank of S.A.*,[135] Goldstone J. explained the duty to give reasons as follows:

> "There is no express constitutional provision which requires judges to furnish reasons for their decisions. Nonetheless, in terms of section 1 of the constitution, the rule of law is one of the founding values of our democratic state, and the judiciary is bound by it. The rule of law undoubtedly requires judges not to act arbitrarily and to be accountable. The manner in which they ordinarily account for their decisions is by furnishing reasons. This serves a number of purposes. It explains to the parties, and to the public at large which has an interest in courts being open and transparent, why a case is decided as it is. It is a discipline, which curbs arbitrary judicial decisions. Then, too, it is essential for the appeal process, enabling the losing party to take an informed decision as to whether or not to appeal or, where necessary, seek leave to appeal. It assists the appeal court to decide whether or not the order of the lower court is correct. And finally, it provides guidance to the public in respect of similar matters. It may well be, too, that when a decision is subject to appeal it would be a violation of the constitutional right of access to

---

[131] *E.g.*, in *Criminal Assets Bureau v. Hunt*, unreported, Supreme Court, March 19, 2003, on appeal from Smyth J.

[132] *E.g.*, Italy and Spain; cf. Art. 455 of the French Code of Civil Procedure and Art. 313 of the German Code of Civil Procedure.

[133] See generally, Ho, "The Judicial Duty to Give Reasons", 20 *I. Legal Studies* 42 (2000).

[134] *English v. Emery Reimbold & Strick Ltd* [2002] 1 W.L.R. 2409.

[135] 6 B.H.R.C. 481 (1999) (S. Africa).

courts if reasons for such a decision were to be withheld by a judicial officer."[136]

Appeal/Review

In most common law countries, statutory rights of appeal from lower courts date only from the middle of the 19th century. This is not to say that, before then, there were no means by which errors and improprieties in the lower courts could be put right. The principal mechanism that then existed, and still exists, is the inherent jurisdiction of the High Court to supervise inferior tribunals through the process which is now known as judicial review; there also was the bill of error and the equity review.

Appeal

An appeal is radically different from judicial review in that the appellate court's function is to consider again the entire merits of the case. As Costello J. pointed out in one instance,[137] there is a distinction between common law powers of judicial review and statutory authority to entertain an appeal. Judicial review is concerned merely with the legality of the lower tribunal's decision; the question is whether that tribunal acted lawfully or unlawfully. But in an appeal, the focus is on the actual merits of the lower tribunal's decision and whether or not it decided correctly in all the circumstances. Appeals from decisions of the District or the Circuit Courts are not addressed in the Constitution. But the Courts Acts provide for appeals from the District Court to the Circuit Court and from it to the High Court; there also is a form of appeal by way of case stated from the District Court to the High Court and from the Circuit Court to the Supreme Court.[138]

As for appeals from the High Court, Article 34.4.4 of the Constitution provides that, not alone are its decisions concerning the "validity of any law" in the light of the Constitution appealable to the Supreme Court, but there is an entrenched right to bring appeals. It is all "cases, which involve (such) questions" that fall within this entrenched right of appeal. In cases where these issues do not arise, the position is two-fold.[139] Any right of appeal from the Circuit Court or from the District Court, or from any other court of first instance as may be established, must be provided for by statute. There is no constitutional right of appeal from those tribunals, be it to the High Court or to the Supreme Court.[140]

---

[136] *Id.*, at pp.484–485.
[137] *Dunne v. Minister for Fisheries* [1984] I.R. 230 at p.237.
[138] See generally, *Delany & McGrath*, Chap.20.
[139] *Supra*, pp.145 and 155.
[140] *Todd v. Murphy* [1999] 2 I.R. 1.

But the position regarding appeals from the High Court is the very opposite. Article 34.4.3 of the Constitution states that, subject to any statutory preclusion of appeals, the Supreme Court has appellate jurisdiction "from all" High Court decisions; thus, there is a qualified constitutional right of appeal from decisions of the High Court.[141] This Article stipulates that this right is "with such exceptions and subject to such restrictions as may be prescribed by law." Consequently, unless the case raises questions about the constitutionality of some post-1937 law, the Oireachtas can prevent various kinds of decisions from being appealed to the Supreme Court. Several provisions to that effect exist; for instance, a decision of the High Court on an appeal from the Circuit Court cannot be appealed further to the Supreme Court.[142] But any preclusion of the right of appeal must be clear and unambiguous, and be contained in a law enacted since (it is not clear) 1937 or 1961.[143]

An issue which occasionally arises in appeals before the Supreme Court is can matters that were not raised in the lower court be considered in the appeal; can fresh arguments be made, new issues be raised and additional evidence be introduced? Most of these questions are resolved by Order 58 of the Rules of the Superior Courts, which deals with these appeals. They are "by way of re-hearing" and the court is authorised to receive further evidence on questions of fact but will only do so when certain criteria are met. Absent exceptional circumstances, parties will not be permitted to make a case that is substantially different from that made before the High Court.

The first time that this issue seems to have arisen was in *Murphy v. Attorney General*,[144] where it was held that provisions of the Finance Act 1967, whereby incomes of husbands and wives should be aggregated for the purpose of income tax, was an unconstitutional attack on the family. The question that then arose was the implications of this decision for the plaintiffs and for all other taxpayers. The Supreme Court gave its judgment on January 25, 1980 and a week later counsel for the Attorney General requested the court to determine the immediate effects of that judgment; in particular, whether the finding should operate retrospectively and, if so, to what extent. These had not been decided by Hamilton J. in the High Court nor had they even been addressed in argument there. But it was not contended before the Supreme Court that it had no jurisdiction to resolve these issues until they had first been determined by the High Court; the Attorney General wanted a speedy and conclusive resolution and, presumably in order to save costs, the plaintiffs were anxious not to have to go back to the High Court. In the event and without canvassing the question

---

[141] *State (Browne) v. Feran* [1967] I.R. 147.

[142] *L.P. v. M. P.* [2002] 1 I.R. 219.

[143] *Supra*, p.155.

[144] [1982] I.R. 241.

of its jurisdiction, the Supreme Court ruled on the retroactive effects of its declaration of invalidity. Where a party objects to a substantially new case from that made at the first instance being made out in an appeal, the court will not consider that case unless it would be manifestly unjust not to do so. As Finlay C.J. put it in *KD. v. M.G.*, "[i]t is a fundamental principle, arising from the exclusively appellate jurisdiction of this Court in cases such as this that, save in the most exceptional circumstances, the Court should not hear and determine an issue which has not been tried and decided in the High Court. To that fundamental rule or principle there may be exceptions, but they must be clearly required in the interests of justice."[145]

In the *Open Door* case,[146] the court refused to consider whether an injunction it previously granted should be vacated in view of the intervening change in the constitutional position, principally because to do so would require it to consider constitutional issues that had not been argued and determined in the High Court. More recently, where arguments about constitutionality had been made in the High Court but were never dealt with in its judgment, the Supreme Court refused to address the constitutional propositions and directed that they should be remitted to the High Court for rehearing.[147] Yet in *Minister for Social Affairs v. Scanlon*,[148] the Supreme Court, perhaps inadvertently, rejected a proposition of unconstitutionality that had never been made in the High Court and where the Attorney General was neither a party nor a notice party to the proceedings.

Another question is what orders can the Supreme Court make on hearing an appeal; is it a *cour de vassation,* which only can set aside verdicts and judgments appealed from, or has it more extensive powers? As well as being able to set aside the decision of the judge or judges being appealed from, it has been held that the Supreme Court can also set aside a jury's award in a civil case, even where that award was not made on the direction of the trial judge. In recent years the Supreme Court has set aside jury awards of damages in personal injuries and defamation cases because the sums awarded were excessive;[149] equally, it will set aside awards for being insufficient.

---

[145] [1985] I.R. 697 at p.701. Compare *Rooney v. Connolly* [1986] I.R. 572, where the court declined to address the point, with *Keenan v. Shield Insurance* [1988] I.R. 89.

[146] *Attorney General (ex rel. SPUC Ir. Ltd) v. Open Door Counselling Ltd (No.2)* [1994] 2 I.R. 333.

[147] *Dunnes Stores Ireland Co. v. Ryan* [1999] 3 I.R. 542 and *Dunnes Stores Ireland Co. v. Ryan* [2002] 2 I.R. 60.

[148] [2001] 1 I.R. 64.

[149] *Holohan v. Donohue* [1986] I.R. 45 and *O'Brien v. Mirror Group Newspapers Ltd.* [2001] 1 I.R. 1.

Judicial Review

Decisions of the lower courts can be challenged in the High Court on the grounds that the lower tribunal denied one party a fair hearing or that it otherwise acted unlawfully.[150] If any such contention is established, the High Court will make an order of *certiorari* that the subordinate tribunal's decision be quashed. Moreover, where it could be shown that the lower court is about to act unlawfully, the High Court can make an order of prohibition forbidding it from acting in that fashion. Where the lower tribunal is refusing to do something which it is obliged to do, the High Court can order that it acts in the manner required by the law.

Post-Appellate Review

There is no statutory mechanism for reviewing the final judgment of a court once handed down and once order in the case is perfected, as exists in several countries. Almost always finality has been given precedence in the common law systems, the principal exception being where it can be demonstrated that the judgment in question was obtained by fraud; in those cases, an aggrieved party may bring fresh proceedings in the trial court to have the judgment set aside. In *Belville Holdings Ltd. v. Revenue Commissioners*,[151] where the High Court had determined a dispute relating to taxation but did not remit (nor refuse to remit) the matters to the Appeal Commissioners, the Revenue subsequently applied to have it so remitted. But the Supreme Court held that, having made up her order in the proceedings, the trial judge had become *functus officio* and no longer had jurisdiction to make further orders in the case. There the court accepted that another order might be made where the order as drawn up did not reflect what was dealt with in the judgment that was handed down, nor were there any "exceptional circumstances" that might warrant departure from finality. Similarly in *Attorney General v. Open Door Counselling Ltd. (No.2)*,[152] an order made by the High Court restraining the defendants from publishing information regarding abortion was upheld by the Supreme Court but subsequently the law on this question was radically changed in a constitutional amendment in 1992. In view of that change, the defendant applied to the Supreme Court to set aside its order. But it refused to do so, asserting that there were no "special or unusual circumstances" warranting departure from the principle of finality. That the ground rules had been entirely reversed in a referendum was not sufficient because the precise import of Amendment no. 14 was not abundantly clear and the court would not adjudicate *de novo* on important questions of constitutionality that were not debated and determined first in the High Court.

---

[150] See generally, *Delany & McGrath*, Chap.21 and *infra*, p.519.
[151] [1994] I.L.R.M. 29.
[152] [1994] 2 I.R. 333.

Where a litigant has not obtained a fair hearing in the High Court, his only remedy would appear to be to appeal to the Supreme Court.[153] Such an appeal was upheld in *Brick v. Burke*,[154] despite the existence of a statutory prohibition on hearing appeals without the judge in question certifying the case as appropriate for an appeal. On account of the manner in which Kelly J. in the High Court had dealt with proceedings concerning a challenge to a compulsory purchase order, it was held that the appellant had been denied *audi alteram partem* by that judge.

The question that arose in *Re Greendale Developments Ltd. (No.3)*[155] and also in *Bula Ltd. v. Tara Mines Ltd. (No.6)*[156] was whether and, if so, to what extent the Supreme Court would reconsider its decision where a party was denied fair procedures in that very court. In *Greendale* it was contended that the court had decided the main issue is an appeal without affording the appellant a fair opportunity to argue his case, which was decided on legal propositions that were never argued before it or in the High Court. In *Bula* it was contended that two of the five judges involved in the appeal had previous professional dealings with one of the parties and, consequently, there existed objective bias. Because what was in issue in both cases was the fairness of the appeal hearing, which is a constitutionally guaranteed right, the court held that in an appropriate case it would intervene but would be very slow to do so, in view of the strong public policy requiring finality and certainty, and also the constitutional stipulation that the Supreme Court's decisions are final. Denham J. in *Greendale* endorsed the position adopted in the House of Lords in the *Pinochet* litigation,[157] where it was said that "the House will not reopen any appeal save in circumstances where, through no fault of a party, he or she has been subject to an unfair procedure."[158] She further agreed with a dictum of Brennan J., that a court "should not pronounce a judgment against a person on a ground which that person has not had an opportunity to argue. However, a sufficient opportunity to argue a ground is given when the ground is logically involved in a proposition that has been raised in the course of argument before the court or is to be considered by the court as an unconceded step in determining the validity of a conclusion which one of the parties contends. Of course the precise ground which a court or judge assigns for a decision will frequently be formulated in terms different from the terms of a submission by counsel but, provided the ground has arisen in one of the ways mentioned, the

---

[153] Except in Circuit Court appeals, *P. v. P.* [2002] 1 I.R. 219, where the remedy is to apply to the High Court to set aside its order in circumstances similar to where such an application may be made to the Supreme Court, as described below.

[154] [2002] 2 I.L.R.M. 427.

[155] [2000] 2 I.R. 514. The background is described in M. Forde, *Company Law* (3rd ed., 1999) at pp.104–107.

[156] [2000] 4 I.R. 412.

[157] *R. v. Bow Street Magistrate, ex p. Pinochet Ugarte (No. 2)* [2000] 1 A.C. 119.

[158] [2000] 2 I.R. 540.

court or judge may properly proceed to judgment without requiring the case to be relisted for further argument and without inviting supplementary submissions to be made."[159] And in *Bula*, the court accepted the "reasonable apprehension" rather than the "real danger" test for objective bias.[160] It was held, however, in both instances that there had been no departure from fair procedures; in the former, that the appellant had been given a sufficient opportunity to argue his case and, in the latter, that the circumstances did not give rise to a reasonable apprehension that the two judges may have been biased.

ADMINISTRATIVE PROCEDURES

Individuals are affected by the decisions of public bodies and officials in a host of ways. It is public bodies and officials who determine, for example, whether planning permission should be granted, whether one should have a passport, whether ones property should be taken for road widening or other purposes, whether a social security benefit should be paid, whether one is entitled to have public housing, whether a driving licence should be issued and the like. One need only contemplate the central government departments (*e.g.* Enterprise, Education, Health, *etc.*), local government, partly autonomous bodies established by the State (*e.g.* the Competition Authority, the Planning Appeals Board, Health Authorities etc.) in order to appreciate the extent to which decisions made by public agencies can directly and seriously affect individuals and organisations.

Separation of Powers

The constitutional scheme for the separation of powers, that prevents the concentration of authority in one organ of state, affects administrative procedures in two principal ways. As has been explained, while the legislature can delegate to others some powers to set standards of conduct, the critical policy choices can only be made by the Oireachtas.[161] In *Cityview Press Ltd. v. An Chomhairle Oiliúna*,[162] the AnCO training levies case, both parties to the action accepted that the governing principles in this regard are "1. Anything clearly identifiable as policy-making should be retained in the control of the Oireachtas. 2. If policy is clearly enunciated in the statute, a legislature can delegate wide powers of implementing the declared policy to a subordinate

---

[159] *Id.* at p.541, from *Autodesk Inc. v. Dyason (No.2)*, 176 C.L.R. 300 (1993).
[160] *Supra*, p.488.
[161] *Supra*, p.179.
[162] [1980] I.R. 381.

agency. (But) there is no universal and apt formula to determine the extent to which legislative power may be delegated."[163]

All criminal cases are reserved to the courts[164] and cannot be decided by administrative agencies or officials, For instance in *Re Haughey*,[165] which concerned an investigation being conducted by the Dáil Committee of Public Accounts under special statutory powers, it was held that those powers were so far-reaching that they transformed part of the investigation into a criminal trial of a non-minor offence, which under the Constitution can only be conducted by a judge and jury.

However, the modern social state, based on a philosophy of frequent economic and social intervention, regulation of property rights and distribution of different categories of welfare benefits, could not function effectively if all decisions, about who should bear particular burdens and who should obtain particular benefits, had to be made by the courts. There are not enough judges to make those decisions and court procedures are not sufficiently speedy or flexible to function effectively in managing the administrative/welfare state. In continental European countries special administrative law courts or tribunals were established in order to deal with many of these questions, for instance labour courts, social security courts, tax courts and cartel courts. It was because of the need for court substitutes that Article 37 of the Constitution was adopted, which permits bodies and individuals other than courts to exercise "limited" judicial functions of a non-criminal nature.[166] However, these bodies are still obliged to act judicially when making decisions. On several occasions it has been held that administrative bodies must observe the principles of constitutional justice. In other words, administrative bodies are partly judicialised in that they must observe certain guarantees of impartiality and certain minimum standards of procedure. Although they are so described, some administrative agencies are not strictly courts, notably the coroners' court and the Labour Court.

Judicial Supervision

Unlike some modern constitutions, the Constitution does not expressly provide that all administrative decisions shall be capable of being reviewed by the courts. Thus, Article 33(3)(a) of the South African Constitution states that "[n]ational legislation must be enacted to ... provide for the review of administrative action by a court or, where appropriate, an independent and impartial tribunal." Insofar as administrative decisions affect persons' "civil

---

[163] *Id.*, at p.389.
[164] *Supra*, p.408.
[165] [1971] I.R. 217; *supra*, p.411.
[166] *Supra*, p.193.

rights and obligations," Article 6(1) of the European Convention and Article 14(1) of the UN Covenant guarantee that they shall be subject to a "fair and public hearing within a reasonable time by an independent and impartial tribunal established by law."[167] What may be regarded as purely administrative decisions that do not affect persons' "civil rights and obligations" are not governed by these guarantees.

Appeal and Review

Where provision is made for appealing an administrative decision to the courts, whether there will be an entirely fresh hearing or whether it will be limited to the record of evidence given to the official or tribunal that is being appealed depends on how the right of appeal is defined.[168] But in any such appeal the court cannot be obliged by law to accept as a proven fact what a particular witness asserts[169] and, furthermore, cannot be prevented from hearing any interested party or any evidence it may regard as relevant depends on how the right of appeal is defined.[170]

Where no right of appeal to the courts is provided for, aggrieved persons can challenge the propriety of administrative determinations by way of application for judicial review.[171] The basis of objection may be either that fair procedures were not complied with or that no reasons were given for the decision being objected to, or that the decision is substantively unlawful. When reviewing administrative determinations, where the decision-maker was given some discretion, the court will not substitute itself for him and set aside his decision merely on the grounds that it would have decided the issue differently; to be set aside, his decision must have some more serious defect than simply being erroneous. Drawing the line between non-reviewable mere error and determinations on the merits that are reviewable can be difficult at times.

Legislative Exclusion

It remains to be determined whether or in what circumstances a provision that certain types of administrative decision cannot be challenged by way of judicial review (formerly described as "no *certiorari* clauses") conforms with the Constitution.[172] No such prohibition appears to exist on the Irish statute book. There are, however, requirements that go some considerable way in this

---

[167] *Cf. R. (Alconbury Developments Ltd) v. Secretary of State* [2001] 2 W.L.R. 1389.
[168] Cf. *Re M.* [1984] I.R. 479.
[169] *State (McEldowney) v. Kelleher* [1983] I.R. 289; *supra*, p.203.
[170] *Cashman v. Clifford* [1989] I.R. 121.
[171] See generally, *Delany & McGrath*, Chap.21, C. Bradley, *Judicial Review* (2000), D. Morgan & G. Hogan, *Administrative Law in Ireland* (3rd ed., 1998), Chap.13 (hereinafter "Hogan & Morgan") and A. Collins and J. O'Reilly, *Civil Proceedings and the State* (2nd ed., 2003), Chaps 4 and 5.
[172] *Cf. Abebe v. Commonwealth*, 197 C.L.R. 510 (1999).

direction, most notably that the Government or Minister "may at its/his absolute discretion" take certain decisions. Stipulating very short limitation periods within which certain decisions may be challenged tends to have a similar effect, as do provisions that either require that no reasons shall be given for a particular decision or their equivalent, a prescribed bland formula of purported reasons that must be recited and left at that. Requirements that certain administrative determinations shall be "conclusive evidence" of particular facts also indirectly exclude judicial review. In *Tormey v. Ireland*[173] it was stated that the Oireachtas cannot oust judicial review of any "justiciable matter," which suggests that there is a category of administrative decisions that are always reviewable but there may be a residual category that can be made judicial review-proof.

Depending on the context, conferring an absolute discretion on an official, or indeed on a Minister or on the Government, to decide a matter that has serious consequences for an individual, would be held to be unconstitutional.[174] Whether such a provision would be "read down" to circumscribe that discretion to a degree is debateable. The express absolute discretion to grant or to withhold naturalisation has been held to be subject to the "principles of constitutional justice."[175] Depending on the context, imposing an unduly short limitation period within which certain decisions may be challenged is also uncon-stitutional.[176] It is debateable whether a statutory embargo on furnishing reasons for particular decisions would be struck down. Where no reasons are furnished and the decision is then challenged by way of judicial review, but even at that stage no reasons for the decision are offered, generally the decision will be set aside on those grounds alone.[177]

In *An Blascaod Mor Teo v. Commissioners for Public Works*,[178] Budd J. upheld the Acquisition of Land (Assessment of Compensation) Act 1919, which contains the mechanism whereby compensation payable for land that has been compulsorily purchased is assessed. Although the assessor there is described as an "arbitrator," that is a misdescription since he is not appointed by the parties but is a Government appointee, albeit on the nomination of a reference committee. Where a claim for compensation is made, this "arbitrator" hears and determines the issue in much the same way as a court or an agreed arbitrator. He is not obliged to give reasons for his decisions, unless requested in advance by the parties to do so.[179] Section 6(1) of this Act states that the "arbitrator's" decision "upon any question of fact shall be final and binding on the parties."

---

[173] [1985] I.R. 289; *supra*, p.148.
[174] *State (Lynch) v. Cooney* [1982] I.R. 337.
[175] *Mishra v. Minister for Justice* [1996] 1 I.R. 189.
[176] *White v. Dublin Corporation*, unreported, High Court, Ó Caoimh J., June 21, 2002 and *Plaintiff S157/2002 v. Commonwealth*, 77 A.L.J.L.R. 454 (2003).
[177] *State (Daly) v. Minister for Agriculture* [1987] I.R. 165.
[178] Unreported, High Court, Budd J., February 27, 1998.
[179] *Manning v. Shackleton* [1996] 3 I.R. 85.

Consequently, in *Doyle v. Kildare C.C.*,[180] it was held that even his manifestly perverse findings of fact are unreviewable. Indeed, that his factual determinations cannot be challenged may justify the absence of any obligation to furnish reasons. In many comparable countries disputes about the amount of compensation to be paid to owners of land that has been compulsorily acquired are determined by the courts and not by administrative agencies; where they are heard by an agency, there is a full right of appeal to the courts, as indeed existed under the former Land Commission scheme. In the event, the Supreme Court upheld the plaintiff's claim that An Blascaod Mór Historical Park Act 1989 was unconstitutional, which rendered it unnecessary then to rule on the appeal about 1919 Act's status.

Among Budd's J.'s grounds for upholding the 1919 Act were that the earlier Supreme Court decisions "sanctioned that [Act's] procedure and implicitly allowed the system whereby the property arbitrator does not give a reasoned judgment."[181] However, in neither of those cases does it appear to have been contended that any part of this Act was invalid on account of the very restricted scope for judicial review and its implicit dispensing with reasoned determinations. In both of them, the court appears to have regarded the "property arbitrator" as indeed an arbitrator subject to the regime governing private consensual arbitrations, when plainly he is more in the nature of a public official deciding a dispute between an individual and the State. But for this misconception, it is likely that the court would have required reasons to be given and permitted a more expansive judicial review of "awards."

Fair Procedures

The concept of fair procedures is sometimes referred to as natural justice or constitutional justice. Traditionally, its ambit was summed up in the maxims *nemo iudex in causa sua* and *audi alteram partem* – meaning that the decision-maker should be unbiased[182] and that the aggrieved individual ought to know the case he has to meet and have a reasonable opportunity to put his side of the case.[183] In recent times courts are beginning to insist on reasons being given for the administrative decision in question.[184] Some administrative adjudications are required to take place in public but there are express *in camera* requirements for others.[185] At times a decision on the basis of written

---

[180] [1995] 2 I.R. 424.

[181] At p.175.

[182] See generally, *Hogan & Morgan*, Chap.10 and D. Galligan, *Due Process and Fair Procedures* (1996).

[183] See generally, Hogan & Morgan, *id.*, Chap.11 and p.437 *et seq.*

[184] *E.g. Orange Communications Ltd v. Director of Telecommunications Regulations (No.2)* [2001] 4 I.R. 159 at pp.211–219.

[185] *E.g. Barry v. Medical Council* [1998] 3 I.R. 368.

representations may suffice; on other occasions, fairness may require oral hearings and even permitting legal representation.[186] Where an individual's detention in custody is being put in issue in administrative proceedings, he may be entitled to be given legal aid if he cannot afford to pay for representation.[187]

Presumption of Compliance

Acts of the Oireachtas are presumed to be constitutional.[188] Accordingly, where an Act confers decision-making powers on an individual or body but does not set out the entire procedures to be followed in reaching the decision, then it will be implied into the Act that the decision must be made through constitutionally fair procedures. That is to say, where they are not excluded by the very terms of the Act, it will be read as requiring adherence to the *audi alteram partem* and *nemo iudex in causa sua* principles, and any other constitutionally-required procedures. Thus in *McDonald v. Bord na gCon*,[189] which concerned administrative powers to investigate alleged improprieties in the greyhound racing industry, Walsh J. for the Supreme Court found that the wording of the statutory provisions did not exclude the application of the principles of natural justice to those investigations. While "the (investigating) Board may determine the manner in which the investigation shall be carried out, the clear words or necessary implication which would be required to exclude the principles of natural justice from such investigation are not present in the sections."[190] And in the *East Donegal Co-op* case,[191] which concerned the scope of the Minister's discretionary powers over the conditions on which bodies are permitted to operate a particular business, Walsh J. observed that "they are powers which cast upon the Minister the duty of acting fairly and judicially in accordance with the principles of constitutional justice .... Therefore, he is required to consider every case on its own merits, to hear what the applicant or the licensee (as the case may be) has to say, and to give the latter an opportunity to deal with whatever case may be thought to exist against the granting of a licence or for the refusal of a licence, or for the attaching of conditions, or for the amendment or revocation of conditions which have already attached, as the case may be."[192]

In *Garvey v. Ireland*,[193] where the Commissioner of the Garda Síochána was removed from office abruptly and without being given any reason, it was

---

[186] Compare *V.Z. v. Minister for Justice* [2002] 2 I.R. 135 with *Commission to Inquire into Child Abuse, re* [2002] 3 I.R. 459.
[187] *M. v. Legal Aid Board* [1994] 3 I.R. 1.
[188] *Supra*, p.43.
[189] [1965] I.R. 217.
[190] *Id.* at p.243.
[191] [1976] I.R. 280.
[192] *Id.* at p.344.
[193] [1981] I.R. 75.

contended that, if the statutory power to remove him did not require compliance with natural justice, then that provision was unconstitutional. According to section 6(2) of the Police Forces Amalgamation Act 1925, the Garda Commissioner "may at any time be removed" by the Government. It was held that this did not authorise removal before the grounds for dismissal were disclosed to the Commissioner and he had an opportunity to reply to them, and accordingly the question of section 6(2)'s constitutionality did not arise. McCarthy J. summarised the authorities in the following terms:

> "Whether it be identified as a principle of natural justice derived from the common law ... or, preferably, as the right to fair procedures under the Constitution in all judicial or quasi-judicial proceedings, it is a fundamental requirement of justice that persons or property should not be at risk without the party charged being given an adequate opportunity of meeting the claim as identified and pursued. If the proceedings derive from statute, then in the absence of any set fixed procedures, the relevant authority must create and carry out the necessary procedures; if the set or fixed procedure is not comprehensive, the authority must supplement it in such a fashion as to ensure compliance with constitutional justice ...".[194]

Legislative Exclusion

In circumstances where the Constitution requires that individuals be afforded some hearing by the decision-maker or that he should be neither biased nor possess the trappings of bias, it would seem that the Oireachtas is not permitted to stipulate that there need not be adherence to these requirements. While there is no reported authority on legislative exclusion of these being struck down, this principle is implicit in the judgments in the *Garvey* case. However, where a statute unambiguously excludes compliance with these requirements, the courts may be inclined to accept the legislature's determination that special circumstances exist that justify departure from constitutional justice.

A particular source of difficulty is what may be described as institutional bias, *i.e.* the designated decision-maker not being entirely independent of the body that may gain or be prejudiced by the decision taken. Under Article 6(1) of the European Convention, if a person's "civil rights and obligations" are involved there should not be bias of this nature or at minimum there should be a right of appeal to a party who is not affected by that bias. This principle is reflected in the scheme for regulating professional discipline among doctors, nurses, dentists and solicitors, where an individual who is severely sanctioned

---

[194] *State (Irish Pharmaceutical Union) v. Employment Appeals Tribunal* [1987] I.L.R.M. 36 at p.40.

by the professional disciplinary body can appeal that decision to the High Court.[195]

It was held in *O'Brien v. Bord na Mona*,[196] concerning the *nemo iudex* principle, that if the decision in question is an administrative as opposed to a judicial one, then there is no constitutional obligation to adhere to the rule that the decision-maker must have no material interest in the outcome. This concerned powers that the Turf Development Act 1946 gives Bord na Mona to expropriate owners of bog land so that the Board can obtain access to the turf in that land. Where land is being compulsorily acquired, the usual procedure is that some individual or body, other than the one needing the land, decides whether it should be acquired for the statutory purposes. But under the 1946 Act, whenever Bord na Mona wants land, it is the Board itself which decides that the owner is to be dispossessed. It was contended that this procedure was unconstitutional because it flew in the face of the *nemo iudex* principle – that the Oireachtas had entrusted the exercise of a function of a judicial nature to a body which cannot be totally impartial, since manifestly the Board had an interest in the outcome, and it had already decided that the land should be acquired. Keane J. concluded that the procedure was unconstitutional on the grounds that, in deciding what land should be expropriated, the Board was exercising a judicial function and it offended fundamental principles of fair procedure for the Board to act as judge in its own cause; moreover, it was not demonstrably impractical to have a procedure which involved a body with no stake in the outcome deciding if particular tracts of land should be taken for the statutory purposes. His judgment was overruled by the Supreme Court on the grounds that decisions to take land, in these circumstances, are exercises of an administrative and not a judicial function and, accordingly, the full rigours of *nemo iudex* do not apply to them. In the light of the 1946 Act's scheme, the Board was "acting in discharge of an administrative function" and, while it had "an obligation to act fairly and properly," it was "not necessarily inhibited from deciding the question as to whether or not to acquire."[197] What this case decides is that public institutions, which have a direct interest in the outcome of particular decisions that gravely affect others, are not, by virtue of their institutional interest, always precluded from making those decisions. Generally, however, such decisions must be capable of being challenged in judicial review proceedings, if not appealed.

Substantive Review

How extensive a reviewing role must be for these purposes depends on the

---

[195] *Infra*, p.783.
[196] [1983] I.R. 255.
[197] *Id.* at p.282.

subject matter of the decision, the manner in which it was arrived at, the context of the dispute, including the basis for the desired grounds of challenge.[198] Where the decision in question is predominantly one of policy, taken within a statutory grant of considerable discretion, the requisite scope for review need be comparatively narrow. A contrast may be drawn with deciding a precise legal issue that requires findings of fact and then the application of the relevant rule, where a more extensive scope for review is required. Compare for instance, deciding whether planning permission ought to be granted for a proposed development with whether a tax assessment should be permitted to stand.

A mantra one frequently encounters in the judgments is a quotation (usually taken out of context) from a 20 years old House of Lords' decision to the effect that "[j]udicial review is concerned, not with the decision, but with the decision making process."[199] Irish judges often cite this as signifying that the substantive merits of the decision being challenged, as contrasted with the procedure adopted in making the decision, is never a concern of the court, which is simplistic and wrong.

Another mantra one frequently encounters is that the role of the court in considering the merits of the decision being challenged is limited to determining whether, in all the circumstances, it is so unreasonable as to be virtually absurd, placing reliance on the Supreme Court's decision in *O'Keeffe v. An Bord Pleanála*.[200] What judges relying on this case frequently overlook is that it concerned the role of the court reviewing a particular type of decision made in a particular decision-making process; it is not a mandate for across the board judicial deference to administrative agencies and tribunals. The issue in *O'Keeffe* concerned whether in the circumstances planning permission for a 300 foot mast for transmitting radio signals should be built in Co. Meath, which had been decided by a tribunal which had special expertise in planning, at which the objectors had been given a full opportunity to present their case at an oral hearing and with legal representation.

How extensive a role the courts should play in reviewing the decisions of administrative bodies cannot be reduced to simple formulae, in view of the enormous variety of such bodies and types of decision being made. Where, however, constitutional rights are in issue, a more intensive scrutiny of the challenged decision would appear to be called for, especially where the individual concerned has not had a full hearing of his case by some specialist administrative tribunal. In this regard, what Lord Cooke of Thorndon said in 2001 about the English equivalent to *O'Keeffe* (the *Wednesbury* case)[201] is

---

[198] See generally, *Hogan & Morgan* chs. 9 (*ultra vires*) and 12 (discretion).

[199] *R. v. Chief Constable, ex p. Evans* [1982] 1 W.L.R. 1155 at p.1160, the most recent reported example being *V.Z. v. Minister for Justice* [2002] 2 I.R. 135 at p.157 (McGuinness J.), "[j]udical review is not concerned with the decision, but with the decision making process."

[200] [1993] 1 I.R. 39.

[201] *Associated Provincial Picture Houses Ltd v. Wednesbury Corp* [1948] 1 K.B. 223.

instructive. He observed that "the day will come when it will be more widely recognised that (*Wednesbury*) was an unfortunately retrogressive decision in English administrative law, in so far as it suggested that there are degrees of unreasonableness and that only a very extreme degree can bring ... invalidation. The depth of judicial review and the deference due to administrative discretion vary with the subject matter. It may well be, however, that the law can never be satisfied in any administrative field merely by a finding that the decision under review is not capricious or absurd."[202]

The overall approach taken in French administrative law may provide helpful guidance.[203] There review for *violation de la loi* has a three-fold perspective, viz. misinterpretation (*erreur de droit*), mistake of fact (*faits matériellement inexacts*) and classification of facts (*qualification juridique des faits*). And the administrative courts interfere with decisions in some areas more than others, being the less willing to do so the closer one comes to "policy;" they differentiate between normal, minimum and maximum control. Maximum control involves *inter alia* applying the test of proportionality.[204] As explained in an English context by Lord Steyn, "there is an overlap between the traditional grounds of review and the approach of proportionality. Most cases would be decided in the same way whichever approach is adopted. But the intensity of review is somewhat greater under the proportionality approach. Making due allowance for important structural differences between various Convention rights, which I do not propose to discuss, a few generalisations are perhaps permissible. I would mention ... concrete differences without suggesting that my statement is exhaustive. First, the doctrine of proportionality may require the reviewing court to assess the balance, which the decision maker has struck, not merely whether it is within the range of rational or reasonable decisions. Secondly, the proportionality test may go further than the traditional grounds of review inasmuch as it may require attention to be directed to the relative weight accorded to interests and considerations.."[205]

---

[202] *R. (Daly) v. Secretary of State* [2001] 2 A.C. 532 at p.549.

[203] Summarised in J. Bell et al, *Principles of French Law* (1998), pp.185–188 and adopted to an extent in Canada, *e.g. Chamberlain v. Surrey School District no. 36*, 221 D.L.R. 4th 156 (2002).

[204] *Ville Nouvell Est*, C.E. Ass. 28 May 1971 [1972] *Dalloz* Jur. 194 and M. Long et al, *Les Grands Arrêts de la Jurisprudence Administrative* (12th ed., 1999), p.170 *et seq. Cf.* H. Delaney, *Judicial Review of Administrative Action, A Comparative Analysis* (2001), pp.87–90 on the status of proportionality in Irish administrative law, which is very much in its infancy.

[205] *Supra*, n.201 at p.547, applied in *e.g. R. (Farrakhan) v. Secretary of State* [2002] Q.B.. 1391.

CONTEMPT

Contempt of court concerns the power of the courts to order punishment of persons in several circumstances because they disobeyed the orders of a court or otherwise offended the court.[206] The rules regarding contempt are almost entirely embodied in case law; in Britain they have been reduced to statutory form, in response to criticism by the European Court of Human Rights of the comparative inaccessibility and the degree of confusion in the case law.[207] The contempt power is extensive and is exercised in accordance with a summary procedure unknown to any other branch of the law. There are two main categories of contempt – civil and criminal.

Civil contempt involves disobedience of an order made by a court in the course of civil proceedings, such as an injunction or refusal without good cause to answer questions in the course of examination or cross-examination, or breach of an undertaking given by litigants or their solicitors. Persons found guilty by a court of civil contempt will be committed to prison *sine die* until they have purged their contempt, *i.e.* until they are prepared to do what they had been ordered to do or to honour the undertaking they gave. What is called criminal contempt is more difficult to define. It involves punishment for interference with the administration of justice in various ways: for instance, publishing matter that interferes with a criminal trial or civil proceedings, direct interference with the course of justice and contempt in the face of a court. Breach of the *in camera* rule falls into this category. Many of the criminal contempt cases involve reconciling the right of freedom of expression with the fair and effective administration of justice.

The principal question of procedure that contempt, especially criminal contempt, gives rise to is whether the person who stands to be punished is entitled to the usual procedural rights of a defendant to be tried with a jury. Where some body other than the courts is given powers equivalent to the contempt power, under the Constitution, those who stand to be punished must be afforded fair procedures, including a jury trial. However, where punishment is being inflicted for contempt of the courts themselves, the individual in question usually has no right to jury trial. Apart from the jury question, the courts have not considered what additional procedural rights are guaranteed by the Constitution when persons are being punished in this uniquely summary manner. Since making statements that constitute an interference with the course of justice is a criminal offence under section 4 of the Offences Against the State (Amendment) Act 1972, it could be argued that conduct, which would amount to an offence under this provision, should be dealt with only by way of a criminal prosecution.

---

[206] See generally, C. Miller, *Contempt of Court* (3rd ed., 2003).
[207] *Sunday Times* case, 2 E.H.R.R. 245 (1980).

Inherent Jurisdiction

Where the court is exercising its inherent jurisdiction, persons are not generally entitled to a jury trial before being punished for contempt of court, be it civil or criminal contempt. But there may be a right to jury trial where central issues of fact are in dispute. It was held that the jury trial guarantee in the Free State Constitution did not extend to civil contempt proceedings[208] and the Supreme Court has interpreted Article 38.5 of the present Constitution to the same effect. Because it had been so clearly and authoritatively established that there was no right to a jury trial in this type of proceedings under the 1922 Constitution, it was held by Finlay P. in *State (Commins) v. McRann*[209] that those who drafted Article 38.5 (on the criminal jury) must have intended that it should not apply to civil contempt proceedings. Furthermore, he reasoned that, if the courts could not of their own motion move against persons who were in contempt and, instead, were dependent on the State prosecuting those persons on a criminal charge, the courts would be deprived of a power which is fundamental to their very independence from the executive; it would contravene the separation of powers if the courts had to depend on the executive in order to take action against those in contempt. If the Constitution were to be interpreted as depriving the courts of their traditional summary jurisdiction in this regard, that would be:

> "depriving the courts of their right to enforce their own orders [which would be] to deny the fundamental tri-partite division of powers which underlies the entire Constitution. In my opinion, it is not fanciful to suppose that a situation could arise in which the Court was obliged to restrain directly the commission of an act by the Executive, or by an agent of the Executive, so as to preserve the right of an individual. If the contention made on behalf of the prosecutor were valid, then by non-activity on the part of a servant of the Executive (the Attorney General or the Director of Public Prosecutions) the Executive could paralyse the capacity of the Courts to enforce their will. Such a consequence would not only be grave but, in my view, would be a vital infringement of the independence of the Courts as guaranteed by the fundamental principle of the tri-partite division of power."[210]

Similar reasoning was adopted in *State (DPP.) v. Walsh*,[211] for concluding that the constitutional right to jury trial does not obtain in criminal contempt of court proceedings, where central issues of fact are not in dispute. Criminal

---

[208] *Earle, Re* [1938] I.R. 485.

[209] [1977] I.R. 78.

[210] *Id.* at p.87.

[211] [1981] I.R. 412, following *Attorney General v. O'Kelly* [1928] I.R. 308.

contempt is not like any other criminal offence: it is *sui generis* in certain respects "[b]ecause the offence strikes at the heart of justice by substantially impeding it, devaluing it, or prejudicing its operation," and "the necessity to come to grips with the offence expeditiously has been recognised for centuries by the summary manner which courts of record have thought necessary to employ in dealing with it."[212] Where the essential facts have been established or are not in dispute, the question of whether a contempt has been committed is one of law to be decided by the judge. It was held that juries are peculiarly inappropriate to decide whether action amounts to contempt because of their lack of legal training and if, as occasionally happens, they gave a perverse verdict that would subvert judicial independence. According to Henchy J., "[t]he ultimate responsibility for the setting, and the application, of the standards necessary for the due administration of justice must rest with the judges. They cannot abdicate that responsibility, which is what they would be doing if they allowed juries of laymen to say whether the conduct proved or admitted amounted to criminal contempt."[213]

But where crucial factual matters are in dispute those should be tried before a jury; the general principles of fair procedures and non-discrimination call for jury trial in those circumstances. According to Henchy J.:

> "When the major offence charged is contempt of court, and if there are live and real issues of fact (such as whether the accused committed the act alleged against him, or whether it was done with his approval, etc.), the accused has a *prima facie* right under Article 38, section 5, to trial with a jury, thus entitling him to have those issues of fact committed to a jury for their determination. As at present advised, I do not find any other provision of the Constitution, which would rebut that presumption. It would not seem to be compatible with the constitutional requirement of fundamental fairness of procedures, or with the equality before the law guaranteed by Article 40, section I, if contempt of court, which carries with it the risk of an unlimited term of imprisonment or an unlimited fine, were the only major offence which is exempt from the requirement of a determination by a jury of the controverted facts."[214]

Statutory Contempt Powers

Some statutory provisions give courts power to deal with persons giving evidence before them, which are analogous to the power to punish for criminal

---

[212] *Id.* at p.433.

[213] *Id.* at p.440. Contrast *State v. Mamabolo*, 10 B.H.R.C. 493 (2001) (S. Africa), condemning this inquisitorial process, which rolls into one the complainant, prosecutor, witness and judge.

[214] *Id.* at p.439, *obiter*.

contempt. Exceptionally, powers analogous to those of punishing for contempt of court are conferred on non-judicial bodies, most notably bodies which conduct investigations into matters of public concern. These powers need to be drafted carefully lest they be struck down as unconstitutional, as happened in *Re Haughey*,[215] which concerned section 2(4) of the Committee of Public Accounts of Dáil Éireann (Privilege and Procedure) Act 1970. This was a mechanism for imposing sanctions on witnesses who refused to testify before the Dáil Committee; any witness who insisted on not giving evidence would have "the offence" certified by the Committee's chairman and the matter would then be sent to the High Court, where it would be dealt with in the same way as if the witness had committed contempt of court. As has been explained, it was held by the Supreme Court that this created a criminal offence and, consequently, the only constitutional way that recalcitrant witnesses could be dealt with was by prosecuting them in the criminal courts.

On account of the presumption of constitutionality, the court was constrained to consider alternative possible constructions of section 2(4) of the 1970 Act but all of them were found also to be unconstitutional. One was that it authorised a finding that disobedience of the Dáil Committee's orders was equivalent to contempt of court. That would be unconstitutional because contempt is a special inherent jurisdiction of the courts, in the interests of safeguarding the due administration of justice; it is a power or jurisdiction, which, under the separation of powers, could not be conferred on any other body. As Ó Dálaigh C.J. put it, "it would not be competent for the Oireachtas to declare contempt of a committee of the Oireachtas to be contempt of the High Court. This is an equation that could not be made under the doctrine of the tri-partite separation of the powers of government."[216] Another possible construction was that the Dáil Committee's certificate to the court was a form of complaint and that the court was empowered to try the witness for the statutory offence of non-co-operation. But because of the potentially limitless sanction, that offence would be of the non-minor category; yet the section did not provide for trial with a jury. Accordingly, this construction would contravene the guarantee of jury trial, which is a right that "is mandatory, it is not simply a right to be adopted or waived at the option of the accused."[217] Another possible construction was that the section created a minor offence and authorised summary trial in the High Court. This too would be unconstitutional because the High Court is not a court of summary jurisdiction; its jurisdiction in criminal matters "is a jurisdiction to try [offences] only with a jury."[218] Another contention was that the section authorised jury trial. But such a construction could not be placed on section 2(4) because it chose the contempt of court-style sanction process,

---

[215] [1971] I.R. 217, *supra*, p.411.
[216] *Id.* at p.253.
[217] *Id.* at p.252.
[218] *Id.* at p.253.

which is a uniquely summary procedure; the section "indicated a particular manner of proceeding against the alleged offender by express reference to contempt of court in terms which clearly indicated a summary manner of disposal of the trial and of the offender, if convicted. ..."[219] Section 10(5) of the Companies Act 1990, which was virtually identical to section 2(4) of the 1970 Act, was declared invalid by the Supreme Court in *Desmond v. Glackin (No.2)*[220] on these same grounds.

The sanction for unlawful non-cooperation with judicial tribunals of inquiry is set out in the Tribunals of Inquiry (Evidence) (Amendment) Act 1979. Any person who disobeys a summons to appear as a witness before such a tribunal, or who refuses to take the oath or to affirm when legally required to do so, or who wilfully gives false evidence, or who obstructs or hinders the tribunal in its functions, or who does not comply with any order made by a tribunal commits an offence. It is also a statutory offence to do any other thing with reference to the tribunal, which would constitute contempt if the tribunal were the High Court. The maximum penalty is two years imprisonment and a £10,000 fine.

---

[219] *Id.* at p.254.
[220] [1993] 3 I.R. 67.

CHAPTER 19

Freedom of Speech and Expression

There are a number of closely related rights that are designed primarily to ensure that persons are free to voice political views, namely freedom of speech and of expression.[1] By political in this context is meant not just the policies of the established political parties but more general views about the nature of society, persons and relations with society. Indeed, these rights have been extended in some countries to the dissemination of predominantly commercial messages. Subject to several restrictions, freedom of expression is guaranteed by Article 40.6.1.i of the Constitution. Speech and expression are also the subject of Article 8, which declares Irish to be "the national language [as] the first official language" but English is "recognised as a second official language."

Some of the older constitutions incorporate various types of expressive activity into the same clause, such as the United States Constitution's First Amendment, which proclaims "freedom of speech," as well as guaranteeing freedom of assembly and of religion, and entitlement to "petition the Government for the redress of grievances." Freedom of thought, conscience and expression are protected by Articles 9 and 10 of the European Convention and by Articles 18 and 19 of the UN Covenant. Although not expressly guaranteed by its provisions, it has been held that freedom of expression is implicitly protected by the democratic nature of the State established by the Australian Constitution.[2] Several modern constitutions make special provision for linguistic diversity where more than one language is spoken by a substantial proportion of the population.

EXPRESSION

Virtually every national constitution and general international human rights instrument guarantees freedom of expression. Thus, according to Article 11 of the 1789 Declaration of the Rights of Man and the Citizen, "(t)he free

---

[1] See generally, E. Barendt, *Freedom of Speech* (1985) and T. Campbell & W. Sadvrski, eds., *Freedom of Communication* (1994).

[2] *Theophanous v. Herald and Weekly Times Ltd*, 182 C.L.R. 104 (1994).

communication of thoughts and opinions is one of the most precious rights of man." Those sentiments are echoed by the US Constitution's First Amendment, which forbids Congress to pass any law that, *inter alia*, "abridg(es) the freedom of speech, or of the press." It is provided in Article 40.6.1.i of the Constitution that:

> "The State guarantees liberty for the exercise, ... subject to public order and morality of ... the right of the citizens to express freely their convictions and opinions. The education of public opinion being, however, a matter of such grave import to the common good, the State shall endeavour to ensure that organs of public opinion, such as the radio, the press, the cinema, while preserving their rightful liberty of expression, including criticism of Government policy, shall not be used to undermine public order or morality or the authority of the State. The publication or utterance of blasphemous, seditious, or indecent matter is an offence which shall be punishable in accordance with law."

Article 40.3.3, *inter alia*, provides that information about abortion services lawfully available abroad may be regulated by legislation.[3] The scope of Article 40.6.1.i of the Constitution has received little judicial consideration, which may suggest that there is in fact extensive freedom of speech in this country or else that highly controversial utterances are not often made.

Historically, the principal argument for affording special protection to freedom of expression has been the importance of open discussion of contentious issues in pursuing the discovery of truth. There are two main versions of this argument. Under one, there is an autonomous truth that ultimately will emerge in the course of open debate; under the other, all truths are relative and can be judged from time to time on the state of the prevailing debate. A variant of the main argument is that free debate is essential for full participation by individuals in a democracy. Another justification sees free speech as an end in itself, as an aspect of the more fundamental concept of human dignity and self-fulfilment.

"Expression"

A vitally important preliminary issue is what exactly is meant by the word expression in this context. It has an obvious core meaning but does it, or can it in certain circumstances, embrace gestures and indeed demonstrative action? Expression is defined in Article 19(2) of the UN Covenant to include freedom "to seek, receive and impart information and ideas of all kinds, regardless of

---

[3] *Infra*, p.726.

frontiers, either orally, in writing or in print, in the form of art, or through any other media of [one's] choice." A common and at times controversial form of expressive activity is burning a national flag, as conveying dissatisfaction with Government policy.[4]

Restrictions on Expression

Absolute freedom of expression is not guaranteed, not even by the US First Amendment, which makes no explicit qualification to the freedom proclaimed there. Article 40.6.1.i significantly qualifies this freedom, as does Article 10(2) of the European Convention which states that, "since it carries with it duties and responsibilities," permits expression to be "subject to such formalities, conditions, restrictions or penalties as are prescribed by law and are necessary in a democratic society, in the interests of national security, territorial integrity or public safety, for the prevention of disorder or crime, for the protection of the reputation or rights of others, for preventing the disclosure of information received in confidence, or for maintaining the authority or impartiality of the judiciary." Article 19(3) of the UN Covenant does not cast the exceptions quite as wide, permitting restrictions on expression "only ... such as are provided by law and are necessary (a) for respect of the rights or reputations of others; (b) for the protection of national security or of public order (*ordre public*), or of public health or morals." Article 20 of the Covenant adds that any "propaganda for war" may be prohibited, as may "[a]ny advocacy of national, racial or religious hatred that constitutes incitement to discrimination, hostility or violence."

Methods of Restricting

Numerous ways exist by which the State can suppress or interfere with freedom of expression and, whether a particular interference constitutes an unconstitutional denial of free speech, can turn on the method used against expression. Legislation for example can criminalise certain kinds of communications, such as section 5 of the Misuse of Drugs Act 1984, which makes it an offence to print, publish, sell or distribute any publication advocating or encouraging the use of a controlled drug, or advertising things used in connection with the taking of the drug. Frequently, forfeiture or confiscation of the item of communication in question will be part of the sanction, when there is a conviction. At times, that item can be confiscated without there being any conviction.

A less drastic restriction is where the communication is a common law or

---

[4] *E.g. HKSAR v. Ng King Siv*, 6 B.H.R.C. 591 (1999) (Hong Kong) and the *Flag Desecration* case, 81 BVerfGE 278 (1990).

statutory tort. In certain circumstances, libel is both a criminal offence as well as an actionable tort. Alternatively, the legislation may require that persons have a licence or some official consent before they can publish in a particular medium, such as by broadcasting, or in order to publish classified official information. Alternatively, the legislation may establish a system of censorship under which an administrative body, on considering the contents of a book or film or whatever, may forbid its being published. The legislation in question may merely impose a tax on particular forms of publication. Or the legislation may permit denial of a privilege to those who express particular opinions, for example, denying them passports or public service jobs, or not allocating publicly funded advertisements to a particular newspaper or other organ of expression that offends the government of the day.

Courts possess an inherent power to punish expression that constitutes contempt of court, including publishing information about court proceedings that is protected by the *in camera* rule. Printers for reward of most kinds of documents that are going to be sold, distributed or displayed are required by section 14 of the Offences Against the State Act 1939, to print their name and business address on the document. And by section 13 of this Act, printers for reward of any document must retain, for six months after printing, a copy of the document and the name and address of the person who required it to be printed. Ireland does not have a body like the Press Council that newspaper owners established in Britain to deal with complaints about what is published in their journals but has a Broadcasting Complaints Commission to monitor complaints about television and radio programmes.

"Prior restraint" means a prohibition against publishing a particular story or item, as distinct from a penalty or liability for having published it. As the celebrated *"Pentagon Papers"* case[5] illustrates, the United States courts have shown a marked reluctance to prevent publication on account of some injury it is claimed that publication will cause. While Irish courts have issued "gagging orders" from time to time, in one instance the Supreme Court expressed its disapproval of such orders. McCarthy J. observed that, in dealing with applications for these orders, "(t)he courts must be vigilant to protect the citizen who also has the right to be informed ...".[6] Orders can be obtained restraining publishing material that is protected by confidentiality, at least for so long as it is actually confidential, and exceptionally persons have been restrained from publishing defamatory statements. Where publication of material would seriously put at risk the fairness of a person's trial, it will be restrained although courts are slow to make such orders. Where publishing certain information constitutes a criminal offence, it would seem that the Attorney General is entitled to have that publication restrained, except of course where the criminal prohibition itself is unconstitutional.

---

[5] *United States v. Nixon*, 418 US 683 (1974).
[6] *Cullen v. Tobin* [1984] I.L.R.M. 577 at p.582.

Justifying Restrictions

Restrictions on freedom of expression should be proportionate to the objective sought, should be a rational means for securing that aim and should interfere with expression as little as is reasonably possible in the circumstances. Article 40.6.1.i stipulates certain permissible objectives for restrictions on expression and permits some of them to be achieved through the criminal law. When considering an objective that is not referred to there, it would appear that the courts ought to judge whether it is constitutionally permissible with reference to the underlying objectives of the free expression guarantee; the more the restricted speech deviates from those objectives, the easier it is to justify the constraint in question. For example criminalising extreme forms of what is described as "hate speech" may perhaps be justified on the basis that expression of that nature is entirely inconsistent with the objectives of finding the truth, of open and equal participation in democracy, and of upholding human dignity.[7] As for the interference with expression being minimal, it should not unfairly discriminate, contrary to Article 40.1, nor should it be over-broad so as to "chill" permissible expression, nor be unduly vague with similar effects. To date, however, it cannot be said that the Irish case law is fully supportive of what has been said here.

Perhaps it is because the constitutional guarantee of expression is so heavily qualified that the courts have demonstrated extraordinary deference to the Oireachtas when confronted with restrictions on free speech, as is demonstrated in two comparatively recent cases where there was no question whatsoever of state security, confidential information or the reputations of others being in any way jeopardised. In *Murphy v. Independent and Radio & Television Commission*[8] and also in *Colgan v. IRTC*,[9] private broadcasting companies were willing to broadcast material supplied by both plaintiffs, in the form of advertisements. In the former case, the advertisement was for an hour long video on a Christian religious theme at the "Irish Faith Centre;" in the latter, the theme was a mildly anti-abortion message. However, under section 10(3) of the Radio and Television Act 1988, broadcasters are not allowed to publish any advertisement "directed towards any religious or political end or which has any relation to an industrial dispute;"[10] there is an identical restriction in the legislation governing the State-owned broadcasting body, Radio Telefís Éireann. In both instances it was held that the proposed advertisements were caught by this prohibition, which raised the issue of its constitutionality. In neither case was evidence led by the State setting out why the Oireachtas adopted section 10(3) of that Act; the only apparent reason was to replicate the provision applicable to the one-time State monopoly broadcaster.

---

[7] *Cf. R. v. Keegstra* [1990] 3 S.C.R. S.C.R. 697.

[8] [1999] 1 I.R. 12.

[9] [2000] 2 I.R. 490.

[10] See *infra*, p.559.

In the *Murphy* case, Barrington J. for the Supreme Court accepted that proportionality had a bearing on the outcome but then immediately concluded that "[a]ll three kinds of banned advertisement relate to matters which have proved extremely divisive in Irish society in the past. The Oireachtas was entitled to take the view that the citizens would resent having advertisements touching on these topics broadcast into their homes and that such advertisements, if permitted, might lead to unrest. Moreover the Oireachtas may well have thought that in relation to matters of such sensitivity, rich men should not be able to buy access to the airwaves, to the detriment of their poorer rivals."[11] In response to the submission that, insofar as those concerns may arise in respect of any individual advertisement, a more finely-tuned prohibition would have sufficed, it was held that "the Oireachtas may well have decided that it would be inappropriate to involve agents of the State in deciding which advertisements, in this sensitive area would be likely to cause offence and which not."[12] A contention that the prohibition infringed the freedom of religious guarantee was rejected too.[13]

In view of what was held there, O'Sullivan J. in *Colgan* felt bound to uphold the blanket ban on political advertising, regardless of what the ad in question may say or its provenance. According to the judge, "[i]f a rational explanation for the wider infringement is available, the court will not condemn it for failing to impair the [constitutional] right as little as possible,"[14] which was the *ratio* in *Murphy*. A contention that the proposed advertisement there was to an extent constitutionally mandated by the "right to life of the unborn" protections in Article 40.3.3, and that section 10(3) of the 1988 Act was thereby unconstitutional, also was rejected in the light of the *Murphy* case. On this logic, it would seem to be constitutionally permissible to prohibit all newspapers from publishing material that fits the description in section 10(3) of the 1988 Act. One would have to travel far to encounter so pusillanimous a defence of freedom of expression and, if the Supreme Court's approach here is to continue, the constitutional guarantee of expression is hardly worth the paper it is written on.

State Security and Authority

One ground that is often invoked to justify interference with free expression is safeguarding the security and authority of the State. Article 40.6.1.i of the Constitution permits restrictions on expression that "undermine(s) the authority of the State" and on seditious expression. The principal legislative measures

---

[11] [1999] 1 I.R. 22.
[12] *Id.* at p.512.
[13] *Infra*, p.622.
[14] [2000] 2 I.R. 512.

restricting expression on these grounds are the Official Secrets Act 1963 and Part II of the Offences Against the State Act 1939. It has not been determined whether the Government are entitled to an injunction to restrain publication of material when publishing it would be an offence under those Acts,[15] nor where the Government can show a proprietary interest in the information that is being divulged.[16] Such publications would most likely be enjoined where it is shown that they would seriously injure the State.

Official Secrets

The prohibitions in the Official Secrets Act 1963[17] against disclosing official information are divided into two parts. Part III (section 9–12) forbids communicating itemised military and Garda information, and "any other matter whatsoever information as to which would or might be prejudicial to the safety or preservation of the State;"[18] communication to a foreign agent or to a member of an unlawful organisation is deemed to be evidence of prejudice to State security.[19] Part II (section 4–8) of this Act is much more extensive and proscribes publication of any matter that is classified as secret or confidential, regardless of its actual content or significance. According to section 4(1), "[a] person shall not communicate any official information to any other person unless he is duly authorised to do so or does so in the course of and in accordance with his duties as the holder of a public office or when ... in the interests of the State to communicate it." Official information is defined in section 2(1) to include any "information which is secret or confidential or is expressed to be either and which is or has been in the possession, custody or control of a holder, of a public office, or to which he has or had access, by virtue of his office. ..." Thus, disclosure of information, which simply has been classified as secret, is proscribed. There is no judicial guidance as to when disclosure is in accordance with an official's "duty in the interests of the State to communicate it."[20]

Offences Against the State

Part II (section 6–17) of the Offences Against the State Act 1939, deals, *inter alia*, with treasonable, seditious and incriminating documents, which are documents emanating from one of the organisations proscribed under Part III (sections 18–25) of this Act.[21] Section 10(1) makes it an offence to "set up in

---

[15] *Cf. Attorney General v. Guardian Newspaper (No.2)* [1990] 1 A.C. 109.
[16] *Cf. Attorney General v. Blake* [2001] 1 A.C. 268.
[17] See generally, P. Charleton et al., *Criminal Law* (1999), pp.757 *et seq.*
[18] S.9.
[19] S.10.
[20] *Cf. R. v. Ponting* [1985] Crim. L.R. 318.
[21] Treason and sedition are considered *infra*, pp.845 and 848.

type, print, publish, send through the post, distribute, sell, or offer for sale any document which is or contains or includes ... an incriminating ... a treasonable ... or a seditious document." It is an offence under section 12(1) for a person to "have any (such) document in his possession or on any lands or premises owned or occupied by him or under his control." Section 11 permits the seizure, destruction and banning the importation of any foreign newspaper containing matter that the Act does not allow to be published.

Former Section 31(1)

Until its repeal in 2001,[22] the Minister for Justice was empowered by section 31(1) of the Broadcasting Authority Act 1960, as amended, to prohibit Radio Telefís Éireann ("RTÉ") from broadcasting matter that might undermine state security or might promote crime. According to former section 31(1), he "may by order direct the Authority to refrain from broadcasting the matter or any matter of the particular class, and the Authority shall comply with the order." This provided for extensive legislative control over the Minister in that every such order had to be laid before each House of the Oireachtas and became ineffective if either House voted to annul it. Moreover, any such order could not remain in force for longer than twelve months, unless it was extended by way of resolutions passed by both Houses, and any extension granted could be for no longer than twelve months unless the order was again extended in the same manner. Several such orders were issued to RTÉ in relation to broadcasting information concerning unlawful organisations. The order in force for many years until 1994 provided as follows:

> "Radio Telefís Éireann is hereby directed to refrain from broadcasting any matter which is–
>
> (1) an interview, or report of an interview, with a spokesman or with spokesmen for anyone or more of the following organisations, namely (Sinn Féin, IRA, INLA, UDA etc).
> (2) a broadcast, whether purporting to be a political party broadcast or not, made by, or on behalf of, or advocating, offering or inviting support for, the organisation styling itself Sinn Féin ...
> (3) a broadcast by any person or persons representing or purporting to represent, the organisation styling itself Sinn Féin ...".[23]

In *State (Lynch) v. Cooney*[24] the Supreme Court upheld the legality and constitutionality of this order. The applicant was one of seven candidates in a

---

[22] Broadcasting Act 2001, s.3.
[23] S.I. No. 13 of 1987. *O'Toole v. Radio Telefís Éireann (No.2)* [1993] I.L.R.M. 458 concerns its interpretation.
[24] [1982] I.R. 337.

general election representing the Sinn Féin party, who sought to make a party political broadcast on RTÉ under the arrangements that the station has for such broadcasts. But under section 31(1) of the 1960 Act, as amended, the Minister had banned all broadcasts connected with that party, which was a lawful political party although it had connections with the Provisional Irish Republican Army, which is an illegal organisation. O'Hanlon J.'s decision to strike down the order was based on the very extensive discretion that section 31(1) gave the Minister, in the light of the authorities dealing with judicial review of decisions where a Minister "is of opinion" that a particular state of affairs exists. In *Offences Against the State (Amendment) Bill, 1940, Re,*[25] the court had held that, where an Act authorises the Minister to do something where he is "of opinion" that certain circumstances exist, the reasonableness of that opinion cannot be challenged in the courts. Consequently, O'Hanlon J. reasoned, section 31(1) empowers the Minister to ban broadcasts on wholly unreasonable and unfair grounds, and the courts are powerless to intervene. Since the Constitution does not permit granting anybody virtually unreviewable discretionary powers, this section was inconsistent with the Constitution and orders made under this section are invalid. However, the Supreme Court held that the section did not confer such extensive powers; in the light of developments in administrative law since the 1940s,[26] decisions made under provisions like section 31(1) can be challenged in the courts on the grounds that there is no factual basis for them. Therefore, section 31 did not purport to give the Minister excessive discretionary powers.

On the question whether it would ever be constitutionally permissible to ban the kind of broadcast that the plaintiff sought to make, O'Hanlon J. concluded that the evidence before him suggested that there were ample grounds for making an order against broadcasts connected with Sinn Féin, which holding was endorsed on appeal. It was held that the power given by section 31(1) to ban broadcasts came within the "authority of the State" qualification in the Constitution's free speech guarantee; that this practically requires the Government to adopt the kind of broadcasting ban envisaged in the Minister's order. According to O'Higgins C.J., for the Supreme Court:

"The basis for any attempt at control(ing expression) must be, according to the Constitution, the overriding considerations of public order and public morality. The constitutional provision in question refers to organs of public opinion and these must be held to include television as well as radio. It places upon the State the obligation to ensure that these organs of public opinion shall not be used to undermine public order or public morality or the authority of the State. It follows that the use of such organs of opinion for the purpose of securing or advocating support for

[25] [1940] I.R. 470.
[26] *Supra*, p.525.

organisations which seek by violence to overthrow the State or its institutions is a use which is prohibited by the Constitution. Therefore it is clearly the duty of the State to intervene to prevent broadcasts on radio or television which are aimed at such a result or which in any way would be likely to have the effect of promoting or inciting to crime or endangering the authority of the State. These, however, are objective determinations and obviously the fundamental rights of citizens to express freely their convictions and opinions cannot be curtailed or prevented on any irrational or capricious ground."[27]

Regarding the order made about Sinn Féin, the court held that, in the circumstances, the applicant was not entitled to the natural justice protection of prior notice and also that the Minister's decision was made *bona fide* and not unreasonably. This denial of *audi alteram partem* was justified on the grounds that "time was short and a decision was urgent; the circumstances of the case dictated that, in the paramount interest of public security, (the) power be exercised promptly and without any formal hearing."[28] And the evidence before the court led the Chief Justice to the conclusion that "any broadcast which sought support for such an organisation could properly be regarded by (the Minister) as being likely to promote or incite to crime or to tend to undermine the State's authority."[29]

Prisoners

How extensive a right prisoners possess to communicate with the outside world, especially with journalists, remains to be determined by the Irish courts. On numerous occasions such a right has been recognised as existing under Article 10 of the European Convention; for instance blanket bans on oral interviews with journalists[30] and very extensive restrictions on communicating on the telephone with journalists[31] have been held to contravene it.

Administration of Justice

Article 10 of the European Convention permits restrictions on freedom of expression aimed at "maintaining the authority and impartiality of the judiciary." Similar powers can be inferred under the Constitution, notably from the provisions that the courts' function is to administer justice and that persons

---

[27] [1982] I.R. at p.361.
[28] *Id.* at pp.365, 383 and 372.
[29] *Id.* at p.366. *Cf. R. (Brind) Secretary of State* [1991] A.C. 696 on a similar restriction in Britain.
[30] *R. (Simms) v. Secretary of State* [2000] 2 A.C. 115.
[31] *R. (Hirst) v. Secretary of State* [2002] 1 W.L.R. 2929.

accused of criminal charges shall be tried in due course of law. The principal source of authority for restricting expression in the interests of maintaining the courts' authority is the inherent power of the courts to punish criminal contempt of court.[32] Any act or omission that is calculated to interfere with the due administration of justice is a contempt of court, including prejudicing or prejudging impending proceedings and what is described as "scandalising the court." There are also some statutory provisions to that end, notably section 4 of the Offences Against the State (Amendment) Act 1972, which prohibits statements and meetings that interfere with the administration of justice:

"(a) Any public statement made orally, in writing or otherwise ... that constitutes an interference with the course of justice shall be unlawful.

(b) A statement ... shall be deemed to constitute an interference with the course of justice if it is intended, or is of such a character as to be likely, directly or indirectly to influence any court, person or authority concerned with the institution, conduct or defence of any civil or criminal proceedings (including a party or witness) as to whether or how the proceedings should be instituted, conducted, continued or defended, or as to what should be their outcome."

Prejudicing Fair Trial

Publication of comment on trials about to take place or taking place, in some circumstances, may jeopardise a fair trial. In the case of jury trials, there is a much greater likelihood of press and other commentary prejudicing the outcome than where the issue is being tried by a judge or judges on their own.[33] It depends on the facts of each particular case whether the publicity is indeed seriously prejudicial and whether any prejudice caused may be alleviated by appropriate directions to the jury or by the "fade factor" arising from the passage of time. Those who publish prejudicial material before or during a trial risk being punished for contempt and that risk exists even if there is no jury involved in the proceedings or in the particular stage of the proceedings. As Barrington J. observed, "it would be unwise to assume that judges are totally immune from frailties commonly held to afflict jurors."[34]

Because their outcome may gravely affect the accused's reputation and even result in substantial deprivation of liberty, there is a greater tendency to proscribe potentially prejudicial publications that deal with criminal trials. It was for this reason that section 17 of the Criminal Procedure Act 1967 was enacted, which curtailed publication of what occurred in a preliminary

---

[32] See generally, C.J. Miller, *Contempt of Court* (3 ed., 2000).
[33] *Supra*, p.452.
[34] *Cullen v. Tobin* [1984] I.L.R.M. 577 at p.580; similarly *Kelly v. O'Neill* [2000] 1 I.R. 354 at p.375.

examination before a District Judge, for the purpose of sending an accused person forward for trial on indictment. This procedure has been abolished and there now is a near automatic sending forward of the accused by the District Court, but section 42 of the Criminal Justice Act 1999 prohibits publication of any information about those proceedings over and above the fact that a named person has brought proceedings against another named person in respect of a specified charge, the court's decision and, where the accused applied to have the charge dismissed, any information that the judge permits to be published at the accused's request. Breach of this restriction may be punished by the High Court in the same manner as if there had been a contempt of court.

Media comment on forthcoming litigation cannot of itself constitute contempt of court until at least some court has seisin of the case.[35] In *State (DPP.) v. Independent Newspapers Ltd*,[36] an article in the defendant's newspaper stated that the Director of Public Prosecutions was about to bring an indecency charge against a local authority councillor, who was not identified, although his political party was named. O'Hanlon J. refused to attach the defendant because "the courts must always have regard to the countervailing importance of preserving the freedom of the press"[37] and also because the publicity surrounding contempt proceedings occurring before the actual trial took place might very well cause undue hardship to the accused. It additionally was held that the very circumstances of the case would not warrant a finding of contempt of court.

It was emphasised by the Supreme Court in *Cullen v. Tobin*[38] that publishing matter about a forthcoming criminal trial should not too readily be prevented. McCarthy J. observed that "(t)he courts must be vigilant to protect the citizen who also has the right to be informed. ..."[39] In this case the plaintiff was appealing to the Court of Criminal Appeal against his conviction for a most brutal murder, where the main evidence against him had been the un-corroborated testimony of an accomplice who was not charged. The defendants, who owned a current affairs periodical, entered into a contract with his accomplice with a view to publishing articles relating to the murder and an injunction was sought to prevent publication of those articles. It was held that, in the circumstances, publication would not jeopardise the appeal and accordingly the injunction was refused.

It depends on all the circumstances whether particular disclosures and commentary would be regarded as likely to prejudice a fair trial.[40] In *Kelly v. O'Neill*[41] it was held that an article in the Irish Times, published between the

---

[35] *The King (Attorney General) v. Freeman's Journal* [1902] 2 I.R. 82.
[36] [1985] I.L.R.M. 183.
[37] *Id.* at p.184.
[38] [1984] I.L.R.M. 577.
[39] *Id.*, at p.582.
[40] *Supra*, p.452.
[41] [2000] 1 I.R. 354.

time the applicant had been convicted in the Circuit Court and when he was due to be sentenced constituted contempt. This article portrayed him as a major criminal, the subject of numerous Garda investigations for many years, and as associate of "some of Dublin's most notorious criminals." There Keane J. pointed out that contempt "is committed ... when a person publishes material *calculated* to interfere with the course of justice: it is not a necessary ingredient ... that it results in such an interference."[42] Had the article in question here been published before or during the trial, it would be an extremely serious contempt. But the fact that the jury's role had ended did not prevent it from still being a contempt. Judges, with their professional training and experience, are not always immune to highly prejudicial and damaging publicity. Even "a rudimentary knowledge of psychology would suggest that a person conscientiously striving to reach a decision free from prejudice might be influenced at a subconscious level in his conclusions by material which he had made every effort to banish from his mind."[43]

Where the pre-trial publicity is not actually prejudicial, it may still amount to contempt. For instance in *Wong v. Minister for Justice*,[44] when the applicant had judicial review proceedings pending, challenging his deportation, the Sunday Times published a sensationalist article about "a triad gang, part of the Chinese underworld" and naming him as appealing his deportation order. Denham J. held that he had thereby been exposed to public obloquy and, while the article would not have prejudiced the hearing of the case because triads were not an issue, it nevertheless was a contempt. Publishing photographs of prisoners under restraint, such as being shackled, can constitute contempt of court[45] because they are capable of undermining the accused's dignity, and also of conveying a prejudicial perception of him.

Censuring Judicial Performance

Criticism of a judge or of the judiciary generally, or of the courts, is protected by the free expression guarantee. But criticism that oversteps the mark may amount to the offence of scandalising the court and be punished as criminal contempt. On several occasions it has been stressed that, while criticism of what judges do is not to be discouraged and indeed can be very much in the public interest, saying that a judge or judges acted for improper motives cannot be tolerated because such assertions undermine the very credibility of the judicial system. As O'Higgins C.J. observed in 1976, "The right of free speech and the free expression of opinion are valued rights. Their preservation, however, depends on the observance of the acceptable limit that they must not

---

[42] *Id.* at p.374.
[43] *Id.* at p.375.
[44] [1994] 1 I.R. 223.
[45] *People v. Davis* [2001] 1 I.R. 146.

be used to undermine public order or morality or the authority of the State. Contempt of court of this nature carries the exercise of these rights beyond this acceptable limit because it tends to bring the administration of justice into disrepute and to undermine the confidence which the people should have in judges appointed under the Constitution to administer justice in our Courts."[46] As Maguire P. put it thirty years earlier;

> "Judges and others in authority are open to criticism. Fair and free criticism is allowable and should be welcomed. We must safeguard the rights of the citizen and the rights of newspaper editors. The last thing I would wish is that citizens should feel that the Courts are too ready to use against legitimate criticism this powerful weapon of attachment for contempt of Court. I would rather err on the other side. In one of these cases cited in the course of these proceedings, it is stated that committal for contempt of Court is obsolete. This, however, is not correct. But in regard to cases which are concluded it is nearly so. The protection of Courts from attacks of this kind where cases are pending is a vital matter, and it is in the public interest in such cases that the Court should intervene and deal severely with the offender. It is different where, as here, the case is terminated."[47]

In a case decided in 1900 O'Brien L.C.J. said that to impute base prejudice to a judge not alone was a contempt of court but amounted to the offence of sedition; that "to say that a judge took a bribe, or that in a particular case a judge pursued his own interests or those of his friends or of his party, or wished to curry favour with the government, or was influenced by fear of the government or by any other motive than a simple desire to arrive at the truth and to mete out justice impartially" amounts to sedition.[48]

It depends on exactly what was said in the circumstances whether criticism is a contempt of court. As was emphasised in a recent decision of the South African Constitutional Court, a contempt prosecution "is a public injury, not a private delict; and its sole aim is to preserve the capacity of the judiciary to fulfil its role under the Constitution. Scandalising the court is not concerned with the self esteem, or even the reputation of judges as individuals, although that does not mean that conduct or language targeting specific individual judicial officers is immune."[49] For instance in the *McHugh* case, the defendant was convicted of contempt because he described the verdict given in a criminal prosecution in Sligo as the verdict of a biased magistrate and a packed jury "who were the hacks of Dublin Castle and by a certain section of bigoted,

---

[46] *Kennedy and McCann, Re* [1976] I.R. 382 at p.386.
[47] *Attorney General v. O'Ryan and Boyd* [1946] I.R. 70 at p.82.
[48] *The Queen v. McHugh* [1901] 2 I.R. 569 at pp. 579–580.
[49] *State v. Mamabola*, 10 B.H.R.C. 493 (2001) at p.513 (S. Africa).

intolerant, narrow-minded, ignorant Tories, who are ever ready to become willing tools to perpetrate a dirty job at the beck of Dublin Castle."[50] In the *O'Ryan v. Boyd* case,[51] it was held to be a contempt to say that the judge was a Protestant, who was not made a judge on account of his legal ability, and that he had insulted a prominent Catholic clergyman. In the *Kennedy and McCann* case,[52] the defendants were attached for contempt of court where they had published information about a family law case that had been heard *in camera*, had made offensive remarks about one of the parties in the case and clearly implied that justice could not be obtained in any Irish court because the courts are part of a "sick society" and are "hypocritical about motherhood, morality and the family." O'Higgins C.J. there described the offence of scandalising the court as "a false publication made which intentionally or recklessly imputes base or improper motives or conduct to the judge or judges in question."[53]

In contrast, in *Desmond v. Glackin (No.1)*[54] where the then Minister for Industry and Commerce in a television interview had criticised the High Court for acceding to an *ex parte* judicial review application, grounded on affidavits that alleged serious wrongdoing but without affording any opportunity to refute then at the time, O'Hanlon J. held that he came very close to the line but, as he did not unquestionably over-step it, a contempt had not been committed.

Public Order, Health and Safety

Article 40.6.1.i of the Constitution permits restrictions on expression in order to preserve "public order" and it cannot be doubted that reasonable restrictions can also be imposed to protect public health and safety. Examples of legislation that comes within the public order qualification to the guarantee include provisions of the Criminal Justice (Public Order) Act 1994; section 11(1) of the Wireless Telegraphy Act 1926, which prohibits broadcasting any "message or communication subversive of public order;" also section 3(1) of the Video Recording Act 1989, that permits the censorship of video recordings that, as being viewed, "would be likely to cause persons to commit crimes, whether by inciting or encouraging them to do so or by indicating or suggesting ways of doing so or of avoiding detection ...".

The extent to which what is described as "fighting words" and "hate speech"

---

[50] [1901] 2 I.R. at 569 at p.574. *The King v. Freeman's Journal* [1902] 2 I.R. 82 is a sequel to this.

[51] [1946] I.R. 70.

[52] [1976] I.R. 382.

[53] *Id.*, at p.387. See also *Hibernia National Review Ltd., Re* [1976] I.R. 388, *Attorney General v. Connolly* [1947] I.R. 213 and *State (D.P.P.) v. Walsh* [1981] I.R. 412.

[54] [1993] 3 I.R. 1. *Cf. R. v. Commissioner of Police, ex. p. Blackburn (No. 2)* 1968] 2 Q.B. 150, where Quentin Hogg Q.C., M.P., P.C. criticised the Court of Appeal in England.

is constitutionally protected remains to be determined.[55] Under section 2 of the Prohibition of Incitement to Hatred Act 1989, it is an offence to publish or display in several ways material that is "threatening, abusive or insulting and intended or ... likely to stir up hatred;" the word hatred is defined as "hatred against a group of persons in the State or elsewhere on account of their race, colour, nationality, religion, ethnic or national origins, membership of the travelling community or sexual orientation." Sections 3 and 4 of this Act prohibit broadcasts that are likely to stir up hatred and also the possession of material likely to stir up hatred. An exception is made for fair and accurate reports of proceedings before either House of the Oireachtas or any of their committees, or if published contemporaneously, such reporting of any proceedings before any court or other judicial tribunal. Video recordings may be censored where, on viewing, they "would be likely to stir up hatred against" any of the above groups.[56]

Restrictions on expression motivated by public health considerations include section 5 of the Misuse of Drugs Act 1985, which prohibits publication of matter supportive of the illegal use of drugs and several sections of the Public Health (Tobacco) Act, 2002. Under section 32 of the Irish Medicines Board Act 1985, the Minister may make regulations concerning, *inter alia*, the advertisement of medical products. Restrictions on publications concerning venereal diseases and contraception are more concerned with obscenity than health, and the Regulation of Information (Services Outside the State for Termination of Pregnancies) Act 1995, has it own distinct constitutional underpinning.[57]

Blasphemy

Blasphemous utterances are expressly excepted from the Constitution's free speech guarantee and have been held not to be protected by the European Convention.[58] Some of the statutory prohibitions against obscene communications also apply to blasphemy, which is a common law offence.[59] Publishing a blasphemous libel is made an offence by section 13 of the Defamation Act 1961. In the only three recorded prosecutions for blasphemy in Irish history, all the defendants were clergymen, two of them Catholic priests

---

[55] Compare *R. v. Keegstra* [1990] 3 S.C.R. 697, the *Holocaust Denial* case, 90 BVerfGE 24 (1994) and *R. (Farrakhan) v. Secretary of State* [2002] Q.B. 1391 with *R.A.V. v. City of St. Paul*, 505 US 377 (1972).

[56] Video Recordings Act 1989, s.3(1)(a)(ii).

[57] *Infra*, p.726.

[58] *Gay News Ltd v. United Kingdom*, 5 E.H.R.R. 123 (1982). *Cf. Olmedo Bustos v. Chile*, 10 B.H.R.C. 676 (2001) (Inter Am. C't H.R.).

[59] See generally, O'Higgins, "Blasphemy in Irish Law", 23 *Mod. L. Rev.* 151 (1960).

and one a Unitarian minister. There is no record of a prosecution for blasphemy since 1922. In *People (Attorney General) v. Simpson,*[60] the *"Rose Tattoo"* case, the defendant was prosecuted for putting on an indecent, obscene and profane performance – profane being another word for blasphemous. But little evidence of that offence was adduced by the prosecution, nor was any definition of the offence suggested, and O'Flynn D.J. allowed charges of obscenity to be substituted for those of profanity.

In the past blasphemy connoted denying the truth of the Christian religion or of the Bible. However, as Barrington J. pointed out in the Supreme Court in *Corway v. Independent Newspapers (Ireland) Ltd,*[61] an offence in these terms does not fit comfortably with a constitution that guarantees *inter alia* equality before the law and freedom of religion. Further, if indeed the mental element required for a conviction is the mere act of publishing the blasphemous material, without any proof of an intention to blaspheme, that too causes constitutional difficulties. Because Article 40.6.1.i makes express reference to the "offence of blasphemy," it must be an offence in Irish law to blaspheme, although in view of the uncertainty about both the *actus reus* and *mens rea*, its essential ingredients are not clear. In *Corway*, the plaintiff was seeking the leave of the court to prosecute the defendant for blasphemous libel, arising from a cartoon published in 1995 during the divorce conroversy; it showed three government ministers rejecting a host and chalice being offered by a priest, over which was the caption "Hello Progress – Bye, Bye Father." Since the task of defining what are crimes is a legislative function and is not for the courts and, in view of the present uncertain state of the law of blasphemy and the absence of any legislative definition that would be consistent within the Constitution, the leave being sought was refused. Consequently, it would appear that, for the time being, there is no offence of blasphemy in Irish law although some blasphemous utterances would be caught by the Prohibition of Incitement to Hatred Act 1989.

Obscenity/Indecency

Article 40.6.1.i permits restrictions on expression in the interests of "public morality;" Article 10(2) of the European Convention and Article 19(3) of the UN Covenant also permit restrictions "for the protection of ... morals." It is not clear what exactly public morality consists of and how exactly its requirements are to be ascertained.[62] Does it mean the conventional morality of the bulk of the population or that of "right thinking people," whoever they may be? To date the Irish courts have not had to answer questions of this

---

[60] 93 I.L.T.R. 33 (1959).
[61] [1994] 4 I.R. 484.
[62] *Infra*, p.657.

nature. In the context of the guarantee of expression, public morality principally concerns obscenity and indecency. Measures against obscenity, of which there is no universally accepted definition, are concerned with guarding persons' moral integrity in a paternalistic manner or protecting some overriding public interest in maintaining moral standards. Measures against indecency focus on protecting persons' sensibilities. In determining the constitutionality of provisions of this nature, the principal concerns are the purpose of the form of expression being restricted, the method used for imposing the restriction and whether it is over-vague or otherwise unduly over-broad. Specialist committees have been established in various countries to review the law in this general area and to recommend changes to bring it into line with current views of what public morality demands but that exercise has not been carried out in Ireland.

The principal laws on all of these questions are over fifty years old and were enacted at a time when some wholly innocuous books and films were regarded as grossly obscene. Apart from the question of abortion-related information, there has been no judicial consideration of the constitutionally permissible techniques that the State can employ in promoting public morality and, in particular, whether prior censorship on those grounds is consistent with freedom of expression. There is a common law offence of outraging public decency and, it would seem, also an offence of conspiracy to corrupt public morals or to outrage public decency. But prosecutions for these are extremely rare, if ever, and they have been described in the leading Irish text on Criminal Law as mainly "out of date and over-vague."[63]

Obscenity and pornography have similar meanings. For the purpose of constitutional analysis, the Canadian Supreme Court[64] has divided pornography into three broad categories, *viz.* (1) explicit sex with violence; (2) explicit sex without violence but which subjects people to treatment that is degrading or dehumanising; (3) explicit sex without violence that is neither degrading nor dehumanising. In this context, violence includes both actual physical violence and threats of such violence. The extent to which obscene or pornographic expression is constitutionally protected remains to be determined.

Censorship of Publications

The principal public morality restriction on publishing and selling books, magazines and papers is the Censorship Publications Acts 1929–1967.[65] A Censorship of Publications Board was established by the 1946 Act,[66] which is

---

[63] P. Charleton et al, *Criminal Law* (1999), p.664.

[64] *R. v. Butler*, 89 D.L.R. 4th 449 (1992); also *Little Sisters Book and Art Emporium v. Minister of Justice*, 193 D.L.R. 4th 193 (2000).

[65] As amended by the Health (Family Planning) Act 1979. See generally, M. Adams, *Censorship, the Irish Experience* (1968).

[66] S.3.

empowered to prohibit the sale, distribution or importation of any book or periodical that the Board considers indecent or obscene, or that advocates the procuring of an abortion.[67] This Board can ban periodicals that devote "an unduly large proportion of space to the publication of matter relating to crime."[68] For these purposes, indecent is defined as "includ(ing) suggestive of, or inciting to sexual immorality or unnatural vice or likely in any other similar way to corrupt or deprave."[69] There is no statutory definition for the term obscene. [70] The Board considers publications that were either seized by customs and excise officers or were submitted to it by any person complaining of the publication. In assessing any book, the Board must have regard to the following matters:

"(a) The literary, artistic, scientific or historic merit or importance, and the general tenor of the book;

(b) the language in which it is written;

(c) the nature and extent of the circulation, which, in their opinion, it is likely to have;

(d) the class of reader which, in their opinion, may reasonably be expected to read it;

(e) any other matter relating to the book which appears to them to be relevant."[71]

This Board has authority to communicate with the book's author, editor or publisher and may take account of representations made. It has been held that the Board has an obligation to make that communication where a plausible case could be made out that the book in question satisfies the above-mentioned considerations;[72] it need not so communicate where the book is manifestly indecent or obscene, or where the editor, author or publisher cannot be traced. There is a right of appeal from the Board's decision to the Censorship Appeal Board but this is confined to a relatively narrow category of persons, *viz.* the author, the editor or the publisher of the work in question, or any five persons acting jointly who are members of either the Dáil or the Seanad.[73] A prohibition order issued on the grounds that the work is indecent or obscene lapses after twelve years unless the Board makes a further order. Section 19 of the 1946 Act gives the Minister a wide discretion to permit publication of material banned by the Board. It is required to keep a register of prohibited publications.

---

[67] Ss.7, 9, 14 and 18.

[68] S.9(1)(c).

[69] 1929 Act, s.2 and 1946 Act, s.1.

[70] *Infra*, p.555.

[71] S.6(2).

[72] *Irish Family Planning Ass'n Ltd v. Ryan* [1979] I.R. 295.

[73] 1946 Act, s.8.

The Board's activities and its constitutional position arose in *Irish Family Planning Association Ltd. v. Ryan*,[74] which concerned a booklet entitled "Family Planning" that was published by the Irish Family Planning Association. A medical doctor was the author, and it contained basic information about different forms of contraception. As O'Higgins C.J. described the booklet, "it was produced as a part of the information services of a family-planning clinic conducted by responsible and qualified people. It reached out to those who might wish to be informed as to the different methods of contraception, which were available. An edition of the plaintiff's book had been on sale freely in Irish bookshops for some three years without let or hindrance from the Board. Far from being pornographic or lewdly commercial or pandering to prurient curiosity, it simply aimed at giving basic factual information on a delicate topic as to which there is genuine concern. It espoused no cause; it advocated no course of conduct; it simply made available basic facts, with necessary diagrams, on which persons so minded could exercise their options."[75] Nevertheless, the book was banned on the grounds that it was "indecent or obscene." Its publishers thereupon launched a full-scale legal and constitutional attack on the entire censorship of publications system. It was contended that the Board's decision here was unlawful because *audi alteram partem* was not complied with; because the ban was unreasonable, was not made *bona fide*, disregarded the criteria in the Act, was based on extraneous considerations and was insufficiently specific about the grounds for the prohibition; because the Board exercised a judicial function that was not limited in the Article 37 sense; because the 1946 Act violated various substantive constitutional guarantees, such as freedom of expression, private property and the second plaintiff's (a doctor and one of the founders of the IFPA) right to practise her profession, *i.e.* to inform her patients and to educate parents and other citizens.

In the event, the Supreme Court did not find it necessary to deal with these intriguing constitutional issues nor, it would seem, were they considered in argument. Instead, the case turned on section 6(3) of the 1946 Act, which empowers the Board to communicate with the book's publishers etc. It was held that the Board was not thereby obliged invariably to communicate with such persons, since the section specially provides for a power to communicate and that power "must, logically, be discretionary in so far as its exercise is concerned."[76] However, constitutional justice requires that the power to communicate and the power to ban books be exercised in a manner that is just and fair; the requirements of fairness depend on the particular facts of each instance and the surrounding circumstances. But where "fair questions or points of view" arise in relation to the matters to be regarded by the Censorship

---

[74] [1979] I.R. 295.
[75] *Id.* at pp.314–315.
[76] *Id.* at p.312.

Board under section 6(2) of the 1946 Act, and the book is not manifestly indecent or obscene, the Board has an obligation to consider whether it should communicate with the book's publishers etc. In the circumstances of this case, the Board should have so communicated and invited representations. Because that was not done, the ban was found to be illegal. As regards the meaning of the words indecent or obscene, Kenny J. observed that those terms in the 1946 Act mean that the book or publication is indecent and obscene in its general tendency and not simply that it contains indecent or obscene passages.

Censorship of Films and Videos

Under the Censorship of Films Acts 1923–1970, exhibiting films in public is subject to a system of comprehensive censorship that is far greater than book censorship. No film may be "exhibited in public" unless the film censor has certified that it is fit for exhibition.[77] Certification will be refused where the censor is of the opinion that the film or part of it is unfit to be publicly exhibited "by reason of its being indecent, obscene or blasphemous or because the exhibition thereof in public would tend to inculcate principles contrary to public morality or would be otherwise subversive of public morality."[78] A similar prohibition exists in respect of extracts from films that are used for advertising.[79] These Acts contain no definition of terms such as "indecent", "obscene" or "public morality". Disappointed applicants for film exhibition certificates can appeal from the censor's decision to an Appeal Board. Unlike the procedure under the Censorship of Publications Acts, the film censor is a single individual who is appointed to a salaried office; no express provision is made for communicating with the film's author, director, producer or distributor;[80] the Minister has no power to permit exhibition of otherwise prohibited films and there is no register of proscribed films. It is doubtful if most exhibitions on television are caught by these Acts. It is provided by section 10 of the 1923 Act that local authorities shall not use their powers to license cinemas in order to determine the character or nature of films that may be exhibited by licensees.

Possessing, importing, selling and exhibiting video recordings is subject to a comprehensive system of licensing and censorship, under the Video Recordings Act 1989. All outlets that sell, let or hire videos must be licensed, subject to certain exceptions, and persons may not supply or cause to be exhibited videos that have not been duly certified by the films censor. He is obliged to certify all videos submitted to him unless he is of the opinion that they are likely to cause persons to commit crimes, they are likely to stir up

---

[77] 1923 Act, s.5.

[78] *Id.* s.7(2).

[79] Censorship of Films (Amendment) Act 1925.

[80] But such duties may be implied by fair procedures.

hatred against specified groups, they depict "acts of gross violence or cruelty ... towards humans or animals," or they "would tend by reason of the inclusion ... of obscene or indecent matter, to deprave or corrupt persons who might view it."[81] When certifying a video, it is to be classified as being appropriate only for persons over specified age groups. Where the censor is of opinion that a video falls within any of the above categories, he may make an order prohibiting its supply. There is an appeal from the censor's decisions in this regard to the same board as deals with film censorship appeals.

Other Restrictions

Various other restrictions have been imposed on expression on public morality grounds. The most recent of these is section 7 of the Criminal Justice (Public Order) Act 1994, which makes it an offence "in a public place to distribute or display any writing, sign or visible representation which is ... obscene with intent to provoke a breach of the peace or being reckless in this regard." There is no legislation dealing specifically with what can be performed in theatres; the Theatres Act 1843,[82] did not apply in Ireland. Accordingly, any public morality constraints on the theatre arise from the general common law. Possessing child pornography is an offence under section 6 of the Child Trafficking and Pornography Act 1998. Part IV (section 16–20) of the Censorship of Publications Act 1929, prohibits certain dealings in books and other printed matter without any reference to the Censorship Board. It is an offence to sell or import or offer for sale an "indecent picture."[83] It is an offence under section 14 of this Act to print or publish in relation to any judicial proceedings "(a) any indecent matter the publication of which would be calculated to injure public morals, or (b) any indecent medical, surgical or physiological details, the publication of which would be calculated to injure public morals." The Dublin Police Act 1842,[84] makes it an offence to "sell or distribute, or offer for sale or distribution, or exhibit to public view, any profane, indecent or obscene book, paper, print, drawing, painting, or representation, or sing any profane, indecent, or obscene song or ballad, or write or draw any indecent or obscene word, figure or representation, or use any profane, indecent, or obscene language, to the annoyance of the inhabitants or passengers."

Among the items that section 42 of the Customs Laws (Consolidated) Act 1876,[85] forbids being imported are "indecent or obscene prints, paintings, photographs, books, cards, lithographic or other engravings, or any other indecent or obscene articles." But imports from EC Member States cannot be

---

[81] Ss.3(1) and 7(1).
[82] 6 & 7 Vic. c.78.
[83] Censorship of Films Act 1923, s.18.
[84] 5 Vic., 2 Sess., c.24.
[85] 39 & 40 Vic. c.36.

excluded unless the article in question contravenes the Community's and not just the State's public morality standards.[86] Where an officer of the customs and excise is of the opinion that a video recording being imported ought to be examined by the censor, he may seize it for that purpose.[87]

The Criminal Law (Amendment) Act 1935, creates the summary offence of public indecency; it is an offence for a person, at or near a place where the public habitually pass, to commit "any act in such a way as to offend modesty or cause scandal or injure the morals of the community. ..."[88] The Indecent Advertisements Act 1889[89] prohibits public advertisement of "indecent or obscene" matter, or "advertisements which relate or refer or may be reasonably supposed to relate or refer to any disease affecting the generative organs of either sex, or to any complaint or infirmity arising from or relating to sexual intercourse, or to the prevention or removal of irregularities in menstruation, or to drugs, medicines, appliances, treatment or methods for procuring abortion or miscarriage."[90] The Health (Family Planning) Act 1979 prohibits publishing any advertisement or notice, or making any display relating to contraception or of contraceptives except to such extent as is permitted by regulations made under that section.[91] Publishing an obscene libel is an offence under the Defamation Act 1961.[92] The Wireless Telegraphy Act 1926 makes it an offence to broadcast matter that is of an "indecent, obscene or offensive character:"[93] The Post Office Act 1908 forbids sending or attempting to send through the post a package which "(b) encloses any indecent or obscene print, painting, photograph, lithograph, engraving, book or card, or any indecent or obscene article, whether similar to the above or not; or (c) has on the packet, or on the cover thereof, any words, marks or designs of an indecent, obscene, or grossly offensive character."[94]

The only reported relatively modern Irish decision of a prosecution for what may be termed public morality offences at common law is *The People (Attorney General) v. Simpson*,[95] where the defendant was prosecuted in the mid 1950s for putting on a theatre performance of Tennessee Williams' "The Rose Tattoo." This is a decision of Flynn D.J. on the question of whether a *prima facie* case had been made out showing that the defendant had put on an indecent and obscene performance. In the event, it was held that he had not. During the course of his judgment, the District Judge considered all the modern

---

[86] *Henn and Darby v. D.P.P.* (Case 34/79) [1979] E.C.R. 3795.
[87] Video Recordings Act 1989, s.17.
[88] S.18.
[89] 52 & 53 Vic. c.18.
[90] S.3. An amendment in 1979 removed the reference to contraception.
[91] Health (Family Planning) Regulations, S.I. No. 248 of 1980.
[92] S.13.
[93] S.11(1)(a).
[94] S.63; see s.17.
[95] 93 I.L.T.R. 33 (1959).

British decisions dealing with questions of obscenity and also decisions of the US Supreme Court, and concluded that those cases indicated in general terms what the common law position was, adding that the common law was "not readily ascertainable" and that it did not have "easily ascertainable standards of guilt."[96] Not one Irish case was found which could assist him. Particular reliance was placed on the decision of the US Court in the famous *Roth v. United States* case in 1957.[97] According to Brennan J.:

> "[S]ex and obscenity are not synonymous. Obscene material is material, which deals with sex in a manner appealing to prurient interest. The portrayal of sex, *e.g.* in art, literature and scientific works is not itself sufficient reason to deny material the constitutional protection of freedom of speech and press. ...
>
> (T)he test in each case is the effect of the book, picture or publication considered as a whole, not upon any particular class, but upon all those it is likely to reach. In other words, you determine its impact upon the average person in the community. ... You judge the (material) by present-day standards of the community."[98]

In order to determine if a *prima facie* case had been made out, Flynn D.J. applied the following test: "[d]oes the play ... tend to corrupt or deprave? Does it lead to certain lascivious thoughts and lustful desires which will affect character and action? Is the play a cloak for something sinister – a camouflage – to render the crudity, the sex ... sufficiently wrapped up to pass the critical standards of the Director of Public Prosecutions."[99]

Defamation

Persons' reputations are protected by the guarantee in Article 40.3.2 of the Constitution, that the State will protect and vindicate the "good name ... of every citizen." This objective is achieved principally through the law of defamation, which makes defamatory remarks that are spoken (slander) or published in some permanent form (libel) an actionable wrong and exceptionally also a criminal offence.[100] As Hamilton C.J. pointed out, "neither the common law nor the Constitution, nor the [European] Convention give to any person the right to defame another person. The law must consequently reflect a due balancing of the constitutional right to freedom of expression and the

---

[96] *Id.* at p.36.
[97] 354 US 476 (1957).
[98] *Id.* at pp.487 and 490.
[99] 93 I.L.T.R. (1959) at p.44.
[100] See generally, B. McMahon & W. Binchy, *Law of Torts* (3rd ed., 2000), Chap.34.

constitutional protection of every citizen's good name. This introduces the concept of proportionality. ...."[101] The tort of defamation applies to what may be defined loosely as statements that tend to lower a person or a body in the esteem of others, by causing them to think less of the individual or organisation being referred to. This term is not defined in the Defamation Act 1961, which regulates aspects of criminal libel as well as the tort. A complaint that is made quite frequently, especially by press interests, is that the Irish law of defamation is far too restrictive and unreasonably inhibits the disclosure of information that the general public interest would justify putting into the public domain. Under the influence of European Convention case law and developments in other jurisdictions, it is likely that defamation law will be made less restrictive, by extending the defence of fair comment and the categories of what kind of statements are privileged.

It would seem that the State itself, the Government and public agencies and bodies are not protected by the law of defamation. Relying, *inter alia*, on the European Convention's freedom of expression guarantee and also on US case law, in England and also in Australia it was held that it is contrary to the public interest that central or local government should have any right at common law to claim damages for defamation, because to do so would inhibit criticism of their activities.[102] What is said in either House of the Oireachtas or in Oireachtas Committees, or reports of what is said there, is absolutely privileged and cannot be the subject of any legal claim.[103] That too is the case for what is said during the course of court proceedings and in reports of those proceedings, subject to narrow exceptions. Even if what is said about a plaintiff is actionable in defamation because it is untrue, the defendant may nonetheless have a defence of qualified privilege or of fair comment. In England in proceedings brought against newspapers, the scope of fair comment has been broadened significantly, most notably in a case brought by a former Taoiseach concerning reports in the Times newspaper concerning political events in Ireland in 1994.[104] But the House of Lords rejected the argument that all publications about political topics should be privileged except where there is malice (*i.e.* knowledge that they are false or recklessness in this regard), as is the case in the United States. Courts in other Commonwealth countries have also wrestled with the question of precisely what criteria should govern *prima facie* defamatory (*i.e.* untrue) statements published in the media about political events, and where should the line be drawn between freedom of the press and the reputation of political actors.[105]

---

[101] *de Rossa v. Independent Newspapers plc* [1999] 4 I.R. 432 at p.456.
[102] *Derbyshire C.C. v. Times Newspapers Ltd* [1993] A.C. 534.
[103] *Supra*, p.108.
[104] *Reynolds v. Times Newspapers* [2001] 2 A.C. 127, applied in *Bonnick v. Morris* [2002] 3 W.L.R. 820.
[105] See generally, I. Loveland, *Political Libels: A Comparative Study* (2000).

Defamation is one of the few kinds of High Court civil cases tried before juries although the parties can agree to a trial by a judge alone; in the Circuit Court there are no juries. It was held by the Supreme Court in *De Rossa v. Independent Newspapers p.l.c.*[106] that the amount of damages a jury can award should bear some proportion to the nature of the defamation but this was a matter for the jury to decide and it is only in a very extreme case that their award would be overturned on appeal. Because the libel there was an extremely serious one – an allegation that the plaintiff, an elected public representative, had been involved in serious crime and supported anti-Semitism and violent communist oppression – and in view of the manner in which the defendant had defended the claim, it was held that an award of £300,000 was not so disproportionate to the wrong done that no reasonable jury would award such a sum.[107]

In the past the courts declined to grant interlocutory injunctions restraining the publication of defamatory material, on the basis that the equity jurisdiction did not permit such orders to be made. But this is no longer the case and, while a court will be very slow to so order, especially where damages awarded in a subsequent trial would be an adequate remedy,[108] in an extreme case publication of *prima facie* defamatory matter will be enjoined, pending the trial of the action.[109]

Confidence and Privacy

There is an implied constitutional right to privacy,[110] which is also guaranteed by Article 8 of the European Convention and by Article 17 of the UN Covenant. Disclosing confidential information without being duly authorised to do so can be an actionable wrong, although disclosure in special circumstances may be justified in the public interest.

Confidential Government information is extensively protected by the Official Secrets Act 1963. In exceptional circumstances this information is covered by executive privilege[111] and consequently can be withheld from legal proceedings notwithstanding its potential relevance. Under the Freedom of Information Acts, 1997–2003, an extensive range of documentation held by Government and other designated agencies can be accessed by anyone, without distinction. Whether there is a constitutional right of access to information

---

[106] [1999] 4 I.R. 432.
[107] In *O'Brien v. Mirror Group Newspapers Ltd* [2001] 1 I.R. 1 a divided (3/2) Supreme Court ordered a re-trial on the amount the jury awarded, £250,000.
[108] *Connolly v. Radio Telefís Éireann* [1991] 2 I.R. 446.
[109] *Reynolds v. Malocco* [1999] 2 I.R. 203.
[110] *Infra*, Chap.23.
[111] *Supra*, p.130.

held by public bodies remains to be decided but it would seem that unduly secretive governmental process would not be compatible with the democratic nature of the State.

The *in camera* principle and several of the statutory prohibitions on publishing the contents of court proceedings[112] are designed to ensure that essentially private matters are kept confidential. But where the confidential information concerns activities of the State, as opposed to a private individual or organisation, the courts will less readily restrain its publication.

It would seem that publication of confidential information concerning the Government will be enjoined only where it is demonstrably in the public interest to do so. In *Attorney General for England and Wales v. Brandon Book Publishers Ltd.*,[113] Carroll J. stated that, whereas equity will readily enjoin publication of private confidences, especially where they are commercial in nature, it is a very different matter with governmental information. She cited the views of an Australian judge that "it can scarcely be a relevant detriment to the Government that publication of material concerning its actions will merely expose it to public discussions and criticism. It is unacceptable in our democratic society that there should be a restraint on the publication of information relating to Government when the only vice of that information is that it enables the public to discuss, review and criticise Government action."[114] In that case, Carroll J. refused to enjoin publication of a book by a former British secret service employee because its contents concerned not alone a government but a foreign government. Because of the publishers' "important constitutional right to publish," the judge refused the application for an interlocutory injunction.

Apart from safeguarding commercial secrets, confidences protected by contract and intimate communications between spouses, in appropriate circumstances the courts will enjoin publication of material that significantly encroaches on a person's private life. But as *M. v. Drury*[115] illustrates, all depends on the particular facts of each case. There, one of the defendants gave newspapers details of his marriage having broken down because he alleged his wife had been having a relationship with a priest. His wife's application for an injunction restraining any further publication on the subject was rejected by O'Hanlon J., on account of the constitutional guarantee of free expression and because generally it is preferable that the ambit of the privacy interest be defined in legislation. Further, the plaintiff did not deny the truth of the core allegation about adultery with a priest and most damage to her and her children's

---

[112] *Supra*, p.503.
[113] [1987] I.L.R.M. 135.
[114] *Commonwealth of Australia v. John Fairfax Ltd*, 147 C.L.R. 39 (1980) at p.52. See also the *"Spycatcher"* case, *supra*, n.15.
[115] [1994] 2 I.R. 8. The leading English cases are *Douglas v. Hello* Ltd [2001] Q.B. 967 and *Campbell v. M.G.N. Ltd* [2003] Q.B. 633.

privacy had already been done in what had been published to date. If she desired to contest the truth of the alleged adultery, she could sue the defendants for defamation.

Political and Religious Advertising

The State-owned radio and television broadcasting organisation, Radio Telefís Éireann, which until 1988 had a legal monopoly of public broadcasting, is prohibited by section 20(4) of the Broadcasting Authority Act 1960, from broadcasting any advertisement "which is directed towards any religious or political end or which has any relation to an industrial dispute." A similar prohibition in section 10(3) of the Radio and Television Act 1988 applies to licensed private broadcasters. In *Murphy v. Independent Radio & Television Commission*[116] the Supreme Court rejected a constitutional challenge to section 10(3), insofar as it affected religious advertising, and in *Colgan v. IRTC*[117] the High Court rejected a challenge to its prohibition on political advertising; in both instances because there was held to be a rational basis for the prhobition. However, the ban on religious advertising was narrowed in 2001, excepting broadcasting a notice of the fact that a particular religious publication (other than, *inter alia*, a book) was available for sale or supply, or that an event or ceremony associated with a particular religion will take place; subject to the proviso that the notice does "not address the issue of the merits or otherwise of adhering to any religious faith or belief or of becoming a member of any religion or religious organisation."[118]

Commercial Speech

Commercial advertising has been held to be protected by the US Constitution's and by the European Convention's free speech and expression guarantees.[119] A question that has not been fully resolved is whether the constitutional guarantee extends to commercial speech. It would seem that the answer is in principle in the affirmative, except that the State possesses very extensive powers to regulate commercial expression. In *Attorney General v. Paperlink Ltd.*,[120] where it was sought to have the Post Office's legal monopoly of carrying letters declared unconstitutional, one of the plaintiffs' arguments was that the monopoly unconstitutionally infringed its right to communicate freely. Costello

---

[116] [1999] 1 I.R. 12; *supra*, p.536.

[117] [2000] 2 I.R. 592, *infra*, p.583.

[118] Broadcasting Act 2001, s.65.

[119] And in Canada, *e.g. Guignard v. City of Saint-Hyacinthe*, 209 D.L.R. 4th 549 (2002).

[120] [1984] I.L.R.M. 373.

J. held that in the circumstances there was no such infringement but appears to have accepted that there is some constitutional protection for commercial communications, when he observed that "the act of communication is the exercise of such a basic human faculty that a right to communicate must inhere in the citizen by virtue of his human personality and must be guaranteed by the Constitution."[121] Although that right is one of the unspecified rights under Article 40.3 and not the freedom of expression protected by Article 40.6.1.i, it would not appear to make any real difference under which Article the protection is granted because it is likely that any legislative interferences with it would be judged on the confusing minimum rationality/proportionality basis propounded in *Murphy v. IRTC*.[122]

COMPELLED EXPRESSION

There are categories of information that are legally privileged and, ordinarily, persons may not be obliged to disclose documents or any other record they have that contains this information, or to answer questions pertaining to it; for instance, what is said to a priest in confession and inter-spousal communications protected by marital privacy, and subject to exceptions, there is a privilege against self-incrimination. On account of the press' vital role in providing news to the public and thereby strengthening democracy, journalists' confidential sources have been held to be similarly privileged under the US Constitution's and the European Convention's free speech and expression guarantees, although their protections against forced disclosure are not absolute.[123]

On the one occasion when the Supreme Court considered this issue in *O'Kelly, Re*,[124] it was held that the Constitution does not confer a privilege of this nature. A prominent journalist was called as a prosecution witness in a criminal trial but he refused to identify the person he had interviewed on a particular occasion. This information was crucial to the outcome of the trial. He genuinely believed that disclosing his interviewee's name would contravene journalistic ethics. It was held that, even though freedom of the press gives journalists a right to gather news and that right may require some confidentiality, nevertheless, journalists do not possess any special evidentiary privileges. According to Walsh J., "journalists or reporters are not any more constitutionally or legally immune than other citizens from disclosing information received in confidence. The fact that a communication was made under terms of expressed confidence or implied confidence does not create a privilege against disclosure.

---

[121] *Id.* at p.381.
[122] *Supra*, p.536.
[123] *Goodwin v. United Kingdom*, 22 E.H.R.R. 123 (1996).
[124] 108 I.L.T.R. 97 (1974).

So far as the administration of justice is concerned, the public has a right to every man's evidence except for those persons protected by a constitutional or other established and recognised privilege. ... The obligation of all citizens, including journalists, to give relevant testimony with respect to criminal conduct does not constitute a harassment of journalists or other newsmen."[125]

In proceedings where Blayney J. held that journalists could be required by a tribunal of inquiry to disclose the source of information they had relevant to the tribunal's terms of reference, it was not suggested that they were entitled to any form of constitutional protection;[126] the only issue was whether the terms of the relevant Act authorised the compulsory disclosure of that information. Indeed, the only person who was penalised by the criminal law in connection with that tribunal was a journalist who was convicted in the District Court for refusing to disclose the source of information she got for a television programme, that was largely responsible for the tribunal being established.

REGULATING THE MEDIA

The print media in Ireland is entirely in private ownership and is not subject to any form of regulation by State agencies; it is governed by the same laws as apply generally. But broadcasting was and remains very different.[127] Prior to 1988, radio and television broadcasting in Ireland was a State monopoly; the State owns and controls Radio Telefís Éireann (RTÉ) which for years was the sole lawful broadcasting station in the country. This station is constituted by the Broadcasting Authority Act 1960, as amended. Overall responsibility for running the broadcasting service is imposed on the RTÉ Authority, a statutory corporation, the members and chairman of which are appointed by the Government for such period as it specifies. However, significant political independence is ensured because a member may be removed by the Government only for "stated reasons" and following both Houses of the Oireachtas passing resolutions calling for removal.[128] Further, the Minister is given very limited say in the operations of the Authority; his approval is required when fixing the total yearly hours to be occupied in TV and radio broadcasts, respectively, and the total daily times to be taken up in advertising.[129] But because RTE's commercial activities do not earn sufficient funds for it to break even, considerable indirect political influence may be exerted since it is the Minister

---

[125] *Id.*, at p.101. Compare *Ashworth Hospital Authority v. MGN Ltd* [2002] 1 W.L.R. 2033 and *Mersey Care NHS Trust v. Ackroyd*, unreported, May 16, 2003.

[126] *Kiberd v. Tribunal of Inquiry* [1992] I.L.R.M. 574.

[127] See generally, M. McGonagle, *Media Law* (2nd ed., 2003), E. Barendt, *Broadcasting Law, a Comparative Study* (1995) and R. Crawford-Smith, *Broadcasting Law and Fundamental Rights* (1997).

[128] Broadcasting Authority (Amendment) Act 1976, s.2.

[129] 1960 Act ss.19 and 20, as amended.

who determines the broadcasting licence fee, which is the main source of the broadcaster's funding.

Privately owned public broadcasting is regulated by the Radio and Television Act 1988, under the authority of the Independent Radio and Television Commission ("IRTC") and the Minister. Members of the Commission are appointed by the Government but may only be removed for "stated reasons" and following both Houses of the Oireachtas passing resolutions calling for removal.[130] Its function is "to arrange ... for the provision of sound broadcasting services ... and one television programme service,"[131] by entering into contracts with broadcasters that entitles and obliges them to provide the service in question. In the case of radio, the broadcaster must have a transmitter licence from the Minister, which may specify conditions under which the service may be provided. Those areas (which may include the whole State) in respect of which sound broadcasting contracts may be awarded are specified by the Minister and the Commission then invites applications for contracts, which are then assessed against criteria set out in section 6(2) of the 1988 Act. In the case of television, on being so directed by the Minister, the Commission will invite applications for the one contract and is obliged to ensure that the broadcaster satisfies criteria set out in section 18(3), (4) of this Act.

The type of service that RTÉ is required to provide is set out principally in section 28 of the Broadcasting Act 2001 and in sections 17 and 18 of the 1960 Act. According to section 28 of the 2001 Act:

> "(1) The ... service ... shall have the character of a public service, continue to be a free-to-air service and be made available, in so far as it is reasonably practicable, to the whole community on the island of Ireland and the Authority shall have all such powers as are necessary for or incidental to that purpose.
>
> (2) Without prejudice to the generality of subsection (1), the Authority shall ensure that the programme schedules of the broadcasting service referred to in that subsection–
>
>   (a) provide a comprehensive range of programmes in the Irish and English languages that reflect the cultural diversity of the whole island of Ireland and include, both on television and radio ... programmes that entertain, inform and educate, provide coverage of sporting, religious and cultural activities and cater for the expectations of the community generally as well as members of the community with special or minority interests and which, in every case, respect human dignity.
>
>   (b) provide programmes of news and current affairs in the Irish and English languages, including programmes that provide coverage

---

[130] Radio and Television Act 1988, Sch., para.3.
[131] *Id.*, s.4(1).

of proceedings in the Houses of the Oireachtas and the European Parliament, and

(c) facilitate or assist contemporary cultural expression and encourage or promote innovation and experimentation in broadcasting."

In performing its functions, RTÉ is required by section 17, as amended in 1976, to:

"(a) be responsive to the interests and concerns of the whole community, be mindful of the need for understanding and peace within the whole island of Ireland, ensure that the programmes reflect the varied elements which make up the culture of the people of the whole island of Ireland, and have special regard for the elements which distinguish that culture and in particular for the Irish language.

(b) uphold the democratic values enshrined in the Constitution, especially those relating to rightful liberty of expression, and

(c) have regard to need for the formation of public awareness and understanding of the values and traditions of countries other than the State, including in particular those of such countries which are members of the European Economic Community."

A special obligation of impartiality is imposed by section 18, as amended in 1976, on RTÉ, to ensure that:

"(a) all news broadcast by it is reported and presented in an objective and impartial manner and without any expression of the Authority's own views,

(b) the broadcast treatment of current affairs, including matters which are either of public controversy or the subject of current public debate, is fair to all interests concerned and that the broadcast matter is presented in an objective and impartial manner and without any expression of the Authority's own views,

(c) any matter, whether written, aural or visual, and which relates to news or current affairs, including matters which are either of public controversy or the subject of current public debate ... is presented by it in an objective and impartial manner."

RTÉ is prohibited from making programmes or broadcasting in such a way as would "unreasonably encroach on the privacy of an individual."[132] And it is prohibited from including in any of its broadcasts "anything which may

---

[132] 1960 Act, s.18(1B), inserted by s.3 of the 1976 Act.

reasonably be regarded as likely to promote, or incite to, crime or as tending to undermine the authority of the State."[133]

In its programming the private television contractor is subject to a regime similar to section 17 of the 1960 Act (as amended in 1976) and also must "include a reasonable proportion of news and current affairs programmes."[134] All private broadcasters are subject to duties similar to those imposed on RTÉ regarding impartiality in the coverage of news and current affairs, privacy, inciting crime and also not doing "anything which may reasonably be regarded as offending against good taste or decency."[135] Radio broadcasters are required to devote a minimum amount of time to news and current affairs programmes, and there is a maximum amount of time during which they are permitted to broadcast advertisements.

Both RTÉ and private broadcasters are prohibited from broadcasting any advertisement "directed towards any religious or political end or which has any relation to an industrial dispute" and constitutional challenges to this ban on religious and political advertising have been rejected.[136] Since 2001, however, religious advertisements may be broadcast simply stating the fact that a particular religious newspaper, periodical or magazine is available for sale or supply, or that an event or ceremony associated with a particular religion will take place.[137] But they may not address the merits or otherwise of adhering to or becoming a member of any particular religion. Party political and other political broadcasting is considered separately below.[138]

Provision is made in sections 22–27 of the 2001 Act for a Broadcasting Complaints Commission, comprised of Government appointees but who may be removed by the Government for stated reasons and following resolutions passed by both Houses of the Oireachtas calling for their removal. Unless the Commission considers it inappropriate to do so, it will publish particulars of its decision on any complaint and it also will require the broadcaster concerned to broadcast that decision.

In the 1980s several European States became concerned about the growth of subscription and pre-pay television services, and the threat that they might gain a monopoly of broadcasting major sporting and cultural events, resulting in a substantial proportion of the interested general public not being able to watch them. These concerns led to the adoption of EC Council Directive 89/552, which was implemented in the State by the Broadcasting (Major Events Television Coverage) Act 1999. Under this, having consulted various interested

---

[133] 1960 Act, s.18(1B), inserted by *id.*
[134] Radio and Television Act 1988, s.18(3).
[135] *Id.*, s.9(1)(d).
[136] *Murphy v. IRTC* [1999] 1 I.R. 12, *supra*, p.536 and *Colgan v. IRTC* [2000] 2 I.R. 490; *infra*, p.583.
[137] Broadcasting Act 2001, s.65.
[138] *Infra*, p.585.

parties and considered the criteria and other factors specified in section 2 of the Act, the Minister may designate one or more events to be broadcast on a free television service.

CHAPTER 20

Freedom of Assembly and Association

A traditional and important mode of expression is organising and taking part in public meetings and demonstrations. Freedom of assembly and association are in large part extensions of freedom of expression; they enable views to be aired by people getting together either informally in assemblies or, with a degree of formality, by joining associations of one kind or another. Article 11 of the European Convention subjects assembly and association to the same regime; in the Constitution and in the UN Covenant, separate provisions govern these.

ASSEMBLY

The central meaning of freedom of assembly is the right to hold meetings and to engage in public demonstrations. In the traditional catalogue of civil rights, freedom of assembly tends to rank next after personal liberty and freedom of expression. Thus, among the rights protected by the First Amendment in the United States Bill of Rights is "the right of the people peaceably to assemble." According to Article 40.6.1.ii and 2 of the Constitution:

> "The State guarantees liberty for the exercise of the following rights, subject to public order and morality – the right of the citizens to assemble peaceably and without arms. Provision may be made by law to prevent or control meetings which are determined in accordance with law to be calculated to cause a breach of the peace or to be a danger or nuisance to the general public and to prevent or control meetings in the vicinity of either House of the Oireachtas.
>
> Laws regulating the manner in which ... the right of free assembly may be exercised shall contain no political, religious or class discrimination."

"Assembly"

Apart from cases dealing with one particular kind of assembly, picketing in the context of a trade dispute,[1] authority on the meaning of constitutional freedom of assembly is sparse. It has not been established, for example, whether the guarantee applies to forms of economic assembly and to sporting and social assembly, or is it confined to meetings and demonstrations with essentially political objectives.

Restrictions on Assembly

Freedom of assembly may be restricted in the interests of "public order and morality", and public order in this context includes state security considerations.[2] Moreover, Article 40.6.1.ii permits laws controlling and prohibiting meetings occurring near the Oireachtas, and also regulating meetings that are calculated to cause a breach of the peace or to be a danger or nuisance to the general public. Article 11 of the European Convention states that assembly may be subject to such restrictions "as are prescribed by law and are necessary in a democratic society in the interests of national security or public safety, for the prevention of disorder or crime, for the protection of health or morals or for the protection of the rights and freedom of others." Additionally, the law may restrict exercise of these rights by members of the armed forces, the police or the public administration. Article 21 of the UN Covenant qualifies the right of assembly in similar terms, but without the caveat for the police, military or public service. To date the Irish courts have not been called on to decide the constitutionality of a law prohibiting or restricting freedom to assemble and demonstrate. In determining the status of any such law, the principal considerations would appear to be similar to those arising when evaluating restrictions on freedom of expression,[3] namely, the objective of the assembly in question, the purpose of the restriction and whether the interference exceeds what is reasonably required in the circumstances.

Irish law does not subject those who are planning to hold public meetings or demonstrations to prior restraint, *i.e.* require the prior consent of the police or of some other authority before the meeting may take place, although organisers of demonstrations often notify the Gardaí in advance in order to reduce inconvenience to the general public. Nor is there any single comprehensive statutory power for banning meetings and demonstrations prior to their occurrence. But meetings held in connection with an unlawful organisation are prohibited. There are numerous provisions that empower officials to proscribe meetings in particular contexts and circumstances. Meetings can become unlawful for being disorderly and the Gardaí have powers to disperse meetings in certain circumstances, and indeed may resort to force in exceptional instances. Section 9 of the Criminal Justice (Public Order) Act

---

[1] See generally, M. Forde, *Industrial Relations Law* (1991), pp.166 *et seq.*
[2] See generally, I. Brownlie, *Law of Public Order and National Security* (2nd ed., 1981).
[3] *Supra*, p.536.

1994, makes it an offence for any person "without lawful authority or reasonable excuse [to] wilfully prevent or interrupt the free passage of any person or vehicle in any public place." There is a statutory right to picket peacefully in support of a trade dispute.[4]

State Security

A meeting connected with an unlawful organisation and any meeting occurring in defiance of a valid prohibition against its taking place or continuing is an unlawful meeting or assembly. Section 27(1) of the Offences Against the State Act 1939, is a blanket prohibition against meetings connected with an unlawful organisation. It provides that it is unlawful to hold a public meeting "which is held or purports to be held by or on behalf of or by arrangement or in concert with an unlawful organisation or which is held or purports to be held for the purpose of supporting, aiding, abetting, or encouraging an unlawful organisation or of advocating the support of an unlawful organisation." Public meeting is defined to include a procession and also a meeting held in a building or on enclosed land to which the public are admitted, whether with or without payment. A senior Garda officer is empowered to prohibit any such meeting but application can be made to the court to annul the prohibition. Mention has already been made of section 4 of the Offences Against the State (Amendment) Act 1972,[5] which makes unlawful any public meeting, procession or demonstration that interferes with the course of justice, *i.e.* is of such a "character as to be likely, directly or indirectly, to influence any court, person or authority concerned with the institution, conduct or defence of any civil or criminal proceedings (including a party or witness) as to whether or how the proceedings should be instituted, conducted, continued, or defended or as to what should be their outcome."

There are several statutory powers for prohibiting public meetings in particular locations. Perhaps the best known of these is section 28 of the Offences Against the State Act 1939, which does not proscribe all meetings occurring in the vicinity of the Oireachtas but which empowers a senior Garda officer to order the dispersal of any such meetings. Those meetings affected by section 28 are "any public meeting to be held in, or any procession to pass along or through, any public street or unenclosed place which or any part of which is situate within one half of a mile from any building in which both Houses or either House of the Oireachtas are or is sitting or about to sit ...".

Public Order

Restrictions on freedom of assembly designed to maintain public order fall

---

[4]   Industrial Relation Act 1990, s.11.
[5]   *Supra*, p.542.

into three principal categories, namely criminalisation *per se*, the power to ban meetings and ordering that meetings of assemblies be dispersed.

Crimes: Assembly in public places is now governed by the Criminal Justice (Public Order) Act 1994,[6] as well as several discrete statutory provisions. Under section 21 of this Act, a member of the Garda Síochána can restrict persons' access to places where an event is or is about to take place, where it is likely to attract a large assembly of persons and intervention appears necessary in the interests of safety or to preserve order. This may be done by erecting barriers at any means of access to the place, no further then one mile from it, and then diverting persons to some other place of access; prohibiting any access where possession of a ticket is required to attend the event; preventing persons from passing through who possess intoxicating liquor, a disposable drinks container or some offensive article. These restrictions do not apply to persons going to their dwellings or place of business in the vicinity of the event, or going for some other lawful purpose to some place in that vicinity.

There used to be a common law offence of unlawful assembly but it was abolished and replaced by section 15 of the 1994 Criminal Justice (Public Order) Act. This new offence of "violent disorder" involves three or more persons being together anywhere, whether public or private, who use or threaten to use unlawful violence and whose conduct would cause a person there to fear for his or for another's safety. Other assembly-related common law offences, namely riot and affray, were abolished by this Act and were replaced by statutory offences.

A meeting or demonstration occurring on the highway or other public place may in the circumstances amount to obstruction under section 98 of the Road Traffic Act 1961, according to which "[a] person shall not do any act (whether of commission or of omission) which causes or is likely to cause traffic through any public place to be obstructed." Under section 60 of the Road Traffic Act 1968, the Minister is authorised to make regulations "for the general regulation and control of traffic and pedestrians in public places" and, in particular, "(a) specifying rules for the use of roads by ... pedestrians; (m) regulating and controlling the conduct of pedestrians on roads...; (o) the control of ... pedestrians by members of the Garda Síochána. ..." Public place for the purposes of these Acts is defined as "any street, road or other place to which the public have access with vehicles whether as of right or by permission ...".[7]

Bans: Statutory powers to ban public meetings include section 9 of the Phoenix Park Act 1925, which authorises the Commissioner of the Garda Síochána to make regulations for various aspects of the park and which are contained in

---

[6] See generally, P. Charleton *et al.*, *Criminal Law* (1990), pp.763 *et seq.*
[7] Road Traffic Act 1931, s. 3(1).

the Phoenix Park Bye Laws 1926.[8] Under general principles of administrative law, restrictions on meetings, adopted under statutory powers, will be declared to be invalid where they are unreasonable.[9]

Ordering Dispersal: There are various circumstances in which, at common law, the Gardaí may order that a meeting or demonstration be dispersed. It remains to be seen whether the constitutional freedom of assembly coupled with the abolition of the offence of unlawful assembly constrains the police powers in this regard.

Many of the reported authorities on public meetings and demonstrations deal with giving orders to disperse and in several of them the persons holding the meeting sued the police officer or justice for trespass. At common law a Garda officer, who reasonably apprehends that the holding or continuance of a meeting will cause a breach of the peace, is entitled to order its dispersal, which can also be ordered where the meeting constitutes an unreasonable user of the highway. However, the Garda officer's mere apprehension of a breach of the peace or mere objection to a particular manner of using the highway is not enough to justify an order to disperse the meeting. Thus in *Queen (Orr) v. Londonderry Justices*,[10] which was a binding-over to keep the peace case, the police had ordered a Salvation Army procession in Derry to disband because they apprehended a breach of the peace. It was held that there was insufficient factual basis for those fears. No single act of hostility by the crowd was proved; the fact that a riot took place four years earlier at a similar procession was held to be too remote to warrant fears of disturbances again and the fact that Catholics had complained that they would not be permitted to march in the city was said to be "not an expression of hostility at all that would cause fear of a collision but was in reality a complaint that in Londonderry, sometimes, the law fluctuated according to circumstances."[11] Similarly in *Lowdens v. Keaveney*,[12] the defendant was a member of a band playing tunes in Belfast streets, which was being followed by a large crowd. A police officer cautioned the band against going down one street because it was so narrow and another street because a riot would be caused. But the defendant proceeded down those streets and he was charged with causing an obstruction. It was held that his conviction should be quashed because, in such cases, a crucial question is whether the defendant's use of the streets was in fact unreasonable. Since the magistrates did not address themselves to that question but accepted entirely the word of the police, the conviction could not stand.

---

[8] S.I. (No. 6) of 1926, regs. 12 and 13.
[9] *Kruse v. Johnson* [1898] 2 Q.B. 91.
[10] (1891) 28 L.R. Ir. 440.
[11] *Id.* at p.449.
[12] [1903] 2 I.R. 82.

A particularly vexed question is what can the Gardaí do when an ordinary peaceful meeting would most likely give rise to violence because it would attract hostile counter-demonstrations, or where it is believed that counter-demonstrations will occur. The reason for not readily banning meetings, that may very well provoke counter-meetings and breaches of the peace, is that such bans make it too easy to suppress expression of unpopular views by objectors threatening violence against those expressing those views. In the *Londonderry Justices* case, O'Brien J. held that "if danger arises from the exercise of lawful rights resulting in a breach of the peace, the remedy is the presence of sufficient force to prevent that result, not the legal condemnation of those who exercise those rights."[13] But this view differs somewhat from those expressed in what is generally regarded as the principal Irish authority on the point, a case decided in the Land War era, *O'Kelly v. Harvey.*[14] Justices ordered the dispersal of a Land League meeting being held at Brookeborough, Co. Fermanagh that was to be addressed by three MPs, including C.S. Parnell. One reason for the dispersal order was that a counter-demonstration of Orangemen from the county had been organised, which the justices believed would end in violence unless the plaintiff's meeting was banned. It was held that in the circumstances there were reasonable grounds for apprehending violence and for believing it essential to proscribe the plaintiffs' meeting, and that accordingly the justices had acted lawfully. In the words of Law C., "even assuming that the danger to the public peace arose altogether from the threatened attack of another body … still if the (Justice) believed and had just grounds for believing that the peace *could only be preserved* by withdrawing the plaintiff and his friends from the attack with which they were threatened, it was … the duty of the (Justice) to take that course."[15]

Use of Force

An issue that is always controversial is when are the Defence Forces, the Gardaí or other State agents permitted to resort to physical force when seeking to suppress an unlawful meeting or demonstration, such as baton charges, water cannons, CS gas and indeed firearms.[16] These questions have arisen on numerous occasions in connection with the conflict in Northern Ireland over the last thirty years,[17] most notably in the "Bloody Sunday" incident in January

---

[13] (1891) L.R. Ir. 450.
[14] (1881) L.R. Ir. 285.
[15] *Id.* at p.110. See also *Humphries v. O'Connor* (1864) Ir. C.L.R. 1 and *Coyne v. Tweedy* [1898] 2 I.R. 167.
[16] See generally G. Humphreys and C. Craven, *Military Law in Ireland* (1997) at p.20.
[17] E.g. *McCann v. United Kingdom*, 21 E.H.R.R. 97 (1995).

1972.[18] Where lethal force is used by the military or the police against civilians, the European Court of Human Rights has held that the incident in question must be properly investigated by the State authorities.[19]

The only modern Irish case on the issue concerns the not quite so notorious Marsh's Yard incident in 1934, which was decided shortly before the present Constitution was adopted. Most of Hanna J.'s lengthy judgment and the judgments of the Supreme Court in *Lynch v. Fitzgerald*[20] deal with the facts. A sale was taking place in an auction yard in Cork of cattle that had been seized from local farmers who had been refusing to pay land annuities. An organisation had been formed to protest against those seizures and sales. Anticipating possible disturbances at the sale in question, there were members of the Garda Síochána present, including members of a special S division who were armed. While the sale was taking place, a lorry filled with men carrying sticks was driven through several cordons of Gardaí and crashed into the sale yard before stopping. As the lorry was coming in through the yard gate the "S men" opened fire and the plaintiff's son was killed.

Hanna J. began his judgment by observing that "(t)his case has a very serious aspect, inasmuch as a civilian has been killed by the armed forces of the State, and it is important that the principles governing the use of firearms against an assembly of civilians should be clearly laid down."[21] He further remarked that "(o)n the subject of involving the loss of civilian life at the hands of armed forces of the State, the law has to be very exact and justice very exacting."[22] Among the authorities cited by the judge were the well known charge by Tindal C.J. to the Bristol Grand Jury in 1832, the Report of the Belfast Riots Commission of 1886, the Report of the House of Commons Select Committee on the Featherstone Riot of 1893 and the Report of the Special Commission on the Bachelor's Walk shooting in 1914. As regards the Marsh's Yard incident, Hanna J. held that the governing principle is "that the armed forces can fire upon an unlawful or riotous assembly only where such a course is necessary as a last resort to preserve life. Force is threatened and it can be repelled by force. ... (I)t is lawful to use only a reasonable degree of force for the protection of oneself or any other person against the unlawful use of force, and ... repelling force is not reasonable if it is either greater than is requisite for the purpose or disproportionate to the evil to be prevented."[23] He concluded that, in the circumstances, the shootings were not justified under this principle and that what the defendants did was "in the most favourable view, a rash act, done in reckless disregard of necessity. ..." He went further

---

[18] January 30, 1972.
[19] *Supra*, p.308.
[20] [1938] I.R. 382.
[21] *Id.* at p.386.
[22] *Id.* at p.400.
[23] *Id.* at p.405.

and found that the evidence before him disclosed a *prima facie* case of manslaughter and he directed the Attorney General's attention to the evidence. In the event, the defendants were never prosecuted.

The following instructions issued to the Gardaí on the use of force were described by Hanna J. as "a correct statement of the law and a perfect instruction":

> "the degree of force to be used must always be moderated and proportioned to the circumstances of the case, and the end to be attained. Hence it is that arms – now at such a state of perfection that they cannot be employed without grave danger to life and limb even of distant and innocent persons – must be used with the greatest of care, and the greatest pains must be exercised to avoid the infliction of fatal injuries, but if in resisting crimes of felonious violence, all resources have been exhausted and all possible methods employed without success, then it becomes not only justifiable but it is the duty of Detective Officers, or other members authorised to carry arms, to use these weapons according to the rules enunciated, and, if death should unfortunately ensue, they will, nevertheless, be justified." [24]

Public Fori

Meetings and demonstrations occurring on private property, without the owner's consent, are actionable trespasses; meetings that do not trespass, but that interfere with the use and enjoyment of property rights, can be actionable nuisances. Private property in the context here includes property that is owned by a public authority or body. It remains to be seen whether the constitutional liberty to demonstrate extends to meetings occurring in publicly-owned areas that are frequented by the general public, such as beaches, airports and parks,[25] and indeed in privately owned areas that the general public use, such as shopping centres.[26]

Those engaged in a meeting or demonstration, who use force to gain access to private property and refuse to leave it, may be guilty of offences under the Forcible Entry and Occupation Act 1971. Entry as a trespasser into any building or its curtilage to interfere with property there, or in a manner likely to cause fear in a person, are offences under sections 11 and 13 of the Criminal Justice (Public Order) Act 1994.

Another question that requires resolution is whether the Gardaí are entitled

---

[24] *Ibid.*
[25] *Cf. The Queen v. Committee for the Commonwealth*, 77 D.L.R. 4th 385 (1991).
[26] *Cf. Hudgens v. N.L.R.B.*, 424 U.S. 507 (1976).

to enter private property, in which persons are meeting, when the purpose of entry is not to apprehend those who are committing, or have committed, an offence but is to prevent the anticipated commission of an offence. It was held in Britain that the police possess such a power. Lord Hewart C.J. once stated that "it is part of the preventive power, and, therefore, part of the preventive duty of the police in cases where there are ... reasonable grounds of apprehension (that offences would be committed) to enter and remain on private premises."[27] He was "not at all prepared to accept the doctrine that it is only where an offence has been, or is being, committed, that the police are entitled to enter and remain on private premises. On the contrary, ... a police officer has *ex virtute officii* full right so to act when he has reasonable ground for believing that an offence is imminent or is likely to be committed."[28] But that decision has been extensively criticised and it does not take account of any overriding guarantee of private property, nor naturally the abolition of assembly-related common law offences in 1994. Morris P. indicated that it does not reflect Irish law, in the light of the Constitution.[29]

ASSOCIATION

In the past there was considerable State hostility to individuals associating, for instance, in political groupings, professional associations and in trade unions, because these formed formidable barriers between centralised State power and the members of the group in question. A general right of freedom of association is a relatively modern phenomenon.[30] No such right is mentioned in the United States Bill of Rights nor in the French Declaration of 1789, although both US and French constitutional law now accept that there is such a right. Freedom of association is expressly guaranteed by Article 40.6.1.iii and 2 of the Constitution; that "[t]he State guarantees liberty for the exercise of the following rights, subject to public order and morality:- The right of citizens to form associations and unions. Laws, however, may be enacted for the regulation and control in the public interest of the exercise of the foregoing right. Laws regulating the manner in which (that) right may be exercised shall contain no political, religious or class discrimination." Freedom of association is protected by Article 11 of the European Convention and by Article 22 of the UN Covenant.

---

[27] *Thomas v. Sawkins* [1935] 2 K.B. 249 at pp.254–255.
[28] *Id.* at p.255.
[29] *D.P.P. v. Delaney* [1996] 1 I.L.R.M. 536.
[30] See generally, A. Guttman ed., *Freedom of Association* (1998)

"Association"

Apart from cases dealing with one particular kind of association, trade unions, authority on the meaning of the constitutional freedom of association is virtually non-existent. It has not been established, for example, whether the guarantee applies to associating for economic objectives, such as forming partnerships and registered companies, and whether it applies to social associations, such as sports clubs, or to the more private intimate associations. In *Private Motorists' Protection Soc. v. Attorney General*,[31] Carroll J. held that the constitutional right of association did not entitle persons to form and to keep in existence corporate bodies, for instance registered companies and industrial and provident societies. She described the constitutional right as "a right of citizens (in the plural) to form an association or associations with each other; it was not intended that it should include the right to form bodies with corporate existence under statute."[32] However, the Supreme court's judgment on appeal suggests that the guarantee has some application to economic associations, although the court did not indicate in what manner and to what effect, other than that the legislation in that case did not contravene the plaintiffs' freedom of association. One of the arguments made in *Norris v. Attorney General*,[33] that criminal proscriptions against certain homosexual conduct contravened the plaintiff's freedom of association, was rejected.

Restrictions on Association

As the Constitution makes clear, laws can be enacted "regulat(ing) and controll(ing)" associations in the public interest. No such law, however, is permitted to contain "political, religious or class discrimination." What class discrimination means in this context has never been judicially determined. Nor has it been decided whether discrimination here means adverse discrimination or does it, as is the case with the freedom of religion clause, include favourable as well as unfavourable distinctions? Article 11 of the European Convention permits association to be restricted on the same basis as freedom of assembly, as does Article 22 of the U.N. Covenant. Freedom of association can be restricted in several ways, most notably, by criminalising the association in question and outlawing the very fact of membership, interfering significantly with an association's internal affairs, denial of State benefits or privileges to those affiliated with certain associations and requiring disclosure of membership lists or the fact of membership of some particular association.

---

[31] [1983] I.R. 339.
[32] *Id.* at p.355.
[33] [1984] I.R. 36.

Proscribed Organisations

Part III (sections 18–25) of the Offences Against the State Act 1939, forbids secret societies in the military or the police force, and it declares certain associations to be unlawful organisations and empowers the Minister to ban them. The constitutionality of this power or of particular exercises of the power has never been challenged.[34] According to section 18, an unlawful organisation is any organisation which:

> "(a) engages in, promotes, encourages or advocates the commission of treason or any activity of a treasonable nature, or
>
> (b) advocates, encourages, or attempts the procuring by force, violence, or other unconstitutional means of an alteration of the Constitution, or
>
> (c) raises or maintains or attempts to raise or maintain a military or armed force in contravention of the Constitution or without constitutional authority, or
>
> (d) engages in, promotes, encourages or advocates the commission of any criminal offence or the obstruction of or interference with the administration of justice or the enforcement of the law, or
>
> (e) engages in, promotes, encourages, or advocates the attainment of any particular object, lawful or unlawful, by violent, criminal or other unlawful means, or
>
> (f) promotes, encourages, or advocates the non-payment of moneys payable to the Central Fund or any other public fund or the non-payment of local taxation ...".

Organisation is defined as "includ(ing) associations, societies, and other organisations or combinations of persons of whatsoever nature or kind, whether known or not known by a distinctive name." Thus, unlawful associations include not merely subversive and criminal organisations in the popular sense but groups that advocate the non-payment of taxes and of other moneys owing to the State or other public body, such as rates. A question that, therefore, calls for resolution is how much support must a body give to those objectives for it to become an unlawful organisation. Membership of any of the above kinds of associations is a criminal offence and the Gardaí can order the closing down of any building used in any way for the purpose of such organisation.

Section 19 of the 1939 Act empowers the Government, if it is of the opinion that any particular association is unlawful, to declare it to be an unlawful organisation that in the public interest ought to be suppressed. The following organisations, *inter alia*, have been banned in this manner the Irish Republican

---

[34] *Cf. Blythe v. Attorney General* [1934] I.R. 266 and *McEldowney v. Forde* [1971] A.C. 632.

Army, the Irish National Liberation Army and the Ulster Volunteer Force. Provision is made that any member of an organisation declared unlawful, within 30 days of that declaration being published in the *Iris Oifigiúil,* may apply to the court for a ruling that the body is not unlawful. Except for this declaratory procedure, the Government's suppression order is "conclusive evidence for all purposes" that the body in question is an illegal organisation.[35]

Limiting Choice of Organisation

Freedom of association includes being free to select between different associations of the same general category, for instance different political parties or interests groups. One of the qualifications that the European Convention puts on Article 11 associational freedom is that the guarantee "shall not prevent the imposition of lawful restrictions on the exercise of these rights by members of the armed forces, of the police or of the administration of the State." There is a like qualification in the UN Covenant but it does not exempt the public service.

In *Aughey v. Ireland,*[36] public order was held by Barrington J to include the security of the State. And it was held there that the statutory prohibition against members of the Garda Síochána joining trade unions was not unconstitutional; that "(b)ecause of their close connection with the security of the State, Gardaí may have to accept limitations on their right to form associations and unions which other citizens would not have to accept."[37]

Freedom of choice was touched on by Gavan Duffy J. in *National Union of Railwaymen v. Sullivan,*[38] another trade union case. But the Supreme Court struck down the legislation in question there because it went further than regulating and controlling choice association in the public interest; it was a flat prohibition on such association. The case concerned Part III (sections 18–40) of the Trade Union Act 1941, which provided, *inter alia*, that in certain circumstances only the majority trade union in the workplace could recruit members, and persons employed there could not join any other union. According to the Supreme Court, the Act "undoubtedly deprived the citizen of a free choice of the persons with whom he shall associate. Both logically and practically, to deprive a person of the choice of the persons with whom he will associate, is not a control of the exercise of the right of association, but a denial of the right altogether."[39]

---

[35] *Sloan v. Special Criminal Court* [1993] 3 I.R. 528.
[36] [1986] I.L.R.M. 206.
[37] *Id*. at p.217.
[38] [1947] I.R. 77; *infra*, p.805.
[39] *Id*. at p.102.

Forced Association

It has been held in a number of trade union cases that the right to associate in unions embodies a correlative right not to be coerced by the State or by others into joining trade unions and that, in particular, economic coercion to establish or to maintain "closed shops" can contravene freedom of association.[40] It can hardly be doubted that legislation forcing individuals to join a particular political party would be unconstitutional and significant, though indirect, pressure by the State to join some political party may also contravene the guarantee. But apart from the trade union cases, there are no Irish authorities on the constitutional right to disassociate. It has been contended in other countries, albeit without success, that legislation and other state pressure on private organisations aimed at stopping them from excluding persons from membership on the grounds of race, sex or religion are unconstitutional because it denies these bodies' existing members of their right to disassociate.

---

[40] *Infra*, p.802.

CHAPTER 21

Political Participation

A group of constitutional rights exist which may be subsumed conveniently under the general heading of political participation.[1] These overlap but differ from the traditional civil liberties in that they guarantee the positive liberty to make a contribution towards the institutional process of self-government; they directly involve the power structure of the State and the distribution of political power within it. These are concerned primarily with participating in elections, voting, standing for elective office and having fair elections in representative constituencies. These supplement the rights which are dealt with in the preceeding chapters, *viz.* freedom of expression, of assembly and of association, which facilitate communication of political views, and equality, which ensures that the State will not discriminate unfairly between individuals. A major concern of many of the rules regarding the political process is to ensure a reasonable degree of equality between all the participants. As Budd J. observed in the *O'Donovan* "constituency boundaries" case,[2] Article 5 of the Constitution provides that Ireland is a democratic State and, in the modern usage of those words, democratic State means "one in which all citizens have equal political rights."[3]

In their treatment of several of the topics considered in this chapter, many national constitutions, and also the Constitution of Ireland, deal with them in the main body of the constitutional instrument and not in the fundamental rights sections. For instance, virtually all aspects of Presidential, Dáil and Seanad elections are regulated by the Articles dealing with the President and with the National Parliament, and not by Article 40 or any of the later Articles. Where the provision in question is located in the text has no great legal significance, although McLoughlin J. (dissenting) in the *McMahon* "secret ballot" case[4] observed that "if the Constitution wished by its terms to confer an absolute personal right as to secret voting at Dáil elections, it would have more appropriately so declared it (according to the scheme of the Constitution) in Article 40 which deals with personal rights rather than in Article 16 which is devoted to machinery for election to and the constitution of Dáil Éireann."[5]

---

[1] See generally, N. Whelan, *Politics, Elections and the Law* (2000).
[2] *O'Donovan v. Attorney General* [1961] I.R. 114.
[3] *Id.* at p.137.
[4] *McMahon v. Attorney General* [1972] I.R. 69.
[5] *Id.* at p.122.

POLITICAL EXPRESSION

Article 40.6.1.i of the Constitution and the freedom of expression guarantees in the European Convention and in the UN Covenant focus principally on political expression. There is also provision in the Convention regarding elections and Article 25 of the Covenant guarantees that:

> "[e]very citizen shall have the right and the opportunity, without any of the distinctions mentioned in Article 2 and without unreasonable restrictions:
>
> (a) To take part in the conduct of public affairs directly or through freely chosen representatives;
>
> (b) To vote and to be elected;
>
> (c) To have access, on general terms of equality, to public service in his country."

These are the only rights in the Covenant that are confined to citizens; all other rights in it are accorded to persons. The potentially controversial issues of restrictions on the political activities of public sector workers and on the sums that individuals and bodies may donate to political parties and candidates have not been considered by the Irish courts. But the regime governing political broadcasting has been the subject of litigation from time to time.

Public Sector Employment

When it places restrictions on what public employees may say or do, the State has a dual role, as sovereign and as employer, and in the latter capacity it has a greater ability as well as an incentive to impose certain restrictions on what may be expressed. By agreeing to work for the State, especially where a restrictive regime already exists, it can be argued that the individual has consented to those curtailments on his freedom of expression and, accordingly, has waived such constitutional rights as he may possess to publicise his own political views or have political affiliations.

Members of the defence forces, of the Garda Síochána and certain other public service office holders and employees are prohibited by law or practice from active participation in party politics. Members of the defence forces are not permitted to "join, or be a member of, or subscribe to, any political organisation or society or any secret society whatsoever."[6] Further, they may not become a member of a local authority.[7] Members of the Garda Síochána

---

[6] Defence Act 1954, s.103.

[7] *Id.,* s.104.

may not become involved in political parties or act in relation to political matters in such a way as would give rise to apprehension about their impartiality.[8] Established civil servants are subject to similar restrictions.[9] None of these are eligible to stand for election to the Dáil, the Seanad, a local authority or the European Parliament.[10]

Where an officer or an employee of a local authority, health authority or one of many other public bodies is elected to either House of the Oireachtas or to the European Parliament, the legislation governing the body in question usually provides that he shall stand seconded from the job for so long as he holds the elected office.[11]

Funding Political Activities

Until recently, political parties and other political actors relied almost entirely on private funding to finance their activities and, with two exceptions, there were no restrictions of any kind on the sources or the amount of funding provided, other than the general law. Since the electoral reforms of the 19th century, it has been a criminal offence to pay a person to vote or not to vote, or to induce another to vote or not to vote.[12] Under the Trade Union Act 1913, "party political" spending by trade unions must come from a separate "political fund" maintained by the union.[13] Individual union members are permitted to "contract out" of this fund, in the sense that no part of their subscription to the union shall be paid into the fund and, further, their union is not permitted to take adverse action against them for choosing to do so. There is no equivalent provision for dissident shareholders of registered companies or for dissident members of building societies or friendly societies.

How political parties and candidates in elections are funded became subject to a strict regime under the Electoral Acts 1997–2002, as has the question of how much parties and candidates may spend on elections. There is a ceiling on the amount that any one person may donate in any year to a political party or to any member of or candidate for election to the Dáil, the Seanad or the European Parliament.[14] In the case of a party it is £5,000 and it is £2,000 for any such member or candidate. No donation may be made by or accepted from

---

[8] *Supra*, p.126.

[9] See generally, M. Forde, *Employment Law* (2nd ed., 2001), pp.305–306. *Cf. Civil Service Loyalty* case, 39 BVerfGE 334 (1975).

[10] Electoral Act 1992, s.41(f)–(h), Local Government Act 2001, s.13(1)(g)–(h) and European Parliament Elections Act 1997, s.11(2).

[11] *Supra*, n.9.

[12] Presently, Electoral Act 1992, s.135(1)(a).

[13] See generally, M. Forde, *Industrial Relations Law* (1991), pp.244 *et seq.*

[14] Electoral Act 1997, s.23A, inserted by Electoral (Amendment) Act 2001, s.49(d).

a non-national resident outside the State or Northern Ireland, or from any body of persons which does not have an office carrying on one of its major activities on the island of Ireland. There are similar provisions for presidential elections.[15]

Where a registered company makes a political donation in excess of £4,000 to a person or party involved in a Dáil, Seanad, European Parliament or Presidential election, details of the amount in question and of the recipient must be published in the directors' annual report to the company's members.[16] An equivalent requirement is imposed on trade unions, building societies, friendly societies and industrial and provident societies. A party member or candidate involved in any of these elections is not allowed to accept an anonymous donation exceeding £100.[17] Further, returns must be made to the Public Offices Commission of all political donations accepted by parties, members and candidates.[18]

Ceilings have been put on the aggregate election expenses that may be incurred by or on behalf of candidates in these elections.[19] In the case of Dáil elections, the ceiling is fixed with reference to whether the constituency in question returns three, four or five members; in the case of European and Presidential elections, it is specified by the Minister.

Annual payments must be made by the State to political parties to fund their activities generally. Additionally, provision is made for the reimbursement by the State of expenses incurred by candidates in Dáil Elections;[20] a similar regime may be promulgated by the Minister for presidential elections and for elections to the European Parliament. In order to qualify for this funding, the party in question must be duly registered. Every such party must be paid £100,000 each year and an additional sum calculated with reference to the total number of first preference votes its candidates secured in the preceding general election.[21] £3 million is allocated to be divided up among all those parties in this manner every year. In addition to this and to any other salary or allowance paid to them, annual allowances are paid to the leader of each party, calculated with reference to the number of TDs or senators the party has, to defray "expenses arising from parliamentary activities, including research."[22] A separate allowance for this purpose is paid to each TD or member of the Seanad.[23] No part of any of these various payments may be applied towards election expenses, which are reimbursed by the State where the individual

---

[15] Electoral Act 1997, s.48A, inserted by Electoral (Amendment) Act 2001, s.49(h).
[16] Electoral Act 1997, s.26.
[17] *Id.*, s.23.
[18] *Id.*, s.24.
[19] *Id.*, ss.27 *et seq.*
[20] *Ibid.*
[21] *Id.*, s.17, amended by Electoral (Amendment) Act 2001, s.50(c). *Cf.* the *Party Finance* case, 20 BVerfGE 56 (1966) and the *Green Party Funding* case, 73 BVerfGE 40 (1986).
[22] Oireachtas (Ministerial and Parliamentary Officers) (Amendment) Act 2001.
[23] *Ibid.*

was elected or where the votes cast for him at any stage in the count exceeded one quarter of the quota.

No provision has been made for funding the protagonists or political parties involved in referenda and in *McKenna v. An Taoiseach (No.2)*[24] it was held to be in breach of Article 40.1's guarantee of equality for the State to provide funding for one side only of the argument in a referendum campaign for an amendment to the Constitution; almost invariably, for the "yes" side.

Political Broadcasting

Formerly, a major technique for conveying political messages was the large public meeting or demonstration but the main participants in the electoral system today rarely rely on such assemblies in order to garner and to manifest support. Advertising and broadcasting have become far more prominent. Political advertising, comment and coverage in the press is not subject to any form of direct regulation; provided that they comply with the general law, owners of newspapers, magazines, billboards and the like may publish whatever political advertisements and other material they choose, and on such terms as they choose.

Advertising Ban

Radio Telefís Éireann ("RTÉ") and private licensed broadcasters may not broadcast any "advertisement ..., which is directed towards any ... political end. ..."[25] In *Colgan v. Independent Radio & Television Commission*,[26] O'Sullivan J. rejected a constitutional challenge to this prohibition, where a broadcaster was being prevented from putting out an advertisement relating to abortion; its tenor mildly discouraged abortion. It was contended that the advertisement did not come within the very terms of this prohibition, not emanating from any political party and not advocating any ideological stance, other than opposition to abortion, a view emphatically endorsed by the Constitution. However, because the advertisement was sponsored by Youth Defence, an anti-abortion organisation that had been involved in referenda on this very question, and because "a listener, ... other than a young Irish mother, might well be induced by this advertisement to offer support to ... a Youth Defence project,"[27] the judge found that it was caught by the prohibition; that securing a "political end" was at least an "ancillary objective." The advertisement was "so closely bound up with the political objectives of Youth

---

[24] [1995] 2 I.R. 1; *supra*, p.394.
[25] Broadcasting Act 1960, s.20(4) and Radio and Television Act 1988, s.10(3).
[26] [2000] 2 I.R. 490.
[27] [2000] 2 I.R. 490 at p.507.

Defence that it would be unrealistic and artificial to shut ones eyes to these objectives and construe the advertisement out of context and severed from its background."[28] In view of the deferential approach adopted by the Supreme Court to the free expression guarantee in *Murphy v. IRTC*,[29] which concerned a religious advertisement, O'Sullivan J. concluded that a "rational explanation" could be supplied for the prohibition and consequently upheld it. However, exactly what explanation existed for the ban is unclear and no evidence was adduced as to its object. According to the judge, "the Oireachtas may well have decided that it would have been inappropriate to involve agents of the State in deciding which advertisements in this sensitive area would be likely to cause offence and which not;"[30] accordingly, the blanket indiscriminate ban on all political advertisements was justified because "a rational explanation for the wider infringement is available to the court."[31]

Commandeering

Section 31(2) of the Broadcasting Act 1960 authorises the Minister to commandeer RTÉ's services in order to make a broadcast. Under this, he "may direct the Authority in writing to allocate broadcasting time for any announcements by or on behalf of any Minister of State, – and the Authority shall comply with the direction." Resort to this provision, so that the Taoiseach could make a broadcast advocating support for the referendum in 1992 on the "Maastricht" treaty, was upheld by Carney J. in *McCann v. An Taoiseach*,[32] where it was held that there was no constitutional or other right to reply to that broadcast. It is debatable whether this remains the law in view of what was held in the *Coughlan* case.[33]

Equality/Fairness

RTÉ and private broadcasters have a general obligation to be "objective and impartial" in their programming, and in their "treatment of current affairs, including matters which are either of public controversy or the subject of current public debate, [to be] fair to all interests concerned. ..."[34] With one possible caveat, no programmer is required to put on party political broadcasts. But

---

[28] *Ibid.*
[29] [1999] 1 I.R. 12; *supra*, p.536.
[30] [2000] 2 I.R. 511-12.
[31] *Id.* at p.512. *Cf. R. (Pro Life Alliance) v. British Broadcasting Corp.* [2003] 2 W.L.R. 1403.
[32] [1994] 2 I.R. 1.
[33] *Coughlan v. Broadcasting Complaints Comm.* [2000] 3 I.R. 1; *infra*, p.586.
[34] Broadcasting Authority Act 1960, s.18(b), as amended in 1976, and Radio and Television Act 1988, s.9(1)(b).

RTÉ is permitted to do so without any express restriction on how those broadcasts may be allocated and presented.[35] Private broadcasting contractors also may do so, provided that "they shall not, in the allocation of time for such broadcasts, give an unfair preference to any political party."[36]

How party political broadcasts are to be allocated was considered in *Madigan v. Radio Telefís Éireann*,[37] where a candidate in a general election complained that inadequate coverage was being given to independent candidates like himself. RTÉ's broad policy in this regard was to take account of the support gained by the various political parties in the previous general election, and it pointed to some coverage that had been given to the applicant. According to Kinlen J., RTÉ's obligation was to be fair to all the interested parties, including independent candidates, and the Authority might be acting unlawfully if it were guided entirely by the results in the previous election. But, it was held, this was not the case here, so that the appropriate legal test was whether the approach taken by RTÉ was so unreasonable and irrational that it flew in the face of common sense, or was made *mala fide*. In view of the evidence, he found that RTÉ's approach could not be faulted in this regard.

It was contended in the *Green Party v. Radio Telefís Éireann*[38] that *Madigan* should not be followed because the parties in that case had taken it for granted that the appropriate standard for review was the *O'Keeffe* "irrationality" standard;[39] that the approach there was incorrect because issues of this nature concern constitutional rights, demanding a somewhat stricter standard of review and, further, a very different kind of decision-making process was involved. Without explaining why, Carroll J. rejected this argument and upheld RTÉ's decision not to broadcast the plaintiff's Ard Fheis. She held that there was nothing unlawful nor irrational about the criteria RTÉ adopted for deciding which parties' Ard Fheiseanna should be broadcast, *viz.* there were at least six TD's representing the party or it obtained at least 5% of the first preference vote in the preceding general election. That the plaintiff had two MEPs and was part of a major European Parliament grouping, whereas two of the parties whose Ard Fheiseanna would be covered had no European representation whatsoever, was held not to invalidate those criteria.[40]

On several occasions endeavours to get interlocutory injunctions relating to broadcasts during referendum campaigns were unsuccessful but those cases never went on to a full trial. The applicant in *Coughlan v. Broadcasting*

---

[35] Broadcasting Authority Act 1960, s.18(2).

[36] Radio and Television Act 1988, s.9(2).

[37] [1994] 2 I.L.R.M. 471.

[38] Carroll J., February 24, 2003.

[39] *O'Keeffe v. An Bord Pleanála* [1993] 1 I.R. 39; *supra*, p.525.

[40] *Cf.* the *West German Media* case, 14 BVerfGE 121 (1962) and the *Radical Groups* case, 47 BVerfGE 198 (1978).

Complaints Commission[41] was not one of those litigants but, some months after the 1995 divorce referendum had been carried, he complained to the Broadcasting Complaints Commission about the manner in which RTÉ had covered that campaign. Over a year later his complaint was rejected and he then challenged that decision by way of judicial review, relying principally on the *McKenna* decision of 1995,[42] which held that Government funding for a "yes" vote and failure to provide any funding for the "no" campaign in that referendum vote contravened Article 40.1's guarantee of equality. His complaint was that a disproportionate amount of broadcasting time was given to advocating a "yes" vote, principally because all the major political parties were in favour of the proposed amendment and all of them were allocated "party political" broadcast time in order to convey their views on the proposal. These uncontested broadcasts in favour of a "yes" vote were approximately 40 minutes in all, whereas the "no" vote got only 10 minutes in total; uncontested transmissions comprised just over 2% of the time devoted to the divorce referendum campaign.

In holding that the "no" side had been unconstitutionally discriminated against in this regard, Hamilton C.J. pointed out that RTÉ were not under any duty to put on party political broadcasts; rather, they were permitted to do so, should they choose and, if so, those broadcasts would not be deemed to contravene their duty of impartiality. Consequently,

> "[I]n deciding to transmit political party broadcasts and all issues in relation thereto [RTÉ] in reaching such decision must have regard to fair procedures and the exercise of the power in that regard will be exercised in a constitutional manner.
>
> In the case of a referendum which has as its objective the amendment of the Constitution, fair procedures require that the scales should be held equally between those who support and those who oppose the amendment.
>
> The party political broadcasts with which we are concerned in these appeals cannot be regarded as normal party political broadcasts but were devoted specifically to the issue to be put to the electorate in the referendum.
>
> Political parties have no right, whether under the statute or under the Constitution, to be afforded the opportunity by [RTÉ] to make party political broadcasts. It is purely a matter for [its] discretion – as to whether or not they will transmit such broadcasts.
>
> In reaching the decision to transmit such broadcasts, [it] is obliged, in the context of a referendum, to hold the scales equally between those who support and those who oppose the amendment.

---

[41] [2000] 3 I.R. 1.
[42] *McKenna v. An Taoiseach (No.2)* [1995] 2 I.R. 1, *supra*, p.394.

The allocation of ten party political broadcasts, to be shared between five political parties, did not hold the balance equally between those who supported the referendum and those who opposed it.

By no stretch of the imagination can that be regarded as maintaining a proper balance and such failure to maintain a proper balance was not in any way compensated for by the allocation of two uncontested broadcasts to *ad hoc* campaigners advocating a 'no' vote in the referendum."[43]

Barrington J., dissenting, supported criteria for allocating broadcasting time that took account of the extent to which political parties supported or opposed a particular proposed amendment, concluding that criteria that took account of this could not be regarded as so unreasonable as to be unlawful. In his view:

"When it comes to advising the people on a major political decision [such as a constitutional amendment] the principal role must rest with their political leaders. A distinguishing feature of a democratic society is that political leadership rests, not on power, but on persuasion. Likewise political authority rests on the consent of the electorate. It is right and appropriate that political leaders should use their authority and the arts of persuasion to lead the people towards the decision which their judgment tells them will best promote the common good. For [RTÉ] to attempt to neutralise the advice of political leaders would be to subvert the democratic values which it is directed to uphold."[44]

But as Barron J. pointed out, in referenda "[t]he contest is not just between political parties. The people are not necessarily split along party political lines. They did not do so in relation to the divorce referendum".[45] Denham J. emphasised that the *McKenna* judgment "illustrate[s] the necessity for fairness and equality in referenda" and concluded that in the circumstances excessive uncontested broadcasting time had been allocated to one side of the argument.[46]

POLITICAL PARTIES

Political parties are an essential feature of the effective operation of a modern democracy. Ireland's political system is dominated by political parties, principally Fianna Fáil, Fine Gael, the Labour Party, the Progressive Democrats,

---

[43] *Id.* at p.25.
[44] *Id.* at p.45.
[45] *Id.* at p.60.
[46] *Id.* at p.31.

Sinn Fein and the Green Party.[47] Unlike some modern constitutions, such as those of France and of Germany, there is no express reference to political parties in the Constitution, nor is there any law resembling the German Political Parties Act 1967, except for the regime on political funding. Entitlement to establish and to conduct the affairs of a political party is guaranteed by Article 40.6.1's rights of freedom of expression, of assembly and of association. In some states the electorate vote only for political parties; there are other systems in which the electorate vote for individual candidates on the one hand and for political parties as well. In Ireland, strictly, the electorate vote only for individual candidates (except for elections for the European Parliament) but in practice it is for and against political parties that many electors vote.

There are no requirements to be satisfied in order to establish a political party, either with regard to the legal form of the party or other preconditions. However, in order to be identified on a ballot paper and also to obtain State funding, a party must be registered under section 25 of the Electoral Act 1992[48] (previously section 13 of the Electoral Act 1963). This does not lay down what a political party's aims shall or shall not be, nor how its internal affairs shall be regulated, nor provide that registration is a prerequisite to functioning as a political party. In order to register, a party must satisfy the registrar (who is the clerk of the Dáil) that it is organised in the State or in a specified part of the State to contest elections for either Dáil, Seanad, European Parliament, local or Údaras no Gaeltachta elections. In place of a requirement that it be a "genuine political party," a minimum membership condition was introduced in 2001, being at least 300-recorded members, or 100 members where it is contesting only local or Údaras elections. This membership requirement does not apply where the party has at least one TD or MEP; similarly, where it is contesting only local or Údaras elections. The party's name must not be too similar to that of an existing registered party and not comprise more than six words; if it operates only in a particular part of the State that must be indicated in its name. A party that is refused registration may appeal to a board, which is chaired by a High Court judge, the decision of which is final. Once registered, the party must keep the registrar informed of the name or names of its officers who have authority to sign certificates authenticating its candidates.

The original version of these provisions was challenged, unsuccessfully, in *Loftus v. Attorney General.*[49] The plaintiffs' application to register a party known as the Christian Democratic Party of Ireland had been rejected on the grounds that it was an organisation, which was almost entirely Dublin-based and was not a genuine party organised to contest elections. They appealed to a

---

[47] See generally, J. Coakley & M Gallagher, *Politics in the Republic of Ireland* (3rd ed., 1999), Chaps 5 and 6.
[48] Amended by s.11 of the Electoral (Amendment) Act 2001.
[49] [1979] I.R. 221.

tribunal, comprised of a High Court judge and the chairmen of the Dáil and the Seanad. It rejected the appeal because their organisation "was not a genuine political party in the sense of having a visible, easily recognisable public image which must include a constitution in which the aims and objects of the party were stated; because the appeal board was not satisfied that the degree of organisation of the party was adequate to contest a Dáil election, even in its best-organised constituency (Dublin North East) in which the first plaintiff had contested a Dáil Éireann election on behalf of his party in May 1963; and because, in the view of the appeal board, the party operated at that time in relation to the city of Dublin, while the name which it sought to register (the Christian Democratic Party of Ireland) did not contain the specific reference to locality required by section 13(5)(c)."[50]

The plaintiffs' claim that this decision went against the weight of evidence was rejected, as was their claim that the tribunal was not properly constituted because the Dáil had been dissolved at the time the appeal was heard. Their main argument was that the absence then of any legislative definition of what is a "genuine political party" gave the registrar an arbitrary discretion to decide which parties should and should not be registered. The Supreme Court's answer was the same as in its subsequent *State (Lynch) v. Cooney*[51] decision, *viz.* that legislative provisions no longer confer virtually unfettered discretion because there is an overriding implied obligation on decision-makers to act fairly and judicially, and decision-makers cannot ignore individuals' constitutional rights. In any event, it was held, the section did not even attempt to prevent disappointed applicants from seeking judicial review of a rejection of their application by the tribunal. The plaintiffs also contended that requiring political parties to register under section 13 of the 1963 Act contravened the guarantees of freedom of association and of expression. But the court's response was that the objective of registration is to regulate the conduct of elections and that, accordingly, it is reasonable to make a political party's electoral aspirations the main test of whether or not it should be registered; moreover, the regulations there did not in fact interfere with the rights of *bona fide* political parties as regards participating in elections. O'Higgins C.J., for the court, observed that some regulation of political parties is constitutionally permissible because "(i)f some control and regulation were not provided, genuine political action might be destroyed by a proliferation of bogus front organisations calling themselves political parties but with aims and objects far removed from the political sphere."[52] Because section 13 permitted political parties, which had representatives in the Dáil in 1963, to be registered automatically, without having to satisfy the registrar that they were genuine political parties, it was argued that the plaintiffs were being discriminated against unfairly. That

---

[50] *Id.* at p.226.
[51] [1982] I.R. 337; *supra*, p.539.
[52] [1979] I.R. 242.

contention was rejected on the ground that the disparity of treatment was neither invidious nor unfair.

As was outlined above, sections 16-20 of the Electoral Act 1997,[53] provide for annual State funding for registered political parties, with £3 million in all allocated for each year. Money so received must be used for the party's general administration, for research, education and training, for policy formation, for co-ordinating party activities, as well as for "the general conduct and management of [its] affairs and the lawful pursuit – of any of its objectives."[54] None of it may be used to defray election expenses. Parties in receipt of these funds must furnish the Standards in Public Offices Commission with annual statements showing how the money was spent. For this purpose and also to comply with other provisions in the 1997 Act regarding the disclosure of political donations and monitoring election expenses, section 71 of this Act requires every registered party to appoint an "appropriate officer." In the absence of such appointment, the party in question's leader is deemed to be that officer.

ELECTIONS

The primary method of government laid down by the Constitution is one of representative democracy in that the President and the members of both Houses of the Oireachtas are chosen in periodic elections.[55] In the case of the President and the Dáil, the electorate are virtually the entire adult population of the State, all of whom have one transferable vote. In addition to the various constitutional rules, electoral law must comply with Article 3 of the European Convention's First Protocol, which requires "hold[ing] free elections at reasonable intervals by secret ballot, under conditions which will ensure the free expression of the opinion of the people in the choice of the legislature." Several other representative decision-making assemblies have been established, notably, Údaras na Gaeltachta, local authorities and various professional bodies. While the Constitution's rules regarding elections do not extend to these bodies, Article 40.1-3.i-iii and the other personal rights apply to them, such as the guarantees of equality, freedom of expression and non-discrimination on religious grounds. Legislation exists which governs elections to the European Parliament sitting in Brussels and in Strasbourg. Because the Dáil is by far the most important representative assembly in the State, the following account deals primarily with Dáil elections. The principal laws regulating them are the Electoral Acts 1992–2002.

---

[53] Amended by s.50(c) (d) of the Electoral (Amendment) Act 2001.
[54] S.18(1)(a), as so amended by *id*. s.50(d).
[55] See generally, B. Chubb, the *Government and Politics of Ireland* (3rd ed., 1992), Chap.8 and *Coakley & Gallagher*, *supra*, n.47, Chap. 4.

Periodic Elections

One of the abuses that the 1689 Bill of Rights[56] sought to remedy was infrequent elections; an increasingly unpopular and unrepresentative government could continue to exercise its powers because at the time the monarch chose not to dissolve the parliament and call fresh elections. Under Article 16.5 of the Constitution, the maximum permissible duration of any Dáil is seven years from the date of its first meeting. The Electoral Act 1992 sets the present maximum duration at five years.[57] Seanad elections are required by Article 18.8 to be held within three months of a Dáil being dissolved at such date as the President fixes. Except where the office is vacated in the various ways set out in the Constitution, elections for the Presidency must take place every seven years.[58]

Where in between elections a Dáil seat falls vacant, the procedure for filling it is by having a writ moved in the Dáil calling for a bye-election. By custom, the writ is moved by the political party whose member gave rise to the vacancy. In *Dudley v. An Taoiseach*,[59] where a vacancy arose and no writ was moved for a protracted period, leave was given to seek judicial review with a view to compelling it being moved. However, on the day before the case was due to be heard, the writ was moved, thereby rendering the issue moot.

Secret Ballot

It was proclaimed in the 1689 Bill of Rights that parliamentary elections "ought to be free" but it was not until 1872 that freedom to vote was significantly protected by the introduction of the secret ballot.[60] That is not to say that open balloting invariably deterred electors from voting for the candidate of their choice: one of the high points in nineteenth-century Irish history was Villiers Stuart's victory over Beresford in the 1826 election in Waterford, when the latter's agricultural tenants openly voted against him. It is stipulated in the Constitution that Dáil, Seanad and Presidential elections shall be by "secret ballot."[61] Much of the Electoral Act 1992 is designed to ensure secrecy; it further expressly obliges all those involved in managing the electoral process to maintain "the secrecy of the ballot" and provides that no one may be required in any legal proceedings to disclose how he voted.

On two occasions the rules regarding the conduct of elections have been

---

[56] 1 W. & M.. 2 sess., c.2.
[57] S.33.
[58] Art.12.3.
[59] [1994] 2 I.L.R.M. 321.
[60] Ballot Act 1872, 35 & 36 Vic. c.33.
[61] Arts.16.4, 18.5 and 12.2.3.

challenged in the courts on the grounds that they did not adequately ensure secrecy. In *McMahon v. Attorney General*,[62] the nub of the plaintiff's case concerned the system of keeping for one year a record of the number of each ballot paper that was issued, in case it should become necessary to count the votes again. Under the then electoral rules, there had to be a ballot paper and also a detachable counterfoil, and each of these were numbered consecutively. When an elector went to vote, his registered number would be recorded on the counterfoil, which then would be stored for twelve months. Since the counterfoil contained both the number of the ballot paper issued and the voter's own number, it was possible to ascertain how an elector voted. This mechanism had been adapted from that in the Ballot Act 1872, and was designed to prevent personation and other forms of unlawful voting. It was conceded that this mechanism did not guarantee absolute secrecy of voting but, in its defence, it was contended that Article 16.1.4 also requires single voting and that it is essential to encroach somewhat on secrecy in order to prevent plural voting.

It was held by Ó Dálaigh C.J., giving the majority judgment in the Supreme Court, that the secret ballot required by the Constitution must not be partly secret but must be entirely secret; that "limited secrecy is not secrecy, it is something less than secrecy." According to the Chief Justice, Article 16.1.4:

> "speaks of voting by secret ballot. The fundamental question is: *secret to whom?* In my opinion there can be only one plain and logical answer to that question. The answer is: *secret to the voter.* It is the voter's secret. It is an unshared secret. It ceases to be a secret if it is disclosed. The Constitution guarantees the voter that his vote will be secret. In my opinion the Constitution therefore requires that nothing shall be done which would make it possible to violate that secrecy. The acknowledged purpose of marking the voter's counterfoil is to disclose how he voted if that should be necessary in order to avoid the inconvenience of a re-poll. But this is what the Constitution says shall not be done–
>
> The Constitution does not require the voting citizen to run the risk of disclosure by accident or breach of the law: it entitles him to shut up within the privacy of his own mind all knowledge of the manner in which he has voted, without fear of disclosure. In my opinion a voting system which permits a state official to note the number of the ballot paper of every voter in the State, and which requires this information to be stored for a full year after the poll, of itself offends against the spirit and substance of the declaration that voting shall be by secret ballot. Under such a system, the fear of disclosure which secrecy is designed to drive away is ostentatiously retained."[63]

---

[62] [1972] I.R. 69.
[63] *Id.* at pp.106 and 111.

Dealing with the argument that secrecy cannot be absolute if plural voting is to be effectively prevented, it was observed that since 1923 there never was a recorded instance of an election petition or of counterfoils being scrutinised in order to prove a charge of personation. Moreover, Part III of the Prevention of Electoral Abuses Act 1923, which allowed personation agents to attend at polling stations, was a much stronger deterrent against personation. Thus, whatever forms of safeguards against plural voting are devised, they must not be such as make it possible for others to ascertain how any elector has voted, subject however to one proviso. If the voter is blind or otherwise physically incapacitated, such that it is necessary to obtain another's assistance in order to vote, the fact that the other person can ascertain how the voter actually voted does not render unconstitutional the legislative provisions that permit giving this assistance. It was contended that, in the light of those provisions, the secrecy required by Article 16.1.4 is not absolute as described above. The court's response was that if secrecy was not breached for these special circumstances, the handicapped voter simply would not be able to vote and making an exception for these circumstances "is no valid reason why the voter should have to share his secret with a state official and with the agents of the candidates".[64]

In *Dillon-Leetch v. Calleary*,[65] the petitioner sought to have the general election result in his Dáil constituency declared invalid because the returning officer had contravened provisions of the Electoral Act 1923, in particular, the Act's detailed rules regarding secrecy, which required, *inter alia*, the returning officer to place the ballot boxes and voting papers under seal during intervals in the course of the count. The two High Court judges who heard this petition found that the boxes and papers had not been sealed during the lunch interval in that constituency; they also found that no actual breach of electoral secrecy had occurred. They therefore concluded that, in the circumstances, the result of the election should not be set aside, a conclusion which was upheld by the Supreme Court. According to Henchy J., for the court, the mere fact that the detailed rules have been broken does not mean that an election must be declared invalid; for this to occur, it must be established that one of the basic principles of the electoral law was contravened and, furthermore, that the breach affected the result of the election. These basic principles include "the right to vote, freedom in the exercise of the vote, secrecy of the vote, and the integrity of the vote or of the count."[66] In the instant case, none of these principles had been broken. But even if there had been such a breach, the election would not have been invalidated unless the breach was "of such a nature as to be fairly calculated in a reasonable mind to produce a substantial effect upon the election." Even though the Constitution guarantees electoral secrecy, to set

---

[64] *Id.* at p.105.
[65] Unreported, Supreme Court, July 31, 1974.
[66] At p.5.

aside an election on account of an "electorally ineffective" breach of that principle would be an improper interference with the vast majority of the electors' constitutional right to vote.

The Right to Vote

As has already been explained, it is only existing members of each House of the Oireachtas and of local authorities, and registered graduates of some Irish universities (TCD and NUI Dublin, Cork, Galway and Maynooth), who can vote in Seanad elections.[67] For Dáil and Presidential elections and referenda, the Constitution lays down a rule of near-universal suffrage. According to Article 16.1.2, which applies to each of these elections, "[a]ll citizens, and such other persons in the State as may be determined by law without distinction of sex who have reached the age of eighteen years who are not disqualified by law and comply with the provisions of the law relating to the election of members of Dáil Éireann, shall have the right to vote at an election for members of Dáil Éireann (and in Presidential elections and referenda)." Women first became entitled to vote in parliamentary elections in 1918[68] and Article 16.1.2 above proscribes sex discrimination as regards voting in Dáil and Presidential elections, and in referenda.[69] Subject to the disqualifications set out below, all Irish citizens aged eighteen years or more are entitled to vote, provided that they reside in the State and are duly registered as electors.

Requirements

In order to be registered for Dáil elections, a person must be either an Irish or a British citizen, or a citizen of a reciprocating state, aged 18 years or more and "ordinarily resident" in the constituency in question.[70] It is only citizens, otherwise eligible, who may vote in referenda and in Presidential elections,[71] and it would appear that the Constitution would have to be amended to permit non-citizens to vote in them. Non-nationals may register to vote in elections for the European Parliament.[72]

Some categories of persons living outside the State are deemed to be ordinarily resident for election purposes and special provisions in this regard are made for patients and inmates of a hospital or a home, persons being held in legal custody and members of the Defence Forces residing in a barracks or

---

[67] *Supra*, p.100.
[68] *Coakley & Gallagher, supra*, n.47, ch.12 on women in politics.
[69] Arts.12.2.2 and 47.3.
[70] Electoral Act 1992, s.8. *Cf. Non-Resident Voting* case, 58 BVerfGE 202 (1981).
[71] Referendum Act 1994, s.2(1) (references to "electoral" as a "presidential elector") and Electoral Act 1992, s.7; Constitution, Arts.12.2.2 and 47.3.
[72] European Parliament Elections Act 1997, s.6.

equivalent premises. Although one can be "ordinarily resident" in more than one place and, consequently, formerly one could be registered as an elector in more than one constituency,[73] dual registration is no longer permitted.[74] Disputes about registration are determined by the Circuit Court, with a right of appeal to the Supreme Court on a point of law.

Deliberately obstructing a person's endeavours to vote is an actionable tort.[75] But in *Graham v. Ireland*,[76] where through inadvertence on the returning officer's part, the plaintiff was prevented from voting, Morris J. rejected his claim for damages on the grounds that negligence had not been established. Both the plaintiff and his father had the same name but, through some error, the father's name was not in the register of electors. Notwithstanding, the father attended at the polling station and was allowed to vote. When later in the day the plaintiff arrived there, he was not allowed to vote because, so far as the returning officer could ascertain from the records, he had already voted.

Aliens

Formerly, only Irish citizens could vote in Dáil elections. In 1983 the Oireachtas sought to grant voting rights to British citizens resident in the State because Britain permits Irish citizens to vote in its parliamentary elections, but that measure was declared unconstitutional in *Re Electoral (Amendment) Bill, 1983*.[77] As has already been explained, it was held that because of its structure, its very nature ("a mechanism by which the people may choose and control their rulers and their legislators") and its context (the analogous Articles 12.2.2 and 47.3), Article 16 was a comprehensive code regarding voting for membership of the Dáil. Accordingly, the franchise, which it gave to citizens, was confined exclusively to them.

Shortly afterwards, Article 16.1.2 was amended and it now permits the vote to be given to non-citizens on such terms as the Oireachtas shall determine. In 1992 the franchise in Dáil elections was extended to resident British citizens and also to citizens of what may be termed reciprocating EC/EU States.[78] These are citizens of Member States of the EC/EU whose laws permit Irish nationals to vote in their parliamentary elections and which have been designated by the Minister as reciprocating States.

---

[73] *Quinn v. Waterford Corp.* [1990] 2 I.R. 507.
[74] Electoral Act 1992, s.11(1).
[75] *Ashby v. White* (1703) 2 Ld. Raym. 938, Electoral Act 1992, s.111 (the Dáil) and Referendum Act 1994, s.2(t).
[76] [1988] 2 I.R. 88.
[77] [1984] I.R. 268; *supra*, p.387.
[78] Presently the Electoral Act 1992 , s.8.

Disqualifications

Article 16.1.2 permits the Oireachtas to "disqualif(y) by law" persons who otherwise would be entitled to vote, provided that sex or being aged eighteen years or more is not used as the basis for disqualification. But this does not give the legislature a virtually free hand to exclude persons from voting, because account must also be taken of the guaranteed personal rights. For instance, disqualification on the basis of religion would be unconstitutional, as would disqualification on the grounds of political views or affiliation, except perhaps where some justification compelled by overwhelming national security exists.

The following categories cannot register to vote in Dáil elections, *viz.*[79] aliens (other than United Kingdom nationals), minors (*i.e.* persons under 18 years of age) and persons not ordinarily resident in the constituency (subject to exceptions). Prior to the introduction of postal voting in 1986, there were certain groups who, although they were entitled under the law to vote, were subject to such circumstances that they could not in fact vote; they may be described as *de facto* disqualified. For instance, some physically handicapped voters could not cast their vote without relying on somebody's assistance at the polling booth and, were they not permitted to cast their vote by post, sailors at sea, some lighthouse men, members of the defence forces serving overseas and many graduates on the university registers would not be able to cast their votes. The question that therefore arises is to what extent does the Constitution require the Oireachtas to adopt voting rules that make it possible for all, or for most, qualified voters to actually exercise the franchise.

This came before the Supreme Court in *Draper v. Attorney General*,[80] where the plaintiff, who was severely handicapped physically, claimed that the Electoral Acts were unconstitutional because they did not allow persons in her circumstances to cast their vote by post. On account of her disability, she could not go to her polling station to vote. She furthermore contended that these Acts discriminated against her unfairly because members of the Gardaí and the defence forces were allowed to vote by post. Rejecting her claim, the court held that giving a postal vote to persons in her circumstances would "obviously contain a very high risk of abuse which could not easily be countered or controlled;"[81] the actual evidence for this conclusion was meagre and far from convincing. For Seanad elections, the Constitution provides that voting shall be by secret postal ballot.[82]

Prisoners being detained under a criminal conviction are not formally disqualified from voting but, on account of their being in detention, are unable to exercise their franchise. In *Breathnach v. Ireland*,[83] the Supreme Court

---

[79] Electoral Act 1992, s.41.
[80] [1984] I.R. 277; *supra*, p.388.
[81] *Id.* at p.290.
[82] Art.18.5.
[83] [2001] 3 I.R. 230.

rejected the contention that this state of affairs infringed the plaintiff's constitutional right to vote. Because some registered electors find it impossible to comply with the existing statutory regime, it does not follow that the Constitution requires the State to so finetune that regime so that they may vote. Indeed, unlike disabled persons in the *Draper* case, prisoners' incapacity to vote is the result of their own voluntary actions and accordingly they have an even weaker case when challenging the existing regime. Additionally, certain constitutional rights of individuals fall into abeyance when they are convicted and incarcerated, in consequence of their voluntary acts. Keane C.J. observed that "[n]o doubt the provision of facilities to enable the applicant to exercise his rights by post or in the precincts of the prison would not be wholly impractical, although it would undoubtedly require legislation. [But] there is no obligation on the State to provide the machinery, since the right remains in suspension or abeyance during the period of … imprisonment."[84] Although remand prisoners enjoy the presumption of innocence, the Chief Justice added that the same principle applied to them as regards exercising their right to vote. They too "are being detained in accordance with law and … accordingly, for so long as they are so detained, some of their constitutional rights, including the right to exercise the franchise, are necessarily in suspension or abeyance."[85]

Single Vote

Article 16.1.4 of the Constitution stresses that plural voting shall not be permitted in Dáil elections; that "(n)o voter may exercise more than one vote –". The same is the case for Presidential and Seanad elections, which are by way of "single transferable vote,"[86] and the one person, one vote rule is implicit in Article 47 regarding referenda. This rule is reiterated in section 111 of the 1992 Act, which stipulates that only persons duly registered are entitled to vote, which is supplemented by section 134, which forbids, *inter alia*, personation and other forms of plural voting. Being registered as an elector in more than one constituency, as being ordinarily resident in both, was held not to contravene this Article,[87] but multiple registration was abolished in 1997.[88]

Transferable Votes and Proportional Representation

Although they are frequently regarded as the same, voting by way of the

---

[84] *Id.* at p.239. *Cf. Sauve v. Attorney General of Canada*, 218 D.L.R. 4th 577 (2002).
[85] *Id.* at p.240.
[86] Arts. 12.2.3 and 18.5.
[87] *Supra,* n.73.
[88] *Supra,* n.74.

transferable vote is distinct from proportional representation (for short, PR). The transferable vote means that the voter is confronted with a slate of candidates and may vote for them in such order of preference – 1, 2, 3, 4, etc. as he chooses. If a voter's chosen first candidate is eliminated in the count, then his vote is transferred on to the next chosen candidate and so on. Proportional representation, on the other hand, connotes electoral constituencies that return more than one candidate. An electoral system can be by way of single transferable vote without it being a PR system and there can be PR without there being the transferable vote. The only other country which uses the Irish combination of PR and single transferable vote is Australia, where it is used for Senate elections and in some of the state elections; this system was also adopted in 1973 for Assembly elections in Northern Ireland and in 1977 for elections to the European Parliament in Northern Ireland.

Under the Constitution, Dáil and Seanad (panel members) elections are by way of single transferable votes and PR.[89] Although the system for Presidential elections is described as "proportional representation by means of the single transferable vote",[90] since only one President can be elected at any one time the reference to PR is inaccurate. In 1959 and 1968 the Governments of the day sought to amend the Constitution so as to abolish PR and the transferable vote system for Dáil elections by introducing a "first past the post" system; both proposals were rejected by the people. How PR is operated in Dáil elections is set out in Part XIX (sections 118–128) of the Electoral Act 1912.[91]

Constituencies

Article 16.2 of the Constitution lays down various rules regarding the constituencies for Dáil elections; the complex constituency system for Senate elections has been explained already.[92] In the first place, the number and size of Dáil constituencies is affected by the stipulated maximum and minimum number of Dáil members (called Teachtaí Dála, or TDs for short). There must be at least one TD for every 30,000 of the population and there must be not more than one TD for every 20,000 of the population. In 2003, there were 166 TDs, which was one TD for approximately 236,144 of the population.

Every Dáil constituency must have at least three seats,[93] *i.e.* it must return at least three TDs. This is to ensure that minority interests get a reasonable opportunity of having candidates of their choice elected, as the greater the

---

[89] Arts.16.2.5 and 19.5.
[90] Art.12.2.3.
[91] Described in *Coakley & Gallagher, supra,* n.47, Chap.4. *Cf.* the *Bavarian Party* case, 6 BVerfGE 84 (1957).
[92] *Supra,* p.100.
[93] Art.16.2.6.

number of Dáil seats there are in any constituency the greater is the opportunity for minority representation. In 2003 there were 42 constituencies in all, 16 of them being three-seaters, 12 more being four-seaters and there were 14 five-seat constituencies.

Equal Representation

Article 16.2.3 stipulates that, so far as is practicable, the constituencies should be arranged in such a way as to ensure that every vote has the same value, in the sense that it takes approximately the same number of votes in every constituency to elect a single TD; that "[t]he ratio between the number of members to be elected at any time for each constituency and the population of each constituency, as ascertained at the last preceding census, shall so far as is practicable, be the same throughout the country." Additionally, the Oireachtas is obliged at least every twelve years to revise the constituencies so as to ensure that the 20,000 minimum – 30,000 maximum representation rule is satisfied and to ensure that all votes have an equal value in the sense just mentioned.

At one time a Government Minister drew up the proposed new consti-tuencies and some gerrymandering occurred. Subsequently, a judge was assigned the task of drafting the proposed revised system. Part II (sections 5–15) of the Electoral Act 1997 established a permanent Constituency Commission for this purpose. It consists of a judge, the Ombudsman, the Clerk of the Dáil and of the Seanad and the Secretary of the Department of the Environment, and is charged with making a report to the Dáil with recommendations as to where boundaries are to be drawn. In making these recommendations, it is required to have regard to the following, viz. the total number of members should be between 164 and 168; each constituency shall return three, four or five members; breaching county boundaries should be avoided so far as is possible; each constituency should consist of contiguous areas; there should be regard for geographic considerations, including significant physical features and the extent of and density of population in each constituency; an endeavour should be made to maintain continuity in the arrangement of constituencies. This Commission also makes recommendations for constituency boundaries in European Parliament elections.

In *O'Donovan v. Attorney General*,[94] the constituency system that was adopted in 1959 was declared unconstitutional because it did not provide the requisite degree of equal representation. The plaintiff claimed that the system of constituencies then in operation was invalid because some of them contained a significantly higher number of people per TD than others and, additionally, because the Oireachtas had not taken sufficient account of changes in population over the previous twelve years. As regards the first of these points, the national

---

[94] [1961] I.R. 114.

average was one TD for every 20,127 persons; but there were four
constituencies in which less than 17,000 persons on average were represented
by a TD and there were three constituencies where more than 23,000 persons
on average were represented by a TD. At the extremes were Galway South
(one TD per 16,575 persons) and Dublin South West (one TD per 23,128
persons). What over-representation as existed was very much in favour of
constituencies along the western seaboard. In an elaborate judgment, which
Budd J. had been told would be appealed to the Supreme Court but in the
event was never appealed, the judge first dealt with the purpose of Article
16.2.3, which is to secure voting equality, and then with the circumstances in
which mathematical equality could be deviated from. His key conclusion was
that only considerations of administrative feasibility must be taken into account
in departing from equality. In particular, the fact that some constituencies are
a long distance from Dublin is no reason why they should be somewhat over-
represented, nor did the fact that those in some constituencies might demand
more constituency work justify giving them greater representation than those
in areas who prefer their TDs to concentrate on legislative affairs. Moreover,
county boundaries should not be virtually inviolable when drawing up
constituencies. Nor is there any special reason why the western seaboard should
be favoured over Co. Dublin with regard to Dáil representation. Budd J.
summed up his general conclusions as follows:

> "First, that the dominant principle of (Art. 16.2.3) is the achievement of
> as near an equality of the parliamentary representation of the population
> as can be attained, paying due regard to practical difficulties. Secondly,
> that there are difficulties of an administrative and statistical nature so
> plain to be seen that it may be safely assumed they, at any rate, must have
> been in the minds of those enacting the Constitution. Thirdly, that these
> difficulties are of themselves alone sufficient to explain and justify the
> qualification of the principle of equality. Fourthly, that there is no
> indication to be found in the Constitution that it was intended that any of
> the difficulties as to the working of the parliamentary system should be
> taken into consideration on the question of practicability. Fifthly, that if
> matters of the kind mentioned as to the working of the parliamentary
> system were to be taken into consideration, the result would be that the
> dominant principle of equality would be departed from so far as to be
> destroyed and the intention of the people in enacting the relevant sub-
> clause would be entirely frustrated. Finally, that this fifth conclusion
> involves rejecting, with one qualification, the contention that the
> difficulties of the operation of the parliamentary system should be
> considered in determining what is practicable. In the result, it would
> seem to me that the difficulties to which the Legislature should have
> regard are those of an administrative and statistical nature, and the
> principal question to decide will be as to whether equality of ratio of

members to population has been achieved in so far as practicable having regard to such difficulties. There is, it seems to me, only one possible qualification of this: that if it be shown that the result would involve the collapse of the parliamentary system that factor would have to be most seriously considered, having regard to the view that I have expressed that our fundamental law must be deemed to have been intended to be workable".[95]

Evidence was given that there were several ways in which constituency boundaries could be drawn so as to secure more equal representation than that obtaining under the 1959 scheme. Accordingly, this scheme was declared to be invalid.

Shortly afterwards, a new constituency system was drafted, which was submitted to the Supreme Court under the Article 26 procedure and was declared not to offend against Article 16.2.3.[96] But the court's judgment, given by Maguire C.J., is very brief and it does not contain any examination of the relevant statistics. The court agreed with Budd J. that, while mathematical parity is not required, parity should be attained "as far as that is capable of being carried into action in a practical way having regard to such practical difficulties as exist and may legitimately, having regard to the context and to the provisions of the Constitution generally, be taken into consideration."[97] Maguire C.J. did not say what these considerations are, other than to instance "well known boundaries such as those of counties, townlands and electoral divisions" and "such physical features as rivers, lakes and mountains."[98] However, the practical considerations which ought to be taken into account and the weight that should be attached to them, it was stressed, are primarily matters for the Oireachtas and should not even be reviewed by the courts unless there is a "manifest infringement" of Article 16.2.3. Accordingly, courts must not readily upset whatever scheme of constituencies the Oireachtas has adopted. Significantly, the court did not say that, in considering the practicalities in the way of achieving equality, only purely administrative difficulties must be taken into account.

Periodic Revision

In order to ensure that voters do not become over or under-represented in consequence of major shifts in population from constituency to constituency, Article 16.2.4 of the Constitution requires that constituencies be revised at

---

[95] *Id.,* at p.138. *Cf.* the *Apportionment II* case, 16 BVerfGE 130 (1963).
[96] *Electoral (Amendment) Bill, 1961, Re* [1961] I.R. 169.
[97] *Id.,* at p.183.
[98] *Ibid.*

least every twelve years; that "[t]he Oireachtas shall revise the constituencies at least once in every twelve years, with due regard to changes in distribution of the population". It was held by Budd J. in the *O'Donovan* case that this clause is mandatory and that it is "the constituencies themselves which have to be revised so as to give effect to the contemplated changes in the distribution of population."[99] The census for 1946 and for 1956 showed major shifts in population from the western counties and into Co. Dublin. Budd J. found that these shifts were hardly reflected in the constituency scheme as drawn up in 1959 and, accordingly, that scheme was also unconstitutional on these grounds.

Several questions arising from the above clause were resolved by the Supreme Court in *Electoral (Amendment) Bill, 1961, Re.*[100] Most importantly, the relevant population figures are those in the last completed census, which is the only way of ascertaining exact figures. Even if more up to date estimates are at hand, the last census must be used and it must be used even if another census has been taken in the meantime and is due to be completed shortly. While revisions must occur at least every twelve years, circumstances can arise which justify allowing a longer period to elapse. In this case it was held that the 1961 Bill, which was passed more than twelve years following the previous revision, was justified because revision had been attempted in 1959 only to be declared invalid by Budd J. in 1961. The Court did not advert to the position that would pertain where a Government did not take a census at the customary period and there are good reasons for believing that the Government's motive was to freeze the constituencies into the mould dictated by the last census. Nor did the court advert to the question of the position where a census is completed shortly after there has been a constituency revision and the new revision could not conceivably be justified under the latest census. Nor has the court been called upon to decide upon the validity of an election that has taken place under a constituency system that has since been declared unconstitutional.

Candidates

Under the Constitution, only Irish citizens are eligible to become members of the Dáil or of the Seanad, or be elected President;[101] accordingly, aliens cannot be candidates in these elections. The Constitution lays down a minimum age of 35 to be elected as President and a minimum age of 21 to be eligible for membership of the Dáil or the Seanad.[102] While the Oireachtas is permitted to declare certain categories of persons ineligible to be members of the Dáil or of

---

[99] [1961] I.R. 151.
[100] [1961] I.R. 169.
[101] Arts. 16.1.1; 18.2; 12.4.1.
[102] *Ibid.*

the Seanad, it is prohibited from excluding persons on the grounds of their sex. Moreover, all exclusionary provisions must be consistent with the Constitution's personal rights guarantees. In addition to non-nationals and persons under 21, the following categories of persons are ineligible for membership of either House of the Oireachtas,[103] *viz.* persons of unsound mind, persons serving a prison sentence of over six months in the State; undischarged bankrupts who were adjudicated bankrupt by an Irish court; members of the defence forces or of the Garda Síochána who are on full pay; permanent civil servants.

Prospective candidates must be duly nominated. Where those standing for Dáil, European Parliament or local government elections are not certified as being affiliated to a registered political party, they must be assented to by registered electors in the constituency in question.[104] The number of assenters required is 30, 60 and 15 electors, respectively, excluding the candidate and any proposer. Formerly, candidates had to deposit money with the returning officer, which sum would be returned after the election if the votes the candidate received exceeded one-third of the quota needed to get elected; otherwise the deposit was forfeited to the State. But in *Redmond v. Minister for the Environment*,[105] Herbert J. declared this system unconstitutional, as incompatible with Article 40.1's guarantee of equality.

The practice whereby candidates' names are placed on the ballot paper in alphabetical order was challenged in *O'Reilly v. Minister for the Environment*,[106] on the grounds that this system unduly favours candidates whose surnames begin with the letters A to G and correspondingly disfavours candidates with surnames beginning with the later letters of the alphabet. Statistical evidence was given supporting this contention and it was argued that it would be relatively easy to devise a system of listing candidates' names that did not produce somewhat biased outcomes, such as the "randomised alphabet" system used in California. However, Murphy J. refused to declare the rules unconstitutional because the somewhat distorted result of elections was more a result of a lack of interest in voters than of defective electoral rules and the suggested alternative rules were also deficient in certain respects. The present rules were constitutionally adequate because they provided the electorate with the essential information needed for voting; every elector was free to vote or not to vote and could vote in the order of choice for all candidates or vote only for some candidates; and the voter was free to select candidates in whatever manner he chose, even by some random procedure. There was "nothing unreasonable about legislation which has the effect of reflecting in one way or another the measure to which the electorate or some part of it is

---

[103] Electoral Act 1992, ss.41–43.
[104] Electoral (Amendment) Act 2002.
[105] [2001] 4 I.R. 61; *supra*, p.396.
[106] [1986] I.R. 143.

indifferent to the effect of the manner in which their votes are cast."[107]

Parts 5 (sections 27–45) and 6 (sections 52–62) of the Electoral Act 1997, place ceilings on the amount of expenses that may be incurred by or behalf of candidates in Dáil, Presidential and European elections. Presently in Dáil elections it is £20,000 for three seat constituencies; £25,000 for four seat constituencies and £30,000 for five seat constituencies.[108] A candidates' party may incur not more than 50% of these sums on his behalf. Election expenses incurred, not exceeding £5,000, will be reimbursed by the State under section 21 of the 1997 Act. Restrictions on election expenses that gave elected members of the Dáil a slight advantage over non-members were held by the Supreme Court in *Kelly v. Minister for the Environment*[109] to contravene Article 40.1's guarantee of equality.

REFERENDA

Referenda are governed by Articles 46 and 47 of the Constitution. Two kinds of referenda are envisaged: one on a proposal to amend the Constitution and one on any other proposal, although the latter type of referendum has never taken place.

Constitutional Amendment

In the case of proposals to amend the Constitution, Article 46.1 provides that this can be done 'by way of variation, addition or repeal ...". Proposed amendments must originate in Dáil Éireann, in the form of a Bill entitled "An Act to amend the Constitution." If the Bill passes or is deemed to have passed both Houses of the Oireachtas, Article 46.2 requires that it "be submitted by Referendum to the decision of the people in accordance with the law for the time being in force relating to the Referendum", which presently are the Referendum Acts 1994-2001. Article 47.3 stipulates that those who can vote in referenda are citizens who are entitled to vote in Dáil elections. The requisite majority for carrying the referendum is stated by Article 47.1 as "a majority of the votes cast ... in favour of its enactment into law", i.e. a simple majority. Subject to the above, "the Referendum shall be regulated by law." Once the President is satisfied that the constitutional and other legal requirements for carrying the referendum have been satisfied, he is required by Article 46.5 to sign the Bill and promulgate it as law.

---

[107] *Id.* at p.163.
[108] S.30, amended by s.50(1) of the Electoral (Amendment) Act 2001.
[109] [2002] 4 I.R. 191, *supra* p.396; resulting in the Electoral (Amendment) Act 2002.

As a result of the *McKenna* case,[110] where it was held to be unconstitutional for the Government to spend money in support of one side in a referendum on a proposed amendment (almost invariably the "yes" side), a Referendum Commission was established in 1998; its functions were altered in 2001.[111]

Procedure

How referenda are to be conducted is regulated by Part II (sections 10-32) of the Referendum Act 1994, and how the votes are to be counted is governed by Part III (sections 33-41) of this Act. It is for the Minister to determine when the referendum will be taken and it is conducted in the same constituencies and polling districts as are Dáil elections, with the same rules for postal voting and "special voters." The form of ballot papers is set out in the 1994 Act's 2nd schedule, which the voter must mark "X" against either yes or no. In *Sherwin v. Minister for the Environment*,[112] Costello J. held that the manner in which the Minister permitted the count in the 1995 divorce referendum to be conducted was unlawful. This was because all the main political parties supported a yes vote but, because appointment of scrutineers was based on Dáil election practice, practically all of the scrutineers were representative of the "yes" interest and very few of them of the "no" interest.

Once the final result of the count is in, the returning officer must issue a provisional referendum certificate, stating the outcome of the poll. If the outcome is not successfully challenged by way of a referendum petition, it becomes final and conclusive.

Challenges

According to section 42(1) of the 1994 Act, the outcome of a referendum "may, and may only, be questioned by a petition to the High Court (a 'referendum petition')" in accordance with Part IV (sections 42–58) of that Act. The basis for bringing such a challenge is set out in section 43(1) as:

"(a) the commission of an [election] offence ...,
(b) obstruction of or interference with or other hindrance to the conduct of the referendum,
(c) failure to complete or otherwise conduct the referendum in accordance with this Act, or
(d) mistake or other irregularity in the conduct of the referendum or in the particulars stated in the provisional referendum certificate."

---

[110] *McKenna v. An Taoiseach (No. 2)* [1995] 2 I.R. 1; *supra*, p.394.
[111] Referendum Acts 1998 and 2001.
[112] Unreported, High Court, Costello J, March 11, 1998.

At the hearing of the petition, the High Court of its own motion may call witnesses, in addition to those called by the opposing sides.[113] Witnesses cannot rely on the privilege against self-incrimination as regards election offences but the court may certify that such answers as they give shall not be used in any criminal proceedings against them, other than for perjury.[114] The court may require that the referendum shall be taken again in any constituency;[115] whether it can require the referendum to be entirely re-run across the State is debatable. But a retaking will not be ordered where the referendum was conducted "in accordance with the general principles laid down in [the 1994] Act and that the non-compliance or error did not affect the result of the referendum as a whole."

The outcome of the divorce referendum in 1995 was challenged in this manner in *Hanafin v. Minister for the Environment*,[116] principally on the grounds that it had been established earlier in the *McKenna* case that the Government had unconstitutionally assisted the "yes" side in that poll, by spending public money on advocating a "yes" vote. Three principal questions arose. First, did section 43(1) of the 1994 Act apply at all to such actions? If the answer were no, Hamilton C.J. pointed out that "this meant that the Oireachtas intended that a constitutional wrongdoing committed by the Government, or any other party, during the course of the campaign and proved to have materially affected the result of the referendum could not be considered by the High Court on the hearing of a referendum petition, which was the only way it could be questioned .... If such was the intention of the Oireachtas, it would have failed in its obligation to respect, and so far as practicable, to defend and vindicate the democratic process ... and the constitutional rights of the citizens."[117] Accordingly, the sub-section had to be given a generous interpretation.

There remained then questions of fact. It was held that the Government-funded advertising campaign for a "yes" vote was an interference with the conduct of the referendum. Although the advertising in itself was not an interference, what made the difference here was that it had been intentionally funded by the State, contrary to its constitutional obligations. Finally, there was the critical question of whether the outcome of the referendum as a whole had been materially affected by that advertising. Those who voted for the proposal were 818,842 and 809,728 voted against. The onus of proof was on the petitioner, which he endeavoured to discharge, *inter alia*, with evidence from professional pollsters. His main difficulty was that voting was secret and it was near impossible to demonstrate that a sufficient number would have

---

[113] S.52(1).
[114] S.52(2).
[115] S.48.
[116] [1996] 2 I.R. 321.
[117] *Id.* at p.424.

voted against the proposal but for the advertising. Blayney J. attached significance to the fact that, once it had been held to be unlawful in the *McKenna* judgment, just a week prior to the poll being taken, the State-funded advertising abruptly ceased; had it continued, that judge might have taken a different view on the question. Further, as O'Flaherty J. pointed out, the court is "bound ... to preserve a proportion between the wrong committed, its possible effect and the remedy proposed to right the wrong – A fresh referendum would have to be held where there would be a different electorate; new voters would have come on the scene and others would have departed for one reason or another. Those who had constituted the *de facto* majority in the void referendum would complain that their rights had not been properly respected. So the setting aside of a referendum must be regarded as an awesome undertaking."[118] It was held by a Divisional Court that the petitioner had not proved that the outcome had been materially affected and the Supreme Court concluded that, on the evidence adduced, it had been entitled to reach that conclusion.

Sherwin v. Minister for the Environment,[119] where a feature of how the count in the divorce referendum was scrutinised was held to be unlawful, was not an election petition. Nor was *Coughlan v. Broadcasting Complaints Commission*,[120] where it was held that the "no" side of the argument in this referendum had been unfairly discriminated against in RTÉ's broadcast coverage of the referendum campaign. If the issues that had been canvassed in these cases had been part of the evidence adduced in *Hanafin*, perhaps his petition would have succeeded. In neither of these cases did the plaintiffs seek to upset the outcome of the referendum but only to demonstrate that some of the procedures under which it was carried out were deficient.

The outcome of a referendum has never been abrogated by the courts: all challenges made to date by way of the petition procedure were unsuccessful, as was a scatter-gun attack by an inveterate lay litigant to both the Act that authorised the 15th Amendment and the legislation that followed it in 1996 providing for divorce.[121] Barrington J. summed up the governing principle as "(t)he role of the President and the courts is simply to ensure that the proposal is properly placed before the people in accordance with the procedure set out in Article 46 and that the referendum is properly conducted as provided by law. They have no function in relation to the content of the proposed referendum. That is a matter for the people. There can be no question of a constitutional amendment properly placed before the people and approved by them being itself unconstitutional."[122]

---

[118] *Id.* at p.438.
[119] Unreported, High Court, Costello P., May 16, 2002.
[120] [2000] 3 I.R. 1; *supra*, p.586.
[121] *Riordan v. An Taoiseach (No.1)* [1999] 4 I.R. 321.
[122] *Id.* at p.335.

An indirect challenge to the outcome of the Fourteenth Amendment of 1992 was made in *Re Regulation of Information (Services Outside the State for Termination of Pregnancies) Bill, 1995*,[123] where the Bill for regulating abortion-related information was referred to the Supreme Court by the President under Article 26. It was contended that, notwithstanding this amendment, the Bill's provisions contravened natural law and accordingly were unconstitutional; further that this amendment "was inconsistent with the terms of the Eighth Amendment – which acknowledged the right to life of the unborn" because "natural law is the foundation on which the Constitution was built and ranks superior to the Constitution."[124] Had this argument been made before the amendment was passed three years earlier, it might at least have carried some weight, although is most unlikely to have succeeded. It was rejected because the Constitution as amended is "the fundamental law of the State to which the organs of the State [are] subject and the provisions of the natural law [are not] superior to the Constitution."[125]

An endeavour very late in the day in *Slattery v. An Taoiseach*[126] to block the referendum on the Treaty on European Union ("Maastricht"), on the grounds that insufficient explanatory material had been distributed to the public and clarification was required on that Treaty's effect on abortion, was rejected. Hederman J. in the Supreme Court endorsed the proposition that there was no constitutional obligation on the Government to provide funds to persons opposing those proposed changes. But it was not contended there that it was unconstitutional for the Government to finance a "yes" campaign and provide no funds for a "no" campaign – a proposition subsequently upheld in the *McKenna* case.[127] It probably is entirely academic to ask whether a referendum would be prohibited if indeed the Government funded only the "yes" campaign or whether the remedy is the post-referendum petition procedure under the Referendum Act 1994.

The actual procedure for giving effect to the proposed amendment was first put in issue in *Riordan v. An Taoiseach (No. 2)*,[128] concerning the then envisaged Nineteenth Amendment to give effect to provisions in the Belfast Agreement of 1998. Under the proposal, once passed in a referendum this amendment would not take effect automatically; its becoming operative was contingent on certain steps being taken by the UK Government with reference to Northern Ireland and those being confirmed by way of a Government declaration. Kelly J. held that it was permissible to have a contingent amendment, which view was upheld by the Supreme Court some months after

---

[123] [1995] 1 I.R. 1.

[124] *Id.* at p.37.

[125] *Id.* at p.43.

[126] [1993] 1 I.R. 286.

[127] *McKenna v. An Taoiseach (No.2)* [1995] 2 I.R. 10.

[128] [1999] 4 I.R. 343.

the referendum had taken place with an overwhelming vote in favour of the proposal. As explained by Barrington J., because "[t]he people have a sovereign right to grant or withhold approval to an amendment –, [t]here is no reason therefore why they should not, provided the matter is properly placed before them, give their approval subject to a condition."[129] This was not really a case of the people delegating to the Government authority to amend the Constitution. Rather, "[t]he people have consented to an amendment – subject to the happening of a particular future event",[130] being the Government's declaration as therein provided.

Barrington J. acknowledged in the *Finn* case[131] that there might be an exception to the principle that the courts will not entertain challenges against proposed constitutional amendments. This arises where the Bill contains not alone the proposed amendment but also some other proposal, because Article 46.4 stipulates that the Bill "shall not contain any other proposal"; although the judge observed that it was "extremely unlikely that the Houses of the Oireachtas would abuse their powers by attempting to incorporate some other proposal with a proposal to amend the Constitution."[132] On appeal, however, the Supreme Court implicitly rejected judicial review in those circumstances. According to O'Higgins C.J., for the court, the jurisdiction to "review legislation on the grounds of constitutionality is confined to enacted laws" and, except where the Article 26 procedure applies, "there is no jurisdiction to construe or to review the constitutionality of a Bill, whatever its nature."[133]

From a purely procedural perspective, the proposed but rejected Twenty-Fifth Amendment to the Constitution in 2002 concerning abortion[134] was the most radical of all such measures, in at least three respects. It took the form of an amendment to Article 46 itself, which is the amending machinery, and purported to disapply that Article's provisions. In addition to the proposed constitutional changes, the Bill providing for the amendment contained in a schedule the text of a Bill that would later be put before both Houses of the Oireachtas and, if enacted into law, could be made operative by an order of the Taoiseach. And if so passed, this Act would have constitutional status, albeit not embodied in the text of the Constitution. Prior to the referendum taking place, the Bill was subject to an unsuccessful challenge in the High Court.

It was argued in *Morris v. Minister for the Environment*,[135] that Article 46 did not permit the adoption of norms having constitutional status but which are not contained in the very text of the Constitution. This, it was said, was

---

[129] *Id.* at p.354.
[130] *Ibid.*
[131] *Finn v. Attorney General* [1983] I.R. 154.
[132] *Id.* at p.161.
[133] *Id.* at p.164.
[134] Twenty Fifth Amendment of the Constitution (Protection of Human Life in Pregnancy) Bill 2001.
[135] [2002] 1 I.R. 326.

because the reference in subs. (i) to amendments by way of "variation [or] addition" could not reasonably be construed as meaning supplementing the Constitution's text with some other text or texts; an analogy was a constitutional Jupiter, which might have one or more constitutional moons revolving around it. Articles 51 and 52 of the Constitution (the transitional provisions) expressly authorised the deletion of certain constitutional provisions from the text and, it was said, if it had been intended that norms having constitutional status could exist entirely apart from that text, a system without any precedent, express provision to that effect would have been made and that free-standing extra-textual constitutional norms were a recipe for confusion and possible constitutional chaos. However, Kelly J. held that the words "variation [or] addition" could embrace free-standing constitutional norms of this nature. This was because the Constitution did "not contain any express prohibition on an amendment in the form in which it (was) proposed here. Neither does it contain any mandatory obligation to the effect that an amendment must be contained in its entirety in the body or text of the Constitution itself."[136] Additionally, he said that previous amendments had been made "by reference to a document or documents which will not be incorporated into the text of the Constitution",[137] instancing the amendments to join the European Communities and for the Belfast Agreement. However, neither of these purported to give constitutional status to the documents in question. All that the 1972 Amendment did was to disapply the Constitution whenever it came into conflict with the EC Treaties or measures adopted under them. And the 1998 Amendment incorporated provisions of the Belfast agreement into the text of the Constitution itself, the only extraneous matter being the question of implementation of that amendment; it could not take effect until certain acts had been done with reference to that Agreement. In the absence of an express prohibition on extra-textual constitutional norms, the judge declined to imply one, "thereby interfering in the legislative process in its most solemn form which will involve the expression of the will of the people."[138] He described the method of amendment being adopted here as "a clever drafting device."[139]

The next point made by the plaintiffs there was that the second schedule to the amending Bill contained the text of a proposal for an Act of the Oireachtas, which contravened Article 46.4's prohibition against that Bill containing "any other proposal"; that the plain literal meaning of this was that no other proposal of any kind should be contained in the Bill, be it a proposed treaty, charter, deed of trust or proposals for legislation. However, Kelly J. held that, in the context, these words should be construed as meaning proposed legislation which, when the Bill is passed, would have "bite" as constituting binding law.

---

[136] *Id.* at p.337.
[137] *Ibid.*
[138] *Id.* at p.339.
[139] *Ibid.*

The envisaged legislation set out in the Bill's schedule II did not fit this description because, even were the referendum to be carried, the Bill would have no force of law until another Bill in identical terms was passed by the Oireachtas, signed by the President and put into effect by order of the Taoiseach. According to Kelly J., Schedule II's text had:

> "*no* legislative effect as a result of its being included in the Second Schedule. The Bill does not propose that the text of the Second Schedule should have legal effect. If the referendum proposal is carried and the Bill is signed into law by the President it will only give effect to the constitutional amendment set out in the First Schedule to the Bill. It does not in any way give constitutional or legal effect to matter contained in the Second Schedule. That will occur if and only if the national parliament passes such a measure into law. There is no guarantee that that will happen. Regardless of the size of the majority achieved in the referendum (if such occurs) there is no legal obligation on parliament to pass the legislation contained in the Second Schedule to the Bill. The Second Schedule merely puts before the People the text of an Act which it is envisaged may, if the referendum is carried, be subsequently passed into law.
>
> The terms of the Second Schedule to the Bill require an entirely separate and distinct decision by the national parliament to enact a law in accordance with those terms before it can have legal effect. The Second Schedule to the Bill is not in my view a "proposal" in the sense in which that term is to be understood where it is contained in Article 46.4 –
>
> In the present case whilst certain parts of the amendment take effect immediately (and that is not contested) the principal and substantial one namely the matter which is dealt with in the Second Schedule to the Bill cannot and does not have any legal effect unless and until it is passed into law in the ordinary way by the Oireachtas.
>
> In other words in this case the People are being asked to adopt a constitutional amendment the principal effect of which will not "bite", to use the Applicants' word until such time as the Act set out in the Second Schedule is independently passed into law on a date subsequent to the referendum. The amendment proposed therefore is one which is substantially subject to a condition subsequent which may or may not be met. Until such time as it is met the material set out in the Second Schedule to the Bill is of no legal effect."[140]

The third argument was that it is not permissible to simultaneously amend the Constitution's amending mechanism and introduce substantive amendments

---

[140] *Id.* at pp.342 and 344.

too; that such a state of affairs requires at least two steps, *viz.* first amend Article 46 and then pass a substantive amendment in the manner allowed by the altered Article 46. If simultaneous amendments to Article 46 and to any other Article were permissible, then one could amend the Constitution without having any referendum as follows, *viz.* by the amending Bill purporting to amend Article 46, by disapplying any provision of that Article which is not compatible (*e.g.* Article 46.2) and setting out the proposed substantive change. Because, however, the proposals here were found not to conflict with the requirements of Article 46.1 ("variation [or] addition") or 4 ("no other proposal"), Kelly J. held that it was not necessary to deal with the third proposition. Although the draftsman designed the proposed changes here as an amendment to Article 46 itself and they commenced with the words "[n]otwithstanding the foregoing provision of this Article", on Kelly J.'s logic all of this was entirely unnecessary; the proposals did not involve any alteration to or deviation from the machinery contained in Article 46. They were a "clever", albeit partly otiose, drafting device.[141]

Other Referenda

Article 27 of the Constitution contains a procedure whereby a Bill, other than a proposed constitutional amendment, may be submitted by the President to the people for what may be described as a consultative referendum, because it "contains a proposal of such national importance that the will of the people thereon ought to be ascertained." All that Article 47.2 of the Constitution states about this referendum process is that the electorate are citizens entitled to vote in Dáil elections; that the contents of the Bill are deemed to be approved unless rejected by a majority of the votes cast, provided that those votes constitute at least one third of the entire electorate; that otherwise the referendum "shall be regulated by law," presently in the Referendum Acts 1994–2001.

Article 47.2 of the Constitution also envisages a referendum on any other proposal of any kind. It has the same requirement about the electorate and when the proposal is deemed to have passed. Otherwise, the procedure is governed by the Referendum Acts 1994–2001.

Non-Extradition and Asylum

Refusal to extradite persons wanted for political offences and granting asylum to political refugees are closely related. Whether genuine fugitives from extreme

---

[141] The plaintiffs there contended that these were too clever by half.

political oppression abroad have a constitutional right not to be sent back there is debatable. An Irish national cannot be deported to another country but may be extradited if wanted there to be tried for an alleged offence or to serve a sentence imposed on him by a court there.

Since the middle of the 19th century the practice grew of states, when concluding extradition treaties either bilateral or multilateral, excluding "political offences" from the obligation to extradite. Until comparatively recently, what was or was not a political offence was not defined and was left to the courts to work out on a case by case basis.[142] With the rise in politically motivated violence and terrorism in the 1970's, steps were taken to narrow the ambit of this exception by courts and by legislatures in many countries, and also by states concluding multilateral conventions on the question of aircraft hijacking and related acts and terrorism generally. When at an early stage the question was mooted of narrowing the political offence exception in the Extradition Act 1965, particularly in the light of the conflict that had broken out in Northern Ireland, the Irish judges (Walsh J. and Henchy J.) and counsel (Doyle SC and Quigley BL) who wrote chapter VIII of the *Law Enforcement Commission Report* in 1973, concluded "there is overwhelming evidence to support the view that both by international custom, as evidenced by the general practice accepted as law, and by international conventions, both general and particular, it is a generally recognised principle of international law that extradition is not granted for political offences."[143] Their advice was that any law that purported to repeal the traditional political offence exception would not be consistent with this principle and would conflict with Article 29.2 of the Constitution.

In the intervening years, however, the international practice with regard to this exception has altered radically and a wide category of politically motivated crimes has been rendered extraditable. Among the offences that are no longer deemed to be "political" for the purpose of extradition to numerous countries are[144] murder, manslaughter, kidnapping, false imprisonment, assault occasioning bodily harm and several other offences against the person; robbery and aggravated burglary, criminal damage, numerous offences involving explosives and firearms, hijacking civil aircraft and other related offences, offences against internationally protected persons. Exclusion of these and other offences from the "political" category followed Ireland's ratification of the European Convention on the Suppression of Terrorism[145] and other multilateral conventions on these topics.

---

[142] See generally, M. Forde, *Extradition Law* (2nd ed., 1995), Chap.5.

[143] Pol.3832, para.50 (p.31).

[144] Extradition (Amendment) Act 1987, 1st schedule; *cf. Quinlivan v. Conroy (No.2)* [2000] 3 I.R. 154.

[145] January 27, 1977, 1137 UNTS 93.

Asylum is governed by the Refugee Act 1996, which gives effect to the Geneva Convention on the Status of Refugees, of 1951,[146] and the New York Protocol of 1967;[147] before 1996, these international agreements were implemented in an *ad hoc* manner. A "refugee" is defined in section 2 of this Act as one who "owing to a well founded fear of being persecuted for reasons of race, religion, nationality, membership of a particular social group or political opinion, is outside the country of his or her nationality and is unable or, owing to such fear, is unwilling to avail – of the protection of that country"; it also covers certain persons who do not have any nationality. Further, deportation is not permitted where the person would be threatened on account of his "race, religion, nationality, and membership of a particular social group or political opinion." There is neither a definition nor an indication of what constitutes a political opinion for this purpose. In determining what comes within this protected category of person, it is most likely that account would be taken of the case law and definitions used for the purpose of extradition.[148]

---

[146] July 28, 1952, 189 UNTS 137. See generally, G. Goodwin-Gill, *The Refugee in International Law* (2nd ed., 1996).

[147] Of January 31, 1967, 606 UNTS 267.

[148] *E.g. T. v. Secretary of State* [1996] A.C. 742 and *Adan v. Secretary of State* [1999] 1 A.C. 293.

CHAPTER 22

Religion

Religious freedom is proclaimed in virtually every national Bill of Rights and general international human rights instrument,[1] although the precise content of protected religious activity varies considerably. For centuries guarantees against discrimination on religious grounds have been inserted into peace arrangements concluded after years of military conflict, such as Henry IV's famous Edict of Nantes, 1598, following the religious wars of the sixteenth century; in the Treaty of Westphalia, 1648, concluded after the Thirty Years' War; in the treaty with Poland signed at Versailles in 1919 and in the post-World War II treaties between the Allied Powers and Italy, Finland, Bulgaria, Hungary and Romania in 1947. Religious tests for public office and the establishment of a religion are prohibited by the U.S. Constitution, which also guarantees the free exercise of religion.[2] Non-interference on account of ones religious opinion is proclaimed in the 1789 Declaration of the Rights of Man and of the Citizen.[3] One of the few individual rights guarantees in the Australian Constitution of 1900 is that the federal Government will not "make any law for establishing any religion, or for imposing any religious observance, ... and no religious test shall be required as a qualification for any office or public trust under the Commonwealth."[4] A somewhat complex set of provisions on religious freedom and Church-State relations, in Articles 136–141 of the 1919 Constitution of Weimar Germany, were carried forward into the present German Constitution.[5]

Article 44 of the Constitution is headed "Religion" and provides as follows:

> "1.   The State acknowledges that the homage of public worship is due to Almighty God. It shall hold His Name in reverence, and shall respect and honour religion.
>
> 2.1°   Freedom of conscience and the free profession and practice of religion are, subject to public order and morality, guaranteed to every citizen.

---

[1]   See generally, M. McDougal et al., *Human Rights and World Public Order* (1980), Chap.11 and Franck, "Is Personal Freedom A Western Value", 91 *Am. J. Int'l L.* 593 (1997).

[2]   Art.VI(3) and 1st Amendment.

[3]   Art.X.

[4]   Art.116.

[5]   Art.140.

2° The State guarantees not to endow any religion.

3° The State shall not impose any disabilities or make any discrimination on the ground of religious profession, belief or status.

4° Legislation providing State aid for schools shall not discriminate
between schools under the management of different religious
denominations, nor be such as to affect prejudicially the right of
any child to attend a school receiving public money without
attending religious instruction at that school.

5° Every religious denomination shall have the right to manage its
own affairs, own, acquire and administer property, movable and
immovable, and maintain institutions for religious or charitable
purposes.

6° The property of any religious denomination or any educational
institution shall not be diverted save for necessary works of public
utility and on payment of compensation."

Religious freedom is guaranteed by Article 9 of the European Convention[6]
and by Article 18 of the UN Covenant; additionally, both of these condemn
discrimination on the ground of religion.

Religious references are also contained in other parts of the Constitution,
notably in the Preamble where "the Most Holy Trinity" and "our Divine Lord,
Jesus Christ" are invoked as the source of all authority and to whom the "people
of Ireland" have obligations. References in Article 44 to several designated
religious denominations and to the "special position" of the Catholic Church
were removed in 1972.[7] The declarations that must be made by the President
and also by judges when assuming office, commence with the words "in the
presence of Almighty God" and conclude with the request, "may God direct
and sustain me."[8]

When the Constitution was enacted in 1937 the State's population was
overwhelmingly and actively Catholic and, until comparatively recently, many
aspects of public administration had a decidedly Catholic ethos. Even at the
time of writing, a substantial majority of the population are Catholic although
religious observance is rapidly falling off, especially among young people. To
an extent defeats in several referenda on issues in respect of which the Catholic
Church had strong views, most notably divorce and abortion, were perceived
by many as reflecting the extent of support for Church influence in public
affairs.[9] Except for the rapidly diminishing Jewish community, until recently

---

[6] See generally, C. Evans, *Freedom of Religion Under the European Convention on Human
Rights* (2001).

[7] *Infra*, p.617.

[8] Arts.12.8 and 34.5.1. A similar requirement was held to contravene the European
Convention on Human Rights: *Buscarini v. San Marino*, 30 E.H.R.R. 208 (1999).

[9] See generally, L. Fuller, *Irish Catholicism Since 1950, The Undoing of a Culture* (2002),
Epilogue.

there have been very few members of non-Christian religions who were citizens or permanent residents of the State. But that changed considerably in the 1990s with the influx of persons with Islamic and other backgrounds. So far, however, the more heterodox religious make-up of the Irish has not given rise to major constitutional difficulties.

RELIGION

Neither the Constitution, the European Convention nor the UN Covenant define what is a religion, for the purpose of their provisions, and neither the Irish courts nor the Strasbourg tribunal have laid down criteria for determining what is religion. A religious belief is a particular way of viewing ones fundamental orientation toward the world; it is how persons define themselves in relation to others and to the cosmos. That belief may be theological, in that it refers to a personalised transempirical source of an unchallengeable message. Or it may be metaphysical, in that it is grounded on non-personalised transempirical conceptions. There are some beliefs that at least their adherents consider to be religious that are founded on varying conceptions of science or of fundamental humanity. Before the modern ideological "isms" took root (*e.g.* nationalism, liberalism, republicanism, capitalism, communism), it was predominantly through religion that individuals understood where they were in the world and what purpose they served in it.

Among the institutions and denominations whose tenets undoubtedly would be regarded as religious are the Catholic Church, the Church of Ireland, the Presbyterian Church in Ireland, the Methodist Church in Ireland, the Religious Society of Friends (Quakers) in Ireland and the Jewish Congregation. These denominations were accorded formal recognition in Article 44.1.2-3 but that clause was removed from the Constitution in 1972. That clause also referred to "other religious denominations existing in Ireland at the date of the coming into operation of this Constitution." There are some statutory references to particular religions, notably section 12(3) of the Adoption Act 1952, which refers to the above-mentioned religions and also to the Baptist Union of Ireland, the Plymouth Brethren and the Salvation Army.[10] Beliefs that are almost universally recognised as religious, such as Hinduism, Buddhism and Islam undoubtedly would also fall within the constitutional protection.

It is mainly the relatively new sets of beliefs and institutions that often tend to be labelled as cults, such as the "Moonies" and the "Hare Krishna," that give rise to difficulty. A considerable body of case law exists in some countries on the question of what is a religion. Many of these cases deal with whether a particular organisation is entitled to a tax exemption that the legislature accords

---

[10] As amended by Adoption Act 1964, s.6.

to religious bodies[11] or whether an organisation is a charity because it is religious,[12] or whether an individual's conscientious objection to compulsory military service has a religious inspiration.[13] A group that has generated extensive litigation on these questions in several countries is the organisation known as the Church of Scientology, or some times as the Church of New Faith. In a case involving the discovery of documents, Geoghegan J. questioned whether this body is indeed a religion, rejecting the view that the question could be decided on the basis of cases concerning tax exemptions.[14]

NON-ESTABLISHMENT OR ENDOWMENT

Some national constitutions provide for a degree of State endorsement of a particular religion. These vary from, for example, Iran (which makes one school of Islam the State's "official religion"),[15] to Greece (which proclaims the Greek Orthodox Church to be the "dominant religion"),[16] to Ireland between 1937 and 1972, during when "(t)he State recognise[d] the special position of the Holy Catholic Apostolic and Roman Church as the guardian of the Faith professed by the great majority of the citizens."[17]

Establishing

In contrast, several national constitutions prohibit the existence of a "State church," or its near equivalent, the "establishment" of any church. An established church is one that has a formal favoured niche in the state apparatus. For example, since … the Church of England has been the established church in England, and in its canon A7, it proclaims that "(w)e acknowledge that the Queen …, acting according to the laws of the realm, is the highest power under God in this kingdom, and has supreme authority over all persons in all causes, as well ecclesiastical as civil." Presumably it was because the Toleration Act 1689[18] secured religious toleration only for Protestants of all sorts that religious freedom does not feature in Blackstone's 1765 catalogue of the "absolute rights of individuals."[19] Under the Act of Union of 1800,[20] the

---

[11] *E.g., Church of New Faith v. Commissioner of Pay Roll Tax*, 154 C.L.R. 120 (1983).
[12] *E.g., Re South Place Ethical Soc.* [1980] 1 W.L.R. 1565.
[13] *E.g., Welch v. United States*, 398 U.S. 333 (1970).
[14] *Johnson v. Church of Scientology* [2001] 1 I.R. 682.
[15] Art.12 of the Constitution of Iran.
[16] Art.3 of the Constitution of Greece.
[17] Art.44.1.23.
[18] 1 W. & M. ch.18.
[19] But ch.11 of his *Commentaries on the Laws of England* (1689), Vol.1 deals with the status of "the clergy", meaning "all persons in holy orders and in eccliastical officers" in

Church of Ireland, which was the Protestant minority's principal church, became the established church for this country but disestablishment was brought about by the Irish Church Act 1869.[21] In view of the Constitution's general proclamation of religious liberty, it is unlikely that the Oireachtas could establish one or more churches; such action would also seem to contravene the separate guarantee against religious discrimination.

Endowing

Although the Constitution permits and to some extent requires the State to adopt measures to facilitate religious practice, Article 44.2.2 draws a line at endowing religion: "(t)he State guarantees not to endow any religion." Endowment in this context is said to mean "the selection of a favoured State religion for which permanent financial provision is made out of taxation or otherwise,"[22] for instance the payment of tithes, which was compulsory for all until the Church of Ireland was disestablished in 1869. This quite restrictive definition of the term would seem to resolve the question posed by Henchy J. In *McGrath v. Maynooth College*,[23] the circumstances of which are dealt with below. It was argued that the public funding for Maynooth College, which was primarily a Catholic seminary, was a proscribed endowment. Only Kenny J. dealt with this point and then very briefly, concluding that the above clause was not contravened on the grounds that Maynooth was not exclusively a seminary. However, the matter was not considered in any depth and indeed was not particularly relevant to the issues in that case. As Henchy J. observed, "(w)hether it is constitutionally permissible for the College, while remaining essentially the seminary of a particular religion, to be financed as it is by the State, and whether in any event its statutes need to be revised to meet its changing academic status and composition, are questions that lie outside the scope of this litigation."[24]

Apart from the question of State funding for denominational schools, there is no judicial guidance as to the circumstances in which providing financial assistance for religious practices and institutions amounts to an unauthorised endowment of religion. State accommodation of religion in various ways, such as endorsing religious teachings or symbols, or exempting religious practices or bodies from the general laws – for instance granting tax exemptions – would

---

the Church of England. At law, the clergy of any other religious denomination constituted part of "the laity."

[20] 40 Geo. 3, c.67 (1800), s.5.

[21] 32 & 33 Vic. c.42; *cf. Le Fanu v. Richardson* [1914] 1 I.R. 321 and *State (Colquhoun) v. D'Arcy* [1936] I.R. 641 on the Church of Ireland.

[22] *Employment Equality Bill, 1996, Re* [1997] 2 I.R. 321 at p.354.

[23] [1979] I.L.R.M. 166.

[24] *Id.* at p.195.

not seem to constitute a prohibited endowment of them. But where that assistance or support is given to only one or a handful of religions, it most likely would fall foul of the separate guarantee against religious discrimination.

Financial Support for Schools

A question that has generated extensive political and constitutional controversy in many countries is the provision of financial support for schools that are owned or managed by religious denominations. In the United States direct public financial assistance for religious education is regarded as a contravention of the non-establishment guarantee. But Article 44.2.4 of the Constitution by its very terms permits the State to provide funds for schools in which there is a significant religious element. Any such funding is subject to three conditions, however. Firstly, there shall be no "discrimination between" schools managed by different religious denominations: that is to say, Catholic schools shall not be preferred over Protestant schools or vice versa, or over schools run by other denominations. Questions that have not yet called for resolution include the meaning of being managed by a religious denomination and what precisely amounts to discriminatory treatment for these purposes. Secondly, the public funding should not be administered in such a way as to prejudice children attending the schools in question but who do not receive religious instruction there. In other words, if the school chooses to admit some children who do not get religious instruction, the conditions under which public funds are granted should not be such as to diminish the rights of those children *vis-à-vis* the school. Thirdly, the funding must not be such as to amount to endowing a religion. In fact, this clause speaks of State "aid" (*cúnamh*) and not merely of funding.

The system whereby chaplains in community schools are paid by the State was upheld in *Campaign to Separate Church and State v. Minister for Education*,[25] as not constituting the endowment of a religion. This system is an endeavour to accommodate intrinsically non-denominational schools with parents' desire that their children obtain some religious "instruction" at those schools, which do not provide religious "education." The plaintiff appears to have accepted that paying the salaries of teachers of religion in these schools was constitutionally non-objectionable but he drew the line there. Chaplains, it was contended, are radically different because their function is predominantly connected with religious worship rather than teaching. For instance, under guidelines published, Catholic chaplains are required, *inter alia*, to say mass twice a term, to arrange for the sacrament of penance to be available to students and to arrange for a retreat for each class at least once a year. Costello J. summed up the evidence adduced as establishing that "the role of catholic

---

[25] [1998] 3 I.R. 321.

chaplains and protestant chaplains is regarded by pupils, parents of pupils and the other staff in the school as a most important one and their help and counsel is constantly sought and given to young people in need of assistance not just in spiritual matters but in one or other of the many moral, social, educational, personal or family problems on which young people may need assistance, guidance and counselling."[26] In other words, outside of formal religious services, chaplains provide guidance on these several matters in line with their own and those students' religious ethos.

This was found by the Supreme Court not to contravene Article 42.2.2, partly on account of the definition adopted for the word "endow"; which was held to mean, "the vesting of property or income in a religion *as such* in perpetual or quasi-perpetual form."[27] Keane J. expressed the view that the concurrent endowment of several religions, in this manner, most likely would be unconstitutional too. But the arrangements being challenged here went no way as far as this. Additionally, they were held to be consistent with Article 42.4, under which, *inter alia*, the State is permitted to "provide other (i.e. other than primary) educational facilities or institutions with due regard, however, for the rights of parents, especially in the matter of religious and moral formation." Chaplains, it was held, contribute significantly to shaping pupils' "religious and moral" sense, which is expressly permitted provided there is no discrimination as between religions. Further, because a major feature of Irish education in the past was the involvement of religious denominations and orders, where many of the teachers were also priests, it was inconceivable that in 1937 the non-endowment guarantee was intended to put an end to some degree of State funding for a religious element in education.

Free Profession and Practice

According to the Treaty of Limerick of 1691,[28] which marked the end of the Jacobite War in Ireland, "[t]he Roman Catholics of this Kingdom shall enjoy such Privileges in the Exercise of their Religion as are consistent with the Laws of Ireland; or as they did enjoy in the Reign of Charles II; And their Majesties, as soon as their Affairs will permit them to Summon a Parliament in this Kingdom, will endeavour to procure the said Roman Catholics such farther Security in that particular, as may preserve them from any Disturbance, upon the Account of their said Religion."[29] However, the pre-Union Irish

---

[26] *Id.* at p.334.

[27] *Id.* at p.365.

[28] Full text reproduced in J. G. Simms, *The Treaty of Limerick* (1961) Ir. Hist. Ser. no. 2, pp. 19-29. *Cf.* Act for the Confirmation of Articles, Made at the Surrender of the City of Limerick, 9 Will. III, 1697.

[29] Art.1 of the Civil Articles.

Parliament prevented effect being given to this undertaking and went to the other extreme of enacting what became known as the Penal Laws, which placed Catholics and other dissenters under considerable legal disabilities.[30] It presumably was with those laws especially in mind that Article 44.3.3 prohibits the State from "impos[ing] any disabilities" on one or more particular religions.

Article 44.2.1's guarantee of the "free profession and practice of religion" goes further than this or than the US First Amendment's condemnation of laws "prohibiting the free exercise" of religion, in that it is couched in affirmative terms. The precise ambit of this Article has been the subject of very little judicial exposition, other than that it forms a justification for putting certain exemptions into laws that facilitate the practice of a particular religion. Tax exemptions enjoyed by religious bodies and institutions, on the basis that they are pursuing charitable objects, may be justifiable on this basis. A person will not be extradited to the UK where there are substantial grounds for believing that the warrant was obtained in order to prosecute or punish him on account of his religion;[31] there is no equivalent stipulation for extradition to other countries. A person with a "well founded fear of being persecuted [for] his religion" in his own country is entitled to refuge status.[32]

Several activities that are protected by Article 44.2.1 also come within the more general guarantees of free expression, assembly and association. Thus in *Murphy v. Independent Radio and Television Commission*,[33] concerning the ban on broadcasting religious advertisements, much of the discussion focused on the guarantee of freedom of expression and the implied guarantee of freedom to communicate information. However, religious opinion, expression and association have always been regarded as something special, perhaps because religious beliefs preceded the various political ideologies to which persons attach themselves in more recent times. Also, religion generally has a significant transempirical element that places it on a radically different plane.

A difference exists between laws designed to prohibit or to inhibit religious practices of one kind or another and laws of general application that have the effect of obstructing those practices. Laws that intentionally target a religious practice require far more justification than laws that indirectly interfere with them. It would be rare, however, to find a modern law especially aimed at any religious practice and it would be difficult to prove that laws which have the effect of banning any such practice were actually motivated by anti-religious sentiments.

---

[30] Around the same time Protestants in France suffered a similar reversal when, in 1685, Louis XIV revoked the Edict of Nantes, ordering the Calvinists (i.e. Huguenots) to leave the country and the destruction of their temples.

[31] Extradition Act 1965, as amended, s.50(2)(bb).

[32] Refugee Act 1965, s.2; *cf. R (Ullah) v. Special Adjudicator* [2003] 1 W.L.R. 770.

[33] [1999] 1 I.R. 12.

A major problem area are laws of general application that have the effect of significantly impeding a particular religious practice; there are abundant examples in US case law, ranging from making polygamy a crime in Mormon territories[34] to refusing to pay unemployment benefit to a Seventh Day Adventist who was dismissed from her job because she would not work on Saturdays.[35] Recently in South Africa a Rastafarian did not succeed in having struck down a law that prohibited smoking cannabis, without any exceptions, even though it infringed his freedom to practise his religion.[36] In another recent instance in England, the prohibition against corporal punishment in schools was upheld, against the objections of nearly 200 independent Christian schools contending that the prohibition contravened their and the parents' freedom of religion and cultural life.[37] And in a recent Canadian case, the question arose of reconciling a statutory provision outlawing discrimination against homosexuals with the demand by an Evangelical college that all teachers sign a "community standards" declaration that, *inter alia*, prohibited homosexual conduct.[38] By what criteria should general laws that considerably encumber a person's ability to practise his religion be judged? In other words, in what circumstances should such laws contain an exception to facilitate the practice in question? Where, however, one or more exceptions for religious practices are provided for, the question then arises whether there has been impermissible discrimination on the grounds of religion.

As with freedom of expression and related rights, freedom to profess and practise religion is not unqualified; it is made "subject to public order and morality." There is the preliminary question of what activities constitute practising one's religion. In the *Murphy* case[39] the Supreme Court appears to hold that a blanket ban on broadcasting all forms of religious advertising did not concern a person's freedom to practise his religion. According to Barrington J., for the court, there was 'no question of any form of discrimination or distinction being made ... on the grounds of religious profession, belief or status", once all religions were being treated equally badly.[40] And because the broadcasting ban was "broad enough to cover not only advertisements tending to favour any or all religions but also advertisements tending to attack all or any religion", it followed that the ban "cannot ... be regarded as an attack on the citizen's right to practise his religion."[41] On this logic, a law that forbade all church attendance would be unobjectionable, provided all religions were

---

[34] *Reynolds v. United States*, 98 U.S. 145 (1878).
[35] *Sherbert v. Verner*, 374 U.S. 398 (1963).
[36] *Prince v. President of the Law Society*, 12 B.H.R.C. 1 (2002).
[37] *R.. (Williamson) v. Secretary of State* [2003] 3 W.L.R. 482.
[38] *British Columbia College of Teachers v. Trinity Western University*, 199 D.L.R. 4th 1 (2001).
[39] [1999] 1 I.R. 12.
[40] *Id.* at p.22.
[41] *Id.* at p.23.

being equally disadvantaged, as well as all comparable anti-religious manifestations being proscribed.

To date, the two qualifications to the guarantee in Article 44.2.1 have not been tested in the courts. With regard to "public order" constraints, a similar question arises as occurs in the freedom of assembly guarantee, *viz.* to what extent may the free practice of a religion be restricted because it attracts the hostility of others who are prepared to cause considerable disruption in order to prevent the practice in question? The Supreme Court's holding in the *Murphy* case suggests that, at least with regard to legislative barriers to religious profession, purely speculative justifications suffice. There the plaintiff was prevented from placing a religious advertisement in a radio broadcast because section 10(3) of the Radio and Television Act 1988, prohibits advertising "directed toward any religious ... end. ..." It is difficult to understand how any reasonable person could take objection to the content of what he proposed to broadcast. Notwithstanding, the blanket ban on every conceivable kind of religious advertising was upheld by the Supreme Court. In Barrington J.'s words, the Oireachtas was "entitled to take the view that the citizens would resent having advertisements touching on [religions] broadcast into their homes and that such advertisements, if permitted, might lead to unrest."[42] An even thinner justification was added, *viz.* the Oireachtas "may well have thought that in relation to matters of such sensitivity, rich men should not be able to buy access to the airwaves to the detriment of their poorer rivals."[43] Additionally, the restriction was found to be proportionate because it did not extend to the print or other media, being confined to radio and television broadcasting. This extraordinary deference to the legislature may be contrasted with the vigorous approach taken by the Strasbourg Court to anti-proselytising laws, that do not pick on any particular religion but undoubtedly create an advantage for the dominant religions in any one State.[44]

Religious profession and practice may also be restricted on grounds of "public morality." Because what is regarded as public morality on certain questions, for example polygamy, is heavily influenced by Christian Church teaching, it would appear that certain religious practices can be prohibited or significantly restricted where they conflict with the Christian ethos.

NON-DISCRIMINATION

As well as prohibiting the imposition of religious "disabilities", Article 44.3 of the Constitution stipulates that "[t]he State shall not ... make any discrimination on the ground of religious profession, belief or status." Unlike

---

[42] *Id.* at p.22.
[43] *Ibid.*
[44] *E.g., Kokkinakis v. Greece*, 17 E.H.R.R. 397 (1993).

the general guarantee of equality in Article 40.1 or the guarantee of free profession and practice of religion in Article 44.2.1, there is no express qualification to this condemnation of discrimination. It is possible, however, that the "public order or morality" limitation in Article 44.2.1 would be applied to this as well.

"Discriminate"

It would appear that all distinctions drawn by the State based on religious grounds are captured by this Article, whether they are discriminations in favour of or against religion generally, or they are against any particular religion or religions, with the caveat that certain distinctions that facilitate religious practice are permissible. According to Walsh J., in a case where certain advantages were conferred on lay teachers that were not given to teachers with a religious background, this guarantee "ensures that, no matter what is one's religious profession or belief or status, the State shall not ... make any discrimination between persons because one happens to be a clergyman or a nun or brother or a person holding rank or position in some religion which distinguishes him from other persons whether or not they hold corresponding ranks in other religions or whether or not they profess any religion or have any religious belief, save where it is necessary to do so to implement the guarantee of freedom of religion and conscience. ..."[45]

It was held in *Quinn's Supermarket Ltd. v. Attorney General*[46] that the term discrimination in this context is not confined to adverse or unfavourable discrimination; that all distinctions made on religious grounds are proscribed when they cannot be justified. Regulations made under the Shops (Houses of Trading) Act 1938, placed restrictions on the opening hours of shops in Dublin that sold meat on any weekday and on Saturdays but, to accommodate Jewish concerns, exempted shops in which only kosher meat was sold. The plaintiffs owned a large supermarket chain and, when their company was prosecuted for selling meat during the prohibited hours on a Saturday, claimed that the regulations were an unconstitutional discrimination on religious grounds. It was held that these did not impose any religious disability on the plaintiffs because the reason why they were not permitted to sell meat after 6.30 p.m. on Saturdays was not their religion. But it was held that these regulations nevertheless discriminated on religious grounds because they used a religious criterion in order to differentiate between shops. Discrimination in the context of Article 44.2.3 is not confined to adverse discrimination. As Walsh J. explained:

---

[45] *Mulloy v. Minister for Education* [1975] I.R. 88 at p.96.
[46] [1972] I.R. 1.

"It is the omission of the word 'against' which confirms me in my view that this portion of the constitutional provision should be construed as meaning that the State shall not make any 'distinction' on the ground of religious profession, belief or status. This is confirmed by the Irish text, which says 'na aon idirdhealú a dheanamh. ...' To discriminate, in that sense, is to create a difference between persons or bodies or to distinguish between them on the ground of religious profession, belief or status; it follows, therefore, that the religious profession, belief or status does not have to be that of the person who feels he has suffered by reason of the distinction created. Indeed it is wide enough to enable the person who might be thought to have profited from the distinction but who did not accept the validity of such distinction, to challenge it by showing that it was based upon the religious profession, belief or status of the suffering party. In such instance the suffering party could avail of the remedies open to him under the 'disability' provision, as well as under the 'discrimination' provision, if in fact he was suffering a disability.

Therefore, I am of opinion that the exception made in relation to the sale of meat killed according to the Jewish ritual is a discrimination on the ground of religious profession, belief or status within the meaning of sub-s. 3 of s.2 of Article 44 and that it is, *prima facie* at least, unconstitutional on its face." [47]

However, the very fact that a law discriminates on religious grounds does not invariably render it unconstitutional.

Adverse Discrimination

Occasionally, distinctions made on religious grounds are explicit in the legislation or rule in question. These distinctions may be unconstitutional where they differentiate between religious and non-religious generally, as well as between different religions. Thus in *Mulloy v. Minister for Education*,[48] the plaintiff challenged an administrative scheme for calculating secondary school teachers' salary increments on the grounds that it discriminated against him on religious grounds. Under this scheme, increments were determined by the length of time teachers had taught in schools; at one time teaching service abroad was not counted for these purposes but that exclusion was withdrawn in respect of "lay", *i.e.* non-religious, teachers. The plaintiff was a Catholic priest and in the past he had taught in Ireland, but he then taught in Africa for several years before returning to Ireland where he again taught. Because he was not a lay teacher, account was not taken of his teaching experience abroad

---

[47] *Id.* at p.16.
[48] [1975] I.R. 88.

in reckoning how much he should now be paid. The Supreme Court held that he was the victim of unconstitutional religious discrimination.

Another provision that so discriminated, section 12 of the Adoption Act 1952, was struck down in *M. v. Bord Uchtála*.[49] It required that the adoptive parents of a non-marital child have the same religion as the child and its mother. The plaintiff gave birth to a child and, when she later got married, she and her husband sought to adopt the child. But because she was a Catholic and the husband was not, section 12 of that Act forbade the proposed adoption. Since it made a distinction on a religious basis and indeed imposed a disability on those grounds, and since it was not shown to be justified on free exercise or on public order or morality grounds, Pringle J. declared it unconstitutional.

Laws that indirectly disadvantage religions or a religious practice are far more common; in other words, measures that do not by their very terms penalise religious beliefs or obstruct religious practices but which nevertheless have the effect of making it significantly more difficult for persons to practise their particular religion. A law that obliged persons to work throughout Sundays might be regarded as indirect discrimination against Christians, who traditionally attend church on Sundays. Laws that have the effect of unduly burdening some religious practice are unconstitutional unless some very strong justification for them exists and, from the terms of Article 44.2.1, it would seem that the only permissible justification is "public order and morality." In the *Quinn's Supermarket* case, Walsh J. observed that if the 1938 Shops Act and regulations had not permitted kosher meat shops to open late on Saturdays, then they may very well be unconstitutional, because they would greatly hamper the practice of the Jewish religion. It remains to be seen what kinds of measures will be regarded as indirect discrimination against religious practice and the grounds on which that discrimination will be upheld.

Subject to some exceptions, discrimination on grounds of "religious belief", which includes "religious background or outlook", is prohibited by the Employment Equality Act 1998 and the Equal Status Act 2000, both of which apply to private sector employers and service providers, as well as to the public sector. It would appear that some form of non-State discrimination against persons on account of their religion is contrary to a more general public policy and that contractual and other stipulations that discriminate in this manner would not be enforced by the courts. Provisions in legacies and in trusts along these lines have been declared invalid on occasion.

Favourable Discrimination

Article 40.6.1.i of the Constitution permits freedom of expression to be curtailed by, *inter alia*, the offence of blasphemy, which in the past meant controverting

---

[49] [1975] I.R. 81.

the truth of the Christian religion or of the bible. But the present legal status of this offence is questionable.[50]

Article 44.2.3 forbids all differential treatment where the actual criterion used is religion; nevertheless, discriminatory measures in favour of religion, or of a particular religion or its adherents, are not unconstitutional where those measures give content to Article 44.2.1's guarantee of the free profession and practice of religion. In other words, discrimination in favour of religion, or of some particular religion, is permissible where the object is to facilitate the practice of religion generally or of a particular religion, provided that the favourable discrimination does not amount to the State endowing religion. In the *Quinn's Supermarket* case[51] the evidence showed that the Jewish Sabbath lasts from sunset on Fridays to sunset on Saturdays and, therefore, Jews would often be prevented from buying meat on Saturdays if kosher meat shops had to close at 6.30 p.m. on that day. Accordingly, exempting these shops from the trading hours restriction facilitates Jewish religious practices. If practising Jews could not lawfully buy meat after 6.30 on Saturday evenings then many of them would be confronted with the stark alternative of either practising their religion and going without fresh meat, or abandoning their religious practices and having fresh meat. The regulations did not give the owners of kosher meat shops any exceptional economic advantage over other meat sellers because there is no legal prohibition against selling meat on Sundays, the Christian Sabbath. Accordingly, the Constitution does not require complete neutrality on religious matters; some encouragement for religion is permitted and indeed may be required. Walsh J. explained the constitutional position of laws that discriminate in favour of religion as follows:

> "Article 44.2.1 ... guarantees freedom of conscience and the free profession and practice of religion in terms which do not confine these to Christianity and Judaism. It appears to me, therefore, that the primary object and aim of Article 44, and in particular the provisions of s. 2 of that Article, was to secure and guarantee freedom of conscience and the free profession and practice of religion subject to public order and morality; and to ensure that the practice of religion and the holding of particular religious beliefs shall not subject the person so practising religion or holding those beliefs to any disabilities on that account, or permit distinctions on the ground of religious profession, belief or status between persons in the State who are free to profess and practise their religion. If, however, the implementation of the guarantee of free profession and practice of religion requires that a distinction should be made to make possible for the persons professing or practising a particular religion their guaranteed right to do so, then such a distinction is not

---

[50] *Corway v. International Newspapers (Ireland) Ltd* [1994] 4 I.R. 484; *supra*, p.548.
[51] [1972] I.R. 1.

invalid having regard to the provisions of the Constitution. It would be completely contrary to the spirit and intendment of the provisions of Article 44, s. 2, to permit the guarantee against discrimination on the ground of religious profession or belief to be made the very means of restricting or preventing the free profession or practice of religion. The primary purpose of the guarantee against discrimination is to ensure the freedom of practice of religion. Any law which by virtue of the generality of its application would by its effect restrict or prevent the free profession and practice of religion by any person or persons would be invalid having regard to the provisions of the Constitution, unless it contained provisions which saved from such restriction or prevention the practice of religion of the person or persons who would otherwise be so restricted or prevented."[52]

Applying these principles to the facts, it was held that excepting kosher meat shops from the normal Saturday night closing time was justified because that was a considerable help to Jews in practising their religion. Walsh J. observed that "(s)o long as the present dietary laws remain a binding part of the Jewish religion, then a sufficient exemption of the type under review would be not merely not invalid but would be necessary if the hours of trading were regulated as at present."[53]

It was confirmed by the Supreme Court in *McGrath v. Maynooth College*,[54] that the Constitution's religious freedom clauses support measures that favour particular religious practices. Maynooth College was founded in 1795 as a seminary for training Catholic priests for all the dioceses of Ireland. Before the French Revolution student priests got their training in Continental Europe, mainly in France, but after 1789 the French religious academies were either shut down or were taken over by anti-clerical interests, thereby compelling the Catholic Church in Ireland to establish its own educational institution. Throughout most of Maynooth's existence the College admitted only student priests and its teaching staff was entirely clerical. But in 1966 it admitted lay students and teachers, and ten years later the lay element in the College outnumbered the clerical element. Maynooth is a Pontifical university and it is empowered to grant degrees from the National University of Ireland. A substantial State subvention is paid to the College every year. The plaintiffs here had been priests and full time teaching officers of the College until they were dismissed at the end of 1976 for breach of various College regulations; their claim was that they had been unlawfully dismissed.

The reasons for dismissing the first plaintiff, it was held, were because, in breach of the regulations, he had published material which was prejudicial to

---

[52] *Id.* at p.24.
[53] *Id.* at p.25.
[54] [1979] I.L.R.M. 166.

ecclesiastic authority and to the interests of the College, and that he had ceased wearing clerical dress. The second plaintiff had been dismissed for not wearing clerical dress, for living outside the College and for not resigning as required by the regulations when he ceased being a priest. Their main argument was that they had not been in breach of those regulations and that the regulations did not authorise their dismissal; this was rejected. They also contended that those regulations discriminated against them on religious grounds in a manner forbidden by Article 44.2.3; that argument was also rejected.

According to Henchy J., the clause must be read in the context of the entire Article, which is "to give vitality, independence and freedom to their religion", and includes the freedom of religious organisations to regulate their own internal affairs. Henchy J.'s reasoning, with which Griffin and Parke JJ. concurred, is as follows:

> "In proscribing disabilities and discriminations at the hands of the State on the ground of religious profession, belief or status, the primary aim of the constitutional guarantee is to give vitality, independence and freedom to religion. To construe the provision literally, without due regard to its underlying objective, would lead to a sapping and debilitation of the freedom and independence given by the Constitution to the doctrinal and organisational requirements and proscriptions which are inherent in all organised religions. Far from eschewing the internal disabilities and discriminations which flow from the tenets of a particular religion, the State must on occasions recognize and buttress them. For such disabilities and discriminations do not derive from the State; it cannot be said that it is the State that imposed or made them; they are part of the texture and essence of the particular religion; so the State, in order to comply with the spirit and purpose inherent in this constitutional guarantee, may justifiably lend its weight to what may be thought to be disabilities and discriminations deriving from within a particular religion.
>
> That is what happened here. The *raison d'etre* of the College, whatever academic or educational accretions it may have gathered over the years, has been that it has at all times been a national seminary where students are educated and trained for the Roman Catholic priesthood. This inevitably means that at least some of its academic staff must not alone be priests but priests with particular qualifications and with a required measure of religious orthodoxy and behaviour. It is part of the purpose of the statutes (which, incidentally, were drawn up by the Trustees, who are all bishops of the Roman Catholic Church, and were not imposed by the State) that due standards are to be observed by those of the academic staff who are priests. Even if it be said that the statutes are, by recognition or support, an emanation of the State, the distinctions drawn in them between priest and layman, in terms of disabilities or discriminations, are no part of what is prohibited by Art. 44, s.2, subs. 3. They represent

no prejudicial State intrusion where priest is advanced unjustifiably over layman, or vice versa. On the contrary, they amount to an implementation of the guarantee that is to be found in subs. 5 of the same section that 'every religious denomination shall have the right to manage its own affairs, own, acquire and administer property, movable and immovable, and maintain institutions for religious or charitable purposes'. These statutes are what the designated authorities of the Roman Catholic Church in Ireland have deemed necessary for this seminary. Their existence or their terms cannot be blamed on the State as an unconstitutional imposition. ..."[55]

Provisions in the Employment Equality Bill 1996 that exempted certain kinds of distinctions on religious grounds from the general ban on religious discrimination were upheld by the Supreme Court on similar grounds. As summed up by Hamilton C.J., for the court, "it is constitutionally permissible to make distinctions or discriminations on grounds of religious profession, belief or status insofar – but only insofar – as this may be necessary to give life and reality to the guarantee of the free profession and practice of religion. ..."[56] Accordingly, where a religious body controls a medical or educational institution, it is permissible to afford some preference in hiring to prospective employees of that religion. And there are limited circumstances where ones religion may be a *bona fide* occupational qualification.

In *Mulloy v. Minister for Education*,[57] where it was held that refusal to recognise clerical teachers' teaching experience contravened Article 44, Walsh J. observed that "(t)here may be many instances where, in order to implement or permit of the full and free exercise of ... freedom of religion ... the law may find it necessary to distinguish between ministers of religion or other persons occupying a particular status in religion and the ordinary lay members of that religion or the rest of the population; but this is not one of those cases."[58]

A panel system for hiring teachers in Catholic-owned secondary schools, which required, *inter alia*, previous experience of teaching in those schools, was upheld by Geoghegan J. in *Greally v. Minister for Education*.[59] This was principally because the relevant criterion was not the teacher's religious belief, profession or status but his previous employment record, which was having previously taught for a specified period in Catholic schools. This criterion did not involve any enquiry into the actual beliefs and practices of the teacher; there was no reason in principle why he might not be a Catholic or a non-practising Catholic. Serious doubts were cast on the constitutionality of a

---

[55] *Id.* at pp.187–188.
[56] *Employment Equality Bill, 1996, Re* [1997] 2 I.R. 321, 358.
[57] [1975] I.R. 88.
[58] *Id.* at p.96. Similarly, *McDaniel v. Party*, 435 U.S. 618 (1978).
[59] [1999] 1 I.R. 1.

criterion based on actual religious belief or practice, which would be "open to considerable doubt, uncertainty and dishonesty."[60] Additionally, account has to be taken of Article 42 of the Constitution, that entitles parents to have their children taught in denominational schools and, arising from this, entitlement of those in charge of those schools to take reasonable steps in order to preserve their own religious ethos.

The only instance of a measure that favoured a particular religion being struck down by the courts was in the *Quinn's Supermarket* case.[61] That was a regulation, which exempted kosher meat shops from the restriction on evening trading between Mondays and Fridays. It was held that this discrimination was unconstitutional because it was not demonstrably necessary to facilitate Jewish religious practices. Indeed, no evidence was adduced to show that giving exemption to kosher meat shops during those hours would significantly help those practices.

AUTONOMY

A right of religious autonomy is proclaimed in Article 44.2.5, according to which "(e)very religious denomination shall have the right to manage its own affairs." Just as trade union freedom requires that trade unions have a degree of internal autonomy, religious freedom signifies that religious denominations' internal affairs cannot be substantially regulated by the State. This does not mean that religious bodies and associations are immune from State regulation but there is a limit to such interventions. The difficult question, of course, is how or by what criteria the line is to be drawn between permissible and unconstitutional State intrusion into the internal affairs of religious denominations. Article 137 of the Weimar German Constitution, which was carried over in 1949, sets out in some detail the scope of the religious autonomy that it guarantees.

Among the grounds for the Supreme Court concluding in *McGrath v. Maynooth College*[62] that the regulations the plaintiffs had broken were not unconstitutionally discriminatory, were that those regulations "amount to an implementation of th(is) guarantee" and were what the Church authorities "have deemed necessary for this seminary."[63]

What a penitent tells a Catholic priest in the confession box is subject to an absolute unwaivable privilege at common law. It was contended in *Cook v. Carroll*[64] that this ancient privilege, which is buttressed by Canon Law, had

---

[60] *Id.* at p.8.
[61] [1972] I.R. 1.
[62] [1979] I.L.R.M. 166.
[63] *Id.* at pp.187 and 186.
[64] [1945] I.R. 515.

not survived the Reformation and consequently no longer existed. But that was rejected by Gavin Duffy J., relying on the then recently adopted Constitution, which at the time guaranteed a "special position" for the Catholic Church, and on the fact that the great majority of the population in the State were Catholics. Furthermore, he found that the priest-penitent relationship satisfied the general criteria for identifying privileged circumstances. It remains to be determined whether this privilege is subject to any exemption – for instance, where the information sought is necessary to save life or to prove a person's innocence – and in what circumstances, if any, it may be abrogated by the Oireachtas. It was held that the privilege is not confined to the confession box but extends to other confidential communications between a priest and one of his parishioners. In an action for seduction, the priest refused to give evidence about a conversation he had at his house with the plaintiff's daughter and the defendant concerning the circumstances of the case. Even if the parishioner in that case was prepared to waive the privilege, Gavan Duffy J. held that the information remained privileged unless the priest too was prepared to waive it.

Later in *Johnston v. Church of Scientology*,[65] Geoghegan J. held that there is a somewhat broader privilege where a parishioner is receiving counselling from his priest but it can be waived entirely by the person being counselled. The contention that counselling within the Church of Scientology was equivalent to the priest-penitent relationship was rejected, however, principally because sufficient evidence to demonstrate that equivalence had not been adduced. In any event, it was found that the plaintiff there had waived whatever privilege she may have had. It also was questioned whether that body was indeed a religious denomination.

Church Property

While rights in respect of property are protected by Articles 40.3 and 43 of the Constitution, the clauses on religion contain a special provision regarding church property. Article 44.2.6; that "[t]he property of any religious denomination or any educational institution shall not be diverted save for necessary works of public utility and on payment of compensation." This suggests that every taking of religious denomination-owned property must be accompanied by payment of compensation and that such property may then be taken only for specific public works.[66] What exactly "works of public utility" are in this context has never been determined by the courts, nor have they indicated what is meant by a religious "denomination."

---

[65] [2001] 1 I.R. 682.

[66] *Cf. Adelaide Co. of Jehovah's Witnesses v. Commonwealth*, 67 C.L.R. 116 (1943).

CHAPTER 23

Privacy and Personality

What exactly is meant by privacy and to what extent privacy should be protected has generated considerable debate in many countries.[1] A number of rights, for convenience, may be subsumed under the heading of privacy. For these purposes, privacy includes not being physically or intellectually interfered with, not being forced to undergo certain tests or to consume substances, or to disclose information, or being brainwashed in some manner. Privacy usually connotes confidentiality in a broader sense; a right not to be searched and not to have ones home or property searched, not to be the subject of clandestine surveillance and not to have information about ones personal affairs disclosed to others. Freedom of choice in relation to sexual identity and activities is often described as an aspect of privacy, although in continental European countries that is classified usually as an aspect of a general right of personality.

Article 40.5 of the Constitution guarantees a degree of privacy in the home but there is no express reference in the Constitution to privacy generally. That also is the case with the United States Constitution's Fifth and Fourth Amendments, which state respectively that "no person ... shall be compelled in any criminal case to be a witness against himself" and that "(t)he right of the people to be secure in their persons, houses, papers and effects, against unreasonable searches and seizures, shall not be violated." Notwithstanding, in the 1960s and 1970s the courts there concluded that, implicit in several of the expressly guaranteed rights that touch on privacy, there is a more general right of privacy, the precise contours of which have been a matter of considerable political as well as legal controversy.[2] Although the Supreme Court has accepted that privacy is protected by the Constitution, there has been very little case law to date delineating its rationale or its ambit. Apart entirely from the Constitution, a degree of protection against undue invasions of privacy exist in the common law – in the torts of trespass to the person and to land, and in liability for breach of confidence which can arise by virtue of the express or implied terms of a contract and also under equity. Privacy interests are also protected by the torts of nuisance and of defamation. To date, however,

---

[1] See generally, B. Markasenis ed., *Protecting Privacy* (1999), D. Solove, "Conceptualising Privacy", 90 *Cal. L. Rev.* 1087 (2002), R. Gavison, "Privacy and the Limits of the Law", 89 *Yale L.J.* 421 (1980) and M. McDougal et al, *Human Rights and World Public Order* (1980), Chap.16.

[2] Culminating in *Roe v. Wade*, 410 U.S. 113 (1973) and the abortion controversy.

it has not been held that there is an over-arching tort of invading privacy, in respect of which claims may be made against private individuals and bodies as well as against public officials and authorities, as exists in the USA and in many continental European countries.[3] On several occasions the English courts have declined to recognise an equivalent general privacy right under the common law, on the grounds that the complexity of the issues and the variety of different interests involved make law reform by way of legislative intervention more appropriate.[4]

Article 8 of the European Convention and Article 17 of the UN Covenant protect everyone's "private and family life, his home and his correspondence;" the latter adds "unlawful attacks on his honour and reputation." But Article 8(2) of the Convention permits restrictions on privacy "in the interests of national security, public safety or the economic well being of the country, for the prevention of disorder or crime, for the protection of health or morals, or for the protection of the rights and freedoms of others." According to Hamilton P. in *Kennedy v. Ireland,*[5] which concerned illegal telephone tapping, "[t]hough not specifically guaranteed by the Constitution, the right of privacy is one of the fundamental personal rights of the citizen which flow from the Christian and democratic nature of the State. It is not an unqualified right. Its exercise may be restricted by the constitutional rights of others, by the requirements of the common good and is subject to the requirements of public order and morality."[6]

Neither the Constitution, the European Convention nor the UN Covenant use the term "right of personality" but such a concept is found in some modern Constitutions, as in the German Basic Law, Article 2(1) of which stipulates that "[e]veryone shall have the right to the free development of his personality in so far as he does not violate the rights of others or offend against the constitutional order or the moral code." Many of the interests that would be categorised as aspects of privacy under the Constitution would be regarded as features of personality under this clause.

PERSONAL SECURITY AND BODILY INTEGRITY

Article 40.3.2 of the Constitution obliges the State to "protect as best it may from unjust attack and, in the case of injustice done, vindicate ... the person

---

[3] See generally, D. Dobbs, *The Law of Torts* (2000), Chap.29 and B. Markesinis, *The German Law of Obligations*, vol.2, *The Law of Torts* (3rd ed., 1997), pp.376 *et seq.* and Markesinis, *supra*, n.1.

[4] Compare *Australian Broadcasting Corp. v. Lenah Game Meats Pty Ltd*, 76 A.L.J.L.R. 1 (2001).

[5] [1987] I.R. 587.

[6] *Id.* at p.592. See generally, B. McMahon & W. Binchy, *Law of Torts* (3rd ed., 2000), Chap.37.

... of every citizen." There is no judicial guidance on the extent to which this imposes affirmative duties on the State and, to such extent as it may do, the remedies available. Laws exist to protect individuals against personal violence, notably the Offences against the Person Act 1861,[7] the Non Fatal Offences Against the Person Act 1997, the Domestic Violence Act 1996, as well as the establishment of criminal courts, a national police force, a central prosecuting service and prisons. Any excessive and non-consensual interference with a person's physical security, which is not authorised by law, gives rise to civil liability in damages for the tort of trespass to the person.

Personal Search

At common law, neither the Gardaí nor any other public official has authority to search an individual or to enter private property for any purpose.[8] Where, however, a person has been arrested, either pursuant to an arrest warrant or if it is a serious offence without a warrant, he may be searched for evidence material to the alleged offence, and also for any concealed weapon or instrument that may facilitate his escape.[9] But that is the extent of the common law power. Thus, when a female detainee suspect being searched by a female police officer forcibly resisted the latter's endeavour to take off the suspect's brassiere, the charge against her of assault was dismissed on the grounds that the search was going beyond what was legally permissible.[10]

More extensive powers to stop persons and search them are given to the Gardaí by statute,[11] most notably section 30 of the Offences Against the State Act 1939, section 8 of the Criminal Law Act 1976 and section 23 of the Misuse of Drugs Act 1977; also customs officers have broad powers to search persons entering and leaving the State. Persons who are being detained by the Gardaí, without having been charged under section 30 of the Offences Against the State Act 1939, section 4 of the Criminal Justice Act 1984 or section 2 of the Criminal Justice (Drug Trafficking) Act 1996 may be searched.

Apart from the question of searching persons' homes, the extent to which statutory powers of search are constrained by the Constitution remains to be determined; for instance, in what circumstances and under which conditions is strip-searching permissible?[12] "Stop and search" powers under section 23

---

[7] 24 & 25 Vic. c.100.

[8] *D.P.P. v. McMahon* [1986] I.R. 393.

[9] *Dillon v. O'Brien* (1887) 20 L.R. Ir. 300 and D. Walsh, *Criminal Procedure* (2002), pp.196 *et seq.* (hereinafter referred to as *Walsh*).

[10] *Lindley v. Rutter* [1980] 3 W.L.R. 660; also *R. v. Naylor* [1979] Crim. L.R. 532.

[11] See generally, *Walsh, supra*, n.9, pp.36 *et seq.*

[12] *Cf. Golden v. R.*, 207 D.L.R. 4th 18 (2001) and *Everett v. Attorney General* [2002] 1 N.Z.L.R. 82.

of the Misuse of Drugs Act 1977 were upheld by the Supreme Court in *O'Callaghan v. Ireland*.[13] According to Finlay C.J., for the court, "the potential damage to society from the use and distribution and, therefore, from the possession of controlled drugs, is so great and constitutes such a pernicious level that the legislature was clearly acting within a reasonable and proper discretion in making lawful" arrests of this nature.[14]

It has been held by the courts in several Commonwealth countries that legally privileged material may not be seized without there being express authority to do so, either in the Act authorising the search or in the search warrant.[15] A question that then arises is whether or in what circumstances is it constitutionally permissible to authorise the search and seizure of material that is legally privileged, such as documentation covered by legal professional privilege.[16]

Persons who have been unlawfully searched have a remedy in damages and, if the search was conducted in a particularly abusive manner, may even recover exemplary or punitive damages. Depending on the circumstances, evidence obtained in an unlawful personal search may be inadmissible in criminal or civil proceedings, especially when it is the unlawful searcher who seeks to rely on the evidence.

Other Infringements

Perhaps the most far-reaching legislative intrusion on bodily integrity is section 2 of the Criminal Justice (Forensic Evidence) Act 1990, which applies to persons being held in custody under section 30 of the Offences Against the State Act 1939, section 4 of the Criminal Justice Act 1984 and section 2 of the Criminal Justice (Drug Trafficking) Act 1996. For the purpose of forensic testing, a Garda officer is permitted to take from the detainee samples of blood, pubic hair and other hair, urine, saliva, a nail and any material found under a nail, a swab from any part of the body including any orifice or genital region, a dental impression and a footprint. This section contains several restrictions on the circumstances in which those samples may be taken. In disputes concerning paternity, Part VII (sections 37–43) of the Status of Children Act 1987, sets out the circumstances in which blood tests can be administered.

Authority to fingerprint a person has been held to be encompassed by the power to search and arrest.[17] Applicants for asylum may be fingerprinted.[18]

---

[13] [1994] 1 I.R. 555.
[14] *Id.* at pp.562–563.
[15] E.g. *Attorney General v. Lavelle, Racket & Heintz*, 216 D.L.R. 4th 257 (2002).
[16] *Infra*, p.650.
[17] *Adair v. M'Garry* (1933) S.L.T. 482.
[18] Refugee Act, 1996, s.9A, as amended by the Immigration Act, 2003, s.7(d).

Persons being detained without having been charged under the above Acts of 1939, 1984 and 1996 may also be fingerprinted and photographed. Persons arrested for certain road traffic offences are required to give breath, blood and/or urine samples.[19]

It was held in *Ryan v. Attorney General*,[20] the "Fluoridation Case," that the right to bodily integrity is one of the "unspecified" rights guaranteed by Article 40.3 of the Constitution. The plaintiff sought to have declared unconstitutional the Health (Fluoridation of Water Supplies) Act 1960, which provides that all health authorities in the country shall be obliged to put a small quantity of fluoride in all public water supplies, with the object of combating tooth decay in children. The evidence was held to demonstrate that there was an alarming incidence of dental decay in Irish children, which could easily cause more general ill health in later life, and that to fluoridate public water supplies would significantly reduce the extent of tooth decay and would not give rise to any harmful effects. It was contended by the plaintiff, a mother of five children who resided in Dublin where public water supplies were to be fluoridated, that the proposed fluoridation would unconstitutionally infringe *inter alia* her right to bodily integrity. But after a 65 day hearing, which consisted mainly of technical evidence, Kenny J. and the Supreme Court on appeal held that fluoridation under the 1960 Act was not unconstitutional. Ó Dálaigh C.J. summarised the plaintiff's case and the evidence as follows:

> "The basis for the plaintiff's complaint that bodily integrity has been violated rests on the probability of mild or very mild mottling in the teeth of up to 10 per cent of the children who drink the fluoridated water and on the small deposition of fluoride ions in the skeletal frames of both children and adults. Neither of these effects is harmful or involves any risk to health. The effect on the teeth is demonstrably beneficial. The purpose and effect of fluoridation is to improve children's teeth and so, indirectly, their health. These benefits to a great extent are carried forward into adult life. Adults by ingesting fluoridated water obtain little or no advantage, but neither do they suffer any disadvantages."[21]

To the question whether these "minute changes, almost imperceptible, usually beneficial, and at worst harmless," contravened bodily integrity, the court's answer was "emphatically, 'no'."[22]

The Supreme Court would not pronounce on the exact meaning of the right to bodily integrity, nor on what would constitute unconstitutional

---

[19] *Cf. R. v. Shaheed* [2002] 2 N.Z.L.R. 377 and *R. (S.) v. Chief Constable* [2002] 1 W.L.R. 3223.

[20] [1965] I.R. 294.

[21] *Id.* at pp.347–348.

[22] *Id.* at p.348.

interferences with that right. It would not even pronounce on Kenny J.'s formulation of the right; he "underst[ood] the right to bodily integrity to mean that no mutilation of the body or any of its members may be carried out on any citizen under authority of the law except for the good of the whole body and that no process which is or may, as a matter of probability, be dangerous or harmful to the life or health of the citizens or any of them may be imposed (in the sense of being made compulsory) by an Act of the Oireachtas."[23] Ó Dálaigh J., for the court, did observe that the State has an obligation to take the necessary steps to protect persons' health; that the State "has the duty of protecting the citizens from dangers to health in a manner not incompatible or inconsistent with the rights of these citizens as human persons."[24] But it was not indicated in what circumstances the court would order the State to adopt measures necessary to protect health.

Whether or in what circumstances a person can be required to submit to a medical procedure on account of general concerns about health was considered by the Supreme Court in *North Western Health Board v. H.W.*[25] However, there was no statutory requirement there that individuals be tested and, additionally, the envisaged test was on an infant child whose parents were opposed to the test. It is a test that is commonly carried out on newborn infants, known as PKU, involving drawing a tiny sample of the infant's blood, which then is analysed for indications of a condition that may cause mental handicap or a serious life threatening disease. There is a minimal risk to the child in carrying out the test. Were it made compulsory by the Oireachtas, the outcome in the case may have been different. But it was held that the Health Authority were not entitled, on the basis of their general responsibilities under the Child Care Act 1991, to obtain a court order against the wishes of its parents requiring that the child be tested. It was held by Budd J. in *J.S. v. C.S.*,[26] which were nullity proceedings, that there was nothing unconstitutional about the court directing that both parties to the petition subject themselves to a psychiatric examination.

Whether the courts would ever require the State to take positive steps in order to protect individuals' bodily integrity is debatable. For instance, if there was no Fluoridation Act on the statute book, in the light of the evidence given in the *Ryan* case, would the court ever declare that such an Act ought to be introduced? Or assuming that a nuclear facility in a neighbouring State posed a significant risk to persons' health in the State, is there any constitutional obligation on the Government to make some reasonable endeavours to counteract that risk? This gives rise to questions about the separation of powers and perhaps the only legal remedy is the granting of a declaration and the

---

[23] *Id.* at pp.313–314.
[24] *Id.* at p.348.
[25] [2001] 3 I.R. 623; *infra*, p.696.
[26] [1997] 2 I.R. 506.

award of damages. A related issue arose in *A.D. v. Ireland*[27] but in the event did not have to be decided because it was held that the constitutional right in question had not been contravened. There Carroll J. rejected the contention that persons are entitled to have a State-funded criminal injuries compensation scheme which would would award sums to victims of crimes for injuries they have suffered in consequence. An *ad hoc* scheme of this nature was introduced in 1972 but in 1980 its ambit was significantly cut back. It was held that the question of paying compensation in these circumstances is one for the Government and the Oireachtas alone, and that there was no constitutional obligation to establish a fund for this purpose, no matter how desirable such arrangements may seem.

A claim for damages against the State for delays in seeking the extradition of a sex offender from Northern Ireland was rejected by Costello P. in *W. v. Ireland (No.2)*.[28] Because, under the general principles of the law of negligence, there was no legal duty on the State owed to the plaintiff to speedily seek the person's extradition, it was held that there was no equivalent constitutional duty. Additionally, it was in the public interest that the Attorney General be permitted to carry out his functions with regard to extradition without threats of civil actions for damages by aggrieved individuals.

Thought and Conscience

An aspect of privacy that so far has not attracted the attention of the Irish courts is the extent to which the State may play a role in determining what persons think and believe, outside the contexts of religious freedom and freedom from State-imposed primary education. A feature of totalitarian societies is intolerance or worse for the unorthodox mind that rejects the official dogma. There is no express reference in the Constitution to freedom of thought and conscience as such but it cannot be doubted that such freedom is an unspecified right. Indeed, freedom of thought is implicit in the Article 40.6.1.i right of freedom of expression and in the unspecified right of privacy; Article 44.2.1 guarantees freedom of religious thought. Article 9(1) of the European Convention guarantees "freedom of thought and conscience" without any express restriction or qualification, as does Article 19(1) of the UN Covenant.

The Covenant's guarantee in Article 18 of freedom of religion extends to freedom to adopt and manifest a "belief" that is not strictly religious. But in *McGee v. Attorney General*,[29] where a prohibition against the importation of contraceptives was declared unconstitutional because it infringed the right of marital privacy, the Supreme Court held that the "freedom of conscience"

---

[27] [1994] 1 I.R. 369.
[28] [1997] 2 I.R. 141.
[29] [1974] I.R. 284.

guaranteed in Article 44.2.1 is confined to freedom of conscience as regards religion. According to Walsh J., "it is not correct to say … that the Article is a constitutional guarantee of the right to live in accordance with one's conscience subject to public order and morality. What (it) guarantees is the right not to be compelled or coerced into living in a way which is contrary to one's conscience and, in the context of the Article, that means contrary to one's conscience so far as the exercise, practice or profession of religion is concerned."[30]

Among the questions that this aspect of privacy poses is whether a mental patient or a prisoner is entitled to refuse behaviour-modification therapy, especially when accompanied by drug treatment or electronic techniques designed to alter his consciousness?[31] Or to what extent may the State prohibit or restrict individuals' use of conscience-modifying substances or other techniques, such as alcohol, caffeine or marijuana? A question that has generated considerable legal controversy in some countries possessing Bills of Rights is whether conscientious objection to military service, on grounds other than religion in the conventional sense, is protected by freedom of conscience. And in countries whose laws permit conscientious objection on religious grounds, the argument has been made that it is unfairly discriminatory to confine legitimate objection to transempirical grounds and not to grant that right to persons motivated by humanitarian and philosophical convictions. Ireland has never had military conscription, not even during World War I. A law that contains what may be called a conscientious objection clause is the Health (Family Planning) Act 1979, which deals with the provision of contraceptives. Section 11 of this Act states that "[n]othing in this Act shall be construed as obliging any person to take part in the provision of a family planning service, the giving of prescriptions or authorisations for the purposes of this Act, or the sale, importation … manufacture, advertising or display of contraceptives."[32]

THE HOME

Incursions into a person's home are restricted by Article 40.5 of the Constitution, and also by Article 8 of the European Convention and Article 17 the U.N. Covenant, respectively. According to Article 40.5, "[t]he dwelling of every citizen is inviolable and shall not be forcibly entered save in accordance with law," which suggests that once there is explicit legal authority to do so, a person's home may be invaded, provided no other constitutional right is being

---

[30] *Id.* at p.317.
[31] *Cf. R. (N.) v. M.* [2003] 1 W.L.R. 562.
[32] S.3 of the Bill in the 2nd schedule to the failed proposed 25th Amendment to the Constitution contained an equivalent conscientious objection clause: Twenty Fifth Amendment to the Constitution (Protecition of Human Rights in Pregnancy) Bill, 2001.

infringed. Under the Convention, in contrast, the home may be invaded only for the reasons specified in Article 8(2); under the Covenant, it may not be "arbitrar[ily]" invaded.

There is comparatively little judicial guidance on the scope of Article 40.5, for instance on the question of what is a "dwelling" and what forms of intrusions constitute "viola[tions]." It remains to be decided whether the "law" referred to there must comply with minimum procedural requirements and also whether it must have a minimum substantive content. In other words, except where a person's life or bodily security is at significant risk, whether laws authorising entry into a person's dwelling must contain certain procedural safeguards (such as requiring warrants) and whether forced entry is permissible only in certain circumstances. Related to this are common law rights of entry and whether some of them are consistent with the Constitution. At common law, it is permissible to enter a dwelling in order to prevent an affray and also to prevent serious injury to a person there.[33] But it is questionable whether the common law authorises entry merely to prevent a suspected breach of the peace.[34] The common law authority of bailiffs to enter a home, in order to take away goods and chattels to defray an occupant's indebtedness, has been described as "a number of confusing rules which are without apparent principle or logic" and that are "based on cases which are in the main, far from contemporary and are founded on medieval authorities."[35]

Search

At common law a person's property cannot be entered in order to be searched without there being a warrant issued authorising the search to be conducted.[36] Whether it is constitutionally permissible for the Oireachtas to allow the search of a person's home, without prior judicial authorisation, is debatable. A strong case can be made that authorisation of this kind is at minimum what Article 40.5 requires, to ensure that there are no arbitrary searches, except perhaps where there is a pressing urgency to conduct the search and it is not practicable to find an appropriate authorising agency in the time available. Otherwise, this guarantee is practically meaningless. The US Constitution's Fourth Amendment has been interpreted as prohibiting warrant-less searches, subject to some exceptions.

---

[33] See generally, D. Walsh, *Criminal Procedure* (2002), Chap.8.

[34] It does, according to *Thomas v. Sawkins* [1935] 2 K.B. 249 at pp.254–255, but in *Delaney v. D.P.P.* [1996] 1 I.L.R.M. 536 Morris P. expressed the view that this would not be followed in Ireland.

[35] Kruse, "The Legacy of Semayne – the Sources of the Present Law on Bailiffs' Rights of Entry", *Civ. Justice Q'ly* 42 (2002).

[36] *D.P.P. v. McMahon* [1986] I.R. 393.

For the purpose of an on-going criminal investigation, there are many statutory provisions authorising property to be searched, including dwellings.[37] For the purpose of tracing the proceeds of crime, section 14 of the Criminal Assets Bureau Act 1996, authorises searches of "any place," including a dwelling.[38] In order to enforce an aliens order or a deportation order, section 7 of the Aliens Act 1935, as amended in 2003, authorises searching any "place", including a "dwelling". Numerous regulatory authorities and administrative agencies are empowered by statute to search a variety of premises, including at times dwellings. The extent to which what is known as the *Anton Pillar* system in England applies in Ireland and, if it does, whether it extends to searches of dwellings is debatable.[39] Under this, in civil proceedings concerning alleged breaches of copyright and the like, a judge may grant an *ex parte* order authorising the aggrieved party to search premises in order to locate material made in defiance of the applicant's copyright, patent or similar right.

Where the Act authorising a search does not allow the use of force in order to gain entry, the question arises whether force can be resorted to. Where an Act authorises a search of premises without express reference to a home or dwelling, there is the question of whether by implication a person's home may be searched. Several of the Acts, that authorise entry onto premises for the purpose of what may be described as business regulation, make express reference to the home. For instance, section 20 of the Companies Act 1990, enables a "designated officer" to obtain a search warrant in respect of any premises, including a dwelling. Under section 13(2) of the Environment Protection Agency Act 1992, an "authorised person" cannot enter a dwelling, without the owner's consent, unless he has obtained a District Court warrant. Under section 94(4) of the Employment Equality Act 1998, a dwelling may not be entered for certain purposes without a Circuit Court warrant and, for other purposes, without the prior authority of the Minister or an officer designated for this purpose.

Where the search of a person's home is authorised under a warrant or otherwise by statute, for the purpose of seizing evidence of an alleged offence or otherwise, are there any restrictions on what may be seized in the course of that search? In particular, can items that are protected by the law of privilege be taken in the absence of express statutory authority to do so? Such case law as exists on this point is concerned principally with legal professional privilege and involves in the main searches of solicitors' officers.[40]

Warrants authorising the search of a person's home must be clearly and

---

[37] *Supra*, n.33.

[38] *Cf. R. v. Southwark Crown Court, ex p.Bowles* [1998] A.C. 641.

[39] See generally, H. Delany, *Equity and the Law of Trusts in Ireland* (2nd ed., 1999), pp.519 *et seq.*

[40] *E.g., Attorney General v. Lavelle, Racket & Heintz*, 216 D.L.R. 4th 257 (2002) and *R. v. Middlesex Crown Court, ex p. Tomosius & Partners* [2000] 1 W.L.R. 453.

unambiguously drawn up. Thus in *DPP. v. Dunne*,[41] which concerned a warrant issued under section 26 of the Misuse of Drugs Act 1977, it did not stipulate that a person in possession of the drugs in question was on the premises. On those grounds, Carney J. held that it was invalid, stating that "the inviolability of the dwelling house is one of the most important, clear and unqualified protections given by the Constitution to the citizen. If it is to be set aside by a printed form issued by a non-judicial personage it would appear ... to be essential that that form should be in clear, complete, accurate and unambiguous terms. It does not seem to ... be acceptable that the prosecuting authority can place reliance on words crossed out by asserting that that was an inadvertence or a slip. Such an approach would facilitate the warrant becoming an empty formula."[42]

Some of the requirements regarding issuing search warrants are dealt with below, on the question of searches generally.[43] The remedy for a warrant-less search of a person's home, or where the authority in a warrant is exceeded, is damages, which may be substantial depending on the circumstances.[44] Also, in an appropriate case the fruits of such searches may be inadmissible in evidence against the accused in criminal proceedings.[45]

Arrest

Section 6 of the Criminal Law Act 1997, authorises a member of the Garda Síochána to enter a premises, including a dwelling, and to search it in order to effect an arrest, using reasonable force "if need be." Where the Garda has an arrest or committal warrant, all that is required to gain entry is that he has reasonable cause to suspect that the person being sought is on the premises. If the Garda does not have a warrant and the person being sought is suspected of being in a dwelling, the Garda may not enter it against the wishes of the occupier or person in charge of the dwelling unless the person sought was observed entering or being in the dwelling, or the Garda has reasonable cause for suspecting that he will either abscond or obstruct justice, or commit an arrestable offence before any warrant can be obtained, or he ordinarily resides there.

Evict

The circumstances in which persons may be evicted from their dwelling, especially by local authorities, and the procedure that must be followed has

---

[41] [1994] 2 I.R. 537.
[42] *Id.* at p.560.
[43] *Infra*, p.647.
[44] *E.g., Hanahoe v. Hussey* [1998] 3 I.R. 69; *infra*, p.653.
[45] *E.g., People v. O'Brien* [1965] I.R. 142; *supra*, p.471.

received little constitutional scrutiny. In *State (O'Rourke) v. Kelly*,[46] section 62(3) of the Housing Act 1966 survived a challenge on separation of powers grounds; it requires a District Judge to issue a warrant authorising repossession in specified circumstances where the house "is not actually occupied by any person." The Landlord and Tenants Acts 1931–94 do not protect tenants of local authority housing.[47]

CONFIDENTIAL INFORMATION

The guarantees regarding the home are part of a wider concept that there shall be no improper intrusion into an individual's private life, such as by compelling disclosure of confidential information and forms of clandestine surveillance. Apart entirely from the Constitution, a degree of privacy is secured by the common law/equitable doctrine that affords protection against the undue disclosure of information that has been obtained in confidence, in the action for breach of confidence. There are numerous contractual and equivalent relationships where, in the absence of express terms to the contrary, the law implies a duty of confidence, for instance between lawyers and their clients, doctors and their patients, bankers and their customers. Apart entirely from the Official Secrets Act 1963, and other statutory provisions on confidentiality, public officials handling confidential information about individuals commit a civil wrong where they unnecessarily disclose that information to others.[48] Information held by the tax authorities is so confidential that there had to be express statutory authorisation for them to disclose it to a member of the Garda Síochána or of the Criminal Assets Bureau.[49] Privacy is also secured by the rules on hearing court proceedings and other proceedings *in camera*.[50] Whether there is a tort of privacy, as exists in the United States and in many Continental European countries, is debatable.[51] It remains to be determined whether the Constitution's guarantee of privacy is more extensive than in the common law and, in particular, whether it applies to non-state action or, in other words, whether it has "horizontal effect;" also, whether it is a right that corporate bodies may invoke.

Where there appears to be sufficient justification for any particular invasion of a person's privacy, fair procedures may still require safeguards in order to ensure that the disclosure in question is indeed warranted and that excessive steps are not taken with a view to securing disclosure. Thus in *Haughey v.*

---

[46] [1983] I.R. 58.
[47] Housing Act 1966, s.62(6).
[48] *The Stepping Stones Nursery Ltd v. Attorney General* [2002] 2 N.Z.L.R. 414.
[49] Disclosure of Certain Information for Taxation and Other Purposes Act 1996.
[50] *Supra*, pp.503.
[51] See generally, B. McMahon and W. Binchy, *Law of Torts* (3rd ed., 2000), Chap.37.

Moriarty,[52] where a tribunal of inquiry made discovery orders relating to documentation concerning the financial affairs of one of the persons being investigated, it was held that they should not have been made *ex parte*. Apart from "exceptional circumstances, such as legitimate fear of destruction of documents if prior notice was given," fair procedures required that prior notice be given to the persons affected.[53] That the discovery orders made there permitted those persons to apply to have them varied or discharged was insufficient in the circumstances.

Searches of Premises

The common law requirement to have a warrant in order to carry out a search on property applies to all kinds of premises and not just dwellings.[54] There are numerous statutory authorisations to conduct searches of persons' property and seize relevant material found there, most notably, for the purpose of a criminal investigation,[55] in order to trace the proceeds of crime,[56] for investigations being carried out by the Revenue[57] or the Department of Social Welfare,[58] and for the purposes of regulatory agencies and bodies. Many of the laws that may be described as concerned with business regulation enable officials of the regulatory agency in question to enter premises without having any warrant, for instance section 60 of the Insurance Intermediaries Act 1989, section 65 of the Investment Intermediaries Act 1995, section 13 of the Environmental Protection Agency Act 1992, section 94 of the Employment Equality Act 1998 and section 34 of the Safety, Health and Welfare at Work Act 1989. Under the latter Act, a District Court warrant is required in order to effect a forcible entry. A District Court warrant is also required before officers of the Competition Authority may enter any premises. Where there is no express authority to use force, it would appear that these and similar provisions do not authorise forcible entry.

It has been held permissible for the Oireachtas to authorise searching a business premises without having a warrant to conduct the search. The constitutionality of extensive powers to search property was contested in *Abbey Films Ltd. v. Attorney General*,[59] in which numerous parts of the Restrictive

---

[52] [1999] 3 I.R. 1.
[53] *Id.* at p.76.
[54] *D.P.P. v. McMahon* [1986] I.R. 393.
[55] *Supra*, n.33.
[56] *Supra*, n.38.
[57] Taxes Consolidation Act 1997, ss.901–908. See generally, K. Corrigan, *Revenue Law.* (2000), Vol.1, pp.415 *et seq.*
[58] Social Welfare (Consolidation) Act 1993, s.212(3) and *cf. Minister for Social Welfare v. Bracken* [1994] 2 I.R. 523.
[59] [1981] I.R. 158.

Practices Act 1972 were challenged, including powers under section 15 of that Act to inspect premises and documents therein, and to take copies of and extracts from the documents. Mc William J. upheld the section, stating that he was "not satisfied that office premises are a dwelling (nor) that entry into a premises cannot be authorised by the Oireachtas in any manner other than by an order of a court or a warrant."[60] Kenny J., for the Supreme Court, confined himself to the conclusion that the section contravened neither the rights of private property nor any other constitutional right.[61]

Because solicitors' offices are most likely to contain legally privileged material, it is possible that the Oireachtas cannot authorise the search of those premises without a search warrant being obtained, as otherwise there is the very distinct risk of privileged material being taken away and inspected.[62] Section 63 of the Criminal Justice Act 1984, under which persons can be required to produce documents and other material needed by the Gardaí when investigating drug trafficking and money laundering, do not apply to legally privileged material;[63] nor may such material be seized in searches carried out under section 64 of that Act.[64] But there is no similar exclusion for searches carried out to trace the proceeds of crime authorised by section 14 of the Criminal Assets Bureau Act 1996.

Provisions for search warrants usually require that a District Judge must issue them; at times a peace commissioner may issue them; exceptionally they may be issued by a senior Gardaí officer; in the case of some Revenue investigations, they must be issued by the High Court.[65] In order to obtain a search warrant, generally the applicant must satisfy the judge, commissioner or senior officer, as the case may be, that he has reasonable grounds for suspecting that the items being sought are on the premises in question. A sworn information merely reciting a suspicion to this effect will not suffice: proper evidence must be adduced supporting the alleged suspicion.[66] Where it is a senior Gardaí officer who issues the warrant, the question is whether there was sufficient information available to him justifying the suspicion.[67] The warrant must describe the items being sought[68] and, when it is being executed, the person in control of the premises must be informed of the legal basis for the warrant.[69]

---

[60] *Id.* at pp.165–166.
[61] *Id.* at p.172.
[62] *Supra*, n.40.
[63] S.63(8)(a).
[64] S.64(5).
[65] *Supra*, n.57 and *cf. Liston v. G. O'C.* [1996] 1 I.R. 501.
[66] *Byrne v. Gray* [1988] I.R. 31, *People v. Kenny* [1990] 2 I.R. 110, *D.P.P. v. Yamanoha* [1994] 1 I.R. 565 and *Trans Rail Ltd v. Wellington District Court* [2002] 3 N.Z.L.R. 780.
[67] *D.P.P. v. Sweeney* [1996] 2 I.R. 313.
[68] *People v. Balfe* [1998] 4 I.R. 50.
[69] *D.P.P. v. Rooney* [1992] 2 I.R. 7.

Where the property to be searched is not under the control of a suspected wrongdoer and there is no good reason for believing that the person in control of the property would obstruct an imminent search, the question arises whether an application for a warrant should be made on notice to that person. Section 63 of the Criminal Justice Act 1984 authorises a District Judge to direct that material relevant to the alleged offence be produced to a member of the Garda Síochána and that he must be given access to it within a specified period, thereby enabling the person in question to apply to the judge regarding his order. Section 64 of that Act, which authorises issuing search warrants for such material, is a fall-back power and ordinarily should not be used where section 63 production orders would suffice.[70]

Forced Disclosure of Information

There are numerous statutory provisions requiring that confidential information be disclosed. For instance, in order to obtain a variety of benefits or advantages from the State, certain facts must be provided to the relevant authorities. Householders are legally obliged to fill in census forms from time to time. Regulatory agencies and public bodies are entitled to demand answers to various questions posed in the course of investigations. Banks, insurers and several other types of financial institutions, and also solicitors, are obliged to disclose to the Gardaí any suspected money-laundering of the proceeds of crime they encounter in the course of their business. Unless it is covered by one or other of the recognised privileges, witnesses in courts and tribunals cannot refuse to answer a question simply because that would involve revealing what otherwise would be legally confidential information.

On several occasions, the courts have rejected privacy-based challenges to provisions requiring the disclosure of confidential information. *Madigan v. Attorney General*[71] concerned the since-repealed residential property tax that was introduced in 1983 to replace domestic rates, which had been abolished some years earlier; it was levied on occupiers of dwellings the net market value of which exceeded £65,000. But households whose aggregate annual income was less than £20,000 per annum were exempted from paying the tax. One of the objections made against this scheme was that it was an unconstitutional interference with privacy because, in order to qualify for exemption, all members of the household were obliged to disclose their annual incomes to the head of the household. O'Hanlon J. gave the argument short shrift, observing that "it had never been considered that such a right of privacy as might be held to exist under the Constitution, extended to the financial affairs of a member of the family," and that it was "quite unrealistic to suppose

---

[70] *Hanahoe v. Hussey* [1998] 3 I.R. 69; *infra*, p.653.
[71] [1986] I.L.R.M. 136.

that a member of a family would leave home to ensure that the burden of tax would not fall on the occupier."[72] The Finance Act 1983, did not oblige all members of the household to contribute towards payment of the tax, nor did it impose any obligation on them to disclose their incomes to the taxpayer. Accordingly, this Act did "not purport to authorise any invasion of the privacy of such members of the household, and a constitutional challenge based on the alleged infringement of the right to privacy cannot be sustained."[73] In any event, it was held that the plaintiffs did not possess the *locus standi* to raise this argument; for that reason the Supreme Court declined even to consider the issue.

In 1992 Murphy J. rejected a similar challenge to the powers of court-appointed company inspectors to demand information about persons' financial affairs.[74] And in 1998 a similar challenge to the Dáil establishing a tribunal of enquiry into substantial payments made to two prominent politicians was rejected by the Supreme Court.[75] In both instances, the intrusions into the plaintiffs' confidences were held to be justifiable in the overriding public interest.

The privilege against self-incrimination, which has been dealt with briefly when considering criminal procedure,[76] is part of a wider principle that in certain contexts persons should not be compelled to disclose confidential information about themselves or others. This privilege has a wider objective than of preserving confidentiality; it also is designed to ensure that witnesses do not tell lies for fear of being prosecuted if they give truthful answers and it provides an incentive for the police to base their case on evidence other than the accused's admissions. Other evidentiary privileges might also be regarded as part of a more general right not to be compelled to disclose information. But the individual's interest in keeping confidences must be balanced against the right of others to have a fair trial, by having all the relevant evidence presented to the court, and the authority of the courts to ensure that justice is done. It was for this reason that, in *Murphy v. Dublin Corporation*,[77] the Supreme Court radically curtailed the ambit of executive privilege.

Some evidentiary privileges, notably regarding communications with confessors[78] and inter-spousal communications,[79] serve separate substantive constitutional ends but it has not been decided whether or to what extent these can be curtailed or abrogated by legislation. Nor has the constitutional status,

---

[72] *Id.* at p.145.
[73] *Id.* at p.156.
[74] *Chestvale Properties Ltd v. Glackin* [1993] 3 I.R. 35.
[75] *Haughey v. Moriarty* [1999] 3 I.R. 1.
[76] *Supra*, p.456.
[77] [1972] I.R. 215; *supra*, p.130.
[78] *Supra*, p.632.
[79] *Infra*, p.669.

if any, of legal professional privilege been determined.[80] Insofar as the Oireachtas seeks to encroach on this privilege, it must do so unambiguously or by necessary implication.[81] Under this privilege, a lawyer and his client are entitled not to disclose communications between them for the purpose of giving or receiving legal advice, whether or not that advice relates to existing or to contemplated litigation. Additionally, communications with third parties, for the purpose of preparing for litigation, are privileged but there is uncertainty about its exact ambit. There are exceptions to the privilege, principally where the communication was part of a criminal or fraudulent arrangement.

Following a comprehensive survey of the case law on the subject, an English judge concluded that, in summary:

> "[T]he common law (1) recognises the right to legal confidentiality which arises as between a person and his legal adviser (save where the client is trying to use the relationship for an unlawful purpose) as a matter of substantive law and (2) regards it as a right of great constitutional importance because it is seen as a necessary bulwark of the citizen's right of access to justice whether as a claimant or as a defendant. Legal professional privilege is an attribute or manifestation of that right. It is also much more than an ordinary rule of evidence, being considered a fundamental condition on which the administration of justice rests."[82]

It remains to be determined in Ireland whether this privilege exists where the information in question would assist a person being charged with an offence to establish his innocence. In England it was held, in this context, that the fundamental principle is "once privileged, always privileged" unless the client waives the privilege.[83] But some Commonwealth courts have rejected this view.[84]

Surveillance

A host of techniques exist for the clandestine surveillance of individuals, such as intercepting letters, telephone tapping, concealed microphones of various kinds, miniature transistorised tape recorders, hidden cameras, closed circuit television, one-way glass, long-distance lenses and infiltrating informers. Resort to some covert surveillance techniques in the absence of any legal regime

---

[80] See generally, H. Delany and D. McGrath, *Civil Procedure in the Superior Courts* (2001), pp.228 *et seq.*
[81] *R. (Morgan Grenfel & Co.) v. Special Commissioners* [2002] 2 W.L.R. 1299.
[82] *General Mediterranean Holdings S.A. v. Pastel* [2000] 1 W.L.R. 272 at p.288.
[83] *R. v. Derby Magistrates Court, ex p.B.* [1996] A.C.
[84] *E.g. Bensons v. Brown*, 210 D.L.R. 4th 341 (2002) at p.487.

regulating them has been held to contravene Article 8 of the European Convention, as an infringement of privacy that is not in accordance with law.[85] The privacy of postal and telecommunications is expressly guaranteed by Article 10 of the German Constitution. Overt surveillance of a person, his house or place of business can be so intrusive as to amount to the criminal offences of coercion or harassment, or the actionable tort of nuisance.

Telephone Tapping

Of these techniques, telephone-tapping has attracted by far the most legal protection. Section 98 of the Postal and Telecommunications Services Act 1983 makes the "interception of telecommunications messages" a criminal offence, but that offence does not exist where, *inter alia*, the Minister has issued a direction, under section 110 of this Act, to intercept conversations in the national interest and also where other lawful authority exists. Section 84 of this Act is a similar prohibition against opening letters and other items that were posted. There may very well be a civil right of action for breach of statutory duty against persons who unlawfully open mail because section 66(1) of the 1983 Act states that "(p)ostal packets and mail bags in course of post shall be immune from examination, detention or seizure except as provided under this Act or any other enactment;" there is no analogous provision for interferences with telephone calls. Section 18(1) of the Official Secrets Act 1963 authorises the Minister to intercept international telegrams.

In *Kennedy v. Ireland*[86] two journalists, whose phones had been illegally tapped on the instructions of a Government Minister, were awarded damages by the High Court for the unlawful invasion of their right to privacy. Hamilton P. posed the question "whether the right to privacy includes the right to privacy in respect of telephonic conversations and the right to hold such conversations without deliberate, conscious and unjustified interference therewith and intrusion thereon by servants of the State, who listen to such conversations, record them, transcribe them and make the transcriptions thereof available to other persons."[87] He had "no doubt but it does." There the State accepted that tapping the plaintiffs' telephones was deliberate, conscious and unjustifiable. Because the State belatedly acknowledged that there was no justification whatsoever for what had been done and that the existing safeguards against unwarranted telephone tapping had been subverted, punitive damages were not awarded. But in view of the entire circumstances, it was held that the plaintiffs should be awarded substantial damages, however these may be described. A curious feature of the judgment is that it makes no reference

---

[85] *Kopp v. Switzerland*, 27 E.H.R.R. 91 (1998) and *Khan v. United Kingdom*, 31 E.H.R.R. 1016 (2000).
[86] [1987] I.R. 587.
[87] *Id.* at p.592.

whatsoever to the several Strasbourg Court decisions that found telephone tapping to contravene the European Convention. Evidence obtained by unauthorised interceptions ordinarily will be ruled inadmissible against an accused.[88]

This entire question is now governed by the Interception of Postal Packages and Telecommunications Messages (Regulation) Act 1993, which permits the Minister for Justice to authorise intercepting postal packages or tapping telephones or faxes on two grounds only. One is to gather evidence in the course of investigating a serious crime, being one that can result in five years imprisonment on conviction, and where there is a "reasonable prospect" that the interception will assist the investigation. The other is for the purpose of gathering information in the interests of the security of the State. Any such authorisation must be by way of the Minister's warrant but, in cases of exceptional urgency, oral authorisation is permissible but must be followed by written confirmation. Provision is made for a High Court judge to review this Act's operation and there is also a Complaints Referee to deal with complaints concerning it.

Data Banks

Another form of surveillance is collecting extensive personal information about individuals in one place, which has been facilitated by the advent of electronic data processing and the greater use of detailed questionnaires in applying for various services and benefits from public and, indeed, private organisations. Behind the very rapid advances in information technology lies the spectre of virtually every piece of information about each individual being collected in one vast State data bank. The compatibility of data banks with the right to privacy has not yet been considered by the Irish courts.[89]

Data collection and retention is governed by the Data Protection Acts 1988–2003, which give effect to the Council of Europe's Data Protection Convention and an EC Directive on the subject.[89] This Act imposes wide-ranging general obligations on data controllers to collect and process personal data fairly. Personal data must be accurate and, where necessary, kept up to date; it must be kept only for lawful and specified purposes, and must not be used or disclosed in any manner that would not be compatible with those purposes. But data can be disclosed for a variety of reasons, *inter alia*, where required to safeguard the security of the State, in order to prevent crime or to assist revenue assessment or collection, where necessary to prevent injury or damage to a person's health, or to prevent serious loss or damage to property. Data controllers must take appropriate security measures against unauthorised access to personal data, or

---

[88] *People v. Dillon* [2002] 4 I.R. 501; compare *Fliss v. R.*, 209 D.L.R. 4th 347 (2002).
[89] Convention of 28 January 1981, 1496 U.N.T.S. 65 and Directive 95/46, O.J.L. 281/38 (1995)

to its alteration, disclosure, accidental loss or destruction. Wide ranging powers of investigation, enforcement, prohibition and supervision are conferred on the Data Protection Commissioner. Certain categories of data controllers must register each year in a register kept by the Commissioner.

Publicising

In the United States and in several continental European countries, the right to privacy includes a right that ones private affairs shall not be the subject of undue publicity – the "private facts" tort.[90] Enforcement of this right often requires a delicate balance of privacy against freedom of the press.[91] At times restrictions on publicity serve a far wider purpose than merely protecting a person's privacy; restrictions are imposed occasionally in order to protect persons' lives, for example individuals in witness protection programmes, or in order to ensure that persons obtain a fair trial.

The closest that the Irish courts have come to imposing liability for unfairly publicising an individual's affairs was in *Hanahoe v. Hussey*,[92] where a member or members of the Garda Síochána tipped off journalists about a search that was about to be carried out on a solicitors' office. A senior Garda officer obtained a search warrant under section 64 of the Criminal Justice Act 1994 to search the files of a leading firm of solicitors for possible evidence about one of their clients, who at the time was wanted for drug trafficking and for murder. When the Gardaí and officers of the Criminal Assets Bureau arrived at the office, there was a large media presence there observing what was going on, which resulted in extensive publicity being given to the search. Kinlen J. awarded damages of £100,000 to the firm's partners on the grounds that "[t]his was a deliberate leaking to the media which caused considerable embarrassment to the [firm]. It was intended to embarrass and distress [the firm] and it most certainly did. It was an outrageous interference with their privacy and their constitutional rights."[93] This is very similar to the tort in U.S. law of publicising a person in a false light.

REPUTATION

Among the rights referred to in Article 40.3 of the Constitution is the right to a "good name." There is no express reference to reputation in the European Convention; Article 17 of the UN Covenant proscribes "unlawful attacks on

---

[90] *E.g. Re C.*, 10 B.H.R.C. 131 (1999) (Germany).
[91] *Supra*, p.557.
[92] [1998] 3 I.R. 69.
[93] *Id.* at p.108.

honour and reputation." A person's reputation is safeguarded principally by the law of libel and slander, which protects the reputation of corporations and other legal entities as well.[94] The right to defend ones reputation is one reason why persons, found guilty of criminal offences, are entitled to challenge their convictions by appealing. It is also why persons are entitled to be heard and to have legal representation before some investigative tribunals. As has already been mentioned, one of the major dilemmas posed by the right to reputation is reconciling this right with freedom of speech and of the press.[95] It may very well be that observations about persons who choose to become prominent public figures, especially in the political field, and which would be defamatory of private individuals, do not invariably give a right of action on account of the constitutional guarantee of freedom of expression.

A major reason why in *Maguire v. Ardagh*[96] the Supreme Court held that an Oireachtas joint committee was not entitled to investigate a fatal shooting incident, involving members of the Garda Síochána, was the threat that this process posed for the individual Gardaí involved. There Murray J. prayed in aid the observation of Blackstone, that "[t]he security of his reputation or good name from the arts of detraction and slander are rights to which every man is entitled, by reason and natural justice; since without these it is impossible to have the perfect enjoyment of any other advantage or right."[97] He went on to explain why a highly politicised tribunal could not be regarded as a reliable instrument for protecting individuals' reputations. This was because:

> "[Parliamentary] Committees of inquiry are, by virtue of their role and function, part of the political process. Evidently, they are composed of public representatives answerable to their constituents, public opinion and with a day-to-day interest in the cut and thrust of everyday politics. I do not say that a public representative by virtue of his or her political role is incapable of acting fairly and objectively. Nonetheless there is the underlying fact that they each have an ever present interest, from one perspective or another, in the political issues of the day including the ever present one of the standing or otherwise of the Government in office and its Ministers. Constitutionally the Government is answerable to members of the Dáil and in a different, but substantive way, may be the subject of support or opposition by members of the Seanad. Unlike other forms of enquiry Oireachtas Committees are not independent of the political process. The question arises whether the Constitution, although silent on the matter, intended that personal culpability of citizens for serious wrongdoing with consequential implications for their good name

---

[94] See generally, B. McMahon and W. Binchy, *Law of Torts* (3rd ed., 2000), Chap.34.
[95] *Supra*, p.555.
[96] [2002] 1 I.R. 385.
[97] At p.592.

should be decided in the course of an enquiry, which was part of the political process. The risks inherent in such a process were adverted to in the document prepared by the Office of the Attorney General (which was submitted to the Court) and contained in the Comparative study into Tribunals of Enquiry and Parliamentary Inquiries published by the Committee of Public Accounts of Dáil Éireann."[98]

How allegations of misconduct in some professions are to be dealt with is regulated by statute, in particular with regard to medical doctors, dentists, nurses, vets and solicitors.[99] Under these, there is a formal adversarial enquiry into the allegations, held by Fitness to Practise Committees, and the practice has been to exclude all persons other than those directly involved in the proceedings; in contrast in some countries, the practice is to hold these enquiries in public unless there are good reasons why in a particular instance they should be held privately. It was held by the Supreme Court in *Barry v. Medical Council*[100] that the effect of the relevant provisions is to give Committees, holding these enquiries, a discretion to exclude whoever the Committee believes should not be admitted; this is to "protect the reputation of practitioners who have not been found guilty of professional misconduct or unfit to engage in the practice of medicine."[101] There the practitioner who was being investigated wanted the enquiry to be held in public but, because of the very nature of the allegations being made and the evidence to be adduced, it was held that the Committee had not abused its discretion by not allowing representatives of the public to attend. The contention that the plaintiff had been denied fair procedures, by being deprived of a public hearing, was rejected. Barrington J. observed that there was no reason why hearings of this nature should not be held in public, provided however "all the parties" and also the Committee were agreeable to doing so.

In *M. v. The Medical Council*,[102] the question arose as to whether the publication by a professional disciplinary body, of the fact that it had found an individual guilty of professional misconduct before that person could contest the body's findings in the courts, contravened his constitutional right of reputation. Allegations that the plaintiff had improperly supplied drugs were investigated by the defendant's Fitness to Practise Committee, which found that they were substantiated; the Medical Council then decided that he should be struck off the register of medical practitioners, as it is empowered to do by the Medical Practitioners Act 1978. Section 45(5) of this Act authorises the publication of an adverse finding against a doctor who has been investigated;

---

[98] *Id.* at pp.598–599.
[99] *Infra*, p.783.
[100] [1998] 3 I.R. 368.
[101] *Id.* at p.391.
[102] [1984] I.R. 485.

publication of the findings is prohibited unless the doctor was found guilty of professional misconduct or unfit to practise by reason of disability. Finlay P. concluded that publication of the findings is not unconstitutional because in the circumstances it is for the common good to publish them; "[i]n the case of a person practising medicine, the public have a clear and identifiable interest to be informed of a responsible view reached by his colleagues with regard to his standard of conduct or fitness."[103] Accordingly, "the absence from the statute of a prohibition on the publication of an adverse finding of the Committee (where they have made a finding of misconduct or of unfitness) can [not] be a failure to protect the good name of the practitioner from an unjust attack. This is particularly true having regard to the fact that neither the finding of the Committee nor any decision made by the Council thereafter can impose any prohibition or suspension on the right of the practitioner to continue practising."[104] Additionally, every doctor who is ordered to be struck off in these circumstances can apply to the High Court for a full hearing on the entire issue and, if there is not sufficient evidence of misconduct or of disability, the Medical Council's decision will be set aside and such a verdict "will necessarily and completely vindicate" his good name and reputation.

SEXUAL CONDUCT AND IDENTITY

Neither the Constitution, the European Convention nor the UN Covenant contain express rights regarding sexual conduct or identity, either in general or in particular circumstances. Article 41 on the family was construed in *McGee v. Attorney General*[105] to include a right of married persons to acquire contraceptives, presumably with a view to having sexual relations between themselves. Relations between married couples are considered in the next chapter on the family. But sexual activity is not exclusive to the family based on marriage and the question that then arises is the extent to which the State is prohibited from restricting individuals' sexual freedom or identity. A closely related political and philosophical question is the extent to which the State in principle ought to intervene in these matters; should the State impose generally accepted standards of sexual morality on all, or should it impose the sexual morality of influential sectors of society on everybody else; or should the State leave sex entirely to individuals' own choice?[106] Controversy about the role of the State in regulating sexual conduct is a dispute about constitutional law because some claim that the guarantees of freedom of expression and of privacy

---

[103] *Id.* at p.500.
[104] *Ibid.*
[105] [1974] I.R 284.
[106] The leading modern exposition of this debate being P. Devlin, *The Enforcement of Morals* (1965) and H.L.R. Hart, *Law, Liberty and Morality* (1963).

mean that individuals should be allowed extensive freedom in sexual matters and that any restrictions, especially where the penalties for their breach are drastic, require convincing justification.

The principal criminal law provisions in force regarding sexual conduct are the Criminal Law (Sexual Offences) Acts 1885-1993; the Punishment of Incest Act 1908, the Sexual Offences (Jurisdiction) Act 1996 and the Child Trafficking and Pornography Act 1998. Non-consensual sexual contact is an actionable trespass at common law, remediable by a civil claim for compensation, which in appropriate circumstances may justify an award of exemplary or punitive damages.

Morality

Everybody has their own moral code but most peoples' moral codes are not fully thought out and, indeed, have numerous inconsistencies and contradictions. Groups also have their own somewhat limited moral codes, such as the cricket community's standards of fair play. Some groups, most notably the major religions, possess far more comprehensive moral codes. The entire community of a State will also share certain common moral values and many of the most important community values will be embodied in legislation, such as the prohibition against theft, the regulation of money-lending, the protection of the environment etc. Although sex is far from the exclusive concern of moralists, much moral controversy in the recent past tended to dwell on state intervention in sexual conduct.

It is generally accepted that the State ought to and indeed has an obligation to regulate sexual conduct that harms others and also sexual conduct involving young persons who are not in the best position to safeguard their own interests. Most of the offences listed above can be justified on these grounds. Philosophical and constitutional controversy arises most often where the conduct in question does not directly harm anybody and young persons are not involved. In many countries in recent years, the extent to which the law should deal with matters such as contraception, homosexual relations and abortion has engendered considerable public debate, as well as constitutional litigation.

Unfortunately, a reading of the Supreme Court's judgments in *McGee v. Attorney General*[107] on contraception, and in *Norris v. Attorney General*,[108] concerning homosexual conduct, throws little light on how, in general terms, the Constitution affects these issues. Most of the judgments given in these cases refrain from any general discussion of the law/morals question. But in

---

[107] [1974] I.R. 284.
[108] [1984] I.R. 36.

the *McGee* case, Walsh J. drew a distinction between public morality and private morality, although he did not indicate how public morality is to be ascertained; that "[i]t is undoubtedly true that among those persons who are subject to a particular moral code no one has a right to be in breach of that moral code. But when this is a code governing private morality and where the breach of it is not one which injures the common good then it is not the State's business to intervene."[109] In other words, the Oireachtas must not impose on the community the moral standards of a few except where such legislation in fact promotes the common good. No guidance is provided, however, as to what exactly is envisaged by the "common good" in this context, where the activity in question is consensual and involves adults who are not mentally handicapped in any way.

In April 1983 O'Higgins J. in the *Norris* case suggested that the criterion for constitutionality here is conventional morality, but did not address the question of how conventional moral views are to be ascertained in an era of changing attitudes to sexual mores. According to the then Chief Justice:

> "the plaintiff ... asserts a 'no go area' in the field of private morality. I do not accept this view either as a general philosophical proposition concerning the purpose of law or as having particular reference to a right of privacy under our Constitution. I regard the State as having an interest in the general moral well being of the community and as being entitled, where it is practicable to do so, to discourage conduct, which is morally wrong and harmful to a way of life and to values, which the State wishes to protect.
>
> A right of privacy or, as it has been put, a right 'to be let alone' can never be absolute. There are many acts done in private, which the State is entitled to condemn, whether such be done by an individual on his own or with another. The law has always condemned abortion, incest, suicide attempts, suicide pacts, euthanasia or mercy killing. These are prohibited simply because they are morally wrong and regardless of the fact, which may exist in some instances, that no harm or injury to others is involved."[110]

A majority of Irish citizens belong to the Catholic Church and that Church, especially in Ireland, had very distinctive views on a host of sex-related questions.[111] *Norris v. Attorney General*[112] is the leading instance where aspects of the sexual activities of unmarried persons were considered by the courts in the light of the Constitution. The plaintiff contended, unsuccessfully, that the

---

[109] [1974] I.R. 313.
[110] [1984] I.R. 64.
[111] See generally, L. Fuller, *Irish Catholicism Since 1950, The Undoing of a Culture* (2002).
[112] [1984] I.R. 36.

criminal sanctions on certain forms of homosexual behaviour were unconstitutional for a number of reasons. What is particularly significant about this case is the Supreme Court's attitude to what may be called unorthodox sexual behaviour in the light of the Catholic Church's teachings on these questions. Briefly, the Catholic view was that sexual relations should occur only between husband and wife in order to conceive children; until the 1960s sections of the clergy castigated "company keeping." Irish law, however, does not entirely reflect Catholic teaching on sexual issues; there are no legal prohibitions for example on pre-marital sex, adultery, the use of contraceptives, prostitution *per se*, masturbation etc. But the law forbade certain forms of sex-related conduct, which was made legal in many Western European and American countries, notably sexual relations between persons of the same sex and abortion.

Because so few cases in this area are heard and since all judges do not share the same views on these issues, and also because attitudes have changed significantly in recent years, it is not possible to generalise about the courts' present attitude to sexual questions and the extent to which constitutional law today reflects Catholic teaching. Although the Papal Encyclical Humanae Vitae in 1968 condemned contraception, in the *McGee* case the Supreme Court (the Chief Justice dissenting) overruled the President of the High Court and held unconstitutional a law that made it virtually impossible for married couples or for anybody else to buy contraceptives. None of the judges in that case discussed religious considerations. But religious views were decisive in the *Norris* case and O'Higgins C.J.'s majority judgment there said as follows:

> "From the earliest days, organised religion regarded homosexual conduct, such as sodomy and associated acts, with a deep revulsion as being contrary to the order of nature, a perversion of the biological functions of the sexual organs and an affront both to society and to God. With the advent of Christianity this view found clear expression in the teachings of St. Paul, and has been repeated over the centuries by the doctors and leaders of the Church in every land in which the gospel of Christ has been preached. To-day, as appears from the evidence given in this case, this strict view is beginning to be questioned by individual Christian theologians but, nevertheless, as the learned trial judge said in his judgment, it remains the teaching of all Christian Churches that homosexual acts are wrong ...
>
> The preamble to the Constitution proudly asserts the existence of God in the Most Holy Trinity and recites that the people of Ireland humbly acknowledge their obligation to 'our Divine Lord, Jesus Christ'. It cannot be doubted that people, so asserting and acknowledging their obligations to our Divine Lord Jesus Christ, were proclaiming a deep religious conviction and faith and an intention to adopt a Constitution consistent with that conviction and faith and with Christian beliefs. Yet it is suggested

that, in the very act of so doing, the people rendered inoperative laws which had existed for hundreds of years prohibiting unnatural sexual conduct which Christian teaching held to be gravely sinful. It would require very clear and express provisions in the Constitution itself to convince me that such took place. When one considers that the conduct in question had been condemned consistently in the name of Christ for almost two thousand years and, at the time of the enactment of the Constitution, was prohibited as criminal by the laws in force in England, Wales, Scotland and Northern Ireland, the suggestion becomes more incomprehensible and difficult of acceptance."[113]

At the time these vigorously confident views were being aired, the European Court of Human Rights had ruled that laws punishing homosexual acts between consenting adults in private contravened Article 8's guarantee of privacy.[114] Little weight was given by that Court to the fact that such acts had traditionally been viewed by law-makers and by several Churches as repugnant. Within ten years of this decision, the Oireachtas repealed the prohibition against homosexual conduct.[115] In the intervening years, the Catholic Church lost much of its influence, largely on account of several scandals that it sought to cover up from public exposure. It is most unlikely today that the Supreme Court would justify the upholding of a criminal law because, traditionally, that Church condemned the acts prohibited by the law in question.

Contraception

The actual use or manufacture of contraceptives was never proscribed by Irish law but it used be an offence to sell, advertise or import them, and information regarding contraception was categorised as obscene by the laws on the censorship of publications, However in *McGee v. Attorney General*,[116] the Supreme Court struck down section 17 of the Criminal Law Amendment Act 1935, which forbade selling, advertising and importing contraceptives. Shortly afterwards the Oireachtas removed references to contraception from the censorship laws.[117] The basis for the decision in the *McGee* case was the constitutional right to marital privacy and that to effectively render contraceptives inaccessible to married couples contravened that right. Whether unmarried persons' constitutional rights extend to being able to acquire contraceptives is an open question. In the *McGee* case Walsh J. based his

---

[113] *Id.* at pp.61 and 64.
[114] *Dudgeon v. United Kingdom*, 5 E.H.R.R. 573 (1983).
[115] Criminal Law (Sexual Offences) Act 1993.
[116] [1974] I.R. 284.
[117] Health (Family Planning) Act 1979, s.12.

judgment on the Article 41 guarantees regarding the family and he stressed that he had "given no consideration whatsoever to the question of the constitutionality or otherwise of laws which would withhold or restrict the availability of contraceptives for use outside of marriage,"[118] and that nothing in his judgment was intended as expressing a view on that matter. But the other judges who found in the plaintiff's favour – Budd, Henchy and Griffin JJ. -based their decisions on the Article 40.3 right to privacy as distinct from Article 41, which suggests that persons who are not married have a constitutional right of access to contraceptives; although those judges emphasised how important it was that married couples should not be denied access to contraceptives. A similar theme runs through several United States cases cited in *McGee*, where anti-contraceptive laws were held to contravene the US Bill of Rights.

Access to contraceptives is now regulated by the Health (Family Planning) Act 1979, which obliges the Minster to "secure the orderly organisation of family planning services" and to "provided a comprehensive natural family planning service." These services may be provided by Health Boards. Where they involve the supply of contraceptives, any private service-provider must have the consent of the Minister and operate within regulations issued by him, and also under the supervision of a registered medical practitioner. There are restrictions on the manufacture, importation and sale of contraceptives and it is forbidden to publish any advertisement or notice relating to contraceptives otherwise than in accordance with regulations issued by the Minister.

Homosexuality

How the law should deal with homosexual relationships has engendered controversy in many countries and the general trend has been towards easing, if not abolishing, draconian prohibitions against such relationships. In the *Dudgeon* case,[119] the European Court of Human Rights held that the criminalisation of buggery, as operated in Northern Ireland, contravened the Convention's guarantee of privacy. However, in *Norris v. Attorney General*,[120] which was decided subsequently, the Supreme Court by a majority of one ruled that identical provisions did not contravene the Constitution. The plaintiff's sexual orientation was and always had been exclusively homosexual. He claimed that the provisions of the Offences Against the Person Act 1861, and of the Criminal Law Amendment Act 1885,[121] contravened his right to privacy and freedom of association, and unfairly discriminated against him on

---

[118] [1974] I.R. 319–320.
[119] *Supra*, n.115.
[120] [1984] I.R. 36.
[121] 24 & 25 Vic. c.100 and 48 & 49 Vic. c.69.

the basis of sex. Although the case was not one where the Constitution's single judgment rule applied, only O'Higgins C.J. (Finlay P. and Griffin J. concurring) gave reasons for upholding the provisions in question. Those were that homosexuality is socially damaging and that, accordingly, the State is entitled to have the relevant provisions on the statute book in order to deter persons from becoming actively homosexual.

No evidence was adduced by the State to show that homosexuality was harmful. The only witnesses to testify – experts in sociology, theology and psychiatry – all disapproved of the prohibition that was being challenged. Notwithstanding, the Chief Justice was persuaded that the evidence led to the following conclusions:

> "(1) Homosexuality has always been condemned in Christian teaching as being morally wrong. It has equally been regarded by society for many centuries as an offence against nature and a very serious crime.
> (2) Exclusive homosexuality, whether the condition be congenital or acquired, can result in great distress and unhappiness for the individual and can lead to depression, despair and suicide.
> (3) The homosexually orientated can be importuned into a homosexual lifestyle which can become habitual ...
> (4) Male homosexual conduct has resulted, in other countries, in the spread of all forms of venereal disease and this has now become a significant public-health problem in England.
> (5) Homosexual conduct can be inimical to marriage and is *per se* harmful to it as an institution." [122]

In other words, homosexuality often causes personal unhappiness and is linked to the spread of venereal disease. While the very same may be said of heterosexual relations, it was held that the important difference was that homosexuality has for centuries been condemned as immoral by all Christian churches. Furthermore, tolerance for homosexuality was said to be a threat to marriage in two ways: it causes men who are somewhat homosexual to "turn ... away from" marriage and it can lead to the "breaking up of existing marriages." Therefore, O'Higgins C.J. reasoned, "no one could regard with equanimity the freeing of such conduct from all legal restraints with the certain result that it would increase and its known devotees multiply."[123] It followed that the sections in question were not an unconstitutional infringement of the plaintiff's right of privacy or his rights to health and association. Nor did they discriminate unfairly on the grounds of sex.

Henchy and McCarthy JJ. disagreed with this summary of the evidence.

---

[122] *Id.* at p.63.
[123] *Id.* at p.72.

As they pointed out with regard to the actual effects in other countries of decriminalising homosexual acts, ten witnesses for the plaintiff testified that decriminalisation did not have significantly adverse effects and was even somewhat beneficial. Not one witness was called on the State's behalf to rebut that evidence. When one considers that the criminalisation of homosexual acts "blights and thwarts in a variety of ways the life of a person who is by nature incapable of giving expression to his sexuality except by homosexual acts ... consensually in private,"[124] the onus is on the State to demonstrate that the provisions in question are required to maintain public order and morality. On the evidence before the court, that onus was not carried. As Henchy J. stated after summarising what each witness had said, "the evidence of all ten witnesses condemned, in one degree or another, and for a variety of reasons, the impugned sections for being repugnant to the essential human needs of compulsive or obligatory homosexuals and as not being required by – indeed, as being inconsistent with public order and morality or any of the other attributes comprehended by the constitutional concept of the common good."[125] In a legal system where courts are supposed to give judgment on the basis of the evidence before them, the only rational conclusion that could have been drawn was that the sections were unconstitutional. In saying that these provisions should be struck down, Henchy J. made it clear that he did not favour abandoning all legal restrictions on homosexual activities and that there were many circumstances where criminal prohibitions should apply, as they do in regard to heterosexual conduct. McCarthy J. endorsed these views that "there was no evidence before (the High Court) upon which [it] could hold other than that the impugned sections were not consistent with the Constitution."[126]

Norris succeeded before the European Court of Human Rights in having the provisions there held to contravene Article 8 of the Convention.[127] The blanket prohibition against buggery was repealed by section 2 of the Criminal Law (Sexual Offences) Act 1993. In recent years the whole legal position regarding homosexuality has changed radically in many European countries and, under the Employment Equality Act 1998, and the Equal Status Act 2000, discrimination on grounds of "sexual orientation" is forbidden.

---

[124] *Id.* at p.36.
[125] *Id.* at p.76.
[126] *Id.* at p.102.
[127] *Norris v. Ireland*, 13 E.H.R.R. 186 (1991).

CHAPTER 24

The Family and Children

Some modern constitutions, such as those of Germany and Italy, refer to the family as a social institution deserving special protection.[1] Articles 41 and 42 of the Constitution were innovative for their time in this regard. According to Article 41:

> "1.1 The State recognises the Family as the natural primary and fundamental unit group of Society, and as a moral institution possessing inalienable and imprescriptible rights, antecedent and superior to all positive law.
>
> 1.2 The State, therefore, guarantees to protect the Family in its constitution and authority, as the necessary basis of social order and as indispensable to the welfare of the Nation and the State.
>
> 2.1 In particular, the State recognises that by her life within the home, woman gives to the State a support without which the common good cannot be achieved.
>
> 2.2 The State shall, therefore, endeavour to ensure that mothers shall not be obliged by economic necessity to engage in labour to the neglect of their duties in the home.
>
> 3.1 The State pledges itself to guard with special care the institution of Marriage, on which the Family is founded, and to protect it against attack."

Article 41.3.2 and 3 deal with divorce and Article 42, which is headed "Education," deals principally with the role of the family and parents in education.[2] Article 42.5 has wider application,[3] beyond education, providing that "in exceptional cases, where the parents for physical or moral reasons fail in their duty towards their children, the State as guardian of the common good, by appropriate means shall endeavour to supply the place of the parents, but always with due regard for the natural and imprescriptible rights of the child."

Articles 8(1) and 12 of the European Convention stipulate that "[e]veryone has the right to respect for his ... family life" and that "[m]en and women of

---

[1] Articles 6 and 29–31, respectively; Article 1 of the Constitution of Chile states that: "[T]he family is the fundamental nucleus of society."

[2] *Infra*, p.698.

[3] *Re Adoption (No. 2) Bill, 1987* [1989] I.R. 656 at p.663.

marriageable age have the right to marry and to found a family, according to the national laws governing the exercise of this right." Article 23 of the UN Covenant states that "[t]he family is the natural and fundamental group unit of society and is entitled to protection by society and the State;" it goes as to guarantee a right to marry and not to be forced to marry, to equality within marriage and that, in the event of a dissolution, the children of the marriage shall be protected. Ireland has ratified the UN Convention on the Rights of the Child,[4] the European Convention on the Legal Status of Children Born out of Wedlock[5] and the European Convention on the Adoption of Children,[6] as well as numerous conventions on the reciprocal enforcement of court orders relating to maintenance obligations and the custody of children.

The general tenor of Articles 41 and 42 of the Constitution were summed up by Murray J. to the effect that "the family as a moral institution enjoys certain liberties under the Constitution which protect it from undue interference by the State, whereas the State may intervene in exceptional circumstances in the interests of the common good or where the parents have failed for physical or moral reasons in their duty towards their children."[7]

It has been held that Article 41.1 and 2 do not purport to "create any particular right within the family, or to grant to any individual member of the family rights, whether of property or otherwise, against other members of the family, but rather deals with the protection of the family from external forces."[8] To what extent Article 41.2 confers legally enforceable rights on the "woman/mother within the home" has engendered some controversy. Married couples' rights regarding sex and procreation, and indeed regarding some other features of family life, are protected by Article 40.3 of the Constitution and not Article 41, although it is usually of little practical importance for married couples which of these provisions embodies the right in question. On the basis of what was held in the *McGee* case,[9] Costello J. in *Murray v. Ireland*,[10] concluded that the rights falling within Article 41 "are those which can properly be said to belong to the institution (of marriage) itself," whereas there are other rights "which each individual member might enjoy by virtue of membership of the family" and which are based on Article 40.3.[11]

---

[4] November 20, 1989, 1577 UNTS 3. See generally, G. van Buren, *The International Law on the Rights of the Child* (1998).
[5] October 15, 1975, 1138 U.N.T.S. 303.
[6] April 24, 1967, 634 U.N.T.S. 255.
[7] *North Western Health Board v. H.W.* [2001] 3 I.R. 622 at p.673.
[8] *L. v. C.* [1992] 2 I.R. 77 at p.108.
[9] *McGee v. Attorney General* [1974] I.R. 284; *infra*, p.679.
[10] [1985] I.R. 532.
[11] *Id.* at p.538.

"FAMILY"

At the outset, there is the question of what comprises a family for the purpose of the constitutional protections; is it the "nuclear" family based on marriage or does the concept have a wider sweep? In the Irish version of these articles, the word used is "*teachlach*," which means the household and not just husband, wife and (their) children. Nevertheless, it has been held on a number of occasions that the family, as contemplated by Article 41 of the Constitution, is that based on marriage – as opposed to male/female and parent/child relationships outside of marriage. In *State (Nicolaou) v. An Bord Uchtála*,[12] where his non-marital child was given for adoption without him being heard by the Adoption Board as to whether it should be adopted, the applicant claimed *inter alia* that his rights under Article 41 had been contravened. But the Supreme Court held that extra-marital relationships do not fall within this Article. According to Walsh J., for the court:

> "It is quite clear from the provisions of Article 41, and in particular section 3 thereof, that the family referred to in this Article is the family which is founded on the institution of marriage and, in the context of the Article, marriage means valid marriage under the law for the time being in force in the State. While it is quite true that unmarried persons cohabiting together and the children of their union may often be referred to as a family and have many, if not all, of the outward appearances of a family, and may indeed for the purposes of a particular law be regarded as such, nevertheless so far as Article 41 is concerned the guarantees therein contained are confined to families based upon marriage .... For the same reason the mother of an illegitimate child does not come within the ambit of Articles 41 and 42 ...".[13]

On later occasions the court has reiterated that it is "well established in case law ... that the family recognised by the Constitution, particularly Article 41, is the family based upon marriage ...;" that a "*de facto* family, or any rights arising therefrom is not recognised by the Constitution ...."[14] But it has been suggested that Article 41.2 applies to all mothers, regardless of their marital status.

This does not mean that persons in comparable extra-marital arrangements have no constitutional protection for their relationships. As with everybody else, those persons benefit from the principles of legality, personal freedom, fair procedures and equality avoid. It was held by the Supreme Court in *I.O'T.*

---

[12] [1966] I.R. 567; *infra*, p.711.
[13] *Id.* at pp.643–644.
[14] *W. O'R. v. E.H.* [1996] 2 I.R. 248 at p.265.

v. B.[15] that "the rights arising from the relationship between a mother and her child born out of wedlock arise from and are governed by Article 40, 3 ... and are not dependent on any other provision of the Constitution."[16] In claims brought by fathers of non-marital children, it has been held that theirs is not a constitutionally protected relationship; such rights and responsibilities as exist between them are dependent entirely on the common law and statute.[17] The European Court of Human Rights treats some extra-marital relationships as families,[18] and there are several legislative provisions that assimilate these relationships to families.[19]

MARRIAGE, DISCRIMINATION AND AUTONOMY

A right to marry, albeit subject to the national laws, is expressly guaranteed by the two major international human rights conventions and, it would seem, implicitly by the Constitution. Those conventions also require "respect" for the family and in Article 41.2 of the Constitution the State guarantees to "protect [it] in its constitution and authority ...."

Right to Marry

Various legal requirements must be met before persons can marry,[20] such as that they are not already married, are of different sexes, have reached a certain age, have the intellectual capacity to marry, are not within the prohibited degrees and that certain formalities are satisfied. Article 41 of the Constitution does not refer expressly to a right to marry but the *Murphy* (Family Taxation) case[21] makes it clear that this right is implicit in that Article.

The extent to which states can impose restrictions or preconditions on getting married has rarely been considered by constitutional tribunals,[22] presumably because the overwhelming view in Europe and America is that there should be very few legal inhibitions against marrying. Restrictions designed to ensure that marriages will endure would most likely be regarded as a means by which the State fulfils its duty under Article 41 to "guard" and

---

[15] *I. O'T. v. B.* [1998] 2 I.R. 321.
[16] *Id.* at p.347.
[17] *J.K. v. V.W.* [1990] 2 I.R. 437.
[18] E.g. *Keegan v. Ireland* 18 E.H.R.R. 342 (1994). *Cf Attorney General of Nova Scotia v. Walsh* 221 D.L.R. 4th 1 (2002).
[19] E.g., "spouse" as defined in s. 2(1) of the Mental Health Act 2001.
[20] See generally, A. Shatter, *Family Law* (4th ed., 1997), ch.4 (hereinafter *"Shatter"*) and G. Shannon (ed.), *Family Law Practitioner* (2000) A (hereafter *"Shannon"*).
[21] *Murphy v. Attorney General* [1982] I.R. 241; *infra*, p.670.
[22] *Cf.* the *Spanish Marriage case* 31 BVerfGE 58 (1971).

"protect" the family. In very recent times, the question of "same sex marriages" has attracted some judicial attention[23] and indeed legislative action[24] in a handful of countries.

Discrimination in Favour of Marriage

There are various legal provisions that facilitate and favour marriage which may even be required by the obligation on the State to "protect" and to "guard" marriage. Formerly, a spouse enjoyed the privilege not to disclose any communication made by the other spouse, during the course of their marriage, in either civil or criminal proceedings. This was abolished in 1992 but subject to the caveat that the change shall not "affect any right of a spouse or former spouse in respect of marital privacy."[25] Accordingly, where the evidence being sought significantly impinges on the partners' privacy, it is privileged and does not have to be disclosed by either of them in any form of proceedings. Whether or to what extent this privilege has constitutional underpinning has yet to be determined.

Other, what may be termed pro-family, provisions include Part IV (sections 47–51) of the Civil Liability Act 1961, by virtue of which a deceased's dependants are entitled to compensation from a person whose wrong caused the death. The Social Welfare (Consolidation) Act 1993, as amended, contains an extensive range of contributory and non-contributory benefits for family members, *inter alia*, pregnancy and maternity benefits, child support payments, carer's allowance, deserted wife's allowance and lone parent family payments. Provisions of tax laws that favour marriage were highlighted by counsel for the State in *Murphy v. Attorney General*.[26] A provision of the Succession Act 1965, that favours inheritance by relatives bound by marital ties over claims by non-marital children, was upheld by the Supreme Court as a justified discrimination in favour of marriage.[27]

Discrimination Against Marriage

Because the question whether an individual is a member of a family can be very relevant to the implementation of various social policies, the law differentiates in numerous ways between persons on the basis of family membership; such discriminatory treatment is not invariably unconstitutional.

---

[23] *E.g. Halpern v. Attorney General of Canada* 215 D.L.R. 4th 223 (2002) and 225 D.L.R. (4th) 529 (2003).

[24] See generally, "Developments in the Law: The Law of Marriage and Family" 116 *Harv. L. Rev.* 1196 (2003), pp.2004 *et seq.*

[25] Criminal Evidence Act 1992, sch. and s.26.

[26] [1982] I.R. 241; *infra*, p.670.

[27] *O'B. v. S.* [1984] I.R. 316; *infra*, p.685.

Discrimination against either men or women on the grounds of their "marital status," in most employments and in the provision of services, is proscribed by the Employment Equality Act 1998 and the Equal Status Act 2000. A *clause célibataire* in a contract most likely would be unenforceable, as contrary to public policy,[28] as very likely would a similar stipulation in a will.[29]

The appropriate way to tax family incomes and family assets has engendered considerable controversy in modern societies.[30] Formerly, the tendency was to pool family earnings and assets for tax purposes because comparatively few married women earned or owned property, but that is no longer the case. Under the Income Tax Act 1967, husbands' and wives' incomes were aggregated for the purpose of determining their liability to income tax; provision was also made whereby either party could have their income assessed separately and there was a married persons' personal allowance which was twice that of single persons. Nevertheless, because husbands' and wives' incomes were aggregated, and especially because income tax in Ireland was distinctly progressive at the time, many married persons with two incomes paid significantly more in tax than they would have paid if they were single and were both in receipt of exactly the same incomes. In *Murphy v. Attorney General*,[31] the plaintiffs were a married couple and schoolteachers and, for the tax year 1977–78 it was estimated that they both would have to pay approximately £2,000 in income tax, whereas if they were not married they both would have been liable for approximately £1,700. They contended that aggregating incomes as it affected them contravened Article 40.1 of the Constitution because it was unfairly discriminatory, and also contravened the guarantees for the family in Article 41. The Supreme Court found that the relevant provisions contravened the latter Article: in the circumstances there was "a breach of the pledge by the State to guard with special care the institution of marriage and to protect it against attack."[32]

Having paraphrased the contents of Article 41 and summarised very briefly the arguments in the case, Kenny J. for the court reasoned that "[t]he Court accepts the proposition that the State has conferred many revenue, social and other advantages and privileges on married couples and their children. Nevertheless, the nature and potentially progressive extent of the burden created by section 192 of the 1967 Act is such that, in the opinion of the Court, it is a breach of the pledge by the State to guard with special care the institution of marriage and to protect it against attack. Such breach is, in the view of the Court, not compensated for or justified by such advantages and privileges."[33]

---

[28] *Fed. de la Mutualite de l'Aube* c. *Dame Forestier*, Cass. Soc., February 7, 1968 [1968] *Dalloz* 429.

[29] See *infra*, pp.892 *et seq.*

[30] See generally, K. Corrigan, *Revenue Law* (2000), pp.625 *et seq.* and *Shannon* BC.

[31] [1982] I.R. 241.

[32] *Id.* at p.287.

[33] *Ibid.* Similarly the *Joint Income Tax Case* 6 BVerfGE 55 (1957).

In other words, section 192 of the 1967 Act discriminated against marriage because it imposed a financial burden on individuals who marry; while the many financial and other benefits the State confers on married couples justify subjecting them to some fiscal burdens, the nature of the burden imposed by s. 192 was such that it could not be justified on those grounds. Precisely why financial advantages in other contexts did not justify the section is not indicated. It might be said it deterred people from getting married and indeed rendered "living in sin" financially attractive. Against that, given the extent of marital breakdown in the country, a measure that had the effect of forcing people to think twice before getting married could be regarded as a measure that supports the family, although section 192 was not enacted with that purpose in mind. In a later case, the court rejected the view that the reason for the *Murphy* decision was because the section "constituted an inducement to men and women to live together without entering into a contract of marriage or, if married, to separate ....".[34] It was held that the plaintiffs could recover the excess tax they should not have been required to pay, but only as from the date they commenced proceedings, and that any others who had instituted comparable proceedings at the time should be similarly treated.

Hamilton J.'s judgment at first instance in *Murphy* focused on the section's discriminatory nature: it aggregated the income of married couples living together but the 1967 Act did not aggregate the incomes of anybody else who lived together. Accordingly, it "discriminated invidiously" against married persons[35] as well as contravening Article 41. However, the Supreme Court rejected the view that s. 192 infringed against the Article 40.1 guarantee of equality.[36] This decision put an end to aggregation for income tax purposes and aggregation does not exist in respect of capital taxes.

Shortly afterwards the tax regime was changed, abolishing joint assessment and substituting two individual assessments. Section 21 of the Finance Act 1980, was retrospective, endeavouring to deal with persons who had not paid tax or who had not been assessed previously. But when applied, married couples still ended up paying more tax than did two single persons. In consequence, in *Muckley v. Ireland*[37] it was declared invalid by the Supreme Court.

That taxes are not invariably unconstitutional because they place some burdens on families was confirmed in *Madigan v. Attorney General*,[38] where Part VI of the Finance Act 1983, which introduced the since-repealed residential property tax, was unsuccessfully challenged. As is explained later, this was a tax imposed on occupiers of what may be termed expensive houses where the aggregate incomes of all those residing in the house exceeded a prescribed

---

[34] *Muckley v. Ireland* [1985] I.R. 472 at p.485.
[35] [1982] I.R. at p.279.
[36] *Supra*, p.379.
[37] [1985] I.R. 472.
[38] [1986] I.L.R.M. 136.

amount. Its constitutionality was contested on various grounds, one being that it contravened Article 41. As regards aggregating incomes, the position was that all occupiers of houses valued at £65,000 or more were liable for the tax but they were exempted if the residents' total income was less than £20,000. Thus, the aggregation did not operate to trigger tax liability; instead it was relevant to exemption from liability. Furthermore, unlike in the *Murphy* case, the incomes of all residents were aggregated regardless of whether or not they were members of the one family.

Social welfare rules have also been struck down on account of their treating family units less favourably than unmarried couples and their children in otherwise comparable circumstances. In *Hyland v. Minister for Social Welfare*,[39] the plaintiff and his wife were unemployed and had one child. Both were paid unemployment allowances of £66.80 in aggregate per week; his was non-contributory assistance while hers was contributory benefit at the lower rate. Had they not been married or had they not been living together, they would have paid a total of £77.98 a week. Relying on the *Murphy* judgment, they contended that this was unconstitutional. For the State it was argued that *Murphy* should be distinguished on several grounds: that there were numerous other social welfare allowances only payable to married persons and, therefore, account should be taken of overall provision for them rather than the one type of benefit/allowance; that the disparate treatment of married and single couples in income tax arrangements was more readily quantifiable than in the present instance; that, unlike with income tax, there was no progressive element in social welfare. More fundamentally, it was said, when it comes to the question of how the State should spend money, the courts ought not get involved or should do so only in the most exceptional circumstances; this was especially so in the social welfare field, which is a most complex area. Nor had it been shown that the Oireachtas had intended any "clear-cut attack on or threat to the institution of marriage ...".

These contentions were not accepted by the Supreme Court. Once the provisions in question substantially penalise marriage, that is sufficient to establish their invalidity; improper motive is unnecessary, again emphasising that the basis for the *Murphy* decision was not that the tax rules there were designed to induce couples not to marry. Nor, it was held, is it relevant that there are some social welfare allowances payable only to persons who are married; Finlay C.J. for the court "reject[ed] the submission that these benefits could compensate for or justify a failure to guard or protect the institution of marriage ...".[40] Nor was the progressive nature of income tax central to the holding in *Murphy*. Finlay C.J. added that, over a one year period, the actual loss of allowances the plaintiff and his wife would suffer by their being married

---

[39] [1989] I.R. 624.
[40] *Id.* at p.645.

was about the same as the plaintiffs would have lost by having to pay additional tax. Indeed, when the overall financial position of both married couples was compared, the hardship on the plaintiff and his wife here was significantly greater than on the couple in the tax case. Provisions in regulations giving effect to an EC Directive on farming in disadvantaged areas were declared invalid in *Greene v. Minister for Agriculture*[41] on similar grounds. Under these, cattle headage payments were to be made to qualifying farmers provided, *inter alia*, their off-farm income, combined with that of their spouses, did not exceed £5,415 per annum. Because this "penalised the married state," Murphy J. held that it contravened Article 41.

A more ambitious attack on perceived anomalies in the tax and social welfare systems was mounted unsuccessfully in *Mhic Mathúna v. Attorney General*,[42] where the focus was on the unmarried mothers' allowance. Over approximately ten years, the married couples' dependent children tax free allowance had been reduced to nil. But unmarried mothers and other categories of parent continued to enjoy a tax free allowance in respect of dependent children. Over the same period, the average weekly support per child through the income tax and social welfare systems increased by 6.8% per annum; for unmarried mothers with a similar number of children it increased by 14.4% per annum. The plaintiffs contended that this disparate treatment of married and unmarried parents with children contravened Articles 40 and 41. They did "not ask the court to rewrite the legislation or to reduce the benefits available to others – [they sought] to establish that to base reductions in support of [their] status as married parents is both unequal treatment and a failure of the State's obligation to the family based on marriage."[43]

This argument created a major difficulty in that if the plaintiffs were to succeed, at most they would obtain was a declaration that the payment of unmarried mothers' allowances was invalid, thereby depriving those mothers of a benefit but acquiring no tangible benefit for themselves. For, if the plaintiffs were to succeed, the courts had no jurisdiction to "direct the legislature to enact new and different provisions in their favour."[44] In any event, the Supreme Court held that the difference in treatment did not constitute invidious discrimination, contrary to the equality guarantee: there were several grounds justifying distinguishing between the needs of single parents and those of married parents living together. As for Article 41, the reason for rejecting the plaintiff's claim seems to have been that success would not have availed them of any benefit, the inter-action between social welfare and taxation is an extremely complex subject, over which the State must have a wide discretion, and there are a variety of other supports the State provides married couples for

---

[41] [1990] 2 I.R. 17.
[42] [1995] 1 I.R. 484.
[43] *Id.* at p.487.
[44] *Id.* at p.495; but *cf. supra* p.403, n.256.

bringing up their children that compensate for such differences as existed in the present case.

Discrimination Within Marriage

There used to be considerable legal discrimination against married women, especially in respect of the ownership of property and employment in the public service. Having summarised the principal legal disabilities borne by married women, Blackstone in 1765 explained that those "are for the most part intended for her protection and benefit. So great a favourite is the female sex of the laws of England."[45] Married women's legal handicaps in respect of property ownership and other related matters were removed by the Married Women's Property Acts 1882-1907, and Married Women's Status Act 1957; the "marriage bar" in the public service was removed in 1973.

Legal provisions that treat persons differently on account of their sex are at times held to be unconstitutional. Equality within marriage is called for by Article 5 of the European Convention's 7th Protocol, according to which "[S]pouses shall enjoy equality of rights and responsibilities of a private law character between them, and in their relations with their children, as to marriage, during marriage and in the event of its dissolution." The common law rule that permitted husbands but not wives to flout ante-nuptial agreements about their children's upbringing was declared unconstitutional,[46] as were the common law rules that a wife was coerced by her husband to commit a criminal offence[47] and that a wife's domicile was always that of her husband.[48] The common law rule that permitted husbands but not wives to sue for damages for loss of consortium was not alone found to be unconstitutional but the Supreme Court held that, in consequence, entitlement to sue in respect of an equivalent loss should be extended to wives.[49]

Other similar anomalies in the common law were repealed by statute. Thus, the rule that, in the event of a dispute between a husband and wife about how their child should be brought up and in the absence of any express or implied agreement between them on the matter, it is the husband's views that prevail,[50] was abolished by the Guardianship of Infants Act 1964. Another such rule, that a husband could not be convicted of raping his wife, was abolished by section 5 of the Criminal Law (Rape) Amendment Act 1990.[51] Some sex-

---

[45] W. Blackstone, *Commentaries on the Laws of England* (1765, Vol. 1) at p.445.
[46] *Tilson Infants, Re* [1951] I.R. 1.
[47] *State (DPP) v. Walsh* [1982] I.R. 412.
[48] *W. v. W.* [1993] 2 I.R. 476; *infra*, p.719.
[49] *McKinley v. Minister for Defence* [1992] 2 I.R. 333; *supra*, p.378.
[50] *Re Frost Infants* [1947] I.R. 3 at pp.23 and 24.
[51] In England this was abolished by judicial innovation: *R. v. R.* [1992] A.C. 599.

discriminatory statutory provisions were repealed in response to international law requirements that outlaw such rules. Thus, the Domicile and Recognition of Foreign Divorces Act 1986 removed the common law rule that married women's domicile invariably followed their husband's domicile; six years later, this rule was also found to be unconstitutional.[52] Under section 1 of the 1986 Act, married women have an independent domicile which is determined by the same factors as obtain regarding everybody else's domicile, Another provision that has been changed is the rule whereby it was possible for wives of Irish nationals to acquire Irish citizenship relatively easily but it was more difficult for husbands of Irish citizens to become nationals.[53] By virtue of the Irish Nationality and Citizenship (Amendment) Act 1986, husbands and wives are treated in exactly the same way as regards becoming Irish citizens.

Many sex-discriminatory provisions in social welfare rules were removed in the general equalisation brought about in order to implement EC Directives in this field.[54]

Spousal Autonomy

The "authority" of the family acknowledged in Article 41.2 of the Constitution and the "respect" for the family proclaimed in the international instruments signifies that spouses are entitled to considerable autonomy in determining how family arrangements should be conducted; that the State should not seek to dictate to them how they should manage their family affairs. As explained below, in 1974 a law that made it practically impossible for married couples to obtain contraceptives was declared invalid.[55] And in 1994 a Bill providing for the joint ownership by spouses of every family home acquired in the future was held to be repugnant, "[h]aving regard to the extreme importance of the authority of the family ... including its right to make decisions within its own authority. ..."[56] An aspect of family autonomy expressly provided for in the Constitution is regarding children's education.

Before 1991 it was not possible to adopt a child whose parents were married but, under the Adoption Act of that year, this became permissible where parents who had "failed in their duty towards the child" are thereby deemed to have abandoned him and, additionally, adoption is found by the High Court to be in the "best interests of the child."[57] The Bill proposing this regime was upheld by the Supreme Court in *The Adoption (No.2) Bill, 1987, Re*,[58] where it had

---

[52] *W. v. W.* [1993] 2 I.R. 476.
[53] Irish Nationality and Citizenship Act 1986; *supra*, p.381.
[54] *Infra*, p.829.
[55] *McGee v. Attorney General* [1974] I.R. 284; *infra*, p.679.
[56] *Re Matrimonial Home Bill, 1993* [1994] 1 I.R. 305 at p.326; *infra*, p.684.
[57] *Infra*, p.708.
[58] [1989] I.R. 656.

been contended that to allow such adoptions constituted an attack on the authority and autonomy of the family guaranteed by Articles 41 and 42, as well as contravening Article 40.3.i and ii. In the statutory scheme, the intending adoptive parent first applies to the Adoption Board and it decides whether there ought to be an adoption. An application is then made to the High Court by the Health Board, in the relevant region, or by the intending adopters for approval of the proposed adoption in view of the criteria summarised above. There is an obligation for the court to hear the child's parents but that can be dispensed with in certain circumstances.

Objections to the Bill were summarised as follows:

"(a) The adoption order contemplated by the bill represents an attack upon the constitution and authority of the family to which the child belonged. The adoption order alters the constitution of that family for all time. It also represents a fundamental attack upon the authority of that family unit eliminating as it must the authority of the family and its members over the child. Additionally, the family as a group are denied their right to progress and exist as a family unit and are denied the right to the intimacy and privacy of their life as a family group. These rights of the family which are infringed by the legislative proposals are rights which are both inalienable and imprescriptible; they cannot be transferred or surrendered.

(b) The contemplated adoption will have the effect of extinguishing the child's right, as a member of the family unit, to belong to that particular family unit; such a right it is submitted it also inalienable and imprescriptible.

(c) The contemplated order further extinguishes other rights the child possesses qua member of the family, namely, the right to the society of the other members of the family unit and the right to be educated by the family group to which he belongs. These rights it is submitted are both inalienable and imprescriptible.

(d) Finally, the proposed legislation if enacted would extinguish the parents' inalienable right to educate and have custody of their children."[59]

For the court, Finlay C.J. stated that Article 42.5 imposed a duty on parents to educate and also to "cater for the other personal rights of the child;" additionally, under Article 40.3, the State is "obliged so far as is practicable, to vindicate the personal rights of the child whose parents have failed in their duty to it."[60] Consequently, it was not "constitutionally impermissible for a statute to restore to any member of an individual family constitutional rights of which he has

---

[59] *Id.* at p.661.
[60] *Id.* at p.663.

been deprived by a method which distorts or alters the constitution of that family if that method is necessary to achieve that purpose."[61] It was concluded that the Bill displayed "a due regard for the natural and imprescriptible rights of the child" to be a member of its parents' family.[62] For instance, failure to safeguard the child's interests on account of poverty would never be a sufficient basis for having it adopted. Nor can it be adopted if it is not shown that the parents' dereliction of duty is unlikely to continue until its 18th year of age. Abandonment here is not confined to literally abandoning the child but, in a later case, was held to have a "special legal meaning," encompassing a failure to fulfil legal obligations to the child to such extent as warrants deeming it to have been abandoned.[63] Nor can the "best interests of the child" be determined on the basis of some "simple material test, but would necessarily involve proper consideration of all the consequences, from the point of view of the child, of bringing it by adoption out of the family into which it was born and into an alternative family."[64]

PROCREATION

It would appear that there is a constitutional right to have children that is not confined to married couples. However, there are no laws that prohibit or that severely disadvantage persons from having children. There are certain legal changes that could be brought about to make it easier for unmarried couples to bring up their children but it is unlikely that there is any constitutional obligation on the State to adopt those measures. To date the Oireachtas has not intervened in areas such as surrogate parenting, *in vitro* fertilisation and other features of reproductive technology.[65] Whether or to what extent the State is permitted to enact laws that discourage procreation or to regulate procreation remains to be determined.

In *McGee v. Attorney General*,[66] which concerned contraception, Walsh J. observed that it is for married couples alone to decide whether they should have children and, if so, when and how many; that "[i]t is a matter exclusively for the husband and wife to decide how many children they wish to have; it would be quite outside the competence of the State to dictate or prescribe the number of children which they might have or should have .. For example, ... (i)f the State were to attempt to intervene to compel (sexual) abstinence, it

---

[61] *Ibid.*

[62] *Ibid.*

[63] *Southern Health Board v. An Bord Uchtála* [2000] 1 I.R. 165.

[64] [1989] I.R. 656 at p.665.

[65] See generally, D. Madden, *Medicine, Ethics and the Law* (2002), Chaps. 4–7 and "Developments," *supra* n. 24, pp.2052 *et seq.*

[66] *McGee v. Attorney General* [1974] I.R. 284; *infra*, p.679.

would be an intolerable and unjustifiable intrusion into the privacy of the matrimonial bedroom."[67] But this does not mean that the State lacks the authority to implement a population policy that discourages or promotes having children. As the judge explained, "the State, when the common good requires it, may ... actively encourage married couples either to have larger families or smaller families. If it is a question of having smaller families then, whether it be a decision of the husband and wife or the intervention of the State, the means employed to achieve this objective would have to be examined. What may be permissible to the husband and wife is not necessarily permissible to the State."[68]

Prisoners

The question that arose in *Murray v. Ireland*[69] was the extent to which the State is obliged to take measures in order to facilitate married couples, in this instance prisoners, having sexual relations for the purpose of procreation. The plaintiffs, a married couple, were in a most exceptional position in that they were both serving life sentences of imprisonment for murdering a member of the Garda Síochána. By the time the wife would be released from prison, assuming the normal practice for remission of sentence, she would be too old to have a child. Both were being held in Limerick prison – the first plaintiff in the women's section and the second plaintiff in the men's section. They had no children and they sought to be provided with facilities so that they could have sexual relations with a view to having children, on the grounds of their constitutional right of procreation. Costello J. held that rights connected with personal liberty, such as having children, must be exercised in ways "which are compatible with the reasonable requirements of the place (of) imprison(ment) or, to put it another way, do not impose unreasonable demands on it."[70] In other words, the right in question must be compatible with the effective administration of the prison. If, as they sought, the plaintiffs were afforded special facilities in order that a child could be conceived, similar facilities would have to be given to other prisoners in equivalent circumstances. But on the evidence before him, Costello J. concluded that it would be administratively impossible for the prison service to make those facilities available; that "it would place unreasonable demands on the prison service to require prison authorities to make facilities available, within the confines of the prison, to enable all prisoners who fall within this category to exercise their right to beget children."[71]

---

[67] *Id.* at pp.311–312.
[68] *Ibid.*
[69] [1985] I.R. 532.
[70] *Id.* at p.542.
[71] *Id.* at p.543. *Cf. R. (Mellor) v. Secretary of State* [2002] Q.B. 13.

Contraception

A law was enacted in 1935 that forbade the importation, manufacture or sale of contraceptives,[72] at a time when contraception, even among married couples, was widely regarded as immoral. In *McGee v. Attorney General*,[73] the Supreme Court held that this measure, which made it practically impossible for married couples to obtain contraceptives, contravened their implied constitutional right to marital privacy. The plaintiff was a married woman, aged 27 years and had four children. Her medical adviser informed her that another pregnancy would have serious consequences for her and would even put her life at risk. She and her husband thereupon resolved that they would not have any more children and decided that she should use contraceptives. Those could not be lawfully manufactured or sold in Ireland, nor imported. She sought to import some but they were seized by the customs authorities and confiscated. She thereupon successfully challenged the constitutionality of section 17 of the 1935 Act on several grounds but principally that it contravened Article 40.3 and Article 41.

Without citing any authority, Budd J. in the Supreme Court approached the issue from first principles – that if the State is entitled to prevent people from determining the number of children they shall have then the constitutional guarantees are virtually meaningless. According to him, "[w]hat more important personal right could there be in a citizen than the right to determine in marriage his attitude and resolve his mode of life concerning the procreation of children? … (I)t is scarcely to be doubted in our society that the right to privacy is universally recognised and accepted with possibly the rarest of exceptions, and that the matter of marital relationship must rank as one of the most important of matters in the realm of privacy."[74] Henchy and Griffin JJ., who cited United States authority on very similar issues, also based their judgments on the right to privacy generally under Article 40.3, rather than Article 41. According to Henchy J., "s 17 of the Act … violates … Article 40(1) … not only by violating her personal right to privacy in regard to her marital relations but, in a wider way, by frustrating and making criminal any efforts by her to effectuate the decision of her husband and herself, made responsibly, conscientiously and on medical advice, to avail themselves of a particular contraceptive method so as to insure her life and health as well as the integrity, security and well-being of her marriage and her family."[75]

Walsh J.'s judgment, on the other hand, is founded principally on Article 41. Since it is "a matter exclusively for the husband and wife to decide how many children they wish to have," and since the State cannot dictate that they shall have a certain number of children, "the husband and wife had a correlative

---

[72] Criminal Law (Amendment) Act 1935, s.17.
[73] [1974] I.R. 284.
[74] *Id.* at p.322.
[75] *Id.* at p.328.

right to have no children."[76] Therefore, "[t]he sexual life of a husband and wife is of necessity and by its nature an area of particular privacy. If the husband and wife decide to limit their family or to avoid having children by use of contraceptives, it is a matter peculiarly within the joint decision of the husband and wife and one into which the State cannot intrude unless its intrusion can be justified by the exigencies of the common good."[77] But no such public interest was established in evidence, and the fact that the majority of citizens may regard contraception as immoral is not sufficient justification for interfering with married couples' choice in this regard. Six years later the Health (Family Planning) Act 1979, was enacted, which permits persons to import contraceptives for their personal use, but which otherwise restricted considerably the supply of contraceptives.

Parentage

An issue that arises from time to time, where a child has been adopted, is whether or to what extent he can obtain information about one or both of its parents' identity.[78] A similar issue arises where some of the modern reproductive technology techniques are used.

The question of who is a child's father arises relatively frequently, especially in relation to claims for maintenance being made against men alleged to be the fathers of non-marital children. Determining who is the father is essentially a matter of fact and of proof. In *S. v. S.*[79] the common law irrebuttable presumption, that any child born to a married woman was fathered by her husband, was declared unconstitutional as being inconsistent with procedural fairness. Rebuttable presumptions are provided for in section 46 of the Status of Children Act 1987, to deal with these and comparable circumstances and Parts VI and VII (sections 33–47) of this Act contain a procedure whereby the identity of a child's parents may be determined in the Circuit Court.

FAMILY PROPERTY

For most purposes, Irish law does not aggregate a husband and a wife's property and treat it as one: each spouse's own property does not automatically become the joint property of their marriage. In the past, a husband on marriage became owner of whatever property his wife owned and also whatever property she

---

[76] *Id.* at p.311.
[77] *Id.* at p.312.
[78] *Infra*, p.707.
[79] [1983] I.R. 68.

subsequently acquired, but the remnants of that system were abolished by the Married Women's Status Act 1957. One of the main principles underlying this Act is that of separate properties; on and after marriage, the husband's property remains his and the wife remains owner of her property. Depending on the circumstances, property acquired during the marriage may belong jointly to both of them. There are several equitable principles and presumptions as to when property purchased by a husband in his wife's name, or purchased by a wife in her husband's name, or purchased jointly, belongs beneficially to one or other of them, or is theirs jointly.[80]

Family Home

Many of the reported cases on this question relate to the family home, where one of the spouses claims a beneficial interest in the home or that part of the home standing in the name of the other spouse. There is no governing principle specific to family homes but the fact that the disputed property is the parties' home tends to have some bearing in the application of the equitable principles concerning beneficial ownership.[81]

Property rights in the family home are not directly affected by the Family Home Protection Act 1976, but it safeguards a spouse's right to reside in the home by rendering ineffective most dispositions by the other spouse of any interest in the home without the prior consent of the aggrieved spouse; accordingly, the latter is usually in a position to veto dealings in the home that would prejudice her right to reside there. The veto that spouses enjoy under this Act is not unqualified and it may be overridden by the court in appropriate circumstances. On several occasions, it has been held by the High Court that the 1996 Act provides no protection against a judgment mortgage registered on the home in respect of one spouse's debts.[82] Whether this implied exclusion of judgment mortgages constitutes unfair discrimination contrary to Article 40.1 or Article 41 has never been determined.

An endeavour to confer property rights in the family home on spouses, especially wives, on the basis of Article 41 was rejected by the Supreme Court in *L. v. L.*[83] Barr J.'s judgment in the High Court eloquently puts the case for the proposition:

"Article 41 contains two fundamental concepts which are interrelated. First, the family is recognised as the natural, primary and fundamental unit group of society which is the necessary basis of social order and it possesses inalienable rights that are superior to all positive law. Secondly,

---

[80] See generally, H. Delany, *Equity and the Law of Trusts in Ireland* (2nd ed., 1999), Chap.7.
[81] *Id.* and *Shatter*, pp.723 *et seq.*
[82] *E.g. Containercare (Ireland) Ltd v. Wycherley* [1982] I.R. 143.
[83] [1992] 2 I.R. 77.

it is recognised that woman's life within the home gives to the State a support without which the common good cannot be achieved. It seems to me that Article 41, in so far as it relates to woman, underscores the pivotal role which she has within the family and recognises that in the day-to-day life of the unit group she plays a crucial part in weaving the fabric of the family and in sustaining the quality of its life. The strongest possible emphasis is placed on the woman's role within the home. Having regard to the terms of s. 2, sub-s. 2, which casts a specific duty on the State to endeavour to ensure that mothers will not be obliged by economic necessity to engage in labour to the neglect of their duties in the home, it is evident that the Constitution envisages that, ideally, a mother should devote all her time and attention to her duties in the home and that it is desirable that she ought not to engage in gainful occupation elsewhere unless compelled to do so by economic necessity. It follows that, if the Article is to be given flesh and meaning in practical terms, a mother who adopts that concept and devotes herself entirely to the family after marriage, has a special place in society which should be buttressed and preserved by the State in its laws. [T]he judiciary has a positive obligation to interpret and develop the law in a way which is in harmony with the philosophy of Article 41 as to the status of woman in the home. It is also in harmony with that philosophy to regard marriage as an equal partnership in which a woman who elects to adopt the full-time role of wife and mother in the home may be obliged to make a sacrifice, both economic and emotional, in doing so. In return for that voluntary sacrifice, which the Constitution recognises as being in the interest of the common good, she should receive some reasonable economic security within the marriage. That concept can be achieved, at least in part, by recognising that as her role as full-time wife and mother precludes her from contributing, directly or indirectly, in money or money's worth from independent employment or avocation towards the acquisition by the husband of the family home and contents, her work as home-maker and in caring for the family should be taken into account in calculating her contribution towards that acquisition – particularly as such work is of real monetary value. In this regard I draw no distinctions between the purchase of the family home entirely or substantially by the husband out of his independent assets and the more usual case where the home is acquired by him subject to a mortgage repayable over a term of years. ...
In either case the right of the wife to a share in the ownership of family property on the basis which I have postulated is subject to any particular arrangement or understanding there may have been between the parties in that regard. In terms of the matter under review it is not necessary for me to consider whether a woman has any constitutional right to a share in the ownership of a matrimonial home which a husband acquired by inheritance or gift or otherwise prior to the marriage and not in

contemplation of it. That may be a matter which should be dealt with by legislation."[84]

But this reasoning was rejected on appeal. While the Supreme Court judges fully sympathised with the predicament of the spouse who stayed at home and the contribution she thereby made to the family's welfare, their concern was that Barr J.'s solution would involve too radical a change in the present law. As Finlay C.J. put it, "the problem which appears to me to arise is a simple question as to whether if this court were to follow [Barr J.'s] reasoning ..., it would in truth ... be developing an existing law within the permissible limits of judicial interpretation, or whether in fact it would be legislating."[85] He added that "to identify this right in the circumstances [here] is not to develop any known principle of the common law, but is rather to identify a brand new right and to secure it to the plaintiff. Unless that is something clearly and unambiguously warranted by the Constitution or made necessary for the protection of either a specified or an unspecified right under it, it must constitute legislation and be a usurpation by the courts of the function of the legislature."[86]

Article 41.1, it was held, does not "purport to create any particular right within the family, or to grant to any individual member of the family rights, whether of property or otherwise, against other members of the family, but rather deals with the protection of the family from external sources."[87] As for Article 41.2.2, the Chief Justice accepted:

> "the contention made the judiciary is one of the organs of the State and that, therefore, the obligation taken by the State to endeavour to ensure that mothers shall not be obliged by economic necessity to engage in labour outside the home to the neglect of their duties is an obligation imposed on the judiciary as well as on the legislature and the executive.
>
> There is, however, I am satisfied, no warrant for interpreting that duty on the judiciary as granting to it jurisdiction to award to a wife and mother any particular interest in the family home, where that would be unrelated to the question of her being obliged by economic necessity to engage in labour to the neglect of her duties. If a court is assessing the alimony or maintenance payable by a husband to a wife and mother, either pursuant to a petition for separation or to a claim under the Family Law (Maintenance of Spouses and Children) Act 1976, it should, in my view, have regard to and exercise its duty under this sub-section of the Constitution in a case where the husband was capable of making proper provision for his wife within the home by refusing to have any regard to

---

[84] *Id.* at pp.98–99.
[85] *Id.* at p.107.
[86] *Ibid.*
[87] *Id.* at p.108.

a capacity of the wife to earn herself, if she was a mother in addition to a wife and if the obligation so to earn could lead to the neglect of her duties in the home. In other words, maintenance or alimony could and must be set by a court so as to avoid forcing by an economic necessity the wife and mother to labour out of the home to the neglect of her duties in it. Beyond that capacity of the judiciary to take part in the endeavour to comply with the provisions of Article 41, s. 2, sub-s. 2 of the Constitution, I do not consider that the transfer of any particular property right could be a general jurisdiction capable of being exercised in pursuance of that sub-section of the Constitution."[88]

Two years later, the Oireachtas intervened to safeguard the position of all spouses in a Bill providing that all family homes acquired in the future would vest in the spouses as joint tenants, regardless of which of them paid for the home. But the Supreme Court in *Re the Matrimonial Home Bill, 1993*,[89] held it to be unconstitutional, as contravening the autonomy of family members to decide how their property rights should be allocated between them. According to Finlay C.J., for the Court, "the right of a married couple to make a joint decision as to the ownership of the matrimonial home is one of the rights possessed by the family ... recognised by ... Article 41.1.1 ... as antecedent and superior to all positive law and its exercise is part ... of the authority of the family which in Article 41.1.2 the State guarantees to protect."[90] What was held to be particularly objectionable about these proposals was their "potentially indiscriminate"[91] interference with decisions spouses had made regarding ownership of their home; in other words, its over-inclusive nature. As described by the Chief Justice:

"The mandatory creation of joint equal interests in the family home also applies to every dwelling occupied as a family home irrespective of when it was first acquired by the married couple concerned and irrespective therefore of the time at which a freely arrived at decision between them may have been made as to the nature of the ownership and in whom it should vest. The provisions of the Bill do not seek to apply to particular categories of cases only, or to particular instances of the acquisition and ownership of matrimonial homes only, but rather are applied to each and every category and instance falling within the time scale provided for in the Bill, with a right of defeasance ....

Having regard to the extreme importance of the authority of the family as acknowledged in Article 41 of the Constitution and to the acceptance

---

[88] *Id.* at pp.108–109.
[89] [1994] 1 I.R. 305.
[90] *Id.* at p.325.
[91] *Id.* at p.326.

in that Article of the fact that the rights which attach to the family including its right to make decisions within its authority are inalienable and imprescriptible and antecedent and superior to all positive law, the Court is satisfied that such provisions do not constitute reasonably proportionate intervention by the State with the rights of the family and constitute a failure by the State to protect the authority of the family."[92]

Succession

In the past members of families were legally free to leave their property to whoever they wished on their death, which was often a cause of considerable hardship for the surviving spouse and the children. Part IX (sections 109–119) of the Succession Act 1965 drastically restricts spouses' testamentary freedom.[93] Where the deceased leaves a spouse and no children, that spouse is entitled to half of the deceased's estate; where there are children of the marriage, the surviving spouse is entitled to one-third of the estate. While surviving children are not given any automatic legal right to share in their parent's estate, they may apply to the court for an order making proper provision for them. Part IX's constitutionality has never been challenged. Although it may appear to be inconsistent with Article 43.1.ii's guarantee of testamentary freedom, it most likely would be upheld as a measure that protects the family and, indeed, that gives recognition to the contribution of married women as acknowledged in Article 41.2.

An individual may bequeath property to his or her non-marital child or children. The 1965 Act's provisions for intestate succession were contested in *O'B. v. S.*,[94] which in effect provide that on intestacy a deceased non-marital child may have no right of inheritance. In other words, if a man dies without having made a will and leaves, on the one hand children or brothers or sisters who were born within marriage, but also one or more non-marital children, under section 67 of this Act only the former are entitled to inherit the property. The deceased died a bachelor, leaving two sisters and as well a non-marital child, but he had made no will. It was held by the Supreme Court that section 67 did not give that child any right to inherit the deceased's property in those circumstances; the term "issue" in that section means children born within marriage. It was, therefore, contended that section 67 was unconstitutional because it infringed property rights and was unfairly discriminatory. As regards property rights, the court held that there was no such thing as a "natural right" to inherit on an intestacy: rights to inherit on intestacy can only be based on

---

[92] *Id.* at pp.325–326.
[93] See generally R. Pierse, *The Succession Act, 1965* (2nd ed., 1986), pp.238 *et seq.* and *Shatter*, pp.808 *et seq.*
[94] [1984] I.R. 316.

common law or statute, and the statutory provision here denied the defendant any right to succeed to the deceased's property.

As for the argument that there was unfair discrimination, Walsh J., for the court, observed that, if Article 41 was not contained in the Constitution, then the statutory differentiation between children and relatives born within marriage and those born outside of marriage might very well be unconstitutional. But it was "unnecessary to speculate upon what would be the position … if Article 41 did not exist."[95] Article 41 requires special protection for the family based on marriage and if a statutory provision can reasonably be regarded as designed to support marital families then it cannot be held unconstitutional because it discriminates against persons outside of the family. As Walsh J. explained:

> "Does a law aimed at maintaining the primacy of the family as the fundamental unit group of society require to come within the words of the proviso (to Article 40.1) to be valid? The Court is of opinion that it does not …
>
> Having regard to the constitutional guarantees relating to the family, the Court cannot find that the differences created by the Act of 1965 are necessarily unreasonable, unjust or arbitrary. Undoubtedly, a child born outside marriage may suffer severe disappointment if he does not succeed to some part of his part of his parents' property on intestacy, but he can suffer the same disappointment if the parent or parents die testate and leave that child no property – an event which could occur even if the Act of 1965 did enable intestate succession on the part of such a child. However, the decision to change the existing rules of intestate succession and the extent to which they are to be changed are primarily matters for the Oireachtas. Even if the present rules were to be found to be invalid having regard to the provisions of the Constitution, it would avail the defendant nothing as the resultant absence of any rules would leave her without any claimable share."[96]

DEPORTATION OF FAMILY MEMBERS

Provided that fair procedures have been followed, that there is no invidious discrimination, that the person's life will not be put at serious risk or that he is not being placed at significant risk of being tortured, there is no constitutional inhibition against deporting an alien. Deportation would also seem to be not permissible where it is a form of "disguised extradition." On the other hand, as a matter of law and also of international law, a citizen cannot be deported.[97]

---

[95] *Id.* at p.336.
[96] *Id.* at pp.334 and 336
[97] *Supra*, p.335.

The question then has arisen, where the State proposes to deport the alien parents of an Irish-born child or children, what if any constitutional constraints apply, because for all practical purposes the deported parents would bring the child away with them rather than leave it in the State in some form of care. As a general rule, to deport an Irish-born child's parents is the equivalent of deporting the child-citizen, who as a matter of law cannot be made the subject of a deportation order.

In 1989, this issue was addressed by the Supreme Court in *Fajujono v. Minister for Justice.*[98] The first two plaintiffs, a Moroccan and a Nigerian citizen, married in London in 1981 and shortly afterwards came to Ireland. They had no legal entitlement to be in the State but their presence here was not detected by the authorities for some years. By that time they had three Irish-born children. The father was then advised by the Minister that he should make arrangements for his family to leave the country or else they would be deported. His response was to commence proceedings seeking to prevent the making of a deportation order, on the grounds that any such order would in substance be one for the deportation of Irish citizens, the children, which was not permissible. In the High Court it was argued that, by virtue of the children's citizenship, their parents could not be deported at all; on appeal, it was accepted that deportation was a possibility in those circumstances but could only take place for "very compelling reasons."[99] Finlay C.J. summed up the constitutional position, that:

> "where ... an alien has in fact resided for an appreciable time in the State and has become a member of a family unit within the State containing children who are citizens, that there can be no question that those children as citizens, have got a constitutional right to company, care and parentage of their parents within a family unit ... *[P]rima facie* and subject to the exigencies of the common good that is a right which these citizens would be entitled to exercise within the State.
>
> [Further], where the parents who are not citizens and who are aliens cannot, by reason of having as members of their family children born in Ireland who are citizens, claim any constitutional right of a particular kind to remain in Ireland, they are entitled to assert a choice of residence on behalf of their infant children, in the interests of infant children."[100]

In view of this, the parents can be deported only "if, after due and proper consideration, [the Minister] is satisfied the interests of the common good and the protection of the State and its society justifies the interference with what is

---

[98] [1990] 2 I.R. 151.
[99] *Id.* at p.162.
[100] *Ibid.*

clearly a constitutional right" of the children.[101] In the case, as here, where a family of five, including three Irish citizens, do not wish to be deported, there would have to be a "grave and substantial reason associated with the common good" to justify any deportation order being made.[102] In the circumstances, the court dismissed the plaintiff's appeal but directed the Minister to give fresh consideration to all the circumstances of the plaintiff's family.

Thirteen years later, this issue again came before the Supreme Court in *L. v. Minister for Justice*.[103] As in *Fajujono*, the parents of the two families involved in these proceedings came from England to Ireland. The main differences were that they had unsuccessfully applied for asylum in England and then applied for asylum in the State, which applications also were rejected. In the meantime, they had children born in Ireland. Additionally, the Minister made an order for the parents to be deported, for which he gave three reasons, *viz.* the length of time both families had been in the State (9 months and 7 months, respectively), the application of the Dublin Convention of 1990[104] (i.e. their previous asylum application in England) and "the overriding need to preserve respect for the integrity of the asylum and immigration systems" (apparently meaning that the only reason why the parents had been permitted to remain temporarily in the State was because they had applied for asylum). There had also been a potentially significant change in the law, namely the amended Article 2 of the Constitution which, the State conceded, placed on a constitutional footing the entitlement of everyone born in the State to Irish citizenship.

As in *Fajujono*, it was accepted by the plaintiffs that parents of Irish-born children could be deported "in exceptional circumstances associated with the common good" but they contended that there were no special circumstances in this instance bringing them within this category. Their failure to secure asylum in England and in the State was not sufficient; they submitted that the Minister must have "specific evidence of the danger to the common good which is related to the illegal immigrant parents concerned, whether as individuals or as members of a class or group," for instance criminal behaviour or involvement in "a class which poses a danger to the common good." Against this, it was contended that there were two major differences from the facts in *Fajujono*. One was the length of time the families were in the State; in that case the family there had lived in Ireland for eight years prior to commencing their proceedings. More important, was the fact that both sets of parents in *L.* had failed to secure asylum first in England and subsequently in the State, and that under the Dublin Convention, the short answer to their Irish asylum applications was their failed applications in England.

---

[101] *Ibid.*
[102] *Ibid.*
[103] Unreported, Supreme Court, January 23, 2003.
[104] Convention of June 15, 1990, presently the Refugee Act 1996 (section 22) Order, 2003, S.I. No 423.

Much of the several lengthy judgments given in *L.* address what exactly had been decided in *Fajujono* because there was ambiguity in the judgment of Finlay C.J. and apparent differences between it and that given there by Walsh J. As summed up by Murray J. in *L.*, "[t]he State may, for reasons associated with the interests of the common good, deport non-nationals who are the parents of a child who is a citizen of Ireland even if that means, *de facto*, that the child is compelled to leave and reside outside the State with its parents. ... [A]ll the parties in the proceedings [accept this]. ... The issues ... focus on the ambit of the power of the State to deport parents in such circumstances."[105] According to Keane C.J., *Fajujono* was not authority for the proposition "in effect" being advanced by the plaintiffs, *viz.* "where a married couple arrive in Ireland in circumstances which render them illegal immigrants and the wife gives birth to a child, the entire family are entitled to remain in Ireland at least until such time as the child reaches his or her majority, that this right derives from the Irish citizenship of the newly born child and the constitutional rights of such a child to the society and care of its parents and that it arises irrespective of the length of time which elapses between their arrival in the State and the birth of the child. It is claimed that the only qualification to which the exercise of those rights is subject is the liability of the non-national members of the family to be deported from the State where the Minister is of the opinion on reasonable grounds that they are engaged in activities inimical to the common good or are likely to be so engaged."[106] Rather, it was authority for the proposition that "in the particular circumstances that arose in that case and which might, of course, similarly arise in other cases, the Minister was obliged to give consideration to whether, in the light of those circumstances, there were grave and substantial reasons associated with the common good which nonetheless required the deportation of the non-national members of the family, having as its inevitable consequences, either the departure of the entire family from the State or its break-up by the departure of the non-nationals alone with the consequent infringement of the constitutional rights of the Irish citizens who were members of the family. Since there was no evidence as to whether the Minister had taken those factors into consideration, the plaintiffs were given liberty to apply to the High Court in the event of his deciding to proceed with their deportation."[107]

Additionally, there had been profound changes in both the actual and legislative contexts since *Fajujono* was decided. That was at a time where there had not been a large-scale influx of aliens into the State seeking refugee status, many of them without success. In the meantime, the whole area of immigration and asylum had been the subject of extensive legislation and administrative activity, including the Dublin Convention designed to deal with

---

[105] At p.1.
[106] At pp.57–58.
[107] At p.61.

multiple asylum applications. In deciding to deport the plaintiffs, it was held that the Minister was entitled to take account of these considerations. That in the meantime the entitlement of those born in the State to Irish citizenship had been put on a constitutional footing was held to be irrelevant.

CUSTODY AND CONTROL OF CHILDREN

When parents fall out they often quarrel about who should have control of their children and, in some circumstances, State agencies seek to deprive one or both parents of custody of their children.[108] Custody is governed primarily by the Guardianship of Infants Act 1964, section 3 of which states that as an overriding principle in deciding all questions arising under that Act, the court "shall regard the welfare of the child as the first and paramount consideration." Welfare in this context is defined as "compris(ing) the religious and moral, intellectual, physical and social welfare of the infant."[109] A considerable number of court decisions have been made under this section and many of those contain strong dissenting judgments, which demonstrates how difficult it is to apply the vague criterion "the welfare of the infant" in various circumstances.

Parent *v.* Parent

Most disputes about custody are between parents; usually, either the parents are not married or they are married but no longer live together. Section 6 of the Guardianship of Infants Act 1964, provides that the father and mother shall be joint guardians and, where one parent dies, the other shall be a guardian. Since 1998 fathers of non-marital children have been entitled to apply to be appointed guardian. In the event of a dispute between parents about custody, section 3 of the 1964 Act renders the "welfare of the infant" paramount. On a number of occasions, claims that section 3 is unconstitutional in those contexts were rejected. Among the constitutional issues that have arisen is whether, in granting custody, an applicant of one sex or of one religion should be preferred over another, or a parent-applicant should be preferred over another. There are no hard and fast rules concerning these issues, although the courts take guidance from what have been called general "rules of prudence," such as that "in most cases the best place for a child is with its parent,"[110] that "(t)he Court is not to prefer one religion to another"[111] and that everything being equal, very young

---

[108] See generally, *Shatter*, Chap.13 and G. Shannon, *Children and the Law* (2001), Chap.1.
[109] S.2.
[110] *J. v. D.*, unreported, Supreme Court, June 22, 1977.
[111] *H. v. H.*, unreported, Parke J., February 4, 1976.

children should be given to the mother but elder children should go to the parent of the same sex.[112] A particularly vexed question has been the relevance of one parent's extra-marital sexual relations to granting custody to that parent.

At times parents disagree about how their children are to be brought up; the dispute may occur during the child's life or at the time it is born, or even before the birth or indeed the marriage. Where the parents have agreed that the child will be brought up in a particular way, it would seem that a parent who later seeks to renege on that agreement will be held to it. At least, so it was held in *Tilson Infants, Re*[113] and in *May Minors, Re*[114] as regards ante-nuptial agreements about religious upbringing, whether the agreement is a formal contract or is implied from the circumstances. In *Tilson* the Supreme Court held that a father is not entitled unilaterally to revoke an agreement made before the marriage and which was acted on, that the child should be brought up in a particular religion. Murnaghan J., for the court, rejected the old common law rule that fathers could not be held to these agreements as archaic and excusing dishonourable conduct. Under the Constitution it is for the "parents" to bring up their children; the rights and obligations regarding upbringing do not fall entirely on the father. Consequently, "[t]he parents – father and mother – have a joint power and duty in respect of the religious education of their children. If they together make a decision and put it into practice it is not in the power of the father – nor is it in the power of the mother – to revoke such decision against the will of the other party .... (A)n agreement made before marriage dealing with matters which will arise during the marriage and put into force after the marriage is equally effective and is of as binding force in law."[115]

Before they got married the parents in *Tilson* agreed that all of their children should be brought up as Catholics; the father was Protestant and the mother was Catholic. They had four children who were baptised and had been brought up as Catholics. But differences arose between the parents regarding the children's upbringing and the father then removed three of them from the family home and put them into a Protestant institution. It was held that his pre-nuptial agreement prevented him from doing this and that he had to give the children back to their mother. In *May Minors* it was held that, where children have been brought up in a particular religion, there is an implied agreement that they should continue to be raised in that manner and one parent cannot resile from the agreement. There, the parents were Catholics when they married and they brought up their children as Catholics but the husband became a Jehovah's Witness and then sought to prevent the children's Catholic upbringing. It was held that, because of their implied agreement, he could not do so.

---

[112] *J.J.W. v. B.M.W.* (1971) 100 I.L.T.R. 45.
[113] [1951] I.R. 1.
[114] [1954] I.R. 74.
[115] [1951] I.R. at p.34.

Where there has been no express or implied agreement on the question it was said in *Frost Infants, Re*,[116] and reiterated in *Tilson* that one or other parent's wishes must prevail and that it should be the father's wishes, which was the old common law rule. Because section 6 of the 1964 Act renders both parents "joint" guardian of the child, the father no longer has the last word on these issues; where the parents cannot agree the governing criterion is the welfare of the child.

The State has entered into international agreements dealing with inter-parental disputes about custody, where a child is taken from one country to another against the wishes of a parent.[117] By the Child Abduction and Enforcement of Custody Orders Act 1991, effect was given to the Hague Convention on the Civil Aspects of International Child Abduction, of 1980,[118] and also the Luxembourg or European Convention on Recognition and Enforcement of Certain Decisions Concerning Custody of Children and on Restoration of Custody of Children, of 1980.[119] A constitutional challenge to the Hague Convention was rejected by Keane J. in *A.C.W. v. Ireland*,[120] where a mother who had been resident in England took her child to Ireland and had been ordered to bring it back to England, where her husband and father of the child resided.

Parents *v.* Child

A question that the courts have not considered in the light of the Constitution is the extent of authority that parents have over their children, with whom they are in dispute. One reason perhaps why no such case has arisen is because section 17(2) of the Guardianship of Infants Act 1964 authorises the courts in guardianship proceedings to consult the wishes of the infant. Moreover, conflicts between parents and their children are usually resolved outside of the courts – often by the child simply leaving the home. Whenever the question does arise, a vital preliminary issue will be who exactly are children within the contemplation of the Constitution? Is it all those under the voting age, or those under the legal age for consent to sexual relations, or those still living with their parents? Presumably, the older and more mature the children are, the greater weight will be accorded to their own constitutional rights when those conflict with their parents' rights.[121]

---

[116] [1947] I.R. 3.
[117] See generally, G. Shannon, *Children and the Law*, Chap.7.
[118] October 25, 1980, 1343 U.N.T.S 89.
[119] May 20, 1980 Eur.T.S. No. 105.
[120] [1994] 3 I.R. 232; *supra*, p.250.
[121] *Cf. Gillick v. West Norfolk H.A.* [1986] A.C. 112.

Parents *v.* Third Parties/State Agencies

There are several ways in which a parent or parents can be denied custody of their children, who will then be handed over to third parties. But whether or to what extent there is an affirmative constitutional duty on the State to intervene and take over the custody of a child, in its best interests, remains to be determined.

Guardianship

Section 16 of the Guardianship Act 1964, empowers the court to decline to grant custody to a parent who has either abandoned or deserted the child, or who has allowed the child for some time to be brought up either at another's expense or with the assistance of a health authority. Nevertheless, the court can grant that parent custody where it is "satisfied ... that he is a fit person" to have custody. On several occasions the constitutionality of section 16 was raised in argument but the courts declined to rule on the issue. Because of the discretion that it gives the courts, it is unlikely to be struck down as invalid: even though it places on the parent's shoulders the burden of proving "that he is a fit person," this would not seem to be a particular onerous burden to discharge.

In *J.H., Re,*[122] the Supreme Court pronounced on how s. 16 should be interpreted when the question involves whether a child should be taken from the custody of its married parents: the principle laid down there applies to all legislative provisions conferring a discretionary power to take children from their parents' control. Before the parents married, the mother handed their child over for adoption but eventually refused her consent, so that the adoption could not then take place. The child was two years of age and for most of its life it had been with the couple who wished to adopt it. Since they could not do so without the mother's consent, the question was who was entitled to look after the child – either that couple or the child's natural parents, who had married some time after it was born. From the evidence, Lynch J. concluded that, in the circumstances and from the point of view of the child, its welfare was best served by the couple who had been looking after it retaining custody, with its parents being given rights of access to it. However, the Supreme Court held that, where the child's parents are married, the child's own welfare cannot then be the overwhelming consideration.

By virtue of its parents' marriage, their child becomes a member of a family within the terms of Article 41 and, consequently possesses imprescriptible rights; it is entitled to protection from the State and to be educated by its family. Any legislative interference with the family's custody of the child must

---

[122] [1985] I.R. p.375.

be consistent with those rights. In particular and as Article 42.5 provides, it is only when the married parents have failed in their duty to the child that the State is permitted to intervene and supplant them. Accordingly, welfare of the child in section 16 of the 1964 Act and similar provisions in other laws must be interpreted in the light of these principles. As Finlay C.J. put it, legislation providing for taking children from their married parents' custody "must be construed as involving a constitutional presumption that the welfare of the child, which is defined in (general terms), is to be found within the family, unless the Court is satisfied on the evidence that there are compelling reasons why this cannot be achieved, or unless the Court is satisfied that the evidence establishes an exceptional case where the parents have failed to provide education for the child and continue to fail to provide education for the child for moral or physical reasons."[123] Applying these criteria and not just the statutory test of the child's own best interests, Lynch J. found that there was no compelling reason why the parents should be deprived of custody and ordered that they should be given their child.

There is a presumption that a very young child's best interests are best served by being with its own married parents and if appropriate circumstances exist that show this to be otherwise in a particular instance, then it will not be acted upon. Neither Finlay C.J. nor Lynch J. indicated the kind of circumstances that would amount to "compelling reasons" why the child's welfare is not best served by being with its natural parents, nor did they elaborate on what is meant by the parents failing to provide an education for their child. But McCarthy J. stressed that any compelling reason or reasons for taking a child from its married parents must be clearly established.

Wardship

There is a long-standing inherent jurisdiction in the High Court to make a person a ward of court.[124] A third party can bring wards of court proceedings to take custody of a child away from a parent or parents, or to have the child otherwise protected from its parent or parents' conduct. Wardship proceedings are most often instituted in order to ensure independent protection for the child's property interests.

At times Health Boards bring proceedings of this nature in order to ensure children's protection against allegedly unsuitable parents.[125] For instance, where a Health Board is of the view that a child should be afforded certain medical treatment, against its parents' wishes, it will often apply to have the child taken into wardship. However, the courts have not laid down general

---

[123] *Id.* at p.395.
[124] See generally, Seymour, "Parens Partria and Wardship Powers: Their Nature and Origins" 14 *Ox. J.L. Stud.* 159 (1994).
[125] *E.g,. Eastern Health Board v. M.K.* [1999] 2 I.R. 99.

principles to govern deciding whether or in what circumstances the parents' wishes should be overridden in cases of this nature.[126] A particularly vexed question is where the parents' objections are founded on genuine religious grounds.[127]

Protection

To what extent the Constitution imposes a legally enforceable right on the State to intervene and protect children from their parents' neglect also remains to be determined. Apart from the substantive legal issue, there are also questions of *locus standi* and of the available remedy.[128] But authority to adopt appropriate measures to that end exists in Article 42.5, "where the parents for physical or moral reasons fail in their duty towards their children ...". Until they were replaced in 2001, those powers were principally the "place of safety" and the "fit person" procedures under the Children Act 1908. The principal basis for State intervention, in order to safeguard a child's best interests, is the powers given to Health Boards and to the Garda Síochána under the Child Care Act 1991, regarding emergencies (Part III, sections 12–15), care proceedings (Part IV, sections 16–23) and special care or protection (Part IVA, sections 23A–23X). In exercising their other functions under this Act, Health Boards are required to "have regard to the principle that it is generally in the best interests of a child to be brought up in his own family,"[129] although it does not define the term "family" for this purpose. It also provides that, "having regard to the rights and duties of parents, whether under the Constitution or otherwise, [health boards shall] regard the welfare of the child as the first and paramount consideration;" additionally, they shall "in so far as is practicable, give due consideration, having regard to his age and understanding, to the wishes of the child."[130]

It has been held that the courts cannot award to another custody of a child and not allow the parents to recover custody where they are in a position to look after the child adequately. In *State (Doyle) v. Minister for Education*,[131] the Supreme Court held that the Constitution "does not enable the Legislature to take away the right of a parent who is in a position to do so to control the education of his child, where there is nothing culpable on the part of either parent or child."[132] Reconciling the rights of parents on the one hand and of the children on the other, and the rights of public agencies to set standards in

---

[126] See generally, D. Madden, *Medicine, Ethics and the Law* (2002), Chap.9.
[127] *E.g., Re A (Conjoined Twins: Surgical Separation)* [2001] 2 W.L.R. 480.
[128] *Cf. T.D. v. Minister for Education* [2002] 4 I.R. 259; *infra*, p.897.
[129] Child Care Act 1991, s.3(2)(c).
[130] *Id.* s.3(2)(b).
[131] [1989] I.L.R.M. 277.
[132] *Id.* at p.280.

the professed interests of the child, has been the subject of controversial cases in Britain and the United States regarding contraception and abortion.[133]

The extent to which, under Constitution, the State may require parents to take steps in order to safeguard what the State perceives to be their child's best interests arose in *North Western Health Board v. H.W.*[134] A screening test, commonly know as the "PKU" test, has been used for over 30 years for testing the presence of certain conditions in children. It is normally carried out on new-born infants, some days after they are born, and involves taking a small blood sample – usually by inserting a lancet into the infant's heel. When the sample is tested, it indicates whether those conditions exist and they can then be treated. Unless early treatment is given, the conditions usually are irreversible. However, these conditions exist only in a very small proportion of children. There is no legislation anywhere requiring this test to be applied. In this instance, when parents refused to permit the test to be carried out on their child, the Health Board sought a declaration and orders requiring that he undergo the test. Initially, the Board relied on the general provisions in section 3(1) of the Child Care Act 1991, that it "shall be the function of every health board to promote the welfare of children in its area who are not receiving adequate care and protection." But during the proceedings, the Board invoked this only to give it *locus standi* and relied entirely on Article 40.3, the general guarantee to vindicate personal rights, and Article 42.5 which provides that, "[i]n exceptional cases, where the parents for physical or moral reasons fail in their duty towards their children," the State may appropriately intervene. The Board's application was rejected by the High Court and also, on appeal, at which stage the only relief it had sought was a declaration that the parents were in breach of this Article.

PKU was a routine test, carried out in many countries for many years, but there was no special reason for testing the infant in this instance. The great majority of infants test positively and a previous test on this infant's sibling had been positive. The parents did not dispute that, from a purely medical perspective, testing would be in its best interests. Their objection was not founded on any particular religious grounds but, in a non-pejorative sense, was irrational. There was evidence that, up to then, approximately six other couples had objected to the test. It was not suggested that the parents were other than careful and responsible parents but they had a deep conscientious objection to this test. Were the child a ward of court, the test would have been sanctioned but the application here was not based on wardship; similarly, if the child were properly in the Board's care under the 1991 Act, where the Board would be in *loco parentis*. The net issue was whether, on the basis of the Constitution's provisions, "a court may enforce on parents who are careful

---

[133] See generally, Bainham, "The Balance of Power in Family Decisions" 45 *Cam.L.J.* 263 (1986).
[134] [2001] 3 I.R. 622.

and conscientious a view of their child's welfare, which is rational but quite contrary to the parents' sincerely held but irrational beliefs;"[135] whether they "have acted in such a manner that exceptional circumstances arise by reason of a breach of duty on their part which would justify the State overriding their personal decision ...".[136]

Apart entirely from the substantive merits, Hardiman J. took the view that, generally, parental decisions "should not be overridden by the State or in particular by the courts in the absence of a jurisdiction conferred by statute,"[137] which was absent here. This was especially so in the circumstances because, for all practical purposes, a ruling in favour of the Board would render the test compulsory; the general principle was in issue and, if the Board succeeded, it and all other Health Boards most likely would rely on the decision against recalcitrant parents. He observed that "[t]he legislature, and not the courts, are in the best position to judge whether such an innovation is necessary, proportionate or desirable,"[138] citing the court's reluctance is *L. v. L.* to devise a solution to the woman-in-the-home's morally justifiable claim to a proprietary interest in the family home. Because they were not dealing with legislation that made this test compulsory, no question of the general public interest arose – as would arise in the case of a compulsory medical treatment to prevent contagious diseases, for example.

As Murray J. emphasised, Article 41.2 requires a high degree of family autonomy; it "provides a guarantee for the liberty of the family to function as an autonomous moral institution within society and, in the context of this case, protects its authority from being compromised in a manner which would arbitrarily undermine the liberty so guaranteed."[139] He concluded that:

> "If the State had a duty or was entitled to override any decision of parents because it concluded, established or it was generally considered that that decision was not objectively the best decision in the interest of the child, it would involve the State and ultimately the courts, in a sort of micro-management of the family. Parents with unorthodox or unpopular views or lifestyles with a consequential influence on their children might for that reason *alone* find themselves subject to intervention by the State or by one of the agencies of the State. Similar consequences could flow where a parental decision was simply considered unwise. That would give the State a general power of intervention and would risk introducing a method of social control in which the State or its agencies would be substituted for the family. That would be an infringement of liberties

---

[135] *Id.* at p.746.
[136] *Id.* at p.740.
[137] *Id.* at p.755.
[138] *Id.* at p.762.
[139] *Id.* at p.737.

guaranteed to the family. Decisions which are sometimes taken by parents concerning their children may be a source of discomfort or even distress to the rational and objective bystander, but it seems to me that there must be something exceptional arising from failure of duty, as stated by this court in *The Adoption (No. 2) Bill 1987* [1989] I.R. 656, before the State can intervene in the interest of the individual child.

It would be impossible and undesirable to seek to define in one neat rule or formula all the circumstances in which the State might intervene in the interests of the child against the express wishes of the parent. It seems however, to me, that there must be some immediate and fundamental threat to the capacity of the child to continue to function as a human person, physically, morally or socially, deriving from an exceptional dereliction of duty on the parts of parents to justify such an intervention."[140]

Education

Article 42 of the Constitution emphasises strongly the prerogatives and duties of parents with regard to educating their children:

"1.   The State acknowledges that the primary and natural educator of the child is the Family and guarantees to respect the inalienable right and duty of parents to provide, according to their means, for the religious and moral, intellectual, physical and social education of their children.

2.   Parents shall be free to provide this education in their homes or in private schools or in schools recognised or established by the State.

3. 1°   The State shall not oblige parents in violation of their conscience and lawful preference to send their children to schools established by the State or to any particular type of school designated by the State.

  2°   The State shall, however, as guardian of the common good, require in view of actual conditions that the children receive a certain minimum education, moral, intellectual and social.

4.   The State shall provide for free primary education and shall endeavour to supplement and give reasonable aid to private and corporate educational initiative, and, when the public good requires it, provide other educational facilities or institutions with due regard, however, for the rights of parents, especially in the matter of religious and moral formation.

---

[140] *Id.* at pp.740–741.

5.   In exceptional cases, where the parents for physical or moral reasons
      fail in their duty towards their children, the State as guardian of the
      common good, by appropriate means shall endeavour to supply
      the place of the parents, but always with due regard for the natural
      and imprescriptible rights of the child."

This Article describes the family as the "natural educator of the child" and
stipulates that parents cannot be obliged to send their children to State schools.
But the State can prescribe minimum standards of education and, where the
parents fail in their duty towards their children, the State can assume certain
parental powers. As well as being obliged to provide facilities for free primary
education, the State is required to provide some support for private education.
The position of parents with regard to their children's education is also the
subject of Article 2 of the European Convention's First Protocol; that "[i]n the
exercise of any functions which it assumes in relation to education and to
teaching, the State shall respect the right of parents to ensure such education
and teaching in conformity with their own religious and philosophical
convictions."[141] When Ireland ratified this Protocol, it entered a reservation
that, in its view, the right to education contained in the Protocol "is not
sufficiently explicit in ensuring to parents the schools of the parents' own
choice, whether or not such schools are schools recognised or established by
the State." Education is addressed in Articles 29 and 30 of the UN Convention
on the Rights of the Child.

It would seem that Article 42, which is headed "Education" (and not "The
Family," as in Article 41) applies to *de facto* families as well as to families
based on marriage. With reference to its requirement to "provide for free
primary education," Keane J. has observed that "while the principal
beneficiaries of the right ... are children in family units, they were not intended
to be the only beneficiaries. Children without parents, natural or adoptive,
whether they grow up in the care of institutions, foster parents or older relatives,
are equally entitled to the right...".[142]

It has been held that education in the context of Article 42 of the Constitution
has a narrow meaning. According to Kenny J. in the *"Fluoridation"* case:

"The word 'education' undoubtedly had [a] wide meaning at one time
but in 1937, when the Constitution was enacted, that meaning had become
obsolete. In the Shorter Oxford Dictionary, issued in 1933, the meanings
given for the word 'education' are: '(1) the process of nourishing or
rearing' (this is marked with a sign to show that this meaning was obsolete
in 1933) '(2) the process of bringing up young persons (3) the systematic
instruction, schooling or training given to the young (and, by extension,

---

[141] Similarly, Art.18(4) of the UN Covenant.
[142] *Sinnott v. Minister for Education* [2001] 2 I.R. 545 at p.630.

to adults) in preparation for the work of life. Also the whole course of scholastic instruction which a person has received'. In other dictionaries the meaning for which Mr. McBride contends is also described as obsolete. Moreover, it seems to me that the terms of the Article show that the word 'education' was not used in this wide sense in the Constitution. Section 1 of the Article recognises the 'right and duty of parents to provide, according to their means, for the religious and moral, intellectual, physical and social education of their children', but in section 2 it is provided that the parents are free to provide this education in their homes or in schools recognised or established by the State. The education referred to in section 1 must, therefore, be one ... of a scholastic nature. It seems to me, therefore, that the fluoridation of the public water supply (even if it be harmful) does not interfere with or violate the rights given to the family and to the parents by Article 42 of the Constitution."[143]

A somewhat broader view of what education comprises was taken by the Supreme Court there, as including training which is not scholastic in the traditional sense. As summed up by Ó Dálaigh C.J. "[e]ducation essentially is the teaching and training of a child to make best the possible use of his inherent and potential capacities, physical, mental and moral."[144]

In the context of the obligation to "provide for free primary education," the term was said by O'Hanlon J. to mean "giving each child such advice, instruction and teaching as will enable him or her to make the best possible use of his or her inherent and potential capacities, physical, mental and moral, however limited these capacities may be. Or, to borrow the language of the United Nations Convention and Resolution of the General Assembly – 'such education as will be conducive to the child's achieving the fullest possible social integration and individual development; such education as will enable the child to develop his or her capabilities and skills to the maximum and will hasten the process of social integration and reintegration'."[145]

Most countries' laws oblige parents to send their young children to a State approved school, although many such laws give parents some option to educate their children privately or at home. The scope of the State's competence to prescribe school attendance was considered in *School Attendance Bill, 1942, Re*,[146] which concerned provisions that, in general terms, would require parents with children aged between 6 and 14 years of age to send them to a national school or to some school recognised by or certified by the Minister for Education. But this obligation would not apply, *inter alia*, where the child was receiving a suitable education as envisaged by the Bill, where there was no

---

[143] *Ryan v. Attorney General* [1965] I.R. 294 at pp.309–310.
[144] *Id.* at p.350.
[145] *O'Donoghue v. Minister for Health* [1996] 2 I.R. 20 at p.65.
[146] [1943] I.R. 334.

State recognised nor funded school accessible to the child. It was contended, successfully, that these provisions were inconsistent with the constitutional guarantees. Dealing with compelling school attendance generally, O'Sullivan C.J., for the court, observed that the State can interfere with parental choice only to a limited extent, viz. it can only require that children have "a minimum standard of elementary education of general application,"[147] although it is not said what precisely this educational standard is. What it means, presumably, is that the State can require that all children be given the very basic education and, while views of what is basic may change over time and those changes can be reflected in legislation, the State cannot require that different children get different basic educations at any one time. The court went on to hold that the State cannot compel parents to send their children to State-owned, recognised or approved schools when the children are in fact being educated, either at home or in some private school, up to the uniform and minimum State standard; that "[t]he State is entitled to require that children shall receive a certain minimum education. So long as parents supply this general standard of education ... the manner in which it is being given and received is entirely a matter for the parents and is not a matter in respect of which the State ... is entitled to interfere."[148] It was held that some provisions of the 1942 Bill were impermissible interferences with parental freedom regarding their children's education.

While most parents are reasonably content to send their children to State schools, occasionally parental concern is caused because of particular features of State education, for instance religious classes or the religious content of courses, corporal punishment or sex education. In many countries the presence or absence of religious elements in education has been a source of considerable controversy.[149] Article 42.3 of the Constitution entitles parents not to send their children to State schools where attending those schools would be "in violation of their conscience." In *School Attendance Bill, 1942, Re*, it was contended that the word "conscience" here means more than religious conscience in the conventional sense but the court found it unnecessary to express a view on the question.

Where parents chose to educate their child at home rather than send it to the national school, they are liable to be prosecuted where the domestic arrangements do not constitute "suitable elementary education."[150] There is no statutory definition for this concept. In *DPP. v. Best*,[151] the Supreme Court held that the absence of any definition is not a defence, although it was not

---

[147] *Id.* at p.345.

[148] *Id.* at p.346.

[149] See generally, Clarke, "Freedom of Thought in Schools: A Comparative Study" 35 *Int. & Comp.L.Q.* 27 (1986) and Coons, "Educational Choice in the Courts: US and Germany", 34 *Am. J. Comp. L.* 1 (1986).

[150] School Attendance Act 1926, s.18(2)(c).

[151] [2000] 2 I.R. 17.

contended there that the prohibition was unconstitutional for failing to comply with the minimum requirements of legality. This was a case stated by the District Court to clarify what that phrase meant but little light was thrown on the subject, other than that it does not mean the existing curriculum for primary schools, that it is not invariably required to teach Irish, and that account should be taken of the child's own circumstances and where the family are living. Teaching the primary school curriculum by methods that are patently inadequate is not sufficient. Subject to this, it is for the District Judge to determine, on the basis of the evidence adduced and his own common sense, whether the requisite minimum is being provided.

It is more convenient to deal with Article 42.4, on the State providing for free primary education and other education facilities, in chapter 27 on education and social welfare rights. The State's obligation in this regard is to the child, regardless of its family situation, and furthermore is unique because, unlike most of the other rights guaranteed in Articles 40-44 of the Constitution, it involves the deployment of large financial resources and logistical provision in terms of personnel, buildings, materials and planning.

DOMESTICATED WIVES/MOTHERS

It has been fashionable to criticise Article 41.2 of the Constitution, whereby the State "recognises that by her life within the home, woman gives to the State a support without which the common good cannot be achieved" and, further, that "[t]he State shall, therefore, endeavour to ensure that mothers shall not be obliged by economic necessity to engage in labour to the neglect of their duties in the home." This has been characterised as an unfair stereotyping of sex roles, the husband being portrayed as the breadwinner in the market place and the wife tied to the home, raising children. That state of affairs was virtually universal in the Ireland of 1937, and indeed throughout Europe and America at the time, and the draftsman hardly could have anticipated the extent to which wives would become part of the non-domestic workforce in the 1970s and later. For those mothers who choose to work in the home rather than outside, especially those who are forced by circumstances to stay at home, Article 41.2 provides a potentially valuable form of protection.

Emphasis was placed on this in *D.T. v. C.T.*[152] which concerned how much financial provision should be made for a wife in a divorce. There a medical doctor married a solicitor, who subsequently built up a lucrative law practice and made shrewd investments. She, on the other hand, became a medical officer with a Health Board and, when their youngest child was born, resigned from the job and worked as a part-time GP, so that she could better look after the

---

[152] [2002] 3 I.R. 334.

children at home. She later found it difficult to establish a full time medical practice. Murray J. pointed out that this guarantee "recognises that work in the home is indispensable for the welfare of the family, husband, wife and children, where there are children."[153] And in determining what financial provision should be made for mothers who chose to work in the home and bring up children, rather than pursue a full-time career, Article 41.2 underscores the value to be attached to her doing so. As is explained above, however, it provides no assistance in establishing entitlement to a share in the ownership of the family home.[154]

O'Flaherty J. expressed the view that this Article is not confined to mothers who are wives but that it extends to all mothers. In his view, what it does is "to require the State to endeavour to ensure that mothers with children to rear or to be cared for are given economic aid by the State. If a mother in dire economic straits were to invoke this Article it would be no answer for the State to say that it did not have to make any effort in her regard at all, though it would be open for it to say that it was doing its best having regard to the State's overall budgetary situation."[155] Accordingly, it ranks alongside the guarantee of free primary education as an economic and social right that is enforceable by the courts against the State. Principally in response to EC obligations, special provision has been made to protect the interests of pregnant women and mothers who are in employment and are breastfeeding.[156]

NON-MARITAL CHILDREN

For much of the last century, comparatively few children were born outside marriage in Ireland and, at least until the 1970s, it was uncommon for couples to live together and have children in much the same way as married couples. All that has changed radically, as has the legal position of non-marital children – formerly referred to as illegitimate children.[157] But the Constitution has been held to exclude the parent and non-marital child relationship from the definition of family,[158] although this is regarded as a family relationship for at least some purposes under the European Convention and the UN Covenant. According to Walsh J. in *G. v. An Bord Uchtála*, "the illegitimate child and its mother do not constitute a family within the meaning of Article 41 of the Constitution."[159]

---

[153] *Id.* at p.407.
[154] *L. v. L.* [1992] 2 I.R. 77; *supra*, p.681.
[155] [2003] 3 I.R. at p.112.
[156] See generally, M. Forde, *Employment Law* (2nd ed., 2001), pp.94–95 and 148–150.
[157] See generally, *Shatter*, Chap.19 and *Shannon*, H.
[158] *Supra*, p.667.
[159] [1980] I.R. 32 at p.70.

Nevertheless, a relationship does exist between a mother and her child that is recognised and supported by the Constitution. As Walsh J. put it in the *G.* case, there are:

> "The natural right or rights of a mother in respect of her child and the natural rights of the child in respect of its mother. These rights spring from the natural relationship of the mother and the child. So far as these particular natural rights are concerned, it is immaterial as between the mother and her child whether the mother is or is not married to the father of the child. ... The mother and her illegitimate child are human beings and each has the fundamental rights of every human being and fundamental rights which spring from their relationship to each other. These are natural rights. ... Rights also have their corresponding obligations or duties. The fact that a child is born out of lawful wedlock is a natural fact. Such a child is just as entitled to be supported and reared by its parent or parents, who are the ones responsible for its birth, as a child born in lawful wedlock."[160]

Discrimination

The extent to which children born outside of marriage suffered disadvantages under the common law was chronicled by Gavan Duffy P. in *Re M.*,[161] where he described the old law as barbarous in many respects. Many of those discriminations have since been removed but some remain. Two related constitutional law questions arise regarding them, *viz.* are they justifiable under the Constitution, especially under the Article 40.1 equality clause, and secondly, whether or to what extent removing such discrimination constitutes an attack on the family. This first question was considered in *O'B. v. S.*,[162] which concerned the provision in the Succession Act 1965, whereby a non-marital child is not regarded as the deceased's "issue" for the purpose of succession in the event of the father dying intestate. The Supreme Court upheld that discrimination on the grounds that the main objects of the 1965 Act and of the provision in question were to protect the family; accordingly, it cannot be said that the measure is unconstitutionally discriminatory.

It was held to be unnecessary to speculate about what the position would be if the Constitution did not contain Article 41. The voluminous United States authority on discrimination against non-marital children was held to be irrelevant because there is nothing like this Article in the US Constitution. Reliance was placed on the Strasbourg Court's decision in *Marcx v. Belgium*,[163]

---

[160] *Id.* at pp.66 and 67.
[161] [1946] I.R. 334.
[162] [1984] I.R. 316.
[163] 2 E.H.R.R. 330 (1979).

which held that provisions of Belgium's inheritance laws contravened the equality guarantee in Article 14 of the European Convention. Under that law, in contrast to the position within a marriage, a child born outside marriage did not have the status of an heir to the mother's estate; only if the mother left no other relative could the child inherit all of the mother's estate and the child had no rights on the intestacy of any of the mother's relatives. Moreover, during her lifetime the mother was prohibited from making a gift of all of her property to the child. According to the court, the Convention should be interpreted in the light of current conditions and, whereas in the past placing non-marital children and their mothers at a legal disadvantage was widely regarded as acceptable, this is no longer the case. The "domestic law of the great majority of member States of the Council of Europe has evolved and is continuing to evolve, in company with the relevant international instruments, towards full juridical recognition of the maxim *mater semper certa est*."[164] The fact that some mothers of non-marital children do not wish to assume any responsibility for their children did not of itself justify a general rule that discouraged mothers from recognising their children, such as the succession law in question. But Walsh J. in *O'B. v. S.* pointed out that the case concerned issues that were significantly different: in particular, Belgian law forbade mothers to transfer all of their property, or leave all of their property, to their non-marital children, which is not the position under the 1965 Act, which in this context simply stipulates who should succeed to the estate, in the event of the mother dying intestate. Moreover, a non-marital child has some succession rights to its mother's estate.

Another instance where a claim of unfair discrimination was rejected is *State (M) v. Minister for Foreign Affairs.*[165] The plaintiff contended that section 40(1) of the Adoption Act 1952 was unconstitutionally discriminatory because it prohibited young children from being taken out of the State in order, for example, to live abroad with their fathers. Finlay P. held that the section was not invalid for that reason because "in the generality of cases the mother of an illegitimate child may be subjected to strains, stresses and pressures arising from economic and social conditions which fully justify the legislature in making special provisions with regard to the welfare of that child, which provisions are not considered necessary for the welfare of a legitimate child."[166] However, he went on to hold the section unconstitutional because, in the circumstances, it was an unreasonable restriction on the child's constitutional right to travel.[167]

O'Hanlon J.'s rejection in *S. v. S.*[168] of the archaic common law presumption

---

[164] *Id.* at p.346.
[165] [1979] I.R. 73.
[166] *Id.* at p.79.
[167] *Supra*, p.335.
[168] [1983] I.R. 68; *supra*, p.484.

that a married woman's child was invariably fathered by her husband, as a rule that was not consistent with the constitutional guarantee of fair procedures, might be rationalised as condemning a rule that unfairly discriminated against non-marital children. Presumably the reason why that rule was adopted originally was to protect family interests.[169] All common law presumptions about "the legitimacy or illegitimacy of any person" were abrogated by section 44 of the Status of Children Act 1987. However, section 46 of this Act introduced a rebuttable presumption where a married woman gives birth to a child while she is married or within ten months of the marriage coming to an end; her husband is presumed to be the father unless the contrary is shown on the balance of probabilities. If, however, she has been living apart from him following a divorce or a separation agreement, he is presumed not to be the father unless the contrary is proved.

In *Johnston v. Ireland*,[170] the Strasbourg Court found that several provisions of Irish law relating to non-marital children contravened the European Convention. The main issue in that case was whether the Constitution's then prohibition against enacting divorce legislation contravened the Convention; it was held that it did not. The first two applicants there wanted to get married but they could not do so because one of them was already married. They had one child of their own, who was the third applicant. It was contended that various statutory provisions operated to deny all three their right to respect for their family life, in that the law did not treat the child sufficiently like a marital child, such as regards the father's lack of parental rights, succession rules, fiscal requirements and the impossibility of the child being legitimated by her parents' subsequent marriage should that ever occur. Observing that the *Marckx* case only concerned the mother/child relationship, the court held that what was said there about integrating the non-marital child within its family is "equally applicable to a case such as the present, concerning as it does parents who have lived, with their daughter, in a family relationship over many years but are unable to marry" because of legal prohibitions against divorce.[171] In those circumstances, the Convention requires that the child "should be placed, legally and socially, in a position akin to that of a legitimate (*i.e.* marital) child."[172] However, Irish law did not treat similarly marital children and children like the third applicant. Accordingly, it was concluded, even though State Parties to the Convention have a wide "margin of appreciation" regarding the details of their family laws, "the absence of an appropriate legal regime reflecting the third applicant's natural family ties amounts to a failure to respect her family life" and also failed to respect her parents' right to family life.[173]

---

[169] *Russell v. Russell* [1924] A.C. 687.
[170] 9 E.H.R.R. 203 (1986).
[171] *Id.* at p.255.
[172] *Ibid.*
[173] *Ibid.*

But the court would not indicate what particular legislative measures should be adopted in order to bring Ireland into line with its obligations under Article 8 of the Convention.

This decision as well as a settlement of an application to Strasbourg following on *O'B. v. S*, led to the enactment of the Status of Children Act 1987, which significantly improved the legal position of non-marital children in a variety of ways. It commences in section 3(1) by stipulating a general principle of non-discrimination, that "[i]n deducing any relationship for the purposes of this Act or of any [subsequent] Act ..., the relationship between every person and his father and mother (or either of them) shall, unless the contrary intention appears, be determined irrespective of whether his father and mother are or have been married to each other, and all other relationships shall be determined accordingly."

Parentage

It was held by the Supreme Court in *I. O'T. v. B.*[174] that a child has an unenumerated constitutional right to know and to ascertain who its parents are but it is a qualified right and is subject to a right of the mother not to have that information disclosed, depending on the circumstances. A child who had been informally but not legally adopted sought an order of discovery against an adoption agency that had handled her placement, in order to ascertain who her mother was. According to Hamilton C.J., "[t]he right to know the identity of ones natural mother is a basic right flowing from the natural and special relationship which exists between a mother and her child .... The existence of such right is not dependent on the obligation to protect the child's right to bodily integrity or such rights as the child might enjoy in relation to the property of his or her natural mother but stems directly from the aforesaid relationship."[175] However, its "exercise may be restricted by the constitutional right to privacy and confidentiality of the natural mothers in respect of their dealings with" adoption societies.[176] It depends on all the circumstances of each individual case which of these rights will be afforded precedence. Where the mother in question wished to retain her anonymity, a procedure was recommended whereby this issue may be determined without her having to disclose her identity to the child, similar to that followed in applications under s. 3 of the Adoption Act 1964.

Part VI (sections 33–36) of the Status of Children Act 1987, permits applications to be made to the Circuit Court to determine who is a child's parent. Part VII (sections 34–47) of this Act authorises the court to direct that

---

[174] [1998] 2 I.R. 321.
[175] *Id.* at p.348.
[176] *Id.* at p.349.

blood tests be taken in order to ascertain parentage, where this is an issue. There is also a jurisdiction in the High Court to determine disputes about legitimacy, which may not be as far reaching. Where, however, an applicant in proceedings of this nature cannot name who most likely is the mother or father, no orders can be made determining parentage – which is how the *I. O'T.* case above arose.

Blood tests cannot be taken without the person in questions consent. In the case of a minor, consent may be given by a person who has charge or control of him; in the case of an adult who is incapable of understanding the purpose of such tests, consent may be given by an equivalent person and a medical practitioner must certify that the test will not be prejudicial to his medical care and treatment. Refusal to consent to a blood test, when directed, permits adverse inferences to be drawn. It was held by the Supreme Court in *J.P.D. v. M.G.*[177] that, in the circumstances there, it was in the child's best interest that the true position of his paternity should be resolved by all parties being blood tested, as directed by the High Court.

Adoption

Adoption is the process whereby a child becomes part of a family and acquires all the rights that a child born within that family possesses or would possess.[178] In 1952 the Oireachtas introduced a statutory mechanism whereby non-marital (then described as "illegitimate") children and orphans could be adopted and that Act has been significantly amended on several occasions. According to section 24 of the Adoption Act 1952, which is headed "effects of adoption orders," once an adoption order is made, "(a) the child shall be considered with regard to the rights and duties of parents and children in relation to each other as the child of the adopter or adopters born to him, her or them in lawful wedlock; (b) the mother or guardian shall lose all parental rights and be freed from all parental duties with respect to the child." The entire adoption process is supervised by An Bord Uchtála, the Adoption Board, which is a State agency established under these Acts for this purpose. It is given a virtual legal monopoly in this area: no other body is permitted to make or attempt to make arrangements regarding adoption, with the exception of registered adoption societies and Health Boards.

Separation of Powers

In the 1970s the question was canvassed as to whether, given the extensive nature of the Board's powers, it in fact exercised what may be termed plenary

---

[177] [1991] 1 I.R. 47.
[178] See generally, *Shatter*, Chap.12 and G. Shannon, *Children and the Law* (2001), Chap.6.

judicial power, which the Constitution provides can only be exercised in courts and by judges appointed under the Constitution.[179] If it did indeed exercise these powers, then all the orders made by it would be invalid. In his judgment in *G. v. An Bord Uchtála*,[180] the circumstances of which are dealt with below, Walsh J. expressed the view that the Adoption Board did not exercise judicial powers:

"Adoption in our law is essentially a consent or voluntary arrangement. The Adoption Board is, in effect, a ratifying agency and a safeguard. The Board ensures that the particular adoption is made in accordance with the Acts of the Oireachtas and that the prospective adopters are suitable. It also preserves the anonymity of the parties to the procedure. Undoubtedly, there have been many cases where the arrangements for adoption have been made directly between the person seeking to have a child adopted and the person seeking to adopt the child but they were routed through the Board for the simple reason that the statute provided that adoption would not amount to legal adoption unless the machinery of the Board was employed and an adoption order was made by the Board.

The Board has no function to settle disputes as to the custody of a child. Neither does it have a jurisdiction to adjudicate upon anything that could be said to be in controversy or dispute between parties, either in the cases where anonymity is maintained or in the cases where the parties are known to each other. The Board is simply concerned with what I am satisfied is the administrative function of seeing that the steps being taken are not contrary to the adoption legislation, are not inimical to the welfare of the child, and that everybody concerned has had a full opportunity of considering the matter carefully. It is quite clear that the Board was not invested with any power to settle or decide any question as to the existence of a right or obligation or duty."[181]

But the other judges there would express no view on the issue. O'Higgins C.J. and Kenny J. stressed that they were reserving their opinions on the question. Parke J. virtually protested against Walsh J. having considered this issue, because it had not been the subject of any submissions or argument before the court, and was not relevant to any of the issues in that case.

In order to resolve uncertainty about the question, the Constitution was amended in 1979 so as to prevent the Board's functions being challenged on these grounds. According to Article 3.2:

"No adoption of a person taking effect or expressed to take effect at any

---

[179] *Supra*, p.195.
[180] [1980] I.R. 32.
[181] *Id.* at pp.71–72. *Cf.* the *Adoption Reference case* 3 D.L.R. 497 (1938).

time after the coming into operation of this Constitution under laws enacted by the Oireachtas and being an adoption pursuant to an order made or an authorisation given by any person or body of persons designated by those laws to exercise such functions and powers was or shall be invalid by reason only of the fact that such person or body of persons was not a judge or a court appointed or established as such under this Constitution."

That is to say, no past or future adoption order made by or with the approval of the Adoption Board is invalid simply because the Board is not a court established under the Constitution.

Discrimination

As is the case with nearly every body of complex legislation, under the Adoption Acts 1952–98, different categories of persons are treated differently for various purposes. Thus, it is not every child who can be adopted; nor is it everyone who can adopt a child. Where the child in question was non-marital, the 1952 Act used to require that both adoptive parents should have the same religion as the child's mother; that provision was declared unconstitutional in *M. v. An Bord Uchtála*[182] as an impermissible discrimination on the grounds of religion. The current position as regards religion is that where the applicants for adoption, the child and its parent or parents are not all of the same religion, an adoption order will not be made unless every person whose consent is needed for the adoption knows about the difference in religion and still consents to the adoption.[183]

These Acts discriminated on the basis of marital status and of sex. Persons who are not and never were married are ineligible to apply for an adoption order – except for the child's own mother or father, or near relatives. Widows generally are entitled to be adoptive parents but, prior to 1991, widowers were not so entitled unless they were within the exceptional circumstances provided for in section 5 of the 1974 Act. An additional requirement that widowers had to satisfy under this section was that they had another child in their custody but that was declared unconstitutional in *O'G. v. Attorney General*,[184] as an unjust and unreasonable discrimination between widows and widowers. According to McMahon J.:

"Where a married couple have received an infant for adoption and the wife dies before the final adoption order is made it is unreasonable and unjust to exclude the widower from being considered as a suitable person

---

[182] [1975] I.R. 81; *supra*, p.627.
[183] Adoption Act 1974, s.4.
[184] [1985] I.L.R.M. 61.

to adopt the child. It is unreasonable because the widower's relationship with the child and his suitability as an adopter from the point of view of the emotional needs of the child is something which a qualified psychologist can readily assess by observing the inter-action between the widower and the child. Disruption of the bond between the child and the widower will in many cases subject the child to emotional trauma. It is therefore unjust to the child as well as unreasonable. I am satisfied that the proviso to s. 5 is founded on an idea of difference in capacity between men and women which has no foundation in fact and the proviso is therefore an unwarranted denial of human equality and repugnant to Article 40(1) of the Constitution."[185]

Another provision that treated men and women differently in the context of adoption was that, generally, there was no statutory obligation on the Adoption Board to consult the father of a non-marital child and the father's consent was not needed for an adoption order to be made, whereas almost invariably the mother must be consulted and must give her consent. This feature of the scheme was upheld by the Supreme Court in *State (Nicolaou) v. An Bord Uchtála*,[186] on the grounds that, as a general rule, there is a significant difference in "moral capacity and social function" between the mothers and fathers of such children. An Irish woman and a Cypriot man lived together in London, where they had a child. The mother returned to Ireland but she kept in touch with the child's father. Throughout, the father was anxious to marry her and he always made it clear to her that he did not want to have his child adopted. Without informing him, she gave the child up for adoption. When he learned of this, he sought to have the adoption procedure declared invalid and to have the child delivered up to him. His principal contention was that, since the Act required the mother's consent for the adoption but not his consent, it discriminated unfairly on the grounds of sex.

   This argument was rejected, firstly, because the 1952 Act did not provide that a father's consent to adoption is never required. Section 14 requires that either the child's mother or guardian, or the person having "charge of or control of" the child, must consent. Circumstances can arise where the father has charge or control of the child and, although a non-marital child's father is not designated its guardian by the Guardianship of Infants Act 1964, the father is not precluded from that Act from applying to be the guardian. Thus, the Adoption Acts did not discriminate outright on the basis of sex as regards consent to adoption. But it gave mothers far more extensive rights than fathers and in most circumstances it permitted adoption without the father's consent. Walsh J. for the Court, held that this differential treatment was not unreasonable and was justifiable because, generally, fathers of non-marital children have a

---

[185] *Id.* at p.65.
[186] [1966] I.R. 567.

very tenuous relationship with the mothers and the children. As he put it:

"Under the provisions of the (Adoption) Act certain persons are given rights and all other persons are excluded. Whether or not the natural father is excluded depends upon the circumstances whether or not he comes within the description of a person who is given a right, and he may or may not come within some such description. If he is in fact excluded it is because in common with other blood relations and strangers he happens not to come within any such description. There is no discrimination against the natural father as such. The question remains whether there is any unfair discrimination in giving the rights in question to the persons described and denying them to others.

In the opinion of the Court each of the persons described as having rights (to consent to adoption and to be heard by An Bord Uchtála) can be regarded as having, or capable of having, in relation to the adoption of a child a moral capacity or social function which differentiates him from persons who are not given such rights. When it is considered that an illegitimate child may be begotten by an act of rape, by a callous seduction or by an act of casual commerce by a man with a women, as well as by the association of a man with a woman in making a common home without marriage in circumstances approximating to those of married life, and that, except in the latter instance, it is rare for a natural father to take any interest in his offspring, it is not difficult to appreciate the difference in moral capacity and social function between the natural father and the several persons described in the sub-sections in questions. In presenting their argument under this head counsel for the appellant have undertaken the onus of showing that in denying to the natural father certain rights conferred upon others s. 14, sub-s. 1, s. 1, and s. 16, sub-s. 1, of the (1952) Act are invalid having regard to Article 40 of the Constitution. In the opinion of the Court they have failed to discharge that onus."[187]

It was also held that the 1952 Act did not discriminate against non-marital children, such as by permitting their adoption without their fathers' consent. "On the contrary," its purpose and effect is "to redress the inequalities imposed by circumstances on orphans and illegitimate children."[188] As Barrington J. pointed out thirty years later, this reasoning was "fundamentally flawed" and "inadequate."[189]

In 1987 the position was relaxed somewhat when it became possible for fathers of non-marital children to be appointed guardians, in circumstances

---

[187] [1966] I.R. 567 at p.641.
[188] *Id.* at p.642.
[189] *W. O'R. v. E.H.* [1996] 2 I.R. 248 at pp.277–280.

where that was in the child's best interests.[190] However, the continuing virtual
exclusion of fathers from any say in the adoption process was held by the
Strasbourg Court in *Keegan v. Ireland*[191] to contravene Article 8 of the
European Convention. The only way in which the applicant could have had a
say in that process was by being appointed the child's guardian but the Supreme
Court refused to appoint him as guardian, on the grounds that it was not in the
child's best interests.[192] It was held by the Strasbourg Court that to allow the
secret placement of a child for adoption without the father's knowledge or
consent constituted an impermissible interference with his right to respect for
family life. In view of this finding, the court concluded that it was not necessary
to consider whether the different treatment of fathers and mothers in these
circumstances contravened Article 14's guarantee of equality.

In 1998 this regime was altered, so that consideration could be given to the
father's position.[193] Under section 70 of the 1952 Act, as then amended, fathers
are entitled to notify the Board of their intention to be consulted about a proposal
by an adoption agency to place their child for adoption, or of any application
by the child's mother or relative for an order that it be adopted. If an adoption
agency is aware of the father's identity, it is obliged to notify him of the proposal
and, if he indicates his objections, the proposed placement must be deferred
so that the father may apply to the court to be appointed a guardian. Where,
however, "having regard to the nature of the relationship between the father
and the mother or the circumstances of the conception of a child, it would be
inappropriate" to involve the father, the Board may authorise the agency in
question not to contact him and, instead, place the child for adoption.[194]

Consent

Section 14 of the 1952 Act provides that, before a child can be adopted, its
mother must consent and, if somebody else is the child's guardian or has charge
or control of the child, his or her consent must also be obtained. In 1987 it
became possible for the child's father to be appointed a guardian and, since
1998, fathers have become entitled to notify the Adoption Board that they
wish to be consulted on a proposal for adoption. Sections 14 and 15 of the
1952 Act lay down various rules regarding consent, which are supplemented
by sections 3 and 4 of the 1974 Act and sections 2 and 3 of the 1976 Act, the
principal purpose of which is to ensure that consents are given freely and not
with undue haste. Thus, the Adoption Board must be satisfied that everybody
whose consent is needed "understands the nature and effect of the consent and

---

[190] Status of Children Act 1987.
[191] 8 E.H.R.R. 342 (1994).
[192] *J.K. v. V.W.* [1990] 2 I.R. 437.
[193] Adoption Act 1998.
[194] Adoption Act 1952, s.7F(2).

of the adoption order;"[195] persons whose consent is needed must be informed that their consent can be withdrawn, that they are entitled to be heard on the application for the adoption order[196] and consent, if given, can be withdrawn before the adoption order is made.[197] If between placing a child for adoption and the making of an adoption order, its mother and father marry and its birth is re-registered, it cannot be adopted.[198] If both parents marry but the child's birth was not re-registered, by virtue of marrying its mother the child's father becomes its parent for the purposes of the Adoption Acts and, accordingly, before an adoption order can be made the father must also have consented to having the child adopted.[199]

Consent of persons who either cannot be found or who are incapable of consenting by reason of mental infirmity may be dispensed with. Furthermore, section 3 of the 1974 Act provides that, where a person (generally the mother) has placed a child for adoption and an application is made to have it adopted, the High Court is empowered to dispense with her consent where she previously consented and then withdrew that consent, or even where she has failed to consent or has refused to consent at all. Therefore, over the mother's (or other party whose consent is required) objection, the court can order that the child be adopted. That order can only be made, however, where the court is "satisfied that it is in the best interests of the child so to do" and the court has the option of granting custody of the child to the applicant for the adoption order but not approving the adoption.

Constitutional aspects of section 3 of the 1974 Act were considered in lengthy judgments in *G. v. An Bord Uchtála*,[200] but none of the judges there suggested that it was invalid. The issue was whether the court should order that the Adoption Board may dispense with a mother's consent to have her child adopted and the criteria for determining this question. It was held that, in addition to her common law and statutory rights to custody of her child, under the Constitution the mother has a personal right to the custody of her child and the child also has a constitutional right to be reared by its natural parent or parents.[201] Nevertheless, the mother can waive those rights; they "can be alienated or transferred in whole or in part and either subject to conditions or absolutely".[202] Additionally, she can be deprived of them due to her conduct: they can be lost by the mother "if her conduct towards the child amounts to abandonment or abdication of her rights and duties."[203] Before a court will

---

[195] Adoption Act 1952, s.15, as amended by 1974 Act, s.8.
[196] Adoption Act 1976, s.3.
[197] Adoption Act 1952, s.14(2).
[198] *Id.*, s.10.
[199] *J.H., Re* [1985] I.R. 375.
[200] [1980] I.R. 32.
[201] *Supra*, p.703.
[202] [1980] I.R. at p.55.
[203] *Ibid.*

order that a child may be adopted, against the wishes of its mother, two hurdles must be overcome. In the first place, she must have agreed to place the child for adoption; without having freely and with full knowledge of the consequences so agreed, authority under section 3 of the 1974 Act to override her wishes in appropriate circumstances cannot even come into operation. Because frequently mothers agree to placing their child for adoption shortly after it is born, in circumstances where they are under considerable stress and worry, the judges in the *G.* case and in subsequent cases emphasised that the mother's agreement must be entirely voluntary and fully informed. As Finlay P. put it in one instance, her agreement "must have been made freely with full knowledge of (the) consequences and under circumstances where neither the advice of persons engaged in the transaction nor the surrounding circumstances deprived the mother of the capacity to make a fully informed free decision."[204] It depends on the entire circumstances whether this test is satisfied. Secondly, where the mother did initially agree to adoption but then withdrew her consent, the criterion to be applied as to whether her veto should be overridden is that contained in section 3 of the 1974 Act, viz. "the best interests of the child." What are the child's best interests again depends on the entire circumstances of the case. While there is a general preference towards letting a very young child remain with its mother, the constitutional rights of the mother *vis-à-vis* her child can no longer have a bearing on the outcome because they have been waived by her when initially she agreed to place the child for adoption.

The plaintiff in the *G.* case, an unmarried civil servant aged 21, gave birth to a child. Nearly three months later she placed the child with an adoption society and signed a form consenting to it being adopted. Shortly afterwards she informed her parents about the child and, when they intimated that they would give her every assistance in bringing it up, she withdrew her consent. The family who had custody of the child at the time, who in all likelihood would have become its adoptive parents, sought an order under section 3 that the mother's consent should be dispensed with. It was held that in the circumstances the order should not be made, the consequence of which was that the mother could have her child back. A majority found that she had freely consented to have it adopted but nevertheless it was not clearly in the child's best interests that its adoption should be permitted by the court.

Where, between the time a mother places her child for adoption and the persons having custody of the child apply to have it adopted, the mother marries the child's father, constitutional considerations affect the second question under section 3 of the 1974 Act. By virtue of the marriage, the child has become a member of a family as contemplated by Article 41; it follows from what was held in *J.H., Re*[205] that the best interests of the child are then to be found within that family, except where "compelling reasons" are given as to why its

---

[204] *S. v. Eastern Health Boa*rd, unreported, High Court, Finlay P., February 28, 1979.
[205] [1985] I.R. 375.

married parents should not get the child or it is proved that its parents have failed in their duty to provide the child with the requisite education. Additionally, the father becomes a "parent" within the Adoption Acts' definition and, accordingly, he too must consent to the child being adopted; if he has not so agreed, then the question of dispensing with his consent as provided for in section 3 of the 1974 Act cannot even arise. Thus in *J.H.*, *Re*, Lynch J. found that the father who married his child's mother after it was born had never agreed to placing the child for adoption and that, since he was resisting any adoption, his veto could not be overruled.

DIVORCE

The circumstances in which a marriage will be dissolved are very restricted in Ireland. If the essential requirements for a valid marriage have not been satisfied, the High Court has power to declare the marriage to be null and void, and the effect of that declaration is that the marriage is deemed never to have taken place; the purported marriage is a complete and utter nullity.[206] The principal grounds on which a marriage will be nullified are lack of capacity to marry, absence of consent to marry and the non-observance of essential formalities. The court can also declare a marriage voidable on the grounds of impotence or inability to enter into and sustain a normal marriage relationship.[207] Alternatively, the court can make a declaration of judicial separation, the effect of which is to separate the husband and wife permanently.[208] Before 1989 that was described as a divorce *a mensa et thoro* but it was not a proper divorce in the sense that the parties were not legally free to marry again so long as the other spouse lived. Catholic Church tribunals exercise a jurisdiction under Canon law to declare marriages null and void. But those tribunals' orders have no legal standing in the law of the State because plenary judicial power can only be exercised by judges appointed in courts established under the Constitution, and legislative power in this country can only be exercised by the Oireachtas.

Until 1995 Ireland shared with Malta the distinction of being the only countries in Europe that did not permit divorce and Ireland was perhaps unique in that the Constitution forbade the enactment of any legislation that would provide for divorce. According to former Article 4.3.2 "(n)o law shall be enacted providing for the grant of a dissolution of marriage." In 1986 a referendum was held on the proposal to remove this prohibition but it was overwhelmingly defeated. In the same year, it was held by the European Court of Human Rights

---

[206] See generally, *Shatter*, Chap.5.
[207] *Id.* Chap.4.
[208] *Id.* Chap.8 and *Shannon* D.

in *Johnston v. Ireland*,[209] that this prohibition does not contravene the European Convention.

In order to deal more effectively with the increasing problem of marriage breakdown, the Judicial Separation and Family Law Reform Act 1989, was enacted, abolishing the divorce *a mensa et thoro* and providing for decrees of judicial separation on grounds of adultery, unreasonable behaviour, desertion, living apart and absence of a normal marital relationship. A challenge to its constitutionality, on the grounds that that it contravened the pledge to guard marriage and the family, and also the ban on divorce legislation, was rejected by the Supreme Court in *T.F. v. Ireland*.[210] It was always accepted that it was in the interests of the "common good" to permit spouses to separate after their marriage had broken down and the 1989 Act was held to be a reasonable endeavour to balance that public interest with the obligation to support and safeguard marriage.

In the same year, 1995, there was another referendum on a proposal to remove this ban and permit no-fault divorces, which was carried by a small majority. Just over a week before that referendum took place, the Supreme Court held that the Government had acted unconstitutionally in spending money on publicity for a "yes" vote[211] but a referendum petition aimed at having the outcome set aside on those grounds was rejected.[212]

Granting Divorces

The only grounds on which a divorce may be granted are set out in Article 41.3.2 of the Constitution, being:

> "i. at the date of the institution of the (divorce) proceedings, the spouses have lived apart from one another for a period of, or periods amounting to, at least four years during the previous five years,
>
> ii. there is no reasonable prospect of a reconciliation between the spouses,
>
> iii. such provision as the court considers proper having regard to the circumstances exists or will be made for the spouses, any children of either or both of them and any other person prescribed by law, and
>
> iv. any further conditions prescribed by law are compiled with."

Under the Family Law (Divorce) Act 1996,[213] an application may be made to

---

[209] 9 E.H.R.R. 203 (1986).

[210] [1995] 1 I.R. 321.

[211] *McKenna v. An Taoiseach (No. 2)* [1995] 2 I.R. 10; *supra* p.394.

[212] *Hanafin v. Minister for the Environment* [1996] 2 I.R. 321; *supra*, p.606.

[213] See generally, *Shatter*, Chap.9 and *Shannon* E.

the Circuit Court or to the High Court for a decree of divorce on the grounds set out in section 5(1) of this Act. It states that, "in the exercise of the jurisdiction conferred by Article 41.3.2" and "[s]ubject to the provisions of this Act," that decree may be granted where the court is satisfied that:

> "(a) at the date of the institution of the proceedings, the spouses have lived apart from one another for a period of, or periods amounting to, at least four years during the previous five years,
> (b) there is no reasonable prospect of a reconciliation between the spouses, and
> (c) such provision as the court considers proper having regard to the circumstances exists or will be made for the spouses and any dependent members of the family."

Sections 6–8 of this Act lay down certain safeguards designed to ensure that the parties are aware of alternatives to divorce and to assist endeavours to secure reconciliation between them, and for adjourning cases to assist reconciliation or to assist reaching agreement on the terms of the divorce. Communications between the parties for these purposes are made absolutely privileged in all legal proceedings.

This Act was passed on November 27, 1996 but did not come into force until three months later. In the meantime, it was held by Barron J. in *R.C. v. C.C.*[214] that adopting new Article 41.3.2 in the referendum conferred jurisdiction on the High Court to grant divorce decrees, subject to whatever restrictions as may be laid down by legislation. Since, however, there were no restrictions in force at that time, it was permissible to grant a divorce where the circumstances were covered by subsection i and ii of this Article and subject to such other provisions as the court deemed appropriate.

Foreign Divorces

The legal status of divorces granted by foreign tribunals is not dealt with in general terms by the Constitution. However, Article 41.3.3 stipulates that "[n]o person whose marriage has been dissolved under the civil law of any other State but it is a subsisting valid marriage under the law for the time being in force within (this State) shall be capable of contracting a valid marriage within (this State) during the lifetime of the other party to the marriage so dissolved." What this says is that a person who is married in the eyes of Irish law and who then gets divorced abroad is not permitted to remarry in Ireland (during the life of the spouse) if the first marriage still subsists in the eyes of Irish law. What it does not say is that foreign divorces, or foreign divorces followed by

---

[214] [1997] 1 I.R. 334.

foreign remarriages, will never be recognised by Irish law. This clause does not squarely address the situation where, under general conflict of laws principles, the foreign divorce would be recognised in most national courts and, accordingly, there is no longer a valid and subsisting marriage in those jurisdictions. Did this clause modify the position under private international law? In a series of decisions, the courts held that there was no such modification.[215]

By section 5 of the Domicile and Recognition of Foreign Divorces Act 1986, it was provided that from July 1986 onwards a divorce granted abroad shall be recognised in Ireland if either spouse was domiciled in the State where the divorce was granted, unless one of the normal bars to recognising the foreign decree exists. This Act also abolished the common law rule that a wife's domicile is invariably the same as her husband's, also as from the date the Act came into force. However, in *W. v. W.*[216] that rule was held to contravene the equality guarantee in Article 40,1, with the result that many more foreign divorces could be recognised in Ireland.

A person's domicile is the place where he has his permanent home, which is predominantly a question of fact. For instance, in *P.K. v. T.K.*,[217] the net issue was whether either party had been domiciled in New York in 1980, when they obtained a divorce decree there. An endeavour to have the basis for recognition significantly extended to decrees granted in any State where one of the parties was resident at the time succeeded in *McG. v. W.*[218] But a similar endeavour failed in *D.T. v. F.L.*,[219] on the basis that *McG.* concerned a divorce that had been obtained before the 1986 Act came into force; that by virtue of this Act, the prerequisite was one of the parties' domicile and not mere residence. Another endeavour to shift the criteria to residence was rejected in *M.EC v. J.A.*;[220] it was held that anything as radical as this called for legislation, not judicial development of the law.

Insofar as divorces granted in EC/EU Member States are concerned, the issue is now governed by the Regulation known as "Brussels II" of 2000.[221] It introduces Community-wide common rules for which states' courts may grant divorces and it is only divorces granted by these courts that will be recognised. It shifts the focus from domicile to habitual residence. A divorce granted in the Member State will be recognised where (1) both spouses are habitually resident; (2) both were previously habitually resident and one of them continues

---

[215] Beginning with *Mayo-Perrott v. Mayo Perrott* [1958] I.R. 336.
[216] [1993] 2 I.R. 476.
[217] [2002] 2 I.R. 187.
[218] [2000] 1 I.R. 96.
[219] [2002] 2 I.L.R.M. 152.
[220] [2001] 2 I.R. 399.
[221] J.O. No. 1347/2000. See generally, *Shannon* E220 and McEleavy, "The Brussels II Regulation: How the European Community Has Moved Into Family Law" 51 *Int. & Camp. L.Q.* 883 (2002).

to reside there; (3) the respondent is habitually resident; (4) the applicant is habitually resident provided he resided there for more than the year preceding the application; (5) either of them is habitually resident, if it is a joint application; (6) the applicant was habitually resident for more than the previous six months and is domiciled there.

THE UNBORN

Apart from the controversial issue of abortion, the legal rights and obligations regarding unborn children, or foetuses, remain largely unexplored territory in Ireland. Among the questions that call for resolution in this regard are whether mothers are entitled to refuse medical treatment or to refuse to give birth by way of caesarean section where their choice presents a serious risk to the life of the baby they are carrying.[222] Some judges have suggested, in the course of legal argument, that a perfectly healthy woman's decision to give birth in her own home rather than in a maternity hospital is somehow legally incorrect, notwithstanding that this process is endorsed by section 62 of the Health Act 1970. Another unresolved question is, where the mother is carrying more than one child, whether or in what circumstances it is permissible to cause the death of one or more of them in order to save the life of the other.[223] A field that requires urgent legislative intervention is assisted reproduction techniques, which presents no end of legal problems and it is difficult to see what real light the words of the Constitution can throw on them.[224]

Legal Personality

In several countries, the unborn is regarded as not having any legal personality. But in *Baby O. v. Minister for Justice*,[225] it was impliedly held by the Supreme Court that this is not so in Irish law. The first named applicant was an unborn baby who, by her mother as next friend, sought to restrain the latter from being deported to Nigeria until after her baby was born. It was contended that the infant mortality rate was far higher there than in Ireland and that, consequently, a far greater risk to that baby's life would be caused if the deportation were permitted to proceed. But it was held that there was no constitutional protection against that measure, Article 40.3.3 being concerned

---

[222] *Cf. St. George's Health Care Trust v. S.* [1998] 2 W.L.R. 936.

[223] *Cf. Re A (Conjoined Twins: Surgical Separation)* [2001] 2 W.L.R. 480.

[224] See generally, D. Madden, *Medicine and the Law* (2002); "Developments", *supra*, n.24, pp.2052 *et seq.*; Garrison, "Law Making for Baby Making: An Interpretive Approach to the Determination of Legal Parentage" 113 *Harv. L. Rev.* 835 (2000).

[225] [2002] 2 I.R. 169.

exclusively with the question of abortion. According to Keane C.J., if the mother "had arrived in this country accompanied by a young infant and both of them had been refused refugee status and ordered to be deported, the life expectation of the infant, and for that matter the [mother], might have been less. That would plainly not be a ground for interfering with the deportation."[226] He added that if the courts were to restrain deportations in these circumstances, the power to deport "would be in a great range of cases virtually negated."[227] This reasoning, he said, makes it "obvious that the rights of the born, in this context, cannot be less than those of the unborn."[228] But no explanation is given for why the power to deport the mother after her baby is born would be "virtually negated" by deferring the deportation until after the birth. Whether an unborn baby can be made a ward of court is debatable.[229]

Abortion

Whether or in what circumstances abortion was constitutionally permitted became a highly controversial issue in the United States and in Western Europe in the 1970s[230] following the US Supreme Court's decision in *Roe v. Wade*,[231] where the Texas anti-abortion statute was declared unconstitutional. In 1974 in Germany and in 1975 in France, the legislatures relaxed the existing bans on abortion, which resulted in challenges before the Federal Constitutional Court[232] and the *Conseil Constitutionnel*,[233] respectively. Challenges to the German abortion law because it was too restrictive[234] and to the English law because it was too permissive[235] were unsuccessful before the European Commission of Human Rights.

At that time, the legal and constitutional position in Ireland was not at all clear.[236] The principal statutory provisions, which remain in force, were sections 58 and 59 of the Offences Against the Person Act 1861;[237] these make it an offence for the mother in question or any third party "unlawfully" to take

---

[226] *Id.* at p.182.

[227] *Ibid.*

[228] *Ibid.*

[229] Cf. *F. (in utero), Re* [1988] 2 W.L.R. 1288 and *Re Unborn Child* [2003] 1 N.Z.L.R. 115.

[230] See generally, M. Glendon, *Abortion and Divorce in Western Law: American Failures, European Challenges* (1989).

[231] 410 US 113 (1973).

[232] 39 BVerf GE 1 (1975); also 88 BVerf GE 203 (1993).

[233] Cons. Const. 15 Jan. 1975 [1975] *Dalloz* 529; also Cons. Const. 27 June 2001 [2001] *J.C.P.* II 10635.

[234] *Bruggeman v. Germany* 3 E.H.R.R. 244 (1977).

[235] *Paton v. United Kingdom* 3 E.H.R.R. 408 (1980).

[236] See generally, J. Kingston & A. Whelan, *Abortion and the Law* (1997), Chap.3.

[237] 25 Vic. c.100.

certain steps in order to procure her abortion but does not indicate what if any steps may be taken lawfully for that purpose. In England it was held in *R. v. Bourne*[238] that the termination of pregnancy in circumstances where the woman would most likely otherwise become "a physical or mental wreck" was lawful and, thus, was not caught by these prohibitions. On several occasions this interpretation of the 1861 Act was followed by the Northern Ireland courts. For instance, in *Northern Health and Social Services Board v. F. & G.*,[239] Shiel J. held that it was permissible for a 14 year old girl in care to have an abortion, where she became pregnant after visiting a disco and, on discovering her condition, refused to take any food and became suicidal. According to McDermott J. in a similar instance, "[l]ife in this context means the physical and mental health or well being of the mother and the doctor's act is lawful where the continuance of the pregnancy would adversely affect the mental or physical health of the mother; the adverse effect must however be a real and serious one and it will always be a question of fact and degree whether the perceived effect of non-termination is sufficiently grave to warrant terminating the unborn child."[240]

It is questionable whether, prior to 1983, courts in the Republic would have followed this interpretation as there were numerous unqualified *obiter dicta* to the effect that abortion was impliedly proscribed by the Constitution. As Keane J. observed in 1997, "[a]ll one can say with confidence at this stage is that the preponderance of judicial opinion would suggest that the *Bourne* approach could not have been adopted in this country consistently with the Constitution prior to the Eight Amendment."[241]

Concern in certain influential quarters that the Supreme Court might follow the US precedent and strike down these sections, resulting in virtual unregulated abortion, or indeed construe these sections in the same way as in *Bourne* and in *F. & G.*, led to the passing of what was then described as the "pro-life" amendment in 1983. Article 40.3.3 (1st paragraph) of the Constitution provides that "[t]he State acknowledges the right to life of the unborn and, with due regard to the equal right to life of the mother, guarantees in its laws to respect, and, as far as practicable, by its laws to defend and vindicate that right." In the twenty years since this guarantee has existed, the Oireachtas has declined to enact any anti-abortion legislation as therein envisaged, an omission that has provoked judicial rebuke on occasion.

But it has been held that legislation is not essential to give effect to this

---

[238] [1939] 1 K.B. 689.

[239] [1993] N.I. 68.

[240] *Northern Health and Social Services Board v. AMNH* [1994] N.I.J.B. 1 at p.4. More recently, *Application of Family Planning Ass'n of Northern Ireland*, Kerr J., July 7, 2003.

[241] *Society for the Protection of Unborn Children (Ireland) Ltd v. Grogan (No. 5)* [1998] 4 I.R. 343 at pp.381–382

provision, that it is "self-executing" and imposes restrictions on private individuals and bodies as well as on the State and its agencies. Whether it empowers the courts to require that the State shall take concrete steps in order to safeguard the life of a particular unborn or the unborn generally has never been put to the test. A paradoxical consequence of this amendment, however, which, *inter alia*, gave express recognition to the "equal right to life of the mother," is that it constitutionally guarantees her entitlement to have an abortion where that is necessary in order to preserve her life. That it had this effect was conceded by the Attorney General in the controversial "*X*" case in 1992 and affirmed by the Supreme Court.[242]

Dissatisfaction with how the court interpreted this amendment in that case led to unsuccessful endeavours in 1992 and again in 2002 to further amend it in a more restrictive manner, rejecting the likelihood of suicide as a permissible grounds for abortion. Against that, this Amendment was supplemented in 1992 by clauses protecting the right to travel to another country to have an abortion and also to enable persons obtain information about abortion facilities in other countries.

"Unborn"

At what exact stage in the development of a foetus does it become an "unborn" for the purpose of these provisions? There is an *obiter dictum* of Hamilton P. that the above guarantee commences from the very moment of conception,[243] although this particular issue was not relevant in that case, which was an application to prevent a pregnancy-counselling service from giving out any information regarding abortion. It would appear that the Catholic Church regards life as commencing at the stage of conception[244] and, if this view were to be accepted by the courts, the above guarantee would apply from then.

In the second unsuccessful (2002) attempt to amend Article 40.3.3 and remove suicide as a justification for abortion, the proposed (entrenched) Act to replace sections 58 and 59 of the 1861 Act defined abortion as an occurrence "after implantation in the womb." Even if this had been adopted in the referendum, it would not inexorably follow that Article 40.3.3 would be interpreted as applying only from the time of implantation and not from the moment of conception.

---

[242] *Attorney General v. X.* [1992] 1 I.R. 1 at p.82.

[243] *Attorney General (Society for the Protection of Unborn Children Ireland Ltd) v. Open Door Counselling Ltd* [1988] I.R. 593 at p.598.

[244] *Cf. R. (Smeaton) v. Secretary of State* [2002] 2 F.L.R. 146, on whether the "morning after pill" contravened ss.58 and 59 of the 1861 Act.

Life of the Mother

Undoubtedly the most difficult medical and legal (and for many persons moral) question arising from Article 40.3.3 is what constitutes a sufficient threat to the mother's life that brings her within the "equal right to life" qualification. Even the medical profession are divided on this very issue, which came to a head in what are known as the *"X"* case and the *"C"* case, concerning two pregnant girls who threatened suicide. In *Attorney General v. X.*,[245] a fourteen year old girl became pregnant after being raped and, with the support of her parents, sought to have an abortion in England. In *A. and B. v. Eastern Health Board*[246] a thirteen year old girl ("C") similarly found herself pregnant after being raped and was then taken into care by the Health Board, which supported her wish to go to England for an abortion. How the matter came before the courts in *"X"* is that, on discovering that the girl had gone to England with her parents to arrange for an abortion, the Attorney General sought an injunction against them restraining them from having the abortion. In *"C,"* the Health Board applied to the District Court under the Children Act 1991, to be permitted to take the child to England for the abortion and this was acceded to but the child's parents then sought to challenge this decision in the High Court by way of judicial review. Both cases raised the question of the risk of the girls' suicide as grounds for permitting the contemplated abortions, the criteria to be applied and whether the evidence satisfied those criteria.

It was contended by the Attorney General in *"X"* that the appropriate test was where it is "established that an inevitable or immediate risk to the life of the mother existed, for the avoidance of which a termination of the pregnancy was necessary ....".[247] But the Supreme Court held that the criterion was whether "it is established as a matter of probability that there is a real and substantial risk to the life, as distinct from the health, of the mother by self-destruction, which can only be avoided by termination of her pregnancy."[248] On the basis of the evidence adduced in *"X"*, it was held that this test had been established. Hederman J. dissented on the grounds that the evidence did not show a sufficiently high probability that the girl would commit suicide, as she never gave evidence, there was no obstetrical or other equivalent evidence adduced and what was offered to the court was a report by a psychologist who had seen the girl once, and had spoken to her parents and to the Gardaí. In his view, the girl required "loving and sympathetic care and professional counselling and all the protection which the State agencies can provide and furnish," "[s]uicide threats can be contained" and, over the several months until the baby is due to be born "it should not be impossible to guard the girl

---

[245] [1992] 1 I.R. 1.
[246] [1998] 1 I.R. 464.
[247] [1992] 1 I.R. at p.53.
[248] *Ibid.*

against self-destruction and preserve the life of the unborn child at the same time."[249]

Having considered the evidence in the "*C*" case, the District Judge concluded that the test in the "*X*" case "has not been met" as she did "not believe that the threat of suicide is imminent". But because "if the pregnancy is allowed to continue the risk will increase substantially,"[250] she permitted the abortion to take place. Her decision was upheld by the Geoghegan J. on the grounds that a full review of the transcript of the evidence showed that the "*X*" case criterion had indeed been satisfied.

Travel

Abortion is lawfully available in many countries in circumstances that would not be permissible in the State under Article 40.3.3. In the "*X*" case Costello P. at first instance made an order restraining the girl from leaving the country in order to have an abortion and restraining others from assisting her to leave for that purpose; he held that her unborn's right to life took precedence over her right to travel abroad. Because in the circumstances there, however, the Supreme Court found that her life was endangered on account of the significant risk of suicide if she remained pregnant, she was held entitled to go to England to have an abortion. Popular concern about more "*X*" cases arising and protracted battles in the courts over whether girls and women finding themselves in comparable circumstances should be permitted to go abroad for abortions, resulted in the Thirteenth Amendment being adopted in 1992.

According to Article 40.3.3 (2nd para.), the 1983 guarantee of the unborn's right to life "shall not limit freedom to travel between the State and another State."[251] Accordingly, a woman cannot be prevented from going to England or anywhere else, in order to have an abortion, even where her life is not at risk by virtue of her pregnancy. It would appear that this is the case even if the contemplated abortion would not be lawful in the country where it is intended to be performed.

In those limited circumstances where permission of a court is required in order to go abroad for an abortion, it was held by Geoghegan J. in the "*C*" case that permission will only be granted in circumstances where the mother's life is at risk as envisaged in the "*X*" case. This he found is because the 1992 amendment "is framed in negative terms and must ... be interpreted in the historical context. ... [I]t was [n]ever intended to give some new substantial right. Rather it was intended to prevent injunctions against travel or having an abortion abroad."[252] Consequently, "the Constitution does not now confer a

---

[249] *Id.* at p.76.
[250] [1998] 1 I.R. 464 at p.479.
[251] See generally, Kingston and Whelan, *supra*, n.238, Chap.7.
[252] *Id.* at p.482.

right to abortion outside of Ireland."[253] But the correctness of this conclusion is debatable for, if a person is constitutionally "free to travel", notwithstanding Article 40.3.3 (1st para.), surely she is then entitled to travel and not be prevented by any agency of the State, including the courts, from travelling in order to obtain an abortion. Because the original version of this amendment was held to be self-executing and not require legislative intervention in order to become effective, surely the post-1992 freedom to travel is equally self-executing? Additionally, even though it was the political impact of the "*X*" case that gave rise to this right, if it had been intended only to stop injunctions of the kind that was granted there by Costello P., para.2 could have been drafted more narrowly in order to achieve this effect.

Information

Before 1992 the Supreme Court upheld orders in several cases enjoining making information available regarding abortion facilities abroad. In the first of these, *Open Door*,[254] which was a relator action by the Attorney General, two pregnancy counselling services were prohibited from giving their clients any information or assistance that would enable them to obtain abortions abroad. In the other, *Grogan*,[255] which was brought by an anti-abortion group, several students' unions were directed not to publish information about abortion facilities available in England. No distinction was drawn by the courts between information that would enable a pregnant woman to save her life, by having an abortion, and other abortion-related information. The sweeping nature of these injunctions was held by the Strasbourg Court to contravene the European Convention[256] which prompted the Fourteenth Amendment to be adopted in that year.

According to Article 40.3.3 (3rd para.), the 1983 guarantee of the unborn's right to life "shall not limit freedom to obtain or make available, in the State, subject to such conditions as may be laid down by law, information relating to services lawfully available in another state."[257] This is a most curious provision because, on its face it would appear to permit legislation that is either extremely liberal or, alternatively, legislation that is very restrictive as to what information may be supplied and in what circumstances, since it contains no qualifications about the contents of any such law insofar as it may prejudice the unborn. In

---

[253] *Ibid.*

[254] *Supra*, n.243.

[255] *Supra*, n.241.

[256] *Open Door Counselling Ltd v. Ireland* 15 E.H.R.R. 244 (1992). *Cf. Society for the Protection of Unborn Children Ireland Ltd (No. 2) v. Ireland*, Case 159/90 [1991] E.C.R. 4685.

[257] See generally, Kingston and Whelan, *supra*, n.238, Chap.7.

the event, a highly restrictive law, the Regulation of Information (Services Outside the State for Termination of Pregnancies) Act 1995, was passed.

In a reference by the President under Article 26 of the Constitution, the Bill which became that Act was upheld by the Supreme Court in the *Regulation of Information (Services Outside the State for the Termination of Pregnancies) Bill, 1995, Re.*[258] Hamilton C.J., for the court, first rejected the contention that, because providing information of this nature somehow contravened natural law, the Constitution could not permit, nor be amended to permit, that information being made available. He further rejected the contention that the decision in the "*X*" case was wrong because it offended against natural law and also because the evidence there did not justify the outcome. Instead, however, of concluding that the 1992 amendment places no restrictions on the contents of what the law envisaged may contain insofar as the unborn is concerned, nor does it require this law to contain any safeguards for the unborn, he proceeded on the basis that the test of constitutionality was "whether the provisions of the Bill represent a fair and reasonable balancing by the Oireachtas of the various conflicting rights and are not so contrary to reason and fairness as to constitute an unjust attack on the constitutional right of the unborn or on the constitutional rights of the mother or any other person or persons."[259]

Because the Bill would prohibit disseminating information that constitutes advocacy of abortion and also making arrangements on behalf of a woman to have an abortion abroad, it was contended that it contravened the rights of the mother. The short answer would seem to be that the rights the mother has in this regard are conferred by the 1983 amendment, which the 1992 amendment states "shall not limit" such provisions as the legislation to be enacted may contain. Instead of so concluding, however, the court found that these restrictions "represent a fair and reasonable balancing of [her] rights. ..."[260] It also was argued that the Bill was constitutionally deficient because, in the case of minors, it made no provision for notifying parents about the information being provided and, in the case of married couples, there was no provision for notifying husbands. On the grounds that there is an overarching constitutional duty to take due account of "the rights of persons likely to be affected by such information, counselling and advice,"[261] and that it is to be assumed that information-providers will have regard to this obligation, it was held that the Bill's provisions "represent a fair and reasonable balancing" of the rights of third parties. Finally, it was held that the comparatively small fine that may be imposed on persons who contravene these provisions did not render the Bill repugnant.

---

[258] [1995] 1 I.R. 1.
[259] *Id.* at p.45.
[260] *Id.* at p.52.
[261] *Ibid.*

CHAPTER 25

Private Property

The right to property is the right to own, acquire, use and dispose of land, chattels and other things that have an economic value. How extensive such a right is varies greatly from country to country; there are some societies where private property rights are regarded as extremely important and others where those rights are barely recognised. Next to personal security and liberty, the eighteenth century jurist Blackstone ranked private property as "[t]he third absolute right inherent in every Englishman ...."[1] Whether rights to private property should be accorded the status of a fundamental right that cannot be taken away by the legislature, or can be taken only in certain circumstances, is a controversial political and moral question.[2] It therefore is not surprising that, while a right to own and to dispose of property is proclaimed by many Bills of Rights, such as in the Fifth Amendment to the United States Constitution and Article 17 of the 1789 Declaration of the Rights of Man and the Citizen,[3] there are numerous constitutions[4] and international human rights instruments that do not protect claims and entitlements to property.

Property rights are guaranteed in three separate parts of the Constitution. Their principal protection is Article 43, which is headed "Private Property":

"1(1). The State acknowledges that man, in virtue of his rational being, has the natural right, antecedent to positive law, to the private ownership of external goods.

---

[1] *Commentaries on the Laws of England* (1765), p.138. According to this author, "there is nothing which so generally strikes the imagination, and engages the affections of mankind, as the right of property; or that sole and despotic dominion which one man claims and exercises over the external things of the world, in total exclusion of the right of any other individual in the universe ...".

[2] Blackstone's view can be contrasted with that of Leon Tolstoy, who contended that "in our time property is the root of all evil and of the suffering of men who possess it, or are without it, and of all the remorse of the conscience of those who misuse it, and of the danger of collision between those who have [it] and those who have it not:" quoted in A. Carter, *The Philosophical Foundation of Property Rights* (1989), p.1. See generally, J. Waldron, *The Right to Private Property* (1988) and J. Harris, *Property and Justice* (1996).

[3] Also Art.51(xxi) of the Australian Constitution, Art.25 of the South African Constitution, Art. 14 of the German Constitution and Art.42 of the Italian Constitution. See generally, Allen, "Commonwealth Constitutions and the Right not to be Deprived of Property", *42 Int & Comp. L.Q.* 523 (1993).

[4] *E.g.*, the Canadian Charter of Rights.

(2). The State accordingly guarantees to pass no law attempting to abolish the right of private ownership or the general right to transfer, bequeath, and inherit property.

2(1). The State recognises, however, that the exercise of the rights mentioned in the foregoing provisions of this Article ought, in civil society, to be regulated by the principles of social justice.

(2). The State, accordingly, may as occasion requires delimit by law the exercise of the said rights with a view to reconciling their exercise with the exigencies of the common good."

But property rights are also guaranteed by Article 40.3.2, which provides that "[t]he State shall, in particular, by its laws protect as best it may from unjust attack and, in the case of injustice done, vindicate the ... property rights of every citizen." Thirdly, property owned by certain religious bodies is protected by Article 44.2.6, according to which "[t]he property of any religious denomination or any educational institution shall not be diverted save for necessary works of public utility and on payment of compensation."

Property rights are guaranteed by Article 1 of the European Convention's First Protocol:

"Every natural or legal person is entitled to the peaceful enjoyment of his possessions. No one shall be deprived of his possessions except in the public interest and subject to the conditions provided for by law and by the general principles of international law.

The preceding provisions shall not, however, in any way impair the right of a State to enforce such laws as it deems necessary to control the use of property in accordance with the general interest or to secure the payment of taxes or other contributions or penalties...".

But the UN Covenant makes no reference to property. Indeed, there was nothing in the Irish Free State Constitution that corresponded to Article 43 of the present Constitution.[5] In a case involving the partial expropriation of land being developed, in order that economically disadvantaged persons may be able to buy affordable housing, the Supreme Court stated that "the tests adopted by the European Court (under the above Article) do not differ in substance from those which have been applied by the courts in this jurisdiction in this area."[6]

There are numerous cases on the constitutional status of State confiscation or restrictions on the use of property but, so far, the existence or ambit of any affirmative obligation to protect property interests has not come before the

---

[5] The only guarantee of property being Art. 8, applicable to the property of a religious denomination or an educational institution (similar to the present Art. 44.2.6). Compare s.5(1) of the Government of Ireland Act 1920.

[6] *Part V of the Planning and Development Bill, 1999, Re* [2000] 2 I.R. 321 at p.356.

courts. Insofar as any such obligation may exist, it is met by, *inter alia*, laws that make theft and other dishonest dealings in property, damaging property and entering property in certain circumstances criminal offences, and the law of tort and principles of equity that protect property rights.

Before examining what constitutes "property" for the purpose of these guarantees and their scope, the relationship between Articles 43 and 40.3 calls for explanation. It was held by the Supreme Court in *Blake v. Attorney General*[7] that Article 43 protects property rights in what may be termed the most extreme circumstances and that for most purposes the appropriate guarantee is that in Article 40.3. According to O'Higgins C.J., for the court, Article 43 gives constitutional protection against legislation seeking to confiscate private property generally or seeking to abolish the general right to transfer, bequeath or inherit property. All other interferences by the State with private property should be considered under Article 40.3, which is a guarantee against all forms of "unjust attack" on property entitlements:

> "Article 43 is headed by the words 'private property'. It defines the attitude of the State to the concept of the private ownership of external goods and contains the State's acknowledgement that a natural right to such exists, antecedent to positive law, and that the State will not attempt to abolish this right or the associated right to transfer, bequeath and inherit property. The Article does, however, recognise that the State 'may as occasion requires delimit by law the exercise of the said rights with a view to reconciling their exercise with the exigencies of the common good'. It is an Article which prohibits the abolition of private property as an institution, but at the same time permits, in particular circumstances, the regulation of the exercise of that right and of the general right to transfer, bequeath and inherit property. In short, it is an Article directed to the State and to its attitude to these rights, which are declared to be antecedent to positive law. It does not deal with a citizen's right to a particular item of property, such as controlled premises. Such rights are dealt with in Article 40 under the heading 'personal rights' and are specifically designated among the personal rights of citizens. Under Article 40 the State is bound, in its laws, to respect and as far as practicable to defend and vindicate the personal rights of citizens.
>
> There exists, therefore, a double protection for the property rights of a citizen. As far as he is concerned, the State cannot abolish or attempt to abolish the right of private ownership as an institution or the general right to transfer, bequeath and inherit property. In addition, he has the further protection under Article 40 as to the exercise by him of his own property rights in particular items of property ...
>
> Article 43 does not state what the rights of property are. It recognises

---

[7] [1982] I.R. 117.

private property as an institution and forbids its abolition. The rights in respect of particular items of property are protected by Article 40, s.3, sub-s. 2, by which the State undertakes by its laws to protect from unjust attack and, in the case of injustice done, to vindicate the property rights of every citizen. It is the duty of the Courts to protect such property rights from unjust attack and the decision as to what is such an attack is to be made by the Courts."[8]

Subsequently, however, it has been held that both of these provisions have a bearing on whether any expropriation is constitutionally valid.[9]

"PROPERTY"

What exactly property comprises for the purposes of these protections is not stated in the Constitution[10] and the question has not been considered in any great depth by the courts. Property, the ownership of which and the free disposition of which is guaranteed by the above Articles, is comprised principally of land, buildings and tangible assets, and documents of title to such property. Rights under contract have been treated as property rights, as have rights to bring an action in tort. Some rights of action for breach of statutory duty may very well be property rights.

But not all entitlements under statutes are regarded as proprietary in the constitutional sense. It was held by Carroll J. in *State (Pheasantry Ltd.) v. Donnelly*,[11] which concerned forfeiture of a wine retailer's licence, that these licences are not protected by Article 40.3. This was because "[t]he licence is a privilege granted by statute and regulated for the public good. It is *ab initio* subject to various conditions, one of which is the inherent possibility of automatic forfeiture ... There is no constitutional right to a liquor licence or a renewal thereof. There are only such rights as are given by statute subject to the limitations and conditions prescribed by statute."[12] Similarly in *Hempenstall v. Minister for the Environment*,[13] where changes to regulations governing taxi and hackney licences were challenged, Costello J. held that those could not be regarded as an attack on property rights because "[p]roperty rights arising in licences created by law (enacted or delegated) are subject to the conditions created by law and to an implied condition that the law may change those

---

[8] *Id.* at pp.135–136.
[9] *Supra*, n.6 at p.351.
[10] See generally, Symposium "The Evolution of Property Rights" (2002) 31 *J. Leg. Studies* 331 (2002) and J. Penner, *The Idea of Property in Law* (1997).
[11] [1982] I.L.R.M. 112.
[12] *Id.*, at p. 516.
[13] 1994] 2 I.R. 20.

conditions. Changes brought about by law may enhance the value of those property rights (as the Regulations of 1978 enhanced the value of taxi-plates by limiting the numbers to be issued and permitting their transfer) or they may diminish them ... But an amendment of the law which by changing the conditions under which a licence is held, reduces the commercial value of the licence cannot be regarded as an attack on the property right in the licence – it is the consequence of the implied condition which is in an inherent part of the property right in the licence."[14] On the basis of EC case law, the Supreme Court held in *Maher v. Minister for Agriculture*[15] that milk quotas allocated under the Common Agricultural Policy are not property rights, at least in the sense that there are substantive constitutional constraints on making significant changes to the quota system without compensating those who incur losses thereby. However, a radical change in a licensing regime that entirely prevents a person from carrying on an economic activity and that deprives him of a return on significant investments made may in the circumstances constitute an unjust attack on property rights.[16]

It would appear that contributory social security benefits are not property rights protected by Article 40.3.1-2, in view of the Supreme Court's decision in *Minister for Social Affairs v. Scanlon.*[17] It concerned disability benefits that had been paid to the defendant for several years until it was discovered that they had been improperly, albeit not-fraudulently, claimed. For most of that time, it was provided in the Social Welfare Acts that improperly claimed benefits could be stopped but there would be no legal obligation to repay benefits already received, unless they had been fraudulently claimed. It was held that this statutory embargo on recovery was not a constitutionally protected property right: it was at most a "statutory concession." Fennelly J. in his judgment added that "[t]he rights to receive benefit in the first place or retain benefit wrongly paid derive from the statute and do not partake of the nature of a property right."[18] This suggests that rights created by statute are not ordinarily, if indeed ever, protected by these Articles, which seems to be an extravagant view if it means that rights under patents and copyright legislation can be compulsory acquired without any provision for compensation. Since rights to land are conferred and defined by law, some of it statutory, it is difficult to understand why some other economic interests created and defined by statute are not protected by Article 40.3.2.

---

[14] *Id.* at p.28.
[15] [2001] 2 I.R. 139.
[16] *E.g., Newcrest Mining (WA) Ltd v. Commonwealth*, 190 C.L.R. 513 (1997).
[17] [2001] 1 I.R. 64.
[18] *Id.*, at p.87.

EXPROPRIATION

The most adverse way in which the State can affect an individual's property is to confiscate or expropriate it, i.e. to deprive the owner of all rights over the property.[19] A person's property may be taken from him only under the express provision of an Act of the Oireachtas or an Act that was carried over in 1937. Absent statutory authorisation, the State cannot expropriate property even during war time.[20] The State has never embarked on across-the-board confiscation, by seeking to abolish the right to own and to transfer ownership of all kinds of property. Any such measure would fall foul of Article 43.1.2. The most extensive programme of expropriation adopted in the last hundred and fifty years was the acquisition of agricultural land under the Land Acts by the Land Commission, principally so that tenant farmers could become owners of the lands they worked and that small holders be given additional land so that they could have economic units.[21] However, the vast bulk of the Commission's programme was completed by 1937 and what then remained to be done has since been finished.[22] Except for the Land Commission scheme, no Irish Government has resorted to nationalisation of the kind and scale once favoured by Labour governments in Britain and the Socialist administration in France.

Legislation exists authorising public authorities to deprive individuals of their land and other property for various purposes:[23] for instance, the Arterial Drainage Act 1945, authorises expropriation in order to facilitate the drainage of land; Part V (sections 75–87) of the Housing Act 1966 permits expropriation so that public authorities can build houses; the Electricity Supply Act 1927 provides for expropriating electricity undertakings and also of land; the Landlord and Tenant (Ground Rents) Acts empower tenants to buy out the ground rents of their houses; section 204 of the Companies Act 1963 enables a company that takes over another company to force minority shareholders, who oppose the take-over, to sell out their shares to the successful bidder. Perhaps the most extensive expropriation provisions enacted since 1937 are those in the Minerals Development Acts 1940-1979. Not alone do these Acts authorise the State to acquire mineral rights and related rights in various

---

[19] See generally, Mann, "Outlines of a History of Expropriation", 75 *L.Q.R.* 18 (1959) and R. Epstein, *Takings: Private Property and the Power of Eminent Domain* (1985).

[20] See generally, G. Rubin, *Private Property, Government Requisition and the Constitution, 1914–1927* (1994).

[21] Commenced with the Land Law (Ireland) Act 1881, 44 & 45 Vic. c.49. See generally A. Lyall, *Land Law in Ireland* (2nd ed., 2000), ch.15.

[22] Irish Land Commission (Dissolution) Act 1992. *Cf. O'Cleirigh v. Minister for Agriculture* [1998] 4 I.R. 15.

[23] See generally, S. McDermott & R. Woulfe, *Compulsory Purchase and Compensation in Ireland: Law and Practice* (1992).

circumstances but they confiscate an extensive range of mineral rights. Thus, section 5(e) of the Minerals Development Act 1940 vests "all mines of gold and silver" in the State and section 5 of the Petroleum and Other Minerals Development Act 1960 vests "the property in all petroleum" in the State. The Minerals Development Act 1979 does not vest the property in other mines or minerals in the State but instead vests in the State the exclusive right to work minerals (*i.e.* to dig, take and dispose of minerals), except for mines being lawfully worked or developed in December 1978.

Article 43 of the Constitution does not expressly authorise the State to take property; it merely speaks of the State "regulat(ing)" and "delimit(ing)" property rights. It therefore has been argued that the Constitution proscribes outright expropriation and confiscation. But that view is incompatible with one of the "directive principles of social policy" in Article 45.2.ii, which calls on the State to expropriate in order to redistribute property somewhat more equitably. According to this principle, "[t]he State shall ... direct its policy towards securing: ... that the owner ship and control of the material resources *of* the community may be so distributed amongst private individuals and the various classes as best to subserve the common good." An argument that the State has no constitutional authority to take private property was rejected in *Attorney General v. Southern Industrial Trust Ltd.*,[24] where it was held that provisions in the Customs Acts, providing for the seizure and forfeiture of chattels that are imported illegally, "must be recognised as a delimitation of the exercise of the general right (of private property) and therefore valid under ... Art. 43.2.2 ....".[25]

In the *Central Dublin Development Ass'n* case,[26] Kenny J. summed up the thrust of the property rights guarantees as follows:

"An analysis of the text of the Constitution and of the decisions on it lead to these conclusions:

The right of private property is a personal right.
In virtue of his rational being man has a natural right to individual or private ownership of worldly wealth.
This constitutional right consists of a bundle of rights most of which are founded in contract.
The State cannot pass any law which abolishes all the bundle of rights which we call ownership or the general right to transfer, bequeath and inherit property.
The exercise of these rights ought to be regulated by the principles of social justice, and the State accordingly may by law restrict their

---

[24] (1960) 94 I.L.T.R. 161.
[25] *Id.* at p.177.
[26] (1975) 109 I.L.T.R. 69.

exercise with a view to reconciling this with the demands of the common good.

The courts have jurisdiction to inquire whether the restriction is in accordance with the principles of social justice and whether the legislation is necessary to reconcile this exercise with the demands of the common good.

If any of the rights which together constitute our conception of ownership are abolished or restricted (as distinct from the abolition of all the rights) the absence of compensation for this restriction or abolition will make the Act which does this invalid if it is an unjust attack on the property rights."[27]

Purpose

As is the case with guarantees of private property in most constitutions, Articles 40.3 and 43.2.2 permit the Oireachtas to order or authorise expropriation in the public interest. These do not in fact use the very term public purpose but that is what the "exigencies of the common good" means, or at least has been regarded by the courts as meaning. It may well be that the public interest justification for taking property owned by religious denominations or educational institutions must be particularly compelling, in order for the expropriation to be valid, because Article 44.2.6 talks of "necessary works of public utility" and not merely of some general public purpose.

Although it is primarily a matter for the Oireachtas to determine what the public interest requires, State deprivations of property must be justified before the courts. In the words of O'Byrne J. in the *"Sinn Fein Funds"* case, "[i]t is claimed that the question of the exigencies of the common good is peculiarly a matter for the Legislature and that the decision of the Legislature on such a question is absolute and not subject to, or capable of, being reviewed by the courts. We are unable to give our assent to this far reaching proposition."[28] How thoroughly the courts will review the factual basis for passing an expropriation measure has not been determined. In particular, will the courts consider the contention that the legislature has erred, that the Act in question will not in fact achieve its professed purpose and that the Act accordingly is invalid to the extent that it interferes with property rights? Article 43 of the Constitution has at times been described as an obstacle to useful social legislation but the Supreme Court has only twice struck down an expropriation law because it contravened the private property guarantee. In both of these instances, the law in question was not truly a general measure but affected

---

[27] *Id.* at p.86.
[28] *Buckley v. Attorney General* [1950] I.R. 67 at p.83.

discrete properties; one of those laws additionally contravened the separation of powers and the other had many of the features of a Bill of Attainder.[29]

In *Buckley v. Attorney General*,[30] legislation was enacted which sought to put an end to litigation before the High Court concerning the ownership of Sinn Fein trust funds; the Act provided that those funds should be handed over to a newly created board which would administer them as directed. It was held to contravene the separation of powers.[31] But it was also struck down because the State neither demonstrated nor even claimed that the power under this Act to take the property was given for a public purpose. As O'Byrne J. stated, "[i]n the present case there is no suggestion that any conflict had arisen, or was likely to arise, between the exercise by the plaintiffs of their rights of property in the trust moneys and the exigencies of the common good, and ... it is only the existence of such a conflict and an attempt by the Legislature to reconcile such conflicting claims that could justify the enactment of (that Act)."[32]

There are two general ways in which property that has been taken by the State can be devoted to a public purpose. One may be called nationalisation, i.e. by some State agency becoming the owner of that property and then using it in order to achieve that agency's general objectives; for instance, bog land acquired by Bord na Mona in order to extract turf and land acquired by a local authority for the purpose of constructing a road. The other way is by redistribution, of which the most outstanding example is the Land Commission scheme. Expropriation called for by the "directive principle" quoted above is of the latter kind. The right of the Land Commission to expropriate, for the general purposes set out in the Land Acts, was never seriously challenged.

Part V (sections 93–101) of the Planning and Development Act 2000 provides for a partial redistribution of building land so that housing can be made available to some persons who ordinarily would not be able to purchase them. Under these provisions, as a condition of obtaining planning permission for a proposed development, the planning authority could require the landowner in question to transfer to it up to 20% of his land, so that housing could be built there for persons who otherwise would not have the means to buy their houses from the developer. Compensation would be paid for this land but at the pre-development market rate. This was part of a national strategy to enable the economically disadvantaged to purchase homes in an era when house prices had risen sharply and also to promote a degree of social diversity where new houses were being built. It was held by the Supreme Court in *Part V of the Planning & Development Bill, 1999, re*,[33] that this scheme was not a

---

[29] *Ibid* and *An Blascaod Mór Teo v. Commissioners for Public Works (No.3)* [2000] 1 I.R. 6.

[30] [1950] I.R. 67.

[31] *Supra*, p.200.

[32] [1950] I.R. 67 at p.83.

[33] [2000] 2 I.R. 321.

disproportionate incursion into property rights. For the court, Keane C.J. concluded that requiring land to be given to a local authority in this context "was rationally connected to an objective of sufficient importance to warrant interference with a constitutionally protected right and, given the serious social problems which they are designed to meet, they undoubtedly relate to concerns which, in a free and democratic society, should be regarded as pressing and substantial [and how] they impair these rights are proportionate to the objectives sought to be attained."[34] Several distinctions contained in this legislation were found not to be "arbitrary, unfair or based on irrational considerations."[35]

It has not been resolved whether the State is permitted to take property merely in order to give it to some other individual or private body, who the State believes will make better use of the property and where that taking is not part of some general scheme for redistribution. In *Roche v. Minister for Industry & Commerce*[36] that question was raised as regards a Ministerial Order purporting to acquire the "Bula" minerals at Navan, but it was held that the order there was *ultra vires* the Minerals Development Act 1940, and accordingly section 14 of that Act's constitutionality did not have to be tested. A variant of this question arose in *An Blascaod Mór Teo. v. Commissioners for Public Works (No. 3)*,[37] where an Act providing for the compulsory acquisition of practically all of the Great Blasket Island provided that the management of that property could be delegated to a designated privately-owned company. In holding this Act to be invalid, Budd J. ruled that a delegation of this nature was otherwise permissible.

Equality in Application

Some modern constitutions, such as Article 25(1) of South Africa's Constitution, provide that "[n]o one may be deprived of property except in terms of law of general application," thereby guaranteeing a degree of equal treatment in expropriations. An expropriation law can be so narrowly focused on an individual or a discrete group of persons that it has many of a features of a Bill of Attainder[38] and contravenes Article 40.1's guarantee of equality before the law. That was held to be the case in the *An Blascaod Mór Teo (No.3)* case,[39] where the Supreme Court found that An Blascaod Mór Natural Historic Park Act 1989 unfairly discriminated in the manner in which it envisaged compulsorily acquiring the plaintiffs' property on the Great Blasket island. As

---

[34] *Id.* at p.354.
[35] *Ibid.*
[36] [1978] I.R. 149.
[37] Unreported, High Court, Budd J., February 27, 1998.
[38] *Supra*, p.293.
[39] *Supra*, p.397.

explained by Barrington J., for the court, differentiating between persons who owned land there before and after 1953 was a classification "at once too narrow and too wide. It is hard to see what legitimate legislative purpose it fulfils [being] based on a principle – that of pedigree – which appears to have no place (outside the law of succession) in a democratic society committed to the principle of equality."[40] That normal compensation would be paid to the landowners there did not save the 1989 Act from invalidity.

Less Drastic Means

If it can be shown that the Oireachtas' object can be achieved conveniently without expropriating the plaintiff's property, it is conceivable that the compulsory acquisition measure would be struck down because it employs unnecessary and disproportionately drastic means. That argument was made in *O'Brien v. Bord na Mona*,[41] where, under statutory powers, the Board compulsorily acquired the plaintiff's land, in order to get turf from it, and where the plaintiff contended *inter alia* that the Board could get all the turf it needed from his land without having to acquire the fee simple in it. That contention was rejected, in the particular circumstances there, by Keane J.,[42] but was not considered in the appeal to the Supreme Court.

Support for a less drastic means criterion can be found in the European Court of Human Rights' decision in the *Sporrong & Lonröth* case,[43] where the court castigated the Swedish planning law for its inflexibility. One feature of that law was expropriation permits which, once issued, remained in force for many years until eventually they were cancelled. It was held that the law was defective because it contained no procedure for considering in the intervening years whether those permits were still necessary: "the law provided no means by which the situation of the property owners involved could be modified at a later date" and the court did "not see why the Swedish legislation should have excluded the possibility of re-assessing, at reasonable intervals during the lengthy periods for which each of the permits was granted and maintained in force, the interests of the city and the interest of the (property) owners."[44]

---

[40] *Id.* at p.19.
[41] [1983] I.R. 255.
[42] *Id.* at p.275.
[43] 5 E.H.R.R. 35 (1983).
[44] *Id.* at p.53 (para.70).

Compensation

Apart entirely from the Constitution, there is a long standing principle of construction that statutes should be interpreted as providing for compensation for property being taken by the State except where the contrary is stated.[45] Most of the statutory expropriation schemes provide that property-owners shall be compensated. The method of assessing the compensation and the criteria governing the quantum of compensation payable are usually the "arbitration" procedures and rules set down in the Acquisition of Land (Assessment of Compensation) Acts 1919-60.[46] These apply where land is acquired by a government department or by any local or public authority, and also where the expropriation Act specifies that these Acts' procedures and rules are to apply. In all other cases, unless the Act authorising expropriation specifies some different mechanism for determining the compensation,[47] the issue is to be decided by a judge and in accordance with common law principles.[48]

Articles 40.3 and 43 of the Constitution make no express reference whatsoever to compensation, which is curious when Article 43 extols property rights in such striking terms. Compensation is mentioned in Article 44.2.6, regarding taking property belonging to religious denominations and educational institutions, and a right to compensation was stipulated in section 5(1) of the Government of Ireland Act 1920. Compensation is expressly guaranteed by the United States Constitution ("just compensation": Fifth Amendment), the 1789 French Declaration ("just and previously determined compensation": Article 17), the Australian Constitution ("on just terms": Article 51 (xxi)) and the German Constitution ("equitable balance between the public interest and the interests of those affected": Article 14(3)).[49] It has been held by the courts that, as a general rule, expropriation and analogous interferences with property rights will be deemed to be unconstitutional unless just compensation is paid to the owner. As Kenny J. put it, "while some restrictions on the exercise of some of the rights which together constitute ownership do not call for

---

[45] *Attorney General v. de Keyser's Royal Hotel Ltd* [1992] 2 A.C. 315, 322 and *Soc. Anon. La Fleurette*, Cons. d'Etat, January 14, 1938, [1938] *Dalloz* 3, 41.

[46] See generally, McDermott & Woulfe, *supra*, n.23.

[47] *E.g.* Minerals Developments Acts, 1940-1979, which give the function to a Mining Board; 1940 Act ss. 16, 17 and 22, and Parts V (ss.33–37) and VII (ss.57–73), and 1960 Act, ss.33–51.

[48] *Comyn v. Attorney General* [1950] I.R. 142.

[49] According to Art.25(3) of the South African Constitution, "[t]he amount of compensation and the time and manner of payment must be just and equitable, reflecting an equitable balance between the public interest and the interests of those affected, having regard to all relevant circumstances, including – (a) the current use of the property; (b) the history of the acquisition and use of the property; (c) the market value of the property; (d) the extent of direct State investment and subsidy in the acquisition and beneficial capital improvement of the property; (e) the purpose of the expropriation". *Cf.* R. Epstein, *Takings* (1985) Ch. 13.

compensation because the restriction is not an unjust attack, the acquisition by the State of all the rights which together make up ownership without compensation would in almost all cases be such an attack."[50] In *O'Brien v. Bord na Mona* the Supreme Court held that, generally, the acquiring authority must "arrive by a fair procedure, at a proper compensation for acquisition."[51]

Even where the interference with property rights does not amount to outright expropriation, there may be a constitutional duty to compensate. In *Electricity Supply Board v. Gormley*,[52] under powers given to it in the Electricity Supply Acts, the Electricity Supply Board (ESB) entered on the defendant's lands and erected on them 220kV power lines in order to take electricity from one part of the country to another. A consequence of placing the transmission lines on her land was to impair its use, for agricultural purposes and for building, and to damage the amenity of the land surrounding her house. The Supreme Court held that the provisions in question were unconstitutional because they did not confer on her the right to be compensated for the interference with her land. In fact, the ESB paid *ex gratia* compensation to persons in the defendant's position and the existence of that practice was held by the court to demonstrate that it would not be unduly burdensome if the ESB were required by law to pay compensation in those circumstances. The court concluded that the law constituted an unjust attack on the defendant's property rights because it authorised extensive interference with her land but without giving her any right to be compensated.

Property-owners are not invariably entitled to compensation for each and every interference with their property, although the courts have not indicated clearly when property can be taken for a public purpose but without compensation being paid. In *Attorney General v. Southern Industrial Trust*,[53] it was held that provisions for forfeiting to the State goods, which were imported unlawfully, did not contravene Articles 40.3 and 43, and it was not suggested that the importer was entitled to any compensation. In *Electricity Supply Board v. Gormley* the defendant also contested the validity of statutory provisions that authorised the ESB to cut trees, shrubs and hedges adjacent to its power lines. But it was held that those were not unconstitutional merely because they failed to provide for compensation. According to Finlay C.J., there did "not appear to be any injustice in the imposition of the relatively minor burden on landowners of the cutting or lopping of trees, shrubs and hedges so as to make and keep safe the existence of a major electricity transmission line ...".[54] The criterion, therefore, of whether or not compensation must be paid is the vague one of "justice." As Walsh J. observed in one instance, "(i)t may well be that

---

[50] *Central Dublin Development Ass'n case*, 109 I.L.T.R. at p. 84.
[51] [1983] 1 I.R. 255 at p.286.
[52] [1985] I.R. 129.
[53] (1960) 94 I.L.T.R. 161.
[54] [1985] I.R. 129 at p.152.

in some particular cases social justice may not require the payment of any compensation upon a compulsory acquisition that can be justified by the State as being required by the exigencies of the common good."[55]

Where the State is constitutionally obliged to compensate, the question then arises of how much compensation must be paid. Must the State pay the property's full market value or the property's replacement cost; should the compensation cover all consequential losses and indeed include some element of bonus as recompense for general disturbance; can compensation be made otherwise than in cash or securities that are easily converted in cash and must the entire compensation be paid at once? Rules for assessing compensation under the Acquisition of Land (Assessment of Compensation) Acts 1919-60 are laid down in section 2 of the 1919 Act[56] and are based on the principle of equivalence, *viz.* not alone is the landowner entitled to be paid the market value of the land taken from him but he must be fully compensated for all losses attributable to him being disturbed, *inter alia* having to move his home or business elsewhere. But the constitutional requirement is not quite as generous. Dealing with claims to be paid the market value for land that is compulsorily purchased, Walsh J., for the Supreme Court in *Dreher v. Irish Land Commission*,[57] said that just compensation is not invariably the property's then market value; that "[i]t does not necessarily follow that the market value of lands at any given time is the equivalent of just compensation as there may be circumstances where it could be considerably less than just compensation and others where it might in fact be greater than just compensation. The market value of any property, whether it be land or chattels or bonds may be affected in one way or another by current economic trends or other transient conditions of society." [58]

Dreher concerned the method of calculating and paying compensation to owners whose property was taken by the Land Commission. Generally, land-owners whose property was taken by the Commission were not compensated in cash but in land bonds, which are government securities that are traded on the Stock Exchange and, therefore, are easily realisable. What was paid as compensation was bonds of a nominal value equal to the land in question's market value; in other words, and as occurred in *Dreher*, where land valued at £30,000 was taken, bonds with a nominal value of £30,000 were J transferred to the landowner. A procedure existed in the Land Acts to ensure that the interest payable on those bonds was around the same rate as can be obtained in the market on comparable government securities; the purpose of this procedure was to ensure that, when issued, the bonds were in fact worth their nominal value. Thus, if the going rate on equivalent government securities at

---

[55] *Dreher v. Irish Land Comm.* [1984] I.L.R.M. 94 at p.96.
[56] *Cf. Dublin Corp. v. Underwood* [1997] 1 I.R. 69.
[57] [1984] I.L.R.M. 94.
[58] *Id.* at p.96.

the beginning of the year in question is 9.75%, the land bonds for that year would be issued carrying that rate of interest. When land was taken by the Land Commission, the owner was credited with the land bonds but those could not be realised until good title was made to the land. Accordingly, because interest rates and stock exchange values can fluctuate rapidly, because bonds may be credited to the landowner some time after they were issued and because there was always some delay between when the bonds were credited and they were sold, the landowner might recover in cash an amount less than what the property was valued at. In *Dreher's* case the plaintiff's land had been valued at £30,000 but when, after making good title, he sold the £30,000 (nominal) bonds he had received, the proceeds came to less than that amount. His contention that the Constitution entitled him to proceeds at least equivalent to the amount which his land had been valued at was rejected by the Supreme Court. The mechanism described above for fixing the rate of interest to be paid on each issue of land bonds was described as ensuring that "the price of the land is to be paid for in land bonds which were to be issued at a rate which made them as near as could be reasonably achieved equal in actual value to the price fixed (for the land)."[59] Accordingly, these provisions "cannot be read as creating any reasonably avoidable injustice or indeed any real injustice. When the statutory provisions ... are observed and carried out they go as far as is reasonably possible to take into account the results of inflation and fluctuating rates of interest so far as they are reasonably foreseeable. If beyond that there are inflationary trends or fluctuations in the rate of interest outside the control of the Minister ... it cannot be said that because the statute does not also take account of that that it is inconsistent with the Constitution." [60]

That landowners are not always entitled to compensation equivalent to the full market price of their property was reiterated by the Supreme Court in *Part V of the Planning and Development Bill, 1999, Re.*[61] Under a scheme whereby, in order to get planning permission, intending developers could be required to give to the local authority up to 20% of the land in question, compensation could be measured in several ways, all "at a level significantly short of its market value."[62] There the court accepted that "a person who is compulsorily deprived of his or her property in the interests of the common good should normally be fully compensated at a level equivalent to at least the market value of the acquired property."[63] However, "[t]here are ... special considerations applicable in the case of restrictions on the use of land imposed under planning legislation,"[64] which on a previous occasion had been held to

---

[59] *Id.* at p.98.
[60] *Ibid.*
[61] [2000] 2 I.R. 321.
[62] *Id.* at p.349.
[63] *Id.* at p.352.
[64] *Ibid.*

warrant restrictions on whether or how much compensation should be paid, because there often is a highly speculative element when land is bought for development purposes without planning permission. Refusing, granting or cancelling planning permission can very significantly alter land values but there is no constitutional obligation to pay compensation on the basis of the owner's most favourable planning outcome.

Milk quotas under the EC's Common Agricultural Policy can be valuable items because they entitle the quota-owner to sell milk at guaranteed minimum prices. In determining the value of land, the size of any milk quota attached to it is a significant feature in fixing the price. It was held by the Supreme Court in *Maher v. Minister for Agriculture*[65] that persons who lose out when there are significant changes to the quota system are not entitled under the Constitution to be compensated for their losses. There the State introduced Regulations giving effect to the "Agenda 2000" policy, whereby the automatic link between quotas and a particular parcel of land was broken, in order to ensure that there would not be an undue number of unused quotas. On account of how these changes were being brought about, the plaintiffs, dairy farmers who owned substantial lands, stood to lose considerably. Their argument that this could not be done without adequately compensating them was rejected. According to Murray J., "when changes are effected to a regime regulating the organisation of a product market ... which are internally rational to the regime and the objectives to be achieved by it, those who participate as economic operators in that market must, in principle, accept such changes as an inherent element in that market in which they participate provided, at least, those changes do not affect other substantive rights independent of the regime and do not offend against fundamental principles such as non-discrimination."[66] Indeed, there are parallels between development land and milk quotas in that both of them are valuable principally on account of how the State regulates their surrounding contexts – being planning permissions and other environmental regulations, on the one hand, and guaranteed prices for outputs on the other.

Procedure

Legislation that authorises expropriation must comply with the constitutional separation of powers, must not preclude all judicial review of the actual decision to take the property in question and the procedure through which the decision to take is made must not be inherently unfair.

---

[65] [2001] 2 I.R. 139.
[66] *Id.* at p.229.

Separation of Powers

None of the major legislative schemes for expropriation provide that the decision to take the property in question must be taken by a judge in court proceedings or that the amount of compensation to be paid must be determined in that manner. But decisions of "arbitrators", acting under the Acquisition of Land (Assessment of Compensation) Acts 1919-60, and decisions of the Mining Board concerning claims for compensation, can be referred to the High Court on questions of law. Given the importance the Constitution attaches to property rights and that the expropriation laws often stipulate that the property may only be taken for certain purposes and in particular circumstances, about which there can be considerable dispute, are not decisions to expropriate frequently exercises of plenary judicial power and, accordingly, should they be decided by judges appointed and in courts established under the Constitution? It could be said that a determination that the State can take one's property, in the appropriate circumstances, is as judicial as a decision about adoption; the argument could be made that, since Article 37.2 of the Constitution expressly permits adoption decisions to be taken by a non-judicial body but no such provision is made for expropriation determinations, the latter ordinarily should be taken only by judges. Against that, the Dáil debates on the proposed Constitution make it clear that Article 37.1 was included principally to ensure that decisions by the Land Commission to take property could continue to be made by the Commission. In *Lynham v. Butler (No.2)*[67] the Free State Supreme Court held that some of the decisions made under the Land Acts were judicial and must be exercised by judges; however the 1922 Constitution contained no provision comparable to Article 37.1.

It has been held that some of the most important expropriation procedures do not involve the administration of justice in the full sense and, therefore, need not be administered directly through the courts. A feature of the Land Commission's procedures was that formerly judges had a direct say in determinations about whether land should be taken, in that aggrieved landowners had a right to appeal to the Judicial Commissioner of the Land Commission, who was a High Court judge. It was held in *Lynham v. Butler (No.2)*, that, when hearing an appeal or an application for a rehearing, the Judicial Commissioneris strictly speaking sitting as a judge of first instance, *i.e.* a judge of the High Court exercising judicial power. But the Land Act 1939 replaced the Judicial Commissioner with Lay Commissioners who were civil servants. In *Fisher v. Irish Land Commission,*[68] it was argued that the ultimate decision over whether land should be acquired is so important that it must be taken by duly appointed judges. But the Supreme Court rejected that contention on the grounds that such decisions were not deciding matters of

---

[67] [1933] I.R. 75.
[68] [1948] I.R. 3.

legal right but were merely implementing statutory policies. Maguire C.J., for the court, reasoned as follows:

> "In making these enquiries and coming to a final decision as to whether the particular parcel of land should be taken, ... these (Land Commission) officials are determining no question of legal right, but are considering and determining whether, for the purpose of effectuating the general purposes and policy of the (Land) Acts, it is necessary to acquire the particular parcel of land ...
>
> (A)ll the steps contemplated ... are steps to be taken in an inquiry of a purely administrative character and (the Act) does not contemplate or intend the determination of any question of legal right .... (However, i)n operating the machinery set up ... the (officials) are, of course, bound to act judicially, just as a great number of purely administrative tribunals are bound so to act ....".[69]

Four years later in *Foley v Irish Land Commission*,[70] the Supreme Court conceded but declined to decide that, in reaching some decisions to expropriate, the Land Commission exercises a limited judicial function or power as contemplated by Article 37.1.

Local government planning authorities were given extensive powers by the Local Government (Planning and Development) Act 1963 to regulate the use of land. In *Central Dublin Development Assn. v. Attorney General*,[71] the plaintiffs launched an extensive constitutional attack on this Act. Among their many contentions was that several sections, authorising the Minister to decide various matters, were an unconstitutional allocation of full judicial powers; notably, the powers to decide what is exempted development, to refuse planning permission because the proposed development would contravene the development plan, to revoke or modify a permission that was granted, to require the removal or alteration of an unauthorised structure, to decide whether a person seeking compensation under Part VI of the Act is entitled to compensation under earlier Acts and to hear appeals. But it was held that these and several other powers either were not judicial powers at all or were limited judicial powers that Article 37.1 permits being delegated to officials.[72] It was stressed, however, in this case and in the three Land Commission cases referred to above that these decision-making powers must be exercised in a judicial manner.

In many comparable countries how much compensation should be paid to persons whose property is being taken from them is decided by the courts.

---

[69] *Id.* at p.25.
[70] [1952] I.R. 118.
[71] 109 I.L.T.R. 69 (1975).
[72] *Supra*, p.194.

And some modern constitutions, such as Germany's, provide that "[i]n case of dispute regarding the amount of compensation recourse may be had to the ordinary courts."[73] In *Madden v. Ireland*,[74] which concerned the Land Commission's procedures for assessing compensation, McMahon J. held that those decisions amounted to administering justice but they, nevertheless, were "limited" judicial decisions which Article 37.1 permits to be consigned to persons other than duly appointed judges. Under current administrative law, reasons would have to be furnished for decisions of this nature and, additionally, they could be challenged by way of judicial review and quashed where it is shown that the sum being awarded is entirely unreasonable.

Although the Acquisition of Land (Assessment of Compensation) Acts 1919-60, in terms do not exempt the "property arbitrator" from giving reasons, they have been interpreted by the Supreme Court to that effect.[75] Decisions by the arbitrator on any question of fact are, by section 6(1) of the 1919 Act, deemed to be "final and binding on the parties ...". In consequence, it was held by the Supreme Court that these decisions cannot be challenged in the courts.[76] But it does not appear to have been contended in that case that a pre-1921 law purporting to exclude all judicial review of such decisions is repugnant to the Constitution. An argument for repugnancy was rejected by Budd J. in the *An Blascaod Mór Teo.* case[77] for reasons that are most unconvincing.[78]

Fair Procedures

As is demonstrated by a considerable body of case law on the Land Commission's activities, persons and agencies making decisions about expropriation and consequent compensation must observe the principles of natural justice or constitutional justice, in particular the maxims *audi alteram partem* and *nemo iudex in cause sua*. Where the legislation is silent on the matter, a duty to observe these principles will be inferred into the relevant statutory provisions. As O'Higgins C.J. put it in one instance, "(t)he constitutional presumption is that the powers ... will be administered with due and proper regard to the requirements of natural justice or justice under the Constitution."[79] As a rule, expropriation decisions must comply with Article 6(1) of the European Convention's requirements of fair procedures, which are "a fair and public hearing within a reasonable time by an independent and impartial tribunal. ..." These requirements are satisfied if there is a right of

---

[73] Art.14(3). Similarly Art.25(2)(b) of the South African Constitution.
[74] Unreported, High Court, McMahon J., May 22, 1980.
[75] *Manning v. Shackleton* [1996] 3 I.R. 85.
[76] *Doyle v. Kildare C.C.* [1995] 2 I.R. 424.
[77] Unreported, High Court, February 27, 1998 at pp.145 *et seq.*
[78] *Supra*, p.520.
[79] *O'Callaghan v. Cmrs of Public Works* [1985] I.L.R.M. 364 at p.368.

appeal from the initial decision-making authority to a body which possesses these attributes.

The circumstances in which it is constitutionally permissible by legislation to exclude compliance with *audi alteram partem* have never been determined, i.e. when would it be permissible to stipulate that a person whose property is being expropriated shall have no hearing whatsoever on the issue. It would be surprising if such a requirement were upheld, although exceptional circumstances may conceivably exist that would justify it.[80] As regards excluding *nemo iudex*, however, it was held by the Supreme Court in *O'Brien v. Bord na Mona*,[81] that there is nothing unconstitutional in providing that the public agency that wants to take land, in order to fulfil its statutory functions, shall be entitled to decide what land it shall have. There is no constitutional obligation that decisions of this nature be made by a wholly independent tribunal or body. In that case the plaintiff's land was taken from him under powers given to Bord na Mona by the Turf Development Act 1946. The Board needed extra turf to supply the electricity power station at Shannon bridge and decided to acquire compulsorily nearly 600 acres of bog, which included the plaintiff's land. However, the procedure in the 1946 Act for making land acquisitions differs considerably from that which exists in most expropriation laws in at least three respects. All that the 1946 Act says is that, if the Board needs land in order to perform any of its functions, it can acquire the land provided that the occupier gets at least one month's notice, and that maps and plans are deposited at the Board's headquarters in Dublin and at the local Garda Station. There is no requirement that the Board give prior notice of the compulsory purchase order being made to persons affected unless and until the Board proposes to enter on the land. Before an order is made, there is no requirement for holding an inquiry – either by the Board or by some other body. And when the order is made by the Board, there is no requirement that it be confirmed by some other body, such as the Minister, before it becomes legally effective.

The Supreme Court held that the absence of these three features from the 1946 Act did not render it unconstitutional. O'Higgins C.J. focused on the Act's basic objective, which is to make available for public use the extensive resources of turf in the country and, to that end, the Act empowers Bord na Mona to acquire bog lands whenever it needs turf. This Act, therefore, "constitut(es) a decision that the common good requires that bogland should be available for compulsory acquisition."[82] It is for the Board itself to decide what lands it needs at any particular time and there is nothing constitutionally objectionable in the Board making that decision, without conducting any formal public inquiry or having its decisions approved by some confirming authority.

---

80 *Cf. id.* at p.369.
81 [1983] I.R. 255.
82 *Id.* at p.283.

It was contended that the 1946 Act denies the landowner an opportunity to make a case against expropriation. But there is a presumption that, in exercising its powers, the Board will afford persons affected some hearing and this Act does not purport to prevent the Board from hearing any objectors. It was contended that, in deciding to expropriate land, the Board is acting as a judge in its own cause and accordingly contravenes the principle of *nemo iudex in causa sua*. But it was held that the Board here exercises administrative and not judicial functions and, in the light of the Act's scheme, the Board was the most appropriate body to decide what land should be acquired.

According to O'Higgins C.J., for the court:

> "The decision as to whether or not any particular area of land should be acquired for the attainment of that objective should be effectively vested in Bord na Mona. There is not any other authority of the State, executive or judicial, which should make the decision in principle as to whether, balancing the desirability of the production of turf on the one hand and the interests of an individual owner of land on the other, the production of turf or the agricultural interests of the land-owner should prevail. Such a view of the purpose and effect of the statute does not vest in Bord na Mona an arbitrary or capricious power. Nor is it exempt in any way from the review by the Courts should it, in any particular instance, act from an indirect or improper motive or without due fairness of procedure or without proper consideration for the rights of others.
>
> This Court is satisfied that, subject to these very considerable restrictions, the making of, or refusal to make, an order for compulsory acquisition is essentially an administrative act.
>
> Having reached that conclusion, the Court is further satisfied that neither the absence of a right of appeal from the decision of Bord na Mona to acquire a particular area of land or property right, as distinct from the right to review the exercise of that right, nor the absence of a scheme for a confirming external authority constitutes a breach of any of the plaintiff's constitutional rights."[83]

Before deciding to acquire land however, the Board must follow fair procedures: it must "give ample and fair notice to the owner of such property of its intention so to do; it must give him an ample opportunity to make representations or objections and then consider such representations or objections in a judicial manner; finally it must reach a decision whether to acquire or not upon the basis of that consideration."[84] The court concluded that the plaintiff had not in fact got an adequate hearing by the Board for his objection and that accordingly the decision to acquire his lands was null and void.

---

[83] *Ibid.*
[84] *Id.* at p.286.

FORFEITURE

A forfeiture is a provision to the effect that one is deprived of all rights to a particular piece of property and that the property shall belong to somebody else. A landlord's common law right of distress is a form of forfeiture, as are the Revenue Commissioners' and rating authorities' statutory rights to distrain in respect of unpaid taxes and rates. Under the Offences Against the State (Forfeiture) Act 1940, the Minister was empowered to declare that certain property acquired or used in a way that prejudiced State security, peace or order shall be forfeited. Several statutes provide for forfeiture of chattels where the owner is convicted of an offence in respect of them, for instance section 23 of the Misuse of Drugs Act 1977, and provisions of the Fisheries Acts 1959-1983.[85] Claims under the Proceeds of Crime Act 1996 have been described by the Supreme Court as "*in rem* proceedings for the forfeiture of property."[86] A penalty that is frequently imposed in regulatory legislation is forfeiture of a licence which is necessary in order lawfully to engage in certain activities, such as driving licences and licences to sell liquor.

In one of the earliest of its decisions on constitutional property rights, *Attorney General v. Southern Industrial Trust*,[87] the Supreme Court upheld a statutory provision for the forfeiture of the defendant's goods to the State. Section 5 of the Customs (Temporary Provisions) Act 1945, provided that, if persons illegally imported or exported specified goods (in that instance, a motor car) proceedings could be instituted against them, which could lead to the court ordering that the goods be forfeited. It was contended that forfeiture contravened the Constitution's property guarantees but the court rejected that argument in a perfunctory manner, characterising it as essentially arguing that the State is never allowed to take private property. Davitt P., at first instance, observed that it cannot be contended that "a person who takes the risk of illegally importing or exporting his own property has any reasonable cause to complain of injustice if it is forfeited in consequence of his offence."[88] The first defendant in this case was not the illegal importer, but a hire purchase company that owned the car in question, and it was contended that it was constitutionally unfair that the property of wholly innocent parties should be forfeited because of another's wrong. That view was rejected by Davitt P. on the grounds that, if forfeiture could not apply in the circumstances there, it would lose much of its effectiveness as a penalty, since virtually every smuggler would use vehicles subject to hire purchase in order to avoid the statutory penalty. It was very much in the public interest to have effective sanctions for breaches of the Customs Acts. Additionally, the legislation there gave the

---

[85] *Supra*, p.426 on whether these are "minor offences".
[86] *Murphy v. G.M.* [2001] 4 I.R. 113 at p.153.
[87] 94 I.L.T.R. 161 (1960).
[88] *Id.* at p.171.

Revenue Commissioners a discretion to mitigate the penalties in the event of particular hardship.[89]

Relying, *inter alia*, on this decision, in *Murphy v. G.M.*[90] the Supreme Court upheld the Proceeds of Crime Act 1966, which permits civil proceedings to be brought against persons for the confiscation of property which is the proceeds of crime, notwithstanding that nobody has been charged or convicted of the alleged crime. The defendants in the appeal there did not dispute the proposition that it was constitutionally competent for the State to confiscate such property but claimed that the Act was invalid on other grounds.

TAXATION

By their very nature, taxes are an interference with private property rights because they require persons to pay specified sums to the State. However, the State has implied authority under the Constitution to levy taxes and the courts are reluctant to strike down tax laws on the basis of the very nature of the tax, as distinct from procedures for assessing and for recovering taxes.[91] Nonetheless, tax laws may be unconstitutional for several reasons. Thus in *Murphy v. Attorney General*,[92] the aggregation of a husband's and a wife's income for the purpose of income tax liability was held to contravene Article 41 on the family. Depending on the circumstances, a tax that singles out the press may constitute an impermissible interference with freedom of expression.[93] A tax at penal rates on activities that are intrinsically criminal may be in substance the imposition of a penalty for the offence.[94] In some circumstances, taxing judges' income may be an impermissible interference with their independence.[95] There are circumstances where retrospective taxes may be struck down.[96] Tax regimes must also take account of the EC Treaty, which forbids fiscal discrimination in a variety of ways.[97]

Virtually every tax discriminates in one form or another. Irish income and capital taxes are progressive and there are varying rates of value added tax for different items. Perhaps the only truly non-discriminatory tax is a poll tax but such a tax could very well be unconstitutional because of its failure to discriminate at all. Taxes are unconstitutional interferences with property rights

---

[89] The company did not seek to have the penalty mitigated: *id.* at p.173. *Cf. Lindsay v. Customs & Excise Cmrs* [2002] 1 W.L.R. 1766.

[90] [2001] 4 I.R. 241; *supra*, p.414.

[91] *Supra*, p.210. and R. Epstein, *Takings* (1985) Ch. 18.

[92] [1982] I.R. 241; *supra*, p.670.

[93] *Minneapolis Star & Tribune Co. v. Minnesota Comrs. of Revenue*, 460 U.S. 595 (1983).

[94] *Dept. of Revenue v. Kurth Ranch*, 511 U.S. 767 (1994).

[95] *Supra*, p.165.

[96] *Doyle v. An Taoiseach* [1986] I.L.R.M. 693 at p.715.

[97] *E.g., Metalgesellschaft Ltd v. Inland Revenue* (Cases 397 and 410/98) [2001] Ch. 620.

where they discriminate in an entirely arbitrary fashion;[98] what may be described as contravening the principle of *egalité devant les charges publiques*. Consequently, taxes are required to have a degree of uniformity but the courts will not readily strike down taxes that discriminate to an extent. As O'Hanlon J. stated in *Madigan v. Attorney General*,[99] "[a]nomalies could arise in any tax legislation and did not render the legislation unconstitutional. ... It has been recognised by the courts ... that considerable latitude must be allowed under the Constitution to taxation statutes, and that absolute equality of treatment of all sections of the community could not be achieved; it could, in fact, be unconstitutional to deal equally with persons where circumstances were unequal."[100] According to O'Higgins C.J. in that case, "[i]t is not for the court to question the choice of imposition which has been made, nor to inquire into the extent to which the desired contribution to the revenues of the State will be achieved. These are matters which belong to the political arena and are for consideration and discussion in the National Parliament."[101]

During the 1970s political parties competed vigorously with each other in advocating the abolition of rates on residential property and that system of raising finance for local government came to an end in 1978. But a variant of rates was introduced by Part VI of the Finance Act 1983, the residential property tax. It was a tax on the owner-occupiers of what may be called expensive houses, based on the value of the house but payable to the Revenue rather than to local government. In brief, the taxpayer was the owner-occupier of residential property with a market value of £65,000 and the rate of tax was 1½%. There were exemptions from the tax where the aggregate incomes of the taxpayer and all others resident in the house was less than £20,000 per annum. These figures were linked to the consumer price index. As well as claiming that features of the 1983 Act contravened their rights to privacy[102] and rights regarding the family,[103] the plaintiffs in *Madigan v. Attorney General*[104] contended that their property rights had been violated, principally by making property valued at more than £65,000 the basis for the tax. As regards selecting the tax base, it was argued that the tax was an unfair discrimination against a minority, *viz.* owner-occupiers of expensive houses. It was contended that in any event the tax base should not be the full market value but the owner-occupier's "equity" in the house, *i.e.*, its net market value; in other words full market value less any mortgage or other charges on the property. But it was held that selecting these houses was not unconstitutionally unfair because the

---

[98] *Supra*, p.399.
[99] [1986] I.L.R.M. 136.
[100] *Id.* at p.145.
[101] *Id.* at p. 161.
[102] *Supra*, p.648.
[103] *Supra*, p.671.
[104] [1986] I.L.R.M. 136.

object of the tax was "exacting (a) contribution from the better off and well-to-do who can be presumed to occupy the more valuable houses."[105] As for using full market value as the tax base, it was pointed out that the method used for valuing houses for domestic rates never took account of charges on the houses, that diminished their value to their owner-occupiers; moreover, domestic rates did not have as generous an exception for low income taxpayers.

The other property-related argument against the tax was that owner-occupiers were exempt from paying it where they demonstrated that the aggregate incomes of themselves and all others occupying the property did not exceed £20,000 per annum; the objection was that it is unjust to use circumstances entirely beyond the taxpayer's control as a criterion when imposing tax – in this case, the incomes of others occupying the house. But it was held that, since a tax based on the market value of expensive houses is not in itself unconstitutional, even if it did not provide an exemption for low-income owners, there is nothing particularly unfair in the form of exemption used in the 1983 Act, especially when in fact the members of most households contribute towards general household expenditure. As O'Higgins C.J. put it, the exempting provision;

> "does not impose a liability for tax. The occupying owner is already chargeable for the tax because he owns and occupies a house with a market value in excess of £65,000. As already stated the court does not consider on any of the grounds open to and relied on by the plaintiff, that the imposition of such a tax lacks constitutional validity. Like any other tax it is bound to affect in varying degrees those who are made liable for its payment depending on the means and circumstances of each such person. For some, no problem may be caused. For others its imposition may have meant a choice between continuing to occupy a house which has become more expensive to reside in and selling or otherwise ceasing to reside therein. While people so affected might feel that they had genuine grounds for complaint against and opposition to the tax they could not challenge its validity merely because they had difficulty in paying .... The court is satisfied that this exemption is based on the common experience in society that members of families and households, to the extent that they can do so, contribute to the expenses and outgoings of the family home. To ignore this fact in framing an exemption to meet cases of hardship or inability to pay would be to act without regard to reality. While there may be situations where the assessable person does not recover a contribution from others who share in the enjoyment of the residence, such situations must be extremely rare and must depend for

---

[105] *Id.* at p.161.

their continuance on a degree of tolerance by the assessable person which borders on foolishness."[106]

Various criteria exist for determining how much tax an individual or body must pay, for instance, the amount of a person's income and the value of a person's assets. The only occasion where a tax measure was struck down for being an unfairly discriminatory interference with property was *Brennan v. Attorney General*,[107] which concerned the way in which agricultural land was valued, primarily for the purpose of levying rates. The basis of valuation was laid down in the Valuation Acts 1852–64[108] and was known as the Griffith Valuation. Briefly, these established a mechanism for valuing agricultural land; there was to be a general valuation of all such land and the main criterion was the average prices obtaining around 1850 for articles of agricultural produce listed. Sir Richard Griffith was put in charge of the entire undertaking, which took 14 years to complete. The work commenced in the South shortly after the end of the Great Famine and the repeal of the Corn Laws, and was completed in the North of Ireland in 1866. Although these Acts provided that the overriding objective was "one of uniform valuation of lands," there always were significant anomalies; most notably, because economic conditions changed greatly during the course of the work, land in the South of Ireland tended to be valued at much less than land in the North. Even as far back as 1902, the Royal Commission on Local Taxation described the agricultural values as "quite out of date" and a Commissioner for Valuation conceded that the system was so antiquated as to be indefensible. What made the values placed on land even more out of date by the 1980s was the huge transformation in economic and social conditions since then.

Farmers in Co. Wexford sought a declaration that the entire system was so anachronistic and riddled with inconsistencies that it was an unconstitutional interference with their rights. Values of their farms affected not alone their liability for rates but also their position as regards income tax on farming profits, resource tax, compulsory health contributions, higher education grants, grants for housing and there was always the prospect of additional financial measures being introduced which would be based on those valuations. But those were not so inconsistent and out of line with current economic conditions that the plaintiffs, for example, would often have to pay much higher rates than would numerous other farmers who owned land that in fact was far more valuable. One plaintiff showed that over several years he paid £1,000 in rates whereas his brother, who had a better farm, paid no rates whatsoever.

Emphasising that the courts' function is not to evaluate the relative merits of different forms of taxation and that the courts "should be extremely slow to

---

[106] *Id.* at pp.162 and 163.
[107] [1984] I.L.R.M. 355.
[108] 15 & 16 Vic. c.63.

interfere" with revenue and fiscal issues, it was held that this system was unconstitutional. From the evidence, Barrington J. found that:

> "1. That the existing valuation system does not provide a uniform system for valuing lands throughout the State.
> 2. That there is no consistency between county and county or with individual counties.
> 3. That the valuation system has failed to reflect changing patterns of agriculture with the result that land which modern agriculturists would regard as good land often carried a low valuation while land which modern agriculturalists would regard as inferior often carries a higher valuation.
> 4. That the whole system is shot through with unnecessary anomalies and inconsistencies."[109]

In particular, the valuations place on the plaintiffs' farms were "hopelessly outdated and unreliable as a guide to the present value of their farms."[110] He then observed that if a Valuation Act were introduced in 1982, providing that property should be valued for taxation and other purposes on the basis of conditions prevailing in the middle of the last century, such a law undoubtedly would be unconstitutional. Consequently, the 1852-66 Acts contravened the guarantee of constitutional equality in Article 40.1 and did not respect the plaintiffs' property rights.

The Supreme Court rejected the view that the valuation system contravened the equality guarantee. But it held that so anachronistic and inconsistent a valuation system gave rise to such unfairly different treatment of farmers that it contravened Article 40.3. According to O'Higgins C.J., for the court, "use of the 1852 valuations was continued as a basis for agricultural rates long after the lack of uniformity, inconsistencies and anomalies had been established, and long after methods of agricultural production had drastically changed. This in itself was an unconstitutional attack on the property rights of those who like the plaintiff found themselves with poor land paying more than their neighbours with better land. When this injustice had become obvious the State had a duty to take action in protection of the rights involved."[111] Taxing laws require a degree of equal or uniform treatment for taxpayers; "[i]n the assessment of a tax such as a county rate reasonable uniformity of valuation appears essential to justice. If such reasonable uniformity is lacking, the inevitable result will be that some ratepayer is required to pay more than his fair share ought to be. This necessarily involves an attack upon his property rights which by definition becomes unjust."[112]

---

[109] [1983] I.L.R.M. at p.361.
[110] *Id.* at p.486.
[111] [1984] I.L.R.M. 361.
[112] *Ibid.* Compare *Browne v. Attorney General* [1991] 2 I.R. 58.

OTHER INTERFERENCES WITH PROPERTY

There are ways other than expropriation, forfeiture and taxation by which the State interferes with an individual's interest in property, some of which have been struck down as unconstitutional. Whether a particular interference is invalid depends on the nature of the property interest being invaded, the character and scope of the interference, its justification, whether there is some uniformity in its application, and the nature and extent of any compensation accruing. For instance, in *Electricity Supply Board v. Gormley*,[113] placing power transmission lines on the defendant's land was held to be unconstitutional because, although the legislation in question was adopted for an admittedly beneficial public purpose, it did not provide for any compensation.

At times compensation may take the form of implicit in kind compensation.[114] By this is meant that a legislative prohibition against a particular use of property may render A, B and C individually less well off but their loss may be compensated for by the fact that all other owners of similar property are also subject to that restriction or prohibition. For instance, environmental planning regulations which prohibit X from putting signs on his property may be fully justified because all other neighbouring property owners are subject to the same prohibition. Account also may be taken of the fact that a variety of State activities significantly benefit individuals and, consequently, State interference in a single use of a person's property is radically different from some private body interfering with that use in an equivalent manner. There can be circumstances where the provision of police, health, educational and transport facilities by the State may be regarded as sufficient compensation for a significant restriction by the State on some uses of property.

Inheritance

Provisions in some modern constitutions guaranteeing property rights expressly refer to inheritance.[115] At one time it was widely accepted that an essential feature of property ownership was absolute freedom to determine who would inherit on one's death. That was the legal position in Ireland until Part IX (sections 109–119) of the Succession Act 1965 required reasonable provision to be made for the deceased's spouse and other family members. Apart from *O'B. v. S.*, which concerned non-marital children, its constitutionality has not been challenged and any such attack most likely would founder on Article 41.

---

[113] [1985] I.R. 129.

[114] See generally, R. Epstein, *Takings* (1985), Chaps 14 and 15.

[115] *E.g.* Art.14(1) of the German Constitution and Art.42 of the Italian Constitution.

Environmental Regulation

By environmental regulation is meant provisions that regulate the uses of land, notably anti-pollution measures and planning laws.[116] These almost invariably contain a significant element of implicit in kind compensation and indeed some planning laws provide for payment of compensation to property owners whose land has been devalued in consequence of planning decisions; notably Part XII (sections 183-201) of the Planning and Development Act 2000. Under this, compensation equivalent to the reduction in the property's value may be awarded to persons who have been refused planning permission, the amount to be determined by "arbitration" under the Acquisition of Land (Assessment of Compensation) Acts 1919–60.

A great number of provisions of the pre-2000 planning regime were challenged, unsuccessfully, on constitutional grounds in *Central Dublin Development Assn. v. Attorney General*.[117] The essentially procedural complaints that Kenny J. rejected were that some decision-making powers under the 1963 Act could only be exercised by the ordinary courts,[118] that this Act placed certain decisions of planning authorities beyond all judicial review[119] and that aggrieved persons were denied a right to be heard in particular circumstances.[120] The principal substantive complaints were that the planning criteria laid down in the 1963 Act were excessively vague and uncertain, and that the Act's following features constituted an unjust attack on property rights, viz. requiring a planning authority's permission in order to develop land, empowering an authority to order that certain uses of land be discontinued, Part VI of the Act's denial of compensation in various circumstances and not providing for reinstatement of buildings formerly owned in an obsolete area. Kenny J.'s general response to these contentions was that "If there is to be planning development, someone must decide whether new or altered buildings are to be allowed in a specified place and whether land should be retained as an unbuilt space. The very nature of town and regional planning requires restriction in the sense that building in a particular area may not be appropriate or that the proposed buildings are not suitable or that buildings may not be used for some purposes. Town and regional planning is an attempt to reconcile the exercise of property rights with the demands of the common good .... The making of a plan will necessarily decrease the value of property, but I do not think that the Constitution requires that compensation should be paid for this as it is not an unjust attack on property rights ...".[121]

---

[116] See generally, Y. Scannell, *Environmental and Planning Law* (1995).
[117] (1975) 109 I.L.T.R. 69.
[118] *Id.* at pp.93–96.
[119] *Id.* at pp.88–89 and 91.
[120] *Id.* at pp.89–90.
[121] *Id.* at p.90.

These views were endorsed by the Supreme Court in the case involving what now is Part V (sections 93-101) of the Planning and Development Act 2000.[122] As Keane C.J. pointed out, that planning "permission for a particular type of development may not be available for the land will, in certain circumstances, depreciate the value in the open market of that land. Conversely, where the person obtains a permission for a particular development the value of the land in the open market may be enhanced."[123] Thus, buying land for development purposes can be an extremely speculative undertaking but there is no constitutional obligation to compensate the disappointed developer on the basis that he did develop those lands because they were then taken from him.

Another type of environmental regulation to withstand a constitutional attack was the National Monuments Acts 1930-54, some provisions of which were the subject of *O'Callaghan v. Commissioners of Public Works*.[124] These Acts were passed to protect national monuments and *inter alia* authorise the Commissioners of Public Works to place a preservation order on particular monuments, the effect of which is to prohibit persons from damaging them in various ways. A promontory fort was designated a national monument in 1970 and, in 1977, the plaintiff purchased a large tract of land on which that fort was located. When he commenced ploughing the land where the fort was, under powers given in section 14 of the 1930 Act the Commissioners immediately ordered that the fort be preserved and that the ploughing cease. It was contended that section 14 was unconstitutional because the plaintiff had not been afforded a fair hearing before the preservation order was made and because part of his property was sterilised economically without any compensation being paid. The Supreme Court rejected these arguments, observing at the outset that "(i)t cannot be doubted that the common good requires that national monuments which are the prized relics of the past should be preserved as part of the history of our people."[125] Accordingly, the 1930-54 Acts regulated the exercise of property rights in the public interest. They were neither "arbitrary nor selective," in that they embraced all national monuments regardless of where they were situated or who owned them. Dealing with the absence of compensation for owners of monuments, the court limited itself to saying that if one buys land in the full knowledge that it contains monuments, one then has no basis for claiming compensation; that "the absence of ... a provision for the payment of compensation to (the owner) in respect of a limitation of use of which he was substantially on notice before his purchase and which is a requirement of what should be regarded as the common duty of all citizens to preserve such a monument, can be no ground for suggesting that

---

[122] *Part V of the Planning and Development Bill, 1999, Re* [2000] 2 I.R. 321.
[123] *Id.* at p.353.
[124] [1985] I.L.R.M. 364.
[125] *Id.* at p.367.

the prohibition or limitation is an unjust attack on his property rights."[126] It therefore would seem that if something on a person's land becomes designated a national monument and as a result that landowner will suffer substantial loss, the Constitution may very well grant a right to be paid compensation in respect of that loss.

Impairing Rights of Action

Rights of action are rights or entitlements under the law which are enforced through the courts. These arise under the common law or derive from statute and also from the Constitution itself. It was held in *Byrne v. Ireland*[127] that impairing common law rights of action, to the extent of granting categories of persons immunity from suit, contravenes the constitutional requirement of legality, except where that immunity can be justified by the express or implied requirements of the Constitution itself. Rights of action have been treated as a form of property right,[128] although the Supreme Court has cast some doubts on that characterisation. Rights of action for direct invasions of property rights in the traditional sense are restricted by at least two measures. One is section 55 of the Air Navigation and Transport Act 1936, which prevents landowners from bringing suit in respect of aircraft flown over their property; it states that "[n]o action shall lie in respect of trespass or in respect of nuisance, by reason only of the flight of aircraft over any property at a (reasonable) height above the ground ... or the ordinary incidents of flight ...." Another is section 1(1)(a) of the Accidental Fires Act 1943, which prevents owners from suing for damages should their property be damaged by accidental fire. According to it, "[w]here any person ... has suffered damage by reason of fire accidentally occurring ... in or on the building or land of another person, then, notwithstanding any rule of law ... no legal proceedings shall ... be instituted in any court by the injured person or ... his insurer ... on account of such damage ...". The precise scope of these provisions is not clear; there are no major reported authorities on their interpretation.

Limitation Periods

One means of impairing rights of action is by imposing brief limitation periods on prosecuting claims in various circumstances.[129] Under the since-repealed Public Authorities (Protection) Act 1893,[130] very short limitation periods

---

[126] *Id.* at p.368.
[127] [1972] I.R. 241; *supra*, p.23.
[128] *Cf. Georgiadis v. Australian and Overseas Telecom. Corp.* (1994) 179 C.L.R. 297.
[129] *Supra*, p.494.
[130] 56 & 57 Vic. c.61, repealed by the Public Authorities (Judicial Proceedings) Act 1954.

existed for actions against public authorities. It was held in *O'Brien v. Keogh*[131] that provisions of the Statute of Limitations, 1957 were unconstitutional because they did not afford adequate protection for infants who had rights of action in respect of personal injuries. And in *White v. Dublin Corporation*[132] it was held that an extremely short period within which certain planning decisions may be challenged was unconstitutional. As is explained earlier in the discussion on civil procedure, several unsuccessful attempts have been made to have limitation periods declared invalid, such as *Moynihan v. Greensmyth*,[133] which concerned an infant victim of a road traffic accident; *Touhy v. Courtney*,[134] which concerned financial loss on account of a solicitor's negligence; *Cahill v. Sutton*,[135] where it was held that the plaintiff did not possess *locus standi* to challenge the provisions in question. In *Moynihan v, Greensmyth*, the Supreme Court cast doubts on the view that rights of action at common law are property rights; but, whatever classification is put on these rights, it cannot seriously be doubted that they are entitled to some constitutional protection.[136]

Ceilings on Damages

Another form of impairing a right of action is by imposing a ceiling, or maximum sum, on the amount of damages which may be awarded to a successful plaintiff. Article 22(1) of the Warsaw Convention,[137] as amended in 1955, was made part of Irish law by section 7 of the Air Navigation and Transport Act 1959. Under it, the liability of air carriers in respect of injury or death caused to their passengers is limited to a maximum of 250,000 *Poincaré* French francs.

Impairment of Contracts

The Constitution contains no provision resembling the United States Constitution's "contracts clause" – that "(n)o State shall pass any law impairing the obligation of contracts."[138] But rights under contract are protected by Article 40.3 as property rights. To what extent the Oireachtas can nullify subsisting contracts between the State or some public body on the one hand and a private individual or organisation on the other has never been considered by the Irish

---

[131] [1972] I.R. 144; *supra*, p.497.
[132] p.755; *supra*, p.449.
[133] [1977] I.R. 55.
[134] [1994] 3 I.R. 1.
[135] [1980] I.R. 269.
[136] *Cf. Smith v. ANL Ltd*, 176 A.L.R. 449 (2000).
[137] Of October 12, 1929, ???.
[138] Article I, 10.

courts. Much of the legislation that affects contractual rights can be subsumed under the general heading of economic regulation and those measures are considered in the next chapter on economic rights.

Rent Restrictions

There are several kinds of legislative provision that deal with relations between owners of property and tenants, be they residential, business or agricultural tenants, for instance the Landlord and Tenant (Amendment) Acts 1980-1984, and the Landlord and Tenant (Ground Rents) Acts 1967–78.[139] Mechanisms for controlling residential rents were adopted in many countries during World War I and survived in one form or another into the 1980s. By the Rent Restrictions Act 1960, what originally were temporary restrictions on the amount of rent that a significant number of residential landlords could charge their tenants were placed on a permanent footing. However, parts of that Act were declared unconstitutional in *Blake v. Attorney General*,[140] as was a replacement measure adopted in 1980.[141]

Objection was taken to three major features of the 1960 Act. One was that it did not embrace all rented residential property; it applied only to "controlled dwellings," which were houses erected before May 1941 and below certain valuations, other than houses where the controlled tenant had surrendered the tenancy. Between 45,000 and 50,000 dwellings in all were controlled. Another focus of objection was the Act's central purpose, which was to place a statutory ceiling on the rent that could be charged for controlled tenancies. The amount of these rents was determined in slightly different ways by reference to rents being charged between 1914 and 1966. Often the actual effect of these ceilings on rents was that landlords had to accept rents that were much lower than what could be charged if controls no longer applied. Evidence showed that in respect of some of the houses owned by the plaintiff, the market rent would have been approximately 9, 10, 11, 13, 14, 17 and 19 times the controlled rent. Thirdly, tenants of controlled premises were given full security of tenure provided that they paid the legal rent; moreover they were entitled to dispose of their leases, except where the landlord could prove that doing so would cause him great hardship. Because landlords of controlled tenancies could not charge anything like the market rent and were effectively precluded from obtaining possession of their properties, the properties' sale values were significantly below their unencumbered market values.

Having set out the history of the 1960 Act and its effect on controlled tenancies, McWilliam J. in *Blake* concluded that it was unconstitutional because

---

[139] See generally, A. Lyall, *Land Law in Ireland* (2nd ed., 2000), Chaps 9 and 20.
[140] [1982] I.R. 117.
[141] *Infra*, p.761.

"a group of citizens arbitrarily selected has been deprived of property for the benefit of another group of citizens without compensation, with no limitation on the period of deprivation, and with no indication of any occasion which necessitates their selection for this purpose from amongst the general body of citizens."[142] In other words, the criteria for ascertaining which tenancies shall be controlled were very much random ones, the principal one being historical accident. The Act deprived those house-owners of most of the economic value of their property and that benefit was transferred to their tenants, who were practically irremovable and no compensation whatsoever was paid for this wealth transfer. On appeal, the same view was taken by the Supreme Court. O'Higgins C.J., for the court, singled out several objectionable features in the legislation. One was that it did not apply to all comparable situations. The only apparent reason why the controlled tenancies were selected by the 1960 Act was because those tenancies had been controlled by the previous temporary legislation. No other explanation was given for choosing the tenancies for permanent control. Related to that, the controls did not apply to the thousands of houses owned by local authorities and let to tenants in need of housing assistance. Furthermore, neither the inability of each tenant of controlled housing to pay the market rent nor the ability of the landlord to let the house for a sub-market rent were ever a criterion for applying rent controls. In other words, rich tenants could hold controlled leases from impoverished landlords. According to O'Higgins C.J. "it is apparent that in this legislation rent control is applied only to some houses and dwellings and not to others; that the basis for the selection is not related to the needs of the tenants, to the financial or economic resources of the landlords, or to any established social necessity ....".[143] Secondly, for most controlled tenancies rents were fixed by reference to rents charged in 1914, which were extremely low, and there was no statutory procedure then in force for adjusting the rents in the light of current economic conditions. According to the Chief Justice, these provisions "restrict the property rights of one group of citizens for the benefit of another group. This is done, without compensation and without regard to the financial capacity or the financial needs of either group, in legislation which provides no limitation on the period of restriction, gives no opportunity for review and allows no modification of the operation of the restriction."[144]

It was intimated that the rent controls might be upheld if landlords were paid adequate compensation and also if they were merely temporary measures or were designed to meet some emergency. But the controls in the 1960 Act did not provide for an "adequate compensatory factor" nor were they "associated with any particular temporary or emergency situation."[145]

---

[142] [1982] I.R. 117 at p.126.
[143] Id. at p.138.
[144] Id. at p.139.
[145] Id. at p.138.

Accordingly, they were "unfair and arbitrary" and an infringement of the plaintiffs' constitutional rights. On the other hand, the Act's security of tenure provisions on their own might not be unconstitutional because "a restriction to this extent of a landlord's right to obtain possession of the rented premises is not in itself constitutionally invalid, provided the restriction is made on a basis that is not unconstitutionally unfair or oppressive, or has due regard both to the personal property rights of the landlord and the rights that should be accorded to tenants having regard to the common good."[146] Because, however, the security of tenure provisions in the 1960 Act were a vital part of an unconstitutionally unfair scheme of rent control, they too were declared invalid. Those provisions were "an integral part of the arbitrary and unfair statutory scheme whereby tenants of controlled dwellings are singled out for specially favourable treatment, both as to rent and as to the right to retain possession, regardless of whether they have any social or financial need for such preferential treatment and regardless of whether the landlords have the ability to bear the burden of providing such preferential treatment."[147]

Almost immediately after this decision was handed down, the Government had a reforming measure, the Housing (Private Rented Dwellings) Bill, 1981, passed by both Houses of the Oireachtas but the President referred it to the Supreme Court under the Article 26 procedure. This Bill, which applied to all tenancies which were controlled at the time the *Blake* case was decided, sought to adjust the balance of landlords' and tenants' rights more in favour of the former. In particular, tenants no longer had a general right to assign their tenancy and the rent payable was to be the going market rate as determined by the District Court. Between 1981 and 1986 the rent was not to be the full market rate but was to be only a proportion of that rate; in 1982, 40%, in 1983, 50%, and so on. This five year transition period between quite low rents and the full market rent was intended to alleviate the hardship that many controlled tenants would suffer if they were obliged immediately to pay the market rate. Nevertheless in *Re Housing (Private Rented Dwellings) Bill, 1981*,[148] the Supreme Court found that obliging landlords to accept sub-market rents for a five year period, in the circumstances, was an unconstitutional interference with their property rights. As O'Higgins C.J. giving the court's judgment put it, "[t]he effect of the rebates ... is that for a period of five years after the enactment of the Bill as law, landlords are to receive an amount which will be substantially less than the just and proper rent payable in respect of their property. In the absence of any constitutionally permitted justification, this clearly constitutes an unjust attack upon their property rights. The Bill offers no such justification for depriving the landlord of part of his or her just rent

---

[146] *Id.* at p.140.
[147] *Ibid. Cf. The Tenancy and Rent Control* case, 37 BVerfGE 132 (1974).
[148] [1983] I.R. 181.

for the period specified in the Bill. This Court has already held that the pre-existing rent control constituted an unjust attack upon property rights. In such circumstances, to impose different but no less unjust deprivations upon landlords cannot but be unjust having regard to the provisions of the Constitution."[149]

Wages/Prices Restrictions

Legislative nullification of contracts between private parties was the subject of *Condon v. Minister for Labour*,[150] and it would seem that the legislation there would have been declared unconstitutional but for its temporary nature. In the mid-1970s most countries experienced high inflation, to which many governments responded by introducing legislation that restricted wage and price increases. The background to the *Condon* case was the national agreements system, i.e.. the system obtaining whereby the major employers' organisations, the Irish Congress of Trade Unions ("Congress" – the national federation of trade unions) and the Government would periodically agree on the levels of wage increases. Those would then be paid to employees of the State and of other employers represented in negotiating these agreements, who would not look for any additional increases for the duration of each agreement. Some employments were not covered by this system, most notably banking: the associated banks were not represented in the negotiations and the bank employees' trade union was not a member of the Congress then. In 1975 and in 1976 the Government decided that, if the national agreements' rates for wage increases were not imposed on the banking sector, the entire system was in grave danger of collapsing. The Regulation of Banks (Remuneration and Conditions of Employment) (Temporary Provisions) Acts 1975 and 1976 were enacted, which empowered the Minister to prohibit banks from paying wage increases that exceeded the rate provided for in the national agreements. In these years the banks had agreed with their employees' trade union to pay its members much higher increases, but the Minister's regulations forbade these payments from being made.

Bank employees, members of the union, contended that by depriving them of their agreed wage increases, their property rights had been contravened. There was no finding that, under their employment contracts, they had an enforceable right to obtain those increases but for the Minister's regulations. McWilliam J. rejected their contention for two reasons. One was that it is for the legislature and not for the courts to decide when the common good requires that property rights be interfered with. The courts' function in regard to this

---

[149] *Id.* at p.191.
[150] Unreported, High, Court, McWilliam J., June 11, 1980.
[151] *Id.* at p.11.

question is to ensure that some reasonable basis exists for the legislature's conclusion – that "there were circumstances which made it reasonable for the legislature to think such measures were for the common good."[151] It was found that there was a reasonable basis for the Oireachtas concluding that the national agreements' rates of wage increase must be extended to the banking sector in order to combat rapidly rising inflation. The other grounds were that the impugned measures were temporary and that no one "was permanently deprived of pecuniary advantage."[152] Nor, in the circumstances, were bank employees arbitrarily selected by the State.

---

[152] *Id.* at p.12.

CHAPTER 26

Economic Rights

By economic rights is meant the right to carry on a trade, business or profession, including the right to work and to involvement in trade unions. Neither the Constitution, the European Convention nor the UN Covenant expressly guarantee any of these rights, with the exception of freedom of association in trade unions. Before the European Union was established, EC law focused almost entirely on economic questions and the Treaty of Rome, and the measures adopted under it may be regarded as safeguarding economic rights, especially activities with an inter-State element. All discrimination against nationals of any EC Member State is forbidden by Article 12 of this Treaty "(w)ithin the scope of application of th(e) Treaty ....". This Treaty contains rules *inter alia* on the free movement between EC States of persons, services, capital and goods, and regarding business competition and also equal pay between men and women. Article 29.4.3 of the Constitution provides for EC rules having effect in Ireland.[1] In 1950 Ireland concluded a Friendship, Commerce and Navigation Treaty with the United States,[2] which confers entitlements on U.S. citizens similar to some of the basic rights granted by the EC Treaties on nationals of EC Member States.

BUSINESS

Freedom to pursue a particular trade or business is partly protected by many of the specified guarantees: for instance, individuals cannot generally be prevented from engaging in a business on account of their sex, their religion or their lawful political affiliations. Economic legislation must respect the separation of powers and the principles of constitutional justice and fair procedures. Furthermore, one of the implied rights under Article 40.3 of the Constitution is the right to earn a livelihood, which has been held to include engaging in a trade or business. In *Cafolla v. Attorney General*,[3] which concerned certain restrictions under the Gaming and Lotteries Acts 1956–1979, Costello J. suggested that this right falls within both sub-clauses 1 and 2 of Article 40.3; that "[g]enerally speaking the right to earn a livelihood can properly be regarded

---

[1] *Supra*, p.258.
[2] January 21, 1950, TS 1950 No. 7; Protocol of November 18, 1992, TS 1993 No. 4.
[3] [1985] I.R. 486.

as an unspecified personal right first protected by Article 40.3.1. But this right may also exist as one of the bundle of rights arising from the ownership of private property capable of being commercially used and so receive the protection of Article 40.3.2."[4]

In Chapters 19 and 20 above, the Constitution's guarantees of freedom of expression, assembly and association were considered and the question was raised whether those apply to economically-motivated activity as distinct from politically or ideologically-motivated activity. This is a question on which the Supreme Court has not yet pronounced. The answer would seem to be that those rights are not confined to the political context except that, when they are being relied on for economic objectives, interference with their exercise does not carry as high a burden of justification.[5]

Statutory regulation of business activities must be in accordance with the Constitution's substantive rights and procedural provisions. But in considering the constitutionality of laws that regulate businesses, account must also be taken of the "directive principles of social policy" contained in Article 45 of the Constitution. As is explained in the next chapter, the courts are not permitted to strike down any post-1937 Act of the Oireachtas on the grounds that it conflicts with any of these principles. Nevertheless, account is taken of them, often in order to demonstrate that the law in question is not unconstitutional because its provisions are consistent with these principles.[6] In the business regulation context the relevant "directive principles" are as follows:

> "2. (iii) That, especially, the operation of free competition shall not be allowed so to develop as to result in the concentration of the ownership or control of essential commodities in a few individuals to the common detriment.
>
> (iv) That in what pertains to the control of credit the constant and predominant aim shall be the welfare of the people as a whole
>
> ...
>
> 3. (i) That the State shall favour and, where necessary, supplement private initiative in industry and commerce.
>
> (ii) The State shall endeavour to secure that private enterprise shall be so conducted as to ensure reasonable efficiency in the production and distribution of goods and as to protect the public against unjust exploitation."

---

[4] *Id.* at p.493.
[5] *Attorney General v. Paperlink Ltd* [1984] I.L.R.M. 373.
[6] *E.g., Landers v. Attorney General*, 109 I.L.T.R. 1 (1975); *infra*, p.796.

Prohibition

There are certain businesses that are outlawed entirely and it is a criminal offence to be involved in them, for instance trafficking in proscribed drugs, prostitution and money-laundering. It would appear that the Oireachtas has a very wide discretion in determining what kinds of economic activity should be outlawed in the public interest.[7] Between 1919 and 1933, the manufacture, sale, transportation, importing or exporting of intoxicating liquors was banned by the 18th Amendment to the US Constitution.

Statutory Monopolies

Certain enterprises enjoyed a statutory monopoly in that, by law, only those enterprises were allowed to supply a particular product or service. All but one of these were owned by the State.[8] Thus, formerly only the Electricity Supply Board could sell electricity to the public, only Radio Telefís Éireann could make commercial radio and television broadcasts, only An Post could provide a postal service and only An Bord Telecom could provide a telecommunication service. Provision was made for private undertakings providing some of these services if given permission to do so in accordance with the relevant legislation. These monopolies no longer exist; under the supervision of "regulators," some of them have been opened up to competition, others have been privatised. A major factor in these developments was old Article 31 of the EC Treaty, which curbed the power of State monopolies "of a commercial character," and Article 86 of that Treaty which applies the EC rules regarding competition policy (Articles 81–82) to "public undertakings and undertakings to which Member States grant special rights."

The monopoly formerly enjoyed by the State, under the Post Office Act 1908 was challenged, unsuccessfully, in *Attorney General v. Paperlink Ltd.*[9] The defendant and its shareholders wished to run a letter and parcel courier business but were prevented by this Act from doing so. When the Attorney General and the Minister sought an injunction restraining them from carrying on the service, they contended that the legislation was unconstitutional in several respects, in particular because it was an unjust interference with their right to earn a livelihood. Costello J. found that, although their business was being run under the aegis of a private company, its shareholders-directors were entitled to assert a constitutional right to earn a livelihood by means of their company.

---

[7] *Cafolla v. Ireland* [1985] I.R. 486. *Cf. Jordan v. State*, 13 B.H.R.C. 203 (2002) (S. Africa), upholding the criminalisation of prostitution and brothel keeping.

[8] The exception being a cement manufacturer; *cf.* Cement (Repeal of Enactments) Act 2000.

[9] [1984] I.L.R.M. 373.

This right, however, is not absolute and is subject to legitimate legal restraints. The defendants' main argument was that the long standing monopoly enjoyed by the Post Office had resulted in a very inefficient and extremely expensive postal service, and that the thrust of one of the directive principles of social policy is to favour private enterprise and to disfavour nationalisation and state monopoly. But it was held that this provision did not require the State to justify before the courts why a particular service or business should be established in the form of a state monopoly. As for the argument based on inefficiency, it was held that it is entirely for the Oireachtas to decide what structures public utilities should have; for the courts to strike down the relevant statutory provisions on the grounds that the Post Office was being run inefficiently would "amount to an unwarranted and unconstitutional interference with the powers of government exclusively conferred on the executive and the Oireachtas. ...."[10] The High Court was not "the forum in which to decide whether a postal service organised on lines advocated by the defendants' experts (accountants and economists) is one which meets the requirements of the common good."[11]

Regulation

Although it existed long before the 1990s, economic regulation in Ireland became far more extensive with the privatisation of many State-owned enterprises and the opening of markets that were previously State monopolies.[12] Economic regulation pursues a great variety of objectives, many of which are responses to what economists call market failure, for instance, controlling monopoly power, proscribing excessive methods of competition, fixing prices either in special circumstances or more generally, requiring that goods and services are of good quality and especially that they do not endanger health and safety, ensuring that financial intermediaries such as banks and insurance companies are sufficiently solvent, rationalising the structures of particular industries and dealing with temporary but severe shortages of products.

Extensive regulation exists in the entire financial services sector, under the aegis of the Irish Financial Services Regulatory Authority, and also in, *inter alia,* aviation, electricity, telecommunications and health provision. A significant feature of the European Communities is the Common Agricultural Policy, under which several aspects of the agriculture industry is made subject to detailed regulation. Milk quotas under the CAP are a frequent source of

---

[10] *Id.* at p.389.

[11] *Ibid. Cf. Government of Malaysia v. Selangor Pilots Ass'n* [1978] A.C. 337, where a statutory monopoly was revoked, and *Soc. United Docks v. Government of Mauritius* [1985] A.C. 585, where one was established.

[12] See generally, M. Forde, *Commercial Law* (2nd ed., 1997), Chap.9 and A. Ogus, *Regulation: Legal Form and Economic Theory* (1994).

litigation. The EC also has a Common Fisheries Policy but the ambit of regulation there is in no way as extensive as for agriculture. A form of regulation that is common in the economic sphere is licensing; in order to carry on numerous business activities, it is necessary to possess an appropriate licence which will contain various conditions about how the business in question is to be conducted.

It was argued in *Pigs Marketing Board v. Donnelly (Dublin) Ltd*,[13] that economic regulation *per se* was unconstitutional; that any law which interferes with the free operation of competition in trade, or interferes with the contractual or proprietorial rights of citizens, is unconstitutional. Hanna J. rejected the contention that the Constitution embodies classic *laissez faire* principles, observing that "it is too late in the day to have that view accepted. The. days of *laissez faire* are at an end ...".[14] Indeed, the Irish courts have never struck down an economic regulatory law because its substantive content was unconstitutional. The closest they came to this was the Supreme Court's finding that part of the Employment Equality Bill 1997, dealing with discrimination on the grounds of disability, unduly intruded on employers' freedom to run their own businesses.[15] An Act of 1975 that placed a ceiling on what wages could be paid to bank employees was upheld by McWilliam J., principally because it was a temporary measure.[16]

The Pigs and Bacon Acts 1935–37, which were the subject of the *Pigs Marketing Board* case,[17] were designed to improve the quality of the bacon industry's product; their object was to ensure that pigs used in the industry should be of good quality, that bacon and pork should be produced under the best conditions by skilled and qualified persons, who would be licensed and registered either as curers or pork butchers, and to regulate the manner in which bacon was to be exported. To that end, a Bacon Marketing Board and later a Pigs Marketing Board were established; these bodies *inter alia* set production quotas for licensed bacon factories and regulated the prices at which pigs and carcases were to be bought and sold. Hanna J. summarised the 1935-37 Acts' objects as "to set up two Boards as the administrative machinery to control, in accordance with the provisions of the statutes, the sale, purchase, price and export of a staple article of food."[18] In addition to the separation of powers complaint, it was contended that these Acts' price-fixing provisions contravened the private property guarantee. But Hanna J. upheld them on the grounds that they simply delimited property rights in the public interest, and

---

[13] [1939] I.R. 413.
[14] *Id.* at p.422.
[15] *Employment Equality Bill, 1997, Re* [1997] 2 I.R. 321.
[16] *Condon v. Minister for Labour*, unreported, High Court, McWilliam J., June 11, 1980; *supra*, p.762.
[17] [1939] I.R. 413.
[18] *Id.* at p.421.

what the public interest requires in the economic sphere is primarily a matter for the legislature to determine:

> "The days of *laissez faire* are at an end, and this is recognised in (Art. 43.2.2) which enacts that the State can 'as occasion requires delimit by law the exercise of (property) rights with a view to reconciling their exercise with the exigencies of the common good'. I am of opinion that the Oireachtas must be judge of whatever limitation is to be enacted. This law does not abolish private ownership in pigs or bacon, it only delimits the exercise of these rights by the persons in whom they are vested, and if the law is contrary to the common good, whatever that may mean, it must be clearly proved ... I have gone through our own statutes from the year 1932, and I find almost fifty statutes that seem to me to delimit the exercise of the rights of private property and of contract, not to mention the Land Acts."[19]

More recent, but unsuccessful, challenges to the substantive nature of economic regulatory measures have been based primarily on Article 40.3 of the Constitution. In *Cafolla v. Ireland*,[20] what essentially was being contended was that financial restrictions on running a particular business, which were constitutionally unimpeachable when they were introduced in the 1950s, in consequence of the great inflation since then had become so onerous that they constituted an unconstitutional infringement on the plaintiff's right to earn a livelihood. His business was operating gaming machines, which he had done for twenty years. This business is governed by the Gaming and Lotteries Acts 1956-1979, which forbid certain forms of gaming entirely but which permit certain other forms provided that the operator of the machine is duly certified by the District Court and licensed by the Revenue Commissioners. What the plaintiff complained of in particular was the limits placed by section 14 of the 1956 Act on all stakes and prizes. The maximum permissible stake at any one time was two and a half pence and the maximum permissible prize at any one time was 50p. Because inflation since 1956 had been very nearly 1,000%, he contended that these limits were so out of line with current economic circumstances that they were unconstitutional. Analogies were drawn with the Rent Restriction Acts cases.[21] But the plaintiff had not been deprived entirely of the opportunity to earn his living with gaming machines. The Supreme Court said that, had the 1956 Act forbidden all use of those machines, such a prohibition would not be unconstitutional: "(t)he validity of that exercise of the (Oireachtas') view of the exigencies of the common good cannot be

---

[19] *Id.* at pp.422–423.
[20] [1985] I.R. 486.
[21] *Supra*, p.759.

seriously questioned."[22] Costello J. conceded that the effect of section 14 combined with thirty years inflation did adversely affect the profitability of the plaintiff's business. Against that, however, the number of licensed gaming halls in the country had steadily increased, which indicated that this business had not been rendered wholly unprofitable even for the plaintiff. The judge rejected the contention that laws making businesses less profitable than they would be under absolute *laissez faire* were unconstitutional, citing as examples the Fisheries Acts, the Intoxicating Liquor Acts and the Prices Acts. In order to succeed, the plaintiff had to demonstrate convincingly that the statutory ceilings on stakes and prizes were not reasonably required by the common good, and that was a particularly onerous task because what the public interest requires is primarily a matter for the Oireachtas to determine. In Costello J.'s words, "(t)his Court has neither the ability nor the jurisdiction to decide what level of restrictions are reasonably necessary to curb gaming in licensed amusement halls; these are matters peculiarly within the jurisdiction and competence of the Oireachtas."[23] From the evidence before him, he found that the plaintiff had not proved "that it would be unreasonable for the Oireachtas to conclude that present-day social conditions required the maintenance of the limits set in 1956, even though the value of money has greatly declined since that time;" nor had the plaintiff shown "that there would be any disproportion between the aims of the 1956 Act and the imposition of controls operating more restrictively than they did (previously)."[24] Upholding this conclusion, the Supreme Court in a brief judgment simply said that, since it would be constitutionally permissible to ban gaming machines absolutely, section 14 of the 1956 Act was not unconstitutional even if its effect was to render operating those machines an entirely unprofitable enterprise. According to Finlay C.J., for the court, "[e]ven if the imposition of these restrictions on the operation of gaming had been proved to be such as to make it wholly unprofitable as part of the business of an amusement hall proprietor, the court is satisfied that, having regard to ... *Private Motorists Protection Soc. v. Attorney General*, such restrictions would not be an unjust attack on the plaintiffs' property rights as they were so clearly imposed with due regard to the exigencies of the common good."[25]

Private Motorists Protection Soc. v. Attorney General,[26] is the Supreme Court's principal authority on the constitutional position of substantive economic regulation. The plaintiffs contested the validity of a law that would compel them after a short period to cease doing their principal business. They were part of the PMPA group of companies that subsequently collapsed in

[22] [1985] I.R. 486 at p.500.
[23] *Id.* at p.495.
[24] *Ibid.*
[25] *Id.* at p.500.
[26] [1983] I.R. 339.

1983 and for which special legislation had to be passed in order to have it run by an administrator.[27] In the mid-1970s the Government became worried about numerous financial intermediaries which were not subject to the Central Bank Act 1971, and which were seriously under-capitalised and held considerable sums on deposit. Most of these were industrial and provident societies and the Industrial and Provident Societies (Amendment) Act 1978, was passed in order to deal with the problem. This Act did not set requisite capital ratios nor provide for a mechanism that would ensure that societies, which took deposits, kept within those ratios. Instead, it forbade all societies from accepting or holding deposits once five years from the time the Act had been passed. However, the Minister could extend this period; also a society was allowed to raise funds if the Registrar of Friendly Societies permitted it to do so. Moreover, the Act did not force societies out of the business of financial intermediaries altogether because they still could obtain any finance they needed from banks or raise money by subscription for shares; they also had the option of converting into a limited company and applying to the Central Bank for a banking licence.

The plaintiff society had about £13,700,000 on deposit, around 87% of that coming from the general public. It had made loans of about £11,700,000, 36% of that going to associate PMPA companies, mainly to finance stocks of cars in PMPA garages. Because of the drastic effect implementation of the 1978 Act would have on the society's business, it was argued that the Act was an unconstitutional interference with property rights under Articles 43 and 40.3. Emphasising that it was not an expropriation measure but merely "regulat(ed) and controll(ed) the range of business which the Society may lawfully transact,"[28] the Supreme Court agreed with Carroll J.'s judgment that the Act was not unconstitutional. Among the relevant facts found by Carroll J. in favour of upholding the Act were that several industrial and provident societies were operating what in fact were banking businesses but many of them had capital ratios that were grossly inadequate under the principles of sound banking practice. When the Central Bank Act was passed in 1971, societies did hardly any banking business, which is why societies were exempted from that Act's stringent requirements. Since then there had been a proliferation of what in reality were banking societies but with capital ratios that presented a danger to the investing public. The 1978 Act was enacted in order to protect investors from these societies. According to Finlay C.J., "the legislation was reasonable, and was in accordance with the public interest and with the requirements of the common good. Therefore, it cannot be regarded as an unjust attack on property rights."[29]

On several occasions, challenges to the Casual Trading Act 1980 were

---

[27] Insurance (No. 2) Act 1983.
[28] [1983] I.R.339 at p.361.
[29] *Ibid.*

rejected, most notably by the Supreme Court in *Hand v. Dublin Corporation*,[30] where it upheld the prohibition on obtaining a street traders' licence for a period, where the applicant has had two convictions of criminal offences; this was held to be neither an unjust nor an unreasonable restriction on the right to earn a livelihood. The test of invalidity, therefore, is whether the Oireachtas acted wholly unreasonably in using the impugned method of advancing what it regarded as the common good, which is similar to the United States Supreme Court's approach to economic legislation.[31]

Entirely or largely de-regulating or re-regulating a particular business can have a significant adverse impact on persons in that very business, as the considerable investment they made in order to enter or remain in the business may be greatly diminished in value, with many new entrants being able to take up a similar business. A challenge to the executive de-regulation of the taxi business was rejected by Carney J. in *Gorman v. Minister for Environment*,[32] who did not accept the argument that existing taxi-licence holders were entitled to be compensated before additional licences could be issued. Many existing licence-holders paid up to £80,000 in order to obtain their licences and, once de-regulation occurred, most of that value would be lost. However, the nature of licences as property is very different from land, chattels and choses in action owned by an individual, and it was held that licence-holders "must have been aware of the risk inherent in the licence that legislative change might affect its value,"[33] in view of major changes that had been introduced earlier in 1978 and 1995. Moreover, the plaintiffs purchased licences in the past usually in order to be able to earn a living, which they did, and they remained free to sell their licences, which had not been expropriated. Emphasis was placed on the fact that property developers affected by Part V (section 93-101) of the Planning and Development Act 2000, were held not entitled to be paid the market value of land they have to surrender under that Act.

Landowners who lost out following a radical reorganisation of the milk quota system in 2000 were held not to be entitled to compensation for the losses they incurred thereby.[34] Where, however, the effect of industry regulation is to cause the closure of the one firm in that market, to the benefit of firms in substitute markets, that may very well require compensation to be paid for the drastically restrictive regime to be upheld.

---

[30] [1991] 1 I.R. 409, followed in *Shanley v. Galway Corp.* [1995] 1 I.R. 396. Also, *Lawlor v. Minister for Agriculture* [1990] 1 I.R. 356, concerning changes in the milk quota regime.

[31] *E.g. Minnesota v. Clover Leaf Creameries Co.*, 499 U.S. 456 (1981). Compare the *Chocolate Candy* case, BVerfGE 13 (1980).

[32] [2001] 2 I.R. 414.

[33] *Id.*, at pp.429–450.

[34] *Maher v. Minister for Agriculture* [2001] 2 I.R. 139; *supra*, p.742.

Regulatory Procedures

Laws and other measures regulating business may be unconstitutional because of some procedural flaw in them, *i.e.* not on account of the substantive restrictions they place on business but by reason of the manner in which those are imposed. One such defect is that the law in question contravenes the constitutional scheme for the separation of powers. While economic regulatory measures tend to give the executive extensive standard-setting, rule-application and discretionary powers, no regulatory law has been struck down on separation of powers grounds or because it contravened the requirements of constitutionally fair procedures. But one provision was declared invalid because it gave the executive a dispensing power.

Separation of Powers

In *Pigs Marketing Board v. Donnelly (Dublin) Ltd*,[35] and in *Cityview Press Ltd. v. An Chomhairle Oiliúna*,[36] it was argued that provisions of the Pigs and Bacon Acts 1935-37, and of the Industrial Training Act 1967, which dealt with prices to be charged and levies to be paid, respectively, were unconstitutional delegations of legislative power to the executive. But those contentions were rejected. Indeed, because of the very nature of economic regulation, it is often well nigh impossible for the Oireachtas to set down very specific standards, so that in order to achieve the statutory objective there is little option but to articulate a general policy and leave it to the executive to implement that policy by appropriate means. Regulations adopted to this end must keep within the terms of the statutory power to regulate, which in some circumstances will be construed narrowly. Thus, for instance, in *Humphreys v. Minister for the Environment*,[37] a significant increase in the fee that was required to hold a taxi licence was held to be in the nature of a tax, not contemplated by the legislation in question, as properly construed. And in *O'Neill v. Minister for Agriculture*,[38] regulations that *inter alia* significantly restricted those who could provide an artificial insemination service to cattle owners were held to be *ultra vires* the legislation there, as it was focused on the desirability of controlling the disease rather than the categories of persons who could provide the service.

When considering the extent to which business regulation is consistent with the separation of powers between the executive and the courts, it should be remembered that for many years the detailed regulation of certain categories of business has been carried out by judges and not by the executive. This

---

[35] [1939] I.R. 413.
[36] [1980] I.R. 381; *supra*, p.180.
[37] [2001] 1 I.R. 263.
[38] [1998] 1 I.R. 539.

direct judicial involvement in business regulation is explained mainly by historic reasons: in the past these businesses were supervised by magistrates, who were the predecessors of District Judges, for instance, selling alcohol, operating betting shops and amusement halls and auctioneering. Most modern Acts that deal with business activities confer regulatory powers not directly on the courts but instead on the appropriate Minister, or on some board or agency which has authority to supervise the industry. The Garda Síochána is the regulatory authority for some businesses, such as taxis until 2003. Several Acts give aggrieved persons a right to appeal to the courts against decisions made by the regulators, for instance section 9 of the Transport (Tour Operators and Travel Agents) Act 1982; several other Acts envisage regulatory decisions being challenged by way of judicial review.

McDonald v. Bord na gCon[39] is the leading case on the allocation of authority between the judiciary and the executive to make particular decisions regarding business regulation. It concerned the Greyhound Industry Act 1958, which provides *inter alia* for the establishment of Bord na gCon, which is given extensive regulatory power over most aspects of the industry. For instance, operators of greyhound racing tracks, those who train greyhounds for profit, persons conducting public sales of greyhounds and bookmakers at greyhound racing tracks must all have a licence or permit from the Board. Additionally, the Board is authorised to conduct inquiries into incidents affecting the industry and, as a result of an inquiry, the Board can ban the persons who were under investigation from all greyhound racing tracks and sales of greyhounds -which it did in the plaintiff's case. He was a greyhound trainer who brought a dog to race at the Cork track but the officials there would not allow the dog to run in the race. Bord na gCon then caused an investigation to be held into this incident. Having heard representations made on behalf of the plaintiff, the Board banned him from attending any greyhound race track, authorised coursing meeting or public sale of greyhounds in the country. Relying principally on *Solicitors Act 1954, Re*,[40] he contended that, in deciding that by reason of his misconduct he should be prevented from earning a living at his chosen occupation, the Board had exercised a power which could only be exercised by judges appointed under the Constitution. His contention was that, on account of the nature of the inquiry into his conduct, the immediate effect and drastic consequence of the exclusion order made against him, and the absence of any right of appeal to the courts on the merits of his case, the Board had been administering justice in the full sense and thus had acted unconstitutionally. He argued that the Board's powers were essentially the same as those of the pre-1960 Law Society Disciplinary Committee, which was found to be unconstitutional, on the grounds that it was exercising what for convenience may be termed plenary judicial powers.

---

[39] [1965] I.R. 217.
[40] [1960] I.R. 239; *infra*, p.781.

A characteristic that Bord na gCon had in common with the pre-1960 Law Society Disciplinary Committee was authority to determine whether individuals in an industry had acted improperly and some power to prevent those against whom an adverse finding had been made from earning a living in that industry. Apart from that, there were significant differences between the two disciplinary systems, although not all of these were emphasised by the Supreme Court. One is that Bord na gCon regulates an industry whereas the Law Society regulates a profession, although the legal profession could also be described as the legal services industry. Another is that solicitors are officers of the court whereas greyhound trainers are not. Another is that the Law Society was given essentially the same powers as the High Court as regards compelling attendance of witnesses, administering oaths, calling for documents and contempt. Furthermore, the Law Society could award substantial compensation to aggrieved parties and it could order that costs be paid in the same manner as High Court costs. But the only difference in powers and procedures of Bord na gCon adverted to was the actual legal consequences of the ultimate disciplinary sanction. Under the scheme considered in *Solicitors Act 1954, Re*,[41] a solicitor who was struck off the roll of solicitors was prohibited from acting as a solicitor; it was a criminal offence, and indeed still is, for a solicitor who is struck off to practise that profession. But all that happens to a greyhound owner or trainer, who is the subject of an exclusion order, is that operators of greyhound tracks or auctions become entitled to remove those persons from the premises if they are ever found there. As Walsh J., for the court, pointed out, often the operator of the track or auction, in any event, would be entitled at common law to exclude the owner or trainer in question and, moreover, the 1958 Act does not oblige the operator to exclude someone who was banned by Bord na gCon. Furthermore, if operators knowingly gave a banned person the legal right to enter their premises, that person could not then be lawfully removed. It is not unlawful *per se* for someone who is banned to be present in these premises. Nor has Bord na gCon any right under the 1958 Act to obtain an injunction ordering a banned person not to trespass on licensed tracks or auction premises. Accordingly, because the body which regulates the industry is not empowered to make a decision, the automatic and absolute effect of which would be to prohibit persons from earning a living in that industry, that body was not exercising plenary judicial powers. Walsh J. did not discuss the question of whether Bord na gCon would be exercising powers of that nature if it had been given the various procedural authorities that the pre-1960 Law Society Disciplinary Committee had.

---

[41] *Id.*

Fair Procedures

Laws or regulations often provide that persons who stand to suffer direct adverse effects consequent on executive decisions shall be entitled to some form of hearing before such decisions are taken. In *McDonald v. Bord na gCon*[42] the Supreme Court stressed that, where a statute is silent on the point, a requirement to give a fair hearing to persons who may be adversely affected will be implied into the Act in appropriate circumstances. Indeed, the constitutional obligation to provide a fair hearing for persons in jeopardy of being deprived of their livelihood was the Supreme Court's answer to the plaintiff's argument that the disciplinary procedure there contravened his constitutional right to work. Having rejected the separation of powers argument, Walsh J. then went on to hold that when a Bord na gCon exclusion order is enforced, "it could affect the rights of the prohibited person in that it might restrict his existing right to trade or his right to enjoy some benefits contracted for. Such a possible result is sufficient to require that the procedure which can lead to that result must conform to the principles of natural justice."[43]

The principal ingredients of a fair hearing are encapsulated in the maxims *audi alteram partem* and *nemo iudex in sua causa*. Additionally, persons are entitled to know the reasons for adverse decisions. Entitlement to a fair hearing applies even where the economic activity in question can only be carried on by persons holding a licence and the executive has a discretion over who should have those licences. Thus, in *Moran v. Attorney General*,[44] the plaintiff was a taxi driver whose licence was revoked under powers entrusted to the Commissioner of the Garda Síochána, on the grounds that he was not a fit and proper person to hold the licence. But he had been given no opportunity to make representations to the Commissioner on the question before that decision was taken. Doyle J. found that his right to natural justice had been infringed and that the Commissioner's decision was thereby invalid.[45] Whether the Oireachtas could stipulate that reasons shall not be given for decisions that significantly adversely affect a person's business is debatable; recent legislation often incorporates on express obligation to furnish reasons.

Even where the administrative decision in question deals not just with one individual's case but involves laying down general rules for a considerable number of persons, the circumstances may require that their entitlement to a hearing be implied into the relevant statute. In *Burke v. Minister for Labour*,[46] which concerned the provisions of the Industrial Relations Act 1946 which authorise Joint Labour Committees to determine what wages employers in

---

[42] [1965] I.R. 217.
[43] *Id.* at p.242.
[44] [1976] I.R. 400.
[45] Also *Doupe v. Limerick Corp.* [1981] I.L.R.M. 456.
[46] [1979] I.R. 354.

particular industries are legally bound to pay their employees, the Supreme Court held that *audi alteram partem* must be observed when fixing the statutory minimum wage. Henchy J. said of the relevant provisions:

> "Where Parliament has delegated functions of that nature, it is to be necessarily inferred as part of the legislative intention that the body which makes the orders will exercise its functions, not only with constitutional propriety and due regard to natural justice, but also within the framework of the terms and objects of the relevant Act and with basic fairness, reasonableness and good faith. The absoluteness of the delegation is susceptible of unjust and tyrannous abuse unless its operation is thus confined, so it is entirely proper to ascribe to the Oireachtas (being the Parliament of a State which is constitutionally bound to protect, by its laws, its citizens from unjust attack) an intention that the delegated functions must be exercised within those limitations."[47]

It was held by the European Court of Human Rights in *Bentham v. Netherlands*[48] that administrative decisions, which have the direct effect of preventing a person from carrying on a business, must comply with Article 6(1) of the Convention, which guarantees "a fair and public hearing within a reasonable time by an independent and impartial tribunal established by law." If the immediate decision-making body lacks some of these features, these requirements are not contravened if there is a right of appeal to a body which possesses those attributes, such as a court.

Investigations

Several laws that regulate businesses empower members of the Garda Síochána to enter premises, to seize and remove documents[49] and to insist on questions being answered. Some Acts even grant search and seizure powers to other duly authorised persons. Under the Restrictive Practices Act 1972 (repealed by the Competition Act 1980) there was established the office of Examiner of Restrictive Practices, the holder of which had extensive investigatory powers, and also a Restrictive Practices Commission, which held inquiries into and conducted studies about various restrictive practices, and could make orders and issue rules on the subject. In *Abbey Films Ltd. v. Attorney General*[50] it was argued, unsuccessfully, that section 15 of the 1972 Act, which gave the Examiner wide powers of investigation, was unconstitutional. The plaintiff's business was distributing films for exhibition in cinemas and its managing

---

[47] *Id.* at pp.361–362.
[48] 8 E.H.R.R. 1 (1986).
[49] *Supra*, p.646.
[50] [1981] I.R. 158.

director controlled a considerable number of cinemas throughout the country. Following complaints made of restrictive practices in the distribution of films, in 1976 the Examiner commenced an investigation into that business. Section 15 empowered him, *inter alia*, to enter and inspect a business premises and to require persons there to produce books, documents and records, and to provide any information sought in connection with the investigation. But the owner of the premises must be informed in advance of the intention to enter it and conduct an investigation there. Moreover, a judicial procedure was laid down to protect businesses from unnecessary or excessive investigation. An owner of a premises, which was about to be entered, could apply to the High Court for a declaration that the Examiner should not enter or demand particular documents or information; the court was given a discretion to make such declaration where "the exigencies of the common good do not warrant" what the Examiner was trying to do.

Section 15 of the 1972 Act was claimed to be unconstitutional on several grounds. It was said to contravene the separation of powers because the authority given to the court, to determine that a particular investigation is not warranted by the exigencies of the common good, was in reality a legislative power. An answer to that might be that legislation means setting general standards whereas the court's decision in this context is an *ad hoc* determination. The answer given by the Supreme Court was that the Constitution does "not adopt a rigid separation" between the three powers and, accordingly, it is not forbidden to delegate broad discretion to the courts.[51] Another separation of powers argument made there was rejected because it was based on a misinterpretation of the section.[52] An argument that the section created an *ex post facto* offence was rejected for similar reasons.[53] And a contention that the section constituted an infringement of the plaintiff's property rights was rejected without comment. It finally was argued that the section was constitutionally unfair because it placed the burden of proof on the shoulders of those seeking to prevent the Examiner from pursuing an investigation. But the court held that there was no unfairness because it is permissible to oblige even defendants in criminal case to prove particular matters; that "(s)ince the legislature may impose on an accused in a criminal prosecution an onus to establish a limited and specified matter, it follows that such an onus may be imposed in a civil action even if this is connected with criminal proceedings."[54] As to whether, in the circumstances of the case, the common good did not warrant the Examiner's entry into the plaintiff's premises, the court found that the Examiner possessed sufficient *prima facie* evidence of restrictive practices

---

[51] *Id.* at p.171.
[52] *Ibid.*
[53] *Id.* at pp.169–170.
[54] *Id.* at p.170.

in film distribution that he was justified in seeking to investigate the plaintiff's affairs.

Discretion

Economic legislation tends to delegate extensive discretionary authority to the executive, for instance, to issue rules and regulations governing various matters, such as fixing the maximum prices to be charged in respect of designated goods and services, or fixing minimum wages for particular industries. Exercises of regulatory discretion must respect the various substantive constitutional rights, including the requirement of equality before the law. Thus in *Cassidy v. Minister for Industry and Commerce*,[55] maximum prices orders issued under the Prices Acts 1958-72, which applied only to the town of Dundalk but not its surrounding areas, and which treated lounge bars and other public house bars on the same footing, were held to have discriminated in an unfair, arbitrary, unjust and inequitable manner.

Frequently, in order to engage in a particular business, it is necessary to possess the appropriate licence and the Minister, or other public agency, is given an extensive discretion to determine what conditions shall govern individual licensees. In *East Donegal Co-operative Livestock Mart Ltd. v. Attorney General*,[56] which perhaps is the *grand arrêt* of Irish economic law, a very broad delegation to the Minister of regulatory power was challenged on the grounds that it contravened the Article 40.1 guarantee of "equality before the law." Under the Livestock Marts Act 1967, which was passed in order to regulate the operation of marts in which cattle and other farm animals are sold, no one can carry on the business of a livestock mart without holding a licence from the Minister. An ostensibly unbounded discretion is given as regards the conditions for granting and revoking licences, although the Act provides for *audi alteram partem* where a licence is refused or revoked, and where a licence is revoked a statement of the reasons must be laid before each House of the Oireachtas. As regards the Minister's discretion, section 3 of the Act provides that "the Minister may, at his discretion, grant or refuse to grant a licence (and) (t)he Minister may ... attach to the licence such conditions as he shall think proper and shall specify in the licence (and) (t)he Minister may, if he so thinks fit, amend or revoke a condition attached to a licence." Breach of any condition in the licence is a criminal offence, which can lead to the licence being revoked by the Minister. O'Keeffe P. held that the extensive freedom given to the Minister to impose conditions on licences, and to amend or revoke those conditions, was so wide as to enable him to impose arbitrary conditions in individual licences, which could not be reviewed by the courts;

---

[55] [1978] I.R. 297.
[56] [1970] I.R. 317.

that a power as extensive as that is unconstitutional. These conclusions, however, were reversed by the Supreme Court.

The main thrust of Walsh J.'s judgment for the court is that the 1967 Act does not grant the Minister quite as extensive a discretion and whatever discretion he possesses under the Act is subject to judicial review, which ensures that all conditions contained in licences are consistent with the Act's structure and general objectives. Thus, the Act did not permit imposing entirely arbitrary conditions or conditions aimed at reducing the actual number of marts in the country. The Act did no such thing – the Minister's powers were constrained by the Act's overall objectives and framework, and by the general principles of administrative law:

> "It is quite true that conditions need not be uniform ... and that in many cases they are by their nature necessarily peculiar to an individual applicant. However, it is not valid to infer that the legislation, because it makes provision for such a scheme of administration or imposition of conditions, authorised the exercise of that function in a manner amounting to a breach of a right guaranteed by the Constitution. The conditions must be ... related to the objects of the Act. ... Any condition which did not conform with th(is) test would be *ultra vires* the Act. Also, ... it is not valid to infer that, because a specified procedure is prescribed (in the Act) for the revocation or the refusal of a licence, the Minister is not bound to act in accordance with the principles of constitutional justice in respect of the imposition, amendment or revocation of conditions attached to the licence ....
>
> (Moreover) there are several ways in court proceedings for reviewing the Minister's decision in any case where it is shown that he has acted outside his powers or upon considerations other than those permitted by the Act. "[57]

However, the court held that a "dispensing power" that the 1967 Act gave to the Minister was unconstitutional. Section 4 empowers the Minister "if he so thinks fit" to exempt any particular business from any of the Act's requirements. In other words, the Minister could decide that several of the 1967 Act's requirements shall not apply to Mr or Ms X's livestock mart. A power of this nature, it was held, is generally unconstitutional; as a rule, the Oireachtas cannot delegate to the executive a power to determine which particular individuals shall not be bound by the provisions of an Act to which they otherwise would be subject.[58] Walsh J. suggested, however, that an executive dispensing power might be valid if its exercise was subject to direct legislative control and he held that this power would be valid where its existence was necessary in order

---

[57] *Id.* at p.348.
[58] *Supra*, p.295.

to prevent an Act being otherwise held unconstitutional. Since neither of these circumstances applied to section 4 of the 1967 Act, it was declared invalid.

PROFESSIONS

There are certain occupations that are commonly described as professions, for instance the legal profession and the medical profession. But not every occupation is so categorised. Many members of professions are employed on a full-time basis and, *qua* employees, they benefit from the constitutional and statutory rights accorded to employees. But a significant number of professionals are self-employed in the sense that, either individually or with partners, they run their own practices or businesses.

Freedom of establishment under Article 43 of the EC Treaty applies to professional activity as well as to setting up and running businesses.[59] Many professionals, who are employees, are members of various trade unions. An "excepted body" is an organisation, other than a trade union, which is permitted under the Trade Union Acts 1941-1975, to negotiate about terms and conditions of employment.[60] Several professional bodies have registered as excepted bodies, notably the Law Society of Ireland, the Irish Medical Association, the Institute of Architects of Ireland and the Veterinary Medical Association.

Statutory Monopolies

There are statutory monopolies in several professions in the sense that, by law, only persons who are duly qualified or registered under the relevant Act may perform particular functions. For example, under section 55(1) of the Solicitors Act 1954, "(a)n unqualified person shall not act as a solicitor."[61] Not alone are unregistered persons forbidden to practise several professions but some regulatory Acts provide that persons, not on the appropriate register, are not entitled to recover fees in respect of any professional advice or services that they have given.[62] Under the Companies Acts 1963-2001 only persons who have duly qualified and are members of recognised accountancy bodies are permitted to act as company auditors.[63] At common law, only barristers and solicitors can represent others in court;[64] in 1971 the barristers' monopoly of representation in the High Court and the Supreme Court was extended to

---

[59] *E.g. Bloomer v. Incorporated Law Society of Ireland* [1995] 3 I.R. 14.
[60] *Infra*, p.797.
[61] *Cf. Incorporated Law Society of Ireland v. Carroll* [1995] 3 I.R. 145.
[62] *Cf.* Solicitors (Amendment) Act 1994, s.68.
[63] Companies Act 1963, s.162.
[64] *Battle v. Irish Art Promotion Centre Ltd* [1968] I.R. 252.

solicitors.[65]

Regulation

Some professions are entirely self-regulatory, in the sense that they run their own affairs without any statutory authority, for instance, architects and barristers. But there are other professions which are subject to extensive direct statutory regulation. For many of these the regulatory authority is established by statute, such as the Medical Council, the Dental Council, An Bord Altranais, the Veterinary Council and the Pharmaceutical Society of Ireland. The solicitors' profession is exceptional in that its regulatory agency is not established by statute but is a chartered body, the Law Society of Ireland, which is given extensive regulatory powers under the Solicitors Acts 1954–2002.[66]

In order to practise most of the regulated professions, a person's name must be enrolled or registered with the relevant professional body; most of these Acts lay down what qualifications are needed in order to register. There are no modern authorities that deal with the thorny question of either the legislature, the executive or the professional bodies themselves restricting entry to particular professions. But it is established that chartered professional bodies that use their powers for essentially economic, as opposed to professional, purposes act *ultra vires* and are in jeopardy of having their charters removed by the writ of *scire facias*.[67]

Several of the regulatory bodies are entrusted with extensive powers over how those practising the profession in question are to conduct themselves in their dealings with clients, with fellow professionals and indeed with the general public. Over and above any express or implied statutory restrictions on exercising these regulatory powers, they are also constrained by substantive constitutional guarantees. For instance, prohibitions or restrictions on professionals advertising their services raise the question of freedom of expression.

Although standards of conduct which are backed by criminal sanctions, are required to be formulated in somewhat specific terms,[68] it is probable that vaguely formulated standards of professional conduct would withstand constitutional challenge. This is partly because professional ethics are not enforced by criminal sanctions and also because it may not be unreasonable to expect professionals to know what, for example, constitutes "professional misconduct" in particular circumstances. Within limits, the courts leave it to

---

[65] Courts Act 1971, s.17.
[66] See generally, P. O'Callaghan, *The Law on Solicitors in Ireland* (2000), Chap.20.
[67] *Dickson v. Pharmaceuticals Soc. of G.B.* [1970] A.C. 402. *Cf. the Pharmacy* case, 7 BVerfGE 377 (1958).
[68] *Supra*, p.284.

each professional body to determine what kinds of action amount to professional misconduct.[69] But an adverse decision of a disciplinary body would be set aside where the court is convinced that, in all the circumstances, what the individual in question did could not reasonably be regarded as misconduct.[70]

Regulatory Procedures

Because long-established professional reputations may be at stake and at times an individual's very livelihood, which has taken years of hard work and extensive investment to establish, may be at risk, professional discipline has been a very contentious question. While the courts allow disciplinary bodies considerable scope in determining what kinds of conduct are to be treated as unprofessional, the courts insist that disciplinary decisions follow proper and fair procedures.

Separation of Powers

There are parallels between professional disciplinary procedures and a trial on a criminal charge, in that the individual in question may be facing accusations of grave wrongdoing and may very well be severely punished if the tribunal decides that there was misconduct. Nevertheless, these procedures do not constitute "tri(al) on a criminal charge" for the purpose of Article 38 of the Constitution nor Article 6(3) of the European Convention. Because professional standards are "directed ... towards a given group possessing a special status," as opposed to being "directed ... towards all citizens" and being of a "general character," disputes concerning alleged breaches of such standards are not criminal trials.[71] On the other hand, professional disciplinary procedures may amount to administering justice in a plenary sense and, where that is the case, must be administered by the courts and not exclusively by administrative tribunals.

It was the exceptional nature of the solicitors' profession, the extensive powers of the old Law Society Disciplinary Committee and the drastic nature of the sanctions that it could impose, that caused Part III (sections 13–23) of the Solicitors Act 1954 to be declared unconstitutional by the Supreme Court in 1958. Under Part III of that Act, which was modelled on the then English legislation and which superseded the Solicitors Act 1898,[72] discipline in the profession was administered by the Law Society, which was authorised to

---

[69] Cf. *O'Laoire v. The Medical Council*, unreported, High Court, Keane J., January 27, 1995.

[70] E.g. *Cahill v. Dental Council*, unreported, High Court, McCracken J., June 15, 2001.

[71] *Ozturk v. Germany*, 6 E.H.R.R. 409 (1984) at pp.423–424.

[72] 61 & 62 Vic. c.17.

appoint from its members a disciplinary committee. That Committee would hear complaints of misconduct made against solicitors. If the Committee found that a solicitor had committed misconduct, it could, *inter alia*, take the solicitor's name off the roll of solicitors and order him to pay the costs of the inquiry and make restitution to persons who had suffered in consequence of the misconduct. The only direct judicial involvement in this scheme was that all members of the Disciplinary Committee had to be approved by the Chief Justice and any solicitor who was found guilty was entitled to appeal against that finding to the Chief Justice. In *Solicitors Act 1954, Re*,[73] this Committee had found the two appellants guilty of misconduct in how they had handled clients' money, and ordered that they should pay the entire costs of the inquiry. In their appeal, they contended that Part III was unconstitutional because it contravened the separation of powers. Maguire C.J. found that the Committee exercised a non-criminal "limited" judicial function, which Article 37 of the Constitution permits to be delegated to bodies other than the courts. But the Supreme Court held that the judicial power given by Part III was not limited and, accordingly, that the entire disciplinary scheme was an unconstitutional allocation of a power that could only be exercised by judges appointed and in courts established under the Constitution.

The criteria Kingsmill Moore J., for the court, adopted to identify "judicial power" and "limited judicial power" are set out above in the general discussion of executive adjudication.[74] Briefly, the fact that the decision-maker is obliged to act judicially, or must decide legal questions, or must adopt some of the trappings of the courts does not always mean that he is exercising judicial power. But a power having the following characteristics is judicial, *viz.* finally deciding a dispute about legal rights or liabilities, or about imposing penalties, having that determination enforced by the State and making the kind of orders that traditionally have been made by the courts. As for what is "limited" non-criminal judicial power, "[t]he test ... lies in the effect of the assigned power when exercised. If (its) exercise ... is calculated ordinarily to affect in the most profound and far reaching way the lives, liberties, fortunes or reputations of those against whom they are exercised, they cannot properly be described as limited."[75] Thus, the test of whether a judicial power is "limited" is how profound an effect it has on individuals. Applied to the Disciplinary Committee under the 1954 Act, its powers had parallels with criminal and civil courts, since the Committee determined individuals' guilt or innocence of charges, decided rights and imposed obligations. As described there, "It partake(s) of the characteristics which ... distinguish both civil and criminal justiciable controversies. (I)t may determine the guilt or innocence of persons charged with offences against a code not indeed directly imposed by the State but

---

[73] [1960] I.R. 239.

[74] *Supra*, p.188.

[75] [1960] I.R. at p.264.

recognised and authorised by it primarily in the interest of its citizens, and may inflict severe penalties for breaches of it, and may determine in a final manner rights and obligations in dispute between parties, which determination will be enforced by the authority of the State."[76] It was the following particular features that led the court to concluding that it exercised plenary and not just "limited" judicial power.

One was the Committee's central concern, which was the special role of solicitors in the administration of justice; solicitors are officers of the court. Kingsmill Moore J. reasoned that "[m]embers of the tribunal when they impose such penalties are in a real sense performing an act of justice in a matter which is a concern of the State as well as of the profession and which the State, by its judges, has hitherto reserved to itself. Historically the act of striking solicitors off the roll has always been reserved to judges. It is necessary for the proper administration of justice that the Courts should be served by legal practitioners of high integrity and professional competence and that the judges should have the power not only of removing those who in their opinion fail to meet the requirements of the office but of retaining those who do."[77]

Another feature was the Committee's very extensive authority in procedural directions. Complaints against solicitors could be heard and determined in their absence, provided that they were notified of the hearing. As regards compelling the attendance of witnesses, the production of documents and examination on oath, the Committee had the same rights, powers and privileges as the High Court. Witnesses before the Committee were to be sworn and then examined, cross-examined and re-examined. Any order made by the Committee was declared to be enforceable as if it were a judgment or order of the High Court. Kingsmill Moore J. concluded that "as far as procedural matters go there have been conferred on the Committee powers assimilated to those of the High Courts and while mere matters of procedure taken by themselves would not necessarily be sufficient ground for declaring a tribunal unconstitutional, it is an element for consideration that the Committee has in many respects been invested with powers equivalent to those of the High Court."[78]

But the "decisive test" was the drastic nature of the orders that the Committee could make. One was to award costs determined in exactly the same way as High Court costs. Another was to order restitution or satisfaction to an aggrieved party, which was virtually the same as awarding damages in tort. According to Kingsmill Moore J.:

> "Presumably restitution or satisfaction could only be made where there had been something in the nature of misconduct, but misconduct would include fraud and negligence. Damages awarded by a Court for fraud or

---

[76] *Id.* at p.264.
[77] *Id.* at p.275.
[78] *Id.* at p.273.

negligence are primarily an attempt to produce *'restitutio in integrum'* and the Court is unable to distinguish the power given to the Committee from the power given to a Court, unless indeed it be that the power given to the Committee, is wider than any that a Court can exercise. The questions which can arise before the Committee are as contentious, as difficult, and as important as the questions which would arise before a Court trying a common law action for negligence or fraud. In the opinion of the Court a tribunal which may make such an order is properly described as administering justice and such a tribunal unless composed of judges is unconstitutional."[79]

Another and more drastic order still was the power to strike a solicitor off the roll of the court, the effect of which was that it became a criminal offence for that person, while struck off, to work as a solicitor – "a sanction of such severity that in its consequence it may be much more serious than a term of imprisonment."[80] Of this power, Kingsmill Moore J. observed that "The imposition of a penalty, which has such consequences, would seem to demand from those who impose it the qualities of impartiality, independence and experience which are required for the holder of a judicial office who, under the criminal law, imposes a fine or short sentence of imprisonment. The only justification for such penalties must be that they are necessary in the interest of the public and of a profession which serves the public."[81]

In the light of all these considerations, the power given to the Disciplinary Committee was held to be of such a nature that, under the Constitution, it could only be exercised by judges duly appointed: "the power to strike a solicitor off the roll is, when exercised, an administration of justice, both because the infliction of such a *severe penalty* on a citizen is a matter which calls for the exercise of the judicial power of the State and because to entrust such a power to persons other than judges is to interfere with the necessities of the proper administration of justice."[82] The fact that the 1954 Act gave solicitors, who were struck off, a right of appeal to the Chief Justice in no way affected this conclusion.

New procedures were adopted shortly afterwards for disciplining solicitors and for striking off veterinary surgeons, and years later similar procedures were adopted for disciplining registered medical practitioners, dentists and nurses. A significant feature of these procedures is that they provide for direct court involvement in the decision whether or not the individual was guilty of misconduct and ought to be prevented from practising the profession. These measures suggest that it is the Oireachtas' view that professional discipline,

---

[79] *Id.* at p.274.
[80] *Ibid.*
[81] *Id.* at pp.274–275.
[82] *Id.* at p.275.

where the potential sanction imposed is prohibition from practice, either temporarily or permanently, is indeed a plenary judicial function. Under the Solicitors (Amendment) Act 1960, there is a Disciplinary Committee of the Law Society whose members are appointed by the President of the High Court from existing or past members of the Society's governing council. That Committee's function is to investigate allegations of misconduct and, on completing its inquiry, it must report to the High Court. It is then for the Court to decide what should be done – whether further evidence is needed, what sanction if any, including striking off the roll of solicitors, shall be applied, and whether restitution shall be made to an aggrieved party. A solicitor who has been struck off can be returned to the roll by the High Court. But as was the case with the disciplinary procedures that were declared invalid in 1958, the Disciplinary Committee has the same powers, rights and privileges as the High Court regarding compelling the attendance of witnesses, the production of documents and examination on oath. That Committee can punish for contempt, in much the same way as the High Court, and witnesses before it have the same privileges and immunities as witnesses before the High Court. In order to practise, solicitors must not only be enrolled but they must possess a practising certificate, which the Law Society issues each year. It has been held that the Society's power to withhold practising certificates must be used for the purpose of protecting the public and clients, and is not exercisable for disciplinary purposes.[83]

Disciplinary authority over nurses, dentists and doctors is exercised by the Fitness to Practise Committees of An Bord Altranais, the Dental Council and the Medical Council, respectively, in accordance with very similar procedures set out in the relevant legislation. For instance, with regard to medical doctors, the supreme regulatory authority is the Medical Council, the composition and powers of which are set out in the Medical Practitioners Act 1978. Investigations into allegations of professional misconduct are conducted by the Council's Committee in accordance with the procedure laid down in section 45 of the 1978 Act. This Committee is given virtually the same extensive procedural powers as the Law Society's Disciplinary Committee possesses. But the actual decision to discipline a doctor is taken by the Medical Council after it has considered the Committee's report on its inquiry. That is not the end of the matter, however, because section 46 of the 1978 Act gives any doctor, against whom an adverse disciplinary decision was made (other than censure), a right to apply to the High Court to have the decision cancelled. There is then a full re-hearing of the evidence.[84] The court has the option of cancelling the decision or declaring that it was properly made and determining the appropriate penalty. Additionally, where the disciplinary sanction is to take the extreme form of

---

[83] *Crowley, Re* [1964] I.R. 106.
[84] *C.K. v. An Bord Altranais* [1990] 2 I.R. 396.

erasure from the register of practitioners, suspension of registration or attaching conditions to being on the medical register, the Medical Council itself does not have the power to impose those sanctions. Instead, the Council must apply to the High Court and it is for the court to decide whether sanctions should be imposed and to order that they be imposed. Thus, it is the court, and not the professional body, which ultimately decides whether in the circumstances the most severe disciplinary sanctions should be imposed.

In *M. v. The Medical Council*,[85] it was contended, unsuccessfully, that this procedure was unconstitutional on separation of powers and unfair procedures grounds. The plaintiff's argument that the powers exercised by the Committee and the Council could only be exercised by judges, duly appointed under the Constitution, was rejected on the grounds that these bodies did not in fact administer justice because they had no authority to order that practitioners shall suffer the severest of the professional penalties. As Finlay P. explained:

> "[T]he powers conferred on either the Council or the Committee under (the 1978) Act are not judicial powers and ... the functions being exercised by them are not the administration of justice. Apart from the right and obligation to hold the enquiry itself, the only powers of the Committee or the Council which could be said to be final, and, in a sense, binding are the publication of a finding by the Committee of misconduct or unfitness to practise and the Council's powers to advise, admonish or censure a practitioner. Even if it could be said that the publication to the public of a finding by a committee of enquiry of misconduct or unfitness was something affecting the rights of a practitioner within the context of the authorities ... or if the same could be said of advising, admonishing or censuring in my view these would be functions so clearly limited in their effect and consequence that they would be within the exception provided by Article 37 of the Constitution even if (contrary to what I believe to be the true legal situation) they constituted the administration of justice."[86]

Principally because they are based on contracts with the members and do not derive from statute, in *Geoghegan v. Instituted of Chartered Accountants in Ireland*[87] the Supreme Court held that the respondent Institute's disciplinary proceedings did not amount to the administration of justice, within the present context. As O'Flaherty J. pointed out, what distinguishes the Solicitors Act 1954 and the Institute's procedures "is that the members of the Institute come together by a form of contract; they agree to be bound by the Charter and bye-laws and there is no question of the Oireachtas giving powers to a body to

---

[85] [1984] I.R. 485.
[86] *Id.* at p.499.
[87] [1995] 3 I.R. 86.

perform judicial functions."[88]

Fair Procedures

Before a formal disciplinary enquiry commences, the professional in question is entitled to be informed that a *prima facie* finding of misconduct may be made against him and be offered an opportunity to address the charges.[89] If an enquiry goes ahead, the professional is entitled to have his expert witnesses and others assisting his defence present at the hearings.[90] Usually, these enquiries are not heard in public but the committee conducting the enquiry has a discretion to permit members of the public to attend. It was held by the Supreme Court in *Barry v. Medical Council*[91] that a professional who is the subject of a misconduct enquiry has no constitutional right to have the proceedings take place in public. Because the Committee's findings of misconduct have no binding legal effect, since any sanction recommended must be imposed by the High Court, its hearings do not constitute the administration of justice. Nor, it was held, was it unfair in all the circumstances that, at the outset the Committee there decided to hear the proceedings *in camera*, retaining a discretion to hold part of them in public in due course. It has yet to be determined the extent to which these committees are required to give reasons for any adverse findings they make.

It was contended as well in *Re M.*[92] that the entire procedure was unconstitutionally unfair in that, having been found guilty by the professional body, the doctor in question was under a distinct disadvantage when appealing to the High Court. But because it is for the Council to prove to the court that the doctor in question is guilty of misconduct and because constitutionally fair procedural requirements will always be implied into statutes, Finlay P. did not see "any want of fair or due procedure arising from the fact that on a previous enquiry, held by a body of persons of the practitioner's own profession, a finding of misconduct or unfitness to practise has been made."[93]

According to one of the classic maxims of fair procedure, *nemo iudex in sua causa,* persons should not judge their own cases. In the administrative law context this means that those who have a distinct stake in the outcome of some dispute should not decide that controversy. An obligation to comply with this maxim will usually be implied by the courts into administrative schemes, including the machinery for professional discipline.[94] A particular aspect of the *nemo iudex* principle, that arises in most professional discipline contexts,

---

[88] *Id.* at p.120.
[89] *O'Ceallaigh v. An Bord Altranais* [2000] 4 I.R. 54.
[90] *O'Cellaigh v. Fitness to Practise Committee* [1999] 2 I.R. 552.
[91] [1998] 3 I.R. 368.
[92] [1984] I.R. 485.
[93] *Id.* at p.499.
[94] *O'Donoghue v. Vetinary Council* [1975] I.R. 398.

is the question of institutional bias, *i.e.* whether the disciplinary tribunal is adequately insulated against potential bias because most members of the tribunal are members of the profession itself and, frequently, politically active members of the profession. In *O'Brien v. Bord na Mona*,[95] a similar question arose in connection with expropriation procedures and it was held that, because the decision to expropriate land in the circumstances there was an administrative and not a judicial decision, it was permissible for the Oireachtas to empower the public body that wants land to decide which particular tracts shall be taken from their owners.

Where, as in the case of solicitors, medical practitioners, dentists, nurses and veterinary surgeons, it is the High Court which ultimately decides whether the gravest disciplinary sanctions should be imposed, questions of institutional bias cannot arise. In *Solicitors Act 1954, Re*,[96] one of the complaints made against the pre-1960 solicitors' disciplinary procedure was of institutional bias. On this question, Kingsmill Moore J. observed that the entire procedure was:

> "Such as to make it difficult for the tribunal to be impartial. In many cases the person against whom a complaint is made will be a solicitor with whom members of the tribunal have had professional dealings which may have predisposed them in his favour or against him. All of the members are liable to contribute yearly to a compensation fund established under the Act to relieve or mitigate losses sustained in consequence of dishonesty of solicitors and the amount of such contribution may be increased if found necessary (ss. 69, 70) so that there might be a tendency to bear hardly on a solicitor charged with dishonesty. Although the character and standing of the members is such that they can be expected to resist and rise superior to any influences which might affect their impartiality, and it is not suggested that they do not so do, the tribunal is not constituted in a manner best calculated to provide the security against bias and partiality which a Court of justice affords."[97]

What conclusion the court drew from this in-built incentive towards bias is not entirely clear. All that was said was "(i)f the Committee are not administering justice the Constitution imposes no restrictions on the composition of the body."[98] But it was found that the Committee did administer justice, which suggests that this aspect of the scheme would have been declared invalid if the entire scheme had not been struck down because the powers there were such as must be administered through the courts.

In *Le Compte v. Belgium*,[99] the European Court of Human Rights indicated

---

[95] [1983] I.R. 255, *supra*, p.746.
[96] [1960] I.R. 239.
[97] *Id.* at p.272.
[98] *Ibid.*

that there must be a significant outside and demonstrably impartial element in a tribunal that makes decisions about professional discipline. But it also held that, where the disciplinary tribunal itself does not contain the requisite assurances of impartiality, Article 6(1) of the Convention is satisfied if there is a full right of appeal from that tribunal to a judicial body, *i.e.* if the disciplinary tribunal is "subject to subsequent control by a judicial body that has full jurisdiction and does provide the guarantees of Article 6(1)."[100]

EMPLOYMENT

Aspects of employment and of trade unions feature in many modern Constitutions and international human rights instruments. Economic security, in the sense of having a job or some other assured source of income, is an essential prerequisite for enjoying most of the constitutionally protected rights; freedom of expression and privacy are of little practical benefit to those who are forced by economic circumstances to go homeless and to starve, or who are economically dependent entirely on others.

At the international level, there is a plethora of human rights norms regarding employment and trade unions. These are the principal subject of the European Social Charter[101] and the UN Covenant on Economic, Social and Cultural Rights.[102] Ireland has agreed to respect the following rights in that Charter, *viz.* to work, to just conditions of work, to healthy work conditions, to a fair remuneration, to protection for married workers and their families, to protection for employed women, to vocational guidance and training and the entitlement of nationals of other State Parties to the Charter to work in Ireland. Employment and trade union questions are the main concern of the International Labour Organisation,[103] which was established in 1919 along with the League of Nations, and which is now an agency of the United Nations, based in Geneva. Ireland is a party to over fifty ILO Conventions, most notably Number 29 concerning forced labour, Number 105 concerning the abolition of forced labour, Number 122 concerning employment policy, Number 182 against the worst forms of child labour, Number 100 on equal remuneration for men and women workers for work of equal value and Number 111 concerning discrimination in employment and occupation.

---

[99] 4 E.H.R.R. 1 (1981).
[100] *Id.* at p.542 (para.29).
[101] October 18, 1961, 529 UNTS 89; revised on May 3, 1996, ETS No. 163.
[102] December 16, 1996, 993 UNTS 3. See generally, M. Craven, *The International Convention on Economic Social and Cultural Rights* (1998).
[103] See generally, G. von Potobski, *International Labour Law* (1995).

Forced and Compulsory Labour

It can hardly be doubted that the Constitution forbids forced and compulsory labour. Ireland is a party to ILO Convention Number 105 on the Abolition of Forced Labour.[104] Since, however, most persons are under some indirect legal compulsion to work – in that if they did not earn a living they might be in breach of their duty to support their families and destitution could ultimately cause them to run foul of the Vagrancy Act – the question arises of what constitutes forced or compulsory labour.

ILO Convention Number 105 prohibits use of any form of forced or compulsory labour for specified purposes, *viz.*:

> "(a) As a means of political coercion or education or as a punishment for holding or expressing political views or views ideologically opposed to the established political, social or economic system;
> (b) As a method of mobilising and using labour for purposes of economic development;
> (c) As a means of labour discipline;
> (d) As a punishment for having participated in strikes;
> (e) As a means of racial, social, national or religious discrimination."

Article 4(3) of the European Convention, by contrast, enumerates certain forms of service that will not be deemed to constitute forced labour:

> "(a) any work required to be done in the ordinary course of detention imposed according to the provisions of Article 5 of this Convention or during conditional release from such detention;
> (b) any service of a military character or, in case of conscientious objectors in countries where they are recognized, service exacted instead of compulsory military service;
> (c) any service exacted in case of an emergency or calamity threatening the life or well-being of the community;
> (d) any work or service which forms part of normal civic obligations."

In other words, forced or compulsory labour does not include work that convicted persons must do while in prison or during their conditional release, compulsory military service or work that is obligatory as a substitute for military service, work that must be done during major disasters and the like, and "normal civic obligations."

---

[104] June 25, 1957, 320 UNTS 291.

The Right to Work

There is no express reference to the European Convention to employment as such (apart from trade union questions) but the rights to work and also to "just and favourable conditions of work" are proclaimed in Articles 6 and 7 of the UN Covenant on Economic, Social and Cultural Rights. The only reference to employment in the Constitution is contained in the "directive principles" in Article 45.2.i which cannot be invoked by the courts in order to strike down post-1937 legislation. It stipules that "[t]he State shall ... direct its policy towards securing: That the citizens (all of whom, men and women equally, have the right to an adequate means of livelihood) may through their occupations find the means of making reasonable provision for their domestic needs." But it has been held that the right to work is one of the unspecified rights under Article 40.3 of the Constitution. Whether this right is enforceable directly against employers who are not agencies or instrumentalities of the State is debatable; this is an aspect of what sometimes is described as the *drittwirtung* question, *viz.* whether constitutional guarantees impose obligations on private individuals and bodies as well as on the State and the public sector.

Dismissal

In the private sector, job security is protected principally by the employee's contractual rights and also by the Unfair Dismissals Acts 1977–93.[105] Many public sector workers hold statutory offices and the relevant Act or regulation usually stipulates the circumstances in which they may be removed from office. Provided they are not removed for unconstitutional reasons or through unfair procedures, civil servants hold their office "at the will and pleasure of the Government;"[106] many local authority officials have far more secure legal tenure. It remains to be determined whether or in what circumstances the Oireachtas may diminish or abolish an officer's existing statutory tenure entitlements, which most likely would be regarded as a form of property within Article 40.3.3.

Unlike the position with certain professions, it is not essential to obtain the approval of a court before a public office-holder may be removed. In *Keady v. Commissioner An Garda Síochána*,[107] where the plaintiff had been dismissed from the Gardaí for fraud, he contended that the procedure under the Garda disciplinary regulations, that preceded his dismissal, was an intrinsically non-limited judicial process, that only could be carried out through the courts. But as McCarthy J. pointed out, a significant feature of the Solicitors Act 1954, absent in the Garda regime, was "the role of the courts as a matter of history in

---

[105] See generally, M. Forde, *Employment Law* (2nd ed,. 2001), Chaps 7 and 8.
[106] Civil Service Regulation Act 1956, s.5 and Forde *id.*, Chap.13.
[107] [1992] 2 I.R. 197.

the supervision and disciplining …".[108] Additionally, unlike Gardaí, if a solicitor "loses [his] certificate and holds himself out as being so qualified he commits a criminal offence."[109] Less persuasive was O'Flaherty J.'s characterisation of the disciplinary hearing as merely "an inquiry" and not "a contest between parties."[110] Additionally, he emphasised, that there no longer is quite the same need for direct judicial involvement in imposing sanctions of this nature because "there is now in place a well charted system of administrative law which requires decision-makers to render justice in the case brought before them and sets out the procedures that should be followed."[111]

A closely related question arose in *O'Cleirigh v. Minister for Agriculture,*[112] where the plaintiff attacked the constitutionality of section 9(1) of the Irish Land Commission (Dissolution) Act 1992, which provided for the dissolution of the Land Commission and authorised the Minister to pay such compensation as he regards reasonable to persons employed there who would become redundant. The plaintiff had been a solicitor in the service of the Commission for over ten years and he contended that the determination of compensation for his loss of office was an intrinsically judicial function that could only be performed by the courts. That claim was rejected by the Supreme Court, which held that ascertaining what rights he lost by virtue of his ceasing to hold office was not "an enormous task requiring judicial enquiry," nor was the "second step of ascertaining reasonable compensation in respect of such lost rights."[113] This was because the principal rights he was being denied were his remaining years of service, up to retirement age, along with the salary and increased pension rights for these years, which he would lose. Valuing these rights was not "an exercise of the judicial power of the State" but was an "administrative function similar to many such functions exercisable by Ministers and other public officials which must be exercised reasonably, conscientiously and fairly and, if not so exercised, is subject to judicial review by the courts."[114]

Persons who are in jeopardy of being dismissed from a public service office or equivalent employment by or under the State, are entitled to a fair hearing before a decision is taken to dismiss them, being principally a reasonable opportunity to refute any allegations of wrongdoing being made against them, and an unbiased hearing into those allegations and reasons.[115] These protections will be implied into all discretionary powers of removal from office and dismissal. To what extent these may be taken away by express legislative provision has not been adjudicated on to date.

---

[108] *Id.* at p.205.
[109] *Ibid.*
[110] *Id.* at p.213.
[111] *Ibid.*
[112] [1998] 4 I.R. 15.
[113] *Id.* at p.30.
[114] *Id.* at p.31.
[115] *Supra,* n.105, Chap.13.

A provision in the Offences Against the State Act 1939, barring from public service employment persons who had been convicted of what may be termed "subversive" offences, was struck down in *Cox v. Ireland.*[116] The plaintiff, a school-teacher, had been convicted in the Special Criminal Court of a scheduled offence under the 1939 Act and received a two-year sentence. On his release, he was informed that he no longer had his job, which had been forfeited; according to section 34 of that Act, persons employed in the public sector forfeited their jobs and also any accumulated pension entitlements on being so convicted. Because that section operated so drastically, without qualification, across the entire public sector, regardless of the gravity or comparative triviality of the offence in question, the Supreme Court held that it violated the implied right to work as well as property rights in respect of the plaintiff's pension. What made section 34 particularly objectionable was that it was entirely within the discretion of the Director of Public Prosecutions to prosecute the offence in question in the Special Criminal Court rather than before the ordinary courts, thereby introducing a peculiarly arbitrary dimension. That in any single instance the Government could waive application of section 34 did not save it from unconstitutionality.

Obtaining Work

In the first case in which the constitutional right to work obtained judicial recognition, that right was not founded on Article 40.3 but on the Article 45.2 "directive principle" quoted above; indeed the outcome of the case could also have been justified under Article 40.1, the equality clause. That was *Murtagh Properties Ltd v. Cleary.*[117] where trade union members picketed the plaintiff's property, a public house, in order to prevent non-union bar staff from being employed there. Since the union's membership was all male and it would not accept women into its membership, the picketers effectively sought to prevent women from being employed. Kenny J. held that Article 45.2 clearly means that "in so far as the right to an adequate means of livelihood was involved, men and women were to be regarded as equal."[118] Accordingly, he concluded, "a policy or general rule under which anyone seeks to prevent an employer from employing men or women on the ground of sex only is prohibited by the Constitution. (And) a demand backed by a threat of a picket that women should not be employed at all in any activity solely because they are women (and not because the work is unsuitable for them or too difficult for them or too dangerous) is a breach of this right (*i.e.* to an adequate means of livelihood)."[119] Since this was precisely the defendants' policy and mode of action, it was

---

[116] [1992] 2 I.R. 503.
[117] [1972] I.R. 330.
[118] *Id.* at p.336.
[119] *Ibid.*

unlawful and their picketing of the plaintiff's premises was enjoined. In subsequent cases, several of them concerning trade unions, it was accepted that the right to work also derives from Article 40.3.5

The existence of such a right does not prevent the State from employing only certain categories of persons or from prohibiting the employment of certain groups of individuals. Nor does it require the state to advertise every vacancy for a post in the public sector.[120] But because earning a living is vital for most persons' contented existence, prohibitions against employment require substantial justification. In *Landers v. Attorney General*,[121] it was held that a statutory prohibition against young persons giving singing performances in public houses was not an unconstitutional interference with young persons' right to work and to earn a livelihood.

Discrimination

The extent to which the Constitution forbids discrimination in employment is largely unexplored territory. Especially in view of EC Directives on the question and with the enactment of the Employment Equality Act 1998, the constitutional debate is no longer of particular practical significance. But the question of confining certain posts in the public sector to Irish nationals or to nationals of EU Member States remains to be addressed.[122] There has not been a history of religious or political discrimination in Irish public service employment, which may explain the virtual absence of case law on this question. In *Greally v. Minister for Education*,[123] a scheme whereby applications for permanent teaching posts in Catholic schools were entertained only from persons who were on a panel, with previous teaching experience in those schools, was held not to constitute unfair religious discrimination.

In the past, women employed in numerous parts of the public service were forced to resign on getting married but that practice does not exist any longer. It not alone contravened the right to work but almost certainly would be deemed to be an unconstitutional interference with the right to marry and found a family. It has never been established whether employers excluding women, or indeed men, from certain jobs is in accordance with the Constitution. The argument for unconstitutionality would focus on the right to work and on the guarantee of equality, and on the fact that Article 11 of the UN Convention on the Elimination of All Forms of Discrimination Against Women[124] proscribes sex discrimination in employment.

---

[120] *Riordan v. An Taoiseach* [2000] 4 I.R. 537; *supra*, p.401.
[121] (1975) 109 I.L.T.R. 1.
[122] See generally, Forde, *supra*, n.105, pp.153 *et seq*. *Cf. Lavoie v. Canada*, 210 D.L.R. 4th 193 (2002).
[123] [1999] 1 I.R. 1; *ante*, p.631.
[124] December 7, 1967, 1249 UNTS 13.

It was held in *Murtagh Properties Ltd. v. Cleary*[125] that the Constitution did not permit trade unions to exert economic pressure on employers in order to prevent women being employed, which is not the same as saying that sex discrimination by employers is unconstitutional. Indeed, counsel for the plaintiffs (the employers) conceded that, under the Constitution, employers are entitled to refuse to employ anyone for any reason whatever. And Kenny J. there appears to have accepted that it would not be constitutionally improper for an employer and a trade union to agree that only males should be employed.[126] He even went so far as to suggest that pay scales in the public service that discriminated on the basis of sex were not unconstitutional. According to the judge, "(i)t was strenuously contended ... that there could be no differences in salary on the ground of sex, and that the remuneration structure of the public service was therefore (unconstitutional). I do not think that this result follows. What is or is not an adequate means of livelihood is a matter for decision by the Oireachtas ...".[127]

Trade Unions

Trade unions are primarily organisations of employees the principal objects of which are to promote their members' interests in the workplace by securing increased wages and better working conditions.[128] A common feature of the Constitution, the European Convention and the UN Covenant is that the clauses guaranteeing freedom of association also embody the guarantee of trade union freedom. According to Article 40.6.1.iii and 2 of the Constitution:

"The State guarantees liberty for the exercise of the following rights, subject to public order and morality: ...
The right of the citizens to form associations and unions. Laws, however, may be enacted for the regulation and control in the public interest of the exercise of the foregoing right.
Laws regulating the manner in which (this) right ... may be exercised shall contain no political, religious or class discrimination."

Article 11 of the European Convention provides that "[e]very one has the right ... to form and to join trade unions for the protection of his interests;" but this right is subject to the usual qualifications and, in addition, it is stipulated that "[t]his article shall not prevent the imposition of lawful restrictions on the exercise of these rights by members of the armed forces, of the police or of the administration of the State." Article 22 of the UN Covenant is in similar vein.

---

[125] [1972] I.R. 330.
[126] *Id.* at p.355.
[127] *Id.* at p.336
[128] See generally, M. Forde, *Industrial Relations Law* (1991).

International Labour Organisation Conventions nos. 87[129] and 98[130] deal with trade union questions, as do Articles 5 and 6 of the European Social Charter and Article 8 of the UN Covenant on Economic, Social and Cultural Rights.

Constitutional guarantees and the international labour standards in this area focus principally on what may be termed the constitutive process of industrial relations, *i.e.* the arrangements for bringing workers' representatives and employers or employers' representatives together for negotiation, with a view to agreeing on terms and conditions of employment and on matters incidental thereto. At common law, employers are permitted to take any form of action, that is not specifically illegal, in order to discourage the growth of workers' organisations in their establishments and to deter demands to recognise and to negotiate with unions, for example, the dismissal of union members, black-listing of activists, excluding union representatives from the establishment etc. By virtue of the Industrial Relations Act 1990, most workers are free to strike and to picket in order to protest against these measures, and to compel employers to bargain with their chosen organisations. Workers, therefore, can be said to possess "negative" protection for their claims to freedom to join trade unions and to take part in union activities, to union recognition and to the free choice of union.

A significant feature of the 1990 Act is that it imposes no obligation on employers to bargain with unions or even to permit their employees to join unions. The view prevalent when that measure's predecessor was being enacted in 1906[131] was that the law should adopt a neutral position in industrial relations; the law should leave both sides free to "fight it out" between themselves and not intervene except where specific wrongs are committed and whether collective bargaining takes place in particular situations should depend on the relative industrial strength of the two sides. In recent years, however, claims for more effective legislative protection for workers' demands on constitutive questions have been recognised by laws and accorded some "positive" protection. The Unfair Dismissals Acts 1977–93 deem unlawful dismissals for anti-union reasons and there are some statutes that require employers to deal with representative trade unions. But the liberty of action conferred by the 1990 Act is largely confined to licensed trade unions and their members, as are the special rights under the 1977–93 Acts, which are shared with members of the "excepted bodies."

---

[129] Convention on Freedom of Association and Protection of the Right to Organise, July 9, 1948, 68 UNTS 17.

[130] Convention on the Right to Organise and Collective Bargaining, July 1, 1949, 96 UNTS 257.

[131] Trade Disputes Act 1906, 6 Edw.7 c.47.

Joining a Union

Freedom of association in the context of labour law connotes freedom to join and to remain a member of a trade union or of an employers' association. The content of this right *vis-à-vis* State or governmental regulation is set out in Articles 3–10 of ILO Convention Number 87. Article 2 of that Convention states that "[w]orkers ... without distinction whatsoever, shall have the right to establish and, subject only to the rules of the organisation concerned, to join organisations of their own choosing without previous authorisation." And it is provided in Articles 1 and 2 of ILO Convention Number 98 that:

"1. Workers shall enjoy adequate protection against acts of anti-union discrimination in respect of their employment.
2. Such protection shall apply more particularly in respect of acts calculated to:
   (a) Make the employment of a worker subject to the condition that he shall not join a union or shall relinquish trade union membership.
   (b) Cause the dismissal of or otherwise prejudice a worker by reason of union membership ...."

Since the dismissal of a person from employment for refusing to join a trade union has been held to be unconstitutional,[132] it should follow that dismissal and other "coercive" action short of dismissal for joining a trade union are an unlawful abuse of right under the Constitution. By "yellow dog" contract is meant an undertaking given to an employer whereby an employee agrees never to become a member of any trade union. Although lawful at common law, such a contract may very well be against constitutional public policy. A variant of it was considered in *Beckton Dickinson Ltd. v. Lee*,[133] the facts of which are outlined below but, in the circumstances, the majority of the Supreme Court deemed it unnecessary "to express any opinion upon the question of how far, or in what circumstances, a person can contract out of a constitutional right or to what extent such an agreement would be enforced."[134]

The international standards regarding trade union membership and activities provide that special arrangements can be made for certain parts of the public service, especially for the police and for the armed forces. In *Aughey v. Ireland*,[135] it was held that the constitutional guarantee of trade union freedom is subject to a similar qualification when applied to bodies and personnel closely connected with the security of the State. That case concerned a dispute about

---

[132] *Meskell v. Coras Iompair Éireann* [1973] I.R. 121; *infra*, p.803.
[133] [1973] I.R. 1.
[134] *Id.*, at pp.41–42.
[135] [1986] I.L.R.M. 206.

employee representation in the Garda Síochána but Barrington J.'s holding is equally applicable to the armed forces. It remains to be seen whether similar considerations would obtain for the prison service and for the top echelons of the civil service. The plaintiffs were detectives who claimed *inter alia* that the statutory machinery for dealing with their employment-related grievances was unconstitutional. Under section 13 of the Garda Síochána Act 1924, no member of the Garda Síochána is permitted to join a trade union or similar organisation. But that Act, as amended in 1977, permits the Government to establish representative bodies to act as intermediaries between members of the Garda and the Garda authorities. A Garda Representative Association and an Association of Garda Sergeants and Inspectors were established by statutory instrument for that purpose. Members of the force are permitted to join these Associations, which function in much the same ways as trade unions except that their rules do not provide for resorting to industrial action.

One contention made by the plaintiffs was that forbidding them to form their own association or union, which would represent detectives' employment grievances, contravened the trade union freedom guarantee in the Constitution; that if they wished to become members of some form of trade union they could only join one of the above-mentioned associations. This was rejected by Barrington J., who held that the right to form and join unions is subject to state security considerations and, since the Garda Síochána "is intimately concerned with the security of the State," section 13 of the 1924 Act was not unconstitutional. According to him, "[t]he right of association is stated in the Constitution to be 'subject to public order.' It appears to me that the Oireachtas is justified in imposing limitations on the extent to which members of the Garda Síochána may organise, even for the purpose of dealing with matters affecting their professional welfare and efficiency. Because of their close connection with the security of the State, Gardaí may have to accept limitations on their right to form associations and unions which other citizens would not have to accept."[136]

Organising and Engaging in Union Activities

State parties to ILO Convention Number 87, in Article 11, "undertake to take all necessary and appropriate measures to ensure that workers and employers may exercise freely the right to organise." The content of this right is spelt out in ILO Convention Number 98, especially in Article 1, which condemns the dismissal of or prejudicing a worker, *inter alia*, "because of participation in union activities outside working hours or, with the consent of the employer, within working hours." The "right to organise" guaranteed by Article 5 of the

---

[136] *Id.* at p.217. *Cf. South Africa Nat'l Defence Union v. Minister of Defence*, 6 B.H.R.C. 574 (1999).

European Social Charter is more narrowly defined: it comprises the "freedom of workers and employers to from ... organisations for the protection of their economic and social interests and to join those organisations ...". The extent to which a trade union's organisational and other activities to advance its general interests are protected by the Constitution from employer retribution has not been considered in the courts. Given the protection afforded to non-trade unionists,[137] it would be inconsistent if "coercive" employer action against persons for their union activities outside of the workplace and working hours were held not be unlawful. On the other hand, it may be that the property right under Article 40.3 entitles the employer, in the absence of legislation to the contrary, to proscribe or restrict in whatever manner he chooses organisational and related activities at the workplace or during working hours.

Union Recognition

Article 4 of ILO Convention Number 98 calls for the encouragement of union recognition and the conclusion of collective agreements; that "[m]easures appropriate to national conditions shall be taken, where necessary, to encourage and promote the full development and utilisation of machinery for voluntary negotiation between employers or employers' organisations and workers' organisations, with a view to the regulation of terms and conditions of employment by means of collective agreements." Article 7(2) of the European Social Charter is similarly worded.

In *Abbott v. Irish Transport & General Workers' Union*[138] it was said by McWilliam J. that, apart from any obligations they may assume under contract or which may be imposed by particular statutes, employers have no legal duty to recognise and bargain with trade unions. It appears that the constitutional right to join the union of ones choice does not oblige employers to deal with their workers' chosen union or to take part in any particular form of negotiations. In that case, the plaintiffs and others quit membership of the Irish Transport and General Workers Union (ITGWU) and joined the Amalgamated Transport and General Workers Union (Amalgamated). The Irish Congress of Trade Unions (Congress) decided that, by accepting these workers into membership, Amalgamated was in breach of Congress' "no-poaching" rules. Up until then, the employer had negotiated exclusively with the ITGWU. But fearing industrial action by ITGWU members and fortified by Congress decision, the employer refused to negotiate in any way with Amalgamated in respect of the latter's members. The plaintiffs claimed that, under the Constitution, their employer was obliged to negotiate with Amalgamated and that the ITGWU accordingly were causing the employer to violate Amalgamated members' constitutional rights. At the trial, however, the question of an affirmative duty to bargain was

---

[137] *Supra*, n.131.
[138] Unreported, High Court, McWilliam J., December 2, 1980.

not pursued. McWilliam J., nevertheless, expressed the view that "(t)here is no duty placed on any employer to negotiate with any particular citizen or body of citizens," and that "it appears to be clear that the plaintiffs have no constitutional right to compel the [employer] to engage in negotiations either with them or with their union ...".[139] He then went on to consider whether there had been any unlawful interference with the plaintiffs' constitutional right not to be compelled to join a trade union and held that there had not.

That an employer has no constitutional or common law obligation to consult or negotiate with a trade union or other body representing some of his employees, was endorsed by O'Hanlon J. in *Association of General Practitioners Ltd. v. Minister for Health.*[140] When determining employment terms and conditions for Health Board personnel, the Minister consulted, *inter alia,* the Irish Medical Organisation, a body that represents approximately 75% of medical practitioners in the State. But he did not consult the plaintiffs, a body that represents a small number of those practitioners. Relying on *Abbott* and several unreported judgments in similar vein, it was held that their rights of freedom to associate and to disassociate had not thereby been infringed.

Closed Shops

A closed shop is an arrangement between an employer and a trade union, or between employers and trade unions, whereby only members of a trade union, or of a particular union or unions, will be employed in an establishment. Unions seek closed shops for a variety of reasons. Their primary function is to assist the recruitment and retention of union members; without closed shops, some workers would not join unions or remain in membership. Also, they ensure that workers obey union rules and leadership, in that disobedience can result in expulsion from the union and consequent loss of a job. A somewhat related function is protecting a union's traditional domain from encroachment by rival unions; a union buttressed by a closed shop in a particular establishment is vulnerable to only the most intense of organisational campaigns mounted by rivals. Another function, of controlling entry to a union and thereby restricting the supply of certain categories of worker, is confined to what are called "pre-entry" closed shops, *i.e.* arrangements whereby persons are required to be union members before they even can obtain certain jobs.

The Supreme Court has held that it is contrary to the Constitution for workers to picket an employer in order to establish or to enforce a closed shop, and also for an employer to dismiss an employee for refusing to join a particular trade union. In *Educational Co. of Ireland Ltd. v. Fitzpatrick (No.2),*[141] the court held that to picket employers, in order to compel them to

---

[139] At pp.7 and 10.
[140] [1995] 1 I.R. 382.
[141] [1961] I.R. 345.

ensure that their non-union employees become members of a union of which the majority of the employees are members, is unlawful, in that the picketing infringed "an implicit guarantee in the Constitution that citizens shall not be coerced to join associations or unions against their will."[142] This right to disassociate was founded on the guarantees of freedom of opinion, of property rights and the freedom of choice of union recognised in the *NUR.* case.[143] The key passage of Kingsmill Moore J.'s judgment is:

> "The right to express freely convictions and opinions ..., must include the right to hold such convictions and opinions and the right not to be forced to join a union or association professing, forwarding, and requiring its members to subscribe to contrary opinions. The undertaking ..., to protect the property rights of every citizen may perhaps include an undertaking to protect his right to dispose of his labour as he wills, and would include impliedly a right not to be forced against his will into a union or association which exacts from him a regular payment. Moreover, I think a guarantee of a right to form associations and unions is only intelligible where there is an implicit right to abstain from joining such associations or unions or, to put it another way, to associate and unite with those who do not join such unions. The *NUR* case emphasised ... the constitutional right of the citizen to a free choice of the persons with whom he would associate and the decision seems to me to establish that a person shall not be coerced, at any rate by legislative action, into forming an association which he is not willing to join."[144]

In *Crowley v. Cleary*,[145] it was held that the threat of a picket to enforce an already established closed shop was unlawful for the same reasons.

The scope of the right to disassociate was extended further by the Supreme Court in *Meskell v. Corás Iompair Éireann*,[146] where it was held that a worker dismissed from his job for refusing to join a trade union was entitled to damages from the employer. For the previous 15 years, the plaintiff had worked for Corás Iompair Éireann (CIÉ), the State-owned road and rail transport company, and throughout was a trade union member. But he objected, as a matter of principle, to his union seeking to enforce a closed shop agreement it had made with the employer in 1958. Believing that it would be unlawful to dismiss all non-trade unionists or to pay them less than unionised employees were being paid, the employer decided on the following strategy. Each and every one of

---

[142] *Id.* at p.396.
[143] *National Union of Railwaymen v. Sullivan* [1947] I.R. 77; *infra*, p.805.
[144] [1961] I.R. 345 at p.395. Compare *Advance Cutting & Coring v. The Queen*, 205 D.L.R. 4th 385 (2001).
[145] [1968] I.R. 261.
[146] [1973] I.R. 121.

its employees would be dismissed but all of them would be offered re-employment in the same jobs if they each signed an undertaking to become and to remain a trade union member. Along with his fellow employees, the plaintiff was dismissed but he refused to sign the undertaking and accordingly did not get his job back. It was held that his employer had treated him unlawfully and that he was entitled to substantial damages for the infringement of his "right to abstain from joining associations or unions, which might be called the right of disassociation."[147] Walsh J., for the court, declined to express any view as to whether the plaintiff would be entitled to reinstatement in the circumstances there, since reinstatement was not claimed. Nor did Walsh J. comment on whether an employer is entitled to insist that, as a condition of getting a job, the aspirant employee must join a trade union or a designated union. Nor did he comment on giving non-trade unionists employment conditions that are not as favourable as those enjoyed by trade union members. Because only the employer was sued in that case, the question of the union's liability did not arise.

It was suggested in the *Educational Co. (No.2)* case that it is not unlawful to condition the acceptance of a job on joining a particular union or to resort to a strike *per se* in support of a closed shop. As regards strikes, Kingsmill Moore J. stated that "the claim to picket and the claim to strike ... involve very different considerations. The right to dispose of ones labour and to withdraw it seems to me a fundamental personal right which, though not specifically mentioned in the Constitution as being guaranteed, is a right of a nature which I cannot conceive to have been adversely affected by anything within the intendment of the Constitution."[148] But in the light of the reasons given in the *Meskell* case — if the Oireachtas cannot compel a person to join a union, no other body can because to do so would be "abusing(ing) the common law right" — closed shop strikes, without being accompanied by any picketing, would seem to fall within the constitutional proscription.

Dealing with hiring workers on condition that they should join a trade union, Kingsmill Moore J. in the *Educational Co. (No.2)* case sought to distinguish "coercion" from mere exercise of "economic pressure", with which "the law has no concern ... in general."[149] Later in *Becton, Dickinson Ltd. v. Lee,*[150] a majority of the Supreme Court deemed it unnecessary in the circumstances to express a view on these arrangements. The plaintiff employer had an agreement with two trade unions that, before being hired, all persons would sign undertakings that they would "agree to become ... and remain a benefit member" of those unions. In the event, some employees, who were hired following signing undertakings, subsequently refused to transfer from

---

[147] *Id.* at p.135.
[148] [1961] I.R. 397.
[149] *Id.* at p.396.
[150] [1973] I.R. 1.

other unions to either of the unions which had the agreement with the employer. Those employees went on strike to secure recognition of their own unions and their action was held to be in furtherance of a trade dispute. Referring to closed shop arrangements, Walsh J., for the majority, said that he had proceeded on the assumption that "the term in the contract of employment with regard to trade union membership is not one which would be held to be void" under the Constitution, adding that it was not necessary to express a view on the question of "how far, or in what circumstances, a person can contract out of a constitutional right; or to what extent such an agreement would be enforced."[151] Henchy J. said that arrangements such as the one in this case could not be constitutionally impeached because they did not amount to coercion; here the matter was one of contract and there was no compulsion, or coercion, and no interference with the citizen's free choice. He left open the question of compatibility with the Constitution of "ensur(ing) by contract that a man must remain indefinitely a member of a particular union ...".[152]

Free Choice of Union

The primary emphasis of ILO Convention Number 87 is the free choice of union. Thus its first substantive provision, Article 2, stipulates that "[w]orkers and employers, without distinction whatsoever, shall have the right to establish and, subject only to the rules of the organisation concerned, to join organisations of their own choosing without previous authorisation." Freedom of choice is emphasised in the European Convention by Article 11 defining the right to form and to join trade unions as being for the "protection of (ones) interests" and in Article 14 by proscribing discrimination on various grounds in the exercise of that freedom; similarly with the UN Covenant.

State Restrictions on Choice

The Constitution's guarantee of the right "to form ... unions" has been interpreted as embracing an extensive freedom of choice. The broadest affirmation of freedom is that made in *National Union of Railwaymen v. Sullivan*,[153] where Part III (sections 18–40) of the Trade Union Act 1941, was struck down as unconstitutional. Those provisions sought to deal with the assumed undue proliferation of trade unions in Ireland by introducing a variant of the United States "majority union represents everybody" system. A union which organised the majority of workers of a particular class, on application to a Tribunal, could obtain the exclusive right to organise those workers. Granting this right could not be contested until at least five years after the

---

[151] *Id.* at pp.40–41.
[152] *Id.* at p.48.
[153] [1947] I.R. 77.

Tribunal's determination and, during that period, no other union could accept into membership workers in the class in question. But the Act did not stipulate that the majority union should have sole bargaining rights for that class, although the mechanism would tend to encourage exclusive representation, in that other unions were prevented from recruiting new members.

The entire Part III was held to be invalid because it was a blanket prohibition against employees joining the trade union of their choice; it gave them the option of either joining the majority union or else not joining any trade union. As Murnaghan J. put it:

> "Both logically and practically, to deprive a person of the choice of the persons with whom he will associate, is not a control of the exercise of the right of association, but a denial of the right altogether .... The (Act) does not prohibit all association, but it purports to limit the right of the citizen to join one or more prescribed associations .... Any such limitation does undoubtedly deprive the citizen of a free choice of the persons with whom he shall associate .... The Constitution states the right of the citizens to form associations or unions in an emphatic way, and it seems impossible to harmonise this language with a law which prohibits the forming of associations and unions, and allows the citizen only to join prescribed associations and unions."[154]

This decision has been criticised and, in the light of *Murphy v. Stewart*,[155] discussed below, the court today might uphold a system similar to that established in 1941. It should not be overlooked, however, that the law as stated in the *NUR* judgment is in accord with Ireland's international legal obligations.

Employer Restrictions on Choice

Dismissing a worker for joining a licensed trade union, other than one approved by the employer, would ordinarily be in breach of the Unfair Dismissals Acts 1977-93, and also would contravene the constitutional guarantee. But more subtle forms of pressure to join a particular union may not contravene those Acts nor fall within the constitutional proscription. One method of employers significantly influencing workers' choice was upheld in *Abbott v. Irish Transport & General Workers Union*,[156] *viz.* refusing to negotiate with the union of which they are members and, instead, recognising another genuine licensed union. According to McWilliam J., "an employer is not prevented

---

[154] *Id.* at p.102.
[155] [1973] I.R. 77; *infra*, p.808.
[156] Unreported, High Court, McWilliam J., December 2, 1980.

from exercising his legal rights merely because this may encourage a workman to join a particular union," which is part of a broader principle that "consideration may be given to the circumstance that there is no right to the advantages which would normally flow from the full enjoyment of a constitutional right."[157]

One of the most effective restrictions that can be imposed on the free choice of union is for employers to induce their workforce to join what are known as "company unions," i.e. unions over which the employer in fact exercises a decisive influence. Significant State tolerance for these unions contravenes Article 2(2) of ILO Convention Number 98, which states that "acts which are designed to promote the establishment of workers' organisations under the domination of employers or employers' organisations, or to support workers' organisations by financial or other means, with the object of placing such organisations under the control of employers or employers' organisations, shall be deemed to constitute acts of interference within the meaning of this Article."

Union Restrictions on Choice

Restrictions on the free choice of union imposed by trade unions include closed shop agreements and the sanction of expulsion for joining rival organisations. In addition, the Irish Congress of Trade Unions' (which is the national federation of nearly all the trade unions in the country) "no poaching" rules are a formidable obstacle to free choice. Of most significance are Congress' rules 47(c) and (d). Under (d), an affiliated union may not organise, or accept into membership, workers in a "negotiating unit" where another Congress affiliate represents a majority, or a "substantial proportion," of the workforce in that unit, except where it has the latter union's consent. And under (c), an affiliate is not allowed to enrol a member of another affiliate who is under discipline, engaged in a "trade dispute" or is in arrears with contributions, without the latter union's consent. Additionally, there is rule 47(b) which requires that an affiliate be consulted before another Congress union accepts one of its members or ex-members into membership. Congress has machinery to ensure compliance with these rules.

The status of these, in the light of the Constitution's guarantee of free choice of union, has been raised on a number of occasions, principally in *Murphy v. Stewart*[158] and in the *Abbott* case.[159] Because of the useful function they fulfil, in preventing many inter-union disputes from erupting into strike action, courts are reluctant to strike down these rules. At the same time, the

---

[157] *Id.* at pp.11 and 9.
[158] [1973] I.R. 77, *infra*, p.808.
[159] *Supra*, p.801.

decision in the *NUR* case[160] stands. On one level, these rules and Part III of the Trade Union Act 1941, are easily distinguishable. Part III was a direct imposition by the State of restrictions on choice while the Congress' rules are merely private contracts and, in addition, would seem to have no direct legal force.[161] The trouble with this analysis is that the courts have rejected a narrow "state action" doctrine of constitutional obligation[162] and in addition, in *McGee v. Attorney General*,[163] it was stated that, in evaluating the constitutional status of laws, what matters is the actual social results they bring about and not the narrow legal position that follows from the impugned provision's terms.

Both the above-mentioned cases were actions by workers against trade unions, of which they were or recently had been members, which refused to consent to their transfer to rival unions, those refusals being upheld by the Congress' disputes committee as being in accordance with rule 47(d) on "negotiating units." The background to *Murphy v. Stewart* was that the disputes committee had said that the acceptance of transfers in the industry in question (car assembly), without the consent of the ex-member's trade union, appeared to be contrary to good trade union practice. Subsequently, the defendant trade union stated that it would never consent to its members, who were employed in the establishment where the plaintiff worked, joining another union. Nevertheless, the plaintiff sought to join another union but his application to the defendant union, of which he had been a member, for consent to transfer was refused. He thereupon claimed a declaration that the defendant's refusal of consent to his proposed joining another union was unconstitutional and an order that consent be granted. Expressing the plaintiff's dilemma as "in order to continue in his present or similar employment (he) must remain a member of the defendant union for the rest of his life,"[164] Murnaghan J. gave judgment for him, but for reasons that are far from clear. Indeed, the dilemma referred to was not quite as stark as posed because, legally in any case, the plaintiff could have refrained from being a member of any trade union whatsoever, or he could have joined a non-Congress-affiliated trade union. The Supreme Court, in a judgment by Walsh J., ruled in favour of the defendants.

Two somewhat separate questions were considered by the court. One concerned the position of the trade union that the plaintiff sought to join; it was held that a union is free to reject any applicant for membership rather than violate the Congress rules and jeopardise its affiliation to Congress.[165] The other issue was the extent to which a union can withhold its consent to the transfer of a member. Here, much depends on whether the union contains in

---

[160] [1947] I.R. 77, *supra*, p.805.
[161] *Spring v. National Ass'n Stevedores & Dockers* [1956] 1 W.L.R. 585.
[162] *Infra*, ch.28.
[163] [1974] I.R. 284.
[164] [1973] I.R. 284.
[165] *Id.* at p.119.

its rules provisions regarding transfers. Where the rule exists, then the union may not act in breach of it, although Walsh J. conceded that the union retains an extensive margin of interpretation in applying such a rule: it "would be entitled to have a view which might objectively be regarded as unreasonable when, in having such opinion, it is not in breach of its own rules."[166] But he did not say what the position was where, as with many unions, there are no provisions in the rules about transfers, apart from stating that any member is entitled to apply to the courts to require their licensed union to insert in the rules provisions regarding the "cesser of membership," as is required by law.[167] It therefore appears that, in the absence of such a rule, a court will not interfere with refusals of consent to transfer from one union to another except where the refusal is actuated only by unlawful motives. But this does not mean that Congress-affiliated unions are at liberty to stifle free choice of union because any refusal of consent to transfer members can be reviewed by Congress' disputes committee in the light of "good trade union practice." On the facts it was concluded that there was "nothing in the circumstances of the present case (that) would warrant the Court in holding that the (defendant's) consent was unreasonably withheld."[168] The implicit broad *ratio decidendi* of the case is that, apart from where a union contravenes its own rules regarding cesser of membership, the fundamental right to free choice of union is subject to the dictates of good trade union practice as determined by Congress under its present procedures.

The constitutional issue was raised again in *Abbott v. ITGWU*,[169] where the Congress' disputes committee had ruled that Amalgamated should not organise and represent workers, who previously had been members of and were represented by the ITGWU, nor accept those workers into its membership. But unlike what happened in *Murphy v. Stewart*, Amalgamated chose to flout the Congress rule by accepting the ex-ITGWU members into its membership and seeking to negotiate on their behalf. The plaintiffs' claim was for an order restraining the ITGWU from interfering with their "effective" freedom of choice by seeking to compel the employer not to negotiate with Amalgamated. It was held, following *Murphy v. Stewart*, that since a refusal to give consent to a transfer of membership ordinarily did not infringe a person's constitutional right to free choice of union, it accordingly, "seems to follow that a refusal to give consent under (the present) circumstances cannot be considered to infringe the constitutional right ...".[170] In other words, since Amalgamated took the plaintiffs into its membership, they could not complain that their freedom to join Amalgamated had been perceptibly interfered with. And in the absence

---

[166] *Ibid.*
[167] *Ibid.*
[168] *Id.* at p.119.
[169] Unreported, High Court, McWilliam J., December 2, 1980.
[170] At p.12.

of a constitutional duty on employers to bargain with trade unions, a union such as the ITGWU here is entitled to claim rights of sole representation for employees and to "endeavour to obtain better terms for its members than those obtained by any other union …."[171]

Industrial Action

The Constitution does not refer to the principal forms of industrial action, the strike and the lock-out. Yet it can be accepted that freedom to resort to these measures is to some extent guaranteed. A right to lock-out could be founded on the Article 40.3 property right. A right to strike could have as its foundation trade union freedom, since often it is essential to strike in order to assert that freedom and also it would be a necessary corollary to any right to lock-out. On a number of occasions judges have referred to a right to strike but they have not indicated what its contents are, apart from saying that "(t)he State cannot by its laws compel (workers to work) when they do not wish to do so," but that it "should protect their right to (work) when they wish to do so and others want to prevent them."[172] An implied constitutionally guaranteed right to strike, therefore, may be confined to prohibiting the State from imposing sweeping restrictions on resorting to strikes. Or it may go further and mean, for instance, that employers should not victimise strikers or their leaders who return to work, or alternatively, that the employment relationship is not terminated by the very fact of the strike taking place, or alternatively again, that the employer may not use strike-breakers, or may use them only in certain circumstances.

Strike action is often accompanied by picketing; those on strike or their sympathisers picket the employer's premises or some other establishment that is connected with the dispute. While picketing, in principle, is not contrary to the common law,[173] most forms of picketing are regarded as unlawful nuisances.[174] The courts take the view that while "it may perhaps be possible to picket a premises so discreetly and unobtrusively as not to (be unlawful), picketing as ordinarily conducted (does not) fall within this category" for it "interferes very seriously with the user and enjoyment of the premises picketed and amounts to a common law nuisance …".[175] Whether the constitutional guarantee of freedom of assembly grants a right to picket that is more extensive than the right under the common law does not appear to have been examined by the courts. But provided this guarantee applies to economic, as opposed to ideologically-motivated, demonstrations, the answer would seem to be in the

---

[171] At p.14.
[172] *Crowley v. Ireland* [1980] I.R. 102 at p.130.
[173] *Hubbard v. Pitt* [1976] 1 Q.B. 142.
[174] *J. Lyons & Son v. Wilkins* [1896] 1 Ch. 255, 811.
[175] *Educational Co. of Ireland Ltd v. Fitzpatrick (No.2)* [1961] I.R. 345 at pp.391 and 389.

affirmative because private nuisance is not one of the express qualifications in Article 40.6.ii. In the context of a "trade dispute," section 11 of the Industrial Relations Act 1990 makes lawful peaceful picketing for the purposes of conveying information or persuasion.

Industrial action also can contravene fundamental rights and accordingly be unconstitutional, as was held to have been the case in the *Educational Co. (No.2)* case[176] and in *Murtagh Properties Ltd. v. Cleary*.[177] In *Crowley v. Ireland*,[178] it was held that the concerted refusal to enrol certain children in primary schools, which was a form of "blacking," was in the circumstances an infringement of their right to education under Article 42.4 of the Constitution. There was a dispute between the teachers' union, the Irish National Teachers Organisation, and a parish priest, in his capacity as manager of a national school, over his appointment of a school principal. In consequence, all but one of the teachers at that school withdrew their services and, on the direction of their union, teachers at schools in neighbouring parishes refused to enrol the children who attended that school. McMahon J. accepted for the purpose of the argument that, in going on strike, the teachers were exercising a constitutional right "to work or not work, or to choose the conditions under which they would work."[179] Nevertheless, he enjoined the union's direction that the children should not be enrolled in neighbouring schools on the grounds that "[t[he character of an act depends on the circumstances in which it is done and the exercise of a constitutional right for the purpose of infringing the constitutional rights of others is an abuse of that right. ... The teachers who refused to enrol the school children in adjoining schools did not act primarily for the purpose of exercising a right to (strike). (T)heir purpose was to deprive (those) children of their constitutional right. Therefore, it is actionable at the suit of the children ...".[180] That is to say, the striking teachers' dominant objective was to prevent the children there from getting any national school education. But taking industrial action, with this objective, is unlawful because of the constitutional guarantee that "(t)he State shall provide for free primary education ...". It does not appear to have been argued that this guarantee is addressed only to the State and not to private organisations and individuals, such as trade unions and their members.

The *Educational Co. (No.2)*, the *Murtagh Properties* and the *Crowley* cases pose a difficult question of principle, which is how the constitutional right to resort to industrial action is to be reconciled with other constitutional rights. Behind this issue of principle lies the very practical one of whether the compromise, reached a hundred years ago in the Trade Disputes Act 1906, is

---

[176] *Id.*; *supra*, p.802.
[177] [1972] I.R. 330; *supra*, p.796.
[178] [1980] I.R. 102.
[179] *Id.* at p.110.
[180] *Ibid.*

to continue, or is it to be significantly modified by the courts by way of constitutional adjudication. A major issue that remains to be resolved is the relationship between the legal freedom to strike and the constitutional rights to property and to work. Employers' rights to land, tangible property and the performance of contractual obligations appear to be adequately protected by the common law and by statute. But if the Article 40.3.2 property guarantee includes some autonomy over business decisions,[181] then virtually all industrial action clashes with that freedom. Similarly with the right to work; industrial action about demarcation, or in order to impose a compulsory retirement age or a minimum age of entry into an occupation, clashes with the right to work.

Internal Union Affairs

Trade unions and employers' associations are treated by the law as essentially private and voluntary associations, and their internal administration is largely in their own hands. Extensive internal autonomy is the principle underlying the international standards. Thus Article 3 of ILO Convention Number 87 on Freedom of Association stipulates that:

(1) Workers' and employers' organisations shall have the right to draw up their constitutions and rules, to elect their representatives in full freedom, to organise their administration and activities and to formulate their programmes.

(2) The public authorities shall refrain from any interference which would restrict this right or impede the lawful exercise thereof."

Statutes impose few minimum standards for unions' internal governance. The Trade Union Acts 1941-1975 require that registered unions provide for a small number of matters in their rule books and establish a very limited amount of administrative supervision of their activities. Some additional obligations are imposed by the Industrial Relations Acts 1946–2001 on licensed union and unions' political expenditure must conform to the Trade Union Act 1913.

Apart altogether from purely legal considerations, courts are somewhat reluctant to intervene in controversies concerning internal union administration, partly on account of judges' distaste of being involved in the "dismal swamp" of ideological and esoteric controversies, their fear of being landed with "hot potatoes," where whatever solution is imposed would raise intense resentment among a significant section of the membership, and their preference for the "living tree" of associated autonomy. The principal exceptions to this pattern

---

[181] *Re Employment Equality Bill, 1996* [1997] 2 I.R. 321 at pp.366–368. *Cf.* the *Codetermination* case, 50 BVerfGE 290 (1979).

are disciplinary issues, where unions can exercise some stranglehold over the livelihood of individual members, and disputes concerning union property.

Trade unions possess a wide degree of autonomy in determining the broad qualifications for membership. It has been held that, apart from constitutional considerations, eligibility for membership rules will not be set aside by the courts merely because they are unfair or unreasonable.[182] In *Murphy v. Stewart*[183] however, the Supreme Court suggested that criteria for admission that unduly impinges upon the right to work might be struck down. Walsh J. observed that "[t]he question of whether [the right to work] is being infringed or not must depend upon the particular circumstances of any given case; if the right to work was reserved exclusively to members of a trade union which held a monopoly in this field and the trade union was abusing the monopoly in such a way as to effectively prevent the exercise of a person's constitutional right to work, the question of compelling that union to accept the person concerned into membership (or, indeed, of breaking the monopoly) would fall to be considered for the purpose of vindicating the right to work."[184]

Following *Murtagh Properties Ltd. v. Cleary*,[185] it may be that eligibility rules that discriminate on the grounds of sex, or perhaps on arbitrary grounds such as race, colour, religion *etc.*, are unconstitutional and contrary to public policy. In any event, admissions criteria that discriminate on a variety of grounds are proscribed by the Employment Equality Act 1998. Additionally, the Trade Union Act 1913, provides that making "contribution[s] to the political fund ... shall not be made a condition for admission ...".[186]

---

[182] *Faramus v. Film Artists Ass'n* [1964] A.C. 925.
[183] [1973] I.R. 97.
[184] *Id.* at p.117.
[185] [1972] I.R. 330.
[186] S.3(1)(b).

CHAPTER 27

Educational and Social Welfare Rights

The various fundamental or human rights provisions that have been considered up to now mostly concern prohibitions against government (principally) acting in a particular manner, such as interfering with personal liberty, suppressing freedom of expression or association and discriminating unfairly. Some of the rights considered, however, require government to take certain positive steps as opposed to merely refraining from acting in some fashion, most notably Article 40.3 (life, person, good name and property, and life of the unborn), 40.1 (equality) and 44.2.1 (religious freedom).[1] Where government action would first require legislation to be enacted, it is inconceivable that the courts would order the legislature to pass the requisite laws; dictating to the Oireachtas what it ought to do, as opposed to striking down laws, would not accord with the constitutional separation of powers. Moreover, the High Court's explicit authority under the Constitution is to declare that laws which are repugnant to the Constitution are invalid and Article 15.4.1 enjoins the Oireachtas not to enact any laws the provisions of which would contravene the Constitution. It is only in the most exceptional circumstances that the courts would direct the Government or a Minister to institute programmes that involve considerable advance planning and funding.[2] But there does not appear to be any reason why, in an appropriate case, a court cannot in principle make a declaration that the Government's failure to have enacted a law contravenes a person's constitutional rights.

A distinction between the rights considered up to now and those addressed in this chapter is that those previous rights do not call for significant Governmental intervention and public expenditure in order to implement its constitutional obligations. Providing legal aid in criminal and in certain other types of case is the right that carries the most obvious price tag. Article 41.2 envisages at minimum the payment of maternity and child benefit to mothers who choose to stay at home in order to rear their children. Making many other rights fully effective requires incidental public expenditure and may even

---

[1] See generally, Currie, "Positive and Negative Constitutional Rights", 53 *U. Chicago L. Rev.* 864 (1986) and R. Alexy, *A Theory of Constitutional Rights* (2002, trans. J. Rivers), Chap.9.

[2] *T.D. v. Minister for Education* [2001] 4 I.R. 259; *infra*, p.897.

impose costs on private individuals. But the rights being considered in this chapter are to things which a person could obtain from other private individuals if only he had sufficient financial means and there were sufficient offers in the market place. These rights call for considerable direct public expenditure, such as on providing educational services, social security and social welfare benefits, and adequate health care and housing for those in need of it.

EDUCATION

Article 42 of the Constitution is headed "Education" and its main emphasis is on the control that parents have over their children's education.[3] Article 42.4 deals with education by guaranteeing free primary education to all and stating an intention to support private education; that "[t]he State shall provide for free primary education and shall endeavour to supplement and give reasonable aid to private and corporate educational initiative and, when the public good requires it, provide other educational facilities or institutions with due regard, however, for the rights of parents, especially in the matter of religious and moral formation." This guarantee complements the State's authority, acknowledged in *School Attendance Bill 1942, Re*[4] to require that all children be given a certain minimum education, which may be provided by the parents themselves but which most parents leave to the national primary school system to provide. Article 2 of the European Convention's First Protocol states that "[n]o person shall be denied the right to education" and this right is proclaimed in the European Social Charter,[5] in the UN Covenant on Economic, Social and Cultural Rights[6] and in the UN Convention on the Rights of the Child.[7] Constitutions of every state in the US contain an education clause in one form or another. As long ago as 1777, the children of Vermont benefited from the stipulation that "a school or schools shall be established in each town by the legislature for the convenient instruction of youth";[8] the Massachusetts Constitution of 1780 contains a similar provision.[9] Since 1868 the people of North Carolina have enjoyed the constitutional "privilege of education and ... the duty of the State to guard and maintain that right",[10] which has been held to embrace secondary as well as primary education.

---

[3] *Supra*, p.698.
[4] [1943] I.R. 344.
[5] October 18, 1961, 529 UNTS 89, Art.10 (vocational training).
[6] December 16, 1966, 993 UNTS 3, Arts.13 and 14.
[7] November 20 1989, 1577 UNTS 3, Arts. 28 and 29.
[8] ch.2, s.40; *cf. Brigham v. State of Vermont*, 692A and 384 (1997).
[9] Part II,Ch.V, s.2; *cf. McDuffy v. Superintendent of Schools*, 653 N.E. 2d 1088 (1995).
[10] Art. 1 s. 15; *Leandro v. State of North Carolina*, 488 S.E. 2d. 249 (1997).

Primary, secondary, vocational and third level education is financed overwhelmingly by the State.[11] The great majority of young children attend free primary schools, but a significant minority of older children attend fee paying secondary schools. In 1995, universities in the State ceased charging fees but subsequently introduced charges that are not radically different from fees, although the sums in question bear no real relationship to the actual cost of providing the education in those institutions.

Although much of Article 42.4 of the Constitution comprises aspiration, it commences with a specific and unqualified guarantee, that the State "shall provide for free primary education ...". This is the only constitutional provision that calls for extensive public expenditure on a social service – the provision of whatever facilities communities need so that their children can obtain primary education. As was emphasised by Murray J. in *Sinnott v. Minster for Education*,[12] which concerned the entitlement of autistic persons to education, the obligation here is "unique in the extent to which it circumscribes the discretion which the organs of State, government and Oireachtas, normally enjoy under the Constitution as to the allocation of national resources."[13]

It was reiterated there that any consideration of the extent of the obligation imposed by Article 42.4 should also not overlook its context, where the emphasis is on parental freedom of choice. As stated by Hardiman J., "[s]ince a child will not himself or herself be capable of making and acting upon decisions as to its own education, these decisions must be made by some person or agency on its behalf. In practice, this could only be a parent or a public body of some sort. The Article accords a primacy to the parent to make his own provision according to his means, to join with others for the purpose of providing private or corporate education, or to avail of State services. Even if the latter option is taken, parental rights must be given due regard."[14]

One aspect of this emphasis is that the State is not obliged to provide the education itself; its duty is to provide what facilities are necessary to ensure that children obtain an education. As O'Higgins C.J. explained in *Crowley v. Ireland*,[15] which concerned problems arising from a national teachers' strike:

> "This Article was intended to avoid imposing a mandatory obligation on the State directly to provide free primary education. Such, if imposed, might have led to the provision of free primary education in exclusively State schools. Rather it was intended that the State should ensure by the arrangements it made that free primary education would be provided ... (i.e.) to see that machinery exists under which and in accordance with

---

[11] See generally, D. Glendenning, *Education and the Law* (1999).
[12] [2001] 2 I.R. 545.
[13] *Id.* at p.681.
[14] *Id.* at p.689.
[15] [1980] I.R. 102.

which (free primary) education is in fact provided. The State discharges this obligation by paying teachers in the national schools owned by the Churches, by making grants available for renovation, repair and, at times, building of national schools, by paying for heating and for school books and by the provision of a proper curriculum and appropriate supervision. It is only when such assistance to the church schools is not possible, or cannot succeed in providing what is required, that the State must act directly to do so."[16]

Exactly what this minimum primary education should consist of is not defined nor indicated and, in determining whether the State has met its obligations under this Article, a considerable amount of deference is shown towards what arrangements the State has devised. As a North Carolina judge, dealing with a similar clause in that State's Constitution put it, "the administration of the public schools of the State is best left to the legislative and executive branches of government."[17] Hardiman J. pointed out in the *Sinnott* case that:

"The duty to provide for free primary education is a complex one, involving enormous annual expense, and requiring for its implementation the taking and constant reviewing of decisions on policy both by the legislature and by the executive. The content of the education provided for, the standard to which that content is to be taught, the mode of teaching, the age at which it is to commence and end, and many other matters must be decided upon and provided for.

Moreover, the enormous expense of educational provision must be provided in the manner laid down by the Constitution. That is to say, monies must be provided under legislation giving effect to the annual financial resolutions. The appropriation of such monies to publicly provided or supported education can only be secured in accordance with Article 17.2 ... of the Constitution. ...

"[T]he constitutional requirements for the conduct of public business, and in particular the expenditure of public monies, as exemplified in this Article and other provisions to be considered later, emphasise that the duty imposed by Article 42 must be discharged in a manner approved by the legislature on the recommendation of the executive. It is true that neither of these organs of government are in a position to disregard a constitutional duty and that the courts have powers and duties in the unlikely event of such disregard. But, excepting that extreme situation, the duty imposed by Article 42 is a duty to be discharged in the manner endorsed by the legislature and executive who must necessarily have a

---

[16] *Id.* at pp.122–123.
[17] *Supra*, n.10.

wide measure of discretion having regard to available resources and having regard to policy considerations of which they must be the judges."[18]

Age

Since 2001, primary education has been compulsory up to sixteen years of age; before then the age limit was fifteen and previously fourteen. The main issue in the appeal in *Sinnott* was to whom was the duty owed; it had been conceded by the State (following a finding against it in the High Court) that its virtually non-existent provisions for educating the first-named plaintiff, who was autistic for most of his life, did not meet the requisite standard. It was held that the obligation here was owed to him only and not to his mother, the other plaintiff. Further, for mentally handicapped persons, the obligation lasts until they are eighteen years of age, when legally they cease to be children and become adults. Had those who framed the Constitution intended that the obligation should last for so long as any individual needs primary education, surely they would have so provided in express terms, and the historical as well as textual context indicated that the intended beneficiaries of the duty were children and not adults. Article 1 of the UN Convention on the Rights of the Child defines a child as "every human being below the age of eighteen years unless under the law applicable to the child, majority is attained earlier." In view of this, the State's constitutional obligation here was held to cease once the person reaches eighteen, no matter how deficient the provision had been prior to then. Keane C.J. dissented on this aspect of the case, on the grounds that "[n]o principled basis exists either in law or in the evidence ... that a person in [that plaintiff's] position ceases to be in need of primary education at age 18, at age 22 or at any age in the future which can now be identified with any precision."[19]

Equality

Because the national public school system is funded by central government rather than local taxation, and the allocation of funding to schools is on a relatively uniform basis nationally, the Irish courts have not had to consider the question of unequal educational provision for children in similar circumstances. However, in the *Sinnott* case, where there had been practically no provision for children with autistic conditions, which was held to contravene Article 42.4, Denham J. was of the view that the plaintiffs there had also been invidiously discriminated against, contrary to Article 40.1. In view of the State's

---

[18] [2001] 2 I.R. 545 at p.660.
[19] *Id.* at p.639.

concession that it had been in breach of Article 42.4 with regard to the boy in question, Denham J. concluded that it had discriminated against his mother's "duty and role, as opposed to that of the mother of a child of average intelligence, in a manner that was unjust and invidious."[20] None of the other judges addressed the argument made for this proposition, other than to find that the duty under Article 42.4 is owed only to the child and not to the parent.

Content

What kind of educational provision for children with an autistic condition is required by Article 42.4 was not determined by the Supreme Court in *Sinnott*, in view of the concession. In a previous case dealing with this issue, *O'Donoghue v. Minister for Health*,[21] although the State appealed to that court, it then withdrew its appeal and settled the dispute. O'Hanlon J. there held that Article 42.4 requires that reasonable provision must be made in accordance with the particular needs of each child, pointing out that in many countries special provision was being made for autistic and other handicapped children, that since 1975 legislation was enacted in the US to this very end and that also in 1975 the UN General Assembly adopted a resolution, declaring the rights of disabled persons to education.[22] He rejected the contention that the child there and other comparable autistic children are un-educable; all of the evidence was to the contrary. Consequently, he concluded:

> "There is a constitutional obligation imposed on the State by ... Article 42. s. 4 ... to provide for free basic elementary education of all children and that this involves giving each child such advice, instruction and teaching as will enable him or her to make the best possible use of his or her inherent and potential capacities, physical, mental and moral, however limited these capacities may be. Or, to borrow the language of the United Nations Convention and Resolution of the General Assembly – 'such education as will be conducive to the child's achieving the fullest possible social integration and individual development; such education as will enable the child to develop his or her capabilities and skills to the maximum and will hasten the process of social integration and reintegration'.
>
> This process will work differently for each child, according to the child's own natural gifts, or lack thereof. In the case of the child who is deaf, dumb, blind, or otherwise physically or mentally handicapped, a completely different programme of education has to be adopted and a

---

[20] *Id.* at p.660.
[21] [1996] 2 I.R. 20.
[22] *Id.* at p.56.

completely different rate of progress has to be taken for granted, than would be regarded as appropriate for a child suffering from no such handicap. ...

Admittedly, it is only in the last few decades that research into the problems of the severely and profoundly physically and mentally handicapped has led to positive findings that education in a formal setting, involving schools and teachers, educational equipment of many kinds, and integration as far as possible in the conventional school environment, can be of real benefit to children thus handicapped. But once that has been established – and my conclusion is that it has been established on a worldwide basis for many years past – then it appears to me that it gives rise to a constitutional obligation on the part of the State to respond to such findings by providing for free primary education for this group of children in as full and positive a manner as it has done for all other children in the community."[23]

This reasoning was endorsed by Barr J. in the *Sinnott* case and, while it was not put in issue in the State's appeal there, Keane C.J. expressed the view that it "is correct"[24] and several other judges indicated their approval. As put by Murray J., "with greater insight into the nature of people's handicaps, the evolution of teaching methods, new *curricula* as well as new tools of education there is no doubt that the nature and content of primary education must be defined in contemporary circumstances. That means where children are capable of benefiting from primary education (however its content is defined) the State have an obligation to ensure that it is provided free to children who can benefit from it including those who suffer from severe mental or physical handicap."[25]

Where significant educational provision is being made by the State, how closely must it be tailored to the preferences of groups of parents or of individual parents? It has never been seriously suggested that free primary education must be specially designed to any unique desires of particular parents or children. In *O'Shiel v. Minister for Education*,[26] parents established their own school in Co. Clare, where teaching was based on what is known as the "Steiner" system or "Waldorf Schools" system, an approach to education devised in Bavaria in the 1920s. There were originally over 100 pupils at this school, at which five full time teachers were employed. Recognition and with it State funding for the school was sought by the parents but was refused, principally because Irish was not being taught and only one of the teachers had the qualifications laid down for recognition by the Minister. In view of Article 44's overall emphasis on parental freedom of choice, Laffoy rejected

---

[23] *Id.* at pp.65–66.
[24] [2001] 2 I.R. at 545 at p.628.
[25] *Id.* at p.682.
[26] [1999] 2 I.R. 321.

the contention that the State could stipulate what it regarded as appropriate for national schools and refuse to fund schools that did not function in that manner. Such a stance "would pervert the clear intent of the Constitution to interpret [its] obligation as merely obliging [it] to fund a single system of primary education which is on offer to parents on a 'take it or leave it' basis."[27] On the other hand, parental freedom of choice "does not mean that the State must accede to an application for financial aid for any group of parents who are united in their choice of primary education which establishes that what is being provided by it is education, that is being provided in a school and that it meets a standard of what can reasonably be defined as primary education ...".[28]

What is constitutionally required is somewhere in between these extremes; the State "must take account of the parental freedom of choice" and its approach "must be based on arrangements which have a rational foundation and prescribe proper criteria for eligibility ...".[29] While account must be taken of budgetary constraints, they are not always determinative and, in any event, those were not an issue there. Because Irish is the first national language under the Constitution, Laffoy J. found that requiring it to be taught was a reasonable prerequisite for State recognition and funding. She had considerable difficulty with the teacher qualifications requirement because the system of training in the State at the time was denominational, it operated under a general ethos not shared by the parents there and, additionally, did not train the Steiner approach to pedagogy. In the event, she was not persuaded that the existing requirements in this regard were so onerous as to be unconstitutional but exhorted "a more searching and pro-active approach" from the State to find a solution,[30] which during the hearing the State indicated would be forthcoming if the parents reapplied for recognition.

In the earliest of the cases concerning Article 42.4, *Crowley v. Ireland*,[31] the issue was what are the State's obligations when national teachers go on strike. It arose out of a protracted industrial dispute between the Irish National Teachers Organisation (INTO) and the management of a national school in Co. Cork. Responding to what they regarded as nepotism in appointing the school's principal, the INTO brought its members, who taught there, out on strike and instructed its members in neighbouring schools not to teach any children who previously had been taught at the school. The plaintiffs were children who had been attending this school but, because of the INTO strike and "blacking", had received no primary education for more than a year. They claimed that their constitutional rights under Article 42.4 had been contravened by the INTO and by Minister for Education.

---

[27] *Id.* at p.347.
[28] *Ibid.*
[29] *Id.* at p.348.
[30] *Id.* at p.358.
[31] [1980] I.R. 102.

Their contention that, in the circumstances, the State was in breach of its obligation under this clause was rejected by the Supreme Court. Previously, McWilliam J. had ruled that, since the children could not be taught at the school where the strike was taking place, the State was obliged to provide buses and to have them sent to national schools in the adjoining area.[32] At first instance, McMahon J. ruled that the INTO's order to its members, not to teach children who were being bused to nearby schools, contravened their constitutional rights. But by the narrowest of majorities, the Supreme Court overruled him in holding that, in all the circumstances, the State had fulfilled its constitutional obligation. While they disagreed about the precise extent to which the State must go in order to satisfy this clause, all of the judges agreed on the general nature of the State's duty, which is not to provide the education but to provide for education, in the sense of providing the buildings and paying the teachers, providing "the means of transport to the school if this is necessary to avoid hardship"[33] and laying down minimum educational standards. According to Kenny J., who gave the majority judgment, in the circumstances the State had done all that could reasonably be expected of it to safeguard the children's educational rights and, since the teachers were refusing to teach, "(t)he State cannot by laws compel (them) to teach when they do not wish to do so…".[34]

SOCIAL WELFARE

Social welfare rights are concerned with how the State deploys resources in order to assist the economically disadvantaged in various ways, such as by having adequate social security and social welfare systems, and by providing adequate basic health and housing care for everyone in need of it. These rights do not feature in the older constitutional instruments, such as the United States Bill of Rights and the 1789 French Declaration. Nor indeed do they feature in every modern constitution;[35] they are not contained in the Federal German Basic Law nor in the Canadian Charter of Rights and Freedoms, for instance. But social welfare rights are proclaimed in the preamble to the French Constitution of 1947, which has been incorporated into the present Constitution of 1958; health care, medical assistance and social security are guaranteed by the Italian Constitution;[36] housing, health care, food, water and social security

---

[32] Referred to *id.*,p.119.

[33] *Id.* at p.126.

[34] *Id.* at p.130. But damages were awarded against the INTO: *Conway v. Irish National Teachers Organisation* [1991] 2 I.R. 305.

[35] See generally, Glendon, "Rights in Twentieth Century Constitutions", 59 *U. Chicago L. Rev.* 519 (1992).

[36] Arts.32 (health) and 38 (social assistance).

are guaranteed by the South African Constitution.[37] Following on the Great Depression of the 1930s, several states in the US incorporated welfare rights into their constitutions, most notably New York.[38]

This difference between that may be termed civil and political rights, on the one hand, and social welfare rights, on the other, is reflected in international human rights law. At United Nations level, there are two major human rights instruments, the International Covenant on Civil and Political Rights and the International Covenant on Economic, Social and Cultural Rights.[39] At European level, there is the European Convention on Human Rights, which deals with the traditional civil and political rights, and the European Social Charter,[40] which is concerned with social welfare rights. Welfare rights in the Constitution are dealt with principally in Article 45, which sets out "Directive principles of social policy", among which are the following:

> "2(v). The State shall ... direct its policy towards securing (t}hat there may be established on the land in economic security as many families as in the circumstances shall be practicable ....
>
> 4.1. The State pledges itself to safeguard with especial care the economic interests of the weaker sections of the community, and, where necessary, to contribute to the support of the infirm, the widow, the orphan, and the aged.
>
> 4. The State shall endeavour to ensure that the strength and health of workers, men and women, and the tender age of children shall not be abused and that citizens shall not be forced by economic necessity to enter avocations unsuited to their sex, age or strength."

It is debatable whether the aspiration in the Preamble to "prudence, justice and charity", and to assuring "the freedom and dignity of the individual" form the basis for an unenumerated right to some minimum degree of welfare provision. Ireland is a party to the European Social Charter, the UN Covenant on Economic, Social and Cultural Rights, and to several conventions of the International Labour Organisation (ILO) that deal with aspects of welfare, most notably Convention Number 102 on minimum standards of social security.[41]

A variety of contributory and also non-contributory social security cash benefits are provided for in the Social Welfare Acts, for instance in respect of

---

[37] Arts.26 and 27; *cf. Minister of Health v. Treatment Action Campaign*, 13 B.H.R.C. 1 (2002) (S. Africa).

[38] Art. 27.1.3; *cf. Tucker v. Toia*, 371 N.E. 2d. 449 (1977).

[39] *Supra*, n.6. See generally M. Craven, *The International Covenant on Economic, Social and Cultural Rights* (1998).

[40] *Supra*, n.5.

[41] Of June 28, 1952, 210 UNTS 131.

disability, unemployment, sickness, old age, pregnancy and maternity, child support, lone parents.[42] Health Boards are required by the Health Act 1970, to provide several medical, nursing and maternity services to eligible persons.[43] Under the Housing Act 1966 loans or grants are payable by the Minister towards the purchase and maintenance of houses, and housing authorities are charged with the provision of houses for persons who cannot afford to buy them.[44]

Except for education and legal aid, and perhaps maternity and child benefits for stay-at-home mothers, the Supreme Court has indicated that it will not read into the Constitution a duty on the State to provide welfare rights because of institutional and other factors. Reluctance to acknowledge the existence of these rights was first articulated by Costello J. in *O'Reilly v. Limerick Corp.*,[45] where the applicants sought redress under the Housing Act 1966, and insofar as this Act was not applicable, under the Constitution. They were members of the travelling community residing on an unofficial halting site, who sought orders directing that the Corporation should provide them with adequate serviced halting sites and also damages for failure to provide those sites. Their claim under the 1966 Act was rejected. They also claimed that, under Article 40.3.2, the State failed in its obligation to vindicate their human dignity by permitting them to live in conditions without water or sanitary services, for which they now should be compensated. This, it was held, raised the more general question whether "the courts with constitutional propriety [can] adjudicate on an allegation that the organ of Government responsible for the distribution of the nation's wealth have improperly exercised their powers. Or would such an adjudication be an infringement by the courts of the role which the Constitution has conferred on them?"[46]

Costello J. concluded that the answer was no, because these determinations raised questions of "distributive justice" as distinct from "commutative justice." As he explained:

> "The traditional academic distinction which is made between the two different types of justice which should exist in a political community, distributative justice and commutative justice. ... There is an important distinction to be made between the relationship which arises in dealings between individuals (a term which includes dealings between individuals and servants of the State and public authorities) and the relationship which arises between the individual and those in authority in a political

---

[42] See generally, M. Cousins, *Social Welfare Law* (2nd ed., 2002) and G. Whyte, *Social Inclusion and the Legal System: Public Interest Law in Ireland* (2002) Chap.4 on judicial treatment of social welfare issues. Cf. A Van der Mei, *Free Movement of Persons Within the European Community: Cross-Border Acesss to Public Benefits* (2003).

[43] See generally, D. Madden, *Medicine, Ethics and the Law* (2002), Chap.2.

[44] See generally, A. Lyall, *Land Law* (2nd ed., 2002), Chap.28.

[45] [1989] I.L.R.M. 181.

[46] *Id.* at p.193.

community (which for convenience I will call the Government) when goods held in common for the benefit of the entire community (which would nowadays include wealth raised by taxation) fall to be distributed and allocated. Different obligations in justice arise from these different relationships. Distributive justice is concerned with the distribution and allocation of common goods and common burdens. But it cannot be said that any of the goods held in common (or any part of the wealth raised by taxation) belong exclusively to any member of the political community. An obligation in distributive justice is placed on those administering the common stock of goods, the common resource and the wealth held in common which has been raised by taxation, to distribute them and the common wealth fairly and to determine what is due to each individual. But that distribution can only be made by reference to the common good and by those charged with furthering the common good (the Government); it cannot be made by any individual who may claim a share in the common stock and no independent arbitrator, such as a court, can adjudicate on a claim by an individual that he has been deprived of what is his due. This situation is very different in the case of commutative justice. What is due to an individual from another individual (including a public authority) from a relationship arising from their mutual dealings can be ascertained and is due to him exclusively and the precepts of commutative justice will enable an arbitrator such as a court to decide what is properly due should the matter be disputed. This distinction explains why the court has jurisdiction to award damages against the State when a servant of the State for whose activity it is vicariously liable commits a wrong and why it may not get jurisdiction in cases where the claim is for damages based on a failure to distribute adequately in the plaintiffs' favour a portion of the community's wealth."[47]

This analysis was endorsed by the Supreme Court in *Sinnott v. Minister for Education*[48] and in *T.D. v. Minister for Education*.[49] As explained above, *Sinnott* concerned the precise ambit of the duty to provide education, in that instance, to persons with autism. *T.D.* involved the questions of *locus standi* and the appropriate remedy where there has been a contravention by the State of its constitutional obligations. Most of the judges in these two cases expressed agreement with Costello J.'s general approach and analysis. Keane C.J. expressed "the gravest doubts as to whether the courts at any stage should assume the function of declaring what are today frequently described as 'socio-

---

[47] *Id.* at pp.193–194. This analysis is criticised by G. Whyte, *supra*, n.42., Chap.1, and is considered by Alexy, *supra*, n.1, pp.334 *et seq. Cf. R.(Q.) v. Secretary of State*, 14 B.H.R.C. 262 (2003)

[48] [2001] 2 I.R. 545.

[49] [2001] 4 I.R. 259.

economic rights' to be unenumerated rights guaranteed by Article 40."[50] As Murphy J. pointed out, "[t]he absence of any express reference to accommodation, medical treatment or social welfare of any description as a constitutional right in the Constitution as enacted is a matter of significance. The failure to correct that omission in any of the 24 referenda which have taken place since then would suggest a conscious decision to withhold from rights, which are now widely conferred by appropriate legislation, the status of constitutionality in the sense of being rights conferred or recognised by the Constitution."[51] This analysis is reinforced by the inclusion of Article 45 in the Constitution.

"Directive Principles"

Article 45 commences by stating that its provisions merely lay down general guidance for the legislature and they do not provide the basis for striking down laws for being unconstitutional; that "[t]he principles of social policy set forth in this Article are intended for the general guidance of the Oireachtas. The application of those principles in the making of laws shall be the care of the Oireachtas exclusively, and shall not be cognisable by any Court under any of the provisions of this Constitution." Not alone are the courts forbidden from striking down laws on the grounds of inconsistency with these provisions but they are decreed "not ... cognisable by any Court." Precisely to what extent the courts are precluded from considering these principles remains to be resolved.

On several occasions the Supreme Court has referred to this very clause in order to demonstrate that Articles 40-44 and indeed other Articles contain rights that the Oireachtas can be obliged by the courts to respect.[52] On a number of occasions the contents of these principles have been the subject of legal argument before the High Court and have even been the subject of several judgments. Some of these cases concerned the right to work, which is one of the implied rights under Article 40.3, but the judges in those cases also referred to Article 45.2.1, which states that the State shall direct its policy towards ensuring that everybody can earn their livelihood. In one of these instances, *Rogers v. Irish Transport & General Workers Union*,[53] the issue was whether a trade union had acted lawfully in introducing a scheme for compulsory retirement, coupled with pensions, for a category of its members who had

---

[50] *Id.* at p.282.

[51] *Id.* at pp.316–317. Compare *Auton v. Attorney General of British Columbia*, 197 D.L.R. 4th 165 (2001).

[52] *E.g.*, *Buckley v. Attorney General* [1950] I.R. 57 at p.83 and *Byrne v. Ireland* [1972] I.R. 241 at p.265.

[53] Unreported, High Court, Finlay P., March 15, 1978.

reached a specified age. Finlay P. observed that a scheme of this nature was consistent with and did not conflict with the directive principles. In *Landers v. Attorney General*[54] it was contended, unsuccessfully, that provisions of the Prevention of Cruelty to Children Act 1904, were an unconstitutional interference with the plaintiff's right to work because they forbade him from earning money by singing in public houses. Finlay P. concluded that the Act's restriction on young persons working in these circumstances was consistent with the directive principles. In *Attorney General v. Paperlink Ltd.*[55] Costello J. interpreted Article 45.3.1 as signifying "that the social order should not be based on a system in which all the means of production are owned by the State," and as preferring private enterprise to state capitalism.[56] But he rejected the contention that it follows that the State is prohibited by the Constitution from establishing State trading companies or public utilities, or even State monopolies.

In *McGee v. Attorney General*,[57] which concerned contraception, O'Keeffe P. stated that it was clear from the Irish language formulation of Article 45's introductory clause that courts are not entirely precluded from considering this Article when deciding if a party's constitutional rights have been infringed. According to him, the effect of this clause is to preclude consideration of the directive principles only when the issue before the court is whether a provision in some post-1937 Act is unconstitutional; the clause's effect is to "exclude from the cognisance of the Courts only questions as to the attempts of the Oireachtas to have regard to the principles laid down in the course of framing legislation, and it may be argued that it does not preclude consideration of these principles by the Courts when a statute of the Oireachtas is not under review."[58] The *Rogers* case (above) did not directly concern legislation, either of the pre- or post-1937 variety; the legislation in question in the *Landers* and *Paperlink Ltd.* cases were pre-1922 Acts and the legislation that was challenged in the *McGee* case was an Act of the Free State Oireachtas.

The only reported instance in which the directive principles were relied on to support a finding of unconstitutionality is *Murtagh Properties Ltd. v. Cleary*,[59] where the defendants, trade unionists, were picketing an employer's premises in order to prevent women workers from being employed there. It was claimed by the defendants that they were acting lawfully because section 2 of the Trade Disputes Act 1906 gave them a right to picket in furtherance of a trade dispute and that they had such a dispute with their employer. Kenny J. rejected this contention on the grounds that Article 45.2.1 recognises a right

---

[54] (1975) 109 I.L.T.R. 1.
[55] [1984] I.L.R.M. 373.
[56] *Id.* at p.386.
[57] [1974] I.R. 284.
[58] *Id.* at p.291.
[59] [1972] I.R. 330

to work, in the sense that there should not be discrimination between men and women regarding obtaining work. Dealing with the general question of whether the courts can take account of Article 45 in constitutional law cases, Kenny J. observed that the introductory clause "does not mean that the Courts may not have regard to the terms of the Article but that they have no jurisdiction to consider the application of the principles in it in the making of laws. This does not involve the conclusion that the Courts may not take it into consideration when deciding whether a claimed constitutional right exists."[60]

Procedures

Procedures for resolving disputes about entitlement to social security and social welfare benefits are laid down in Part VII (sections 246–276) of the Social Welfare (Consolidation) Act 1993; disputes about eligibility for health services under the Health Act 1970 are resolved in the manner provided for in s. 47 of that Act; there is no equivalent arrangement for housing loans and grants under Part II (sections 13–49) of the Housing Act 1966, or for obtaining local authority housing under Part III (sections 53–62) of this Act. It has been held that, under the separation of powers, decisions to retrospectively disqualify a person for social welfare benefits paid to him over many years and, consequently, to oblige him to repay an equivalent sum, may be made be made by administrative bodies.[61]

Where the procedures to be followed are not laid down in an Act of the Oireachtas, the courts will insist that the procedures used comply with the principles of constitutional justice or natural justice, especially the maxims *nemo iudex in sua causa* and *audi alteram partem.*[62] Where the procedures to be followed are set out in an Act, then if possible the statutory provisions will be interpreted as requiring compliance with these principles. Because, however, most disputes arising under social welfare laws concern how some publicly financed benefit is to be allocated, as contrasted with depriving persons of something of value that they already have (i.e. a "giving" as contrasted with a "taking"), the courts did not insist on quite as high procedural standards in this context as are required when the State sought, for example, to acquire compulsorily an individual's land or deprive someone of their permanent job in the public service. But the courts now insist that applicants for social welfare benefits are given a fair hearing.[63] The Oireachtas is constitutionally competent to stipulate that particular administrative procedures shall not be in accordance with the *nemo iudex* principle to the extent that the body or agency put in

---

[60] *Id.* at pp.335–336.
[61] *Minister for Social Affairs v. Scanlon* [2001] 1 I.R. 64.
[62] See generally, Cousins, *supra*, n.42, ch.18 and Whyte, *supra*, n.42, Chap.4.
[63] *E.g., McLoughlin v. Minister for Social Welfare* [1958] I.R. 1.

charge of administering the benefit in question is itself entitled to resolve disputes about whether those claiming a particular benefit are indeed entitled to it.[64] Whether or to what extent *audi alteram partem* can be excluded entirely by legislation remains to be decided.

Article 6(1) of the European Convention on Human Rights lays down minimum standards of fair procedure when disputes about persons' "civil rights" are being decided; there must be a "fair and public hearing within a reasonable time by an independent and impartial tribunal established by law." One of the contested questions regarding this Article was whether it applies to deciding disputes about entitlements to social welfare benefits. The argument against applying it to such disputes is that the term "civil rights" connotes rights under the ordinary civil law, or private law, and was never intended to include decision-making processes in the administrative or public law field. It nevertheless was held that certain social security benefits can possess a predominantly "private law" character and, in those instances, disputes concerning them must comply with Article 6(1).[65]

Non-Discrimination

Unfair discrimination in the provision of welfare benefits can fall foul of Article 40.1 of the Constitution. So far, however, the courts have not struck down as invalid any provision of a Social Welfare Act because it discriminated unfairly. A challenge on this basis to the payment of deserted spouses' allowance to wives who have been deserted, but not to husbands in equivalent circumstances, was rejected by the Supreme Court.[66] However, provisions in several statutory instruments that discriminated arbitrarily as to who was not entitled to particular benefits have been held to be *ultra vires*.[67] A provision that allowed unmarried cohabiting couples to claim significantly more in benefits than a married couple could in comparable circumstances, was struck down as unfairly discriminating against families.[68] In order to comply with EC Directives, social welfare provisions that discriminated in that manner were repealed, but there remain disparities on that basis that are outside the EC Regime.[69]

---

[64] *O'Brien v. Bord na Mona* [1983] I.R. 255; *supra*, p.746.
[65] *Cf. Adan v. Newham. L.B.C.* [2002] 1 W.L.R. 2120.
[66] *Lowth v. Minister for Social Welfare* [1998] 4 I.R. 321; *supra*, p.382.
[67] See generally, Whyte, *supra*, n.42, Chap.4.
[68] *Hyland v. Minister for Social Welfare* [1989] I.R. 624; *supra*, p.672.
[69] See generally, Cousins, *supra*, n.42, ch.9 and M. Bolger & C. Kimber, *Sex Discrimination Law* (2000), ch.7.

Substantive Entitlements

In view of the Supreme Court's observations in the *Sinnott*[70] and in the *T.D.*[71] cases, endorsing the distinction between "commutative" and "distributive" justice, it is unlikely that the Irish courts would hold that the State should introduce a welfare scheme because some particularly deserving group is in great need of income, health care or housing. Faced with such claims, the courts' most likely response would be that what the plaintiffs seek are essentially political demands and that, under the separation of powers principle, it is not for the courts to order the Oireachtas that costly schemes be introduced. Thus, in *A.D. v. Ireland*,[72] it was held by Carroll J. that the unenumerated right to bodily integrity did not oblige the State to introduce a scheme to compensate victims of criminal offences for the pain and suffering they were forced to endure. Whether there should be a criminal injury compensation system was entirely "a matter of policy for the Government and the Oireachtas ... no matter how desirable such a policy might seem ...".[73]

Nevertheless, the Constitution has been held to oblige the State to embark on one particular public spending scheme, the provision of free legal aid to persons who have no funds and who are being tried on criminal charges.[74] Whether or to what extent Article 41.2 requires making financial provision for mothers, who otherwise are "obliged by economic necessity" to work outside the home, remains to be determined.[75] The most far reaching decision in this general area is that of Geoghegan J. in *F.N. v. Minister for Education*,[76] concerning appropriate provision for children who cannot be controlled by their parents and who are a risk to both themselves and others. On the basis of *obiter dicta* in a case concerning adoption, it was held in *F.N.* that "where there is a child with very special needs which cannot be provided by the parents or guardian there is a constitutional obligation on the State under Article 42.5 ... to cater for those needs in order to vindicate the constitutional rights of the child."[77] How extensive or absolute this duty was did not call for elaboration, other than that in the instant case the State was obliged "to establish as soon as reasonably practical ... suitable arrangements of containment with treatment for that child."[78] No mandatory nor even declaratory order was made there; instead, the proceedings were adjourned to ascertain what measures the State

---

[70] [2001] 2 I.R. 541.
[71] [2001] 4 I.R. 259.
[72] [1994] 1 I.R. 369.
[73] *Id.* at p.373.
[74] *Supra*, p.439.
[75] *Supra*, p.702.
[76] [1995] 1 I.R. 409.
[77] *Id.* at p.416.
[78] *Ibid.*

would take in the light of what had been held to be its duty. Subsequently, several Supreme Court judges indicated that this decision was wrong insofar as it may require the State to detain in secure conditions young persons who have not been convicted of any offence.[79]

Withdrawal or cancellation of welfare benefits, on the other hand, could very well fall under Article 40.3 of the Constitution's property rights clause, especially where the benefit in question contains a significant contributory element. Fennelly J. stated in *Minister for Social Affairs v. Scanlon*[80] that there was no constitutional infirmity with the mechanism for recovering social welfare benefits that had been improperly claimed. But this question was never pursued in argument before the court; it had not been raised in the High Court, no notice had been given to the Attorney General that the point might be made in the Supreme Court and, in view of that court's practice of confining argument to issues that had been dealt with in the court below, it is puzzling why the judge addressed the issue at all and then did so in a manner that would appear to contravene the Constitution's own "single judgment" rule.

---

[79] In the *T.D.* case [2001] 4 I.R. at p.345, Hardiman J.
[80] [2001] 1 I.R. 64.

CHAPTER 28

Non-Government Conduct

Most of the obligations arising under the Constitution are imposed on the State or on some public body, agency or officer. And the vast bulk of constitutional cases concern one party claiming that some governmental entity has acted unconstitutionally. Occasionally, however, it is claimed that some private or non-governmental individual or body has contravened the Constitution, which raises the general question of whether, or to what extent, the Constitution imposes obligations on individuals and organisations who are not part of the State machinery. In other words, when if ever must non-governmental action comply with the constitutional provisions? When if ever does the Constitution have "horizontal" effect? A related question is whether and, if so, to what extent the Constitution imposes obligations on individuals in favour of the State that the State can enforce directly, without any express legislative authority to do so.

National constitutional laws vary considerably in this regard.[1] In the United States there is what is known as the "state action" doctrine,[2] which holds that most provisions in the US Constitution impose obligations only on public officers and bodies, and not on private individuals and entities. If what is alleged to have occurred or is happening does not involve state action, then the Constitution has no bearing on the dispute. A similar approach is taken in Canada[3] and was taken under the interim Constitution of South Africa.[4] By contrast, in France the guarantees contained in the 1789 Declaration and some of the Constitution's provisions have been held to bind private parties.[5] In Germany, where this issue is referred to as the *drittwirkung* question,[6] the courts have adopted a somewhat in-between position. Generally, the Basic Law does not impose duties on private parties. However, the Civil Code contains

---

[1] See generally, R. Alexy, *A Theory of Constitutional Rights* (2002, J. Rivers trans.), pp.351 *et seq*. and D. Friedman & D. Barak-Erez, *Human Rights and Private Law* (2002).

[2] See generally, L. Tribe, *American Constitutional Law* (2nd ed., 1988), Chap.18.

[3] *Retail, Wholesale & Department Store Union v. Dolphin Delivery Ltd*, 33 D.L.R. 4th 174 (1985).

[4] *Du Plesis v. De Klerk* [1997] 1 L.R.C. 637 (S. Africa).

[5] See generally, M. Frangi, *Constitution et Droit Prive* (1992) and Lamy, "Les Principles Constitutionnels dans la Jurisprudence Judiciaire", *Rev. Dr. Public* 781 (2002).

[6] See generally, Alexy, *supra*, n.1, and Markesinis, "Privacy, Freedom of Expression and the Horizontal Effect of the Human Rights Bill: Lessons from Germany", 115 *L.Q.R.* 47 (1999).

two "general clauses," which provide that a "juristic act which is contrary to good morals (*güte Sitten*) is void" and a "person who inflicts damage to another in a manner contrary to good morals is obliged to compensate the other," and the courts often look to the Basic Law to determine what in particular instances is required by *güte Sitten*. South Africa's Constitution squarely addresses this question by stipulating that its Bill of Rights "binds a natural or a juristic person if, and to the extent that, it is applicable, taking into account the nature of the right and the nature of any duty imposed by the right."[7] Perhaps the principal academic debate generated by the British Human Rights Act 1998, is whether or to what extent it has "horizontal effect."[8]

From their very nature, the vast majority of the Constitution's clauses do not impose duties on private individuals and bodies. It is usually in respect of fundamental rights that the non-governmental action question arises. Some employers, professional organisations and other bodies discriminate on the grounds of politics. The press and private police forces occasionally infringe on privacy. At times employers and trade unions interfere with individuals' freedom to work. Conduct such as this can give rise to three related questions, *viz.* is that conduct unlawful, would the courts grant an injunction against that conduct and would the courts award damages in those circumstances? If a constitutional guarantee has been breached, there is no doubt that the courts will fashion an appropriate remedy. The question therefore is whether particular guarantees, such as the right to fair procedures, equality, freedom of expression, religious freedom and the like, apply to what a private individual or body has done or is doing.

Some judges take the view that, as a general rule, the Constitution's fundamental rights provisions impose obligations on private individuals and bodies as well as on the State, public bodies and officials. Costello J. has observed, as regards Article 40.3.1, that "to succeed in a claim that the exercise of a personal right referred to in Article 40.3.1 has been infringed it is not necessary for the plaintiff to establish that the infringer is the State or an organ or agent of the State. Article 40.3.1 certainly imposes obligations and duties on the State. But it also recognises that the citizen enjoys personal rights. So, if within the State the exercise of any of their constitutionally protected rights is invalidly infringed (whether or not the wrongdoer is an agent of the State) a [remedy] may lie."[9] If, however, Article 40.3.1 indeed has horizontal effect, surely a remedy must lie rather than "may lie," on the assumption that a constitutional right has been infringed; at the very minimum an aggrieved plaintiff would be entitled to a declaration to that effect. Other judges have

---

[7] Art.8(2).

[8] *E.g.* Markesinis, *supra*, n.6 and Beyleveld and Pattison, "Horizontal Applicability and Horizontal Effect", 118 *L.Q.R.* 623 (2002).

[9] *Moyne v. Londonderry Port & Harbour C'mrs* [1986] I.R. 299 at p.316.

suggested that some of the fundamental rights obtain only against the State. At least in *McGrath v. Maynooth College*,[10] where it was alleged that the defendant contravened the plaintiff's right to religious freedom, Kenny J. took the view that the prohibition in Article 44.2.3 "is confined to the State" and does not even "apply to bodies which receive public moneys from the State whether they be grants for income or capital purposes."[11]

In disputes between private individuals or bodies, what may seem to be a violation of one person's constitutional rights may very well constitute an assertion of the other's own constitutional rights. An employer's refusal to hire an individual on account of that person's political activities might be viewed as the employer asserting a fundamental right of political freedom and of non-association. In contrast, it cannot be constitutionally permissible for the State to exclude persons from public sector employment on account of their lawful political activities, although there are certain categories of public sector work where the State may be justified in prohibiting those employed there from engaging in certain political action, as is the case with the Defence Forces, the Garda Síochána and parts of the civil service.[12] In the *Maynooth College* case, for instance, even if the plaintiffs' religious freedom was *prima facie* violated, the College could claim that, by virtue of the explicit guarantee of religious autonomy in Article 44.2.5, it was perfectly entitled to discriminate on those grounds.

There are two principal ways in which constitutional rights affect relations between private individuals. One is that effect will not be given to existing common law rights insofar as they are incompatible with the Constitution. Thus, for example, liability for defamation may have to be restricted somewhat in view of the guarantee of free expression. On several occasions directions in wills were disregarded by the courts where they were incompatible with constitutional values. The other way is that certain activities by individuals will be remedied by either granting an injunction to restrain them or an award of damages to compensate for such losses as were caused.

DECLARATION OF INVALIDITY

At common law, contracts that are contrary to public policy will not be enforced and a court could easily find that the fundamental rights reflect public policy for these purposes, in much the same way as *güte Sitten* embraces the values declared in the German Basic Law. How this question is approached in Canada and in South Africa is that the courts develop the common law in the light of

---

[10] [1977] I.L.R.M. 166.

[11] *Id.* at p. 214.

[12] *Supra*, p.580.

values contained in their Constitutions.[13] On several occasions the Irish courts have declared common law rules to be invalid because they contravened the Constitution, especially rules pertaining to family relationships.[14] So far, no contractual provision has been declared invalid on the grounds that it contravenes some constitutional guarantee. In *Murphy v. Stewart*,[15] it was held that certain contractual restrictions on freedom to choose a trade union are not unconstitutional where somewhat equivalent statutory restrictions on this freedom have been declared invalid.[16]

Directions in wills regarding children's education and religious upbringing have been declared void because they conflicted with Article 42, which provides *inter alia* that children's parents have the principal authority and responsibility for educating them, including their religious upbringing. In *Burke and O'Reilly v. Burke and Quail*,[17] the testatrix left property in trust for a child, with a direction that the trustees should select which Catholic school the child should attend. Gavan Duffy P. struck down that direction on the grounds that "the will at this point would override the sacred parental authority and defy the parental right and duty of education" under this Article and, although the clause was well-meaning, it was "inoperative and must be ignored."[18] A similar provision was struck out in *Re Blake*,[19] a legacy with the condition that the beneficiaries be brought up in the Catholic faith. Dixon J. held that this requirement probably contravened public policy at common law[20] but that Article 42 puts the matter beyond any doubt. According to the judge, any attempt to restrict or fetter the parents' rights regarding their children's upbringing "would be contrary to the solemnly declared policy and conceptions of the community as a whole and therefore the courts ... could not and would not lend their aid to securing"; the condition was "void as against public policy and cannot be given effect to."[21]

INJUNCTION

On several occasions the courts have issued injunctions against private individuals and bodies because what they were doing, or were proposing to do, was deemed to be in contravention of the Constitution's guarantees. To date, those orders have been prohibitory as opposed to mandatory, *i.e.* they

---

[13] *Cf. Khumalo v. Holomisa*, 12 B.H.R.C. 538 (2002) (S. Africa).
[14] *Supra*, p.378.
[15] [1973] I.R. 97; *supra*, p.808.
[16] *National Union of Railwaymen v. Sullivan* [1947] I.R. 77.
[17] [1951] I.R. 216.
[18] *Id.* at p. 222.
[19] [1955] I.R. 69.
[20] *Cf. Blathwayt v. Baron Cawley* [1976] A.C. 397.
[21] [1955] I.R. 69 at p.97.

forbade specified action as opposed to requiring persons to take certain action. And the successful applicants have all been private individuals and bodies rather than the State or public agency.

Non-Governmental Applicants

The general principles concerning when injunctions will be granted are part of the law of equity. Orders of that nature will be made, *inter alia*, to restrain the commission or continuance of a tort. All of the injunction cases to date have concerned the implied right to work and earn a livelihood, and Article 40.3.3 on abortion. In those right to work cases, however, there was a significant element of "state action." Several of them involved persons who were in breach of the criminal law in a manner that prejudiced plaintiffs' ability to earn their livelihood. Generally, an individual will not be granted an injunction to restrain the commission of a criminal offence, except where the offence would also amount to a tort in the ordinary law. However, in *Parson v. Kavanagh*,[22] it was held by O'Hanlon J. that an injunction may be granted to restrain the defendant's breach of the Road Transport Act 1932, that had the effect of undermining the plaintiff's transport business, on the grounds that his constitutional right to work and to carry on business was being unlawfully interfered with. An injunction was upheld in similar circumstances by the Supreme Court in *Lovett v. Gogan*,[23] where it was emphasised that the penalty for persons convicted of contravening the relevant provisions of this Act was so low as to not discourage offenders. On account of this flaw in the legislation, it was held that the only practical means of protecting the plaintiff's constitutional right to earn their livelihood was to restrain any further commission of the offence. In contrast, in *O'Connor v. Williams*,[24] Barron J. refused to grant an injunction restraining breaches of the regulations on taxis and cabs because the penalties in them were substantial and, accordingly, constituted an adequate protection for the plaintiffs' right to earn their livelihood.

Several more of the right to work cases concerned trade unions, their officers and members who were picketing an employer's establishment, and who were held to be making demands that conflicted with constitutional provisions. An element of state action was involved there because picketing, as it is normally practised, is an unlawful nuisance at common law. But the legislature intervened by passing section 2 of the Trade Disputes Act 1906,[25] giving persons a right to picket peacefully in furtherance of a "trade dispute." Picketing to prevent

---

[22] [1990] I.L.R.M. 560
[23] [1995] 3 I.R. 132.
[24] [2001] 1 I.R. 248.
[25] Presently, Industrial Relations Act 1990, s.11(1).

non-union members and women from being employed, for example, was accordingly *prima facie* authorised by section 2 of that Act. There was never a direct constitutional challenge to section 2. Because, however, picketing carried out under it was aimed at infringing employees' constitutional rights, their employers got orders enjoining the picketing – in *Educational Co. of Ireland Ltd. v. Fitzpatrick (No.2)*,[26] where the picketers sought to prevent non-trade union members from being employed, and in *Murtagh Properties Ltd. v. Cleary*,[27] where they sought to prevent the plaintiff from employing women. Most forms of arbitrary discrimination in the areas of employment and the provision of services are now outlawed by the equality legislation of 1998 and 2000.

A similar element of "state action" obtained in *Crowley v. Ireland*,[28] where the second defendant, a trade union, was enjoined from organising the "blacking" of school children, *i.e.* from instructing its members not to teach any of the children who had been attending a national school, at which the union's members were on strike. Blacklisting is unlawful at common law but this practice too was made non-actionable by section 3 of the Trade Disputes Act 1906.[29] McMahon J. there did not spell out in any detail why he made the order against the union, other than to say that the union's members were "abusing" their right to strike and were using "unlawful means" to deprive the children of their right to primary education under Article 42. This aspect of the judgment was not appealed to the Supreme Court.

At least as regards some constitutional rights, it has been held that there need be no State involvement of any kind whatsoever in what is being done for an injunction to be issued on the grounds that persons are violating those rights. In the *Educational Co. of Ireland Ltd.* case Budd J. said that:

> "If an established right in law exists a citizen has the right to assert it and it is the duty of the Courts to aid and assist him in the assertion of his right. The Court will therefore assist and uphold a citizen's constitutional rights, obedience to the law is required of every citizen, and it follows that if one citizen has a right under the Constitution there exists a correlative duty on the part of other citizens to respect that right and not to interfere with it. To say otherwise would be tantamount to saying that a citizen can set the Constitution at nought and that a right solemnly given by our fundamental law is valueless. It follows that the Courts will not so act as to permit any body of citizens to deprive another of his constitutional rights and will in any proceedings before them see that

---

[26] [1960] I.R. 345; *supra*, p.802.
[27] [1972] I.R. 330; *supra*, p.797.
[28] [1980] I.R. 102; *supra*, p.811.
[29] Presently, Industrial Relations Act 1990, s.10.

these rights are protected, whether they be assailed under the guise of a statutory right or otherwise."[30]

But this *dictum*, which other judges have endorsed, begs the central question, of against whom does the right in question run, *i.e.* is it a right against state action or it is a right against the entire world. If it falls into the latter category, then it must follow that the courts will enforce the right against private individuals and bodies as well as against the State.

Article 40.3.3 of the Constitution provides that the State "guarantees in its laws to respect and ... by its laws to defend and vindicate" the right to life of the unborn as provided for therein. One would expect that, in the twenty years since this was adopted, the Oireachtas would have passed a law delineating the ambit of this guarantee, over and above the measure on abortion information made necessary by the amendment adopted in 1992.[31] A comparison could be drawn with the Civil Rights Act 1871, enacted by Congress following adoption of the 13th and 14th Amendments to the US Constitution. And if an individual was doing something that endangered the unborn, one might expect that the courts would not be able to intervene on its behalf until this guarantee was implemented by the envisaged law being enacted. This, however, is not how things evolved, as the guarantee was held to apply to private activities in default of legislative intervention.

In *Society for the Protection of Unborn Children Ireland Ltd v. Open Door Counselling Ltd*,[32] the defendants were enjoined from contravening this Article where the State was not implicated in any way. Pregnant women were being counselled by the defendants, who gave advice and some assistance regarding obtaining abortions in Britain. The plaintiff sought a declaration that their action contravened the Constitution and also an injunction against the counselling. One of the defences was that the guaranteed right to life was primarily protection against "state action"; that if abortion-related activities of private individuals were to be proscribed, the appropriate procedure was for the Oireachtas to enact legislation outlawing specific practices and conduct; that the constitutional guarantee was not self-executing and, in the absence of legislative intervention, injunctions should not issue against the defendants. Hamilton P.'s answer was that the court's function is as described in Budd J.'s dictum (*supra*) and in dicta in several other cases to the same effect. Accordingly "[t]hese and many other statements clearly establish that the Courts will provide a procedure for the enforcement and protection of personal rights and the powers of the Courts in this regard do not depend on legislation."[33] He further observed that "under the Constitution ... the State's powers of government are exercised

---

[30] [1972] I.R. 368.
[31] *Supra*, p.726.
[32] [1988] I.R. 593.
[33] *Id.* at p.606.

in their respective spheres by the legislature, executive and judicial organs established under the Constitution and the Courts will act to protect and enforce the rights of individuals and the provisions of the Constitution. ... [T]he judicial organ of Government is obliged to lend its support to the enforcement of the right to life of the unborn, to defend and vindicate that right and, if there is a threat to that right from whatever source, to protect that right from such threat, if its support is sought."[34]

The grant of this injunction was upheld on appeal, where it does not appear to have been contended that the actions in question could not be enjoined on the grounds that they were being performed by private individuals and bodies. Nor was it found that what was decisive about the remedy (as distinct from *locus standi*) was that the nominal plaintiff was the Attorney General, at whose relation the action was being brought. In later proceedings concerning the abortion issue, an injunction was obtained by a private anti-abortion group to restrain students disseminating information about abortion facilities available abroad[35] and, again, no issue appears to have been made about the absence of any "state action" in the disputed activities.

Governmental Applicants

Injunctions will be granted to the Attorney General in certain circumstances where they would not be obtained by private individuals, in particular to protect what are described as public rights. In the first of the many *"SPUC"* cases,[36] as described above, the plaintiff was the Attorney General, who permitted an anti-abortion group to bring the action on his behalf. Subsequently, in *Attorney General v. X.*,[37] Costello J. granted the Attorney General an injunction restraining a teenager who had been raped from having an abortion in England. That order was set aside, on appeal, on the grounds that the abortion was necessary in order to save her life but the Supreme Court did not question the appropriateness of an injunction if her life had not been endangered.

An application by a health authority for a mandatory injunction was refused by McCracken J. in *North Western Health Board v. H.W.*,[38] where parents would not consent to their infants being subjected to the PKU "pin prick" test. On appeal, the Board sought only a declaration that those parents were failing to vindicate their child's rights, by not consenting to this test. But it too was refused, on the grounds that Article 42 of the Constitution guarantees them considerable autonomy as to how best to bring up their child. Hardiman J.

---

[34] *Id.* at p.599.
[35] *Society for the Protection of Unborn Children Ireland Ltd v. Grogan* [1989] I.R. 753.
[36] *Supra*, n.32.
[37] [1992] I.R. 1 I.R. 1; *supra*, p.724.
[38] [2001] 3 I.R. 622; *supra*, p.696.

there expressed separation of powers concerns about relying on the Constitution as a basis for creating obligations on individuals that can be enforced directly by the State, when it may be entirely open to the State to enact legislation providing for those obligations that, in practical terms, will have general application.[39] Another concern is the policy underlying Article 15.5, against imposing liabilities on persons where none exist under existing law.

DAMAGES

Many private infringements of bodily integrity, personal liberty, family rights, property and economic rights, and freedom to vote are actionable as common law torts, such as trespass, defamation, interference with contract and breach of statutory duty. In such cases, it is of no particular relevance whether a remedy lies in the Constitution as well. If, say, a law were enacted abolishing any of these torts, the State would then be directly implicated and that law could very well be unconstitutional.[40] But there are several fundamental rights that the common law does not adequately protect, most notably equality and privacy, although the deficiency in the former case has been largely made up by the equality legislation of 1998 and 2000 concerning employment and the provision of services..

Where a private individual or body does something that, had the State done something similar it would be acting unconstitutionally, has the person prejudiced by such action a remedy in damages where there is no statutory protection or obvious common law remedy? At the outset, the actions being complained about may constitute the actor's assertion of his own constitutional rights. Subject to this and depending on the nature of the right in question and the type of breach involved, the answer would appear to be yes. The leading authority on the question of "constitutional torts" is *Meskell v. Córas Iompair Éireann*.[41] Even though the first defendant in that case was a public body (the state-owned transport company) and the subject matter of the dispute was surrounded by legislative provisions (the sections in the Transport Acts dealing with industrial relations), the case is widely regarded as laying down principles that obtain equally to entirely non-governmental defendants. Briefly, the plaintiff had worked for Córas Iompair Éireann (CIÉ) for many years and had been a trade union member. When his union and CIÉ concluded a closed shop agreement, he left the union in protest. Because he was no longer a member of that union, he lost his job. It had already been established that the Constitution guarantees a right not to associate and, in particular, a right not to be compelled

---

[39] *Id.* at pp.761–4.
[40] *Cf. Hanrahan v. Merck Sharpe and Dohme* [1988] I.L.R.M. and *Sweeney v. Duggan* [1991] 2 I.R. 274.
[41] [1973] I.R. 121.

to be a member of a trade union. Walsh J., for the Supreme Court, held that this right obtains against all employers just as much as it obtains against the legislature, because "[i]f the Oireachtas cannot validly seek to compel a person to forego a constitutional right, can such a power be effectively exercised by some lesser body or by an individual employer? To exercise what may be loosely called a common law right of dismissal as a method of compelling a person to abandon a constitutional right, or as a penalty for him not doing so, must necessarily be regarded as an abuse of the common law right because it is an infringement, and an abuse, of the Constitution which is superior to the common law and which must prevail if there is a conflict between the two."[42] In other words, where there is a conflict between an individual's common law right (*e.g.* not to hire or to dismiss) and a constitutionally protected interest (*e.g.* to work and not to join a trade union), it can be an unlawful abuse of the common law right if exercised in a manner that defeats that interest. This reasoning is a variant of the "abuse of rights" principle that exists in many continental European countries but was rejected in Ireland and Britain one hundred years ago, although accepted to some extent in the US in the doctrine of the *prima facie* tort.

In *Crowley v. Ireland*,[43] another trade union case, McMahon J. held that a trade union contravened the plaintiff children's right to primary education as guaranteed by Article 42, and that it was liable to them in damages.[44]

---

[42] *Id.* at p. 135.

[43] [1980] I.R. 102.

[44] Applied in *Conway v. Irish National Teachers* Organisation [1991] 2 I.R. 305.

CHAPTER 29

State Security, Emergencies and War

Most national constitutions and many international human right instruments contain special provision for dealing with state security and with public emergencies, including war. At the very least, many of the fundamental rights guarantees are made subject to some broad security or emergency qualification. At the other extreme, provision is often made for the virtual suspension of the constitution in times of war and during the gravest of public emergencies. In between these extremes, the Constitution of Ireland provides for the Special Criminal Court, when the ordinary courts are regarded as inadequate for dealing with particular categories of crimes and also for military courts and for the suspension of *habeas corpus*. Additionally, the Oireachtas has enacted various laws for the purpose of protecting the security of the State, including laws which permit the administrative detention of individuals without trial. Under Article 28.3, the State may not participate in a war without the assent of the Dáil.

STATE SECURITY QUALIFICATIONS TO RIGHTS

Several of the rights contained in the Constitution, and also in the European Convention and the U.N. Covenant, are subject to what may be called state security qualifications, in that the scope of these rights is expressly made subject to the interests of state security. Article 40.6.1's guarantee of freedom of expression does not extend to publishing or uttering sedition. That Article also provides that the organs of public opinion "shall not be used to undermine ... the authority of the State." In *State (Lynch) v. Cooney*,[1] it was held that a directive issued by the Minister to Radio Telefís Éireann under former section 31(1) of the Broadcasting Act 1960, which forbade election broadcasting on behalf of the Sinn Féin Party, not alone was consistent with Article 40.6.1 but was a method of giving effect to the State's obligation to prevent broadcasts that are aimed at, or that may have the effect of, supporting organisations that seek to overthrow the State by violence. The rights contained in Article 40.6.1

---

[1] [1982] I.R. 337; *supra*, p.539.

to expression, to assemble, and to associate and form trade unions are formulated as being 'subject to public order'. In *Aughey v. Ireland*,[2] it was held that the restriction in the Garda Síochána Act 1924, on members of the Garda's choice of trade union was justified 'because of their close connection with the security of the State ...".[3] On account of the Constitution's strong emphasis on the 'common good', notably in Article 6, it is most likely that the scope of various other rights would be narrowed somewhat where that is deemed necessary in the interests of state security.

The Nature of State Security

What precisely constitutes state security for the purpose of the above qualifications was not stated in the *Lynch* case nor in the *Aughey* case. In particular, does that concept embrace economic security? At least as regards rights, the exercise of which are subject to considerations of public order, measures designed to alleviate economic insecurity might be treated as being aimed at protecting public order and, accordingly, within the qualification.

An instance where issues of this kind were raised was *Campus Oil Ltd, v. Minister for Industry & Commerce,*[4] which concerned the "public security" exception in the EC Treaties. The Government adopted regulations to ensure that what then was the country's only oil refinery at Whitegate remained open, and importers of petroleum into the country were obliged to buy a proportion of their product from the State oil company, which got its supplies from Whitegate. That requirement contravened the EC rules on the free movement of goods unless it could be justified under then Article 36 of the Treaty, which permits derogation from free movement in the interests of *inter alia* "public security." Advocate General Slynn's conclusions include the following definition of public security in the context of the case, viz. "'[p]ublic security' is clearly not limited to external military security ... Nor in my view is it limited to internal security, in the sense of the maintenance of law and order, falling short of 'serious internal disturbances affecting the maintenance of law and order' ... The maintenance of essential oil supplies is in my view capable of falling within 'public security' in that it is vital to the stability and cohesion of the life of the modern State."[5] The Luxembourg Court reached a similar conclusion, that "in the light of the seriousness of the consequences that an interruption in supplies of petroleum products may have for a country's existence, the aim of ensuring a minimum supply of petroleum products at all times is to be regarded as transcending purely economic considerations and

---

[2] [1986] I.L.R.M. 206; *supra*, p.799.
[3] *Id.* at p.217.
[4] Case 72/83 [1984] E.C.R. 2727.
[5] *Id.* at p.2764.

thus as capable of constituting an objective covered by the concept of public security."[6]

Of course in order to be entitled to benefit from this somewhat extensive concept of national security, it must be demonstrated that the measure in question is in fact needed on those grounds and that no other less restrictive measure could have adequately protected public security. While several articles of the EC Treaty and regulations permit deviation from their strict requirements on grounds of national security, public order or public safety, it has been held that the Treaty does not embody an overriding proviso that all EC-source obligations are subject to a public safety or similar qualification.[7]

Judicial Review of State Security Assessments

The full extent to which the Oireachtas or the executive are required to substantiate their determinations that measures are needed for reasons of state security has not been resolved by the Irish courts. Prior to the Human Rights Act 1998, in Britain those determinations were virtually unreviewable. According to the House of Lords, although the courts would require some evidence to show that the decision in question was taken on national security grounds, the courts would not decide if those considerations provided adequate justification for what was done. As Lord Scarman put it, "[o]nce ... the court is satisfied that the interest of national security is a relevant factor to be considered in the determination of the case, the court will accept the opinion of the (government) as to what is required to meet it, unless it is possible to show that the opinion was one which no reasonable minister advising the (government) could in the circumstances reasonably have held."[8] On this basis the courts there declined to judicially review decisions of the government, taken on national security grounds, to locate nuclear bombers at an RAF station[9] and to ban trade unions at an intelligence collection facility.[10] For the courts there to re-examine those decisions at the time was held to be inconsistent with the separation of powers. Since 1998, however, the courts there have not been quite so deferential.[11] As commentators on the law of *habeas corpus* point out, "[t]he Australian courts are not prepared to be as awestruck by the mantra of national security."[12]

---

[6] *Id.* at p.2752.
[7] *Johnston v. Chief Constable RUC* (Case 222/84) [1987] Q.B. 129.
[8] *Council of Civil Service Unions v. Minister for the Civil Service* [1985] A.C. 374 at p.406.
[9] *Chandler v. DPP.* [1964] A.C. 763.
[10] *Supra*, n.8.
[11] *Secretary of State v. Rehman* [2003] 1 A.C. 153.
[12] D. Clark & G. McCoy, *The Most Fundamental Legal Right* (2000), p.122. *Cf. Operation Dismantle Inc. v. The Queen*, 18 D.L.R. 4th 481 (1985) and the *Cruise Missile* case, 66 BVerfGF 39 (1983).

The principle of legality and the authority of the courts to safeguard constitutional rights by reviewing laws and executive action, require the courts to examine more thoroughly the executive's and even the Oireachtas' assertion of state security as a reason for acting. In *State (Lynch) v. Cooney,*[13] the former section 31(1) of the Broadcasting Act case, it was held that there must be an objective basis for the Minister's decision to ban particular forms of broadcasting and that the Minister's view on danger to the State "must be one which is *bona fide* held and factually sustainable and not unreasonable."[14] A similar standard would probably be applied where the Oireachtas restricts exercise of the personal rights on state security grounds, although the courts may be somewhat more prepared to accept its assessment of factual situations. As is explained below, in 1996 the Supreme Court demonstrated extreme reluctance to review acts of the Government with reference to dis-establishing the Special Criminal Court in circumstances where it appeared that the ordinary criminal courts were functioning entirely adequately and it was not shown that there was any special reason why the applicant there should be tried other than in those courts.[15]

MEASURES TO PROTECT STATE SECURITY

State security is protected by legislation in numerous ways. Under Article 15.6 of the Constitution, only the Oireachtas can "raise and maintain military or armed forces" and there is a constitutional prohibition on all forms of private armies. The organisation, status and function of the defence forces is regulated in extensive detail by the Defence Acts 1954–98.[16] Ireland has never had legislative and executive inquisitions into alleged subversive penetration of the civil service, the theatre, schools and the like; nor has Ireland experienced systematic dismissal of alleged subversives from public office. Ireland has not joined NATO, nor is it a member of any other military alliance. The principal provisions aimed at protecting state security in the narrow sense call for brief mention.

Treason

By far the most important of these provisions, perhaps, the Treason Act 1939, is based on Article 39 of the Constitution, which comprises a restrictive definition of treason. Under it, "[t]reason shall consist only in levying war

---

[13] [1982] I.R. 337.
[14] *Id.* at p.361.
[15] *Kavanagh v. Government of Ireland* [1996] 1 I.R. 321; *infra*, p.852.
[16] *Supra*, p.123.

against the State, or assisting any State or person or inciting or conspiring with any person to levy war against the State, or attempting by force of arms or other violent means to overthrow the organs of Government established by this Constitution, or taking part or being concerned in or inciting or conspiring with any person to make or take part or be concerned in any such attempt." There have been no reported court decisions on the scope of this offence. In *Quinn v. Wren*,[17] an extradition case dealing with the "political offence" exception in the Extradition Act 1965, the Supreme Court said that the Irish National Liberation Army, an illegal private army, was a treasonous organisation and that accordingly its members were not entitled to benefit from that exception. But that unconvincing rationale for granting extradition was subsequently repudiated by the Supreme Court.[18] No alleged member of the INLA, nor of any of the comparable illegal private armies, has ever been prosecuted for treason, let alone convicted of that offence.

Official Secrets

Getting or disclosing information "to the prejudice of the safety or preservation of the State" is forbidden by Part III (sections 9–12) of the Official Secrets Act 1963. According to section 9(1), a person "shall not in any manner prejudicial to the safety or preservation of the State – (a) obtain, record, communicate to any other person or publish, or (b) have in his possession or under his control any document containing, or other record whatsoever of information relating to (the enumerated matters)." It is a defence to have acted with a Minister's authority or to have acted "in the course of and in accordance with (ones) duties as the holder of a public office."[19] Communicating such information to a foreign agent or to a member of an unlawful organisation is deemed to be evidence of prejudice to the safety or preservation of the State.[20]

Offences Against the State

According to its preamble, the Offences Against the State Act 1939, was adopted principally in order to combat "actions and conduct calculated to undermine public order and the authority of the State." That Act, as amended, contains the principal statutory measures for protecting state security. Some of its provisions have already been considered above, notably Part III's (sections 18–25) rules on suppressing unlawful organisations,[21] the sections in Part II

---

[17] [1985] I.R. 322.
[18] *Finucane v. McMahon* [1990] 1 I.R. 165.
[19] S.9(2).
[20] S.10.
[21] *Supra*, p.576.

(sections 6–17) that curtail freedom of expression,[22] prohibitions on certain categories of meetings,[23] forfeiture of property under the 1985 Act,[24] searches under section 29 of the Criminal Law Act 1976,[25] and arrest and extended detention of suspects under section 30.[26] The most direct threats to the State's security are proscribed by the following provisions, only one of which has received judicial interpretation.

Section 6 of the 1939 Act declares usurping the functions of government to be an offence that carries a maximum penalty of 20 years imprisonment. Usurpation is defined as "usurp(ing) or unlawful exercis(ing) any function of government, whether by setting up, maintaining or taking part in any way in a body of persons purporting to be a government or a legislature but not authorised in that behalf by or under the Constitution, or by setting up, maintaining or taking part in any way in a purported court or other tribunal not lawfully established, or by forming, maintaining or being a member of an armed force or a purported police force not so authorised, or by any other action or conduct whatsoever ...".

There are several provisions that outlaw interfering with public administration. Section 7 of the 1939 Act makes obstruction of the Government an offence, with a maximum penalty of 20 years imprisonment. This offence is defined as "prevent(ing) or obstruct(ing), or attempt(ing) or (being) concerned in an attempt to prevent or obstruct, by force of arms or other violent means or by any form of intimidation the carrying on of the government of the State or any branch (whether legislative, judicial or executive) of the government of the State or the exercise or performance by any member of the legislature, the judiciary or the executive or by any officer or employee (whether civil (including police) or military) of the State of any of his functions, powers or duties ...".[27]

Section 8 of this Act makes it an offence to obstruct the President in the performance of his duties. Section 9, which forbids interference with State employees' performance of their functions, will require some reconciliation with the Constitution's implied right to strike:

> "(i) Every person who shall with intent to undermine public order or the authority of the State commit any act of violence against or of interference with a member of a lawfully established military or police force (whether such member is or is not on duty) or shall take away, injure, or otherwise interfere with the arms or equipment or any part of the arms or equipment, of any such member shall be guilty of a misdemeanour. ...

---

[22] *Supra,* p.538.
[23] *Supra,* p.568.
[24] *Supra,* p.748.
[25] *Supra,* p.636.
[26] *Supra,* p.321.
[27] *Cf. People v. Keogh* [1983] I.R. 136.

(ii) Every person who shall incite or encourage any person employed in any capacity by the State to refuse, neglect or omit (in a manner or to an extent calculated to dislocate the public service or a branch thereof) to perform his duty or shall incite or encourage any person so employed to be negligent or insubordinate (in such manner or to such extent as aforesaid) in the performance of his duty shall be guilty of a misdemeanour ...".

Other provisions include section 15 of the 1939 Act, which forbids unauthorised military exercises, section 16, which proscribes secret societies in the army and the police, and section 17, which makes it an offence to administer unlawful oaths. The Special Criminal Court and the powers of prolonged detention or internment are dealt with separately below.

Sedition

A number of what may be termed state security offences exist at common law, most notably sedition. According to *Archbold*,[28] which is the practitioners' principal treatise on criminal law, sedition "consists in conduct whether by word, deed or writing, which directly tends (i) to raise discontent and dissatisfaction among or promote ill will between the (State's) subjects; (ii) to incite persons to use or attempt to use any unlawful means and in particular physical force in any public matter connected with the State; (iii) to bring into hatred or contempt ... the government, the laws or the Constitution." Several commentators have remarked that this definition is too wide and is not supported by case law.[29] A Canadian judge has remarked that "probably no crime has been left in such vagueness of definition as that with which we are here concerned, and its legal meaning has changed with the years."[30] There is no reported instance of a prosecution for common law sedition in Ireland since 1921[31] and prosecutions have been extremely rare in Britain in the last century. Although the Constitution's guarantee of freedom of expression may cut back the scope of sedition, seditious speech and writing is one of the express exceptions to that guarantee.

Several offences in respect of seditious documents are created by the Offences Against the State Act 1939. Seditious documents are defined in section 2 as including:

---

[28] P.J. Richardson (ed.), *Criminal Pleading, Evidence and Practice* (2000 ed.), p.2128.
[29] I. Brownlie, *Law of Public Order and National Security* (2nd ed., 1980), p.234.
[30] *Boucher v. R.*, 2 D.L.R. 2d 369 (1951) at p.382.
[31] The last reported ones being *McHugh* [1901] 2 I.R. 569 and *Freeman's Journal* [1902] 2 I.R. 83.

"(a) a document consisting of or containing matter calculated or tending to undermine the public order or the authority of the State, and

(b) a document which alleges, implies, or suggests or is calculated to suggest that the government functioning under the Constitution is not the lawful government of the State or that there is in existence in the State any body or organisation not functioning under the Constitution which is entitled to be recognised as being the government of the country, and

(c) a document which alleges, implies or suggests or is calculated to suggest that the military forces maintained under the Constitution are not the lawful military forces of the State, or that there is in existence in the State a body or organisation not established and maintained by virtue of the Constitution which is entitled to be recognised as a military force, and

(d) a document in which words, abbreviations or symbols referable to a military body are used in referring to an unlawful organisation ...".

It is an offence under the 1939 Act to set up in type, print, publish, send through the post, distribute, sell or offer for sale any such document.[32] The Minister may take action against foreign newspapers that contain seditious material,[33] and the mere possession of any such document is an offence.[34]

Inciting Disaffection

Inciting State employees to disaffection is proscribed by section 9(2) of the Offences Against the State Act 1939.[35] Section 254(1) of the Defence Act 1954, contains a parallel provision for causing disaffection among members of the armed forces. It is an offence for "[a]ny person who by any means whatsoever incites or attempts to incite any person subject to military law (a) to mutiny, or (b) to refuse to obey lawful orders given to him by a superior officer, or (c) to refuse, neglect or omit to perform any of his duties, or (d) to commit any other act in dereliction of his duty ...". That Act further proscribes, *inter alia*, inducing members of the defence forces to desert and interfering with persons performing their military duties. Section 14 of the Garda Síochána Act 1924, applies a similar rule to inciting disaffection and the like among members of the Garda. It is an offence "[i]f any person causes, or attempts to cause, or does any act calculated to cause, disaffection amongst the members of the Garda Síochána, or induces or attempts to induce, or does any act

---

[32] S.10.
[33] S.11.
[34] S.12.
[35] *Supra*, p.538.

calculated to induce any (such) member ... to withhold his services or to commit a breach of discipline, he shall be guilty of a misdemeanour...".

Surveillance

Tapping persons' telephones or faxes or opening their post may be authorised by the Minister to obtain information in the interests of national security.[36] Restrictions in the Data Protection Acts 1998–2003, on obtaining access to personal data do not apply where, in the opinion of a senior Garda or army officer, the information is "required for the purpose of safeguarding the security of the State."[37]

Deportation

An alien may be deported if, in the Minister's "opinion," that would be conducive to the common good and, when determining whether to make a deportation order, the Minister must have regard to "considerations of national security and public policy."[38] Nationals of EC Member States may also be deported for reasons of, *inter alia*, "national security."[39]

SPECIAL CRIMINAL COURT

In contrast with many otherwise comparable constitutions, the Constitution of Ireland expressly authorises the establishment of special courts when the ordinary criminal courts cannot function properly. According to Article 38.3 and 6:

> "Special Courts may be established by law for the trial of offences in cases where it may be determined in accordance with such law that the ordinary courts are inadequate to secure the effective administration of justice, and the preservation of public peace and order.
>
> The constitution, powers, jurisdiction and procedure of such special courts shall be prescribed by law.
>
> The provisions of Articles 34 and 35 of this Constitution shall not apply to any court or tribunal set up under section 3 ... of this Article."

---

[36] Interception of Postal Packages and Telecommunication Messages (Regulation) Act 1993, ss.2(1) and 5.

[37] S.8(a).

[38] Immigration Act 1999, s.3(2)(i) and (6)(k). *Cf. Secretary of State v. Rehman* [2001] 3 W.L.R. 877.

[39] EC Treaty, Article 39.3.

Whereas it took over 20 years for the ordinary courts as contemplated by Article 34 of the Constitution to be established in 1961, legislation providing for special courts was enacted just over two years after the Constitution was adopted, viz. Part V (sections 35–53) of the Offences Against the State Act 1939.[40] A Special Criminal Court was established for the first time in August 1939 and remained in existence until 1962. It was established again in May 1972,[41] since when it has been in existence, although it has not been as active in recent years as it was in the 1970s. While the 1939 Act permits more than one Special Court to exist at any one time, only one such court has ever been established.

This Act empowers the Government to establish the court whenever it comes to the conclusion that the existing courts cannot function adequately and it makes a proclamation to that effect. As section 35(2) of the 1939 Act puts it, the court acquires jurisdiction when the Government proclaims that it is "satisfied that the ordinary courts are inadequate to secure the effective administration of justice and the preservation of public peace and order" and that it is necessary that Part V of the Act shall come into force. Once the court is in existence, it retains its jurisdiction until the Government issues a proclamation declaring that it is satisfied that the ordinary courts can do their job effectively.[42]

Persons can be tried before this court for any criminal offence. Its jurisdiction is principally in respect of scheduled offences as defined by section 36 of the 1939 Act; those are offences of one or more classes that the Government has declared can be tried by this court because it is satisfied that the ordinary courts cannot satisfactorily try persons charged with those offences. But the court has also jurisdiction in respect of any other criminal offence when the Director of Public Prosecutions certifies that, in his opinion, the ordinary courts are not adequate for trying the accused on the charge.[43] Section 43 of the 1939 Act defines the court's jurisdiction as "to try and to convict or acquit any person lawfully brought before (it) for trial under this Act;" the court can sentence persons duly convicted, require a person before it to enter into recognisances, order persons' detention or admit them to bail, administer oaths to witnesses and exercise the same powers of punishment for contempt as are possessed by the High Court.

Various procedural features of the Special Criminal Court are set out in Part V of the 1939 Act, such as regarding preliminary proceedings in the District Court in relation to a scheduled offence and in relation to a non-scheduled offence that can be tried by the court, charging persons in the court itself instead of in the District Court, transferring trials from the ordinary courts

---

[40] See generally, D. Walsh, *Criminal Procedure* (2002), Chap.20.
[41] S.I. No. 142 of 1972
[42] S.35(4).
[43] S.46.

to the court,[44] defendants standing mute of malice and refusing to plead, orders and sentences of the court, and members' of the court's immunity from suit. The court decides questions before it by way of majority verdict and it is given extensive power to "control its own procedure in all respects …".[45] Undoubtedly the court's most significant feature is its composition and the terms on which its members serve. Its members are appointed by the Government and, when being appointed, must be either a serving judge, a barrister or a solicitor of more than seven years' standing or a member of the defence forces not below the rank of commandant. In the 1940s the court was comprised entirely of army officers but since 1972 it has been staffed only by judges.

Challenges to the court on constitutional grounds are confronted by a formidable obstacle, in that Article 38.3 expressly provides for the establishment of such courts with such jurisdiction, powers and procedure as are "prescribed by law"; Article 38.6 stipulates that the provisions of Articles 34 and 35 of the Constitution (i.e. on the administration of justice in the courts and by judges duly appointed) do not apply to the court; and Article 38.5 exempts the court from the requirement of jury trial. Unlike the position during the emergencies as described below, the court on the other hand, remains subject to the fundamental rights and other clauses of the Constitution.

In *McCurtain, Re*,[46] where the applicant had been tried by a Special Court comprised of army officers and sentenced to death for murder, several arguments against the legality of that court were made without success. The strongest of these, perhaps, was that when the Government proclaims that the ordinary criminal courts are inadequate, in the sense laid down in the 1939 Act, it should give reasons. That contention was rejected on the grounds that it is impossible to imply such a requirement into the Act when there is no express provision to that effect.

On the two occasions when the court was established, it was not contended that the Government's proclamation under section 35(2) of the 1939 Act was *ultra vires* on the grounds that there was insufficient factual basis for it being satisfied that the ordinary courts were not functioning adequately. It remains to be seen how much evidence the Government would have to adduce in order that its proclamation be upheld in those circumstances. In *Kavanagh v. Government of Ireland*,[47] where the question was whether it was permissible to continue operating the court when for many years the ordinary criminal courts continued to function satisfactorily, these issues were described by the

---

[44] S.48. In *O'Reilly and Judge v. DPP.*, unreported, High Court, Carroll J., May 5, 1983, it was held that this was not an unconstitutional interference with the administration of justice.

[45] S.41(1).

[46] [1941] I.R. 83.

[47] [1996] 1 I.R. 321.

Supreme Court as "primarily a political question and, for that reason is left to the legislature and the executive."[48] Barrington J. held that this analysis was supported by section 35(5) of the Act, which empowers the Dáil at any time to pass a resolution annulling the proclamation. Accordingly, "[p]rovided these powers have been exercised in a *bona fide* manner the ordinary courts have no function in relation to them,"[49] leaving some opportunity for judicial review.

Having been arrested in 1994 in respect of offences committed during a bank robbery, the applicant in *Kavanagh* was charged and returned for trial before the Special Court. He then contended, *inter alia*, that, because there had been a radical change in the circumstances that caused the court to be established in 1972, there was an obligation on the Government to either dis-establish it or at minimum, conduct a review to ascertain whether its continued operation remained necessary. In 1972 there was the serious breakdown of law and order in Northern Ireland, the effects of what had spilled over into the State. Insofar as intimidating jurors may have been a concern, it was argued that this problem was significantly alleviated by the majority verdict system and also there was practically no evidence of jurors being intimidated. But it was held that these did not warrant the Supreme Court intervening because, when making a decision in this area, the Government "is making a political judgment on the adequacy of the ordinary courts to secure the effective administration of justice and the preservation of public peace and order. It is natural that such a political decision should be primarily subject to political control."[50] But as Keane J. pointed out, "a decision of this nature ... cannot be regarded as for ever beyond the reach of judicial control" because, save in a time of war or for the emergency as is described below, "the courts at all times retain their jurisdiction to intervene so as to ensure that the exercise of these drastic powers to abridge the citizens' rights is not abused ...".[51] He observed that, even when the proclamation was made by the Government in 1972, the ordinary courts continued to function satisfactorily. It was of no significance that the Act required the Government to be "satisfied" as to their inadequacy rather than merely have an opinion that they are inadequate. A subsequent endeavour to challenge the continuation of the Special Court, on much the same grounds, was rejected by the Supreme Court.[52] It was held that any such contest should be formulated in plenary summons proceedings and a stay was refused on that applicant's forthcoming trial pending the outcome of any such proceedings. In the event, they were not pursued.

Between 1972 and 1985, the practice in the Special Court had been that

---

[48] *Id.* at p.354.
[49] *Ibid.*
[50] *Id.* at p.355.
[51] *Id.* at pp.355 and 366.
[52] *Gilligan v. Ireland* [2000] 4 I.R. 579.

some of the judges sitting were retired judges, who were on pensions, rather than existing serving judges with tenure as guaranteed by the Constitution. That was challenged in *Eccles v. Ireland*,[53] where the plaintiffs had been convicted of capital murder and were sentenced to death by a court comprised of a serving judge and two retired judges. Because Part V of the 1939 Act states that judges of the court are removable at will by the Government and that their remuneration shall be such as the Minister shall determine, it was argued that the court lacked the requisite degree of independence from the executive. But any suggestion that the judges had failed to act independently was disclaimed. Undoubtedly, if it were shown that the judges had not acted independently, the convictions would be set aside. Dealing with the potential given by Part V of the 1939 Act for the Government to interfere with judicial independence, by removing judges who do not give verdicts that pleased the Government and rewarding judges who give satisfactory verdicts, it was held that Article 35.5, (which provides that certain of the constitutional guarantees do not apply to the court) does not exempt it from the general requirements of judicial independence and from the obligation to try cases in due course of law. However, statutory provisions must be construed in a constitutional manner. Accordingly, it was held that the statutory power to remove and to remunerate these judges cannot be used in order to subvert their independence when performing their judicial functions. As explained by Finlay P., for the Supreme Court, "if either the Government or the Minister were to seek to exercise its power in a manner capable of interfering with the judicial independence of the Court, in the trial of persons charged before it, it would be attempting to frustrate the constitutional right of persons accused before that Court to a trial in due course of law. Any such attempt would be prevented and corrected by the courts established under the Constitution. Whilst, therefore, the Special Criminal Court does not attract the express guarantees of judicial independence contained in Article 35 of the Constitution, it does have, derived from the Constitution, a guarantee of independence in the carrying out of its functions."[54] This unconvincing reasoning is not consistent with the general approach to testing judicial bias.[55] It also fails to address the practical difficulty that it is only in very exceptional circumstances that an accused would become aware of endeavours by the State to interfere with a judge's independence.

It is for the prosecuting authorities to decide whether an accused should be charged before this court. In the case of "non-scheduled" offences, the DPP must certify that the ordinary courts are not adequate to try the accused on the charge. On several occasions attempts to go behind this certificate have failed.

---

[53] [1985] I.R. 545.
[54] *Id.* at p.549.
[55] *Supra*, p.488.

In *Savage and McOwen v. DPP.*,[56] the plaintiffs sought a declaration that the certificate was void. But it was held by Finlay P. that the Director's opinion as to the adequacy of the ordinary courts would not be reviewed by the High Court. This was because, firstly, his functions in this regard had formerly been exercised by the Attorney General, whose opinion on such issues was unreviewable. Furthermore, there were practical objections to judicial review because, if the Director was obliged to reveal in open court why the ordinary courts were not adequate to try the defendant on the charge in question, it would become impossible to operate Part V of the 1939 Act in relation to non-scheduled offences. Five years later, however, that same judge accepted that the Director's decision in the context was reviewable if "it can be demonstrated that he reaches a decision *mala fide* or influenced by an improper motive or an improper policy,"[57] but no such motive or policy was demonstrated to exist there.

Another of the arguments made in *Kavanagh v. Government of Ireland*[58] was that the applicant was being unconstitutionally discriminated against because there was no suggestion that the offences with which he was charged had any connection with the violence in Northern Ireland; that they were "non-political crime" and, to date, offences of that nature were prosecuted entirely in the ordinary courts. Nor was any evidence adduced to suggest that there was some basis for the Director being of the view that those courts were not suitable to try the accused. Because, however, there was no evidence before her of *mala fides*, Laffoy J. held that the Director's decision to prosecute the accused was not reviewable. On appeal, the Supreme Court did not address this point to any extent, probably on the basis that it accepted that the only good grounds of review here was *mala fides*. However, an application arising from the case to the UN Committee on Human Rights succeeded,[59] where it was held that prosecuting the applicant in the Special Court was *prima facie* discriminatory and, since no reason of any kind had been furnished for treating him differently from other accused persons in comparable circumstances, he had been denied equality before law as guaranteed by Article 26 of the UN Covenant.

PROTRACTED DETENTION WITHOUT TRIAL

In times of grave public emergency, when the security or the very continued existence of the State is in jeopardy, governments tend to look for powers to

---

[56] [1982] I.L.R.M. 385; also *State (Ballard) v. Special Criminal Court*, unreported, High Court, Kenny J., September 20, 1972.

[57] *State (McCormack) v. Curran* [1987] I.L.R.M. 225 at p.237.

[58] [1996] 1 I.R. 321.

[59] *Kavanagh v. Ireland*, UNCHR, April 4, 2001.

detain indefinitely and without trial enemies of the State or persons whom governments regard as threats to the State, Thus, during World Wars I and II the British Government interned numerous people without trial on the grounds that they might endanger national security if they remained free.[60] In the United States thousands of citizens of Japanese origin were interned following the attack at Pearl Harbour.[61] In the early 1970s in Northern Ireland hundreds of persons, with nationalist backgrounds or connections, were interned without trial under the Special Powers Act 1922.[62] At present, a number of non-UK nationals are being detained without trial in England[63] and the United States Government has interned hundreds of alleged terrorists in a military base at Guantanamo Bay, Cuba.[64]

It was largely to prevent Governments from detaining persons for long periods, without ever having any intention of trying them for criminal offences, that Article 5(1) of the European Convention enumerates five grounds on which a State may detain individuals. It is only where a State has properly derogated from this provision, in accordance with Article 15 of the Convention, that persons may be detained on other grounds (such as that they pose a grave threat to national security).[65] Accordingly, use of the internment power, given by the Offences Against the State (Amendment) Act 1940, would contravene the Convention in the absence of a proper derogation. Whether, in the absence of a derogation, the seven days detention powers under the Emergency Powers Act 1976, are consistent with Article 5 is open to question.

Seven Days Detention

As has already been explained, section 30 of the Offences Against the State Act 1939, authorises arrest and detention of a suspect for 24 hours and for up to 72 hours maximum.[66] When section 2 of the Emergency Powers Act 1976 is operative, it replaces section 30 of that Act and permits the arrest and administrative detention of suspects for as long as seven days. Gardaí possess the power to arrest under section 2 of the 1976 Act only when the Government has ordered that those powers shall come into force. Any such order cannot

---

[60] See generally, A. Simpson, *In the Highest Degree Odious: Detentions Without Trial in Wartime Britain*, (1992).

[61] Upheld in *Korenatsu v. United States*, 323 U.S. 214 (1944).

[62] See generally, Spjut, "Internment and Detention Without Trial in Northern Ireland, 1971–1975", 49 *Mod. L. Rev.* 712 (1986).

[63] Upheld in *A. v. Secretary of State* [2003] 2 W.L.R. 564.

[64] *Cf. R. (Abbasi) v. Secretary of State*, 42 I.L.M. 358 (2003) and *Hamdi v. Rumsfeld*, 42 I.L.M. 197 (2003).

[65] *Ireland v. United Kingdom*, 2 E.H.R.R. 2 (1978) and *A. v. Secretary of State* [2003] 3 W.L.R. 564.

[66] *Supra*, p.321.

last for more than 12 months, although those powers can he renewed for a further 12 month period. At present, no such order is in force. The constitutionality of the 1976 Act was upheld by the Supreme Court in *Emergency Powers Bill 1976, Re,*[67] because it was an exceptional emergency measure which was adopted under the time of emergency procedure contained in Article 28.3.3 of the Constitution, as explained below.

An initial arrest by any Garda under section 2 of this Act can be for as long as two days and then a Chief Superintendent can direct that the suspect be detained for a further period not exceeding five more days. However, the Act does not authorise arrest and detention merely because the person concerned is regarded as an enemy of the State. Persons can be arrested under it only where the arresting Garda "suspects with reasonable cause" that they have committed certain, what may be called, quasi-political offences. These offences are any offence under the Offences Against the State Act, 1939, any scheduled offence for the purpose of Part V of that Act, possessing information relating to such an offence or carrying a document or article related to such an offence.

The Supreme Court stressed that its decision upholding the 1976 Bill's validity did not mean that there would be no constitutional protection for those who are stopped and arrested under section 2. According to O'Higgins C.J., the section does not purport to override detainees' constitutional rights and should not be construed as doing so:

> "a person detained under section 2 ... may not only question the legality of his detention if there has been non-compliance with the express requirements of section 2 but may also rely on provisions of the Constitution for the purposes of construing that section and of testing the legality of what has been done in purported operation of it. A statutory provision of this nature which makes such inroads upon the liberty of the person must be strictly construed. Any arrest sought to be justified by the section must be in strict conformity with it. No such arrest may be justified by importing into the section incidents or characteristics of an arrest which are not expressly or by necessary implication authorised by the section ...
>
> (T)he section is not to be read as an allegation of the arrested person's rights (constitutional or otherwise) in respect of matters such as the right of communication, the right to have legal and medical assistance, and the right of access to the Courts. If the section were used in breach of such rights the High Court might grant an order for release under the provisions for *habeas corpus* contained in the Constitution."[68]

---

[67] [1977] I.R. 159.
[68] *Id.* at p.173.

Internment

In addition to this detention power, which can only be used during a time of emergency as defined in the Constitution, the State possesses far more extensive powers to hold persons without trial for prolonged periods. Use of these powers is consistent with the European Convention only where Ireland has properly entered a derogation on the grounds that a public emergency exists. So far as the Constitution itself is concerned, exercise of the internment power is not contingent on there being a time of emergency in the constitutional sense in existence. Moreover, resort to these powers is not *per se* invalid because the 1940 modified statutory scheme for internment was upheld by the Supreme Court in *Offences Against the State (Amendment) Bill 1940, Re.*[69]

Part VI of the 1939 Act

In *State (Burke) v. Lennon,*[70] internment powers under Part VI (sections 54–59) of the Offences Against the State Act 1939, were held to be unconstitutional. According to section 55(1) of this Act, following a proclamation by the Government that internment powers were necessary to secure peace and order, the Minister could direct a person's arrest and indeterminate detention, whenever he was "satisfied that (the) person is engaged in activities calculated to prejudice the preservation of the peace, order or security of the State ...". The applicant, who was arrested and interned by order of the Minister, in *habeas corpus* proceedings, sought his release on the grounds that several requirements laid down in the 1939 Act had not been followed and that, furthermore, section 55 was unconstitutional. It would seem that in September 1939 a Garda sergeant searched the applicant's home and found what appeared to be seditious and incriminating documents within the terms of the 1939 Act. Suspecting him of an offence under this Act, the sergeant contacted a Chief Superintendent in Dublin, who in turn contacted the Department of Justice. Shortly afterwards, the Minister issued a warrant for the arrest and indefinite detention of the applicant. But Gavan Duffy J. held that section 55 of the Act was invalid on the grounds that it contravened the constitutional separation of powers and also the right to personal liberty.

Emphasis was placed by the judge on two fundamental considerations. One was that the law in question was not a law enacted under Article 28.3.3 of the Constitution, which deals with emergency measures (unlike section 2 of the 1976 Act). Therefore, Part VI of the 1939 Act had no special constitutional exemption, which even that Act's provisions on the Special Criminal Court enjoy. In other words, the Constitution nowhere expressly gives the State a

---

[69] [1940] I.R. 470; *infra*, p.861.
[70] [1940] I.R. 136.

power to intern without trial. Secondly, there were the circumstances of the arrest, which Gavan Duffy J. found meant that the warrant was signed because seditious or incriminating documents were found in the applicant's possession. This led to the 'inescapable conclusion' that, instead of prosecuting him under Part II of the 1939 Act, the Minister had decided "to take the alternative course of directing indefinite imprisonment without trial for the 'activity' of possessing seditious or incriminating documents."[71] In deciding to order a person's internment, the Minister must be satisfied of certain facts and some of those, in essence, were that the person had contravened the criminal law. Because internment encroached on personal liberty, the Minister's decision required careful consideration and, not alone was it a judicial decision but it was held to amount to administering criminal justice, which is a matter reserved for the criminal courts.[72] Separation of powers considerations aside, section 55 was held to be inconsistent with the State's constitutional obligation to defend, protect against attack and vindicate the personal rights, especially that most vital of personal rights, the right to liberty and not to be made subject to protracted administrative detention.

As regards the criminal nature of what the Minister must be satisfied about, Gavan Duffy J. observed that:

"First, the Constitution (Art. 9) declares fidelity to the nation and loyalty to the State to be fundamental political duties of all citizens; there is, I think, much to he said for the view that the citizen engaged in activities conflicting with that fidelity and loyalty commits a misdemeanour, for which he is liable to prosecution under the criminal law. Secondly, and quite apart from that consideration, it would be difficult, and I think impossible, for a man to engage in activities calculated to prejudice the preservation of the peace, order or security of the State without offending the ordinary criminal law. Thirdly, I am further of opinion that the activities contemplated by section 55, if not otherwise unlawful, are made unlawful by this very enactment, authorising internment as their reward; if such activities are not in terms forbidden by our laws, they are at least prohibited by necessary implication in section 55, under pain of internment. Fourthly, the activities described by the section make the subject matter of Part VI of the Act one 'which, by its very nature, belongs to the domain of criminal jurisprudence'. Fifthly, I am of opinion that indefinite internment under Part VI of the Act is indistinguishable from punishment for engaging in the activities in question ...".[73]

It therefore followed that the Minister's decision to intern amounted to

---

[71] *Id.* at p.153.
[72] *Supra*, p.408.
[73] [1940] I.R. 151.

administering criminal justice and "the document which the Act calls a warrant is really a combination of a conviction, an order to arrest and a warrant of committal."[74]

Internment in the manner provided for, moreover, contravened the State's duty to safeguard the individuals personal liberty. As explained by the judge:

> "Article 40, if I understand it, guarantees that no citizen shall be deprived of liberty, save in accordance with a law which respects his fundamental right to personal liberty, and defends and vindicates it, as far as practicable, and protects his person from unjust attack; the Constitution clearly intends that he shall be liable to forfeit that right under the criminal law on being duly tried and found guilty of an offence. In my opinion, a law for the internment of a citizen, without charge or hearing, outside the great protection of our criminal jurisprudence and outside even the special Courts, for activities calculated to prejudice the State, does not respect his right to personal liberty and does unjustly attack his person; in my view, such a law does not defend his right to personal liberty as far as practicable, first, because it does not bring him before a real Court and again because there is no impracticability in telling a suspect, before ordering his internment, what is alleged against him and hearing his answer, a course dictated by elementary justice." [75]

After referring to Magna Carta and the United States Constitution, he concluded that "the power to intern on suspicion or without trial is fundamentally inconsistent with the rule of law and with the rule of law as expressed in the terms of our Constitution."[76]

The 1940 Act

World War II had broken out when the 1939 Act's internment provisions were held to be unconstitutional in the *Burke* case. The State's immediate response was to enact a similar law and have it referred to the Supreme Court under Article 26 of the Constitution. The principal differences between Part VI of the 1939 Act and the Offences Against the State (Amendment) Act 1940, are that the latter is headed "powers of detention," instead of "powers of internment," the Minister can order indefinite detention when "of opinion" that the specified circumstances exist, as opposed to being "satisfied" that they exist. Those specified circumstances are that the person in question is "engaged in activities which, in (the Minister's) opinion, are prejudicial to the preservation of public peace and order or to the security of the State ...".

---

[74] *Id.* at p.154.
[75] *Ibid.*
[76] *Id.* at pp.155–156.

In *Offences Against the State (Amendment) Bill 1940, Re,*[77] the arguments against the measure were essentially the reasons given by Gavan Duffy J. in the *Burke* case. In support of the measure, stress was placed on the various safeguards in the Bill that prevent the executive from abusing the detention power, and on the argument that the whole object of detention is to prevent occurrences from happening rather than to punish persons for what they have already done. Speaking for the majority who upheld the measure, Sullivan C.J. observed that it was of particular significance that provision for detention without trial had existed under the law before 1922 and in the law of the Free State[78] but the Constitution, which proscribes various practices, does not expressly condemn indefinite detention. This he said, "is a matter to which we are bound to attach considerable weight."[79] He found that detention, as envisaged by the 1940 Bill, was essentially preventive rather than punitive and, therefore, the Minister's decision to intern could not be regarded as administering criminal justice; that "neither section 4 nor section 5 ... creates or purports to create a criminal offence. The only essential preliminary to the exercise by the Minister of the powers contained in section 4 is that he should have formed opinions on the matters specifically mentioned in the section. The validity of such opinions is not a matter that could be questioned in any Court. Having formed such opinions, the Minister is entitled to make an order for detention; but this court is of opinion that the detention is not in the nature of punishment, but is a precautionary measure taken for the purpose of preserving the public peace and order and the security of the State."[80]

Even if internment is not administering criminal justice, it was contended that this method of preserving peace and order and the security of the State contravened Article 40.3. But the court in effect held that this clause is not a source of specific constitutional rights, a view that would not be upheld today.[81] While a strong argument could be made that this case would not be decided in the same way if it came before the courts today, the effect of Article 26 of the Constitution may be to insulate the 1940 Bill's detention powers against future constitutional challenge.[82] However, since the decision upholding this Act was made by the former, not the present, Supreme Court, it is possible that the decision is not insulated by Article 34.4.4 of the Constitution from judicial review because, on several occasions, it has been held that the Supreme Court referred to in Article 34.4 is the one which was established in 1961.

Indefinite detention under the 1940 Act was re-activated in July 1957 and one of the first persons arrested and held under that Act challenged it. In *Ó*

---

[77] [1940] I.R. 470.
[78] See generally, C. Campbell, *Emergency Law in Ireland, 1918–1925* (1994).
[79] [1940] I.R. 478.
[80] *Id.* at p.479.
[81] *Supra*, p.314.
[82] *Supra*, p.91.

Láighléis, Re,[83] one of the principal arguments used against the validity of this Act was that, in the light of the European Convention on Human Rights, it was unconstitutional. But the Supreme Court held that, under the Constitution, international treaties cannot override legislation enacted by the Oireachtas. The applicant then complained to the European Commission of Human Rights that his detention violated his rights under the Convention. In *Lawless v. Ireland,*[84] the first case before the court at Strasbourg, two main questions called for resolution. One was that referred to in Chapter 15 on personal liberty, *viz.* whether detention, which is not for the purpose of charging an individual with a particular offence or for any of the other purposes enumerated in Article 5(1) of the Convention, contravenes that Article. The court's answer was an unqualified "yes". However, in July 1957 Ireland had entered a derogation from provisions of the Convention, claiming that detention under the 1940 Act was necessary because of the political and security situation obtaining then. It was contended by the Government that, at the time of the applicant's detention, there existed a grave public emergency threatening the very life of the nation; consequently, it was claimed, the State was entitled to derogate. By a narrow majority, the court held that the situation in Ireland in July 1957 justified the conclusion that there was "a public emergency threatening the life of the nation" and, in the circumstances, the 1940 Act's powers were "strictly required by the exigencies of the situation."[85] Consequently, "administrative detention ... of individuals suspected of intending to take part in terrorist activities, appeared, despite its gravity, to be a measure required by the circumstances"[86] and the procedures laid down in the 1940 Act provided adequate safeguards against abuse in the circumstances.

Section 4's detention power is formulated as follows:

> "(1) Whenever a Minister of State is of opinion that any particular person is engaged in activities which, in his opinion, are prejudicial to the preservation of public peace and order or to the security of the State, such Minister may by warrant under his hand and sealed with his official seal order the arrest and detention of such person under this section.
>
> (2) Any member of the Garda Síochána may arrest without warrant any person in respect of whom a warrant has been issued by a Minister of State under the foregoing sub-section of this section.
>
> (3) Every person arrested under ... section shall be detained in a prison or other place prescribed, ... by regulations made under this Part of

---

[83] [1960] I.R. 93; *supra*, p.238.
[84] 1 E.H.R.R. 15 (1961).
[85] *Id.* at p.33.
[86] *Ibid.*

> this Act until this Part ... ceases to be in force or until he is released ..."

In other words, the Minister may order that a person be arrested and detained indefinitely whenever he forms the view that the person in question is doing something which, in the Minister's opinion, prejudices public peace and order or prejudices State security. The Garda officer who makes the arrest need not possess a warrant, although the Minister must have issued a signed and sealed warrant in respect of that person. The form of the Minister's warrant is set out in the schedule to the Act and a copy of the warrant must be served on the person arrested, at least by the time he arrives at the prescribed place of detention. A detention lasts until the Minister orders the person's release but cannot last after Part II of the 1940 Act ceases to have effect. A person arrested and detained under section 4 can be searched, photographed and fingerprinted, and must give his name and address to a Garda.

When seeking to challenge the legality of an individual's detention in *habeas corpus* or other proceedings, the question arises whether the Minister's opinion that certain circumstances exist and justify detention can be reviewed by the courts. In the *1940 Bill* reference the Supreme Court observed that "'(t)he validity of such opinions is not a matter that could be questioned in any Court."[87] It was contended in *Ó Láighléis, Re*[88] that the Minister's opinion was not entirely unchallengeable and reference was made to the famous dissenting judgment of Lord Atkin in *Liveridge v. Anderson*,[89] an action for false imprisonment arising out of the plaintiff's internment in England during World War II. This argument was rejected on the grounds that the analogy with the English case was not complete. The relevant provision in the English regulation was that the Home Secretary could order internment "if he had reasonable cause to believe" that specified circumstances existed, whereas detention can be ordered under the 1940 Act once the Minister is "of opinion" that certain things have happened and may happen. According to Maguire C.J., this difference in terminology is crucial; that "Lord Atkin regarded reasonable cause for a belief as an objective fact, examinable and triable like any other fact. The contrast he drew was between 'reasonable cause' for belief and 'mere belief' that a fact exists ... to have 'reasonable cause' for his 'belief': he is authorised to act on his opinion. 'Mere belief' is enough. Lord Atkin clearly regarded 'mere belief' as a subjective state which was not examinable or triable by a Court."[90]

More recently, however, the Supreme Court has disagreed with the proposition that the exercise of a statutory power cannot be reviewed when

---

[87] [1940] I.R. 470 at p.479.
[88] [1960] I.R. 93.
[89] [1942] A.C. 206.
[90] [1942] I.R. 112 at p.128.

the only condition for exercising that power is that the Minister is of the opinion that certain facts exist. That was in *State (Lynch) v. Cooney*,[91] which concerned an order made under former section 31(1) of the Broadcasting Act 1960, and where the approach to the question in the above two cases was described as out of line with modern developments in administrative law. It therefore would seem that the Minister's opinion, when ordering arrest and detention under the 1940 Act, must be held *bona fide* and factually sustainable, and not unreasonable. It remains to be seen how far the Minister must go to rebut allegations of *mala fides*, acting on a misconception of the circumstances and unreasonableness. Because one of the relevant circumstances concerns danger to the State's security, the exercise of judicial review will have to be reconciled with claims to evidentiary privilege on the grounds of national security.

The 1956 Act

Section 2 of the Prisoners of War and Enemy Aliens Act 1956, empowers the Minister to intern not alone prisoners of war but also any "enemy alien" whose detention he is "satisfied … is absolutely necessary for the security of the State …". While these persons are being so detained, they are protected by the Geneva Convention Relative to the Protection of Civilian Persons in Time of War.[92]

NATIONAL EMERGENCIES

When confronted with the most extreme emergencies, such as civil war or invasion, governments seek to rule by decree, by-passing the legislature.[93] Often most constitutional protections for individuals are suspended for the duration of grave emergencies, which in some countries are referred to as states of siege. The actual scope of a government's powers to deal with serious emergencies will depend on what each national constitution permits and also on international law minimum standards. Thus, under Article I.9(2) of the United States Constitution, the right to *habeas corpus* can be suspended "when in cases of rebellion or invasion the public safety may require it." Article 16 of the French Constitution gives the President sweeping powers to deal with grave emergencies, provided that the Constitutional Council is consulted and the National Assembly remains in session; also the Government can declare a

---

[91] [1960] I.R. 131.

[92] August 12, 1949, 75 UNTS 287.

[93] See generally, D. Bonner, *Emergency Powers in Peacetime*, (1985), Wood, "The Rule of Law in Times of Stress", 70 *U. Chicago L. Rev.* 455 (2003) and Gross, "Chaos and Rules: Should Responses to Violent Crises Always be Constitutional?", 112 *Yale L.J.* 1011 (2003).

"state of siege" but it cannot last longer than twelve days without the legislature's consent. Articles 115a-1 of the German Constitution, which were adopted in 1968, lay down a detailed code for a "state of defence." Article 37 of the South African Constitution similarly is a detailed code for "states of emergency." How the state dealt with emergencies under the Free State Constitution was to amend it in 1931 and to insert in it Article 2A.[94] This comprised sweeping powers that were to be given to the Gardaí and the military, and provided that the remainder body of the Constitution was to be read and construed as subject to those emergency powers, which were to prevail in case of any inconsistency.

Emergency situations are dealt with by the Constitution in several ways. Under Article 15.8.2 either House of the Oireachtas may hold a private sitting "in cases of special emergency", provided two thirds of the members present consent. Article 24 provides for abridging/removal time for enacting legislation where in the government's opinion ... the Bill is urgent and immediately required for the preserve of the public peace and security, or by reason of the existence of a public emergency, whether domestic or international. In the event of actual invasion, Article 28.3.2 authorises the Government to "take whatever steps they may consider necessary for the protection of the State." If the Dáil is not sitting it should be summoned to meet at the earliest practicable date. Where the State is not being invaded but there exists a "state of war or armed rebellion," Article 38.4 provides that military tribunals may be established and the Constitution's *habeas corpus* provisions shall not be invoked to interfere with any act of the defence forces.[95] Article 28.3.3 renders Constitution-proof laws enacted during a time of emergency, in order to secure public safety and preserve the State, but the death penalty cannot be re-introduced.[96]

Within two years of the Constitution being adopted, World War II broke out and the Government promptly declared an emergency.[97] When the War ended, that declaration was not revoked, and since 1945 the State remained in a legal state of emergency. Eventually in 1976 the Dáil and Seanad declared that this emergency had ceased but, at the very same time, they resolved that, on account of the "armed conflict" in Northern Ireland, an emergency would remain in existence. Eventually, in 1976, it was revoked.[98]

Time of Emergency

Originally the Constitution did not define the term "time of war or armed

---

[94] *Supra*, p.8.
[95] Art.40.4.6.
[96] As amended in 2002.
[97] Declared on September 2, 1939.
[98] August 31, 1976.

rebellion," so that it was not entirely clear when the Oireachtas could enact Constitution-proof emergency laws. But if the State is in fact directly involved in a "war or armed rebellion," then the Oireachtas undoubtedly was and is empowered to enact such laws. Laws have never been enacted under this particular branch of Article 28.3.3. It has been held that where the Oireachtas passes a law for the purpose of preserving the peace etc. during a deemed emergency, as described below, that law would not apply when a war or armed rebellion to which the State is a party actually occurs.[99]

The first two amendments made to the Constitution in 1941 sought to define the terms "war" and "armed rebellion" in this context. These were defined, not by reference to matters such as how intense or widespread any conflict is, but instead by reference to the contents of a resolution of both Houses of the Oireachtas. According to Article 28.3.3 "'time of war" *includes* a time when there is taking place an armed conflict in which the State is not a participant but in respect of which each of the Houses of the Oireachtas shall have resolved that, arising out of that conflict, a national emergency exists affecting the vital interests of the State" (First Amendment). And "'time of war or armed rebellion' *includes* such time after the termination of any war or of any such armed conflict, as aforesaid, or of an armed rebellion, as may elapse until each of the Houses of the Oireachtas shall have resolved that the national emergency occasioned by such war, armed conflict, or armed rebellion has ceased to exist' (Second Amendment)." Under the first of these amendments, the term "time of war" is defined as including whenever there is taking place an "armed conflict" to which the State is not a party and both Houses have resolved that, arising from such conflict, an emergency exists "affecting the vital interests of the State." In other words, there must in fact be an armed conflict in which the State is not directly involved and both Houses must have passed the appropriate resolution.

It was the second amendment that greatly expanded the definition of emergency under this clause. For it provides that, even if an actual war or armed rebellion in which the State was directly involved has ended, or if an armed conflict which has been the subject of a resolution as just described has ended, the time of emergency shall continue until both Houses have resolved that the emergency ceased to exist. In other words, as well as for the duration of a war or armed rebellion to which the State is a party, "time of emergency" includes when an armed conflict to which the State is not a party is taking place but the Dáil and Seanad have resolved that that conflict affects the State's vital interests. This time of emergency continues during the period following a war or armed rebellion, or following an armed conflict in respect of which both Houses have passed the above-mentioned resolution, and ends only when both Houses resolve that it has ceased to exist.

---

[99] *Emergency Powers Bill, 1976, Re* [1977] I.R. 159 at p.175.

Following adoption of the 31 August 1976 emergency resolutions, the Emergency Powers Act 1976, was passed; its provisions on extended arrest are described above.[100] When considering the constitutionality of this measure, the Supreme Court suggested that legal recognition would not be accorded to a time of emergency resolution where the facts clearly demonstrated that no real emergency existed. In the words of O'Higgins C.J., "[t]he last matter to be considered is the question of the existence of the state of affairs necessary to permit the application of Article 28.3.3. ... (T)hese are the matters or statements of fact which are contained in the resolutions of the two Houses .... It was submitted by the Attorney General that there is a presumption that the facts stated in the resolutions are correct. The Court accepts the existence of that presumption and the corollary that the presumption should be acted upon unless and until it is displaced."[101] But in the next paragraph he said that the court "expressly reserves for future consideration the question whether the courts have jurisdiction to review such resolutions."[102]

Constitution-Proof Laws

Laws that are enacted for the purpose of dealing with an emergency, as defined in Article 28.3.3, cannot be struck down because they are unconstitutional, except one providing for the death penalty. According to this Article, "[n]othing in this Constitution shall be invoked to invalidate any law enacted by the Oireachtas which is expressed to be for the purpose of securing the public safety and the preservation of the State in time of war or armed rebellion, or to nullify any act done or purporting to be done in time of war or armed rebellion in pursuance of such law ...". That is to say, where there is an actual emergency or where it is resolved that an emergency as defined above exists, and a law is enacted with the express purpose of securing public safety etc, that law or any of its provisions cannot be declared unconstitutional, other than a provision for the death penalty. As Gavan Duffy J. explained in a case concerning legislative provisions for military tribunals:

> "Perhaps the phrase "Nothing in this Constitution shall be invoked" would be better rendered "no provision whatever in this Constitution shall be invoked," though the meaning is substantially the same. This veto makes no exception in favour of the "fundamental rights." The universality of the injunction against invoking anything in the Constitution seems effectively to dispose of the suggestion of repugnancy between this enactment and other provisions of the Constitution making stipulations of their own for military exceptions in turbulent times.

---

[100] *Supra*, p.856.
[101] [1977] I.R. at p.175.
[102] *Id.* at p.176.

The meaning of the words "Nothing in this Constitution" has been discussed. I recognise, on the one hand, that an exceptional enactment, in derogation of the regular Constitution, ought not to be read as disturbing the national polity further than the language selected and the times in contemplation really require; on the other hand, an enactment expressly devised for use in a grave emergency is meant to become an efficient weapon, when the time comes for its use, and must not be so blunted and contracted by a narrow construction as to fail in its purpose ...

So long as the jurisdiction of this Court to enforce ... constitutional rights remains in abeyance in pursuance of an Article in the Constitution, persons ... cannot justify an application to this Court by reference to the guarantees in the Constitution."[103]

Nevertheless, the Supreme Court in *Re Emergency Powers Bill 1976*, observed that laws enacted under and covered by Article 28.3.3 will be construed with the utmost strictness and persons being dealt with under such laws do not lose all their constitutional rights.[104] It would seem that a law passed under this Article could suspend the Article 40.4.2 form of *habeas corpus* procedure but none of the emergency measures that were enacted so far have sought to do that.

Military Tribunals

During grave emergencies, governments may decide to by-pass entirely the ordinary courts and even the special courts, and administer law through military tribunals, *i.e.* tribunals comprised entirely of members of the defence forces. Thus, during the War of Independence the British authorities placed certain parts of the country under martial law and administered a form of justice through military tribunals and, during the Civil War, the Free State Government resorted to military tribunals.[105] As has already been explained, the Special Criminal Court or Courts can be comprised of officers of the defence forces not below the rank of commandant; during World War II that court was made up of army officers.

Apart entirely from that court, the Constitution authorises establishing military tribunals during a state of emergency. According to Article 38.4.1 "military tribunals may be established ... to deal with a state of war or armed rebellion." This clause (and also Article 40.4.6, which suspends *habeas corpus*) does not apply whenever the time of emergency as envisaged in Article 28.3.3 is in existence. The country must in fact be in a state of war or there must be an

---

[103] *State (Walsh) v. Lennon* [1942] I.R. 112 at p.119.
[104] [1977] I.R. 159 at p.173.
[105] See generally, Campbell, *supra*, n.78.

actual armed rebellion taking place, before these exceptional tribunals may be established. Not alone does this clause not refer to the extended concept of "time of war and armed rebellion" used in Article 28.3.3, but there is a significant difference in both clauses' Irish versions. This clause speaks of *"le linn nó le ceannairc faoi arm"* whereas Article 28.3.3 speaks of *"in aimsir chogaidh nó cennairc faoi arm."* The meaning of *eisithe* is more extensive than war, meaning conflict, quarrel, dissention or strife. Military tribunals have never yet been established under Article 38.4.1 but were set up under the time of emergency legislation envisaged by Article 28.3.3.

Tribunals Established by Emergency Law

Tribunals established by legislation under Article 28.3.3 are Constitution-proof, in that whatever powers or procedures are provided for in the Act in question cannot be struck down as invalid because they are inconsistent with any of the constitutional guarantees (except for the death penalty). But as was made clear in *Emergency Powers Bill 1976, Re*,[106] all such legislative provisions will be strictly construed. Powers and procedures that otherwise would be unconstitutional will not be upheld unless they come within the strict terms of the Act in question. It is not clear what the position is where the Act establishing the tribunal simply states that it shall possess such powers and shall function in such manner as the Government or the Minister directs. In other words, the Act does not lay down what exceptional powers and procedures the tribunal shall have but, at the same time, makes it clear that it can go further than is normally constitutionally possible and that the Government or the Minister is authorised to stipulate precisely what those powers and procedures are. Unless the relevant legislation provides otherwise, these tribunals are subject to the supervisory jurisdiction of the High Court.[107]

On two occasions constitutional challenges to military tribunals failed. The Emergency Powers Act 1939, expressly disclaimed any intention of establishing military courts. But the Emergency Powers (Amendment) (No. 2) Act 1940 empowered the Government by order to establish such courts with jurisdiction to try persons for offences specified in the relevant order. By the Emergency Powers (No. 41) Order 1940, the Government set up a military tribunal comprised of the three army officers who at the time also made up the Special Criminal Court. In *McGrath and Harte, Re*,[108] the applicants had been convicted of murder and been sentenced to death by the tribunal. Most of the arguments there were on technicalities; it does not seem to have been contended that the 1940 Act gave the Government too wide a discretion as regards the

---

[106] [1977] I.R. 159.
[107] *Cf. State (O'Duffy) v. Bennett* [1935] I.R. 70 and *State (Hughes) v. Lennon* [1935] I.R. 128 on judicially reviewing Article 2A tribunals.
[108] [1941] I.R. 68.

composition, jurisdiction and powers of the tribunal. Perhaps the most substantial argument was that, since the murder of which the applicants were convicted had occurred before the tribunal was established, the Order contravened the fundamental principle against retrospective criminal legislation. The Supreme Court's answer was not that there had been no violation of Article 15.5 but that the 1940 Act, which authorised establishing the tribunal, by its terms gave the tribunal power to try charges of offences committed before the tribunal was established and this was a complete answer to complaints founded on any of the Constitution's provisions.

In the second case, *State (Walsh) v. Lennon*,[109] the four applicants had also been tried for and convicted of murder, and sentenced to death. There were several exceptional features about their trial. They had been charged and sent for trial before the Special Criminal Court for the murder in question but, before the trial commenced, the Attorney General entered a *nolle prosequi*. Prior to that, the Government had made an order that they should be tried by the military tribunal and that all four of them should be tried together, although the Special Criminal Court had decided that some of them should be tried separately. Thirdly, the Government made an order that excluded several long-established rules of evidence from applying in trials by the military tribunal and which gave the tribunal a wide discretion to ignore any other rule of evidence, whether statutory or common law. But the Supreme Court refused to quash the convictions, on the grounds that Article 28.3.3 stands in the way of any argument that the applicants' constitutional rights had been contravened. As Gavan Duffy J. observed, '(s)o long as the jurisdiction of this Court to enforce … constitutional rights remains in abeyance in pursuance of (this) Article … persons in the position of the applicants cannot justify an application to this Court by reference to the guarantees in the Constitution."[110] According to Sullivan C.J., it was "impossible to invoke any other Article of the Constitution to invalidate this or any other order made in pursuance of an Act passed by the Oireachtas and expressed to be for any of the purposes mentioned in" Article 28.3.3 and that "(m)any of the arguments addressed to us would be more fittingly addressed to either House of the Oireachtas …".[111] In the light of what was said in *Emergency Powers Bill 1976, Re*,[112] however, it may very well be that the order changing the rules of evidence would be declared invalid today because its contents were not necessitated by the actual terms of the Emergency Powers Acts and it is only what is contained in the Acts themselves that is immune from invalidation.

---

[109] [1942] I.R. 112.
[110] *Id.* at p.122.
[111] *Id.* at pp.129 and 131.
[112] [1977] I.R. 159.

Martial Law

At times of extremely serious civil disturbances, some governments resort to what are termed martial law courts.[113] During civil wars and international wars, military authorities themselves establish *ad hoc* tribunals to administer a very rough form of justice in the field. Tribunals of this nature were used during the War of Independence and the Civil War and, as *Wolfe Tone's* case[114] and other cases of that earlier era illustrate, such tribunals have often been used in order to suppress uprisings against the government of the day. It is tribunals of this nature which Article 38.4.1 envisages. Because an actual "state of war or armed rebellion" must be in existence before they may be established, these tribunals function in far more difficult circumstances than do the statutory tribunals which have just been considered.

These tribunals are rendered Constitution-proof in only two respects. Articles 34 and 35 and the requirement of trial by jury do not apply to them. But apart from that, they are not exonerated from respecting the other constitutional guarantees. As was made clear in the *Eccles* case,[115] Article 38.6 of the Constitution does not exempt them from provisions such as regarding trial "in due course of law," that there shall not be retroactive crimes and the like. To an extent that remains to be determined, these tribunals cannot be controlled by the Article 40.4 *habeas corpus* form of procedure. According to Article 40.4.6, "[n]othing in this section, however, shall be invoked to prohibit, control, or interfere with any act of the Defence Forces during the existence of a state of war or armed rebellion." This clause has never been construed by the courts but it would seem to mean that the actions of courts martial during a war or an armed rebellion cannot be scrutinised by way of judicial inquiry under Article 40.4.[116]

Article 40.4.6 does not by its terms preclude judicial review by way of the other procedures through which the High Court has traditionally exercised its supervisory jurisdiction, notably through orders in the nature of *certiorari*, prohibition and *mandamus*. But the common law position has been that courts martial are not amenable to judicial review through any of these procedures. As was explained in *Clifford and O'Sullivan, Re*,[117] where the courts refused to issue prohibition against a military tribunal, these tribunals are not courts in any legal sense but are merely committees of military personnel who advise commanders in the field of battle. While these committees may mimic criminal procedure, that is to the advantage of prisoners brought before them but does

---

[113] See generally Keane, "The Will of the General: Martial Law in Ireland, 1535-1924", 25–7 *Ir. Jur.* 150 (1990–1992) and Bowman, "Martial Law and the English Constitution", 15 *Mich. L. Rev.* 93 (1916).

[114] (1798) 27 St. Tr. 614.

[115] *Eccles v. Ireland* [1985] I.R. 545; *supra*, p.854.

[116] See generally, Clarke & McCoy, *supra*, n.12, Chap.3.

[117] [1921] 2 A.C. 570.

not turn them into criminal courts. Because martial law tribunals, as envisaged by Article 38.4.1, have never yet been established, the precise extent of their Constitution-proofing and immunity from judicial review is a matter of speculation.

Of great relevance to the questions under discussion is the extent to which the common law rules regarding martial law tribunals have been carried over by Article 50 of the Constitution. One of the submissions in *State (Walsh) v. Lennon*[118] was that Article 38.4.1, which authorises martial law tribunals when there is a war or an armed rebellion, is "declaratory of the law, and is based on the right of the State to repel force by force, and to employ military tribunals."[119] The vast majority of the modern authorities on the common law regarding martial law arose in three contexts, *viz.* the Boer War, the Irish War of Independence and the Irish Civil War. Of the common law, Keir and Lawson have observed that "(o)n this subject there is no universal consensus of opinion, and the authorities are few and inconclusive."[120] At least there is agreement on one fundamental point, which is that the courts will not interfere with decisions of these tribunals where it is proved that a state of war exists in the community, be it an international war or a civil war. The fact that the ordinary courts still sit does not of itself demonstrate that there is no war[121] but the existence of war must be established to the court's satisfaction. Once the war is ended, however, the military authorities will be held responsible for any excess of the powers the legislature had given them. It is on account of this principle that Acts of Indemnity are frequently passed when conflicts have ended – for instance, the Indemnity (British Military) Act 1923, the Indemnity Act 1923, and the Indemnity Act 1924. One of the 1798 Rebellion cases, *Wright v. Fitzgerald*,[122] is authority for the proposition that an Act of Indemnity is no defence where the conduct in question was not done *bona fide* to repel the invasion or to suppress the insurrection. Indeed some indemnity laws, such as the Acts of 1923 and 1924, expressly apply only to what was done in good faith; they added that good faith is to be presumed unless the contrary is proved. They also expressly validated sentences which were passed by the Civil War military tribunals.

A particularly vexed question about military tribunals, although not confined to that topic, arises when the legislature has adopted measures in order to deal with an insurrection or civil war; for instance, where the Oireachtas passes legislation under Article 28.3.3 establishing military courts. Does this legislation operate to deprive the military authorities of their common law power to establish *ad hoc* courts martial in the most drastic circumstances? What makes

---

[118] [1942] I.R. 112.

[119] *Id.* at p.126.

[120] D. Keir & F. Lawson, *Cases in Constitutional Law* (6th ed., 1979), p.217.

[121] *R. (Childers) v. Adjutant General* [1923] I.R. 5.

[122] (1798) 27 St. Tr. 759.

the question so important is that the statutory military tribunals may have been given specific authority and been required to follow set procedures so that, if the legislative provisions displace the common law, the individual in these circumstances cannot be judged other than in accordance with the statutory requirements and by a tribunal that is subject to the Article 40.4.2 form of *habeas corpus*.

Under the Restoration of Order in Ireland Act 1920, the British military were given extensive powers to deal with the conflict in Ireland and, by a proclamation on December 10, 1920, the counties of Cork, Kerry, Limerick and Tipperary were placed under martial law for the purposes of this Act. In *R. v. Allen*,[123] the applicant had been sentenced to death by an informal court martial for unlawful possession of arms. But the military tribunals established under the 1920 Act were not empowered to pass sentence for that particular offence. Nevertheless, it was held by an unanimous King's Bench Division that, since a war was actually taking place, the military were entitled to exercise their customary court martial powers and the existence of statutory provisions for dealing with the conflict did not deprive the military of their full common law authority. It would have been different if the 1920 Act expressly curtailed the traditional court martial powers. But in *Egan v. Macready*,[124] where the facts were very similar, O'Connor M.R. reached a contrary conclusion. Disagreeing with the Kings Bench judges, the Master of the Rolls found that the 1920 Act created a code which was to regulate all measures that the military might take in dealing with the uprising, to the exclusion of all other rules of law. The military's traditional powers during wartime derive from the royal prerogative but, when matters normally subject to the prerogative are regulated by legislation, the Act in question supersedes all those prerogative powers. Moreover, it could not be said that conditions in Ireland had changed so much since the 1920 Act was passed that the state of affairs was not contemplated by Parliament when it enacted the law. In support of this view, it could also be said that a state of war exists when the military are compelled to resort to measures that are not within their ordinary legal powers. But because the 1920 Act gave the military the most extensive powers to deal with the situation in Ireland, the Act postponed the necessity to resort to extra-legal powers and, accordingly, there was no "state of war" to permit acting by way of the traditional *ad hoc* court martial.

WAR

Article 28.3 prevents the State from declaring war "save with the assent of [the] Dáil ...". Additionally, the State "shall not participate in any war save

---

[123] [1921] 2 I.R. 241.
[124] [1921] 1 I.R. 265.

with the assent of [the] Dáil ...". Accordingly, the Government may not significantly involve itself in any war without first obtaining the Dáil's acquiescence. The difficult question here is what exactly is meant by the word "participate"; in particular, how involved must the State get in another State's war for it to amount to participation. In *Horgan v. An Taoiseach*[125] Kearns J. declined to answer this question because the Dáil resolution of March 20, 2003, authorising certain assistance to be given to the United States in prosecuting its war in Iraq, expressly stipulated that it was not a resolution authorising any participation in that war. It was contended by the plaintiff that such assistance as had been given to the U.S. military was so extensive as to amount to the State participating in that war and, accordingly, was *ultra vires* the resolution. But it was held that, except where the State's involvement in a war plainly amounts to participating in it, it was principally a matter for the Dáil to characterise such involvement as it sanctioned as participation or otherwise. It was incorrect to assume that the court is better suited than the Dáil for deciding what constitutes "participation in a war" except in "quite exceptional circumstances. ..."[126]

---

[125] [2003] 2 I.L.R.M. 357.
[126] *Id.* at p.400.

CHAPTER 30

Procedure and Remedies

The Constitution consists in the main of a series of commands and prohibitions, along with several declarations that some ethical principles constitute fundamental rights. Its requirements are implemented principally by Acts of the Oireachtas, for instance governing the conduct of elections, the rules of criminal law and procedure, family law, raising taxes and distributing benefits, and the regime for equality in employment and in the provision of services. If an individual is aggrieved about conduct that is inconsistent with many provisions in the Constitution, there is already a law giving effect to many of those requirements which he can enforce in the courts. Article 40.3.1 and 2's guarantee with regard to persons' life, person, good name and property are rendered effective partly by the criminal law and also partly by the common law of tort and of contract.

Where a requirement in the Constitution is not being met then, subject to certain exceptions and provided that certain procedural steps have been followed, the aggrieved individual will usually be granted a remedy. Two remedial measures are provided for in the Constitution itself. Article 34.3 empowers the High Court to declare invalid a law that contravenes the Constitution. And a procedure in the nature of *habeas corpus* is set out in Article 40.4 for questioning the legality of an individual's detention. Over and above these, there are other remedies that the courts regularly grant in all types of cases, principally, a declaration of right or invalidity, an injunction and the award of compensation.

Several of the leading cases contain ringing declarations of the extent to which the courts will go to ensure that a constitutional violation does not go unremedied, most notably Walsh J.'s judgment in *Byrne v. Ireland*,[1] particularly the observation that "[w]here the People by the Constitution create rights against the State or impose duties upon the State, a remedy to enforce these must be deemed also to be available."[2] There is also Ó Dálaigh C.J.'s statement in *State (Quinn) v. Ryan*[3] that "It was not the intention of the Constitution in guaranteeing the fundamental rights of the citizen that these rights should be set at nought or circumvented. The intention was that rights of substance were being assured to the individual and that the courts were the custodians of these

---

[1] [1972] I.R. 241.
[2] *Id.* at p.281.
[3] [1965] I.R. 70.

rights. As a necessary corollary it follows that no one can with impunity set these rights at nought or circumvent them, and that the courts' powers in this regard are as ample as the defence of the Constitution requires. Anyone who sets himself such a course is guilty of contempt of the courts and is punishable accordingly...".[4] The governing principle, as stated by Finlay C.J. in *State (Trimbole) v. Governor of Mountjoy Prison*[5] is that the:

> "courts have not only an inherent jurisdiction but a positive duty (i) to protect persons against the invasion of their constitutional rights; (ii) if invasion has occurred, to restore as far as possible the person so damaged to the position in which he would be if his rights had not been invaded; and (iii) to ensure as far as possible that persons acting on behalf of the Executive who consciously and deliberately violate the constitutional right of citizens do not for themselves or their superiors obtain the planned results of that invasion ....
>
> This jurisdiction and direct duty arising from the Constitution and the position of the Courts created by it is ... more ample and dominant than [the] inherent jurisdiction recognised by the common law in courts to prevent an abuse of their own processes."[6]

STANDING

Before litigants may raise a constitutional claim in the courts, they must have *locus standi*, or "standing," to do so; otherwise and in the absence of special circumstances, their claim will not be entertained.[7] Standing requirements vary considerably from country to country. At the one extreme there is France, where only a very limited category of individuals are entitled to challenge the validity of legislation, and then only prior to its coming into force. In contrast, Article 38(d) of the South African Constitution extends standing to make claims under its Bill of Rights to "anyone acting in the public interest." There is no provision in the Constitution that addresses this question other than Article 26 which enables the President to refer Bills to the Supreme Court in order to determine whether they are consistent with the Constitution.

Standing could be confined to circumstances equivalent to where private law rights are infringed, namely where the plaintiff contends that he has a definable constitutional right that is being violated to his own material prejudice.

---

[4] *Id.* at p.122.
[5] [1985] I.R. 573.
[6] *Id.* at p.122.
[7] See generally, A. Collins and J. O'Reilly, *Civil Proceedings and the State in Ireland* (2nd ed., 2003), Chap.6 and G. Whyte, *Social Inclusion and the Legal System: Public Interest Law in Ireland* (2002), pp.62 *et seq.*

Or standing can be more extensive: for instance, where a plaintiff seeking declaratory relief has a tangible interest in the impugned governmental action but no definable right of his is being infringed, or even where he does not have that tangible interest but complains of a substantive breach of the rule of law. Requirements for standing reflect the role of the judiciary in the overall constitutional scheme of things. As the Chief Justice of Israel once remarked, "a judge whose judicial philosophy is based merely on the view that the role of the judge is to decide a dispute between persons with existing rights is very different from a judge whose judicial philosophy is enshrined in the recognition that his role is to create rights and enforce the rule of law."[8] Standing therefore is just one aspect of the more general question of justiciability considered earlier.

There are different kinds of constitutional provisions and the standing requirements for cases concerning some of these are different from those for others. Furthermore, parties in cases who raise constitutional questions appear in court in varying roles - as either plaintiffs or defendants in civil actions, or as the accused in criminal prosecutions. It may well be that the standing requirement should vary somewhat with whatever role the person raising the constitutional issue plays in the case. Whether an aggrieved person or body has standing can turn on the remedy he is seeking; it is when the remedy sought is a declaratory order that the question of standing – and also of ripeness and mootness – can be become particularly acute. At times, lack of standing is invoked by the courts as a pretext for not addressing some issue that would be inconvenient for them to rule on. At other times, strong *prima facie* standing objections are rejected where the court is anxious to rule on a particular matter. Accordingly, the regime governing *locus standi* in constitutional cases is not written in stone and there is some inconsistency in judicial decisions on this question.

Adverse Effect

As a general rule, plaintiffs must be able to demonstrate that they suffered, are suffering or are about to suffer a distinctive loss due to the impugned measure. This is because it has been held that, under the Constitution, the function of the courts is to administer justice and not to resolve hypothetical issues of constitutional law. Requiring plaintiffs to have a distinctive stake in the issue being raised ensures that scarce judicial resources are not wasted in resolving theoretical and moot points, and should guarantee that both sides of the case

---

[8] *Ressler v. Minister for Defence*, 42(2) P.D. 441 at p.458. Compare *Union de Pequenos Agricultores v. Council* (Case C–50/001) [2003] 2 W.L.R. 795 on standing to challenge E.C. rules and decisions.

are adequately prepared and presented. As O'Higgins C.J. stated in the leading case, *Cahill v. Sutton*:

> "Without the exercise of (the courts') jurisdiction, the checks and balances of the Constitution would cease to operate and those rights and liberties which are both the heritage and the mark of free men would be endangered. However, the jurisdiction should be exercised for the purpose for which it was conferred — in protection of the Constitution and of the rights and liberties thereby conferred. Where the person who questions the validity of a law can point to no right of his which has been broken, endangered or threatened by reason of the alleged invalidly, then, if nothing more can be advanced, the Courts should not entertain a question so raised. To do so would be to make of the Courts the happy hunting ground of the busybody and the crank. Worse still, it would result in a jurisdiction which ought to be prized as the citizen's shield and protection becoming debased and devalued."[9]

As was explained by Henchy J. "[t]he primary rule as to standing in constitutional matters is that the person challenging the constitutionality of the statute, or some other person for whom he is deemed by the court to be entitled to speak, must be able to assert that, because of the alleged unconstitutionality, his or that other person's interests have been adversely affected, or stand in real or imminent danger of being adversely affected by the operation of the statute."[10] Requiring such impact ensures that the question at issue is decided against the background of actual events, which usually facilitates reaching the correct conclusion on the net point; it "ensures that normally the controversy will rest on facts which are referable primarily and specifically to the challenger, thus giving concreteness and firsthand reality to what might otherwise be an abstract or hypothetical legal argument."[11] In the absence of circumstances showing loss inflicted or pending, cases tend to lack the force of urgency and reality. Furthermore, impact as described guarantees that the case will be argued thoroughly and vigorously; it lessens the likelihood of a situation arising where persons, who in fact suffer loss in consequence of a particular Act or regulation, have a grievance because some busybody previously conducted an inept constitutional challenge against its provisions. A challenge based on one set of facts may fail while a challenge to the same measure but based on a very different set of facts may subsequently succeed. Not requiring adverse impact, it was said, could result in a great waste of scarce legal resources; it would be an irresistible attraction for the "litigious

---

[9] [1980] I.R. 269 at pp.277–278.
[10] *Id.* at p.286.
[11] *Id.* at p.282.

person, the crank, the obstructionist, the meddlesome, the perverse, the officious man of straw and many others" to indulge in constitutional litigation rather than simply observing the law.[12] Finally it was said that there are important separation of powers considerations; it "would be contrary to the spirit of the Constitution if the courts were to allow those who were opposed to a particular legislative measure, inside or outside Parliament, to have an unrestricted and unqualified right to move from the political arena to the High Court once a Bill had become an Act."[13]

Assuming, however, that the Government is acting in breach of the Constitution, it subverts the very rule of law to reject a plaintiff's challenge to that action on the grounds that he is a meddlesome crank and a man of straw. On the basis of this assumption, it is difficult to understand how the separation of powers would be subverted if the courts were to entertain proceedings that could result in that unconstitutionality being established and the rule of law being maintained. A particular difficulty that arises here is where the plaintiff seeks to conduct his case without legal representation and is not doing so in a competent manner.

Application

The courts adopt a generous view of what is an "adversely affected" set of circumstances for the purpose of standing and, in appropriate cases, will permit constitutional issues to be raised where the party to the proceedings is not personally prejudiced in any manner. A party has standing to challenge the validity of a law where its operation or effect deprives him of a right that is protected by the Constitution or appreciably diminishes its enjoyment. That right may be the same as that protected by the law of tort, such as personal integrity and bodily security, enjoyment of property and engaging in economic activity. Or it may be one of the other rights, such as to vote, freedom of expression, privacy and family relations. A party has also standing where his constitutionally protected right is about to be interfered with or is in significant jeopardy of being contravened. Thus, in the *East Donegal Co-Op* case,[14] where a recently enacted law regulating the livestock marketing business was challenged, the plaintiffs were organisations that were involved in that business and some of their shareholders. Although no losses had yet been inflicted on them by the new Act, it was held that they had standing because they were "engaged in the type of business which is directly affected, and subject to control, by provisions of the Act ...".[15] In the *Norris* case[16] the plaintiff, who

---

[12] *Id.* at p.284.
[13] *Ibid.*
[14] [1970] I.R. 317.
[15] *Id.* at p.339.
[16] [1984] I.R. 36.

challenged an Act that criminalised several homosexual practices, was a homosexual but had never been prosecuted under that law, nor could he prove any particular discrimination against him by the State on account of his sexual orientation. Nevertheless, it was held that he had the requisite standing. According to O'Higgins C.J., "as long as the legislation stands and continues to proclaim as criminal the conduct which the plaintiff asserts he has a right to engage in, such right, if it exists, is threatened and the plaintiff has standing to seek the protection of the court."[17]

Individuals also have standing to bring claims against measures concerning the functioning of the general political process. In *McMahon v. Attorney General*,[18] the leading case on electoral boundaries, the successful plaintiff was not even registered to vote in Dáil elections. Persons have been permitted to challenge the constitutionality of international agreements that the State proposed to make[19] and also to contest international agreements that the State had signed and was proposing to ratify.[20] Even the allocation of public funds for an alleged unconstitutional objective has been held to be a fit subject for a constitutional challenge by an individual.[21] On the other hand, where civil servants were adversely affected by a decision of the Government to cease collecting the farm tax, it was held that they did not have the standing to obtain an order declaring this decision to be invalid.[22] But they were granted other reliefs in consequence of the manner in which this decision had prejudiced them.

Exceptions and Qualifications

There are exceptions to this "rule of judicial restraint," which is not absolute. One arises where "those prejudicially affected by the impugned statute may not be in a position to assert adequately, or in time, their constitutional rights."[23] A very old example is an individual being held in detention, in breach of the Constitution, and physically prevented from instituting proceedings: for many years, any person with a genuine interest could commence Article 40.4/*habeas corpus* proceedings in order to secure the release of a person being unlawfully detained.[24] A more recent instance is a group established to defend the right to life of the unborn, who were permitted to take proceedings against aspects of abortion.[25]

---

[17] *Id.* at p.339.
[18] [1972] I.R. 69; *supra*, p.592.
[19] *Boland v. An Taoiseach* [1974] I.R. 338; *supra*, p.229.
[20] *Crotty v. An Taoiseach* [1087] I.R. 713; *supra*, p.230.
[21] *McKenna v. An Taoiseach (No.2)* [1995] 2 I.R. 10; *supra*, p.394.
[22] *Duggan v. An Taoiseach* [1989] I.R. 713; *supra*, p.209.
[23] *Cahill v. Sutton* [1980] I.R. at p.285.
[24] *Supra*, p.338.
[25] *Society for the Protection of the Unborn Child (Ireland) Ltd v. Coogan* [1989] I.R. 734.

Another exception is where the Act or provision in question "is directed at or operable against a grouping which includes the challenger, or with whom the challenger may be said to have a common interest particularly in cases where, because of the nature of the subject matter, it is difficult to segregate those affected from those not affected by the challenged provision."[26] What exactly Henchy J. had in mind here is not entirely clear, but probably he was considering laws affecting categories of companies or of organisations or associations.

Over and above any of these situations, the courts will waive the normal standing requirement in order to ensure that justice is done; that requirement will be waived "if, in the particular circumstances of a case, the court finds that there are weighty countervailing considerations justifying a departure from the rule."[27] Thus a serving judge was held to have standing to challenge the manner in which the Minister exercised his power to grant remission of sentences handed down by the courts.[28]

A procedure exists at common law whereby, if someone is about to contravene some statutory provision and thereby inflict loss or damage on an individual, that person can call on the Attorney General to bring suit in order to have the breach of statutory duty enjoined. Usually, in those circumstances, the Attorney will permit the individual to proceed with the action in the Attorney's name – at the relator of the Attorney; hence the description "relator action." It was held by the Supreme Court in *Attorney General (Society for the Protection of Unborn Children Ireland Ltd) v. Open Door Counselling Ltd*[29] that an organisation, the main aim of which was to challenge abortion-related activities, was entitled to bring an action in the Attorney General's name with the object of having certain practices enjoined for contravening the right to life of the unborn as guaranteed in Article 40.3.3.

Corporations

Many of the rights in the Constitution are described as "personal rights" and indeed the terms "human person," "man," "woman," "mother" and "child" appear in the formulation of some of these rights. The question therefore arises whether or to what extent can corporations assert rights under the Constitution and, in particular, bring proceedings to have an Act of the Oireachtas declared invalid. Some of the Constitution's provisions have plainly no direct application to corporate bodies, such as statutory corporations and registered companies, and consequently they would not have *locus standi* to assert those rights. Where, however, they are formed in order to vindicate individuals' particular personal

---

[26] *Cahill v. Sutton* [1980] I.R. at p.285.
[27] *Ibid.*
[28] *Brennan v. Minister for Justice* [1995] 1 I.R. 612.
[29] [1988] I.R. 593.

rights, generally they will be permitted to institute constitutional claims for that purpose – for example the Society for the Protection of Unborn Children.[30]

Formerly, there was a view that the guarantees regarding private property did not directly benefit corporations and, in consequence, where a particular measure affected a corporate financial interest, the practice was that one or more of its members would bring the proceedings. This practice does not appear to have been objected to, on the grounds that the corporation's lack of a constitutional right should not be circumvented in that manner. Eventually in *Iarnród Éireann v. Ireland*,[31] Keane J. held that the guarantee of private property covered corporate as well as individuals' property.

In *Quinn's Supermarket v. Attorney General*,[32] the Supreme Court held that Article 40.1's formulation of the equality guarantee precluded corporations from invoking that right in an action to have regulations issued under an Act of the Oireachtas struck down on the grounds that they discriminated unfairly. But in the light of Keane J.'s reasoning in the *Iarnród* case, it is unlikely that this is the position today. There appears to be no sound practical ground for holding that the ban on unequal treatment should not apply as much to corporations as to individuals, although the potential scope for invidious discrimination is much greater in the case of individuals.

Non-Nationals

With regard to non-nationals or aliens one question is whether they are entitled to rights which are expressly guaranteed to "citizens," *e.g.* to vote, to stand in elections for the Oireachtas, equality, fair procedures, personal liberty, inviolability of the dwelling, freedom of expression, assembly and association, and freedom of conscience. These are by implication extended to non-nationals except for rights which traditionally have been confined to citizens, such as to stand and vote in parliamentary elections and, by definition, to nationality and citizenship. Indeed, it was held that citizens had such a strong constitutional interest in their vote in Dáil elections that this right could not be diluted by the Oireachtas extending the franchise to certain aliens;[33] the Constitution had to be amended in order to permit selective extension of the franchise to non-nationals.[34]

In the *Nicolaou* case,[35] which concerned the Adoption Acts, it was held that the plaintiff, a non-national who resided in England, was entitled to challenge those Acts' validity in the light of Articles 41 and 42, which do not

---

[30] *Ibid.* and *supra*, n.25.
[31] [1996] 3 I.R. 321.
[32] [1972] I.R. 1.
[33] *Electoral (Amendment) Bill, 1983, Re* [1984] I.R. 268; *supra*, p.387.
[34] *Supra*, p.595.
[35] [1966] I.R. 567; *supra*, p.711.

refer to citizens. In the *L'Henryenat* case,[36] a non-national sought to have provisions of the Fisheries (Consolidation) Act 1959 declared unconstitutional for violating Article 38.1 and the personal liberty guarantees. But it appears that his *locus standi* was not questioned there. Non-nationals have been permitted to challenge the constitutionality of measures that uniquely affect them, such as the law on nationality and citizenship, and procedures for deportation and extradition. Presumably it is because they are almost invariably permitted to raise constitutional arguments, as if they were citizens, that it has never been argued that nationals of States with which Ireland has Friendship, Commerce and Navigation Treaties should have favourable treatment as regards standing in constitutional actions. Nor does it appear to have been argued that nationals of EC Member States should enjoy advantages in that regard, especially when the Treaty of Rome outlaws discrimination against nationals of Member States within the scope of the Treaty, and Article 29.4.3 of the Constitution virtually subjects the entire Constitution to that Treaty.

Ius Tertii

The *ius tertii* question, which is closely related to that of standing, concerns whether a particular argument is open to a litigant who is seeking to have a law declared invalid because it operates in an unconstitutionally unfair manner but who is not directly affected by that very unfairness. Thus in the *Norris* case,[37] the plaintiff challenged prohibitions on certain homosexual practices, including buggery, and argued *inter alia* that the law in question contravened marital privacy. Because he was not married and, by his own declaration, would never be married, it was held that an argument based on the constitutional rights of married persons was not open to him. O'Higgins C.J. reasoned that "it is *nihil ad rem* for the plaintiff to suggest, as a reason for alleviating his own predicament, a possible impact of the impugned legislation on a situation which is not his, and to point to a possible injury or prejudice which he has neither suffered nor is in imminent danger of suffering ...".[38]

In rejecting the *ius tertii* argument, the court was following *Cahill v. Sutton*,[39] where a similar contention was raised for the first time during the appeal. The plaintiff claimed that she had suffered injury in 1968, as a result of negligent medical treatment administered by the defendant, and sought damages. One of the defences was that the action was out of time under section 11(2)(b) of the Statute of Limitations 1957. Her reply was that this provision was unconstitutional because it operated most unjustly in particular circumstances, notably where it shut out persons who never even knew or

---

[36] [1983] I.R. 193.
[37] [1984] I.R. 36; *supra*, p.661.
[38] *Id.* at p.58.
[39] [1980] I.R. 269.

could know that they had a right of action within the three year period following the injury. Because the plaintiff had always been fully aware of the facts entitling her to sue for damages, it was contended that this argument could not be made by her — that she could not "conjure up, invoke and champion the putative constitutional rights of a hypothetical third party so that the provisions ... may be declared unconstitutional on the basis of that constitutional *ius tertii* ...".[40] The Supreme Court held that she should not be permitted to make such an argument because, if constitutional challenges could be mounted on the basis of the *ius tertii*, there was the grave danger that the courts would be flooded with a multiplicity of constitutional actions based on hypothesis, and it could offend the spirit of the Constitution and indeed damage the courts if those claims were readily entertained. As Henchy J. stated, for the court:

> "Were the Courts to accede to the plaintiff's plea that she should be accorded standing merely because she would indirectly and conse-quentially benefit from a declaration of unconstitutionality, countless statutory provisions would become open to challenge at the instance of litigants who, in order to acquire standing to sue, would only have to show that some such consequential benefit would accrue to them from a declaration of unconstitutionality – notwithstanding that the statutory provision may never have affected adversely any particular person's interests, or be in any real or imminent danger of doing so. It would be contrary to precedent, constitutional propriety and the common good for the High Court or this Court to proclaim itself an open house for the reception of such claims."[41]

Whether the defendant in a criminal prosecution would be permitted to raise the *ius tertii* against the statutory offence alleged to have been committed has not been determined. But in the *Norris* case,[42] McCarthy J., dissenting, refused to reject the plaintiff's argument that the law being challenged there contravened family rights, on the grounds that the *Cahill* case was not binding on this particular question. He demonstrated absurdities that could arise if criminal defendants were debarred from arguing the *ius tertii*, citing United States cases where those arguments have been relied upon in order to strike down criminal statutes.

Intervention

Another question related to standing, is that of third party intervention in ongoing proceedings. In ordinary private law litigation, the circumstances in

---

[40] *Id.* at p.280.
[41] *Id.* at p.286.
[42] [1984] I.R. 36.

which a non-party can participate in a trial are strictly limited.[43] But in judicial review applications the court has a wide discretion to permit sufficiently interested parties intervene.[44] There is a strong tradition in some countries of non-parties intervening in constitutional litigation, where the outcome of the proceedings will affect a significant number of individuals who are not directly implicated in the dispute. But that is most unusual in Ireland, except for instances where the Attorney General seeks to intervene in the broader public interest. Unlike in the USA and Canada, and indeed more recently in the UK,[45] bodies representing civil liberties, environmental, consumer and other equivalent interests rarely seek to intervene in constitutional cases before the Irish courts. This may change and indeed the Human Rights Commission is expressly authorised to involve itself in proceedings as *amicus curiae*.

RIPENESS

Where the underlying issue in proceedings has not crystallised into an outright dispute between the parties and circumstances may very well evolve to prevent a full blown dispute arising, or to structure it in a manner significantly different to that presently envisaged, a court may decline to adjudicate on that issue because it is not "ripe" for determination. Where it appears that future events will or may very well affect the parties, with regard to the underlying issue, a balance must then be struck between the undesirability of dealing with it prematurely and the hardship the parties will encounter if its resolution is deferred to another day. Like standing, the question of ripeness is another aspect of the more general issue of justiciability considered earlier. There are no definite principles or rules setting out when an issue becomes sufficiently ripe to warrant a trial taking place and, at times, a finding of unripeness may be a convenient device to avoid having to resolve a difficult issue.

In *Blythe v. Attorney General (No. 2)*,[46] the plaintiffs had formed a political organisation, the Young Ireland Association, which the Free State Government declared illegal. They then formed an entirely new organisation, the League of Youth, and on the very same day instituted proceedings claiming a declaration that, under the 1922 Constitution's guarantee of free association, they were entitled to form that body. Johnston J. held that, since the Government had taken no action whatsoever to suppress the new association, which according to the plaintiffs was wholly unconnected with the previous one, he had no jurisdiction to make the binding declaration being sought; or if he had jurisdiction, he exercised his discretion to dismiss the action because the

---

[43] *Barlow v. Fanning* [2002] 2 I.R. 593.
[44] RSC, O.84, r.22(6) and 26(1). Cf. Whyte, *supra*, n.7, pp.92 *et seq.*
[45] *Northern Ireland Human Rights Commission, Re* [2002] N.I. 236.
[46] [1936] I.R. 549.

plaintiffs "have not been attacked."[47] In contrast, in the *East Donegal Co-Op.* case,[48] it was found that the prospect of economic loss was sufficiently immediate in the circumstances for the plaintiffs' case to be heard. And in *Norris*[49] it was held that, where there is a criminal prohibition against conduct arguably protected by the Constitution, it is irrelevant that the plaintiff has not been prosecuted or indeed, for one reason or another, is most unlikely to be prosecuted.

MOOTNESS

Mootness is the very converse of ripeness; instead of the issue being deemed to be too premature for adjudication, mootness concerns circumstances where it is too late to hold a trial because, for all practical purposes, the issue between the parties has already been resolved in another manner. It may be that the underlying legal framework has changed to such extent that the plaintiff can no longer have a live grievance, calling for a remedial court order, or that the underlying facts have changed to a similar extent. Alternatively the relief being sought may have been provided by a party before the case is due to be heard. For instance in *Eastern Health Board v. E (No. 1)*,[50] at the very commencement of *habeas corpus* proceedings the defendants surrendered custody of the child in question and thereafter did not claim any entitlement to its custody. The Supreme Court held that the issue between the parties had then become moot and that should have been the end of the High Court proceedings. Some of the arguments for restrictive standing requirements support the courts not deciding a constitutional controversy that, as between the parties, has become moot.

There are circumstances, however, where the courts are willing to resolve constitutional questions notwithstanding that they have become moot as between the parties to the action. One of these is where the very same question is very likely to recur and will require resolution sooner or later. Thus in *Sherwin v. Minister for the Environment*,[51] where the plaintiff sought a declaration that part of the regulations under which the 1995 divorce referendum was conducted were invalid, she succeeded even though the referendum had long passed and nothing could then be done about its outcome. In response to the contention that her claim should be dismissed for being moot, Costello P. said that "[t]he possibility that other referenda will take place in circumstances similar to those (in 1995) is not a fanciful one and the issue raised by the plaintiff may very

---

[47] *Id.* at p.554. See too *Lennon v. Ganly* [1981] I.L.R.M. 84.
[48] [1970] I.R. 317.
[49] [1984] I.R. 36.
[50] [2000] 1 I.R. 430.
[51] Costello P. , November 11, 1997; *supra*, p.607.

well arise again. It therefore is proper that the court should clarify the Minister's legal powers'.[52] Because a person's conviction in a criminal case has serious collateral consequences, his challenge to that conviction does not become moot merely because he has served his prison sentence.[53]

Where, in between a case being decided and the time an appeal against it is to be heard, the issue becomes moot, that appeal may still be determined if there is a strong public interest in having the question resolved. In *Application of Zwann*,[54] the Attorney General sought to appeal against an order of *habeas corpus* where several foreign fishermen had been ordered to be released. They had left the jurisdiction and there was no real prospect of them ever returning. Nevertheless, it was held that the appeal should be heard because it raised a matter "of real concern" to the Attorney. In *Condon v. Minister for Labour*,[55] the plaintiffs appealed the High Court's dismissal of their claim that temporary legislation regulating wages in the banking industry was unconstitutional. But in the meantime the duration of the impugned Act's term expired. It was held that once a cause of action existed when the proceedings commenced, the court was not deprived of jurisdiction to hear it merely because the Act which was being challenged was no longer in force. Kenny J. stressed the temporary nature of the Act there, the likelihood that identical measures would be reintroduced and, if the constitutionality of measures that had expired could never be tested, the Government would have a very simple device to contravene constitutional values in a perfectly lawful manner. The governing principle is whether similar legislation is likely to be reintroduced: that "[w]hen an issue arises as to whether the court should decline to entertain a case because the legislation attacked is no longer in force, the question to be asked is whether similar legislation is likely to be introduced in the future. Unless the court is satisfied that such legislation will not be introduced again, it should decide the case even though the Act is not in force."[56] In the event, the plaintiffs did not continue with their case.

A more recent instance is *Sinnott v. Minister for Education*,[57] where the High Court had held that the guarantee in Article 42.4 of free primary education lasts beyond eighteen years of age and the State sought to appeal that determination. Notwithstanding, the State paid damages to the first plaintiff on the basis of the High Court's ruling. In view of this, Keane C.J. felt that the appeal had become moot,[58] adding that he would have agreed with the High Court if it weren't moot. But the other judges concluded that the circumstances

---

[52] At p.22. *Cf.* Whyte, *supra*, n.7, pp.101 *et seq.*
[53] *S. O'C. v. Governor Curragh Prison* [2002] 1 I.R. 66.
[54] [1981] I.R. 395.
[55] [1981] I.R. 62.
[56] *Id.* at p.72.
[57] [2001] 2 I.R. 541
[58] *Id.* at p.636.

warranted the central issue there being decided and they held that the guarantee lasts only up to that age.

Where a plaintiff is seeking a mandatory or prohibitory order, his claim for that relief may become moot but he may have an outstanding claim for damages to be decided.

DELAY/LIMITATIONS

Where a plaintiff in any kind of proceedings seeks a mandatory or prohibitory order from the court, he may be refused it on account of undue delay on his part. Regardless of the relief he is seeking, he may be defeated by the Statutes of Limitation 1957-2000.

Where the nature of the constitutional claim being made closely resembles one of the categories provided for in these Acts, they are applied by way of analogy to the action. In *McDonnell v. Ireland*,[59] where the plaintiff sought damages for being deprived of his job as a civil servant twenty years previously, the Supreme Court held that he had an adequate remedy under the common law for his grievance, being that of the tort of misfeasance in public office or else breach of contract. Consequently, it was held that the appropriate limitation period for his claim was that prescribed in the 1957-2000 Acts for those causes of action. That in the proceedings he sought declarations of unconstitutionality added nothing of substance to his claim as its real focus was financial redress for losing his job. As Barrington J. explained:

> "Constitutional rights should not be regarded as wild cards which can be played at any time to defeat all existing rules. If the general law provides an adequate cause of action to vindicate a constitutional right it appears to me that the injured party cannot ask the court to devise a new and different cause of action. Thus the Constitution guarantees the citizen's right to his or her good name but the cause of action to defend his or her good name is the action for defamation. The injured party, it appears to me, has to accept the action for defamation with all its incidents including the time limit within which the action must be commenced. Likewise the victim of careless driving has the action for negligence by means of which to vindicate his rights. But he must, generally, commence his action within three years. He cannot wait longer and then bring an action for breach of his constitutional right to bodily integrity."[60]

It remains to be determined what principles apply where the gist of the case

---

[59] [1998] 1 I.R. 134.
[60] *Id.* at p.148.

does not have a near equivalent provided for in the 1957–2000 Acts. It was suggested in *McDonnell* that all breaches of constitutional rights are torts for these purposes but the court there declined to decide that issue, since it did not strictly arise.

EVIDENCE

The very same rules of evidence apply in constitutional actions as in all other legal proceedings but two particular questions call for brief comment. In references by the President to the Supreme Court under Article 26, evidence is not taken. There is no actual rule that prevents evidence being adduced in proceedings of that nature but the practice has been not to admit evidence. There can be a serious flaw in evidence not being available in cases where a Bill has been passed which is premised on assumptions that are not factually sustainable.

Travaux preparatoires in drafting the Constitution are not taken into account when interpreting its provisions. Nor ordinarily are they taken into account when interpreting the provisions of an Act of the Oireachtas.[61] But it was held by Budd J. in the *An Blascaod Mór (No.2)*[62] case that it is permissible to look at earlier versions of an impugned Act, when the provision in question is ambiguous. He concluded that "the Court is entitled to look at the wording of the Bill relevant to [the] section as the court is concerned with constitutional litigation and the application of the double construction rule and severability principle and as it may assist interpreting the Act and the section."[63]

DECLARATION

A declaratory judgment is a formal statement by the court of the existence or non-existence of a legal state of affairs.[64] Where a dispute is decided by the court making a declaratory order, it is usually taken for granted that the losing party will abide by the law, as pronounced in the order, especially where that party is the State or one of its agencies. Questions of *locus standi*, and of ripeness and mootness, and also the desirability of putting other potentially affected persons on notice, most frequently arise when a party seeks declaratory relief.

By far the commonest remedy sought in constitutional litigation is a declaration that the Act, regulation, action or whatever in question is invalid

---

[61] *Controller of Patents v. Ireland* [2001] 4 I.R. 229.
[62] [2000] 1 I.R. 1.
[63] *Id.* at p.4. Similarly, *Wilson v. First County Trust Ltd (No.2)* [2003] 3 W.L.R. 568.
[64] Woolf, *The Declaratory Judgment* (3rd ed., 2002), p.1.

by virtue of the Constitution. Sometimes that is the only remedy claimed; at other times declarations are sought merely to formulate the legal basis to a claim for damages or an injunction. For instance, in *McDonnell v. Ireland*,[65] the plaintiff sought declarations that he had been unconstitutionally removed from his office and unconstitutionally denied his salary, superannuation and other benefits, as well as payment of damages for these alleged violations.

Article 15.4.2 of the Constitution stipulates that the provisions of any law enacted by the Oireachtas which contravene the Constitution are invalid and Article 34.3.2 empowers the High Court to declare those provisions invalid. Article 50 carried over into the post-1937 legal system the provisions of pre-1937 laws which are not inconsistent with the Constitution. Whether declaring a pre-1937 law unconstitutional is a declaration of invalidity depends on what definition is being used for the term invalid.

Retroactive Effect

Constitutional laws differ significantly with regard to the temporal effect of a decision that the provisions of a measure are unconstitutional. Under some systems, a finding of invalidity operates only prospectively from the date of the judgment; in other systems, the law is deemed to have been invalid from the very time of its purported enactment; other systems again adopt solutions somewhere in between these two extremes.[66] On account of the very terms of Article 15.4.2, Article 50 and Article 34.3, it has been held that declarations of unconstitutionality under the Constitution operate retroactively. In the case of laws enacted by the post-1937 Oireachtas, it was held in *Murphy v. Attorney General*[67] that an Act which conflicts with the Constitution is invalid and, consequently, was never truly capable of creating rights and imposing obligations. As Henchy J. put it, "a statute of the Oireachtas which incurs judicial condemnation for its repugnancy to the Constitution has invalidity attached to it from the time of its purported enactment by the Oireachtas."[68] Although the matter has never been conclusively determined, it would seem that pre-1937 laws which are deemed to have been legally ineffective since 1937 because they were never carried over into the new State by Article 50 of the Constitution, have been invalid since that date.

However, laws which are found to be unconstitutional will not be treated as never having any effect whatsoever from the time of their purported enactment or since 1937, as the case may be. Because of the chaos that could result from absolutely comprehensive retrospective invalidity, constitutional

---

[65] [1998] 1 I.R. 134.
[66] See generally, M. Cappelletti, *Judicial Review in the Contemporary World* (1971), pp.85 et seq. Cf. *Percy v. Hall* [1997] Q.B. 924.
[67] [1982] I.R. 241.
[68] *Id.*, at p.313.

systems that opt for retroactive invalidation qualify this principle in various ways; conversely, some systems which opt for prospective invalidation also qualify that principle to allow for a degree of retroactive nullity. The implications of retroactive invalidity were considered in detail in *Murphy v. Attorney General*,[69] which concerned one aspect of this general question, *viz.* the extent to which taxes which have been found to be unconstitutional can be recovered from the State by those who had paid them. Before dealing with that particular issue, Henchy J. emphasised that foreign authorities dealing with the temporal effects of findings of unconstitutionality are of little assistance due to the significantly different constitutional provisions in this regard. By virtue of the above-mentioned Articles, the position here is that "once it has been judicially established that a statutory provision enacted by the Oireachtas is repugnant to the Constitution, and that it therefore incurred invalidity from the date of its enactment, the condemned provision will normally provide no legal justification for any acts done or left undone, or for transactions undertaken in pursuance of it …".[70]

Circumstances nevertheless can arise where this principle cannot be applied at all. For instance, it was held in *McMahon v. Attorney General*[71] that the system of voting, which obtained before 1972, was unconstitutional because it did not adequately safeguard secrecy. If retroactive invalidity were to be carried to its logical conclusion there, it would mean that all pre-1972 Dáils were not properly constituted and, accordingly, all laws enacted between 1937 and 1972 were not properly adopted and therefore are null and void. For obvious practical reasons, therefore, the principle of retroactive invalidation cannot always be fully applied. As Henchy J. explained in the *Murphy* case:

"For a variety of reasons the law recognises that in certain circumstances, no matter how unfounded in law certain conduct may have been, no matter how unwarranted its operation in a particular case, what has happened has happened and cannot, or should not, be undone. The irreversible progressions and by-products of time, the compulsion of public order and the common good, the aversion of the law from giving a hearing to those who have slept on their rights, the quality of legality – even irreversibility - that tends to attach to what has become inveterate or has been widely accepted or acted upon, the recognition that even in the short term the accomplished fact may sometimes acquire an inviolable sacredness, these and other factors may convert what has been done under an unconstitutional, or otherwise void, law into an acceptable part of the *corpus juris*."[72]

---

[69] [1982] I.R. 241; *supra*, p.670.
[70] *Id.* at p.313.
[71] [1972] I.R. 69; *supra*, p.592.
[72] *Id.* at pp.314–315.

Beyond these observations, neither he nor the other judges would be drawn into giving a general answer to the questions of "when, and to what extent, acts done on foot of an unconstitutional law may be immune from suit in the Courts?"[73] As to the specific issue of unconstitutional taxes, it was held that parties are entitled to be reimbursed taxes they have paid as from "the first year for which they effectively objected to the flow of those taxes into the central fund."[74]

Where declaring an Act or statutory provision invalid will have immediate and drastic consequences for public administration, courts in some countries direct that their declaration shall be suspended for a specified period, in order that the legislature may adopt appropriate alternative provisions, in line with the constitutional requirements.[75] To date, that has not occurred in Ireland. But on a few occasions the Government anticipated declarations of invalidity being made by having ready Bills for amending the legislation in question, which were rushed through both Houses and signed within days of the court's decision.

Severance

Where only some provisions in a contract, a will or a deed are unlawful, the entire instrument is not thereby rendered unlawful: clauses which are not unlawful and can stand on their own will be severed from the illegal ones and will be enforced by the courts. A similar approach is adopted where the nature of the illegality is unconstitutionality. Thus, in *Blake, Re*,[76] where it was held that provisions in a will directing that the testator's grandchildren be brought up as Catholics contravened the guarantee of parental authority, the question that most preoccupied Dixon J. was how to sever the unconstitutional direction from the remainder of the will; in particular, whether the gifts of the income and the capital that were tied by the unconstitutional condition failed. It was held that, although attempting to fetter parents' discretion regarding the religious upbringing of their grandchildren is not a crime nor an offence of any kind, and is neither *malum in se* nor *malum prohibitum*, it is "opposed to the policy of the law [which is] written into the fundamental law of this country" and accordingly is void and unenforceable.[77] Consequently, the gifts which were made subject to that condition were also void and unenforceable.

Where it can be done conveniently, the courts will sever the unobjectionable

---

[73] *Id.* at p.315.
[74] *Id.* at p.318. See generally, Pannam, "The Recovery of Unconstitutional Taxes in Australia and the United States", 42 *Texas L. Rev.* 777 (1964).
[75] *E.g. Trocuik v. Attorney General of British Columbia* 14 B.H.R.C. 563 (2003) at pp.573–574.
[76] [1955] I.R. 69.
[77] *Id.* at p.105.

parts of statutory instruments and other regulations from the clauses which are found to be unlawful, because they exceed the statutory grant of delegated authority or they contravene the provisions of the Constitution.[78] In *Cassidy v. Minister for Industry and Commerce*,[79] where the Supreme Court found unconstitutional parts of a statutory instrument that purported to regulate the prices to be charged for liquor in Dundalk, the question then arose of severing the valid provisions from the objectionable ones. It was held that, since those regulations by their terms applied to all categories of bars, both "public" and "lounge," it was not possible to declare them invalid with regard to prices in lounge bars and to sever the provisions regarding public bars. Because of how they were drafted, they did "not lend themselves to verbal severance."[80] However, the court ruled that the regulations should be interpreted as not applying to lounge bars but only to public bars and that, as thus construed, they were not *ultra vires*. In other words, because of their drafting, the offending features of the regulations could not be abstracted in an almost physical sense, the regulations should be construed as not applying in the offensive manner.

There are numerous instances of provisions in Acts of the Oireachtas being severed from those which were found to be unconstitutional. The governing principle is that where the offending provision can be neatly excised, without doing violence to the legislative intentions underlying the measure, the courts will sever. But where severance would result in a meaning that differs significantly from what the Oireachtas intended, the courts will not sever: in that event, the entire section, or entire part of the Act or the entire Act itself, as the case may be, will be declared invalid. As FitzGerald C.J. explained in *Maher v. Attorney General*,[81] where the Supreme Court refused to sever a section in the Road Traffic Act 1968, regarding the conclusive evidentiary nature of a certificate of blood/alcohol content:

> "The application of the doctrine of severability or separability in the judicial review of legislation has the effect that if a particular provision is held to be unconstitutional, and that provision is independent of and severable from the rest, only the offending provision will be declared invalid. The question is one of interpretation of the legislative intent. Article 15, section 4, subs. 2, of the Constitution lays down that every law enacted by the Oireachtas which is in any respect repugnant to the Constitution or to any provision thereof shall, but to the extent only of such repugnancy, be invalid; therefore there is a presumption that a statute

---

[78] See generally, G. Hogan & D. Morgan, *Administrative Law in Ireland* (3rd ed., 1998), pp.473 *et seq.*; *e.g. DPP. v. Hutchinson* [1990] 2 A.C. 783.

[79] [1978] I.R. 297.

[80] *Id.* at p.312.

[81] [1973] I.R. 140.

or a statutory provision is not intended to be constitutionally operative only as an entirety.

This presumption, however, may be rebutted if it can be shown that, after a part has been held unconstitutional, the remainder may be held to stand independently and legally operable as representing the will of the legislature. But if what remains is so inextricably bound up with the part held invalid that the remainder cannot survive independently, or if the remainder would not represent the legislative intent, the remaining part will not be severed and given constitutional validity."[82]

In *King v. Attorney General*,[83] where the court declined to sever section 4 of the Vagrancy Act 1824 in the manner sought by the Attorney General, Henchy J. pointed out that:

"The power of severance is but an aspect of the power of judicial interpretation in the light of the Constitution; it does not amount to a legislative power which, in effect, would allow the Courts to enact that which the legislature did not enact. It is one thing to strike down a particular statutory provision on constitutional grounds. It is quite a different thing, and one for which there is no constitutional warrant, for the Courts to attempt to breathe statutory and constitutional life into a set of words which acquires a new and separate existence after the severance, but which was never enacted as law. That would be a legislative function which the Constitution expressly reserves to the Oireachtas."[84]

There, the court would not excise the words "suspected" and "reputed thief" from section 4 of the 1824 Act, so that it would then read "every person etc.;" to do so would "so unwarrantably extend what was enacted by parliament that it would not be possible to say that the result would represent the enacted will of parliament."[85] To sever in this manner would result in the court extending the scope of criminal liability.

Findings of Inequality

Where a measure which confers some benefit or advantage improperly discriminates against someone, consequent declarations of invalidity can give rise to particular difficulties. If declared invalid, persons who benefited from the measure may be deprived entirely of that benefit even though morally

---

[82] *Id.* at p.147.
[83] [1981] I.R. 233.
[84] *Id.* at pp.259–260.
[85] *Id.* at p.261

there are no good grounds for saying that they should not enjoy that benefit. But because the measure is impermissibly under-inclusive, they may have to bear the brunt of any such invalidation.[86] A solution to this dilemma is to "equalise up" and bring the victim of the discrimination within the scope of the impugned measure. Although that has been done in the case of an archaic common law rule that discriminated against wives,[87] the courts decline to similarly rectify unconstitutional discrimination in Acts of the Oireachtas.[88]

INJUNCTION

An injunction is a court order directing the defendant either to do or not to do something in particular.[89] It is traditionally regarded as an equitable remedy. Refusal to comply with the terms of an injunction is punishable as a contempt of court. At least outside of the constitutional context, there are circumstances where an injunction will not be granted notwithstanding that the plaintiff's rights will be contravened. In brief, these are principally where damages are an adequate remedy, where there has been undue delay in bringing the proceedings, where the courts would have to take an active part in supervising compliance with the order and where it would be impossible to perform the order if made.

Where a party is likely to breach another's constitutional rights, generally the courts will grant an injunction restraining that breach.[90] For instance, in the abortion litigation in the 1980s, the High Court ordered a girl who had become pregnant after being raped not to have an abortion; it also ordered pregnancy counselling bodies and student organisations not to disseminate information concerning abortion facilities available abroad.[91] Sometimes the courts will not grant an injunction, restraining the State from contravening a plaintiff's constitutional rights, on the assumption that making an order simply declaratory of those rights should suffice. On at least one occasion, namely the *McKenna (No.2)* case,[92] the Government disregarded the declaration that was made and did what the Supreme Court had held to be unconstitutional,

---

[86] *E.g.* graduates of university law schools in the Republic, in *Bloomer v. Incorporated Law Society* [1995] 3 I.R. 14; *cf. Abrahamson v. Incorporated Law Society* [1996] 1 I.R. 403.

[87] *McKinley v. Minister for Defence* [1992] 2 I.R. 333; *supra*, p.378.

[88] *MhicMathuna v. Attorney General* [1995] 1 I.R. 484 and other cases considered, *supra*, p.673.

[89] See generally, H. Delany, *Equity and the Law of Trusts in Ireland* (2nd ed., 1999), Chap.13.

[90] See generally, B. McMahon & W. Binchy, *Law of Torts* (3rd ed., 2000), pp.4 *et seq.*

[91] *Society for the Protection of Unborn Children (Ireland) Ltd v. Grogan (No.5)* [1998] 4 I.R. 343.

[92] [1995] 2 I.R. 1.

viz. pay a PR agency £500,000 for pro-divorce publicity generated prior to the 1995 referendum on divorce.[93]

Interlocutory Injunctions

An interlocutory injunction is a temporary order enjoining certain action pending the ultimate resolution of the parties' dispute at the trial. In an appropriate case and on the basis of the conventional criteria, courts will grant such orders restraining unconstitutional activity. Where the constitutionality of an Act of the Oireachtas is the basis for the plaintiff's case, that is an additional factor to include in the balance. Apart from the presumption of unconstitutionality that an Act enjoys, to temporarily restrain enforcing it could severely prejudice many individuals who stand to benefit from its terms and for whom the usual undertaking as to damages is not sufficient protection in the event that the challenge does not eventually succeed. Exceptionally, however, implementation of an Act's provisions will be enjoined pending the trial of the action.[94]

Mandatory/Structural Injunctions

At times, plaintiffs seek mandatory injunctions, compelling the State or other defendant to do something, in order to vindicate their rights. Traditionally, courts have been reluctant to grant such orders because of difficulties arising in supervising them. Those problems might be alleviated somewhat by the court retaining seisin of the case in order to monitor compliance with its directions.[95] Where it is shown to be impossible for a public body to discharge its clear statutory duty, it will not be ordered by the courts to carry out that duty.[96]

In several countries, courts grant what have been described as "structural injunctions," obliging State authorities to carry out a programme that requires some time and significant finance to complete, and possibly even legislation.[97] Perhaps the best known of these are the endeavours to end race segregation in public schools in the US following *Brown v. Board of Education*.[98] Comparable

---

[93] *The Irish Times*, January, 1996.

[94] *Pesca Valentia Ltd v. Minister for Fisheries* [1985] I.R. 193; compare *Controller of Patents v. Ireland* [2001] 4 I.R. 229 and *Grange Developments Ltd v. Dublin C.C.* [1989] I.R. 377.

[95] *E.g. Auton v. Attorney General*, 197 D.L.R. 4th 165 (2001), but disapproved of by Keane C.J. in *Sinnott v. Minister for Education* [2001] 2 I.R. 541 at p. 640 and in *Attorney General v. Doucet-Boudreau*, 203 D.L.R. 4th 128 (2001).

[96] *Brady v. Cavan C.C.* [1999] 4 I.R. 9.

[97] See generally, D. Dobbs, *Law of Remedies* (2nd ed., 1993), pp.641 *et seq.*

[98] 347 U.S. 483 (1954).

orders were made by the South African Constitutional Court to force the Government to deal more effectively with the HIV/AIDS epidemic there.[99] In *Crowley v. Ireland*,[100] McWilliam J. ordered the Minister for Education to provide buses so that school children could be "bused" to schools in the parishes adjoining Drimoleague; McMahon J., who subsequently tried the case, made no further order against the Minister. But on the basis of what the Supreme Court held in *T.D. v. Minister for Education*,[101] it would appear that similar orders would not now be granted because, it was held, to do so would contravene the separation of powers. In view of what was done in those other countries, separation of powers is a most unconvincing explanation for this decision. The true reason would appear to be either the view that the High Court's earlier decisions on the merits in the *F.N.*[102] and in the *D.B.*[103] cases were wrong, or else plain unwillingness to endeavour to force the Government to comply with its constitutional obligations.

In 1995 Geoghegan J. held in the *F.N. v. Minister for Education*[104] that, where children have special needs, there is an affirmative constitutional obligation on the State to take the necessary steps to cater for those needs, including establishing suitable arrangements for containing and treating them. No final order was made and, within a week of the decision, it appears that the Minister satisfied the judge that appropriate steps were in the process of being taken. But those proposals were then substantially departed from and, three years later, "little concrete progress" had been made in preparing appropriate legislation to deal with the problem and progress was extremely slow on the administrative side.[105] There was "uncontroverted evidence ... that 60 places [we]re required to accommodate children with needs [of this nature]."[106]

Later, in *D.B. v. Minister for Justice*[107] proceedings were commenced on behalf of a 15 year old boy in need of institutional care for an injunction directing the Minister to "build, open and maintain a secure 24 bed high support unit at Portrane in Dublin." On account of the protracted delays and frequent changes of policy by the Minister, even on the very day preceding the hearing of this motion, it was contended that the only way of ensuring that the applicant's rights would be protected was by making the mandatory order. Kelly J. held that the court had jurisdiction to make the order sought and, in all the

---

[99] *Minister of Health v. Treatment Action Campaign*, 13 B.H.R.C. 1 (2002), The Canadian Supreme Court did not go quite as far as this in *Re Language Rights under section 23 of the Manitoba Act, Re*, 19 D.L.R. 4th 1 (1985).
[100] Unreported, High Court, McWilliam J.; referred to in [1980] I.R. 102 at p.108.
[101] [2001] 4 I.R. 259.
[102] *F.N. v. Minister for Education* [1995] 1 I.R. 409.
[103] *D.B. v. Minister for Justice* [1999] 1 I.R. 29.
[104] [1995] 1 I.R. 409.
[105] [1999] 1 I.R. 29 at p.36.
[106] *Id.* at p.38.
[107] [1999] 1 I.R. 29.

circumstances, that it ought to be made. On the jurisdiction question, he observed that "in carrying out its constitutional function of defending and vindicating personal rights, the Court must have available to it any power necessary to do so in an effective way. If that were not the case, this Court could not carry out the obligation imposed upon it to vindicate and defend such rights. This power exists regardless of the status of a respondent. The fact that in the present case the principal respondent is the Minister for Health is no reason for believing that he is in some way immune from orders of this Court in excess of mere declarations if such orders are required to vindicate the personal rights of a citizen."[108] Dealing with the contention that making such an order would implicate the courts in questions of policy, the judge's response was that "[i]f such an intervention were required in order for this Court to carry out its duties under the Constitution in securing, vindicating and enforcing constitutional rights, then, in my view, it would be open to it to so do. One would hope that such a situation would not arise. However, I need not decide this question nor do I purport to do so since any order I make will not involve the Court being involved in questions of policy."[109]

These conclusions were implicitly endorsed by the Supreme Court in *D.G. v. Eastern Health Board*,[110] another "troubled child" case, where Kelly J. had *inter alia* ordered the Health Board to provide suitable care and accommodation for the applicant and, additionally, that he be arrested and detained for the purpose of receiving such care. The only issue raised in the appeal was the order for detention and it was conceded that the court had jurisdiction to so order in the circumstances, but not to direct that the boy be held in St. Patrick's institution because no other suitable place was available at the time. Although Denham J. dissented, none of the five judges suggested that there might be any difficulty with the core order that suitable accommodation be provided.

Five years on from the *F.N.* decision, there remained a dearth of accommodation for "troubled children." This led to an application on behalf of several such children in *T.D. v. Minister for Education*[111] for an injunction against the State and the Minister for Health and Children "to take all steps necessary to facilitate the building, opening and maintenance of secure and high support units." Kelly J. concluded that there had been "culpable delay" on the part of the State in doing what previously it had assured the court would be done in this regard. In those circumstances and because no undertaking was being offered to adhere to the State's own selected time-scales, the judge made orders, specifying in detail what was required in order to ensure compliance, observing that not to do so "would be to continue to allow the [children's] entitlements to be subjected to a real risk of even more delay by

---

108 *Id.* at p.40.
109 *Id.* at p.42.
110 [1997] 3 I.R. 511.
111 [2000] 3 I.R. 62.

the administrative branch of government."[112] But it was held by the Supreme Court that these orders contravened the separation of powers.[113]

Keane C.J. described the orders as "without precedent in that they do not merely find the Executive to have been in breach of their constitutional duties: they also require the executive power of the State to be implemented in a specific manner by the expenditure of money on defined objects within particular time limits."[114] This of course overlooks comparable decisions in other countries notwithstanding that their constitutions also provide for the separation of powers. Having then emphasised the desirability of making only declaratory orders in the expectation that the State will honour its constitutional obligations, the Chief Justice immediately concluded that he was "satisfied that the granting of the order [here] is inconsistent with the distribution of powers between the legislative, executive and judicial arms of government mandated by the Constitution."[115] No reason is given for this conclusion, other than the absence of precedents and the desirability of resolving such issues through the declaratory mechanism. He added that the orders also were objectionable because they involved directing the State in how "to deal with a particular social problem,"[116] which overlooks the fact that, on the basis of the law as it then stood, children in the position of the applicants there had a constitutional right to the form of secure accommodation envisaged by Kelly J. Two of the appeal judges expressed the view that *F.N.* had been wrongly decided and the Chief Justice did so obliquely, in expressing concern about "the criteria by which the unenumerated rights are to be identified."[117]

Murphy J.'s judgment consists almost entirely of disagreement with the legal basis for *F.N.*, being the concept of social rights. That theme also pervades that of Hardiman J., who expressed puzzlement at why *D.B.* had never been appealed by the State, especially when it was being contended by the State's counsel that there was no jurisdiction to make the order that had been granted there.[118] He also warned against the court making orders that "can bring the

---

[112] *Id.* at p.85.

[113] [2001] 4 I.R. 259.

[114] *Id.* at p.285.

[115] *Id.* at p.287. Compare, Barak, "Foreword: A Judge on Judging: The Role of a Supreme Court in a Democracy", 116 *Harv. L. Rev.* 17 (2002) at p.121: "The separation of powers means that every branch is independent within its sphere, so long as it operates lawfully. The judiciary ultimately decides whether an action is lawful. ... [T]he role of the judiciary is to adjudicate disputes and in doing so to give a binding interpretation of the constitution and statutes. In the words of Chief Justice Marshall, "[i]t is emphatically the province and duty of the judicial department to say what the law is." By defending the constitution ... the court is restoring the constitutional balance that underlies the principle of the separation of powers — a balance that was undermined when the unlawful decision was made."

[116] *Ibid.*

[117] *Id.* at p.281.

[118] *Id.* at p.366.

courts into unwarranted and unjustifiable conflict with the political branches of govern-ment,"[119] which suggests that if there is a real risk of the executive refusing to give effect to a recognised constitutional right, it would be preferable for the courts to "back off" rather than risk provoking a constitutional crisis. Where, however, the State made no endeavour of any kind to give effect to a constitutional right, both he and Murray J. accepted that a mandatory order could then be made in the nature of the one granted here. What particularly concerned Murray J. was the detailed form of the order, which stipulated the very programme of action that the Minister had disclosed to the court, observing that in incorporating the policy programme as part of the High Court order, the policy is taken out of the hands of the Executive, which is left with no discretionary powers of its own. A consequence of this, he held, was to "undermine the answerability of the Executive to Dáil Éireann and thus impinge on core constitutional functions of both those organs of the State."[120] But as Denham J. dissenting pointed out, the court had to accept the legal principle, as articulated in *F.N.* and in *D.B.* and, in the light of the entire history of the "troubled children" litigation, making further declaratory orders was most unlikely to vindicate the rights of the children there, before they reached eighteen years of age.

DAMAGES

Another remedy for breach of a party's constitutional rights is to award damages, either as compensation for the plaintiff's loss or as restitution for the defendant's unjust gains, or exceptionally as exemplary/punitive damages.[121] Rights such as to bodily integrity, reputation, property and earning a livelihood are extensively protected by the law of contract and tort, and by statute, which may be viewed as the principal manner in which the State gives effect to these rights. In circumstances where the common law or statute provides a remedy for the aggrieved individual, that is his exclusive basis for obtaining compensation and the existence of equivalent constitutional rights adds nothing to his claim. As Costello J. pointed out in *W. v. Ireland (No. 2)*, where a remedy exists under the ordinary law, there is "no need to construe the Constitution as conferring a new and discrete cause of action for damages in those cases ...".[122]

But where there is no comparable cause of action, damages will usually be

---

[119] *Id.* at p.371.

[120] *Id.*, at p.335.

[121] See generally, McMahon & Binchy, *supra*, n.90; Hogan & Morgan, *supra*, n.78, at pp.819 *et seq.*; Binchy, "Constitutional Remedies and the Law of Tort" in J O'Reilly ed., *Human Rights and Constitutional Law* (1992), pp.201 *et seq.*; J. Wright, *Tort Law and Human Rights* (2001); D. Fairgrieve, *State Liability in Tort* (2003).

[122] [1997] 2 I.R. 141 at p.167. Cf. *Cullen v. Chief Constable of the R.U.C.* [2003] 1 W.L.R. 1763.

awarded where loss has been inflicted by the constitutional violation.[123] It was held in *Meskell v. Coras Iompair Éireann*[124] that "a right guaranteed by the Constitution or granted by the Constitution can be protected by action or enforced by action even though such action may not fit into any of the ordinary forms of action in either common law or equity and that the constitutional right carries within it its own right to a remedy or for the enforcement of it."[125] There the plaintiff was awarded damages for not being able to retain his job, on account of a "closed shop" agreement. Other examples include *Kearney v. Minister for Justice*,[126] where letters sent to the plaintiff, while in prison, were never given to him; *McHugh v. Commissioner An Garda Síochána*,[127] where the plaintiff was compelled unnecessarily to incur costs and expenses in proceedings against the State; *Kennedy v. Ireland*,[128] where the plaintiff journalists' telephones had been "tapped" for an extended duration; and *Hayes v. Ireland*[129] and *Conway v. Ireland*,[130] on account of a teachers' union boycott of children who had been attending a national school. In *McKinley v. Minister for Defence*,[131] the Supreme Court held that confining entitlement to damages for loss of a spouse's consortium to husbands discriminated unlawfully and, in consequence, that the wife of a seriously injured soldier should be compensated for her equivalent loss. It does not appear to have been contended that to so extend liability in damages might be inconsistent with Article 15.5 of the Constitution, perhaps because the defendant employer was the State.

It was held by Budd J. in the *An Blascaod Mór Teo (No.4)* case[132] that, where enacting an Act of the Oireachtas causes direct loss to individuals and that Act is then declared invalid, generally they are entitled to compensation from the State in respect of their losses. In the circumstances there, however, he found that there were "a number of imponderables in respect of the heads of damage and that there is a lack of the type of direct causal link necessary,"[133] principally because the plaintiffs had not actually been dispossessed of their property on the Great Blasket Island. The declaration that the 1989 Act, providing for nationalising most of that island, was unconstitutional and the award of costs to the plaintiffs was held to be a sufficient vindication of their rights to property and to equality.

On the other hand, there may be some constitutional provisions, the breach

---

[123] Compare *Kruger v. Commonwealth*, 190 C.L.R. 1 (1997).
[124] [1973] I.R. 121.
[125] *Id.* at pp.132–133.
[126] [1986] I.R. 116.
[127] [1986] I.R. 228.
[128] [1987] I.L.R.M. 651.
[129] [1987] I.L.R.M. 651.
[130] [1991] 2 I.R. 305.
[131] [1992] 2 I.R. 333.
[132] [2000] 3 I.R. 565.
[133] *Id.* at p.590.

of which do not sound in damages even where the plaintiff does suffer financial loss directly in consequence of the State's failure to comply with the requirement. In *Green v. Minister for Agriculture*,[134] the plaintiffs obtained a declaration that, in making regulations for headage payments, the Minister discriminated against farmers who were members of families, as against single farmers. But Murphy J. held that, because their "personal constitutional rights have not been infringed" and there was "no evidence of damage suffered" by them, they were not entitled to be paid damages.[135]

A question that remains unresolved is "whether an action [for damages] does lie for failure on the part of the Oireachtas to legislate in protection of personal rights, as distinct from the action to set aside or invalidate legislation which fails adequately to protect or vindicate them."[136] Other unresolved questions include the criteria for assessing how much is to be paid in compensation; the applicability of emerging principles of restitutionary damages; when if ever should punitive damages be awarded outside the existing categories under common law; whether the State is always liable where a public official or agency acts outside the scope of their authority; whether the courts can uphold legislation and instead award damages to persons adversely affected where, otherwise, the law would be unconstitutional if no compensation were paid; whether there are special defences open to the State which are not available to defendants in tort cases, such as executive necessity.

Nullification

Where agents of the State deliberately resort to unconstitutional action, the State may be debarred from taking advantage of that action. Thus a person whose arrest has been obtained in clear breach of his constitutional entitlement to personal liberty will be ordered to be released.[137] There are several circumstances where criminal proceedings may be stayed.[138] Unconstitutionally obtained evidence may be held to be inadmissible in a prosecution of the person whose right has been contravened.[139]

---

[134] [1990] 2 I.R. 17.
[135] *Id.* at p.29.
[136] *Pine Valley Developments Ltd v. Minister for Environment* [1987] I.R. 23, at p.38.
[137] *Supra*, p.324.
[138] Cf. *H.M. Advocate v. R.* [2003] 2 W.L.R. 317.
[139] *Supra*, p.469.

CRIMINALISATION

In *Attorney General (ex rel. Society for the Protection of Unborn Children Ireland Ltd) v. Open Door Counselling Ltd*[140] it was held by Hamilton P. that, in certain circumstances, persons who contravene constitutional rights could incur criminal liability, even though their actions are not prohibited by any criminal law, on the grounds that such action may constitute the offence of conspiracy. That case concerned giving advice regarding abortions in England and the judge observed that the defendants' action may very well amount to the offence of conspiracy to corrupt public morals, an offence which "may be committed even when the agreement between two or more persons is to assist in the commission of a lawful act."[141] In no comparable country has contravention of constitutional rights been held to be a criminal offence *per se*. Any such development in constitutional remedies would require to be consistent with the principle of legality, in particular the maxim *nullum crimen sine lege*. However, in many countries the legislature has intervened in support of constitutional guarantees by providing that certain kinds of constitutional violations shall also be punishable as criminal offences.[142]

---

[140] [1988] I.R. 593.

[141] *Id.* at p.613.

[142] *E.g.*, the U.S. Civil Rights Act 1871, 42 U.S.C. s.1983; also 18 U.S. Code ss. 241, 242 and 245.

Index